H. G. Schaller

THE GROWTH OF THE AMERICAN ECONOMY

THE AUTHORS

Robert G. Albion
Professor of History
Harvard University

Joe S. Bain
Professor of Economics
University of California

Richard M. Clewett
Assistant Professor of Marketing
Northwestern University

Thomas C. Cochran
Professor of History
University of Pennsyvania

Wesley Frank Craven
Professor of History
Princeton University

Clarence H. Danhof
Assistant Professor of Economics
Woodrow Wilson School
Princeton University

Carroll R. Daugherty
Professor of Business Economics
Northwestern University

Catherine Ruggles Gerrish
Cambridge, Massachusetts

Max Gideonse
Professor of Economics
Rutgers University

Constance McLaughlin Green
Chief Historian
Ordnance Section
Historical Division
Department of the Army

Kent T. Healy
Professor of Economics
Yale University

Muriel Hidy
Business History Foundation, Incorporated

Edgar M. Hoover
Staff Economist
Council of Economic Advisers

Louis C. Hunter
Professor of American History
The American University

William C. Kessler
Professor of Economics
Colgate University

Charles Byron Kuhlmann
Professor of Economics
Hamline University

Theodore Marburg
Professor of Economics
Hamline University

Richard B. Morris
Professor of American History
Columbia University

Margaret Myers
Professor of Economics
Vassar College

Philip H. Overmeyer
Professor of History
Lewis and Clark College

Richard C. Overton
Professor of Business History
Northwestern University

Kenyon E. Poole
Professor of Economics
Northwestern University

Samuel Rezneck
Professor of History
Rensselaer Polytechnic Institute

Carl C. Rister
Research Professor of History
University of Oklahoma

Earle D. Ross
Professor of History
Iowa State College

Harold M. Somers
Dean
School of Business Administration
University of Buffalo

Harold F. Williamson
Professor of Economics
Northwestern University

THE GROWTH OF THE AMERICAN ECONOMY

EDITED BY

Harold F. Williamson

NORTHWESTERN UNIVERSITY

SECOND EDITION

NEW YORK

Prentice-Hall, Inc.

1951

PRENTICE-HALL ECONOMICS SERIES

E. A. J. Johnson

EDITOR

PRINTED IN THE UNITED STATES OF AMERICA

PREFACE

THE GUILD of economic historians sets no rigid qualifications for membership within its ranks; it welcomes and, indeed, must draw extensively upon the contributions offered by students and scholars of the most diverse interests and talents. It asks of its fellows only that they remember the main objective of their association: to promote a clearer understanding of how man's struggle for material existence has been carried on through time. By this standard the economic historian's claim to journeyman's or master's status will be judged. In this book on the economic history of the United States, the authors have consistently followed the precepts of honest craftsmanship. They have subordinated all other considerations to the main task of describing and analyzing the changes that have occurred in the wealth-getting and wealth-using activities of the American people. Only incidentally has attention been given to the influence of our economic development upon allied fields of legal, political, intellectual, or general social history—matters which, while of great interest, should not be considered in detail in an introduction to economic history.

In its entirety, American economic development has been exceedingly complex, extending over roughly three centuries and encompassing the lives of millions of persons whose economic activities subdivide into dozens of major occupations, hundreds of specialized branches, and thousands of enterprises. The manifold changes in these various phases of American life have been so uniquely conditioned that only specialized study can give an adequate explanation of their evolution. For this reason it is doubtful if any one person can ever treat with authority all the topics that should be included in a survey book on the economic history of the United States. A really adequate treatment must draw upon the knowledge of scholars who have worked intensively in particular areas. Such is the plan followed in this volume. Each author has been chosen because of his special competence in the field about which he has written. Each chapter represents the balanced judgment of a person who has made a careful monographic study of his subject and who is therefore intimately acquainted with its details.

A wealth of material necessitates careful choice of subject matter for an introductory text on American economic history. It is impractical to include anything more than those topics that give the beginning student a knowledge and understanding of the major trends in the evolution of our economic institutions. Emphasis has therefore been placed upon the analysis and interpretation of the more important trends. The facts of our economic history have been lifted from their resting places in documents, census reports, monographs, and the like, and their meaning and significance illuminated. Finally, developments in the major subdivisions of our economic life have been synthesized by giving specific attention to measuring the adaptation and performance of the economy as a whole.

Within this general framework the present edition has been thoroughly revised. The original chapters were carefully checked by their respective authors and rewritten in part or in whole wherever more recent scholarship gave a clearer understanding of the subject matter. Two chapters covering the important subject of marketing have been added to the topics treated in the first edition. The major chronological divisions have also been changed: the first period ends with 1789, the second with 1865, the third with 1918, and the last with 1950. This arrangement makes it possible to give better perspective to developments since World War I. Short introductions have been added to each of the major chronological divisions in an attempt to point up the major trends discussed in more detail in succeeding chapters.

I take this opportunity to thank those users of the first edition who made constructive criticisms; many of those criticisms have been incorporated in the revision. I am deeply indebted to the authors, for both their original work and their patience in revising material to conform to the general plan of the revision. Special acknowledgment must be made to Dr. E. A. J. Johnson for his suggestions concerning the structure of the present volume. Responsibility for the general organization and for the content of the book must, of course, be assumed by the editor.

HAROLD F. WILLIAMSON

Northwestern University

TABLE OF CONTENTS

Part 3 • *Early National Period 1789-1865*

Part 4 • *1865-1918*

PART 1

INTRODUCTION

1 · THE PROCESS OF ECONOMIC DEVELOPMENT

EXCEPT IN THOSE RARE COUNTERPARTS of the Garden of Eden, found principally in the realm of imagination, human beings have always faced the stern reality of limited resources with which to satisfy their seemingly endless needs and wants. Economic history tells the story of the ways by which men have attempted to overcome these limitations imposed by nature, and describes the uses made of the products of their efforts. Discovery of new resources and development of more effective methods of utilizing those already known have made possible an existence well above a subsistence level for a considerable part of the human race; moreover, this improvement has challenged man's ingenuity to extend these benefits to a larger proportion of mankind. But the record of economic history is often less roseate: exhaustion or waste of resources and failure to discover ways of relieving scarcity have reduced or kept incomes below comfort levels for great masses of people and have brought on the tragedies of malnutrition, starvation, and associated evils.

Interest in economic history naturally centers upon the factors that make for change. What are the dynamic elements in economic development? What are the conditioning circumstances that encourage or inhibit change? What forces lead to particular forms of economic institutions? Answers to questions of this type are the principal concern of the economic historian.

In its entirety, the process of economic development is complex. The factors that influence and shape economic institutions appear at first glance so numerous that any attempt to analyze their cause-and-effect relationships seems hopeless. No one, in fact, has been able to suggest any acceptable single factor or independent variable that gives *the* key to understanding the historical process. This does not mean, however, that economic history must be confined to description; that it is impossible to show that some forces have relatively greater influence on the character of the economy than others. Keeping in mind the fact that the relationships involved are reciprocal or interdependent, it is possible to analyze economic development in terms of the combined effect of three sets of factors: the physical environment, innovation, and social institution. Each of these plays a distinctive part in the process of historical evolution.

The Physical Environment

Physical environment may be described as the stage upon which men work and live, and within the limits set by this stage the problems of material existence must be worked out. So apparent are the conditioning effects of physical environment upon the economic organization of societies that it is easy to exaggerate its influence. Some physical variations, like long-run weather cycles, a receding or expanding shore line, the melting of a polar ice cap, or an earthquake, arise out of circumstances quite divorced from human action and may have significant effects on economic organization.

For the most part, however, the physiographic environment is, *in itself,* relatively stable: Its influence on economic development may best be described by saying that geography sets the boundaries within which economic development *can* take place. Man is no passive agent, forced to adapt himself to circumstances rigidly determined by his physical surroundings. He has the power to choose among existing alternatives; even more important, he has been able to mold his environment to meet his needs. One eminent geographer has stated the issue very clearly: "There are no necessities, but everywhere possibilities; and man, as the master of these possibilities, is the judge of their use." [1] Thus, an understanding of the limits imposed by physical environment on economic development and of the range of possibilities within those limits is especially helpful in accounting for the economic relations between regions and in explaining the details of organization within areas at particular periods. An analysis of the relative industrial growth shown by countries at specified dates, for example, can best be approached by reference to the geographic potentialities involved. But the most comprehensive understanding of the physiographic elements in a region will not shed much light on the question as to why a particular set of economic institutions emerged, nor will it explain the timing of their appearance. Only by reference to other material can a more complete explanation be obtained.

The Role of Innovation

It is principally through innovation that men have been able to utilize and adapt their physical environment more effectively to satisfy their material needs. Innovation must be broadly defined. It includes the activities of explorers, certain functions undertaken by entrepreneurs, and the work of inventors. Down to about the 17th century, it is probable that geographic exploration exerted the most influence on economic organization. As the geographic frontiers were pushed back discoveries

[1] L. P. V. Febvre, *Geographical Introduction to History,* p. 236. New York: Alfred A. Knopf, 1932.

relating to technology and management assumed a more predominant role in bringing about modifications in economic life; indeed, it has been claimed that invention is the greatest single cause of change in our modern society.

While motivations vary between individuals, all innovators share a common interest in exploring the unknown; curiosity about what lies over the ocean or beyond the next range of mountains is closely akin to the desire to know the results that may be obtained from a new combination of chemicals or from experiments with the properties of the atom.

In general, the process of invention has been less clearly understood than the actions of the geographic explorers. Until fairly recent times, it was supposed that improvements in technology sprang fully developed as a result of a mysterious mental activity on the part of a few highly gifted persons whose appearance in society was quite unpredictable. Modern studies have shown this older view to be incorrect in several respects. The mental processes involved in innovations are quite similar to those exercised by most people in the ordinary business of living. It is probable that all populations contain a considerable number of individuals with the innate capacity to solve the more complex problems connected with inventions. Furthermore, innovation is a cumulative process: inventions are closely related to previous discoveries, and are therefore a result of an evolutionary rather than a revolutionary process.

Technical innovation or invention consists in the establishment of relations that did not previously exist. Essentially it is a new combination of old ideas. Many problems connected with everyday life require mental activity of this sort for their solution. Most persons, however, limit their innovating activity to a fairly simple level—to areas where the problems are not very complex and where the immediate objectives are fairly obvious. Considerable effort is involved in deviating very far from established channels of thought. Hence, the solution of more difficult problems requires the attention of a relatively small group whose imagination and training are more highly developed.

Although the psychology involved in the process of invention is by no means simple, some of the principal steps may be distinguished. The initial step comes with a feeling of dissatisfaction with the results of techniques currently in use. This feeling may arise out of a recognition that contemporary methods are providing an inadequate supply of familiar kinds of goods, or that they are incapable of being used for the production of new products. If the sense of dissatisfaction is sufficiently strong, a second phase of the inventive process will occur in attempts to solve the problems involved in improving current methods of production. In all but the simple situations, this second step will necessitate the attention of persons especially qualified by training or experience to solve the particular kind of problems involved. This is why inventors often tend to specialize in certain types of work; this is why improvements are often made by workmen intimately acquainted with certain technical processes.

The total experiences of many inventors suggest a third step in the mental process of innovation. Numerous firsthand accounts tell of the "flashes of inspiration" that have marked the successful solution of the particular problems. As Professor Usher has indicated, some "stage setting" is necessary before the new combination of old elements can be visualized.[2] Such a setting may involve the use of physical properties or it may consist entirely in mental images. In either case, the proper combination may suggest the sought-for solution.

There may be a considerable interval between the moment that an invention takes form in the mind of its creator (or is embodied in a working model) and the time that it begins to have any effect on economic life. Practically all important technical innovations have had to go through a long period of testing and modification before the basic ideas could be put into workable form. Difficult mechanical problems must often be solved; moreover, in some instances, successful operation may have to wait until allied techniques have developed.

As a rule, the lines along which technology develops will depend to a considerable extent upon the nature of the problems facing innovators. Their attention will be directed to overcoming those obstacles that seem most important and urgent. Where raw materials are scarce and labor abundant, as in Germany, efforts are likely to be turned toward methods of obtaining greater or improved production from such raw materials. Where labor is relatively limited, as in the United States, attempts will be made to economize on its use by seeking "labor-saving" improvements. War or its threat turns the attention of scientists and inventors to the creation of instruments of destruction, although it should be noted that these may have important peacetime applications.

The Social Environment

The customs, mores, and institutions that form the social environment of a nation constitute the third set of factors that affect economic life, and they are, in turn, influenced by changes in technology and physical background. Like the physical background, the social environment may impose limits or may present opportunities for economic change. If it reflects a general attitude of veneration toward tradition and past accomplishments, the incentives for modifying current economic arrangements will be weakened merely because the attention of potential innovators will be directed toward channels less likely to disturb existing conditions. If, on the other hand, the prevailing philosophy accepts

[2] See A. P. Usher, *History of Mechanical Inventions,* pp. 18-19. New York: McGraw-Hill Book Company, 1929.

the idea that material advancement is both possible and desirable, encouragement will be given to forces making for improvements in existing techniques: inventors and innovators will be held high in public esteem; positive aid may be given in the form of patent rights, bounties, land grants, and other governmental assistance.

Disturbances in economic organization almost inevitably affect some groups in society adversely; others find their positions improved by the changes. Should those members who feel a strong vested interest in maintaining the *status quo* be able to translate their sentiments into legislation or social conventions, serious limitations will be imposed on change. This conservative effect, however, may be offset by those social groups whose interests appear to be best served by the adoption of innovations.

Even if there is a general aceptance of the idea that progress and change are closely associated and on the whole desirable, economic development will be influenced by the skill with which laws and customs are adapted to meet the requirements imposed by technical change. A legal framework that is well suited for an agricultural or commercial economy may work badly when applied to an industrial organization. New techniques, like the introduction of railroads or the generation and distribution of electric power, may present problems of social control unknown to previous generations of lawmakers. The part played by legislators and statesmen in economic development is especially significant. Their actions will determine to a very considerable extent the usefulness that any particular innovation or series of technical changes has for a society. Specifically, their function is to see that the potentialities of innovations are directed toward given social goals. The principal mental quality needed is that of judgment: the ability to choose from among a given range of possibilities the alternative that seems most desirable.

The interrelations between the social environment and economic factors present an extremely complex problem of analysis. Some scholars have attempted to explain the general character of society principally if not exclusively in terms of economic or technical considerations. This position seems untenable. That economic influences are important is obvious, inasmuch as a great part of man's social life is occupied with the problems of getting and spending a living. But it is fully as clear that social institutions are also influenced by intellectual and ethical concepts that are not dominated by material considerations. Political and religious philosophies, for example, are no simple reflection of economic organization, and hence their evolution may follow a relatively independent pattern.

A knowledge of the social environment will aid in understanding the type of economic organization to be found at a particular period of time as well as in explaining why particular forms came into existence. But it is important to bear in mind that social factors are only partly deterministic in their effect on economic life, since they are subject to modification by geography and technologies.

The Changing Significance of the American Physical Environment

For the original settlers in the New World, the forests, the sea, and the soil were the most significant features of their new physical environment. The Colonists were able to transfer many of the techniques, crops, types of capital equipment, and attitudes from Europe and thus develop an economy quite different from that of the native Indians. But geographic factors offered new opportunities and set physical and economic limits to the accustomed kinds of activities. Fishing in the ocean probably presented the fewest difficulties of adaptation to the Colonists. Long known and used by Europeans, the fishing banks furnished an important food supply and an early export product, especially for New England. The forests presented both problems and opportunities. They had to be cleared away before any extensive agriculture could be undertaken; but the trees furnished materials for buildings, ships, tools, and the like, on a scale impossible in the mother country. In addition, charcoal supplied the fuel for the small but flourishing iron industry, and within the woods lived an abundant animal life that formed the basis of a profitable, if short-lived, fur trade.

Agriculture, by far the principal occupation of the Colonists, soon showed regional differences closely associated with localized soil and weather conditions. New Englanders found their land ill-adapted to the production of wheat and consequently turned to the indigenous Indian corn for their chief cereal crop. Corn, in fact, became a leading product throughout the Colonies; but in New York, Pennsylvania, Maryland, and Virginia, wheat production became increasingly significant. In the Southern Colonies, especially in Maryland and Virginia, circumstances so favored the raising of tobacco that it became a staple at an early date.

One distinctive feature of life in the New World was the considerable degree of economic self-sufficiency that was practiced. Besides growing a large proportion of their own food supplies, most households provided the major part of their other wants, including clothes and manufactured articles. Physical features were partly responsible for this high degree of self-sufficiency. In the absence of a cheap method of providing inland transportation, only those who had easy access to the sea could engage in any advanced degree of economic specialization.[3]

[3] It should be emphasized that "self-sufficiency" was only relative. Even the pioneers, cut off from most traffic, depended upon others for important items such as metal products, gunpowder, and the like.

By the end of the colonial period, the significance of the American physical environment for economic activity had undergone considerable modification and expansion. New crops, testing of new production methods, further exploration, all combined to widen the range of choices to which physical resources could be put.

Even more striking changes were to occur after the establishment of the national state. The Louisiana Purchase in 1803 added an "empire" to the original territory. By 1850, expanded coastal trade, highways, canals, and the newly constructed railroads had decreased the comparative isolation of the previous period and had ushered in a new era of geographic and occupational specialization. Now the farm lands beyond the Appalachians could send their staples in increasing amounts to Eastern markets. In the South, tobacco, still an important staple, had abdicated in favor of the new "king cotton," which was expanding its domain to the Southwest. Agriculture continued to claim the services of the largest part of the population, but its domination had been weakened by the growing significance of industry. New Englanders, borrowing and developing the power-driven machinery of England, had taken the lead in American industrial development. The numerous streams in that area had acquired an added meaning as the source of power for operating the new apparatus. Already the potentialities of steam power were beginning to be appreciated, and experiments with coal pointed the way to the use of this energy-producing mineral on a scale but dimly perceived by contemporaries. Important advances had been made in the production of iron and its fabrication, which in turn further encouraged the exploration for new sources of raw materials.

Another half-century saw further advance along both old and new lines. By war, negotiation, and purchase, the country's continental boundaries had been rounded out. Both industry and agriculture had been vitally affected by the expanded transport system. Agricultural regions far distant from waterways could now send their products to markets. Older producing areas in the United States and even Europe were feeling the effects of the newly cultivated land in the American "West" as wheat, cotton, and meat products poured into their markets in increasing quantities. Industry, too, was able to draw its raw materials from sources located hundreds of miles away from processing points and markets.

Probably the most outstanding changes in respect to resource utilization were connected with the expansion of industry and commerce and involved the growing use of minerals, especially coal and iron. Steam power generated by coal now drove most of the factory wheels and the locomotives. It supplied heat for factories, office buildings, and homes, and in the form of coke it had almost entirely supplanted charcoal as the fuel used to refine the iron ore and to produce steel. Iron production had also expanded greatly. Low-cost iron and steel made possible a wide use of machinery on the farms and in the factories.

By the end of the fifth decade of the twentieth century, Americans were not only using previously known resources on a greatly expanded scale compared with the exploitation a half-century before, but in addition they had tapped a bewildering array of materials unknown to earlier generations. The transportation system had received significant additions. Private automobiles, aided by buses and airplanes, moved millions of individuals from place to place; moreover, motor transport had led to shifts in population that were worrying the urban landowners and city officials.

The expansion in the use of the internal combustion engine was made possible by the development of a new source of energy, petroleum. This product, which a few decades before was principally used as a hair restorer, was not only the principal source of lubricating materials, but supplied an estimated 30 per cent of the energy consumed in the United States in 1939, although coal was still the principal source of power.

Iron and steel likewise retained their dominant position as the chief mineral products used in the construction of machines and finished products. But other materials were being utilized, of which aluminum probably represented the most important. Its use now gave economic value to the deposits of bauxite. Meantime, the science of chemistry had added other products to our economy, such as rayon, cellophane, and plastics, and in so doing either expanded the employment of previously used raw materials or brought new resources into use.

American Technology

The principal differences between Colonial economic organization and the modern American scene are attributable to a large extent to the application of new techniques to resources. Americans have long recognized the leading part that technology has had in shaping their economic development. They have taken a justifiable pride in the accomplishments of native innovators and inventors, and the names of Whitney, McCormick, Howe, Bell, Wright, and Edison, to mention only a few, stand high on the list of honored national figures. While there has been some tendency to neglect the lesser figures whose accomplishments were not so spectacular or so well publicized as those of the popular heroes, the ability to solve technical and economic problems has been quite widespread among the population. "Yankee ingenuity" is not thought to be confined to the New England region; it is expected to show itself in the factories, on the farms, or wherever new problems are faced. National pride should not hide the extent to which we have borrowed ideas from other countries. The first settlers brought with them invaluable knowledge and techniques developed in the Old World, and this source has never been cut off. Yet Americans can rightfully claim an important part in adapting borrowed ideas to meet local conditions and in contributing new techniques and discoveries to the world's knowledge.

Conditions in the New World favored the advance of technology and discovery. Frontier life presented many new problems for which there was little precedent to indicate the proper solution. Large supplies of raw materials offered the possibility of high rewards to the successful inventor who could make them available. The general character of American contributions to technology reflects the kind of problems that were met. Great distances to traverse, large unused resources, and a scarcity of labor give the key to much that has been typical of our technology. Whitney's epoch-making cotton gin is an example of a labor-saving device that was devised to reduce the great amount of effort that had formerly been required to separate the cotton fiber from the seeds. American contributions in the field of agricultural implements—plows, cultivators, reapers, harvesters—all helped to reduce the time and work required to prepare and cultivate the soil and harvest the crops. Technical advances in the field of transport have shown a response to a major need. With resources widely separated from markets or processing points, this country has had a particular interest in a cheap and flexible system of transportation. By the beginning of the nineteenth century, the problem of improving the existing road, river, and canal systems had become acute. Credit for the original combination of the railway and the steam locomotive goes principally to British innovators. But Americans quickly recognized the potentialities of this new type of transport and developed the railroad along lines that differed from the English and Continental roads. A comparative scarcity of capital and labor in America prompted an economy in construction. Whereas the British railways were free from severe curves and their roadbeds were nearly level, the engineers in this country initially built their lines much more to the contours of the country, and so-called hairpin turns were commonplace. America's contribution of a swivel truck to permit cars and locomotives to negotiate sharp curves grew out of the nature of our roadbed construction.

Probably America is best known for its contributions to the development of mass-production methods. This development also shows the desire to conserve on labor. Eli Whitney, Simeon North, Samuel Colt, and other Americans share the credit with certain British inventors for the early use of the system of interchangeable-parts manufacture, which is the basis of large-scale production. Begun in the field of firearms, this method of manufacture spread to other parts of industry, receiving one of its most notable results in the manufacture of automobiles and, more recently, of airplanes.

Much of the experimentation by early American innovators was done on an empirical basis. Many improvements in technique were made by mechanics, laborers, and farmers working largely without the benefit of theoretical background. Even well-known inventors like McCormick and Hussey apparently brought little more than a native mechanical ability to the problems of developing a mechanical reaper. But this lack of scientific knowledge should not be exaggerated. Whitney, for example, brought to his work a formal education that included a familiarity with scientific principles; Oliver Evans was familiar with the current literature dealing with the theoretical aspects of the steam engine; and Thomas Jefferson is credited with working out a mathematical formula that could be used to give an efficient contour to the mold board of the plow. As educational opportunities expanded, experimentation tended more and more to gravitate into the hands of specially trained operators and away from the workshops, factories, and farms and into the laboratories. In this change, the individual inventor began to lose his identity. Modern research is carried on chiefly by specially trained scientists working as teams in laboratories supported by educational institutions, research foundations, industry, and government. The millions of dollars spent annually by these organizations and the extensive interchange of newly discovered scientific information have no doubt speeded up the rate at which innovations can occur.

The American Social Environment

The American social environment has evolved out of many diverse influences. Native or indigenous aspirations have combined with ideas drawn by successive generations from Europe. The resulting philosophies have affected the nature of American institutions and have, in turn, been greatly modified by the economic and physical environment of the New World. On the whole, it may be said that our social environment has been favorable to a rapid expansion of the economy and to a vigorous exploitation of our resources. There has been rather little in the congeries of customs, institutions, and philosophies that would discourage the activities of explorers, innovators, or inventors, or of that larger group, the entrepreneurs or businessmen, that turned the former's discoveries to account.

It should not be supposed, however, that resistances or impedimenta have been absent from the American scene. New processes and ideas not uncommonly had to overcome prejudice and inertia or the antagonism of vested interests. But throughout our history the influence of those who favored change has generally outweighed the elements that favored maintaining the *status quo*.

Among the many ideas that have formed the philosophic or ideological background of Americans, two are of special interest through their relation to our economic development. These two lines of thought are found in our attitudes toward material prosperity and individualism. Most Americans have maintained little doubt that material progress is possible and desirable. This belief has its roots deep in our past. The original settlers were attracted to this country by the possibilities of improving their social, political, or economic status. The abundant resources of their new physical environment gave the promise of unusual opportunities for economic advancement, and there was little in their religious or political thinking incompatible with the idea of material progress. Indeed, to labor hard at one's earthly calling was one of the tenets of the Puritan faith. A few generations later Benjamin Franklin's "Poor Richard" was pointing out to an appreciative audience the virtues of thrift and hard work as leading to the good and successful life. With variations, the theme has continued to occupy a leading place in our thinking. As one competent observer has noted, we have had "a people imbued with a passion for work and regarding 'business' not only as the absorbing concern of life, but as the social activity most worthy of emulation and reward." [4] In the absence of a nobility or a strong military caste, the chief road to social distinction has been through economic success. With the possible exception of the *ante-bellum* planter aristocracy, there has been no stigma attached to being "in trade," as has been the case in other countries.

Economic progress has been considered the normal course of events in America. To be sure, doubts might be raised, especially during one of the many business depressions that have affected the economy, but these disturbing thoughts have given way to a reaffirmation of a faith that the future promises even more than has been realized in the past. The examples of the Astors, Vanderbilts, Carnegies, Rockefellers, and Fords, as well as of a large number of less well-known figures, have helped to perpetuate the Alger tradition that success in America was open to anyone who had the ability and the willingness to work hard. Not only could every American boy aspire to become President: even better, he might become a millionaire.

A belief in the importance of the individual was also evident early in our history. The doctrine drew its early inspiration from such sources as the pronouncements of the prophets of the Reformation, the experiences of the Colonists in drawing up their own "social compacts," and the writings of Roger Williams and John Locke. These ideas were in turn supplemented by the naturalistic philosophy of the French Physiocrats and the development of English liberalism in the late eighteenth and early nineteenth centuries.

The philosophy of individualism found an especially congenial environment in this country. The relative scarcity of people tended to raise

[4] See Edwin F. Gay's introduction to *Recent Economic Changes in the United States*, p. 7. New York: McGraw-Hill Book Company, 1929.

the social and economic importance of individuals. Conditions in the New World put a premium on the qualities of self-reliance and personal aggressiveness. Very often it was not only economic success that depended on these qualities, but survival itself. Under frontier conditions, or even in more settled areas, social and economic problems were handled on a local basis by the joint action of individuals and with little reference to the central government.

It should not be supposed that this emphasis on individualism was carried over immediately following the Revolution into the economic sphere. The Colonists' objections to the British government's regulation and participation in economic affairs were primarily directed against particular acts or operations and not against the principle involved. Recent studies have shown that in both Massachusetts and Pennsylvania, for example, there was no inclination to exclude the state from taking an active part in the promotion and regulation of economic activities.[5] Nor was this attitude confined to Massachusetts and Pennsylvania. The populace in all of the former colonies had been long conditioned to mercantilistic regulation and were aware from first-hand experience of the power of group association. It seemed proper and natural to look to the government, at least at the state level, for active aid and direction of the economy.

It was not until after the Civil War, when the economies of the states became more inextricably a part of the national pattern and individual business concerns grew strong enough no longer to need state aid, that the principles of *laissez-faire* began to find wide acceptance. Developed principally by English classical economists, the basic ideas of *laissez-faire* may be summarized briefly as follows:

The principal responsibility for economic activity, it was felt, should be in the hands of the individual, who, in the absence of interference by the Government, would exercise his talents to the best of his ability. In seeking his own best interests he would, to use Adam Smith's famous phrase, "be led by an invisible hand" to contribute to the good of the group as a whole. Economic competition between members of society would prevent the practice of any major abuses. Individuals, of course, could not be expected to put forth their full effort unless they were reasonably sure of receiving and keeping the results of their activity. It was, therefore, one of the principal functions of the Government to protect property rights. In addition, the Government might properly extend positive aids to farmers and businessmen in the form of subsidies, tariff protection, and the like. Otherwise, it should largely confine its attention to seeing that "the rules of the game" were enforced; but, other

---

[5] See Handlin, Oscar and Mary, *Commonwealth: Massachusetts, 1774-1861*. New York: New York University Press, 1947; and Hartz, Louis, *Economic Policy and Democratic Thought: Pennsylvania, 1776-1860*. Cambridge: Harvard University Press, 1948.

than in an exceptional case like the post office, the Government should not take any direct part in the economic process itself.

As long as the economy was composed of farmers and small businessmen, the system of minimum Governmental controls apparently operated with reasonable success; competition among individuals and firms worked to keep prices within tolerable limits, prevented undue discrimination, and tended to reward people on a basis of their ability and energy. To be sure, our not infrequent business depressions were probably more severe than they would have been under stronger social controls, especially over the monetary and banking system. The "planless" exploitation of natural resources resulted in much unnecessary waste. But real agitation for stronger Governmental controls did not come until technical factors, along with a growing use of the business corporation, had resulted in large business and industrial units, which in turn might be combined into even larger organizations. "Big business," as represented by the railroads and industrialists, was increasingly under attack toward the end of the nineteenth century. But for the most part, the goal of the "reformers" was to restore the balance in the competitive system that had been disturbed by the rise of large business units. There was little agitation for the state to engage directly in economic production. Even the direct participation by the Government during the First World War was quickly abandoned in the "return to normalcy" of the 1920's. The decade ending in 1929 gave promise of achieving a new "era" in the drive toward material progress, which still had a great appeal to Americans.

The impact of the depression following 1929, however, brought renewed demands for centralized regulation over the economy. The "emergency" was the occasion for participation by the Government in economic activity on a fairly substantial scale. The continued failure of the economy to recover its expected vigor led to an extensive re-examination of our economic policies and institutions. The issues involved had not been resolved when the Second World War brought the state into all phases of our social and economic life on a scale unprecedented even in the previous world contest. Nor have the years since the end of that conflict shown any clear-cut trend. It is for the future to determine the characteristics of our economic policies and institutions in the postwar period.

Selected References

GEOGRAPHY AND RESOURCES

East, Gordon, *The Geography Behind History*. London: Thomas Nelson and Sons, 1938.

Ely, Richard T., and George S. Wehrwein, *Land Economics*. New York: The Macmillan Company, 1942.

Fairgrieve, James, *Geography and World Power*. London: University of London Press, 1932.

Febvre, Lucien P. V., *Geographical Introduction to History*. New York: Alfred A. Knopf, 1932.

Huntington, Ellsworth, *Civilization and Climate*. New York: Charles Scribner's Sons, 1924.

de La Blache, P. Vidal, *Principles of Human Geography*. New York: Henry Holt and Company, 1926.

Smith, J. Russell, *Industrial and Commercial Geography*. New York: Henry Holt and Company, 1928.

Zimmerman, Erich W., *World Resources and Industries*. New York: Harper & Brothers, 1933.

TECHNOLOGY AND INVENTION

Gilfillan, S. C., *The Sociology of Invention*. Chicago: Follett Publishing Company, 1935.

National Resources Committee, *Technological Trends and National Policy*. Washington, D. C.: U. S. Government Printing Office, 1937.

Rossman, Joseph, *The Psychology of the Inventor*. Washington, D. C.: The Inventor's Publishing Company, 1931.

Usher, Abbott Payson, *A History of Mechanical Inventions*. New York: McGraw-Hill Book Company, 1929.

SOCIAL INSTITUTIONS

Brady, Robert A., *Business as a System of Power*. New York: Columbia University Press, 1943.

Cochran, Thomas C., and William Miller, *The Age of Enterprise*. New York: The Macmillan Company, 1942.

Farnam, Henry W., *Chapters in the History of Social Legislation in the United States to 1860*. Washington, D. C.: Carnegie Institution, 1938.

Gabriel, Ralph H., *The Course of American Democratic Thought*. New York: The Ronald Press Company, 1940.

Handlin, Oscar and Mary, *Commonwealth: Massachusetts, 1774-1861*. New York: New York University Press, 1947.

Hartz, Louis, *Economic Policy and Democratic Thought: Pennsylvania, 1776-1860*. Cambridge, Mass.: Harvard University Press, 1948.

National Resources Committee, *Energy Resources and National Policy*. Washington, D. C.: U. S. Government Printing Office, 1939.

Schumpeter, Joseph A., *Capitalism, Socialism, and Democracy*. New York: Harper and Brothers, 1947.

PART 2

THE COLONIAL PERIOD

SOME 169 years intervened between the founding of the first permanent English settlement at Jamestown in 1607 and the start of the American Revolution. It was not until a generation or so after political independence had been achieved that the economic bonds that connected this part of the New World with the Old were seriously disturbed. Thus, for the better part of two centuries American economic development was carried on under colonial conditions.

Despite the modifying influence of the physical environment, this long association with Europe had a marked effect on the economic as well as the social life of the colonies. The settlers brought with them a civilization or culture that included such elements as the institution of private property, a considerable reliance on individual initiative, a knowledge of the advantages of division of labor, the use of money, and a European standard of living.

Of these, the last is of special significance in explaining certain basic features of the Colonial economic organization and development. One of the principal concerns of the Colonists was to establish conditions that would permit them to enjoy and improve their "imported" standard of living. They could and did provide for the bulk of their basic needs, such as food, shelter, and clothing, from resources near at hand. But a sparse population and a relative scarcity of capital, coupled with abundant natural resources, made it impossible or impractical to produce the manufactured articles, the tea, the silk, and the other items that marked the difference between a primitive existence and the kind of a consumption income desired. For these "conventional necessities" the Colonists were largely dependent upon trade. Although some considerable progress was made in overcoming the scarcity of both labor and capital, throughout the entire Colonial period there was a constant seeking for exportable products or activities that would yield foreign exchange that could be used to purchase imports.

These points are brought out in more detail in the chapters that immediately follow. Chapter 2 describes the problems that had to be met in the colonizing process; Chapter 3 shows the character and development of Colonial commerce; Chapter 4 tells of the principal economic activities followed by the inhabitants; and Chapter 5 gives a brief summary of the economic growth prior to 1790.

2 · THE EARLY SETTLEMENTS: A EUROPEAN INVESTMENT OF CAPITAL AND LABOR

THE ECONOMIC HISTORY of America has its beginning in an investment of European capital and labor. The Colonial settlements were inspired by a wide variety of motives, but in a very large degree the accomplishment of the purposes of settlement, whatever their nature, depended upon the solution of a basic economic problem—to enlist the capital necessary for underwriting the venture and to recruit a labor supply possessed of the requisite endurance and skill. This necessity, in turn, called for some plan of settlement assuring an adequate return on the investment made. The adventurer, as the European promoter who risked chiefly a capital investment was commonly described, demanded a reasonable assurance that merchantable commodities could be produced in sufficient quantity to provide a profitable return of the capital sum invested. The colonist who adventured his life and labor in the settlement naturally insisted upon a share in the produce of his efforts that would permit him either to return to the old country after a few years with his fortune made, or to remain in America in the enjoyment of an economic and social position superior to any he could command at home. It follows that the infant economy of an American community was measured chiefly by its capacity to meet the demands and potentialities of a European market. For only through the establishment of credit in an Old World market could the adventurer be assured of the return of his capital, the homeward-bound fortune hunter of the means for a fuller enjoyment of Old World life, and the permanent settler in America of an ability to purchase essential supplies in Europe. On the primitive frontiers of the New World, it must be understood, there was no hope of an advanced standard of living save through imports from abroad.

Such basic considerations, rooted in the very conditions of original settlement, were through many generations to shape the developing economy of America. Upon successive frontiers new communities were established, each representing an investment of capital and labor drawn from older communities, and each in its turn tied to a dependence upon established markets. The point of departure for most of the settlements here dealt with was London; but with the passage of time, such cities as

Boston, New York, or Philadelphia were to assume a role in the westward advance of settlement not unlike that originally held by Britain's metropolis. And while, with the passage of time, the growing complexity of the American scene compels attention to the many separate chapters into which the story breaks down, the over-all picture has been subject to only a gradual modification. Only lately has America's status in relation to Europe changed from that of a debtor to a creditor. Over large areas of the nation men have continued to count up their wealth in terms of the production of such primary staples as tobacco or cotton for a European market. The liberal rules of immigration that characterized our national policy until recent years trace their origins to the earliest attempts of Colonial promoters to meet the problem of an adequate labor supply in America. In brief, our dependence upon European capital, European immigration, and European markets outlasted our political dependence by many years.

Other features of the story are no less suggestive of a pattern familiar in our later history. The awakening interest in America that marked the dawn of modern Europe was first directed to exploration of the uncharted Atlantic. Next came establishment of footholds upon continental America, or on islands just off it, to serve, among other purposes, as outposts for a more careful study of the potentialities of the continent and its coastal waters. Such early projects of settlement as Raleigh's Roanoke Island venture and the first Colony at Jamestown were largely exploratory in character. Once the foothold was made secure, often a task of extraordinary difficulty, the early Colony served as a base from which explorers, traders, and farmers fanned out in an expanding field of endeavor. The original settlement, or a more fortunately situated base that took over its functions, was not unlike a bridgehead, its fortifications holding open a line of communication with the home base in Europe, from whence it received the tools and other equipment a young and undeveloped community must perforce obtain from abroad, as well as a yearly influx of immigrants offering their skill, their brawn, and on occasion a welcome contribution of capital.

Thus was the way prepared for an overland march destined to cross a continent. The explorer now traveled by land and inland waterway; a river bed or a mountain pass shaped his route instead of the wind and current at sea. But the work was essentially the same and the order of the advance unchanged. New outposts were established to hold open a line of communication with the coast and to aid in bringing up the supplies required for the next move forward. Well nigh three hundred years were needed for completion of the job, and at St. Louis and other such points men were to re-enact again and again in the nineteenth century scenes first associated with Jamestown, Boston, Philadelphia, or Charleston. In the story of American exploration and colonization, the break that terminated the so-called Colonial period in 1776 represents chiefly a change in the higher command.

A New World and New Opportunities

Europe's early interest in America presents a complex question. It is necessary, on the one hand, to understand that the New World offered aid to a solution of some of Europe's oldest problems. The western European states, whose leadership in trans-Atlantic adventure was a notable feature of the movement, were for climatic and other reasons dependent upon the East for supplies essential to an advancing standard of living. They produced only limited quantities of goods that were acceptable in exchange and the resulting necessity of making payments to the East in bullion occasioned a drainage of specie, a circumstance that helps to explain Europe's eager hopes for American gold and silver. In America, too, there might be found fresh sources of supply and an opportunity to provide additional commodities acceptable in eastern markets. On the other hand, it is even more important to recognize that the forces at work in this new age of discovery were dynamic, and that the energies of western Europe that now launched the most impressive era of expansion in human history had been long in the gathering. Those who study closely the processes in this modern movement of expansion will readily grasp the essential factors in the less dramatic growth that had prepared the way. Expansion, in a sense, had fed and was now to feed upon expansion.

Each new advance, in business technique as in geographical discovery, opened up new possibilities to challenge the ingenuity of men. Explorers in search of solutions for old problems not infrequently discovered instead hitherto unsuspected opportunities. America itself affords the classic example. Made known by a man who set forth in quest of a new route to the East Indies, it was to provide no satisfactory stepping stone to the Orient, as many at first hoped, but instead a distinctly new and major field for Europe's developing imperialism. Here the way lay open especially for the development of that phase of modern imperialism we know as colonization. The essential services of supply for New World colonies created in Old World centers fresh and expanding fields of business activity. The commodities the colonists sent back in return not only enriched the life of European communities, but increased the opportunities for exchange among themselves, facilitated their payments on new frontiers of trade in other parts of the world, and altered at points the very habits of life. Perhaps the most suggestive example is that provided by the modern tobacco industry. Built upon a weed unknown to the Europeans prior to the discovery of the New World and based on a habit borrowed from the social and ritualistic usages of the American Indian, it served to promote some of the most important experiments in colonization, quickly became a staple of worldwide trade, a means to the employment of increasing numbers of people in mercantile and industrial establishments, and a bond of unity wherever men have occasion to exchange smokes. Of such things is the story of discovery and of Europe's expanding interest in America.

England and America

The economic origins of the United States, like its political traditions, trace back largely to a chronicle of English adventure.[1] It is appropriate at this point, therefore, to turn to England in search of a more exact estimate of the forces that shaped the settlement of America. Reliance upon private initiative and agencies was a distinguishing feature of English colonization. Nevertheless, men moved from the first in response to national needs, and through their efforts made England a party to the international contest that from the sixteenth through the eighteenth centuries marked the economic and political history of America. In the promotional efforts attending early overseas adventure nothing is more impressive than the constant changes rung on the theme of national interest. Many a man contributing to the support of experimental ventures overrode his business judgment in the desire to render a patriotic service. In this very service to the commonweal, however, lay an opportunity that appealed to the hard business sense of men. A successful venture strengthening the national position offered the surest promise of ultimate profit; and this assurance was reinforced by the very policies of the state. Private investment was often encouraged by the granting of royal charters guaranteeing a monopoly of the benefits accruing and offering, implicitly at least, such other aids as a tariff preference in the home market over all foreign competitors.

This union of individual and national interests arose from certain practical considerations of which was born an ideal of national self-sufficiency. England's commercial prosperity, and hence in large degree her domestic economy, depended upon the marketing of her great staple, woolen cloth.[2] In the latter half of the sixteenth century her established markets were beset with many uncertainties. The trouble arose in part because of increasing production of woolens on the continent, competition that could be met only through improved techniques of processing and dyeing. Another source of concern was the international tension, fed partly by the conflict between Protestantism and Catholicism, that repeatedly threatened or brought wartime disturbances of trade. These

---

[1] For the earlier chapters in this chronicle, outstanding studies are those of J. A. Williamson: *Maritime Enterprise* (Oxford: Clarendon Press, 1913); *Sir John Hawkins* (Oxford: Clarendon Press, 1927); and *The Age of Drake* (London: A. & C. Black, 1938).

[2] An especially valuable discussion of the relationship of the cloth trade to English expansion is Sir William Foster, *England's Quest of Eastern Trade* (London: A. & C. Black, 1933.)

risks also beset England's imports of sugar, silk, wine, and other commodities increasingly essential to a rising standard of living. Significant was England's dependence upon Spain as a major market and a hardly less important source of dye materials and vegetable oils required for the processing of cloth. Under Elizabeth, England had emerged as the foremost Protestant power, while Spain under Philip II became the leading Catholic champion. Their relations were marked by a growing tension that broke into war with the sailing of the Spanish Armada of 1588. As war approached, many Englishmen felt an increasing concern over the extent of their dependence upon the nation's arch-foe. National security clearly required the opening of new markets and the assurance of alternative sources of supply for essential materials not produced at home.

Overseas adventure offered an obvious solution, and such a plan of action was encouraged by a common disposition to attribute much of Spain's threatening power to her extensive possessions in America. Of the several proposals advanced, chief interest for us is found in those that directed attention to the possibilities of North America.[3] The way there from England was relatively short and, provided key positions were promptly fortified, promised to be free from foreign interference. The hope for a market was twofold. In the first place, a passage through or around North America might lead to Cathay (northern China), where by reason of the country's climate and reputed wealth a profitable sale of woolens could be expected. Moreover, the North American climate itself was favorable and the native inhabitants, through a judicious mixture of missionary and business enterprise, might learn to value English clothing—a hope that was not altogether misplaced. The Indian, it is true, proved slow to adopt English habits of dress, but an exchange of woolen blankets for furs and skins became so important throughout the colonies that the modern American has difficulty in dissociating the Indian and the blanket. As the history of this great trade indicates, and as contemporary students on the basis of observations made at Roanoke Island and other points estimated, the market was potential rather than real and depended upon some form of English settlement in America. The primitive state of the Indian's economy dictated a similar conclusion regarding the exploitation of natural resources; while the results of exploration by men like Frobisher, Gilbert, and Davis argued that whatever passage might exist, its discovery would require a closer search that might be better undertaken from some established base in America itself. Opinion, in fact, increasingly favored the hope of discovering a river on the Atlantic side of

---

[3] An unusually valuable collection of source materials is found in E. G. R. Taylor, *Writings and Correspondence of the Two Richard Hakluyts,* Vols. I and II. London: Hakluyt Society, 1935.

the continent that could be joined by means of a short overland portage to some other waterway having its outlet in the Pacific.[4] And this called, of course, for the kind of exploration, much of it overland, to which the Virginia Colonists were repeatedly to direct their attention in the hope of reaching the "South Seas." At the same time, Spain's sugar, tobacco, cattle, and ginger-producing plantations in the West Indies, together with Portugal's success with transplanted woad [5] in the Azores and wine in Madeira, had suggested an agricultural type of settlement for the supply of essential materials that England was forced to acquire by imports.

And so did basic geographical and ethnological considerations, together with the full range of England's needs, suggest that her hopes of the New World could be realized only through military and political occupation of the American continent, at any rate to the extent necessary for its control and the exploitation of its diverse opportunities. In the opinion of the two Richard Hakluyts, relatives and close consultants of Raleigh in his Roanoke Island ventures, such an occupation might with time make of North America a center of well-rounded agricultural, pastoral, industrial, and commercial activity, reinforcing England's economic independence and affording settlers every opportunity through a true exchange of goods to profit by England's peculiar needs.[6] Their plan set the following objectives, some immediate, others to be realized over a long term: (1) establishment of outposts for exploration and experimentation, a necessary preliminary to all other effort; (2) exploitation of fisheries and of natural dyes, medicinal herbs, mineral deposits, naval stores, and other readily collected products, especially as a means of meeting immediate and unavoidably heavy overhead costs; (3) location and development of the plantation type of settlements producing sugar, wine, silk, hides, olive oil, dyes, and other such staples; (4) further development of such extractive industries as the resources of America and the requirements of England dictated—shipbuilding and the repeated attempts at iron manufacture, for example; and (5) development of a native market, to be achieved first through a sale of beads and inexpensive trinkets that might well be manufactured in the Colony itself, and to be joined ultimately to the cloth trade through the civilizing influence of English settlement. It was not expected that all these opportunities were to be centered in any one place. Plans took account of the entire coastal region extending northward from Spain's defensive

---

[4] The hope came partly from a knowledge of the riverways of Russia, where English agents of the Muscovy Company had passed from the White Sea by way of the Dwina to within reach of the Volga, and then by it to the Caspian Sea and so to Persia.

[5] A plant serving as a major source of blue dye, a favorite color then as now.

[6] On the highly significant work of the Hakluyts, see G. B. Parks, *Richard Hakluyt and the English Voyages* (New York: American Geographical Society, 1928), and again E. G. R. Taylor's collection of their writings.

outpost in Florida, and envisioned a series of settlements effectively joined through control of the intervening navigation.

Problems of Finance and Organization

The program outlined by the Hakluyts was obviously a long-term one requiring heavy investment. Only the great merchants of England possessed the capital, experience, and equipment essential in so hazardous an undertaking. But the wealthier merchants, preferring instead the promise of a more immediate advantage through new trades with Russia, the Levant, and in time with the East Indies by way of the Cape of Good Hope, were slow to respond. No small part of the explanation for the unhappy results of initial attempts in America is found in this reluctance. As the latest student of Gilbert's ventures has emphasized, the most significant of Sir Humphrey's failures marked his attempt to secure the backing of a first-rate mercantile community.[7] He won, it is true, limited help from the second-rate outport of Southampton, but the great merchants of London, who alone, with the possible exception of Bristol merchants, had the necessary means, remained indifferent. And though little exact information exists regarding the financing of Raleigh's subsequent projects, it appears that he was little if any more successful.

There were early projects of American adventure, of course, that did enlist the support of mercantile interests. Examples of these are found in the great fishing fleets annually sent out from the western ports of England to exploit the rich fisheries of North America, in frequent expeditions for the plunder of Spanish trade and possessions, and in occasional voyages of discovery or other such speculative adventures. But the initiative and leadership in projects that were designed to effect a permanent occupation of the continent came largely from the landed classes. Indeed, as the names of outstanding figures from Gilbert and Raleigh to William Penn repeatedly testify, the leadership of this group remained a highly significant feature of the movement. The explanation is not difficult to find. A complex transition through which English society was passing produced pressures that bore with especial acuteness on all who lived by the land, and turned their thoughts increasingly to the well-nigh limitless expanse of fertile soil in America. Hard-pressed tenants and farm laborers glimpsed a vision of independence through the acquirement of their own land in the new world, while the landed aristocracy saw an opportunity to meet a rising standard of living through an extension of its feudal forms of proprietorship to America. It was to this latter interest that Gilbert most successfully appealed for support of those projects of 1582–1583 that are generally accepted as marking

7 D. B. Quinn, *Voyages and Colonising Enterprises of Sir Humphrey Gilbert*, Vol. I, pp. 1-104 (2 vols., London: Hakluyt Society, 1940), provides the best study of Gilbert's ventures. Among the documents included are important promotional tracts.

the genesis of American settlement. The agreements he entered into with several gentlemen, agreements embracing millions of acres and plans for a feudal type of jurisdiction, stamped the American venture at its very outset with the qualities of a gigantic speculation in land. And so it was long to remain, its principal impetus the hope of men to gain possession of some part of the land.

The land in itself, however, was of little practical use unless it could be joined through established channels of trade to the markets of Europe. Those who settle on the land must first give thought to ways and means of reaching a market, a necessity that is apparent in the tendency of settlement in America to cling to riverways affording ready access to markets as late as the very eve of the railway construction that in the nineteenth century "opened" new lands. Theoretically, it would have been possible to finance a purely agricultural experiment in America over the long term that would be required to prove the soil and produce marketable commodities in sufficient quantity to justify the regular dispatch of shipping from Europe. Actually, the resources available were altogether too limited, and in any case it seemed better business to rely upon other and more varied hopes. If settlement of the land could be combined with a prosperous trading venture, the farmer could feed the trader, acquiring a share in the return of his goods to the European market and enjoying meanwhile favorable freightage as a means of testing agricultural experiments that might themselves with time support a flourishing trade. Such was the reasoning that guided the earliest projectors of American settlement. Although trading and exploratory ventures were often sent to America independently of colonizing efforts, it is significant that early projects of settlement usually embraced the hope of finding a passage to Cathay, gave emphasis to other prospects for trade, and counted upon some tie-up with the fishing industry. In its simplest form, the hope was that the farmer might share in the returns from fish; in its grandest conception, men saw, with the discovery of a passage, unlimited opportunities for profitable settlement along a main artery of England's Oriental trade. So great was the need, and so emphatic the effort in promotional literature, to convince the great merchants of this full promise of America that modern students are easily misled as to the essential nature of a movement that was no more concerned with trade than with colonization except insofar as the one may have appeared to be on occasion on indispensable step toward achievement of the other.

A Joint-Stock Experiment in Virginia

It was not until after the Anglo-Spanish war, which to its end in 1604 naturally directed attention to projects offering more immediate aid, that the great merchants became seriously interested. In 1606 the first Virginia Charter was issued in behalf of two groups of gentlemen and merchants, one representative of interests centering around the western port of Plymouth, the other with headquarters in London and including among its leaders Sir Thomas Smith, governor of the recently established East India Company and the greatest merchant prince of his day. The charter authorized exploratory, trading, and colonizing activity along the American coast from Carolina to Maine, with the northern region assigned to Plymouth, and the southern to London—a division indicative of the influence of prospects for sugar, silk, wine, and other staples indigenous to southern climates in gaining the support of the London merchants. Two settlements were promptly undertaken in 1607, one at Sagadahoc in modern Maine, the other at Jamestown. The former was soon abandoned, but the latter lived on to become the first permanent English settlement.[8]

The difference is largely explained by the fact that the Jamestown experiment had behind it the resources of London. The initial effort in Virginia is properly regarded as an exploratory field expedition that actually achieved much of what it was intended to accomplish. Hopes of a passage, an occasional thought for gold, and a much stronger interest in rich copper mines reported by Raleigh's agents on their return home in 1586, all came to nought. But iron was discovered, valuable experience in dealing with the natives was gained, and exploration revealed a rich and fertile region traversed by the most marvelous system of inland waterways to be found on the Atlantic Coast. Here, indeed, was a promise for settlement and trade broad enough to stir men to great endeavor. It came in 1609. The London adventurers were reorganized and their membership enlarged under a second Virginia Charter. This and a third charter in 1612 created the usual organization of an English commercial company. Powers vested in a governor, council, and general assembly or court of the adventurers provided an administrative pattern for the government of the Colony that has left its mark on the structure of American state government even to the present day. The joint-stock device, whereby the contributions of many individuals were pooled as one large fund for investment under the direction of the company's officers, was used to provide one of the most impressive sums ever invested in any English maritime venture. Not only was the wealth of London enlisted, but heavy drafts had been

---

[8] The leading authority on economic as well as other phases of early American settlement is C. M. Andrews, *The Colonial Period of American History* (4 vols.). New Haven: Yale University Press, 1934-1938. A more recent study is W. F. Craven, *The Southern Colonies in the Seventeenth Century, 1607-1689*. Baton Rouge: Louisiana State University Press, 1949.

made on its tested business experience for the organization and management of the enterprise.[9]

The Virginia Company, however, was no ordinary commercial corporation. The landed gentry were largely and influentially represented in its membership, and like many other land-grant companies that were to follow it in American history, its purpose was colonization. More than 500 settlers immediately set sail for Virginia, and plans were laid for another thousand promptly to follow. Hope for an agricultural experiment with staples like wine, sugar, tobacco, and silk was especially strong, and as the history of a sister colony planted in Bermuda by the Virginia adventurers after 1612 clearly indicates, this hope tended increasingly to overshadow all others.[10] The plan of settlement was adjusted to the peculiar requirements of a task largely exploratory, experimental, and otherwise preparatory. In tackling the problems of frontier settlement, Americans thereafter were frequently to have occasion to resort to community enterprise, as in clearing new ground or in raising a house, and so went the decision now. It was agreed that for a seven-year term all would work together in a communal effort, with men assigned to such tasks as circumstances or special aptitude might suggest. At the end of the term the common rewards of their labors were to be proportionately divided. Through an interesting adaptation of the joint-stock principle, adventurers and planters were at the same time joined in a similar community of interest.

The joint-stock of 1609 was no mere capital fund, but rather a pooling of both capital and labor. The colonists were recruited under an agreement with the adventurers (its form undoubtedly influenced by the share-right practices under which crews were at times recruited for fishing, piratical, and trading voyages) to divide on a share-and-share-alike basis all returns from the joint investment. The personal adventure of the colonist was rated as equivalent to £12 10s., the value of one share of stock, with provision for a higher rating being made for those bearing a special responsibility or offering a specialized skill. Separate contracts for wages, charged against the joint-stock before division, were possible for those who did not care to go on adventure, as it was termed. That most of the colonists went on adventure, however, there can be little doubt. And there is no difficulty in reconstructing the hopes they followed. At the end of the specified term in 1616 large areas of the land would, with good fortune, have been cleared and made secure; the soil would have been tested and marketable crops proved; essential ex-

[9] Comprehensive in scope is W. R. Scott's *English, Scottish and Irish Joint-Stock Companies to 1720* (2 vols.). Cambridge: The University Press, 1910-1912.

[10] For discussion of the many experiments of the Virginia adventurers, see W. F. Craven, *Dissolution of the Virginia Company* (New York: Oxford University Press, 1932); and *Introduction to the History of Bermuda* (reprinted from *William and Mary Quarterly,* Vols. XVII-XVIII, 1937-1938).

plorations completed; extractive industries tried and some established; and a profitable trade with the natives organized. Then would come, as promised, a division of both the land and the capital returns accumulated to the credit of the joint-stock, with dividends assigned to each adventurer and colonist according to his shares. Possessed thus of an individual title to the land, the colonist would take his share of cattle from a common herd that had been shepherded together for a seven years' natural increase to offset the high cost of their shipment from England, put his land to such crops as had been proved under expert guidance, and draw upon his monetary dividend for the purchase of essential equipment. The company, still possessed of countless acres of undivided land for further colonization, might press such trades as circumstances directed, relying upon periodical joint-stock subscriptions for the purpose, and in the regular supply of the colony could look forward to an expanding business opportunity.

The results, it hardly needs saying, were extremely disappointing. So much ill fortune beset the company that by 1616 its resources were exhausted, and disillusionment threatened the very existence of the colony. Yet, as men soon recognized, the effort had actually met with a modest success. Some of the land had been won, and though other experiments had failed those with tobacco now gave assurance of at least one marketable staple that had the advantage of maturing for the market within one season. There was in this success alone enough to stir anew the hopes of men, and the promise that beckoned again was made more attractive by the chance that where one valued staple had taken root others might still be proved. By 1618 the great migration, as historians have described it, was under way—a migration that was to carry thousands into Virginia where before only hundreds had gone; that was to spread out over the British West Indies, and in its mounting force to effect the occupation of Maryland and New England.[11] From this point on few factors in our story bear greater import than a growing willingness of Englishmen to migrate to America. Their readiness to settle in a new land points not only to the familiar economic, religious, and political causes of unrest, but to the increasing promise of America itself. The Virginia Company, earliest beneficiary of this folk movement, never really recovered from the heavy weight of debt incurred in its first experiments. After a final attempt to prove at one stroke the Hakluyt program of diversified settlement, it went down in bankruptcy in 1624, and Virginia passed under the direct supervision of the crown as the first royal Colony.

Though a failure by business standards, the Virginia Company had nevertheless rendered a great service. In 1606 Englishmen knew the

11 A useful summary of the full story is found in A. P. Newton, "The Great Migration, 1618-1648," *Cambridge History of the British Empire*, Vol. I, 136-182.

Chesapeake only by report and probably not even that much of such neighboring regions as Delaware Bay; they had yet to test the alternative sailing routes across the Atlantic with reference to the actual problems of transporting men, women, children, livestock, seeds, and plants; and they depended chiefly upon the limited experience of Raleigh's people at Roanoke Island to guide them in their relations with the native Indians. To such preliminary and financially unprofitable tasks the Virginia Company had directed its energies, and all men who subsequently settled in America stood in its debt.

Land Policies and Immigration

The policies of the company's later years gave shape and form to the further development of the American experiment. Of chief importance after 1616 were those policies governing the distribution of its land. In accordance with an obligation under previous contracts to issue land dividends, and prompted by a lack of other assets, the company awarded a dividend of 100 acres per share to all those holding full rights in the joint-stock. A comparable grant was also offered to any who would now invest £12 10s., a move that virtually reduced the company to a real estate corporation dealing in undeveloped lands. In another move to provide revenue, an annual quitrent of 2s. per 100 acres was reserved by an act that marks the beginning of a quitrent system continued by the Crown and borrowed by other American proprietors as a source of revenue incidental to their overlordship of the land. To encourage a development of the land, the company promised an additional grant of 50 acres for every person settled in the colony. Thus might a man who had received an original grant of 100 acres double it by sending or bringing into the colony two men for its cultivation; or, to use another example, a man able to finance his own migration with a wife and three children might move his family to Virginia with the ultimate assurance of acquiring 250 acres of his own land. This was the famous headright system under which a man's claim to the land was figured in proportion to the number of laborers he provided for its development. The essential administrative principle involved, it will be seen, was a use of land reserves to underwrite immigration. And though Virginia's headright system was not exactly reproduced in all colonies, the principle in some form or other underlay the economic development of each and all.

By such policies increasing numbers of Englishmen of modest means and position were induced to settle in America. Selling or mortgaging their property at home, and on occasion drawing upon the generosity of relatives, they brought to the settlements both capital and labor, not to mention a very helpful contribution to the tone and quality of Colonial society. There is no way of estimating accurately their numbers, but in all colonies they constituted an important segment of the population.

These same policies opened up opportunities as well for those who had only their labor to offer. Thus was shape given at an early date to a system of indentured labor that was especially important to the Middle and Southern Colonies, and that survived even the growing competition of Negro slavery, itself encouraged at points by the master's privilege of claiming a headright for every African imported. The indentured servant, or redemptioner, as he was at times identified, migrated under a contract, written or merely understood, to work out the cost of his passage by several years' labor in the colony. The contract was usually with a shipmaster sailing for America, or with someone for whom he acted as agent, and it was understood that it would be sold on arrival. The farmer, or local merchants who found it profitable to deal in such labor contracts, paid in produce, and the exchange quickly developed into a main feature of the commercial transactions between England and America. The recruiting of servants at home became a large-scale business in itself, with agents extending their activity far inland from the seaport towns in which it first centered.[12] Indeed, an export of labor through this and other devices, including the contract labor scheme of the nineteenth-century industrialist, was long to remain the principal item in Europe's supply of the American market.

Though this early trade was obviously open to abuse, that part of the story may easily be overemphasized. Public authority on both sides of the Atlantic moved to regulate its operation. The institution borrowed heavily from the law and custom of English apprenticeship, and was used to provide the colonists with schoolmasters and other professional aids as well as farm hands. In fact, it is properly viewed as offering to thousands of young people whose outlook at home was limited by economic and social conditions an opportunity to serve an apprenticeship in American undertakings that might lead, and more often than not did lead, to a better life.

As the role of the recruiting agent forcefully indicates, the function of the promoter in the later period of settlement was no less important than in its earliest stages. Of especial value was his continued contribution to the opening of new areas of settlement; and even immigrants to older centers often required the assurance of participation in some organized group action to overcome their natural reluctance to take the hazard. The land policies of the Virginia Company, accordingly, had been framed principally with a view to the encouragement of co-operative efforts, and were closely joined to a scheme of settlement in well-knit town communities that would provide among other attractions the inestimable advantages of comradeship and company. To these con-

12 A valuable study of this trade is A. E. Smith, *Colonists in Bondage, White Servitude and Convict Labor in America, 1607-1776*. Chapel Hill: The University of North Carolina Press, 1947.

siderations were added other problems. It was commonly recognized that much agricultural experimentation remained to be done, since few Englishmen, despite their ambition to extend their landed estates into America, were willing to hazard large sums on the possible returns from tobacco alone. To share the cost and spread the risk of this experimental work appeared now as before a reasonable procedure. And since men were willing to risk only a modest individual investment, a question of how best to provide supervision of overseas labor arose as a serious administrative problem. It is not astonishing, therefore, that many of the first English proprietors of land in America sought its development through co-operative associations.

Joint-Stock Associations on a Smaller Scale

The Virginia adventurers after 1616, drawing heavily on their experience in Bermuda, pooled their land claims against the company to secure a common patent in evidence of title to one large acreage. For the development of such plantations, or "hundreds," as they were at times called, the joint proprietors subscribed to a common fund, met as occasion required in courts and committees, negotiated through designated officers with shipowners and prospective settlers, and drafted plans for a communal type of effort to be executed under the direction of such overseers, captains, or governors as might be designated for the command in America. These subsidiary agencies of colonization, in other words, represented reasonably faithful reproductions of the parent company. Each group was in large measure autonomous, and plans might thus vary, but fragmentary records indicate that the communal effort was to continue only for such a term, apparently seven years, as was required to accomplish those tasks of original settlement that had dictated the earlier community scheme of 1609. Trading truck sent out to Berkeley Hundred in Virginia shows a purpose to rely upon the financial aid of trade in meeting heavy costs of settlement. There is evidence, too, that contracts with settlers were often made on terms of adventure that included a share in the land upon its later division. In other instances, a system of half-share tenancy, an adaptation of the original share-and-share-alike principle, was borrowed from the custom of Bermuda and the usage of the company in Virginia in the development of plantations of its own for the benefit of the joint-stock and for the support of public charges. In either case, servants might be sent on simple terms of indenture without reference to the share rights of other and more responsible settlers, except insofar as the cost might become a common charge. The adventurers were free, of course, to divide the land as they saw fit, and it should be noted that under rules of the company the plantation would be by the very act of its occupation doubled in acreage. It would be increased, too, by the increment of headright claims for all persons settled thereon. The major effort of the Virginia adventurers after 1616 was thus broken down into a number of smaller projects patterned essentially after the original scheme of 1609.

Historically, the most interesting of these projects was that which brought the Pilgrim Fathers to America.[13] Having in 1608 found refuge in Holland from religious persecution at home, they became interested by 1617 in emigrating to America, and entered into negotiations with the Virginia Company. Because they had little to offer except their labor, they made a contract with a group of adventurers who held a patent from the company. The agreement reproduced all essential features of the 1609 joint-stock. The unit of investment for the adventurers was £10, and the personal adventure of the settler was rated at an equal figure. As was customary, the settler might invest in additional shares of the stock. A community of property, funds, and effort was to hold for a seven-year term. For reasons not too clear, the Pilgrims landed in New England instead of Virginia, but few other changes in plans resulted immediately. A patent obtained in 1621 from the newly established New England Council reproduced even the phraseology of the usual form of Virginia patent and left unchanged the existing arrangement between adventurers and Colonists. The experiment proved disappointing, however, especially to the adventurers. Accordingly, through negotiations of 1625–1626 the Pilgrims undertook to buy out the claims of their partners, and subsequently organized the trade of the Colony to provide funds for the purpose. Their ultimate success is a further reminder of the relationship of trade to colonization.

The Virginia plantations present a different story. Experiencing all the misfortunes, including epidemic sickness and Indian massacre, that beset the colony, they went down in the general bankruptcy of 1624. Their liquidation left little to bother the Colonists who survived to carry on their individual efforts, not even an absentee title to the land. Yet, brief as was their existence, they hold for the student more than passing interest. They were succeeded by somewhat similar joint-stock projects of adventure in American settlement; some of their instruments, like share-crop tenancy, took root in the plantation economy of America; and their history lends special emphasis to those basic problems of settlement that were so often to invite some form of community effort. Striking parallels in the early history of the Dutch patroonships in New York, private projects of settlement and trade backed by adventurers in and under patents from the Dutch West India Company, suggest that this phase of the Virginia experiment was shaped principally by the conditions governing the early settlement of America rather than by ideas peculiar to the London adventurers.

[13] The best discussion is Andrews, *Colonial Period,* Vol. I, pp. 249-299.

The Proprietary Pattern of Settlement

The later history of the patroonship shows an even closer relationship to the vast landed proprietorships that after the 1620's became a highly significant feature of English settlement.[14] As early as the time of Gilbert's ventures, gentlemen of the landed classes had been eager to acquire extensive grants with a view to their development under a feudal type of landlordism. The practical problems of getting people onto the land and into a position to produce rents had, however, forced a postponement of these hopes. A leading factor in their revival was the increasing number of Englishmen willing to venture both their lives and fortunes in America. Here, in brief, was an opportunity for a gentleman of wealth and position to assume the role of promoter and to direct some part of a growing body of emigrants to his own lands under a feudal scheme of settlement. His social and political position gave him a decided advantage in securing a title to the land, and there was nothing anomalous to the contemporary Englishman in proposals for a feudal type of settlement. Its forms of land tenure were the familiar ones. The lord proprietor's claim to jurisdiction over his tenants was no less familiar, and in practical terms meant an assumption by him of a primary responsibility for the establishment of law and public authority, absolute prerequisites to orderly settlement. Nor should it be forgotten that most Englishmen were by habit and experience more disposed to place their confidence in a gentleman than in any other leader.

The story has its beginning in the New England Council. This association of gentlemen secured in 1620 a charter to the New England area. Much in the organization and activity of the body reminds us of the forms of joint proprietorship then being tried in Virginia, but even more forcefully does the record look forward to the later phases of proprietary settlement. The council's ideas of colonial administration were feudal in character, and its most significant activity through a decade marked chiefly by the failure of its plans was the issuance of land patents. Some of these, notably the Mason and Gorges grant to New Hampshire and Maine, remained important to New England's history for several decades beyond the brief life of the council itself.

More pertinent to the discussion is Lord Baltimore's grant to Maryland. The recipient in 1632 of a royal charter granting 10,000,000 to 12,000,000 acres on upper Chesapeake Bay, he established his first settlers at St. Mary's in 1634. These and others who followed were recruited through a well-conceived promotional campaign that offered individual land grants in proportion to the investment to be made. This

[14] Especially useful is Andrews' introductory discussion of the proprieties, *Colonial Period,* Vol. II, pp. 199-240.

investment was measured by the number of persons equipped and settled by the grantee on the land. That the larger grantees, their acreages designated as manors, might be created manor lords with many of the traditional prerogatives and responsibilities of that dignity at home, should not becloud the far more significant point that Lord Baltimore's land policy was essentially little different from that in Virginia. He sought to use the land, a form of headright serving as an equitable unit of apportionment, to underwrite a settlement that would in turn enhance the over-all value of his holding. From quitrents, licensing fees for trading privileges, and other prerogatives incidental to his lordship of the land, together with the direct returns from certain proprietary manors cultivated by his own immediate tenants and servants, he hoped to recoup, with a benefit extending down through successive generations of his family, a very considerable investment made in the promotion of the Colony.

The same general hope inspired his equally famous successors—the Carolina proprietors in 1663; the Duke of York, proprietary lord of New York on its conquest in 1664; Lord John Berkeley and Sir George Carteret, joint proprietors of Jersey by grant from York; and after 1681 William Penn in Pennsylvania. It is unnecessary to recount here the history of each proprietary colony. The objective is not to relate the full chronicle of settlement, but rather to show a developing pattern of settlement that reveals the nature of those interests that inspired its promotion and the technical arrangements through which men sought the accomplishment of their several purposes in America. The list is in itself a sufficient indication of the extent to which a proprietary type of management dominated the later phases of the movement. Such additional grants as are represented by the Fairfax estate, which did not include the usual powers of government but covered a very large portion of the modern state of Virginia, emphasize the point even more strongly.

All of the great proprietors looked upon their extensive grants as private estates from which they expected not merely a revenue for public administration, but a personal income commensurate with the lord proprietor's position and responsibilities as well. They were no more indifferent than earlier promoters to opportunities for trade; but their principal asset was obviously a prior title to the land and their chief prospect of profit was in turning this asset to advantage through the promotion of settlement. All in some measure adopted feudal ideas of settlement, though none clung so stubbornly to an exact pattern of this sort as did the lords Baltimore. Feudalism, in fact, put out few roots in America, and such of its vestiges as survived proved to be more of legal than of economic significance. Proprietors were usually ready to turn the land to account as the occasion offered, and to deed it away on several terms of grant, lease, and even sale. Quitrents were usually, though not always, reserved. Sections of the land were often set aside as a proprietary reserve to be held for future use or disposal when development of surrounding areas had brought an increase in its value. The essential interest, in short, was a land-office business, and much of it was of a speculative nature.

One of the promotional devices was to enlist the aid of subsidiary promoters, who assumed a role in the development of a single province not unlike that played by the greater proprietors in the larger field of English settlement. Generous grants to individual settlers made in anticipation of, and as an inducement to, a subsequent development, served, too, the useful political purpose of allying the more energetic and wealthy members of the community with the proprietary interest. One of the better examples is found in the manorial grants made in New York that had the ultimate effect of incorporating leading Dutch families in a landed aristocracy of great importance to the social, economic, and political life of the Colony. Some of these grants merely confirmed, as with the vast patroonship of the Van Rensselaer family, titles tracing originally from grants by the Dutch West India Company. Such proprietary assignments followed a policy essentially no different from that of the home government in England, which offered extensive grants to individuals or corporate groups as an inducement to undertake their development. The same practice was often followed in Colonies other than the proprietary ones, frequently at the instance of a colonial legislature, for the promotion of frontier settlement. That many grantees took their promotional duties none too seriously, and used them merely as an excuse for speculative ventures, illustrates how prodigal men can be with the land where there is so much land. The widespread influence of these practices forces upon us the conclusion, too, that for the average settler there could not have been as much "free land" as popular tradition would have us believe.

When, after the line of settlement had finally reached the Appalachians, men looked across them upon the fertile region of the Ohio, they followed but the established customs of American settlement in seeking extensive grants as individual adventurers or for the several Ohio and Mississippi companies that vied with one another in a bewildering confusion through the era of the American Revolution. Nor did this race for awards of lands by any means mark the end of the land-grant system. Whatever significance others may attach to the great land grants with which railway construction and colonization in the West were subsidized in the nineteenth century, they speak to the student of colonial history primarily of a very old and a very American way of getting on with the country's development.

Corporate Settlements in New England

No less important to later chapters of our history is the Puritan settlement of New England. The Pilgrim community at Plymouth was but one of several projects undertaken in the 1620's under patents from the New England Council. The more significant of them focus attention once more on the relation contemporaries saw between the fishing industry and possibilities for settlement. The waters of the North Atlantic had early attracted the fishermen of Europe. And though some of them on occasion remained in America for a winter or more, thus contributing in advance of organized colonization to a growing European population of fishermen and traders, they normally came out and returned with the fishing fleets each year. Some observers felt that it would be more economical to settle the fishermen in America and center their activities here except for the final marketing. With this proposal was tied up the hope of building a colony upon the diverse opportunities for profit in supplying and equipping the fishing fleets. It was expected that salted codfish would thus serve the Colony as an exportable staple guaranteeing, like the tobacco of Virginia or the wool of later Australia, an essential supply of European goods.

The full co-operation of the fishing interests would have given such a project more than adequate financial backing. But the great fishing interests, like the great fur-trading and cattle-raising interests of another day, tended to oppose rather than favor colonization. Not only were its leaders disinclined to undertake the expensive work of settlement such a transfer would have involved, but the fishing ports of western England that annually profited by outfitting the fleets and marketing their catch naturally could see in the idea no advantage for themselves. Moreover, they viewed with apprehension any move to establish an authority in America that might impose restrictions or exactions of a sort already suggested by plans of the New England Council on essential privileges of the shore for drying, salting, and repairing operations. It is to be noted that in Newfoundland, where these interests were able to maintain control, a normal development of the colony was retarded until well into the nineteenth century. As a result of this attitude early colonizing efforts in New England were small in scale. The most important of them, representing a joint-stock association of Dorchester, moved by way of several disappointments to the establishment of the famous old town of Salem in 1626, but its people were a mere handful and the future of New England's settlement still appeared to lie along a way of slow and painful progress like that of the struggling Pilgrims at Plymouth.[15] But just at this point the spiritual force of Puritanism

[15] Especially valuable is Frances Rose-Troup, *The Massachusetts Bay Company and Its Predecessors.* New York: The Grafton Press, 1930.

endowed the New England experiment with resources and energies unmatched in the story of English colonization.

The Puritans, increasingly perturbed over the trend of ecclesiastical policy at home and alarmed over the future of a parliamentary cause with which their security as a religious minority was closely united, made plans in 1628 for a settlement in America. Economic disadvantages sharpened the discontent of a religious group, and the search for a solution to the problem was greatly influenced by the wide experience of prominent Puritans in the commercial life of the nation. Puritanism was strong among the middle classes of England's commercial centers and over the eastern counties that depended heavily upon a woolen industry still faced with difficulties. As the writings of John Winthrop and other sources indicate, the continuing problems of landowners in England helped to win the support of gentlemen of means, background, and experience in public affairs. There can be no question, however, that the inspiration of the movement was essentially religious, and its primary purpose to establish in America the true church as the Puritan understood it. His thought was not merely of his own salvation, but of a purpose to found in the New World wilderness a City of God that might ultimately by its demonstration of the true way serve even to redeem England from a false leadership. The Colony thus represents the earliest of many projects of settlement, great and small, extending through the Quakers of Pennsylvania to the Mormons of Utah, in which a religious purpose gave strength and shape to an economic effort no less than to a political and social order.

It is this religious purpose that explains the unusual advantages of leadership enjoyed by the Puritan Colonies.[16] Though it has become a popular fallacy to regard them as impractical "Biblical commonwealths," the plain fact is that no other Colonies in the first years of settlement equaled them in the background, education, and hard-headed experience of their leaders. The appeal of a great religious undertaking attracted, too, an unusually large number of men of substantial means. As the flow of migration to New England increased—a migration estimated at no less than 20,000 persons in the years before the outbreak of the English civil wars in 1642 brought a revival of Puritan hopes at home—there passed each year through Boston more than the normal complement of men having, in addition to a will to settle, the capital reserves to serve the purpose. The economic life of New England for a time fed principally upon an annually renewed investment of capital and labor. Just as the settlement of Maryland extended the range of economic opportunity for the neighboring Colonists of Virginia, so did the unbroken stream of immigration into New England provide an expanding market

[16] A very readable and suggestive study is S. E. Morison's *Builders of the Bay Colony*. Boston and New York: Houghton Mifflin Company, 1930.

for agricultural produce and the output of such other activity as there had been time to organize for the supply of newly arriving Colonists. Indeed, no other chapter of our story reveals so clearly the importance to the accomplishment of the original purposes of settlement of a continuing investment of capital and labor. A lag in this essential provision, occasioned by disappointment and doubt following promptly upon an original enthusiasm, often meant the difference between success and failure.

When the slackening of this migration threatened depression after 1642, the Colonists were sufficiently well established, and possessed among themselves enough skill and business experience, to take advantage of those commercial and industrial opportunities on which the prosperity of the region was thereafter to rest. The means were at hand for an increasingly successful experiment with a locally based fishing industry that stimulated allied industrial efforts like shipbuilding, and so provided an expanding market for agricultural produce. A further outlet was found in the supply of meat and grain to the West Indian plantations, where from about 1640 more and more land was put to sugar at the expense of food crops. The New England Colonies had come closer than any other to realization of that combination of interrelated agricultural, industrial, and commercial endeavor that had inspired English hopes for settlement since the days of the Hakluyts. And as the record repeatedly suggests, the earliest promoters of the American venture had been correct in their estimate of the commercial advantages that might proceed from settlement, but had overestimated the aid to be expected from trade in the initial stages of settlement.

When the Puritans took charge of the Massachusetts Bay Company, an organization fundamentally no different from the Virginia Company except for the smaller scale of its ventures as heir to the Dorchester project at Salem, they took also the extraordinary step of carrying the company and its charter with them to New England. Accordingly, there was left in England no superior promotional organization holding a prior claim to the land and the benefits of its settlement. The leading investors in Puritan colonization, in fact, migrated with their capital to New England, and by this act transferred the chief claims against the enterprise to the Colony itself. Necessary promotional work in England was effected through associations that sprang principally from a community of religious interest and purpose. An integral part of many such associations was the congregation, and the same unique collaboration of ministerial and lay leaders that so distinguished the political and religious life of the Puritan Colonies. It was not uncommon for a large part of a congregation by agreement among its members to migrate and settle in America under the leadership of its minister and elders. It is interesting to note that Edward Gibbon Wakefield, leading figure in the much later colonization of Australia and New Zealand, found in the organization and promotion of the Puritan settlements virtually the only model in the entire earlier story of English colonization that was in his judgment worth copying.[17] In New Zealand he even relied upon a similar community of religious interest as the foundation for two of his most interesting experiments. He viewed with particular approval, also, the diverse benefits of New England's town or village type of settlement.

The early projectors of English settlement had never had any other thought than that their people would settle in relatively compact communities, permitting and perpetuating many advantages for the commercial, religious, and cultural life of the Colony. It was the familiar pattern of life at home, and considerations of security from Indian attack alone were enough to recommend such procedure. Indeed, many of the communal features of earlier experiments, none of which bears any relation whatsoever to modern communism, had been shaped by a desire to assure the fullest enjoyment of the rewards of individual endeavor by establishing first the manifold opportunities and services of community life. Elsewhere, however, misfortune, the failure of ill-conceived plans of settlement, loosely administered land policies encouraging speculative holdings, the quickly demonstrated superiority of European weapons and military organization over the native, the imperious demands upon the soil of a crop like tobacco, or such influences as the easy access to marketing facilities provided by the Chesapeake waterways, had encouraged a dispersal of settlement that promptly made of the isolated farmhouse a familiar feature of the American scene. In New England the cohesive forces of community life proved stronger. The congregation was often older than the town in which it settled. Much more frequently did men migrate to America, and from Massachusetts to Connecticut, as members of a group bound together by a compact among themselves that presents subtle and significant differences from the type of individual contract commonly made with some promoter for settlement in the other areas. The New England Colonists, moreover, had well conceived and faithfully administered a plan of town settlement that fortunately proved well adapted to the economic opportunities of their geographic location.

In a very real sense the community under this plan was first organized and then settled. Since the charter had been brought to Massachusetts, the control of land grants rested entirely in the hands of local authorities. Grants were issued to groups organized for settlement in townships. In

[17] Students of American settlement will find much of interest and value in the story of later English settlement in these and other Dominions. Some of the best accounts, and for the most part by Dominion scholars, are found in the *Cambridge History of the British Empire*.

keeping with the usages of Puritan migration, the leaders of the projected settlement assumed a primary responsibility in negotiating the necessary arrangement with the Colony's authorities, and it was only natural that for the sake of legal clarity the grant should be issued in the names of these men, who as the "proprietors" of the town were charged with superintending the actual work of settlement. Under the direction of this committee, allotments of land were made to the several members of the community. Grants were based on the size of a man's family, his social station, the extent of his investment in the project, and other considerations, including the general rules of the Colony. Voluntary joint-stock associations frequently proved here, as they had in Virginia, a convenient instrument of group settlement, and were especially common in Connecticut. Where such joint-stock agreements existed, they governed in great degree the division of the land. The transplanted Massachusetts Bay Company served primarily as the framework of a commonwealth, and lacked the usual profit-seeking motives of other such corporations. Elsewhere in New England, settlement was commonly undertaken without a royal charter and often in defiance of prior chartered rights. Land policies, therefore, were shaped principally by the desires of the settlers themselves, and men usually held their land free of quitrents and other encumbrances of the sort. Aside from this point, however, a more orderly and equitable distribution of the land rather than an underlying difference in principle distinguishes New England's settlement from those of other sections.

Wherever settlers from New England migrated thereafter, they were inclined to transplant the town organization so characteristic of their Puritan background. In Puritan procedure, too, is found the pattern of the attempt to write into the Northwest Ordinances of the 1780's principles of orderly and progressive settlement in the West. That these very ordinances were enacted partly because of speculative hopes rooted in New England itself need occasion no astonishment. Though the earliest town proprietors administered their offices with a real sense of community responsibility, the form of organization was easily corrupted in later days to serve the familiar purposes of speculation in frontier lands. Associates might procure a town grant on the legal assumption that they would promote its settlement; but, as with grantees in other Colonies, a loose administration did not demand it.

Promotional Policies

So much of America's land fell into the hands of speculators that it is easy to accept the mistaken assumption that the promoter's role throughout was essentially parasitical. In closing, therefore the very real promotional work they accomplished and its great importance to American settlement should be recalled. In colonization as in other undertakings, someone must take the initiative and assume the responsibilities of leadership. No surer discipline in the exercise of such responsibilities has been found than to join them with a hope for personal gain. On this principle rested the administrative arrangements for American settlement, and, whatever faults of human nature may have appeared, a magnificent achievement stands too in the record. Though that record is written in a language that today seems quaint, the student of history finds there principally a chronicle of business acumen and skill. The Elizabethan adventurers, returning from America with an Indian or two to parade in the market place and on Sunday to church, could teach our modern advertising expert more than one lesson in the stimulation of popular interest and the presentation of a project in the most favorable light. Broadsides, ballads, and skillfully composed tracts were distributed by printers employed by the promoters for the purpose. The aid of playwrights was enlisted, and Raleigh in 1585 even sent a first-class artist to Roanoke Island to paint the life and scenes of "Virginia."[18]

By such methods countless numbers of persons were made aware of a new opportunity and a new hope. The terms of settlement offered were necessarily favorable—social, religious, and political barriers to advancement in the old world were repeatedly ignored—and in this necessity is found a root cause of that political and religious liberalism that was to become so characteristically American. Much of the story is summed up in the career of William Penn. A great advocate of political and religious freedom, he is perhaps even more significant as a promoter possessed of consummate skill. He was the first to extend a well-organized promotional campaign to the continent of Europe to enlist the aid of thousands of persons of non-British stock in the English settlement of America. And his effective joining of political and religious guarantees with the promise of economic opportunity represents, at one and the same time, the perfection of a promotional technique and the enunciation of a public policy no less important to our economic than to our political development.

Selected References

Andrews, C. M., *The Colonial Period of America* (4 vols.). New Haven: Yale University Press, 1934-1938.

Beer, G. L., *Origins of the British Colonial System*. New York: The Macmillan Company, 1908.

Bond, B. W., *The Quit-Rent System in the American Colonies*. New Haven: Yale University Press, 1919.

Brebner, J. B., *Explorers of North America*. London: A. & C. Black, Ltd., 1933.

[18] John White, possibly the same John White who served as governor of the "lost colony" of 1587.

Craven, W. F., *Dissolution of the Virginia Company*. New York: Oxford University Press, 1932.

———, *The Southern Colonies in the Seventeenth Century, 1607-1689*. Baton Rouge: Louisiana State University Press, 1949.

Foster, Sir William, *England's Quest of Eastern Trade*. London: A. & C. Black, Ltd., 1933.

Hull, William I., *William Penn and the Dutch Quaker Migration*. Swarthmore, Pa.: Swarthmore College Press, 1935.

———, *William Penn: A Topical Biography*. London and New York: Oxford University Press, 1937.

Johnson, E. A. J., *American Economic Thought in the Seventeenth Century*. London: P. S. King & Son, 1932.

Matthews, Lois K., *The Expansion of New England*. Boston: Houghton Mifflin Company, 1909.

Morison, S. E., *Builders of the Bay Colony*. Boston: Houghton Mifflin Company, 1930.

Osgood, H. L., *The American Colonies in the Seventeenth Century* (3 vols.). New York: The Macmillan Company, 1904-1907.

Parks, G. B., *Richard Hakluyt and the English Voyages*. New York: American Geographical Society, 1928.

Rose-Troup, Frances, *The Massachusetts Bay Company and Its Predecessors*. New York: The Grafton Press, Inc., 1930.

Smith, A. E., *Colonists in Bondage, White Servitude and Convict Labor in America, 1607-1776*. Chapel Hill: The University of North Carolina Press, 1947.

Weeden, William B., *Economic and Social History of New England* (2 vols.). Boston: Houghton Mifflin Company, 1890.

Wertenbaker, T. J., *The First Americans*. New York: The Macmillan Company, 1927.

———, *The Planters of Colonial Virginia*. Princeton: Princeton University Press, 1922.

Williamson, J. A., *Maritime Enterprise, 1485-1558*. Oxford: Clarendon Press, 1913.

———, *Sir John Hawkins, The Time and the Man*. Oxford: Clarendon Press, 1927.

———, *The Age of Drake*. London: A. & C. Black, Ltd., 1938.

3 · COLONIAL COMMERCE AND COMMERCIAL REGULATION

In the old days, it was the customs ledger, rather than the map, that determined the desirability of a colony. The time was far distant when whole deserts or vast stretches of wilderness would be annexed simply to bolster national pride by map-coloring. The choicest colonial possessions were often mere dots upon the map; but as long as they furnished their mother country with exotic goods that she could not produce at home and in turn consumed her exports, they were bones of contention in war and rich sources of profit in peace. For that reason England, at the close of her second naval war with Holland in 1667, almost took a tiny spice island instead of New York and New Jersey. That was also why, a century later, after the Seven Years' War with France, she debated long over the relative value of the little sugar island of Guadeloupe as compared with the whole of Canada.

The potential offerings of America were one of England's chief reasons for planting colonies across the Atlantic. Although these might not match the rich spice trade that the Portuguese had found in the East or the silver flood that poured into Spain from her mines in Mexico and Peru, her hopes ran high of obtaining other non-European products to render herself commercially independent of her rivals and to give her a surplus for sale abroad, to the enrichment of the nation. The glowing prospectuses of Virginia contained long lists of such economic dreams, while even the Puritans who came to more northern homes "for the good of their souls" anticipated profits from the sale of their Colonial products.

Dutch Commerce and Empire

During the half-century from 1600 to 1650, when England was establishing the foundations of her American empire, she was thoroughly overshadowed on the seas by Holland, a nation in her heydey as a maritime power. Those years of Dutch ascendancy must be taken into account, because in several ways they influenced deeply the growth of England's colonization. Holland and England had fought together to break Spain's monopoly of overseas activity; but once the Armada was shattered, Holland got off to a much quicker start. Not only did she crowd the English out of the spice islands, but all over the known world the Dutch were soon trading all things with all people. On the whole, it was by energetic and intelligent business methods rather than by coercion and regulation that the Dutch grew rich. Other nations traded with them, not because they had to, but because the Hollanders would generally sell goods or carry them for fully a third less than could their own countrymen.

Amsterdam quickly rose to first place among seaports by developing the entrepôt game: that is, concentrating many routes of commerce at one port, so that the offerings of every land passed briefly over its docks and through its warehouses, to the great profit of its enterprising merchants, who naturally collected revenues from such handling. This device was ever the surest road to wealth for a maritime community. Furs and lumber from the Baltic, currants and fruit from the Levant, wines and silks from France, woolens from England, tobacco from Virginia, and the products of the German interior all paid toll to the Dutch in the form of commissions, insurance, freight, and the numerous other levies of commerce. Even when such wares did not actually reach Amsterdam, the chances were that they would be carried by the ubiquitous ships of the Dutch merchant marine. Nor was this simply selfish exploitation on the part of the Dutch: they gave service and helped others to profit in the process. With an uncanny nose for scenting new opportunities for profit, they showed the English settlers of Barbados how to gain wealth by introducing sugar from Brazil, and taught other Englishmen in Virginia an easier way to grow tobacco by selling them their first Negro slaves, while for themselves they transplanted coffee from Mocha to their own plantations in Java.

In actually settling beyond the seas, they lagged behind the English during that half century. The spice islands were colonies of exploitation, where a handful of whites dominated large numbers of natives; they differed from colonies of settlement, with their transplanted European population and society, such as England established along the American Seaboard. Even in America, the Dutch settlements at New Amsterdam, Curaçao, Surinam, and the like were but sparsely settled trading posts from which they could exploit the neighboring colonies of other powers. Holland, of course, was a small country, and there were, besides, too many good opportunities at home for many Dutchmen to emulate the wholesale overseas migration of the English.

England chafed at a situation that allowed the profits of her own trade and the trade of her new Colonies to go across the North Sea to enrich the merchants of Amsterdam. For the time, however, she was too much distracted internally by political and religious disputes and too greatly outmatched at sea by the powerful Dutch navy to be able to hold her own in straight commercial competition, and could merely hope for a future day when London might replace Amsterdam as the world's entrepôt and when the red ensign of the English merchant marine might lure away the lion's share of cargoes from Dutch bottoms. By the middle of the century, with internal opposition crushed and with a good navy developed at last, England was ready to challenge Dutch maritime supremacy. Her method would not be underbidding for cargoes and freights, but government regulation to restrict foreign competition; and she was prepared to back her program with armed force if necessary.

England's Navigation Acts

It was in such circumstances that Parliament in 1651 passed the celebrated Navigation Act, designed to liberate England's own trade, at least, from the Dutch stranglehold. Earlier centuries had seen similar parliamentary legislation, but it had not come to much. Now England was ready to enforce a definite commercial system based on the general principles of government regulation to promote the nation's economic well-being. England would not thoroughly discard this system until two centuries later, when she would be in a position to dispense with regulation and embrace a policy of *laissez-faire* or free trade. Like much else in English government and law, the Navigation Laws were subject to constant modification to meet specific situations; by the time that they were finally repealed in 1849, Parliament had passed some 340 other laws modifying the policy in detail. The most important of those changes came in 1660 and 1663; by that time the broad framework had been worked out by bringing the Colonies into the picture and defining their role in England's trade.[1]

As far as the Colonies were concerned, three basic principles in the Navigation Acts limited their freedom of action. The first involved shipping. All trade to England from America, Asia, and Africa had to be carried in English (or Colonial) ships with crews at least three-fourths Englishmen (or Colonists). That barred from Colonial ports all foreign vessels, particularly those of the ever-present Dutch, who had been taking a heavy share of those lucrative long hauls.

Second, all Colonial imports, except wine and salt from southern Europe, had to come from England. One of the chief uses of colonies was conceived to be their function as an outlet for a mother country's manufactures; England, like most of the other colonizing powers, was reserving that market for herself by this regulation. If any products of other European nations were to reach the Colonies, they must at least come by way of England to swell the profits of the new London entrepôt.

1 The Navigation Acts were fairly anonymous measures—not the work of Cromwell or any other person, but rather the combined work of numerous London merchants and officials.

Finally, the acts enumerated or listed certain Colonial products that could be shipped only to England. These were, for the most part, commodities that could not be produced in England itself and would, therefore, help to round out a self-sufficient empire that would depend as little as possible upon outsiders. Official opinion called for a favorable balance of trade, with an excess of exports over imports; consequently, the role of colonies, especially of those with a climate different from the homeland, was obvious in such a system of "sell more than you buy in foreign trade." All sugar, all tobacco, all indigo, and, as years passed, all of various other American products that were added to the "enumerated" list were allowed to be shipped only to England. If, as generally happened, a colony produced more than England herself could consume, the mother country could make a tidy entrepôt profit by re-exporting the surplus to European countries that were not blessed with a supply of their own. The Colonists, however, were denied the extra profits, which would have been theirs had they been permitted to ship their products directly to European ports where prices were higher than in England. On the other hand, many Colonial products, such as flour and fish, which would compete with England's own products and which she did not need, might be shipped anywhere, in order that the Colonists would be able to buy English wares in return.

Naturally, the interests of the Colonists were subordinated to those of England in such an arrangement. Had the Americans been free to buy and sell wherever they pleased around the world, they could certainly have made more money. There were, however, certain compensations that have been too often overlooked in the general American condemnation of the system. The Colonists and their ships were granted the free run of the empire, virtually on a par with the English themselves—a privilege so valuable that Scotland voluntarily gave up its separate government in 1707 in order to secure it. And a look at the story of American commerce in the dreary decade following the Revolution shows the former Colonists appreciating, to their sorrow, what it meant to have to look at the British Empire from the cold outside.[2]

The Navigation Acts fell unevenly upon the Colonists as far as restrictions and privileges were concerned. The Southern Colonies, which, like the West Indian colonies, were regarded as the most desirable in English eyes, had more legitimate cause for grievance than did the Middle and Northern Colonies. Products of the latter appeared less frequently upon the "enumerated" list, and those Colonies were, therefore, freer to export to regions outside England, and they took full advantage of the shipping opportunities. Moreover, while the latter purchased from England almost exactly as much as the Southerners, they sent only a quarter as much to England in return. The balance of

[2] See Chapter 12.

the Northern cargoes came from their bartering of cargoes in other ports. This is evident from the following brief summary of what the customs ledgers had to tell of the trade with England herself:

COMMERCE OF AMERICAN CONTINENTAL COLONIES WITH ENGLAND *

(Annual Averages, in Thousands of Pounds Sterling)

Colony	Exports to England			Imports from England		
	1701–1710	1731–1740	1761–1770	1701–1710	1731–1740	1761–1770
New England	37	64	113	86	197	358
New York	10	16	62	28	92	349
Pennsylvania	12	14	35	9	52	295
Maryland-Virginia	205	394	468	128	207	491
Carolinas	14	177	330	22	94	262
Georgia	..	..	36	..	3	40

* Compiled from D. Macpherson, *Annals of Commerce, passim;* American figures tabulated in J. S. Homans, *Historical and Statistical Account of the Foreign Commerce of the United States* (1857), pp. 6-7.

The relative importance of the continental or mainland Colonies (they did not number 13 until 1733) in relation to British trade as a whole is shown in the second table, which indicates that, although constantly overshadowed by the British West Indies, their commerce was increasing at a faster rate than was any other part of British trade, just as England's trade with the empire (including Ireland at that time) was overtaking her commerce with the foreign nations of Europe:

ENGLISH COMBINED IMPORTS AND EXPORTS

(Annual Averages, in Thousands of Pounds Sterling)

Area	1701-1710	1731-1740	1761-1770
American continental	556	1,313	2,843
British West Indies	942	1,781	3,406
India	582	1,179	2,516
Ireland	579	1,045	2,850
Total Empire	2,802	5,751	12,651
Total Europe	7,673	10,555	11,740
Grand Total	11,069	18,919	25,930

From the English standpoint, none of the continental colonies could compare with the Caribbean sugar islands—Jamaica, Barbados, Antigua, St. Kitts, and others. Those islands concentrated upon a single activity, the raising of cane from which came sugar with its by-products of rum and molasses. Furnishing England with her most important "enumerated article," sugar, they were able in return to purchase large quantities of English offerings. On the eve of the Revolution, the commerce of Jamaica alone totaled more than that of all the continental colonies combined. This direct trade is not of immediate concern here, but the sugar islands, as will be seen, helped to fit into the picture of imperial self-sufficiency through their heavy purchases from the Middle and Northern Colonies.

The Southern Colonies

On the mainland, the closest counterpart to the islands, from the standpoint of imperial desirability, was the Chesapeake region with its tobacco. The initial shipment of that "noxious weed" made by John Rolfe from Jamestown in 1614 was the beginning of America's most important Colonial offering. At first, the Dutch carried off a considerable part of the supply, but England was quick to "enumerate" it, and thus she forced all tobacco to London, Bristol, or some other English port. The English, to be sure, could not smoke all that Virginia and Maryland produced. In 1773-1775, their annual tobacco imports averaged 99,000,000 pounds and their re-exports 83,000,000 pounds, supplying a heavy entrepôt profit as a result of the monopoly.[3] Tobacco could be raised in southern England, but that was discouraged by the government, which wanted the customs duties on the American product.

The Colonial planter was generally content with what he made in raising the crop; the further profits of distribution he left to others. He ordinarily consigned his tobacco to some London merchant and ordered whatever imports he wanted in return. Factors or commission agents, generally Scots, resided in the Colonies to handle the business for the English merchants. Frequently, the planter's purchases outweighed his sales, so that his account was in arrears, but heavy interest charges made even his debt profitable to the merchant, and only in extreme cases would a local Scot foreclose. The same situation was repeated with the cotton planters in the early nineteenth century, when New York houses, with Connecticut Yankees resident in the South as factors, carried on much the same sort of business, making such heavy profits in interest, commission charges, freight, insurance, and other tolls that it was claimed that they got 40 cents of every dollar the planter received for his cotton. Such a state of affairs, comparable to the condition of the English wool trade in the early Middle Ages, could be called a passive commercial economy in contrast to the active economy practiced in New England.

Another unique feature of the Chesapeake trade was the absence of commercial centralization such as existed in the busy ports to the northward. Norfolk carried on a modest amount of business and was the

[3] *Massachusetts Historical Society Proceedings,* Vol. 44, p. 369.

chief habitat of the Scottish factors, but much of the trading took place locally throughout the region. A ship or brig, generally English but sometimes from New England, would poke its way up the James, York, Rappahannock, Potomac, or some other arm of the sea to a little plantation wharf, unload the desired imports, and take on the big tobacco hogsheads. It was not until the Revolution that Baltimore, at the upper end of the bay, began to gather that loose trade into its hands and to develop the flour trade, which was gradually overtaking tobacco in importance.

Further to the southward, Charleston was doing a better job in concentrating the trade of the region in a single port. Established long after the Chesapeake trade was well under way, it took a while to gain momentum; but by the middle of the eighteenth century, Charleston was doing a flourishing business. It felt the impact of "enumeration" from the outset, for indigo, valuable for blue dyes, was on the original list, while rice, which was successfully transplanted to the adjacent swamp land, was also "enumerated" for a considerable period. The third offering of South Carolina, deerskins obtained in trade with the Indians, escaped such restrictions until the end. North Carolina, cut off from the open sea by the long sand spit culminating in Cape Hatteras, and approachable only by a few dangerous inlets, lagged far behind its proud neighbors to the north and south. Its only important export consisted of naval stores (whence the nickname "Tarheels"), and these too were added to the "enumerated" list early in the eighteenth century. Georgia, the last of the Thirteen Colonies to be established, had developed only a very modest trade by the time of the Revolution, with Savannah serving as a small-scale counterpart of Charleston. It should be remembered that the cotton "enumerated" by the English came from the Caribbean at that time—in fact, it was not produced by any Southern states until after the Revolution.

While the South was caught by "enumeration" at almost every turn, and thus restricted in its choice of markets, it was able to make money because England wanted what it had. Under such conditions, it was possible to develop a shuttle trade. A vessel might profitably spend all its time sailing back and forth between London and the Chesapeake or between Bristol and Charleston because of the availability of cargoes at each end of the route that could be sold at the other.

"Triangles"

Farther northward, the situation was different. The Middle and New England Colonists also wanted English textiles, hardware, and other manufactures, but England had small use for what they could send in exchange. Consequently they had to use their ingenuity to find other markets for the nonenumerated produce for enough money to enable them to get what they wanted from England. As a result, instead of a simple shuttle trade, the vessels from those colonies prowled around on all sorts of mongrel voyages, trading and retrading until they eventually got what they desired. Out of this practice of following lines of barter came several triangular patterns, among others too complex for any such geometrical description. Each region had its own particular staple products—flour from the Middle Colonies; livestock from Connecticut; fish, lumber, and ships from eastern New England. With such products as a start, those mariners ranged far and wide until they came back with legal ladings from England, together perhaps with illicit cargoes from no one knew where—the customs officials discreetly forebore to inquire too closely.

The principal outlet for these products of the Northern Colonies was found in the English sugar islands in the West Indies. The concentration of those islands upon sugar made them a good place in which to exchange such goods. Jamaica had—in addition to sugar—coffee, pimento (pepper), and other semitropical commodities; she also carried on enough irregular trade with the Spanish colonies to provide a supply of silver dollars. Luckily for the Yankee traders, the planters found it more profitable to buy their flour, fish, and lumber from the "continent" than to spend the time of their slaves in producing such necessities themselves. Out of that situation grew the sugar triangle, which became one of the mainstays of Colonial commerce. This triangle involved three-cornered reciprocal support within the empire, with the mainland colonies, the sugar islands, and the mother country each offering something of value and each receiving something in return. The mainland colonies found a market for products that England herself did not want; the islands were free to concentrate upon raising cane; and England could receive payment for her manufactures, which otherwise the Americans might not have been able to purchase. The triangular trade did not assume a single, standardized pattern. Sometimes a fair-sized brig or ship might carry a cargo from Philadelphia, New York, or Boston, swap it at Jamaica or Barbados for sugar and molasses, and proceed on the long haul to London or Bristol, returning home with English wares, unless the vessel itself was sold there. At other times, small schooners or sloops would carry cargoes to the Caribbean and return to their Colonial home port, whence the surplus sugar might be carried across the Atlantic in larger vessels. But those two alternative patterns by no means exhausted the possibilities: tramp voyages of various sorts, with frequent "swapping" and "re-swapping," were common.

It did not take the Colonists long to discover that the English islands were not the only ones that would take their offerings in exchange for sugar. A skipper might arrive at Jamaica or Barbados to discover that previous arrivals from the northward had so glutted the market that his cargo could be sold only at a loss, especially since in those days of slow communication every voyage was, of course, literally a venture. Rather than sell within the empire at a sacrifice, he might slip over to Martinique, Guadeloupe, Haiti, or some other foreign island and sell his wares at a substantial profit, for none of the other nations had such good supply sources. This practice, however, ran counter to the English plans for a self-sufficient empire. To check it, Parliament in 1733 passed the Molasses Act, which imposed a very heavy duty upon sugar from the non-English islands. Effectively enforced it might have curbed such wanderings outside the imperial fold, but complaisant customs officials winked at it for years. In 1750, more tonnage arrived at New York from the foreign islands than from the English ones. Finally, in 1764, the new Sugar Act increased the duty on foreign sugar but lowered it on molasses, and put more teeth into the collection, to the anger of the Yankee traders who had violated the old regulation so long that they felt the new one was an infringement of their vested rights.

The Navigation Laws, however, did permit a moderate amount of trade outside the empire. Nonenumerated commodities might be shipped to Spain and Portugal and their Atlantic islands near by. Catholic restrictions on meat meant a good market for fish in those regions. Staves and headings for wine casks also found customers, and so, too, did flour. Consequently, trade with the Straits (of Gibraltar) flourished. Most of the money received from such transactions had to be spent in purchasing return cargoes from England, but exceptions were made in the case of salt, especially from the Portuguese Cape Verdes, and of wine, from Madeira in particular, which could be brought home directly without paying toll to the English entrepôt. Legal trade with Europe north of Spain, however, was extremely rare. France, Holland, Germany, and Scandinavia would have been glad to receive tobacco and other "enumerated" articles direct, but had scant use for the rest of the Colonial exports.

A third branch of trade that did not show on the English import and export list was the exchanging of commodities up and down the coast among the various Colonies. In particular, eastern New England presented a constant market for flour from the Hudson, the Delaware, or the Chesapeake, to which it sent its fish and lumber in return. Sometimes, more ambitious coastal traders saw that Eastern produce reached Carolina, while occasional vessels ventured northward to the Maritimes, Quebec, or Newfoundland. Now and then, a port developed local entrepôt functions of its own. It would distribute English imports up and down the coast, and receive in return materials that could be shipped back across the Atlantic. Early in the eighteenth century much of New York's commerce and financial transactions with England were routed for a while by way of Boston, which took the profits inherent in such an arrangement.[4]

Altogether, it is easy to appreciate the discrepancy between exports and imports in the trade of the Middle and Northern Colonies with England. Between trade with the sugar islands, trips to the "Straits," the coasting trade, and occasional less conventional voyages, they disposed of enough of their unenumerated goods to pay for what they wanted from London or Bristol. But, while most of the voyagers from Pennsylvania up to Maine followed those general patterns, the initial cargoes varied widely among the different regions.

Trade of the Middle Colonies

The flour barrel was the chief symbol of the trade of the Middle Colonies—New York, New Jersey, and Pennsylvania (Delaware was often reckoned as the "three lower counties" of that third Colony). Scores of little mills throughout the hinterland ground their wheat into flour, or their corn into meal, to be carted or floated to New York or Philadelphia; although New Jersey produced its fair share, most of its seaborne trade went through the big ports just across the Hudson or the Delaware. Flour was seldom needed in England, which was still relatively self-sufficient in agriculture, but it found a constant market in the Caribbean and a fair demand in southern Europe. The casks of salted beef or pork, also offered in generous quantities by the Middle Colonies, competed with the Irish product. Ireland, with its linen industry, absorbed a fair amount of Colonial flaxseed, while one of the few products marketable in England were the potashes and pearlashes (used in the making of soap and glass) that came from the burning of logs incidental to clearing away forests. Like most of the other Colonies up and down the coast, those in the middle region shipped modest amounts of furs obtained from trading with the Indians. Since the trade of a port depended somewhat upon the hinterland that it served, Philadelphia profited by the rapid growth of Pennsylvania with its liberal land policy. Its commerce took a sudden jump in 1749, and although New York was ahead in the 1760's, Philadelphia was clearly in the lead by the time of the Revolution and maintained that position for the next 20 years.[5]

The Middle Colonies were less desirable members of a self-sufficient empire than were the tobacco and sugar regions; they found, neverthe-

---

[4] Invaluable source material, illustrating the complexities of these Colonial routes and cargoes, is contained in the details of thousands of voyages in the mid-eighteenth century, from the records of the custom house "Naval Officers" at various American and West Indian ports, assembled by Professor L. A. Harper of the University of California.

[5] Tables indicating the commerce of the principal ports around 1770 are included in the Appendix of V. D. Harrington, *The New York Merchant on the Eve of the Revolution.* New York: Columbia University Press, 1935.

less, more favor in English eyes than did New England, which was called by one writer in 1695 the "most prejudicial" part of England's possessions. Instead of filling a "passive" commercial role allowing a maximum of profit for British merchants and shipowners, the New Englanders developed a decidedly "active" commerce that frequently competed with that of the mother country. They declined, as will be noted later, to develop a product that would have contributed to the empire's self-sufficiency. On the other hand, they persisted in manufacturing to meet their own needs instead of buying manufactures from England. They profited more than any other Colonists by the provisions of the Navigation Laws, and at the same time they probably evaded those laws more persistently than any other Colonists. Altogether, their commerce paid them well, and contributed to the prosperity of numerous thriving ports.

The commerce of southern New England was not impressive in its volume, but it developed two specialties. The distinctive offering of the Connecticut ports was livestock: for more than a century, deckloads of horses and cattle, along with miscellaneous agricultural produce, were carried from New Haven and New London to the sugar islands and other parts of the Caribbean. Newport handled another type of livestock—slaves from the Guinea Coast. These were taken to the sugar islands and traded there for molasses, which, in turn, was converted into rum, to be exchanged for more Negroes. This business was the profitable innovation of Rhode Island in triangular trade.

New England Cod and Pine

It was the territory north of Cape Cod, however, that soon became the most active commercial region of the Colonial period. Boston clearly led all other American ports during the first century after settlement, although the 100-mile stretch eastward up to Portland (then called Falmouth) also participated in a lively manner. The climate of northern New England was too bleak for the effective use of Negro slaves, and its farms were often more prolific in stones than in crops, so that the produce of the Southern or Middle Colonies could not easily be duplicated. By hard labor, however, profitable initial shipments could be wrested, with small capital investment, from the fishing banks and the pine forests. With those as a start, the Yankees wandered far and wide, swapping and re-swapping until they came back with generous profits.

It is very appropriate that the "sacred cod" hangs in the legislative halls at Boston, for, like the woolsack on which the Chancellor sits when presiding over the House of Lords, it represents the original economic foundation of the region's prosperity. Geography gave New

England an advantage over old England, as far as the fisheries were concerned. Ever since the Cabots discovered the Grand Banks south of Newfoundland teeming with codfish, hardy mariners from the western ports of England had gone out there for the fishing season. The distance was too far, however, for them to return home with every fresh catch of fish, and, consequently, they had to go ashore on Newfoundland to salt and dry their fish, which they would eventually carry home at the end of the season. The fishermen of Marblehead, however, could easily return with each haul during the season to their home port, where the fish could be split and dried while the fishermen were off for another load. Massachusetts fishermen did not always have to go as far as the Grand Banks, for the Georges Bank not far off their own coast often yielded rich hauls. The finished products of this strenuous work were frequently divided into three grades. The best was reserved for local consumption or traded down the coast in exchange for flour or tobacco. The next best was carried over to the Catholics of southern Europe in return for salt and wine. Finally, the "refuse" was shipped to the sugar islands to feed the slaves. This business often ran afoul of the French in those regions, and in the many years of war French privateers were wont to prey upon the Yankee fishermen. This was one reason why New Englanders participated eagerly in the capture of Louisburg in 1745.

If fishing was the specialty of eastern Massachusetts, lumbering was the prime activity of the narrow strip of New Hampshire coast and the long, indented coast of Maine, then part of Massachusetts. Portsmouth was the lower limit of the great belt of virgin white pines, trees often reaching a tremendous size, with a texture so soft that they were sometimes called "pumpkin pine." Scarcely had settlements spread into the southern part of that region, when primitive little sawmills began to convert the huge logs into timber, planking, and boards, while the settlers during spare hours split the wood into shingles and clapboards. The tougher white oak of the region was likewise converted into staves and headings for sugar and wine casks. There was a steady demand for these Eastern forest products in the Caribbean, while the staves also found a market in Madeira and the other wine islands. Yankee ingenuity anticipated the modern prefabricated house by sending whole ready-to-assemble house frames to the West Indies. Although England was experiencing an ever-increasing shortage of timber, it drew only a moderate amount from New England, depending more generally upon the nearer Baltic supply.

In one particular product of these pine forests, however, England had a very keen interest. None of the great maritime powers of that day—England, France, Spain, or Holland—produced within its borders any trees suitable to serve as great masts for their warships. Along with tar, pitch, and other "naval stores," masts were almost the only "strategic materials" for war that were not obtainable at home in that relatively self-sufficient era. The Baltic supplied medium-sized firs that could be pieced together to form masts for ships-of-the-line, but the New England forests produced great, pliant single sticks even up to the maximum mast-size of 40 yards long and 40 inches in diameter. From 1652, when the first Dutch war threatened the Baltic supply, until 1775, when the news of Lexington led the Colonists to break off the trade, the Royal Navy received all its great masts from Portsmouth, New Hampshire, and, after 1727, from Portland. The comings and goings of the "mast ships" were the principal maritime events at those Eastern ports. To preserve those great trees for the navy, Parliament reserved all pines over two feet in diameter and instructed royal forest officials to cut the "broad arrow" upon them, but the Colonial lumbermen time and again disregarded those regulations that would have deprived them of much good potential lumber. Masts and naval stores were "enumerated" shortly after 1700, but that legislation did not prevent the Colonists from selling them to France and Spain, even while those nations were at war with England.[6]

While the masts went regularly to the naval dockyards across the Atlantic, the New Englanders showed little interest in producing naval stores, which would have given them a very useful niche in the scheme of a self-sufficient empire. From those pines could have been extracted tar for preserving ropes and pitch for calking seams in hulls. England required large amounts of both tar and pitch, and made heavy annual purchases from Sweden and other Baltic nations. Around 1700, the government realized that this Baltic dependence was bad, both from a political point of view and with respect to strategic considerations: that it led to an "unfavorable balance" of trade with the Baltic, while the bottleneck entrance to that sea meant that an enemy might cut off those essential supplies as England herself was cutting off the supplies of her rivals. Here was an obvious opportunity for "prejudicial" New England to play a useful role in remedying both those evils. Parliament offered a bounty on naval stores and sent over an agent to stimulate their production, but its representative found that the Yankees would rather spend their time spinning and weaving homespun woolens, to the detriment of the English export trade. Only in North Carolina did the naval-stores business gain any headway, but the Royal Navy rejected its output as of "too hot a nature" and injurious to the ropes—a thought that arouses added sympathy for the poor devils who were from time to time tarred and feathered.

[6] R. G. Albion, *Forests and Sea Power: the Timber Problem of the Royal Navy*, Chapters V-VI. Cambridge, Mass.: Harvard University Press, 1926.

Colonial Shipbuilding and Shipping

Perhaps the most profitable product of those Yankee pines and oaks went out in the form of ready-made vessels that could be produced in almost any harbor or tidal creek. The abundant supply of timber close at hand made Colonial construction far cheaper than construction in England, which was running short of oak and lacked domestic masts. In addition, any vessel built on Boston Bay or along the Merrimac or Kennebec was rated under the Navigation Laws as virtually English, just as if it had been built on the Thames: it had the free run of the empire (except India), and it could be sold in England. By the time of the Revolution, about a third of all the shipping in British registry had been built in the American Colonies, mainly in eastern New England. English merchants were usually glad to snap them up as bargains, for they were cheaper than those built at home. The privileged position of Colonial shipping meant that in one respect, at least, the Navigation Laws were an asset rather than a liability to Colonial commerce.

Those Colonial vessels fell into two main categories. The larger, "square-rigged" ships and brigs sometimes ran as large as 500 tons and were capable of transatlantic voyages. The smaller schooners and sloops were generally used for coastal, fishing, and West Indian trips. Unlike other types, which followed English models to a considerable extent, the schooner was a distinctive American invention. Its for-and-aft rig required fewer men to handle it than the square rig of the brig, which likewise had two masts, and it was also better for keeping off a lee shore—an important consideration in the coasting trade. In 1771, the Colonies produced 128 square-rigged vessels and 291 schooners and sloops, totaling 24,068 tons.

From the very beginning, the New England vessels began to undertake "tramp" voyages that showed a considerable amount of ingenuity and imagination, quite different from the "passive" shuttle trade of the Chesapeake region, which was largely in English hands. The 200-ton ship *Tryal*, for instance, built in Boston in 1642, made her first voyage to the Canaries and then to the sugar islands of St. Kitts and Barbados, on her next trip the long haul to Malaga and Bilbao in Spain, then journeyed up the coast to Canada, and in 1645 sailed to London and Holland, for the Navigation Laws had not yet restricted the legal scope of such activity. Whereas the business in the Chesapeake fell pretty much into the hands of factors from the English houses, the merchants of Boston, in particular, and later those of New York, Philadelphia, and other ports kept most of the initiative in their own hands. Generally, they owned both the vessels and the cargoes that they carried, and developed regular commercial contacts with "correspondents" along many of the principal sea lanes. Such an arrangement naturally was less desirable to the English than the more "passive" commercial role of the Colonies to the southward. The New Englanders preferred to keep the commissions, freight money, and other profits in their own hands; but at least these activities of the Middle and Northern Colonies enabled them to buy as heavily from England as did the Southerners with their "enumerated" goods.[7]

Commercial relations between the Colonies and the mother country ran a fairly placid course, without too much interference with irregularities, until the close of the Seven Years' War in 1763. Then George Grenville, Chancellor of the Exchequer, worried by the sudden jump in the national debt, began to tighten up some of the former leakage that had proved so profitable to the Colonial traders. The new Sugar Act, the increased vigilance of customs officials, and an extension of the "enumerated" list to include many new articles coincided with the Stamp Act to provoke widespread opposition in the Colonial ports. The Colonists were quick to play their highest commercial trump in return: they refused to import from England, and thus cut off an important share of the mother country's markets. This blow fell particularly upon the British merchants, who were heavily interested in the American trade.

This nonimportation agreement, as was anticipated, produced enough pressure in Parliament to result in the repeal of the Stamp Act within the year. The Colonial merchants co-operated in nonimportation, but most of them were reluctant to follow the radicals toward further steps that would jeopardize the constantly growing commerce among various parts of the empire.[8] The trade statistics, which suddenly became more ample with the increased customs activity, showed a fairly steady increase until the eve of the Revolution, when the Continental Congress declared its economic independence of the imperial bond months before it declared political independence. Even in 1775, when fighting had actually started around Boston, and a new nonimportation agreement cut off shipments from Britain once again, exports were permitted for several months longer; this produced the heaviest total of cargoes to England in the course of the whole Colonial period. Eight years later, after independence had been won and recognized, the Americans suddenly began to realize that membership in the British Empire had its economic advantages as well as its burdens. But their adjustment to the new problems of independence is another story.

---

[7] Detailed analysis of these methods will be found in Harrington, *The New York Merchant on the Eve of the Revolution*. New York: Columbia University Press, 1935.

[8] This whole situation is ably analyzed in A. M. Schlesinger, *The Colonial Merchants and the American Revolution*. New York: Columbia University Press, 1918.

Commerce in the Colonial Economy

Commerce and shipping were the closest approach to "big business" in Colonial America, except perhaps for a few large land companies. They were responsible for the principal accumulation of active capital and for the growth of the major cities and towns. This activity affected not only those who were immediately engaged in it, but also most of the rest of the Colonial population. The trade with England, the West Indies and other parts of the world enabled the agriculturist to swap his surplus "cash crops" advantageously for what he wanted from beyond the seas. This applied not only to the Virginia planter exchanging tobacco for luxury imports but also to the fairly self-sufficient pioneer out on the edge of things, whose surplus potashes or pearlashes enabled him to procure salt, rum, an axe, or a rifle. The English Colonies went out and got what they wanted, instead of being dependent, as were the Spanish Colonies to the southward, upon the inadequate flow of goods that the mother country doled out to them at exorbitant prices.

Selected References

Albion, R. G., *Forests and Sea Power: the Timber Problem of the Royal Navy.* Cambridge, Mass.: Harvard University Press, 1926.

Andrews, C. M., *The Colonial Period of American History* (4 vols.; see especially Vol IV). New Haven: Yale University Press, 1934-1938.

Beer, G. L., *The Old Colonial System, 1664-1754.* New York: The Macmillan Company, 1912.

———, *British Colonial Policy, 1764-1765.* New York: The Macmillan Company, 1907.

Bridenbaugh, C., *Cities in the Wilderness.* New York: The Ronald Press Company, 1938.

Harper, L. A., *The English Navigation Laws.* New York: Columbia University Press, 1939.

Harrington, V. D., *The New York Merchant on the Eve of the Revolution.* New York: Columbia University Press, 1935.

Macpherson, D., *Annals of Commerce* (4 vols.). London: 1805.

Morriss, M. S., *Colonial Trade of Maryland, 1689-1715.* Bryn Mawr, Pa.: Bryn Mawr College, 1914.

Schlesinger, A. M., *The Colonial Merchants and the American Revolution.* New York: Columbia University Press, 1918.

Sellers, L., *Charleston Business on the Eve of the American Revolution.* Chapel Hill, N. C.: University of North Carolina Press, 1934.

Semmes, R., *Captains and Mariners of Early Maryland.* Baltimore: John Hopkins Press, 1937.

4 · THE ORGANIZATION OF PRODUCTION DURING THE COLONIAL PERIOD

IN THE TASK of subduing the wilderness and organizing economic activity in the Seaboard Colonies, both the promoters who financed settlement and the early generations of pioneers, brought over largely as the result of promotional efforts, played important roles. Nevertheless, as late as 1680, in answer to the query, "What obstruction do you find to the improvement of the trade and navigation of your Corporation?" the governor of Connecticut replied: "The want of men of estates to venture abroad, and of money at home for the management of trade, and labor being so deare with us." With an economy of words scarcely typical of the period the governor thus succinctly stated the problem of Colonial production. The lack of capital and the scarcity and high cost of labor were principal obstacles to the rapid expansion of Colonial productive enterprise.

Actually, large-scale industrial organization on a capitalistic basis was first achieved in the South in the field of agriculture. The North lagged behind, but, by the early eighteenth century, shortages of labor and capital had been in part overcome in that area in such fields as mining, milling, lumbering, fishing, and whaling, where rapid expansion occurred. It is proposed at this point to examine some of the major problems business men and farmers faced in organizing and expanding Colonial productive capacity.

Agriculture

Although handicapped by scarcity of capital and labor, by poor marketing and transportation facilities, and by political regulation, Colonial productive enterprise was given impetus and sustained by the abundant natural resources of the Atlantic Seaboard. Colonial production centered chiefly in the extractive industries requiring little machinery and using, in the main, unskilled or semiskilled labor. The soil provided crops and minerals, the forest furnished timber, fur-bearing animals, and game, and the coastal waters, rivers, streams, and lakes yielded a wide variety of fish.

Of Colonial productive enterprise, agriculture was the leading occupation and principal source of wealth; and down to the end of the Colonial period the population remained predominantly rural. On the eve of the Revolution, Boston and New York each had approximately 20,000 inhabitants; Newport 9,000; Philadelphia, the largest Colonial town, 35,000; and Charleston, the largest city in the South, under 15,000. Other towns averaged between 1,000 and 4,000 inhabitants, and the greater proportion of the population lived in villages, on farms, or on plantations.[1]

The organization of the Colonial farm was determined far less by traditional European practices than by such factors as topography, climate, rainfall, fertility of the soil, and specialization. Little of the New England land was level or especially fertile. Great stretches of it were strewn with boulders. Hence, the bulk of the land did not lend itself to remunerative farming or to as intensive specialization as did the plantation economy. At least superficially, New England villages resembled medieval English farming communities. Much of the English village economy was transplanted, each family having its own home lot of three to five acres with outlying fields, generally several small tracts totaling from 50 to 200 acres, of which only a very small portion was as a rule arable. The common, or pasture land available to all freeholders, was copied from the English village plan. For generations the uneconomical three-field system of crop rotation was practiced in New England. The same ground might be planted to corn or sowed to flax and oats year after year until it "ran out." But improvements in farming methods followed the development of town and city markets. New England turned to the growing of diversified crops. Among these, Indian corn was the favorite since it could be cultivated by hand labor, whereas wheat could be grown only after the land had been thoroughly plowed. In addition, oats, rye, and barley were raised, and some attention paid to dairy farming and sheep raising.

The region between the Hudson and Potomac possessed advantages in soil and climate that soon made it the outstanding area for general farming along the entire Atlantic Seaboard. Wheat instead of corn was the important staple, but rye, oats, barley, and other cereals were raised in abundance, as well as fruit and vegetables. In addition, potatoes were extensively grown. The region was also famous for the excellent quality of its livestock and horses. While subsistence farming prevailed in New England, the "bread colonies" exported most of their crops. Flour was produced for foreign sale, together with other foodstuffs from wheat. In the seventeenth century the manufacture of flour and bread was the chief industry of New York City, where for a time

[1] See E. B. Greene and Virginia D. Harrington, *American Population Before the Federal Census of 1790*. New York: Columbia Univ. Press, 1932.

all flour exported from the province had to be bolted or sifted, thus giving the local merchants control of the flour trade. Finally, this monopoly was broken, but as a consequence of the spread of fraudulent practices, such as the mixing of flour with Indian corn and the false "taring" (marking the weight) of bread and flour casks, the reputation of New York products suffered in foreign markets. Pennsylvania's provision industry was the chief beneficiary of New York's loss of prestige and customers.

In the South, where agricultural staples were produced primarily for a commercial market, farming was more of a capitalistic enterprise. The planter raised a specialized crop for export—in Maryland and Virginia tobacco, in South Carolina rice. He himself did not work the soil, but employed an overseer who managed the labor first of indentured servants and ultimately of Negro slaves. His economy was highly sensitive to the world price of his staple, and he became largely dependent upon credit from merchant capitalists in England and Scotland. Such credit made it possible for him to purchase new lands as his soil gradually became exhausted, to maintain the large labor supply that capitalistic agriculture demanded, and to preserve a conspicuously high standard of living. As production was sometimes limited to a fixed number of plants per laborer, old grounds would be abandoned when their declining yields increased labor costs. Hence, geographic shifts westward marked tobacco production, and by the mid-eighteenth century the industry was beginning to expand beyond the Fall Line. Notwithstanding the decline in the price of tobacco, production expanded rapidly. Average exports from Virginia to London around 1640 amounted to 1,395,063 pounds, not including a considerable quantity carried directly to Holland, whereas on the eve of the Revolution the exports to Great Britain exceeded 100,000,000 pounds. Capitalistic agriculture and the plantation system were also successfully instituted in the Carolina rice fields, where Negro slave labor was soon found to be more successful than indentured servants in coping with the hot, pestilential swamplands. The planters maintained residences in more healthful locations, leaving management in the hands of overseers. By the beginning of the Revolution, South Carolina and Georgia exported annually 165,000 barrels of rice.

While production on the plantations was in large measure centered upon staples, attention came to be devoted to diversified crops raised on partly exhausted lands. In the eighteenth century the Southern Colonies showed a large increase in the production of corn, wheat, and other cereals, and in the raising of cattle, sheep, and hogs. In addition, a good deal of manufacturing was done on the plantation. Many plantations supported their own tanneries, and produced cloth from flax, wool, and cotton, both for home consumption and for neighborhood exchange. Hogsheads, barrels, and tierces were manufactured for exportable products. Other industrial activities, such as brewing and the manufacture of bricks, rope, salt, powder, potash, and hardware, were undertaken. As a result, many of the slaves on the plantations were employed in nonagricultural labor and manufacturing processes.

The organization of agricultural production was reflected in the real-property law of the Colonial period. The Colonial charters granted tenure in free and common socage. In general, farmers sought freehold grants, since their primary purpose in coming to this country was to secure holdings relatively free of feudal obligations. Where, as in New York, the manorial system and tenant farming were practiced, immigration lagged. Elsewhere feudal services were generally limited to the reservation of a specific quitrent. Everywhere quitrents were resented and, though the amounts were nominal, their collection proved to be a formidable task. After the Revolution most feudal incidents, including quitrents, were abolished by statute, and a fee simple vested in the freehold tenant. The small holdings of New England were reflected in laws that provided for divisible succession among the male heirs, saving a double portion for the eldest son. This was a substitute for the English system of primogeniture, by which the eldest son was the exclusive inheritor of the land. Pennsylvania, which encouraged immigration and built up a prosperous farm population by generous freehold grants, followed New England's suit, but New York and the South clung tenaciously to primogeniture until the Revolutionary period. Virginia, under the leadership of Thomas Jefferson, was first of the group to abandon this method of descent. Holdings in the Middle Colonies and the South were frequently entailed, so that the large plantations were preserved intact for generations. Abolition of entails or barring them by deed or will was another achievement of the social legislation of the Revolutionary period.[2] Finally, throughout the Colonies confiscation of the great Loyalist estates, such as the holdings of the Penn family, of Pepperell, Philipse, De Lancey, Fairfax, and Granville, led ultimately to a more equitable distribution of landholdings in all the Seaboard states.[3]

Deposits of furnace clay, sand, and lime in certain areas made possible the glass industry in the Colonies. The location of brick and tile yards and potters' kilns was determined by the availability of suitable deposits. Bog ores found in eastern Massachusetts and along the New Jersey coast were well adapted for making castings and hollow ware.

[2] See R. B. Morris, *Studies in the History of American Law,* Chapter II. New York: Columbia Univ. Press, 1930.

[3] Recent investigations have shown that in a number of states the confiscation of Tory property was less democratizing in its immediate effects than has been supposed. See H. B. Yoshpe, *The Disposition of the Loyalist Estates in the Southern District of New York.* New York: Columbia University Press, 1939.

Rock ores, found principally in northern New Jersey, eastern Pennsylvania, and the South, gave rise to the furnace and forge industries of those regions.

Forest Resources and Industries

From the virgin forests of Colonial times sprang such enterprises as the fur and lumber industries, shipbuilding, and the production of naval stores and potash. Fur-trapping remained largely in the hands of the Indians. The white traders in exchange for pelts offered guns, axes, knives, ammunition, blankets, and gewgaws at such inland trading posts as the Dutch frontier post of Fort Orange, which later became the English fur center of Albany. Here furs were obtained from the Iroquois, who acted as middlemen in procuring pelts from Indian hunters and trappers of the interior of the country. In the eighteenth century, Albany traders traveled all the way to Oswego on Lake Ontario to procure furs obtained from remote Indian tribes. In the South, Charleston and later Augusta were important trading posts to which huge quantities of deerskins were brought. The rivalry between the English and the French over the trans-Appalachian fur trade broke out in the contest between the French fur merchants and the Hudson's Bay Company in Canada. This rivalry was ended by the Treaty of Paris of 1763, which assured Britain's supremacy. In the eighteenth century, traders and trappers could no longer obtain furs along the coast, but found it necessary to penetrate the area of the Great Lakes, the upper waters and tributaries of the Ohio, and, in the South, as far west as the Mississippi. Most of the furs of the Thirteen Colonies were of the cheaper sort—muskrat, marten, and raccoon. Far more valuable were the otter, beaver, mink, fox, wolf, bear, and wolverine obtained from Canada. With Britain's acquisition of that area the fur industry of the Colonies declined in importance. Something less than 5 per cent of the beaver skins shipped to Britain in 1773 came from the Thirteen Colonies, and but slightly over 40 per cent of the total of other furs.

The timber resources of the Colonies fed a flourishing lumber industry—shipbuilding, the production of naval stores, and potash. In New England white pine supported the shipbuilding industry, prize trees serving as masts, yards, and spars for the royal navy, which was hard-pressed to get timber from the Baltic countries. The white oak of the Middle Colonies provided valuable stock for the cooperage industry as well as excellent ship timber; and other hard woods of that area, such as walnut, cherry, and red maple, supported the cabinetmakers' trade. In the South yellow pine was the principal source of tar, pitch, and turpentine. The commercial manufacture of lumber was confined to the Fall Line in New England and the Middle Colonies, the most important centers being Maine and New Hampshire.

Fishing and Whaling

The resources of the land were supplemented by the bounties of the sea. Fish, notably cod, caught off the banks from Newfoundland to Long Island, found a ready market. The better grades were shipped to Europe; the inferior went to the West Indies for the slave population. "Our ancestors," declared a Marblehead fisherman, "came not here for religion. Their main end was to catch fish." By the eve of the Revolution a fleet of well over 100 vessels employing over 1,000 men and shipping half the dried codfish of New England was based in Marblehead. This control of almost a sixth of all the vessels engaged in the New England cod fishery and a quarter of all the crews, represented a relative degree of centralization of the industry. Whaling competed for the attention of the seamen of New England and New York. Offshore fishing first provided the Colonies with oil, but ultimately deep-sea whaling took the vessels out into the Atlantic Ocean from Hudson's Bay to the Falklands and from Africa to Brazil. Nantucket, New Bedford, and Sag Harbor led the Colonies in this industry by the time of the Revolution, when a fleet estimated at 360 ships accounted for some 45,000 barrels of sperm oil and 75,000 pounds of whalebone. Declared Edmund Burke in the House of Commons: "Neither the perseverance of Holland nor the activity of France nor the dexterous and firm sagacity of English enterprise ever carried this most perilous mode of hard industry to the extent to which it has been pushed by these recent people."

Until the end of the Seven Years' War, the French competed with American and English fishermen off the Great Banks, but the acquisition by the Treaty of Paris of all French territory in that area except the little islands of St. Pierre and Miquelon left Britain in control. As a result of the removal of a foreign rival, Britain and her colonies now entered into such fierce competition that in 1775 an English writer asserted that "the Northern colonies have nearly beaten us out of the Newfoundland fisheries, that great nursery of seamen; insomuch that the share of New England alone exceeds that of Britain." While New England sold a goodly portion of her fish and other products to the British West Indies, she was forced to turn to the French West Indies for molasses to be made into rum in the New England distilleries and shipped to Africa in exchange for slaves. The British West Indies could no longer provide supplies of molasses adequate to the demands of the Northern Colonies. A more rigid enforcement of the Navigation Acts and the passage of the Molasses Act in 1733 and the Sugar Act in 1764 were intended to counteract the trade with the French. The former act imposed duties on foreign sugar, rum, and molasses entering the Colonies. The latter reduced the duties on foreign molasses, but increased the duties on foreign sugar and prohibited foreign rum. Henceforth, serious attempts were made to check smuggling. The attempt to curb New England's commercial expansion centering about her fishing industry was one of the basic factors leading to the American Revolution.[4]

The Labor Problem and Colonial Production

The productive capacity of the American Colonies was materially affected by the power of the labor market. Because of the scarcity of labor, particularly of skilled workmen, this market favored the laborer rather than the employer. Colonial workmen commanded wages from 30 to 100 per cent higher than the wages of contemporary English laboring men.

Economic nationalism entered into the problem of the labor market as well as other problems of economic enterprise, and created a policy marked by sharp contradictions. Colonies were favored, but at the same time an effort was made to maintain a large labor supply at home in order to assure low wages and manufacturing costs. The home authorities sought to encourage early colonization. Master guildsmen and merchants sponsored the settlement of Virginia. It was widely believed, although now we know erroneously, that England was overpopulated, and that the unemployed, poor, and vagrant class should be shipped to the Colonies to produce the raw materials needed at home and to consume England's surplus manufactured products.

Following the Civil War and the Stuart Restoration, the official attitude gradually changed. As England rose to great commercial and industrial power, she was not anxious to encourage the emigration of good workmen, preferring instead to export convicts. For many years Parliament was loath to encourage the activities of recruiting agents by giving them immunity from civil actions for damages brought by persons claiming to have been transported to the Colonies against their will. Reluctantly such immunity was granted, provided that the agents had secured from such persons and had properly recorded testimonials of their willingness to depart. In 1765, as a means of preventing the spread of closely guarded industrial secrets and of maintaining an adequate supply of highly trained labor at home, Parliament forbade the emigration of skilled workingmen.[5] This act anticipated the British statutes of

[4] By the Treaty of 1783 New England fishermen were given the right to fish off the Great Banks and other banks of Newfoundland, and in the Gulf of St. Lawrence as well as permission to dry or cure fish in specified unsettled areas in British Canada. For a recent thorough treatment of the problem, see H. A. Innis, *The Cod Fisheries.* New Haven: Yale University Press, 1940.

[5] Only a few years later General Gage, commander-in-chief of the British military forces in the Colonies, wrote to the home authorities: "It would be well, if the Emigration from Great Britain, Ireland and Holland, where the Germans embark for America, were prevented; and our new settlements should be peopled from the old ones, which would be a means to thin them, and put it less in their power to do Mischief." From C. E. Carter, ed., *Correspondence of General Thomas Gage* (2 vols.), Vol. II, p. 450 (1768). New Haven: Yale University Press, 1931, 1933.

1774, 1781, and 1782 forbidding the exportation of textile machinery, plans, or models.

Because of restrictions imposed by the home government and certain other difficulties, chief of which was the formidable transportation problem involved in populating the Atlantic Seaboard with European workingmen, it was necessary for Colonial production to draw upon sources of labor other than the free workingmen. Bound white labor and Negro slavery filled the huge gap in the labor market.

Indentured Servitude

Bound laborers were contracted under articles of indenture to serve for specified terms, generally from three to seven years, in return for maintenance and certain "freedom dues" at the expiration of service. These freedom dues were established both by law and custom and generally amounted to working tools and clothing. Of the various sources of bound labor, the recruiting of immigrants, British, Irish, and German, was numerically the most important.

The financing of imported labor came either from the planter, as in Virginia and Maryland, who received a headright or land grant for each immigrant brought into the country, or through recruiting agents in England and on the Continent who were employed by merchants specializing in the sale of servants' indentures. Zealous recruiting agents went through the Rhineland areas—devastated by the Thirty Years' War and the War of Legitimacy—and gained the name of "Newlanders," a term of opprobrium. English recruiting agents sent drummers through various inland towns to cry publicly the voyages to America, or distributed extravagant literature at annual fairs with the help of a piper who drew the crowd. These agents were often guilty of sharp practices. After securing the signature of the immigrant to the indenture, the agent would frequently confine him in a "cookes house," or actually imprison him aboard ship to prevent his breaking his contract before sailing time. This treatment led to frequent charges of "spiriting," which, while unquestionably exaggerated, were unfortunately true in the case of unscrupulous agents who were not above kidnapping children and "trepanning" or shanghaiing adults.[6]

The average cost of transporting a passenger across the Atlantic was £10. To pay his passage, the immigrant workingman signed an indenture. This indenture was assigned to the ship's captain, who would sell the passenger on his arrival at a Colonial port. Immigrant workingmen coming into the Colonies in this way were known as *redemptioners*. South of New England, which was largely Anglo-Saxon, some 50 per cent of the population was of non-English stock at the time of

[6] See A. E. Smith, "Indentured Servants: New Light on Some of America's 'First' Families," *Journal of Economic History*, Vol. II, (May, 1942), pp. 40-53.

the Revolution. In general, this meant that the majority of the Scottish, Scotch-Irish, Irish, German, and Swiss immigrants came to this country as indentured workingmen bound for their passage money. Pennsylvania received the lion's share of this immigration.

A numerically smaller but still important element in the unskilled labor market was the British convict, exported principally to Maryland and Virginia. Parliamentary acts of 1662 and 1717 specifically authorized this disposal of convicts. Under the first act "rogues, vagabonds, and sturdy beggars" might, if adjudged incorrigible, be transported. The second authorized the transportation of persons convicted of lesser crimes for seven-year terms of servitude, and of those guilty of offenses punishable by death to fourteen-year terms. In addition, a great many political prisoners convicted of participation in the Monmouth rebellion and in the uprisings of 1715 and 1745 to establish the Pretenders upon the throne were sent to this country. All told, about 50,000 convicts were shipped to America, of whom 20,000 went to Maryland. Women of the Moll Flanders type, men from out of Hogarth, still other characters, like the notorious university book-thief, Henry Justice, barrister and bookseller, made up the motley throng of convicts. They aroused a general feeling of insecurity in the Colonies to which they were transported and added immeasurably to the crime problem. Moreover, the bulk of them were unskilled workers, not distinguished for industry and obedience. Despite Colonial opposition, manifest in laws imposing prohibitive duties upon the importation of convicts—all of which were disallowed by the Crown, which favored wholesale convict dumping—marginal farmers and frontiersmen who could not afford to purchase slaves found convicts to be a cheap source of labor and doubtless made it profitable for this practice to be continued right through the Colonial period.

Besides the British convicts, American Colonists convicted of such criminal offenses as larceny might be permitted to serve as indentured servants to pay the damages or fines assessed. Extra service was regularly exacted also of runaway servants and of women servants bearing illegitimate children. Finally, orphans and child-paupers could be bound out by the courts to save communities the expense of their maintenance. A further source of bound labor in the Colonies was the judgment debtor. In England imprisonment for debt had long been the fate of impecunious debtors; but in this country, where labor was scarce, such confinement served little purpose. Hence, very early in Colonial history courts began the practice of discharging debtors from prison provided they would serve their creditors or assigns for a period of time deemed sufficient to satisfy their debts.

The indenture by which the labor of immigrants was contracted usually did not carry an obligation on the part of the master to instruct them in a particular craft or "mystery." Bound servants worked at miscellaneous jobs about the household and farm. Indentures that did bind the master to give the artisan instruction in reading, writing, and accounting, as well as training in a particular trade, were known as "articles of apprenticeship." These were entered into by minors with their parents' consent. In return for their training, the apprentices were bound normally until their eighteenth or twenty-first birthday to live with and work for the master. In the absence of vocational schools, this was the only method of producing skilled workers, and the provisions of apprenticeship were in the main carefully guarded by the courts.

Slavery

Bonded servitude preceded slavery in the South. Slavery became firmly established, however, within a generation after the first Negroes were brought to Virginia in 1619. Slaves were generally first landed at the West Indies and seasoned before being sold in the mainland colonies. By the end of the seventeenth century, the slave population had rapidly mounted. They were confined in the main to employment in the Southern plantation economy. While the bulk of them were used for field and household labor, others were trained in a variety of trades and often were farmed out by their masters. The skilled Negro artisan was, therefore, a serious threat to the free Southern workman in such towns as Charleston. Ultimately he entirely replaced the free workman in the supply of skilled labor in the South. The increase in rice and indigo production in the South boosted the price of slaves. The average price in 1650 was £20 a head, in 1700 £25, and by the eve of the Revolution between £50 and £80. The tobacco planters, harassed by the declining profit margin from their product, by soil exhaustion, and by the mounting burden of fixed charges and debts, found the high price of slaves a serious strain on their economy. Yet the Carolina planters felt that slave labor paid. The author of American Husbandry observed in 1775:

> The price of labour is incomparably cheaper in Carolina than in Britain: a negro costs 2£ 13s. per annum, to which if we add 2£ 10s. the interest of his prime cost, the total is only 5£ 3s. and as the common calculation is, that one English labourer does as much work as two negroes, a labourer to the planter costs 10£ 6s. a year, whereas to a farmer he costs from 20£ to 25£. The difference is 125 per cent; this article therefore is very decisive in favor of the planter.[7]

The Control of Wages

This advantage did not hold in the case of white labor. All authorities agreed that relatively high wages prevailed in the Colonies. One discouraged New Englander wrote in 1660 that "help is scarce and hard

[7] Harry J. Carman, ed., *American Husbandry*, p. 302. New York: Columbia University Press, 1939.

to gett, difficult to please, uncertaine, etc." "Poor People," wrote Gabriel Thomas of Pennsylvania workingmen, "can here get three times the wages for their Labour they can in England." This high level of wages curbed to some extent the ability of Colonial producers to compete with English manufacturers; it rendered competition with Continental producers in some fields virtually hopeless without subsidies. It was reported in 1694 that in Sweden and Denmark, "Labour costs but one-sixth of the price as it does in New England." William Byrd 2nd abandoned plans for the introduction of hemp, because, he wrote in 1737, "Labour being much dearer than in Muscovy, as well as the Freight, we can make no Earnings of it."

It might be assumed that high wages should have attracted many immigrants, and thus lowered the wage scale by glutting the labor market, but this was not the case. Agriculture, not industry, lured the Colonial workingman. As soon as he had accumulated a small amount of money he could, and in many cases did, take up a tract of land and settle on it as a farmer. The opportunity to acquire good land in freehold tenure rather than the prospects of high wages attracted immigrants to the American Colonies.

Early Colonial governments attempted to cope with this problem. Endowed with broad powers of supervision over strangers, vagrants, and the idle, with authority to establish compulsory labor, and the right to impress men to pursue fugitive servants on land and over water, they also experimented for several generations with a program of fixing maximum wages. Virtually every Colony sought such a solution, but the New England group was the most persistent. To prevent a fixed wage base and a runaway price scale from throwing the labor system out of equilibrium, early statutes included elaborate regulations of the prices of basic commodities. The early settlers accepted in general the medieval doctrine of the "just price." The assize of bread was the most persistent regulatory measure employed in American towns down through the eighteenth century; but other price, quantity, and quality regulations included the assizes of casks, leather, wood, and bricks. The attempt to control wages, either by legislative fiat or the administrative discretion of local officials was generally abandoned, even more rapidly than in England where the system had become largely ineffective by the latter part of the seventeenth century.

In the face of the rapid depreciation of paper money during the American Revolution, the various state governments once more attempted to set maximum wages and prices. Regulations drawn up by state legislatures and regional conventions relied for sanctions primarily upon the boycott and social ostracism. They failed, not because of the impossibility of regulation *per se,* but rather because of the failure of the Continental Congress and the states to stem the currency crisis.

Without a stabilized currency, control of wages and prices proved impossible.

Because of this failure, economic thinkers of the "critical period," such as Pelatiah Webster, were generally committed to a hands-off business policy. Abolishing internal restrictions on business, while at the same time effectively regulating commerce between the states and protecting home industry from foreign competition would, according to early American entrepreneurs, assure a revival of prosperity. This view was reflected in the framing of the Constitution, a document enthusiastically endorsed by the industrialists and city workingmen of the time.

Concerted Action Among Workers

After 1689 British workingmen began to act in concert to secure better working conditions. Doubtless owing to the fluid character of the Colonial labor market, workingmen's combinations in Colonial times were at best temporary affairs, generally confined to the licensed trades, such as those of the carters and porters whose fees or wages were set by the town authorities, or of the master bakers who frequently acted in concert to protest against the town assizes. During the Revolutionary era, a perceptible momentum toward labor combinations and concerted action along class lines was effectively diverted from economic into political channels. Masters and journeymen joined in protest against British imperial policy and supported the nonimportation agreements, which were a great boon to local industry. The foundations of permanent trade-unionism were not really laid until the post-Revolutionary period.

Nor were combinations of master craftsmen of permanent nature. The guild system never was successfully transplanted to Colonial soil. In 1644 the Massachusetts authorities placed shipbuilding under the supervision of a chartered company, following the English pattern, and four years later the shoemakers of Boston and the coopers of Boston and Charleston were given a charter of self-government conferring upon them the power to "suppresse" craftsmen not approved by the guild. But in neither case does it appear that the charters were renewed at the expiration of the three-year period. Beginning with the Philadelphia house carpenters in 1724, master carpenters in most of the Colonial towns agreed upon a scale of prices for their work, and the practice of entering into and publishing such agreements was widely followed in the post-Revolutionary and Federal periods. By the "critical period" master silversmiths, coopers, wigmakers, and others were organized by crafts. Master mechanics were combining in the leading towns to establish inter-craft organizations for economic as well as philanthropic ends.

For a long time Colonial towns strove to maintain the monopoly of the crafts by making the completion of a term of apprenticeship a prerequisite to opening up one's own shop, or by limiting practice in trades and crafts to inhabitants admitted to the freedom of the town. In 1675 a group of ships' carpenters were find by the county court for riding an interloper out of Boston on a rail because he had worked in the yard before completing his full seven years' apprenticeship. By the mid-eighteenth century, however, *laissez-faire* tendencies led to a noticeable slackening in the enforcement of these restrictions. New York, which had been vigilant in protecting its coopers against outsiders from Boston in 1675 refused flatly to intervene when in 1747 building-trades workers complained that carpenters, bricklayers, and others coming in from New Jersey not only worked at much lower wages but brought in their own building materials. The South was unable to prevent Negro slaves from driving the more highly paid white artisans out of the labor market.

The Investment of Capital in Productive Enterprise

Capital invested in Colonial productive enterprises was drawn both from European and from Colonial sources. The Lynn iron works was started in the seventeenth century with English as well as Colonial money. British ironmasters organized the Principio Company in Maryland and Hasenclever's short-lived undertakings in New York and New Jersey. English merchants supplied the initial capital for the New England fishery, but control rapidly passed into the hands of resident settlers. English capital also underwrote a large part of the New England shipbuilding industry.

In the American Colonies the capitalist class was not comprised principally of manufacturers. Merchants, landed proprietors, and office-holders made up its ranks. They found safer and more attractive types of investment than manufacturing. They invested their surplus incomes in real estate or else in British Government securities, which were considered more conservative than industrial enterprises. In the course of time, however, Colonial merchants saw the possibilities of profit from lumber and flour mills, sugar refineries, breweries, distilleries, potash and pearlash works, iron furnaces and bloomeries. The entrepeneur of the type of Robert Morris, who financed shipping ventures, merchandising, road and canal building, and land speculation, was rarely found in the Colonial period. With the advent of the Revolution, however, industrial promoters rose to considerable prominence. William Duer was probably chief among them. His financial ventures included a timber project, financing of supplies to the Continental troops, promoting land and stock speculation in the "critical period," and joining with other promoters in backing the Society for Establishing Useful Manufactures, founded in 1791, one of the pioneer industrial enterprises of this country.

As compared with modern times, relatively more capital was needed in the Colonial period for operating a manufacturing enterprise than for fixed investment. The large amount of working capital was necessary because of the slow processes of manufacture and the delayed return from sales resulting from transportation problems and long credits. Handicraft trades lacking capital were never expanded beyond the point of producing for the local community. The "putting-out" system of textile manufacture involved relatively little capital, while the factory system, which had not extensively developed at that time, required far more. Until a substantial merchant-capitalist group had been firmly established in America, surplus capital for manufactures continued to be scarce and productive enterprises accordingly restricted in scope. The capital invested in productive enterprises might vary between $500 and $1,000 for a sawmill to $250,000 for an iron works.

The scarcity of capital encouraged high interest rates. Nevertheless, it must be kept in mind that the first call on the printing press was not made to satisfy the needs of productive enterprise but rather to meet public budgets increased by war emergencies and later by local fiscal conditions. The attempt to satisfy the desire for more money by issuing paper currency failed and brought with it rapid depreciation. Private paper-money issues were declared illegal in 1741. Ten years later Parliament forbade the New England Colonies to issue any bills of credit in the future and ruled that thereafter no bill of credit should be made legal tender. In 1764 this prohibition was extended to the rest of the Colonies. Coming at the end of a war and the beginning of a depression, this action was badly timed and aroused widespread resentment. Franklin stated that the restraints on paper money were one of the principal causes of Colonial disaffection.

Had the joint-stock company or corporation been employed more widely, capital for financing industrial ventures in the Colonies would undoubtedly have been available to a greater extent. But the individual investor rather than the corporation normally underwrote productive enterprises. Even when factories were started by public subscription, as were some of the textile companies set up during the nonimportation agreements, the public was suspicious that the entrepreneurs might seek to enrich themselves unduly rather than to carry out the major objective —the employment of the poor.

The principal public corporations chartered in the Colonies were the Colonial municipalities. The private corporations set up were mainly concerned with such nonprofit objectives as religious worship, philanthropy, and education. Business corporations were few in number. Land companies made up the majority, but a few commercial companies were chartered, such as the trading corporation set up in Connecticut in 1723, the wharf companies chartered in that Colony in 1760 and in Massachusetts in 1772, and a number of fire insurance and water supply companies. There were few industrial corporations. Some of the early mining companies, notably that of the Simsbury mines in Connecticut, were incorporated. The Revolutionary era witnessed the rise of a number of joint-stock companies for manufacturing. Of these the United Company of Philadelphia for Promoting American Manufacturers, founded in 1775, was probably the most successful, but, by and large, the joint-stock company was not the medium for financing productive enterprise in the Colonial period.

While the corporate type of organization was not usual in industry, the risks of enterprise were at times shared by the entrepreneur with the workers. Fishing, whaling, and privateering are the best examples of this type of business organization; the seamen by waiving their claims to regular wages in reality contributed substantially to the financing of the enterprise. The financial return to the seaman took the form of a "lay," or a fractional share in the net proceeds of an entire voyage. In fishing voyages the master and men customarily received one-third of the fish, and the remaining two-thirds went to the owners. In whaling expeditions a green hand commonly started with a lay of 1/200 of the catch, and captains received as much as one-tenth. But the workers had no part whatever in the functions of ownership or management. They shared to the full the risks of enterprise without being allowed the slightest part in the determination of those risks.

The Organization of Colonial Manufacturing

In the Colonial and Revolutionary periods, three stages of manufacturing existed side by side: household manufacturing, the prevailing system; the domestic or putting-out system, well entrenched by the middle of the eighteenth century; and the factory, developed under the stress of Revolutionary conditions. For goods produced mainly for local consumption and not requiring elaborate equipment, household manufactures or workshop crafts prevailed. Spinning and weaving of woolen, linen, or cotton cloth were common in most households, as was the making of homespun garments. As Victor S. Clark points out, as long as an operative was required for every spindle, as was the case of the hand-wheel or the Saxon wheel operated by a treadle, there was no economy in applying water power to spinning or any incentive to the setting up of factories. On the other hand, weaving required more mechanical equipment and greater skill, and therefore cloth making tended to become specialized and to be produced in workshops or factories. The farmers slaughtered their own cattle, cured and salted their meats, and, as by-products of this activity, produced tallow, soap, lard, and candles. To the total volume of production in the Colonies household manufactures contributed a respectable proportion.

The Workshop Crafts

The prevailing mode of production in the Colonial towns was the workshop crafts. Normally making their products on order for customers, the master craftsmen did not require large inventories or stocks of raw materials. Because of failure to establish a permanent craft guild system, shortage of skilled labor, and the rise of *laissez-faire* tendencies, workers frequently performed more than one industrial process: the blacksmith was a toolmaker; the soap boiler a tallow chandler; and, despite restrictive legislation, the tanner often acted as a currier and shoemaker. Such versatility was attained often through the sacrifice of quality. When John Julius Sorge advertised in the New York newspapers in 1755 that he could make artificial fruit, do japan work, manufacture cleaning fluid, toilet water, soap, candles, insecticides, and wine,[8] there is no reason to believe that New Yorkers were taken aback by this display of diverse talents. Aside from the Jack-of-all-trades who was master of none there was also the highly skilled craftsman who was enterprising enough to branch out into other related fields. Paul Revere, renowned for carrying the messages of the Committees of Correspondence and the Sons of Liberty, was also a distinguished silversmith by trade. His sugar bowls and creamers, spoons and sugar tongs, medals and buttons amply demonstrate to posterity his mastery of his craft. But in addition, he was a well-known copperplate engraver, although not a very good one, a dentist who set false "foreteeth," a manufacturer of clock-faces for clockmakers, of branding irons for hatters, and spatulas and probes for surgeons. After the Revolution, while continuing his workshop craft of silversmithing, he branched out into large-scale industry, setting up a foundry, making brass cannons, casting bells—at which he was most proficient—and making hardware for ships, the most famous of which was the *Constitution*. Finally, in 1800 he set up a mill for rolling copper into sheets that is now one of the great copper establishments of the country.[9]

The Domestic System

The putting-out or domestic system developed in a few industries, notably in weaving and in shoe manufacturing. The weaver or shoemaker worked at home but was dependent for stock upon an entrepreneur who in some cases furnished implements as well. Spinning and weaving received a great impetus during the period when nonimportation agreements were in force. The Colonial towns began to concentrate intensively on the production of woolen, cotton, and linen goods. It is clear

[8] *New-York Gazette or the Weekly Post-Boy,* June 16, 1755.

[9] For an interesting biography of the famous craftsman and patriot, see Esther Forbes, *Paul Revere: The Man and His Times.* Boston: Little, Brown and Company, 1942.

that in some cases the workers produced fabrics in their own homes from raw materials that they had raised themselves.[10] In other instances, raw material appears to have been provided by an entrepreneur. The spinners of New York were notified in May, 1766 "that due Attendance will be given, every Tuesday, Thursday, and Saturday, in the Afternoon, to give out Flax and receive in Yarn" at the factory of Obadiah Wells in Mulberry Street. Apparently Wells not only engaged in the putting-out system, but also hired factory operatives to work in his own plant, as he was compelled to announce that "to prevent Trouble, no Person who has not been an Inhabitant in this City ever since May last, will be admitted as a Spinner in the Factory." [11] Finally, spinning wheels and looms were occasionally assembled in factories, as was the case with the "Manufactory House" opened by William Molineaux in Boston in 1769 and with two establishments set up in Philadelphia a few years later for the manufacture of cotton and woolen goods.

Shoes, also manufactured under the domestic system during the latter part of the Colonial period, were being produced for a wholesale market. By 1760 there were sufficient workers in the shoe trade as well as adequate capital to justify ventures on a larger scale in the domestic and foreign markets. Lynn, Massachusetts, was the most highly organized center for the domestic system in shoe manufacturing on the eve of the Revolution.

Mills and Factories

Lumber mills and gristmills, as well as the manufacture of glass and paper, early required the use of considerable machinery and the establishment of plants. The availability of water power was a factor in determining the location of such plants, although windmills were not uncommon. Power was used in a number of industries. For example, in paper mills it propelled two rollers that ran over an iron bed-plate containing macerating knives. By the eve of the Revolution power was applied to milling. The machinery perfected by Oliver Evans of Philadelphia for cleaning, grinding, cooling, bolting, and barreling grain without manual operation represents an early instance of complete mechanization of manufacturing, from raw materials to finished commodity. Under such a system, six men, mostly employed in closing barrels, could annually convert 100,000 bushels of grain into flour. Fulling and powder mills also employed water power.

By the eve of the Revolution, factories and mills were growing larger in size. Gristmills and iron works were employing greater numbers of workers. In New York City a small linen factory with 14 looms, a

[10] For example, in 1767 three individuals made in their homes in Woodbridge, New Jersey, 599 yards, 567 yards, and 414 yards, respectively, of woolen and linen cloth.

[11] *New-York Gazette or the Weekly Post-Boy,* May 8, 1766 (Supplement).

paper mill, a beaver hattery, a glass house, two breweries, a spermaceti candle works, and a number of shipyards were at work. A Trenton tannery had, in 1778, 64 vats, 5 limes, 2 water pools, a bark house, currying and skin dresser's shops, and facilities for making leather breeches. The mill and furnace industries, probably to a greater extent than other types of Colonial manufacturing enterprises, involved a considerable concentration of labor of a semiskilled character working along rather specialized lines under one employer. In addition, they required a heavy investment in plant and equipment. While almost any country blacksmith might improvise a bloomery, the expansion of iron manufacture demanded considerable capital for the building of ore furnaces employing water power, furnaces for remelting iron and making steel, and steel works, including steel furnaces, refining forges, slitting mills, and plating forges.

The fact that by 1775 the American Colonies had more blast furnaces and forges than England and Wales combined was largely due to the pioneering enterprise of Colonial ironmasters. These ventures were not always crowned with success. With the help of British capital and imported workmen, the scientifically minded John Winthrop, Colonial governor of Connecticut, eldest son of the governor of Massachusetts Bay, and first member of the Royal Society resident in America, set up in the 1640's a furnace at Lynn and another at Braintree. Later he expanded his ventures in New Haven Colony. He also developed lead and salt works, but none of these prospered despite liberal subsidies of land conferred by friendly Colonial governments, exemptions from all taxes, and exemptions of workers from muster duty. This small-scale development (the Lynn plant turned out eight tons a week in 1648) contrasts strikingly with the far more ambitious iron works established prior to the Revolution by Peter Hasenclever, who, reared in Prussia and trained in long hours of toil of a Continental steel mill, brought to his forge and furnace enterprises a broad commercial and industrial experience. Upon becoming a British subject, he formed a company with an initial capital of £21,000 and, coming to this country in 1764, set up in Morris County, New Jersey, Orange County, New York, and elsewhere mining and smelting works and potash plants. He supplemented these activities with raising hemp and flax. He tested mineral deposits, invested in extensive equipment, and constructed bridges and dams. As a result of careful preparation and intelligent organization, his company produced the best iron ever exported to England from America up to that time. Controversies with his English directors and long-protracted litigation led, however, to the failure of the Colonial enterprise, and Hasenclever spent his declining years in manufacturing activities in Silesia.

Even more glamorous was the career of Henry William Stiegel, ironmaster and glassmaker. Arriving in Philadelphia from Cologne in 1750, he was employed by an ironmaster in Lancaster County, married the boss's daughter, and after his father-in-law's death went into partnership with Charles and Alexander Stedman of Philadelphia to develop the Elizabeth Furnace. There he manufactured stoves and iron castings, and by 1760 had become the most prosperous ironmaster in the region. He invested in thousands of acres of woodland, erected tenant houses, laid out the town of Manheim, and gained the sobriquet of "Baron" because of his lordly manner of living. Upon his return from a visit to England in 1764 he brought back a number of skilled glassmakers, and erected a glass factory at Manheim. In a second factory erected by him in that town in 1769, and known after 1772 as the American Flint Glass Manufactory, was turned out the renowned Stiegel glassware, in addition to window and sheet glass. But his extravagant and happy-go-lucky manner of living led to his financial undoing; and after going through bankruptcy in 1774 and spending some weeks in debtors' prison, he was reduced in his last years to working as a country schoolmaster and music teacher.

Similar to the factories of the industrial towns were the somewhat smaller works set up on numerous plantations in the Southern Colonies. George Washington had an establishment for the manufacture of woolen, cotton, and linen cloth employing at least one white woman and five Negro girls, and producing in 1768 some 2,000 yards of linen, woolen, and cotton cloth. Diversified economy, as it was developed on the plantations on the eve of the Revolution, turned many planters into mill and factory operatives as well as agriculturists. Epitome of these men of many affairs was the Virginia planter, Robert Carter, who, in addition to his holdings of 300,000 acres of land, held an interest in the Baltimore Iron Works organized in 1731. The partners either sold the iron produced or used it on their own plantations. Carter did both, manufacturing various iron implements in his own smithy, offering axes, broad hoes, plows, and nails for sale. He set up a fulling mill and employed ten Negro women at spinning wool in a tobacco house converted for the purpose. During the Revolution he engaged six white workers who were expert spinners and weavers, and proceeded to manufacture cloth, for which he erected a building 77 feet in length and 26 feet in width. Gradually Negro workers were trained to replace white artisans in that enterprise. A stocking weaver made hosiery which Carter offered for sale. When the depression of the 1750's and 1760's forced many planters to produce such other staples as wheat, corn, rye, and barley, Carter engaged in milling on an ambitious scale. He built a grain mill designed to grind 25,000 bushels of wheat a year and requiring £5,000 annually for its operation; in his two ovens 100 pounds of flour could be baked at one time. He also set up complete equipment for the manufacture of salt. So wide a variety of occupations throws out of perspective the traditional picture of the planter solely dependent upon the vagaries of the tobacco market for the livelihood of family and workmen.[12] "I have a large Family of my own," wrote William Byrd 2nd of "Westover" in 1727, "and my Doors are open to Every Body, yet I have no Bills to pay, and half-a-Crown will rest undisturbed in my Pocket for many Moons together. Like one of the Patriarchs, I have my Flocks and my Herds, my Bond-men and Bond-women, and every Soart of Trade amongst my own Servants, so that I live in a kind of Independence on every one but Providence."

Economic Nationalism and Colonial Production

The British policy expressed in the imperial program of trade regulation was a manifestation of the intense economic nationalism of the period. Colonies were looked upon as sources of raw materials and outlets for the manufactured products of the mother country, whose export trade was to be encouraged by protecting manufacturers against high wages or excessive raw materials costs and by providing subsidies to home manufacturing or to Colonial enterprises deemed essential to the home economy.

Some aspects of this program proved advantageous to Colonial productive enterprise. Shipbuilding benefited only slightly from the Navigation Acts, which discouraged, but did not forbid, the use of foreign-built vessels in the English merchant marine. Certainly even without this legislation Colonial shipbuilding could have held its own in free competition. By the time of the American Revolution, one-third of the ships in the British merchant marine were launched in the Thirteen Colonies, which were then turning out close to 30,000 tons of shipping per year.

Bounties to noncompeting industries served to stimulate Colonial production somewhat unevenly. Raw-silk production did not thrive in the Colonies, Georgia, the largest producer, shipping a little over 1,000 pounds of silk to England in 1773. Bounties also directed a quantity of lumber to Britain, although the chief market for American lumber products remained the West Indies. Production of naval stores showed the greatest response to bounties granted it. These bounties totaled £1,471,719; but, while the production of tar, pitch, rosin, and turpentine was appreciably advanced, that of hemp gained little momentum. The cultivation of indigo in Carolina and Georgia was unquestionably stimulated by a bounty totaling £145,032 for the years 1749-1773. After the Revolution, the competition of the British East Indies led to the

[12] See Louis Morton, *Robert Carter of Nomini Hall*. Williamsburg, Va.: Colonial Williamsburg, Inc., 1941.

virtual abandonment of the cultivation of indigo. The prohibition on the planting of tobacco in England was designed to encourage American production, but it does not seem to have achieved anything noteworthy in this direction.

Generally speaking, the restraints that British policy imposed upon Colonial productive enterprise outweighed the bounties and monopolies granted certain favored industries. The Navigation Laws, which required that tobacco be sent through Britain instead of directly to the Continental markets, worked hardship on the tobacco planters, since the greater part of the world price of tobacco now went to English middlemen. In 1773 Britain consumed less than 4,000,000 pounds of the 100,000,000 pounds imported, the remainder being re-exported, mostly to Holland and Germany.

The restrictions on Colonial industry were in the main as detrimental as were the controls placed upon the tobacco trade. The British Government paid premiums on masts, yards, and bowsprits, but at the same time its legislation forbade any cutting of white pine suitable for masts. In practice the King reserved for his own use all pines measuring 24 inches in diameter at a height of three feet. Such trees were to be marked with the king's broad arrow by the surveyor-general of the woods. Respect for the royal mark was not too conspicuous among lumbermen. Loggers cut down reserved trees with impunity. The ensuing litigation was not advantageous to the lumber industry. The Colonists felt that to substitute a doubtful trade in naval stores for the profitable industry of timber-cutting and board-making was poor business.

The act of 1699 forbidding shipment of Colonial wool or woolen manufactures outside the border of a colony does not seem to have restrained Colonial producers seriously. But this industry was throughout Colonial times largely confined to the production of homespun garments for local consumption. The act of 1732 barring exportation of hats, limiting each manufacturer to two apprentices, requiring a seven-year apprenticeship, and excluding Negroes from the industry appears to have hindered Colonial enterprise. Violations of the act were prosecuted in New York in the mid-eighteenth century. After the Revolution, the United States, freed from the restrictions of this act, began once again to export hats to foreign countries. Prohibitions on the erection of any additional slitting mills in the Colonies (1750) or on the exportation of Colonial iron outside the empire (1757) were openly defied, at least in Pennsylvania. Nevertheless, conservative investors were indubitably discouraged from entering a field of illegal activity. It must be borne in mind that, while the British Government opposed the Colonial manufacture and exportation of finished iron and steel products, it favored the production of Colonial pig and bar iron and granted these products preferential treatment when entering England.

Resentment on the part of manufacturers and workingmen over British policy was but one of the numerous causes of the final break with the mother country. Actually the regulations were never systematically enforced. But no other single issue was as well-calculated to unite master and workingman in opposition to the British Government. The non-importation agreements beginning with the Stamp Act were a great stimulus to Colonial production and the expansion of the domestic and factory systems.[13] The Revolution served to foster production at home for military uses. Colonial and Revolutionary producers blazed the way for the artisans and entrepreneurs of the next generation, such as Samuel Slater, who successfully developed and expanded the use of power-driven machinery and consequent mass-production methods.

In considering the role of agriculture and industry in the Colonial economy, it should be borne in mind that the Colonial economic scene embraced other important elements. In many parts of the Colonies real estate and commercial activity constituted the mainsprings of wealth, and throughout the Colonial period the Colonies may properly be considered an integral part of the European economic world. As was noted in the preceding chapter, the Colonial producer was often intimately involved in problems of large-scale distribution and marketing.

Selected References

Bining, A. C., *British Regulation of the Colonial Iron Industry.* Philadelphia: University of Pennsylvania Press, 1933.

Bishop, J. L., *History of American Manufactures, 1608-1860* (3 vols., 3d ed. rev.). Philadelphia: Edward Young, 1866-1868.

Clark, V. S., *History of the Manufactures in the United States, 1607-1860* (3 vols.). New York: McGraw-Hill Book Company, 1929.

Cole, A. H., *The American Wool Manufacture* (2 vols.). Cambridge, Mass.: Harvard University Press, 1926.

Commons, J. R., ed., *History of Labour in the United States,* Vol. I. New York: The Macmillan Company, 1936.

Commons, J. R., *et al., A Documentary History of American Industrial Society* (11 vols.). Cleveland: A. H. Clark Company, 1911-1919.

Davis, J. S., *Essays in the Earlier History of American Corporations,* Vol. I. Cambridge, Mass.: Harvard University Press, 1917.

Gras, N. S. B., and H. M. Larson, *Casebook in American Business History.* New York: F. S. Crofts and Company, 1939.

Gray, L. C., *History of Agriculture in the Southern United States* (2 vols.). Washington, D. C.: Carnegie Institution, 1933.

Harper, L. A., *The Navigation Laws.* New York: Columbia University Press, 1939.

———, "The Effect of the Navigation Acts on the Thirteen Colonies," in R. B.

[13] A London paper of this period, reporting on some beautiful samples of cotton goods made in Philadelphia for export to London, as well as on American progress in other branches of manufacturing, commented: "by which it should seem, that our American colonies intend to shake off, by degrees, what they have long called a slavish dependence on the mother country." *Lloyd's Evening Post,* August 10, 1764.

Morris, ed., *The Era of the American Revolution: Studies Inscribed to Evarts Boutell Greene*. New York: Columbia University Press, 1939.

Hazard, Blanche E., *Organization of the Boot and Shoe Industry in Massachusetts before 1875*. Cambridge, Mass.: Harvard University Press, 1921.

Johnson, E. A. J., *American Economic Thought in the Seventeenth Century*. London: P. S. King and Son, Ltd., 1932.

Morris, R. B., *Government and Labor in Early America*. New York: Columbia University Press, 1946.

Nettles, Curtis, "The Menace of Colonial Manufacturing, 1690-1720," *New England Quarterly*, Vol. IV (1931), pp. 230-269.

Phillips, U. B., *American Negro Slavery*. New York: D. Appleton-Century Company, 1918.

Schafer, Joseph, *The Social History of American Agriculture*. New York: The Macmillan Company, 1936.

Smith, A. E., *Colonists in Bondage*. Chapel Hill: University of North Carolina Press, 1947.

Tryon, R. M., *Household Manufactures in the United States, 1640-1860*. Chicago: University of Chicago Press, 1917.

5 · THE PERFORMANCE OF THE AMERICAN ECONOMY TO 1789

From the handful of settlers who barely survived the first few years at Jamestown, the number of inhabitants in the thirteen colonies had grown to an estimated 2.5 million on the eve of the American Revolution. Beginning about 1660, a high domestic birth rate and a rising number of immigrants had combined to increase the population by approximately one-third every ten years. Nor did the Revolution disturb this trend. In 1790, at the time the first census was taken under the new government, the total number of people was reported at slightly in excess of 3.9 million. By this date there was a continuous line of settlements, between the mountains and the sea, extending from Maine to the northern boundary of Florida; and pioneers had already pushed their way across the Alleghanies and established themselves in Tennessee and Kentucky.

This growth and spread of population is a good index of a rapidly expanding economy. Unfortunately, however, it is not possible to give any very specific information about how well the economy operated during this period. It is doubtful if anyone has even ventured a guess at the rate of growth of "national" income, but, on the not unreasonable assumption that average *per capita* income was no smaller during the late 18th century than it had been during the 17th, it may be concluded that the expansion in total income was at least proportional to the increase in population. Actually it was probably greater. The increase in population itself and a slowly growing supply of capital made it possible to secure the advantages of greater specialization and division of labor, at least on a limited scale. Nor, as has been pointed out in the preceding chapters, was the period without important improvements in knowledge and techniques. Numerous experiments had revealed which crops and methods of cultivation were best suited to the soil and climate and available markets. The extent to which manufacturing and industry could be carried under the limitations of British colonial policy and relatively high labor and capital costs had also been discovered. The potentialities of commerce and the carrying trade had been vigorously exploited. In sum, there seems little doubt that the inhabitants in the area of the original colonies had made material progress by 1789 in their ability to get larger amounts of goods and services, either directly or indirectly through trade, from their resources.

The extent of this progress should not be exaggerated. The economy was still largely based upon agriculture with the export of staples and the merchant marine supplying funds for much needed imports. In the days before mechanization was applied to agriculture and prior to the time that industry would utilize energy other than that generated by humans, there were severe limits to the capacity to increase output *per capita.*

Even the simple agrarian and commercial economy of the colonial period suffered from fluctuations in its economic activity. The earliest recorded depression in America came in New England in 1640.[1] The colonial economy, being but a European offshoot, was open to all the cyclical and wartime upheavals of the countries of the old world. Its prosperity and depression were but a reflection of similar conditions abroad, except where peculiarly natural conditions, such as drought, impaired the functioning of the economy. It was not until the Revolutionary War, however, that a major burden was placed on the economy and its performance in the face of seriously disruptive forces was tested.

The American Economy During the Revolutionary War [2]

The diversion of a large part of the national income to the prosecution of the war with England was extremely onerous for an economically immature and relatively unorganized group of Colonies.[3] Men, materials, and money were scarce. Lack of men resulted from the small population, division of loyalties, and unsatisfactory methods of recruiting and maintenance. Lack of materials arose from the British blockade, the undeveloped state of the country's manufactures, and the policies adopted to obtain supplies. Lack of money—money that could effectively assist in the prosecution of the war with a minimum of economic disruption—was a consequence of decentralized authority, shortsighted fiscal policies,

1 See Willard L. Thorp, *Business Annals,* p. 112. New York: National Bureau of Economic Research, 1926.

2 See: Edmund Cody Burnett, *The Continental Congress.* New York: The Macmillan Company, 1941. Robert A. East, *Business Enterprise in the American Revolutionary Era.* New York: Columbia University Press, 1938. Arthur Meier Schlesinger, *The Colonial Merchants and the American Revolution, 1763-1776.* New York: Columbia University Press, 1918.

3 The earlier wars had involved a relatively small economic effort. "Our wars during the first half of the eighteenth century were somewhat desultory, in the nature of intermittent skirmishes in the wilderness. The American Revolutionary War was the first example in our history of a concentrated military effort, involving armies and financial outlay that placed a heavy burden upon the pioneer civilization of that time." Norman J. Silberling, *The Dynamics of Business,* p. 52. New York: McGraw-Hill Book Company, 1943.

poor credit standing of the Colonies, and the makeshift central Government. All these factors were, of course, closely connected.

The manpower problem was less acute in fact than it appeared on paper. Considering the population on which England could draw and the force she could and did put into the field, the Colonies were indeed at a serious disadvantage. But England had to watch France and other countries, and had to fight at a great distance from her home base. Moreover, the fact that some of the American armed forces could be engaged in both agricultural and military pursuits at the same time made for a fuller utilization of the available manpower. But the existence of an openly hostile Tory group substantially reduced potential manpower. The inadequate provision for the army, and the low and depreciating army pay reduced the size and the effectiveness of the American fighting force.

The problem of obtaining materials might have been fatal had it not been for outside assistance. Because of natural advantage and by specific dictate of the mother country, the Colonies had emphasized agriculture and neglected manufacturing. Consequently, the Colonies were well stocked with food but deficient in clothing and munitions. Fortunately France was willing and able to act as an arsenal of democracy and aid the Colonies in their fight. Also, some leaks were found in the British blockade. But far from the fullest use was made of available resources. The Continental Congress soon found itself unable to obtain supplies and had to call on the separate states, sometimes on private individuals, for assistance. Rivalry, selfishness, and lack of co-ordination combined to reduce efficiency; and sometimes, as in the case of embargoes on exports from one state to another, the different units worked at cross purposes. Further unnecessary confusion resulted from competition among various purchasing units: the Congress, the states, and the various foreign governments. Only after 1781, when some semblance of centralized control of purchasing was attained, did the situation improve. The price policy adopted also reacted unfavorably on the availability of supplies. With the rapidly rising market price level, attempts at price-fixing led to hoarding and even to sales to the enemy. Although some groups of states adopted price conventions, general laxity of enforcement and the irresistible appeal of the printing press soon made shambles of attempts at control; and variations in the degree of enforcement among the various states disrupted the flow of commodities.[4]

Monetary problems were the most spectacular. Lacking the power to tax, the Continental Congress had to depend on its own credit and on the munificence of the states to finance the war. Through foreign loans

[4] See Anne W. Bezanson, "Inflation and Controls, Pennsylvania, 1774-1779," *Journal of Economic History,* Supplement (1948), pp. 1-20.

the Congress was able to raise some money.[5] But this source of funds soon proved inadequate, and the Congress had to resort to printing-press money to so great an extent that the paper dollar depreciated rapidly in value. The general disinclination to taxation prevalent in the Colonies forced the states likewise to seek help from the printing press. The weak central Government, whose military prowess far exceeded its economic power, seemed to have no alternative. Attempts to enforce legal-tender provisions merely had the effect of driving specie out of circulation. The young economy experienced an upward rush of prices not to be equaled in its most mature years. The general level of wholesale prices rose to high points in 1779 and 1780, and then began to fall.[6]

The fiscal problems of the Revolution and the unsatisfactory methods employed to solve them had repercussions throughout the economy.[7] Uneven effects fell on different groups of people and on different individuals within those groups. Contractual obligations fixed in monetary terms redounded to the advantage of the debtor against the creditor, since the money payment represented a much smaller quantity of goods and of effort than at the time when the obligation was undertaken and prices were lower. Persons with fixed incomes whose monetary earnings changed only slowly, and therefore lagged behind prices, suffered a decline in real income and standard of living. On the other hand, those engaged in selling goods could take advantage of the rise in prices and the lag in costs to earn large profits, and were mainly responsible for the atmosphere of extravagance and luxury that prevailed in some quarters. The price rise reacted back on the governments that had to pay for the war and raised the cost of equipping and maintaining the armed forces. Ultimately, good money in the form of specie brought over by the French and British drove out bad; Gresham's law seemed to reverse itself since the paper money that at first was accepted below par soon was not accepted at all. Since the supply of specie was neither sufficient nor widely distributed, barter replaced monetary transactions in many instances. The successful conclusion of the war owed much to military prowess and considerably less to wisdom of economic policy.

Economic Changes Following the War

The economic changes that followed the Revolutionary War were of two sorts: those that affected general activity and those that affected the

---

[5] Bills of exchange were drawn on France and sold even before the French loans were assured. See Burnett, *The Continental Congress,* pp. 375-377, 419.

[6] See Arthur H. Cole, *Wholesale Commodity Prices in the United States, 1700-1861.* Cambridge, Mass.: Harvard University Press, 1938.

[7] It should perhaps be pointed out that the desirability of imposing heavy taxes to prevent inflation was generally recognized in enlightened circles. See Burnett, *The Continental Congress,* pp. 376, 408, 417, 424.

distribution of wealth and income among various groups of the population. The first type of change operated in both domestic and foreign trade. The wartime depreciation of the currency and the inflationary rise in prices were followed by a sharp deflation in the post-war period, particularly in 1785 and 1786. The sharp rise in prices caused by the war was matched only by the precipitous fall when peace was proclaimed. During the immediate post-war period, the price system as a whole settled back to its pre-war level. By 1785 wholesale prices had fallen to the level of 1776. Deflation, which thus continued to 1789, discouraged domestic trade and business activity, although business began to recover after 1787. In foreign trade the infant industries created by the emergency conditions of the war now lost their artificial protection. Goods of British manufacture flooded the market and depressed business. At the same time the export industries that had been encouraged during the Colonial period now lost their preferential treatment in the British market. Immediate economic advantages of the break with England were not apparent. Although the country had met with military success, the gains on the economic front appeared empty.

A significant redistribution of wealth and income and in the economic power of various groups took place within the country. The confiscation of Tory property effected such redistribution to some extent, but the uneven impact of Government war expenditures and of price changes were of more profound importance. The sharp price rise during the war had favored the debtor classes but the deflation of the post-war period placed at a disadvantage those who had undertaken contractual obligations during the period of high prices. The war had brought with it the inevitable crop of *nouveaux riches*. While some branches of economic activity suffered during the war others benefited from high profits. Some people had won and some had lost on the economic front. In the individual states post-war deflation, particularly in the year 1785-1786, stirred up strong agitation for "easy money." The state governments were subjected to pressure for an increase in the issue of paper money. This pressure was the expression of a popular movement of the debtor classes, mainly rural and agricultural, against the creditor classes, mainly urban. In some cases mob violence broke out, notably in Shays' Rebellion. In many states the governments yielded to the pressure and issued large amounts of paper money that was made legal tender. The fiscal condition of the central Government became worse, if possible, in the post-war period than it had been during the war. Requisitions on the states, sale of public lands, and even loans from abroad provided insufficient funds to meet expenditures. The Continental Congress even had to default on its interest payments. By the end of the period it was on the verge of insolvency, and a drastic enlargement of the economic powers of the central Government was required.

Selected References

GENERAL WORKS

Morris, Richard B., *Historiography of America, 1600-1800.* New York: Columbia University Press, 1933.

Silberling, Norman J., *The Dynamics of Business.* New York: McGraw-Hill Book Company, 1943.

Thorp, Willard L., *Business Annals.* New York: National Bureau of Economic Research, 1926.

SPECIAL TOPICS

Bezanson, Anne W., "Inflation and Controls, Pennsylvania, 1774-1779," *Journal of Economic History,* Supplement, 1948, pp. 1-20.

Burnett, Edmund Cody, *The Continental Congress,* New York: The Macmillan Company, 1941.

Cole, Arthur H., *Wholesale Commodity Prices in the United States, 1700-1861.* Cambridge: Harvard University Press, 1938.

East, R. A., *Business Enterprise in the American Revolutionary Era.* New York: Columbia University Press, 1938.

Schlesinger, A. M., *The Colonial Merchants and the American Revolution, 1763-1776.* New York: Columbia University Press, 1918.

PART 3

1789-1865

IT IS NOTEWORTHY *how little the American Revolution affected the basic structure of the economy. Even taking into account the disturbance and readjustment in commercial relations brought about by the conflict and its aftermath, there was little change in the organization of production and in the importance of trade with the outside world.*

The forces that were to change this structure, however, were already gathering strength. Following the War of 1812 the country began to move slowly but perceptibly away from an economic dependence upon Europe and foreign trade. Increasing attention was given to developing domestic sources of commodities previously imported and to exploring the possibilities of the regions beyond the mountains. Just as the Atlantic seaboard had attracted settlers from across the ocean, now the West began to pull increasing numbers from the Atlantic coast states. The trickle of westward migration that began in the late 18th century swelled into a flood that, by 1860, had reached the Pacific coast and had begun to spread into the most promising areas in between. Like the Colonists, the population in the West brought with it a standard of living that under frontier conditions could not be satisfied except by producing commodities that could be exchanged for articles manufactured in the East. Internal trade began to replace foreign trade as the object of concern and lay back of the intense interest in improving the means of inland transportation. The well springs that fed this westward migration were in turn replenished by a rising tide of immigrants and a continued high domestic birth rate. For each successive decade until 1860 the over-all population grew at the rate established during the Colonial period.

Both the total growth and the westward movement of population opened up new economic opportunities for the Eastern states, especially the Middle Atlantic and New England groups. A larger population meant a larger market for manufactured articles; the location of a considerable portion of that market in the West meant that it could be supplied more easily from domestic than from foreign sources. A larger population also meant a larger labor supply, which, in conjunction with continued imports of capital from Europe, augmented by increasing savings from domestic sources, served to change the proportionality of the factors of production. More capital and labor relative to natural resources made it economically feasible to undertake ventures that had formerly been impossible or impractical. But this was not all. England during the late 18th century was in the midst of the Industrial Revolution. Involving use of inanimate sources of energy, power driven machinery, and new methods of refining and fabricating metals, the techniques developed proved especially adaptable to the American setting and gave an added stimulus to the development of the industrial segment of the economy. The interaction and cumulative effects of these various elements for the period ending in 1865 are brought out in the succeeding twelve chapters.

ꕥ 6 · WESTWARD EXPANSION BEFORE THE HOMESTEAD ACT

THE MOVEMENT OF THE PEOPLE from the Eastern Seaboard to the Pacific Coast is of tremendous significance to the student of American economic history and provides one of the keys for an adequate understanding of why American institutions resemble and yet are different from the European institutions from which they originated. This great movement, involving millions of persons and spanning nearly three centuries of time (1607-1890), contains all the drama, comedy, and tragedy that one would expect in a play so sweeping in scope and with a theme of such grandeur. But more important than this, it provides answers to some of the perplexing questions as to how and why adjustments were made, and finally, how Americans conquered the wilderness and set in motion those forces that are dominant in our economic life today.

Moving Frontiers

The frontier, or the area where the actual pioneering process took place, may be defined in a number of ways: as a point behind which were cities, culture, and civilization and ahead of which were forests, Indians, and wild animals; or as a "line marking the fringe of white settlements that was constantly moving westward." [1] But more than this, the frontier was an area in which the settler had to readjust himself to primitive conditions, where he had to test old institutions, and, if these failed as they did in the area of the Great Plains, he had to invent new ones that would stand up under a different or altered environment. At first the rigors and newness of frontier life tended to drag the pioneer down near the level of the Indian but, with the establishment of secure agriculture and market outlets and the increased use of capital, the later generations climbed again the hill of civilization and culture. Only an optimist would venture to the frontier; thus it was a selective process that left its indelible stamp.

Almost from the earliest settlements a certain rather clearly marked

[1] Dan E. Clark, *The West in American History*, pp. 80-81. New York: Thomas Y. Crowell Company, 1937.

sequence in the westward movement is discernible. First came the hunter, then the fur trapper, the trader, and the missionary, and the accounts of their travels often provided the information that guided the actual settlers to their destination on the frontier. The activities of men of this class led to the founding of fur-trading posts such as Albany, Pittsburgh, and many other places that later developed into important cities. Closely following the trails blazed by these wanderers came the ranchers, or the pioneers who planted a patch or two of grain or vegetables in the wilderness, bore the brunt of Indian attacks (and often fomented them as well), and laid the basis for the coming of the next group of settlers—the farmers. The farmers often bought out the ranchers or the professional pioneers for a few dollars, settled down on the partially cleared land, improved it, and began the orderly processes of living and building a more permanent civilization. With them came more capital for the development of the natural resources, and soon gristmills appeared, attracting skilled workmen; towns sprang up and presently industries and cities. This sequence in the subduing and development of the wilderness appeared again and again, and this pattern has left its indelible imprint on American habits, thought, culture, and institutions. It was this constant recurrence that made for the difference between American and European life—and underlying it was the rich, relatively free land. Sometimes there were local variations from the usual pattern of settlement, such as a gold rush, when all of the groups seem to have arrived at about the same time.

The areas in which the westward movement took place are fairly well defined and can be traced chronologically. For the first century and a half, the chief area of settlement stretched from Maine down to Georgia, and extended from the Atlantic Coast inland to the Appalachian Mountains. Culturally as well as economically, this area was divided into two parts; the first part was the Tidewater region, inhabited mainly by people controlling large land grants, aristocratic in bearing, and looking to England and Europe for guidance and commercial connections; the second part, above the Fall Line in the Piedmont area, was populated by frontiersmen or backwoodsmen who possessed relatively small land plots, were democratic in outlook and action, and looked to themselves for guidance, but who were nevertheless ruled by and somewhat dependent on the Tidewater area for capital, goods, and services. Naturally, conflicts soon arose between the peoples of the two areas.

In the last quarter of the eighteenth century, a second area stretching from the Appalachians to the Ohio River and westward to the Mississippi was being settled. It was peopled mainly by pioneers of diverse nationalities, and its settlement was patterned after the third (farming) type of frontier. From it were carved the states of Kentucky, Tennessee, and, later, West Virginia.

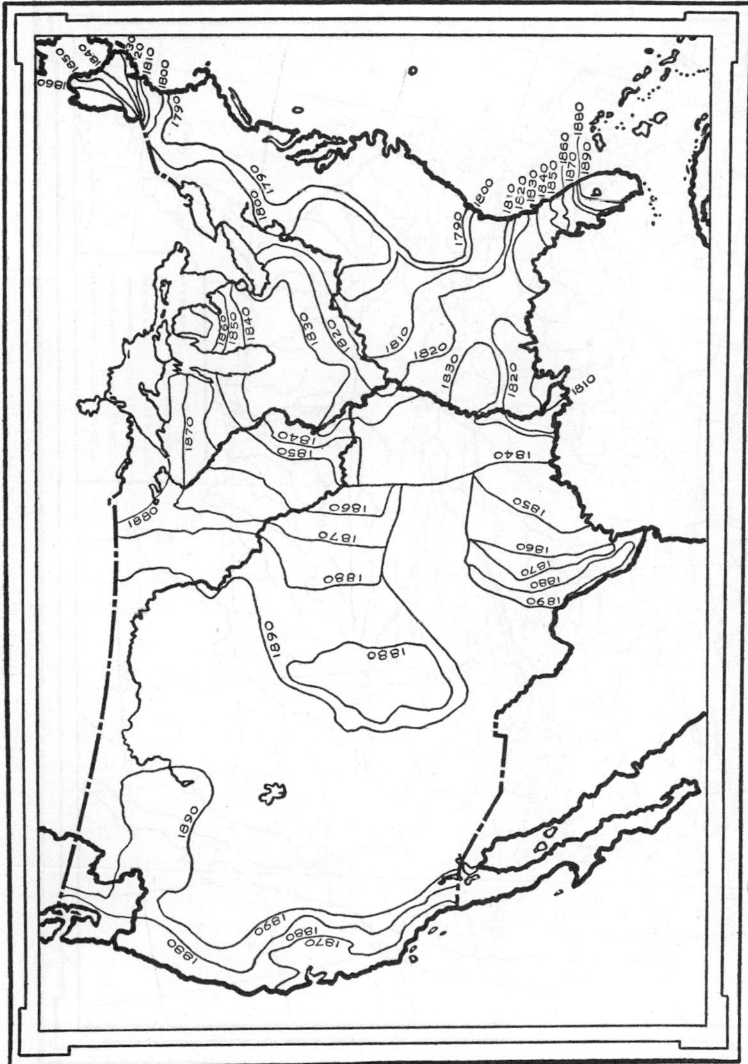

Fig. 1. *Frontier Lines, 1790-1890.* (According to Report of the Director of the Census, 1890)

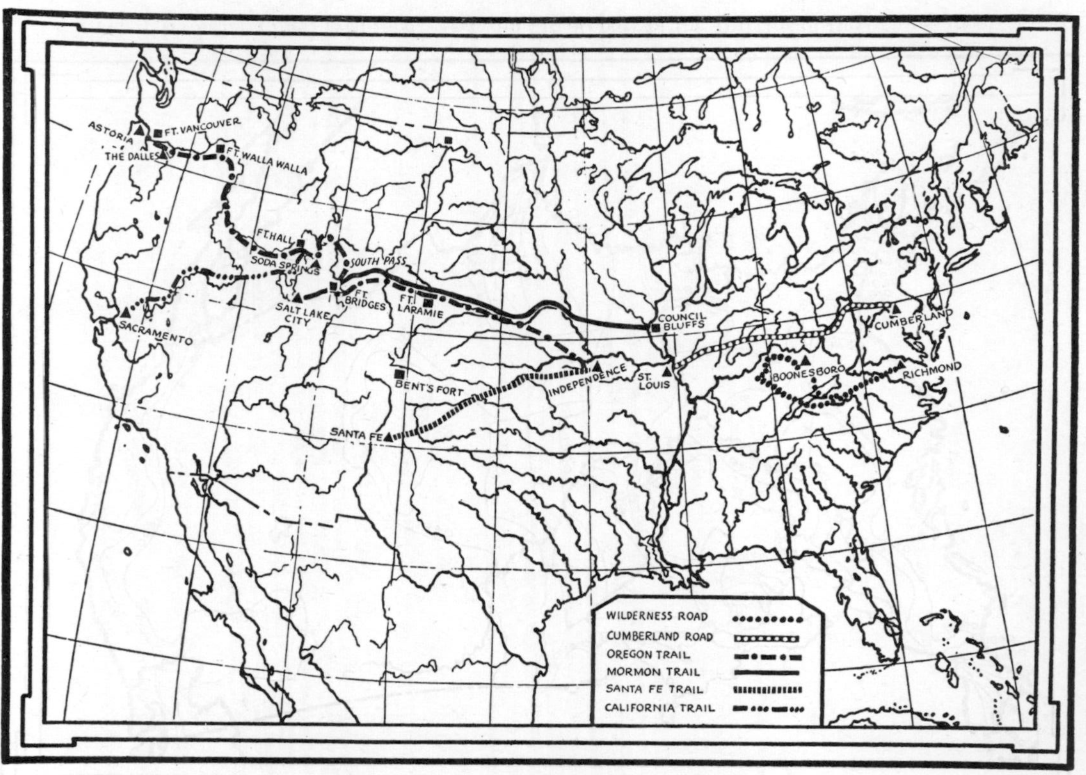

FIG. 2. *Main Roads and Trails to the West.*

A few years later, and following the same general scheme, came the settlement of the area of the Old Northwest, comprising the states of Ohio, Indiana, Illinois, Michigan, and Wisconsin. This region was peopled by typical pioneers, and settlement followed the same sequence and developed in much the same way, so far as the natural resources permitted, as the area bounded by the Appalachians, the Ohio, and the Mississippi. At first the occupants were mainly pioneers pushed out of the South by the pressure of the large landowners, but before the middle of the nineteenth century New Englanders and pioneers from the Middle Colonies helped to swell the numbers inhabiting the region.

Early in the nineteenth century, explorers, fur traders, trappers, and missionaries roamed over the rich area lying west of the Mississippi River. Here new and terrifying problems arose to plague the settlers, accustomed to moist land, to water and timber; for the farther west they went, the dryer and more open the region became, until, when a point west of the 98th meridian was reached, but one factor was left—the land. Here, too, were the fiercest and most warlike of all Indians, perhaps the world's best horsemen, who successfully defied the white man for many years. Furs, grains, minerals, and beef each played a role in the settlement of this vast plain that stretched from the Mississippi westward to the Rocky Mountains and from the Rio Grande northward to the Lake of the Woods.

Finally, there remained the region of the Pacific Coast, extending from the ocean eastward for a thousand miles to the watershed of the Rocky Mountains. Furs, rich farm land, gold, grain, timber, and fish have all contributed to the economic and historical development of this rich area. In point of time, many settlers crossed the region of the Great Plains and settled on the Pacific Coast before the Middle West was filled up, and hence the development of the two regions took place at about the same time, roughly from 1840 onward.

The Routes of Westward Travel

From ancient times man has used rivers as means of ingress and egress to continents, and the New World proved no exception. The French and the Spanish, the former to the north and the latter to the south of the English settlements, utilized the rivers as highways in their advance into the interior of the country. The St. Lawrence led to the Great Lakes, which constituted in effect a great inland sea; this route was early used by the French, beginning with Champlain, who early in the seventeenth century ascended this great waterway and discovered Lakes Huron and Ontario as well as Lake Champlain. Easy portages connected Lake Superior with the St. Croix River; Lake Michigan was connected *via* Green Bay and the Fox River with the Wisconsin River, *via* the Calumet (near Chicago) and the Des Plaines with the Illinois River, and *via* the St. Joseph River on the eastern end of Lake Michigan and the Kankakee with the Illinois River. From Lake Erie short portages led from the Maumee to either the Wabash or the Miami, from the Sandusky to the headwaters of the Scioto and down that stream to the Ohio, from the Cuyahoga to the Muskingum or from French Creek to the Allegheny; another route led *via* Lake Chatauqua. These easy paths permitted the French to establish themselves on the upper Mississippi long before their English antagonists entered this rich land of peltry.

The English, too, used the rivers as a convenient and cheap means of transportation, beginning as early as 1627, when James Claiborne of Jamestown pushed up the Potomac and the Susquehanna Rivers in search of furs. The Dutch in New York had established themselves up the Hudson as far as Albany by 1623, and by 1661 had a post at the rapids of the Mohawk, the site of present-day Schenectady. In New England the story was much the same: Springfield on the Connecticut was established by 1636. From the Hudson *via* Lake George, Lake Champlain, and the Richelieu River was the usual route to Canada. The East was connected with the Ohio Valley by means of short portages between the Susquehanna and Allegheny Rivers near Kittanning, between the Juniata and the Allegheny, and from the Potomac to the Monongahela by way of Wills Creek. Lake Ontario could be reached from the upper Mohawk by way of a portage to Oneida Lake and then down its outlet to the present Oswego, or by portaging to the headwaters of Black River and going down that stream to connect with the Lake and the St. Lawrence and Canada.

There were land or land-and-water routes that led through the great Appalachian barrier, some of which were early used by the Americans in their westward journeys. The best route, up the Hudson and the Mohawk and thence to the Susquehanna or to Lake Erie, could not be used until the late eighteenth century because the powerful and warlike Iroquois blocked the path. The second led from the Mohawk to the Allegheny, while the third led across southern Pennsylvania by a western branch of the Susquehanna and over a long land trail to the Allegheny; another route made use of the westward-reaching Juniata and then the upper Conemaugh and the Ohio. The route later known as the Forbes Road led through southern Pennsylvania and became in time one of the most important of the Appalachian crossings. But the most important of all the routes led southward down the Great Valley to what is now the extreme western tip of Virginia, and there crossed the divide by means of the famous Cumberland Gap. The route south of the great Appalachian barrier was blocked by the Cherokee Indians. Present-day railroads have utilized many of these routes, thus testifying to the soundness of the pioneers' engineering approach. Although these routes were long known to the early fur traders, they were but little used until near the end of the eighteenth century, when the settlers began to push across the mountains in great numbers to the new, rich lands of Kentucky and Tennessee and later to the Old Northwest Territory north of the Ohio River.

Red Man and War Whoop

Three courses of action were followed by the white man to solve the Indian problem. The first, employed by the Spanish, was to enslave the Indians, thus keeping them as a source of labor on the large Spanish land grants; the second, used by the French, was to intermarry with the red man (some French traders had a dusky wife in each tribe with which they exchanged goods!) and to carry on trade with them; the third, based largely on the wish of the English to occupy and cultivate the land, was mostly a policy of annihilation. "There is much truth in the old saw, that the early colonists first of all fell on their knees and then fell on the aborigines. Equally true is the saying that the colonists approached the native with a deed of sale for land in one hand, which the native was voluntarily to sign; while in the other hand and under the arm were a Bible, a bottle of rum, and a gun." [2] Each new group on the frontier believed and practiced the same adage: "The only good Indian is a dead Indian." As the frontier was pushed farther and farther westward, the older areas, forgetting their own experiences and deeds, looked upon the Indian problem with kinder and more tolerant eyes, but to the frontiersman the Indian was a menace to be eradicated as soon as possible.

By the end of the Revolutionary War, except in the Southern Colonies, the Indians had either been pushed westward or their ranks had been so thinned that they were no longer a menace. As the frontier moved westward so did the Indian problem. By the late nineteenth century, the red man, his ranks depleted by war and the white man's diseases, could no longer muster the strength to raise the war whoop and tomahawk. The Indians finally went down to defeat before a combination of the superior guns and organization of the whites, whiskey, diseases, destruction of their food supply, and sheer weight of numbers. A lesser and inferior civilization gave way before a greater and superior one.

Settlement

By 1800 all of New England, with the exception of northeastern Maine and the northern tip of New Hampshire, was populated. The Middle Colonies, with the exception of a wild tract in upper New York and the extreme western portion of that state, along with the adjacent northern and western part of Pennsylvania, had been brought under the sway of the white man. Southward to almost the eastern half of Georgia, the land was occupied for nearly 150 miles inland; and on the Virginia-

[2] William C. MacLeod, *The American Indian Frontier,* page vii. New York: Alfred A. Knopf, 1928.

North Carolina border, settlement had penetrated over the watershed and into Tennessee. Owing to large land grants, much of what was later West Virginia was still unsettled, although a thin line extended from the head of the Ohio down almost to the southern tip of Kentucky, and the central part of that state was fairly well populated. One branch of this settlement even dipped down into north central Tennessee. A small area just west of Pennsylvania, in the Old Northwest Territory, and isolated outposts in what was soon to be the state of Ohio, completed the settlements. The heaviest settled belt of population extended from central New England down through Virginia, barely touching North Carolina, although around Charleston, Louisville, and Pittsburgh small areas were well populated.

By the outbreak of the Civil War, the frontier line ran westward along the northern half of Maine, across the northern half of Michigan and Wisconsin, turned southward at the eastern corner of Minnesota, bulged a little at the eastern end of Nebraska and Kansas, then went down the western border of Arkansas, and, following the Red River westward, took in almost all of the eastern third of Texas. The southern tip of Louisiana and the southern half of Florida were still unsettled, as was a fair-sized spot in upper-central New York. The hardy pioneers had traversed the area of the Great Plains and, lured by free land, timber in Washington, rich farm lands in Oregon, gold in California, and the romantic Orient across the broad Pacific, had established themselves aiong Puget Sound, the Willamette River, and San Francisco Bay. Nearly 2,000 miles of semiarid plains and rugged mountains separated the two regions. By far the greatest density of population stretched from Massachusetts southwestward through the center of Connecticut past the mouth of the Hudson into the region lying between the Delaware and Susquehanna Rivers. Most of the settlements were within 50 miles of the seaboard, with the exception of those extending along the Connecticut Valley in Massachusetts, along the Hudson and a few miles westward on the Mohawk in New York, and up the Delaware in eastern Pennsylvania. Beginning along the Potomac River and continuing southward through the present confines of Virginia was the widest single area of settlement, gradually narrowing as the Roanoke was reached. Nearly a third of the people lived in New England, a similar number in Virginia and Maryland, with most of the balance in the former Middle Colonies, with the exception of perhaps 5,000 persons in North Carolina and twice that number in and around Charleston, South Carolina. Atlanta and New Orleans completed the well-populated urban centers in the South. That the population was quite unevenly distributed is illustrated by the fact that approximately 90 per cent of the population lived east of the Mississippi, while the remaining 10 per cent were to be found on the Great Plains and along the Pacific Coast.

Sectionalism

A thorough knowledge of sectionalism is necessary for any real appreciation of American economic history and is a key that unlocks many of the riddles of our national life. Sectionalism stems from a feeling of economic inferiority on the one hand and from local economic or class interests on the other. It is opposed to any exaggerated or oppressive form of centralization. Its roots are found in the prevailing geographical and climatic conditions that underlie settlement in any specific region. Thus, long before the Revolutionary War, sectionalism had arisen because of the existence of one or more of the factors listed above.

As the pioneers pushed steadily southward or westward, subdued the Indians, and brought the land under cultivation, they gradually lost touch both culturally and economically with those older establishments situated in the Tidewater area. In addition, the frontier itself imposed a new and more democratic outlook on its inhabitants. As Professor Turner has said, "The frontier regions stressed the rights of man, while the statesmen who voiced the interests of the East stressed the rights of property." [3] This conflict first became manifest in 1676, when Nathaniel Bacon, representing the frontier, led a rebellion against the aristocratic Governor Berkeley of Virginia. Although Bacon died at the height of his power, and even though Berkeley took a terrible revenge on the western leader's followers, the revolt showed that sectionalism had reared its head in the Colonies; future events were to prove that the same problem was to continue until the present time.

In the Regulator Movement in the Carolinas, nearly a century later (1769-1771), the frontiersmen, tired of delays in obtaining a voice in the Tidewater-dominated government, desiring lower taxes, agencies of local government, and, most important of all, protection against the Indians, rose in rebellion and actually fought a pitched though losing battle with the forces raised by the planter aristocracy; "These episodes, however, were only the more spectacular events in the unceasing conflict which imbued the individualistic, liberty-loving westerners with a deep-seated distrust of governments remote from them and unsympathetic with their interests and needs." [4]

From time immemorial a frontier region has been a debtor region, and the American frontier was no exception. The outlook of the debtor frequently clashes with that of the creditor, and this play of forces between the creditor of the conservative East and the debtor of the more liberal and democratic West provides American economic history with some of its most illuminating interpretations. The struggle for free

[3] Frederick J. Turner, *The Significance of Sections in American History*, p. 24. New York: Henry Holt and Company, 1932.

[4] Clark, *The West in American History*, p. 341.

land, cheap money, agrarian revolts, third party political movements, more liberal state constitutions, and opposition to a centralized banking system all had their origin in and were expressions of the sectional interests of their day.

Settlement and the Old Northwest

At the close of the Revolutionary War the boundaries of the United States were, roughly, the Mississippi River on the west, Florida on the south, the Atlantic on the east, and the Great Lakes and the St. Lawrence on the north. In the unsettled region lying north of the Ohio several states had western claims, but these were finally resolved, New York first ceding her claims in 1781 and Georgia ending the state cessions in 1802. Thus, with the exception of certain small areas reserved for special uses, the western lands had been ceded to the Government of the United States.

As a result of the war, many vestiges of European feudalism that had secured a foothold in the Colonies were swept away. Such institutions as quitrent (a small fee collected by the Crown or by proprietors), primogeniture (a system whereby the land was granted to the eldest son), and entail (a legal provision that made it almost impossible to alienate an estate) were removed either as a result of the fight against England or through the earnest efforts of the Jeffersonian party. In addition, many large estates formerly in the hands of wealthy Tories were broken up and sold for the benefit of the Colonies. A more democratic system of landholding replaced the former aristocratic, semifeudal form of land tenure.

One of the most serious consequences of the Revolutionary War was the relatively large public debt that faced the country at the end of the war. The chief asset that the Government possessed was the public domain or land ceded by the states to the Federal Government, especially that portion located north of the Ohio River. In general, the older states believed that the public lands should be held as an asset for the future, should be made hard to obtain, and should be kept fairly expensive. The South believed that the public lands offered serious competition to its tobacco and cotton lands, while the East feared that the cultivation of new, rich soil would lower the value of its older, somewhat worn, and only fairly productive fields. In addition, the Eastern manufacturers saw the West draining away an all-too-scarce supply of labor, and feared that this would result in higher wages for workers. Western sentiments prevailed, however, and the public domain was parceled out on comparatively easy and generous terms.

In order to reimburse her soldiers whose homes had been burned by the British raids during the war, Connecticut reserved in the Old Northwest a strip of land 120 miles wide in the northeast corner of Ohio, while Virginia reserved 6,000 square miles between the Scioto and Little Miami Rivers in order to redeem her military bounty certificates. Congress reserved, for the same reason, bounty lands between the Scioto and the Seven Ranges. All the rest became the basis [5] of the 1,441,-436,160 acres that the Federal Government has owned at one time or another.

Under the Articles of Confederation, Congress passed the justly famous Ordinance of 1787. From a background dark with greed and land speculation there emerged one of the truly great land laws of all time. The chief provisions of the act stipulated that not less than three nor more than five states could be created from the Northwest Territory; that slavery and involuntary servitude should be prohibited; that after a period of rule by Congressional appointees any region, upon attaining 5,000 adult, free, male citizens, could have a separate territorial government; and that, upon achieving 60,000 free inhabitants, the region might be granted statehood with full equality with any state in the Union. The last provision was revolutionary in its extension of the democratic principle. But economically the prohibition of slavery was the most important feature of the Ordinance.

The Ordinance of 1787 was passed largely in response to the machinations of a group of land speculators headed by the Reverend Manasseh Cutler, who, with his henchmen, some of whom were in Congress, had formed the Ohio Associates. They purchased nearly 2,000,000 acres of land with depreciated soldiers' scrip worth about 12 cents on the dollar, and, coupling their scheme with the Scioto Associates, which secured a grant of nearly 5,000,000 acres, were able to bring pressure to bear on Congress. In the spring of 1788 the Ohio Associates settled Marietta, Ohio, at the mouth of the Muskingum River and near the protecting guns of Fort Harmar. A few months later Judge John Cleves Symmes acquired a grant of nearly 1,000,000 acres between the Great and Little Miami Rivers, and set about founding the city of Cincinnati. The Scioto Associates, without having secured title to their grant, sold about 3,000,000 acres to a French company, and in 1790 the duped Frenchmen settled Gallipolis on land that William Duer hastily purchased from the Ohio Associates. Six years later, Moses Cleaveland bought most of the Connecticut Reserve and founded Cleveland on Lake Erie. Meantime Congress had provided the first territorial governor in the person of Arthur St. Clair, a former companion-in-arms of Washington. After an initial setback suffered by St. Clair at the hands of the Indians but later rectified by "Mad" Anthony Wayne at the battle of the Fallen Timbers in 1794, settlement rapidly got under way. The rate of growth of the

[5] The public domain was enlarged greatly during the nineteenth century as new additions were made by conquest or by purchase. See below, pages 104-107.

population in the area is indicated by the admission, as states, into the Union of Ohio in 1803, Indiana in 1816, Illinois in 1818, Michigan in 1837, and Wisconsin in 1848.

Settlement in the Southwest

Until 1800 most settlers drifting to the frontier went south of the Ohio River rather than up into the Old Northwest. The main reasons for this were that the regions of Kentucky and Tennessee had an earlier start; moreover, land titles were cleared in the southern region earlier than they were to the north. Then, too, as the land of the older Southern Colonies began to show the ravages of too constant cropping, the wealthier landowners began to exert economic pressure on the poorer tenants and slowly forced them up into the hill country. Although the Cherokee, Choctaw, Creek, Chickasaw, and Seminole Indians were a barrier, they were not so formidable as the Indians in the Old Northwest. A real obstacle and irritant to settlers and to settlement in this region was the presence at the mouth of the Mississippi at New Orleans of the Spanish, who denied to the casual settler and trader the right of deposit of his products. Not until 1795, when Pinckney obtained that right for a three-year period, were the frontiersmen placated. But whoever controlled the mouth of that stream held the stopper to the great bottle of the Mississippi Valley.

The settlements of Boone, Henderson, Robertson, and Sevier bore fruit, within a few years, for by 1792 Kentucky became a state and four years later Tennessee was granted statehood. Shortly after 1800 these settlers began to move northward to the Old Northwest and to a new "frontier." Those who remained were forced toward the mountains, and some became the familiar "Hill Billies" celebrated today by song, feud, and the radio.

Georgia, the last settled of the original Thirteen Colonies, also comprised in the eighteenth century what are now the states of Alabama and Mississippi. In 1795 the Georgia Legislature sold to four land companies, at an average price of 1½ cents an acre, some 50,000,000 acres of land located in and around the Yazoo River. Many of the grantees were legislators, who hastened to unload their unsavory titles, and none too fast, since the next legislature repealed the grants. Before this happened, however, many unwary investors had purchased land in good faith, and even the Supreme Court and Congress were hard pressed to unscramble the mess. Settlers were attracted to Mississippi earlier than they were to Alabama, so that Mississippi was admitted as a state in 1817, while Alabama had to wait two years longer. Indian trouble accounted for a part of this delay; indeed, the Seminole War dragged on until 1842, and a few aborigines who took to the Everglades are still technically at war with the United States. But the migration of Seminoles to Florida did not save them from the advancing frontier; Florida, which had been sold to the United States by Spain in 1819, was admitted as a state in 1845.

Land Problems and the Public Domain

During Colonial times no good system of land survey existed; a great deal of land was granted under the old haphazard system of "metes and bounds." As the land became more thickly settled, this led to innumerable difficulties and to many legal suits and disputes. Indeed, "law" became a verb in New England! The Continental Congress proceeded to deal with the problem of land survey by passing the Ordinance of 1785, which provided for the system of rectangular survey, a system that was extended to all new lands acquired except the original states, Kentucky, Tennessee, and Texas. In short, all land that became part of the public domain was and is surveyed under an exact and regular system.

Although the system of rectangular survey possesses great merit, it did not operate effectively and efficiently in the region between the 98th meridian and the Rocky Mountains, for here water, not land, was the controlling factor. In the dry and arid region of the Great Plains, the size of the land unit defined by this system was too often too small to be of any practical value. For most regions possessing a plenitude of land, wood, and water, the act has been of incalculable value, inasmuch as it permits of precise and exact definition of each parcel of land.

The Ordinance had political as well as economic implications; the creditor of the East thought that the size of the land unit granted to settlers should be large and costly enough to prevent the "little fellow" from getting a cheap "stake in the country," while the debtor of the West believed that the unit at worst should be small and cheap and at best should be altogether free. As the years rolled on, the Western viewpoint slowly but surely was adopted, and its complete victory was signalized by the passage of the Homestead Act of 1862.

The rectangular system of land survey operated as follows: a base line running east and west and an intersecting principal meridian running north and south were first established in the wilderness by the surveyors. From these lines, perpendiculars were run out by the surveyors at six-mile intervals. Thus the land was divided into squares containing 36 square miles each. Each square was a township, which was in turn divided into 36 squares of one square mile each and containing 640 acres (commonly called a "section"). Section 16 was reserved for the support of the public schools, and after 1842 most states reserved section 36 as well. The squabble between the East and the West raged over the size of the minimum unit offered for sale, the terms of payment, and matters of a like nature.[6] The following table tells the story of the development of the Government land policy and the increasing victory of the Western attitude.

Act	*Minimum Unit in Acres*	*Minimum Auction Price per Acre*	*Terms of Sale*
1785	640	$1.00	Cash, ½ by township; ½ by sections
1796	640	$2.00	[½ cash, ½ credit (1 yr.)]
1800	320	$2.00	(¼ cash; ¼ 2 yrs.; ¼ 3 yrs.; ¼ 4 years.)
1804	160	$2.00	Same as in 1800
1820	80	$1.25	Cash
1832	40	$1.25	Cash

Thus, while in 1785 it took $640 to purchase a Western farm, by 1832 a start could be made for only $50. In general it can be said that, while the public land policy of the Federal Government has not been financially successful, it has been of great value in getting the land settled quickly and getting land into the hands of a large number of people, although not all of them lived on the land. Indeed, speculation in Western lands has been a game for the American people almost from the beginning of settlement.

Rounding Out the Borders

As a result of the Pinckney Treaty of 1795, the cork was pulled from the bottleneck of the Mississippi and Ohio Valleys and the trans-Appalachian region as well. Within a few years the pressure of European affairs brought to the United States the tremendous empire of Louisiana. As a result of the French and Indian War, France had transferred this great region to Spain; but with the rise of Napoleon, Spain retroceded it to France by the secret treaty of San Ildefonso in 1800. When news of this action reached the United States, great uneasiness was felt; it was one thing to have Louisiana in the hands of a comparatively weak power like Spain, but—from the American standpoint—it was quite another matter to find it in the hands of the expanding imperialistic power of France, then under the sway of the "Little Corporal." Girding for war and fearful that the prize might fall into the hands of England, his archenemy and nemesis, Napoleon offered the whole region to the astonished American Minister Livingston for the paltry sum of $15,000,000, an offer that was soon taken. The purchase

[6] Settlement quickly pushed ahead of the surveys. Squatters technically were lawbreakers; but, as they improved the land and added value to it, Congress in 1841 passed a Pre-Emption Act that allowed the squatter to have first right to purchase his holding at the minimum price per acre. Certain lands were regarded by the pioneers as unsuitable for settlement; in 1854 Congress passed a Graduation Act, which reduced the price of such land according to how long it had lain unpurchased. Thus, land unpurchased for 30 years sold by law at 12½ cents per acre.

in 1803 had vast significance for the future power and greatness of the United States; although the boundaries were somewhat indefinite, the addition of Louisiana doubled the land area of the nascent world power.

The acquisition of Florida from Spain was the next episode in the history of our expanding public domain. In 1810 the United States took possession of the territory from West Florida to the Pearl River, and three years later added the small strip that included the area from Mobile Bay to the Perdido River. Then in 1819, Spain, fearful of losing all the rest to the young giant of the north, sold the balance of Florida to the United States for about $5,000,000. Part of the treaty consummating this transaction was devoted to a definition of the western boundaries of Louisiana, and under it Spain gave up her claims to any territory north of the 42nd parallel, thus removing herself as one of the contestants for the region later known as the Oregon Country.

Louisiana, settled since early in the eighteenth century, was admitted to statehood in 1812, and from this area a constant stream of Americans invaded the region to the west, the present state of Texas. Beginning in 1821, when Moses Austin obtained a land grant, which was conferred at his death on his son Stephen, land-hungry pioneers streamed into the rich agricultural and grazing lands in Mexican Texas. Although the movement had all the characteristics of a regular extension of our frontier, it caused considerable repercussions at the time, New Englanders and Abolitionists accusing Southern slaveholders of a plot to extend the boundaries of their "peculiar institution." By the year 1836 the Texans, after a series of bloody battles with Mexico, had secured their independence, and Texas stood as a free nation of slaveholding Americans, a status that she maintained for the next nine years. Then in 1845, as a result of politics, the sale of Texan scrip and bonds, and the natural workings of "Manifest Destiny," Texas was admitted as a state. Because of her former national existence and because of her public debt, most of the public lands were retained by Texas and were never a part of the public domain. Owing to the huge size of the state, Texas was given the right to form herself into as many as five states.

Still another chapter in the history of our public domain needs to be recounted. Shortly after the Revolutionary War, and just at the time when the struggling young nation needed new markets to replace those lost by severance from England, hardy New England shipmasters began to send their ships around Cape Horn and up to the Northwest coast for furs. This maritime trade (Indian trinkets for furs, furs for Chinese goods for the New England market), based first on the sea otter and later on the fur-bearing seal, made known the Oregon Country to the Americans. Four nations had claims to this region—Spain, Russia, England, and the United States. The Spanish and Russian claims were based on discovery and occupation. Spain relinquished her claims by treaty in 1819, and Russia agreed to stay north of 54° 40′ by the treaty of 1824. Meantime, in 1818, as part of the treaty agreement drawing the northern boundary between Canada and the United States along 49° and west to the "Stony" mountains, England and the United States had agreed to occupy jointly the Oregon Country. The region, embracing what are now the states of Oregon, Washington, Idaho, and parts of Montana and Wyoming, was rich in furs (mainly beaver), fine valley farm land, and timber. The area was first exploited by fur traders, but in the 1840's missionaries and American settlers came in increasing waves. The sheer weight of numbers, plus a declining fur market, tended to swing the scales in favor of the Americans. By the treaty of 1846, England agreed to draw the northern boundary westward from the Rocky Mountains along the 49th parallel to the sea, Vancouver Island excepted.[7] Thus, by the middle of the nineteenth century the United States had an unbroken sweep across its northern border from the Atlantic to the Pacific. Oddly enough, settlers traveled clear across the former Louisiana Purchase to settle in Oregon. Henceforth the United States had both an eastward- and westward-moving frontier line.

Just at the time that the Americans were getting interested in Texas, Mexico declared her independence from Spain (1821). Since the Mexican Government had never recognized Texan independence, the admission of Texas as an American state made war inevitable. In 1848, after two years of sharp fighting during which Mexico was invaded, Mexico, by the treaty of Guadalupe Hidalgo, ceded to the United States the region west of the Texas boundary and south of the 42nd parallel to about the 33rd parallel.[8] It was agreed that the sum of $15,000,000 should be paid to Mexico and that certain American claims for damages should be canceled. There were few Americans in this whole region, and the acquisition of this territory did not generate the usual pioneering process or any comparable extension of the westward movement.

Almost as a footnote to the Mexican cession came the Gadsden Purchase of 1853. A small strip of territory lying just south of the cession territory was desired by the United States for a better railroad route across the mountains. The Mexican maps showed the southern boundary of New Mexico to be south of the boundary drawn in 1848. Hence James Gadsden made this purchase for the United States for $10,000,000, the highest price per acre ever paid by the United States for any considerable extension of its boundaries.

There also occurred, in the northeastern part of the United States,

[7] Strictly speaking, the only part of the Oregon Country that was in dispute between England and the United States was that part lying west and north of the Columbia River.

[8] Although gold had been discovered in California early in 1848, neither the American nor Mexican commissioners knew it at the time the treaty was signed.

another extension of the frontier; here the direction was east and north rather than west or south. The northeastern boundary between the United States and Canada was finally settled by the Webster-Ashburton Treaty of 1842 after a humorous "Battle of the Maps" in which the American maps showed the boundary to be farther south than the Americans claimed while the British maps showed it to be farther north than the British insisted.

As a result of all these events, in the short space of 50 years the United States carved from the continent of North America by purchase, war, and diplomacy a country whose land area totaled over 3,000,000 square miles, a territory 15 times the size of France and about 25 times the size of the United Kingdom. Giant strides were made in those 50 years. But the political expansion was only the beginning; under the heading of unfinished business came the exploration and development of this vast new region.

Exploration and the Great Western Trails

In order to learn something about the climate, topography, and resources of the newly purchased Louisiana region, President Jefferson, in 1804, sent out the Lewis and Clark expedition to explore and report its findings. The expedition ascended the Missouri and wintered at Fort Mandan, then continued westward over the Rockies and down the Snake and Columbia Rivers and spent the second winter at Fort Clatsop in the Oregon Country. They returned in 1806 to make their report. Previous to this, in 1792, Captain Robert Gray, of the ship *Columbia,* had discovered and entered the great river that bears the name of his ship. These explorations provided the basic claims of the United States to the Oregon Country.

Then came systematic exploration of the Great Plains. Early in the nineteenth century fur traders and explorers roamed over the vast expanse of territory lying west of the Mississippi. John Colter, Robert Stuart, Jim Bridger, N. J. Wyeth, the Sublette brothers, Jedediah Smith, and a host of others contributed to local knowledge of the areas they explored. Missionaries such as Jason Lee, Marcus Whitman, and Father De Smet soon followed, carrying Christianity in the wake of the fur trader. These intrepid pioneers made known many of the mountain passes, the rivers, and the ranges of the region. Most important among the mountain passes was South Pass at the head of the North Platte, in the southwestern corner of what is now the state of Wyoming; over this pass thousands of settlers crossed on their way to the rich farm lands of the Willamette Valley in Oregon or to the gold fields of California.

The army, too, had a large share in making known the new wilderness. Lieutenant Zebulon M. Pike explored the headwaters of the Mississippi in 1805-1806, and in 1806-1807 went westward from St. Louis over to the head of the Colorado and on to the peak that now bears his name. John C. Fremont, "the Pathfinder," traversed much of the region west of the Rockies between 1842 and 1844, revealing new information and putting on a scientific level the facts obtained in his journeys. By 1853 Congress ordered and provided the funds for a scientific railroad survey to determine the most practicable route that would connect the Mississippi with the Pacific Coast. Five surveys from the 49th down to the 32nd parallels were made between 1853 and 1855. The result was a series of well-organized, scientific expeditions, carried out for the most part under army leaders, that not only brought to light new information but also co-ordinated old but little-known geographical facts. The southernmost route was recommended by Secretary of War Jefferson Davis as the most practicable; but, owing to sectional differences between the South and North, no action resulted until the approaching war removed one of the contestants. That the work was well done is illustrated by the fact that the transcontinental railroads, when built, largely followed the paths indicated by the surveys.

As the American frontier pushed west of the Mississippi, great trails began to appear over which lumbering men and beasts proceeded westward, sometimes ahead of but usually behind the explorers. Early in the 1820's American traders began to supply the Spanish outpost of Santa Fé with such trading goods as were capable of withstanding the rigors and the cost of the long, slow journey. Trinkets, beads, and cloth, both fabricated and coarse, made up the bulk of the goods going to Mexico, while mules and beaver skins, plus silver and gold bullion from the rich Mexican mines, made up the return load.

At about the same time that the Santa Fé trading trail was coming into prominence, trappers, traders, missionaries, and finally settlers began to cross the Great Plains *via* the Platte River and South Pass over what became known as the Oregon Trail. Starting at Independence, Missouri, the trail ran in a northwesterly direction until it struck the southernmost bend of the Platte; then it followed along that stream to the Sweetwater, over the Rockies by means of the wide gateway known as South Pass, and thence up to the Snake River and along that stream until near the present site of Boise, Idaho, where it branched off to strike the Columbia. Nearly 2,000 miles long, it was perhaps the greatest trail and carried more settlers to new homes than any other American pathway. People rather than goods moved over this trail, and the first large migrations, beginning in the 1840's, soon marked a broad path for the thousands who were to follow. Near Fort Hall in southeastern Idaho a southern branch, the California Trail, led across Utah, Nevada, and California. During 1849 literally thousands jammed the trail in their efforts to get to the gold fields. Indians and disease dogged the path of the homemaker and miner, and thousands of graves and skulls gave mute testimony to the toll exacted by nature and the red men. On the north bank of the Platte ran a famous counterpart of the Oregon Trail, for here was to be found the Mormon Trail, which paralleled the former until it reached South Pass, where it branched southward to Salt Lake City, founded in 1847 by the great leader of the Mormon Church, Brigham Young. In the valley of the Great Salt Lake, the Mormons, employing irrigation from the neighboring streams, settled and found a thriving colony. This desert outpost, established miles from any regular settlement, was engaged mainly in agriculture and cattle raising, although trading with the "forty-niners" and later comers was profitable to both parties. South of the Santa Fé trail, the Overland Mail trail led from St. Louis, *via* Fort Smith, El Paso, Tucson, and Fort Yuma, up through the interior of Califonia to San Francisco. Mail and people were carried west or east in about 25 days by lumbering mail coaches. This slender communication thread was superseded in 1869 upon the completion of the Union and Central Pacific railroads. But even before the railways came, the region west of the Mississippi was fed by several great arteries that carried goods and people into the West from the settled East.

Beginning in 1825 under President Monroe, the Indians in the Old Northwest Territory and in the old Southwest (east of the Mississippi) were removed from their old homes and settled west of the river; by 1841 many of the most formidable tribes had been relocated in what is now Oklahoma.[9] Gradually, as the whites pushed westward and inevitable clashes occurred, the Indians were squeezed southward and northward into smaller and smaller tracts that soon became known as "reservations." In the 1860's and 1870's Indian wars from Minnesota to California resulted in defeats for the red men, who were rounded up and put on reservations throughout the West. As time went on and the covetous whites encroached on the Indian lands, even these reservations were decreased in size. In addition to the toll caused by the white man's whiskey and by his diseases, the destruction of the buffalo, which had been the Indian's chief source of food supply, so depleted the Indian ranks that by 1880 they could no longer contest by any show of force the land that once was theirs.

Economic Activities and Frontier Life

The great incentive to the fur trade in North America was the beaver, inasmuch as his pelt commanded a good price in England and on the European continent. Until the middle of the nineteenth century, many articles of men's clothing were made from beaver fur, especially men's hats; but, about 1840, stylists decreed them no longer fashionable and

[9] Today, one-fifth of the Indians are located in Oklahoma.

dealt a death blow to this great activity. In addition, settlement and agriculture put an end to trapping as a profitable occupation. While other furs such as marten, muskrat, and fox, to say nothing of buffalo hides, were also gathered and sold, the beaver was always the backbone of the trade.

Although many individuals engaged in trapping as individuals, presently great fur companies arose to exploit the trade more efficiently and effectively. John Jacob Astor, a German immigrant, began to operate his companies in the latter part of the eighteenth century and expanded his activities in the nineteenth, founding his fortune on this trade. His business extended from New York across the continent to Astoria (Oregon), which he founded in 1811. British companies, too, engaged in the fur trade in what is now United States territory; the most prominent of these companies were the Northwest Company and the great Hudson's Bay Company, and these firms contested the rich Oregon Country in the early years of the nineteenth century. The Great Plains and the Rockies were dominated by the American Fur Company; early in the century this company began to send out trapping parties. It evolved a new trading institution, the *rendezvous,* which was a meeting place for traders and trappers, usually in some small valley in the Rockies. There, in the late spring, trappers, traders, and friendly Indians met for a week or ten days to carouse, swap furs for trinkets, goods, whiskey or metheglin, and to forget the cares and dangers of a hard and uncertain life. Great profits were made for both the fur trade in general and the managers of the *rendezvous* in particular.

Whether the frontier was in Indiana or Idaho, the process was much the same. Close on the heels of the trapper came the pioneer or early settler, who in wooded regions built the familiar cabin or "lean-to" and scratched a few acres of ground and planted his scanty crop of corn, beans, pumpkins, and grain. He combined fishing and hunting with his agricultural pursuits, wresting a precarious living from his surroundings. Within a few years he was usually bought out—normally he moved west again and his place was taken by the familiar farmer—and the old process of settlement and introduction of capital and industry was begun. In the region immediately west of the Mississippi, on the open and rolling plains, only the turning of a furrow and the planting of a crop was needed, and here the sod-house frontier began an existence all its own.

The early pioneer, owing to lack of cash and transportation, was forced to make most of the things he used in everyday life. Tables, chairs, dishes, houses, and a host of other articles were fashioned by hand mostly from the convenient timber surrounding him on every side. The Ohio and Mississippi Rivers, with their tributaries, furnished a waterway upon which to float his trading goods to market. Certain necessities, such as salt, lead, iron, and gunpowder, were usually purchased in town or city; but except for these, the pioneer was largely self-sufficient. "Homespun," although now merely a type of cloth, had a literal meaning for most people on the frontier. Because life was rough, crude, hard, and dangerous, few people of culture and means were attracted to the frontier, and hence the pioneers in general were, for the most part lower middle class, some of whom through their own efforts were able to amass comfortable fortunes. The bullets of the Indians respected neither wealth nor social position, and this helped to make the frontier a great leveling institution; all had to face the same hardships and dangers, and a man stood out above his neighbors because he possessed the virtues of hardihood, fortitude, knowledge of woodlore, leadership, and hunting sense. The great heroes of the frontier were successful Indian fighters and early trail blazers, rather than cultured aristocrats or financiers.

Although the westward movement was primarily an agricultural advance, certain regions west of the Mississippi owed their settlement to unforeseen and unusual reasons. Gold was one of these. Early in 1848, the precious metal was discovered in the American River on the land grant of John Sutter near Sacramento, California. The news soon leaked out, and in 1849, thousands came to the diggings. Some came around the Horn on the all-water route; some by boat to Panama and by land across the Isthmus and again by boat up the coast; but most, for economic reasons, chose the longer, slower land route over the Oregon and California Trails—40,000 are estimated to have crossed the plains in 1849 alone. By 1850 more than 100,000 miners were the basis for the admission of California as a state. Gold was discovered in Oregon three years later, and in 1858 the precious metal was discovered in the Pike's Peak region; thousands now joined the rush to this last strike, many bearing signs on the sides of their wagons "Pike's Peak or Bust," only to return a few years later with the sad news "Busted By Gosh" painted under their former hopes. In the early 1860's gold was discovered in Idaho and western Montana and thousands rushed to the new diggings. A "take" of $3 to $5 per day was considered ordinary while a day's panning of $10 was enough to start a new rush or boom. Tents, rude shacks, saloons, and bawdy houses made their appearance at about the same time, and street fights, brawls, knifings, and shootings were commonplace.

The mining frontier engendered lawlessness and attracted the most dissolute men and women into the towns that mushroomed with each reported strike. Economically the miners furnished a growing market for the foodstuffs produced by the more prosaic farmer. Before the advent of United States law and order, the better elements evolved an extralegal organization known as the "Vigilantes" to take care, in summary fashion, of robbers, brigands, and highwaymen. Near Carson City, Nevada, in 1859, was found the marvelously rich silver strike, the Comstock Lode, and inspired miners traversed most of the mountainous regions in their search for gold and silver. As time went on, the rich placer or gravel bars gave out, and the great amount of capital needed to exploit the quartz or hard-rock mines led to their coming into the hands of large mining interests. Meantime, however, the mining fever gave great impetus to an eastward-moving frontier from the Pacific Coast.

Influence of the Westward Movement

The movement of the population westward has had great effect on the political, economic, and social development of the United States. The state constitutions of the Western states were almost invariably more liberal than those of their Eastern neighbors, although many of their provisions were copied from by the more conservative East. The West gave rise to new political parties, and Jackson's concept of democracy typified the spirit of the pioneer and frontiersman in his disregard for form, in his attack on the Second Bank of the United States, and in his strong nationalistic stand with regard to South Carolina and nullification. Lincoln, too, with his tolerance, his simple ways, and his great humanity, was to become a symbol of the democratic spirit, fostered and nurtured in the cabins of the frontier. As the time grew closer for the trial by arms of the Republic, the West held the balance of political, especially Senatorial power, between the North and the South, and this enabled Western statesmen to secure many advantages for their respective regions.

Economically, the westward extension of the population has meant a great consuming market for Eastern manufactured goods; Henry Clay's "American System" embodied this idea in an effort to promote harmony among the sections of the nation. Then, too, as new regions were settled under the jurisdiction of the United States, old international boundaries were no more, and trade barriers were destroyed. As population spread westward, new regions came into production, increasing immeasurably the diversity of products and leading to greater exchange among the sections. Although, at first, most Western products were floated down the rivers to New Orleans, by the time of the outbreak of the Civil War a great deal of the West had been firmly united to the East by bands of railroad iron and gave its weight in men, material, and productive capacity to the North in that struggle. As a sponge for Eastern capital, the West provided an attractive field for investment (and speculation) and turned American capital toward internal improvement rather than to European or world markets. The constant draining of manpower from the East to the West tendered to maintain or even to increase the wages granted to the Eastern laboring classes. Finally, the demand on the part of the West led to better transportation facilities in the matter of roads, river improvements, canals, and railroads.

Socially the West has stood for democracy, and the pioneering process has tendered to level the extremes in wealth and to break down the caste barriers engendered by older and more stable societies. The basis of this attitude is intimately connected with the public domain, and, as Professor Turner has well said, "The free lands of the United States have been the most important single factor in explaining our development." [10]

Selected References

WESTWARD MOVEMENT

Bankcroft, H. H., *Works* (39 vols.). San Francisco: A. L. Bancroft & Co., 1882-1890.

Billington, Ray A., *Westward Expansion, A History of the American Frontier.* New York: The Macmillan Company, 1949.

Clark, Dan E., *The West in American History.* New York: Thomas Y. Crowell Company, 1937.

Coman, Katherine, *Economic Beginnings of the Far West* (2 vols.). New York: The Macmillan Company, 1912.

Donaldson, T. C., *The Public Domain.* Washington: Government Printing Office, 1884.

Goodwin, C. L., *The Trans-Mississippi West, 1803-1853: A History of its Acquisition and Settlement.* New York: D. Appleton and Company, 1922.

Hulbert, Archer B., *The Paths of Inland Commerce* (in *Chronicles of America*), Vol. 21. New Haven: Yale University Press, 1920.

Ogg, F. A., *The Old Northwest* (in *Chronicles of America*), Vol. 19. New Haven: Yale University Press, 1919.

———, *The Opening of the Mississippi.* New York: The Macmillan Company, 1904.

Paxson, Frederick L., *History of the American Frontier, 1763-1893.* Boston: Houghton, Mifflin Company, 1924.

———, *The Last American Frontier.* New York: The Macmillan Company, 1910.

Smith, Justin H., *The Annexation of Texas.* New York: The Macmillan Company, 1919.

———, *The War with Mexico,* 2 vols. New York: The Macmillan Company, 1919.

Turner, Frederick J., *The Frontier in American History.* New York: Henry Holt and Company, 1920.

Webb, Walter P., *The Great Plains.* Boston: Ginn and Company, 1931.

LAND POLICY

Akagi, R. H., *The Town Proprietors of the New England Colonies.* New York: D. Appleton and Company, 1924.

[10] F. J. Turner, *The Significance of Sections in American History,* p. 17. Inherent in the Turnerian thesis is the concept of the West as a "Safety Valve," that is, that so long as free (or nearly free) land existed, almost anyone could and would remove himself to the frontier when economic or social conditions became depressed at home. In recent years scholars have assailed this idea with considerable vigor and partial success.

Bond, B. W., *The Quit-Rent System in the American Colonies*. New Haven: Yale University Press, 1919.

Hibbard, B. H., *A History of the Public Land Policies*. New York: The Macmillan Company, 1924.

Sakolski, A. M., *The Great American Land Bubble*. New York: Harper & Brothers, 1932.

Stephenson, G. M., *The Political History of the Public Lands, 1840-1862*. Boston: R. G. Badger, 1917.

Treat, P. J., *The National Land System, 1785-1820*. New York: E. B. Treat & Company, 1910.

IMMIGRATION

Faust, A. B., *The German Element in the United States* (2 vols.). Boston: Houghton, Mifflin Company, 1909.

Ford, H. J., *The Scotch-Irish in America*. Princeton: Princeton University Press, 1915.

Hanna, C. A., *The Scotch-Irish* (2 vols.). New York: G. P. Putnam's Sons, 1902.

Stephenson, G. M., *A History of American Immigration, 1820-1924*. Boston: Ginn and Company, 1926.

SPECIAL TOPICS

Abernethy, T. P., *Western Lands and the American Revolution*. New York: D. Appleton-Century Company, 1937.

Alvord, C. W., and Lee Bidgood, *The First Explorations of the Trans-Allegheny Region by the Virginians, 1650-1674*. Cleveland: The Arthur H. Clark Company, 1912.

Bidwell, P. W., and Falconer, J. I., *History of Agriculture in the Northern United States, 1620-1860*. Washington: The Carnegie Institution of Washington, 1925.

Bridenbaugh, C., *Cities in the Wilderness; The First Century of Urban Life in America, 1625-1742*. New York: The Ronald Press, 1938.

Chittenden, H. M., *The American Fur Trade of the Far West* (3 vols.). New York: F. P. Harper, 1902.

Commager, H. S., *Documents of American History*. New York: F. S. Crofts & Company, 1938.

Dick, E., *The Sod-House Frontier, 1854-1890*. New York: D. Appleton-Century Company, 1937.

Edwards, E. E., *References on the Significance of the Frontier in American History*, Washington: Dept. of Agriculture, Bib. Contributions No. 25, 1935.

Hawk, E. Q., *The Economic History of the South*. New York: Prentice-Hall, Inc., 1934.

Indexes or issues of *The American Historical Review, The Mississippi Valley Historical Review, The Pacific Historical Review*.

Leupp, F. E., *The Indian and His Problem*. New York: C. Scribner's Sons, 1910.

Macleod, W. C., *The American Indian Frontier*. New York: A. A. Knopf, 1928.

Semple, E. C., *American History and Its Geographic Conditions*. Boston and New York: Houghton, Mifflin and Company, 1903.

Thwaites, R. G., ed., *Early Western Travels, 1748-1846* (32 vols.). Cleveland: The A. H. Clark Company, 1904-1906.

———, *Original Journals of the Lewis and Clark Expedition, 1804-1806* (8 vols). New York: Dodd, Mead & Company, 1904-1905.

Turner, F. J., *The Significance of Sections in American History*. New York: Henry Holt and Company, 1932.

Turner, F. J., and F. Merk, *List of References on the History of the West*. Cambridge: Harvard University Press, 1922.

Wissler, C., *The American Indian*. New York: Oxford University Press, 1938.

7 · AMERICAN TRANSPORTATION BEFORE THE CIVIL WAR

SEPARATION FROM ENGLAND radically changed the political and economic demands for transportation in the newly freed American states. Transatlantic commerce had been dominant, and maximum use had been made of the cheapest type of transportation then available—namely, by water, with the wind as motive power. Each colony had had its ports, either on the ocean or on navigable rivers, to and from which the long-haul foreign traffic was carried by economical sailing vessels. Land traffic to the hinterlands of the many ports had till then been confined to narrow zones because of the low density of population in those parts of the country and the great expense of land transportation.

After the Revolution both political and economic factors prompted an interest in the promotion of freer intercommunication between the former Colonies. Such connections would further political unity, and would make the varied resources of the several states accessible for the benefit of all. In addition, there was the urge to make available the wealth of the Western areas of the North American continent. A unified system of transportation required increased use of north-and-south coastwise water routes to take advantage of the economical water transportation and indicated the need for parallel inland highways wherever topography did not permit the use of water routes. Contact with the West called for greatly increased use of land transportation, except in the areas adjacent to the larger rivers flowing into the Atlantic or the Gulf of Mexico.

Characteristics of Early Land and Water Transportation

It is hard to realize today the limitations that a forced dependence upon land transportation for interior communications imposed on the new republic. Pack animals, which were used in the earliest trans-Appalachian traffic had limited capacity and were expensive. It has been estimated that on level ground a horse can move but one-tenth as much by pack as by wagon. Nevertheless, pack animals were used extensively because the improvement of roads required resources that, except for a few key routes, could not be spared. Clearly, then, roads were a necessity if horses were to be used in the most effective way. Even where roads were built, however, wagons or sleds could be used only during part of the year, in the drier season or when the ground was solidly frozen but not obstructed with snow. Compared to water transportation, wagon-borne traffic was fabulously expensive. This fact was dramatically illustrated by the route and rates for shipment of grain from Northampton, Massachusetts, to Boston. Though the direct overland distance was only 100 miles, it apparently paid to use the circuitous water route of over 300 miles around Cape Cod to take advantage of the cheapness of the water transport. The water part of the route of some 250 miles (from Windsor down the Connecticut River to Hartford, thence to Long Island Sound and around Cape Cod) involved a cost of but 6 pence, whereas the short 36-mile land journey from Northampton to Windsor cost 12 pence, about 13 times as high a rate per ton-mile.

Although water transportation in those days was comparatively cheap, another characteristic was as important in its economic implications. The boats of that period, whether they were for coastwise or for ocean shipping, were relatively small and drew little water. Twenty-ton sloops were standard vessels used in coastwise service, for instance. This meant that harbors and rivers were navigable to an extent not possible for the larger vessels of today. It also meant that even a fairly small-scale industry used large enough quantities of goods to make use of a substantial portion of a boat's cargo or even a complete shipload. The combination of these two factors enabled many places, not now commercial ports, to rate as such and to support seaport industries. Essex, Connecticut, near the mouth of the Connecticut River, for instance, was able to maintain the piano-key industry in its hinterland, to be a port of import for ivory direct from India, and to warrant the complementary operation of a shipyard. Today such an arrangement would not be conceivable, because modern steamers could not reach Essex nor could unloading facilities be supported on so small a flow of commerce.

The War of 1812 demonstrated how important the low-cost coastwise water routes were to our economy. With the British dominating the seas, our coastwise traffic was reduced to a trickle. The result was that flour purchased in New York for use in Boston, which had in peacetime cost but 75 cents a barrel more in Boston as a result of transportation cost, suddenly became $5 a barrel more when it had to be moved overland. Likewise, cotton from the South doubled in price on a delivered basis at Providence, Rhode Island.

Development of the Highway Systems

The dangers that threatened the nation because of lack of adequate north-and-south highways in case an enemy cut off coastwise transport, together with the need for developing areas of the country where water transportation was not available, compelled the Government to give more serious thought than ever before to developing a network of inland highways, regardless of the high cost of land transport. Furthermore, the post roads and "King's highways" which had been bequeathed the country by the Colonies were not laid out in a pattern that catered to the needs of a society that was pushing westward and developing Eastern lands far more intensively. While private interests assumed some of the responsibility for the provision of highways, there was a feeling that private enterprise could never be profitable in the face of normal coastwise competition from boats that would take most of the traffic. A belief that governmental subsidy was needed led Secretary of the Treasury Gallatin to propose in 1807 that a Federal canal and highway system be constructed parallel to the Atlantic Coast. Constitutional objections to activity of this sort by the Federal Government, however, were a major deterrent to the carrying out of any such projected plans.

Moreover, the development of routes to open up the West received more interest than the north-and-south highways. Again there was a question of what institutions should undertake the development of this expanding transportation system. Many people thought that until the frontier areas became more populous, private enterprise could not be relied upon to project the country's highway system rapidly enough into the West, and they urged that the Federal Government should contribute heavily to the work. The loudest champions of this proposal hoped that the headwaters of each of the major rivers flowing into the Atlantic would be connected by highways reaching westward to the headwaters of corresponding rivers tributary to the Mississippi. Here again it was Albert Gallatin who put forth a plan contemplating four major east-and-west Federal roads. But actual Federal appropriations were to fall far below expectations. The Cumberland Road, or National Pike, initially extending from Cumberland, Maryland, to Wheeling, West Virginia, some 130 miles, was the sole project to surmount constitutional difficulties and to rise above the bitter jealousies between states as to what route such a Federal highway should take. This highway was a notable achievement. Finished to Wheeling in 1817, it was built on an ample basis, being 80 feet wide over all with a 30-foot surfaced center. It cost the Government some $7,000,000.

The failure of the Federal Government to become an active agency in the building of highways in either the East or the West, did not, however, prevent the development of a comprehensive highway system in the country. Local interests, both state and private, in the end acted more effectively than had been anticipated toward creating such a network. One of the most interesting parts of this history is the regional variation in the type of economic institution used in this development. Pennsylvania, plus the states to the north, constituted an area in which the work was left largely in the hands of private enterprise operating on a profit motive. In this area the private corporation with charter rights and obligations given by the states came into extensive use in the highway field. The famous Philadelphia and Lancaster Turnpike Company was the first highway corporation, but by 1800 there were 72 such corporations in the Northern states. A decade later, turnpike and bridge corporations were numbered in the thousands. The corporation provided a vehicle whereby the states could pass on their responsibility for providing highways to an organization which, in return for a promise of interest and dividends, could attract sufficient capital to meet the communities' highway needs. The states, in turn, believed that they had adequate control through charter provisions limiting tolls and rates of return to prevent any injustice to their citizenry. That such an arrangement was usually justified during this period is evident; by 1820 all the major cities in the Eastern and Northern states were interconnected by a reasonably good system of surfaced roads. Yet, active as the promotion of highway development by private corporations was in this period, after 1825 this institution gradually died out. The roads reverted to Governmental custody, under which came a long period of quiet hibernation.

In the South the public turnpike with public trustees or local road commissioners was given preference over roads built by private corporations, in part at least because of the fear that the delegation of state responsibility to private interests might result in the exaction of monopolistic profits. The meager evidence available as to the results of this arrangement tends to indicate that the technical standards of the highway system of that area were not so high as they were under the corporate systems of the North. The reasons for the existence of a less effective organization for road building in the South are difficult to ascertain. In 1800 the total population of the Southern area was practically as large as that of the North; moreover, the most energetic movements to the territory west of the mountains had been from the South rather than from the North. On the other hand, the population of the South was less dense; there were no large cities, and greater emphasis was given to agricultural production. In addition, the local inland settlements appeared to have been organized on a much more self-sufficient basis than those of the North, although this may have been as much a result of the poor transportation system as a cause for it.

The history of highways before the Civil War can hardly be complete without mention of the plank road companies promoted in Pennsylvania and the Middle Western states during the late 1840's and early 1850's. The proposal to make all-weather farm-to-market roads by using the readily available wood planks as a surface on ordinary roads seems to have made an extraordinary appeal. Small private companies by the hundreds were organized to raise the necessary capital. The speculative incentives for such promotion, building upon the hope of improved local roads, apparently far outran technological possibilities; in fact, by 1860 this whole corporate activity had disappeared with scarcely any trace and with little word as to why it had come to grief.

The actual operation of vehicles over all these various types of highways was carried on by simpler forms of business organizations: individuals, partnerships, or, in some cases, small companies had under their control a number of coaches or wagons. Operations were generally competitive, although on some routes the coach proprietors obtained charters or other special privileges restricting other operators. The general competitive nature of express and freight enterprises contrasted with the monopoly of the highways themselves, which existed because the states refused to charter parallel highways, or because the topography of the countryside prevented closely parallel lines.

Canals

Simultaneously with road building, great activity was shown in making the more economical water transportation available in inland regions not served by navigable waterways. The English had shown the feasibility of large canal projects, particularly in the case of the Duke of Bridgewater's successful canal joining Manchester with Liverpool. As was the case with roads, private corporations were used in New England, and initially in New York State, to carry on the construction of canals, while public organizations undertook the work in Pennsylvania and in the South. By 1800 a scattering of successful canals had been built, including the private Middlesex Canal joining the Merrimac River in New Hampshire to the Boston area, several small private canals in New York State along the route of what was later to be the Erie Canal, the Potomac Canal, and one or two others in the South.

Between 1800 and 1840 canal building became almost a mania. In New York, Pennsylvania, Ohio, and Indiana comprehensive networks of canals were laid out, with trunklines running mostly east and west, joining principal navigable bodies of water and equipped with feeder lines projected into productive areas remote from the trunklines. New York State was one region where these grandiose schemes were carried most nearly to completion. After the private canal construction in the Mohawk Valley area of New York State had failed, the state government took over and proceeded to build the famous Erie Canal. The initial act of the state legislature was passed in 1817, and in 1825 the whole line from the Hudson River to Lake Erie was open for navigation. This canal was 363 miles long, 40 feet wide at water level, and 4 feet deep. It was provided with 84 locks to overcome the rise of 630 feet from the Hudson River to the highest point on the route and the fall of 62 feet from there to Lake Erie. The total expenditure ran to something over $10,000,000. Somewhat earlier, in 1819, the 76-mile Champlain Canal, providing water transportation to northern New York State, had been finished. As soon as the Erie Canal itself was completed, the construction of branches proceeded. The principal components of the secondary system were a 97-mile canal from Utica to Binghamton, a short branch from a point near Syracuse to Lake Ontario on the north, a series of canals and lakes joining Elmira with the Erie Canal, and a branch 120 miles long from Rochester to Olean in the southwestern part of the state. New York, favored by aggressive leadership, completed its main canal system in the early phase of the commercial development arising out of Western settlement, thus garnering a profitable share of the transportation revenues involved in that commerce. Also the topography of the state was such that the engineering problems of these canals could be readily overcome with the engineering and managerial techniques then available. The whole system in the state was built for less than $20,000,000. The immediate success of the Erie Canal was the guiding light for the canal exponents of other states.

Pennsylvania was a follower rather than a leader, and did not begin its activities until 1826, one year after New York put its principal canal into operation. In contrast to the topography of New York, the mountainous nature of much of Pennsylvania made canal construction far more difficult and operation more expensive. It was, in fact, impossible to complete a through east-and-west canal in Pennsylvania, and only when the Allegheny Portage Railroad, some 36 miles in length, had been completed did Pennsylvania have a relatively efficient through transportation route from its eastern to its western border. The disadvantages of this route, compared to the Erie Canal, are indicated by the 690-foot rise necessary to reach the portage railroad from the east and the 500-foot fall from the western end of that railroad to the Ohio River.

The young State of Ohio, admitted to the Union in 1802, undertook its program of internal improvement by canal building in 1825, and, the topography being relatively favorable, it was able to forge ahead rapidly. By 1830 it had finished the Miami Canal, running north from Cincinnati 178 miles to a junction with the Wabash and Erie Canal (which completed the route to Lake Erie at Toledo); by 1832 the state had finished a 307-mile canal from Portsmouth on the Ohio River to Cleveland. In addition, in the eastern part of the state, short sections of canals ran west from the Ohio River to the main north-and-south canal going to Cleveland.

This brief account of the canal development should also mention the projected Wabash-Erie Canal that was to join Lake Erie through the State of Indiana to the navigable section of the Wabash River on the western border of the State of Indiana, and the completion by the State of Illinois of the 96-mile Illinois and Michigan Canal, which enabled commerce to flow from Lake Michigan up the Chicago River, then through the canal, and thence down the Illinois River to the Mississippi.

The canal era, covering as it did the first half of the nineteenth century, saw the expenditure, largely by state governments, of something like $100,000,000. Some of these canals proved to be self-supporting enterprises, whether constructed by private corporations or by the states. The most notable example was the state-built Erie Canal, the tolls from which reached $1,500,000 in the best years, enabling $1,000,000 a year to be paid back to the state for interest and for retirement of the canal debt. The secondary feeder canals seldom proved self-supporting, and the later-built main-line canals either were constructed through such adverse territory that expenses were excessive or were undertaken so shortly before the coming of the railroad that they never had a chance to prove their worth.

As on the highways, the vehicles were privately owned. The operators paid tolls for the use of the various sections of the canals and added this expense to the cost of boats, animal motive power, and their labor to determine what should be the profitable charge for passengers and shipments of goods.

Charges for Turnpike and Canal Transportation

A review of the price structure of highway and canal transportation will complete the picture of this phase of inland transportation during the era before the Civil War. Speaking broadly, the charges for wagon transportation in heavy-traffic routes on highways in good condition were in the neighborhood of 20 cents per ton-mile. When road standards were poor or weather bad, the charges were as high as 40 cents. In the direction of light traffic, rates were not uncommonly below 20 cents. The tolls assessed for using the highways varied with the type of vehicle and the breadth of its wheels. In the case of the larger four-horse wagons with broad tires, the charges seemed to have varied from 2 to 6 cents per vehicle-mile. Translated into a ton-mile unit, this range would represent a charge of from ½ cent to 2 cents per ton-mile in addition to the wagoner's charges. In the case of the canal boats, the boatman's charges were about 1 cent per ton-mile, to which had to be added the canal toll, which was based on a classification of the freight carried rather than on a uniform ton-mile charge. Summarized in very general terms, the canal tolls varied from ½ cent to ¾ cent per ton-mile for raw commodities such as coal and hay, up to 3 cents for more valuable articles such as dry goods and furs. A differentiation was also made between traffic moving in the direction of light flow as compared to that moving in the direction of heavy flow, the latter having to pay frequently twice as much as the former. A third factor in rate making was evident on those canals that were part of through routes from the Atlantic Coast to the Middle West: lower rates were charged for through business than for that which originated or terminated locally. This last differentiation in rate making was obviously in response to the competition provided by the Mississippi River-Gulf-Atlantic Coast routes which had provided a main artery for commerce to the Middle West before the advent of the canal.

The Steamboat

In the midst of the canal-highway era, experiments were made with steam engines as motive power for transportation. Beginning in 1786, a group of inventors which included John Fitch, Robert Livingston, John Stevens, Oliver Evans, and Robert Fulton experimented for some 20 years with the application of steam motive power to boats. In 1807 when the *Clermont* steamed up the Hudson, the steamboat gained general public acceptance. Within a few years steamboats appeared on the Ohio River and shortly thereafter on the Great Lakes, but their adoption into general usage was slow, partly for technical reasons, but primarily for legal ones. Quite early, Fulton and Livingston had obtained a monopoly of steamboat transportation in the waters of New York State and had then extended their power to control steamboats in the rest of the United States. In addition, along the Atlantic Coast, the well-entrenched operators of sailing packets were able to arouse such public opposition that for a time it was almost impossible for steamboat operators to enter a number of the coastal ports. These troubles continued until an aggressive steamboat owner, a Mr. Gibbons of New Jersey, pressed his fight against the Livingston monopoly up to the Supreme Court. In the famous case of *Gibbons vs. Ogden,* written by Justice Marshall in 1824, the navigable waters of the country were finally opened to all.

With the final disappearance of the restrictions to steam navigation and with improved techniques of construction, facilities for building steamboats at the more important points on the Atlantic Coast and inland waterways were soon provided. The whole business of steamboat building and operation was encouraging testimony to the ingenuity and enterprise of American mechanics and businessmen. From 1821 to 1830 some 385 steamboats totaling 65,000 tons were built; while in the decade following 1830, the figure jumped to over a thousand steamboats, with an average tonnage of 175. An inventory taken in 1838 indicated some 700 vessels in operation, with half of the tonnage on the Atlantic Coast or Gulf of Mexico, a third in the Mississippi Valley, and the rest on the Great Lakes. In the next decade the tonnage constructed was tripled, and during the decade just prior to the Civil War the output was doubled again. Technical improvements took place rapidly; more efficient high-pressure engines replaced the earlier low-pressure ones, and in the 1840's the screw propeller was first introduced. The speed and size of ships increased rapidly. The highly competitive nature of the steamboat business brought great pressure to bear on builders to produce fast and luxurious vessels. The best Hudson River boat came close to making 30 miles an hour, and those on the Mississippi River traveled 25 miles an hour downstream and 16 miles an hour upstream.

FIG. 1. *Inland Navigation About 1848.* (After Tanner). Place names indicate heads of navigation on principal rivers.

The vessels were operated by individuals or by associations of share-owners whose holdings sometimes grew to be substantial. Rates and fares were subject to severe competitive pressure, and, particularly in the case of passengers, there was keen rivalry to provide the best service. The better operators were able to make sufficient profit to increase their fleets by reinvestment and to amass substantial fortunes on the side. Some of them, of whom Cornelius Vanderbilt was possibly the leading example, used every means at hand to establish monopolistic control in certain areas. Although strong-arm methods were frequently used to perpetuate such control, it was never lasting because of the relatively small amount of capital necessary for a new competitor to enter business and because there seemed always to be an entrepreneur ready to fight his way into the field. Meantime there developed a clear differentiation in the various types of construction, primarily in terms of size and methods of propulsion and draft. By the 1850's, the usual Great Lakes boat was of 400-odd tons, with some boats reaching 1,000 tons. Boats for the larger rivers ranged around 300 tons, with some as much as 700; while for the smaller rivers, a type of craft drawing not much over a foot was developed and was able to penetrate into the upper regions of these waterways to a degree difficult to realize today.

The historical importance of the initial domination over the commerce of the Middle West of boats operating on the Mississippi and on the 14,000 miles of its tributaries can be no better demonstrated than by the distribution of the centers of population in that area in 1850. Cincinnati, with a population of 115,000, was the biggest city. St. Louis came next with 78,000 and Louisville third with 43,000. Of the western Great Lakes ports, Chicago had reached but 30,000 and Detroit, Milwaukee, and Cleveland were in the neighborhood of only 20,000. New Orleans, the outlet of the Mississippi system, could boast of 116,000 inhabitants, whereas Buffalo at the eastern outlet of the Great Lakes had only 42,000. The population of New Orleans was only slightly smaller than that of Baltimore or Boston.

At the middle of the century about two-thirds to four-fifths of the outbound commerce from the Middle West seems to have moved *via* the southward route of the Mississippi. The inbound traffic, totaling less in tonnage but some 50 per cent more in value than the outbound, seems to have been divided in reverse proportions, the large share moving westward over the canal, rail, and lake routes and the small share up the Mississippi.

Early Railroad Development

Just after the beginning of the nineteenth century, three of the men closely connected with the development of the steamboat, Evans, Stevens, and Fulton, began investigations of the technical problems of the railway and the steam locomotive. They gave only slight thought to the use of steam-driven vehicles on the highways; hence the trend of development in the United States entirely by-passed the era of the steam highway carriage that monopolized attention for a number of years in England. It may have been that the existing roads were of such poor quality and our severe winters made them so difficult to traverse for a substantial part of the year that there was little to recommend them for steam coaches. As early as 1810 a number of railway advocates began voicing their opposition to current canal proposals, pointing out that the railroad, though not in an operable state of development, would soon be superior to the canal. Interestingly enough, however, the first steam railroads were brought into operation in conjunction with the canals, the railroad performing the function of traversing the heavy grades that the canal could not undertake.

Early discussions of the relative advantages of railways as compared with turnpikes and canals frequently pointed out that the railway probably could not carry freight for less than 3 or 4 cents a ton-mile, and therefore could not compete with the canals, except for those few goods whose quick delivery justified high rates. On the other hand, since passengers were obviously interested in speed and would be willing to pay for the saving of time, it was expected that they would provide the principal business for railroads. A partial explanation of this minimization of the freight-moving possibilities of railroads may lie in the fact that a number of railway advocates had connections with the canal companies. The stand taken by the people interested in the Baltimore & Ohio Railroad was quite different. That railroad was designed to compete with the Chesapeake and Ohio Canal, and hence the promoters of the Baltimore & Ohio Railroad argued that at speeds over three miles an hour, a given pull would move so much more of a load in a freight car than was possible with a canal boat that there could be no question that the railroad was superior of the two even for freight service.

Another basic question that initially arose in connection with the railroads was whether they would, from the start, be public highways over which anyone could run his vehicles, as was the case with the turnpikes and canals. If the state was to build railways or to delegate its authority in a charter to some private company, it seemed as though it might be desirable to continue the traditional public-highway concept to prevent possible discrimination. This problem was quickly settled, however, by the physical difficulties that arose. It was soon found impracticable to allow a number of users to provide their own motive power and vehicles and operate them at the same time on a single-track railroad.

The Beginning of the Railroad Era

The first common carrier railroad for the movement of general traffic to be opened in the United States was the Baltimore & Ohio in 1830. Such estimates as have been made of the annual rates of construction indicate that 40 miles of lines were built in 1830; by 1835 the annual average was around 200 miles, and by the last years of the decade about 400. All together, in the first 10 years, some 2,200 miles were constructed, of which one-seventh was in New England, nearly two-thirds in the Middle Atlantic States, and the rest in the South. A guess would place the total cost of these facilities at $75,000,000. During the 1840's something over 6,000 more miles were added to the railroad system with an investment of some $200,000,000—more, probably, than had been invested during the previous 40 years in turnpikes, canals, and steamboats. The following 10 years saw 22,000 more miles of line, representing possibly from $600,-000,000 to $700,000,000 more of capital expenditures. Thus, by 1860 the railroads had become a billion-dollar industry.

Initially, most of the railroads were built as feeders or extensions to existing lines of water transportation. The ports on Long Island Sound and Narragansett Bay, to which steamers from New York plied, had their railroads running inland to tap the hinterland. New York, Philadelphia, Baltimore, Norfolk, Charleston, and Savannah each feverishly projected lines westward to gain control of such commerce as might be developed in the interior. Other feeders were built from the Great Lakes ports of Detroit, Monroe, Toledo, and Buffalo, as well as from river points, such as Madison on the Ohio River, Frankfort on the Kentucky River, Florence on the headwaters of the Tennessee River, and a town on the Illinois River close to Springfield. As the technical improvement of railroads progressed rapidly, their services became more reliable and their range of operation extended. They quickly demonstrated that they were to be something more than subsidiaries to the existing water transportation network. By 1850 a through line had been completed from Albany to Buffalo and another from Detroit to Chicago. Cleveland and Sandusky were tied to Cincinnati by rail, the Erie Railroad reached from the Hudson River at Jersey City to the western part of New York State, and the lines west from Philadelphia and Baltimore extended well into the Alleghenies. Both Charleston and Savannah were connected with Atlanta. By 1855 through train service was available between Boston and New York, and New York was joined by a continuous line of rails to Chicago. Thus by 1860 a substantial network of railroad lines covered the country east of the Mississippi.

Early Technological Developments

The very early technological development of the railroad had been carried on largely in England. American railway promoters had kept themselves informed of these developments by sending agents to that country to make reports on progress, and they relied initially upon England for their first locomotives, although soon after 1830 locomotives were constructed in the United States. Initially, the locomotives used by the American builders were greatly divergent in design. Railway tracks also were built according to widely varying patterns, and it took some 10 or 15 years for the varying schools of thought on design to come to agreement on generally desirable fundamentals. The acceptance of the cross-tie as a rail support, and the "T" section rail with large heads to take the wear of the flanged wheels came first. By the late 1830's the four-wheel bogie truck provided with metal springs became standard for passenger cars. By 1840 early experiments with compartment and seating arrangements had given way to the "American" type, with two rows of upholstered double seats without compartmentation, seating some 50 passengers. Longitudinal bunks or berths in tiers had been introduced for sleeping accommodations by 1840, and by 1858 Pullman had introduced his ideas in two experimental cars on the Chicago and Alton. By the early 1850's locomotive design crystallized on the horizontal fire-tube boiler, the front end of which rested on a saddle supported by guiding wheels. Horizontal cylinders rather than the earlier sloping variety became standard design. The cab, attached to the rear of the firebox to protect the engine crew, had already become an accepted fixture. Car axle bearings or journals of the present outside type were universal by 1845, and bearings of soft metal oiled by waste packing were generally adopted by the 1850's. The extent to which the first 30 years of practical operation experience with the railroads was technologically able to produce a basically standardized pattern of design that was to last to the present is astonishing.

Financing the Railroads

While some of the first railroad construction was carried on directly by state governments, notably in the cases of Pennsylvania and Michigan, the economic institution used primarily was the private business corporation. The use of the corporation did not mean that the state immediately lost all hold on the railroads. On the contrary, the concept of the relation of the state to its highways was carried over into the railroad field from the earlier turnpike experience, inasmuch as the early railways were regarded as specialized highways. The state retained such charter control over rates, profit, and other matters as seemed necessary, although railroad promoters in turn were pressing for as free a hand as they could obtain. By 1850, however, railroad promoters had become strong enough to have this check on their companies pretty much removed, and hence general charter acts were passed making the grant of the privilege to construct a railroad almost automatic and stripping the state of most of its actual control.

The state governments and local governments played a further role in the early promotion of railroads: they frequently made substantial contributions to the initial capital of railway companies. These contributions might take the form of specific grants of cash or land or purchases of stock or bonds. In Virginia, the state went so far as to apply a standard rule that it would subscribe two-fifths of all railroad stock. In some cases the railroads were granted banking privileges tantamount to a private form of the deficit financing so much discussed today.

In spite of important state aid, the major part of the capital for railroad construction seems to have come from private sources. Because so much of the railroad construction was designed to control the trade from the hinterland of the port cities, it is not astonishing that the commercial interests of these cities as well as the manufacturers located there contributed capital in substantial amounts. Moreover, the important influence that transportation had on land values made land speculators more than ready to supply credit; in fact, some railroad companies seemed to be primarily land-speculating organizations rather than railroad builders. Not all the capital, by any means, came from American investors; the promised rates of interest and dividends were high enough to attract not only local capital but sizable amounts of European capital. The promoters of these enterprises did not worry much about whether their money came from government or private sources just as long as the flow was ample.

Quite early in railroading, the professional promoter played an important part in bringing about railroad construction. He was not interested primarily in developing the commerce from the hinterland or in improving the communications of the country; he was concerned with making a fortune for himself in the course of the initial financing and the construction of a railroad. His influence was especially felt in the Middle West, although there were instances of his operations in the Eastern states, even Massachusetts, where railroad financing was generally on the most conservative basis. His operations did much to upset the theoretical notion that stock represented the holdings of entrepreneurs who took the big risks in developing new projects and who therefore should be given ample return. For, actually, the promoter was quite careful to see that the bondholders were the ones who put up the cash and, to a considerable extent, unknowingly carried the real risk, for which they received a relatively low and fixed return. He, the promoter, got most of the stock for supplying temporary working capital, and thus he acquired a claim to whatever profits might be forthcoming, at little or no expense or risk to himself. Procedures of these types were sometimes concealed by creating a promoter-controlled construction company which took both bonds and stock as payment for the work that it did, selling the bonds at a discount to raise cash to cover construction expenses and holding the stock for itself as a bonus. It was this sort of manipulation that made for instability of railway finances and, unfortunately, attracted the financial manipulator after a railway had been put into operation.

The meteoric rise of the railroad to the position of the largest single industry in the country, together with the promotional and manipulative weaknesses that it fostered, made the railroads a key factor in the rise and fall of business activities. Undoubtedly, the discovery of concealed losses in the Eastern Railway of Massachusetts and of the defalcations of the president of the New York and New Haven Railway, both coming in 1854, precipitated the financial panic of that year. Railroad building certainly produced a dangerous expansion of credit, a fact made abundantly clear three years later in the panic of 1857.

Charges for Railroad Service

The charges which the railroads made for their services in the first 10 or 20 years of their history varied widely between different companies. About 1840 the average revenue per ton-mile ranged from 4 to 10 cents, and passenger fares from 3 to 8 cents a mile. The higher charges seem to have been made under conditions of little competition. A number of quarters felt definitely that high rates should be exacted even to the point where some adverse feeling was created. It was only begrudgingly admitted that "to a certain extent, reduction of cost of freight and travel does stimulate increase of receipts in income." A few scattered companies, primarily in the East, believed that low charges would in the long run stimulate sufficient traffic to justify reduction; a leader in the latter school of thought was the Baltimore & Ohio.

The theory of rate making held most widely during these years followed the principle of "charging what the traffic will bear." Actually, the nature of railroad growth, especially as lines became longer and came into competition with one another and with steamboats and canal operators, had more influence on the trend of rates than did any rate theories held by railway executives. By 1855 competitive pressure had reduced freight rates to a figure centering around 3 cents per ton-mile, while passenger fares were in the neighborhood of 2 cents per mile. The downward trend in freight rates continued gradually, reaching levels in many cases of approximately 2 cents by 1861.

Transportation in Relation to Location of Economic Activity

As already noted, transportation was quite primitive and expensive, compared with modern standards, during the first 50 years of our history. Traffic moved slowly and uncertainly, compared to present standards. Yet during these same years water transportation, available first on natural waterways and later on canals (supplemented by high-cost highway operations), made possible an astonishing redistribution of population and economic activity. Migration to the West and the development of resources in that area proved quite possible with transport facilities existing at that time. Indices of the distribution of population show, for example, that in 1790 a negligible proportion of the population lived west of the Appalachians. Yet 50 years later, before a single railroad had penetrated that area from the coast, some 40 per cent of the nation's people lived west of New York, Pennsylvania, and the coastal states of the South. The center of population had moved during these years from a point 25 miles east of Baltimore to a spot almost on a line with the western border of Pennsylvania.

The limitations of early modes of transportation appear in respect to the specific location of economic activity rather than in the general dispersion of population. Within the western area, for instance, commercial centers before 1850 were founded almost exclusively on the waterways. In 1820 Cincinnati, on the Ohio River, was the only city with a population of over 1,000 in the state. By 1840, largely as a result of the development of Ohio's canal system, Dayton and Toledo, on the Maumee Canal, and Cleveland, Columbus, and Canton, on the Ohio-Erie Canal and its tributaries, could all boast of populations over 1,000. Another indication of the importance of water transport for urban growth was the fact that in 1840, of the country's largest cities, the first five in order of size were coastal ports and the next five were river ports—four on the Mississippi system and one 150 miles up the Hudson.

Technical factors associated with water transportation were effective before 1850 in changing the direction and channels along which long-haul traffic moved. During the first quarter of the century, the products of the Middle West moved chiefly along the Mississippi River and its tributaries. The Erie Canal diverted a major part of this traffic to an east-west channel. That it did not make even greater inroads may be attributed to the development of the Mississippi River steamboat.

In spite of the opposition of vested interests in water transport, most of the localities owing their original development to navigable water facilities were among the first centers to attract railroad service. Much of the Erie Canal route was paralleled by a railroad at an early date. The first railroads of Ohio were laid out to join already established points like Cincinnati, Columbus, and Cleveland. The first railroad across Michigan started from the Great Lakes ports of Monroe and Detroit. Railroads in theory might well have led to the establishment of important dry-land intermediate centers, but the practice of quoting lower rates for centers served by water than were quoted for dry-land points placed definite restrictions on any such development.

Selected References

GENERAL WORKS

Dunbar, S. A., *History of Travel in America*. Indianapolis: The Bobbs-Merrill Company, 1915.

Magill, C. E., *History of Transportation in the United States before 1860*. Washington, D. C.: Carnegie Institution, 1917.

Poor, H. V., *History of the Railroads and Canals of the United States*. New York: J. H. Schultz & Company, 1860.

Ringwalt, J. L., *Development of Transportation Systems in the United States.* Published by Author, Railway World Office, 420 Liberty St., Philadelphia, 1888.

SPECIAL TOPICS

Davis, J. S., *Essays in the Early History of American Corporations.* Cambridge, Mass.: Harvard University Press, 1917.

Dixon, F. H., *A Traffic History of the Mississippi River System.* Washington, D. C.: U. S. Government Printing Office, 1909.

Gephart, W. F., *Transportation and Industrial Development in the Middle West.* New York: Columbia University Press, 1909.

Gould, E. W., *History of River Navigation,* St. Louis: Nixon-Jones Printing Company, 1889.

Lane, W. J., *Commodore Vanderbilt.* New York: Alfred A. Knopf, 1942.

———, *From Indian Trail to Iron Horse.* Princeton: Princeton University Press, 1939.

Morrison, J. H., *History of American Steam Navigation.* New York: W. F. Sametz & Company, 1903.

Phillips, U. B., *A History of Transportation in the Eastern Cotton Belt to 1860.* New York: Columbia University Press, 1913.

Roberts, C., *The Middlesex Canal 1793-1860.* Cambridge, Mass.: Harvard University Press, 1938.

8 · AGRICULTURE

THE STORY OF THE SETTLEMENT of the American landed domain told in a preceding chapter is a dramatic one. From the point of view of our own times, however, an even more important aspect of the growth of the American economy is the story of the development of the agricultural industries. For vastly increased productivity of agriculture is the basis upon which we have built our vast industrial and urban civilization. The settlement of the American land alone could not have supported such an economy. The story is one of an ever-increasing effectiveness in the use of land, animals, and plants by farmers to produce ever-increasing quantities of food and fibers.

At the time of colonization, the continental United States provided precarious subsistence for an estimated one million aborigines. By 1865 that same territory, much of it still remaining to be settled, supported 31 million people at levels unexcelled anywhere else in the world. This achievement was based largely upon changes in the implements that farmers used, and to a lesser extent upon better animals and improved strains of plants. As one change followed another, a revolution in agriculture developed no less significant for the future course of economic society than similar changes that occurred in industry and transportation. The process was by no means complete in 1865; indeed, it was still continuing in the middle of the 20th century. But by 1865 the foundations had been firmly laid and its effects were already clearly apparent.

The Background

European emigrants coming to these American shores brought with them the crops, animals, tools and the agricultural knowledge of the native cultures of Northwestern Europe. Because of the similarities of climate, these introductions were well adapted to the New World. The settlers found in the possession of the aboriginal inhabitants of this continent an agricultural economy far more primitive than their own. It possessed, however, certain cultivated plants unknown to Europe, particularly corn, cotton, tobacco, peanuts, squashes and sweet potatoes, that were of such economic value as to be quickly incorporated in colonial farming.[1] The Colonists also adopted some Indian techniques, such as

[1] The potato and tomato were Andean crops that came to the United States via Europe.

those of clearing land and the hill culture of corn. Thus began a process of selective absorption, accommodation, and innovation that, under the pressure of the problems posed by the exploitation of a new land, gave to American agriculture almost from its beginnings a character sharply divergent from that of either of its principal sources. This distinctiveness was early recognized, for new arrivals from Europe were frequently admonished to observe carefully and copy American methods if they wished to be successful in agriculture in this new world.

The tools with which the Colonial age went about its tasks were those that had been in use for many centuries in Europe; indeed most of them were very little changed from Roman and earlier times. In its domesticated animals, American agriculture was particularly dependent upon European sources, since the American Indian had no domesticated animals save the dog. American importations from Europe supplied the original livestock and continued borrowings were the basic source of improvements. In the case of cultivated crops, Indian contributions were very important. Though the small grains of Europe—oats, barley, rye and particularly wheat—occupied large acreages, corn was the chief food crop as tobacco and cotton were the foremost market products.

The American farmer approached the problems of exploiting a continent in a spirit of adventure. The qualities and abilities of its soils were unknown; every farm carved out of the wilderness was a speculative venture. Private ownership of land, little known in Europe, could be achieved much more easily in the Colonies. Though even here the principle of private ownership was not accepted without a struggle with other systems of tenure, by the opening of the 19th century it was clearly established.

With the exception of the plantations of the South, cultivated at first by indentured servants and later by slaves, the family-sized farm became characteristic. Large holdings cultivated by tenants or by wage earners were not uncommon in the North, but on the whole they possessed no advantages over smaller operations while labor shortages plagued them. On the other hand, the agricultural wage earner was a common figure. Until harvesting operations were mechanized he was indispensable, and the labor force of the average farm was certainly larger than it is today.

There lay upon the American farmer few of the restraints that centuries of traditional practices had placed upon the European. This is not to say that farmers as a class were not conservative. There was a general distrust of "book farming" and skepticism of innovations. On the other hand, America was fortunate in the presence of a class of agricultural leaders, many of them farmers in name only, who were eager in their search for improvements and new opportunities and aggressive in their exploitation of their discoveries.

The farmer was likewise an active participant in economic and political movements that held out to him the hope of improving his market position. The demand for new agencies of transportation, such as the turnpikes, canals, and railroads, came in large part from agricultural interests. This receptive state of mind extended also to activities more immediately concerned with the cultivation of land. The lessons in open-mindedness that were forced upon the early settlers and resulted in their adoption of Indian plants and techniques were not forgotten. European tools and methods were employed, modified, or abandoned to suit the requirements of the American situation. European methods of crop rotation and of soil fertilization were not long continued by European farmers on American soil; such practices were abandoned to reappear only when changing conditions encouraged their development in a form adapted to American needs.

Markets and Specialization

On the frontier of settlement throughout its history, the men who undertook the arduous task of converting a piece of wild land into a farm accepted the fact that they would have to produce their own food and many other necessities. But there always existed the hope and expectation that some product would be found that could be shipped to distant markets, or that towns and cities would develop nearby with industrial populations providing a cheaply accessible market for farm products and a nearby source for the increasingly long list of things farmers desired but could not readily produce for themselves.

The search for crops that could be profitably marketed was constant. During the Colonial period success was determined by the nature of the demands of foreign markets, since the non-farm population of the colonies provided only a very small market. About 1775 the products that found readiest acceptance abroad were tobacco and wheat together with some meat products and work animals. Climate and soil conditions gave the South the advantage, and by this date tobacco had become the dominating crop in Maryland, Virginia, and the Carolinas. Rice and indigo were also important in the Carolinas, and wheat in Virginia and Maryland. Long staple cotton early achieved importance on the sea islands of Georgia.

Out of tobacco culture emerged the plantation system with its dependence upon indentured servants and, later, slaves as its labor supply. It remained, however, for the development of textile machinery in Great Britain and the cotton gin in the United States to make short staple cotton a profitable crop.

Prior to the invention of the gin, cotton had been a luxury fiber more expensive than wool or linen. Its costliness followed from the amount of labor needed to remove the seed from the fibers. The gin reduced this cost to a negligible figure and cotton became the cheapest clothing material available anywhere. The growing mechanized textile industry of Great Britain provided a market, and the South turned from unprofitable tobacco and indigo to the short-staple upland cotton. The crop increased from 73,222 bales in 1800 to 1,347,640 bales in 1840; by 1860 it had reached 3,841,416 bales. At that date Southern cotton was the raw material for the growing textile industry of New England as well as of Great Britain. This staple alone accounted for over 60 per cent of the value of all exports from the South.

Cotton was a merciless King. Its profitability led plantation operators to an unyielding cotton-corn rotation, with cotton occupying all the acreage that could be harvested by the available labor. As a clean crop, carefully cultivated, its presence quickly destroyed the thin soils of the Southeast. It was not only a matter of the loss of fertility of the soil but the disappearance, in some places almost complete, of the top soil. Proper soil use practices, rotations, and protection against excessive erosion were attempted by some, but in general cotton moved to the fertile lands of the West. In 1820 Georgia and South Carolina were the principal producers. In 1850 Alabama took the lead, and in 1860 leadership had been assumed by Mississippi. By the latter date, Texas was producing more cotton than South Carolina.

Though small family-sized farms with no or very few slaves accounted for the larger part of the Southern agricultural population, the large plantation with its slave labor dominated the production of the great Southern staple.

The climate and soil resources north of the Potomac were too similar to those of Northwestern Europe to permit the development of profitable export staples. Some wheat, salted beef and pork, and a few other products found overseas markets, chiefly in the West Indies. On the whole, the development of agriculture in this area was dependent upon the growth of the cities. The development of Baltimore, Philadelphia, and New York, along with numerous smaller towns, permitted the development of a market-focused agriculture in the Middle States. In New England, markets were more restricted and the harsher climate and poorer soils hindered the development of a commercial agriculture. The opening of the Erie canal and the development of railroad transportation a few decades later exposed the agriculture, not only of New England but also of the eastern areas of the Middle States, to competition that it could meet with difficulty, if at all. In the Middle States rapidly expanding urban populations permitted a shift to dairying, fruits, and truck crops, but in New England after 1840 agriculture began a long period of slow decline.

With the development of adequate markets, self-sufficient farming tended to disappear. Farmers continued, of course, to consume at home some of their product as they do today. But the objective of farming was to maximize money income, because only in that way could farmers participate fully in the advantages of specialization. Farm industries, such as the spinning and weaving of wool and the preparation of garments, disappeared quickly with the growth of the textile industry. Tools and furniture were increasingly purchased rather than made at home. Before 1850 New England farmers were eating bread made of midwestern wheat and, to a lesser extent, eating beef raised in Illinois. Gradually the farmer became completely absorbed into the pecuniary-market system. Exceptions existed in isolated areas, but only at levels of consumption that fell increasingly below those of the population generally because of their inaccessibility to markets.

West of the Alleghenies, where transportation was available, agriculture began with wheat as the basic export crop. Elsewhere corn was the crop, converted to marketable commodities in the form of whiskey or pork. Cincinnati and Louisville early became marketing centers for both these products. Since it could be shipped by water to New York, wheat was the early cash crop of the area about the Great Lakes. Later as the farmers accumulated capital, cattle and hogs partially displaced wheat. Further south, wheat, corn, hay and livestock moved down the Mississippi to be marketed to the cotton plantations or in New Orleans.

Interest in New Crops and Methods

Already in Colonial times, but more especially after 1800, there appeared a group of men deeply interested in improving agriculture's resources and techniques. The ordinary farmer had little time or ability to experiment or to explore the possibilities for improvements. But individuals and groups did devote themselves to experimenting with crops, animals and techniques. For the purpose of improving American agriculture, some of them engaged in explorations of European agriculture and imported techniques, new plant strains, and, particularly, improved animal breeds. Others searched more broadly in Asia and Africa with similar objectives. Such individuals organized agricultural societies and wrote for the agricultural periodicals that appeared after 1820 and that constituted a vigorous group of publications in 1860. State governments supported such activities by grants of funds to agricultural societies and by establishing Departments of Agriculture. The Federal government entered the field of agricultural promotion in the 1840's when the Commissioner of Patents undertook the collection and publication of agricultural information and began the distribution of seeds and plants collected from abroad.

The working farmer on the whole entertained a deep interest in new plants, new breeds of livestock, and new equipment. His concern with such innovations was generally tempered with caution and conservativeness, but occasionally he became the victim of one of the series of speculative fervors that swept the country. In some cases the enthusiasm became so intense as to take on the character of a mania. Among the first of these speculative eruptions was that centering upon the importation of Spanish Merino sheep in the years 1810–1815 and upon the Saxon Merino during the years 1822–1826. Interest in the importation of improved European breeds of cattle developed after 1820, although this wave of enthusiasm followed a more moderate course. More absurd than most of the speculations was the "fowl mania" or "hen fever" that ran its course from 1849 to 1855 and that raised to fantastic heights the prices paid for specimens and sometimes for single eggs of the larger breeds of Asiatic poultry. Although individuals occasionally lost small fortunes in the speculations, on the whole substantial public benefit followed them in the establishment of superior breeding stocks.

Similarly, in the plant world speculation moved from one newly introduced plant to another. Public enthusiasm focused its attention upon the mulberry from 1832 to 1839. The credulous purchased and planted broom corn in 1837 and Chinese tree corn in 1839–1841. With the encouragement of the United States Patent Office,[2] they planted Chinese sorghum during the early fifties for the purpose of producing sugar for home consumption. In the same decade the Osage orange became the object of much public enthusiasm as a substitute for wooden fences, which were difficult to provide on the prairies. Excitement of a speculative character frequently attached to the introduction of new varieties, alleged as well as real, of old staples. Among these may be mentioned the Rohan potato, Petit Gulf cotton, Mediterranean and Russian wheats, and several varieties of clover. Some of these were failures if not frauds; others proved additions of the greatest economic significance.[3]

The Soil

If the American farmer was somewhat conservative in his techniques he was characteristically careless and exploitative in his attitude towards

---

[2] Prior to 1862, promotion of the interests of agriculture by the Federal Government was carried on by an office within the United States Patent Office. In that year President Lincoln approved the establishment of a new office, that of the Commissioner of Agriculture, which became a federal Department in 1889. See T. Swann Harding, *Some Landmarks in the History of the Department of Agriculture*. Washington, D. C.: U. S. Department of Agriculture, Agricultural History Series No. 2, 1942.

[3] For an interesting account of speculative fads in agriculture prior to the Civil War, see Arthur H. Cole, "Agricultural Crazes, a Neglected Chapter in American Economic History," *American Economic Review*, Vol. XVI (1926), pp. 622-639. For factual accounts of plant and animal improvement work, see: Carleton R. Ball, "The History of American Wheat Improvement," *Agricultural History*, Vol. IV (1930), pp. 48-71; Charles T. Leavitt, "Attempts to Improve Cattle Breeds in the United States, 1790-1860," *Agricultural History*, Vol. VII (1933), pp. 51-67; E. Parmalee Prentice, *American Dairy Cattle, Their Past and Future* (New York: Harper & Brothers, 1942); Knowles A. Ryerson, "History and Significance of the Foreign Plant Introduction Work of the United States Department of Agriculture," *Agricultural History*, Vol. VII (1933), pp. 110-120.

land. He was not behind the other elements of the population in exercising a propensity towards speculation. The attractions of western lands and of timber and mining claims were as great to him as to his urban relatives. Much pioneering on the frontier was motivated chiefly by the hope of increased land values. Throughout the nation farms and plantations commonly comprised acreages greatly in excess of what the operator could reasonably hope to cultivate with the available manpower.

In his use of the soil the farmer was profligate. Although new land for cultivation had to be reclaimed from virgin forest and grassland, and although the difficulties and costs of clearing were great, efforts to maintain soil fertility were considered uneconomical by most settlers. On new land, planting of the same crop was generally repeated until the inevitable decline in production was so great that the profitability of continued cultivation of the field was questionable. The process of exhaustion might take twenty years; it sometimes occurred in five. Declining productivity encouraged migration to the fresh lands of the West.

As an alternative to migration, the methods employed in Europe to renew and maintain soil fertility were borrowed and adapted to American conditions in many of the affected areas. These methods included rotation of crops, cultivation of legumes, the use of fertilizing agents, and the control of soil erosion.[4] Simple rotation of crops was practiced very early in eastern Pennsylvania, was common in New England by 1800, and in eastern New York, New Jersey, Virginia, and the older South by the 1840's.[5] The same technique was followed to a limited degree in many parts of the West by the 1860's and became common in the ensuing decades. Animal fertilizers were regarded as a worthless nuisance so long as the soil retained its pristine fertility. It was, for example, quite generally the fashion in the earlier years of cultivation in a given area to "compute the expense of moving the barn or the manure and very frequently the barn was moved as the lightest job; and that was only done when the cattle were likely to mire in the dung." As the yield of the soil declined with continued cultivation, the value of applying manure to the soil came to be recognized. At first, only the readily available manure was utilized. Later, care was exercised to conserve and to increase the supply, and eventually attention turned to the use of artificial fertilizing agents.

---

4 For a brief résumé of the work of the pioneers in this field, see Angus McDonald, *Early American Soil Conservationists.* Washington, D. C.: U. S. Department of Agriculture, Miscellaneous Publication No. 449, 1941.

5 For detailed analyses of developments in restricted areas, see Arthur R. Hall, *The Story of Soil Conservation in the South Carolina Piedmont 1800-1860,* (Washington, D. C.: U. S. Department of Agriculture, Miscellaneous Publication No. 407, 1940); and Avery O. Craven, *Soil Exhaustion as a Factor in the Agricultural History of Virginia and Maryland 1606-1860,* (Urbana: University of Illinois Studies in the Social Sciences, Vol. XIII, No. 1, 1925).

The introduction of such supplementary fertilizing materials was not the least important innovation in agricultural practice in this period.[6]

The utilization of lime, marl, gypsum, and other calcareous materials commenced in the late 1830's. Credit for calling the attention of the public to the utility of these agents belongs to Edmund Ruffin of Virginia.[7] In the late forties, guano was introduced and found wide use in the next decade along the Atlantic Coast north of Virginia. Chemical fertilizers, such as superphosphates, were also coming into use in the fifties. A significant development that became important in the South in the late forties was the practice of using cottonseed as a fertilizer instead of destroying it as a waste material.

The Growth of Mechanization

The period 1820–1850, which witnessed so much experimental activity with new plants and animals and during which artificial fertilizers came into use, did not neglect the improvement of tools and the possibilities of mechanizing agricultural operations. Indeed, these years were a period of remarkable inventive activity in the field of agricultural implements.[8] Prior to 1820 a small sum invested in a few hand tools completed the equipment needed to operate a farm. Included were a hoe, rake, axe, scythe, sickle, flail, and perhaps a plow.[9] Most of these in the early nineteenth century differed little in appearance and effectiveness from their prehistoric prototypes. The years from 1820 to 1860 were years of transition to an era when the capital required in farm operation came to be measured by hundreds of dollars, when the farmer in order to carry on his work efficiently had to have, in addition to the simple tools, such machines as drills, planters, reapers, mowers, horse rakes, threshers, feed grinders, and plows and cultivators of many descriptions. Each one of these was the product of the period before the Civil War in origin and in varying degrees of perfection. Some of these implements performed new tasks; some of them performed old tasks better; some of them lightened labor; some of them displaced labor. The new implements were made

---

[6] Of particular importance was the publication of Justus Liebig's *Organic Chemistry and Its Applications to Agriculture and Physiology*, Cambridge, 1841. See also: Charles A. Browne, "Justus van Liebig—Man and Teacher," pp. 1-9 in Faust Ray Moulton, ed., *Liebig and After Liebig: An Analysis of Progress in Agricultural Chemistry*. Washington, D. C.: Publication of the American Association for the Advancement of Science No. 16, 1942.

[7] Edmund Ruffin, *An Essay on Calcareous Manures*. Petersburg: 1832.

[8] The factual record is to be found in James T. Allen, *Digest of Agricultural Implements Patented in the United States from 1789 to July, 1881* (New York: 1886), and in Robert L. Ardrey, *American Agricultural Implements, A Review of Invention and Development in the Agricultural Implement Industry of the United States* (Chicago: privately published, 1894).

[9] Colonists sent to Virginia by the London Company were equipped with a box of tools for each family of six members. Along with axes and building tools were included five broad and five narrow hoes, three shovels, and two spades. No plows were sent.

of iron and steel instead of wood; the tools were highly perfected; the machines brought to bear upon agricultural tasks a degree of nonhuman power previously unknown and hitherto unattainable. They also increased the tempo of operations, as is evidenced by the fact that the horse gradually displaced the slower-moving ox as the draft animal. As a group, these innovations inaugurated the modern age of agricultural technology. By 1860 the foundations for a mechanized farming economy had been securely laid. The agriculture of the twentieth century is more highly advanced in its reliance upon artificial power and the more common use of steel, but it is based upon the machinery introduced, perfected, and brought into common use in the nineteenth century.

The tasks involved in producing desired plant products from the soil divide themselves into five groups: preparing the soil, seeding, cultivating the immature plants to protect them from weeds and to conserve moisture supplies, harvesting, and preparing the harvested crops for market. A well balanced farming operation attempts to produce as much of a desirable market crop as possible, the limiting factor, if adequate acreage is available, being the amount of labor needed for the operation in which time is the most critical factor. Thus in the case of cotton and tobacco, the amount of labor available for harvesting determined the acreage that was planted in these crops. The same was generally true of wheat and sometimes of corn. But in the case of corn, the crop could be harvested by turning animals loose in the fields and the amount planted might be determined by the land that could be plowed in the proper season or perhaps by the amount that could be cultivated. The important point is that any change in the technique or machinery available for one of the five operations affected all the rest. Change in one area thus produced pressure for improvements and greater efficiency in others.

Thus, improved plows made possible the preparation of greater acreages for a crop such as wheat than could be conveniently harvested with scythe or cradle, and there followed great interest in mechanization of the harvesting operation. Such machinery could not be operated on soils as they were commonly prepared, however, and from this followed need for harrows, rollers and clod pulverizers.

The Development of the Plow

The implements used to prepare the soil for seeding in the period preceding 1820 included the hoe and various forms of simple wooden plows. Complete dependence upon the hoe in soil preparation was by no means unknown in these years; indeed, plows were very scarce in the early years of settlement. In parts of the cotton- and tobacco-growing South, the hoe was the basic and, in some areas, the only agricultural implement in use at the beginning of the nineteenth century, a condition that persisted in some regions until the Civil War. The shovel plow, a V-shaped piece of iron without a moldboard, was in various forms the most common type of plow in the Middle States and in the South.

The moldboard plows used in the North were generally constructed entirely of wood save for the "share," which was of wrought iron. It varied considerably in details, since it was usually made by the farmer or the local millwright with the help of the village blacksmith. Compared to later models, all the "improved plows" of this period were heavy, clumsy, and inefficient and, although their performance was distinctly superior to that of the old shovel plows, they were able to penetrate the soil only for four or five inches.

The history of the cast-iron plow in the United States begins with an implement patented by Charles Newbold in 1797 which failed to win popular acceptance. Other patents on iron plows followed. Most successful were those of David Peacock, recorded in 1807 and 1822, which achieved popularity particularly in the Middle Atlantic States, where they continued to be used until the eve of the Civil War. Jethro Wood in 1819 introduced a cast-iron, three-piece plow of special significance because the shape of its moldboard was based on extensive analysis and experiment to improve performance and lessen draft.[10] In addition, the Wood plow possessed a great advantage in that its three parts were cast from standardized patterns and hence were interchangeable and easily replaceable. The Wood plows were widely and successfully used during the 1830's and for decades thereafter. Further improvements in the shape of the plow were incorporated in the Eagle plows of Joel Nourse, which were sold during the forties at a rate of from 25,000 to 30,000 annually.

The plow of the 1820's and earlier was an all-purpose instrument. In the East a one-horse cultivator had been introduced about 1820 and achieved some success, although it displaced the shovel plow only slowly. In the forties a form of cultivator known as a "gang plow," with two or more light shovels, had appeared, and by 1865 it was said that "such implements are known and employed by all." The five- or six-tooth cultivator made of iron replaced the shovel plow in the forties, and by the fifties it had become popular in the West. It was in turn being displaced in the fifties by the more satisfactory steel-tooth cultivator. In the South, cultivation of corn, cotton, and similar "clean" crops was commonly carried on by hand hoeing, sometimes with the assistance of the one-horse shovel plow. After 1840, however, specialized cultivating implements considerably reduced the amount of hand hoeing required.

Western soils posed a special problem to farmers. Cast iron did not

---

[10] Thomas Jefferson experimented with the application of mathematical principles to the design of the moldboard. Although his experiments did not result in success, his work was significant in placing plow design upon a scientific basis. Another important political figure who contributed to the development of the plow was Daniel Webster, whose experiments with very large breaking plows attracted wide attention.

take a high polish and sticky soils clung to its pitted surface. Although these plows were satisfactory upon the virgin soils of the Mississippi Valley, as continuous cropping reduced the humus in the soil the plows scoured poorly. By 1830, working these soils with cast iron plows was considered a "sad trial" to the patience of the farmers of Illinois and Indiana.

The importance of the problem to the West was recognized by a Vermont blacksmith, John Deere, who had emigrated and settled in Grand Detour, Illinois, where he carried on his trade. In 1847 Deere produced the first all-steel plow.[11] It was far superior to the cast-iron instruments and, in Illinois soils, had only half their draft. The plow was an immediate success. By 1860 the steel plow had become standard throughout the West, although, because of its relatively high cost it did not immediately displace the cast-iron plow.

It is difficult to assess the importance of the development of the plow in quantitative terms because of the higher quality of the work done by the improved implements. Unquestionably the new instruments increased the acreage that could be worked in a given period of time. The old wooden plow generally required two men and four oxen to plow an acre per day; the cast-iron instrument plowed from one to one-and-one-half acres in the same time but required only one man and only one yoke of oxen or a team of horses to operate it. The steel plows and likewise the gang and sulky plows also increased productivity. Aside from increasing the rate at which plowing was done the new implements enabled a far more effective job to be performed. The development of the plow compensated in a considerable degree for the destructive exploitation of the soil which resulted from the agricultural methods employed. In the period of first settlement the poor quality of the work done by the plows available was not particularly serious since pulverization of the soil was not an essential requirement in new soils. Early inventors were less concerned with the manner in which plows operated than in reducing the effort required, because newly cleared soils are full of humus and thus fall apart very easily. But the decrease in the amount of vegetable matter after long cultivation tended to make the soil clod easily when plowed. The decrease in fertility likewise required a more complete mixture of the soil elements if productivity was to be maintained; hence the need for more efficient implements. The ability of American agriculture to secure sustained production for long periods from the same soil, despite decreasing intrinsic fertility and the reluctance with which American farmers turned to fertilization and crop rotation, was in part a result of the increased efficiency of the plow.

---

[11] In 1833 John Lane discovered that steel would scour in the sticky soil, and made a plow with a share cut from an old saw blade. He apparently did not attach great significance to his discovery.

Seeding

The improved plows and harrows available by the forties made a well prepared seed bed over a large area economically possible. The older wheat-producing sections, well beyond the farmmaking stage, were experiencing a decline in wheat yields. The wheat-growing areas were, moreover, moving to the smooth clear grasslands of the West, and these regions likewise felt declining yields after some ten years of cultivation. At the same time, the European markets for wheat became increasingly attractive. All these factors called attention to any method that would increase yields, decrease the loss of winter wheat by winterkilling, and save seed.[12]

After 1850, grain drills slowly displaced broadcast sowing of wheat in Pennsylvania, and their use spread to the wheat areas of Virginia and Maryland and north into the wheat regions of New York. As the agriculture of the Mississippi Valley passed out of the farmmaking stage, the drill appeared there also. The machines were in use in Ohio by the late forties, common in the late fifties, and familiar throughout the wheat areas of the Midwest prior to the Civil War.

In the South, cottonseed was generally planted by hand, although mechanical "planters," drills modified for this purpose, were available and in use by 1860. A "planter" operated by one man could do as much work as four men and two mules in hand planting. Cotton was generally planted in rows and thinned by hoeing after the plants were established. Corn, in contrast, was planted in hills that had to be accurately located so that the crop might be cultivated in both directions. For this purpose the early drills were of no value, but a corn planter that gave the operator direct control over the dropping of the seed, placed on the market in 1853, partially solved the problem. The ideal of a one man machine that would plant accurately and rapidly in the desired row was not developed until after the Civil War.

Harvesting

Early Methods

The ultimate benefit of improvements in plowing, cultivating, and planting implements depends upon the degree of development of those implements useful to the farmer in harvesting. In the case of most crops the labor of harvesting is, of all agricultural tasks, the most arduous as well as the most crucial. The capacity to harvest has been and still remains the bottleneck of agricultural production; the labor the farmer is able to apply at harvest time determines his product for the season, par-

[12] Economy in seed was important, since an acre which might yield on an average of from 10 to 20 bushels required from 2 to 2½ bushels of seed if sown broadcast, but only half that amount if it were drilled.

ticularly in the case of wheat, hay, cotton, and tobacco. Because of the longer harvesting season, the problem was less acute in the case of corn. The inventions of the nineteenth century contributed immeasurably to increasing the productivity of labor in harvesting.

At the beginning of the nineteenth century the harvesting of hay and the small-grain crops presented the greatest labor problems because of the slow and difficult work in reaping, mowing, and raking; because of the brief period during which these crops are ripe and must be harvested; and because of the danger of loss from untimely rains. The primitive method of harvesting the grass crops was by sickle, or scythe, and rake; that of the small grains, by sickle, rake, and hand binding. The first advance in wheat harvesting was the introduction of the cradle, a heavy form of scythe with fingers parallel to the blade to hold the cut grain.

Reapers and Harvesters

The concept of a mechanical device to mow and reap is European and very old. Nevertheless, such implements were first brought to mechanical practicability, to popular utilization, and to large-scale commercial manufacture in the United States. The period of successful and useful reapers began in 1831, when Obed Hussey of Maryland patented the first successful machine. Cyrus H. McCormick, a Virginian, patented another reaper in 1834, and these two pioneers were succeeded by numerous other inventors and imitators. Although the reaper was the product of many minds, both in its origins and in the perfection of its details, the credit for placing the machine in the hands of the public in large numbers, in constantly improved form, and upon favorable terms belongs to McCormick.

The adoption of the reaper did not wait upon its ultimate perfection. Crude though the early machines might be, they were to a progressive farmer far better than the cradle or the scythe. Harvesting by the early machines was only slightly cheaper than hand labor; yet the economy was less important than the fact that they increased harvesting capacity. Popular adoption of the machines began about 1855, the date when the first satisfactory McCormick was produced. In that year some 15,000 machines valued at about $2,000,000 were manufactured and sold. Twenty thousand of the machines were said to have been used in the 1856 harvest in Illinois alone. Probably 100,000 were in use by 1860, and during the Civil War some 250,000 additional machines were placed in operation.

To cut, bind, and shock from one-half to three-quarters of an acre of good wheat was an average day's work with the sickle. A cradler could cut approximately two acres in the same time, but the grain had yet to be raked, bound, and shocked. One binder following each cradler was the minimum; more generally, three binders were required to follow two cradlers so that the output with this implement was actually one acre or less per man. The productivity of the cradle was thus little greater than that of the sickle although the occasional employment of women in binding did increase the labor force available for the task. The early Hussey and McCormick reapers cut from 12 to 15 acres per 10-hour day. The reaping machine was thus equivalent to four or five cradlers. Four to six binders—but generally five—were employed behind each reaper so that a saving of some five men was made by the reaper and of six men by the self-raker over the sickle. The harvester still further reduced the labor required, since only two or three binders were necessary, and thus only four men were needed to harvest 10 or more acres per day.

Harvest wages were always high and harvest labor always scarce in the wheat and hay fields. The period of rapid adoption of the reaper began about 1855 but was greatly accelerated during the sixties, coinciding with the Civil War. Although the scarcity of labor during the war no doubt stimulated the sale of reapers, the satisfactory quality of the machines then becoming available must be considered the determining factor in their rapid acceptance.

Mowers

Until the eighties one of the specifications considered essential for a satisfactory harvesting machine was that it be quickly interchangeable to cut either grain or grass. The problems of mowing are, however, dissimilar to those of reaping, and the perfection of a machine that would do close and economical mowing required that the two functions be distinguished. Close cutting, although important in a reaper, was essential in a mower; it was nearly impossible with the type of machines that were manufactured. The first definite distinction between the two objectives was made in 1854, when the Ketchum mower was patented. Improvements that appeared within a few years made this a practicable machine, and the perfected mowers such as the Kirby and the Buckeye were well established by 1860 in a form essentially like the present one.

Although hay was still mostly cut by scythe in 1840, it was generally raked by the "revolver," a horse-operated, wheelless rake consisting of two sets of wooden teeth set on opposite sides of a wooden shaft. Progressive farmers in the fifties were turning to a two-wheel rake which came into use rapidly after 1853. It was estimated that this rake did the work of from eight to ten men, whereas the "revolver" was capable of doing the work of about six men equipped with hand rakes.

Attempts were also made to develop mechanical devices to harvest other crops. A cotton picker was patented as early as the fifties. It was unsuccessful, as were hundreds of subsequent efforts. Experiments with the mechanical harvesting of corn began as early as 1820. These early machines were patterned largely after the grass mower and grain reaper.

The Cotton Gin

A large part of the weight of picked cotton bolls is contributed by the seed, to which the fiber adheres tenaciously. It required a day for a man to clean from one to a maximum of six pounds of the fiber from its seed, depending upon the variety and the length of the staple. The cost of the cleaning operation was such that cotton remained a luxury textile higher in price than other available fibers.

In the Colonial period a simple machine, the roller mill, had been introduced from East India into the Sea Island cotton areas. This machine added little to a man's productivity in the short staple cottons, but it proved valuable in the long staple fibers, increasing the production of clean cotton to as much as 25 pounds per man per day. Cotton remained too costly, however, to find general use. It was upon this scene that Eli Whitney in 1793 introduced his "saw" gin, which solved the problem of separating the seed and fiber. Because his device was simple and could be easily and cheaply reproduced, it met with a degree of immediate success accorded to few other inventions.[13]

The cotton gin, more than most new machines, was the product of one man's inventive skill. It was the first important agricultural invention produced in this country, and its significance in the development of American economic life is second to that of no other technological innovation. Because it made the production of cheap cotton profitable, the cotton gin, along with the inventions within the textile industry in England, helped to fasten the plantation system and slavery upon the South. The more fundamental significance of the gin lies in the fact that, combined with these other textile innovations, it made possible the cheapest source of clothing materials the world has enjoyed. Only the recently developed synthetic fibres can challenge cotton's supremacy.

Threshing

Preparing harvested small grains for market requires that they be threshed to loosen the kernel from the head, that the grain be separated from the straw and chaff, and that the grain be winnowed to clean it of chaff and dust. The threshing methods brought to this country from Europe were the age-old flail and treading floor. After the grain was threshed by either of these methods, the straw was raked aside, the grain gathered and cleaned of its dust, dirt, and chaff by winnowing. The

---

13 The roller mill consisted of two wooden rollers which revolved against each other, but lacked any device to pull the fiber from the seed. The Whitney gin consisted essentially of two cylinders, one, equipped with teeth, turning to enter a hopper containing the seed cotton, the teeth pulling the fiber through holes in a screen too small to permit the passage of the seed. The fiber was then removed by brushes on the second cylinder which rotated in the opposite direction and at a greater speed.

crudest method of winnowing was that of tossing the grain into the air on a windy day so that the light dust and chaff were blown away. Winnowing was the first threshing operation to be mechanized. Simple, hand-operated fans designed to blow a current of air through the grain as it was fed through a hopper were imported from England and were in use by 1770.

Credit for the first permanently successful American thresher belongs to Hiram and John Pitts of Maine, who introduced their machine in 1837. The early Pitts machine was not so much a new contribution as it was a combination of an old fanning mill and the established "groundhog" thresher. With the addition a few years later of an endless apron separator that removed by vibration the grain not removed in the concave, the Pitts machine became the prototype of all subsequently developed threshers.

These early threshing machines were powered sometimes by water, but more frequently by large stationary sweeps operated by horses or oxen. Hand power was quite inadequate, although at least a few of the early machines were intended to be crank-operated. The introduction of the endless belt or railway power, operated by horses, represented a distinct advance and made possible portable threshers. It was, indeed, in working on the perfection of such a power that the Pitts brothers' attention was so successfully turned to the thresher.

Working with a flail and winnowing with a sheet a man could thresh from five to eight bushels of wheat per day, depending in large part upon the quality of the grain. Five to six bushels were probably the usual product early in the century. The fanning mill had a productivity of some 100 or more bushels per day and increased threshing productivity as a whole slightly. Where treading was the method employed, the product was about 15 bushels per man. The early threshing machines had a capacity of about 50 bushels per day. Merchant threshers such as were in use in the fifties employed five men and two horses. The product of such a combination varied considerably, ranging from a low of 20 bushels per man to as much as 100 bushels. Perhaps 30 bushels per man per day can be taken as representative under good conditions. The machines that became available about the time of the Civil War increased this figure materially and steam-operated machinery may have doubled the results suggested.

The preceding pages have described the development of agricultural implements from simple, hand-operated tools, made largely of wood, to machines of considerable complexity that employed animal power. Only a part of the story, albeit the most important, has been told. No mention has been made of improvements in such simple tools as axes, shovels, hoes, and forks, nor of the development of such machines as hay and feed cutters, grinders, shellers, hand planters and broadcast seeders, and clover seed harvesters, Neither has there been any discussion of one particular industrial product of the greatest importance to agriculture—the barbed wire for use in fencing that was invented in the sixties.[14]

Summary and Conclusions

The development of the agricultural economy prior to 1860 differed very substantially between North and South. In the Colonial period in both areas there was conflict between the agricultural organization based on large land holdings and operated by tenants, wage, or slave labor, and the small holdings, frequently owned by the operator who supplied much of the labor and who was assisted by no more than a few hired hands. In the North the large holdings gradually gave way to the small, and the family-type farm achieved dominance. In the South, though the larger part of the white population operated small holdings of land, the large slave-operated plantation dominated the market and determined the character of the entire area. In the South, aside from the cotton gin which fastened the cotton plantation-slave complex upon agriculture, few other technological innovations occurred. The slave-owning plantation operator did not readily put improved implements into the hands of his slaves, and preferred removal to the West to changing his agricultural techniques and practices. The capital he accumulated went into slaves or land and not into improved machinery. Cotton production per hand did increase somewhat in the first half of the 19th century but the gain is to be attributed to the movement of the cotton region to the more fertile lands of the West and to the introduction of more prolific varieties from Mexico.

In the North, the growth of towns and cities gradually provided a market for a diverse group of products, an outlet of much greater importance than the foreign demand for northern staples. Both the farming areas and the cities and towns sought to integrate their economic interests by developing cheaper and more widely available means of transportation.

If the growth of the cities provided a market, the expansion of employment opportunities in commerce, industry, and transportation also proved to be a source of competition with agriculture for the available labor supply. The expansion of transportation facilities, moreover, tended to destroy the monopolistic and semi-monopolistic positions enjoyed by many farmers in their local markets. Such pressures served to force farmers to give their attention to methods by which costs of production could be cut. It was in response to forces such as these that Northern agricul-

[14] See Early W. Hayter, "Barbed Wire Fencing—A Prairie Invention," *Agricultural History,* Vol. XIII (1939), pp. 189-207. On the importance of the problem see Clarence H. Danhof, "The Fencing Problem in the Eighteen-Fifties," *Agricultural History,* Vol. XVIII (October 1944), pp. 168-186.

ture underwent a transformation to emerge in a form much as we know it today.

About 1800 "a clumsy ax, a miserable kicking plow with a wooden moldboard, a wooden-tooth harrow, a coarse shovel, a heavy hoe, an imperfectly tempered scythe and sickle, flail and a hand grain fan were about all the implements that the best farmers then thought necessary for them to possess." The progress of mechanization up to the 1850's is well illustrated by the editor of the *Scientific American,* who wrote in 1857 that "every farmer who has a hundred acres of land should have at least the following: a combined reaper and mower, a horse rake, a seed planter, and sower; a thresher and grain cleaner, a portable grist mill, corn-sheller, a horse power, three harrows, a roller, two cultivators, and three plows." The total cost of the tools described as adequate for 1800 may be estimated at $15 or $20. The investment required by the implements described as necessary in 1857 and which actually were commonly owned within a few decades was many times as much. A reaper-mower cost about $135; a seed drill, about $60; a portable thresher, from $100 to $200; a sweep or tread mill horsepower, about $85 to $150; a gristmill, perhaps $15 to $30; while plows, cultivators, and harrows were on the market at from $5 to $20 each. The new implements were expensive. In view of this fact it is surprising that they were adopted so quickly and in so imperfect a form. This is particularly true when considered in light of the fact that land could be purchased from the Federal Government at $1.25 an acre, that the wages of common labor were less than a dollar a day, of skilled labor, perhaps $1.25 to $2.00, that farm hands received from $100 to $150 per year, that Eastern farmers considered a year's efforts not unsatisfactory if they made profits of from $50 to $100 above their own wages. A low estimate of the investment in implements necessary to the operation of an average Northern farm was $500. Before the Civil War many and perhaps most farms fell short of such outlays in implements but the trend was nevertheless toward heavier investments in mechanical equipment.

The effect upon the ability of an economy to produce is the most important measure of technological advance. In those areas where the mechanical changes already described were adopted, the changes in productivity were great. A man with a two-horse team and equipped with the machines available about 1860 could perform about 10 times as much work as he could have done by hand. Consequently a greatly expanded acreage could be cultivated in fewer hours and with less human effort.

At the beginning of the century, in the wheat-producing areas of Virginia, Maryland and New York, it required from 65 to 80 hours of work in the various operations from plowing the soil to the final sacking of the threshed grain to produce an acre of wheat, or from 15 to 25 bushels. By 1860 in the same states, the employment of the improved plows, drills, reapers, and threshers reduced the labor time required to perhaps 40 hours. Wheat production had become, however, primarily a western industry. In Indiana and Illinois the time required had been reduced to as little as 30 hours. Whereas one day of labor at the beginning of the century had yielded from 3 to 4 bushels of wheat, by 1860 twice that much was not unusual.

MAN-HOUR REQUIREMENTS IN WHEAT PRODUCTION
(PER ACRE) *

Date	*Preparation and Seeding*	*Harvesting*	*Threshing*	*Total*
Prior to 1830	26	20	29	75
1850	13	10	8	30

* Data given are highly generalized in character and indicate minimum hours required with the use of the best available equipment.

The author is particularly indebted for assistance in preparing this table to Miss Catherine Corson, and for the use of her unpublished manuscript, *Technological Changes in Wheat Production as a Factor Affecting Labor Inputs.*

The technological progress and the economy in labor achieved in wheat production only slightly exceed in importance the less spectacular changes that had taken place in the cultivation of corn. By 1865 every phase of corn production except that of harvesting could be conducted by horse-powered implements and machines. With a wooden plow and a hoe, only a few acres of corn could be cultivated by one man, whereas with an improved iron or steel plow and with horse-operated planters and cultivators a man could care for perhaps 40 or more acres. The application of the mower and the horse rake to the production of hay had similar results on productivity in the dairy and beef producing industries. Not to be overlooked in this area was the widespread sowing of meadows and pastures to domesticated grasses as a substitute for the far less productive native grasses.

The ultimate effect of mechanization was to reduce greatly the proportion of the population that had to devote itself to the production of food and fibers. This fact is well illustrated by the changes that were taking place in the distribution of the population. In 1790 there were in the United States only 24 towns and cities of more than 2500 population. These accounted for 6 per cent of the people. Ninety-four per cent were rural and, while some of these lived in small towns and villages not recognized by the Census, most of them were undoubtedly closely associated with agricultural activities. In 1860 less than half of the population (48 per cent) lived on farms; the 392 cities by the Census definition accounted for 20 per cent of the population. The other 32 per cent of the population lived in small towns and villages or in the open country, but not on farms. Some of them were no doubt closely associated with agriculture, but it is probable that most of them were engaged in some industrial, commercial, or transportation activity. So greatly had the conditions of agricultural activity changed that this greatly reduced proportion of the population not only supplied food and fibers to the nation's population in greater abundance than ever before, but also provided large quantities for export. The difference in these two situations is a rough measure of the increased productivity of mechanized agriculture.

Selected References

GENERAL WORKS

Bidwell, Percy Wells, and John I. Falconer, *History of Agriculture in the Northern United States, 1620-1860*. Washington: Carnegie Institution, 1925.

Carrier, Lyman, *The Beginnings of Agriculture in America*. New York: McGraw-Hill Book Company, 1923.

Clark, Victor S., *History of Manufactures in the United States* (3 vols.). New York: McGraw-Hill Book Company, 1929.

Edwards, Everett E., "American Agriculture—the First 300 Years," *Yearbook of Agriculture, 1940*. Washington: U. S. Department of Agriculture, 1941.

Gras, N. S. B., *A History of Agriculture in Europe and America*, New York: F. S. Crofts & Company, 1925.

Gray, Lewis Cecil, *History of Agriculture in the Southern United States to 1860* (2 vols.). Washington: Carnegie Institution, 1933.

Kaempffert, Waldemar, *A Popular History of American Invention*. New York: Charles Scribner's Sons, 1924.

McCormick, Fowler, *The Development of Farm Machines*. Princeton, N. J.: Newcomen Society, 1941.

Schafer, J. K., *The Social History of American Agriculture*, New York: The Macmillan Company, 1936.

Schmidt, L. B., "Agriculture in the United States," *Encyclopedia of the Social Sciences*, New York: The Macmillan Company, 1930.

SPECIAL TOPICS

Anderson, Russell H., "Grain Drills Through Thirty-Nine Centuries," *Agricultural History*, Vol. X (1936), pp. 157-205.

Clark, Neil M., *John Deere, He Gave to the World the Steel Plow*. Moline, Illinois: Privately printed, 1937.

Deering Harvester Company, *Official Retrospective Exhibition of the Development of Harvesting Machinery for the Paris Exposition of 1900*. Paris. n.d.

Demarree, A. L., *The American Agricultural Press, 1819-1860*. New York: Columbia University Press, 1941.

Elliot, J., *Essays Upon Field Husbandry in New England, and Other Papers, 1748-1762*, ed. by Harry J. Carman and Rexford G. Tugwell. New York: Columbia University Press, 1934.

Hutchinson, William T., *Cyrus Hall McCormick* (2 vols.). New York: D. Appleton-Century Company, 1930, 1935.

———, "The Reaper Industry and Midwestern Agriculture 1855-1875," in *Essays in Honor of William E. Dodd*, ed. by Avery Craven, pp. 115-130. Chicago: University of Chicago Press, 1935.

Quaintance, H. W., *The Influence of Farm Machinery on Production and Labor*, Publications of the American Economic Association, Vol. 5, No. 4, 3rd Series, 1904.

Rogin, Leo, *The Introduction of Farm Machinery in Its Relation to the Produc-*

tivity of Labor in the Agriculture of the United States during the Nineteenth Century. University of California Publications in Economics, Vol. 9. Berkeley, Calif., 1931.

United States Census, 1860, 8th Census, *Preliminary Report,* pp. 90-100.

———, 1860, 8th Census, *Agriculture,* Vol. I, pp. xi-xxiv.

Van Wagenen, Jared, Jr., *The Golden Age of Homespun*. New York State Dept. of Agriculture and Marketing, Bulletin 203. Albany, 1927.

9 · PROCESSING AGRICULTURAL PRODUCTS IN THE PRE-RAILWAY AGE

PROCESSING means subjecting materials to a process of manufacture, development, or preparation for the market; converting something into marketable form, as livestock by slaughtering, grain by milling, cotton by spinning, milk by pasteurization, fruits and vegetables by sorting and packing. There are four main types of processing. (1) In some industries, such as the refining of sugar, an *extractive* process is involved in which, mainly by the application of heat, the refined product is extracted from the raw. (2) Meat packing is an *analytical* process in which a basic raw material is disintegrated or decomposed into several different products. These end products may consist of one or more main products and dozens, or even hundreds, of by-products. (3) In the *synthetic* or assembly process several elements are combined to make a single product. The baking of bread serves as an example of this type of manufacture, for flour, sugar, dry milk, solids, and shortening are combined with other ingredients to produce the end product. (4) Finally, there are industries engaged mainly in changing the shape, texture, form, or size of the material on which they operate. These are called *converting* industries. A creamery, churning cream into butter, would fall into this classification.

Extent and Variety of the Agricultural Processing Industries

A quick survey will show the extent and variety of these industries. Some are based on the cereals: wheat, corn, oats, barley, rice, and so forth. These provide raw materials for flour milling, baking, the manufacture of cereal breakfast foods. From corn come whiskey and alcohol, as well as starch, corn syrup, and a multitude of other products. Second, there are the industries based on animal husbandry, including the production of dairy products: creameries producing butter, cheese factories, plants producing condensed and powdered milk, and ice cream factories. Wool from sheep and goats provides raw material for textile mills. Cattle hides form the basis of the leather industry; and cattle, hogs, and sheep of the meat-packing industry. Poultry and eggs must undergo some processing before they are ready for the market, and so also must fruits and vegetables, which have in recent times become the mainstay of the canning industry. Third are the vegetable fibers, cotton and flax especially, that form the basis not only of textile industries but of the manufacture of other products: linseed oil from flax, cottonseed oil from cotton, and various other vegetable oils. Still other crops give rise to such industries as the refining of sugar, the roasting of coffee, the manufacture of cigars and cigarettes, as well as to the making of various alcoholic and non-alcoholic beverages.

Some of these activities did not exist 200 years ago; most of them were carried on quite differently from those of today. The development of the more representative industries, important between 1789 and 1865, will be analyzed in this chapter.

Stages of Development in the Agricultural Processing Industries

On the pioneer farm grinding grain into meal, baking bread, slaughtering livestock to provide meat, preserving vegetables, making clothing, cutting firewood, and sawing logs into lumber were at first all carried on for household consumption. The farmer provided his own raw material, performed the processing activities, and owned the finished product.

Most of these processes were carried on in the home by members of the family. As settlements grew, skilled workmen came to devote all their time to processing. They were often itinerants who traveled from one farm to another to make shoes or clothes, or to slaughter the farmer's meat supply. Even when the need for mechanical power was met by the erection of a village gristmill, the pioneer farmer often had to assist the miller in grinding the grain. The miller took his toll and gave back the remainder to the farmer who carted it home for his family's use.

As villages grew into towns, many itinerant workers settled in them, built small shops, and began to purchase raw materials and sell the finished products. They worked mainly with hand tools and sold most of their products directly to the consumer.[1]

At the time of the Revolution most production was in one of these two stages. Those industries or producers that had reached the point of manufacturing for export were in a third stage in which "goods are made by one set of persons, marketed by another, and consumed by a third." [2] Manufacturing was still typically by hand, but the processed goods were sold to wholesalers, who in turn sold to distant retailers. Wholesalers were to be found in the principal seaports of all the Colonies at the close of the Colonial period. They sold products imported from Europe, the

---

1 V. S. Clark, *History of Manufactures in the United States,* Vol. I, p. 164. New York: McGraw-Hill Book Company, 1929.

2 N. S. B. Gras, *Industrial Evolution,* p. 25. Cambridge, Massachusetts: Harvard University Press, 1930. The first four chapters of this book provide an interesting and valuable analysis of the evolution of manufacturing in England and America up to the pre-factory stage of development.

West Indies, and other Colonies to the country stores, and purchased from them the commodities that the country storekeeper had accepted from the farmers and that were suitable for sale in the coastal towns, or in Europe and the West Indies. The miller, the tanner, or the meat packer who had surplus products that he was unable to sell in his immediate locality, was also glad to avail himself of the services of these merchants. For example, the Brandywine millers at the close of the Colonial period were manufacturing mainly for export and were marketing their flour through exporters.

Rise of the Meat-Packing Industry

Animals had provided an important part of the American food supply throughout the Colonial period. At first, in every community, each farmer was his own butcher. After the harvest was over and the cold weather had set in, several hogs and perhaps a steer were killed to provide the winter's supply of meat. The meat that was not eaten fresh was smoked or cured with salt, a procedure followed by pioneer farmers, and, indeed, by many families beyond the pioneer stage, all the way from the Atlantic to the Pacific.

As population increased and villages grew into towns, men began to specialize in the butchering trade. Itinerant butchers traveled from farm to farm to slaughter for the farmers. After a time many settled in the growing towns and became meat dealers as well. They set up slaughterhouses at the edge of the inhabited area, bought animals from the farmers, and sold fresh meat to the community over the counters of their little shops. Sometimes they peddled it from house to house.

Much of the meat had to be cured in some way because it could not be sold fresh. Moreover, in seaport towns quantities of meat had to be prepared for the crews of fishing boats and other sailing vessels, and for export to foreign markets. The farmer had preserved his winter's supply by smoking the meat or salting it. For the overseas trade, however, it was necessary to pickle the meat in brine and pack it in barrels. Thus there arose the term "packer": one who packs meat in barrels. It is still customary to speak of the men who furnish our meat supply as "packers," although today packing in its exact sense is a minor branch of the meat industry.

Packed meats for the export trade came from a variety of sources. Farmers and planters who slaughtered their own animals brought to market the excess not needed by their families. Merchants took livestock in exchange for foods and had it killed and packed by men who made a specialty of this business. Some packers were themselves dealers in cattle and provisions, combining in their own hands both manufacturing and merchandising.

In cities like Boston, growth of population combined with growth of shipping and exporting to enlarge the meat trade. The Boston market demanded a larger supply of animals than the farms of the neighborhood could supply. As early as 1654 William Pynchon drove cattle overland from the Connecticut Valley to Boston.[3] Thus the cattle drovers originated. Their functions arose from the fact that the principal areas of livestock production were so far removed from the centers of population, since then, as in later times, cattle raising flourished where unoccupied lands offered free range. The drovers therefore traveled from farm to farm, collecting cattle and hogs until they had obtained a sufficient number to drive to market where the animals were sold to the butchers and meat packers.

Originating in New England, this practice was soon adopted in the Middle and Southern Colonies, where cattle and hog raising flourished most in the back country, in the Great Valley of Pennsylvania, the Shenandoah Valley, and the Piedmont region of the Carolinas. In this territory the settlers created cattle ranches, an open range, and a cow country similar to the later development of the Great Plains. New York, Philadelphia, and Baltimore became packing centers and live cattle began to be exported from Charleston.[4]

Concentration of meat production in these cities brought the rise of related industries, such as leather tanning, soap making, and the molding of tallow candles. Marketing methods changed as markets and fairs were organized to assure a meat supply for the larger cities, such as Philadelphia, Hartford, New Haven, Providence, and Boston. Drawing livestock from distant farms and ranches, they caused a growing centralization of slaughtering and meat packing. Outside of Boston stockyards and cattle pens were built where sellers could show their animals and buyers could inspect them, but Faneuil Hall in the business district provided a meeting place for the sale of livestock.

When cattle and hog raising developed beyond the Alleghenies after the Revolution, this system of markets and fairs was copied. All through the Ohio Valley fairs served as points of concentration at which drovers or packers might obtain a sufficient number of animals for their needs. The farmers of the Ohio Valley early developed a surplus of cattle and hogs that they disposed of in several ways. Some of them did their own slaughtering, selling the meat in near-by towns. A country storekeeper might gather a boatload of animals from farmer-packers to ship downriver to the New Orleans market.

---

[3] William Pynchon was also the first regular packer, packing hogs for export to the West Indies. R. A. Clemen, *The American Livestock and Meat Industry,* p. 323. New York: Ronald Press, 1923.

[4] Joseph Schafer, *The Social History of American Agriculture,* p. 96. New York: The Macmillan Company, 1936. A good description of the development of cattle ranching from Colonial times is found on pp. 90-106.

Before the development of the canals and railroads, however, most of the cattle and hogs raised for distant markets were driven "on the hoof" to Atlantic Coast markets. During the summer along the main lines of travel "so many drovers passed, that an observer a mile or more away, could know of the passing of the stock, for up in the air he could see long moving lines of rising dust." [5] Seldom were there less than one hundred head of cattle in a drove; droves of hogs were often many times as large. Fat cattle could cover seven miles a day, hogs somewhat less, so that the journey was often a protracted one. Frequently the cattle were sold, just before they reached the market, to farmers who fattened them and sold them again at a profit.

This system of droving declined somewhat when slaughtering and meat-packing centers arose in the West. By 1850 it was said that there were a hundred towns in Ohio, Indiana, and Illinois engaged in the business. Of these, Cincinnati offered outstanding advantages. Large supplies of capital were available through Cincinnati banks. Fortunes acquired in Boston packing houses were invested in Cincinnati establishments.[6] The Ohio River and its tributaries provided transportation into the live-stock areas and to distant markets. River navigation was supplemented by canals and railroads. As early as 1818 Cincinnati had become a recognized center; and by 1832 a contemporary writer could state, "Cincinnati is decidedly the largest pork market in the United States." In a new country, it was found that hogs could be raised more easily than cattle: they reproduced more rapidly, needed less care and attention, and could protect themselves against wild animals better than cattle and sheep, although they were unable to stand long journeys over mountain roads as well as cattle. Hogs could be slaughtered and their meat smoked or cured by relatively unskilled labor; moreover, the meat was as palatable in the form of salt pork, bacon, or ham as when it was fresh. All this favored the establishment of pork packing west of the mountains for supplying eastern markets.

In Cincinnati in the earlier years, and generally in other centers, the slaughtering was done by farmers. Meat was sent to commission merchants in the city who packed and marketed the products. As the trade developed, merchants found it safer to buy live hogs because the farmers often handled the meat carelessly so that much of it was spoiled. Rather than do the slaughtering themselves, the merchants turned over the animals to butchers operating slaughterhouses on the outskirts of the city. From the slaughterhouses the carcasses were hauled across the city to the

---

[5] King, "The Coming and Going of Ohio Droving," *Ohio State Archives and Historical Society Quarterly*, Vol. XVII (1908), pp. 247-253. Quoted in P. W. Bidwell and J. I. Falconer, *History of Agriculture in the Northern United States*, p. 178. Washington: The Carnegie Institution, 1925.

[6] Clark, *History of Manufactures in the United States*, Vol. I, p. 482.

packing houses on the river bank, where the meat was smoked, cured, or pickled, and packed in barrels.

The slaughterhouses had, by 1840, developed a considerable division of labor and were also learning to profit from by-products. The cheaper fats were rendered into lard oil, which superseded whale oil as the illuminant in poor men's homes. Soap and glue factories were established, as were plants for making hog bristles into brushes.[7] In 1849 the cooperage industry in Cincinnati and its environs employed 1,500 men, most of whom were engaged in making kegs, pork barrels, and bacon hogsheads for the packing industry. By 1850 concentration of ownership had brought packing and slaughtering under a common management. Hand labor still predominated, and much working capital was required because of a delay of from six to eight months between the purchase of the livestock and the sale of the finished product. It was for this reason that Cincinnati's banking facilities were so important. The length of time that elapsed between purchase of livestock and sale of finished product, together with the unpredictability of prices, made the business highly speculative. For the packers the transition from prosperity to absolute bankruptcy could be very sudden. Special talents were needed to achieve lasting financial success.

The market that Cincinnati built up for its products was catered to with great discrimination. England, Germany, New England, the merchant marine, the navies of America and Europe, and the plantations of the South and of the West Indies consumed the varied products that Cincinnati prepared for them. The city's rapid growth in population provided an ample labor force. Subsidiary industries and services—trucking, cooperage, and so forth—also developed. Although their nearness to supplies of livestock and their transportation advantages led such other cities as Louisville, Alton, and St. Louis to take up meat packing, Cincinnati remained without a peer up to 1850. In 1833 Cincinnati firms packed 85,000 hogs; in 1848 nearly 500,000. There was both humor and admiration in the statement of a contemporary writer that Cincinnati was "the most hoggish place in the world." [8]

The Leather Industry

From the hides and skins that were by-products of the packing industry arose the leather industry so important in Colonial days. In every Colony pioneer farmers found it necessary to preserve hides and skins for clothing and for other uses. Leather was used not only for shoes, but

[7] In 1847 it was stated that Cincinnati packers could pay higher prices for hogs than those at other places because of their income from by-products. Clark, *History of Manufactures in the United States,* Vol. I, pp. 483-484.

[8] *DeBow's Review.* Quoted in Edward C. Kirkland, *A History of American Economic Life* (rev. ed.) p. 299. New York: F. S. Crofts Company, 1939.

for coats and breeches, for gloves, belting, harness, upholstery, bookbinding, and a multitude of other purposes.

Hides in the natural state are fairly durable if kept dry. But centuries ago savages discovered that if the brains and fats of the animal were rubbed into a skin, it could be preserved for a far longer period.[9] Later it was discovered that tannic acid derived from the bark of hemlock, oak, or chestnut trees worked the same effect. At the outset most pioneer farmers doubtless did their own tanning, since equipment and processes were simple and inexpensive. From the leather they made their own shoes and leather garments as well.

But although "almost any pioneer could manufacture leather, it took a skilled man to produce good leather." [10] In response to the great need for a superior product artisans soon set up tanneries and engaged in leather manufacture in every Colony. Most of these tanneries were on a very small scale. Even the more successful establishments represented but a small investment—two or three thousand dollars in raw materials, much less in buildings and equipment. A site alongside a running stream, a number of vats sunk in the ground and others (for liming) above ground, an open shed for a beamhouse, and a bark mill in which water or animal power was used to grind the bark were all that was necessary. Processes, too, were simple. The vats were filled with alternate layers of bark and hides and then covered with water. The tannic acid leached from the bark and impregnated the hides, which were turned from time to time and moved into other vats so as to expose the hides to liquor of varying strength. Since the process required almost a year, a considerable amount of capital was tied up in the hides. The bark used depended on the locality. New England tanneries used hemlock; the Southern tanneries, oak. Hemlock produced a lighter leather so that a considerable interchange arose between the Colonies.

In most of the Colonies the Government encouraged tannery and related industries by laws forbidding the exportation of hides; other laws provided for public inspection of leather.[11] An effort was made to prevent men from carrying on a combination of tanning, currying (finishing leather), and shoemaking in one enterprise. Apparently such laws were not successfully enforced.

Salem and Lynn, Massachusetts, have been looked upon as the birthplaces of leather manufacture in this country. There were, at the end of the Colonial period, many small tanneries in or near those cities. As the

---

9 And this was good leather. As made by the American Indian, it has never been surpassed by the white man in spite of his superior technical knowledge. Malcolm Keir, *Manufacturing,* p. 428. New York: The Ronald Press, 1928.

10 Keir, *Manufacturing,* p. 429.

11 In some Colonies the export of leather was also prohibited for the protection of the shoemakers. See Clark, *History of Manufactures in the United States,* Vol. I, pp. 53-56, for a summary of these regulations.

supply of bark ran low in this area the industry moved westward into regions of undepleted timber, since the availability of the bark rather than of the hides determined the industry's location in those days. Hides, after being partly dried, could be transported long distances, whereas bark crumbled easily and was hard to transport without waste and loss. So the tanning industry spread westward into the hardwood regions of Pennsylvania and the Ohio Valley.

Other than this westward movement, no important changes took place in the industry until after the Civil War. Some new tanning materials were developed; imported hides and skins were depended on more and more. Meantime, tanneries multiplied rapidly until by 1870 there were 4,500 in operation. But the great changes that were to modernize the industry in technique, scale of operations, and organization came after that date.

The Development of Flour Milling

Long before the end of the Colonial period the grinding of grain by hand mills or, Indian fashion, with a hominy block and wooden pestle, had given way to power mills. These early mills were small and crudely constructed with the limited capital available.[12] Only the smallest streams could be dammed. Sometimes an undershot wheel set in the current of the stream made a dam unnecessary, although such a wheel gave but a small amount of power. Many of these mills had no machinery other than the millstones. A farmer dependent on such a mill had to carry home his meal and sift out the flour by hand. A definite advance came when the mills installed cylindrical bolting machines to do the sifting. Often this apparatus was turned by hand and the farmer who brought in his grist had to do the turning. One man, the miller himself, usually constituted the labor force of such mills as these. Because the stream might dry up during the drought of summer, or freeze up in winter, the miller often fell back on other occupations and other sources of income. A famous Philadelphia miller, for example, operated a farm, a distillery, and a sawmill, as well as his flour mill.[13]

The typical Colonial mill took the farmer's grain and ground it, returning the identical grain to the farmer minus a toll to cover the cost of grinding. The miller might consume the toll-flour himself or he might sell it. Once he got into the way of selling flour it was natural for him to take the next step: buying wheat and manufacturing for sale. Then the gristmill became a "merchant-mill." Many of these merchant-mills

---

12 For a description of milling processes and machinery in Colonial times see C. B. Kuhlman, *Development of the Flour Milling Industry,* pp. 93-96. Boston: Houghton, Mifflin Company, 1929.

13 François de la Rochefoucauld, *Travels Through the United States,* Vol. I, pp. 101-104.

catered especially to the export trade. By 1792 American mills exported 824,000 barrels of flour, mainly to the West Indies and to southern Europe.[14]

By that time power mills were common in all the Colonies. Almost every farmer grew some grain for his family food supply, if not for a cash crop. The difficulty and high cost of transportation multiplied the number of mills. Said Thomas Jefferson in 1786, "There is no neighborhood in any part of the United States without a water gristmill for grinding the corn of the neighborhood.[15] There had developed, however, a fairly distinct wheat belt in which wheat was grown as a staple crop so that a large surplus was made available for export. In this belt, reaching from the Mohawk Valley southward through Pennsylvania into Maryland and Virginia, was the largest concentration of merchant-mills. In Philadelphia and on the Brandywine Creek near Wilmington were located the chief mills of that period. Hundreds of Conestoga wagons hauled grain to them from distant farms. Large shipments of wheat were floated down the Delaware, the Schuylkill, and the Susquehanna Rivers to the millers' docks.

Just after the Revolution a period of rapid technical improvement in flour milling was induced by the inventions of Oliver Evans. He tells how he undertook to build a mill on Brandywine Creek in 1782: "I then began," he says, "to study how I could make the mill exceed all others. I first conceived the grand design of applying the power that drives the millstones to perform all the operations which were hitherto effected by manual labor." And so he developed a series of improvements: a conveyor that moved the meal horizontally from one machine to another, an elevator that moved it vertically from one floor of the mill to another, and a "hopper-boy" that spread the flour for cooling. In 1791 he was granted a patent on his inventions. They were installed in some of the Brandywine mills where they quickly demonstrated their usefulness and whence their fame spread to other mills over the country. Their main advantage was that they saved labor. A mill that made 40 barrels of flour a day had required four men and a boy to operate. Now, with Evans' improvements, two men were sufficient.[16] But the new machinery required larger amounts of power and cost more to construct. More capital was therefore needed, and this tended to transform the industry to a capitalistic basis. The larger merchant-mills using the Evans equipment could operate at a lower cost per barrel, and thus the large mills flourished and the smaller mills failed.

---

[14] Tench Coxe, *View of the United States,* 413-417. Philadelphia, 1814.

[15] Andrew A. Lipscomb, ed., *The Writings of Thomas Jefferson,* Vol. V. Washington, D. C.: Thomas Jefferson Memorial Association, p. 403.

[16] Oliver Evans, *The Young Millwright and Miller's Guide,* 9th ed., p. 239. Philadelphia: Carey & Blanchard, 1836.

This trend, in turn, led to the localization of the industry in favorably situated milling centers. The mills of the Brandywine lost the leadership to those of Baltimore early in the national period. Possibly the Baltimore millers were somewhat more progressive than those of the Brandywine and therefore more easily persuaded to adopt the Evans inventions. At any rate, the most famous Baltimore millers—the Ellicotts—were soon won over to their use. Then, too, Baltimore had valuable water power and access to the finest wheat supplies of Maryland, Pennsylvania, and Virginia. After the Baltimore and Ohio Railroad was built, the mills of Baltimore could secure cheap wheat from the Ohio Valley. Baltimore was then the country's leading seaport for trade with South America, and large shipments of flour were sent annually to Brazil as well as to Great Britain and the West Indies. At home, Baltimore developed a flourishing flour trade with the cotton states to the south. By 1850 the mills of the city were producing 500,000 barrels of flour and an equal amount came to the Baltimore market from mills in the surrounding area.

Richmond, gaining importance as a milling center about 1820, ranked second to Baltimore. Its activities centered in the mills of Gallego and Haxall. Its chief advantages were the water power provided by the James River and the wheat supplies of the interior valleys of Virginia. The Richmond mills were the largest of the time. The Gallego mill could turn out 900 barrels of flour a day; the Haxall, 700. Thus they were the first to prove the advantages of large-scale production in milling. But Richmond lacked the fine harbor and the foreign trade organization that Baltimore had developed so successfully. The Civil War cut off her foreign markets, while the competition of the Western millers delayed recovery of lost ground.

Rochester rose as the third milling center of the East. The Genesee River afforded plenty of water power for many mills. When the Erie Canal was put into operation, it supplied an outlet to the New York City market, and, in addition, enabled the Rochester mills to supplement their local wheat supplies by drawing from the Ohio Valley. Moreover, the Rochester mills were large, efficient, and well equipped. By 1850 they were producing almost as much flour as the mills of Baltimore, and more than those of Richmond. After 1870, however, they too began to feel the pressure of competition from the Western mills. Even the local wheat supplies were failing the Rochester mills, as Genesee Valley farmers turned from staple wheat growing to diversified farming.

As wheat growing spread westward, milling centers developed in the Mississippi Valley. By 1870 St. Louis had become the most important milling center. In 1841 there were but two mills in the city; by 1851 there were 19. This growth was all the more remarkable because St. Louis has no water power. No other city, however, is better situated for river navigation, which, combined with a network of railroads, forms a superlative transportation system. St. Louis millers took advantage of their location to secure very low rates for their flour shipments. The Gulf States became a subsidiary market. St. Louis flour rapidly conquered the New York market as well. The soft red winter wheat produced in the territory tributary to St. Louis was conceded to make the best bread flour, and the marketing organizations set up by the St. Louis Exchange enabled her mills to get the best wheat at lowest prices.

Beginnings of the Canning Industry

The art of preserving food by sterilizing it with heat and enclosing it in airtight receptacles is generally said to have been perfected by a Frenchman, Nicholas Appert. (Canning in his day would have been a misnomer, since he used glass jars; tin cans came somewhat later.) For centuries man had tried to preserve foods by drying, salting, and smoking. They had been successful only with meats, fish, and a few fruits. Sailors on long voyages ate little but hardtack and salt meat. The shortage of vitamins caused many deaths from scurvy. To supply the needs of the French Navy for a more adequate diet, Napoleon had offered a prize for a successful method of food preservation, with the stipulation that the winner explain his process in a book so that the public could learn how it was done.

Appert had devoted a lifetime to preparing foods. He had worked as a pickler, preserver, wine-worker, confectioner, brewer, distiller, and army contractor at various times. Although he had had no scientific education, he worked out a process that was scientifically sound. Its axiom was that food sterilized with heat and enclosed in airtight receptacles would keep for long periods of time. Heat is the great natural sterilizer.

Appert's treatise, "The Book for All Households or the Art of Preserving Animal and Vegetable Substances for Many Years," was published in 1810. An English translation some years later spread the knowledge of the new method to English-speaking countries. One of his successors developed a closed vessel for steam-pressure cooking and a gauge for measuring the temperature that greatly improved the process. By 1820 canners were beginning to use tin cans instead of glass jars, and canning as it is now known came into being.

Even before Appert's book was published American experiments were being made.[17] It was in England, however, that the new process made the most rapid progress, which may explain why the first important canneries in the United States were started by men of English birth. William

[17] The Swedish traveler, Peter Kalm, who visited the American Colonies about 1750, described a process used in New York to preserve oysters and lobsters. According to his account, they were washed and boiled and put up in glass or earthen jars, "well stoppered to keep out the air." *Travels into North America,* Vol. I, pp. 185-187.

Underwood is said by some to have been the first American canner. English-born, apprenticed in his youth to the pickling and preserving trade, he came to America and settled in Boston in 1819. By 1821 he was shipping fruits and berries in glass jars to South America and the Orient. The bottles had to be imported from England. Lobsters and tomatoes were put up, as well as fruit. Apparently Underwood at first met with little success in his home market, which preferred English canned foods. Even his shipments to foreign ports are said to have carried a London label.

At about the same time, another Englishman was getting a start in New York City. Thomas Kensett came to America after acquiring some experience in pickling and preserving food in England. Settling in New York City, he formed a partnership with his father-in-law, Ezra Daggett. As early as 1819 they canned oysters, lobsters, and salmon. In 1822 the firm was advertising in a New York newspaper, "meats, gravies and soups put up in tins, warranted to keep fresh for long periods, especially during protracted sea voyages." [18]

In the next two decades canning became an established industry at various points on the Atlantic Coast, but especially in the neighborhood of Baltimore. Supplies of shellfish were superior in that area, and workers were easily obtained for the canning season. These advantages, together with Baltimore's facilities for distribution, made the city America's canning center.

About 1840 the canning of corn was begun in Maine, largely as a result of the persistent experiments of an old sea captain, Isaac Winslow; and gradually other vegetables as well were canned. To the original purpose of preserving food for long voyages was now added the prevention of waste of surplus fruits and vegetables. The California gold rush gave impetus to the canning industry: tinned meats and fruits were used extensively in the boom towns. In the Middle West the first cannery of which we have record was set up in Cincinnati in 1860. In the following year the Van Camp Company, now famous in this field, started operations in Indianapolis.[19] But it is conservative to say that prior to 1860 this method of preserving food was still largely confined to sea food and most of the canneries were located along the Atlantic Coast.

By 1860 tin cans crudely made by hand were in general use; machine-made cans were not developed until 1885. Tinsmiths (cappers) sealed the cans after they were filled by hand. The cans were both expensive and undependable. Boiling water was used to sterilize the product; the proc-

---

[18] Clark, *History of Manufactures in the United States,* Vol. I, p. 485.

[19] The Van Camp Company at the start packed fruits and vegetables in five-gallon tins. The grocers opened them, retailed the contents and sent the cans back for refilling. William V. Cruess, *Commercial Fruit and Vegetable Products,* Chapter 3. New York: McGraw-Hill Book Company, 1924.

ess was slow; the canneries small (the largest processed only 2,000 to 3,000 cans a day); and the market limited. Prices of canned goods were high: a small can of tomatoes, corn, or peas, might sell for 50 cents at retail.

The decade 1850–1860 witnessed the beginning of fruit canning in California and of salmon canning in the Pacific Northwest. But the most striking development was the invention by Gail Borden of a successful method of canning milk. Borden was a lovable and romantic figure, in some ways the typical Yankee inventor. Born in 1801 of Puritan ancestry, brought up on the frontier of Indiana Territory, he spent much of his life in the South as schoolteacher, surveyor, newspaper editor, and collector of customs at Galveston. As a pioneer who felt the need of concentrated food for long marches in the wilderness, he invented a "meat biscuit" that he manufactured in large quantities for the men who joined the California gold rush. A trip across the Atlantic impressed him with the sufferings of immigrant children for lack of fresh milk, and set him to experimenting with the preservation of milk. Others, including Appert, had attempted to find a process before him. Borden's experiments were carried on in the dairy region of New York. In 1853 he applied for a patent "on a process of evaporating milk in a vacuum." The patent was held up for three years until the Patent Office was satisfied that the vacuum performed a really important function in protecting the milk from air and in keeping it clean while it was being condensed.

There are no census figures on the canning industry before 1870, but estimates put the total output before 1860 at about 5,000,000 cans a year. Ten years later it had risen to 30,000,000 cans. The Civil War had undoubtedly brought a great impetus to the industry. The Union Army purchased large quantities of canned foods, of which thousands of men got their first taste in the army. Gail Borden's condensed milk became popular. Oysters attained a prominent place on menus inland as well as on the coast. Growing popularity and widening demand for canned food thus laid the foundation for future advance.

Beginnings of the Liquor Industry

European travelers who visited America at the end of the Revolutionary period were wont to make unfavorable comments on the poor quality of American tea and coffee and the excessive fondness of the country people for intoxicating liquors.[20] In Colonial times the healthfulness of alcoholic beverages was universally believed, in part no doubt because of painful experiences resulting from drinking impure water. The brewing of beer was carried on both in the home and in specialized plants.

[20] See, for example, André Michaux, *Travels to the Westward of the Allegheny Mountains* (1905), R. G. Thwaites, ed. Cleveland: Arthur H. Clark Company, 1917.

Many a pioneer family made its own supply, but in the larger towns breweries were soon established in which beer and ale were brewed for local consumption, as well as "strong porter" for ships' use and for export. Such plants were usually small in scale according to present-day standards: "Some country breweries represented an investment of less than $1,000, and what were accounted considerable establishments sold for twice or three times that sum." [21] Breweries usually had their own malt houses, although often malting was a separate industry. Barley, wheat, Indian corn, and rice were all used as raw materials, giving considerable variety to the finished products.

Rum was long popular for domestic consumption as well as an export commodity. During the Colonial period it was the poor man's drink; the well-to-do preferred their imported wines. The Scotch and Irish immigrants of the eighteenth century brought a taste for whiskey, and after the Revolution it began to displace rum in public favor. Made from corn or rye "as commonly as grain was ground," whiskey became the drink of farmers as rum was the liquor preferred by mariners and the people of the seacoast. As the farming population spread westward grain distilling moved west just as had flour milling. In the undeveloped state of Western transportation before the canal and railroad era, the transportation of grain to Eastern markets was impracticable. Concentrated in the form of whiskey, it could stand high-cost transportation. At first whiskey distillation was most prominent in the western valleys of Pennsylvania, Maryland, and Virginia. After 1810 Ohio became the chief seat and Cincinnati "the largest whiskey market in the world."[22]

About that time an effort was made to promote the sale of malt liquors in order to check the excessive consumption of rum and whiskey. Intemperance was beginning to cause alarm to thoughtful people, though it was still regarded with a degree of tolerance that seems strange to many persons today. This campaign was successful in part, but it was not until 1860 that the manufacture of fermented liquors exceeded that of spirituous. Meantime, however, the influence of German immigration had caused a switch from English ale and porter to lager beer.

Tobacco Manufacturing

Though in Colonial times tobacco was grown primarily for the export market, domestic consumption was large. This domestic demand grew after 1776, with pipe-smoking absorbing much of the output, although cigars were common and cheap, the retail price in the early days of the

[21] Clark, *History of Manufactures in the United States,* Vol. I, p. 167.

[22] *Ibid.,* pp. 318, 480. For some interesting sidelights on the Colonial liquor industry, see also Lyman Carrier, *Beginnings of Agriculture in America,* Chapter XXIV. New York: McGraw-Hill Book Company, 1923.

Republic being two for a cent or even less. Cigarettes were not commonly used until after the Civil War; but tobacco chewing was even more prevalent before the war than in later times.

The simplest and crudest processing involved leaf stemming, pressing the tobacco into plugs for those who chewed, grinding to produce snuff, and shredding to make fine-cut smoking tobacco. Once the household stage was passed, these operations were carried on in small shops, except for snuff making which required mechanical power. The preparation of chewing and pipe tobacco stayed close to the tobacco-growing areas, but snuff and cigar making were widely scattered. About 1812 New Orleans was prominent as a center of cigar manufacture. Fifteen years later some of the seaport towns in Massachusetts took an important place in the trade, making cigars for export to the West Indies. In 1846, when tariff duties on imported cigars were lowered, American manufacturers began to feel the effects of Cuban competition, and domestic consumers learned to prefer the Cuban tobacco in cigars. American cigar makers met this situation by making cigars with Cuban tobacco filler and a domestic-grown wrapper. Most of the wrapper tobacco was grown in the North, particularly in Connecticut, hence the larger part of the cigar industry was kept in the Northern states. By 1860 Philadelphia was probably the leading cigar-making city.

The rest of the tobacco industry was more largely concentrated in the South. In 1840 Richmond was said to carry on 41 per cent of all tobacco processing, much of the work being done by Negro slaves hired from their owners to work in the factories. By 1860, 40 tobacco houses in Richmond employed 2,500 slaves. At the same time Louisville and St. Louis were becoming important centers of manufacture, aided by the westward spread of tobacco growing in Kentucky and Tennessee.[23]

The Dairy Industries

In Colonial times butter and cheese were made on all farms for home consumption. As much greater skill is required to turn out a good product than the average farmer possessed, the quality was apt to be poor.[24] Since there were no refrigerators, the butter had to be heavily salted. When there was a surplus above family needs, however, it could be sold at the general store. A cool springhouse and extra care sometimes produced superior butter that could be sold to selected customers at prices higher than the general store offered, and dairying might then become a business of producing for the market. By 1750 many farmers

---

[23] Clark, *History of Manufactures in the United States,* Vol. I, pp. 486-488.

[24] As late as 1843 a Richmond newspaper declared that much of the butter brought to that city would "hardly be thought good enough to grease a cart-wheel." L. C. Gray and E. K. Thompson, *History of Agriculture in the Southern United States,* Vol. II, p. 838. New York: Peter Smith, 1942.

in Connecticut and Rhode Island were producing considerable quantities of both butter and cheese, some of which was exported.

After 1800 the farmers of New York State, particularly those of Orange and Ulster Counties, began to build up a reputation for high-grade butter and cheese. With the opening of the Erie Canal dairying on a large scale arose in the Mohawk Valley. By 1835 large quantities of butter and cheese were being shipped to Eastern markets, by way of the Erie Canal, from central and western New York and from the Western Reserve in northern Ohio. Before the Civil War the Western Reserve had acquired the name of "Cheesedom." The census of 1860 showed that New York was producing 46 per cent of all cheese manufactured in the United States, and Ohio 20 per cent. Butter production was less concentrated, but New York, Pennsylvania, and Ohio together produced almost half the American output.[25]

By that time the growth of cities had created a considerable market for fresh milk. At first, this was supplied by near-by dairies that could make direct deliveries. As transportation systems developed, the cities were enabled to draw their milk from more distant areas, and the "milk shed" of New York and those of other states covered a considerable area. Middlemen took over distribution.

About 1850 the first attempts were made to establish the factory system of cheese making. These earliest factories were located in western New York. Jesse Williams, a farmer in Oneida County who had had unusual success with his own dairy, undertook to supervise cheese making on neighboring farms. To simplify supervision, milk was delivered from the other farms to his dairy. The success of the plan, known as the "associated dairy system," doubtless led to the establishment of the first cheese factories. From New York State they spread into Ohio, Indiana, and Illinois, and thence into Wisconsin and Minnesota. Progress was slow, however; in 1860 there were only 17 cheese factories in New York State. The big developments in this field, together with the rise of the creamery and other plants using milk and cream as raw materials, came after the Civil War. The milk condensory has a long history, but milk-powder plants, ice cream factories, and chocolate factories are comparatively recent developments.

Conclusion

This brief survey has shown the close link between the agricultural processing industries and the growth and spread of agriculture, from which they stemmed. Agricultural changes necessarily brought changes in the agricultural processing industries. A shift from tobacco growing to wheat growing helped to build up Richmond as a milling center. A

[25] For an account of butter and cheese making before 1850 see Bidwell and Falconer, *History of Agriculture in the Northern United States,* pp. 424-430.

new and superior type of wheat grown successfully in the territory tributary to St. Louis helped to make that city a milling center. The westward progress of hog raising developed new packing centers in the West.

Other factors helped to determine the final result. New markets in foreign lands may build up an industry and establish new manufacturing centers. This was the case with the Baltimore flour mills; their growth was a result of the development of Brazilian markets. Conversely, the closing of markets may ruin an industry, which is what happened when the Civil War shut off Richmond's flour trade. New techniques of production have their influence on the spread of an industry, as was the case after the introduction of Oliver Evans' flour-milling inventions. Favorable transportation may help to build up an industry in one locality and help to destroy it in another. And the business ability (or lack of it) of the enterprisers who organize the market for an industry's product and set up controls for its supplies of raw materials may play a large part in causing the growth or decline of an industry in a given locality.

Selected References

GENERAL WORKS

Alderfer, E. B., and A. E. Michl, *Economics of American Industry*. New York: McGraw-Hill Book Company, 1942.

Bidwell, P. W., and J. I. Falconer, *History of Agriculture in the Northern United States (1620-1860)*. Washington, D. C.: The Carnegie Institution, 1925.

Clark, V. S., *History of Manufactures in the United States*, Vol. I (1607-1860). New York: McGraw-Hill Book Company, 1929.

Malott, D. W., and B. F. Martin, *The Agricultural Industries*. New York: McGraw-Hill Book Company, 1939.

SPECIAL TOPICS

Canning:

"Gail Borden," *Dictionary of American Biography*.

Collins, J. H., *The Story of Canned Foods*. New York: E. P. Dutton & Company, 1924.

May, E. C., *The Canning Clan*. New York: The Macmillan Company, 1937.

Dairy industries:

Alvord, H. E., "Dairy Development in the United States," *Yearbook of the United States Department of Agriculture*, 1899, pp. 381-398.

"Dairy Industry," *Encyclopedia of the Social Sciences*.

Schafer, Joseph, *Social History of American Agriculture*, pp. 134-139. New York: The Macmillan Company, 1936.

Flour milling:

"Oliver Evans," *Dictionary of American Biography*.

Evans, Oliver, *The Young Millwright and Millers' Guide* (9th ed.). Philadelphia: Carey & Blanchard, 1836.

Kuhlmann, C. B., *The Development of the Flour Milling Industry in the United States*, Chapters 1 and 2, Boston: Houghton, Mifflin Company, 1929.

Leather:

"Leather Industries," *Encyclopedia of the Social Sciences.*

Keir, Malcolm, *Manufacturing,* Chapter 18. New York: Ronald Press Company, 1928.

Warshow, H. T., ed., *Representative Industries of the United States,* Chapter 12. New York: Henry Holt & Company, 1928.

Liquor manufacture:

Carrier, Lyman, *The Beginnings of Agriculture in America,* Chapter 24, "The Influences of Alcoholic Beverages on Colonial Agriculture." New York: McGraw-Hill Book Company, 1923.

Meat packing:

"Meat Packing and Slaughtering," *Encyclopedia of the Social Sciences.*

Clemen, R. A., *The American Livestock and Meat Industry.* New York: Ronald Press Company, 1923.

Keir, Malcolm, *Manufacturing,* Chapter 18.

Warshow, H. T., ed., *Representative Industries of the United States,* Chapter 13.

Stages of development in manufacturing:

Gras, N. S. B., *Industrial Evolution,* Chapters 1-4. Cambridge: Harvard University Press, 1930.

Tobacco manufacture:

Jacobstein, M., *The Tobacco Industry in the United States.* New York: Columbia University Press, 1907.

Malott, D. W., and Martin, B. F., *The Agricultural Industries,* Chapter 7.

10 · THE HEAVY INDUSTRIES BEFORE 1860

THE HEAVY INDUSTRIES in this country, as in Europe, are largely a development of the past century. Their growth has been consequent to the introduction and spread of the techniques and organization of production associated especially with the Industrial Revolution and stemming particularly from the indirect method of manufacturing that steadily replaced the older face-to-face relation between fabricator and consumer. So long as manufacturing was organized on the basis of fireside industries, handicrafts, small shops, and local markets, the term "heavy" could hardly be applied either to the capital investment, to the products of manufacture, or, with a few exceptions, to the equipment used. Even in certain mill industries the often massive equipment of mill wheels, gearing, and so forth, incidental to the use of water power was customarily constructed on the spot by local craftsmen and gave rise to no specialized branch of heavy industry.

With the introduction and spread of steam power, machine production, and the factory system, all this was changed. The emphasis on mass production on an ever-expanding scale called for larger and stronger equipment, higher speeds of operation, and more massive power plants not only in the fabrication but also in the handling and transportation of raw, semifinished, and finished materials. To handle things in large volume was to handle them more efficiently and cheaply, and the whole scale of industrial equipment moved upward. A new group of industries arose to supply and equip, not consumers, in the ultimate sense, but producers with goods ranging from raw materials at one end to intricate machinery at the other. Ores and coal, the major nonferrous metals, iron and steel manufactures in their primary forms, the rails and rolling stock of railroads, and the more massive forms of industrial machinery and equipment, including that of the heavy industries themselves—all these are properly described as products of heavy industry. Together they form the backbone of an industrial economy.

The Iron Industry in an Agrarian Economy

The basic heavy industry of the new industrial age was, of course, the manufacture of iron and steel.[1] Even as organized and conducted in the pre-industrial era, iron manufacturing, puny as its scale of operations appears by modern standards, may quite properly be described as a heavy industry, with respect to both the size of the equipment used and the weight of the masses manipulated during the processes of manufacture. The blast furnaces of the eighteenth century, with their equipment of waterwheel and bellows or blowing cylinders, were much the largest industrial mechanisms to be found in the country at the time. The iron industry provided the basic materials for the new heavy industries and in scale of operations and size of equipment it set their pace as well.

At the opening of the nineteenth century the great bulk of the iron manufactured in this country was produced by the two-stage process of smelting and refining.[2] The quantity of iron made directly from ore in bloomery forges was not large and its production was confined increasingly to a limited section of the country. The iron ore was reduced by smelting in the blast furnace, with charcoal as fuel, and except for hollow ware, that is, kettles, cooking utensils, and other articles made by casting directly from the furnace, the product was crude cast iron in the heavy lumps known as "pigs."

While some pig iron was remelted in the cupola furnaces of foundries for recasting into various articles, the greater part of the product of the blast furnace was subjected to a second refining process in an open forge. In this process more of the impurities contained in the iron were eliminated and the amount of carbon was reduced. At the same time the crystalline structure of pig iron gave way to a fibrous, striated structure of near-pure iron, intermingled with slag, that possessed the essential qualities of malleability and capacity for welding. The refining process consisted of repeated heatings in a forge and beatings under a water-driven trip hammer, which, with its head of several hundredweight, was the principal mechanical equipment. The resulting product was drawn out under the trip hammer into wrought-iron bars or plates of the various sizes and shapes in current demand. Iron plates were of distinctly sec-

---

1 The principal older work in this field, J. M. Swank, *The History of the Manufacture of Iron in All Ages* (2nd ed., Philadelphia: The American Iron & Steel Association, 1892), has many limitations for the present-day student. The best general source for the study of heavy industry, including iron and steel, in this period is V. S. Clark, *The History of Manufactures in the United States* (1929 ed.), Vol. I (1607-1860).

2 The best detailed description of the old rural iron industry is found in A. C. Bining, *The Pennsylvania Iron Manufacture in the Eighteenth Century*. Harrisburg: Publications of the Pennsylvania Historical Commission, 1938.

ondary importance, owing to the smaller demand for them and to the difficulty and expense of hammering them out.

Almost invariably the ironmaster depended upon local sources of ore and fuel, owning or leasing the land on which they were found or contracting for supplies. Ore, with few exceptions, was obtained from surface or near-surface deposits through stripping and open pit operations. Charcoal was prepared in the traditional manner from cordwood. The huge quantities of this fuel required—between 175 and 250 bushels per ton were used in the smelting process alone—necessitated access to cheap and abundant timber. Poor roads, limiting the radius within which ore and fuel could be obtained, served as a check on the scale of operations and periodically forced the abandonment of old furnace stacks as accessible raw materials were exhausted.

The production of the typical blast furnace did not exceed several tons a day during an annual season often of no more than 20 to 30 weeks. The rest of the year was spent in gathering and preparing stocks and in idleness enforced by a lack of water power during the driest and coldest portions of the year, as well as by seasonal labor scarcities caused by the pressure of agricultural needs. The pre-industrial character of the iron manufacture conducted in this manner is suggested not only by its small scale of operations and rural environs but by the nature of its market and the uses to which its products were put. Production was geared primarily to the needs and requirements of an essentially agricultural economy.

The local market served by most iron works was a rural one and the products made were largely those indispensable to the farm. The principal cast-iron wares were articles in demand in the typical rural household—pots, skillets, and other utensils for cooking; kettles for making soap, rendering lard, and washing; heavy pans for boiling down syrup and salt brine; andirons, sadirons, and various other articles in the same class. The bar iron of assorted sizes that was the leading product of the refinery forges was also made to meet the requirements of a predominantly agricultural population. Known as merchant bar, it was regularly stocked in innumerable country stores for blacksmiths, the principal iron fabricators of the time. The sizes of bar iron in greatest demand were those most suitable for making into wagon tires, horseshoes, chains, nails, and a wide variety of tools, implements, and other articles in use about the farm and home that the blacksmith—and frequently the farmer with his Jack-of-all-trades ingenuity—ordinarily made and repaired at his forge.

In many ways the typical blast furnace and forge of the eighteenth and early nineteenth century closely resembled the local mill industries that loomed so large in the agricultural economy of the period. Drawing its supplies from and often disposing of its products in the immediate vicinity, it devoted its operations to the needs of the rural communities that it served. The early ironworkers, however, stood apart in important respects from the fulling and carding mills, the gristmills and sawmills, early established in every frontier area. The operations performed at such works were at no time conducted by the individual farmer, as was the grinding of grain, sawing of wood, and so forth. Even had iron ore been readily available, the high degree of skill and elaborate equipment required would have made individual production impractical. Moreover, the ironworks, with its extensive ore and timber properties and heavy equipment, represented a far greater investment of capital than other types of mill industry. Whereas the typical gristmill or sawmill was owned and operated on a one-man (family) basis, the rural ironworks, which even in the eighteenth century called for an investment of thousands of pounds sterling, was conducted by a partnership. Although the ironmaster was usually the principal owner, capital was put up by merchants, professional men, planters, well-to-do farmers, and many others with funds to invest.

In the first stage of its development, iron manufacture was distributed throughout the country, as the result of the widespread availability of ores in workable amounts and the active if limited demand for iron in the settled regions. Iron was made in all but one of the Colonies, and prior to 1860 ironworks were in production for a time, at least, in every state east of the Mississippi, except for three in the Deep South, as well as in several states of the trans-Mississippi West. The greatest concentration of the industry prior to 1800 centered in Pennsylvania, Maryland, New Jersey, and eastern Massachusetts. This range of activities had not changed greatly by 1860, save for the development of important Western areas of production, especially in the Ohio and Cumberland Valleys. Works conveniently situated near transportation facilities disposed of a portion of their products outside of their immediate localities.

Revolution in the Iron Industry

The story of what might be called the industrialization of iron manufacture and its transformation into the basic heavy industry is one in which a number of major changes occur: the introduction of the newer techniques of making iron; the concentration of the industry in large urban centers; the shift from wood to coal as fuel and from local to assembled supplies of ore and crude iron; and, of particular importance, the steady replacement of an essentially agricultural demand for iron by one stemming from the advance of industrialization in all branches of American manufacturing.

The technical innovations of the period from the close of the eighteenth century to the decade ending in 1860 followed in reverse order those established by the revolution in iron manufacturing in England: rolling, puddling, and the replacement of charcoal by mineral coal as fuel in the several processes. In England the original impulse to change was given by scarcity of timber, but in this country the primary factor was scarcity of labor. The first of the new processes to be adopted in the United States was rolling, and the last the use of coal in the blast furnace. The method of reducing slabs or blooms of iron to bar iron by means of grooved rolls in place of trip hammers was first introduced in this country at a rural ironworks in western Pennsylvania in 1817 and was quickly taken up by the rising iron industry at Pittsburgh and other centers of iron manufacture. The adoption of the refining process of puddling was not slow to follow. Puddling differed from the traditional method of refining pig iron in the open forge not so much in the essential character of the refining process (which was little changed) as in the scale of operations and the equipment used. The open forge, in which the pig iron was heated and worked in direct contact with the fuel, was replaced by the closed furnace of the reverberatory type, in which the metal was worked by hand tools on a hearth out of contact with the fuel, which burned in a separate firebox.

The reverberatory furnace not only permitted the working of larger charges of metal more rapidly and with less consumption of fuel, but, by separating fuel from metal, made possible the substitution of mineral coal for charcoal, heretofore impractical because of the harmful effect on the finished product of the sulphur and phosphorus present in coal. The advantage of coal lay not only in its lower cost (despite the abundance of timber in this country), but in its concentrated character. It was pointed out about 1850 that, whereas from 2,000 to 5,000 acres of timber were required to supply an ordinary charcoal furnace, a coal mine with a 6-foot seam, covering half an acre, would yield a sufficient supply. The centralization of the iron industry was made possible by coal.

With the introduction of rolling and puddling, primary iron manufactures lost their once wholly rural character, and the industry was gradually reorganized on the basis of rural blast furnaces smelting iron with charcoal, and urban rolling mills refining and reducing pig iron by the new techniques, in most cases with mineral coal as fuel. The course of centralization is well illustrated by its development in Pittsburgh.[3] The first iron manufacturers there were blacksmiths who fashioned wrought bar from the rural ironworks of central Pennsylvania into finished articles to supply demands arising from commercial activity centering at this strategic point of transfer between the transmontane routes of travel and the Western river system.

---

3 The economics and technology of centralization at Pittsburgh are described in Louis C. Hunter, "Influence of the Market upon Technique in the Iron Industry of Western Pennsylvania up to 1860," *Journal of Economic and Business History,* Vol. I, pp. 241-281.

From this initial stage, Pittsburgh's iron industry took over successive steps in the making of iron from the rural sources of supply until finally all processes, beginning with smelting, were conducted in the city. Hammered bar was early replaced by slab iron or blooms as the raw material of the industry, and, with the improvement and spread of the puddling process, blooms in turn were displaced by pig iron. As their scale of operations expanded, Pittsburgh's rolling mills drew pig metal from a steadily widening radius of territory. Depending at first chiefly on crude iron brought by wagon and flatboat from central and western Pennsylvania, by 1840 Pittsburgh manufacturers were using pig iron carried by steamboat and canal as well as by flatboat from blast-furnace districts as widely separated as western Tennessee and eastern Pennsylvania, with western Pennsylvania, Ohio, and Kentucky supplying the bulk of the needs.

Beside Pittsburgh must be placed the other rolling-mill centers of the country in the years preceding the Civil War: Cincinnati, St. Louis, and Wheeling in the West; Philadelphia, Scranton, and Phoenixville in eastern Pennsylvania; Boston; the Troy-Albany district; and, in the South, Baltimore and Richmond.[4] Single plants of outstanding size were occasionally found in smaller places, such as the Cambria plant at Johnstown and the Great Western works at Brady's Bend, western Pennsylvania. More than half the rolled iron in the country in 1856 was made in Pennsylvania.

The final stage in the centralization of the iron manufacture, the establishment of blast furnaces at the rolling-mill centers of the country, was dependent on two factors: the adaptation of mineral coal as a smelting fuel and access to new and ampler ore supplies. The substantial beginnings of this stage date from the forties and fifties, but it was not until the decades following the surrender at Appomattox that the transition gained momentum. The shift from charcoal as a blast-furnace fuel got under way first in the iron region of eastern Pennsylvania during the thirties, stimulated by the growing scarcity of charcoal and the availability of anthracite coal, and was made technically practical through the use of the hot blast. By 1860 nearly 100 blast furnaces in eastern Pennsylvania used anthracite coal as fuel and in the country as a whole the output of anthracite iron had passed that of charcoal iron.

The introduction of bituminous coal proceeded more slowly in the trans-Appalachian region. The delay in its adoption was not due simply to the abundance of timber (contrary to the accepted view, cheap timber did not mean cheap charcoal), nor to prejudice of consumers and producers but, above all, to the fact that wrought iron made from coal or

[4] The Virginia iron industry centering at Richmond is admirably handled in Kathleen Bruce, *Virginia Iron Manufacture in the Slave Era,* Published for the American Historical Association. New York: D. Appleton-Century Company, 1931.

coke pig iron was not so well adapted to the agricultural uses to which iron was put in the West as the charcoal-smelted product. For general blacksmithing purposes, the toughness, malleability and capacity for welding of charcoal-smelted iron made it much preferred to that made from coal or coke pig iron. The latter product first found general acceptance in rolling mills engaged in the manufacture of rails. By 1860 bituminous coal and coke were well established as blast furnace fuels in the major pig-iron districts of the West.

The successful introduction of coal in blast-furnace practice removed a major obstacle to the scale of operation heretofore imposed by both technical and transportation difficulties connected with the use of charcoal. Typical weekly yields of 25 to 30 tons of iron from the old-style charcoal blast furnaces were before 1860 dwarfed by yields of as high as 300 tons from the much larger furnaces developed to make use of mineral coal. With greatly enlarged furnace capacity and the trend toward centralization of pig-iron production in rolling-mill centers, the problem of supply of raw material shifted from fuel to ore. The widely distributed but shallow deposits of ore that served the rural pig iron industry were quite inadequate to the great and expanding needs of the coal and coke blast furnaces. At first the enlarged blast-furnace plants were located near the more extensive ore deposits of the older iron districts, but an industry capable of meeting the needs of a nation in process of industrialization could not attain permanency until the great ore ranges of the Lake Superior country were discovered and made accessible. Not only was the ore of the five great ranges from Marquette to Mesabi present in masses of near-mountain proportions, some of which were admirably adapted to exploitation by opencut and stripping methods, but its metallic content was much above that of the ores of the older iron districts, often half to twice again as large.

The problem of transporting the ore to the rising iron districts of eastern Ohio and western Pennsylvania some 600 to 1,000 miles away was solved by two major innovations: the development of specialized ore steamships and extraordinarily efficient ore-handling equipment at loading and unloading docks on the Great Lakes, and by the construction of ore-carrying railroads to and from the lake ports. Not until the completion of the original Soo Canal in 1855 did the development of the Superior ores get under way. By 1860 nearly one-tenth, 10 years later fully one-fourth of the pig iron manufactured in the United States was made from Lake Superior ore. The center of iron production, which had long rested in eastern Pennsylvania, moved gradually to the trans-Appalachian region. Pittsburgh, with inexhaustible supplies of unsurpassed coking coal at its doorsteps, prepared to assume the dominant position in the nation's iron industry. The erection of its first blast furnace in 1857, using coke fuel and ore drawn by water and rail from the distant ore fields of Missouri and Lake Superior, marked the beginning of a new era in the iron manufacturing of the entire country.

Associated with the changes in technique of production were changes in the use of and demand for iron.[5] Blacksmith's bar and nail iron receded steadily in importance before iron in the variety of forms and shapes required for industrial purposes, above all those growing out of the introduction of steam power in transportation. By 1850 if not earlier the railroad had become the leading industrial outlet for iron and within 10 years after the Civil War one-half of the iron consumed in the United States was employed in railroad construction and maintenance. The manufacture of rails for the rapidly expanding railway network of the country led to a virtual revolution in blast-furnace and rolling-mill practice. Early rails were merely heavy strap iron, differing only in size from the ordinary run of merchant bar turned out by the typical rolling mill. As the demand for rails assumed vast proportions and strap rails gave way to rails with U- or T-shapes, specialized rail mills on a large scale were established to meet the demand. The rolling of shaped rails called for new and specialized rolling equipment and enlarged power plants as well as iron of a quality better adapted to the manufacture of rails and more economical than that suited to merchant bar. Some of the largest rail mills operated their own blast-furnace plants to supply them with crude metal.

The first rail mills were erected in the middle forties and 10 years later a full score were in operation, of which the largest were located in Pennsylvania, where two-thirds of the total product in the country was rolled prior to 1860. West and south of Maryland the rail mills were small in number and capacity and were engaged chiefly in rerolling worn rails. In 1860 the annual output of these mills totaled 235,107 tons, absorbing close to one-fourth of the pig iron of the country and surpassing bar iron in importance. Outstanding among the rolling mills of the fifties were the Phoenix Rolling Mills in eastern Pennsylvania, and the Cambria Iron Works in western Pennsylvania. Of the three rolling mills comprising the Phoenix plant, the rail mill with its 36 heating and puddling furnaces and three trains of rolls quite overshadowed the other two works, turning out 18,592 tons of rails in 1856. The Cambria Works at Johnstown, Pennsylvania, was the largest integrated rail mill in the country. Its 30 puddling furnaces were supplied with pig metal by one charcoal and six coke furnaces, and from its four trains of rolls in 1857 came 17,808 tons of rails.[6] The first wrought-iron girders were rolled in the decade before the Civil War, but the age of structural iron was still in the future.

---

[5] This matter is discussed in some detail in the Hunter article cited above.

[6] An interesting cross-section view of the iron industry in all its branches in this year is given in John Peter Lesley, *The Iron Manufacturer's Guide*. New York: John Wiley & Sons, 1859.

Heavy Machinery: Steam Engines

Prior to the new age of iron, heavy industrial equipment was made largely of wood, owing to the difficulty of shaping and working iron. In mills in which water power was employed for grinding flour, operating trip hammers, and providing air blast, the ponderous wheels, shafts, and gearing were made entirely of wood except for such iron as was used for fastenings and at points of bearing. The trip hammers themselves were made largely of wood, as were the blowing tubes for making the blast and even the cylinders and boilers of the first clumsy steam engines. Alongside the blast furnaces and rolling mills of the industrial era now arose works for the production of heavy machinery and other industrial equipment. Employing pig-iron and wrought-iron bars and slabs as their chief raw materials, the products of these heavy industries were given their rough form in foundry and forge shop and were finished to exact dimension and fitted in the machine shop. Blowing engines for blast furnaces, machinery for rolling mills, mills for crushing sugar cane, heavy shafts, car wheels and axles, gears, flywheels, and a variety of other mill machinery and equipment were turned out by these works, but their most important products were steam engines—stationary, marine, and steamboat—and locomotives.

The development of steam engines merits special mention. Amounting to only a handful in this country before 1800, the beginning of their commercial production may be said to date from the establishment of the works of Oliver Evans in Philadelphia about 1805 and in Pittsburgh a few years later. Evans has received increasing recognition as one of the great mechanics and engineers of our industrial infancy. In the years immediately following the Revolutionary War, he devised a system of continuous flour milling that completely mechanized the process and effected a radical change in the conduct of the industry. Thereafter his attention was directed chiefly to the improvement of steam power and its application to industrial purposes, especially transportation by water. The steam engine as improved by Watt and manufactured by Boulton and Watt used steam of low pressure; it was a heavy and complicated mechanism, costly to build and difficult to maintain and keep in repair. Spurred on by the need for a power plant of light weight suitable for driving boats, Evans built a high-pressure steam engine which in proportion to its weight was many times as powerful as the prevailing low-pressure type. By perfecting a simple, powerful, and cheap engine, Evans popularized the use of steam power in this country for manufacturing and transport purposes alike.[7]

---

[7] For an outstanding work in its class, see Greville and Dorothy Bathe, *Oliver Evans: A Chronicle of Early American Engineering*. Philadelphia: Historical Society of Pennsylvania, 1935.

Navigation was the most important of the early uses to which steam power was applied. What the railroad was to the iron industry after 1850, the steamboat had been in large measure during the preceding generation. Despite the almost universal use of wooden hulls, the hundreds of steamboats launched each decade from the shipyards along the Atlantic Seaboard and the Western rivers absorbed great quantities of iron in their construction. The production of engines with cylinders ranging up to nine feet in diameter, batteries of as many as eight boilers 30 feet and more in length, smokestacks that often towered 75 feet above the main deck, hog chains, tie rods, walking beams, chain cables, gallows frames, anchors, steam and water pipes, kept foundries and forge shops, the boiler works and machine shops humming in the steamboat-building centers of the country. On the Western rivers alone more than 3,500 steamboats were built prior to the Civil War. By 1850 the construction of the massive power plants of ocean steamships had become an important industry in several of the larger northern seaports.

Due to the wide distribution, low cost, and mechanical simplicity of small water powers, the steam engine made relatively slow progress in manufacturing during the early decades of the century. A Treasury Department survey in 1838 showed that even at this advanced date steamboat engines accounted for nearly three-fifths of the total steam power of the nation, possessing an average power rating three and one-half times as great as that of engines used in industries and by railroads. Iron rolling was the only branch of industry using engines of comparable power.[8] With the improvement of and growing familiarity with steam engines, the increase of manufacturing in the larger urban centers where water power was not available, and the desire to be free from the seasonal limitations of water power, steam power grew steadily in popularity and use. The manufacture of stationary engines to meet industrial needs became an important branch of manufacturing.

The building of locomotives in this country dates from the beginning of the railroad period; comparatively few were imported from England.[9] The first locomotives were built in general foundry and machine-shop works but specialized locomotive works were soon established, among them the well-known firms of Baldwin (1832) and Norris (1834) in Philadelphia, leading center of the industry. So successful were American locomotive builders that their products were being exported to Europe in substantial numbers even before 1840. The Norris firm sold 41 of its first 145 locomotives in Europe, and another American company built

[8] This "Report on the Steam Engines in the United States" (House Ex. Doc. 21, 25th Congress, 3rd session) is one of the most interesting documents of our early industrial history.

[9] Much the best work available on the evolution of the American locomotive is Angus Sinclair's *The Development of the Locomotive*. New York: A. Sinclair Publishing Company, 1907.

162 locomotives for a Russian railroad. The early locomotives were small affairs, frequently weighing only from 5 to 10 tons and using much wood in their construction; by the middle of the century locomotives of from 20 to 25 tons were common. According to the census of 1860, 19 establishments were engaged chiefly or wholly in the manufacture of locomotives, employing a capital of nearly $500,000 and 4,174 hands. The three largest concerns, located in Philadelphia and Paterson, New Jersey, built 258 of a total output of some 470 locomotives for the entire country.

Foundry and Forge

Foremost in the equipment of the plant making steam engines and other heavy machinery was the foundry, where were made those parts that because of their size or peculiarities of shape could not be produced under the forge hammer. Such parts as engine cylinders were always cast; other parts such as boiler heads, shafts, girders, pillars and other supporting members were early made of cast iron and later forged from wrought iron. With the machines available in the early years, the forging of heavy shafts, connecting rods, and the like was often impractical and the products of forging with inadequate equipment were frequently imperfect, breaking under strain. Recourse was sometimes had to wood as in the case of paddle wheel shafts, pitmans, and flywheel arms in steamboats, and of spokes and felloes in locomotive driving wheels; but when iron was necessary or desirable, castings were long used. Every foundry had one or more cupola furnaces, similar to blast furnaces in construction and operation, in which the pig metal was melted down for casting. A wooden facsimile of the part or piece desired was carefully constructed by the pattern-maker as a model for making molds of damp sand, into which molten metal from the cupola was poured. Upon cooling, the casting was given the necessary finish by lathe, file, and chisel. In this manner there were made not only intricate shapes quite beyond the limited range of the trip hammer but simpler pieces such as shafts in which size and strength were the main feature.

As late as 1828 castings weighing four tons aroused comment, but within a few years others weighing 30 to 40 tons were being made, and about 1850 a 60-ton bedplate for a steamship engine had been cast by a New York firm. On the other hand, a 6½-ton shaft made forging history in 1841 and 20 years later 23-ton shafts marked the peak of forging technique. Such work was exceptional, the regular forging of heavy pieces waiting upon the general introduction at forge shops of the steam hammer and of heating furnaces of large capacity. Prior to 1861, according to Clark, a 6½-ton Nasmyth steam hammer and a 7½-ton Condy hammer were the largest in use in the United States. The railroad gave rise to a specialized branch of foundry work for the manufacture of car wheels, running four or five to the ton. The largest establishment of the kind in the United States in 1860 was a Wilmington foundry where 30,000 of a national total of 142,000 car wheels were made, with a value of approximately $500,000.

The Early Copper Industry

Of the nonferrous metals, only copper and lead attained in the *antebellum* years a position deserving notice. As in the case of iron, the early history of copper is marked by the wide distribution of the industry. Copper has been mined at one time or another in nearly every Seaboard state from Maine to Alabama. The oldest mines in the country are the Simsbury (or Newgate) mines in Connecticut; the Ely mine in Vermont was at one time the nation's largest producer. The record of the Eastern states in copper production is one of numerous small-scale mines opened, worked for a time, then abandoned, to be reopened in many instances years later under favorable market conditions, and again operated for a time. The failure or limited success attending most of these enterprises has been due to the relatively small extent of the deposits and the difficulty and expense of their extraction. Annual outputs even of the larger mines did not often exceed one or two thousand tons of ore. The most productive of the Eastern mines in the years before 1860 were those of the Ducktown district in the extreme southeastern portion of Tennessee, and extending across the line into Georgia. This development got under way in the fifties when a number of mines were opened and a "copper fever" ruled temporarily. First worked in 1852, the total output of the mines in this district to July, 1854, was something over 18,000 tons of ore, averaging 32 per cent copper.[10]

The Eastern copper deposits were reduced to a position of quite minor importance by the discovery and active exploitation in the middle forties of the rich resources of the Lake Superior copper deposits in northern Michigan. The presence of copper in the Superior country was known to missionaries and explorers as early as the seventeenth century but it was not until in 1841 that the rich possibilities of the district were made public by the report of Dr. Douglass Houghton, state geologist of Michigan. When the Government opened lands for location in 1843, speculators and their agents swarmed in and started a copper boom that reached its climax in 1846. Then a reaction set in, to be followed shortly by a soberer and a more substantial growth. By 1860, fully three-fourths of

10 For the early history of the copper industry, consult J. W. Foster and J. D. Whitney, *Report on the Geology and Topography of a Portion of the Lake Superior District in the State of Michigan* (Washington, D. C.: Printed for the House of Representatives, 1850-1851); A. S. Piggot, *The Chemistry and Metallurgy of Copper* (Philadelphia: Lindsay and Blakiston, 1858); and W. H. Weed, *Copper Deposits of the Appalachian States* (Washington, D. C.: U. S. Government Printing Office, 1911). An interesting popular account of the Lake Superior copper industry is Angus Murdoch, *Boom Copper: The Story of the First U. S. Mining Boom* (New York: The Macmillan Company, 1943).

the 8,000 tons of copper in the United States came from the Michigan mines, which were concentrated in three districts.

From the beginning, mining operations in the Superior fields were dominated by a few large companies. The heavy expenses of exploration and development, of sinking shafts hundreds of feet deep and opening levels often miles in length, together with the cost of the heavy machinery for raising and concentrating the ore, called for amounts of capital that only large organizations could supply. The capital investments of the larger companies ranged from $100,000 to $500,000 and up. The copper deposits were, however, extraordinarily rich, and with care in development, the best properties paid handsome returns. A distinctive feature of the Superior fields was the large amount of native copper present in many of the veins. Masses of solid copper weighing from several hundred pounds to several tons were common, and others weighing 20 to 50 tons were not infrequent. In 1853 a mass of native copper measuring 40 by 20 by 2 feet, with an estimated weight of between 150 and 200 tons, was dislodged.

The first large-scale copper mining operations in the United States got under way in 1844 at the Cliff mine of the Pittsburgh and Boston Mining Company. By 1850, this mine employed 160 men and shipped 1,500,000 pounds of ore, yielding nearly half its weight in copper. On an original paid-in capital stock of $111,000 dividends were first declared in 1849 and for the years 1849–1856, inclusive, reached a total of more than $700,000. Equally extensive were the operations of the Minnesota Mine, which in 1855 employed 471 workers and produced 1,434 tons of copper.

Even in the larger developments, mining operations were at first conducted by near-primitive methods, with hand tools. The great masses of native copper frequently encountered could be removed only with great difficulty because of the meager equipment available. Such masses had first to be laboriously cut into pieces that could be moved by the tedious and expensive use of hand chisel and sledge hammer. In the early years clumsy horse-driven whims employing large wooden winding drums hoisted copper and ore from depths of as much as several hundred feet. Steam power was necessary, however, to operate the massive stamp mills in which the ore, after roasting in ovens or open heaps, was crushed before its separation from waste rock by washing. The early stamp mills consisted of vertical wooden beams or pestles with iron heads weighing 100 to 300 pounds that were raised and dropped by cams fixed in a revolving horizontal cylinder. Within a few years mills of this type were superseded at the larger mines by stamps built on the plan of a steam hammer with each stamp leg bearing a total weight of 2,500 pounds and making 90 to 100 strokes a minute.

With few exceptions smelting and refining operations were not conducted near the ore fields, owing in part to the early establishment of these branches of the copper industry in the leading Eastern seaports of Boston, New York, and Baltimore, where imported raw materials and cheap fuel were available and the manufacture of sheathing and fastenings for ships afforded a market. As a consequence of the lack of cheap fuel in the mining districts, smelting and refining operations were relegated to the Eastern centers and to works later established at Pittsburgh and the lake ports of Cleveland and Detroit. At these points, too, were rolling mills for the reduction of the refined metal to the shapes in demand, chiefly sheet copper for sheathing, boilers, stills, pipes, and the like. Sacks of copper ore from a southern Appalachian mine were wagoned 40 miles to a railroad for shipment hundreds of miles north to smelting works. Lake Superior copper in the several forms of mass copper, barrel work (small lumps of mass copper with associated rock), and stampwork was regularly shipped as far as Pittsburgh and Boston for further treatment.

Smelting and refining operations were carried on for the most part in reverberatory furnaces similar in character to those in which iron was puddled. Charges of several hundredweight, together with flux and later additions of charcoal or wood, were reduced to a molten state in which the earthy gangue rose to the top in the form of slag and was removed. With minor differences in treatment this process was repeated several times until the sulphur, arsenic, iron, and other impurities found in copper were completely eliminated. The resulting ingot copper was reduced to the desired shape and size in the rolling mill. These crude methods of refining were tolerated chiefly because of the richness of the ore; there were heavy losses of copper in the slag, to recover which it was sometimes reduced in the cupola furnace. Although sheet copper was the most important product, increasing amounts were made into brass to supply the rapidly expanding industry centering in the Naugatuck Valley of Connecticut.[11]

From Wood to Coal

During the first quarter of the nineteenth century, the coal industry of the United States was of minor importance.[12] From the late eighteenth century coal was used for domestic purposes increasingly in the Seaboard cities, the Virginia mines being the chief source of supply. In

[11] The standard monograph on the brass industry is W. G. Lathrop, *The Brass Industry in Connecticut.* Shelton, Conn.: W. G. Lathrop, 1909.

[12] Despite widespread interest in the coal industry during the past generation and an extensive literature dealing with its problems and ailments, the industry still awaits its historian. Much useful material on the development of the anthracite industry is found in Eliot Jones, *The Anthracite Coal Combination in the United States* (Cambridge, Mass.: Harvard University Press, 1914). For statistical material on the early industry, see R. C. Taylor, *Statistics of Coal* (2nd ed., Philadelphia: J. W. Moore, 1855). A wealth of historical data on the coal industry is contained in Howard N. Eavenson, *The First Century and a Quarter of American Coal Industry* (Pittsburgh: privately printed, 1942).

the East men were slow to recognize the value of the rich anthracite deposits of northeastern Pennsylvania and active exploitation of the bituminous fields, long confined to a small district in western Pennsylvania, awaited settlement and industrial growth in the West. Difficulties of mining development and of transportation of coal combined with the abundance of cheap and easily accessible timber to make wood the basic fuel for domestic and industrial purposes until well into the nineteenth century. As late as 1850 railroads and steamboats as well as the metal industries used wood as their principal fuel, but with the growth of urban centers exhaustion or scarcity of near-by supplies of wood made it increasingly difficult to rely on this source of fuel. Coal was adopted as more compact and economical. Manufacturers and home-owners alike turned more and more to its use as improvements in transportation facilities made it more generally available.

The Rise of Anthracite

Prior to 1850 there were two major centers of coal production in this country, both of them in Pennsylvania: the anthracite district of the northeastern part of the state and the bituminous district of the Pittsburgh-Connellsville area. More than 95 per cent of the rich anthracite resources of the country are concentrated in five Pennsylvania counties, the workable beds occupying some 480 square miles, divided among several fields. Although it was known well before the eighteenth century that coal was present in these fields, its development was retarded partly by the difficulties attending the use of this fuel but to a greater extent by its remoteness from the principal urban markets of the Seaboard. Some was floated down the rivers in flatboats at flood stages but the risks and difficulties involved slowed the growth of the trade. Businessmen who became interested in the exploitation of the anthracite fields, finding themselves first obliged to provide transportation facilities for carrying their product to market, undertook ambitious programs of canal building and river improvement. Between 1820 and 1830 a number of important canals were built, notably the Delaware and Hudson, the Lehigh, the Morris, and the Schuylkill.[13] These canals were supplemented by short connecting railroads running to the mines.

The significant consequence was that in two of the three major anthracite fields, mining properties and transportation facilities were in the same hands. Only in the Schuylkill district did the canal company leave the mining of the coal open to independent operators. The union of transportation and mining in the same companies led to various abuses, loud complaints, and eventually in 1833 to an investigation by a state commission. The recommendation of the commission that the mining and

[13] The standard work on this subject is C. L. Jones, *The Economic History of the Anthracite-Tidewater Canals*. Philadelphia: University of Pennsylvania, 1908.

transportation of coal be separate enterprises was not acted upon. The next 40 years saw the gradual decline in the importance of the canal systems as dominant factors in the anthracite industry and their replacement by railroads. The progress of railroad construction, the purchase of coal lands, and the concentration of ownership by mergers and consolidations continued until by 1870 a handful of railroad corporations, headed by the Lackawanna, the Lehigh Valley, and the Philadelphia and Reading, owned the greater part of the anthracite district. These railroads bought up large areas of the coal regions, not only to assure traffic for themselves but to shut out new and competing lines. The combination of coal mining and transportation in the anthracite district greatly increased the normally high capital requirements of the industry and corporate enterprise dominated the field from the beginning.

The development of the industry, slow before 1840, proceeded rapidly thereafter, stimulated by the widening use of anthracite, especially in the manufacture of iron and in steamboat transportation. Shipments of coal from the anthracite region mounted from 376,000 tons in 1834 to about 1,000,000 tons in 1842 and 10,000,000 tons in 1864.

The Bituminous Industry

The existence of coal in western Pennsylvania was known prior to the War for Independence and mining privileges in Pittsburgh's Coal Hill were sold in 1784. From this time on, the exploitation of the rich bituminous coal resources underlying the region went hand in hand with Pittsburgh's industrial development, which from the beginning relied almost exclusively upon coal as a source both of heat and power. The great Pittsburgh seam that was long the chief source of coal in this region lay exposed on the hillside for miles along the Allegheny, Monongahela, and Ohio Rivers. Its thickness of six to 10 feet and its horizontal position made mining operations simple. Expensive shafts and hoisting equipment were usually unnecessary and there was no drainage problem. The coal was easily reached by horizontal drifts driven into the face of the hillside and the cars in which it was brought out were in some instances routed directly into the yards of mills and factories along the waterfront at a cost to the consumer in the fifties of as little as 80 cents a ton. Concentration of ownership in the Pittsburgh-Connellsville district was eventually to develop to almost as great a degree as in the anthracite region but before 1860 the abundance of cheap coal lands and the relatively small capital investment required for mining operations under highly favorable physical conditions kept the fields in the hands of small-scale enterprise.

During the early decades of development, mining operations were carried on most actively along the banks of the Monongahela for some distance above Pittsburgh and were greatly facilitated by the improvement of navigation on this stream by locks and dams, operated privately on a toll basis. This slackwater system permitted coal to be mined and loaded in flatboats much of the year and insured an uninterrupted supply to meet Pittsburgh's rapidly expanding industrial needs. Large fleets of coal boats assembled in the lower pools of the Monongahela awaiting the flood stages that would carry them down the Ohio River to the markets below. The early industrial growth of Cincinnati, Louisville, and, in less degree, St. Louis was largely dependent upon Pittsburgh coal. By 1845 nearly 2,000,000 bushels of coal were consumed at Pittsburgh and exports down the river from the lower Monongahela mounted from over 2,500,000 bushels in this year to more than 16,000,000 bushels in 1855.

Although mining operations were most intensive in the Pittsburgh district, bituminous fields were worked in a number of other districts in the Appalachian region and the Mississippi Valley, especially in the Wheeling and Kanawha districts and on and near the Ohio River in Kentucky, Ohio, and Indiana. Anthracite rather than bituminous coal was the primary industrial fuel of the *ante-bellum* years. The average annual production of bituminous coal in the fifties was under 5,000,000 tons, and it was not until the seventies that it assumed the leadership it has since held.

Significance of the Rise of Heavy Industry

The rise and expansion of heavy industry was a major factor in the industrialization of the American economy. It laid the foundations of an age in which iron, coal, and steam power played primary and indispensable roles. Although distinguished in the main as industries which served other industries, the heavy industries had numerous and far-reaching repercussions upon the lives and standards of living of the ultimate consuming public. Steam navigation, rail transportation, the progressive mechanization of manufacturing and agriculture, the replacement of wood by metal as a raw material not only in machinery but for many articles of common utility, and the use of coal as a domestic fuel were all made possible by the rise of the heavy industries. If these industries prepared the way for a higher standard of living by facilitating economic specialization and the emancipation of the agricultural population from the limitations of subsistence farming, they also gave rise to new industrial hazards and occupational diseases and contributed their full share to the many other grave social problems which were the by-product of industrialization.

Selected References

GENERAL WORKS

Bining, A. C., *The Pennsylvania Iron Manufacture in the Eighteenth Century*. Harrisburg: Publications of the Pennsylvania Historical Commission, 1938.

Bruce, Kathleen, *Virginia Iron Manufacture in the Slave Era*. New York: D. Appleton-Century Company, 1930.

Clark, V. S., *The History of Manufactures in the United States* (1929 ed.), Vol. I, 1607-1860. New York: McGraw-Hill Book Company, 1929.

Eavenson, H. N., *The First Century and a Quarter of American Coal Industry*. Pittsburgh: privately printed, 1942.

Jones, Eliot, *The Anthracite Coal Combination in the United States*. Cambridge, Mass.: Harvard University Press, 1914.

Swank, J. M., *The History of the Manufacture of Iron in All Ages*, 2nd ed., 1892.

SPECIAL TOPICS

Bathe, Greville and Dorothy, *Oliver Evans: A Chronicle of Early American Engineering*. Philadelphia: Historical Society of Pennsylvania, 1935.

Foster, J. W., and J. D. Whitney, *Report on the Geology and Topography of a Portion of the Lake Superior District in the State of Michigan*. Washington, D. C.: Printed for the House of Representatives, 1850-1851.

Hunter, Louis C., "Influence of the Market upon Technique in the Iron Industry of Western Pennsylvania up to 1860," *Journal of Economic and Business History*, Vol. I, pp. 241-281.

Ingalls, W. R., *Lead and Zinc in the United States*. New York: Hill Publishing Company, 1908.

11 · LIGHT MANUFACTURES AND THE BEGINNINGS OF PRECISION MANUFACTURE

The Initial Impetus

AT THE END OF THE REVOLUTION the United States was not only politically disrupted but was in economic straits. The difficulty of obtaining manufactured goods from abroad during the war had inevitably encouraged some new domestic manufactures, though most households had made shift with what could be contrived at home. But with the peace came a flood of European goods to meet the accumulated demand, and the country soon found itself faced with the prospect of being tied economically to Great Britain or France as tightly and helplessly as before the war. Hard money was scarcer than before, and peacetime production of foodstuffs and goods for export was slow in gaining headway. And still European manufactures came pouring in.

At the first session of the Federal Congress a petition for protection of American manufactures was presented by a group of artisans and mechanics of Baltimore. Similar appeals from New York and Boston followed almost at once. Congress promptly effected some relief by placing duties on a number of articles, among them candles, soap, cables and cordage, leather, hats, slit and rolled iron, iron castings, nails, unwrought steel, paper, cabinet ware, carriages, tinware, wool cards, and anchors. This act, virtually the first passed by the new Government, inspired confidence in the future, and American manufacturing enterprise began to feel its way haltingly, and with many experiments, toward a capacity calculated to meet domestic needs.

The extent of Colonial manufacturing and the expansion of American productivity before 1785 has been discussed in Chapter 4. Luxuries were the chief items of import after, as before, the Revolution. Most household necessities continued to be made at home, at the village smithy or wheelwright's shop, or, in parts of the South, in plantation workshops. Usually every community in the North had its tanworks, its sawmill and gristmill, and often its fulling mill as well. Pottery, salt, firearms, paper, and the small amount of glassware in use were frequently of American manufacture; but as these articles could not be made without special equipment and skilled workmen, the number of establishments for these manufactures was limited. Yet by 1791 Hamilton could report considerable progress in American manufacture of a long list of consumers' goods, in making many of which he believed the country, given proper encouragement and protection, might soon be self-sufficient. There were in the thirteen states some 70 paper mills, a cotton-yarn mill operating with American-made approximations of Arkwright's spinning frames, a woolen mill in Connecticut that made the broadcloth worn by George Washington when he delivered his first annual message to Congress, several successful glassworks and potteries, numerous brick kilns, and a great many small forges and blast furnaces for iron smelting.

The early development that was to have the most marked effect upon American manufacturing, the introduction of power-driven machinery for cotton manufacture, had started in 1789 in response to the rewards for workable spinning or weaving machines offered by state legislatures and the Pennsylvania Society for the Encouragement of Manufactures. To the accomplishment of Samuel Slater, whose ingenuity was largely responsible for the success of this undertaking, it will be necessary to return later. Suffice it here to point out that the determination of Americans to be free of dependence upon European manufactured goods proved a constant stimulus to the inventive in every line; the Government bounties and subsidies that were established after Alexander Hamilton's report had made clear the wisdom of such a policy helped the financially weak enterpriser and encouraged the launching of many manufacturing attempts. The creation of the patent office in 1792 was a further step in the right direction. During the last decade of the eighteenth century dozens of mills sprang up, many of them doomed to shut down in the course of a few years, more often for lack of adequate financing, owing to inexperience of the owner, or for scarcity of trained labor, than for want of ready markets.

Although unpopular in many sections of America, the Embargo in 1807 intensified efforts to produce American manufactures, and the War of 1812 further accentuated the necessity for goods made at home. Merchants who would perhaps have preferred to import commodities of known quality were obliged to finance and abet in every possible way manufacturing in this country in order to obtain adequate supplies of goods to sell.[1] The impetus thus given by harsh circumstance as well as by patriotic sentiment was not again to be lost, and although some of the great mercantile houses were later to divert their interest in American manufacturing back to foreign trade, many continued the financial support begun of necessity.

---

1 See F. W. Taussig, *Some Aspects of the Tariff Question*. Cambridge: Harvard University Press, 1915.

The Rise of the Textile Industry

The strides made in manufactures before 1816 were most notable in two fields, of which the earlier and most immediately outstanding was textiles. Because in England the introduction of power-driven machinery had been most effective and complete in yarn and cloth manufacturing, it was logical that the Industrial Revolution should find its first foothold in America in the same enterprise. All through the 1780's attempts had been made in this country to build carding and spinning machines, patterned either after English inventions or original drawings. But full success had to await the arrival in Pawtucket, Rhode Island, of Samuel Slater in 1790.

Slater, a gifted and ambitious mechanic, had been employed for several years in Arkwright and Strutt's plant in Milford, England, when reports of the money offered by an American society for models of textile machinery induced him to emigrate. Since British law strictly forbade export of drawings or models of the revolutionizing machines, and indeed emigration of mechanics, Slater spent some time in studying the details of Arkwright's frames, and only when he felt competent to reproduce them from memory did he sail incognito for America. Contact with two men of means in Providence, William Almy and Moses Brown, quickly produced an agreement that Slater build necessary machinery and supervise the erection of a mill, in which he himself was to have one-half interest. The neighborhood of Providence had already a fairly well-established handicraft cotton industry, producing chiefly candlewicks and yarn made upon hand jennies. But Slater refused to use the spinning frames Almy and Brown had endeavored to make work, and built new ones. By 1793 the firm of Almy, Brown & Slater was operating a 72-spindle mill, and the patenting of Eli Whitney's cotton gin the next year insured ample supplies of cotton. By the end of the century, the success of the Slater mill had been duplicated by several others, and before 1810 Gallatin reported some 50 cotton-yarn mills north of the Potomac River. A memorial to Congress in 1815 stated that there were within 30 miles of Providence 140 cotton manufacturers employing 26,000 hands and operating 130,000 spindles. The American textile industry was launched.

Cotton manufacturers, rather than woolen, were the first products of the new machine-equipped plants, doubtless because homespun woolens (albeit frequently machine-carded) were easier to produce by the old process than were cottons. Nevertheless, factories for woolen manufacture soon followed. Interest in growing wool was slower to make headway in the United States than interest in cotton raising, and the woolen industry may well have been affected by the problem of procuring adequate supplies of the raw material. But wool-carding machines had been built in America before the end of the Revolution and the spread of factories for carding and dressing wool for home weaving was rapid after 1795. Even carpet manufacturing was begun in Philadelphia about 1791.

Arms Manufacture

The other industry in which America made extraordinary progress before 1816 was the manufacture of firearms. The advance was less generally recognized, and it less promptly affected the whole American economy than did the new textile mills, although ultimately, changes in methods of small-arms manufacture were to be of even greater consequence. For in this enterprise was developed the system of interchangeable parts, a technique acknowledged many decades later to be the key to mechanized mass production.

The desperate need for American-made firearms had been obvious all through the Revolution, and small gunsmithies had multiplied and continued to turn out muskets after the war was over. But Congress, early aware of the urgency of making the country completely free of reliance on foreign arms, in 1792 authorized the creation of two national armories and a few years later generously subsidized several private contractors to make muskets, pistols, and rifles for the Government. The superintendents of the national armories in Springfield and Harper's Ferry and the half-dozen private enterprisers engaged in this manufacture from the beginning pooled their experience. It is impossible to assign to any one of them exclusive credit. To perfect machines accurate enough to turn out parts wholly interchangeable was an ambition common to them all, and each man probably contributed something to the final achievement.

Eli Whitney, best known as inventor of the cotton gin, had attained some success in interchangeability as early as 1800; [2] and Simeon North of Berlin and Middletown, Connecticut, working independently, arrived at the same goal before 1808.[3] Crude screw augers, power-driven trip hammers for barrel-welding, and drilling jigs were the earliest machine tools devised for arms making, and both Whitney and North, as well as Asa Waters in Millbury and the Government armorers, had each his

[2] Interchangeability in manufacturing firearms had originated in France and Thomas Jefferson in the 1780's, having visited the shop where the scheme was being tried, wrote home with enthusiasm of its possibilities. But in France it was soon dropped as impractical. French and British armament makers derided the idea of interchangeable manufacture as visionary. Skepticism began to prevail in the United States War Department also. To prove the feasibility of his methods Whitney, late in 1800, took to Washington the parts for ten complete muskets. In a dramatic demonstration before the Secretary of War and chief Ordnance officers he selected at random from the piles of parts and before the eyes of the doubting officials assembled ten perfectly fitted guns.

[3] North wrote to the Secretary of the Navy in 1808, "I find that by confining a workman to one particular limb of the pistol untill he has made two thousand, I save at least one quarter of his labour, to what I should [otherwise have] provided I finished them by small quantities; and the work will be as much better as it is quicker made.... I have some seventeen thousand screws and other parts nearly finished and the business is going on brisk and lively."

own variation of workable machinery. North's contract of 1813 for Government pistols, based upon his success with this interchangeable method of production from 1808 on, is the first contract known to have stipulated expressly that the arms were to be manufactured with wholly interchangeable parts.

Eli Whitney, one of the first great inventors and gunsmiths of America, was born on a Massachusetts hill farm in 1765. At the age of 15, he persuaded his father to allow him to start a shop for making iron nails, and until the end of the Revolution he carried on a thriving business. With money earned by this and later undertakings, he went in 1788 to Yale College and acquired the education earlier denied him. During a sojourn in Georgia in 1792 he learned of the problem confronting Southern cotton growers, namely the need of mechanical means of removing the green seeds from short staple cotton. In a few weeks he had built with self-made tools a workable gin, the basic principles of which have never been altered. The immediate and far-reaching consequences of this invention cannot be overestimated, but its pirating and the ruinous law suits that followed so discouraged Whitney that in 1798, backed by a Government subsidy, he turned his mechanical genius to gun making. His bitter experiences in vainly trying to protect his patent rights in the cotton gin led him thereafter to seek no patents for the machines he built in his armory in Whitneyville, but there is ample testimony to the importance of the automatic devices he installed for arms making. His educated bearing and personal charm won for him a host of admirers, while his fame as the inventor of the gin made him a national figure. His influence among men of affairs at the time of his death in 1825 was enormous.

Simeon North, on the other hand, was comparatively little known. Born in Berlin, Connecticut, in the same year as Whitney, he never acquired an education comparable to that of Whitney and until late in life he had few outside contacts. His great native gifts, his tenacity of purpose, and his deep-seated patriotism alone enabled him to make outstanding contributions to American mechanical development. This lean, taciturn, Connecticut Yankee, like Whitney, took out no patents and gave freely the benefits of his skill and experience to his Government and to his fellow contractors. Over a period of 53 years he constantly improved upon his own methods of production, and at his death in 1852 he had perhaps done more to place American interchangeable manufacture upon a mass-production basis than any other one man.

Connecticut clockmakers, following closely in the wake of the gunsmiths, were the first to apply the interchangeable part system to another line. In fact, Eli Terry and Seth Thomas are believed to have made some 4,000 grandfather clocks between 1807 and 1810, starting work upon 500 at a time. While the wooden works of these clocks were far easier to reproduce exactly in quantity than the steel or iron parts of guns, the necessity of accuracy in producing interchangeable parts of timepieces makes the tooling accomplishment of these early clockmakers notable.

Problems of the Manufacturer Before 1816

Despite the early enthusiasm for national self-sufficiency the difficulties attending the development of manufacturing upon any scale were overwhelming. Not only were the patterns of the first machines for factory production hard to acquire, but the necessary capital to start even a small mill was not easy to command. Unlike the armament makers, ambitious enterprisers in other lines could not rely upon Government subsidy to supply the initial funds needed. Mercantile capital was naturally the most ready source, but merchants were frequently loath to risk their resources in a comparatively unfamiliar field, and not until trade was cut off by threat of war or war itself were many persuaded to invest in industrial ventures. The story was nearly universal; it was repeated in New England, in the Middle States, and in the West. Men of means, and they were not numerous at best, preferred to speculate in land purchases or to enlarge their spheres of trade rather than to back manufacturing projects. Banking facilities were meager and managerial experience in any kind of manufacturing was virtually nonexistent. The generation of Americans between 1785 and 1815 moved cautiously and rather reluctantly into industrial investment. Small mills on small streams were the rule, with little capital, local workmen, and localized markets.

The initial problem of finding capital was complicated by that of obtaining labor. Indeed, even with ample financial backing, success was frequently dubious because of the difficulty of keeping trained workmen in the plant. Skilled men could be imported from Europe and apprentices and journeymen bound to learn a craft, but with the lure of free opportunities in the West it was impossible to keep them long. Baron Stiegel, who had poured money into his glassworks in Pennsylvania in the 1770's, had been obliged to close down largely because the hands he brought from Europe at great expense worked out their passage and then, without exception, departed. Labor supply was often a wholly insuperable problem. Dependence upon trained men and women living on farms or in homes in the immediate neighborhood to some extent solved the problem.

Two other difficulties confronted the manufacturer all through the experimental period: lack of power to drive machinery, and want of transportation facilities for shipping raw materials and finished goods. Before 1815, and in fact generally before 1835, water had to supply the power, and few were the streams that never ran dry in summer or froze up in winter. Occasionally, on great rivers like the Connecticut, construction of wing dams could divert enough water even in midsummer to turn mill wheels, but it involved a costly and hazardous engineering feat. Even the great Government armory at Springfield relied exclusively for power upon a small tributary to the Connecticut, a source that gave out usually for several weeks in July and in most years for much of December, January, and February. Similarly, before the days of steam, transportation generally waited upon the weather because, even where carting cross-country was not prohibitively expensive, ox teams and horses could not draw heavy loads over snow-drifted roads in the winter or muddy morasses in the spring. Unless the mill were located very near the coast, shipments in and out were confined to spring, summer, and fall. The transportation problem served one useful purpose in this early period, however. It raised around the local enterprise a protective barrier that enabled many a small concern to build itself into financial security because it could market its goods locally on a virtual monopoly basis. When improved roads and waterways opened up the local market to competition, the original safeguard of monopoly was no longer essential.

Effect of the War of 1812

The end of the War of 1812 introduced a new phase in American industry. Just as European goods came pouring in after the Revolution, so during 1815 British and French manufacturers dumped quantities of goods into the hungry American markets. American merchants who had supported American manufacturing began to return to their Old World suppliers, and capital, only recently and very tentatively diverted to industry in this country, was in many cases withdrawn to finance an extension of foreign markets for American agricultural products. But public indignation was aroused and the outcome was the passage of the tariff of 1816, a measure supported by the South as well as the North, doubtless for sentimental rather than economic reasons. The protection was sufficient to stem the tide somewhat, and American mechanical ingenuity was spurred to find means of competing with foreign goods. Improvements in all types of machinery began to multiply; the power loom was introduced in textile manufacture, lathes and screw-cutting machines were patented, Fourdriniers or the more newly invented cylinder machines began to appear in paper mills.[4] Native mechanics and skilled

[4] The Fourdrinier, invented by a Frenchman during the French Revolution, was built commercially and first put into operation in Great Britain. Its principle was really an adaptation to a machine of the old hand process of screening. The liquid pulp, "half-stuff," was fed by gravity onto one end of a moving, vibrating screen that meshed the fibers. The wet, matted sheet was picked up at the other end of the screen by a felt-covered roller and fed between two other rollers that squeezed out more of the excess water than could be shaken out through the screen. The paper that emerged might be one continuous sheet, provided the machine tender could maintain the machine in smooth operation. The cylinder machine picked up the half-stuff from a shallow pan direct onto a roller, but it could not achieve the evenness and fineness of the papers made by the screening of the Fourdrinier.

artisans in every field increased in numbers, and the movement toward effective industrial development slowly gained momentum.

The most marked progress was shown, as before, in cotton manufacture and small-arms production. Before 1815 cotton mills had been almost exclusively yarn mills, with the weaving "put out" to women in the neighborhood to be done on hand looms at home. Only a few manufacturers had undertaken to have cloth woven in the factory, and under the old system there was no urgent reason for such an arrangement. But the power loom, first set up in Francis Lowell's mill in Waltham in 1814, changed this situation. This Boston merchant had visited English cotton factories and brought back a description of the power loom. His memory of its details, however, proved too inaccurate to be reliable and his new company, the Boston Manufacturing Company, depended rather upon looms built and installed by an American mechanic, Paul Moody. Accustomed to dealing in large sums of money, accepting great risks, and expecting huge profits, Lowell envisaged a wholly new form of the industry, in which a large initial capital and complete mechanization, and therefore full factorization, of all the processes of cotton-cloth making should place the American industry upon a large-scale basis. The new era in cotton manufacture that Lowell's company and its imitators inaugurated was important not only because it marked the creation of vertically integrated mills, but because the whole system was predicated upon extensive fluid finances.[5] The improved methods of manufacturing cottons so lowered prices that the domestic market was enormously expanded. In large areas of the back country, where homespun woolens and home-woven cottons had served, the marketability of cheap cotton goods rose quickly as people discovered that their time was more profitably employed in other ways than in household manufacturing. As early as 1822 building of cotton mills had assumed such proportions that Colonel Lee, writing from the Springfield Armory about the threatened exodus of skilled mechanics to Rhode Island, declared that he could not keep his best workmen without pay increases—"the rage for manufacturing cotton prevails to such a degree."

But woolen manufacturing also took a forward leap during the 1820's. New shearing machines and better cards and looms turned out finer materials in the bigger mills. The power loom was adopted more slowly for woolen manufacture than for cotton, partly because the woolen industry as a whole was less quickly established upon a full factory basis of production and partly because woolen warps were less readily adapted to the strain of mechanized weaving.[6] However, by the 1830's power looms

[5] See Caroline Ware, *The Early New England Cotton Manufacture.* Boston: Houghton Mifflin Company, 1931.

[6] The development of fabrics with cotton warps and wool fill early provided one way around this difficulty.

had been installed in the plants of most successful manufacturers. Meanwhile, through the century small woolen mills sprang up, often equipped with makeshift machinery, but locally financed, locally supplied with wool, and operated by the children and older daughters of local farmers.[7] Although many of these undertakings were in time abandoned as improved transportation brought wider competition, the increase in numbers before 1830 served to strengthen the growing conviction in the United States that America had important industrial possibilities.

Meantime, an extraordinary advance was made before 1832 in developing machines accurate enough to eliminate many hand processes in gun manufacture. It was not by chance that the services of machinists of the armories were in demand. Although in the years before and during the War of 1812 arms manufacturers had been experimenting with various types of power-driven tools, belt-driven trip hammers for welding, screw augers for boring, and lathes for turning barrels, reasonably satisfactory results were not reached much before 1820. As in any exacting science or mechanical art—while the principle may be clear, it is upon the perfection of the instruments or tools that the adequacy of the outcome must rest—it was primarily in making more accurate the performance of earlier crude machines that the progress of the next decades was to come. As yet nothing had been achieved that in any modern sense could be labeled precision manufacture, but constant improvement and refinement was pointing the way. Probably the only really new invention of note in the twenties was Thomas Blanchard's gun-stocking lathes, machines that in about a minute and a half turned the stocks and cut in the locks, with great improvement in accuracy and with considerable saving of operating costs. Blanchard's stocker with only minor improvements was to be used in all important American armories down to the Civil War and was manufactured for export to Great Britain during the Crimean War.

Achievements of the Experimental Period

Thus, by 1830 the potentialities of America as a manufacturing nation were beginning to be seen. In consequence, the apprehensions of far-sighted men in the South were aroused and the long-drawn-out struggle between the advocates of free trade and the proponents of protection was born. In order that Congress might have authentic information about the extent of manufacturing in the United States from which to judge the wisdom of tariffs, the Secretary of the Treasury was instructed in 1831 to make a careful survey of manufacturing enterprises in the states and territories. The McLane Report is the first detailed census of manufactures in the United States and, though by no means exhaustive, it

[7] An interesting detailed account of woolen manufacturing is to be found in Arthur H. Cole, *The American Woolen Manufacture.* (2 vols.) Cambridge: Harvard University Press, 1926.

gives a clear idea of the character and extent of American industry at the end of the nation's first 42 years. The reports of manufactures came in from only 11 states, the activities of the West being included in the report from Ohio. As manufacturing areas, the seven Southern states could be utterly disregarded.

The outstanding achievements were largely those of four states: Massachusetts, Connecticut, Rhode Island, and Pennsylvania; the New England states led in textiles, clocks, boots and shoes, woodenware, and tools, Pennsylvania in glassware, iron, and paper. But already Ohio and the West were making headway, as the population grew and as local markets expanded more rapidly than river transport could supply them. Household manufacturing lingered on in the back country, but after 1824 cheap cotton goods rapidly supplanted all but homespun woolens. In the Miami River valleys alone there were three cotton mills, five woolen mills, and eight paper mills. Cincinnati had begun to manufacture hats, chairs, and cabinetware for export to the South; and in Kentucky were hemp-bagging mills for Southern cotton. In this region steam power was early put to use, as the ready accessibility of wood and coal would make logical, and iron manufacture for nails, agricultural tools, and other consumers' goods developed rapidly.

As the questionnaires appended to the statistical data called for by the Federal marshals were designed to provide evidence for and against the need of continued tariff protection, a considerable mass of information comes to light about the financial status of American manufacturing enterprises. In the Eastern states some firms professed to find domestic as well as foreign competition so great that their profits were cut to a meager 6 or 7 per cent; whereas in Ohio and the West, where distance and poor communications served as natural protection, capital generally demanded a return of 15 to 20 per cent on any industrial investment, since manufacturing was there still considered speculative. But every report dwelt upon the disasters that would befall if the tariff were lowered. By modern standards, most of the concerns were small, with capitalization of a few thousand dollars, frequently less; proprietorships and partnerships greatly outnumbered corporations, and the number of employees rarely exceeded 50, save in the textile mills. American industry could still be termed supplementary to agriculture and commerce.

Spread of the Factory System Before 1850

But the experimental period was over. Overwhelming problems had been solved, reverses weathered, and manufacturing was soon to be universally accepted as a legitimate, nonspeculative business. Not until the middle forties, to be sure, were industrialists to feel sure of their place in the American scene, but just as the twenties brought the widening of merchants' interest in manufactures as an investment, so the thirties saw the spread of factories, the beginnings of mechanization in many fields, and the multiplication of kinds of manufacture undertaken in America. Money for new textile mills was easier to enlist, paper makers began to install machinery made in American shops, some Massachusetts bootmakers and shoemakers established small plants for partly mechanized production, and tool-making began to emerge from the local blacksmithy into shops equipped with trip hammers and power-driven forges.

The reasons for this acceleration are not hard to find. Years of profitable mercantile ventures had increased by many times the amount of money available for investment. Banking facilities and new insurance companies eased financing for the newborn enterprises, and, although the panic of 1837 hampered manufacturers like everyone else, the ensuing wariness of capital about land speculation probably shortly redounded to the benefit of manufacturing interests. Furthermore, the unquestioned success of many mills naturally led to the building of others, sometimes by attracting new money, not infrequently by the process of reinvestment. Of the stockholders in the New England cotton mills of the thirties, there were few who had not been among the backers of mills built in the twenties.

Success in one field quite naturally led to experiment in another. For example, the early textile concerns generally built in their own shops at least part of the machinery for their expanding plants. In time the machine shop was detached from the parent company and, as an independent unit, might produce many kinds of goods besides shafting or textile machinery. Tools, various household wares, cutlery, all could be and often were made during the thirties in shops originally developed by textile capital. Indeed, the capitalists of the cotton industry promoted industrialization in many ways. Because of the extent of the funds necessary to build great dams and canal systems, to secure title to the adjacent land for mill sites, and then to finance the erection of the factories, the original group of enterprisers not infrequently acted primarily as a power and real estate company whose manufacturing interests were largely subsidiary.[8] Finally, backers of the railroads in the thirties and forties were eager to see more than agriculture developed in the country through which the new roads ran. To create freight for these roads many a new factory was launched in what had been inaccessible back country, not necessarily because the mills were sure investments, but because they guaranteed the investment in the railways. The problem of finding capital for manufacturing was pretty well solved.

[8] The development upon the Merrimack of Lowell and Lawrence and upon the Connecticut of Holyoke are outstanding examples. In the last instance, the investors overreached themselves by tying up so much capital in the power development and in slow-selling real estate that they were unable to weather the financial storm of 1857. See Constance M. Green, *Holyoke, Massachusetts*. New Haven: Yale University Press, 1939.

Meanwhile the textile industry was aided by a notable technical advance in weaving. In the late thirties the invention of the Crompton loom permitted mechanical weaving of elaborate patterns and eased much of the pull upon the warp yarns, enabling woolen weavers as well as cotton manufacturers to put it to use. With the greater complexity of construction of these new looms and the use of metal frames and parts instead of wooden, production of textile machinery after the mid-forties became the province of specialized machinery companies rather than of subsidiaries of cotton or woolen concerns.

The increase in numbers of mills and diversification of kinds of mechanized shops served to train an ever-growing group of skilled workmen, although, of course, the demand for such men was growing even faster than they could be trained. In wheelwright shops in remote Vermont or in bigger machine shops nearer the business centers, country boys apprenticed to masters had by the middle thirties already been schooled in the use of water-driven lathes, and, armed with Oliver Evans' *Young Millwright,* were acquiring a sound, technical education that was to produce a host of able mechanics and inventors to revolutionize American industry in the course of a generation. Evans' notable contributions as the inventor of the high-pressure steam engine are discussed in Chapter 10, but equally important, perhaps ultimately more significant, was his service as a teacher of the theory and techniques of hydraulics. His book, published in 1795, went through 15 editions before 1860 and before mid-century was in the hands of nearly every competent millwright in America. One of the least appreciated and most gifted men the United States has produced, Evans profited little from his work, but he spoke truly of the value of his book when he said:

> . . . the Millwrights' and Millers' Guide, containing some eternal truths, true theories, which will, like Euclid's Elements, stand the test of time, and lead no practitioner into an expensive error. I supposed it would have sold most rapidly, but was disappointed. . . .
>
> Two thousand copies were published. . . . My agents carried them to show the millers and millwrights, and gave a great proportion of the edition to them, by orders from me, for the purpose of getting my improvements introduced. One of my agents traveled for thirteen years, to instruct millwrights and millers to make and use the improvements . . . ; he often declared his belief that he rode 100,000 miles.[9]

It was not until long after his death that the benefits of Evans' knowledge and inventions were widely spread.

Apart from the specially skilled, the labor situation was also eased by the greater readiness of respectable farmers' daughters to undertake mill work. Francis Lowell, in launching his cotton mill in 1814, insisted upon

---

[9] Greville and Dorothy Bathe, *Oliver Evans, A Chronicle of Early American Engineering,* p. 47. Philadelphia: Historical Society of Pennsylvania, 1935.

proper living conditions for the help, and accordingly he had boarding houses built where careful supervision could be maintained over the young women who came in from the New England farms to work for a winter or two in the factory. The Waltham system spread through much of the New England cotton industry and unquestionably helped to banish doubts about the propriety of mill work for any healthy country girl. In consequence, the labor supply was tremendously augmented by this management innovation.

Furthermore, transportation and power problems were greatly lessened by the end of the thirties. Steam engines were no longer a rarity, and in the Middle States and accessible parts of New England coal was coming into use. Factories no longer depended upon water power alone, and year-round operation, unaffected by drought or frozen streams, could insure a success thitherto doubtful. Steamboats plied regularly on all the navigable rivers, and railroads were building. The coming of the railroads not only opened up markets in the back country, often incidentally destroying local monopolies, but accelerated industrialization in various ways. As has been said, railroad money was ready to launch new manufacturing communities, while, with the spread of the railway network, resources of power or raw materials earlier too inaccessible for exploitation became available. It is not without significance that in 1837 Massachusetts, the leading manufacturing state in the Union, issued its first census of industry, a statistical survey that showed scarcely a town without some small manufacturing establishment. By 1845 when the second industrial census was made, the advance in numbers of plants, in numbers of hands employed, and, most of all, in value of goods produced, was impressive. In this progress the railroads had played an important part.

Mill Labor Before 1850

Although the "putting-out" or "domestic" system as it had been organized in Great Britain had no substantial counterpart in America, and the establishment of factories therefore necessitated no similar drastic readjustment of the national economy, still the spread of factories for the manufacture of consumers' goods involved, as time went on, a sharpening differentiation between employer and employee. Improved transportation and communication, through destruction of the purely local monopoly market, abolished some of the small mills and fostered a keener competition that made the question of wage rates for factory hands more acute. Whereas mill owners in the early thirties had paid their help whatever was necessary to induce the neighborhood farmers' sons and daughters to work in the plant, by the forties employers might draw labor from a much wider radius. Furthermore, the extraordinarily close interconnection of all the New England cotton textile concerns standardized wage rates and working hours, leaving the workers comparatively helpless in bargaining.

A native American labor movement had sprung up in the late twenties and flourished for a decade or more, but its strength derived from urban artisans rather than from mill hands, and its program was concerned not with wages but with hours, educational opportunities, and mechanic's lien laws. The introduction in 1836 of the 10-hour day in the Government navy yards and its later extension to all Federal employees made no dent upon the regime of private employers, and the fairly widespread use of gas illumination in mills after 1840 made a 12-hour day as general in winter as in summer. During the forties a new labor movement arose, this time sponsored by mill workers. As long hours were easily the most vulnerable point of attack, it was first and foremost a 10-hour movement, although success would doubtless have quickly inspired attempts to secure better wages. Corporations, creations of the state legislatures, were logically subject to regulation, but the political power of mill owners sufficed to defeat suggested reforms. By 1848 the operatives had largely abandoned the attack.[10]

Nevertheless, factory work was not considered hopelessly degrading, as it had been in England. In 1840 the girls in the Lowell mills began the publication of the *Lowell Offering*, a collection of essays, romantic and realistic, written by members of their own "Improvement Circles." The tone of these papers is, to be sure, defensive, constantly reiterating the dignity and value of factory employment.[11] And, it is true, conditions in the mills that adopted Lowell's pattern were distinctly better than in the Rhode Island factories, which, following Slater's English conception, made no attempt to supervise the workers' lives. The latter *laissez-faire* arrangement had none of the annoying paternalistic features of the Puritan Massachusetts system, but child labor was more extensive and mill agents tended to consider their operatives as part of the machinery; and a Fall River manager frankly stated, "So long as they can do my work for what I choose to pay them, I keep them, getting out of them all I can." But until the general influx of Irish and French Canadian immigrants into the mills in the late forties and fifties, the character of labor in American industry was of a singularly high order. Massachusetts in 1837 required for all child employees under 15 years of age three months'

[10] The best compact discussion of the condition of mill workers of this period is contained in Norman Ware, *The Industrial Worker, 1840-1860*. Boston: Houghton Mifflin Company, 1924.

[11] Harriet Martineau, that shrewd English observer and essayist, after visiting the Waltham mill in 1834 wrote a most eulogistic account of the industrial community she found. "I saw a whole street of houses built with the earnings of the girls; some with piazzas and green Venetian blinds, and all neat and sufficiently spacious." The contrast to English mill towns was inevitably sharp, but had Miss Martineau observed the American scene a decade later she must have noted much to trouble her. See Martineau, *Society in America*, especially Volume II. London: Saunders and Otley, 1837.

schooling a year, and although for another 30 years there was to be no system of factory inspection to see that the law was enforced, the humanitarian gesture was a source of pride to Massachusetts employers.

Industry Outside the Factory System Before 1850

It would be a mistake to think of American manufacturing enterprise before 1850 as functioning fully on a factory basis. Although complete home manufacture had largely died out before 1850 even in the West, many products were made on a partial "putting-out" system. And, indeed, there is evidence of this system's enduring long after the Civil War, when modern industrial methods are frequently supposed wholly to have superseded the less centralized regime. It could be used, of course, only in fields not fully mechanized. But these were still numerous. Even in paper making the introduction of machinery was slow, although ever since the seventeenth-century beginnings of the industry in America a power-driven mill with special equipment and trained workmen had been necessary. In the middle forties a number of small paper mills still relied upon hand processes. The "putting-out" system, as such, prevailed primarily in the manufacture of boots and shoes, of palm-leaf and straw hats, and, after the invention of the sewing machine in 1846, of ready-made clothing. In rural New England quantities of "tops, taps, and fixings" for boots were distributed to farm families by the entrepreneur who in time collected the finished work at so much a pair. The invention of shoemaking machinery in the fifties only very gradually drove out this system. The same scheme obtained in hat making, in some localities in the sewing together of machine-knit stockings, and in the finishing of men's ready-to-wear shirts, caps, and pants. It was leisure-time occupation—if leisure in rural America before 1870 be not a total misnomer—and men, women, and children alike gladly supplemented returns from farm or country store [12] with earnings in real money. In urban communities, however, such homework tended to become the main source of livelihood, and the shockingly low rates of pay necessitated appallingly long hours.

Era of Industrialization, 1850-1865

By mid-century, then, manufacturing, whether in factory alone or in factory plus home, had earned a secure place in the American economy. The agrarian South, intent upon the defense of its "peculiar institution," watched with increasing alarm the growth in wealth and population of the North and Northwest, but neither sentimental disapproval nor gradually lowered tariff schedules could check industrial development. Abundant raw materials, greatly improved transportation, far-flung markets, an ever more highly skilled force of mechanics, increasing use of machin-

12 In many remote sections barter between country merchant and country customer endured longer than is sometimes realized.

ery that made feasible employment of unskilled labor, accumulating capital—all pointed to industrial progress. Every year added new mills and new types of manufactures until the agricultural Arcadia envisaged by Jefferson was doomed.

One evidence of the rapid multiplication of factories, requiring considerable machinery and hence larger capital than individuals or partners could generally command, was the passage in most Northern states of general incorporation laws in lieu of the special legislative acts formally resorted to. Save in the cotton industry, capitalization was still comparatively small, and manufacturing corporations could start operations on financial shoestrings.

To man these new mills more hands were needed than even prolific America could provide. The potato famine in Ireland and the political upheavals on the Continent brought to the New World in the late forties and early fifties great numbers of immigrants, of whom the Germans in particular were often skilled workmen. But the lure of the unsettled West, let alone the discovery of gold in California, made it difficult to hold the mill hands in the manufacturing East. The device of importing labor under contract was therefore hit upon, and agents began to scour European cities and French Canadian villages to engage workers for American manufacturing concerns. The agent, paid so much a head for every person signed on, was usually instructed to bring, if possible, hands with some experience in operating machines. Frequently, however, this was impossible, and raw boys and girls from Irish or Canadian farms were brought into the United States, bound to work out their passage money and any other cash advances made them by months of labor in the mills.

It is easy to exaggerate the hardship this scheme imposed upon the immigrant. Apparently most people so brought to the States were eager to come and did not regret it later. But it is also easy to comprehend the wrath of the Southern slaveholder who, cut off from the African slave trade and subject to attack from Northern abolitionists, reviled the hypocrisy of the slave traders in Northern industry. Had the increased efficiency of the machinery in manufacturing plants not lessened the need for trained operatives, such wholesale importation of unskilled labor could scarcely have been economical for the employer. As it was, manufacturers recruited hands by this method until unsolicited immigration reached volume proportions after the Civil War.

But resentment of the system was by no means confined to the slave states. Native American mechanics and artisans viewed this flood of cheap immigrant labor first with distaste and shortly with outright hostility. Workingmen's Leagues, composed almost exclusively of native Americans, in the early fifties renewed their efforts to get state legislatures to enact 10-hour laws, and with the failure of that attempt angrily threw their political weight into Know-Nothingism, a short-lived endeavor to freeze out the immigrant from participation in the economic and political benefits of American democracy. The earlier concept of the community of interest between employer and employee gave way before the idea of every group for itself, and the general Trades' Union movement of the thirties was not revived. Before 1860 some four craft unions appeared, of which the typographical union was the first and most permanently vigorous. But factory labor remained largely unorganized. Though unions in the transport and building trades were formed during the war under the stimulus of the acute labor shortage, among mill workers unionization was to emerge only a full generation later, and then it was to be limited to the specially skilled. Meanwhile, with the influx of foreign workers into the mills, American farmers' daughters ceased to regard factory work as "pleasant" and "honorable." The *Lowell Offering* dropped from sight, and the educated "female operative" of the forties was rarely found by the end of the fifties.

Precision Manufacture, 1832-1865

The rapidity of expansion and early efficiency of American industry was conditioned on the development of machine tools. The machine shops that supplied these tools before mid-century were usually adjuncts of manufacturing corporations for which the tools were custom-built. Machine tool making as a separate industry, each company specializing in making tools of its own design, was a development of the fifties and sixties. In the perfecting of interchangeable manufactures, however, the general machine tool played a lesser part than the introduction of precision gauges. Interchangeability of parts of mechanisms, a matter quite different from the production of articles virtually identical but not fitting permanently into a mechanism, grew in exactness with every decade. But it must be remembered that the meaning of the term itself grew: "The interchangeability of 1813 would not have been considered satisfactory in 1855."[13]

Numerous improvements upon the machines of the earlier period were constantly introduced into the armories, public and private, during the thirties and forties—elaborated millers, grinding machines, and others. Clockmakers abandoned wooden works in favor of brass, a change that necessitated more carefully constructed tools and machines. But it was

[13] Joseph Wickham Roe, in his valuable book *English and American Tool Builders* (New York: McGraw-Hill Book Company, 1926), pp. 140-141, illustrates this statement: "When Hall completed his first hundred rifles at Harper's Ferry in 1824, it is said that 'the joint of the breech block was so fitted that a sheet of paper would slide loosely in the joint, but two sheets would stick.' This system of gauging will have a familiar sound to the older mechanics who grew up before the days of the micrometer. When Colonel North was given his first contract for rifles and furnished two models to work from, these models were so unlike that he asked to have one set aside and that he be allowed to gauge his work from the other."

the *vernier caliper,* first made in America in 1851, that inaugurated true precision manufacture in the United States. Its maker, Joseph R. Brown, had been a clockmaker, repairman, and small producer of mathematical instruments in Providence for some years. In 1850 he had invented and turned out in his shop, where only 14 men were employed, an automatic linear dividing engine for graduating rules. Improved upon somewhat in the course of the decade, this machine was still in use in the 1920's, meeting modern standards of accuracy.

The new caliper, reading to thousandths of an inch, was the first practical tool for exact measurements that could be sold at a price within the reach of ordinary machinists. Its importance, therefore, can scarcely be overestimated, although its general adoption was astonishingly slow. The *"vernier,"* named for the seventeenth-century French inventor who first evolved the principle, is an auxiliary scale, made to slide along the divisions of a graduated instrument, for indicating parts of a division. The *vernier caliper* is an ordinary rule fitted with two jaws, one rigidly fixed to the rule, the other attached to the vernier scale that slides along the rule. The instrument has both British and metric scales and is provided with devices to measure internal depths and also diameters of cavities. For the first time gunsmiths, watchmakers, sewing-machine manufacturers, anyone closely concerned with interchangeable manufacture, could measure the accuracy of their work without costly equipment.

Brown and his partner, Lucien Sharpe, shortly produced other valuable precision tools: vernier protractors, the American wire gauge for clock springs, and, soon after, a precision gear-cutter for clocks. With the coming of the Civil War, the firm embarked upon the building of a whole series of important machine tools. In the invention and construction of precision instruments, however, Brown's greatest contribution, other than the vernier caliper, was the micrometer, put upon the market in 1867. Without these minutely exact gauges American interchangeable manufacture could never have achieved its high degree of efficiency. Other men and companies, of course, took up the making of precision gauges and tools. Most advances in mechanical invention are the work of many persons, and a great number of gifted mechanics carried further the contributions of Brown and Sharpe.

No account of the beginnings of American precision manufacture would be complete without mention of the Colt workmen. Samuel Colt had invented his revolver as early as 1836, but his pistols were not widely accepted as practicable until the Mexican War. In 1853 Colt built his own armory just south of Hartford, Connecticut, and there a corps of extraordinarily able workmen began the production of small arms on a basis of interchangeable manufacture in which machine work almost wholly superseded hand work. Under the superintendence of the ingenious Elisha K. Root, modern machine tools were developed and standards of precision achieved that spelled a new era in American manufacturing. From this shop a succession of men went forth to start many of the great machine companies whose products completed the industrialization of America. The progress well begun in the fifties was hastened by the demands of the Civil War. Manufactures of the postwar period were to be produced with a speed and an accuracy unattainable before.

Shop and Factory Organization Before 1865

Armories and specialized machine shops were organized somewhat differently from mills producing textiles, paper, shoes, or ordinary household wares. In the former, highly skilled workmen were necessary and the so-called contract system, established early in the nineteenth century, was generally maintained until long after the close of the Civil War. Under this arrangement, a competent master workman entered into a contract with the shop whereby, supplied with raw materials, tools, and power, he undertook to turn out the product of his department for a settled sum. He engaged his own workmen and set his own wage rates. The contract might run for a year or until the completion of a given job. Frequently, particularly in the early years, there was a kind of apprenticeship system that enabled the inexperienced boy to acquire a technical education under the direction of a skilled workman. One needs but look at the long list of eminent American mechanics and tool makers who got their training at Whitney's, or Robbins and Lawrence's, or Colt's, or Brown and Sharpe's, to realize the value of the system. Whether or not it was because it created intimate association between contractor and men, the fact remains that in the nineteenth-century armories and precision machine shops, probably more than in any other industry in America, innate capacity had opportunity to express itself and to reap its rewards.

Occasionally the textile mills, at least the finishing departments, resorted to the contract type of employment. But usually the foreman or superintendent hired and fired, and the employee's name was entered upon the mill register with the department to which he or she was assigned. Pay days came monthly in the more adequately financed mills, but in some factories only every three or every six months. Nor were wages always in cash. The wages of the single employee, obliged to live in the company boarding house, had deductions for room and board, while married men and women might have to take payment in tokens redeemable only in goods at the company store.

Because textile mills employed greater numbers of persons than other manufactures, personal contacts between owners and operatives were fewer. The spread of corporate ownership also early involved absenteeism in the cotton industry, and even before mid-century many mill hands never knew the heads of the company by sight. Financial control and ultimate managerial responsibility was centered in Boston with underlings as "agents" in charge of the plants scattered through New England. The agent had to refer important decisions to the company treasurer in his Milk Street office, but to the mill employee the agent was the representative of all authority. That labor disputes and other paralyzing managerial difficulties were fairly few is surprising until one recalls that in the early decades the whole system was too new to seem immutable, and later the immigrant mill-population was too ignorant and too unfamiliar with the American scene to make protest appear possible.

In other fields of manufacturing, financial and administrative reorganization was less complete. Few paper companies employed more than 40 hands, and management was almost always vested in the principal owner. Absentee ownership was rare, for paper making was still considered an art that demanded careful supervision Although labor turnover in paper mills was higher than in other lines, its rate was apparently largely attributable to a paper makers' tradition that able men roamed from one mill to another, always sure of getting jobs. Proprietorships and partnerships in the paper world were common long after they had virtually disappeared in the textile industry. Machinery had fully supplanted hand methods of paper making before 1860, but makeshift second-hand equipment could be bought with no great capital outlay, and a small mill faithfully tended could always sell its product at a profit.[14] Less highly mechanized industries producing various household wares—"Yankee notions," pots and pans, pins and needles, woodenwares, and the like—needed comparatively little capital to function successfully, and here small local concerns drawing on neighborhood labor still predominated.

The Civil War, like every great conflict, brought many changes, a speeding up of production, an intensification of effort. Industrialization in much of the North and in sections of the settled West was an accomplished fact by 1865, but an industrial society had not as yet arisen. Agriculture or commercial undertakings still supplemented factory employment in many communities. In the cotton-textile industry alone were there evidences of conditions that were later to become general. Not until the nineties was the skilled factory worker to realize that the increasing weight of America's capital structure had limited the opportunity for every man to creep up the ladder to economic security by his own efforts. Machines, and therefore factories in which to run them by water or steam power, existed in every branch of manufacturing in the *ante-bellum* period. But great concentrations of wealth, a conscious proletariat, elaborate marketing schemes, and all that an industrial society spells to the modern world, had not yet come into being.

[14] In 1851 the failure of a small paper mill in Massachusetts elicited the horrified comment from Joel Munsell in his *Chronology of Paper and Papermaking* that no paper manufacturer in America need ever go bankrupt.

Selected References

Bathe, Greville and Dorothy, *Oliver Evans, A Chronicle of Early American Engineering*. Philadelphia: The Historical Society of Pennsylvania, 1935.

Bishop, J. Leander. *A History of American Manufactures from 1608-1860* (2 vols.). Philadelphia: Edward Young and Company, 1864.

Clark, Victor, *History of Manufactures in the United States, 1607-1914* (3 vols.). Washington, D. C.: Carnegie Institution of Washington, 1916.

Cole, Arthur H., *American Wool Manufacture* (2 vols.). Cambridge, Mass.: Harvard University Press, 1926.

———, and Harold Williamson, *The American Carpet Manufacture*. Cambridge, Mass.: Harvard University Press, 1941.

Green, Constance M., *Holyoke, Massachusetts, A Case History of the Industrial Revolution in America*. New Haven: Yale University Press, 1939.

Hazard, Blanche, E., *The Organization of the Boot and Shoe Industry In Massachusetts before 1875*. Cambridge, Mass.: Harvard University Press, 1921.

Lippincott, Isaac, *A History of Manufactures in the Ohio Valley to the Year 1860*. New York: The Knickerbocker Press, 1914.

Martineau, Harriet, *Society in America* (2 vols.). London: Saunders and Otley, 1837.

North, S. N. D. and Ralph H., *Simeon North, First Official Pistolmaker of the United States*. Concord, N. H.: The Rumford Press, 1913.

Roe, Joseph Wickham, *English and American Tool Builders*. New York: McGraw-Hill Book Company, 1926.

Schlakman, Vera, "Economic History of a Factory Town," *Smith College Studies in History,* Vol. XX. Northampton, Mass.: 1936.

Taussig, F. W., *Some Aspects of the Tariff Question*. Cambridge, Mass.: Harvard University Press, 1915.

Ware, Caroline, *The Early New England Cotton Manufacture*. Boston: Houghton Mifflin Company, 1931.

Ware, Norman, *The Industrial Worker, 1840-1860*. Boston: Houghton Mifflin Company, 1924.

12 · FOREIGN TRADE IN THE ERA OF WOODEN SHIPS

FOR THE 40 YEARS after the outbreak of the Revolution in 1775, American shipping faced abnormal conditions. Its hectic hide-and-seek existence during the Revolution was followed by a dismal decade of trade dislocations resulting from the imperial divorce; then it entered upon its exciting and profitable "heroic age" during the long Anglo-French wars. With the end of those wars in 1815, the situation became more normal, while new cargoes and new sea lanes developed alongside the old. Commerce and shipping gradually expanded into the "golden age" of the clipper ship era around 1850. After that, American cargoes still continued to increase; but at the time of the outbreak of the Civil War American shipping was already showing traces of its coming long decline that was to continue until the outbreak of World War I.

Although the Revolution offered Yankee shipping new opportunities to break loose from the restrictions of the Navigation Laws, it also confronted American trade with a tremendous and serious task. For the only time in our maritime history, the nation faced a desperate need for munitions from beyond the seas; and the mighty Royal Navy blocked the way. But that navy, for various reasons, proved to be far less dangerous in the conflict than its size and reputation had indicated. As a result of its ineffectiveness and the astuteness of the American mariners, an adequate supply of munitions arrived from France and Holland to save the desperate situation after Bunker Hill, when Washington had almost no gunpowder left. Part of the munition supply came in French ships directly across the Atlantic, and part of it in small American vessels by way of the French, Spanish, Danish, or Dutch islands in the West Indies. Once that immediate need was met, the Yankees turned to the development of commercial contacts with England's enemies. At times war risk insurance rates on American vessels rose to 50 per cent, but on the whole supplies came through safely more often than not, and our ports were kept well stocked with salt, spirits, and luxury goods.[1]

---

[1] R. G. Albion and J. B. Pope, *Sea Lanes in Wartime,* Chapter II. New York: W. W. Norton & Company, 1942.

Post-Revolutionary Readjustments

Peace was a less roseate story, for it brought new problems. The decade from 1783 to 1793 was one of the dreariest in the annals of American commerce. Although William Pitt and some other British statesmen indicated a willingness to grant the Americans generous commercial terms, opinion was turned in the opposite direction by the appearance of Lord Sheffield's *Observations on the Commerce of the United States.* Sheffield argued that, since the Americans were now foreigners by their own volition, they deserved no special privileges under the Navigation Laws, which should be kept in full force. He pointed out, moreover, that force of habit and superior service would undoubtedly keep the Americans coming to British ports, whatever discriminatory steps England might take, and that no serious alienation of trade by the French or the Dutch need be feared.

As a result, the Americans found to their consternation what it was like to be forced to view the British Empire from the outside. Particularly galling was the barring of their vessels and some of their exports from the British sugar islands, which had played so important a role in Colonial economy. The rich merchants of the big ports were less affected by this loss of the lucrative "sugar triangle" because they could participate in the profitable new trade around the Cape of Good Hope to the Far East. That new sea lane had been inaugurated in 1784 with the voyages of the *Empress of China* from New York to Canton and of the *United States* from Philadelphia to India; these pioneer ventures were soon followed by the spectacular exploits of Salem vessels in the Eastern seas. But voyages of that sort tied up capital for longer periods than the "little fellows" could stand; and many of these, who had been accustomed to load some local produce upon a small sloop for a voyage to the Caribbean found that business was not what it used to be before the Revolution had closed the door to the privileges of trading within the British Empire.

As far as the sugar trade was concerned, the inconvenience was temporary, for France, Holland, Denmark, and even Spain soon opened at least some of their Caribbean ports to American vessels. Not until 1830 was trade with Jamaica, Barbados, and the other British islands fully reopened for the Americans, but they found Haiti and later Cuba to be fairly adequate substitutes. The real victims of British commercial policy were Britain's own Caribbean planters and their slaves; they were now cut off from their previous abundant and cheap supply of flour, fish, and lumber, which could not be obtained in sufficient amounts from the remaining British North American colonies.

Although some Caribbean ports were thus still open to the Yankee vessels and cargoes, the "sugar triangle" as such was gone, since its profitable side, the "long haul," was closed to them. American cargoes could still be swapped for sugar, molasses, and rum at French and other non-British ports, but the Americans themselves had to consume all return cargoes, since the rich freight earnings from the "long haul" across the Atlantic of such surplus cargoes were reserved by European nations for themselves. Consequently, Yankee schooners and sloops, which flocked to those foreign islands in considerable numbers during the postwar years, found that the pre-Revolutionary good sources of shipping profits were now much reduced.

Sheffield had been correct in predicting that, despite the harsh British prohibitions, the Americans would soon gravitate back to London, Bristol, and the fast-growing port of Liverpool. During most of the next century, England and the United States were to be each other's best customer. The French tried to follow up their Revolutionary contacts and good will with the establishment of regular official packet sailings between Lorient and New York, but the hoped-for luring of American trade did not materialize. The differences in language and in weights, measures, and materials, along with less generous credit arrangements offered by French merchants, drove the Yankees back to the familiar ports where they knew what they were getting and where they would be given ample time to pay. The beginnings of the Industrial Revolution, moreover, made England's offerings more attractive than ever, and the British went more than half-way by dumping cargoes at bargain rates in the American ports vacated by the redcoats.

A gloomy tone ran through the letter books of the American merchants during the middle and late 1780's. British goods would not, of course, keep coming forever unless they were paid for, and payments were becoming increasingly difficult with the British West Indies cut off, the grain crops ruined, the state currencies in a jumbled condition, and debts everywhere.

One Scot residing in New York as a factor wrote to his correspondents, soon after the British left: [2]

> Every week day has the appearance of the Holidays in old times. Money scarce and daily draining, trade dull; in short, nothing but vendues and commission stores seem now to be in vogue. The gentlemen of the army form a considerable part of these, but one-half of them must soon either starve or become bankrupts at the expense of their neighbors.

The new Federal Constitution in 1789 was welcomed by the merchants as a means of presenting a united front for international bargaining purposes, but that could not remedy everything.

---

[2] *Macgregor Letter Book*, N. Y. Public Library, quoted in *N. Y. History*, Vol. 21 (1940), p. 396.

Neutral Opportunities

April, 1793, brought a British mail packet to New York with the long-desired answer to the American merchants' prayers. England and France were again at war; and, as a neutral, the United States was on the threshold of a tremendous maritime boom. This boom was created chiefly by the opportunities in trade for neutral vessels where belligerents dared not sail. Such voyages risked seizures and other complications, but until the end of 1807 neutrality meant increased prosperity; between 1807 and the final fall of Napoleon, however, those same seagoing ventures involved more trouble than profit.

Most important of the new opportunities was the recovery of the profitable long haul of West Indian sugar across the Atlantic. With the British Navy pretty well controlling the seas, French vessels ran great risks in voyaging between Haiti and Bordeaux or between Martinique and Nantes. France threw open the long haul to the Americans. England interfered and started to restrict the trade altogether, but finally winked at the subterfuge of breaking the voyage at some American port. By this "broken voyage" system, a Yankee brig would load sugar and coffee at Haiti, for example, and carry it to New York. There the cargo would be unloaded and the customs duties paid. The next step was the reloading of the same cargo while most of the duties were refunded! Now the vessel could proceed eastward on a "neutral" voyage to a French port free from the hazards of seizure. The return voyage would be of the same sort, with French goods brought to the islands by way of New York. Out trade statistics became suddenly inflated by the entry and quick withdrawal of hundreds of such cargoes, in which we had only a fleeting but very profitable interest. During several years around the end of the century, such re-exports outweighed the domestic exports of our own products.

Meantime, other American vessels were making rich earnings in diverse ways. Good profits came from the freight money in "tramp" voyages between foreign ports where it was not safe for belligerents to enter. Concurrently the British West Indian ports had been opened to our smaller vessels, which were not large enough to carry sugar across the Atlantic. There was also steady business in the shuttle between America and England, while the number of vessels on the run to the Far East increased.

With vessels able to pay for themselves in a voyage or two, shipbuilding boomed along the coast, so that our tonnage doubled and then trebled over the prewar level. This state of affairs reached its climax in 1807, when American imports reached a total of $138,500,000 as compared with $31,500,000 in 1792, a higher figure than any attained until 1835.

Then came, in turn, Embargo, Non-Intercourse, and finally the War of 1812 to shut down seagoing adventures. Despite the popular impression of our "humbling the pride of the Royal Navy" in that war, the effect upon the United States' shipping was serious if not disastrous. That same navy was able to impose such a strangling blockade of every seaport along our whole coast in 1814, that almost nothing came or went by sea. At times it was not even safe to sail between New London and New Haven on Long Island Sound.[3]

Luckily we were not long at war, and the coming of peace to the world's sea lanes in 1815 brought more normal trade conditions in place of the artificial stimuli, the dangers of neutral trading, and the crop of wartime regulations. The time had come for the new nation to settle down to the establishment of regular sea routes in a fairly normal world.

The Return to Normal Trade

The most important features of American commerce for the next 30 years were to be the continued increase of our trade with England; the development of substantial business with France and Germany; the emergence of cotton as the chief American export; and the rapid development of Cuba as a substitute for the other old Caribbean markets. Later, increased immigration, the final willingness of England to buy American grain, and the new trade with California were to provide the added stimuli for pushing our shipping to its climax. That story is summarized in the table on the following page.

The tea cargoes from Canton and the pepper from the "Salem East Indies," representing the most glamorous part of the nation's trade, have received more than their rightful share of attention. In volume and value, they amounted to only a fraction of the prosaic products of the Industrial Revolution that were brought month after month from Liverpool to New York across the stormy 3,000 miles of North Atlantic in the teeth of the "westerlies." England's time-honored woolens from Yorkshire generally headed our list of imports in value, but the newer cotton goods from Manchester and other places in Lancashire surpassed them in yardage and were fast catching up in value. These textile imports went far in clothing those Americans who did not wear homespun. The domestic textile industry was not doing well; it had blossomed briefly during the war interruptions but had been stifled by England's heavy dumping over here of textiles that had been accumulating in wartime while the world markets were unavailable. Huge quantities were rushed to the American ports to be sold at very low prices. Hardware from Birmingham and cutlery from Sheffield likewise crammed the holds of the freighters from Liverpool. Later, when the railroad boom was under way, iron rails were to be a further stimulus to British exports.

Throughout the world, England was profiting from her long head start with industrial machinery, but the United States was the best of all her

[3] For a thorough description, see A. T. Mahan, *Sea Power in its Relations to the War of 1812* (2 vols.). Boston: Little, Brown & Company, 1905.

FOREIGN COMMERCE OF THE UNITED STATES, 1821-1860 *

(In Millions of Dollars)

	1821	1831	1841	1851	1860
Total Imports	62	103	127	220	362
Total Exports	64	81	121	218	400
Grand Total	127	184	249	438	762
Combined Imports and Exports:					
United Kingdom	46	77	96	211	340
France	10	17	41	55	105
Cuba	11	13	17	23	46
British North America	2	4	8	18	46
Germany (Hanse)	3	5	6	16	36
Brazil	1	4	9	18	27
China	7	4	4	9	22
Imports, by Ports (state totals):					
New York	23	57	75	111	248
Boston	14	14	20	32	41
Philadelphia	8	12	10	14	14
New Orleans	3	9	10	12	22
Baltimore	4	4	6	6	9
Exports, by Ports:					
New York	13	25	33	86	145
New Orleans	7	16	34	54	107
Mobile		2	10	18	38
Boston	12	7	11	12	17
Philadelphia	7	5	5	5	5
Baltimore	3	4	4	5	9

(In Thousands of Tons)

	1821	1831	1841	1851	1860
Total Documented Tonnage	1,298	1,267	2,230	3,772	5,353
Total Registered Tonnage	619	620	945	1,726	2,546
Total Steam Tonnage	..	68	175	583	867
Total Shipbuilding Tonnage	55	85	118	298	212
Total Documented Tonnage (by states):					
New York	248	300	490	1,050	1,661
Massachusetts	334	342	531	694	835
Maine	136	163	304	536	784
Maryland	126	73	113	204	254
Tonnage Cleared, Total	880	1,244	2,371	5,130	8,789
Per Cent American	(91%)	(77%)	(69%)	(62%)	(71%)
For British North America	118	174	852	2,139	4,465
United Kingdom	173	341	421	952	1,557
Cuba	107	150	208	391	695
France	38	68	155	184	360

* From annual *Report on Commerce and Navigation.* Partial summaries in J. S. Homans, *Foreign Commerce of the U. S.* (New York: G. P. Putnam's Sons, 1851) and R. G. Albion. *Rise of New York Port* (New York: Charles Scribner's Sons, 1939). For a 1793-1815 statistical summary, see R. G. Albion and J. B. Pope, *Sea Lanes in Wartime* (1942).

customers—better, by far, than in the days when the Navigation Laws had forced Americans to buy from her. That fact was not lost upon the economic-minded "Little Englanders," who were ready to let their colonies of settlement break loose after pointing out that England did more business with New York, which cost them only a consul's salary, than with Canada, Australia, New Zealand, and South Africa combined, which took millions to defend.

Trade with France, which had failed to materialize after the American Revolution, came into its own about 1840. Silks and other luxury goods vied with wines for space in the packets from Havre; Paris fashions even then meant much to Americans. The ships from Havre were generally smaller than those from Liverpool, but they came often because of the constant demand for the very latest styles. Heavier and coarser wares, in ever-increasing quantities, arrived from the old Hanse ports of Bremen and Hamburg, through which passed most of our trade with Germany.

French and German trade combined, however, did not amount to half of the British total, while none of the other European countries came anywhere near their separate totals. Boston did a moderate amount of business in the Baltic and Mediterranean, but it was only a trickle compared with the heavy volume of traffic on the Anglo-American main line, which increased further in volume in the fifties as women began to swathe themselves in more and more cloth.

Cuba was the outstanding new field of exploitation during the period, generally ranking third in American markets, preceded by England and France. Along with Puerto Rico, which developed a respectable trade with us also, it was all that Spain retained after 1825 of her former vast American colonies. Ironically, it was worth more to Americans commercially than all the newly freed republics of Spanish-America, where we entertained such high hopes of commercial opportunities. Close to our shores, Cuba was easily accessible in its new role as successor to Jamaica as a source of sugar and as an outlet for our offerings. At Havana, Matanzas, and elsewhere along the Cuban coast, American businessmen advanced money to the Cuban planters, catered to their various wants (all the way from food to coaches and railroad cars), and brought back huge quantities of sugar. The island was thoroughly brought within our sphere of economic influence more than half a century before we finally pried it loose from Spain. By the time that England eventually permitted us to trade freely with Jamaica and her other sugar islands, we no longer had any particular interest in doing so. Those islands, which were soon to be deprived of their slaves, were falling rapidly from their former proud position.

The United States did a fair business with Mexico and the struggling little Spanish-American republics of the Caribbean. England, on the other hand, had the bulk of the trade with the more remote parts of

South America, which were as near to London as to New York; their commodities, moreover, fitted better with England's for a mutual exchange. Trade with Buenos Aires, Montevideo, and Valparaiso thus remained on a modest scale, although with the forties a new trade began in guano, or bird-dung, brought in odorous cargoes from islands off Peru for use as fertilizer. With Portugal's former great colony of Brazil, trade went better. Its rapidly-growing coffee output was an accessible and economical substitute for imports from distant Java, and our vessels flocked to Rio for coffee. However, American products did not find there a ready market.

Although the coffee from Brazil was worth more than the tea from Canton, the Chinese were better customers than our neighbors to the southward. At first, to be sure, the Americans were hard pressed to find something with which to pay for the teas, silks, and chinaware brought around the Cape of Good Hope. The always-acceptable silver dollars were scarce in our seaports, and the initial cargoes of ginseng—a drug supposed to restore vigor to old men—quickly glutted the market. Yankee ingenuity soon developed, without too much outlay of capital, offerings of furs obtained by trading with Indians on the Northwest Coast or by killing seals in the Antarctic. Sandalwood from Hawaii likewise went well at Canton, and, for a short while in the thirties, opium could be carried over from India. Eventually the Chinese, who had originally shipped cheap cotton "nankeens" to us, began to purchase some of the products of our cotton mills. Salem continued to do a thriving pepper business with Java and Sumatra for a while. Boston kept up a good trade with India, even sending out ice, while various ports traded with Spanish Manila.

American shipping statistics at this point tend to be distorted, unless regarded with caution, by a fast-growing trade at our very doors. A glance back at the table on page 216 shows that by 1841 more tonnage cleared for British North America than for any other country. Some of it resulted from little coasting voyages up to the Maritime Provinces, but the bulk of it consisted of freshwater trips across the northern frontier. These even included the constant comings and goings of little craft on the Detroit and Niagara Rivers. The tonnage, it will be noted, was out of all proportion to the value of the cargoes sent and received.

New Commodities and Opportunities

More striking than any other change in commerce during those years was the sudden development of cotton exports. Absent from Colonial offerings, the cotton bale quickly overshadowed every other commodity in our foreign commerce, as the table on the following page indicates. The invention of the cotton gin, just as the Anglo-French wars were starting, gave the Southern states a staple export for which the demand increased steadily as the Industrial Revolution gained headway. What was more, by means of it the nation kept a closer balance in foreign trade

PRINCIPAL EXPORT AND IMPORT COMMODITIES, 1821-1860 *
(*In Millions of Dollars*)

	1821	1830	1840	1850	1860
Exports:					
Cotton	20.1	29.6	63.8	71.9	191.8
Wheat and flour	4.4	6.1	11.7	7.7	19.5
Tobacco	5.6	5.5	9.8	9.9	15.9
Lumber and wood manufactures	1.5	2.0	2.9	4.8	14.6
Cotton manufactures	..	1.3	3.5	4.7	10.9
Imports:					
Woolens	7.2	5.9	10.8	19.6	43.1
Cotton manufactures	7.3	7.8	6.5	20.7	33.2
Coffee	4.4	4.2	8.5	11.2	21.8
Sugar	3.5	4.6	5.5	7.5	31.0
Hides, skins, and furs	1.1	2.7	3.1	5.8	12.3

* *Reports on Commerce and Navigation,* summarized in *U. S. Statistical Abstract,* 1941, pp. 528-531.

by offering something that England and the rest of Europe would take in exchange for what they sent westward across the Atlantic.

Out of that situation grew one of the most original and impudent patterns in the story of America's foreign trade—New York's "cotton triangle." Along with the establishment of sailing packet lines for regular transatlantic service, the development of an auction system for the centralized sale of European imports, and the building of the Erie Canal, it was one of the main steps by which New York shot ahead of Boston, Philadelphia, and Baltimore in the years immediately following 1815 to become "the great commercial emporium of America." By its excellent packet lines the port was able to attract to Sandy Hook most of the incoming cargoes of European manufactures, but it had no adequate local offerings to fill the holds of the returning vessels. It therefore took advantage of the chronic commercial passivity of the South, which might perfectly well have developed a direct shuttle trade from the cotton ports of Charleston, Savannah, Mobile, and New Orleans to England. Instead, the enterprising New Yorkers dragged the cotton shipments 200 miles out of their normal course to bring them to their own docks and there transship them in other vessels, while the South's imports from Europe were influenced to take the same roundabout course.[4] Like Amsterdam and London before it, New York thus derived heavy entrepôt profits from this routing of the trade of others by way of its own wharves. Its commission agents—mostly, as it happened, Connecticut Yankees, established themselves in interior Southern cities, just as the Scottish factors had set-

[4] In 1822, New York's domestic exports amounted to $9,228,000, of which cotton stood first at $3,925,000, while Southern products as a whole amounted to 55 per cent of the total.

tled in the Chesapeake region before the Revolution. New York banks loaned money on the crops; New York vessels carried the cotton; and the sum total of commissions and profits, it was reckoned, amounted to 40 per cent of the value of the cotton. If any one man may be credited with developing this system, it would be Jeremiah Thompson, who came to New York to sell the woolens from the family factory in Yorkshire. The cotton exports developed from the need for return cargoes; and so, too, did Thompson's establishing of the Black Ball Line, whose packet ships soon began to carry those shipments between New York and Liverpool on regular schedules.

Between 1846 and 1848, three events gave a tremendous new stimulus to American shipping and carried it to its peak in the next five years: the potato crop failed in Ireland; Germany had an epidemic of unsuccessful revolutions; and gold was discovered in California.

As a result of the potato famine, a steady demand developed in Britain for the wheat of the Middle Atlantic and Mid-Western states. England had wanted little of this, it will be recalled, during the Colonial period, and from 1815 on the Corn Laws had closed the market except in emergencies. Now, the victory of the industrial over the agricultural interests in Parliament, culminating in the repeal of the Corn Laws, opened the way for new possibilities in this trade. Whereas the Caribbean islands and Brazil generally imported their breadstuffs already ground into flour, the British preferred to purchase the grain and thereby keep the extra processing profits for themselves.

Not only did this new market for American wheat bring a new demand for shipping on the Atlantic shuttle, but the potato famine also was responsible for providing new passenger business for the return voyage. The population of Ireland fell off by one-fourth during those terrible years. Many starved to death, but many more migrated to America in the overcrowded between-decks of Yankee square-riggers at about $20 a head. The immigration from Ireland rose from 52,000 in 1847 to 163,000 in 1851. During the next three years, it was topped by the arrivals of Germans leaving their homeland because of political and economic conditions. Their numbers jumped from 69,000 in 1851 to 176,000 in 1854. That was the peak year when the newcomers from all countries reached a total of 460,000.

The grain and the immigrants swelled the burden of traffic upon what was already the most important of the world's sea lanes; the news of gold in California, on the other hand, suddenly opened a spectacular new route, 16,000 miles around Cape Horn to San Francisco. Passengers, mails, and gold moved by steamships that landed them on each side of the Isthmus of Panama or on Nicaragua. Then they were taken overland to the other ocean to complete their journey by sea. General cargo, on the other hand, was carried in swift square-riggers around the stormy Horn.

Shipbuilding and Shipping

So much for cargoes and trade routes. As for the vessels that handled the business, the National Government did something to stimulate and protect the American merchant marine, but it did not have to do a great deal. It should be borne in mind, in connection with shipping policy, that the interests of the shipper, the shipowner, and the shipbuilder are not always identical. The shipper is apt to want the cheapest freight rates possible, regardless of whether his cargoes are carried in American or foreign vessels. The shipowner (who was less and less apt to be carrying his own cargoes as time went on) wants to have the government discriminate against vessels under foreign flags, but would be glad to be able to buy foreign-built ships at times when they might be cheaper than home-built ships. The shipbuilder, whose demands are the most extreme, wants all the privileges reserved to American-*built* vessels. Congress, throughout our history, has generally given the shipbuilders that desired protection, in the same spirit in which Parliament had legislated in favor of English-built ships in the Navigation Laws. Incidentally, the application of those Navigation Laws after the Revolution broke up the old practice of selling American vessels in the English market; indeed, not until the final repeal of the Navigation Laws in 1849 was that possible again.

Very real protection was extended our vessels by the Government in 1818, through granting them a monopoly of our coasting trade. This amounted to more here than did similar measures in England and other European countries, because the coasting voyages were generally longer and consequently involved heavier freight earnings than the shorter hauls in other countries. The important route between New York and New Orleans, for instance, was 1,711 miles, which was more than half the length of the transatlantic run. The technical extension of the principle to the route around Cape Horn from East Coast ports to California, in order to bar foreign vessels from that long "coastal" voyage, helps to account for the heavy profits in the early clipper period. Even a half-century after that, when our shipping was in decline, similar "coastal" protection to the trade with Hawaii, Alaska, and Puerto Rico kept alive most of the few flourishing units in our merchant marine.

Discriminatory port dues and similar devices, especially in the earlier period, were occasionally employed in order to extract concessions from foreign nations. Our interrupted trade with the British West Indies saw several cases of this practice, as did American trade with France in the years immediately following 1815. Subsidies, that later common form of Government aid to shipping, however, were not granted by Congress except to some lines of mail steamships, around 1850, and to the fishing fleets in the form of bounties.

As for the ordinary sailing vessels, they did not need such financial aid to hold their own against foreign competition, because they enjoyed a decided advantage in construction costs. Thanks to an abundant supply of oak and pine close at hand, wooden vessels could be built along our coast much more cheaply than in England, where much of the timber and all the masts had to come from either the Baltic or from America. Transportation was the principal item in timber costs; a log delivered in England cost 15 times as much as the value of the tree itself growing in a Polish forest. That condition explained the English readiness to buy American-built vessels in the Colonial period, and this advantageous position of American shipbuilding lasted for much of the era of wooden ships. In 1791 the best new American ships cost about $34 a ton, while similar vessels built in England cost from $55 to $60 a ton. A similar differential lasted as late as 1830. Naturally the American shipbuilder could fully hold his own in competition with the British in freight rates. It might cost more to feed and pay American crews, but the superior operating efficiency of the average American captain tended to offset that.

By 1840 some of that early advantage in construction cost was being lost. The American builder was having to go further and further afield for his timber, while England was beginning to buy cheap vessels from Quebec and the Maritimes. After the repeal of the Navigation Laws, the English once more turned to our builders for ships to compete with vessels flying our flag. Later, when steam and iron began to replace wood and canvas, the construction advantage passed to the British shipyards.[5]

Most of the freighters of those days were bluff-bowed, "burthensome" tubs, in which speed had been deliberately sacrificed in order to secure maximum cargo capacity. At times, however, when speed was essential for particular purposes, the Americans led all competitors in turning out fast vessels. The speedy little Baltimore "clipper" schooners and brigs proved particularly useful in dodging inquisitive British warships during the Revolution and in later troubled periods at sea. Their streamlined design was later to influence the construction of pilot boats and other fast craft. The climax in speed, however, came with the China and California clipper ships built around 1850. With sharp, concave hull lines in place of the bulges of earlier ships, and with lofty masts designed to carry a tremendous amount of sail, they made remarkable records on long runs where speed was important enough to offset the loss in carrying capacity. For ordinary runs, however, less extremely specialized vessels were still built.

Along with those developments went a gradual increase in the size of the larger vessels. The average full-rigged ship of 1800 measured about 250 gross tons, equivalent to the capacity of eight modern railroad freight

[5] These economic aspects are thoroughly analyzed in J. G. B. Hutchins, *The American Maritime Industries and Public Policy*. Cambridge, Massachusetts: Harvard University Press, 1941.

cars. By 1850, ships of 1,000 tons were frequently launched, while a few of the bigger clippers exceeded 2,000 tons. For the lesser runs to the Caribbean and along the coast, however, 200-ton brigs and 100-ton schooners continued to carry the bulk of the business.

On the quantitative side, shipbuilding was decidedly sensitive to external stimuli. The first great boom came during the neutral trading between 1793 and 1812, with the merchant marine reaching a peak of 1,124,000 tons in 1810. For some time after 1815, the tonnage slumped; and not until the mid-forties did the totals begin to climb substantially. In 1854, the peak year of building, the American yards turned out 361 ships and barks, 126 brigs, 605 schooners, 669 sloops and boats, and 253 steamers. This total of 2,034 vessels measured 583,000 tons, or ten times the tonnage built in 1830. In the same year, 1854, our merchant marine almost equaled the British in tonnage. Its total continued to increase until 1861, when it reached 5,539,000 tons. The British, however, had drawn still further ahead by that time. At an estimated average value of $40 a ton, our shipping was thus worth about $500,000,000.

Except for steamers and occasional whalers, the corporate form of ownership was rare. The title to the average vessel was divided into eighths, sixteenths, or even sixty-fourths. Occasionally, a wealthy merchant like John Jacob Astor or Stephen Girard would own a considerable fleet outright. Very frequently the partners in a commercial house might own one or more vessels between them. In very many cases, however, the shares were divided among the shipbuilder, the sailmaker, the captain, merchants—sometimes those in various ports—and casual investors who had nothing to do either with the building, the lading, or the sailing of the vessel. One of the owners would generally serve, for a commission, as the operating manager or "ship's husband."

Functionally, there were three classes of merchantmen: the "transient" or tramp; the "regular trader"; and the packet or liner. Most numerous were the transients, which went wherever freights were to be had, not restricting their movements to particular ports. They were the marginal ships, useful in handling seasonal movements of cotton, wheat, sugar, and the like, but never at all certain of business between seasons. The regular trader generally plied between two or more particular ports, primarily engaged in carrying her owners' cargoes, but ready to utilize any extra space for general shipments. The packet, forerunner of the liner, went a step further in regularity by sailing on specified days of the month, instead of waiting around port until she was full.

The packet line service attracted not only passengers but also the bulk of the "fine freight" and less-than-shipload business. Even in the eighteenth century, British Government mail packets had maintained service on schedule, but line sailings by a group of private vessels as common carriers for cargo began in the first week of January 1818, when the first ships of the Black Ball Line sailed from New York and from Liverpool. New York, which had taken the initiative in this business, soon had weekly sailings to Liverpool, with less frequent service to London and to Havre. Closely correlated with this transatlantic shuttle were its coastal packet lines to Charleston, Savannah, Mobile, and New Orleans. These brought cotton for the eastbound ocean voyages from New York and distributed southward part of the merchandise brought from beyond the seas. Lesser lines of schooners or brigs performed similar functions on the shorter coastal runs.

By the time that steamships came on the scene, line service had been thoroughly and successfully established by those "square-riggers on schedule," the sailing packets. The steamers took over line service almost from their beginning, for they had the distinct advantage over sail in that their date of arrival, as well as their day of departure, could normally be predicted in advance.

The lone voyage of the auxiliary steamer *Savannah* to England in 1820 did not lead to immediate results. Regular transatlantic service dates from 1838, when the *Sirius* and *Great Western* arrived at New York from England within a few hours of each other. In 1840, Samuel Cunard began his celebrated line. By the late forties, Congress began to subsidize competition under the American flag. The initial mail lines to Bremen and Havre did not come to much, but the Collins Line to Liverpool gave Cunard severe competition in speed and luxury during the early fifties until, after two severe disasters resulting from excessive speed, Congress withdrew its subsidy. From that time on, liner traffic on the Atlantic shuttle has been for the most part under foreign flags, whereas formerly the Yankee sailing packets had had the field pretty much to themselves.

Whatever the flag, however, New York was generally the western terminus of the cream of the transatlantic trade. Its geographically central position, its excellent harbor, and the various products of its initiative gradually lured business away from its rivals until, by the eve of the Civil War, it was pretty much monopolizing the import business from Europe and handling a substantial share of the nation's exports.

Although New York has thus had definite primacy among our ports for more than a century, no single port has enjoyed a clear-cut second place. Boston ranked second to New York in imports, thanks to its special initiative in the Baltic, the Mediterranean, and the Far East. New Orleans, on the other hand, stood second in exports to New York (for a brief period around 1840 it was actually first), as it was an important outlet for the cotton trade; not all of its cotton by any means traveled up the coast to New York in the "cotton triangle," although most of it was carried in New York vessels. Mobile eventually came third in exports, but imported almost nothing. Philadelphia and Baltimore came next, with the Maryland port gradually catching up with its once-distinguished rival on the Delaware. Gradually, the lesser ports suffered from the tendency toward concentration, accentuated by the railroads, which the major ports pushed westward in competition for the trade of the hinterland. In shipping, as distinct from commerce, the South played a negligible role. New Yord led, as in other fields, with Boston a strong second, while Maine built and sailed ships in a volume out of all proportion to its relatively meager trade. The unequal distribution of shipping was to have an important influence upon the maritime aspects of the Civil War.

Relation to the National Economy

Commerce and shipping gradually lost the high relative position that they had held in the Colonial and early national economy. The half billion dollar investment in shipping in 1860 was overshadowed by investments four or five times that size in railroads, with similarly substantial amounts invested in industrial establishments and banks. Ironically, the money made in commerce and shipping did much to build up those rival forms of economic activity. The lists of the early railroad promoters bristle with names long familiar in the maritime world.[6] John Murray Forbes, for instance, invested his fortune from the China trade in developing the Michigan Central, while the money that Moses Taylor made in Cuba helped to establish the Lackawanna and the City (later National City) Bank. Likewise, the names of Lowell and Lawrence in Massachusetts reflected the transfer of sea-earned capital to the new textile industry. As time went on, the busy spindles and looms of those cities would multiply, while the wharves of nearby Salem lay empty and neglected.

By 1861, the high tide of the early fifties had already begun to ebb, as far as shipping was concerned. Although the total tonnage in that year was higher than ever before, and higher than it was again until the First World War, elements of decay were already apparent. The profits of the early clippers had led to overproduction of ships, so that there was not business enough for all those fast and beautiful vessels, too slender for profitable service on ordinary runs. The panic of 1857 aggravated the situation, while England, which was already using much steam and iron, was once more drawing ahead. The ravages of the Confederate raiders, such as the *Alabama,* upon our shipping in the Civil War ended by frightening great numbers of shipowners into foreign registry for their vessels; but that transfer simply aggravated a decline that had already set in. The half century after the Civil War was the dark age of the American merchant marine.

Shipping, however, was no longer so closely tied up with commerce as it had been in earlier days, when the merchant carried his own cargoes

6 E. C. Kirkland, *Men, Cities, and Transportation,* Vol. I. Cambridge, Mass.: Harvard University Press, 1948.

in his own ships. The nation's imports and exports, therefore, continued merrily upward in volume, even while the American tonnage figures were shrinking away. Importers and exporters could find plenty of foreign vessels to carry their cargoes. While this new state of affairs spelled trouble for the shipping districts of eastern New England, New York was still able to carry on a thriving business along those set lanes that had been developed between the Revolution and the Civil War.

Selected References

GENERAL WORKS

Albion, R. G., *The Rise of New York Port, 1815-1860.* New York: Charles Scribner's Sons, 1939.

Clauder, A. C., *American Commerce as affected by the Wars of the French Revolution and Napoleon.* (Privately printed.) Philadelphia: The University of Pennsylvania, 1932.

Cutler, C. C., *Greyhounds of the Sea: The Story of the American Clipper Ship.* New York: G. P. Putnam's Sons, 1930.

Hutchins, J. G. B., *American Maritime Industries and Public Policy, 1789-1914.* Cambridge, Mass.: Harvard University Press, 1941.

Morison, S. E., *Maritime History of Massachusetts, 1783-1860.* Boston: Houghton Mifflin Company, 1921.

Tyler, D. B., *Steam Conquers the Atlantic.* New York: D. Appleton-Century Company, 1939.

SPECIAL TOPICS

Albion, R. G., *Square-Riggers on Schedule: The New York Sailing Packets to England, France and the Cotton Ports.* Princeton: Princeton University Press, 1938.

———, and J. B. Pope, *Sea Lanes in Wartime: The American Experience, 1775-1942.* New York: W. W. Norton & Company, 1942.

Buck, N. S., *The Development of the Organisation of Anglo-American Trade, 1800-1850.* New Haven: Yale University Press, 1925.

Dulles, F. R., *The Old China Trade.* Boston: Houghton Mifflin Company, 1930.

Homans, J. S., *An Historical and Statistical Account of the Foreign Commerce of the United States.* New York: G. P. Putnam's Sons, 1857.

Johnson, E. R., *et al., History of the Domestic and Foreign Commerce of the United States* (2 vols.). Washington, D. C.: Carnegie Institution of Washington, 1915.

Kirkland, E. C., *Men, Cities, and Transportation* (2 vols.). Cambridge, Massachusetts: Harvard University Press, 1948.

13 · MONEY AND COMMERCIAL BANKING, 1789-1865

The Background

AT THE TIME OF THE ADOPTION of the Constitution the country already had a long acquaintance with monetary and credit problems. During the early Colonial period a scarcity of circulating media had forced a dependence on barter, but the obvious inconveniences involved soon led to the use of various commodities such as tobacco, corn, beaver skins, and Indian wampum as money. By the beginning of the 18th century, coins came into more general circulation. The English pound, shilling, and pence, served as the money of account, but an adverse balance of payments with the mother country limited the supply of this kind of money, and Spanish, Portuguese, and French coins formed the principal specie circulation of the colonies.[1]

Experiments had also been made with paper money issues.[2] Some of these, such as the ones carried out by Pennsylvania between 1723 and 1760, were highly successful in remedying an inadequate monetary supply, without an undue effect on prices.[3] In other instances, especially when used in connection with the financing of military expeditions, the issuance of paper money led to considerable inflation.

The new government founded in 1789 had immediately behind it the monetary experiences during and following the Revolution. Pressed for funds, the Continental Congress had resorted to the printing press to help finance the struggle. Prices rose to a point where the Continental paper money became practically worthless. During 1785 and 1786 this trend was

[1] The original use of English money arose, of course, from the fact that most of the Colonists came from Great Britain and traded almost exclusively with the mother country and with one another. The lack of unity among the Colonial monetary systems and the continued importance of trade with Britain made it convenient to keep accounts in pounds, shillings, and pence, even though this kind of money was rarely seen. An examination of store records for a number of Connecticut merchants shows that in this area, at least, British units were still being used for accounting purposes as late as 1816.

[2] "The first paper money issued by any government in Europe or America was issued by Massachusetts." Richard A. Lester, *Monetary Experiments, Early American and Recent Scandinavian,* p. 7. Princeton, N. J.: Princeton University Press, 1939.

[3] *Ibid.*, pp. 56-111.

sharply reversed and by the end of the latter year, the general level of prices had dropped to approximately the 1776 level.[4]

These experiences served to sharpen more than to resolve the basic issues of monetary standards and policies. Everyone agreed that the country needed an adequate supply of money and credit, but opinion was divided over the advantages of "cheap" versus "sound" money. With the development of commercial banking this argument was carried over into the relative merits of a strong central banking system as opposed to local banking autonomy. While some of the questions raised were settled between 1789, and 1865, others were only temporarily compromised and were a source of bitter dissention in later years.

The Establishment of a Monetary Standard

Among the important tasks undertaken by the First Congress was the establishment of a national coinage system. Under the Constitution, the Federal Government was given the exclusive right "to coin money, regulate the value thereof, and of foreign coins." There was a need for uniformity, especially since the current monetary system was a hodge-podge, the circulating media consisting largely of foreign coins of various types, mostly clipped or worn, together with some bank notes and various kinds of paper money issued by individual Colonies and by the Continental Congress.

In the third of his famous reports to Congress, Alexander Hamilton early in 1791 recommended the establishment of a mint and a national coinage system. Under his plan, which was designed to disturb existing conditions as little as possible, the official unit of account was to be the dollar, with both silver and gold acceptable for coinage into "lawful money." The metallic content of the dollar was fixed at 371.25 grains of silver (the average weight of silver in the Spanish milled dollars currently in circulation). Gold was to be coined at a ratio of 1 to 15, which was about the prevailing market ratio.

Congress accepted Hamilton's recommendations with only minor variations. The mint was established in 1791, and a year later legislation was passed that implemented his suggestions concerning the coinage system. Under the new law, gold eagles ($10), half eagles ($5), and quarter eagles ($2.50) were coined in addition to silver dollars and subsidiary coins. Foreign coins were given legal-tender status for a period of years, after which it was presumed that domestic coins could effectively supplant them.[5]

In view of the bitter controversy that later developed over the merits of bimetallism, it is noteworthy that the First Congress was largely unconcerned by either the ratio or the choice of metals. Hamilton had

[4] See above, Chapter 5.

[5] The Spanish dollar and its subdivisions continued to have legal-tender qualities until 1857.

earlier indicated a preference for gold, but finally recommended the dual standard, because "to annul the use of either of the metals as money is to abridge the quantity of circulating medium, and is liable to all the objections which arise from a comparison of the benefits of a full with the evils of a scanty circulation." [6] This opinion apparently was accepted by most members of Congress. But a fierce debate arose over the question of whether the coins should be stamped with a figure of the head of the Goddess of Liberty or the incumbent president.

The expectation that American coins would soon supplant the foreign money in circulation was not realized. The adverse trade balance with Great Britain that had characterized the pre-Revolutionary period reappeared after the cessation of hostilities. British goods were still prized in American markets; and trade relations, which had been based largely upon personal contacts, were not seriously damaged by the war. Merchandise imports reassumed much of their former importance, and gold and silver again tended to flow out of the United States as payment for the excess of the value of imports over export items.

During the succeeding years, such events as the monetary inflation of 1811–1816 and changes in the market ratios of gold and silver tended to limit the circulation of American coins. The country continued to depend on miscellaneous foreign currencies for its specie circulation.

The general situation began to improve during the early 1840's. Although the trade balance was still adverse, an increasing flow of foreign investments into the United States made it possible to keep gold in circulation, and this metal began to flow into the mint in increasing quantities. With the gold discoveries of 1849, the problem of a specie standard was settled for the remainder of the period before the Civil War.

Some of the principal difficulties connected with establishing a monetary system had thus been solved by 1861. The dollar, with its convenient subdivisions, was established as the monetary standard. To be sure, little success had been achieved in keeping a bimetallic standard in operation. The country operated upon a *de facto* silver standard (using foreign coins) until the change in the mint ratio in 1834, together with the increasing supplies of gold, caused a shift toward a monometallic gold basis, which was maintained until January 1862, when the government abandoned specie payments. The fact that the legal status of silver remained unchanged was, of course, to lead to much controversy at a later date.

Government Paper Money: The Greenbacks

Congress made a tentative gesture toward issuing paper money in connection with the War of 1812. Between 1812 and 1816 something over $36,000,000 of Treasury notes were issued by the Government in payment

[6] *The Works of Alexander Hamilton* (editor, H. C. Lodge), Vol. IV, p. 16. New York: G. P. Putnam's Sons, 1904.

for needed war supplies and services. Only about $4,000,000 of these, however, were of denominations less than $100, and consequently the issues had only a limited general circulation. Furthermore, none had full legal-tender qualities, and they were promptly redeemed after 1815. There is some reason to believe that if the war had lasted longer, subsequent issues of these notes would have acquired further characteristics of government paper money.

Government operations during the Civil War gave a different story. Delay in imposing taxes combined with difficulties in floating sufficient loans to carry on the financial burden of the struggle led to the issuance, beginning in 1862, of some $450,000,000 of United States notes or greenbacks. The issuance of these notes began to drive up prices, which, coupled with the abandonment of specie payments by the government, brought about a premium on gold and silver and drove metallic money out of circulation.[7]

Shortly after the suspension of specie payments a gold exchange market was established in New York near the stock exchange. Here it was possible for individuals and firms to purchase gold at prices in greenbacks that reflected the premium on gold. These prices fluctuated widely, depending in part upon the fortunes of war, but the general trend was upward until the summer of 1864, when it took $285 of greenbacks to purchase gold worth $100 according to prewar standards. After that date the trend was reversed but it was not until just before resumption of specie payments in January 1879 that the premium on gold disappeared.

Banking Development

The Setting

American banking development between 1789 and 1865 revealed many of the basic differences existing between sections and between economic classes. Opposing interests were often closely matched in economic and political strength, and this fact made the controversies all the more vigorous and the results uncertain. Agitation for cheap money, which had been given little expression in the establishment of a national currency, found its outlet in the banking field; meantime a fear of a centralized money monopoly became widespread and persistent. The fact that banking privileges could be granted by the states as well as by the Federal Government made possible a variety of experiments and was still another influence that added greatly to the complexities of the banking structure.

These controversies over the proper functions and scope of banking institutions had their roots in certain features of the general economic setting. This was especially true of the demands for cheap money. Sup-

---

[7] The absence of subsidiary coins was especially exasperating and resort was had to privately coined fractional money and government paper money in 5 cent and 25 cent denominations.

port for such a policy arose basically out of the fact that the country was new and growing rapidly. Population was increasing by over one-third every ten years, and new areas and resources were fast coming into use. There was a continuing desire for capital and a real need for institutions that could mobilize the savings of the community. The possibilities of securing a competence, if not a fortune, engendered a speculative spirit that prompted large numbers of the people to go into debt on a scale that made their financial position precarious in times of economic adversity.

In agriculture the situation was probably the most critical. This branch of the economy occupied by far the largest percentage of the population, and the desire for capital funds to purchase land, stock, and equipment was almost insatiable. It was in the field of agricultural credit that the capital markets were most poorly organized. Commercial houses, in contrast, could not only secure credit from commercial banks, but customarily had foreign connections, especially with English firms, that made borrowing relatively easy. Transportation and industrial ventures were able to call increasingly upon both foreign and domestic sources of investment funds. The farmers, however, found it difficult to borrow for their intermediate and long-term capital needs from banks that were lending on short-term business and commercial paper. Nor could the agriculturists offer the kind of securities that would appeal to the purchasers of stocks and bonds.

Many people saw a close connection between large supplies of money and abundant capital. As a result, a substantial part of the population was quick to resist any attempts that would introduce deflationary elements into the monetary system. To these groups a reduction in the supply of money would bring stabilization or a fall of the price level, which in turn would threaten not only increased debt burdens but a reduced supply of capital funds as well.

Banks apparently offered an easy solution to these various needs and desires. They could issue notes that would add to the circulating media of the country and at the same time contribute materially to the supply of loanable funds. Popular opinion on these matters had no small merit. Banks can be important energizing agencies, especially in communities with little money or without credit facilities. So many American areas approached this description, especially in their earlier history, that probably the introduction of banks made an unusually important contribution to our growth and expansion. Admittedly, ignorance and inexperience led to many unfortunate experiments; but, as one of the pioneer writers on this subject has pointed out, "It is well . . . to remember that while there were undoubted losses from the imperfections inherent in the diverse banking systems well-nigh inseparable from the primitive conditions of those times, the State banks existing before the Civil War were, nevertheless, of great benefit to the commerce and industries of the country.

The 'red dog' and 'wildcat' currency of these banks is generally held up as an example of the impropriety of permitting banks to issue notes, but the banks which redeemed their notes, even after the government suspended specie payments, seem to have been forgotten." [8]

Unincorporated Banking

It would be a mistake to date the beginning of banking operations with the establishment of formally organized institutions. Many communities possessed important banking facilities prior to the introduction of incorporated banks.[9] Commonly these functions were performed by local merchants or storekeepers, who sold goods on a fairly long-term credit basis and accepted in payment the goods and services of their customers. By keeping open accounts for long periods of time, extending in many cases to several years, they greatly economized the use of cash. Furthermore, the merchants contributed to clearing operations within the communities by accepting promissory notes drawn between their customers and by transferring debits and credits on their books. Not infrequently storekeepers combined these services with savings bank or investment banking functions. This was done by lending the proprietor's own capital, and by borrowing and relending surplus funds from other members of the community.[10]

How important this type of country store may have been for American development is impossible to determine, but there is reason to think that it was not uncommon, especially in the earlier stages of our economic development. One of the principal handicaps under which these "cracker-barrel" bankers operated, however, was the limited area within which their credit was acceptable. By contrast, the privilege of note issue enabled incorporated institutions to circulate their credit much more widely. This feature, coupled with limited liability of investors, gave the incorporated banks a considerable advantage over the unincorporated type. As a result, the chartered banks played a much more important part in American economic development.

Growth of State-Incorporated Banks

The country began its national existence with but three chartered banks. The number grew slowly in the succeeding two decades, and not until 1802 were there banking facilities in all of the Seaboard States. Only after that date did they begin to appear in the hinterland. The best esti-

[8] John Jay Knox, *A History of Banking in the United States,* pp. 305-306. New York: Bradford Rhodes & Company, 1900.

[9] Investment banking, which was largely conducted by individuals and partnerships, is discussed below in Chapter 14.

[10] The foregoing information has been gathered from an examination of a number of account books of Connecticut and Massachusetts stores operating in the later eighteenth and early nineteenth centuries.

mate puts the total number at 88 in 1811. The failure in that year to recharter the First Bank of the United States [11] was the occasion for a sharp increase, nearly 250 banks being reported in 1816, the year in which the Second Bank of the United States went into operation. Expansion was again slow down to 1830, reaching an estimated figure of 330 at that date.

An impression of the growth and distribution of banks for the period 1834-1861 is given in the following chart. The record is one of rapid increase in totals up to 1839; then follows a decline for approximately four

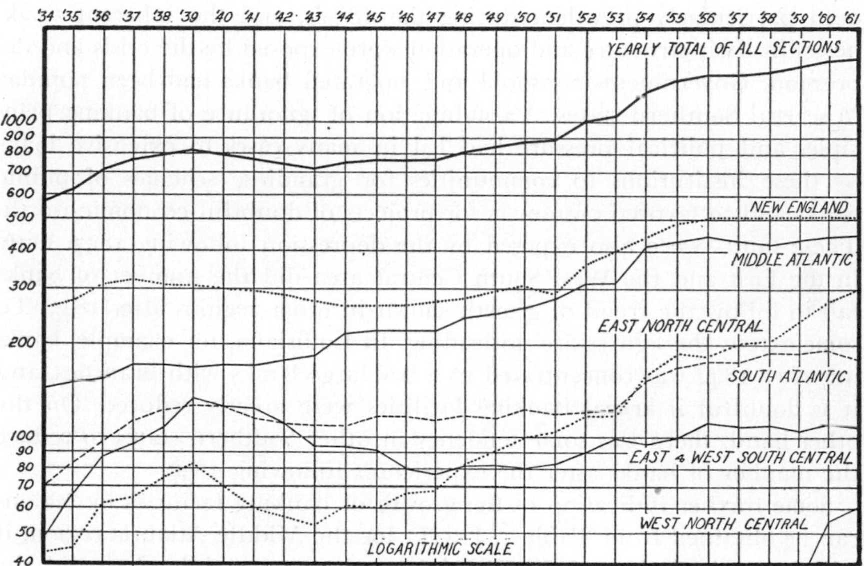

FIG. 1. *Number of State Banks, 1834-1861.* Classification by areas follows the census. Based on Report of the Comptroller of the Currency, 1876.

years, after which there is an almost uninterrupted expansion until 1861. The initial growth following 1834 was closely associated with the failure to recharter the Second Bank of the United States.[12] The decline between 1839 and 1843 was due principally to the panic of 1837 and the subsequent period of depression. After 1843 the increase reflected not only the general expansion that was occurring in the American economy, but a somewhat more lenient legislative attitude toward the granting of charters as well. Prior to the late 1830's, bank charters were granted only by special acts of the state legislatures. This system tended to limit the number of banking institutions and was subject to considerable abuse. In many cases charter privileges became prizes to be handed out to the sup-

[11] See below, pp. 246-247.

[12] See below, pp. 250-251.

porters of the political party in power or in return for compensation of various kinds. New York took the lead in changing this system in 1838 by enacting legislation that permitted the formation of a bank by any group that could meet the requirements set forth in the law. Known as the "free banking act," this measure was copied by a number of other states.[13]

The regional pattern shows some variations from the general picture. It will be noted that the decline in the number of banks was most severe following 1839 in the East North Central and the East and West South Central areas. In the former section the "wildcat" [14] type of banks had been particularly prevalent during the 1830's, and the inherent weaknesses in their structure and operation were exposed by the crisis and depression. Government-sponsored and -operated banks had been popular in several Southern states. A combination of ignorance of banking principles and political pressure had led in many cases to extensive loans by these institutions to communities for grandiose schemes of public works and to favored customers for projects of doubtful economic worth. These faults were also exposed by the depression following 1837. Only in the East and the West South Central area did the number of banks fail to follow the trend of growth shown in other regions after 1843. To some extent the figures are misleading. In Louisiana, for example, banking after 1842 was concentrated in a few large banks with branches, and it is doubtful if actual banking facilities were greatly reduced. On the other hand, there was some tendency in other Southern states to reduce the number of banks after the experiences following 1837.

Some further indication of the growth of banking facilities by regions can be obtained from Table 1. Except for the Middle Atlantic region, it will be noticed that population increased more rapidly than did the number of banks between 1830 and 1850, but that banks again grew faster than population in the following decade. In the Southern states, especially in the Deep South, there were fewer banks for a given number of persons in 1860 than there had been 20 years before. By contrast, the Northern sections all show sharply increased facilities per capita for the same period. Most striking is the relatively large number of banks in New England in comparison to the population. This condition reflects

---

[13] The enthusiasm for banks, however, was by no means universal. Experiences, especially during the panic and depression following 1837, led to a strong anti-bank feeling in several regions. In some states the legislatures refused to renew the charters of existing institutions or to authorize new banks; and in one or two cases, state constitutions explicitly prohibited the establishment of banks. According to Sumner, "In 1852, there were no banks in Florida, Texas, Arkansas, Illinois, Wisconsin, Iowa, Minnesota, Oregon, California, and the District of Columbia." William Graham Sumner, *A History of Banking in the United States*, p. 415. New York: The Journal of Commerce and Commercial Bulletin, 1896.

[14] See below, p. 236.

the extent to which New England had developed transportation, commerce, and manufacturing during the years under consideration. These activities not only stimulated a desire for banking facilities, but, coupled with "Yankee thrift," furnished funds for their establishment.

TABLE 1

ESTIMATED POPULATION PER BANK

(In Thousands)

Year	New England	Middle Atlantic	East North Central	South Atlantic	East and West South Central	West North Central
1840..	7.4	26.0	42.0	24.0	22.0	..
1850..	8.8	23.5	45.0	37.0	54.0	..
1860..	6.3	17.0	25.0	28.0	48.0	35.0

Source of basic data: Report of Comptroller of the Currency, 1876; *Statistical Abstract of the United States,* 1938.

Note. The classifications by areas follow those used by the census.

Bank Promotion

The initial steps in the promotion of banks during the period before 1865 were undertaken either by individuals, by states, or by some combination of the two. The majority of banks probably owed their organization to groups of individuals, but a considerable number were formed and managed by the states, in addition to many that were jointly financed and directed. The privately promoted institutions were established generally in the Eastern and more settled areas, while the state-sponsored banks were located in the South and West. The privilege of investment and partial control by the states was fairly common, although the rights were not always exercised.

Success or failure of the banks apparently had little to do with the form of their original promotion. The state-operated banks of Kentucky, Illinois, Tennessee, Florida, Mississippi, and Alabama were on the whole dismal failures, whereas Ohio and Indiana could boast of well-run and successful systems. The mixed form and the privately organized institutions showed similar variations. The need for banking facilities and the general intelligence with which they operated apparently had more to do with their success than did their institutional form.[15]

The specific motives for establishing banks varied considerably. The state-operated systems usually received their support on the grounds that

---

15 A similar observation may be made concerning legal restrictions. Knox points out that "A banking system succeeded well in Louisiana under almost identical laws with those of banking systems in Alabama, Mississippi, and Florida, which were most ridiculous failures. The banking laws of Michigan were very similar to those of New York, but the banks in the latter state were generally successful while those of Michigan became a by-word and a hissing." John Jay Knox, *History of Banking in the United States,* p. 314. New York: Bradford Rhodes & Co., 1900.

they would make important contributions to general welfare.[16] Not infrequently a need for a special type of credit, particularly for agriculture, was an important factor in their promotion. Individuals were attracted to banking for a variety of reasons. To some the opportunities for speculation or for fraud had special appeal. General ignorance of banking procedures, coupled with laxity in the enforcement of laws, gave rise to a number of amusing and sometimes tragic episodes; the term "wildcat" banking, for example, arose from the practice of locating redemption offices in inaccessible spots such as the depth of a forest where there were few human habitations "but plenty of wildcats." Promoters of such ventures had no thought of conducting a regular banking institution; their actions were little more defensible than those of counterfeiters. The failure of these schemes fell most heavily upon the innocent and gullible who were left holding worthless notes.[17] While each area had its own experiences of this sort, their importance should not be exaggerated, since quantitatively they probably were not of great significance.

The investment opportunities offered by banks made an appeal to a sizable number of persons. How profitable banking actually was during this period is not known, but it seems clear that bank stock stood high among investment outlets. The faith in the soundness of such investments is shown by the provision by some states that religious and educational groups be allowed to subscribe to a certain portion of the securities of newly established banks.[18]

While available evidence is by no means conclusive, it seems probable that the people most active in the promotion and management of the average bank were groups and individuals primarily interested in developing sources of credit. In view of the great demands for capital, it is not astonishing that the possibilities offered by banking institutions should be developed in this manner. In some instances the establishment of a bank merely formalized a practice that had been carried on previously: namely, the pooling of resources, which would be loaned to the various participants. In other cases, the purpose was to secure a preferential position in respect to the funds contributed by others or created by

[16] Thus, the preamble of the charter of the Bank of the State of Alabama stated that the object of its establishment was "to provide for a safe and profitable investment of the funds of the State and to secure an extended and undepreciating currency." It might be added that salaries and privileges of the officials of this bank were such that appointments became a part of the political "spoils" system of the state.

[17] W. G. Sumner, *History of Banking in the United States,* contains numerous examples of fraudulent and highly speculative banking.

[18] The high standing of the stock of an established bank is illustrated by the following names selected from among the list for 1839 of stockholders of the Canal Bank of Portland, Maine: Charity Fund, First Parish; Female Orphan Asylum; Trustees, School Fund, North Yarmouth; Trustees, Portland Academy; Lodge Charity Fund; Trustees, Ministerial Fund; Mutual Fire Insurance Company, Saco; Institution for Savings for Portland and Vicinity; Proprietors of Atheneum.

the institution.[19] As a result, several interesting and fundamental questions having to do with the functions and responsibilities of bank officials were raised by contemporaries. The issues became focused upon the propriety of loans to officers and stockholders. Opponents of any but nominal loans to officials insisted that the officers should manage the bank for the benefit of the stockholders. The privilege of doing business under a public charter was stressed, and it was felt that the advantages should be open to the public on a more impersonal basis. On the other hand, there were the obvious difficulties of getting officials who "would inspire the confidence of the community" and at the same time not be logical candidates for large loans. Ordinarily no salaries were paid to members of the boards of directors, and even the presidents usually received only a nominal compensation.

In general, the matter was compromised. Most states eventually put specific limits on the amounts that could be borrowed in this fashion. But evasion was not too difficult,[20] and the situation seemed to be governed by the circumstances affecting the individual bank. Like many other features of American banking during its early history, the practice was not in itself unsound. The danger lay in the excessive or unscrupulous use of the privilege.[21]

Banks often found it difficult, especially in newer areas, to raise capital, as surplus funds that could be used for this purpose were limited. One of the commonest devices used to meet this deficiency involved the use of stock notes. Under this arrangement purchasers of bank stock would make a small "down payment," and the unpaid balance would then be borrowed from the bank on personal notes, with the stock as collateral. In some cases even the "down payment" was omitted, the entire amount being advanced by the bank. The extent to which banks were founded in this way varied considerably. Most institutions started with more or less capital contributed by stockholders, but probably only a small fraction of

---

[19] Even public officials were sensitive to this possibility. Dewey points out that one of the reasons why many bank charters contained the proviso that the State should be permitted to own part of the stock was "... because ownership would place the State in the light of a favored customer when it wished to borrow." Davis R. Dewey, *State Banking Before the Civil War,* p. 33. Washington, D. C.: The National Monetary Commission, 1910.

[20] The Maine Bank Commissioners, for example, commented in their Annual Report for 1849, "The Commissioners have again to regret, that in several of the banks the limitation of the law in relation to the indebtedness of the directors, is very little heeded; and as this is the rock most dangerous to banking institutions, it might be well to mark it by more severe penalties. Who ever knew, or heard of the failure of a banking institution, except through excessive loans to the directors? The public seldom, if ever, suffer from any other cause."

[21] Even the conservative Massachusetts Bank as late as 1860 permitted loans to directors to the amount of $450,000, or about one-third of the total loans of the Bank at the time. N. S. B. Gras, *The Massachusetts First National Bank of Boston, 1784-1934,* p. 122. Cambridge, Mass.: Harvard University Press, 1937.

the banks established during the period before 1861 began operations with their stock fully paid. The practice was clearly open to abuse. In extreme form, it permitted individuals to start banks with no financial risk to themselves. If the venture proved successful, the stock could be paid for out of earnings; if it failed, the incidence was borne by others. But the fact that a great many of the institutions founded during these years continued to operate successfully is evidence that the procedure was not necessarily bad.

TABLE 2

STATE BANKS' RATIO OF SPECIE HOLDINGS TO DEPOSITS AND CIRCULATION

(*Figures Are in Millions.*)

Date	*Deposits*	*Circulation*	*Total*	*Specie*	*Percentage*
1836	$115	$140	$255	$40	17.0
1837	129	149	276	38	13.7
1840	76	107	183	33	18.2
1845	88	90	178	44	24.8
1850	110	131	241	45	18.5
1855	190	187	377	54	14.3
1860	254	207	461	84	18.0

Source of basic data: John Jay Knox, *History of Banking*, p. 312. New York: Bradford Rhodes & Co., 1900.

Lack of specie presented another difficulty that frequently faced our early banking institutions. Charters commonly provided that a portion of the funds subscribed for bank stock was to be paid in specie. It will be recalled, however, that there was a chronic shortage of specie well down into the 1840's. Resort was made to various schemes that would meet this deficiency. On occasion, specie would be paid in and kept in the vaults long enough to satisfy the legal requirements, after which it would be promptly withdrawn, possibly to serve in a similar capacity for another institution. The bank examiners for Michigan complained at one time that "Gold and silver flew about the country with the celerity of magic; its sound was heard in the depths of the forest, yet like the wind, one knew not whence it came or whither it was going." The examiners soon began to recognize individual coins that would turn up each time they examined a new bank.[22]

In some instances specie certificates were acceptable instead of specie. These, too, could be borrowed, for a consideration, by those who wished to start banks, and returned when the ordeal of examination by bank commissioners was safely passed. But these examples of attempts to do banking with little or no specie reserves should not be given undue importance. The accompanying tabulation (Table 2), while based upon

[22] John Jay Knox, *History of Banking*, p. 734. New York: Bradford Rhodes & Co., 1900.

incomplete data, shows that, after 1836 at least, the banks had on the average a considerable amount of specie reserves against their liabilities.

Banking Operations

The New York Bank Commissioner's Report for 1831 states, "The common operations of banking are receiving deposits for safe keeping, loaning the floating balance of such deposits, borrowing large sums at a reduced rate of interest upon deposits, and employing the average balance in productive investments, loaning capital upon real estate, accommodation, or business paper, purchasing and selling bills of exchange, circulating bank paper as currency upon the credit either of a portion of capital received for redeeming it, or upon the floating balance of deposits."

This list of operations, probably typical of most of the state systems of the time, gives clear evidence of the diverse activities engaged in by the American banks. To be sure, not all banks engaged equally in each of these types of business. Specific institutions tended to reflect their economic environment. This was especially true of banking done in the cities as contrasted with that in the towns or rural districts.

The first banks were established in urban centers, and the three that were operating in 1789 are typical of later banks in the larger cities. These were the Bank of North America, the Bank of New York, and the Bank of Massachusetts, located, respectively, in Philadelphia, New York, and Boston. Doing business in the principal business and commercial cities of the country, these institutions had certain common characteristics. Their establishment represented a response to the growing need for banks that could furnish short-term commercial loans; and to a considerable extent their operations only formalized an earlier practice of pooling resources, which had for some time been carried on by merchants in these cities.[23] They functioned according to the accepted standards of European commercial banks; loans were chiefly on short-term commercial paper and customers were principally merchants and businessmen.

Banks were not long confined to commercial centers, however. Typical of the conditions leading to the establishment of banks in many other parts of the country is the following description of the situation in western New York State in the late 1830's: "Here was concentrated the demand for new banks, an expression of the need for capital to improve farm lands, to build flour, grist, and saw mills, to buy up real estate for speculating purposes. Cotton, woolen, grass, rope, paper, oilcloth, leather factories, and iron works were being established and required capital accumulation not available to promoters. The aid of banks was enlisted. Even city merchants, whose credit requirements were suited to the in-

[23] See Bray Hammond's interesting article, "Long and Short Term Credit in Early American Banking," *Quarterly Journal of Economics,* Vol. XLIX (1935).

terests of commercial banks, began to ask for longer maturities, under the pressure from their country purchases." [24]

To meet such demands the banks were forced to do a somewhat different kind of business from that carried on by those operating in commercial centers. The principal variation concerned the nature and length of their loans. Much borrowing was done, not for the purpose of financing short-term, self-liquidating projects, but with the object of meeting intermediate or long-term capital needs. Since both bank notes and most bank deposits were payable on demand, the banks were placed in the position of having to pay out of immediate-order funds that were not collectible until a considerable time period had elapsed. Some attempt was usually made to preserve the form of commercial loans by accepting paper repayable within a short term, and then renewing such loans as they came due, actually furnishing long-term capital funds.

The dangers to the banks involved depended upon the circumstances under which they were operating. As long as the loans were sound, the banks could be reasonably certain of repayment. Furthermore, the fact that most loans were taken by customers in the form of bank notes made long-term lending less embarrassing to the banks than might otherwise have been expected, for, in contrast with checks drawn against deposits, bank notes tend to remain in circulation for much longer periods of time. In times of uncertainty, however, when the solvency of particular institutions or of the banks as a whole was questioned, banks that had made long-term loans were especially vulnerable (although their loans were not necessarily inherently unsound) and were likely to be thrown into bankruptcy as depositors or holders of their notes presented their claims for redemption into cash.

Security of Note Issues

Almost without exception the states, through the provisions in individual bank charters or in their general banking laws, made some attempt to protect the holders of bank notes. The plans varied a great deal as different areas attempted to work out satisfactory solutions. Among the many schemes that were tried a few, however, deserve special mention because of their importance for later American banking policies or because of their fairly widespread use before 1861. Because notes rather than deposits continued to be the most important item in bank liabilities until well after the middle of the nineteenth century, legislative interest centered primarily on the protection of all persons who received bank notes in the ordinary course of business.

One plan allowed banks to issue notes against general assets, usually according to some ratio between the volume of notes and the amount of

---

[24] This quotation is from an unpublished manuscript by Anna Jacobsen, *Commercial Banking in New York Before 1863*, p. 17.

the bank's capital. This plan was especially important in New England, where, in conjunction with the Suffolk System, it worked quite successfully, under the supervision of state bank commissions and because it was aided by a comparatively conservative economic environment.

Meantime New York, in 1829, had put in its Safety Fund System, which called for a total contribution of three per cent of the capital of the participating banks to form a protective fund administered by the State Treasurer. As originally passed, the Safety Fund was designed to protect both depositors and noteholders of failed banks. The State Treasurer was therefore authorized to dip into the safety fund to make up any deficit that remained after the assets of an insolvent bank had been liquidated. As it turned out, before all the payments to the creditors of failed banks between 1840 and 1842 could be made, the "safety fund" was exhausted, and the State of New York was forced to advance enough funds to make up the deficiency. As a result, the law was changed in 1842 to provide protection only for noteholders.[25] Later safety fund contributions by the banks repaid the State for its advances. In principle the safety fund had much to recommend it as a device for the protection of the public against bank failures: it was an early version of our present guarantee of bank liabilities.[26] The system, however, was not popular outside New York, owing in part at least to the difficulties that that state experienced with the administration of the safety fund.

The first statutory emphasis upon reserves as a way of insuring the quality of deposits and notes occurred in Louisiana. By legislation passed in 1842, the banks of the state were required to operate under the following principal provisions: at least one-third of each bank's deposits and circulation had to be backed by specie, with the rest protected by short-term, non-renewable commercial paper. Renewal of paper at maturity was forbidden, and anyone who requested such a renewal was to have his account closed and his name sent to all the banks as delinquent. Finally, a statement of the condition of the banks in New Orleans had to be published weekly.

Strictly enforced, these provisions carried the Louisiana banks through business crises in the forties and fifties and allowed them to weather the outbreak of the war in 1861 without suspension. In many respects, however, the situation in Louisiana was unique. Five institutions with central offices in New Orleans and with branches throughout the state did all the banking for the state. At that time, New Orleans was one of the world's most important commercial centers and the chief market through which

25 The logic of this provision lay in the fact that noteholders, unlike depositors, usually had little choice whether they would accept bank notes offered in payment. This was especially true of the more uninformed members of the community.

26 Canada adopted a similar system in 1890, which has operated quite successfully. The Federal Deposit Insurance Corporation established by Congress in 1935 also follows this principle in respect to bank deposits.

gold and silver from Mexico made their way into the United States. These conditions contributed to the system's success, and obviously were not the typical circumstances that characterized most American areas. While the plan was subsequently followed in part by New York and Massachusetts, it found little acceptance elsewhere.

New York's free banking system provided the most popular but by no means the most effective plan for safeguarding the issue of bank notes. This legislation, it will be recalled, was passed in 1838, and permitted any person or group of persons to start a bank provided the stipulations of the law were met. Under the act, no bank could circulate notes until it had first deposited approved securities equivalent in value to 100 per cent of the note issues with the comptroller of the state. In case of default by any bank, the securities thus deposited were to be sold and the proceeds applied to the redemption of the notes.

The New York law was widely copied; indeed, some 16 states eventually adopted similar legislation. Nor are the causes for the popularity of free banking hard to explain: free banking fitted in well with the generally accepted doctrine of equal rights; security-backed bank notes promised to provide abundant circulation; and banks could collect interest from the securities that they had deposited as well as from lending their notes. From the standpoint of banking operations, however, the system had a serious limitation. Banks could be established with little or no regard for the existing credit needs of the communities in which they were located. Any person or group of persons, no matter how inexperienced they might be in financial matters, could start a bank. As a result, many institutions originally formed under this type of legislation were organized chiefly for the purpose of issuing currency, with little or no thought given to the proper functions of banking.[27] Without care in making loans, many of these banks were soon forced to default on their notes, and it was then discovered that the securities pledged were often as worthless as the claims issued against them. It was only when the laws were modified and when state officials became more careful in their administering, and the banks on their part recognized the necessity of doing a banking

[27] The following description illustrates how a number of "banks" were established under the free banking act adopted by Indiana in 1853. "A thousand or two dollars in cash was all that was required to start a bank. This was needed to pay for engraving the plates and printing the bills. An embryo banker would go to New York with a thousand dollars, order an engraver to make the plates, and print $50,000 in bills. He would next visit a broker and negotiate for $50,000 of the bonds of some State, get them at a discount, and instruct the broker to send them to Indianapolis in care of the Auditor of State, the price to be paid on their delivery at Indianapolis. He would then go to Indianapolis with his $50,000 of new bills, get the Auditor to countersign them, and pay for the bonds with the bills and have a surplus left. *Thus a new bank would be established, without banking-house, furniture or anything else.*" John Jay Knox, *History of Banking*, p. 702.

business, that the security-backed bank note system began to operate more effectively and with fewer hazards to noteholders.

Interbank Relationships and Centralized Banking

Once established, American banks tended rather quickly to develop certain interbank relations. These connections took a number of forms and in their more advanced stages involved a centralization of those functions that concerned the operation of the banking system as a whole.

Development of Clearing

Clearing of accounts was one of the first interbank relations to develop. This operation began on an informal basis, with each bank in a town or city sending its claims by messenger to all the other banks. Settlements of balances were customarily made by the payment of cash on a daily or weekly basis. The scheme greatly economized on the use of specie, since the balances to be paid ordinarily amounted to only a small fraction of the total liabilities to other banks. With an increase in the number of participants, the use of messengers grew more complex and wasteful of time. As a result, several formal clearing house associations were formed in the principal financial centers. New York led the way with the establishment of its association in 1853, and was followed by Boston in 1856 and Philadelphia in 1858.

Clearing between communities was accomplished by the development of correspondent relations. The primary purpose of such an arrangement was to avoid the expense of sending out-of-town checks and notes directly to each of the banks at which they were payable. A simpler way to handle this problem was to arrange with some centrally located bank to accept these items and provide for their collection. Hence it presently became the practice for country banks to maintain balances with correspondent banks in the chief commercial and business centers, and to allow the correspondent bank to use these funds as compensation for the expense involved in clearing interbank accounts of the country banks participating in the plan. The services of the city institutions were not confined to the handling of collection items. Country banks were able to call upon their urban correspondents for a number of important financial services. Thus the city banks acted as agents in investing country-bank funds in security markets, they furnished information regarding credit ratings of firms and individuals, and they gave advice regarding future business trends.

Centralization of Reserves

As was noted above, the development of correspondent relations between banks tended to concentrate funds in the principal commercial and industrial centers. This trend was accentuated as country banks began lending their surplus funds to city institutions. The incentive for such loans arose from several circumstances. In the first place, much of the business done by country banks was seasonal in nature, a fact that left them periodically with idle funds; hence, investment in the metropolitan areas was one way of increasing earnings in off seasons. Second, many banks had a lending capacity that exceeded local demands at current or customary rates, a situation that also resulted in urban lending.[28] Finally, as many payments made by banks for their customers were payable in centers like Boston, New York, Baltimore, and Philadelphia, it was convenient to maintain balances in those cities for such purposes. Banks in the commercial centers, on the other hand, had sufficient opportunity for relending to make it worth while to pay interest on these deposits of the country banks.

This trend toward centralization of funds had important implications for the American banking structure as a whole. Country banks began to treat their deposits with the city banks as the equivalent of reserves in their own vaults. In case of emergency they expected that such deposits could be quickly withdrawn.[29] By 1850 such concentration had reached important proportions. One difficulty resulting from this arrangement was that banks in the urban centers, especially New York, held the main banking reserves of the country without having accepted the responsibility which that concentration implied.[30] If these reserves were to serve the purpose of meeting an emergency, there had to be skillful and united action by the holders, but this task the urban institutions were unable or unwilling to assume. As a result of the freezing of accounts in New York, the panic of 1857 was much more serious than it otherwise would have been. This crisis heralded a series of collapses in the banking system that were to plague the American economy throughout the remainder of the century and into the first decade of the next.

Central Banking

The absence of a strong centralized banking organization constituted the principal structural weakness of the American banking structure for some 80 years after 1833. In no other country has the unit system occupied such an important place. This peculiarly American institution came to dominate American banking after a heated controversy over the rela-

---

[28] In some instances state laws set maximum rates of interest that were below what could be obtained in unregulated markets.

[29] In 1852, for example, the Bank Commissioners of Vermont, in explaining the relatively small amount of specie reserve held by the banks in that state, accused their critics of overlooking the fact that "our deposits remaining in the city banks, and now amounting to $1,265,000, are, to all intents and purposes, so much specie laid by for the redemption of our circulation; and that too, at a place altogether more convenient for the public, than at the counter of each Bank." Bank Commissioner's Report for Vermont (1852), p. 84.

[30] See below, Chapter 28.

tive merits of centralized versus decentralized banking and after some 40 years' experience with the operation of the First and Second Banks of the United States.

As will presently be made clear, the withdrawal of the Government's deposits from the Second Bank in 1833 and the failure to extend the life of that bank beyond 1836 were events which, together with the enthusiastic adoption of the free banking principle a few years later, opened the way for the spread and triumph of a unit system of banking. It is, therefore, the abandonment of the principle of central banking that lends special interest to the history of the First and Second Banks, institutions that had actually performed the major functions of central banks from 1791 to 1811 and from 1816 to 1833.

The First Bank of the United States

Under the terms of a 20-year charter granted by Congress in 1791, the First Bank of the United States was organized along lines suggested by Hamilton the preceding year. Total capital was set at $10,000,000, three-quarters of which was open to purchase by the public, the rest having been reserved for the Government. Its note issues, which were limited to the amount of its capital, were receivable for public dues as long as the Bank maintained the ability to redeem its notes in specie on demand. Provision was made for the establishment of branches in the important commercial and financial centers.

The Bank was closely connected with the fiscal operations of the United States Government. Some $13,500,000 was lent to the Treasury over the 20-year period; moreover, the Bank, acting as general fiscal agent for the Government, was the principal holder of Government accounts and through its eight branches facilitated the transfer of Government funds from place to place without charge. For the Government, the participation in the banking venture proved to be very remunerative: some $700,000 profit was realized from the sale (between 1796 and 1802) of the original $2,000,000 subscription. The lending operations of the Bank and its branches were extensive. Its loans were made customarily for 60 days, and were secured chiefly by commercial paper. As a result, merchants, manufacturers, and occasional wealthy landowners were its principal customers.

The First Bank performed important functions and services for the community as a whole. Its notes, issued in denominations of $5 and upwards, had general acceptance throughout the country; they provided a standard type of money at a time when the Government was having difficulty keeping its coins in circulation.[31] Total circulation was kept at moderate levels, well within the limits set by the charter. The branches

[31] See above, pp. 228-229.

acted as clearing agencies for their respective districts and to some extent provided a national clearing system for state bank notes. Since the Bank held the principal specie reserves for the country, one of the reasons for limiting note issues was the desire to protect these reserves. By conservative issue and loan policies, the Bank maintained a general creditor position with respect to the state banks. This enabled it to check overexpansion on the part of the state banks, since it might threaten to call for payment in specie of these balances owed to it whenever the state institutions appeared to be exceeding the bounds of sound banking practices. Many of these activities, it will be noted, are of the kind usually associated with the operations of a central bank: holding specie reserves, serving as a lender of last resort, exercising control over the quality and quantity of the currency, and centralizing clearing for the banks as a whole. It is more than likely that these functions would have been expanded had the Bank's life been extended beyond 1811.

In spite of its accomplishments, however, and to some extent because of them, the renewal of the charter of the First Bank met strong opposition. Part of the opposition came from the state banks. These institutions felt that they would secure several advantages if they could prevent a recharter of the Bank. Thus they thought that they would become the recipients of the Government deposits if their large and powerful rival could be eliminated from competition. In this connection, it should be understood that the First Bank's refusal to accept the notes of non-specie-paying state banks had created bitter antagonism inasmuch as this policy had restricted the profits of "wildcat" banks.

The obvious advantages of the First Bank as a financial institution would probably have been sufficient to offset this opposition had not personal and political considerations come into the picture. As an institution established by the Federalists, it was under fire from the Republicans. Personal antagonism to Secretary Gallatin by certain disgruntled spoilsmen intensified the opposition. In the course of the debates on recharter, the possibility of foreign control was raised. Actually, even though a large block of stock was held by Englishmen, the danger of foreign control was nonexistent, for the reason that under the charter foreign stockholders had no vote. The final decision on recharter was made early in 1811. The vote in the House was 65 to 64 against recharter. In the Senate there was a tie, 17 to 17, which was broken by a vote against the Bank by George Clinton, the vice-president. By such a narrow margin was the decision made.[32]

---

[32] In a most illuminating article James D. Wetterau suggests that the directors of the Bank were particularly inept in political matters. Their chief lobbying agent in Washington was "tactless and uncompromising." See James O. Wetterau, "New Light On The First Bank of The United States," *Pennsylvania Magazine of History and Biography* (July, 1937), pp. 284-285.

The demise of the First Bank was a signal for a sharp increase in the number of state banks. Within five years they expanded almost threefold—from 88 to 246. Meanwhile those officials charged with Governmental finances had much cause to regret the failure to recharter the National Bank: faced with the necessity of financing the war that began in 1812, the Treasury sorely missed the services of the First Bank. In the absence of the clearing mechanism formerly supplied by that establishment, Government funds, now deposited with a selected group of state institutions, were difficult to transfer from one area to another. Moreover, since the notes of the state banks could not be circulated beyond a limited geographical area except at a discount, the Treasury suffered from a loss of purchasing power whenever Governmental receipts could not be equalized within each of the regions, a situation that often occurred.

For various reasons, the War of 1812 was financed chiefly through loans,[33] and here again the absence of a national bank was unfortunate. Such a bank could have been of great assistance in the distribution of Government securities. State institutions, to be sure, bought large amounts of Government issues, but paid for them with notes of limited acceptability. To make matters worse, the securities were then used by the state banks as a basis for further note issues, and in this way the banking system contributed markedly to the price inflation accompanying the prosecution of the war. In the autumn of 1814, all the banks outside New England suspended specie payments, an action that in turn made their notes subject to further depreciation.

The Second Bank of the United States

In spite of these difficulties, no agreement about the re-establishment of a United States Bank could be reached until after the close of the war, when Congress faced the problem of restoring some order to the highly disturbed monetary and banking system. Opposition came from the same elements that had brought about the end of the First Bank. Arguments against the new institution followed familiar lines: too much power would be concentrated in the hands of a few; the Government's connections with the bank would be dangerous; all these and many other objections were raised. Proponents of the new bank were successful, however, in getting a bill through Congress early in 1816.[34]

Like its predecessor, the new institution was given a 20-year charter. Capital was set at $35,000,000, four-fifths of which was open to public subscription, the remainder being reserved for the Government. Provision was made for 25 directors, 5 to be appointed by the President of the

[33] See below, Chapter 16.

[34] After a bitter debate, the measure was passed by the House by a margin of 80 to 71. Little opposition was met in the Senate. See Ralph C. H. Catterall, *The Second Bank of the United States,* pp. 19-21. Chicago: University of Chicago, 1903.

United States and the rest by the stockholders residing in the United States. The Bank's notes were to be receivable for all payments to the United States. Both notes and deposits were to be redeemable in specie, failure to make such redemption being punishable by a levy of 12 per cent per annum on the amount of the unpaid claims. Government deposits were to be made with the Bank, while the Bank on its part was to effect the transference of these funds without charge. Branches were to be established wherever the directors thought desirable.

The Second Bank began operations in July, 1816. A combination of ignorance, ineptness, and chicanery almost wrecked the institution during the first few years of its existence. Its first president, William Jones, was a political appointee who had no very clear conception as to how the Bank should be operated. The officers of the parent bank and the board of directors of many of the branches were likewise incompetent; consequently, the Bank entered into an unwise policy of expansion, especially in the Southern and Western portions of the country. By pledging the Bank's own stock for loans, several officials engaged in extensive stock speculation. In one case fraudulent practices were used to cover up the speculative activities of the president and cashier of the Baltimore branch. These events served to put the Bank into a precarious financial position by the latter part of 1818. At this point officials at the parent office in Philadelphia began hastily to contract its loans and note circulation. This action occurred at a most inopportune time, since the country was just recovering from the disturbances that had accompanied the recent war with England. The contraction by the Bank initiated a panic, leading one contemporary to observe that "the Bank was saved, but the people were ruined." Nor was it only the immediate effects that were unfortunate; the Bank incurred the ill will of thousands of people in the Western and Southern sections of the country, which proved to be an important factor in the later struggle over recharter.

In 1819 a new president, Langdon Cheves, was appointed. He immediately set about to improve the Bank's financial position by reducing loans and note issues and by arranging for imports of borrowed specie from Europe. These and other actions put the operations of the Bank on a more conservative basis. Because Cheves felt that his job was accomplished, and because the low dividends resulting from his cautious administration had caused dissatisfaction among the stockholders, Cheves resigned his position, and in January, 1823, Nicholas Biddle assumed the presidency.

It was under the management of its third president that the Bank began to develop its potentialities. A member of a prominent Philadelphia family, Biddle, when he assumed office at the age of 37, had already distinguished himself as a scholar, lawyer, and student of banking and monetary questions. He set about to increase the business done by the

Bank without endangering its financial position: close supervision was exercised by the parent bank in Philadelphia over the operation of the various branches; loans on short-term commercial paper were increased; and dealings in domestic and foreign exchange were greatly expanded. Within a few years Biddle had clearly demonstrated his ability and skill as an executive.

The Bank's greatest importance stemmed from its position in the general monetary and credit structure of the country. Its notes, which were acceptable "from Montreal to Mexico City," added a much needed unity to the nation's monetary circulation, and the Bank's issues furnished an "elastic" currency, as a considerable volume of loans was made on short-term paper for seasonal needs. With branches in the important commercial centers, the Bank provided a convenient clearing system for the country. Its large dealings in domestic exchange further facilitated the interregional movement of funds. One of the most important accomplishments of the Second Bank was the practical elimination of discounts on state bank notes. Two devices were used to achieve this result. According to law, state bank issues were acceptable for Government debts provided that the notes were redeemable in specie. The Second Bank was given the power to certify whether any state institution was meeting this requirement. To have its notes made unacceptable for Government debts was a serious blow to the prestige of any bank. Should this method prove ineffective, the Second Bank, which consistently maintained a creditor position in relation to the state banks, could present a collection of notes to the doubtful institutions for specie payment and thereby threaten their solvency.

The Second Bank also held the principal reserves of the banking system. It was in a real sense "the lender of last resort" in that it had to meet any large and unexpected demands for specie. Its policy under Biddle was to maintain a high ratio of specie to its liabilities. As added protection, the bank kept favorable balances with its European correspondents, upon which it might call for aid in times of emergency. The Bank handled all Government accounts and provided for quick and easy transference of funds between areas. Further aid was extended the Treasury in financing, and repayments of Government debts were handled through the Bank without disturbance to the money market.

From the foregoing account it may be seen that the Second Bank occupied a most important place in the national economy. This position was not achieved, however, without arousing animosity and antagonism in many quarters. Criticisms stemmed from many sources, ranging from complaints by disgruntled politicians over alleged discrimination in regard to loans, to the honest convictions on the part of many people regarding the constitutionality of the Bank. More fundamental was the popular distrust of a powerful private institution, especially in the banking field, and the dislike of the restrictions on monetary expansion, especially in the Southern and Western parts of the country. The latter point merits special attention. There can be little doubt that the Bank was operated on a conservative basis after 1819 and would have continued to act as a restraining influence upon expansion of bank credit in those areas that were most eager for an "easy money" policy.

Yet, in spite of criticism for its conservatism, under the guidance of Biddle the Bank had expanded its business, especially in the South and West, where credit demands were most urgent. In July, 1821, total discounts and holdings of domestic exchanges stood at some $30,000,000, while the circulation of notes was around $4,000,000. Ten years later, the corresponding items were something over $57,000,000 and $19,000,000.[35] To some extent these increases were at the expense of state banks, but on the whole the data indicate a considerable expansion. Had this policy been continued, there is no reason to suppose that the banking structure as a whole would have been placed in a financial straightjacket through the operations of the Second Bank.

The year that Andrew Jackson became President, in 1829, the prestige of the Bank was such that contemporaries were quite sure it had taken a permanent place in the American scene. But this opinion underestimated the strength of the opposition, which came from a number of sources: from those who doubted the Bank's constitutionality, from states that resented any infringement on their rights, from banks whose activities had been restrained, and from persons who felt that democracy was being threatened by the existence of a great "money monopoly."

The succeeding struggle over the question of recharter almost inevitably centered around the personalities of Biddle and Jackson. It would be difficult to imagine two persons more divergent in background, interests, and philosophy than the aristocratic gentleman from Philadelphia and the man of the people from the backwoods of Tennesese. Yet at the outset there seemed to be no differences between the two in respect to the Bank that could not be compromised. Jackson apparently had genuine doubts about the constitutionality of the institution, and he displayed some concern over its monopoly position. But on the whole he was not unfriendly to either Biddle or the Bank, and as a practical administrator he was quite aware of its services to the Government. Biddle, on his part, was willing to make concessions on many points in order to secure favorable action. The great danger lay in the possibility that the question would become a political issue and then fail to be decided upon its merits. This contingency Biddle resolved at first to avoid; but partisans on both sides tended to show a regrettable lack of restraint in their arguments, and, moreover, Jackson's public statements appeared less conciliatory in tone

[35] These data are from Ralph C. H. Catterall, *The Second Bank of the United States*, p. 501.

than Biddle had expected them to be. Biddle was under increasing pressure from opponents of the President to push for recharter and in this way make the Bank an issue in the presidential election of 1832. After much consideration, Biddle finally decided on this policy. A bill for recharter was passed by Congress in July, 1832, and was promptly vetoed by Jackson, who by this time was thoroughly convinced that the Bank was a dangerous institution. The question of the recharter became one of the principal isues in the political campaign. Jackson's overwhelming victory left no doubt concerning the final decision, and the Bank ended its existence as a national institution with the expiration of its charter four years later, a victim principally of political ineptness on the part of its proponents.[36]

The Independent Treasury

In 1833 Jackson decided that the Government's deposits in the Second Bank should be withdrawn and placed in selected state institutions. Accordingly, contracts were made with a group of state banks which agreed to perform the same services for the Government that formerly had been rendered by the Second Bank. Meanwhile, as has been noted, the number of state banks was rapidly increasing. Unfortunately, a large proportion of the funds from these newly created institutions went into speculation, especially for the purchase of land. The "speculative bubble" burst early in 1837, and was followed by a restriction in the money markets, a sharp drop in prices, and other events associated with panic conditions, including a general suspension of species payments by banks throughout the country.

As a result of the panic, the Federal Government suffered much inconvenience and some losses on the deposits it had made in the state banks. Agitation was started in Congress to provide some way of safeguarding Government funds. In response to a sort of financial atavism, it was proposed to establish a number of "strong boxes" throughout the country in which Government funds should be kept. In order to divorce Federal finances completely from the banking system, all payments to the Government were to be made in the form of specie or the Government's own obligations. This system, called the "Independent Treasury," was first put into effect in 1840, only to be repealed the following year. But in 1846 the plan was again adopted by Congress, and, beginning in January, 1847, the provision regarding payments in specie or Government notes went into effect.

---

[36] In 1836 the Second Bank secured a charter from Pennsylvania. Although Biddle continued to act as president, the institution entered into several speculative ventures and finally failed in 1841. While creditors were fully paid, the stockholders received nothing on their entire investment. Biddle, who lost his personai fortune, died three years later.

From the standpoint of the financial and banking structure of the country, a less promising institution can scarcely be imagined. The difficulties arose from the fact that unless payments into the Treasury happened to coincide with disbursemetns of equal amounts, there would be a drain upon the commercial banks, principally in the form of specie drawn from their reserves. To the extent the banks customarily kept some sort of fixed relationship between their loans and their specie holdings, this "hoarding" of specie by the Treasury could easily cause a wholly arbitrary stringency in the total volume of bank credit. On the other hand, an unwarranted expansion of bank credit could occur if the Government's disbursements exceeded its receipts. By its very nature, the Independent Treasury exercised certain functions of a central bank but without necessarily assuming any responsibility for the effective operation of the monetary and banking system. Fortunately, the potentialities of the institution for disturbances were neutralized to some extent by various Secretaries of the Treasury, who violated the spirit of the original law by keeping a substantial portion of the Government's deposits with the banks and by occasionally making disbursements to ease a stringent monetary situation.[37]

The National Banking System

In 1861, some 1600 state banks did the main banking business of the country. Despite considerable improvement, the notes of these banks varied in value, chiefly reflecting the quality of the securities (principally state and industrial bonds) upon which they were based. The advent of the Civil War impaired the value of many of these bonds and brought on a number of bank failures, which in turn reduced the volume of notes in circulation. This situation prompted Salmon P. Chase, Lincoln's Secretary of the Treasury, to urge Congress to establish a bank note currency based upon United States bonds. The need for financing the war was an added consideration, since such a measure would widen the market for government securities.[38]

The bill that finally established the National Banking system was not passed until June 1864, too late to give much of a market for government bonds during the war. The legislation did, however, create a system of unit banks chartered by the federal government. The notes of these banks were secured by a deposit of United States government bonds, and in addition were backed by the general assets of the banks, double liability on the part of stockholders in case of bank failure, and by the government's direct guarantee. These safeguards insured a bank note issue of unquestioned soundness and uniformity of value. Furthermore, the de-

---

[37] See David Kinley, *The History, Organization, and Influence of the Independent Treasury of the United States*. New York: Thomas Y. Crowell Company, 1893.

[38] See A. M. Davis, *The Origin of the National Banking System*. Washington, D. C.: U. S. Government Printing Office, 1910.

positors in the National banks were protected by the requirement that substantial reserves be held against deposits.

Contrary to expectations at the time the legislation was passed, the state banks were not especially eager to convert themselves into National banks. In order to bring pressure to bear on the state institutions Congress in 1865 placed a prohibitive tax of 10% per annum upon the notes of state banks, thus giving sole privilege of bank note issue to the National banks. The immediate effect was to decrease the number of state banks and increase the number of National banks.

Conclusion

To make an accurate appraisal of the operations of the American banks during the period between 1789 and 1861 is difficult. The great variety of experiments carried on at different times and in different regions makes any generalization subject to numerous exceptions. There is little doubt, however, that the "easy money" policy that found almost universal expression in our banking institutions led to a more rapid economic development than would have occurred under a more conservative regime. The ability to "create" credit without much regard for specie reserves made possible the promotion of large numbers of undertakings that would otherwise have been delayed. This development did not take place without some losses in economic efficiency. Numerous ill-conceived projects resulted in a wastage of labor and materials. The burden of such failures fell largely upon the holders of depreciated or worthless bank notes or deposits, who in many instances were least able to bear the losses, and who indirectly contributed the capital to many business enterprises.

Yet it can be argued that, except for the inflationary outbursts that accompanied the War of 1812 and the Civil War and the rapid rise in in price between 1835 and 1837, the monetary and banking system functioned on the whole in a fairly effective manner. To be sure, borrowing for purposes of speculation was never absent from the scene, but credit, which came principally from the banks, was expanded largely for the purpose of financing the production and marketing of goods and services. With the exceptions noted, fluctuations in general prices were not beyond the limits expected from the operation of an economic system of free private enterprise.[39] By 1861 the "wildcat" type of banking, which had something of the zonelike development that has characterized so much of American history, had largely disappeared. Apparently each region had to learn its own lessons from experience before reforms were put into effect. Except in areas like that served by the Suffolk System, bank notes continued to circulate at different values, a fact that added somewhat to

[39] For a detailed account of the operations of the American economy during the period, see Walter B. Smith and Arthur H. Cole, *Fluctuations in American Business, 1790-1860*. Cambridge, Mass.: Harvard University Press, 1935.

the difficulties of doing business. But after the end of the Second Bank, the greatest deficiency of American banking was the absence of any central control over the banking system as a whole; a deficiency which the National Banking system failed to remedy. There was no institution to post storm warnings of threatened financial difficulties, to take positive steps to prevent booms from reaching dangerous proportions, and to stand ready to extend assistance in times of economic distress. The banking structure rested upon a foundation that was subject to periodic collapse.

Selected References

Brown, Kenneth L., "Stephen Girard, Promoter of the Second Bank of the United States," *Journal of Economic History,* Vol. II, No. 2 (November, 1942).

Catterall, Ralph C. H., *The Second Bank of the United States.* Chicago: University of Chicago Press, 1903.

Chaddock, Robert E., *The Safety Fund Banking System in New York.* Washington, D. C.: National Monetary Commission, 1910.

Dewey, Davis R., *Financial History of the United States,* 12th ed. New York: Longmans, Green & Company, 1934.

———, *State Banking Before the Civil War.* Washington, D. C.: National Monetary Commission, 1910.

Dunbar, Charles F., *Chapters on the Theory and History of Banking,* rev. ed. New York: G. P. Putnam's Sons, 1901.

Federal Reserve, *Banking Studies.* Washington, D. C.: The Federal Reserve Board, 1941.

Gras, N. S. B., *The Massachusetts First National Bank of Boston.* Cambridge, Mass.: Harvard University Press, 1937.

Hammond, Bray, "Long and Short Term Credit in Early American Banks," *Quarterly Journal of Economics,* Vol. XLIX.

———, "The Louisiana Banking Act of February 5, 1842," *Monthly Review, Federal Reserve Bank of Atlanta,* Vol. XXVII. No. 1.

Hepburn, A. Barton, *A History of Currency in The United States.* New York: The Macmillan Company, 1915.

James, F. Cyril, *The Growth of Chicago Banks* (2 vols.). New York: Harper and Brothers, 1938.

Kinley, David, *The History, Organization, and Influence of the Independent Treasury of the United States.* New York: Thomas Y. Crowell Company, 1893.

Knox, John Jay, *A History of Banking in the United States.* New York: Bradford Rhodes & Company, 1900.

Laughlin, J. Laurence, *The History of Bimetallism in the United States,* 4th ed. New York: D. Appleton-Century Company, 1897.

McGrane, R. C., *The Correspondence of Nicholas Biddle, 1807-1844.* Boston: Houghton, Mifflin Company, 1919.

Miller, Harry Edward, *Theories of Banking in the United States Before 1860.* Cambridge, Mass.: Harvard University Press, 1927.

Smith, Walter B., and Arthur H. Cole, *Fluctuations in American Business, 1790-1860.* Cambridge, Mass.: Harvard University Press, 1935.

Sumner, William Graham, *Andrew Jackson.* New York: Houghton, Mifflin Company, 1882.

Sumner, William Graham, *A History of Banking in The United States.* New York: The Journal of Commerce and Commercial Bulletin, 1896.

Wetterau, James O., "Branches of the First Bank of the United States," *Supplement of Journal of Economic History* (December, 1942).

———, "New Light on The First Bank of the United States," *The Pennsylvania Magazine of History and Biography* (July, 1937).

White, Horace, *Money and Banking, Illustrated by American History,* 2nd ed. Boston: Ginn & Company, 1904.

14 · THE CAPITAL MARKETS, 1789-1865

WITHOUT THE NECESSARY CAPITAL, the rapid growth of agriculture, manufacturing, commerce, and transportation during the years 1789 to 1865 would have been impossible. Men with plans for new enterprises or the extension of those already established needed funds. At times American governments were also large borrowers. The supply of capital came from the surplus accumulated in Europe and from the increasing savings in the United States, supplemented by the working of the credit mechanism, a subject discussed in the preceding chapter. Businessmen of the period employed both old and new methods and evolved new institutions to finance economic enterprises in the momentous years of the nation's early political independence. Although there was growth of capital throughout the period to 1865, the rate of increase was interrupted by crises and wealth was diverted into different channels by the wars of the period.

The term capital has been used to mean somewhat different things by different people. The word *capital* as a factor in production is often employed as an abbreviation for capital goods, those material products of man's labors that are used for further production. In other cases the term *capital* is used in a broader sense to refer to all property that is used to obtain income rather than for the immediate enjoyment of the owner. A businessman referring to his desire for capital might mean that he needed funds to purchase not only capital goods, such as machinery, but to buy land on which to build a factory and to pay wages in advance of the return from his products. In this case he is including not only investment capital, which is to be converted into capital goods, but also "working" capital, to provide him with funds to cover current costs.

To meet these demands various markets evolved in the period under discussion. In analysing the functioning of our economy, some writers limit the term capital markets to those institutions where investment funds are obtained for extended periods of time; a distinction is made between these and short-term credit or commercial credit markets.[1] While

[1] See Margaret G. Myers, *The New York Money Market*, Vol. I, *Origins and Development*. New York: Columbia University Press, 1931; Melchior Palyi, *The Chicago Credit Market Organization and Institutional Structure*. Chicago: University of Chicago Press, 1937.

this differentiation of function is important to keep in mind, it should be remembered that in the early development of these markets the differentiation of function was not very clear. Not only did the same firms perform many different functions, but the markets were closely interrelated. The role of commercial banks has already been discussed. They lent money from deposits, or credit that they were able to create. The present chapter is concerned, not with capital markets, in the narrower meaning of that term, but with several ways in which credit was obtained either for a short or long period in the years before 1865. The practical questions that it plans to answer in part are: "How did an entrepreneur finance his business? Where and how did the Federal, state and municipal governments borrow? What institutions were developing to meet these needs?"

Variations in the conditions of demand for capital covered a wide range. Those needing funds included individuals, partnerships, corporations, and governments. The amounts desired ranged from small sums which businessmen could supply themselves from savings, or meet by informal loans from friends, to the unprecedented total borrowed by the Federal government during the Civil War. The time-span of need ranged from a few days to several years; so-called short-term credits, for example those to finance the export of cotton, were extended for a number of months in a period when transportation and communication were slow; long-term credits for the purchase of capital goods, such as for building a railroad, were often required for two decades or more. Evidence of having obtained capital included everything from a handshake and an oral promise to promissory notes, bills of exchange, stocks, and bonds.[2] The uses of capital and the conditions of obtaining it were numerous in a rapidly growing economy where dynamic individuals were freely choosing their respective fields of endeavor and their methods of attaining their goals.

The demand for long-term loans to provide investment capital increased, especially after 1815. Until this date there were few securities besides Federal bonds to attract investors or to require the services of financial middlemen. In the years that followed, the promising opportunities of the West and the need for capital to finance internal improvements provided the incentive. Especially during the twenties and thirties the states and municipalities borrowed money to aid private companies building turnpikes, canals, or railroads and to forward banking. Banks, canals, and insurance companies all issued securities in large amounts. The railroads, particularly in the 1850's, raised capital by large flotations of stocks and bonds. The Federal government entered the mar-

[2] See Harold G. Moulton, *Financial Organization and the Economic System.* New York: McGraw-Hill Book Company, Inc., 1938. The reader will find this book a useful reference for financial terms and functions.

ket several times during the first half of the nineteenth century, and became in the 1860's a heavy borrower.[3]

At the same time, the money markets were called upon for short- or intermediate-term loans. Often these were to finance foreign or domestic trade. Evidences of such debts took the form of promissory notes and bills of exchange. Sometimes businessmen used techniques now considered desirable only for obtaining short-term credit in order to acquire funds for long periods of time; through renewals and re-drawing, short-term credits were extended from months to years.

Financial Centers and Institutions

Although several cities and institutions served special financial needs, even a full description of these markets would not give the complete story of raising funds. In this period the individual proprietorship and the partnership were very common types of business units in both commerce and manufacturing. In many cases only a small amount of capital was needed to start a business, and that could be provided by the owner. Even fairly large firms made no public appeals for capital but called on relatives and friends to invest in the firm, and enlarged their resources by ploughing profits back into the business. When a small corporation was organized, although the form of the business was changed, there was often no dependence on financial centers or financial middlemen. Merchants, wealthy retired persons, rich widows, or others with a surplus to invest bought the securities directly from the incorporators. The local market absorbed stocks and bonds issued to finance small manufacturing enterprises and local public improvements.

The total flow of capital is not easy to trace. For example, although the promissory notes signed by Western debtors and the sale of bonds in the East were evidences of indebtedness by individuals or firms in the newer parts of the country, these do not fully represent the large aggregate of capital that was taken West by the many settlers who individually carried with them small quantities of tools, other equipment, food, and money.

A few cities were important centers for those who needed large amounts of capital. Although the United States was developing her own financial markets, foreign capital was a significant part of the supply throughout the whole nineteenth century. London was already a well-developed financial center, and Americans in need of money frequently solicited funds in the English city. Through the methods used, some of the profits of British trade and industry flowed through London to the United States. The promises of the rapidly growing economy of a new country, the

[3] William J. Shultz and M. R. Caine, *Financial Development of the United States.* New York: Prentice-Hall, Inc., 1937. This is a useful reference to study the development in shorter periods.

high interest offered on bonds, and the pleasing returns realized by owners of early issues of stocks attracted both British and Continental investors. American agents wishing to raise funds might appeal to houses in Amsterdam, Rotterdam, Paris, and Hamburg, but throughout this period the United Kingdom was the leading exporter of capital to the United States and the rest of the world.

In the United States itself some cities outstripped others as financial centers. At the beginning of this period Philadelphia stood out in the country's financial affairs. The early development of banking and the establishment of the First and later of the Second Bank of the United States in that city gave it considerable advantage. Philadelphia was also an important center for both domestic and foreign trade. New York City, however, had attractions that soon gained for it financial leadership. It surpassed Philadelphia in the quantity of imports and exports of merchandise before 1800. With a good harbor at the mouth of the Hudson, New York benefited from the developing manufacturing industry of New England and from the growth of the West. Transportation facilities were improved by the opening of the Erie Canal and by the building of the railroads. The first line of regular packet ships began operation from New York in 1818, thus giving to the city advantages in foreign trade, while the aggressive new techniques of New York businessmen attracted merchants who came East to purchase goods.[4] The financial supremacy of New York, based on its commercial leadership and the resulting accumulation of wealth, developed it as a real national center in investment and commercial credit.[5]

Important as New York had become by the second quarter of the nineteenth century, the sum total of financing in other markets must not be ignored. The financial business of several cities was very important for their respective hinterlands: in Philadelphia, Boston, New Orleans, and, later, St. Louis, Chicago, and many smaller cities, firms were developed to serve local needs. In New England accumulated wealth from foreign trade was ready to flow into manufacturing and Western railroads. In the growing cities of the West and South new houses were set up and branches of others established to help facilitate the movement of capital to these sections from Europe and the East.

The expanding volume of business during this period stimulated the evolution of financial middlemen to serve persons who wished to obtain funds and those with a surplus to invest. Many of the houses established were not specialized but carried on a variety of undertakings, sometimes combining financial activities with mercantile pursuits. Some firms grad-

---

4 Robert Greenhalgh Albion, *The Rise of New York Port,* pp. 13-15. New York: Charles Scribner's Sons, 1939.

5 Margaret G. Myers, *The New York Money Market,* Vol. I, *Origins and Development,* pp. 3-9. New York: Columbia University Press, 1931.

ually became specialists, devoting most of their attention to some particular lines, but for the most part this was an age of diversification and business opportunism, not of specialization. At the same time the early development of methods of performing certain financial functions may be recognized, and the evolution of several institutions is foreshadowed in the activities of these pioneer firms. Some houses of the period can be considered investment banking firms, or other types of specialized financial establishments in embryo, even though at the time they dealt in merchandise as well as bonds, sold lottery tickets as well as commercial paper, or performed some of the functions of a commercial bank in addition to marketing issues of new securities.

The Importation of Capital

In Europe a number of firms participated in the export of capital to the United States, but it was through Great Britain, especially London, that most of the capital moved. To this center Americans turned, especially in the early part of the century, to market stocks and bonds. In Great Britain, a nation in which there were many importers of raw materials and exporters of manufactured articles, facilities were developed to finance foreign trade, including that with the United States. Among the firms that evolved techniques to facilitate the export of capital was a group of houses known as the Anglo-American merchant bankers.

These houses performed a variety of functions. In most cases the partners had been merchants and they continued to deal in goods, either on their firm's own account or on commission for buying or selling. In addition, however, the reputation that they had established fitted them well to carry on financial functions for others as well as for themselves. Through them new issues of securities were marketed, especially bonds, and short-term credits were arranged.[6]

Although a number of houses performed some of the services in this field of Anglo-American merchant banking, a few firms achieved prominence. In the 1830's there were eight houses that stood out, but failures among them left openings for new firms and enterprising merchants were attracted to the opportunities. Throughout this whole period, the leading firm was Baring Brothers & Company, London. Also prominent was W. & J. Brown & Company of Liverpool (Brown, Shipley & Company after 1839), which had allied partnerships in American centers, and N. M. Rothschild & Sons.

In a field in which knowledge of the United States was so important it could be expected that citizens of that country would play a part in providing leadership. Baring Brothers & Company had two New Eng-

---

[6] R. W. Hidy, "The Organization and Functions of Anglo-American Merchant Bankers, 1815-1860," *The Journal of Economic History*, Vol. I, Supplement (December, 1941), pp. 53-55, 65-66.

landers among its partners: Joshua Bates from Boston and Russell Sturgis, who had had experience as a merchant in Manila and Canton. Another native of Massachusetts, George Peabody, established a new house in London. He had gained experience, capital, and reputation while exporting European dry goods to his firm in Baltimore, Maryland. In 1854 George Peabody & Company took into partnership a dry goods merchant from Boston, Junius Spencer Morgan, and thus the first Morgan entered banking.

Contacts between firms in England and those in the United States were maintained in several ways. In some cases the British house acted for others, earning only a commission for its efforts. Often, however, the firm in England preferred to take the risk itself in return for the profit on a financial operation. In order that the chance of loss should be at a minimum, adequate information and guidance was required from the United States. One of the methods of obtaining this was for the house abroad to operate on a joint account for designated transactions with houses in the financial centers of the United States. This was a flexible device that made possible the sharing of knowledge, risks, and profits. W. & J. Brown & Company of Liverpool operated through a system of interlocking family partnerships in New York, Philadelphia, and Baltimore, and through agents in Boston and the South.[7] Thomas Wren Ward served Baring Brothers & Company as a special agent in Boston for twenty-three years. He was succeeded by his son, who in the 1860's moved the office to New York. August Belmont came to that city in 1837 to look after the interest of Rothschild & Sons. To this growing financial center Junius Spencer Morgan sent his son, J. Pierpont, for training. The young man became the American agent of the firm in London, and on this foundation the American house of Morgan was established.

The flotation of long-term loans was an important service performed by these Anglo-American merchant bankers. Through them many securities were purchased during this period by both British and Continental investors. Sometimes the selling in Europe was done entirely on a commission basis; if no advance of money was involved, the charge was only 1 per cent. The English firms, however, benefited from other commissions on the payment of interest and principal on the American securities held in Europe. In some instances a house in London purchased an issue on joint account with a firm in the United States and shared the profit or loss that resulted. In other cases the London concern undertook to market the whole of a small issue at its own risk.[8]

---

[7] John Crosby Brown, *A Hundred Years of Merchant Banking*, pp. 3, 8, 23, 25. New York: privately printed, 1909.

[8] For an example see R. W. Hidy, "The Union Bank of Louisiana Loan, 1832: A Case Study in Marketing," *The Journal of Political Economy*, Vol. XLVII, No. 2 (April, 1939), pp. 232-253.

Several methods of appealing to the investing public were developed. By the 1850's advertisements in newspapers, appealing circulars, and other publicity devices were quite common. A firm in London would also make offers to houses on the Continent if the issue was of such a type and floated at such a time that German, Dutch, French, and other investors might be attracted.

The Anglo-American merchant bankers served the security market in further ways. They facilitated the buying and selling of old issues of securities. Often discretionary orders were sent to them to buy in the European market; in other instances they dealt on their own initiative through their agents in various markets. When securities were depreciated, or the conduct of the borrower was in doubt, the houses attempted to safeguard their clients' interests in the United States.[9]

Although the trans-Atlantic capital movements in the form of long term loans often attracted more attention, the flow of capital in the form of short-term credits was also significant. Whether the merchant was American, British, or of some other nationality, he often depended, at least in part, on the British money market to finance his export or import trade with the United States. Over this period the rates charged and the conditions governing credits changed frequently, but certain generalizations can be made about some sections of the trade.

When a merchant in the United States wished to import British goods he turned, particularly during the second quarter of the nineteenth century, to the London money market to provide his working capital. In some instances he was granted credit on the books of the manufacturer or merchant from whom he made his purchases. If the American merchant visiting England was well established and favorably known, he might ask the creditor to draw a bill of exchange on him, and so postpone the date of payment for the three or four months that would pass before the draft reached maturity.[10]

More often the short-term credit was arranged through the services of an Anglo-American merchant banker and the London money market. Granted a credit on a merchant banker, the American importer either drew against it himself or authorized his creditor to draw. The British firm accepted the bills, expected to be remitted funds by the American merchant upon or before the maturity of the drafts, paid the bills when due, and charged a commission for accepting and paying. By accepting drafts the merchant bankers lent their names and credit, and the bills became negotiable in the London money market. The actual funds

---

[9] Reginald C. McGrane, *Foreign Bondholders and American State Debts,* pp. 72-81, 96-98. New York: The Macmillan Company, 1935.

[10] *Peabody Papers,* 1830-1839, *passim.* Salem, Mass.: unpublished mss., Essex Institute; Norman Sydney Buck, *The Development of the Organisation of Anglo-American Trade, 1800-1850,* pp. 114-116, 133. New Haven, Conn.: Yale University Press, 1925.

to convert the acceptances into cash usually were provided by bill brokers and discount houses which by the beginning of the century were well qualified to perform this function. These specialists in the bill market provided an outlet for the surplus funds of banks in manufacturing and other districts of Great Britain. Firms such as Overend, Gurney & Company, the leading house dealing in bills during this period, paid interest to banks for the use of deposits and advanced the money on drafts at a discount from the maturity value. In turn, if necessary, they could appeal to the Bank of England for rediscounts.[11] The merchant banker lent his credit; the discount house acted as a reservoir for the British capital; the seller of the goods was reimbursed; and the American merchant was given several months to meet his payments.

The terms and charges of the merchant bankers varied with the goods involved and the country to which the merchant was making his shipments. For the importation of British dry goods to the United States, especially during the 1830's, an "open" revolving credit was granted for a definite sum without the merchant's putting up security. Against this credit the merchant or his agent could draw in Great Britain in bills at three or four months' date for a charge of 1 per cent. Thousands of tons of railroad iron were shipped to the United States under similar arrangements, but the importer was usually given the right to draw on the merchant banker only for a specific operation. The terms further stipulated that a bill of lading bearing evidence of the amount of metal shipped should accompany the draft.

Exports of goods from the United States also were financed in large part by the British money market. Farmers received little direct credit in this period, but the producers of the export staples obtained indirect financial aid in marketing their produce abroad. The case of cotton may serve as the example. The plantation owner directly, or more likely a merchant or factor acting for him, would draw a bill of exchange on the English importer. Immediate payment was obtained in the United States by turning over to an agent of an Anglo-American merchant banker evidence of the shipment of cotton in return for payment of the bill.[12] Since New York was the great import center and New Orleans was the port from which most cotton was shipped, the demand and supply of bills of exchange on England was matched by three-cornered operations in exchanges between New Orleans, New York, and London. The reader need not be concerned with the intricacies of this device other than to note that money was to be lost as well as made by those who grasped the opportunity to operate in the fluctuating exchanges. Both

[11] W. T. C. King, *History of the London Discount Market,* pp. 5-14, 117-128, 264-265. London: George Routledge & Sons, Ltd., 1936.

[12] Norman Sydney Buck, *The Development of the Organisation of Anglo-American Trade, 1800-1850,* Chapters 3 and 4. New Haven, Conn.: Yale University Press, 1925.

domestic and foreign exchanges showed not only a propensity to fluctuate widely but also irregular seasonal patterns. Many firms were attracted by the possibility of profit; but, after the Second Bank of the United States ceased to dominate the field of foreign exchange, the houses of the Browns, with their agents in Southern cities, were the most active operators in this field.[13]

Not only were the other exporters of American produce, including wheat, flour, and tobacco, financed in this way, but also American merchants in various parts of the world found short-term credits available to aid their business. A merchant shipping coffee from Brazil to the United States could obtain the right to draw drafts covered by bills of lading. Especially after 1825 an American merchant who shipped tea or silk from China to Europe or to the United States was likely to finance the shipment by drawing against a credit on an Anglo-American merchant banker.

These credits received in the British market were the basis for a further extension of credit in the United States. The case of dry goods importations is one in point. The importer in New York, Philadelphia, or Baltimore, financing his imports by means of three- or four-months bills on a London merchant banker was able to extend credit facilities to the jobber or wholesaler. In turn they gave the retailer lenient terms. The final purchaser of the goods, who might well be a farmer who paid his debts from the annual proceeds of his crop, was at the end of this long chain of credit.

Banks in the United States also benefited by credits extended by Anglo-American merchant bankers. The purposes for which they borrowed varied, but credits were often arranged to facilitate dealings in foreign exchange. Although even in the 1840's some merchants balanced imports of goods with exports, or bought exchange directly from another merchant, some time before that date certain merchants were known to make a specialty of such dealings and chartered banks had also undertaken the function.[14] To supply American merchants with pounds sterling for the payment of foreign debts, the bank or merchant-banking firm drew against a credit granted in London; later it remitted to cover by sending bills of exchange drawn by Americans on British importers. The Bank of the United States was active in this field, especially between 1831 and 1836, when it held a credit of £250,000 on Baring Brothers & Company for this purpose.

Similar institutions obtained credits in London for other reasons. The

---

[13] John Crosby Brown, *A Hundred Years of Merchant Banking*, pp. 280-281. New York: privately printed, 1909. The book contains a brief discussion of the seasonal changes of domestic and foreign exchange rates.

[14] Arthur H. Cole, "Evolution of the Foreign Exchange Market of the United States," *Journal of Economic and Business History*, Vol. I, No. 3 (November, 1928), pp. 385-390.

Second Bank of the United States negotiated several large loans there; in 1819, for example, to tide it over a difficult period, a $2,000,000 three-year loan was arranged in Europe.[15] In 1822 the Bank of New York and Trust Company, having been refused by the legislature the right to increase its capitalization, turned to the London market to negotiate a loan.[16] In this way the American market was supplied with funds from England indirectly through the facilities accorded to banks.

The flow of capital from Europe to the United States fluctuated a great deal in the period 1789 to 1860. These years opened with a foreign debt and with a new flow of funds from Europe. Borrowing was interrupted by the War of 1812 and did not amount to much in the postwar years. During the 1830's, however, the total of both long- and short-term loans grew rapidly. The bonds of Eastern states issued to aid public works and the securities of Southern and Western states to promote banking and internal improvements found a ready market in Great Britain. Stocks and bonds of private corporations, banks, insurance companies, mining companies, canals, and railroads were also owned abroad. In addition to the securities marketed by the Anglo-American bankers many others reached Europe. When American merchants wishing to make payments found pounds sterling high, they often remitted securities. In 1836 and later, Samuel Jaudon, agent of the Bank of the United States, took a large volume of securities abroad as collateral for needed loans. Other firms in the United States sent smaller quantities of stocks and bonds to the European market.[17] Various estimates have been made of the total of securities, short-term obligations, and direct investments in land held abroad. A total of $225,000,000 may be said to give a reasonable picture of the foreign indebtedness of Americans in 1843.[18]

The panic of 1837 was followed by a brief recovery in 1839, and after that came a long depression during which the credit of Americans in Europe suffered. Three Anglo-American houses failed in 1837 and others were embarrassed. The Bank of the United States, now a state bank, tottered and finally fell. The European holders of its stock suffered losses. In 1841 and 1842 eight states and one territory stopped payment of interest. Whatever the causes of the defaults—overexpansion, a sudden break in the flow of funds, inadequate taxes, irresponsible leadership—the European investors were discouraged. Conditions for the granting of short-

15 Ralph C. H. Catterall, *The Second Bank of the United States*, p. 71. Chicago: The University of Chicago Press, 1903.

16 Josephine Mayer and R. A. East, "An Early Anglo-American Financial Transaction," *Bulletin of the Business Historical Society*, Vol. XI, No. 5 (Nov. 1937).

17 Leland Hamilton Jenks, *The Migration of British Capital to 1875*, pp. 64, 85, 92, Chapter 3. New York: Alfred A. Knopf, 1927.

18 Cleona Lewis, *America's Stake in International Investments*, p. 520. Washington, D. C.: The Brookings Institution, 1938. See Appendix B, "Estimates of Foreign Investments in the United States."

term credits were tightened and American securities remained depreciated on the market. An attempt was made to persuade the Federal Government to assume the debts of the states but without success. In 1842, when an agent of the United States visited Europe, he found the merchant bankers unwilling to market Federal bonds because of the investing public's lack of interest.

Within six years, however, the credit of Americans was reinstated. All but two of the states were prepared to meet their obligations, economic conditions in the United States had improved, the development of the old Northwest, particularly the building of railroads there, offered a fresh investment opportunity. By the end of the 1840's, short-term credits were increasing and had become very important in financing the purchases of rails. Europeans again were willing to invest in enterprises in the United States. French, Dutch, Swiss, and especially German investors looked from the disturbed conditions of Europe to the rapidly developing economy of a young nation.[19] Although the flow of capital was interrupted by the Crimean War and financial crises in 1854 and 1857, the total exportation of capital grew from 1848 to 1865. One estimate of the aggregate foreign indebtedness of the United States by 1857 is $375,000,000.[20]

During this period of renewed interest in investments in the United States there was a change in emphasis on the techniques of financing them. The Anglo-American merchant bankers continued in some cases to market an issue at their own risk in the European market. Very often, however, a house in the United States took over the securities and arranged for sale of part of them by English firms either on commission or for a share in the profits. Furthermore, with improved communication between Europe and the United States, more foreign investors were sending their orders for securities directly to the New York market.[21] The United States still looked to Europe for capital. Large blocks of American bonds and stocks, even of those issues floated in the United States, reached the British market, but the domestic money market had been developing and was able to take more of the initiative. Agents continued to visit Europe to sell securities, and foreign short-term credits directly aided in the building of railroads as well as in the financing of imports and exports, but by the fifth decade of the century the American money market had achieved a new maturity, ready to assume a growing role in supplying our capital needs.

---

[19] R. W. Hidy, *The House of Baring in American Trade and Finance, 1763-1861,* pp. 406 ff. Cambridge: Harvard University Press, 1949.

[20] Cleona Lewis, *America's Stake in International Investments,* p. 522. Washington, D. C.: The Brookings Institution, 1938.

[21] *Peabody Papers,* 1850, *passim.* Salem, Mass.: unpublished mss., Essex Institute.

Investment Market in the United States

Within the United States between 1789 and 1865 a variety of firms and techniques emerged to implement the flow of capital. In the early period, merchants were almost the sole representatives of finance in the American money market. Chartered banks were very few, and their boards were made up almost entirely of merchants. Thus both long- and short-term credit was in the hands of the merchantile community. As time passed some of these merchants became private bankers; others retained their diversified interests, leaving their security and exchange operations to secondary importance. Unlike the chartered banks, these private firms were not restricted as to the area in which they might operate and some of them extended their branches or agencies over the country. They were also free to perform, and did perform, a variety of functions, including dealings in both foreign and domestic exchange, operations in old issues of stocks and bonds, and the flotation of new securities.

Before the issue of securities became the predominant method of raising long-term capital to finance new enterprises, some private banking firms handled lotteries to aid in raising funds, a method not uncommon at the end of the eighteenth and in the early nineteenth century. The purchaser gambled on a prize, the project obtained capital, and the house that sold the tickets received for its service a percentage of the money raised. By 1833 there were 200 lottery offices in Philadelphia alone. S. & M. Allen and Company, which had grown out of a general business established in Albany in 1808, was one of the firms carrying on this type of business, among other activities, through its branches in several cities of the North and South. In 1817, for example, it contracted to sell lottery tickets for the Union Canal Company of Pennsylvania.[22] Other means of financing developed, and both public opinion and legislative action hastened the decline of this method of raising capital in the 1830's.

During the early years of this period, some chartered banks made long-term advances directly to borrowers. Through long-dated and frequently extended notes, banks made loans that in reality provided investment capital, although the form was that of a short-term credit.[23]

With the increase in the number of issues of new securities many individuals and firms competed for the handling of stocks and bonds. Stephen Girard, John Jacob Astor, and David Parish were associated with the Federal issue of 1813 and with the promoting of the Second Bank of the

---

[22] Henrietta M. Larson, "S. & M. Allen—Lottery, Exchange and Stock Brokerage," *Journal of Economic and Business History,* Vol. 3, No. 3 (May, 1931), pp. 424, 430-432.

[23] Bray Hammond, "Long and Short Term Credit in Early American Banking," *Quarterly Journal of Economics,* Vol. XLIX, No. 1 (November, 1934), pp. 83-84, 88, 89; Ralph C. H. Catterall, *The Second Bank of the United States,* pp. 160-161. Chicago: The University of Chicago Press, 1903.

United States. In the 1830's the private banking houses of Prime, Ward & King, Nevins, Townsend & Company, Astor & Sons, and Brown Brothers & Company competed with such chartered banks as the Bank of the United States and the Bank of Manhattan Company in floating the many new issues of that decade. New houses and men played significant roles in the following years.[24]

Securities were placed on the market by various methods. Small issues were handled by an incorporated or local private bank, which disposed of its holdings through correspondents in other centers if the immediate market would not absorb all the securities. Larger issues were usually negotiated in a city such as New York, Boston, or Philadelphia. Sometimes the bank acted as an agent selling on commission; at other times the middleman contracted to buy the securities at an agreed price and market them at his own risk, and in some instances he obtained his block of securities competitively as a result of answering a call for sealed bids.

A few houses devoted their attention to special types of securities. W. W. Corcoran of Washington, D. C. played the leading role in handling the large Mexican War loans of the Federal Government in 1847 and 1848. Corcoran had established his house of Corcoran & Riggs in the national capital in 1840. Prior to that time this son of an Irish settler in Georgetown, D. C., had been a businessman on a small scale. He had entered the mercantile field, and then, after a failure in 1823, had turned his attention to real estate and domestic exchange. Next he formed a partnership with George Washington Riggs, the young son of Elisha Riggs, a New York financier. Land and securities became the chief interest of Corcoran & Riggs. Pleased with its success in outbidding the New York houses for the greater part of the $18,000,000 Federal loan of 1847, the firm submitted a sealed bid to buy the new issue of 1848 at a 3.02 per cent premium. It was awarded $14,065,550 of the $16,000,000 20-year 6 per cent bonds. Even before making the bid, Corcoran and Riggs had arranged to share it with others. Of the approximately $5,000,000 to be taken by other houses, $1,250,000 went to Baring Brothers & Company. Further sales were made in the United States; but when the market lagged, Corcoran visited Great Britain and disposed of about $4,000,000 more in the foreign market. The premium offered was high, and it was fortunate for the Washington house that the end of the Mexican War and the improvement in the European market for American securities both came in time to forward the undertaking.[25] It was a big transaction for the period, and the house of Corcoran & Riggs made a good profit from its operations, but not without some months of uncertainty.

---

[24] Margaret G. Myers, *The New York Money Market,* Vol. I, *Origins and Development,* pp. 23-24. New York: Columbia University Press, 1931.

[25] *Riggs Papers,* 1847-1848, *passim.* Washington, D. C.: unpublished manuscripts, Library of Congress.

In addition to the Mexican War loans many other issues of securities provided business for the private bankers in this period. The growth of railroads, the development of Western states, municipal borrowing, and the general incorporation laws of the States all gave rise to a large flow of securities, especially during the 1850's. The number of private bankers had grown in the previous decade, and by 1854 the American *Bankers Magazine* listed 18 in New York, 10 in Boston, 20 in Philadelphia, and 15 in St. Louis.[26] The increase in the issue of stocks and bonds offered business opportunities for these and other houses.

Financing the Civil War was an unprecedented operation demanding new methods. In the early stages of the conflict, the Secretary of the Treasury, Salmon P. Chase, marketed Federal bonds by offering issues directly for competitive bids as had been the practice in earlier Federal financing. The credit of the northern government, however, was not high either at home or abroad, and the government's rejection of those bids considerably below par resulted in the failure to place all of some issues in 1861. In the course of making other attempts the Secretary became well acquainted with a financier, Jay Cooke, to whom in 1862 he turned for special aid in marketing $500,000,000 of five-per-cent, twenty-year bonds.

Jay Cooke had already had considerable experience in financial affairs. Born in Ohio, he had received his training in the firm of E. W. Clark & Company of Philadelphia, and there he had established his own firm in 1861. To a varied assortment of functions the new house added that of marketing government securities. In company with the firm of Drexel & Company, Jay Cooke & Company had acted as general agent for the sale of an issue of Pennsylvania bonds for defense; the issue had been marketed by appealing to the buyers' patriotism. In February, 1862, a few months before he was called on by the Secretary to aid in marketing the large Federal issue, Cooke had organized a new firm in Washington, D. C.

Jay Cooke accepted the tremendous task and accomplished it by using new marketing techniques. From his commission of one-half of one per cent on the first $10,000,000 sold and three-eighths of one per cent on the remainder, he paid all the expenses of what at that time was the most ambitious marketing organization ever used. He employed 2,500 sub-agents and started an active campaign. To make a patriotic appeal to the small investor, he advertised in newspapers, circulars, posters, and handbills. More comprehensive than ever before was this approach in the retail selling of securities, and bonds were bought by many small investors.

There was an interruption to Jay Cooke's agency, and other men and methods aided in the financing of the war, but it was largely through this

[26] Henrietta M. Larson, "E. W. Clark & Co., 1837-1857. The Beginning of an American Private Bank," *Journal of Economic and Business History,* Vol. IV, No. 3 (May, 1932), pp. 442-443.

financier's ingenuity that the large loans were raised.[27] The war was financed, the Federal debt was increased about $2,400,000,000, and the American capital markets were further developed.

As the quantity of securities already issued grew, the dealings in stocks and bonds increased. At first merchants acted as agents for those wishing to buy or sell securities but specialists in handling these transactions emerged. For fear of being accused of considering interests other than those of their clients, the more conservative among them refused to assume any functions beyond the buying and selling of securities for others.

Institutions were developed to facilitate the exchange of previously marketed securities. As early as 1792 the brokers in New York had agreed on the commissions they would charge, but at that time the limited number of securities did not justify more formal organization. In 1817 a committee was formed to report on methods of procedure and the New York Stock and Exchange Board was organized. At first the president of the association read once each day the list of securities and gave an opportunity for trading. Actual transactions were registered and rules were made governing the dealings on the Exchange.[28] Unless otherwise stipulated, sales had to be settled for on the next day succeeding the date of sale, but for some time many transactions were contracted for on longer credit.

As experience was gained and the volume of trading grew, new rules were imposed. The transactions of one of the early stock manipulators, Jacob Little, is credited with causing the adoption of one policy. In 1840 Little sold a number of Erie Canal shares at seller's options running from six months to a year. Atttempts to corner him failed because he held Erie bonds that could be converted into stock. The affair hurt the prestige of the Exchange, and the duration for seller's options was limited thereafter to 60 days. With the exception of one act of New York State designed to prevent short selling and later repealed, the voluntary unincorporated association of the Exchange set its own rules.[29]

Important as was the New York Exchange, a sizable volume of business was carried on outside of its jurisdiction. A rival board existed in the city from 1836 to 1848 and again from 1864 to 1869. Outside of the Exchange brokers engaged in buying and selling, and operations in other cities were not negligible. The brokers of Philadelphia had organized early. The Boston Stock and Exchange Board was formally established in 1834; it played an important part in security transactions of the New

---

[27] Henrietta M. Larson, *Jay Cooke, Private Banker,* Chapters 7, 8 and 9. Cambridge: Harvard University Press, 1936.

[28] J. Edward Meeker, *The Work of the Stock Exchange,* rev. ed., pp. 63-65. New York: The Ronald Press Company, 1930. In 1865 the New York Stock Exchange moved to its present location on Wall Street.

[29] N. S. B. Gras and Henrietta M. Larson, *Casebook in American Business History,* pp. 328, 329. New York: F. S. Crofts & Company, 1939.

England manufacturing companies, and by 1863 the volume of business justified two sessions daily.[30] As other cities grew, exchanges were set up; San Francisco had one by 1862.[31] In spite of this competition, New York became and remained the great center for operations in securities. The mail service of the railroads, the development of the telegraph, and the progress of the steamboat increased the speed with which clients could send orders to this active market. Foreign dealers sent orders directly to New York, especially after 1850.

Another advantage offered by New York was the ease of borrowing in that city through the call-loan market. The Stock Exchange was well developed before the growth of the call-loan market, but the new mechanism increased the facilities for obtaining funds for operations in securities, especially in the city.[32] Funds were available and the temporary nature of their deposit determined that the loans should be payable on demand.

The supply of the funds came mainly from the deposits of bankers' balances in incorporated banks and with private bankers and brokers in New York. There were several reasons why sums accumulated in this commercial and financial center. Payments had to be made there for the purchase of imports and domestic goods. The fact that commercial paper with names of well-known merchants of the city was a good investment also attracted funds, while the premium on New York money and the need of banks to retain balances to redeem their own notes in that city encouraged institutions to allow deposits to pile up. Other cities also attracted these balances and the pull of Boston resulted in comparatively small deposits by Massachusetts banks in New York during this period, but the flow of funds from banks in other states was preponderantly to New York.

The institutions holding these funds on interest were eager to invest them in such a way that the money would be available if the deposits were demanded. Thus the call loan developed. The purchasers of securities were attracted by the low interest charged on loans subject to call on demand and the stocks and bonds themselves afforded the collateral security.

At the same time other developments began to affect the operations of the stock market. More rapid transfer of shares was facilitated by the fact that registered shares could be assigned in blank, and because the tele-

---

[30] Clarence W. Barron and Joseph G. Martin, *The Boston Stock Exchange,* no paging. Boston: Hunt & Bell, 1893.

[31] Jos. L. King, *History of the San Francisco Stock and Exchange Board,* p. 1. San Francisco: Jos. L. King, 1910.

[32] For a detailed discussion of the call-loan market see Margaret G. Myers, *The New York Money Market,* Vol. I, *Origins and Development,* Chapters 6 and 7. New York: Columbia University Press, 1931; and Joseph Edward Hedges, *Commercial Banking and the Stock Market before 1863,* Chapters 3 to 6. Baltimore: The Johns Hopkins Press, 1938.

graph increased the speed of communication with traders in other regions. By 1857 the most frequent method of dealing on the New York Stock Exchange was by daily settlement; funds were provided by the call-loan market.

Although the difficulties arising from this close connection between bankers' balances and the operations on the stock market were strongly felt in this period, no successful remedy was achieved. When country banks required large funds for the seasonal needs of an agricultural nation, they placed a demand on New York. To meet these wants the New York bankers and brokers called their loans. Securities were forced on the market and prices declined. As the deposits grew and call loans expanded, the manifestations of this weakness became more marked. The crises in the decade 1850 to 1860 occasioned much criticism of the call-loan market. It was accused of attracting funds from other activities and regions and encouraging stock market speculations. After the crisis of 1857 reformers sought to reduce the connection between bank reserves and call loans. None of the changes proposed, however, brought any significant result and the importance of the call-loan market grew. The mechanism that helped to develop the New York Stock Exchange also contributed to the instability of the market.

Although there were no specialized houses for the man with funds to consult concerning his investments, there were firms that performed this function along with many others. A well-informed, retired merchant might devote his energies to studying the security market as he transferred his capital from trade to stocks and bonds. In the ranks of rich men of New York were several who devoted the knowledge and judgment acquired in commerce to enlarging their fortunes in this new avenue of profit. On the other hand, some of them depended heavily on the advice of private bankers and sent discretionary orders for purchase or sale through these channels so as to gain the advantage of an opinion nearer the market before the orders were given to a broker. Others preferred to pass the whole matter of decision over to a trusted house or individual. John P. Cushing, a retired China merchant, for example, entrusted the management of his investments to his friend, William Sturgis of Boston.[33]

Commercial Credit Market in the United States

Developments in the field of short-term credit paralleled those in long-term operations. In addition to the facilities granted by banks, mercantile credit played its part in the provision of working capital for the wholesaler, retailer, and other businessmen. Terms differed with the trade, locality, and date, but throughout these years payments were post-

---

[33] See "John P. Cushing as an Investor, 1828-1862," in N. S. B. Gras and Henrietta M. Larson, *Casebook in American Business History*, pp. 119 ff. New York: F. S. Crofts & Company, 1939.

poned for a relatively long time. A wholesaler in Cincinnati might obtain credit in an Eastern city for 6 months or more and gain protracted extensions. In turn, he might grant the retailer from 6 to 12 months' credit. New England manufacturers gave their customers from 2 to 12 months to pay; later the terms were shortened to 60 or 90 days and some buyers were eager to take advantage of cash discounts.[34]

This mercantile credit was significant in volume, and in periods of crises collections were difficult to make. Usually the length of credit was shortened after such an experience and in general the time allowed was lessened as transportation and communication improved.

As the volume of credit spread over an expanding area, specialized agencies were needed to gather information on which to base decisions as to the merit of various merchants. Early in the century each importer and wholesaler whose volume of business was appreciable sent agents to tour the country, visit customers, make collections, and judge the standing of those to whom their firms were extending credit. Their reports were long, comprehensive, and often very discerning. The agents of foreign firms, in turn, examined the position of the importers and sent elaborate credit ratings to their houses in Europe. This confidential information was in some cases shared with a few others, but there was a considerable duplication of effort in the gathering of material. It was natural that out of credit analyses of innumerable firms a specialized service should grow. From the experience gained by a New York dry goods firm, Arthur Tappan & Company, Lewis Tappan organized The Mercantile Agency in 1841, to collect and disseminate information on the standing of business houses. In 1854 Robert Graham Dun joined the firm. Branch offices were opened in Eastern cities in the 1840's and by 1857 the house had expanded to London and Montreal as well as to the South and growing West. Another credit agency originated in St. Louis, where John M. Bradstreet, a dry goods merchant and lawyer, had begun to sell his credit information to others. In 1855 Bradstreet's Improved Commercial Agency was set up in New York and the two original components of a well-known credit rating agency were well established.[35]

Commercial credit, although it sometimes took the form of book credit, was often arranged by promissory notes or domestic bills of exchange. Mere entry of accounts receivable on the books of the seller did not give rise to a negotiable instrument. A wholesaler who received a promise to pay signed by the debtor held an evidence of debt that could be dis-

---

[34] See Fred Mitchell Jones, *Middlemen in the Domestic Trade of the United States, 1800-1860*, pp. 17-18. Urbana: University of Illinois, 1937; Lewis Atherton, *The Pioneer Merchant in Mid-America*, p. 113. Columbia, Mo.: *The University of Missouri Studies*, Vol. XIV, No. 2 (April 1, 1939); Roy A. Foulke, *The Sinews of American Commerce*, pp. 101-114, 153-156. New York: Dun & Bradstreet, Inc., 1941.

[35] Roy A. Foulke, *The Sinews of American Commerce*, pp. 283-297. New York: Dun & Bradstreet, Inc., 1941.

counted to pay the manufacturer or importer before its date of maturity. In some cases the creditor drew on the debtor and these drafts or bills of exchange when accepted by the drawee were likewise negotiable. A draft drawn by a Southern planter on a firm in the North that purchased his cotton illustrates one device for obtaining advance payment. In like manner manufacturers in New England drew on their agents in New York and Western commission agents drew on buyers of wheat and cattle in the East. Time drafts drawn on a reliable purchaser could be discounted; the seller received funds and yet the date of payment was postponed for the purchaser. Both promissory notes and bills of exchange varied in the length of time that they had to run; usually the terms ranged from ten days to six months.

As business expanded and more commercial paper made its appearance, another financial service was organized. During the eighteenth century the volume of such paper was small and merchants disposed of such negotiable instruments by selling them to other merchants who had money to invest or who wished to remit funds to the locality on which the bills of exchange were drawn. Even before 1800, however, brokers operating in negotiable paper were established in the commercial and financial centers of the Eastern states.

In the first half of the nineteenth century, the field for such operations expanded. Not only was there more business paper in which to operate, but there was more capital to be invested in it. Bill brokers operated in the growing cities of the West as well as in Eastern centers. New York gained leadership and the houses established there served more than a local market. New England with its growing manufacturing community put Boston into second rank in the decade before the Civil War.

Although some firms made a specialty of this particular financial activity, they usually performed other functions as well. In Boston, Gilmore, Blake & Ward, established in 1850, became one of the leading dealers in commercial paper, but the firm also sold foreign exchange, granted credits on a London merchant banker, and aided in the marketing of securities. Other private bankers combined similar financial functions with their commercial-paper business.

For the most part in this period commercial-paper houses acted as agents. Brokers procured paper, usually promissory notes from importers, wholesalers, and other merchants. They charged those who wished to dispose of the paper a commission that varied from 0.25 to 1 per cent, and undertook to find a person or institution to discount it. Banks, both incorporated and private, often provided the market found by these middlemen in business paper, but merchants with surplus funds, retired businessmen, and others also made discounts. Some firms, especially after 1850, began to operate on their own acocunt and quoted rates for commercial paper; they were willing to assume the risk and responsibility of finding a market for their purchases. Henry Clewes, who stated that he began to deal on his own account in bills by 1857, became the best known dealer in commercial paper during the Civil War.[36]

As this discount market evolved, it became better systematized. By the 1830's rates on commercial paper were being quoted in the financial periodicals of the leading cities. In the decade before the Civil War the market in New York was well developed. Paper was classified according to a regular system and discounts for different types of paper were quoted at rates that fluctuated only with changes in the conditions of the money market.[37]

Institutional Investors

There were other types of middlemen in the capital market. In addition to commercial banks, several other institutions acted as reservoirs for funds, accepting money from a large number of individuals and investing it in short-term credits or securities. Among these firms were the savings banks, which grew in number and the size of their deposits. The first mutual savings bank in the country, The Philadelphia Savings Funds Society, was established in 1816, the same year in which the Provident Institution for Savings in Boston was chartered. By 1860 deposits in these and similar banks totaled $150,000,000. These funds flowed indirectly into credits for business, loans on mortgages, and securities. As the activities of these firms increased, the states passed general laws governing the investment of their funds. Massachusetts in 1834 put a limit of $1,000 on a deposit by an individual in one bank and stipulated that annual financial statements should be made.[38]

Trust companies developed and usually took larger sums for investment. Although in most cases before 1850 contractual interest was paid on trust deposits, in some instances funds were kept separately and invested for an individual. The Massachusetts Hospital Life Insurance Company, established in 1818, at first followed another practice. The beneficiary did not receive income from the specific trust property, but his share of the income derived from all the funds of the company, in a manner similar to the policy of the modern investment trust. As the financial affairs of corporations became more complex, the trust companies also developed agency functions, paid dividends and interest, and in other ways served corporations.[39]

Insurance companies accumulated funds available for investment. By 1841 there were 131 domestic mutual and stock fire and marine insurance

---

[36] Henry Clewes, *Fifty Years in Wall Street*, p. 78. New York: Irving Publishing Company, 1908.

[37] Albert O. Greef, *The Commercial Paper House in the United States*, pp. 3-37. Cambridge: Harvard University Press, 1938.

[38] Franklin J. Sherman, *Modern Story of Mutual Savings Banks*, pp. 49, 55, 69. New York: J. J. Little & Ives, 1934; Roy A. Foulke, *The Sinews of American Commerce*, p. 178. New York: Dun & Bradstreet, Inc., 1941.

[39] James G. Smith, *The Development of Trust Companies in the United States*, pp. 239-246, 273, 276, 290-291, 316. New York: Henry Holt and Company, 1928.

companies that not only sold insurance but granted short-term loans on promissory notes or mortgages. Life insurance got its real start early in the nineteenth century. The Pennsylvania Company for Insurance on Lives and Granting Annuities was chartered in 1812. New companies were organized and such institutions as the Massachusetts Hospital Life Insurance Company, and the New York Life Insurance and Trust Company brought together an increasing volume of funds that were invested in securities, loans on collateral and mortgages on real estate.[40]

Conclusion

While the foregoing changes in the capital markets were taking place, many events, political and economic, foreign and domestic, had exerted a disturbing influence. Strained national and international relations and exchanges had complicated dealings between creditors and debtors. Changes in the tariff, the struggle over the Second Bank of the United States, the establishment of the Independent Treasury—these and minor events agitated the business world. In the 1850's the flow of gold from California added a new feature to be considered, and uncertainty was increased by the disturbed political conditions of that decade. The Civil War both disturbed the money markets and stimulated their development. During the period 1789 to 1865, several crises and ensuing periods of depression occurred. At such times the weaknesses in the financial system were widely discussed. Caught in the current, many men and firms failed, and even the successful struggled through many stormy years of economic uncertainty.

The opportunities offered during the first three-quarters of a century of national life, however, had induced the development of the capital markets. The nation continued to depend on the importation of capital from Europe, but financial facilities in the United States had been expanded. Men and institutions in many cities had played their part in providing enterprises in their vicinities with credit institutions, and New York had developed into a national financial center. The issue of stocks and bonds had become an important means of bringing together large amounts of capital. Security markets had been organized and their volume of business had grown. Commercial credits had been increased. Specialists had emerged to deal in domestic bills of exchange and promissory notes. Intermediary institutions had appeared to serve those who only indirectly invested savings in long-term or short-term loans. Several types of firms had evolved to serve special needs; in the years that followed, many were to build on the houses founded and the techniques developed during these formative years.

---

[40] Roy A. Foulke, *The Sinews of American Commerce*, pp. 122 ff. and 162 ff. New York: Dun & Bradstreet, Inc., 1941; J. Owen Stalson, *Marketing Life Insurance, Its History in America*, pp. 46-49, 285-286. Cambridge, Mass.: Harvard University Press, 1942.

In the period before 1865 the growth of the capital markets had aided in the development of the nation. Facilitated by the new methods, the flow of funds had made possible the building of canals and railroads and the development of banking. Both export and import trade had been increased. Internal trade, expanding with the opening of Western areas and a growing population, had been financed. Funds had been supplied for new manufacturing and mining enterprises. In the rapid growth of the United States credit already had played a dynamic role.

Selected References

GENERAL WORKS

Edwards, George W., *The Evolution of Finance Capitalism.* New York: Longmans, Green & Company, 1938.

Foulke, Roy A., *The Sinews of American Commerce.* New York: Dun & Bradstreet, Inc., 1941.

Gras, N. S. B., and Henrietta M. Larson, *Casebook in American Business History.* New York: F. S. Crofts & Company, 1939.

Jenks, Leland Hamilton, *The Migration of British Capital to 1875.* New York: Alfred A. Knopf, 1927.

Lewis, Cleona, *America's Stake in International Investments.* Washington, D. C.: The Brookings Institution, 1938.

Moulton, Harold G., *Financial Organization and the Economic System.* New York: McGraw-Hill Book Company, Inc., 1938.

Myers, Margaret G., *The New York Money Market,* Vol. I, *Origins and Development.* New York: Columbia University Press, 1931.

Schultz, William J. and M. R. Caine, *Financial Development of the United States.* New York: Prentice-Hall, Inc., 1937.

SPECIAL TOPICS

Albion, Robert Greenhalgh, *The Rise of New York Port.* New York: Charles Scribner's Sons, 1939.

Brown, John Crosby, *A Hundred Years of Merchant Banking.* New York: privately printed, 1909.

Brown, Kenneth L., "Stephen Girard, Promoter of the Second Bank of the United States," *The Journal of Economic History,* Vol. II, No. 2 (November, 1942), p. 125.

Buck, Norman Sydney, *The Development of the Organisation of Anglo-American Trade, 1800-1850.* New Haven: Yale University Press, 1925.

Catterall, Ralph C. H., *The Second Bank of the United States.* Chicago: The University of Chicago Press, 1903.

Cole, Arthur H., "Evolution of the Foreign-Exchange Market of the United States," *Journal of Economic and Business History,* Vol. I, No. 3 (November, 1928), page 384.

Greef, Albert O., *The Commercial Paper House in the United States. Harvard Economic Studies,* Vol. LX. Cambridge, Mass.: Harvard University Press, 1938.

Hammond, Bray, "Long and Short Term Credit in Early American Banking," *Quarterly Journal of Economics,* Vol. XLIX, No. 1 (November, 1934), p. 79.

Hedges, Joseph Edward, *Commercial Banking and the Stock Market before 1863. The Johns Hopkins University Studies in Historical and Political Science, Series* LVI, No. 1. Baltimore: The Johns Hopkins Press, 1938.

Hidy, R. W., *The House of Baring in American Trade and Finance, 1763-1861.* Cambridge, Mass.: Harvard University Press, 1949.

———, "The Organization and Functions of Anglo-American Merchant Bankers, 1815-1860," *The Journal of Economic History,* Supplement (December, 1941), p. 53.

———, "The Union Bank of Louisiana Loan, 1932: A Case Study in Marketing," *The Journal of Political Economy,* Vol. XLVII, No. 2 (April, 1939), p. 232.

King, W. T. C., *History of the London Discount Market.* London: George Routledge & Sons, Ltd., 1936.

Larson, Henrietta M., *Jay Cooke, Private Banker.* Cambridge, Mass.: Harvard University Press, 1936.

———, "S. & M. Allen—Lottery, Exchange and Stock Brokerage," *Journal of Economic and Business History,* Vol. III, No. 3 (May, 1931), p. 424.

McGrane, Reginald C., *Foreign Bondholders and American State Debts.* New York: The Macmillan Company, 1935.

Meeker, J. Edward, *The Work of the Stock Exchange,* rev. ed. New York: The Ronald Press Company, 1930.

Peabody Papers. Salem, Mass.: unpublished manuscripts, Essex Institute.

Riggs Papers. Washington, D. C.: unpublished manuscripts, Library of Congress.

Sherman, Franklin J., *Modern Story of Mutual Savings Banks; a narrative of their growth and development from the inception to the present day.* New York: J. J. Little & Ives, 1934.

Smith, James G., *The Development of Trust Companies in the United States.* New York: Henry Holt and Company, 1928.

15 · BUSINESS ORGANIZATION AND THE DEVELOPMENT OF AN INDUSTRIAL DISCIPLINE

The Day of the Merchant

IN THE UNITED STATES in 1790 business was organized and business activities generally were conducted in the fashion that had been traditional in Europe for centuries. Business in this country consisted mainly of shipping, brokerage, wholesaling and retailing. There were but three banks in the United States of 1790, three bridge companies, a handful of insurance associations, and a dozen canal companies.[1] Of several manufacturing enterprises attempted on a factory basis, only one had succeeded. There was no labor force skilled in handling machinery, nor any executives experienced in managing complex business structures. Lack of inland transportation, save on occasional rivers, confined the market to the seaboard cities, and left the farmers of the interior largely self-sufficient. The city merchant was the typical business figure. From a small shop in downtown Boston, New York, Philadelphia, or Baltimore he carried on both wholesale and retail trade in various commodities, receiving his wares from and dispatching them to all parts of the world. Since he stayed in his office directing his agents, supercargoes, and ship captains, letting buyers come to him, he has been called the "sedentary" or "resident" merchant.

By 1860 American business had assumed almost all the varied forms and functions with which we are familiar in the twentieth century. Great railroad, telegraph, shipping, and canal companies employing thousands of men maintained metropolitan offices with scores of clerks, copyists, accountants, and executives. Banks and insurance companies had imposing buildings in every city. A thousand traveling salesmen drummed the wares of large factories devoted to textile, iron, leather, hardware, furniture, and many other kinds of manufactures. The modern type of corporation with hundreds or thousands of stockholders was the usual form in transportation, commercial banking, and insurance and had even ap-

[1] See Joseph S. Davis, *Essays in the Earlier History of American Corporations* (2 vols.). Cambridge, Mass.: Harvard University Press, 1917.

peared in some lines of manufacturing. The Industrial Revolution had come to America, and created the modern world of business.

While the ventures of the eighteenth-century merchants, with their large fleets of ships and their supercargoes buying and selling in all the ports of the seven seas, might be no less complex than modern business dealings, their administrative organizations were simple. A chief clerk and two or three apprentices constituted the entire "central office" staff, and among these the only permanent employee might be the clerk. Field ventures were intrusted to resident agents in foreign ports, to captains, or supercargoes, all of whom generally worked on commission, and could not be considered as part of a permanent hierarchical organization. Many merchants owned their ships, the crews in that case being employees, who should not, however, be classed as part of the mercantile staff, since the owners had no contact with them nor control over them once they had left the home port. Furthermore, in the business of trading in goods, the ship's crews performed only the auxiliary service of transportation.

The supercargo—the usual type of traveling commission agent—was generally a young relative or family friend of the merchant who accompanied the goods in transport and negotiated the necessary exchanges. This post was the best job for one wishing to learn the more important details of the business, and ordinarily it was used by the young man to amass enough capital from his commissions to enter business for himself. Similarly, a bankrupt merchant might recoup his fortune by a voyage or two as a supercargo for one of his more fortunate relatives. This reliance on family connections seems to have rested partly on the fact that honesty and diligence were more indispensable than skill or experience in conducting business thousands of miles away from the home office. But it was also a reflection of the patriarchal character of the prevailing system. Sons were trained to succeed fathers, and places were made for cousins, nephews, and relatives by marriage in preference to outsiders. As Professor Kenneth W. Porter puts it: [2]

> The Massachusetts mercantile group was apparently, during this period, pretty much of a closed corporation. In the Jackson-Cabot-Lee circle one does not encounter barefoot farm boys, who come to Boston, secure a warehouse job, study nights, get promoted to the countinghouse, become junior partners, and make their fortunes. It was not, nevertheless, impossible for a poor boy to work himself up to the position of an independent merchant, but his route would be by way of the fo'c'sle and quarter deck, and even here his chances would be considerably improved by being at least a distant and poor relative of the shipowner.

---

[2] See Kenneth W. Porter, *The Jacksons and the Lees* (2 vols.), Vol. I (Cambridge, Mass.: Harvard University Press, 1937), for a good description of the activities of the old style merchants. Reprinted by permission of the President and Fellows of Harvard College.

New York and Philadelphia business was probably less bound by family ties than Boston business. At all events, the greatest of the sedentary merchants, John Jacob Astor, succeeded in New York without benefit of any local family connections.[3] Astor's differences from the typical merchants of his day, however, may have accounted for his unusual degree of success. After only one or two voyages as an agent, he turned his major attention to the fur trade of the interior, and invested more of his money in New York City real estate than in merchant ships. Yet in other ways his activities were identical with those of Cabots or Lees, Derbys or Willings. Once he was well established, he stayed in his New York countinghouse, dispatching agents to trade in China, Hawaii, the Pacific Northwest, South America, and Mediterranean ports, as well as to gather furs from around the Great Lakes.

Typical also of the great merchant of the early nineteenth century was Astor's range of activities. He was a leader in the chartering of the Second Bank of the United States, and he became one of its directors as well as president of the New York branch. He owned the principal theater in New York, and later built the city's largest hotel. Retiring from active business in the early 1830's, he devoted the last dozen years of his long life to finance: buying and selling bonds, making loans, and acquiring more and more New York City real estate. It was this last field more than any other that helped him to accumulate $25,000,000 by the time of his death in 1846, more than twice the amount of capital that any American had so far amassed.

Never in all of Astor's extensive activities had he personally organized a large office or labor force, and the same was true of his great contemporaries. The conditions of the business seemed to have placed distinct limits on the expansion of the individual firm. Keen competition, due to the small amount of capital necessary to enter into trading ventures, kept profits reasonably low, and frequent failures made the successful merchant fearful of delegating responsibility. There was a time, to be sure, from about 1790 until 1807 when the rate of profit was steadily high, perhaps as much as 15 to 20 per cent a year for the abler operators, and it seemed as though some great houses like those of Girard, Astor, Derby, Gray, or Perkins might develop and perpetuate dominant positions in ship owning and foreign trade. But at the very peak of the movement, Government policies—trade restrictions, war, and tariffs—and after 1815 the rise of peacetime foreign competition put a deadly pressure on the rate of profit. One after another, between 1812 and 1830, the bigger houses abandoned world trading and shifted their capital to internal ventures such as banking, transportation, acquiring of western land, and manufacturing. Thus the most successful sedentary merchants became

[3] Kenneth W. Porter, *John Jacob Astor* (2 vols.) (Cambridge, Mass.: Harvard University Press, 1931), is the best business biography on this period.

manufacturers or financiers without ever having trained junior executives to assume part of the responsibility or having built up any great commercial organizations like the India companies of Europe. As railroad executives or manufacturers, they had to learn to handle the problems of large-scale management from the ground up.

The Rise of the Corporation

Partnerships, such as these old mercantile firms, were simple contracts governed by the common law. No partner might dispose of his holdings without the consent of all of the others and the death of any one of them terminated the whole agreement. Offsetting these inflexibilities in ownership, however, was the power of each partner to speak or make contracts for the firm, to handle the company business as simply as though it were his own.

Investments in shipping, trading, or small-scale manufacturing were regularly made on the basis of partnership agreements subscribed to because of faith in the other men involved, and usually the ability to keep an eye on what went on. The joint-stock company with its transferable securities or the corporation with its specially chartered privileges seldom appeared in American mercantile ventures. But new enterprises brought the need for new business forms. The capital necessary for large-scale operations in western land, turnpike, and canal companies made it necessary to go beyond the immediate locality for financing, and to seek investors who, being busy elsewhere, required the protection afforded by a governing board and freely salable shares of stock. The success of the joint-stock company in attracting the capital of merchants into large ventures gradually made it popular for small manufacturing operations as well. Even when only six or eight local capitalists were associated in an enterprise flexibility both as to size and ownership was assured by setting it up as a company rather than a partnership.

Several factors led to the increasing use of the chartered corporation rather than the joint-stock company in the second and third decades of the nineteenth century. The risks of manufacturing on the factory scale in America made the advantage of limited liability, when it could be secured by a charter, a great help in raising capital.[4] Turnpikes, canals, and railroads required increasingly large amounts of capital. To raise these sums, low par-value shares were offered in appeals to hundreds or even thousands of small investors who would not risk their money in distant enterprises unless protected against unlimited assessments. Furthermore, these ventures and many others such as bridge, power, and

---

[4] New York led the way by an act of 1822 in the establishment of limited partnerships. The limited partners took no part in management, and incurred no risks beyond the cost of their shares. But the ordinary rules of partnership governed withdrawal from the agreement. Connecticut soon passed a similar law.

water supply companies had to have franchises for the use of public property.

Consequently, the wave of corporate business rose steadily, in spite of the many difficulties accompanying incorporation by special act. To get a charter passed by the state legislature involved delays, lobbying expenses, and possible exposure to public attack by journalists and politicians. It cost Colonel Neilson and other promoters of the Delaware and Raritan Canal Company, for example, $3,100 and two years of work to get a charter from the New Jersey Legislature. Special acts might have, of course, some compensating advantages. Skillful legal arrangements or wise expenditure of money often won the company special right or privileges. Railroads like the Boston and Lowell, and the Camden and Amboy were granted monopoly privileges, while Southern lines like the New Orleans and Carrollton were allowed to issue paper money and conduct banking businesses.[5]

Two distinct concepts spurred the movement for general incorporation acts. Laws like that enacted by New York in 1811 for the incorporation of certain kinds of manufacturing concerns with less than $100,000 capital, or by Connecticut in 1817 and Massachusetts in 1830 granting limited liability, were passed to encourage incorporation. The later wave of general incorporation acts after the panic of 1837 and the long depression that followed was inspired largely by the fear that corporations were gaining too many dangerous privileges through special acts. Led by Connecticut in 1837, Maryland, New Jersey, New York, Pennsylvania, Indiana, Massachusetts, and Virginia all passed some type of general incorporation statute before the Civil War. In all cases save those of Connecticut and Virginia, the laws had certain restrictions as to types of companies not found in modern general acts, but they were all alike in striving to bring about uniformity and to protect the public from special privileges in the establishment of corporations. Yet the ease of incorporation under these laws was in the long run a great stimulus to "big" business and the increasing use of the corporate form of organization.

The rise of the large corporation introduced a division between ownership and control that had not existed in the partnership or small company. The old conception of the entrepreneur as the man who ventured his money and energies, and, if successful, took the rewards no longer applied. When the directors—those who made the business decisions—held but little stock in the company they were inevitably risking "other people's money" more than their own, while the larger group that had ventured their savings had no direct control over the conduct of the business. This form of organization, minority ownership by the directors, has been

[5] See: F. A. Cleveland and F. W. Powell, *Railroad Promotion and Capitalization*. New York: Longmans, Green and Company, 1909.

called by Berle and Means the "modern" corporation.[6] It first appeared in America with the establishment of banks at the close of the Revolution. The Bank of North America, the Bank of New York, the Massachusetts Bank, and the First Bank of the United States were all "modern" corporations. The large amount of capital required for transportation enterprises produced a division between ownership and control from the start, but not until the later 1820's did it appear in manufacturing, where investments were smaller and dependence on skill management greater. As this type of corporation spread in the thirties and forties, and as examples of occasional mismanagement by directors whose own fortunes were not deeply involved were brought to light, economic thinkers became disturbed by the situation. Even Nathan Appleton, himself one of the greatest directors of "modern" corporations, wrote in 1841:

> There is, in the nature of things, greater danger of mismanagement in such an institution, where the interest of the managers is comparatively small, than in institutions of less capital immediately under the direction of parties more deeply interested.

The capital needs of banking and transportation brought state participation in business organization. Few such pioneer enterprises seemed possible without substantial state, county, or municipal purchases of stocks and bonds. The credit of the state was generally substituted in part for that of the private company by issuance of state bonds and use of the proceeds to buy the company's securities. The states in this way piled up debts of $100,000,000 for the securities of banks, railroads, and canals during the twenties and thirties, and new Western states repeated the process in the fifties. In a few instances transportation systems were constructed by the states themselves and operated under state ownership. New York by 1825 had finished the Erie Canal at a cost of nearly $8,500,000; Pennsylvania by 1834 had built a rival canal, rail, and cable system from Philadelphia to Pittsburgh at a cost of more than $33,000,000. The problem of crossing the southern Appalachians was finally solved in 1851 by the Western and Atlantic Railroad, owned by the state of Georgia. The determining factor leading to state enterprise in all of these cases seems to have been high initial costs in relation to expectations of an immediate, profitable return.

Free and secret transferability of corporate ownership encouraged grave abuses on the part of unscrupulous financiers. It was possible for managing groups to profit personally by ruining great companies and then selling out before the situation became known. Daniel Drew was perhaps the outstanding example of this kind of entrepreneur in the period before the Civil War. He bought and sold, built up or ruined properties solely

---

[6] A. A. Berle and G. C. Means, *The Modern Corporation and Private Property*. New York: The Macmillan Company, 1932.

for the purpose of extracting the maximum personal gain. But in the long run the more conscientious men, who mixed pride in productive efficiency with the quest for wealth, were better rewarded. Cornelius Vanderbilt, Nathan Appleton, and Erastus Corning all branched out from the successful conduct of one enterprise to the control of many through strategic stock ownership.

The best-known of this trio of general entrepreneurs is Vanderbilt, who amassed the largest fortune, but much of whose fame and wealth rest on his railroad activities following the Civil War.[7] Never a pioneer in new industries, he had a keen sense of when to interest himself in a company, and when to sell out. Specializing first in steamboat and steamship lines, his basic principle seems to have been either to establish a monopoly or sell control to someone who could. One of the great competitors, his aim was always to eliminate competition. So successful was he in bringing competitive pressure against the Government-subsidized steamship lines between New York and San Francisco that after 1856 they paid him first $40,000 and later $56,000 a month not to engage in the business. He boasted that if he couldn't operate a steamboat line 20 per cent cheaper than a competitor, he would get out of the business, and he averaged 25 per cent a year on his investments. Abandoning the shipping business for railroading during the Civil War, he put together the New York Central system from New York to Chicago, and in the course of the operations increased his fortune from perhaps $20,000,000 to $100,000,000.

Nathan Appleton illustrates most clearly the possibilities of widespread influence opened to the financier by the modern corporation. Turning from mercantile pursuits in 1813, Appleton, together with some of the Lowells and Jacksons, put his capital into large-scale textile manufacture. As the efficiently run business prospered the profits were invested in new textile companies, and many other forms of enterprise. Appleton came to be looked upon as the business leader of Massachusetts, sometimes sitting in Congress, at other times coaching Daniel Webster to look after his interests, and always writing and lecturing on the value of the protective tariff and sound banking. By 1840 he and his Boston associates had created in eastern Massachusetts a miniature of the corporate industrial society of the twentieth century. They controlled banking, railroad, insurance, and power companies, as well as great textile mills scattered all over the state.[8] It was the large "modern" corporation controllable by strategically organized blocs of shares, and virtually self-

---

[7] See Wheaton J. Lane, *Commodore Vanderbilt*. New York: Alfred A. Knopf, Inc., 1942. A general entrepreneur is one who controls many ventures, usually without assuming the duties of routine management.

[8] See Vera Shlakman, *Economic History of a Factory Town*. Northampton: Smith College, 1935.

perpetuating boards of directors that made this concentration of power possible, but it must be remembered that it was also this device for gathering together the savings of thousands of small investors that had produced the great development.

Management and Labor

The merchant, the master worker, or the owner of the small mill or foundry was scarcely conscious of "management" as a separate task. There was no managerial hierarchy or managerial departmentalization beyond the distinction between laborers, overseers, and clerks, and more often than not the books were kept by the proprietor.[9] Only on ocean-going ships was there a truly hierarchical business organization, and there the captain rather than the merchant was in charge. The captain faced many of the personnel problems of modern management, but the traditional rules of the sea and the routine nature of most of the tasks made his job a relatively simple one. Even at this early date, however, success in trade probably depended more on the choice of able captain-managers than on any other single element, and it was here that the great merchants like Astor, Girard, Derby, and Gray showed their executive ability.

The growth of the large company between 1790 and 1860 brought with it the necessity for more complex structure in management. Expansion gradually forced canal, railroad, and even large manufacturing companies to departmentalize their staffs. The chief executive came to have less contact with actual operations, and more frequent relations with lesser officers, clerks, and foremen. Usually these trends were resisted both by presidents and directors, and many large mills employing hundreds of workers were run with negligible office forces. As late as 1851 the Eastern and Portland Railroad out of Boston, one of the chief suburban lines, employed only one clerk. But some of the new forms of business already demanded large office staffs. The Delaware and Hudson Canal Company, for instance, required a whole building in New York City to house the administrative force that controlled its 4,200 employees. Banks and insurance companies needed relatively large numbers of white-collar workers and junior executives. As early as 1814 the Massachusetts Bank had, besides a president and vice-president, nine employees, ranging from cashier to assistant clerk.

The supply of new executives for these growing enterprises came not only from the existing mercantile class, but also from the agricultural yeomanry, the skilled hand workers, and the successful small operators. When, for example, Zadoc Pratt decided to establish his great tannery at Pottsville, New York, in 1824, he recruited his labor from the surround-

9 See Robert G. Albion, *The Rise of New York Port*. New York: Charles Scribner's Sons, 1939.

ing countryside, and hired the owner of a small tannery at Northampton, Massachusetts, to serve as manager. As managerial positions multiplied rapidly with the spread of banking, insurance, manufacturing, and transportation, the development gave to our whole business society a dynamic and optimistic aspect. The new superintendents, agents, cashiers, and even clerks had skills that commanded good pay. Compared to laborers or most farmers, they could be called "high-level consumers." This new consumer demand stimulated the growth of service industries such as newspapers, theaters, large retail stores, and the passenger business of rail and boat lines that, in turn, provided still more administrative jobs. In prosperous times, positions multiplied more rapidly than the supply of men of proved ability to fill them. Hence, advancement was rapid and fairly certain for industrious men with the right qualifications.

Within the new companies, even as late as 1860, managerial problems were solved simply by experience or rule of thumb. No books had yet analyzed the functions of the executive, personnel management, or staff and line co-ordination. Yet, as the organizations were small enough for effective one-man supervision, results were, on the whole, tolerably satisfactory. Dr. J. S. Davis, to be sure, thinks that the failure of most of our early manufacturing establishments may have been due to weaknesses in management; but once the pioneering stage was passed and certain lessons had been learned, American industry seems to have been well run. A good president in almost any company could keep track of all branches of the business and know all the lesser administrators and even the older workmen. Thus, there was a natural co-ordination of departments and functions that has been duplicated in modern big business only, if at all, by careful study reinforced by psychological and efficiency-engineering techniques.

Fully as scarce in 1800 as competent executives were properly skilled workers. At that time there was only a handful of shops in the whole country using any kind of complicated machine processes. But when trade difficulties and eventual war with England between 1807 and 1815 cut off imports, hand workers and farmers had to become skilled mechanics. The transition has never been easy, either in America or elsewhere. Not until 1814 was there a power loom in this country, and one constructed then by F. C. Lowell cost more than four times as much as the contemporary Scottish models. Yet, every one of the hundreds of factories that sprang up during these years needed machinery and skilled mechanics.[10] Foreign technicans, good, bad, or indifferent, sold their services at a premium, and

---

[10] See: Arthur H. Cole, *The American Wool Manufacture* (2 vols.). Cambridge, Mass.: Harvard University Press, 1926. Arthur H. Cole and Harold F. Williamson, *The American Carpet Manufacture*. Cambridge, Mass.: Harvard University Press, 1941. Caroline F. Ware, *The Early New England Cotton Manufacture*. New York: Houghton Mifflin Company, 1931.

firms employing such workers advertised the fact as a guarantee of the quality of their products. Not until the 1830's, when a new generation familiar with machinery had grown up, and more foreign workers had developed the habit of seeking their fortunes in America, did the skilled labor supply begin to catch up with the demand.

The early railroads, in particular, suffered from lack of both skilled workers and executives. Safe and efficient railroading depends upon a high level of reliability that comes only with experience and the development of traditional routines. The switchman must realize that hundreds of lives depend upon his continuous vigilance; the men responsible for train dispatching must keep in mind that there can be no mix-ups in their orders; maintenance men must understand that they cannot afford to take chances with slightly weak equipment. The development of all these disciplines and the experience and information necessary to them took time. To one accustomed to the smooth efficiency of railroading in the mid-twentieth century, the annals of the 1830's, forties, and fifties have an unreal, nightmarish quality. Terrific wrecks due to the most elementary errors, and delays of hours or even days because of the simplest kind of carelessness in the upkeep of equipment were common.[11] These and similar wastes were endured over and over again as machines spread continuously to new areas, recruiting employees from among men brought up on farms.

Finding unskilled labor for factories and mills, railroads, and canal construction was a less difficult problem. While the big textile mills in the New England area had to recruit workers by sending agents with wagons into the back country, the supply of men, women, and children from surrounding farms was adequate for ordinary enterprises. By 1816 cotton manufacturers employed 66,000 women and girls, 24,000 boys, and 10,000 men; and there are no records of business ventures being seriously handicapped by lack of common labor.[12] From the 1830's on, large numbers of Irish and German immigrants swelled the supply of unskilled workers. In the forties and fifties these earlier Europeans were augmented by French Canadians seeking relief from the hard farming conditions of Ontario, Quebec, and the Maritime Provinces. So great was this flood of immigrant labor after 1845 that native workers joined in ineffectual movements to restrict immigration and naturalization. By 1860 more than one-third of the population of New York and one-quarter of the population of Rhode Island and Massachusetts was foreign born.

Many German immigrants, having money, went into the Western farming areas, but the impoverished Irish had to stay in the cities, forming a

---

[11] See F. C. B. Bradley, *The Eastern Railroad*. Salem, Mass.: Essex Institute, 1922.

[12] See James L. Bishop, *A History of American Manufacturing from 1608 to 1860* (3 vols.). Philadelphia: E. Young, 1868; and Victor S. Clark, *History of Manufactures in the United States* (3 vols.). New York: McGraw-Hill Book Company, 1929.

cheap but undisciplined working force.[13] Riots of Irish stevedores, porters, and construction crews seem to have been frequent. Often, as in 1834, when striking workmen killed several contractors on the Washington railroad, these disturbances led to bloodshed and the calling out of police or militia. In the factories employing large numbers of men, strikes over wages and hours seem to have been frequent during the periods of prosperity. But none of these activities prior to the Civil War led to any permanent organization of unskilled labor.

In this period the skilled craftsmen, producing mainly for city consumption, were the only workers to form effective unions. Cooperation among these urban craftsmen dates back to the eighteenth century associations for mutual aid in sickness and death. But the associations to better wages and working conditions formed by the shoemakers (called cordwainers) and the typographers in New York and Philadelphia at the end of the century are the earliest ancestors of modern trade unions. The increasing size of urban markets, leading to more workers and keener competition, spread organization to other skilled groups such as stone cutters, masons, carpenters, and tailors. These unions sought both higher wages, during the period of rising prices from 1790 to 1815, and maintenance of the system that denied workers the status of journeyman, or fully qualified worker, until they had served a term of apprenticeship.

Meanwhile the employers, or master workers, tightened up their own local associations, formed initially to control prices and selling practices, and used them to present uniform resistance to the demands of the workers. In 1816 the employers successfully prosecuted the striking Journeymen Cordwainers of Philadelphia for common-law conspiracy in restraint of trade. But since, in most cases, it was quicker and cheaper to meet strikes by lockouts, strikebreakers, or direct negotiation, the courts were not as much of a deterrent to labor action as might be presumed from a reading of the occasional decisions.

In the mild business upswing of the mid-eighteen twenties the local craft organizations increased in numbers and strength. Led by the building workers of Philadelphia in 1827, the crafts in the major cities established Central Unions of Trade Associations. While these regional federations devoted their energies largely to reform through political action, they also served to unite the workers on such issues as the ten-hour day.

The inflationary boom from 1834 to 1837 gave a great impetus to trade union activity in the urban crafts. The union ranks widened to include such skilled journeymen as painters, cabinet makers, hat finishers, basket makers, locksmiths, coopers, carpet weavers, and coach makers. After 1834 the trades associations of the cities held national conventions, and

---

13 See Marcus L. Hansen, *The Atlantic Migration, 1607-1860.* Cambridge, Mass.: Harvard University Press, 1940; and Oscar Handlin, *Boston's Immigrants, 1790-1865.* Cambridge, Mass.: Harvard University Press, 1941.

a few of the crafts attempted national organization. From 1834 to 1836 the number of trade unionists, it was claimed, increased from 26,500 to 300,000. Even if half the latter figure is correct, it indicates a high percentage of unionization among the skilled handworkers in the cities.

The rise of union militancy gave new vitality to the older master's associations. Strikes for the ten-hour day and higher wages were fought by seven employer's organizations in Philadelphia, and eight in New York. As in earlier years, the employers successfully appealed to the courts against the right of unions to picket or attempt to enforce the closed shop. Only in Massachusetts, in Commonwealth vs. Hunt, a case not decided until 1842, did a judge uphold the right of peaceful picketing. But it was the long depression after 1837, more than employer or legal opposition, that broke the strength of the unions.[14] During the forties, increasing mechanization, immigration of skilled workers from Germany and England, and general depression reduced the craft unions to regional organizations for co-operative insurance, education, and social functions.

Prosperity in the early fifties brought new militancy and strikes, but once again successful organization was confined to the highly skilled trades. And, whereas the unionists of the twenties and thirties had been interested in political and social reform for the benefit of labor as a whole, those of the fifties confined their attention rather strictly to apprenticeship rules, the closed shop, higher wages, and shorter hours. Led by the efforts of typographers in 1850, half a dozen of the strategically situated skilled crafts formed some type of national organization before 1860.

In the factory industries where the employers were stronger, labor remained unorganized. The blacklist from 1829 on, at least, proved a most effective weapon for preventing union activity. No worker, it was said, after dismissal from one of the "boarding house" mills of Massachusetts could get another job in this type of factory. The railroads were able to pursue similar policies through their regional managers' associations. By 1860 virtually every trade in every locality had some kind of association for dealing with labor, but none of them had as yet perfected national organizations equal to those of the strongest trade unions.

The movements of real wages and their effect on American productivity and living standards prior to the Civil War are highly uncertain. Reliable statistical series are lacking and different standards of consumption vitiate comparisons. The unions appear to have been responsible for fairly rapid advances in the wages of skilled workers during the periods of rising prices, but, since only a small and specialized fraction of the labor force was unionized, it is impossible to measure the effect of craft organization on the general wage level.

---

[14] John R. Commons and Associates, *History of Labor in the United States,* Vol. I. New York: The Macmillan Company, 1936.

Wage and hour standards were regarded by most employers and many workmen as fixed by the demands of competition. No manager thought of studying the problem of whether shorter hours and better working conditions might lead to greater productivity. If an employer paid the traditional or prevailing rate, and asked for the usual number of hours of labor he was dealing "justly" with his employees. He would, almost without exception, be convinced that any departure from these wage standards in an upward direction would be ruinous, and in some cases, where a truly competitive market existed, he was right. Unless a regional union could enforce equal conditions on all competitors it was dangerous for any individual employer to meet the delegates' demands. Perhaps even more important was the employer's feeling that he could not run his business efficiently if he were "dictated to" by labor leaders outside his plant.[15] Unionism with its demands for fixed arrangements menaced the flexibility in costs and the high degree of managerial opportunism that, in the minds of the management, were necessary factors in competitive success.

Another major reason for the slow growth of both managerial organization and trade unions was the paternalism of many employers, and the existence in a real form of "personal relations" between the older worker and the "big boss." By the 1830's cotton manufacture was the most advanced factory industry, yet there were, on the average, less than a hundred employees per establishment in New York and Massachusetts. Even by 1860 only six industries averaged more than 100 employees per plant, and of these only cotton textiles (with an average of about 120) consisted of many establishments. The McCormick plant in Chicago, the largest agricultural machinery factory, employed 300 workers in the mid-fifties, but it was managed personally by Leander McCormick, Cyrus's brother, and four foremen. The very biggest plants were the marine iron works in New York City employing up to a thousand men, but even here contact between the managing partners and the skilled workers seems to have been fairly close. In the great majority of cases the plant manager was also a heavy investor in the enterprise. Under such conditions he could dispense a sort of compensation insurance out of his own pocket. Knowing the lives of his permanent employees, he could aid them when sickness came or care for them or their families in case of injury. Unconsciously the older workers and the boss entered into semifeudal relations. The workers gave the boss loyal support in his battles with competitors and he in turn regarded them as "his" men.

The pleasant personal relations and working conditions of the owner-run plant were, to be sure, not universal. Railroads, shipping, and New England textile manufacture in particular presented pictures of low-paid,

[15] See T. C. Cochran and W. Miller, *The Age of Enterprise,* Chapter XI. New York: The Macmillan Company, 1942.

overworked operatives who were left to shift for themselves in case of sickness or injury. Top executives in railroad and shipping lines were necessarily out of touch with local "shop" conditions, and the large corporate organization of most Massachusetts cotton mills brought them under the same handicap. In all these industries the dictatorship of the "little boss" or foremen began to assert itself and produce the mixture of evils and occasional benefits that was to present such problems to the big companies of the twentieth century.

The Problems of Competition

The self-sufficient, agricultural society of inland America at the end of the eighteenth century was from the business standpoint largely non-competitive. As long as transportation was prohibitively expensive, the local gristmill, tannery, sawmill, smithy, or general store represented a regional monopoly. The rapid spread of turnpikes, canals, and railroads in the first decades of the nineteenth century, however, rudely shattered these stabilized business relations in one community after another and ushered in a period of intense competition between local and "outside" products. The cheaper transportation became, the more certain was the conquest of the market by outside factory-made wares; and the broader the market became, the greater were the advantages of mass production. When Zadoc Pratt, for example, invested $250,000 in "the world's largest tannery" at Pottsville, one may be sure that scores of local tanners in central New York were driven out of business. The rise of Dun's and Bradstreet's mercantile credit agencies after 1840, making it possible safely to extend credit to strange or remote merchants, removed one of the major handicaps to doing business at a distance. Thus, by 1860 local monopoly or duopoly survived chiefly in the selling and service trades such as storekeeping, barbering, horseshoeing, building, or banking.

As new machine processes cut the cost of an article and moved its production from the home or small shop to the factory, a favorable or "sellers' " market would be opened for the product at new low prices that nevertheless paid a high return to the factory owner. Organization of additional manufacturing companies would follow, until the demand for the article was more than supplied and sellers were forced into cutthroat competition. As soon as this situation appeared in any of the mechanized fields, those firms suffering most from the competition invariably took steps to bring it under control. An attempt to distinguish their products from those of their competitors by brand names or special features was often the first step. In such ways makers of clocks, metal ware, firearms and even sheet brass were able to maintain special markets for their products at prices somewhat above their competitors, or else were able to convince their rivals that nothing would be gained by price warfare. Where the product, such as flour or tobacco, was hard to "differentiate," recourse might be had to fancy sacks or other distinctive packages.

But with advertising still local and generally limited to a few lines of type, and with consumers accustomed to buying goods in bulk and haggling over prices, "price maintenance" through brand names, packaging, or other differentiation proved in many cases to be ineffective. Formation of a regional trade association, similar to those created locally by the old master workers in the handicrafts, was usually the next recourse for dealing with competition. Through this organization attempts were made to fix prices at a point that would allow a profit to all competitors, and, if possible, to limit production so as to avoid surpluses that would endanger the market. Such co-operation seemed necessary to preserve price stability whenever large amounts of invested capital were at stake in either manufacturing or transportation. One of the earliest trade-association agreements was that of the upper Ohio River steambot operators in 1818 regulating rates and schedules, but in general the decade of the fifties marked the spread of the large regional or national associations such as The New England Railway Managers Association, The American Brass Association, and The American Iron Association.[16]

As written agreements for price fixing or limitation of production fell within the usual common law interpretation of conspiracy in restraint of trade, all bargains rested on verbal or "gentlemen's" agreements that could not be enforced by law. The trouble with such agreements was described by a speaker at a convention of New England railroad executives in 1851:

> We make solemn bargains with each other to be governed by certain principles and rules, and violate them the same day, by a secret bargain with an individual, to obtain a small pittance of freight from another road.

As soon as one party started to sell below the price agreed upon, the whole arrangement, of course, broke down. Pooling of goods or traffic and sale through a central agency offered a better guarantee of fair dealing, but the quotas were very difficult to arrange and normally had to be re-negotiated each year. The final solutions, reached even as early as the forties, were either consolidation of the principal firms into a single company or control of the various competing companies by a single stockholder interest. The first type of solution is illustrated by New York Central in the railroad field, Western Union in telegraphy, and the Kanawha River Salt Association in manufacturing; the second type by the enterprises of the "Boston Associates" in Massachusetts, discussed on page 285. But in most cases these final steps were not taken until many years

---

16 For early beginnings see Louis Hunter, *Studies in the Economic History of the Ohio Valley*. Northampton: Smith College, 1934; for general discussion, see Cochran and Miller, *Age of Enterprise*, pp. 59-63.

after the Civil War, and meanwhile "gentlemen's agreements" or pools were made, broken, and remade year after year.

Business on the Eve of the War

Within the first 60 years of the nineteenth century a competent industrial labor force had been created from a nation of farmers. National trade unions had grown up in the most skilled crafts, and from 1859 on there were annual conventions of national trade union leaders. Rapid immigration to Eastern cities in the two decades before the war provided an abundant supply of unskilled labor, while those immigrants who went West seeking farms broadened the markets for industrial products.

Although business organization as a whole was still regional and small-scale, a railway net stretching from Boston, Charleston, and New Orleans to LaCrosse, Wisconsin, St. Joseph, Missouri and Wynne, Arkansas, invited mass production for a national market. Some products such as Colt arms, McCormick farm machinery, Baldwin locomotives, Pratt leathers, American screws, or New England textiles already occupied this market, coming by rail and steamboat to distribution centers like Chicago, St. Louis, Memphis, or New Orleans. But the protection afforded by transportation costs and the absence of widespread national advertising preserved the existence of thousands of local enterprises. Most firms sold only in certain natural geographic regions, shipping only limited distances and depending upon consumer satisfaction and local advertising for the spread of their wares. New Jersey and New York were dotted with small iron works that sold locally in competition with Pittsburgh firms, and almost every state had textile mills that held their regional customers against the pressure from New England.

Management had already faced, in embryo form at least, most of the problems of large-scale business organization. The co-ordination of big office staffs had been learned, particularly in finance and transportation, and fixed habits or disciplines were developing among the underlings that made it safe to delegate to them authority over routine matters. While no important fields of production had been monopolized by a single company, managers had experimented with almost all the modern techniques of limited competition. The rise of the "trust" and the railroad "ownership system" in the succeeding decades were already clearly foreshadowed in the trends of Eastern business.

Selected References

GENERAL WORKS

Albion, Robert G., *The Rise of New York Port.* New York: Charles Scribner's Sons, 1939.

Clark, Victor S., *History of Manufactures in the United States,* Vol. I. New York: The McGraw-Hill Book Company, 1929.

Cleveland, F. A., and F. W. Powell, *Railroad Promotion and Capitalization*. New York: Longmans, Green & Company, 1909.

Cochran, T. C., and William Miller, *The Age of Enterprise*. New York: The Macmillan Company, 1942.

Cole, Arthur H., *The American Wool Manufacture*, Vol. I. Cambridge, Mass.: Harvard University Press, 1926.

———, and H. F. Williamson, *The American Carpet Manufacture*. Cambridge, Mass.: Harvard University Press, 1941.

Commons, John R., and associates, *History of Labor in the United States*, Vol. I. New York: The Macmillan Company, 1936.

Dulles, Foster R., *Labor in America*. New York: Thomas Y. Crowell Company, 1949.

Gras, N. S. B., and H. M. Larson, *Casebook in American Business History*. New York: F. S. Crofts & Company, 1939.

Green, Constance M., *Holyoke, Massachusetts*. New Haven, Conn.: Yale University Press, 1939.

Handlin, Oscar, and Mary Flug, *Commonwealth, A Study of the Role of Government in the American Economy: Massachusetts, 1774-1861*. New York: New York University Press, 1947.

Hansen, Marcus, L., *The Atlantic Migration, 1607-1860*. Cambridge, Mass.: Harvard University Press, 1940.

Hertz, Louis, *Economic Policy and Economic Thought: Pennsylvania, 1776-1860*. Cambridge, Mass.: Harvard University Press, 1948.

Kirkland, Edward C., *Men, Cities and Transportation* (2 vols.). Cambridge, Mass.: Harvard University Press, 1948.

Lane, Wheaton J., *Commodore Vanderbilt*. New York: Alfred A. Knopf, Inc., 1942.

Porter, Kenneth W., *John Jacob Astor* (2 vols). Cambridge, Mass.: Harvard University Press, 1931.

Shlakman, Vera, *Economic History of a Factory Town*. Northampton, Mass.: Smith College, 1935.

Ware, Caroline F., *The Early New England Cotton Manufacture*. New York: Houghton Mifflin Company, 1931.

SPECIAL TOPICS

Appleton, Nathan, *Introduction of the Power Loom and the Origin of Lowell*. Lowell, Mass.: B. H. Penhallow, 1858. (See also many other writings by Appleton.)

Bishop, James L., *A History of American Manufacturing from 1608 to 1860* (3 vols.). Philadelphia: E. Young, 1868.

Commons, John R., and others, eds., *A Documentary History of American Industrial Society* (11 vols.). Cleveland: A. H. Clark, 1910-1911.

Porter, Kenneth W., *The Jacksons and the Lees* (2 vols.). Cambridge, Mass.: Harvard University Press, 1937.

16 · PUBLIC FINANCE AND FISCAL POLICY, 1789-1865

CIVILIZED SOCIETIES have all had some sort of government even as did the Egyptians who banded together to maintain their dikes and irrigation trenches along the Nile. The need for protection has been the most important motivating factor in the establishment of governments; protection against nature, against outsiders or foreigners, against members of the society itself. As civilization has become more complex other needs have pressed to the fore, and governments have undertaken to protect their people from the results of social and economic forces as well as from the direct action of natural forces. They have endeavored, also, to contribute to the positive development of men and society as well as to guarantee the more negative end of protection. The form and structure of governments have varied greatly, from monarchies and dictatorships to democracies. In all, including America, serious disputes have arisen over the proper scope of the activities of government. In all of them the question of how the government should be supported has been of great moment; whether the necessary exactions have been in direct labor, agricultural produce, military service, or monetary payments, who should be required to pay them and in what amount have been major problems.

The Colonial Background

Actually these problems were relatively unimportant during the greater part of the American Colonial period. The fiscal activities of Colonial governments were narrow in scope and their expenditures were accordingly small. The support of the governor frequently accounted for one of the largest items; the expenses of the militia, which were sometimes met by the individual members, were not great, and no navy was maintained. The Colonies benefited substantially, of course, from the protection afforded them both on land and sea by the British government. There were no costly public improvements and no expenditures for welfare purposes. Unemployment was practically unknown and families looked after their own poor or unfortunate. Taxation for the support of churches, however, was common in many of the Colonies; although the desire for religious freedom played a part in the settling of the new continent, the separation of church and state and religious toleration came only as a later development. While private schools were numerous, education was not generally considered a public function, although some expenditures for schools were made in New England. In fact, Massachusetts towns were required as early as 1642 to give public instruction, but the law was far from being universally observed.

The sources of Colonial revenue were various. In New England the Colonies levied a poll tax and a tax on the gross produce of land, the latter finally developing into a general property tax. A faculty tax, or a tax on individuals according to the incomes assumed to result from their occupations, was added later. During the Revolutionary War more than a third of the Colonies were moved to impose faculty taxes by the appearance of profits that were not subject to the property tax, but most of these taxes were discontinued after the War. In the South, where there were many large estates, the property tax was not so well received, and, although the poll tax had been the chief source of revenue in the beginning, it lost favor with the importation of slaves and indirect taxes became the main source of revenue. Indirect taxes or excises were also the mainstay of revenue in the middle Colonies where the traders were influenced by their Dutch background. Custom duties and excises were used by nearly all of the Colonies to some extent, but there was an early decline in the use of export duties, and these had practically disappeared by the middle of the eighteenth century. A large amount of revenue was also derived from issues of paper money, which assumed greater importance after the Revolution when the restraints of the royal governors and the British government were removed. The economic and social significance of fiscal policy could be seen at an early date in a number of states where farmers were influential in securing large issues of paper money that raised the prices of agricultural products and made it easier for them to pay their debts.

The situation that gave rise to the Revolutionary War necessitated a more centralized form of government, and in this development the Continental Congress was the first step. The Congress could not regulate commerce among the states, it had no authority to establish a uniform system of currency, and it could not interfere with state issues of paper money. While it could vote money for certain purposes, it had little power to raise revenue either in its early days or after the adoption of the Articles of Confederation. The sale of land in the Northwest Territory proved disappointing as a source of revenue, and only small contributions were forthcoming from the states. Since the Congress was not empowered to levy taxes, it obtained most of its funds from the issue of paper money and from borrowing at home and abroad.

Federal Finance: Powers Under the Constitution

It was obvious from the experience of the Continental and Confederation Governments that a Federal Government could not function satisfactorily unless financially independent of the states. Fear of a strong central government was still so great, however, that the powers given the new government established in 1789 were carefully defined and circumscribed in the Constitution. Congress was authorized "to coin money" and "regulate the value thereof," to borrow, "to lay and collect taxes, duties, imposts, and excises, to pay the debts and provide for the common defense and general welfare of the United States." Taxes on exports were prohibited, and direct taxes were to be levied in proportion to population. Furthermore, all taxes were to be uniform throughout the United States —a provision that has been interpreted to mean geographical uniformity. The Constitution also laid restrictions upon the states, prohibiting them from coining money or emitting bills of credit, from taxing interstate commerce, and from levying import or export duties or tonnage taxes without the consent of Congress, as well as forbidding the Federal and state governments from taxing each other's instrumentalities.[1] In the years since the adoption of the Constitution the power to tax has been further defined by court decisions.[2]

Fiscal Operations

There was no immediate expansion of governmental operations, which, as a matter of fact, did not even include the functions that Adam Smith, the great exponent of laissez-faire, had held to be the province of government—protection, justice, and public works for facilitating commerce and for eduction. The appropriation bill of 1789 was a brief document, with four items pertaining to civil expenses, military expenses, the payment of the public debt, and pensions. It is not surprising that protection was the largest item of expenditure for the new government. The

---

[1] An exception to the prohibition against the levying of import and export duties by states is made in the case of duties absolutely necessary for the enforcement of inspection laws.

[2] The due process clause of the Fifth and Fourteenth Amendments has been held applicable to taxation. The Constitution contains other restrictions that apply indirectly to the taxing power of the states. State legislation cannot contravene federal treaties or impair obligations of contracts. The citizens of each state are entitled to the privileges and immunities of citizens in the several states, and no state is to "deny to any person within its jurisdiction the equal protection of its laws." The states have always been allowed to levy certain taxes on national banks. There has been some change, however, in the Supreme Court's position on the taxation of Federal and state instrumentalities. In 1938 the Supreme Court affirmed the right of the Federal Government to tax salaries paid by the Port of New York Authority, and a year later it approved Federal taxation of state and local salaries. The way was thus cleared for Congress to pass in 1939 the Public Salary Tax Act, which permitted the Federal Government to tax salaries of state employees and states to tax salaries of Federal employees.

skirmishes with the Indians in the Northwest Territory, and the possibility of conflict with France and Spain emphasized the need for an adequate army and navy. Interest payments on the Federal debt were second in size inasmuch as civil expenditures were a relatively small part of the total.

Alexander Hamilton, the Secretary of the Treasury, an advocate of a strong central government, was influential in determining many of the policies of the new government. Assumption by the Federal Government of the debt of the Continental and Confederation Governments and the interest payments that had been in default for some time was a major issue. It was argued that it was not only unwise to burden the new government with a heavy debt, but also unfair since bonds that had seemed practically worthless had passed out of the hands of the original holders in many cases into those of speculators. Hamilton argued, however, that funding the debt would help to preserve the Union by establishing the credit of the government on a firm basis. He maintained that it would strengthen the new government by giving bondholders a common stake in its Treasury and he believed that it would have the happy result of providing circulating capital for trade and industry in the form of government securities. The winning of the case for assumption is to be attributed not only to Hamilton's persuasive powers but also to the fact that many members of Congress were holders of the debt and stood to gain thereby.

The assumption of the state debts by the Federal Government was even more hotly debated. Considerable sectional feeling was involved inasmuch as the debts of the Northern states were much heavier than those of the Southern states. Furthermore, most of the state bonds were held by speculators in the North while practically all Federal revenue came from customs duties that fell on all consumers. But, as in the case of the Confederation debt, Hamilton maintained that assumption would strengthen the new government and would have the beneficial effect of providing more circulating capital for business and industry. He argued also that it was only just that the state debts be assumed since they had been incurred in a common cause, the fighting of the Revolution. It was hardly proper, he further insisted, that state bondholders should be left in a worse position than Federal bondholders, as they now would be with the states giving up one of their main sources of revenue, the taxation of imports. The outcome was a compromise that involved a trading of votes on this issue for votes on the location of the nation's capital. Hamilton finally persuaded Jefferson, his most formidable opponent, of the necessity for assuming the state debts. Thereupon Jefferson arranged a dinner for both factions at which it was finally agreed, on the one hand, that the state debts would be assumed by the Federal Government, and, on the other hand, that the national capital would be moved to the banks of the Potomac River after a ten year interval in Philadelphia.

Revenues and Expenditures

In view of the strife that had been engendered by the imposition of various kinds of taxes it is not surprising that the new government was supported almost entirely by customs duties. From the beginning both Washington and Hamilton were concerned over giving encouragement to home industry and commerce. In fact, as his personal contribution to the encouragement of the infant textile industry Washington had worn a dark brown suit entirely made in America for his first inauguration. After passing a tariff bill in 1789 that afforded moderate protection, Congress requested Hamilton to submit a report showing how the government could foster manufacturing with a view to making the country self-sufficient in regard to necessary materials. This Hamilton did in his famous "Report on Manufactures," a protectionist document. But Congress paid little heed to his recommendations, and although tariff rates were increased from time to time during the next two decades, industry had no significant protection until the War of 1812.

When it became apparent that revenue from the Tariff Act of 1789 was inadequate, internal taxes were levied in spite of great opposition. An excise tax was imposed on whiskey in 1791, to be used exclusively for paying interest on the debt, or for repaying principal if there was a surplus above interest requirements. This excise, bitterly decried as a tax on one of the necessities of life and never very productive, led to the Whiskey Rebellion in Pennsylvania in 1794. As the need for revenue became greater, additional excises were imposed in 1794 on carriages, snuff, refined sugar, and auction sales. The increase in military expenditures because of troubled relations with France accounted for the imposition of stamp taxes on legal transactions in 1797. Included among the latter was a tax on legacies and probates of wills, sometimes called the first Federal tax on inheritances. The following year a direct tax was imposed for the first time when a levy of $2,000,000 on houses, land, and slaves was apportioned among the states on the basis of population. Houses were taxed at a progressive rate, every slave was taxed at 50 cents, and after the sums assessed on houses and slaves were deducted from the sum assessed on each state the remainder was assessed on land according to its valuation. Collections of this tax were poor, almost one-third of it being still unpaid in 1801.

When Jefferson became president in 1801 a change was inevitable. Unlike Hamilton, he was opposed to a powerful national government and believed an agrarian society of small landholders to be the most felicitous. His administration, accordingly, was marked by retrenchment in both civil and military expenditures, except during the years overshadowed by the Embargo Act and trouble with England and France. Whereas expenditures had about doubled during the 1790's, they were reduced from almost $11,000,000 in 1800 to $8,000,000 in 1811. The tax on whiskey was repealed and all excises were abolished in 1802, except the tax on salt, which was eliminated in 1807. Customs duties, to which Jefferson did not object since he believed them to be paid by the rich, remained the principal source of income and were so productive that Federal revenue, four times greater in 1802 than in 1792, fluctuated around $15,000,000 during the decade before the War of 1812. Large surpluses reduced the debt almost 50 per cent from its 1803 peak to $45,000,000 in 1811.

Although Jefferson was opposed in principle to a strong central government, and held that the powers of the Federal Government were strictly limited to those enumerated in the Constitution, his policies frequently reflected a broad interpretation of that document. In spite of the fact that there was no specific authorization in the Constitution for the acquisition of more territory, he approved the Louisiana Purchase in 1803, thereby greatly enhancing the wealth of the country and its opportunities for expansion and development. Nor was there any Constitutional authorization for such an undertaking as the Lewis and Clark expedition to the Pacific, which was organized at his behest and was financed by Federal funds. Although he was generally opposed to public industries, as was to be expected from his laissez-faire leanings, he believed that the government should go into the business of manufacturing salt. He was always a staunch advocate of government support of education, a function that in his day was most often considered a matter for private initiative. Although the Constitution said nothing about highways or public works, he approved the construction of highways and had plans made for more extensive public improvements. He would have urged many more internal improvements had he not had grave doubts as to their constitutionality. For this reason he strongly urged a constitutional amendment that would clarify the authority of the Federal Government.

Receipts from customs duties dropped sharply when war broke out in 1812, and although direct taxes were imposed, with greater success than in 1798, and internal taxes were levied again, revenue was far from adequate. The government encountered great difficulty in borrowing, however, because of the lack of support for the war in New England where commerce was badly hit, and because of the poor military outlook. Further contributing factors were the absence of any banking organization to assist in floating loans and the ineptitude of the Treasury. The increase of almost 200 per cent in the Federal debt reflected the impossibility of borrowing on other than very unfavorable terms; loans of over $80,000,000 netted the Treasury only about $34,000,000 in specie.

Treasury Surpluses

In the quarter of a century following the War of 1812, revenue policy was little influenced by fiscal considerations. Eighteen of the twenty-one years between 1815 and 1836 showed an annual surplus in the Federal Treasury. The level of the tariff, the principal source of revenue, depended primarily on the strength of the protectionist forces rather than on the government's need for income. After the war the demand for increased protection on the part of the new industries that had sprung up during the conflict was met by the Tariff Act of 1816, which was definitely protective. Succeeding acts of the next decade were even more protective, until duties reached their highest level before the Civil War in the Act of 1828. When the Act of 1832 modified the latter Act only slightly, the South rose up in protest and a national crisis was precipitated by the threatened secession of South Carolina. As a consequence, more moderate duties were put into effect in the 1830's, although tariff rates were still high enough to be very protective to domestic industries. Sales of public lands, the only other source of revenue, were not significant until 1830, in spite of a reduction in price in 1820 from $2 to $1.25 an acre, but thereafter they began to increase as westward expansion got under way, and in 1836 even exceeded customs receipts. After the country recovered from the crisis of 1819, Federal revenue began a gradual ascent from about $20,000,000 in the early 1820's to $35,000,000 in 1835 and $51,000,000 in 1836.

The scope of the Federal Government was still quite narrow, however, and expenditures did not keep pace with the growth in revenue, in spite of more liberal granting of pensions to Revolutionary veterans after the disability qualification was removed in 1818. Interest charges declined as the debt was reduced and finally paid off completely. A small amount was spent on roads and canals, but, although there was a great clamor for internal improvements, the tradition against the Federal Government's entering upon such undertakings was overwhelming. Between the War of 1812 and the crisis of 1837 Federal expenditures, which were less than $18,000,000 in most years, varied from $15,000,000 to $37,000,000. Madison vetoed legislation for internal improvements in 1817, even though he was favorably disposed towards such measures, because he doubted their constitutionality. Monroe shared Madison's attitude, and, like Jefferson, argued for a constitutional amendment to clarify the authority of the Federal Government. In the matter of the Florida Purchase, however, which he signed in 1819, he ignored the question of constitutional authority as Jefferson had in the instance of the Louisiana Purchase. John Quincy Adams favored internal improvements and believed Congress did have authority to undertake them. But in spite of the fact that he was a less ardent exponent of laissez-faire than most of the founding fathers, he was unsuccessful in persuading Congress to authorize the internal improvements he desired to see undertaken. As for Jackson, he had voted for internal improvement bills as a senator, perhaps, it has been suggested, because in his frontier campaigns he had been impressed with the importance of roads from a military point of view. Nevertheless, by the time he became president he had come to feel that internal improvements were the province not of the Federal Government but of the states.[3]

After the Federal debt was paid off in 1835, funds began to accumulate in the Treasury, and by 1836 the surplus was so large that pressure to do something with it could be resisted no longer. As already noted, Jackson opposed the expenditure of surplus revenue on internal improvements. He also opposed gifts to the states on the grounds that they lacked a contitutional basis. But there was much agitation for the distribution of the surplus to the states, and a bill was finally passed which avoided the Constitutional question by providing that the surplus should be deposited with the states according to their representation in Congress. Although these deposits were made in the form of loans, it was understood that they would never be called for, and that they were really gifts. They are still carried, however, on the books of the United States Treasury. The solution to the problem was a compromise and did not give complete satisfaction. The Whigs favored an outright distribution, while some of the southern states, which were very much opposed to the protective tariff, "received their share with protests and received them only because if they refused the North would get them. . . ." [4] The distribution was to be made in four instalments, only three of which were made before the crisis of 1837. The fourth instalment was never paid.[5]

Revenue declined sharply after the crisis of 1837, the most severe the country had yet experienced. The depression that followed was not the occasion for large relief expenditures, inasmuch as Van Buren did not

[3] The interpretations of the reversal of Jackson's attitude are various. Dewey, *Financial History of the United States,* 11th ed., p. 255. New York: Longmans, Green and Company, 1931. The change in Jackson's political convictions "was due to a sincere belief that democratic government was threatened by great moneyed interests rather than to fine-spun interpretations of the Constitution." P. W. Gates, "Internal Improvements," *Dictionary of American History,* Vol. III. Jackson's opposition as president to internal improvements may have been due in part to the fact that Clay favored them. John S. Bassett, *The Life of Andrew Jackson,* Vol. II, p. 486. New York: Doubleday, Page and Co., 1911. In fact the Maysville Road, provided for in the bill that Jackson vetoed in 1830, was to have been located in the state in which Clay lived, and "was supposed to be a kind of challenge from that gentleman...." William MacDonald, *Jacksonian Democracy,* p. 140. New York and London: Harper and Brothers, 1906, "Jackson based his veto partly on constitutional grounds," and reconciled his veto with his earlier votes for internal improvements by stressing the local character of the project. See Bassett, *op. cit.,* p. 491.

[4] E. G. Bourne, *The Surplus Revenue of 1837,* p. 25. New York: G. P. Putnam's Sons, 1885.

[5] "The uses made of the funds distributed were various. Massachusetts distributed them among the towns; Boston used the money for current expenses; Salem built a town hall; Groton repaired a broken bridge. The State of Maine made a per capita distribution; some States used the money for internal improvements, while a few saved it and use its income today for educational and other purposes." Dewey, *Financial History of the United States,* p. 222.

believe that the government should assume responsibility for the misfortunes of the people or that the Constitution gave it authority to extend aid to industry and to the unemployed. Nevertheless the position of the Federal Government was difficult as most ordinary expenditures remained large and some increased with the expansion of the country. The protectionists lost no time in taking advantage of such an opportune situation, and, since the case of the opposition was greatly weakened by the need for revenue, pressed successfully for higher tariff rates in 1842. When more prosperous conditions shortly thereafter brought a surplus into the Treasury again, free traders demanded a lowering of the tariff, but, while duties were reduced somewhat in 1846, they were not reduced as much as fiscal requirements would have allowed. The Mexican War, which was financed entirely by borrowing, caused the Treasury little trouble, and the deficits of the war years were soon followed by surpluses. The country remained very prosperous until the crisis of 1857. Customs duties poured into the Treasury, and together with sales of public lands, which were especially large in the middle fifties, led to surpluses in eight successive years from 1850 to 1857. Federal revenue exceeded $70,000,000 in both 1854 and 1856. The national debt, which had increased from $15,500,000 in 1846 to over $68,000,000 in 1851, had been reduced by 1857 to $28,500,000. Pressure on the part of protectionists to distribute revenue from the sale of public lands to the states was strenuously opposed by free traders, who saw that such a distribution was merely intended to further the case for high customs duties by decreasing Federal revenue. When recurring surpluses finally made existing tariff rates no longer defensible, the reduction of customs duties in 1857 practically coincided with a serious financial and industrial crisis. Revenue declined more sharply than anticipated, and a period of deficits began that was to last until after the Civil War.

Various differences on matters of national policy had arisen during these years between the North, which was largely mercantile and industrial, and the South, which was almost wholly agricultural. For many years the North had favored a more rapid distribution of public lands, while the South wanted the public domain preserved and had been apprehensive for fear distribution might upset the balance of slave and free states in Congress. The North, where trade and industry flourished, was much more anxious for internal improvements than was the South. Likewise, the North felt much more urgency for some sort of centralized banking system than did the South. But it was over the issue of slavery that the North and South split when Civil War broke out in 1861. The seriousness of the conflict was not appreciated in the beginning, and it was generally believed that the war would soon be over. The struggle lasted four years, however, and left enduring marks on the economic, political, and social life of the country.

Fiscal Aspects of the Civil War

It was apparent almost immediately that customs duties, which had been the main source of Federal revenue until this time, would be inadequate to meet the necessary expenses of war. Chase, the Secretary of the Treasury, believing that the war would not last long, planned to finance it mainly by borrowing, although he hoped to obtain some revenue from increases in the tariff and from sales of public lands. But when it soon became obvious that other measures would be necessary, Congress took the initiative in levying a broad variety of miscellaneous excises and a direct tax of $20,000,000 on real property, to be apportioned among the states according to population.[6] This latter tax, which was not very productive, yielding less than $2,000,000 in 1861 and less than $1,500,000 the next year, was suspended in 1864.

The general public was more than willing for heavier taxation. Furthermore, the feeling had been growing that a direct tax, or a tax on real estate unaccompanied by a tax on personal property, was unjust. Therefore, to round out what it considered a defensible program, Congress levied an income tax in 1861 and an inheritance tax in 1862. So strong was the feeling that real estate should not be the sole object of taxation that the inheritance tax applied only to transfers of personal property, and transfers of real estate did not become taxable until the law was revised in 1864. Inasmuch as Secretary Chase did not favor the income tax, he took no steps toward collecting it for some months. The law of 1861 provided for a flat rate of 3 per cent on all incomes over $800, but by the time the measure was made effective in 1862, progressive rates had been introduced. Later revenue acts raised the rates until they extended from 5 per cent on incomes between $600 and $5000 to 10 per cent on incomes above $5000. This tax produced almost 20 per cent of Federal revenue in 1865, and during the four years of war it accounted for about 10 per cent of Federal revenue.

But taxation fell far short of providing sufficient funds. Expenditures increased almost twenty times from 1861 to 1865, when they passed the $1,000,000,000 mark, a level they were not to reach again for half a century. The government relied for most of its funds, therefore, on the issue of paper money and on loans. Beginning with the autumn of 1861, non-interest bearing notes, which were legal tender, were issued to the amount of $450,000,000. These notes, known as greenbacks, underwent a very rapid depreciation, and the question of their redemption in specie was

[6] A tax was levied in 1862 upon liquor, tobacco, carriages, auction sales, the gross receipts of railroads, steamboats, bridges, insurance, telegraph, and express companies, and various other businesses and industries. License taxes were imposed on thirty-three occupations and professions, and a $10 license fee was imposed on all unenumerated occupations in 1864. There were few articles or businesses, in fact, not subject to an excise tax.

one of the great political and economic issues of the next decade. The difficulty encountered in trying to market bonds was one important reason for the establishment of the national banking system, although the new bond-secured currency did not provide a large market for government securities. The method of financing the war improved as the struggle wore on. Taxes, which had furnished less than one-eighth as much as loans in 1861, were furnishing almost one-fifth in 1862, and by 1864 were furnishing over one-third as much as loans. From $65,000,000 in 1860, the debt increased to $2,322,000,000 in 1866, a figure not to be equalled again until World War I.

State and Local Finances

From the formation of the Union until the War of 1812 the states had no serious financial problems. For their Revolutionary debts they received Federal bonds, which they set aside as capital funds, invested in bank stock, or used for current expenditures. The sale of public lands also provided them with revenue, some of which was treated as capital funds bust most of which was used currently. The ease with which revenue was obtained encouraged them to spend freely on their civil governments, militias, and roads, without any great need for taxation.

Deficits incurred by many states as a consequence of direct tax requisitions during the War of 1812 were not a problem for long because of reimbursement by the Federal Government for war expenditures and returning prosperity in the 1820's. The construction of the Erie Canal in New York, completed in 1825, proved to be a very profitable venture, contrary to popular expectation, and from that time until shortly after the crisis of 1837 the states indulged in an orgy of improvements. The construction of highways, canals, and railroads, and the improvement of rivers were undertaken on a large scale, while many states, especially those in the South, invested in bank stock. The distribution of the Federal surplus in 1837 gave further encouragement to this lavish spending. The depression that followed the crisis of 1837 found the states, therefore, in poor financial condition. Many of the projects undertaken proved unprofitable, and nine states defaulted.[7] A movement for the Federal assumption of state debts, based on the theory that the internal improvements for which the debts were incurred were of benefit to the whole country, developed into an issue in the campaign of 1842, but nothing came of it. The situation improved with heavier state taxes and the prosperity of the 1840's, but the period of defaults had its legacy in con-

---

7 Dewey, *Financial History of the United States,* p. 244-45. "... and in some of the newer commonwealths particularly there was not an honest determination, even where there was the ability, to meet the maturing obligations of interest and principle." See also Ratchford, *American State Debts,* p. 87. "... The New England states, North Carolina, and Georgia did not participate in the borrowing of this period."

stitutional amendments imposing limitations on state borrowing, which, although unknown before 1840, were in effect in nineteen states a decade and a half later. State borrowing increased again in the 1850's and, while not quite so reckless and speculative, it resulted, nevertheless, in large losses. With the exception of New York, the borrowing of this period, which was principally for railroads, was undertaken by southern and western states, none of the states that defaulted in the 1840's participating.

As the states expanded their activities during the 1820's and 1830's, taxation became more necessary, in spite of the fact that there was still a tendency to look upon investments as the primary source of revenue and taxation as merely supplementary. An effort was already being made in these years to meet some of the problems incident to the general property tax, the principal source of state revenue, through the creation of county and state boards of equalization. Income taxes were levied in a number of states, but none of them was very productive of revenue. Pennsylvania and Maryland levied such taxes in the 1850's largely because of the need for more revenue, but in some of the southern states, in Virginia, Alabama, Florida, and North Carolina, income taxes were to be accounted for in larger measure by a movement for greater equality in taxation.[8] A number of states also made use of inheritance taxes at an early date, especially in the South. While Virginia had had a probate duty ever since 1687, Pennsylvania levied the first inheritance tax in 1826, and Louisiana the second in 1828. In 1855 North Carolina had the distinction of being the first state to tax direct heirs.[9] Taxes were also levied on various kinds of businesses, such as that imposed by Virginia on railroads and public service corporations in 1842, and that levied by Pennsylvania in 1844 on the capital stock of all corporations.

During the Civil War expenditures of state and local governments increased both because of the offering of bonuses to volunteers and the outfitting of military units, and also because of the effect of the inflated price level on civil expenditures. The system of taxation was not capable of expanding to meet the increased expenditures, however, and the consequence was a great increase in state and local debts.

Conclusion

The fiscal policy of the Federal Government before the Civil War showed no well defined objective. Budgetary considertions did not bulk

[8] Land taxes had never been so important in the South as in the North because of the influence of large landowners. But gradually a new group appeared made up of merchants and professional people. Income taxes and license taxes on occupations were an effort to put part of the burden of government on this new group.

[9] Ratner, *American Taxation*, p. 51. New York: W. W. Norton and Company, 1942. "The receptivity of the southern planter aristocracy to advanced ideas in taxation has not received the attention it deserves."

large in the determination of revenue and expenditure policies during much of the period, although there was more inclination to remedy deficits than surpluses. Except during wars and the periods immediately following the crises of 1837 and 1857, the Federal Treasury showed an annual surplus in most years. The level of customs duties, the mainstay of Federal revenue, varied primarily with the strength of protectionist forces, and, although surpluses were so large on occasion as to force some reduction in tariff rates, duties remained higher, on the whole, than the needs of the Federal budget would have required. The dominance of the laissez-faire attitude toward government meant that expenditures were affected by few factors other than the territorial growth of the country and the increase in population, and that the scope of Federal activities underwent little change. Recurring surpluses might have had a more restricting effect had it not been that the economy was undergoing a very rapid industrial and commercial expansion as well as a widening of its geographical boundaries.

The Declaration of Independence had declared "that all men are created equal," but the political rights of men were far from being equal in 1789. The right to vote was so hedged around with various property and other qualifications that only a minority of the male population, ten per cent in some states, was eligible to vote. When the constitutions of the western states were written most of them provided for manhood suffrage from the beginning, and the constitutions of the older states were gradually revised until, by the middle of the century, practically all white men could vote. The number voting in the presidential election of 1828 was three times greater than in 1824, and in 1840 it was seven times greater. It is not surprising, therefore, that the nature of presidential campaigns changed completely, with the candidates "going to the people," and doing almost anything to get attention, rather than conducting themselves in a sedate manner and expending their energies upon a somewhat extended correspondence as had been the custom previously.

It was no more coincidence that the same period that saw a widening of the electorate also saw the extension of public education. Public assistance for education had been provided for in the Northwest Ordinance of 1787, according to which a section of land in each township was to be devoted to the support of schools. But there was little further progress for many years in spite of the fact that Washington had recommended the establishment of a national university in his first message to Congress and that Jefferson favored the use of public funds for education. As new states were created in the West, certain lands were set aside for the support of schools, and local units were required to maintain public schools. Gradually, permissive laws in the older states became mandatory. With the 1830's the movement gained momentum, and by the time of the Civil

War free public education was general in the northern and western states.

Although the extension of manhood suffrage had practically no effect as yet on expenditures other than those for education, it had some bearing on the introduction of an income tax and an inheritance tax during the Civil War. The public was receptive towards higher taxes and the average man was not reluctant to pay his share. But the introduction of these taxes reflected the desire for less reliance on indirect taxes, which were especially burdensome to the lower income groups, and for greater emphasis on taxation according to ability to pay.

While there had been from the beginning those who believed that it was hardly proper for a democracy to put a price on its public lands, free settlement of the western lands had been opposed both by the southern planters, who feared that an increase in the population of the West would cause free states to outnumber slave states in Congress, and by northern manufacturers, who saw that free settlement in the West would reduce their supply of factory labor. The stake of the common man, however, had been very well put forth by Walker, the Secretary of the Treasury, in his annual report for 1845. "The reduction of the price of public lands in favor of settlers and cultivators would enhance the wages of labor. It is an argument urged in favor of the tariff that we ought to protect our labor against what is called the pauper labor of Europe. But whilst the tariff does not enhance the wages of labor, the sales of public lands at low prices, and in limited quantities to settlers and cultivators, would accomplish this object . . . because when these lands were thus reduced in price, those who live by the wages of labor could purchase farms at these low rates, and cultivate the soil for themselves and families, instead of working for others twelve hours a day in the manufactories. Reduce the price which the laborer must pay for the public domain; bring thus the means of purchase within his power; prevent all speculation and monopoly in the public lands, confine the sales to settlers and cultivators in limited quantities; preserve those hundreds of millions of acres, for ages to come, as homes for the poor and oppressed; reduce the taxes by reducing the tariff and bring the prices which the poor are thus compelled to pay for all the necessaries and comforts of life, and more will be done for the benefit of American labor than if millions were added to the profits of manufacturing capital by the enactment of a protective tariff." Although the laboring class did not like the tariff, it felt less sure of its ground in this controversy because of the oft repeated contention that the tariff protected the level of American wages. But the lines were more solidly drawn for the free settlement of public lands, both among the laboring classes of the East and among all westerners, and when southern opposition disappeared from Congress after the beginning of the Civil War, the Homestead Law was passed in 1862. Thus the public domain, which had been a significant source of federal revenue in some years, became every man's heritage and his opportunity for economic improvement.

Selected References

Beard, Charles A. and Mary R., *A Basic History of the United States.* New York: Doubleday and Co., Inc., 1949.

———, *The Rise of American Civilization.* New York: The Macmillan Company, 1947.

Bolles, A. S., *The Financial History of the United States, 1774-1885* (3 vols.). New York: D. Appleton and Co., 1886.

Bourne, E. G., *The History of the Surplus Revenue of 1837.* New York: G. P. Putnam's Sons, 1909.

Dewey, D. R., *Financial History of the United States,* 11th ed. New York: Longmans, Green and Co., 1931.

Grayson, T. J., *Leaders and Periods of American Finance.* New York: John Wiley and Sons, Inc., 1932.

Ratner, Sidney, *American Taxation.* New York: W. W. Norton and Co., Inc., 1942.

Secretary of the Treasury, *Annual Report.* Washington, D. C.: U.S. Government Printing Office.

Shultz, W. J., and M. R. Caine, *Financial Development of the United States.* New York: Prentice-Hall, Inc., 1937.

Sumner, W. G., *The Financier and the Finances of the American Revolution* (2 vols.). New York: Dodd, Mead and Co., 1891.

17 · THE PERFORMANCE OF THE AMERICAN ECONOMY: 1789-1865

AN ECONOMY may be judged by its performance—its record in utilizing the resources at its disposal in the satisfaction of material wants. A critical examination of the performance of the American economy can throw valuable light on the factors that have governed its past behavior and may assist in understanding and solving current problems.

The performance of an economic system is to some extent a consequence of the positive steps that the authorities take in creating or neutralizing disruptive forces. It is not necessary to believe that the Government should, or could, prevent peacetime fluctuations in business activity. But it is not to be denied that the Government can influence such activity for better or for worse. In wartime, moreover, the Government by unanimous consent is entrusted with the task of mobilizing and then demobilizing resources; by appropriate action it can maximize the war effort and mitigate wartime and post-war adjustments. A study of the performance of the American economy will indicate how effective it has been in satisfying both wartime and peacetime needs.[1]

In trying to gauge and evaluate its performance, it is necessary to examine the system's record of behavior under ordinary and extraordinary conditions and under the impact of both internal and external shocks; to study the extent to which it has shown wide fluctuations in its ability to satisfy material wants; and to examine its resilience in the face of disruptive forces. It is also necessary to go deeper, and try to disentangle the transient adjustments from the permanent, thus disclosing underlying tendencies of long-term development indicative of its ability to perform its functions.

A study of the performance of the American economy may therefore conveniently be broken up into three parts: (1) A consideration of how it has behaved under peacetime conditions—the fluctuations in the national income during prosperity and depression. (2) An analysis of how it has withstood the impact of war—the mobilization of a large part of the national income for military purposes and then reversion to peace-

[1] See W. B. Smith and A. H. Cole, *Fluctuations in American Business: 1790-1860*, p. xxi. Cambridge, Mass.: Harvard University Press, 1935.

time conditions. (3) An investigation of the trends that have been in operation and, perhaps far more cautiously, of the tendencies that may be expected to manifest themselves in the future.

American economic development before 1865 was mainly dependent upon the increasing power of the central Government and the geographical expansion of the country. These two factors controlled the economic fluctuations of the period. Before the Revolutionary War, the separate Colonies possessed their own economic and political organizations, which were tied very closely to those of the motherland. The Revolutionary War reduced somewhat economic dependence on England and strengthened considerably the interdependence of the nation's individual units. It also set up a new political and economic organization, the United States of America, which, as time went by, grew more powerful in its relations both with the individual states and with the rest of the world. Economic independence lagged considerably behind political independence, as the events leading up to the War of 1812 demonstrated so fully. Extension of territory made available vast natural resources and created a demand for facilities and workers to exploit those resources. Manpower, machines, and money were required. The increase of the central Government's power was interrelated with this increase in size of the economy.

Wartime Booms and Post-War Reactions

A period of war necessarily involves serious adjustments in the economic organization of a society, since part of the national income must be diverted to the production of war materials and part of the population must be removed completely from production and placed in the armed forces. The utilization of previously unemployed resources and manpower in the early stages of a war might give the impression that it is possible to have both guns and butter, both soldiers and workers. When a high level of production and employment is attained, however, civilian sacrifices are made more apparent by shifts from civilian to war production or service. Even when the transition from peace to war is effected gradually, some disruption must take place; when it is not carried out gradually, disruption may become so widespread as to resemble chaos. The transition may be made difficult, and the departure from normal conditions may be intensified, by the cessation or curtailment of foreign trade or by harmful fiscal or other economic policies adopted by the government.

In the post-war period problems of adjustment are even more serious because the change is usually made suddenly and proceeds from more hectic economic conditions. The economy is opened up, trade is resumed; meanwhile wartime production becomes obsolete. Yet the fiscal policies of wartime leave their legacy of overexpanded credit and currency. War workers and soldiers must be fitted into civilian production again. It is thus not astonishing that severe economic disturbances usually characterize post-war eras. Such wartime booms and post-war reactions were numerous in the period before 1865. Willard Thorp quotes John Adams as saying: "I am old enough to remember the war of 1745 and its end, the war of 1755 and its close, the war of 1775 and its termination, and the war of 1812 and its pacification. Every one of these wars has been followed by a general distress, embarrassments of commerce, destruction of manufactures, fall of the price of produce and lands." [2]

Peacetime Crises and Cycles

From the time of the earliest settlements, this country has experienced peacetime economic fluctuations.[3] In the period before the Civil War these fluctuations may be traced mainly to agriculture, which was influenced primarily by world conditions, including wars in Europe. Dependent as the country was on the product of the soil, it is not astonishing that its economic fluctuations stemmed partly from agricultural variations. Periodic changes in demand—perhaps because of war—or supply—perhaps because of drought—led to violent fluctuations in price and resulted in further changes in supply. The rapid growth of the economy coupled with monetary instability completed the environmental conditions conducive to wide swings in business activity. In Colonial days, particularly, the peacetime fluctuations of the economy were exogenous in origin. Only in the later period of nationalistic development did crises and cycles of internal origin become evident. Until some time after the War of 1812, the influence of domestic and foreign wars was so great that it seems best to restrict the discussion of *peacetime* crises and cycles to the period 1817-1860.

During this period many internal changes made the United States more sensitive to disruptive forces. The extension of resources through the development of the West took place so rapidly and was generally accompanied by such boom conditions that the rate of change here exceeded that of other parts of the economic system. Maladjustments inevitably arose when different parts of the economy were progressing at different rates. Speculation was rife in Western lands. Every so often the economy, stopping to catch its breath, so to speak, burst the speculative bubble. The resulting reaction on the whole economic organization often precipitated a general crisis. Another sensitive feature was the heavy capital investment in specialized equipment required by the country's growing industrialization. The time span for which decisions and plans had to be

---

[2] Willard L. Thorp, *Business Annals*, p. 112. New York: National Bureau of Economic Research, 1926.

[3] Dr. Thorp finds that the earliest recorded depression in America came in New England in 1640. See his *Business Annals*, p. 112.

formed was greatly lengthened. It was easier to make mistakes; and mistakes when made were more costly. A wave of mistakes might precipitate general deflation and depression.

Finance, too, was characterized by a very delicate constitution. Capital expansion and widespread speculation greatly increased the use of credit and extended monetary and banking facilities. Here again a cumulative process was always potentially at hand, and a slight disruptive force could set the whole organization toppling. Meantime, the internal organization of the country became more and more complex and greater interdependence resulted from the extension of market areas and increased specialization.

Economic Activity During the European Wars: 1789-1814 [4]

Economic activity in the period 1789-1811 showed the effects of war, but no gaping wounds appeared until after 1806. Early in the period, the country gained from the European wars. Production and trade were stimulated.[5] The situation was similar to that prevailing later in the First World War and the Second World War in the years before this country actually began hostilities.[6] The economy still bore many marks of its Colonial origin; hence it was mainly agriculture and shipping that experienced the higher level of activity.

The Non-Importation Act of 1806 and the Embargo of 1808 put this profitable period to an end.[7] The country was cut off from many foreign manufactures, and in turn was restricted in its exports. As a result, commerce, shipping, and agriculture were hard hit. Increased self-sufficiency was the only alternative. Advantages of international specialization were lost. But the development of interregional specialization within the confines of the United States compensated in part for this loss and reduced to some extent this nation's dependence on other countries for the maintenance of its living standards.

The outbreak of the War of 1812—which had been encouraged by the expansionist aims of inland groups rather than for the redress of griev-

---

[4] See Thorp, *Business Annals,* pp. 113-117; and Smith and Cole, *Fluctuations in American Business, 1790-1860,* pp. 3-33.

[5] The merchant tonnage more than doubled between 1793 and 1805. See Vernon G. Setser, *The Commercial Reciprocity Policy of the United States, 1774-1829,* p. 161. Philadelphia: University of Pennsylvania Press, 1937.

[6] Also a considerable amount of speculative activity in 1791 and 1792 followed the success of Hamilton's funding plan for the national debt. See Richard Brandon Morris, *Historiography of America 1600-1800,* p. 13 (New York: Columbia University Press, 1933); Margaret G. Myers, *The New York Money Market,* Vol. I, p. 12 (New York: Columbia University Press, 1931); and Joseph Stancliffe Davis, *Essays in the Earlier History of American Corporations,* pp. 332 ff. (Cambridge, Mass.: Harvard University Press, 1917).

[7] For an extremely interesting account of this period the reader is referred to Herbert Heaton, "Non-Importation, 1806-1812," *The Journal of Economic History,* Vol. I (November, 1941), pp. 178-198.

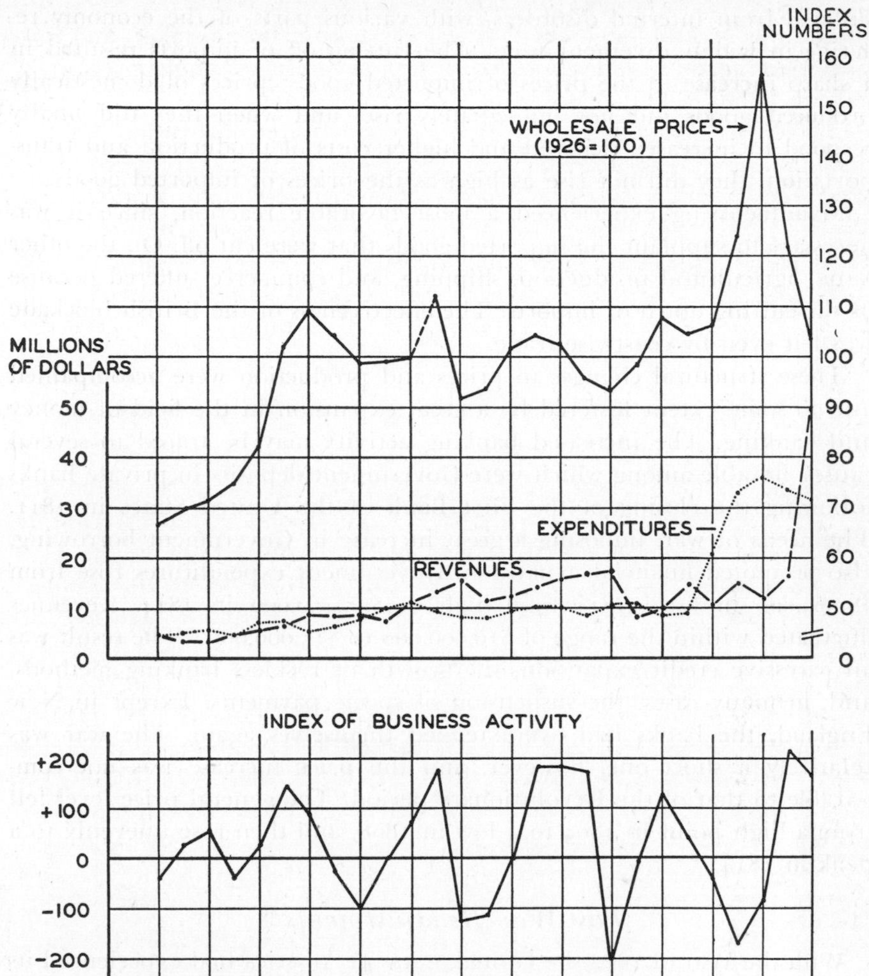

FIG. 1. *Fiscal Policy and Business Activity: 1790-1816.* (Note: The fiscal year is the same as the calendar year in this period.) Sources: "Expenditures" and "Revenues," United States Treasury Department (*Annual Report of the Secretary of the Treasury,* 1937, pp. 346-349); "Wholesale Prices," 1801-1816, United States Bureau of Labor Statistics (Jesse M. Cutts, "One Hundred and Thirty-Four Years of Wholesale Prices," *Monthly Labor Review,* July, 1935); "Wholesale Prices," 1790-1806, based on Bezanson, Gray, and Hussey, *Wholesale Prices in Philadelphia, 1784-1861,* Vol. I, p. 392 (Philadelphia, 1936); "Business Activity" based on Cleveland Trust Company monthly index.

ances of the maritime section [8]—completed the closing of the American economy. The effects on economic activity within the country were immediate and widespread. The price structure and the structure of industry

[8] See Julius W. Pratt, *Expansionists of 1812,* esp. pp. 17-62 (New York: The Macmillan Company, 1925; Peter Smith, 1949).

suffered from internal disorders, with various parts of the economy reacting in widely divergent ways. The cutting off of imports resulted in a sharp increase in the prices of imported goods; prices of domestically produced goods did not immediately rise, and when they did finally respond to increased demand and higher costs of production and transportation, they did not rise as high as the prices of imported goods.

Manufacturing experienced a most favorable reaction, since it was necessary to supplant the imported goods that were cut off. On the other hand, agricultural production, shipping, and commerce suffered because of the cutting down of imports. The effectiveness of the British blockade was felt even by coastwise trade.

These structural changes in prices and production were accompanied and to some extent fostered by a great expansion in the field of money and banking. The increased banking activity may be traced to several causes, notable among which were Government deposits in private banks following the closing of the First Bank of the United States in 1811. The needs of war, imposing a great increase in Government borrowing, also promoted financial expansion. Government expenditures rose from $8,560,000 in fiscal 1811 to a high of $35,450,000 in 1814. Revenues fluctuated within the range of $10,000,000 to $15,000,000.[9] The result was an excessive credit expansion, the growth of reckless banking methods, and, in many cases, the suspension of specie payments. Except in New England, the banks had overextended themselves again. The war was relatively a short one, however, and the price increase was not comparable to that of the Revolutionary period. The general price level fell from a high point in 1805 to a low in 1808, and then rose unevenly to a peak in 1814.

Post-War Readjustments [10]

With the War of 1812 the United States of America had experienced its first major shock. Considering the country's dependence on foreign trade and the instability of its financial structure, it is perhaps no exaggeration to say that the shock was greater in relative terms than it has ever experienced since that time. The depression of agriculture, shipping, and commerce, the expansion of manufacturing output, and the rise of prices left their mark. The end of the war opened up the economy again and upset the price relations established during the struggle. Prices of imported goods fell sharply, while prices of domestically produced goods continued high until 1817, owing to the sustained European demand for foodstuffs. Both dropped, however, with the panic of 1818-1819 and

[9] U. S. Treasury Department, *Annual Report of the Secretary of the Treasury, 1937,* pp. 346-349.

[10] See Thorp, *Business Annals,* pp. 117-118; and Smith and Cole, *Fluctuations in American Business, 1790-1860,* pp. 3-33.

reached the low level that had prevailed before the outbreak of the European War in 1792. The hopeless situation that beset banking by the end of the war reached a breaking point. Provision was finally made for a new Bank of the United States, which was to have a 20-year lease on life from 1816 to 1836. Lagging Government revenues finally caught up with and overtook expenditures in 1816, when revenues were $48,490,000 and expenditures $31,390,000.[11] The general level of wholesale prices fell from a high point in 1814 and continued downward for some years. The usual pattern of wartime boom and post-war reaction had reasserted itself.

The Crisis of 1819 and the Period 1817-1832 [12]

The crisis of 1819 may be traced to an interplay of monetary overinvestment with the exogenous factor of a decline in the export demand for foodstuffs. Investment in Western land had been stimulated by high prices brought by agricultural staples during the War of 1812 and the sustained demand during the post-war period. Land values soared and the turnover was rapid. The transactions involved required large amounts of money and these were supplied by a rapidly expanding banking system. But the investment could not be supported indefinitely by the banking system, and a point was reached where a contraction in the monetary supply became necessary. This reduction was made in 1817 and 1818. Banknote circulation declined from about $110,000,000 in 1816 to $65,000,000 in 1819.[13] In 1817 an attempt had been made to force resumption of specie payments on the note issues of the banks and this movement brought about some contraction in the amount of loanable funds. Then in 1818 difficulties besetting the Second United States Bank aggravated the general financial stringency. The inability of the banking system to sustain the prevailing rate of investment any longer prepared the way for the bursting of the speculative bubble.

A circumstance entirely unconnected with the economy helped to precipitate a crisis.[14] The European demand for foodstuffs, which had been maintained at a high level during the reconstruction period following the Napoleonic Wars, fell off sharply in 1819. Prices fell correspondingly. Wheat, cotton, and corn led the way in 1819, and a general drop in

---

11 U. S. Treasury Department, *Annual Report of the Secretary of the Treasury, 1937,* pp. 346-349.

12 See Thorp, *Business Annals,* pp. 118-121; and Smith and Cole, *Fluctuations in American Business, 1790-1860,* Sections I and II.

13 See Albert Bolles, *Financial History of the United States,* Vol. 2, p. 329. New York: D. Appleton-Century Company, 1891.

14 The interaction of the two sets of factors was graphically described by a Philadeldelphia publication in 1818: "A great crisis approaches—slow in its march, but deadly and relentless as the yellow fever which desolated your cities—and like it compounded of foreign contagion acting upon internal predisposition." (From Smith and Cole, *Fluctuations in American Business, 1790-1860,* p. 21.)

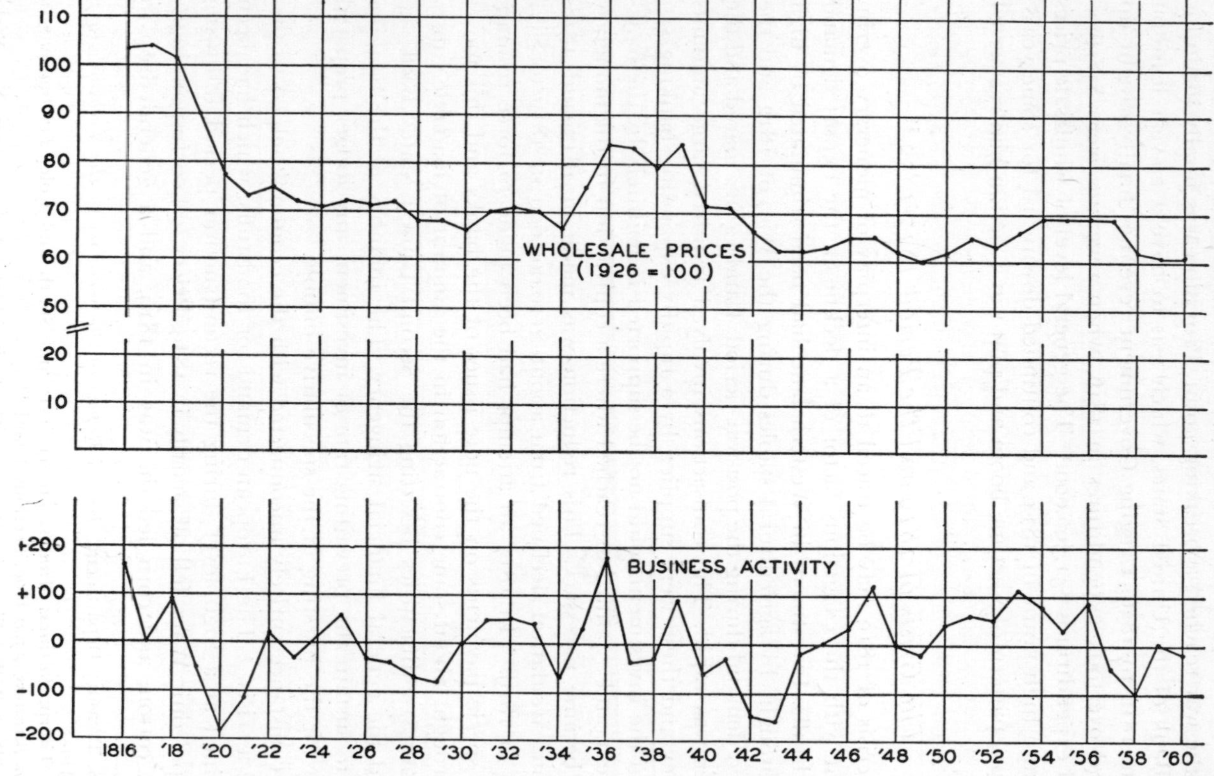

FIG. 2. *Wholesale Prices and Business Activity: 1816-1860.* (Sources: "Wholesale Prices," United States Bureau of Labor Statistics (Jesse M. Cutts, "One Hundred and Thirty-Four Years of Wholesale Prices," *Monthly Labor Review*, July, 1935); "Business Activity" based on Cleveland Trust Company monthly index.)

prices followed in 1820. The index of wholesale prices (1926 base) fell from 102.2 in 1818 to 89.7 in 1819, 76.6 in 1820, and 73.2 in 1821.[15] The result was a general depression affecting both industry and agriculture.

The depression was characterized by a rise in interest costs, a fall in property values, and a growth of bankruptcies and unemployment. The rise in interest costs grew out of the general scarcity of loanable funds that accompanied the contraction of note issue and the suspension of specie payments by the banks. The fall in property values took place in both urban and rural areas. With the general deflation of values and scarcity of funds, debts remained unpaid and bankruptcies resulted. Production and trade fell off and unemployment became widespread, requiring a great extension of poor relief.

The West suffered the most severe consequences of the depression and, as has been usual in this country's history, adopted the most radical measures for meeting the situation. Debt moratoria of various degrees were declared in several states. In some places laws were passed preventing foreclosure and seizure. Monetary measures were also adopted to increase the supply of loanable funds. In a number of states new banks were established to issue notes and make loans to debtors. But, as is typical in such cases, the increase in note issue was excessive. Loans were extended too freely, spending increased more rapidly than supply, and hence commodity prices rose. The scales now turned, and creditors were at a disadvantage. In the 10-year period from 1823 to 1833 conditions generally improved with only a few minor recessions. The country had suffered a sharp crisis and had come out of it with the aid of an expansionary monetary policy.

The Crisis of 1837 and the Period 1833-1848 [16]

The crisis of 1837 represents another instance of monetary overinvestment coupled with unfavorable exogenous developments. The main cause of the crisis was the speculation in land in the new Western territories that were opening up. Urban land values also rose, particularly in rapidly growing metropolitan communities like Chicago and New York.[17] The upward movement was encouraged by internal improvements,

[15] Jesse M. Cutts, "One Hundred and Thirty-four Years of Wholesale Prices," *Monthly Labor Review,* July, 1935. The figures for this period are based on the work of Professor Alvin H. Hansen.

[16] See Thorp, *Business Annals,* pp. 121-124; and Smith and Cole, *Fluctuations in American Business, 1790-1860,* pp. 37-84.

[17] "The craze was not confined solely to the West and the public-land sales. The rise in the value of real estate in New York was one form the speculative spirit assumed in the East. From $250,000,000 in 1830, the valuation of real property in New York rose to $403,000,000 in 1835, being an increase of 50 per cent in five years." (Reginald C. McGrane, *The Panic of 1837,* p. 45. Chicago: University of Chicago Press, 1924.)

mainly canals and railroads. The new lands were thereby made more accessible and their actual and potential value increased. The high point in this development came in the year 1836, when the sale of land reached a peak.[18]

Speculation was made possible and encouraged by the great increase in the supply of loanable funds of both domestic and foreign origin. The number of banking institutions increased after 1832 and the bank-note circulation consequently rose.[19] The availability of loanable funds, indispensable to Western territories for financing speculative activity and real investment, was enhanced by the transfer of the assets of the defunct United States Bank to Western banks. A large influx of foreign capital, to some extent in the form of a specie inflow,[20] increased the availability of loanable funds and tended to ease the terms of borrowing. It found its way directly into speculative and business activity and also absorbed state bonds issued to finance internal improvements.

The business boom that could trace its origin largely to monetary factors could likewise trace its end to monetary factors. The supply of loanable funds could not increase without limit; a stage of complete inelasticity of the monetary supply was reached and a severe contraction resulted. Both domestic and foreign factors contributed to this stoppage and reversal in the flow of loanable funds for speculative and business investment. A primary domestic factor was Jackson's Specie Circular of 1836, which required payment in specie for public lands purchased. This provision inevitably reduced speculative activity because the available supply of specie, even with the current inflow from abroad (which, as will be indicated below, also ceased), was inadequate to sustain operations at the previous level.[21] To make matters worse, there was the embarrassing Government surplus of 1836 that had arisen largely out of the sale of public lands and thus was represented by deposits in Western banks. In

[18] "It was all-absorbing, that engrossing desire to catch the golden opportunity, whose swelling tide wafted to wealth. The physician, intent upon some proferred bargain, when asked by his anxious patient how his medicine was to be taken, answered abstractedly, 'one quarter down, balance three annual installments.'" (Guy H. Salisbury, *The Speculative Craze of '36,* p. 323. Publications of the Buffalo Historical Society, Vol. 4. Buffalo: The Peter Paul Book Company, 1896.)

[19] In the decade, 1829 to 1839, the number of banks increased from 329 to 840. Their capital grew from $110,000,000 to $327,000,000 and their loans rose from $137,000,000 to $492,000,000. See Davis R. Dewey, *Financial History of the United States,* p. 225. New York: Longmans, Green and Company, 1918.

[20] The reduction of the public debt to practically nothing in 1835 was an important factor in improving the country's credit standing and inducing an inflow of foreign capital. See W. G. Sumner, *History of American Currency,* pp. 128 ff. New York: Henry Holt and Company, 1874.

[21] The Treasury refused to redeposit with the banks the coin received in payment for land. "The treasury would insist upon receiving specie for itself, but how the banks were to get it was none of its concern." (Margaret G. Myers, *The New York Money Market,* Vol. I, p. 169. New York: Columbia University Press, 1931.)

distributing this surplus to the states in quarterly installments in 1837, a transfer took place from Western banks to Eastern banks. Since Western banks had to contract their loans, the total money supply was restricted. At the same time, a financial stringency developed in England and resulted in the repatriation of capital that had been invested in the United States.

In addition to these monetary difficulties, agricultural conditions were affected directly by a drop in the price of cotton in the English market. And as if this were not enough, crop failures occurred here. These developments had repercussions in the banking centers where agricultural production was financed. The New York banks had to suspend specie payments and it was not long before most of the other banks in the country followed suit. Nor was this the end. In the early part of 1839 specie payments were resumed, but another reaction soon set in. In the latter part of 1839 the tottering United States Bank (chartered as a state bank by Pennsylvania) finally collapsed, the proximate cause being an unsuccessful attempt to keep up the price of cotton in order to protect the Bank's investment, thereby setting loose a string of specie suspensions in the Western and Southern parts of the country.

A general deflation followed these crises. The Cotton Belt suffered most severely, and perhaps even more in the second crisis than in the first. The disturbed condition of the banking system intensified a depressed situation that expressed itself in the low level of production, sales, employment, land values and rents, and prices of commodities. The index of wholesale prices (1926 base) fell only slightly in the crisis of 1837, the decline being from 83.5 in 1836 to 82.8 in 1837 and 79.4 in 1838, but after a recovery to 83.5 in 1839 it fell sharply to 71.1 in 1840 and reached a low point of 61.8 in 1843.[22]

The recovery was associated with two radically different policies. In New York and in the New England states, Nature was allowed to run its course. Credit contracted severely, and improvement had to start from a low level of activity. In other parts of the country, relief measures were adopted and credit expansion was undertaken. Business activity reached its low point in 1842 and then started to improve, but not before steps had been taken to guard against a recurrence of the events of the past few years. Some state governments incorporated into their constitutions a prohibition against state borrowing for the purpose of financing either internal improvements or banks. Banking laws were also reformed to keep a stricter rein on the growth of banking institutions. To guard against the inflationary and deflationary effects of redistribution of Treasury funds held in private banks (and partly for other reasons), the independent Treasury system was established in 1840. This measure made

[22] Cutts, "One Hundred and Thirty-four Years of Wholesale Prices," *Monthly Labor Review,* July, 1935. (Based on work of Hansen and Senate Committee on Finance, 1893.)

economically innocuous its distribution of funds from one section of the country to another.[23]

After 1845 a consistent recovery resulted from these measures and from an exogenous factor, an increase in exports of foodstuffs, induced by the Irish potato famine and the repeal of the English Corn Laws. A minor recession in 1847 and 1848, also caused by exogenous factors, namely, banking difficulties in England and depressed conditions on the Continent, had little retarding effect on the generally improved course of business.

The Crisis of 1857 and the Period 1849-1860 [24]

The crisis of 1857 again was dominated by monetary overinvestment, with both domestic and foreign exogenous factors operating. During the first part of this period, business activity took an upswing that has become known as the "Golden Age." This upswing was characterized by large investments promoted and accompanied by an expansion in the money supply, a rise in the price level, and a general improvement in business activity. The increase in investment took the form primarily of railroad construction that opened up new territories to commercial exploitation.

Increased demand led to an expansion of manufacturing, agriculture, and trade, accentuated by increased foreign purchases of foodstuffs arising from a crop failure in Europe in 1853 and the Crimean War. This increased demand brought about a rise in prices of commodities such as cotton, of slaves, and of land. Once more land speculation played a prominent part in the boom. This boom, in turn, was geared to an expansion in the supply of money and credit. The discovery of gold in California, the growth of banking, and the influx of capital from abroad (mainly into railroad companies [25]) increased the supply of loanable funds and facilitated the investment and business activities of the country.

The supplies of capital turned out to be inadequate to maintain the investment projects undertaken. Most of the railroads were completed, but revenues lagged, since the development and exploitation of the territories served by the railroads was a slow process. Continued supplies of capital would have been required to maintain the railroads in this early phase. But the expansion of the monetary supply was stopped and a

[23] A serious disadvantage, however, was that the funds held by the Treasury became sterilized as long as they were so held. Thus, Treasury operations in acquiring and spending funds resulted in a net absorption or release of funds in the economy at times that were not guided by considerations of sound fiscal policy.

[24] See Thorp, *Business Annals*, pp. 124-127; and Smith and Cole, *Fluctuations in American Business, 1790-1860*, pp. 87-138.

[25] England alone had some $400,000,000 invested. In the period 1848 to 1859, railway mileage increased from 5,996 to 28,789. See Ira Ryner, *On the Crises of 1837, 1847 and 1857 in England, France and the United States: An Analysis and Comparison*, p. 14. Lincoln, Neb.: University of Nebraska Studies, Vol. 5, 1905.

restriction of capital precipitated by developments outside the immediate sphere of operations.

A panic on the New York Stock Exchange in 1854 restricted finance and caused many business failures, but a quick recovery took place and speculation continued to a high point in 1857. Then followed a sharp credit contraction traceable to several factors.[26] A capital outflow took place, partly as a result of a withdrawal of foreign funds to meet financial difficulties in Europe and partly to offset an unfavorable trade balance left by a failure of the Louisiana sugar crop and an increase in imports. Worst of all, the capital outflow took the form of a loss of specie, which immediately created difficulties for the banks. At the same time, railroads were forced into failure through an inability to obtain further credit accommodation to meet interest obligations. The banks, in turn, had heavy stakes in the railroads. The sudden collapse of the Ohio Life and Trust Company, considered a pillar of sound finance, gave the first alarm. Many banks failed and the suspension of specie payments spread widely.[27]

In the resulting period of depression, railroad building ceased completely, and concomitantly employment and business activity in general

---

[26] The acuteness of the financial situation is suggested by a Wall Street doggerel of 1857:

> "Rushing around the corners,
> Chasing every friend
> Plunging into bank—
> Nothing there to lend—
> Piteously begging
> Of every man you meet."

From Samuel Rezneck, "Depression and American Opinion, 1857-1859," *Journal of Economic History*, Vol. II, No. 1 (May, 1942), p. 12.

[27] An apparently able contemporary writer places the major share of the blame for the financial crisis on the poor management of bank officers:

"It is a false notion, that panic comes from mysterious and unmanageable causes. So long as we give credence to this commercial fatalism, and accept it as an excuse for the incapacity of financial managers, we shall be liable to a recurrence of panic whenever an adverse wind sweeps the ocean.

" 'If there had only been an able man among bank officers, in whom the others had confidence, to take the lead, the panic might have been crushed in the bud.'

"This was a common and freely-expressed opinion among all classes of merchants. It is a singular fact, that must occupy the foreground in any history of the suspension of 1857, whatever part different writers may assign to accessory causes. In the fright and confusion which succeeded the failure of the Ohio Life Insurance and Trust Company, our bank officers fell back, each to his separate place, to 'fortify' his institution, though at the expense of every private and common interest of the market. They did not recognize, in any one of their number, that superiority of intelligence and capacity in management, which in times of anarchy and doubt never fails to be felt—never fails (where it is known to exist) to be called on *to lead*. Never, in the whole course of our commercial history, did the public distress cry louder for the ability that can unite separate interests for a common purpose; and for the want of it, no common purpose was created. Everything went by chance, or by necessity." (J. S. Gibbons, *The Banks of New York and the Panic of 1857*, pp. 387-388. New York: D. Appleton-Century Company, 1858.)

fell. Commodity and land prices fell sharply and speculative activity ceased. The index of wholesale prices (1926 base) dropped from 68.5 in 1857 to 62.0 in 1858, 61.0 in 1859, and 60.9 in 1860.[28] The depressed conditions provoked widespread and growing unrest among the working classes. Since the crisis of 1857 had originated to a large extent in financial overexpansion, the sharp credit contraction and financial reorganization seemed to remedy the situation and bring about recovery. At any rate, business improved and by the end of the period before the Civil War reached a prosperous condition.

Impact of the Civil War on the American Economy: 1860-1865 [29]

In the Civil War, the American economy was broken in two, and each incomplete part had to try to mobolize its resources for war against the other; then, after the war, the two parts had to be knit together again and jointly readjusted to peacetime conditions. Except for the stimulus given to mass-production industries and the corporate form of business organization,[30] the North underwent no profound structural changes during the war, although there were some short-run changes of considerable importance.[31] At the beginning of the war, there was the peculiar phenomenon of a business decline instead of the usual improvement. Both businessmen and the public were cautious in their buying, with a resulting reduction in the income flow. Then, when the die was cast and Government spending began on a large scale, there was an increase in income, a fuller utilization of resources, and a general state of prosperity. All branches of industry and trade gained in this early stage of the war: manufacturing and farming, mining and commerce.[32] Even trade with the South persisted in some degree by means of smuggling. Banking suffered disruption in the early stage of the war, as did other branches of economic activity, and some banks even had to suspend specie payments. In the subsequent period of prosperity, however, especially after the establishment of the national banking system, there was an expansion and improvement in banking organization.

The financing methods of the Federal Government constituted a disruptive element. Expansionary elements existed in the expenditures financed by an unsatisfactory tax structure and borrowing program. This

[28] Cutts, "One Hundred and Thirty-four Years of Wholesale Prices," *Monthly Labor Review,* July, 1935. (Index for this period based on report of Senate Committee on Finance, 1893.)

[29] Thorp, *Business Annals,* pp. 127-129.

[30] This structural change is emphasized in Edgar W. Martin, *The Standard of Living in 1860,* p. 5. Chicago: The University of Chicago Press, 1942.

[31] E. D. Fite, *Social and Industrial Conditions in the North During the Civil War.* New York: The Macmillan Company, 1910.

[32] For a full discussion of the developments that took place in each of these industries during the war, see Fite, *Social and Industrial Conditions in the North During the Civil War.*

was bad enough, but the outright printing of money in the form of "greenbacks" [33] constituted an expansionary influence in its entirety and contributed greatly to the inflationary rise in prices that took place.[34] This rise in prices exceeded the peak reached in the War of 1812 but fell short of that reached during the Revolutionary War. Fiscal policy as a whole had the effect of releasing purchasing power through Government expenditures in excess of the absorption of purchasing power through taxes and loans that cut down spending. The difficulty involved in obtaining supplies was an additional aggravating factor. The price increase that took place had the usual effect of creating disparities in the distribution of national income—an increased income that was created by the Government expenditures and by the resulting stimulus to private spending. In the international sphere, the position of the North was strengthened, if anything, by the war. Exports of foodstuffs were substantially maintained [35] and imports declined a little. At first there was a net capital outflow, but during the course of the war, when it became evident that the South could not win and the North could not lose, a capital inflow took place. The relation between fiscal policy and business activity during these years is indicated in Figure 3.

The South suffered serious dislocations during the war, much more so than the North, since the South had typically had an open economy, specializing in the production of exportable staples and dependent on

---

33 The following excerpt from a letter written by President Lincoln to his friend Colonel Taylor deserves a place in the theory as well as the history of money:

"My dear Colonel Dick, I have long determined to make public the origin of the greenback and tell the world that it is Dick Taylor's creation. You had always been friendly to me, and when troublous times fell on us, and my shoulders, though broad and willing, were weak, and myself surrounded by such circumstances and such people that I knew not whom to trust, then I said in my extremity: 'I will send for Colonel Taylor; he will know what to do.' I think it was in January, 1862, on or about the 16th, that I did so. You came, and I said to you: 'What can we do?' Said you: 'Why, issue treasury notes bearing no interest, printed on the best banking paper. Issue enough to pay off the army expenses and declare it legal tender.' Chase thought it a hazardous thing, but we finally accomplished it, and gave the people of this republic the greatest blessing they ever had—their own paper to pay their own debts." (Taken from Emil Ludwig, *Lincoln*, pp. 448-449. Boston: Little, Brown & Company, 1930.)

34 At the same time that the greenbacks were issued, the Government was "hoarding" gold. "The first step we are bound to take is to relieve the Government from the mischievous position of being a hoarder of gold. It cannot afford to be an instrument in the hands of its enemies, a participator in the depreciation of its currency, a party to the speculations of the sea-board . . . The second step should be to allay the public fears as to the value and extent of the legal-tender issue. The amount is but $400,000,000, not $1,000,000,000. Instead of an unlimited issue hereafter, not one dollar more should be added; but, on the contrary, the amount in circulation should be reduced, and a more enlarged system of taxation established." (From a speech by the Hon. Henry G. Stebbins in the House of Representatives, March 3, 1864, reprinted in *Finances and Resources of the United States*. New York: Loyal Publication Society, 1864.)

35 In 1860, 1861, and 1862 there were crop failures in Great Britain, and in one of these years a crop failure in Europe. See Fite, *Social and Industrial Conditions in the North During the Civil War*, p. 17.

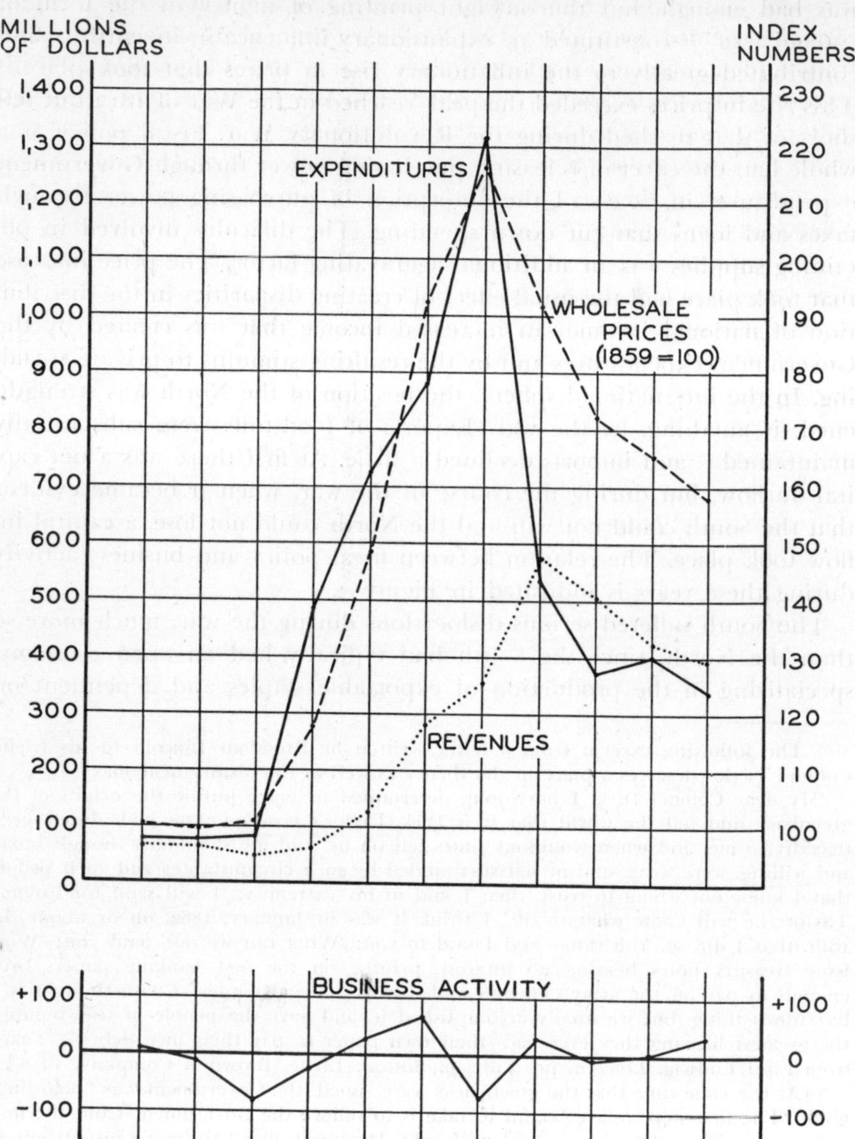

FIG. 3. *Fiscal Policy and Business Activity, 1859-1869.* (Expenditures and revenues in fiscal years; wholesale prices and business activity in calendar years.) Sources of basic data: "Expenditures" and "Revenues," United States Treasury Department; "Wholesale Prices," United States Bureau of Labor Statistics; "Business Activity," Cleveland Trust Company.

international trade. The products exported, mainly tobacco and cotton products yielded by a plantation-slave economy, were traded for foodstuffs and manufactured goods, in which this area was deficient. With the outbreak of war, the exports of the South were cut off and depressed industries immediately appeared. From the point of view of the war effort, the curtailed exports, taken by themselves, were desirable in hastening diversion of men and resources to military service and production. The diversion to war production took place very slowly, however, because the slaves were not readily adaptable to nonplantation methods. The Government's purchasing policy, involving requisitions below the market price, had the effect of discouraging production. Since the major part of imports for both civilian and military purposes was cut off, the development of diversified farming and manufacturing became an absolute necessity. The only redeeming feature in the South's situation was the prevalence of smuggling through the North's blockade.

The financial methods adopted by the South did not tend to reduce the economic disruption, and in this respect they were similar to those of the North. Resort was had to excessive currency issues, and the Confederacy lacked the power and the will to use taxes to absorb the purchasing power that it released through its expenditures. This, taken together with the restricted supply of goods, resulted in a rise in price and a decline in the buying power of the Confederate currency.

Economic Trends

The long period extending from the earliest Colonial days to the end of the Civil War saw the growth of the country from an undeveloped satellite of Europe to a mature nation that, like Europe, met serious internal difficulties of its own. The country was still heavily dependent on the rest of the world, but it had at least achieved some diversification of its output and had removed some of the earlier impediments to progress. The growth of the economic power of the Federal Government had progressed to a considerable extent, but the banking situation was still little more than hopeless when it came to dealing with financial crises.

The open nature of the American economy, the weakness of the central Government, and its unwillingness to impose strong fiscal and other measures under emergency conditions, led to wide wartime and post-war fluctuations in this period. The wartime booms were of an extremely mixed variety with far greater sectors suffering sharp curtailment than is true today. This difference is attributable to the greater dependence on foreign trade that existed at that time. The wartime difficulties might still have been mitigated if more effective measures had been pursued to divert depressed industries and workers to war production and service. But the measures taken frequently defeated their purpose and the fiscal methods adopted interposed the additional disruptive factor of rapid fluctuations in price levels.

The post-war reactions were allowed to run their course with virtually unbridled severity. Foresight was lacking in bridging the transition from war to peace. The sudden resumption of foreign trade, the sudden cessation of demand for military supplies, the sudden release of soldiers and war workers inflicted an even greater shock than war itself. The post-war maladjustments in business activity and employment might have been prevented, partly if not wholly, by adequate planning designed to swing the economy gradually back onto a peacetime basis.

The vulnerability of the American business community to unbridled credit expansion and to external influences, even under peacetime conditions, is also demonstrated amply in this period. Given a readily expansible monetary supply and a growing economy, speculative activity became dominant and overinvestment took place. So weak was the foundation of the credit supply, however, that the slightest breath of ill wind could topple the whole superstructure. A withdrawal of foreign capital, a reduction of exports, or the failure of a large house could bring nationwide deflation and depression. The fault lay in the weak banking system and in the absence of basic regulatory measures controlling credit expansion. Unpredictable exogenous factors could not have wreaked such disaster if, even with a rapidly growing economy, the monetary situation had had some basic elements of stability.

In relieving the crises two opposing schools of thought prevailed. Expansionary monetary and fiscal remedies were adopted mainly in the Western and Southern parts of the country, while sharp credit contraction and deflation were allowed to take place in the "sound-money" Eastern states. If avoidance of subsequent crises be the criterion of success, neither policy has a record of which it can be very proud. Again, the basic instability of the monetary situation suggests the source of the difficulty. Whether the recovery is "healthy" or "unhealthy" makes little difference if it can soon turn into a speculative craze.

The physical and economic growth of the country intensified the complexity of the problems attending progress free from excessive, albeit temporary, setbacks. In spite of setbacks, a review of the developments of the period as a whole indicates that favorable achievements were made. These gains may be measured by the national income and its composition, and by the length of the working day and the average length of life. Estimates of national income reveal the quantity of commodities and services available for current consumption or future production, while length of the working day and of the average life span indicate the effort required to produce these goods and the length of time in which they might be enjoyed. Whether people were happier at the end of the period than at the beginning no one can say—no successful utilometer or index of the soul has yet been devised—but with respect to material matters there is a substantial record of favorable progress.

National Income and Its Composition

Estimates of national income begin with the year 1799 and are available only by decades for the period under review. A necessarily rough estimate of the national income in this period places the real income per capita in 1799 in the neighborhood of $211.[36] By 1859 it had reached $300. This rise indicates fairly well the growth in the economy's productivity per capita during the 60-year interval, as the two years were in roughly the same cycle phase, namely, that of "revival." [37] The figures for the intervening decades show very clearly the effects that wars and financial crises had on the country's growth. In 1809, a year of "depression," real income per capita was $202 and in 1819, a year of "severe depression; financial panic," it was only $168. Likewise in 1829, which saw first "depression" and then "revival," the real income per capita was at a low level, $166. In 1839, which is characterized by "revival; panic; recession," the figure was just under $200. The year of "prosperity," 1849, saw a real income per capita of $241. The growth of approximately 50 per cent from 1799 to 1859 suggests the rapidity with which expanding population and resources were brought into economic production. However, by 1869 it had dropped to $233, perhaps a reflection of the war years.

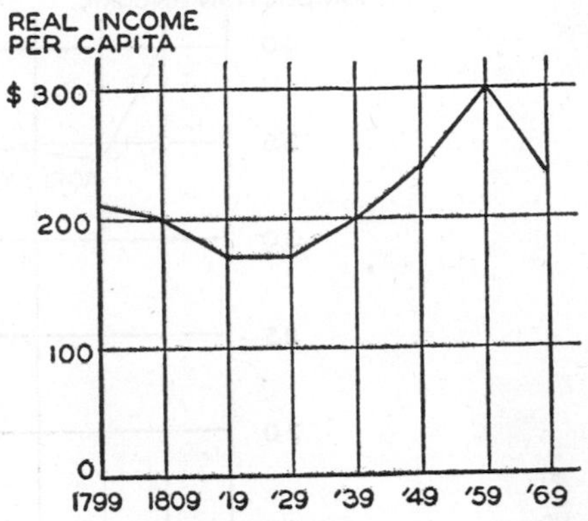

FIG. 4. *Real Income Per Capita, 1799-1869 (Decade Figures)*. (Source: Robert F. Martin, *National Income in the United States, 1799-1938,* p. 6. New York: National Industrial Conference Board, 1939)

The industrial composition of the national income demonstrates the tendency, however unspectacular, toward greater diversification in the country's production. From 1799 to 1859 the importance of agriculture in the national income fell from 39.5 per cent to 30.8 per cent while manu-

---

[36] Owing to the paucity of primary statistical series in this early period the national income estimates must necessarily be to a considerable degree approximate. The estimates presented here are those of the National Industrial Conference Board. The "realized national income" is used to approximate national income. The monetary figures are deflated by an index of the general price level. The deflated figures are in terms of 1926 dollars. See Robert F. Martin, *National Income in the United States, 1799-1938,* pp. 6-7. New York: National Industrial Conference Board, 1939.

[37] See Thorp, *Business Annals,* pp. 114-127, for the cyclical phase of all the years discussed here.

facturing rose from 4.8 per cent to 12.1 per cent. The trend was accentuated greatly in the war decade, the figures being 24.1 per cent for agriculture and 15.9 per cent for manufacturing in 1869.[38] Although the country was still far from self-sufficient it was gradually becoming more nearly capable of maintaining its living standards in case of a break-down in its relations with other parts of the world.

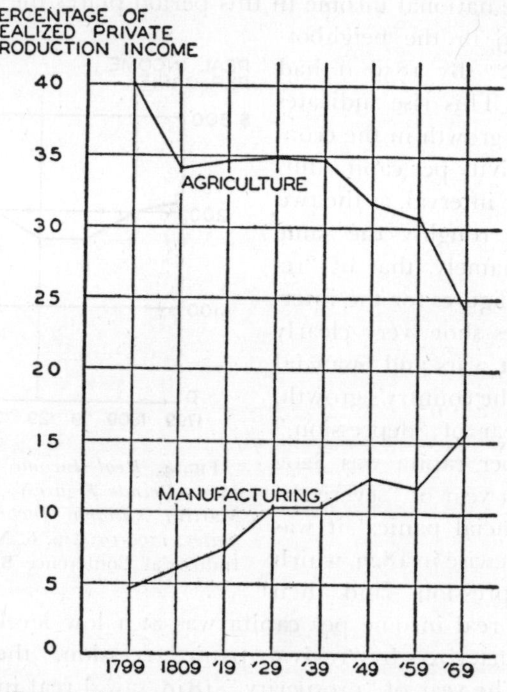

Fig. 5. *Percentage Shares of Agriculture and Manufacturing in Realized Private Production Income, 1799-1869.* (Source: Robert F. Martin, *National Income in the United States, 1799-1938,* p. 60. New York: National Industrial Conference Board, 1939)

Length of Working Day and Length of Life

In a country in which the main industry was agriculture, little could be done to reduce the length of the working day since "sunrise to sunset" was, and is, the agricultural working day. In manufacturing, the deplorable conditions that prevailed in England set the standard for this country at first. The hours were the same as in agriculture. In summer this meant 14 to 16 hours a day, with two hours or less off for meals. In winter it meant 9 to 12 hours, with one hour or less off for meals. There were few holidays other than the Sabbath. Early efforts by workers' organiza-

[38] Martin, *National Income in the United States, 1799-1938,* p. 60.

tions to obtain a 10-hour day met strong opposition in a public opinion that seemed to accept sunrise to sunset as the standard of "industrious habits." Concerted action began in 1833, led by building tradesmen and followed by blacksmiths, mechanics, tailors, ship-workers, and others in skilled crafts. By the autumn of 1835, after strikes in Boston, Philadelphia, and Baltimore (and several smaller towns) most city craftsmen had won the 10-hour day. The less highly skilled workers, especially in the cotton and woolen mills, worked longer hours. Worker agitation persisted, and in many states laws were passed setting a 10-hour legal day except where contracts specified otherwise. These laws, however, were largely ineffective in practice. In 1840 the President of the United States declared the 10-hour day for Federal employees.[39] Widespread and co-ordinated effort to reduce hours of work in this country dates back only to about 1850.[40] The achievements were clearly not very great in this period but in certain narrow fields considerable progress had been made.

Systematic records of current mortality in any large area of the United States were not compiled until the beginning of the present century, but there were a few early attempts to prepare life tables for the populations of American communities. It is necessary to piece the available fragments together in order to obtain some indication of the trend. Among the first of these was a life table based on the mortality for part of Philadelphia in the years 1782, 1788, 1789, and 1790.[41] According to these observations, the expectation of life at birth in Philadelphia seems to have been about 25 years. In 1789 a table gave an expectation of life for Massachusetts and New Hampshire of about 35 years. A table compiled in 1850 gave a life expectation of 38.3 years for males and 40.5 years for females. The estimate was 39.8 years for both sexes in a table for 1855 and became progressively higher with the publication of later tables. Allowing for incomplete statistics there would seem to have been an increase of 10 to 15 years in length of life from the end of the Colonial period to 1865.

Basic Conditions of Future Growth

The transition from Colonial to National status, the increased diversification of production, and the growth in power of the central government showed their effects on the standard of living during the period ending in 1865. The increased real income per capita and the reduction in the length of the working day were tangible evidences of material progress; and the improved conditions of health that resulted in a longer

---

39 See *The Five-Day Week in Manufacturing Industries,* p. 9. New York: National Industrial Conference Board, 1929.

40 L. T. Beman, *Five Day Week,* p. 43. New York: The H. W. Wilson Company, 1928.

41 See Louis I. Dublin and Alfred J. Lotka, *Length of Life,* pp. 44, 54, 65. New York: Ronald Press, 1936.

life were indications of better living conditions. Nevertheless, the progress that took place was not by any means spectacular, in material terms at least. The reason for this must be found in the severe shocks to which the economy was subjected in war and peace. With every step forward it apparently had to take more than half a step backward.

More fundamental developments than those reflected in statistical data occurred. The basic conditions were laid for future economic growth. The same economic system that encouraged crises also built canals and railroads, opened up the West, improved agricultural techniques, and laid the groundwork for heavy industry. Unbridled freedom of enterprise and an unstable monetary system left in their wake monetary deflations, bankruptcies, and heartaches. They also left a legacy of important benefits—physical capital, institutional improvement, hard-won experience, and a tradition of large profits for large risks.

Conclusions

The history of American economic development to 1865 reveals the origin of those conditions and institutions that later made possible the political and economic pre-eminence of the United States. It also demonstrates the hazards of relying entirely on the "invisible hand" to maximize economic welfare. Repeated speculative booms and "busts" in peacetime and serious dislocations in wartime indicate that a visible hand must guide the invisible. Otherwise the general level of activity suffers and with it private enterprise and individual well-being.

The crises of 1819, 1837, and 1857 show that some regulatory measures would have promoted rather than hampered the long run growth of the free enterprise system. Individual zeal led to overinvestment that ran far ahead of real values and outstripped the capabilities of the country's weak financial mechanism. To dampen such zeal a little by restricting speculative activity and credit expansion would have increased rather than diminished individual achievement and would have strengthened rather than weakened individual enterprise. The benefits of dynamic growth could have been gained at less cost. The real and permanent losses in the period of deflation and depression nearly equaled the apparent and transient gains of speculative inflation and artificial prosperity. The country's record of canal, railroad, and farm building in this period was based on individual and state enterprise but owes little to excessive and speculative inflation and deflation of security and land values.

The economic experience of the Revolutionary War, the War of 1812, and the Civil War shows that short-term estimates of individual or national well-being may be extremely misleading. The natural reluctance to pay increased taxes and the apparent advantage (if only of expediency) of other methods of war finance led to such severe inflation, depreciation, and finally deflation and depression that in the end the individual and the nation were worse off in both war production and post-war income than if a more realistic and farsighed fiscal policy had been pursued. At the same time, when a freely operating price mechanism was suddenly supplanted by price-fixing, there were serious effects on the production and flow of commodities and services because full recognition was not given to the requirements of the private sector of the economy. This process was demonstrated convincingly in the effects of the abortive price conventions and fixed-price requisitions of the Revolutionary War. Although the precise degree of control necessary to establish a sound economy can never be accurately determined, the dangers to be avoided seem to be indicated by the experience of this period.

Selected References

GENERAL WORKS

Burton, Theodore E., *Financial Crises.* New York: D. Appleton-Century Company, 1931.

Martin, Robert F., *National Income in the United States, 1799-1938.* New York: National Industrial Conference Board, 1939.

Mitchell, Wesley C., *Business Cycles, The Problem and Its Setting.* New York: National Bureau of Economic Research, 1927.

Morris, Richard B., *Historiography of America 1600-1800.* New York: Columbia University Press, 1933.

Silberling, Norman J., *The Dynamics of Business.* New York: McGraw-Hill Book Company, 1943.

Smith, Walter B., and Arthur H. Cole, *Fluctuations in American Business, 1790-1860.* Cambridge, Mass.: Harvard University Press, 1935.

Thorp, Willard L., *Business Annals.* New York: National Bureau of Economic Research, 1926.

Warren, George F., and Frank A. Pearson, *Prices.* New York: John Wiley & Sons, 1933.

Wright, Chester W., *Economic History of the United States.* New York: McGraw-Hill Book Company, 1941.

SPECIAL TOPICS

Angell, James W., *Investment and Business Cycles.* New York: McGraw-Hill Book Company, 1941.

Beman, Lamar T., *Five Day Week.* New York: The H. W. Wilson Company, 1928.

Cole, Arthur H., *Wholesale Commodity Prices in the United States, 1700-1861.* Cambridge, Mass.: Harvard University Press, 1938.

Davis, Joseph S., *Essays in the Early History of American Corporations.* Cambridge, Mass.: Harvard University Press, 1917.

Fite, Emerson D., *Social and Industrial Conditions in the North During the Civil War.* New York: The Macmillan Company, 1910.

Gibbons, J. S., *The Banks of New York and the Panic of 1857.* New York: D. Appleton-Century Company, 1858.

Hansen, Alvin H., *Fiscal Policy and Business Cycles.* New York: W. W. Norton & Company, 1941.

Heaton, Herbert, "Non-Importation, 1806-1812," *The Journal of Economic History,* Vol. I (November, 1941), pp. 178-198.

Martin, Edgar W., *The Standard of Living in 1860.* Chicago: University of Chicago Press, 1942.

McGrane, Reginald C., *The Panic of 1837.* Chicago: University of Chicago Press, 1924.

Myers, Margaret G., *The New York Money Market,* Vol. I. New York: Columbia University Press, 1931.

Rezneck, Samuel, "Depression and American Opinion, 1857-1859," *Journal of Economic History,* Vol. II (May, 1942), p. 12.

Ryner, Ira, *On the Crises of 1837, 1847 and 1857 in England, France and the United States: An Analysis and Comparison.* Lincoln, Neb.: University of Nebraska Studies, Vol. 5, 1905.

Salisbury, Guy H., *The Speculative Craze of '36.* Publications of the Buffalo Historical Society, Vol. I. Buffalo: The Peter Paul Book Company, 1896.

PART 4

1865-1918

THE END *of the Civil War brought different problems to the major sections of the country. For the South there were the difficulties of reconstruction, which required a generation or more for solution. For the North and West it was a different story. Largely untouched by the physical destruction of combat, these parts of the country actually emerged from the conflict with an enlarged industrial plant, with agricultural methods advanced, and, aside from minor post-war adjustments, ready to take the lead in the challenging task of developing the better part of a continent. This was an undertaking that absorbed the major energies of the nation for the succeeding half century. Economically as well as politically our attention was centered on the domestic scene. Although economic ties with the outside world remained important we moved further and further away from the position where domestic prosperity depended upon Europe and foreign trade; on the contrary many parts of the world economy became increasingly sensitive and responsive to economic conditions within the United States.*

In many respects the development of the domestic economy followed the trends established before 1865. Population continued to grow rapidly, although at a slower rate. Each of the three decades following 1860 witnissed an expansion of a little over 25 per cent; but by 1920 the decennial increase had dropped to approximately 15 per cent. Even with this decline in the rate of growth, the total of over 105 million inhabitants in 1920 was nearly three and a half times the figure reported 60 years earlier. Judged by this standard alone, the United States had become one of the world's great nations. It was during this period that over 28 million foreign born made their way to our shores. Mostly between the ages of 17 and 45, approximately two-thirds male, these immigrants added an important element to America's labor force.

Migration affecting the United States was by no means confined to crossing international borders. Aided immeasurably by an expanding railway network, the extensive internal movement of people, so characteristic of the period before 1860, continued on an even larger scale. In many respects this movement reflected the dynamic character of our economy. In so far as knowledge and means permitted, most of those who changed their places of residence were seeking to better their economic and social positions. For many, the West with its cheap or free land still offered the brightest opportunities. Others sought occupations in the growing urban centers, which were responding in their expansion to increasing industrial activity or to commercial and associated activities, the concomitants of an ever thriving trade. Indeed this movement to the cities brought about a significant change in the structure of our society. In 1860 only one out of five persons lived in a town or city with 2,500 or more inhabitants; by 1920 the ratio was approximately one to one. America was beginning to lose its predominantly rural-agrarian character and was becoming more of a nation of city dwellers.

Some of the basic changes in the pattern of economic opportunities between 1870 and 1920 are revealed in the major shifts in the distribution of the labor force. The total number gainfully employed during these years grew from around 12.9 million workers to 41.6 million, but Agriculture, which employed some 50 per cent of the total in 1870, absorbed only 25 per cent in 1920. In contrast, Manufacturing and Construction increased their proportions from 21 per cent to 32 per cent, and Transport, Public Utilities, Trade and Finance, which together claimed 11 per cent of the labor force in 1870, took in some 22 per cent a half century later. An emerging "servant problem" is revealed in the decline from 7.3 per cent to 4.1 per cent in employment in Domestic Services. On the other hand, Personal Services outside the homes expanded from 2.1 per cent to 4 per cent. Of special interest was the expansion of employment in Government which grew from less than 1 per cent to around 2.4 per cent.

These figures point up the major changes in the structure of the American economy that came during the half century ending in 1920. They reveal the growing importance of industry, transportation, and trade relative to agriculture. The increasing number of government employees reflected some of the growing complexities of our economic and social life. Not so apparent, but implicit in these changes, was a greater division of labor and specialization; geographically, along product lines, and in the functions of labor, management, and capital. The combined result of these developments was a remarkable increase in the production of goods and services; an increase that was scarcely appreciated either at home or abroad until brought out dramatically by America's participation in World War I.

In the succeeding seventeen chapters these major trends are described and analyzed in more detail. In general the organization follows that of the previous sections: the first two chapters discuss the westward movement of the population and the development of transportation; the next fourteen deal with agriculture, industry, marketing, foreign trade, commercial policy, financial institutions, business organization, the "trust" problem, and the role of public finance. The section is concluded with a summary of the performance of the economy.

18 · WESTWARD EXPANSION SINCE THE HOMESTEAD ACT

Westward Expansion and the Frontier

THE LOCATION, VOLUME, AND SPEED of our westward expansion since 1860 can be measured most simply by comparing the density of population for that year with that, for example, of 1890. Except for a sizable projection into eastern Texas and a smaller extension into Kansas and Nebraska, the frontier lines of 1860—beyond which the population was less than two persons to the square mile—followed the 95th meridian almost exactly from the Gulf of Mexico to central Minnesota. From there it ran slightly south of east to Lake Huron, leaving the northern parts of Minnesota, Wisconsin, and Michigan beyond the fringe of settlement; northern Maine and southern Florida were likewise beyond the two-per-square-mile line. Thus, except for the settlements on the Pacific Coast and in New Mexico, the people of the United States in 1860 lived in a compact diamond-shaped mass with its sharpest points in Maine and Texas and its greatest density in its northeastern quarter. Within the short span of one generation the frontier as a distinguishable unbroken line had disappeared. Furthermore, those states beyond the frontier line in 1860 added more people to their population in the 30-year period following 1890 than they did between 1860 and 1890. The relatively rapid growth of the West in contrast with other parts of the nation, particularly between 1850 and 1910, is revealed in the chart on page 339.

Since the Civil War there have been two distinct forms of native white migration: one agricultural in nature, the other industrial. The former has been characterized by a steady westward flow of population from a reservoir that has itself gradually shifted west (it is probably true that this movement, representing the traditional advance of the general farmer, was largely complete by 1910, although the continuing expansion into the Pacific Coast states since then has been partly agricultural). The migration accompanying industrial expansion, on the other hand, has been toward manufacturing centers in the Great Lakes region and on the North Atlantic as well as on the Pacific coasts. Throughout the period since 1860, foreign immigrants, first from the northwestern and then from the southeastern part of Europe, have swelled the stream of city-bound

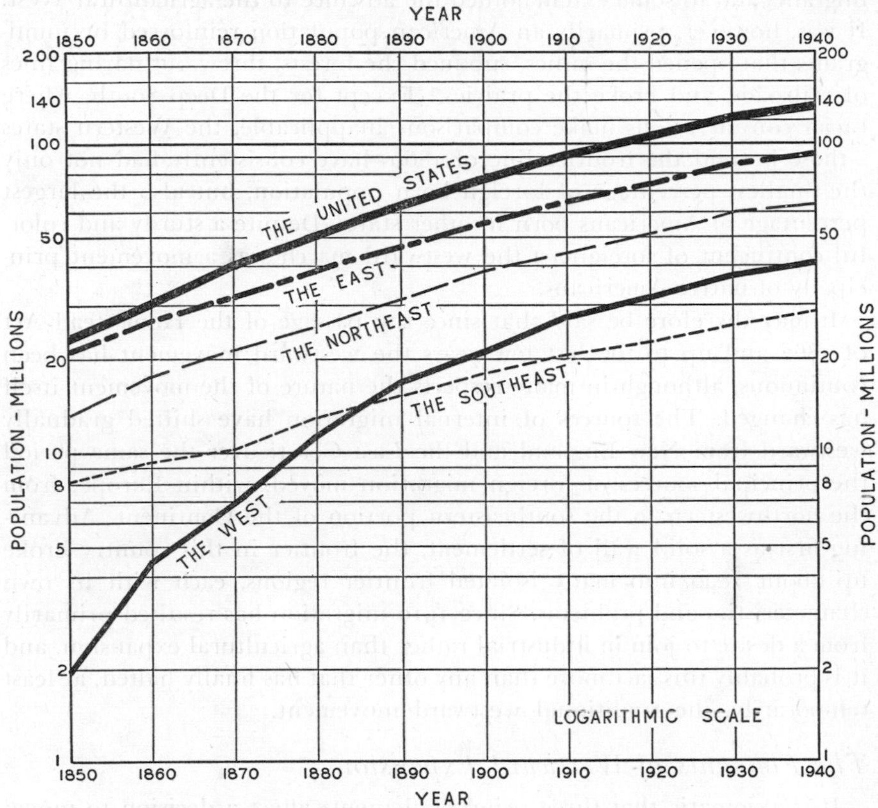

FIG. 1. *Relative Population Increase of the Several Sections of the United States, 1850-1940.* (Source: Sixteenth Census, 1940.) States included in sections shown on chart (dates after Western states indicate year of admission to the Union):

The West: Arizona (1912), Arkansas (1836), California (1850), Colorado (1876), Idaho (1890), Iowa (1846), Kansas (1861), Louisiana (1812), Minnesota (1858), Missouri (1821), Montana (1889), Nebraska (1867), Nevada (1864), New Mexico (1912), North Dakota (1889), Oklahoma (1907), Oregon (1859), South Dakota (1889), Texas (1845), Utah (1896), Washington (1889), Wyoming (1890).

The Southeast: Alabama, Delaware, District of Columbia, Florida, Georgia, Kentucky, Maryland, Mississippi, North Carolina, South Carolina, Tennessee, Virginia, West Virginia.

The Northeast: Connecticut, Illinois, Indiana, Maine, Massachusetts, Michigan, New York, New Hampshire, New Jersey, Ohio, Pennsylvania, Rhode Island, Vermont, Wisconsin.

The East—The Southeast plus The Northeast.

The United States—The East plus The West.

migrants and to some extent joined the advance to the agricultural West. It was, however, primarily an American population reinforced by immigrants that opened the mines, subdued the forests, threw out daring lines of railroads, and broke the prairies.[1] Except for the Deep South, where racial considerations make comparisons inapplicable, the Western states —those beyond the frontier line of 1860—have consistently had not only the smallest percentage of foreign born population, but also the largest percentage of Americans born in other states. Despite a sturdy and colorful contingent of foreigners, the westward march was a movement principally of native Americans.

It may therefore be said that since the passage of the Homestead Act of 1862 and up to the last few years the westward movement has been continuous, although in many respects the nature of the movement itself has changed. The sources of internal migration have shifted gradually westward from New England and the East Coast; over the same period the principal sources of foreign migration moved, within Europe, from the northwestern to the southeastern portion of the Continent. Advancing first as a solid wall of settlement, the frontier in this country broke up about 1890 into many isolated frontier regions, each with its own characteristics and problems. Since 1910 migration has resulted primarily from a desire to join in industrial rather than agricultural expansion, and it is probably this fact more than any other that has finally halted, at least temporarily, the traditional westward movement.

The Elements of Westward Expansion

It is axiomatic that three primary elements affect a decision to move: (a) reasons for going to a new home, (b) reasons for leaving an old home, and (c) a practical means of transportation. Obviously these factors affect any individual decision to move in different ways, but they are all inevitably present to some degree. Hence, for the sake of clarity, at first they will be discussed separately. The second step will be to analyze the combined agencies of pull, push, and transport, the obstacles limiting their operation, and the interaction of such forces to produce a net shift of population.

The West and Its Possibilities

The development not only of mining, lumbering, cattle raising, and agriculture but also of trade, industry, transport, and professional services has been determined in the West by the possibilities and limitations of the land. Thus the key to westward expansion lies in the physiographic character of the region beyond the Mississippi (see map, pages 342 and 343).

[1] W. J. Trimble, "The Influence of the Passing of the Public Lands," *Atlantic Monthly,* Vol. CXIII (June, 1914), p. 775.

If an intending migrant, poised on the threshold of the Great West in 1862, could have been omniscient, he would doubtless have been overawed by the vastness and variety of the land and the opportunities laid out before him.[2] In that year, the frontier line north of Arkansas lay near the western boundary of the broad Interior Lowlands, a level, humid area extending from the Appalachians roughly to the 20-inch rainfall line that bisects the Dakotas, Nebraska, and Kansas in a north-and-south direction. The western portion of this province, then still to be settled, embraced some of the nation's best land for corn and wheat raising; Wisconsin offered an ideal situation first for lumbermen, then for dairy farmers. Some coal existed in Iowa, and more in Missouri, Kansas, and what is now Oklahoma; oil lay beneath the surface of the two last-named states.

The Ozark Plateau and Ouachita Mountains, in southern Missouri and northern Arkansas between the Interior Iowlands and Coastal Plains, presented a rugged and relatively uninviting prospect to the farmer, although hogs, cattle, sheep, and corn could be raised, if only for local use. Timber and the lead deposits of southern Missouri were more stable assets.

The western reaches of the Coastal Plain embracing Louisiana and eastern Texas lay near the edge of settlement in 1862 and furnished an area of expansion for the cotton culture of the South. Rice and sugar cane could be grown in Louisiana, while the southern portion of Texas was well-fitted for cattle raising, truck gardening, and growing of citrus fruits. Oil, so vitally important to our present-day economy, underlay large sections of northeastern Texas.

Like a great swath cut across the West from Canada to Mexico, the almost treeless Great Plains extended westward from the 20-inch rainfall line to the Rockies. Although the terrain was generally level, rainfall was both scanty and irregular, so that the province offered more inducements to the cattleman than to the farmer. In the northern portion where evaporation was less rapid, however, agriculture, especially when aided by irrigation, was potentially profitable. Like a huge isolated citadel in this province rose the Black Hills of South Dakota, with their abundant timber and varied mineral resources.

As Lobeck described it, the high, rugged area west of the Great Plains as far as the Pacific could be considered as three belts running from north to south. The easternmost included the Rocky Mountain chain, attractive to the immigrant primarily for its minerals and timber. West of the mountains lay the Interior Plateau country, subdivided into three easily distinguished sectors. On the north was the Columbia Plateau of eastern Washington and Oregon and southern Idaho. In central Wash-

---

2 The physiographic provinces described in the following pages are those set up by A. K. Lobeck in the text accompanying his physiographic map published by The Geographical Press, Columbia University, New York, 1932.

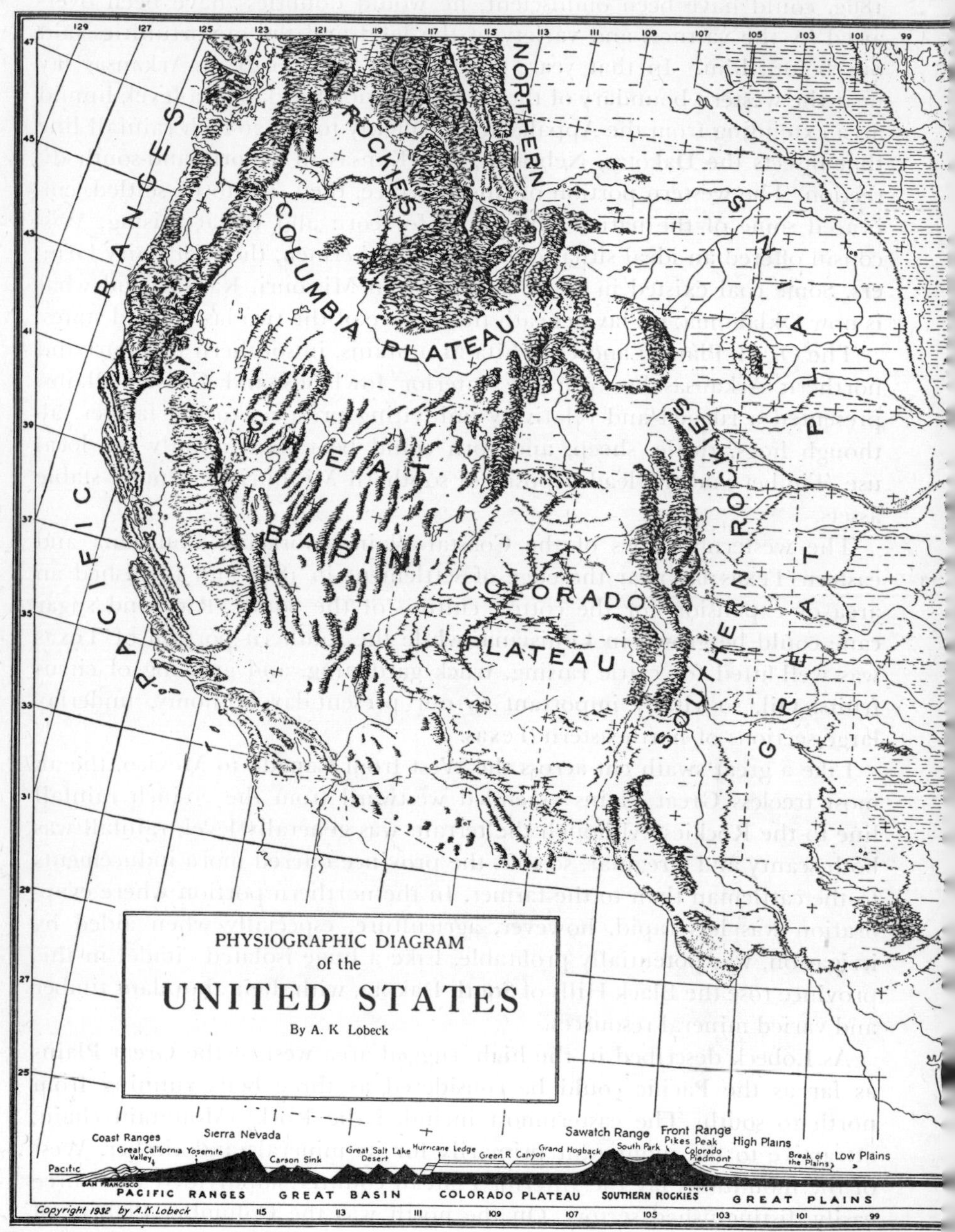

Copyright, 1932, by A. K. Lobeck. Published by The Geographical Press,

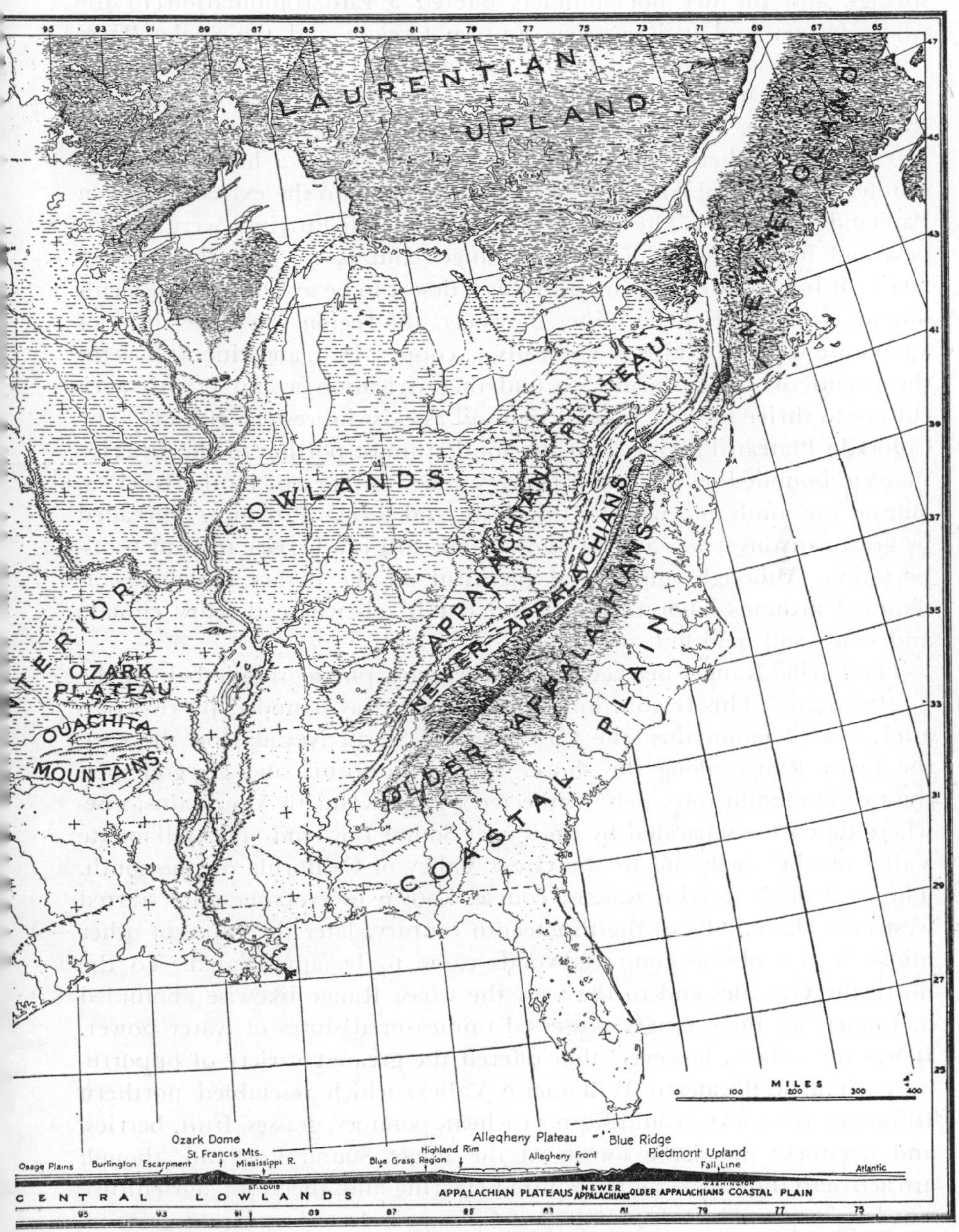

Columbia University, New York. Reprinted by special arrangement.

ington the rich soil formed by decayed basalt, the moist winters and springs, and the dry hot summers offered a rare combination to the wheat farmer and fruit grower. Eastern Oregon and the Snake River region, on the other hand, with far less moisture, were primarily suitable for ranching. Directly south of the Columbia Plateau lay the Basin and Range Province, its northern half roughly coterminous with the state of Nevada, its southern half extending like the tip of a horn along the southern portions of Arizona, New Mexico, and into the extreme western Panhandle of Texas. The unifying features of this Province were its dryness and its succession of isolated ranges and basins. To the pioneer farmer it held out few charms and was a desert to be avoided or a difficult obstacle to cross. For the miner, however, the region was little short of a paradise with its wealth of gold, silver, copper, lead, and zinc. It was for the twentieth-century farmer to find that irrigation would permit agriculture to thrive in such areas of rich soil as exist in western Nevada. The Colorado Plateau Province was the southernmost portion of the Interior Plateau, bounded on the north by Wyoming, on the east by the Rockies, and on the south and west by the Basin and Range Province. Threaded by great canyons it was and to some extent still is a barrier to land transportation. Although timber was plentiful on the higher tablelands, it required arduous labor to reach and cut it; elsewhere the dry climate and sandy soil held few attractions.

The Pacific Ranges marked the westernmost physiographic belt in the United States. This region, long and narrow, was bounded by two parallel rows of mountains: the Cascades and Sierra Nevadas on the east, the Coast Range along the shore. Where California and Oregon met, the two mountain rows were connected by the Klamath Mountains; elsewhere they were separated by the Puget Sound Lowland and Willamette Valley on the north and by the Great Valley of California on the south. The gold of the Sierras was, of course, known to everyone who started west after the middle of the nineteenth century; later the value of other minerals and of the giant redwoods came to be appreciated. To the north the Cascades and to the west the Coast Range likewise abounded in timber; all three ranges possessed unmeasured stores of water power. It was the valleys, however, that offered the greatest variety of opportunities. The well-watered Willamette Valley, which resembled northern Illinois or Kentucky, would support wheat, potatoes, grasses, fruit, berries, and livestock; the dense forests of the Puget Sound Lowland, though attractive to the lumberman, required clearing and, therefore, agriculture was less simple. The Great Valley of California, however, would grow almost any type of vegetable or fruit, wheat, barley, rice, and alfalfa; it was likwise suitable for cattle raising and possessed vast stores of oil beneath its surface. The southern California coast, in addition to its horticultural possibilities, offered a climate and landscape that, after 1890, were to prove a veritable magnet for retired farmers, businessmen, health-seekers, as well as farmers, oil men, and, eventually, the movie-makers.

In the early sixties the possibilities of this prodigious area west of the line of continuous settlement were not, of course, fully or accurately known, but—and this was important—they were suspected. Ever since the mid-forties the Oregon Trail had witnessed a steadily growing stream of farmer-pioneers filing into the fertile Willamette Valley. Late in that decade, Kearney's march to southern California and the world-famous gold rush to the Sacramento region drew world attention to some of the assets of the fabulous state that Spanish and Mexican settlers had utilized quietly for almost three quarters of a century. Meanwhile, the Mormons, astride the Overland Trail, were beginning to demonstrate what could be done with irrigation in the desert. In 1853, Jefferson Davis, then Secretary of War, initiated a survey of five transcontinental rail routes. When the War Department, in 1855, published its findings in thirteen thick volumes that described parallel bands of territory running east and west from the Canadian border to Mexico, a new storehouse of information was available to the curious. In the late fifties a second gold rush brought bands of wealth-seekers to the Pike's Peak region, and from these came enticing tales of the Rocky Mountain area. Nearer the East, the steady advance of the trapper and lumberman in Wisconsin and Minnesota, of the dirt farmer in Iowa and Kansas, and of the cotton grower and rancher in Texas served as a more substantial if less romantic indication of westward expansion.

The opportunities in the West, both actual and potential, were legion. Naturally, the appeal was primarily to trappers, miners, cattlemen, lumbermen, and farmers. But the activities of these men created the need for the soldier to subdue the wild tribes, the teamster to serve the army posts, mines, and ranches, the ubiquitous general storekeeper, the carpenter, the miller, the tanner, the printer, the packer, and the preacher. And, as settlement progressed, the stage driver, the freighter, the banker, the lawyer, and the schoolteacher were soon regarded as necessities. To the railroad builder, the West presented a superb promise as well as a mighty challenge. Save for such rivers as the Missouri, Arkansas, Sacramento, and lower Columbia, navigable streams were few and the opportunities for the provider of land transportation were boundless.

This was the country the migrant of 1862 faced; the golden opportunity of developing its primary mining, lumbering, agricultural, and pastoral resources was the basic cause of our westward expansion. Without these advantages, railroads would never have been built across its wide acres, the Indian would have remained undisturbed, and certainly the industrial development of the nation would never have reached its present proportions. The opportunity existed; westward expansion was inevitable.

The Occupation of the West: A Summary

By 1862 the trapper had marked out his trails, the Santa Fe traders had developed a major highway to the Southwest, and the mining advance had already penetrated into California, Colorado, Nevada, Arizona, Idaho, and Montana.[3] Soon after the Civil War, mines were opened in Wyoming as well. Operations were first carried out on public land where an extra-legal code of procedure was enforced in the absence of effective public law. Aside from producing gold and silver to fill the nation's expanding commercial needs, this mining advance stimulated the agricultural development of the Rocky Mountain and California areas; stock raisers, seeking new grasslands upon which to graze and fatten part of the huge surplus of longhorn cattle that was pouring out of Texas, eagerly took up large areas of Kansas, Nebraska, the Dakotas, New Mexico, Colorado, Wyoming, and Montana. Furthermore, transportation facilities, especially in Colorado, were built in response to mining needs. Thus, this one phase of expansion had a cumulative effect on the movement as a whole. One counteracting result was the provocation of Indian wars, which served, temporarily at least, to retard settlement. Eventually the mining industry, following the pattern of big business elsewhere, became largely a corporate rather than an individual undertaking and its effect on expansion became even more marked.

The lumber industry that blossomed in the West after 1865 turned first to the extensive white pine stands in upper Michigan, Wisconsin, and Minnesota. Transportation by way of the Mississippi or the Great Lakes was readily at hand, and by 1870 the established mills of Maine and Pennsylvania began to feel the pinch of falling prices brought about by competition from the West. Meanwhile, lumbering began on the West Coast. Until well after the turn of the century, however, the center of the industry was in the northern portions of the old Northwest Territory. Thereafter the operations of the Far Northwest began to assume major proportions. As the lumber trade flourished it attracted to it a steady stream of newcomers. Like the mining advance, it often blazed the trail for the agriculturist and contributed positively to westward expansion.

Texas, even before the Civil War, was a breeding ground for cattle. After that conflict ended and as the Indian tribes were concentrated on reservations in the late sixties, the practice of driving cattle northward for grazing and eventual shipment to the East came into vogue. Such towns as Abilene, Ellsworth, Fort Dodge, Ogallala, and Glendive sprang up as receiving centers for stock driven north. By the mid-nineties, breeding on the northern ranges and the advance of settlement in the Central Plains ended the colorful long drive. Cattlemen began instead to fence in large areas of public domain for their herds, though not without en-

3 See Chapter 6 above.

countering the strenuous opposition of farmers and, eventually, of the Government. Closed-range ranching, with stock grazing on owned and leased land, has characterized the industry since the turn of the century. Throughout its development the prospects offered by cattle raising have proved a potent factor in westward expansion.

The lure of the West, however, has always operated most strongly on the farmer. By 1870 the northern portions of Michigan and Iowa, the eastern part of Kansas and Nebraska, and many regions in Colorado—all largely vacant in 1860—had felt the plow. A decade later most of Nebraska, northern Wisconsin, and the Red River Valley of the North had been occupied; Oklahoma—the Indian territory—was virtually surrounded by farmers. By 1890, as the director of the census duly noted, the frontier line had disappeared under the impact of this agricultural advance.

In large measure this expansion was based on grain production. The Winter Wheat Belt eventually spread from southwestern Illinois and southern Iowa across Missouri and Kansas into southern Nebraska and central Oklahoma. To the north, principally in the Red River of the North Valley, spring wheat was the principal crop. Between these areas, in Indiana, Illinois, Iowa, and eastern Nebraska, lay the Corn Belt. The possibilities of these crops were doubtless more responsible than any other one factor for expansion westward; emigration from the older farming areas of northern Illinois and Wisconsin forced those regions to turn to dairying, a readjustment that contributed, in part, to the discontent culminating in the Granger Movement. In the eighties, wool raising was attracting men to Montana, Wyoming, Texas, and the Far West. By the turn of the century, the opporunities for fruit growing in the coastal states were being steadily developed.

Inevitably, this mighty advance led to the rise of milling, meat packing, and other processing industries in such centers as Chicago, St. Louis, the Twin Cities, Omaha, Kansas City, and Denver, Steel mills were built at Pueblo and on the Pacific Coast. Along with these activities grew the businesses of supply, construction, banking, transport, and professional service. Meanwhile, the advance of pure and applied science made more easily available the economic resources of the West. Such inventions as the chilled plow, barbed wire, the combine, the double-rotary saw, the windmill, the hard-surfaced road, and the tractor—to mention only a few—have lightened man's labor. Improved processes, such as high-speed milling and gradual reduction of wheat, mechanical loading of ore boats, the refrigerator car, dry farming, and high-pressure pipelines, have given man greater returns for his labor. Construction of huge dams, long aqueducts, and the extension of irrigation have opened new areas for development. The basis for these developments and their substantial contribution to the westward movement lay, however, in the original potentialities of the land.

Such, in the briefest terms, was the nature of America's western expansion. But whence did the people come who answered the call of the West? How did they get there? What were the obstacles that qualified the attraction of the region and what attempts were made to overcome them? How, in short, was westward expansion possible?

The Reservoirs of Emigration

In view of the basic fact that American economic life of the late nineteenth and early twentieth centuries was characterized by the concurrent rise of the city and the development of the agricultural West, internal migration on a large scale was inevitable. Two important and obvious distinctions, however, must be made at the outset: (1) Although the pulling factors of the trans-Mississippi area, when they operated successfully, resulted exclusively in expansion to the West, the pushing forces in the areas of emigration did not necessarily result in a move Westward. In other words, as some emigrants left a given region for the West, others were leaving, in varying numbers, to grasp the countless industrial and commercial opportunities of the city. (2) Much of the westward expansion of Americans, particularly into the great central agricultural area, was accomplished by a long succession of very short moves.

In 1870, Illinois, for example, whose surplus of native-born Americans from other states over locally born emigrants was the highest in the Union, counted 1,461,522 new-comers born in neighboring states of the East North Central district of which it was a part; the next largest contingents came, in order, from the Middle Atlantic, East South Central, and New England regions. In 1880 and 1890, Kansas showed the nation's highest surplus in the same respect; in both decades, its newcomers had been born principally in neighboring states; the next ranking contirbutory districts were the East North Central and Middle Atlantic states. When, in 1900, Texas showed the greatest surplus, the largest number of immigrants had been born in Arkansas and Louisiana; the next largest in the East South Central states, and the next in the South Atlantic states. Even the states on the periphery of the westward movement, though not at first adhering to the general trend of short moves, eventually fell in line.

Why did farmers, small tradespeople, and the like wish to move still further west from the fertile, level plains of Illinois and Iowa, and from the still-growing Midwestern centers of trade? Why, in the 1890's and 1900's did they wander into the sandhills of western Nebraska, the flats of Oklahoma, and the dreary plains of the Dakotas? Why, in other words, did the reservoir of emigration move toward an area that in preceding decades had been the prime object of westward expansion, particularly when pushing factors in the East and Europe were as strong as or stronger than before?

The movement took place, primarily, because of the pull of a new country, the vision of ever better opportunities, and the chance to begin life anew in denser forests, richer mines, wider fields, and busier towns. Yet there were elements of push in these Midwestern areas that became operative soon after the first settler arrived. Good lands near adequate transportation were often entirely taken up by the first breathless influx; physiographic, marketing, and social conditions frequently turned out to be far less agreeable than the visionary migrant expected; the prospect of tenancy, when it appeared, was a possible deterrent; and the competition of forests, mines, and farms farther west many times presented almost immediate problems. Furthermore, such periods of acute agricultural distress as occurred in the Midwest during the seventies and nineties as a result of overexpansion, drought, land monopoly, and other causes not only made the prospective migrant hesitant, but bred discouragement leading to a countermigration back East or to a movement even farther west. Finally, it must not be forgotten that Midwesterners were themselves the children of people who had once moved; the tradition of moving westward was strong among them. They were also the first to receive reports of new regions and new resources, and being less firmly established than people in the East or in Europe had fewer connections to sever. And, of course, they were geographically nearer to the areas to which they wished to move; consequently, the labor and expense of migration was proportionately less. Whatever the reasons—and they are as yet by no means fully explained—the westward expansion in America has consistently drawn its greatest numbers from the nearest sources. The exceptions to this general rule, however, are important. This same westward expansion has throughout its history been strongly reinforced and leavened by contingents from areas in the East and from Europe.

Prior to the Civil War the small farms and pastures of New England, upstate New York, southern New Jersey, western Pennsylvania, and Ohio produced grain, sheep, and cattle as well as dairy products and vegetables. Small mills and shops, foundries, distilleries, tanneries, and the like nestled by countless waterfalls and produced a wide variety though small quantity of manufactured articles. Each township center boasted, on a miniature scale, a well-rounded commercial and professional existence. Yet could such an economy withstand the post-war developments? Could the Vermont farmer, hoeing by hand the corn on his tipped, rock-studded fields, compete with his Illinois or Iowa counterpart whose teams could pull labor-saving cultivators across broad level acres? Could the tiny specialty mills and foundries of Maine, western Connecticut, northern New York, or central Pennsylvania compete with even the forerunners of mass production in the large urban centers? Could the banker, the lawyer, the doctor, the maker of furniture and of carriages, even the preacher find as promising an outlet for his talents or as pressing a need for his services at home as in the lustily growing counties of the West? The answer, particularly plain to the young farm hand, mill apprentice, or law clerk, was "no"; in increasing numbers he yielded to the pull of the city or to the lure of the West. In a sense he was impelled—pushed—into moving.

For certain classes the economic outlook in the Old South was even less promising than in the Northeast, Middle Atlantic, or East North Central states. The collapse of the plantation system based on slave labor removed the traditional stabilizing element of Southern economic life. Capital was scarce and the small-scale white farmer was ill equipped by training and too few in numbers to create and maintain an independent agricultural society. Too often the alternative was to become a tenant farmer or to move, either to such near-by industrial centers as Birmingham or Atlanta, or farther west.

By and large, then, the choice offered the Eastern farmer or small townsman was to move to the city or to go west. Often he chose the latter course. In fact, though he made many stops on the way—sometimes for years or for a generation—it was he who formed the backbone of the Eastern contingent in the West, Within this movement from the East, from the close of the Civil War onward, the Northerner was in the great majority even though his lot to begin with was probably better than was the Southerner's. The reason probably lay in higher per capita savings enabling the Northerner to move and start anew, his experience as farmer, "mechanic," or small businessman that was readily adaptable to conditions in the West, his innate energy and restlessness and, particularly before 1885, his far superior means of transportation. Nevertheless, after that date, movement from the Old South to the Southwest was of considerable proportions.

The basic urban and industrial development of the East that partly induced so many of the stresses in other regions and occupations itself generated, from its own excesses, a centrifugal force. This force, however, was not directional; it did not necessarily propel the persons on whom it operated into the West or any other particular region or occupation. It was merely an explosive agency tending to blast people loose from where they were.

Obviously, the chief cause of movement from industrial centers was economic depression, yet there are almost no data to indicate that the unemployment that was a logical prelude to emigration was discoverably mitigated by movement to the so-called free lands of the West. Despite the urgings of Horace Greeley and in the face of the plausible if unsupported "Safety-Valve Doctrine," [4] contemporary evidence from the

[4] For a discussion of this doctrine, see Carter Goodrich and Sol Davidson, "The Wage Earner in the Westward Movement," *Political Science Quarterly,* Vol. L, No. 2 (June, 1935), p. 161; and Vol. LI, No. 1 (March, 1936), p. 61; also Shannon, "The Homestead Act and the Labor Surplus."

West, fragmentary though it is, casts heavy doubt on the theory that the common laborer or skilled worker solved his difficulties by moving westward, unless he settled in other industrial centers. The principal reason for this immobility of the laboring population—and it applied with equal force to the factory émigrés from abroad—was that subduing the forests, breaking the prairie, and herding cattle were not occupations easily learned. Nor could such activities be undertaken with any assurance of success without enough financial backlog to provide food and other necessities until the first returns came in. Finally, it cost money to move west and, in most cases, to acquire land or a base of operations.[5] Lacking both experience and ready cash it is not astonishing that the factory worker, despite his hardships, stayed with his trade however much he shifted his scene of operations. Of course, the growing industrial importance of the Pacific Slope after 1910 offered a fresh start to the discontented Eastern or foreign laborer who could move. To the extent that he availed himself of this opportunity he fed the stream of westward expansion.

In contrast with America, there were, even after 1860, stronger elements of push on the European than on the native of the Eastern United States. To the New World's pulling demand for labor, the promise of free lands, and the increasing availability of low-cost ocean transportation was added the inability of many of the migrants to find employment at home in agriculture or industry that would enable them to live properly. This situation in Europe was, in the latter part of the nineteenth century, due to many causes; among the more potent were technological changes, the existence of large estates and the tenancy system, and the reduction of the death rate. Such elements of push were offset to some extent by sentimental ties to the old home and by legislative restrictions or social hostility against emigration. As letters from America reached relatives abroad, however, the break became easier and, notably in the case of Germany under Bismarck, governmental obstacles to migration were, for the time being, at least, removed. Thus the elements of push figured prominently in the causes of the enormous migration from Europe following the mid-sixties.

As in the case of native Americans, the West laid claim principally to farmers, although immigrants from Europe rarely moved to the outer frontier; exceptions to this rule were Welsh miners and livestock specialists from Scotland and England. As emigrant guides and some of the more conscientious colonizing companies stressed, pioneering was a highly specialized occupation and one that was manned principally by Americans seasoned by years or even generations of frontier experience. The Scandinavian, Swiss, or Russo-German Mennonite, for example,

[5] Burlington and Missouri River Railroad, News Sheet, March, 1873. (Quoted in Overton, *Burlington West*, p. 349.)

turned his attention toward a more intensive secondary frontier. Occasionally, a factory worker would test his fortune in the West, but the class most desired were farmers.[6]

Transportation and Its Relation to the Westward Movement

Transportation affected westward expansion in two principal ways: it afforded a means of reaching the West in the first place, fulfilling an indispensable function in the process of migration, and it provided a channel of trade and communication for those already in the West, adding another element of pull toward that region. Since these two advantages were arrived at simultaneously, though in different degrees, their achievement may be traced together.

Domestic Transportation

In 1860 the railway network of the United States reached into virtually every county where population had attained a minimum density of 18 to the square mile (see page 338). A decade later the railroads north of the 37th parallel (which divides Kansas and Oklahoma) had caught up with the frontier line of two persons per square mile; the first transcontinental had struck boldly across sparsely settled plains and mountains to reach San Francisco while a second independent line was approaching Denver. In the South, because of the war, progress had been less rapid; Texas was still isolated from the national network. During the seventies the railways actually outstripped the solid farming frontier and carried even the trapper, miner, and lumberman far along their paths. During the following decade, the South, and Texas in particular, joined the North in the nation's greatest era of rail construction. A vast steel gridiron with lines approximately 14 miles apart was laid down in the area extending westward roughly to the 20-inch rainfall line at about the 100th meridian. Meanwhile, an adequate system was built in Colorado, in the Pacific Northwest, and along the coast; by 1911 no less than seven transcontinental routes, each with numerous feeders, connected the Midwest with the Far West.[7]

The census reveals beyond any doubt that the participants in the traditional westward expansion of the farming frontier were principally natives of the New England, Middle Atlantic, and East North Central states, or foreigners who entered through northeastern ports. Did these people, after 1865, dominate western expansion because railroads made the West particularly accessible to them, or were the railroads built, among other reasons, to carry a stream of migration already in existence?

---

[6] See statement of Henry Wilson, Agent General of B. & M. R. R. R. in England to district agents, January 1, 1872, as quoted in Overton, *Burlington West,* p. 365.

[7] See Chapter 19 below.

Both alternatives were partly true. A comparison of the railway network and population density over a period of years suggests that until about 1865 the rails generally followed population. Thereafter, however, particularly in the case of the Western land-grant roads, they preceded the area of continuous settlement and actively participated in expansion and colonization. Thus, quite aside from the many economic, social, political, and religious factors pushing and pulling Americans and foreigners alike to the West, it is reasonable to assume that the existence and development of an East-West railway network that was predominantly in the North played a substantial part after 1865 in determining the origin of settlers of the American West.

The rise of the American railroads after 1865 brought about a sharp decline in river and canal traffic. After the Civil War passengers turned almost in a body to the rails. Although the shift in freight traffic was slightly less abrupt, it was eventually as definite and, from a revenue basis, more decisive. There was, however, one important exception to this shift away from inland water carriers. Beginning in the 1880's the Great Lakes began to witness the growth of their technically superb fleet; although the effect on westward-bound passenger travel was temporary, a new outlet to the East was provided for the ore and, to a lesser extent, for the grain and lumber of the Northwest. At the same time, the West was provided with a cheap method of obtaining Eastern fuel. All these improvements in transportation inevitably made the West more attractive.

The traditional westward agricultural expansion, which preserved its identity as a cohesive, unified movement until about 1910, was accomplished primarily by the railroads. Partly because of the location of these roads, migration was principally from Northern states. The frontier, in the sense of a single transitional border region, was punctured and then virtually obliterated by the iron horse; in its place were left countless patches of land, either wholly unsettled or sparsely populated, that had been by-passed by the rails. These areas were reached by the automobile and truck as they shouldered the task of the intensive settlement of the West.

Foreign and Ocean Transportation

Just as the location and accessibility of transportation in the United States helped determine the reservoirs of emigration, so the status and development of European and transatlantic transport facilities affected the complexion of the overseas contingent bound for the American West. By 1860 the British, Germans, Norwegians, and Swedes could reach their seaports easily by rail, river, or canal; passage thence to the New World by the recently-developed iron steamship was relatively speedy and cheap. This set of circumstances undoubtedly contributed to the preponderance of northwestern Europeans reaching our shores. By the same token, the progressive expansion of the rail networks in Austria-Hungary, Italy, and Russia after 1890 (thus making it easier for natives of those countries to reach points of embarkation) certainly accelerated the shift in the sources of emigration to southeastern Europe.

The Limitations on Westward Expansion and the Agencies for Overcoming Them

So far attention has been directed to the broad questions of why westward expansion took place and who, in general terms, participated in that movement. The elementary answers to these questions lay in the attraction of land and its possibilities, economic difficulties in the reservoirs of emigration, and a feasible means of mass travel by land and by sea. These basic elements moved into the American West a vast army composed principally of Americans dependent upon the primary possibilities of the land. Consideration must now be given first to some of the limitations that have restricted and qualified this expansion, and second to the means by which man has endeavored to offset these limiting factors.

The Limit of Inaccessibility and Governmental Aid to Transportation

To the intending migrant of 1862, who still had before him a wondrous choice of places to go, the most immediate drawback was probably the lack of transportation. Technically, even at that date, there was no reason why railroads—the obvious solution to the problem—could not be built. The War Department's surveys of 1855 indicated at least five mechanically feasible transcontinental routes. Yet what railroad builder who had traditionally laid his rails to tap existing sources of traffic could be expected to throw his lines into country with less than two persons to the square mile? And even assuming he would enjoy steady patronage from the outset of operations, how could he expect to meet current expenses, let alone to recover his original investment, until the farming and trading communities along his line became settled and productive? The answer was that he could not unless he were helped.

As it happened, a means and precedent for the necessary aid was at hand in the Federal land grants to railways. The first grant had been made in 1850 to aid construction of the Illinois Central. By 1871, when the practice was discontinued, Congress had granted a total of about 158,000,000 acres to aid railroads in every state west of the Mississippi River except Texas, where the United States owned no lands, and except in Oklahoma and South Dakota, then wholly or largely occupied by Indian reservations. East of the Mississippi, grants had been made to speed development of the then unsettled portions of Illinois, Michigan, and Wisconsin in the North, and of Florida, Alabama, and Mississippi in the South. All these lines had to agree to carry mail, troops, and all

Government property at rates fixed by Congress, usually at a level of from 20 to 50 per cent below prevailing commercial railroad rates. Furthermore, unaided competing lines in the same territory had to offer these lower land-grant rates if they wished to participate in moving traffic subject to such rates. Thus the land grants have proved to be a shrewd bargain for the Government.[8] Eventually, a sixth of the total granted acreage was returned to the United States because certain railroads failed to build their lines according to the terms of the grants. Approximately 130,000,000 acres, however, were patented by the railroads and aided in the construction of some 21,500 miles of line in the new South and West. Roads built with the help of grants from states swelled this total. Since the land-grant states now contain 133,243 miles of road, it is obvious that most of the mileage was eventually built principally by private capital. Nevertheless, when most of the Federally-aided lines were completed, they represented the more important part of the western mileage then existing, and provided a skeleton network reaching into much of the region that lay beyond the frontier line of 1862.

The mere completion of these roads would have given a lively stimulus to westward expansion. As it was, the highly organized and far-reaching colonization activities undertaken by many of the railway land departments speeded the entire process. To such companies, whose lines pushed into sparsely settled territory, the most important objective was the permanent development of the region as a source of traffic; a second logical objective was the sale of their granted lands. Thus, during the half century following 1854, such roads as the Illinois Central, Burlington, Union Pacific, Rock Island, Northern Pacific, Santa Fe, and Southern Pacific—to mention only the more active—launched extensive advertising campaigns in both this country and Europe in an effort to attract permanent settlers. These colonization activities reached their peak in the seventies and eighties. Lands varied in price depending on topography, water supply, timber, and accessibility; average prices were about $4 or $5 an acre, although marginal lands sold as low as fifty cents an acre and better farm tracts sold for as much as $35 an acre. Townsite property sometimes brought even higher returns. Almost all the large companies offered long credit, and some added such special inducements as reduced rates for immigrants and their goods, discounts from long-term prices as the reward for improvements, and the like.

---

[8] Land-grant rates on Government property over lines subject to land-grant deductions were 50 per cent of the commercial rail rates; mail rates were 80 per cent of regular commercial rail rates. Under the Transportation Act of 1940, application of land-grant rates was restricted to troops and government property, although the total volume of traffic moving under such rates increased enormously with the outbreak of World War II. Through Equalization Agreements induced by competition, the Government obtained the benefits of these reductions also from non-land-grant roads serving land-grant territory until Congress abolished all land-grant rate preferences in 1946.

Because granting of public lands to the railroads withdrew millions of acres from private entry, because it favored corporate interests allegedly at the expense of the community at large, because fraud and mismanagement characterized the disposal of certain individual grants, and because the most publicized references to land grants in general have been made by critics of big business, the entire policy has often been the object of sweeping condemnation. Yet the only full-length studies so far made of individual grants reveal that indiscriminate condemnation of the policy is not warranted;[9] final judgment must be reserved until further studies are made. In any event, whatever the defects of the land-grant policy, it did result in the construction of lines essential at the time to westward expansion and national unity, and it prompted organized colonization that, when conscientiously carried out, immeasurably speeded western settlement. Whether, in some cases, it led to what twentieth-century hindsight regards as overdevelopment of marginal areas is a moot point; so far research has not revealed any particular correlation between areas of rail colonization and of economic distress. When the grants were settled, no development seemed too rapid or too intense for the buoyant Westerner. Probably at least a million persons bought land from railroads; if half of them were heads of average families, some three million migrants must have been directly affected by the policy.

In addition to lands received from the United States, railways in Western and Southern states received considerable land, as well as varying financial support usually in the form of security subscriptions, from town, county, or state sources. Competition to obtain railways was strong between communities whose access to market was essential, and these aids, usually exchanged for a definite promise to build on a specified route, were in effect bids for adequate transportation. In so far as these aids were actually extended, they speeded construction, but their frequent failure to materialize made their net effect problematical.

Railroads were by no means the only carriers to receive Government aid in the West. Highways and waterways had been assisted almost from the beginning of the Republic, and after 1862 such assistance continued and grew. Until about 1910, however, only the railroads could conveniently carry people in large numbers and goods in bulk; by that time the expansion of the agricultural West was nearly complete. Since 1910 Federal and state aid to highways in the states west of the Mississippi has continued. And, particularly since 1926, the United States has spent many millions to aid airway development in the same area. These newer forms

---

[9] Paul W. Gates, *The Illinois Central Railroad and Its Colonization Work*. Cambridge, Mass.: Harvard University Press, 1934; James B. Hedges, *Building the Canadian West; the Land and Colonization Work of the Canadian Pacific Railway*. New York: The Macmillan Company, 1939; Overton, *Burlington West*. Other studies are under way.

of transportation, both by carrying people west and offering them service when there, have undoubtedly contributed to the westward movement; Federal subsidy has helped them perform this function. Yet Governmental aid to highways, waterways, and air lines has been nationwide and has not generally involved public lands. Thus, although it has facilitated the intensive development of the West, it has done so incidentally. In contrast, the railway land-grant policy was formulated for the specific purpose of settling the West and the New South. That is why it is of prime importance in any consideration of westward expansion.

The Indians and Government Policy

Until 1860, American Indians were constantly pushed westward on the easy assumption that there would always be enough room for them in the vast open spaces beyond the Mississippi. During the early years of the sixties it was apparent that this assumption was no longer valid. The wave of western expansion encouraged by more liberal land laws and the growing rail network was already reaching and in some cases overwhelming the red man. The mining rushes, for example, frightened away the Indian's game; railroad surveys and the opening of new army roads cut through some of his best hunting grounds. In 1862 the Sioux, and later the Arapahoes and Cheyennes, took the warpath to protect themselves against further encroachment.

Such outbreaks as these confirmed the Westerner's feeling against the Indians as both a physical menace and an economic obstacle, for in addition to their occasional—and often comprehensible—resort to war, they laid claim to some of the most desirable land in the West. Partly to solve these problems and partly to protect the Indians, Congress in 1867 adopted the reservation system for all western tribes, and proceeded to concentrate the Indians on lands set aside from the public domain in almost every western territory and state. This task, accomplished none too gently, was supposed to be jointly handled by the departments of Interior and War, the latter taking control of "warlike tribes." Actually the conflicts over jurisdiction between the two departments aggravated the entire situation until in 1879 Congress gave the Department of the Interior full authority.

The reservation system, combined with the extinction of the buffalo, eventually ended the military phase of Indian history. It did not, however, solve the land problem to the Westerner's satisfaction nor did it offer either social or economic stability to the Indian. In 1870 all but the Panhandle of Oklahoma, all of the western part of South Dakota, nearly a fifth each of Montana and Colorado, one-eighth of Arizona, and extensive areas in Minnesota, Wyoming, Idaho, Washington, Oregon, and New Mexico were barred to the white man except for restricted transit and trading privileges. Apart from the sizable reduction of Indian reservations in Colorado and Montana, the situation was virtually the same in 1880.

The Dawes Act, approved in 1887, opened a new chapter in Indian policy. The President of the United States was given authority to subdivide tribal reservations among individual Indians; each head of a family was to receive 160 acres, and other members a smaller proportion; surplus land was to be purchased by the Government, the proceeds to form a trust fund for the tribes; no Indian could alienate or mortgage his land for 25 years, but upon receiving title, he became a citizen. The Five Civilized Tribes, originally exempted from the act, elected to follow its provisions in 1906.

This act which, in general, has worked to the benefit of the white settlers and the detriment of the Indians paved the way for the occupation by Westerners of hundreds of thousands of acres hitherto unavailable. The most spectacular advance was into Oklahoma, which had long been the objective of neighboring whites. When, at noon on April 22, 1889, a cannon signalized the opening of part of Indian Territory to settlement, some 50,000 persons rushed across the border. By night the town of Guthrie was founded; by 1890, the Territory had over 100,000 white citizens. The occupation of other former Indian lands was not so precipitate; but as the policies of the Dawes Act were carried out, reservations shrank rapidly. These reservations continued, however, to be sources of continuous irritation to both the white man and the Indian. As the pressure of population increased, during the second decade of the twentieth century, repeated attempts to infringe upon the remaining Indian lands resulted in scores of legal battles in both state and Federal courts, and in attempts to secure passage of new legislation to restrict and further confine the red man. Changes in Indian administration have gradually brought a reversal of the trend toward extinction in many parts of the West, and once again the various tribes have increased in both birth rate and population.

The Problem of Land Ownership and Public Policy

As 1862 opened, almost all the land except Indian territory beyond the frontier line was available for settlement; on the other hand, virtually none of it could be obtained free by the intending settler; he, like anyone else, was obliged to pay varying prices according to the particular law applicable to each tract. Land, the common treasure of the nation, was not yet the free heritage of the landless. Although its acquisition had become progressively easier in certain respects, public land remained what it had been since the nation was founded: an asset that was generally sold, and never given away except in exchange for some special service, past or prospective.

Western land could be acquired by purchase in a variety of ways:

for cash from the United States; from states that had received land for internal improvement, swamp reclamation, education, or other purposes; from holders of scrip and military warrants; from railways; and, of course, from individuals. The homestead principle of free land in exchange for permanent settlement, however, was not strange to America; it had existed in the colonial policies of France and Spain and in the English headright system. Agitation for its revival had occurred time and again in the early days of the Republic, and the principle emerged as a major political and social issue in the mid-forties. Indeed, between 1842 and 1854 the United States offered from 160 to 640 acres free to settlers who would occupy, improve, and, if need be, defend remote portions of Florida, Oregon, Washington, and New Mexico. Yet during the fifties, as sectional lines hardened, it became apparent that the South, fearing a virtual Northern occupation of the West, would defeat, either in Congress or through the Presidency, a general homestead measure. Thus, it was not until May 20, 1862, that Lincoln signed the Homestead Act, passed by a Congress unencumbered by Southern opposition.[10]

By its provisions, this act offered to any citizen or intending citizen who, among other things, was head of a family and over 21 years of age, 160 acres of surveyed public domain after 5 years of continuous residence and payment of a registration fee varying from $26 to $34. The law applied to all lands subject to purchase at $1.25 under the Preemption Act, and to 80-acre lots within the lateral limits of railway grants. As an alternative, the homesteader could buy the land he had entered after 6 months' residence, at the regular price.[11]

Once the homestead principle was adopted, Congress logically, though sometimes with questionable wisdom, sought to apply it to special situations. In 1866, for example, mineral lands were thrown open freely for occupation, although within a decade many of these tracts were classified and restricted to cash disposal at prices varying from $1.25 to $20 an acre. In 1873 the Timber Culture Act promised 160 acres to anyone eligible for a homestead who for 10 years would keep trees growing not more than 12 feet apart on 40 acres. Five years later the minimum tree-growing area was reduced to 10 acres. In 1909, after twenty-five years of pressure by Western live stock interests, Congress increased the maximum permissible homestead entries to 320 acres in portions of Colorado, Mon-

[10] In 1860 a bill containing most of the features of a free homestead act was passed by both branches of Congress only to be vetoed by Buchanan.

[11] During the next decade various amendments were added to hasten disposal. In 1864, for example, soldiers with 2 years' service were permitted to take title after 1 year's occupancy; in 1870 soldiers with 90 days' service could "enter" 160 acres within railway grants; 2 years later soldiers were allowed 6 months after "entry" before beginning residence, and their term of service in the Army, up to 4 years, was deducted from their residence requirements. Thus the Homestead Act was employed as a substitute for a perilous universal land bounty and at the same time soldiers were encouraged to move westward.

tana, Nevada, Oregon, Utah, Washington, Wyoming, and Arizona. A quarter of the area was to be cultivated and no commutation for cash was allowed. In 1916 a further encouragement was given cattle and sheep raisers by the enlargement to 640 acres of the tracts that they could acquire.

Meanwhile, Congress continued to dispose of public domain that could be acquired by the individual, if at all, only by purchase. In the same year the Homestead Law was enacted, Lincoln signed the Morrill Act, which granted to each loyal state for endowment of at least one agricultural college 30,000 acres of land for each senator and representative then in Congress. These lands were to be sold by the beneficiary states. Railway grants were continued until 1871, the largest being that of nearly 39,000,000 acres to the Northern Pacific. Three other measures, designed to accelerate disposal of nonagricultural land, should be noted. One, the Desert Land Act of 1877, permitted purchase at $1.25 an acre of 640 acres of arid land provided the buyer irrigated and cultivated at least one-eighth of the area; the maximum amount that could be bought was halved in 1890. The other two measures, both passed on June 3, 1878, were the Timber Cutting Act and the Timber and Stone Act, which together allowed for the first time the legal cutting and purchase of timber from the public domain. The West vigorously supported these laws. Under the first, bona fide settlers and mining interests were permitted to cut timber free for their legitimate use. Under the second, surveyed lands in California, Oregon, Nevada, and Washington, chiefly valuable for timber and stone but presumably unfit for cultivation, could be purchased in 160-acre lots at $2.50 an acre.

Unquestionably the guiding principle of national land policy, at least until the last decade of the nineteenth century, was to promote the settlement of the nation by the disposal of the public lands to those private individuals or corporations who could and would use them. From the first years of the Republic, another principle, at times dormant and often reversed, had influenced land legislation. This was conservation of the nation's assets on, under, and above the public lands. The rush for lands between 1850 and 1890, however, made it physically impossible if not politically inexpedient for the Government to classify its vast holdings or to enforce what restrictions there were, such as those against removing timber and minerals. Even the West, which eventually stood to lose by the indiscriminate disposal of land, was lukewarm if not coldly opposed to measures that would conserve resources and favor the small settler at the expense of speedy occupation. Inevitably, then, a law such as the Homestead Act, which had originally been designed to aid the actual settler, was abused by agents of large holders or companies serving as dummy entrymen until title could be secured, while the acts that might have led to some conservation were openly flaunted. Titles under the Swamp, Timber Culture, and Desert Land acts all too often passed, frequently through speculators or hired agents, to wealthy individuals or companies whose prime interest was the exploitation rather than conservation of resources. The resulting concentration of ownership tended to make land purchase in the West more difficult for the small, independent buyer.

The general result was to speed land disposal not wisely but too well; by the time Cleveland came to the Presidency this fact, highlighted by the rapid disappearance of the best farming and timber lands, the rise of tenancy, and the emergence of land monopolies, began to be realized. Eventually, on March 3, 1891, an act was approved repealing the Preemption and Timber Culture acts, reducing the maximum entries under the Desert Land Act, extending from 6 to 14 months the period that must elapse before homesteads could be commuted, and authorizing the President to set aside timber areas as national parks. Three years later the Carey Act authorized granting about a million acres to certain states provided they undertook settlement and irrigation, and in 1902, under the Reclamation Act, the Federal Government itself began to subsidize irrigation projects on public domain. Beginning spectacularly under Theodore Roosevelt, steady progress has been made during the twentieth century toward reclamation, conservation, and scientific use of land. At present no less than 176,000,000 acres are reserved in national forests (not only to protect their timber resources, but, even more important, to guard vital watersheds); mineral, water power, and oil reserves (mostly in the form of subsoil rights) affect another 47,948,454 acres; and about 20,000,000 acres are under irrigation. National land policy now emphasizes planned development rather than indiscriminate disposal and settlement. The activities of the Federal Government in resettling submarginal agriculturists must be considered a part of the program of conservation and land classification.

In most general terms, then, during the period from 1862 to 1891, rapid disposal was the prime object of Federal land legislation. Thereafter increasing attention was paid to adapting the laws to special physiographic conditions, to discouraging land monopoly, to conserving our natural resources, and, finally, to promoting intelligent land classification and use.

There is, of course, no doubt whatever that the land itself was the greatest single pulling factor in our westward expansion. In 1862 over a billion acres remained unreserved and unappropriated out of the original 1,441,436,160 acres in the 29 public land states. By 1904 a mere 473,836,402 acres remained unclaimed; today there is none, although powerful and frequently vociferous pressure groups demand new legislation that would force the Federal Government to dispose of public lands suitable for grazing, timbering, or mineral exploitation to private purchasers. But which policies, which particular laws in our past history have encouraged and made practicable the occupation of the Great West?

Traditionally, the Homestead Act has been eulogized as the concentrated wisdom of legislation for the settlement of the public lands and as the greatest democratic measure of all history.[12] Certainly it did climax the long struggle for free lands, and undoubtedly the promise it offered provided a psychological stimulus to the prospective migrant. Its immediate effect on the urban worker, however, was negligible; the mere fact that Congress provided no means for the laborer to reach the free lands would probably have been fatal apart from the occupational diffi-

TABLE 1

THE PUBLIC DOMAIN, 1789-1904

Disposition		Acres	
A. Acquired by or available to individuals by purchase only:			
1. Cash sales:			
Before June 30, 1880	196,755,216		
Since June 30, 1880	79,803,004		
Former Indian lands	1,116,038	277,674,258	
2. State grants:			
School lands	69,058,443		
Swamp lands	65,739,266		
Internal improvements	20,587,863	155,385,572	
3. Railroad, state and corporation grants patented, certified, or withdrawn		117,550,292	
4. Private claims		33,440,482	
5. Private wagon roads, canals, river improvements		9,712,425	
6. Agricultural colleges (Morrill Act)		7,672,800	
7. Timber and Stone Act		7,695,078	
8. Mineral lands		1,731,276	
Total lands acquired or available by purchase only			610,763,183
B. Acquired by or available to individuals free (except for fees):			
1. Homesteads:			
Patented	96,495,030		
Pending	39,525,840	136,020,870	
2. Timber Culture Act		9,745,434	
3. Scrip to Veterans, individuals, Indians, etc.		1,585,066	
Total lands acquired free			147,351,370
C. Reserves unavailable to individuals:			209,485,205
D. Unappropriated			473,836,402
Total public domain, United States			1,441,436,160

12 For summaries of eulogistic references to the Homestead Act see Roy M. Robbins, *Our Landed Heritage,* p. 209. Princeton: Princeton University Press, 1942; and P. W. Gates, "The Homestead Act in an Incongruous Land System," *American Historical Review,* Vol. XLI, No. 4 (July, 1936), pp. 652-681. See esp. pp. 652-654.

culties already noted. But what effect did the law have on those who turned West?

Over twice as many lands were acquired by purchase as were obtained free. After June 1862, the willing buyer was generally able to crowd out the seeker of free lands, since no specific acreage in the West was reserved for the homesteader. What free lands there were near towns or railroads were generally snapped up in the first rush; in fact, they were claimed the moment a town site or railway route was staked out, often by squatters and land agents. Consequently, the settler who followed the initial influx was usually faced with the choice of buying from a speculator, a railroad, or a state on the one hand, or of going further afield where opportunities for social and economic intercourse were limited.[13] However anxious these

TABLE 2

Public Domain Available for Purchase, 1789-1904

	Acres	
	Before June 30, 1862	After June 30, 1862
Cash sales	178,649,737 actual	97,908,483 actual
Former Indian lands	616,038 estimate	500,000 estimate
School lands	14,058,443 "	55,000,000 "
Swamp lands	15,739,266 "	50,000,000 "
Internal improvements	4,587,863 "	16,000,000 "
Railroad grants	15,962,813 actual	101,587,479 actual
Private claims	25,440,482 estimate	8,000,000 estimate
Private wagon roads, canals, river improvements	5,426,885 actual	4,285,540 actual
Agricultural colleges	....	7,672,800 "
Timber and Stone Act	....	7,596,078 "
Mineral lands	....	1,731,276 "
Total	260,481,527	350,281,656
		260,481,527
Grand total		610,763,183

selling agencies may have been (and many were not) to attract actual settlers to the land by advertising, easy credit schemes, and aid to the settlers, and however justified their acquisition of the public domain had been in the first place, the fact remains that, at least between 1862 and 1904 when the traditional frontier line was disappearing, they barred most of the land, especially the best portions of it, from free settlement under the Homestead Act. As one authority has suggested, the famous Homestead Act merely "imposed an unharmonious principle on an old system." [14] And, at least until the turn of the century, the two systems clashed.

[13] "The Homestead Act in an Incongruous Land System," *American Historical Review,* Vol. XLI, No. 4 (July, 1936), p. 652.

[14] Gates, "The Homestead Act in an Incongruous Land System," *op. cit.,* p. 654.

Even so, the effect of the Homestead law during the first generation of its operation must not be underestimated. As early as 1874, homestead patents began to exceed cash sales, and in 1904 they exceeded disposals under all other acts combined. Paradoxically enough, in the light of the widely accepted notion to the contrary, more acres were patented under the Homestead Act after 1904 than before that date, although most of the lands thus patented were distinctly inferior to those taken up in the earlier period. The Homestead Act, particularly while the frontier line still existed, usually has been regarded as a prime cause of westward expansion, yet in view of the facts its efficacy must be fully qualified.

Selected References

Billington, Ray A., *Westward Expansion.* New York: The Macmillan Company, 1949.

Brayer, Herbert O., Vol. I, *William Blackmore: The Spanish-Mexican Land Grants of New Mexico and Colorado 1863-1878*; Vol. II, *William Blackmore: Early Financing of the Denver and Rio Grande Railway and Ancillary Land Companies 1871-1878.* Denver: Bradford-Robinson, 1949.

Buck, Solon J., *The Agrarian Crusade.* New Haven: Yale University Press, 1920.

Donaldson, Thomas C., *The Public Domain.* Washington: U. S. Government Printing Office, 1884.

Faulkner, Harold U., *American Political and Social History* (esp. Chapter XXV). New York: F. S. Crofts & Company, 1937.

Ferenczi, Imre, *International Migrations.* New York: National Bureau of Economic Research, 1929-31.

Gates, Paul W., "The Homestead Act in an Incongruous Land System," *American Historical Review,* Vol. XLI, No. 4 (July, 1936), pp. 652-681.

——, *The Illinois Central Railroad and Its Colonization Work.* Cambridge: Harvard University Press, 1934.

Goodrich, Carter; Bushrod W. Allin; C. Warren Thornwaite, et al., *Migration and Economic Opportunity.* Philadelphia: University of Pennsylvania Press, 1936.

Hansen, Marcus Lee, *The Immigrant in American History.* Cambridge: Harvard University Press, 1940.

Hedges, James B., "The Colonization Work of the Northern Pacific Railroad," *Mississippi Valley Historical Review,* Vol. XIII, No. 3 (December, 1926), pp. 311-342.

Hibbard, Benjamin H., *A History of the Public Land Policies.* New York: The Macmillan Company, 1924.

Lokken, Roscoe L., *Iowa Public Land Disposal.* Iowa City: The State Historical Society of Iowa, 1942.

Merk, Frederick, *Economic History of Wisconsin during the Civil War Decade.* Madison: State Historical Society of Wisconsin, 1916.

Olson, James C., *Sterling Morton.* Lincoln: University of Nebraska Press, 1942.

Overton, Richard C., *Burlington West: A Colonization History of the Burlington Railroad.* Cambridge: Harvard University Press, 1941.

Paxson, Frederick L., *History of the American Frontier, 1763-1893.* Boston: Houghton Mifflin Company, 1924.

Priest, Loring B., *Uncle Sam's Stepchildren: The Reformation of United States Indian Policy, 1865-1887.* New Brunswick: Rutgers University Press, 1942.

Quiett, Glenn Chesney, *They Built the West*. New York: D. Appleton-Century Company, 1934.

Robbins, R. M., *Our Landed Heritage—The Public Domain, 1776-1936*. Princeton: Princeton University Press, 1942.

Sandoz, Marie, *Old Jules*. Boston: Little, Brown & Company, 1935.

Schmeckbier, Laurence Frederick, *The Office of Indian Affairs*. Baltimore: The Johns Hopkins Press, 1927.

Seymour, Flora W., *Indian Agents of the Old Frontier*. New York: D. Appleton-Century Company, 1941.

Shannon, Fred A., "The Homestead Act and the Labor Surplus," *American Historical Review*, Vol. XLI, No. 4 (July, 1936), pp. 637-651.

Turner, Frederick J., *The Frontier in American History*. New York: H. Holt & Company, 1920.

United States, 58th Congress, 3rd Session, Senate Document No. 189, *Report of the Public Lands Commission*. Washington: U. S. Government Printing Office, 1905.

United States, National Resources Planning Board, *Land Classification in the United States*. Washington: U. S. Government Printing Office, 1941.

19 · DEVELOPMENT OF A NATIONAL TRANSPORTATION SYSTEM

THE YEAR 1870 found the country with a well-formed network of railroads east of the Mississippi and north of Washington and the Ohio River. Through railroad routes extended from Boston to the West, *via* Canada, or *via* Albany and New York State. New York City was connected with Chicago by railroads operating over the present routes of the New York Central and the Pennsylvania. The Erie and the combination of the Central of New Jersey and the Baltimore & Ohio furnished additional service as far west as Ohio.

The railroads of the South were still far from complete. While local lines connecting the Atlantic ports to the hinterland were well developed and had served military needs during the war, the present-day through north-and-south routes of the Southern, the Atlantic Coast Line, and the Seaboard Airline east of the Appalachians were hardly in evidence. Coastwise water carriers still moved an amount of the north-south traffic. In the interior, the Louisville & Nashville had pushed as far south as Decatur, Alabama; while the Nashville, Chattanooga & St. Louis had a connection with Atlanta. The one through line from the large cities of the East came from Roanoke diagonally through the mountains to Knoxville and Chattanooga along the present route of the Norfolk & Western and the Southern railways. North and south in the Mississippi Valley there was only a partially completed route, for here again the water carriers were dominant, and the bridging of the lower Ohio offered engineering difficulties.

In the West a number of railroads had been built across Illinois and southern Wisconsin; a few had pushed west to the Missouri River, and one extended north through Wisconsin to Minneapolis. Although the Mississippi River had been first bridged, in 1856, at Rock Island, it was not until 1865 that a second bridge was built at Clinton, and not until just before 1870 that bridging was general. The Union Pacific alone had pushed beyond and crossed the continent to the Pacific. In the Southwest, one line reached from the Mississippi across into Arkansas, and another in Louisiana extended toward the eastern edge of Texas. As for the remainder of the West, there were a few short lines in operation, such as those radiating from Galveston and from Houston in Texas, and those in the San Francisco Bay area.

In total there were about 53,000 miles of railroad in the entire country, nearly four-fifths of which was east of the Mississippi River. The water-transportation system of the country still occupied a position of great importance. Coastwise lines in the East still handled the major part of the freight moving north and south. The ports of call were joined with the interior by rail. Inland water transportation had not decreased in magnitude, even though its proportion of the total was lessened. One-half of the western grain movement coming east on the northern route was moving over the Erie Canal; one-third of St. Louis' commerce was moving on the Mississippi River.

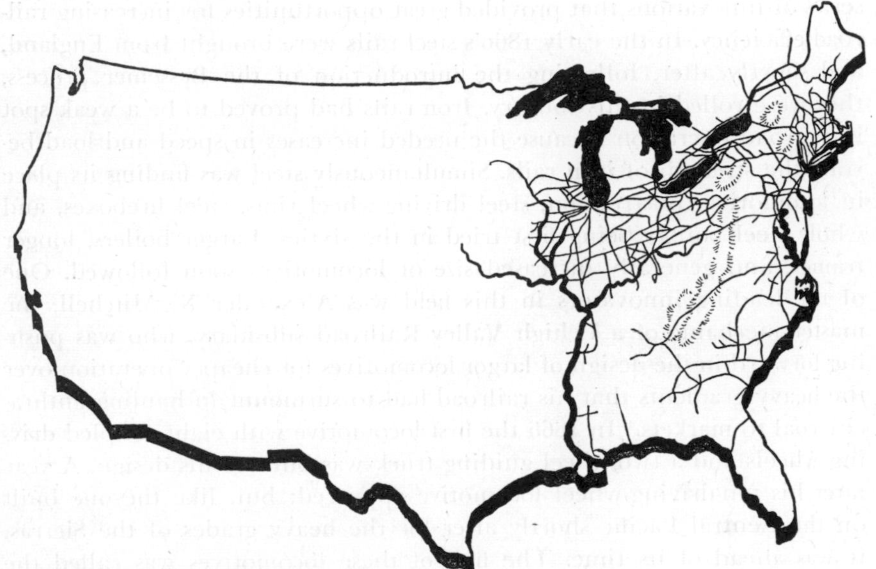

FIG. 1. *The Railroad System About 1860.*

The country's highways were in a stagnant state, having been left to the various local government agencies after the promotional phases of the turnpike and plank-road companies of the earlier period. Highway traffic was of a local character and its economic significance was overshadowed by the interest in railroad developments.

Railroads

For the next four decades after 1870, the development of railroad transportation was to be the country's most dramatic enterprise. Rapid technological progress was made in the physical tools with which the railroad companies operated. New sections of the country were to be opened up, and older ones provided with a more intensive coverage by extension of railroad lines. The financial phases of the economy, both private and governmental, were to be profoundly influenced by the methods and tactics of railroad promoters and manipulators. The whole economy was to feel the impact of changing levels of rates as well as changing relations between particular rates. The problems arising in the course of all this activity were to lead to a restriction of the railroad companies' private position, and the imposition of some degree of Government controls. At the end of the four decades, the period of extensive development was over and the field for the promoter was gone.

Technological Developments in the Railroads

The decade from 1860 to 1870 had witnessed the introduction of a series of innovations that provided great opportunities for increasing railroad efficiency. In the early 1860's steel rails were brought from England, and shortly after, following the introduction of the Bessemer process, they were rolled in this country. Iron rails had proved to be a weak spot in railroad operation because the needed increases in speed and load beyond the strength of iron rails. Simultaneously steel was finding its place in locomotive construction, steel driving-wheel rims, steel fireboxes, and whole steel boilers being first tried in the sixties. Larger boilers, longer frames, and generally increased size of locomotives soon followed. One of the leading innovators in this field was Alexander X. Mitchell, the master mechanic of a Lehigh Valley Railroad subsidary, who was pushing forward in the design of larger locomotives for cheaper operation over the heavy gradients that his railroad had to surmount in hauling anthracite coal to markets.[1] In 1866 the first locomotive with eight coupled driving wheels and a two-wheel guiding truck was built to his design. A year later his ten-driving-wheel locomotive appeared; but, like the one built on the Central Pacific shortly after for the heavy grades of the Sierras, it was ahead of its time. The first of these locomotives was called the "Consolidation," which became the type-name for a class of heavy freight engines, the use of which spread widely over the country during the next 40 years. The urge to develop such increased pulling power as these locomotives represented was a definite response on the part of aggressive personalities to the particular handicaps that they faced.

The basic technological development of the railroads continued in the direction of stronger, heavier rails and larger locomotives with higher boiler pressures and with increased wheel loads, all made possible by im-

[1] Alexander Mitchell was one of those little-heard-of figures, who, as an ingenious mechanic, responded constructively to the needs apparent in his environment. He had the good fortune to develop something almost immediately acceptable to his industry: the "Consolidation"-type locomotive. He also had the misfortune, often encountered by men of his type, to develop equipment far ahead of practical use. His ten-driver, "Decapod," fell in the latter class.

proved rails. This improvement was to lead to heavy freight train loads. In 1868 maximum steel rail weights were 65 to 67 pounds per yard; while three pairs of driving wheels with the loads per axle approaching 20,000 pounds represented the most advanced locomotive size. This axle load produced a pull of some 15,000 pounds available for hauling trains. By 1876 the Consolidation locomotive with its four pairs of drivers had become generally accepted as the heavy freight motive power, and axle loads had increased to 25,000 pounds, making possible a maximum pull of 25,000 pounds. In 1884 the first 80-pound rail was laid; the 95-pound rail was introduced in 1891 and the 100-pound came in 1892. By 1900 axle loads had increased to 40,000 pounds, and draw-bar pull to 40,000 pounds. Just after the turn of the century, lomocotives with five driving axles were adopted as standard on the Santa Fe, and they became generally used within the succeeding 15 years in heavy freight service on other roads. For heavy grades the Mallet type, introduced from Europe, with two sets of cylinders and drivers, followed closely on the heels of the Santa Fe type. Complementing this was the development of the automatic air brake and the friction draft gear, together with a strong and automatic coupler; all three were necessary to handle the fifty and then the hundred or more cars in a train, which it now came within the power of the locomotive to haul. The ineffectiveness and expense of stopping a long freight train with hand brakes made necessary a device that would automatically and powerfully apply the brakes from the locomotive. The impossibility of starting a long train as a unit made necessary a device that would allow slack between the cars so that they could be started serially, but at the same time would absorb the excessive shocks otherwise arising from the slack running in and out. George Westinghouse, more than anyone else, was responsible for developing the automatic air brake to meet the first need and the draft gear for the second.

Parallel with the foregoing development came the increased size of freight cars. The standard coal car of 1870 was a drop-bottom car weighing 16,000 pounds, about 22 feet long, with two four-wheel trucks, and with a capacity of 10 to 12 tons. The load per axle on this car was 10,000 pounds. As a result of improved rails and better car materials and construction, the capacity of cars was increased 50 per cent within the next 10 or 15 years. By 1895, 35-ton capacity hopper cars had been adopted, and 10 years later 50-ton capacity cars had been introduced. Thereafter followed the 70-ton car and, for special operations, a 100-ton capacity car, both having two four-wheel trucks; they had axle loads, respectively, of 45,000 and 65,000 pounds. This particular development is significant not only because of the sevenfold increase in carrying capacity of the standard coal cars, but also because the heavier cars and loads do not require an increase in pull (on level tracks) corresponding to the increase in loads.[2] Thus the heavier car enabled a locomotive of a given pull to carry decidedly more freight on the level stretches of the railroads.

Physical Growth of the Railroad System

In the East. The rate of development of the country's railroad system after the Civil War varied widely as between periods and regions. The reasons for construction also showed considerable divergence. East of the Mississippi and north of the Ohio most of the new mileage after the war grew from the competitive desire on the part of existing railroads to secure greater bargaining power in respect to traffic. For example, in the 1870's the Pennsylvania built its own lines from Baltimore to Washington to avoid using the Baltimore & Ohio, and the Boston & Maine built from Portsmouth, New Hampshire, to Portland, Maine, rather than use a competitor's line. In the same decade the Baltimore & Ohio projected its system west from Ohio to Chicago, in order to be on more nearly equal terms with the Pennsylvania and the Vanderbilt systems in competing for western traffic. The Baltimore & Ohio had earlier obtained access to St. Louis, but it did not want to miss the growing Chicago traffic. In the 1880's the Erie followed suit and built its line to Chicago. In a less extensive way, the Delaware, Lackawanna & Western and the Lehigh Valley attempted to provide traffic for themselves by reaching west from the anthracite regions of eastern Pennsylvania to the Buffalo gateway. The desire of business interests in Minnesota and Wisconsin to insure the best possible rates to the East led to the projection in the 1880's of two lines across northern Wisconsin to the Soo. With the Canadian Pacific east of the Soo, these lines formed strategically important routes, joining the West with Atlantic ports. The period between the panic of 1873 and the depression of 1884 represented the peak of building.

The 1873–1884 period also witnessed the greatest amount of purely promotional railroad construction in the East. The 1,000 odd miles of the West Shore Railroad from New York to Buffalo and the New York, Chicago and St. Louis ("The Nickel Plate") from Buffalo to Chicago were the biggest projects with this background. Finished in 1881, closely parallel to Vanderbilt's New York Central and Lake Shore and Michigan railroads, the promoters of the West Shore and "Nickel Plate" seem to have had in mind a possible sale to the latter for nuisance value.[3] The

[2] Because the elements of friction in ordinary bearings do not increase with an increased weight on the bearing, there is surprisingly little more pull required to move a heavily loaded car than to move an empty car on level track. A coal car loaded with 50 tons of coal takes 210 pounds of pull to move it at 10 m.p.h. compared to 140 pounds when it is empty.

[3] The New York, Chicago and St. Louis was reputed to have acquired the name "Nickel Plate" when Vanderbilt remarked on paying an exorbitantly high price for it, that the price would warrant his expecting to have it all nickel plated.

unfinished South Pennsylvania project of the same period, now the route of the Pennsylvania motor turnpike, represented something of the same sort of thing in the Pennsylvania Railroad territory. Numerous abortive attempts of this kind continued through the early 1900's.

The relative position of railroad construction east of the Mississippi and north of the Ohio after the Civil War was, however, essentially a declining one. Whereas the construction of new lines in the Middle Atlantic states had accounted for 15 per cent of the country's total from the war to 1873, the share fell rapidly, so that between the depressions of 1887 and 1892 it accounted for but 6 per cent. The proportion of building in the north central states from Ohio to Illinois and Wisconsin likewise hit its peak of 26 per cent before 1873 and fell by the turn of the century to but 15 per cent.

In the South. After the Civil War, there was still much basic coverage to be provided in the South, east of the Appalachians, and the tendency was for the construction to be carried out as it had been earlier: by local lines, which were later combined to form more sizable operating systems. West of the Appalachians, the larger properties appeared earlier. But the amount of construction undertaken in the years from the war to the panic of 1873 was small compared to the other parts of the country; from 1873 to the depression of 1884 it still lagged, but from 1884 to the depression of 1892 some 15 per cent of the country's new mileage was laid in the South, and during the following 10 years the same proportion was maintained.

It is astonishing how the well-developed coastwise water carriers and the barrier of the Appalachians delayed the opening of many of the final links in the long-haul railroad routes of the South. The first post-war rail crossing of the Appalachians south of the Baltimore & Ohio was that of the Chesapeake & Ohio in 1873. The second was a full nine years later, when the line west from Asheville, N. C., was completed. The third did not come until 10 more years had passed, when the Norfolk & Western reached over to the Ohio River Valley in 1892. In 1900 the Clinchfield finished its crossing from North Carolina to Tennessee, and the Virginian in 1907 built the last transmontane route. The delay in the opening of through north-and-south routes east of the mountains was equally great. The present main line of the Southern was completed to Atlanta in 1873. Not until 20 years later was the last gap of the present Atlantic Coast Line main route finished in North Carolina. Not until 1900 was the Seaboard Airline's through route completed.

The last large-scale construction in the South occurred in Florida. While the northern part of the state had had railroad lines as early as the 1850's, the heart of the state was not reached until the 1880's, and it was not until a decade later that the southern parts were reached by the Florida East Coast.

During the 1880's and 1890's competitive building similar to that in the East accounted for an important part of the new construction in the South. The predecessors of the Southern Railway reached from Atlanta to Cincinnati in 1880 and pushed west to Mississippi in 1889, all in Louisville & Nashville territory. The Seaboard Airline's predecessors along the Atlantic Coast developed their western connection to Birmingham in 1892, reaching Montgomery also in 1891. The early 1900's witnessed the struggle for control of traffic in Florida by way of the competitive building of new railroad lines.

In the Prairie states. In the Middle West, the roads that had reached the Mississippi River before the war pushed on through the plains. The nature of construction changed rapidly from that of providing clearly necessary lines of communication to that of wild competitive and promotional building. In the 1880's particularly was the construction in this category.[4] It was this stage that provided the prairie states with the highest mileage per capita of any part of the country and left its impress of the most closely knit web of lines on the railroad map of the United States. Each system extended its branches into every section of rich farm land within reach and attempted to reach its share of the major commercial centers: Chicago, St. Louis, Omaha, Kansas City, Minneapolis, or Denver; as well as the minor ones, Sioux City, St. Joseph, and the like. The Santa Fe, which originally had its eastern terminus at Kansas City, projected a line to Chicago to protect its bargaining strength in the Eastern markets with the Eastern railroads. One of the predecessors of the Chicago, Milwaukee & St. Paul pushed in the reverse direction westward to Kansas City. The Chicago, Burlington & Quincy built west to Denver to insure its bargaining strength. The Burlington in these years also forged northward from Illinois to St. Paul, in order to enter the northwestern region. The Chicago, Rock Island & Pacific also built across the prairies to Denver to keep up with the rest. Denver, which had been dependent for its eastern communications upon a branch of the Union Pacific and the Kansas & Pacific line from Kansas City, found itself the terminus of two other main-line railroads. In the same period both the Burlington and the Chicago & Northwestern reached into southeastern Wyoming with long branches.

By 1873 Texas had been connected with both St. Louis and Kansas City by a single railroad line. The push of competing roads from the north into this territory, to tap possible riches and gain outlets on the Gulf, was very active in the 1880's. The Fort Worth & Denver City joined

[4] The contemporary view of this kind of building is provided by J. L. Ringwalt in his *Development of Transportation Systems* (Philadelphia: The Author, 1888): "Illustrations of the tendency to expand systems, interwoven with the disposition to invade contiguous or preoccupied territory, which is one of the notable features of modern railway development, were furnished by a considerable proportion of the new construction in the Middle States." (P. 352.)

Texas with Colorado. The Santa Fe constructed a line across the middle of Oklahoma to Fort Worth, and another to the center of the Texas Panhandle. The Frisco reached from western Missouri to Dallas. Later the Rock Island and the Kansas City Southern entered the Texas area. Activity in new construction continued till the First World War.

Construction in the Great Plains states, between the Mississippi and the Rockies, and between the Gulf of Mexico and Canada, accounted for 36 per cent of the country's total from 1864 to 1873. In the next period to 1884 its proportion was 44 per cent, and it retained almost as high a share through to 1900. During the early 1900's the Southwest in particular was one of the remaining areas of the country where extensive construction continued.

In the Western states. The first railroad to cross the Rocky Mountains and the Sierra Nevadas was finished by the juncture of the Union Pacific and the Central Pacific in 1869. Close on the heels of this initial construction came the period, from the panic of 1873 to the depression of 1884, in which the greatest number of routes across the Rockies, Coast Range, and Sierra Nevadas were opened. (See map following.) First an outlet from southern California to the East *via* the Central and Union Pacific was opened by the completion in 1876 of the Southern Pacific line from San Francisco to Bakersfield and over the mountains to Mojave and Los Angeles. Then came a direct route from Los Angeles to the East with a peculiar combination of two competing lines: the Santa Fe, having crossed the Rockies in 1880 to Albuquerque, reached south almost to Mexico in 1881 to join the Southern Pacific route built west from the Los Angeles area. The following year the Texas & Pacific made connection with the same Southern Pacific line at El Paso, and in 1883 the Southern Pacific's own lines east of El Paso were placed in operation. In that year the Santa Fe itself had reached west from just south of Albuquerque to the California line at Needles, to join with a Southern Pacific branch from Mojave. In 1885 this branch was turned over to the Santa Fe, and with a new line over Canjon Pass the latter railroad reached Los Angeles and then San Diego.

In the Northwest equally energetic railroad construction was under way. The Oregon Railway & Navigation Company finished a line along the southern bank of the Columbia River in 1882. The Northern Pacific was pushed across the Rockies in 1883, so that Portland, Oregon, had its eastern connection almost as soon as did Los Angeles. In 1883 the Northern Pacific also finished its connection from Portland to Tacoma, to give Puget Sound its first through eastern service. In 1884 the Oregon Shortline, extending north from the Union Pacific to the Oregon Railway & Navigation Company, was completed, and Portland had a second outlet eastward. In those lush years of railroad building the pattern for the mountain Pacific area was pretty well established.

In the next period, from 1884 to the depression of the 1890's, the Great Northern was the only over-all, east-west addition. The Northern Pacific in 1888 added a line across the Cascades directly to Puget Sound without passing through Portland. In a north-and-south direction, however, the line joining Oregon with California was finished, and the Santa Fe reached north to San Francisco.

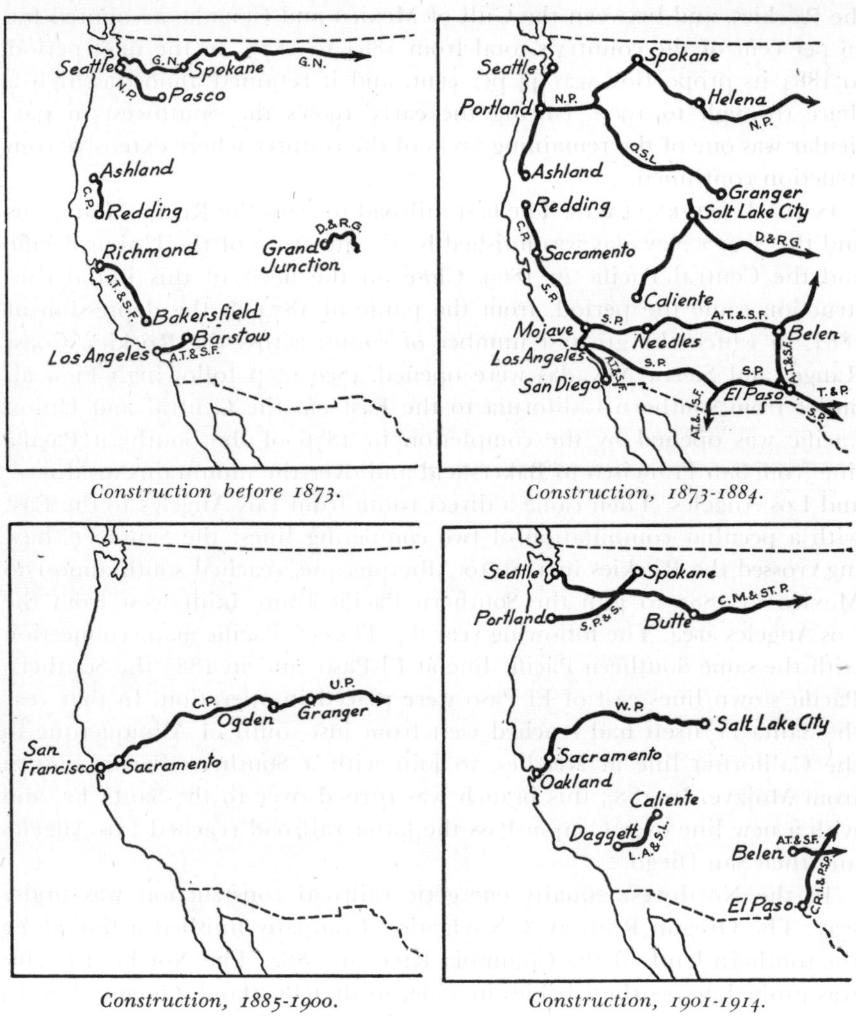

FIG. 2. *Growth of the Transcontinental Railroad System.* Lines are shown schematically, identified by principal controlling carriers.

In the first decade of the twentieth century there was a flare-up of transcontinental construction, largely to protect traffic for parts of already existing routes. (See adjoining map.) A Middle Western railroad, the Chicago, Milwaukee & St. Paul, projected its system west from the

Missouri River to Puget Sound in 1909, in order to insure that it could get a reasonable amount of transcontinental traffic.[5] The city of Los Angeles and the Union Pacific Railroad both improved their bargaining positions by the completion of a line from Salt Lake City to Los Angeles in 1905. Those persons interested in the Denver & Rio Grande promoted the construction of the Western Pacific from Salt Lake City, the western terminus of their line, to San Francisco Bay, with operation starting in 1909.

THE COUNTRY AS A WHOLE. In 1870 the country had started the railroad era with 53,000 miles of line, a large share of which was east of the Mississippi. By 1882 the mileage had doubled, and by 1904 it had doubled again. By 1914, after the addition of 39,000 more miles, the country's network reached its approximate peak with 252,000 miles of railroad, nearly one-half being west of the Mississippi. The investment in roadway and equipment stood at some $15,000,000,000. The end of extensive development of the railroad system was not, however, to mean the marked reduction of investment in facilities. Reductions in grades and curvature, strengthening of track, and betterment of equipment had even before 1914 become a major factor in capital expenditures, so that despite reduction in building new lines, a level of about $500,000,000 a year was maintained throughout the early 1900's, except for depression years.

Railroad Finance and Consolidation

The history of railroad finance encompasses the promotion and raising of capital for new construction and the security transactions involved in consolidation and manipulation, as well as the whole matter of reorganization of those companies that found themselves in financial difficulties. Most of the techniques of corporate finance, such as the separation of stock between common and preferred, procedures for reorganization after receivership, and the use of the construction company as an intermediary between the operating company and its promoters, had been developed before the Civil War. It remained to carry them to a far greater degree, to magnify their use and abuse, and to add further refinements in the subsequent years.

---

5 A graphic picture of how such construction was motivated is given in the Interstate Commerce Commission's report on the affairs of the Milwaukee: "Everything indicates that the project was the result of rivalry between powerful groups. Miller, Rockefeller and others controlling the St. Paul felt that they could not tolerate its being bottled up in South Dakota with the Hill lines to the north controlling the Burlington, and the Harriman lines to the south working closely with the North Western. It is obvious that the stockholders in general had no voice in the momentous decision, and as it was not necessary to secure a certificate that the public convenience and necessity required the construction of such a line under provisions of law such as are now a part of section 1 of the interstate commerce act, personal rivalries and ambitions were free to do as they willed with a great property." (131 I.C.C. 615, 618, 1927.)

Railroad promotion. The post-1865 railroad era was characterized by wide and extreme abuse of the construction company.[6] One of the most notorious of these, the Crédit Mobilier, was used by the Union Pacific in constructing the eastern part of the first "transcontinental" railroad in the later 1860's. The Central Pacific's promoters had a similar company for the western section. In contrast to the earlier period, there was now an important new factor in railway promotion, namely, Government subsidy in the form of land grants and, in the case of the Union and Central Pacific, the loan of Federal credit by turning over Government bonds to the companies. The land grants were an attractive bonus either to the railroad companies, which could use the land as lien for mortgages, or to the promoters, who, by means of a construction company or some other intermediary, could siphon off the better land unto themselves for speculative purposes. In the case of the Pacific railroads the principal money for construction was supplied by Government bonds and by first mortgage bonds having a lien on the donated land. The promoters furnished relatively small amounts of working capital, for which they were quickly reimbursed. They garnered very substantial cash profits and also, for nominal contributions, acquired the common stock that would give them claim on future profits. In the case of the Union Pacific, the promotional arrangements were so outrageous that the road became the center of a great public scandal; indeed, one of the intermediate companies, the Crédit Mobilier, became a byword of financial evil. What the Pacific railroads represented on a gross scale was duplicated in one phase or another by numerous, less spectacular, small developments for many years thereafter.[7]

The cyclical variations in economic activity during those years must, to an important extent, be attributed to such railroad activities. The tremendous surges of financing of new projects, followed by sharp contractions when it became obvious that progress had been too rapid, characterized financing from the 1860's to the 1890's. In the early 1870's a peak of $500,000,000 a year of new railroad securities was issued, and in 1871 alone over 7,000 miles of new line were built. The recession of 1873 was precipitated by the insolvency of Jay Cooke, the banking firm particularly interested in the Northern Pacific project. In the year 1875 only 1,700 new miles were added. But recovery from the depression brought another period of feverish activity, with $800,000,000 of new securities issued in 1882. In that year construction reached 11,500 miles. The financial difficulties of the West Shore, in early 1884, and the Ward

---

[6] See above, p. 129.

[7] *Poor's Manual's* comments in 1900 were to the effect, "There was never a period in our history in which, in the construction . . of railroads, the good sense of our people was so thoroughly at fault as in the period from 1879 up to and including 1892." (*Poor's Manual,* 1900, p. xliv.)

banking house failure in May, marked the beginning of another slump. In 1885 building dropped to but a fourth of what it had been in 1882. After a short depression another boom of financing followed in 1887 and 1888. The all-time record of 12,900 miles of new construction was reached in 1887. This was to lead to still another depression, that of the 1890's, which proved to be the last one closely connected with railroad enterprise.

The financing of this era was characterized by substantial amounts of stock "watering," that is, the issuance of stock with no more than a nominal cash contribution by the holder thereof, but with the full par value shown on the books as a liability and an equivalent amount added to the investment account on the assets side. *Poor's* estimate in 1900 was that $1,250,000,000 of the $3,100,000,000 par value of common stock outstanding in the hands of the public was "watered."

REORGANIZATION. The emphasis on promotional profits led both to construction of railroads far ahead of any markets for their services and to the undertaking of financial obligations that could not be fulfilled. The results were regular waves of financial reorganization for numerous companies in each depression period. The depression of the seventies saw the receivership of the Erie, Northern Pacific, Kansas Pacific, and many other less well-known companies. In the eighties an even larger group of companies succumbed. The slump of the nineties saw 30 per cent of all railroad securities then outstanding subject to receivership proceedings. More prominent in the array this time were the Baltimore & Ohio, the Norfolk & Western, the "Santa Fe," the "Frisco," the Union Pacific, the Northern Pacific, the Central of Georgia, and most of the predecessors of the Southern. From 1884 to 1900, some 60,000 miles of line were involved. The last wave of this type was from the panic of 1907 to the depression of 1914–1915, when the Pere Marquette, the Chicago & Eastern Illinois, the Rock Island, the Missouri Pacific, the Missouri, Kansas & Texas, and the "Frisco" were involved. The financial record of these years was not one to inspire confidence in the judgment of many of the railroad leaders or their banker associates.

EMPIRE BUILDING. While there had been a preview of the building of railroad empires in such instances as the formation of the New York Central out of numerous small connecting lines in 1858, the great surge in this direction did not get under way until after the Civil War. Empire building was to be a major factor in the railroad industry from then until the First World War. It was responsible for much of the competitive building and many of the financial difficulties already discussed. It was also behind the trend toward loss of the separate existence of many railroads through purchase, lease, or other means of obtaining control. The basic motive behind this consolidation movement was the "scotching" of competition and the control of traffic so that as much revenue as possible could be brought to a system. The more subtle urge of a sheer will-to-power also played an important part. In particular instances, the possibility of great profits from financial manipulation carried on in the process of consolidation was an additional incentive.

Jay Gould's kaleidoscopic passage over the railroad map of the country represented the high point of the latter motivation. Gould's first major operations in the railroad field involved the Erie in the late 1860's. He had joined the board of directors of the Erie in 1867, made a small fortune selling the company's stock short in 1868, obtained control of the connecting Albany & Susquehanna in 1869, and was finally forced out of the Erie in 1872.[8]

Gould next appeared in 1873 with temporary control of the Union Pacific, in the course of which he made some speculative profits. A few years later he purchased the Denver Pacific and the Kansas Pacific, which were potential competitors of the Union Pacific, with a view to selling them for nuisance value to the latter road. To establish that value, he was finally forced to buy the Missouri Pacific, the Missouri, Kansas & Texas, the Denver & Rio Grande, the Texas & Pacific, and several other less well-known lines, so that the former two would have connections with which to interchange traffic and so control its routing. This situation forced the Union Pacific to buy the two competing roads as Gould had originally planned, and left him with both a handsome profit at the expense of a competitor and a very substantial railway system in the Southwest made up of the latter lines. With the purchase of the Wabash as an eastern connection for this system, extending to Buffalo, Gould entered the field of competitive construction. He fought the Burlington with the extension of the Wabash to Council Bluffs, with the Missouri Pacific as he built northward into Nebraska, and again with the Wabash when he pushed into Chicago. He allied himself with the Huntington-Southern Pacific group to stave off the threats of the Santa Fe's extension to the Pacific Coast by jointly buying control of the "Frisco." The financial burden of all this, together with the devious devices he employed to unload his holdings on others with a profit to himself, while he still held control, led to financial difficulties after 1884 that were to leave serious scars on almost every company that came under his wing. In the depression of the late 1880's his empire shrank and his power was drastically curtailed, but with little loss to his own personal profit.

[8] The operations of Gould and his colleagues and opponents revealed, in the words of Charles Francis Adams, "the deep decay which has eaten into our social edifice. . . . The stock exchange revealed itself as a haunt of gamblers and a den of thieves; the offices of our great corporations appeared as the secret chambers in which trustees plotted the spoliation of their wards; the law became a ready engine for the furtherance of wrong, and the ermine of the judge did not conceal the eagerness of the partisan; the halls of legislation were transformed into a mart in which the price of votes was higgled over, and laws made to order were bought and sold; while under all, and through all, the voice of public opinion was silent or was disregarded." Quoted in F. C. Hicks, *High Finance in the Sixties*, p. 114. New Haven: Yale University Press, 1929.

On the other hand, systems like that of the Burlington were built up during the same years with most conservative financing and no scandal, even though they were forced into competitive building that their better judgment might have rejected had it not been for the presence of more speculative elements in the field. In between the two, in varying degrees of responsibility, lay the other of the early empire builders—the Huntington-Southern Pacific group, Commodore Vanderbilt, and Joy in the Middle West.

In the period just after 1900, the country witnessed many dramatic episodes in large-scale railroad empire building. In contrast to the earlier emphasis on construction of new lines, this period stressed the acquisition of control of already existing systems. There seemed no limit to size or to the lust for power.[9] Harriman welded together the Union Pacific and the Southern Pacific and dominated the Illinois Central, thus providing a railroad dominion covering a rectangle with its corners in San Diego, Portland, Oregon, Chicago, and New Orleans. In New England, J. P. Morgan and C. S. Mellon, through the New Haven Railroad, controlled substantially every transportation agency. The younger Gould was building a system extending from Baltimore to San Francisco. The questionable financial transactions, the increase in rates, and the abuse of political and economic power that were associated with much of this manipulation led to the congressional and judicial action that broke much of it apart in the following decade or so. Proceedings under the anti-trust laws were an effective means of breaking down the largest combinations.

GOVERNMENT CONTROL DURING THE FIRST WORLD WAR. An interlude to the normal financial history of the railroads occurred during the First World War. As a result of serious congestion on the railroads in the fall of 1917, it was deemed necessary for the Federal Government to take possession of the country's railroads, compensating the companies for their use by a guarantee of a net operating income at the level of the average for the preceding three fiscal years. Owing to a rapid increase in average hourly wage rates and material prices, both during and after the war, the earned income of the railroads well-nigh disappeared by the end of the period of Government control. From the entrance of the

---

[9] That there was no limit to the desire to grasp properties was indicated in the Interstate Commerce Commission record in the investigation of the Harriman acquisition of the Union Pacific, Southern Pacific, and other carriers in the early 1900's. Questioned by the Commission as to where his policy of acquisition was to stop, Mr. Harriman said:
A. I would go on with it. ***

***

A. ** If you (the Commission) will let us, I will go and take the Santa Fe tomorrow.

***

A. I would go on as long as I live.
Q. Then after you had gotten through with the Santa Fe and had taken it, you would also take the Northern Pacific and Great Northern, if you could get them?
A. If you would let me. 12/ICC/277, 280 (1907).

United States into the War in April, 1917, to the cessation of Federal control in March, 1920, the hourly wage rates increased roughly 100 per cent and costs of materials similarly. Rates and fares did not increase proportionally, nor did technological factors change sufficiently to compensate for the increase, so the proportion between operating expenses and revenue jumped from between 70 per cent in 1917 to nearly 100 per cent in the first months of 1920, thus leaving in the end a negligible income. In all, for the two years and three months of Federal control, nearly $900,000,000 was contributed by the U. S. Treasury to the companies in lieu of earned income. The continuance of the guarantee for six months after the cessation of the control necessitated further Treasury aid of over $500,000,000 to company income, the higher rate of this contribution being accounted for by further inflation that caused expenses still further to exceed revenue.

Railroad Charges

The difficulty in uncovering the history of railroad charges before 1907 lies in the lack of information as to the net rates actually paid for the movement of specific commodities. This is principally owing to the fact that there is no knowledge of the extent of rebates that were or might have been granted. One of the characteristics of the early system of payment for transportation service was that discounts below published rates were widely available to shippers with bargaining power. Large, favorably situated shippers could threaten a railroad with withdrawal of business to a competitor unless special discounts were given. Political pressure could be brought to bear where grants of special charters or other privileges were concerned, or any number of other pressure tactics were usable. The historian is thus left with the general figures for revenue per ton-mile, which provide only a limited basis for a general review of rates.

General rate levels. (a) *History of rate-level changes.* Revenue per ton-mile figures varied widely between various railroads because of the differences both in commodities hauled and in the degree of competition. In New England, 4 cents a ton-mile was quite usual in 1860, yet the Boston & Albany predecessors had a unit revenue of only 2.3 cents at that time. The trunk lines going to the West kept closely to a 2-cent level. In the South, the tendency was for the revenue to be in the higher brackets. During the period of the Civil War, there was a general rise throughout the country of from 25 to 50 per cent. Thereafter there was a continuous drop until the early 1900's. The first and most spectacular part of this decline, from 1865 to the middle 1870's, can be attributed to a combination of three basic developments: the increased pressure of competition that drastically reduced the margin of profit, the post-war deflation that reduced the price of materials and labor and in turn lowered expenses, and the technological advances and changes in the nature of traffic that decreased the effort needed to produce a ton-mile of freight service. The second and more gradual drop in rates followed on down to 1900. The important forces appeared to be the continued pressure of competition and the lessened effort needed to produce freight service, both working against slightly rising material and labor prices.

The following graph of data for the Lake Shore & Michigan Southern during this period is indicative of some of the factors involved, for a typical railroad. In this case, from 1870 to 1900 the average freight charge

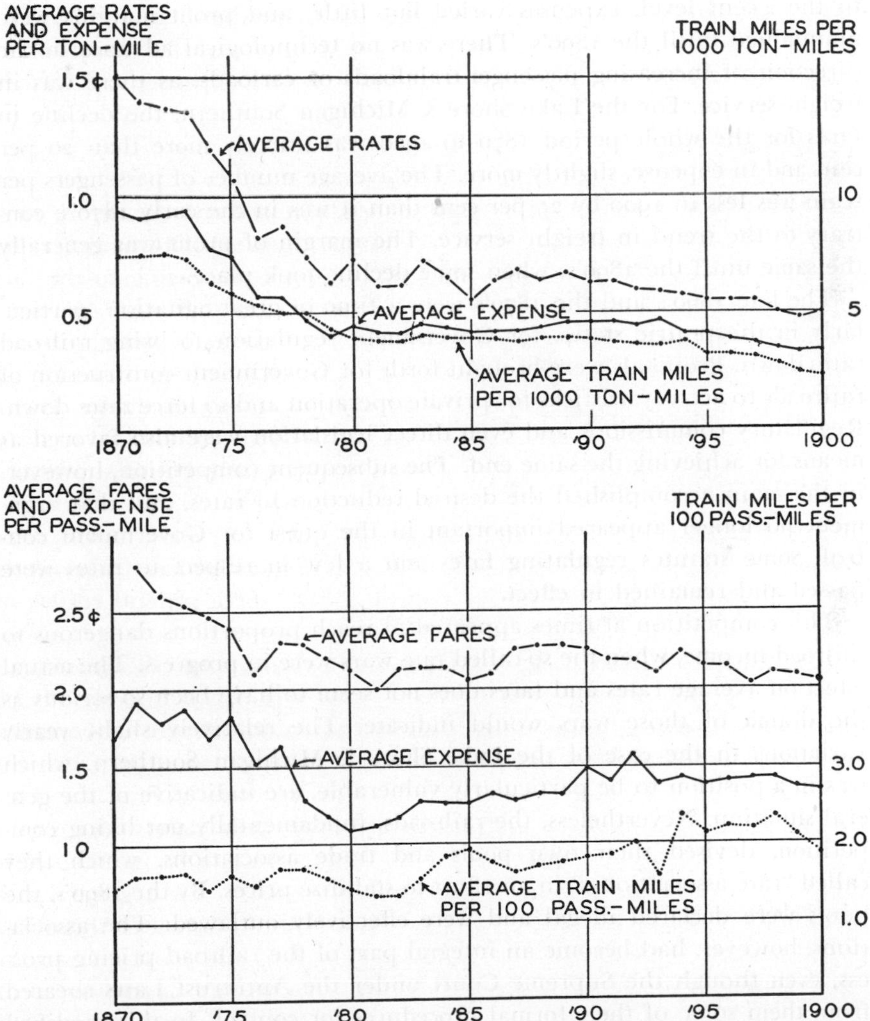

FIG. 3. *Trend of Prices, Expenses, and Trainload on a Typical Railroad.* (Source: L. S. & M. S. Annual Reports)

per ton-mile dropped approximately 65 per cent, expenses 55 per cent, and, a general index of improving physical efficiency, train-miles per 1,000 ton-miles, 69 per cent. Profit per ton-mile dropped 50 per cent in the first five years after 1870, held fairly constant to 1890, and dropped further during the 1890's. Almost the entire drop in rates and expenses after 1875 could be justified by the technological advances of the type mentioned earlier and the changes in traffic characteristics that allowed a train to haul a greater tonnage of freight.

The parallel history of passenger fares and expenses has quite a different trend. After the deflation just after the Civil War fares held closely to the 2-cent level, expenses varied but little, and profit margins were maintained until the 1890's. There was no technological advance in the direction of increasing passenger-trainloads or carloads, as there was in freight service. For the Lake Shore & Michigan Southern, the decline in fares for the whole period 1870 to 1900 was scarcely more than 20 per cent and in expense, slightly more. The average number of passengers per train was less in 1900 by 25 per cent than it was in the early 1870's, contrary to the trend in freight service. The margin of profit was generally the same until the 1890's, when some decline took place.

The late 1860's and the 1870's were a time of great agitation, particularly in the prairie states, for Government regulation to bring railroad rates down. Proposals were brought forth for Government construction of railroads to act as yardsticks for private operation and so force rates down. Regulatory commissions and even direct legislation were also favored as means for achieving the same end. The subsequent competition, however, in the main accomplished the desired reduction in rates, and that argument no longer appeared important in the quest for Government control. Some statutes regulating fares and a few in respect to rates were passed and remained in effect.

This competition at times appeared to reach proportions dangerous to railroad income, when the so-called rate wars were in progress. The actual effect on average rates and fares does not seem to have been so serious as the drama of those wars would indicate. The relatively slight yearly variations in the case of the Lake Shore & Michigan Southern, which was in a position to be particularly vulnerable, are indicative of the general situation. Nevertheless, the railroads, fundamentally not liking competition, devised their own pools and trade associations, which they called "rate associations," in an effort to stabilize prices. By the 1890's, the pools were declared illegal and were effectively outlawed. The associations, however, had become an integral part of the railroad pricing process, even though the Supreme Court under the Anti-trust Laws sheared from them some of their formal procedures for control. In this modified form they have remained an important indirect restriction on freedom of rate change by individual carriers down to the present.

After 1900 average rates for the country as a whole stayed close to 0.75 cent per ton-mile, and fares remained at about 2.0 cents per passenger-mile until our entrance into the First World War.

(*b*) *Government regulation of rate levels.* As the rates decreased in the eighties and nineties, the railroad companies showed more active interest in the general rate level. The railroads were particularly concerned about any downward pressure that the newly formed regulatory commissions might exert on rates. The basic legal premise involved was that rates should be fixed so as to avoid taking property without due process. In a long-echoing decision, the Supreme Court in 1898 established the doctrine "that the basis of all calculations as to the reasonableness of rates . . . must be the fair value of the property . . ." [10] and that any company is "entitled to ask" for a "fair return" on that value. Out of this decision grew a feeling, beyond the probable intent of the Court, that the railroads virtually had a right to earn a fair return on a fair value almost irrespective of the laws of supply and demand. No matter what judgment had been used in locating railroads, or what their expenses were, or what their prices and services were in relation to other prices and services, this fair return should be forthcoming.

GOVERNMENT REGULATION OF RATE RELATIONSHIPS. From the point of view of those directly interested in rates, the most important fact is the relation of what one shipper pays to what another pays. For that reason, the rebates mentioned above, together with other forms of discriminatory charging, quite early attracted public attention more than did the general level of rates. The policy of favoring powerful shippers and discriminating against the weaker ones was carried to extremes in the 1870's and 1880's. The Standard Oil interests went so far as to get a share of the rate paid by independent oil companies for transportation of their oil.[11] In spite of railroad protests against Government interference with their private business affairs, the public's interest finally prevailed upon numerous state legislators to pass laws and form commissions that would be directed toward the eradication of discriminatory pricing. Finally the major responsibility was assumed by the Federal Government, with the passage of the Interstate Commerce Act and formation of the Interstate Commerce Commission in 1887. There proved, however, to be a long legal and congressional battle before the public's objective was reached. The railroads were successful in evading much of the effort of state regulation by arguing that they were involved in interstate commerce, which could

10 *Smyth* vs. *Ames*, 169 U. S. 466, 546 (1898).

11 The Senate Report of 1874 keynoted "the evils of unjust discrimination against one locality in favor of another, or in favor of one description of trade at the expense of another . . . and of uncertainty and favoritism by means of special contracts, rebates, drawbacks and the thousand and one other means by which a rich and powerful company may, by the secret adjustment of rates, impose upon the public." *43rd Cong., 1st Session, Sen. Report No. 307, Part I*, p. 137.

not be impeded by the state orders. They further persuaded the courts to so interpret the provisions of the Interstate Commerce Act that they became almost worthless in controlling the discriminatory rate practices. In the early 1900's, rebates and discrimination were still prevalent. It was not until Theodore Roosevelt's presidency and his advocacy of effective legislation in the form of the Hepburn Act of 1906 and the passage of the Mann-Elkins Act of 1910, together with a change in the attitude of the Supreme Court toward recognition of the administrative function of the Interstate Commerce Commission, that Government regulation really began to operate at all effectively to eliminate the abuses that had long characterized the industry.

Water Transportation

Common Carriers of General Commodities

Water transportation by common carriers of the general run of commodities continued at slightly declining levels for some time after the close of the Civil War. Operations on the Mississippi River and the Erie Canal remained largely a matter of independent enterprise, but on the Atlantic Coast, on the Great Lakes, and on the smaller rivers in the South the railroads gradually gained a substantial degree of control over their competitors for this general type of business. The Louisville & Nashville Railroad interests quite early dominated water carriers in their territory in the South. By the turn of the century the railroads in the Atlantic Coast section of the South had established an important degree of influence in the business and they used it as a bargaining device with Northern roads. The Southern Pacific exercised extensive power over intercoastal ship routes, whether operating *via* Texas ports, by the Isthmus of Panama, or around South America. The peak of this type of control was reached in the earlier 1900's along with the peak in the building of large-scale railroad combinations. The New York Central, the Lehigh Valley, the Lackawanna, and others all had their boat lines on the Great Lakes. The New Haven owned practically every coastwise line in New England. The Illinois Central, through its subsidiary, the Central of Georgia, had extended its operations into New York by acquiring a Savannah-New York line. The increase in water carrier rates, along with restrictions on competition that generally resulted from all this, led Congress to limit railroad control over common carrier boat lines by the Panama Canal Act of 1912. Joint water-rail rates were subjected to the power of the Interstate Commerce Commission, and continuance of railroad control of lines that were potentially competitive to the controlling railroads required Commission approval. These moves served to abate the major abuses that had grown out of railroad control over water shipping.

Carriers of Specialized Cargoes

The other part of the water carrier picture, involving specialized vessels for hauling particular bulk products that can be unloaded easily, has had a different history. Their growth started with the shift in origin of certain of our primary resources from areas relatively near the point of use to more remote ones. The use of Minnesota and Wisconsin iron ore in place of Eastern ore, the use of West Virginia in addition to Pennsylvania coal, oil production in Texas as well as in Pennsylvania and Ohio, all led to the development of heavy water-borne flows of traffic. The first locks between Lake Superior and Lake Huron were opened in 1855 to make the initial developments possible. The Great Lakes movement of iron ore, and of coal in the reverse direction, did not begin in volume, however, until the 1880's. From 1880 to 1895 it increased tenfold, and by 1910 it was five times as much again.

Pipe Lines

Similar to the development of specialized water carriers has been that of pipe lines. The first long pipe line was built in 1878 from Pennsylvania to the Atlantic Coast in defiance of high rail rates. The saving in transportation cost to the oil companies led to rapid building of a pipe-line system in Pennsylvania and Ohio and, by 1891, as far west as Chicago. By the depression of the 1890's, there were about 3,000 miles in the system. By 1914 it had expanded to 10,000 miles, with construction west of the Mississippi starting soon after 1900.

Street Railways

That phase of the history of transportation that covers the street railway is unique in that it covers the birth, promotion, maturity, and, in a wide area, the death of an undertaking. Just before the Civil War the street railway had been introduced as an improved form of urban transportation. It did not come without some protest, but its possibilities were too patent to allow any but superficial resistance.[12] With horses and then with the cable as motive power, it developed slowly but consistently in the cities of the country. With the invention of the electric dynamo and motor and their application to railway traction in the 1880's, a real spur was given to the advance of the street railway. This innovation had provided the background from which all the promotional forces, so

12 A contemporary observed of the horse car as a new means of transportation: "It is hardly too much to say that the modern horse car is among the most indispensable conditions of modern metropolitan growth. It is to a city what steam car and steamship lines are to the state and the country. In these modern days of fashionable effeminacy and flabby feebleness, which never walks when it can possibly ride, the horse car virtually fixes the ultimate limits of suburban growth." (M. McClintock, *Report on San Francisco City-Wide Traffic Survey*, 1937, p. 39.)

prominent in steam railroad development, could launch forth. From 1890 to the First World War, the investment value recorded on the books of the street railway companies (including considerable "water") increased from $400,000,000 to over $5,000,000,000. Construction companies, stock watering, manipulation, competitive building, and consolidation were in even greater evidence here than in the case of the railroads. The leading street-railway promoters would easily match the railroad magnates for wealth and fame. Widener, Whitney, and Thomas Fortune Ryan were comparable to Harriman, Gould, and Huntington. Nor was the street railway confined to urban operation, for it spread into interurban lines to a remarkable degree. As such it appeared as a competitor of the railroads, and the attempt of the latter to buy control was to add another, not too successful, phase to empire building in the case of the New Haven and the Southern Pacific.

In the midst of all this, during the First World War, the motor vehicle appeared as a threat, in the form of the "jitney." It was resisted by attempts at franchise restrictions, but in the long run such means could not stop the progress in the direction of flexibility, speed, service, and passenger comfort that the final improvements of the bus could offer.

Highway Transportation

The long period of quiet in the field of highway transportation was broken by the outcrop of a "Good Roads" movement in the 1890's. The combined interest of bicylists' organizations, farmers, and the Post Office Department, with its rural free delivery program, pushed this movement into prominence. The avenues of promotion lay in several directions. The existing institutions for road building and maintenance were local government units which had taken little initiative and had been far from efficient. The advocates of good roads sought to change this by obtaining the transfer of at least the main rural roads to state highway departments, which, it was expected, would be progressive and far more competent. Thus the new institution, the state highway commission or department, was started in New Jersey in 1891, had spread to several other astern states by 1900, and by the First World War had become a general thing. Increased funds for highway construction were obtained by initiating the sale of the state and country road bond. By 1914 some $450,000,000 of such bonds had been issued, roughly one-third of which were state obligations. Simultaneously, Federal activity was started, first in the field of education and promotion and, by 1916, expanded to actual appropriation of funds on a small scale. Parallel with this movement were important technological advances. The use of oil and bituminous materials to improve road surfaces was being developed, concrete surfaces were introduced, and road-building machinery was being improved.

From 1890 to 1910 was the period in which the "spade work" was being done in developing the motor vehicle, taken for granted today. While the invention of the internal combustion engine and automobile had taken place in the preceding decade, there were, at the turn of the century, many who believed that the electric automobile was to be the accepted type of car. The early 1900's were to settle the question, as well as to see the final objective reached—a low-priced, reasonably reliable vehicle. In 1909, 100,000 new cars were produced, and by 1912 Ford had reduced the price of his Model T to $600. By 1917 the annual rate of production had reached nearly 2,000,000 passenger cars, and truck manufacture had also reached large-scale proportions.

Selected References

GENERAL WORKS

Daggett, Stuart, *Principles of Inland Transportation*. New York: Harper & Brothers, 1941.

Hadley, A. T., *Railroad Transportation*. New York: G. P. Putnam's Sons, 1885.

Healy, K. T., *The Economics of Transportation in America*. New York: Ronald Press, 1940.

Locklin, D. P., *Economics of Transportation*. Chicago: Business Publications, 1938.

SPECIAL TOPICS

Baker, G. P., *The Formation of the New England Railroad Systems*. Cambridge: Harvard Univ. Press, 1937.

Bogen, J. I., *The Anthracite Railroads*. New York: Ronald Press, 1927.

Chatburn, G. R., *Highways and Highway Transportation*. New York: Crowell, 1923.

Cleveland, F. A., and F. W. Powell, *Railroad Promotion and Capitalization in the United States*. New York: Longmans, Green, 1909.

Daggett, Stuart, *History of the Southern Pacific*. New York: Ronald Press, 1922.

———, *Railroad Reorganization*. Cambridge: Harvard Univ. Press, 1908.

Grodinsky, Julius, *Railroad Consolidation*. New York: Appleton, 1930.

Hedges, J. B., *Henry Villard and the Northwest Railroads*. New Haven: Yale Univ. Press, 1930.

Hines, W. D., *War History of American Railroads*. New Haven: Yale Univ. Press, 1928.

Interstate Commerce Commission, *Valuation Reports* (Corporate Histories), Special Series, Vol. 22 to 47 and special volumes in regular series.

Mason, E. S., *The Street Railway in Massachusetts*. Cambridge: Harvard Univ. Press, 1932.

Sharfman, I. L., *The Interstate Commerce Commission*, Vol. 1. New York: Commonwealth Fund, 1931.

U. S. Army, U. S. Shipping Board, *Transportation on the Great Lakes*. Washington: U. S. Government Printing Office, 1930.

20 · THE EXPANSION OF AGRICULTURE

Agriculture Becomes a Modern Business

DURING THE HALF-CENTURY between the close of the Civil War and the outbreak of the First World War American agriculture changed from an occupation that was still largely primitive in its technique and organization, and to a considerable extent self-sufficing in its economy, to a modernized business, mechanized, standardized, and commercialized.[1] These changes, interrelated with those in other divisions of the national economy, made the farmer a direct participant in modern industrialism. Agriculture, like the nation, was coming of age. The modernizing of the basic interest was due to the same underlying influences that were leading to national consolidation and the emergence of the United States as a world power. The period was marked by the occupation and utilization of the country's remaining land resources (as has been outlined in Chapter 18). From 1860 to 1910 the number of farms was tripled and the number of acres brought into cultivation was more than doubled.[2]

The settlement of the Prairies and the Great Plains provided a great opportunity for large-scale, systematized use of machinery. Introduced in the thirties and increasingly adopted during the Civil War, by the seventies basic implements for cultivation and harvesting had come to supersede traditional hand methods. In the following years mechanical techniques were extended to the raising of new crops, and the construction and operation of agricultural machinery was progressively perfected. By the First World War the gasoline tractor was beginning to supply the long-sought power element. As in other industries, mechanization resulted in a continuing displacement of labor, an acceleration of

1 The term "agricultural revolution" that historians and economists have applied to these changes, when tested by the evidence, seems inaccurate and inappropriate. For a brief critique on the use of the term, see E. D. Ross and R. L. Tontz, "The Term 'Agricultural Revolution' as Used by Economic Historians," *Agricultural History,* Vol. 22, pp. 32-38.

2 The fullest and most scholarly synthesis of the agricultural development of the latter half of the nineteenth century is organized about the occupation and utilization of the last frontier. F. A. Shannon, *The Farmer's Last Frontier.* New York: Farrar & Rinehart, Inc., 1945.

operations, and a greater standardization of products. The extent and elaborateness of technical devices and processes varied with the requirements of different regions and their special crops and systems, but the "mechanical man" found a place in all branches of cultivation and husbandry until the expression "the farm, a factory" had an essential justification.[3]

With the extension of farming into new regions of varied adaptability and the accelerated and systematized operations made possible by machinery, there was a steady, if gradual and uneven, improvement in methods. Basic applications of the principles discovered in the biological and physical sciences during the first half of the nineteenth century now brought a trend toward what the English have termed "high farming" as contrasted with the extensive methods of cultivation and husbandry previously used. Here again the advances varied with the region and commodity involved, but the applications of the findings of botany, chemistry, physics, genetics, and bacteriology were in many cases of determining influence. The applications of the social sciences, seriously entered upon in the opening years of the new century, were to be no less influential upon the farming business and upon rural life and institutions. Thus privately endowed and publicly maintained research institutions, intelligent and progressive agricultural journalism, and competent and alert individual enterprise all had a share in the advance of farming.

The extension and co-ordination of a national system of transportation provided the means for commercialized marketing of the surplus of the farm and ranch. Increased speed and size of trains, specialized stock and provision cars, and systems of through shipments widened the area of competition for many commodities and thus hastened regional specialization on the basis of the most profitable utilization of land and labor.

Along with modernized transportation there developed the modern marketing organization. The primary grain markets improved their physical equipment and marketing system. The produce-exchange with its price-stabilizing function came into full operation; the great cotton exchanges were developed in Liverpool and New York City.

These modernized utilities and trading agencies were indispensable in marketing at home and abroad the enormous volume of produce. The statistics of sales, so far as available, reflect the requirements of the modern factory and its workers. Agriculture made a major contribution to the mounting volume of internal trade. Population tripled in the half century, and industrial specialization and urban concentration brought

[3] All contemporary records indicate that hand equipment was replaced very gradually in the East and South. For the progress of the invention and manufacture of farm implements down to the time of the Columbian Exposition, see R. L. Audrey, *American Agricultural Implements*. Chicago: The Author, 1894. The best general survey is Leo Rogin, *The Introduction of Farm Machinery*. Berkeley, California: University of California Press, 1931.

steadily increasing demands for food. By 1900 agricultural production was also providing more than four-fifths of the raw materials manufactured.[4]

In these years the export trade in grain and meat reached its peacetime height. From the increasing demand in the sixties the food trade grew steadily until it reached a peak in the first decade of the new century. It is reliably estimated that the United States exported more wheat from 1875 to 1883 than in all the previous 50 years. It is small wonder that the Austrian economist, Dr. Alexander Peez, described the trade in this agricultural surplus as the "greatest economic event of modern times." [5] Moreover, by the seventies the South had fully recovered the European cotton trade.

Special Limitations of Agriculture as a Modern Business

Unfortunately, this impressive volume of trade did not bring good times for the farmers. On the contrary, the three decades following the Civil War were times of stress and strain for most of those engaged in the occupation of agriculture and a period of acute distress for many. Farmers labored under limitations and disabilities in both the production and the disposal of their surplus. In spite of all the advances in farming, the census of 1880 shows that the proportionate share of agriculture in the nation's income was becoming steadily smaller. Thus, early in the new era problems of parity sprang up.

Physical limitations, always an unsettling factor in agricultural production, appeared with increasing effect when farming became a commercial enterprise. The extension of cultivation into the semiarid region of the Great Plains brought recurring seasons of crop failure or ruinous shortage. In addition, deforestation, extreme drainage, and improper tillage led to destructive floods in humid areas. Shortsighted cropping practices exhausted soil fertility, while extreme specialization and careless methods heightened the destructive ravages of plant and animal diseases. In general, adjustments of commodities and systems to the resources of a given region and the selection of the most profitable varieties and breeds for particular purposes were achieved at the cost of much wasteful trial and error. As Gras has emphasized, the "business" type and function of farming has been the latest to develop and the most difficult to maintain.[6]

Financial problems were no less serious and complicated. The farmer of the period following the Civil War had his problems of surplus pro-

---

[4] E. G. Nourse, *American Agriculture and the European Market.* New York: McGraw-Hill Book Co., 1929; S. W. Malott and B. F. Martin, *The Agricultural Industries.* New York: McGraw-Hill Book Company, 1939.

[5] Quoted by William Trimble, "Historical Aspects of the Surplus Food Production of the United States, 1862-1902," American Hist. Assoc., *Report,* Vol. I (1918), p. 227.

[6] N. S. B. Gras, *History of Agriculture in England and America,* 2nd ed., pp. 356-357. New York: F. S. Crofts and Co., 1940.

duction, just as did the farmer following the First World War. Lavish and unplanned disposal of the public lands had not only taken settlement into the subhumid area but had led to the increase of grain and meat production in excess of available market needs. In addition to the problems of relative overproduction, the appreciated gold standard caused a general fall in the price level from about 1875 to 1897. The farmer, by the nature of his investment, was unable to adjust his production to the depressed marketing conditions to the degree that other businesses could. Before adequate regulatory supervision, the farmer was the exploitable victim of discriminatory utilities and of fraudulent salesmen and promoters.

All regions faced their special difficulties. Eastern farmers had to compete with the cheaper production of the West or restrict their undertakings to narrow specialties. Western farmers were carrying a heavy burden of mortgage indebtedness to Eastern creditors. With the taking up of the available portions of the public domain, the price of land, influenced by speculation, increased disproportionately to the returns that could be obtained from its use. New farmers were seriously handicapped by the necessity of investing a large proportion of their funds in land rather than in equipment and improvements.

Relatively small returns upon investment and meager compensation for labor and managerial services restricted living conditions on the farm more than those in the cities or even in the larger villages. Educational and recreational opportunities were especially limited. Although social and intellectual standards and outlook varied between regions, there is abundant evidence to indicate that in all rural settlements they showed a decline from former days and an increasing disparity with town conditions. Moreover, in determining state and national policies the farmer was much less influential than he had been before the Civil War. Policies seemed to be shaped more and more in the interest of the industrialists and financiers, and the abuses of big business were not effectively restrained.

Formative Agricultural Organization

Conditions called for organization; in fact in a society in which all other interests were organized more or less effectively such a policy became a necessity if the farmers were to secure and maintain a relatively favorable position in the economy. But organization presented numerous difficulties; not only were the traditions of American agriculturists opposed to common action, but the nature and diversities of the occupation created serious obstacles. The very large number of farmers involved, their varied and competing commodity interests, the dispersion of the agricultural population, and the lack of developed leadership were all retarding and inhibiting influences. Agricultural societies, more often than not led and controlled by professional and "business" men, had been in no way class conscious, and farmers' clubs in their discussion of current issues had been drawn into the sectional controversy.

Whatever the difficulties of organization, the distress was real and pressing to the point of desperation. Out of the hard times of the years of deflation and transition came the first class-conscious farmers' movements in American history—desperate, inexperienced, emergency ventures that were to inaugurate the permanent organization of American farmers. Each of the successive movements reflected the particular need and the special center of distress of the time.

The Granger Movement

The basis of the first class-conscious farmers' movement was the Patrons of Husbandry, founded in 1867 as a purely fraternal organization by a group of clerks in Federal bureaus. It was originated by Oliver H. Kelley, a native of Massachusetts who had pioneered in Minnesota. On an inspection trip through the South as an agent of the new Department of Agriculture Kelley became impressed with the need for an organization to bring together farmers of the different regions and to improve the social and intellectual conditions of rural communities. In 1867, with the aid of associates in Washington, he drew up a constitution and ritual for a new order that was to be open to both men and women, and that was to have aims, titles, and ceremonies drawn from farm life. The local branches were known as *granges*. It is a symptom of the temper of the American farmer of that day that such a purely social and benevolent lodge as the Patrons of Husbandry should have been seized upon as the agency for an action-program to bring redress of grievances and relief from prevailing distress.

Although the order was established in all regions, the fullest and most aggressive program was carried on in the upper Mississippi Valley—the "Granger West"—the main center of agrarian distress in the seventies. In addition to the common causes of dissatisfaction, these states had suffered special aggravations. Wheat cropping was bringing the inevitable effect of diminished yields in comparison with the new lands farther to the west whose overextended acreage was tending to depress the market. A heavy volume of indebtedness had been contracted during the period of high prices that accompanied the war boom. These debts became an increasing burden with the approach of resumption of specie payments by the Government and the consequent lowering of the price level. Under the pressure of promotive zeal and regional desire, railroads had been overextended in the Northwest. Without adequate planning and with no regulation of their capital structure, methods, and charges, the railroads indulged in such abuses as watering of stock, unfair reorganizations, discrimination between shippers and between shipping points, and the fixing of rates at what the traffic would bear in the more prosperous seasons.

It was their grievance against railroad rates that the aroused farmers most emphasized and attacked most directly. Between 1873 and 1876 "independent reform" or "antimonopoly" parties, organized among the grange members, obtained control of state legislatures and enacted laws to fix the charges of railroads and of warehouse and elevator companies. Railroad commissions were created to administer the regulatory laws. The most complete of these so-called granger laws were put through in Illinois, Wisconsin, Iowa, and Minnesota.[7]

Lack of precedents and adequate information as a basis for operations doomed these regulatory ventures to ineffectiveness. The railroad corporations involved sought to discredit the whole program by exaggerated complaint and reduced service. In any case, it was soon decided that the main responsibility and authority for the regulation of transportation utilities belonged to the Federal Government and not to the states. There was, however, a real achievement in these state enactments: crude, premature, and inadequate as they were, they established the precedent, confirmed by the Supreme Court of the United States, that such corporations were of a public nature and thus subject to governmental regulation.

Hardly less irritating were the farmer's grievances against the middleman—the commission merchant, the wholesaler, and various distributive and credit agencies. Co-operation, it was felt, would eliminate superfluous or predatory charges imposed by these groups. Buying and selling agencies were set up by local granges with a fair degree of success. The first of the large general mail order houses, Montgomery Ward and Company, was organized to sell to the granges. Stores were established on the Rochdale plan of distributed profits, but this system did not appeal to the Middle Western American farmer as it had to the English workingman. Credit associations and fire insurance companies, however, when well managed and kept within conservative limits, rendered moderate service.

Especial hostility was felt toward the manufacturers of harvesters, who concertedly refused to cut their prices for grange buying agencies. Again a remedy was seen in co-operative action. In Iowa the state grange bought a patent for a harvester that could be put on the market for a price estimated at half that of other machines, and undertook quantity production. With accumulating funds, the national grange bought up patent rights for a full line of farm and household implements and planned to establish factories in seven states. Such a pretentious industrial program was ill considered. Trouble developed in the operation of the machines, and litigation arose over the infringement of patents. The Iowa factory failed in its second year and brought ruin to the treasury

[7] The fullest account of the movements of the 1870s is still S. J. Buck, *The Granger Movement*. Cambridge, Mass.: Harvard University Press, 1913.

of the state grange, and most of the other ventures in productive co-operation were soon suspended with disastrous liabilities. Nothing did more to discredit and hasten the decline of the grange movement in the Northwest than the failure of these co-operative undertakings. With all their cost, however, these experiences afforded valuable lessons at the time and later in showing the possibilities and the limits of a co-operative modification of wholly private business institutions.

The social and educational activities and influences of the granger movement were generally wholesome and inspiriting. Local meetings provided an opportunity for regular social relaxation; and lectures and discussions furnished information and stimulated thinking. The state and national granges advocated improved rural schools and the increased support of agricultural colleges, according to their rather narrow conceptions of the methods and curricula of such institutions. But these activities, although they were to be the most enduring, attracted the least public attention.

Premature or ill-considered political and economic programs adopted by the granges brought a drop in membership as rapid as its growth had been. Political dissolution was hastened by the greenback issue, which divided farmers no less than laborers. The independent agrarian parties, formed primarily to regulate corporations, were confronted in the national election of 1876 with the alternative of returning to the old parties or merging with the national greenback organization.[8]

The Alliances

In contrast to the initial movement of the granges, the organized effort of the eighties was characterized by the number and spontaneity of farm organizations. The difficulties of the small farmers and tenants of the Southwest and of the wheat farmers of the new Northwest, who were experiencing the perils of settlement beyond the line of adequate normal rainfall, led to a variety of local organizations that were eventually combined in two regional societies. The Northern groups were merged into the National Farmers' Alliance (generally known as the Northwestern

[8] From the late sixties there was political agitation to check deflation by preventing the contraction of the supply of greenbacks and by redeeming war bonds in legal tender. The proposal for this type of price stimulation was directed mainly to the Mid-western debtor-farmers and to the Eastern laborers. This extreme inflationist panacea, however, never made a wide appeal to the farming interests, and most of the independent parties were opposed to it. Two of the three Presidential candidates (1876-1884) nominated by the Greenback party represented labor rather than agriculture; only James B. Weaver, the standard-bearer in 1880, could be classed as an agrarian. In spite of distress that at times reached the point of desperation, such intransigent proposals failed to gain the general support of a basically conservative proprietary class. But the distress grew acute and cumulative. A price recovery in the early eighties proved temporary and illusory. Organized effort, consequently, appeared imperative; and, whatever the form of such combined action, increasing consideration must of necessity be given to the vital problems of currency, credit, and the marketing system.

Alliance) and the Southern into the National Farmers' Alliance and Co-operative Union of America (the Southern Alliance). Efforts to bring the two combinations together failed. They differed somewhat on economic and political proposals; the Southern Alliance was regarded as more aggressive and extreme. There were, however, serious competing commodity interests, as those between lard and cottonseed oil.

The Alliance programs placed main emphasis upon co-operative activities, but it was increasingly evident that such limited correctives and palliatives were wholly inadequate to deal with the central problem of steadily falling purchasing power. The most original and constructive of the proposals of the Southern Alliance was for a Federal system of county warehouses and elevators where the leading crops might be deposited in return for negotiable certificates and in exchange for loans in legal tender up to 80 per cent of the local price of the products. Interest on the loans was to be one per cent per annum and the farmer was to be given a year in which to market his products. The scheme of the Northwestern Alliance for increasing the currency proposed a Federal land-loan bureau that would make loans upon agricultural land up to one-half of its appraised value at two per cent per annum, with the privilege of payment at any time within 20 years. Both proposals were too far in advance of public thinking on Governmental policy and economic theory to get any serious consideration.[9]

While the leaders of both of the alliances emphasized that their function was business and not politics, the memberships, under stress of the times, participated more and more in elections, either in third-party demonstrations with labor groups or in coalition with one of the main parties. As a result of such policy, in the landslide election of 1890 the Alliance forces helped to secure the election of half a hundred representatives in Congress, four United States senators, and three governors and obtained the balance of control in a dozen state legislatures. Eventually, too, the national organizations formulated the equivalent of a party platform; in fact, the resolutions of the St. Louis convention of 1889, at which both alliances were represented, were an anticipation of the basic issues of the People's party. The transition thus prepared the way for the greatest of agrarian political efforts in the Populist movement.

People's Party

The economic status of the American farmer in the era before the Great Depression of the 1930's reached its nadir in the early nineties when farm prices fell far below the cost of production and when farm incomes could not meet obligations of indebtedness. As in the case of labor in times of depression, the farmers turned from economic organization to direct political action. The situation, they felt, called for drastic

[9] J. D. Hicks, *Populist Revolt.* Minneapolis: University of Minnesota Press, 1931.

reform and for relief by the national Government. The answer was the most influential third party in our history before the Progressive revolt in 1912. The People's party, shortened to Populists in common usage and to "Pops" in journalistic derision, reflected the denunciations and demands of the farmers, the disparity in security between farming and other occupations, the plight of the homesteader on the "Last Frontier" caught between the millstones of deficient crops and falling prices, and the distress of the Southern tenant held in the vicious share-crop cycle. So great and general was the protest in the disaffected sections that in the election of 1892, the party, under the leadership of the "grim, gray, and deadly serious" General Weaver, polled over 1,000,000 popular and 22 electoral votes. Two years later, with hardship intensified by the panic, the new party elected seven representatives and six senators to voice their protest and to urge the passage of the farmers' charter in Washington.[10]

The economic platform of the Populists had three main planks: reform and regulation of the disposal of the public domain in the interest of the actual settler; strict corporation control with public ownership and operation of transportation and communication utilities; and, mainly, the raising of the price level through an exclusive and liberal system of Federal note issue and the restoration of the free coinage of silver at the old ratio of 16 to 1. Under existing conditions of production of the metals this step would have meant in effect not bimetallism, but rather the substitution of a cheap silver for a dear gold standard.

On this paramount issue the party staked its life in coalition with the dominant element of the Democratic party under the leadership of William J. Bryan in the "battle of the standards" in the campaign of 1896—the Populists lost. The determining cause of the defeat of the young leader who was able to voice so eloquently and sympathetically the cumulated protests and prejudices of his section has not been generally understood. The heated, not to say hysterical, opposition of the industrial regions by all of the ingenious resources known to current political manipulation, augmented by those of the new business organization, was to be taken for granted. But most of this effort and expenditure resulted in making assurance doubly sure in the creditor-minded areas. The rejection of Bryan and his program was due not to the strength of the financial East, but to the candidate's failure to hold his own territory—the states that previously had shown a strong sympathy for his cause and that from natural interest might have expected to profit by the program. In the crucial showdown, the border state of Kentucky, the Western farm states of California, Oregon, North Dakota, and Minnesota that had hitherto strongly favored the Populist doctrines veered to the

[10] J. D. Hicks, *Populist Revolt;* F. E. Haynes, *Life of James B. Weaver*. Iowa City: State Historical Society of Iowa, 1919. The description of Weaver in the text is from William Allen White.

side of "sound money."[11] Evidently the West, especially the Middle Border and the Pacific Coast areas, lost its "radicalism" in growing up and was becoming conservative.[12]

The Farmer in the "New Prosperity"

For about a decade and a half from the closing years of the old century and the first of the new, the price level steadily mounted, and general business activity made appreciable advance. Previous influences were largely reversed. The monetary standard was cheapened through the increased production of gold, and at most points demand for farm products came abreast or forged somewhat ahead of available output. Primitive natural abundance of the virgin frontier and the open range went the way of exploited mines, depleted forests, and fished-out waters. Cheapened production for the future was dependent upon technological processes and business management. For the time being the problem of the high cost of living (the "H.C.L." of the journalist) replaced that of falling prices; indeed, it became a tonic to the whole business situation, giving it an optimistic outlook in spite of alleged abuses and recurring financial flurries. Agriculture shared in *Our New Prosperity* that Ray Stannard Baker pictured so vividly and attractively in 1900. Even the Populist West, through more understanding adjustments and adaptations and by aid of the recurrence of a seasonal recuperative cycle, attained to greater stability and security, with consequent effect upon regional attitude and outlook. In the prevailing good times, agriculture, like labor, emphasized political action less and economic organization more. There remained, to be sure, the under-privileged and submarginal small holders and tenants to whom the co-operative programs of the Farmers' Union and the Society of Equity made an especial appeal. The tendency toward adjusted production of commodities and controlled marketing significantly foreshadowed future policy. No less significant were the efforts at federation along general or allied commodity lines.[13]

The Problem of Future Organization

By reason of inexperience and the pressure for immediate emergency action, the agrarian movements had been largely episodical in emphasis and opportunist in aims. Their spokesmen, concerned with this or that panacea, had failed to face squarely and realistically the fundamental issue as to whether agriculture in the new industrial age was to be in a

11 See the detailed map in C. O. Paulin and J. K. Wright, *Atlas of the Historical Geography of the U. S.*, Plate 108. Washington, D. C.: Carnegie Institution, 1932.

12 Compare the suggestive contemporary essay (Sept., 1896) by Frederick J. Turner reprinted in *The Frontier in American History*, pp. 205-221. New York: Henry Holt and Company, 1920.

13 Edward Wiest, *Agricultural Organization*. Lexington, Ky.: University of Kentucky, 1923.

position of relative parity with other interests or was to be definitely and permanently subordinated to them. With extended and costly findings of trial and error during the lean years, and with the opportunity in the relatively fat years to plan for the future, it remained to be seen if a far-and-broad-visioned leadership would develop, and on what basis and to what extent the varied and at times competing interests within the occupation could be united. In any case, it was already becoming evident that the effectiveness of organized groups, general and special, would depend to no small degree upon their ability to ally and harmonize their programs with those of public agencies that were expanding in response to an awakened public opinion.

Governmental Activities

Early Neglect

The agricultural well-being of a nation with abundant natural resources increased by each successive addition of territory was long taken for granted. Consequently, public aid to agriculture was slow and retarded. Factories had to be established and maintained by special effort and sacrifice; transportation, home and foreign, must, it was felt, be subsidized. In contrast, land was regarded as almost in the nature of a free good, and Americans were given the confident assurance that Uncle Sam was rich enough to provide all of his children, native-born and adopted, with family-size farms. A yoke of oxen, a clumsy wagon, a crude plow, and hand implements of neighborhood fabrication were all that the tough-muscled and stronghearted pioneer presumably required. As late as 1862, in the debate on the land-grant college bill, Senators argued that all the Western farmer desired from Government was to be given a homestead, and to be left alone. In full accord with this view, Federal policy up to that time had been devoted mainly to furthering exploitive efforts by a system of land disposal as loose as it was liberal. With a settlement system adjusted increasingly to regional desires and with imperial grants to corporations, the domain was alienated, with no safeguard against speculation and with a total lack of scientific classification of land areas or of other forms of planning.[14]

State Policies

The aid of the states before the Civil War was limited mainly to modest grants to agricultural societies for conducting their exhibitions. By the fifties a few states had appointed boards that collected, with more or less care and competence, statistics and other bits of information supposedly of interest and pertinence to the farmers. The extension of regulatory supervision of the dairy, canning, meat and other food production and processing industries, and the systematic combating of animal and

[14] See chapters 6 and 18.

plant diseases necessitated a more definite and permanent type of administrative authority. Accordingly, state departments of agriculture began to be created in the seventies.

United States Department of Agriculture

Similar needs in the realm of national jurisdiction gave to the Federal department its first important functions. Before the Civil War the only national agency for agricultural improvement had been a clerkship in the Patent Office for which small appropriations were made, from 1839 on, for collecting and distributing seeds and assembling statistical and other more or less informative material to be put into the annual report.

In 1862, as a part of the free-soil economic program, a separate Department of Agriculture with restricted functions and headed by a commissioner was created. The early activities of the Department were devoted manly to introducing and establishing new products, such as sorghum and beet sugar, tea, silk, hemp, and jute. Old abuses in seed distribution lingered, and much of the statistical and advisory material collected and published was of doubtful authenticity and availability. The Department's chief contribution in the early years lay in the research projects inaugurated by certain technically trained members of the staff, even though their work was hampered by hesitant administrators and rapacious politicians. With the establishment in 1884 of the Bureau of Animal Industry to administer the meat inspection laws, the regulatory powers of the Department became of first importance.[15]

By 1889 the increase of functions and the potential threat of agrarian unrest and party disaffection led to the raising of the Department to full executive rank and the creation of a Secretary with membership in the cabinet. Such a change was opposed by Senators who felt that the proposed Department, in contrast to all the others, would be concerned exclusively with technical matters and not at all with determination of policy [16] and it is highly significant that in the creation of clientele departments, as in the initiation of regulatory functions, agriculture should have taken the lead.

From the start experience proved that there was no lack of policies of material concern and of provocative nature clamoring for the attention of the Department, and that the Secretary and his expanding staff were in no danger of wasting their time with trivialities.[17] The rapid and profound changes in the farming occupation brought a multiplication of

[15] E. D. Ross, "The United States Department of Agriculture During the Commissionership." *Agricultural History,* Vol. 20 (1946), pp. 129-143.

[16] H. B. Learned, *The President's Cabinet,* pp. 335-338. New Haven: Yale University Press, 1912.

[17] J. M. Gaus and L. O. Wolcott, *Public Administration and the United States Department of Agriculture* (Chicago: Public Administration Service, 1940) is a thorough administrative study that gives unusual attention to historical origins and backgrounds.

bureaus and agencies having to do with the promotion and protection of all aspects of the agricultural enterprise and with the conduct of state relations. The latter in the early years very largely involved Federal aid for education and research.

Agricultural Education and Research

The foundation of serious instruction in agriculture was laid by another of the free-soil measures of the notable Congressional session in the spring and summer of 1862: the Morrill Act, granting land endowments to state colleges offering courses in agriculture and mechanic arts. Half a dozen states had already made provision for colleges of agriculture, and in at least three instruction was being given in an elemental manner. But the Federal grant gave the needed incentive for the founding in each state of the peculiarly American institution, the land-grant college.[18]

Great and far-reaching as the achievements of these colleges were to be, they were slow in finding their particular place and function. A long and heated controversy ensued between the advocates of practical training of farmers and artisans, with required manual labor as the central feature of the course, and those who would train leaders in technology upon a broad basis of science inculcated by the laboratory method introduced from European universities. In either case there were lacking an organized body of knowledge and teachers capable of imparting it.

Experiment Stations

The turning point came with the organization of experimental work, started in the states and systematized and standardized by the Hatch Act of 1887.[19] Such aids and incentives by the Federal Government to the creation of better varieties, breeds, methods, and techniques were in part an offset and a corrective influence to the wasteful and disorderly practices of cultivation and husbandry encouraged and promoted by the careless and prodigal alienation of the public lands culminating in the Homestead Act of 1862 and its supplemental extensions. A nucleus of teachers and research workers was recruited from the body of native scientists educated in old-line colleges and medical schools, from among American students trained in European universities, immigrant scholars, and, gradually, graduates of the first of the new colleges.

The research carried on at the stations more than any other of the activities of the land-grant colleges won recognition from scientists and from farm leaders. The working farmers were slowly reconciled and con-

[18] The fullest history of the land-grant college movement is in E. D. Ross, *Democracy's College*. Ames, Iowa: Iowa State College Press, 1942.

[19] A. C. True, *A History of Agricultural Experimentation and Research in the United States*. Washington, D. C.: U. S. Department of Agriculture, 1937; T. S. Harding, *Two Blades of Grass: A History of Scientific Development in the Department of Agriculture*. Norman, Okla.: University of Oklahoma Press, 1947.

ciliated to the program by the presentation of practical short courses and farmers' institutes. The beginnings of systematic extension work appeared during the first decade of the century in club work in the South and the emergence of county agents.[20] In the same period vocational education was finding an assured place in the rural high school.

Federal-State Cooperation

Meanwhile, the technical and administrative personnel of the Federal service was being drawn more and more from the student groups of land-grant colleges, and forces were getting under way that would lead to the large inclusive programs of Federal-state cooperation. The revolution in social and political opinion that would make possible such an extension of public functions and such a degree of centralized control awaited the pressure of modern agricultural distress; in extent and complexity this change of thought was as radical as the nature and degree of the relief sought. In the broader realms of regulation, research, and education, basic foundations had been laid, although the problems of more positive aid—credit, marketing, price-fixing, rural living, and social security—were hardly more than glimpsed and no concerted demand for action had been made.

Without the visions of spectacular enrichment that attended the fabulous inflations and imputations of the First World War, American agriculture by the time of the first Wilson administration had come of age. The promises of the frontier were gone; elementary adjustments had been made; and the main occupational groupings with their special needs and opportunities had become fixed. In the process, agricultural production had become increasingly localized.

The Main Agricultural Regions[21]

From the adaptation of systems of production to environment, in agriculture as in manufacturing, a geographical specialization had slowly been reached, one that had proceeded from haphazard trial and error to careful experimentation and planning, both by private initiative and

---

[20] A. C. True, *A History of Agricultural Extension Work.* Washington, D. C.: U. S. Department of Agriculture, 1928; J. C. Bailey, *Seaman A. Knapp: Schoolmaster of American Agriculture.* New York: Columbia University Press, 1945; S. G. Smith, *The People's Colleges: A History of the New York State Extension Service in Cornell University and the State.* Ithaca, N. Y.: Cornell University Press, 1949.

[21] The most usable and available description of the different regions is a series of articles by O. E. Baker, "Agricultural Regions of North America" in *Economic Geography,* Vols. II-VI (1926-1930). *The Atlas of American Agriculture* (Washington, 1936), prepared by the Department of Agriculture under the direction of Dr. Baker, provides an elaborate and minute representation of all the environmental influences involved. A convenient summary description is in *Distribution of Types of Farming in the United States,* Farmers' Bulletin No. 1289. Washington, D. C.: U. S. Department of Agriculture, 1923.

public aid. New varieties, new crops, wars, unexpected disasters or opportunities might demand shifts and readjustments from time to time, but compared with the earlier tentative and unstable areas the modern belts of production were to prove relatively fixed and enduring. Each was to be dominated by one commodity, grown in connection with subordinate products and with limited areas in which some specialty had local preference. As in the case of the localization of manufacturing industries, regional dominance of agricultural commodities has resulted from the most strategic combination of advantages in production and distribution, advantages that were both physical and social. In this regional adjustment and adaptation the number of new products introduced was relatively small. Localization involved readjusting and sytematizing the old enterprises in accord with scientific methods, mechanization, and market demands.

Subtropical Belts

The distinctive geographical features of the Gulf Plain from southeastern Texas to southern Florida—high humidity, mild climate, fertile soil in the delta and coastal prairie of Texas and Louisiana and thin sandy soils in the rest of the area—have determined the characteristic crops and systems of this subordinate, largely undeveloped belt.[22]

Rice

The coastal prairie of southeastern Texas and southwestern Louisiana, an area of from 25 to 50 miles in width and some 250 miles in length, proved uniquely suitable to the cultivation of rice. Its advantages were to establish the industry much more securely than it had been in the old Carolina-Georgia Tidewater area of production. In the 1880's settlers from the grain-growing Northern Prairies invaded these Southern Prairies and started growing rice on a large scale. Irrigation was easily and naturally provided by artesian wells or pumping stations. A Japanese variety of rice introduced by the United States Department of Agriculture flourished. The labor-saving machinery of the grain area was utilized in the cultivation and harvesting of the crop, and the cost of production was so reduced that the surplus could be sold in the Orient in competition with the native product. A student of human geography has strikingly summarized the relocation and reorganization of production of an old staple: "A fortunate complex of geographic factors thus made possible the adjustment of the steel robots of the wheat field to an aquatic plant in a startling agricultural development. . . . If the tradition of slavery once

[22] E. Q. Hawk, *Economic History of the South.* New York: Prentice-Hall, Inc., 1934. A. E. Parkins, *The South.* New York: John Wiley and Sons, 1938. R. B. Vance, *Human Geography of the South.* Chapel Hill: University of North Carolina Press, 1935.

clung to the rice farming of the Carolina coasts, it was long since removed by wheat farmers from the Northwest."[23]

Sugar Cane

Sugar cane remained strictly localized in the Mississippi delta of Louisiana. In slavery days the production of this staple was undertaken on the largest plantations, and after the Civil War cultivation continued on a large-scale capitalistic basis. Equipment for a large plantation or a unified group of production units included a central mill and a private railway line to transport the cane. The unusual seasonal labor demand was supplied largely by roving Negro and immigrant workers.

Since the proportion of the domestic consumption provided by the home-grown cane was very small, the large, if concentrated, enterprise was closely dependent upon tariff rates. The duty of 2½ cents per pound on unrefined sugar from 1873 to 1890 had a stimulating effect. The McKinley Act of 1890 put the product on the free list, but compensated with a generous bounty for the native producer. This direct subsidy was replaced in the Wilson Act four years later by an ineffective *ad valorem* duty, and with markets glutted from tropical sources a ruinous competition ensued. The Dingley "high tariff" of 1897 brought protective rates to a new peak but further difficulties came with the admission of sugar from the country's new possessions, Puerto Rico and the Philippines, and as a result of a reciprocity agreement with Cuba. From this cumulative depression the sensitive industry was rescued for several seasons by the First World War. The Sugar Bowl area was thus unique in its concentration, organization, and insecurity of market. By the first decade of the new century the production of beet sugar in the lakes and plain areas exceeded that of cane by an increasing margin, thus creating a new interest to be protected.

Fruit and Vegetable Areas

Less spectacular but of increasing importance were the fruit and trucking crops. Winter vegetables and citrus fruits flourished throughout the Gulf and lower coastal areas, and the trucking belt extended up the coast to New Jersey. The citrus fruits of Florida provided the chief competition to those of southern California, whose irrigated "sun-kissed" valleys, after trial of more general staples, were concentrated on these specialties as the most effective utilization of their precious soils. Such specialties entailed their own problems of marketing—of grading, advertising, merchandising, and shipping. The growing demand for them reflected a far-reaching change in national dietary habits.

---

[23] R. B. Vance, *Human Geography of the South,* pp. 216, 219.

The Cotton Belt[24]

The strong demand for cheaper textiles in the years following the Civil War, and the transformation of cottonseed from waste material to a valuable by-product in the manufacture of fertilizer, feed, and oil expanded the borders of the old Cotton Kingdom westward into Texas to the subhumid line, and northward into Oklahoma, Arkansas, Tennessee, and Missouri to the frost line. At the same time the application of commercial fertilizers in increasing amounts revived old areas in the Carolinas and Georgia.

Localization in the expanded region was by 1880 paralleled and encouraged by the establishment of cotton manufacturing in the southern Piedmont. With the advantages afforded by easily accessible raw material, natural power, and cheap labor supply, the Southern mills took the lead in the production of the cheaper grades of cloth, and, in striking contrast to former times, fabricated more than half of the cotton crop in the region of cultivation. Indeed, the integration of cotton fields and cotton mills was one of the essential features of the "New South." But both fields and mills were subject to limiting and disturbing influences. In the decade following Appomattox, the transition was made from cotton growing under the plantation organization to the production of the staple upon small units of land operated under a share-cropping system. This rather desperate expedient was resorted to only after the failure of efforts to keep the plantation organization intact by the use of the hired labor of freedmen or immigrants. The tenant's share of the return from the main crop—almost as varied as the apportionments of the catch to the whalers in *Moby Dick*—ranged in practice from one-fourth to two-thirds, depending upon the share-cropper's investment in the farm enterprise. In some cases the landlord supplied everything but the labor. Thus the cotton-growing tenant often occupied a position midway between crop tenancy proper and hired labor service—hire in many cases for most uncertain wages.

An essential and determining characteristic of the new tenancy was the crop lien by which the landlord-merchant staked the cropper his necessary living supplies—the "pawn-shop system" of credit, as Kendrick and Arnett term it. The owner in turn was carried by the country banker. The procedure was uneconomical and in the long run unsatisfactory to all

[24] In addition to the references on the South already cited, see E. E. Edwards "Historical Background of the Present Situation in Southern Agriculture," Southeastern Economic Association, *Proceedings*, 1930, pp. 78-93; B. B. Kendrick and A. M. Arnett, *The South Looks at Its Past* (Chapel Hill: University of North Carolina Press, 1935); and the older standard studies of M. B. Hammond, *The Cotton Industry* (New York: The Macmillan Company, 1897); and "Cotton Production in the South," in *The South in the Building of the Nation*, Vol. VI, pp. 87-103 (Richmond, Va.: Southern Historical Publications Society, 1909). The spectacular large-scale cotton growing enterprise in Southern California belongs to the recent period.

the parties concerned. The tenant paid high prices for inferior goods and was often bound to the landlord by accumulated annual deficits. Diversification either for the market or for subsistence was discouraged, as cotton represented a standardized marketable commodity and generally kept the tenant dependent. Share cropping as a system provided no agricultural ladder up which a farmer could climb to higher and more secure status. The enterpriser, in spite of his exploitive exactions, found his returns fluctuating and uncertain. Production was inefficient, the cotton market wavered from unsteady to weak, while costs remained relatively high. The banker charged exorbitant interest rates for risks that he found ruinous in times of depression. Falling prices and restricted credit in the eighties and nineties hit the cotton grower of the South as hard as they did the wheat grower of the West.

Diversification of crops in the cotton region was an objective that antedated, attended, and followed the Civil War, but the peculiarities of cotton growing under both slave labor and cropper labor made systematic and planned rotation difficult. There were and always had been subordinate crops and enterprises throughout the region, it is true: corn and pork were the most general stand-bys. Corn was used not only for feed but to an unusual extent for human consumption. In times of special depression of the cotton market, the corn acreage was markedly increased.

The greatest challenge to the dominance of cotton and the most severe threat to the existence of the Cotton Belt came neither from competing areas without nor from rival crops within, but from the ravages of a devouring beetle that imperiled cotton growing on a commercial scale. The boll weevil crossed the border into Texas in the nineties and in the following years became such a menace to the cotton plant that M. B. Hammond, the historian of the cotton industry, wrote in 1909 that "the future of cotton production in the Southern States is threatened unless means are discovered of reducing the losses caused by this pest." [25]

To offset the losses inflicted by the insect, cotton growers turned to a substitution and diversification of crops that have been publicized out of proportion to their importance for regional economy. The main attack sought to protect the dominant crop by introducing hardier varieties of cotton and improved methods of cultivation. In this campaign for agricultural improvement in the Cotton Belt, the foundations of modern extension service were laid by Dr. Seaman A. Knapp, agent for the United States Department of Agriculture, and representative of the General Education Board. Innovations and defensive compulsion brought diversified rotation into certain areas; for the region as a whole, however, the staple retained its dominant position and cotton still ruled its particular kingdom.

---

25 M. B. Hammond, *The South in the Building of the Nation,* Vol. VI, p. 101. Richmond, Va.: Southern Historical Publication Society.

Tobacco Area [26]

Tobacco, the oldest of the Southern staples, continued to be grown widely according to the local adaptability to varieties sought by the trade. The cultivation of the main types, however, came to center in a limited area that was to constitute a subregion of the Winter Wheat and Corn Belt. The location was in one case an extension of the production area of 1860 and in another the development of a new area of cultivation. The heavier dark burley tobacco demanded by foreign markets became more firmly entrenched in western Kentucky. The bright-leaf, flue-cured variety, the natural cigarette tobacco, became the major crop in expanding fields in northern and eastern North Carolina. Liberal use of fertilizer produced fairly satisfactory yields upon thin or partially depleted soils. Meantime, the great centers of manufacture at Durham and Winston-Salem sprang up in proximity to the supply of the leaf.

The steady demand for all forms of tobacco put production on a high and mounting level, but the business had its drawbacks and limitations. Cropping involved risks; the tobacco plant is exacting in its cultivation and soil-depleting in its effects. In large portions of the area share tenancy and crop lien prevailed. Concentration of the manufacture of tobacco products in a few large corporations set controls on standards and price. Certain varieties suffered from foreign competition. But by the time of the First World War—during which the demand for cigarettes was to reach phenomenal proportions—the tobacco staple in its leading commercial types was as definitely and firmly localized as was the cotton.

Hay and Pasture Regions—The Dairy Belt [27]

Specialized transportation—and through routes—brought the bulk-food products of the West, raised at relatively low cost, into competition with the limited supplies grown in the East. The farmers of New England and the Middle Atlantic states were thus forced into specialized branches of cultivation and husbandry that demanded a greater amount of labor and a more intensive use of the available land in producing commodities with an assured and expandable market. Something of the same

[26] Joseph C. Robert, *The Story of Tobacco in America*. New York: Alfred A. Knopf, 1949; U. S. Department of Agriculture, *Yearbook, 1919*, pp. 151-175. For a thorough history of an important variety, N. M. Tilley, *The Bright-Tobacco Industry, 1860-1929*. Chapel Hill, N. C.: University of North Carolina Press, 1948.

[27] There are very few reliable studies on the history of dairying. *Successful Farming's* "Ten Master Minds of Dairying" (Des Moines, Ia.: Meredith Publishing Company, 1930) is a convenient summary of leading figures in the industry. Edward Wiest, *The Butter Industry in the United States* (New York: Columbia University Press, 1916) is in part historical. E. P. Prentice, *American Dairy Cattle* (New York: Harper and Brothers, 1942) is the most convenient work on the subject. The first-hand story of the efforts to regulate marketing in a leading market-milk state is told in J. J. Dillon's *Seven Decades of Milk*. New York: Orange Judd, 1941.

problem confronted the tier of states to the westward along the Great Lakes and north of the prairies proper—central Michigan, Wisconsin, northeastern Iowa, and central Minnesota. Hay and forage crops flourish naturally in this region; its climate and situation is admirably suited to dairying, in which its Eastern and Scandinavian settlers excelled. The entire region from New England to Minnesota, with scattered special areas intervening, became predominantly a Dairy Belt. With the growth of industrial centers the eastern portion of the belt gave increasing attention to the production of fluid milk for the metropolitan markets. Wisconsin, which after the decline of wheat growing had turned to dairying, became the leading cheese-producing state. Dairymen in Iowa and Minnesota specialized in butter making.

The progress of the industry between 1880 and the First World War was attended by notable achievements in production, processing, and marketing. The experiment stations in the dairy states conducted extensive studies of the problems of dairy husbandry and industry. Special dairy breeds were introduced and highly developed for the qualities sought. The efforts to breed "dual purpose" cows, profitable both for milk and beef, proved ineffective, although breeds like the Milking Shorthorns have been profitable in a supplemental way in areas of other specialties. Instead of trying to develop "milk strains" in breeds primarily of the beef type, dairymen introduced dominant milk breeds. From widely scattered dairy centers of Europe they imported Channel Island Jerseys and Guernseys, Scotch Ayrshires, Brown Swiss, and the increasingly popular Dutch breed of Holstein-Friesians. The experiment stations worked out problems of feeds and feeding methods for milk as well as for beef production. By 1890, after a decade of experimenting, farmers accepted the ensiling process as the most effective method for the complete utilization of the corn plant. New forage crops, especially clovers, were introduced to supplement the corn ration and for soiling purposes where pastures were deficient.

The handling and processing of milk and its products were revolutionized by the findings of chemistry and of bacteriology. The perfecting of the condensing process invented by Gail Borden and the production of milk powders gave rise to major industries. Two epochal inventions have affected the development of all phases of the industry: the first centrifugal cream separator brought out in 1878 by the Swedish scientist, Carl G. P. DeLaval, and a simple, dependable butter-fat test perfected by Dr. Stephen Babcock at the Wisconsin experiment station in 1890. Like other branches of agriculture in these years, dairying was lightening and speeding up by machinery its most laborious operations. During the labor shortage of the Civil War, Orange Judd, prominent agricultural editor, replied facetiously to a correspondent that he knew of no machine for milking except the human hand. Before the First World War this most burdensome and exacting task of dairy routine was successfully performed by mechanical means.

Dairying has been notable for early organization of producers in the different branches of the enterprise and for relative success of co-operation in processing and marketing its products. Early enactment by state legislatures and by Congress of laws for establishing standards and for affording protection against substitute products attests to the standing and influence of the industry.

In spite of the exacting and confining nature of the work and the fluctuations in return for labor and investment, caused chiefly by difficulties in the adjustment of the cost of feed to the prices of the products, the dairy business enjoyed distinct economic advantages and security. Returns were regular and more dependable than those of a one-crop staple. The rotation involved in feed production maintained soil fertility. The dairy region was characterized by a relatively advanced and stabilized economy with enlightened social standards and institutions.

The industry in general could point not only to its achievements but to its great possibilities. The market for its products was growing and extending. The new national dietary habits referred to in connection with citrus fruits and vegetables placed a high value on the products of the dairy and were to rate them even more highly as nutritional studies already well under way in the laboratories of Babcock, Hart, Steenbock, and McCollum were popularized, and as the average consumer became concerned with vitamin content and calorie balance. As it was, the dairy lunch became increasingly popular, and the household larder was replenished from the creamery at the expense of the butcher and the miller and the growers of meat and grain.

The Wheat Belts

An invariable accompaniment of the settlement of each successive frontier has been the movement of the characteristic frontier crop, wheat. By the Civil War the center of production had shifted from the Appalachian Valley to the Prairies. In the census returns from 1859 to 1879, Illinois was first in production. But with the growing diversification of the Prairies and the northwestward movement of spring wheat, Minnesota led in the returns of 1889 and 1899, in turn to be superseded by North Dakota in 1909. Following the gang plows' encroachment on the grazing area during the First World War, Kansas took the lead decisively in 1919.

Two main wheat belts developed in accordance with the composition of the grain and the conditions necessary for its growth. In the Corn and Winter Wheat Belt, the staple was combined with a corn and livestock economy. This belt occupied in general the border region between the

Cotton and Corn belts, at points overlapping them. California, following a spectacular wheat boom, was by the nineties changing to the cultivation of fruits and other specialties.

A newer and more extended region was that of hard spring wheat stretching from the northwest border of the Prairies to the furthest limit of requisite humidity and occupying detached irrigation areas and the valleys of the Pacific Northwest. The extension of the Wheat Belt westward and northward followed upon development of new varieties of wheat and innovations in methods of cultivation. In the late nineties Mark Alfred Carleton, cerealist for the Department of Agriculture, introduced from Russia strains of durum wheat that proved unusually resistant to drought and rust. Early in the new century, after long trial, the Canadian scientists, William and Charles Saunders, developed the Marquis cross, which was of unusual hardiness and ripened earlier than varieties previously grown.[28] Dry farming, tried empirically in various early settlements in the semiarid region and later exploited by charlatan and visionary promoters, was given systematic testing by the experiment stations of the states concerned. When and where minimum precipitation was sufficient, paying crops might be obtained every two or three years from lands previously unproductive.

In all such extensions of the cultivable areas, whether due to selected varieties or adapted methods, there remained always the danger of unjustified encroachment upon the grazing area beyond the line of safety in farming. On the other hand, if the new area proved highly productive, there was the risk, in the case of a product as widely grown as wheat, of oversupplying the market. The wheat farmers of the Populist West had to compete with those of Canada, South America, and other new areas. Consumption of the staff of life decreased as a result of the competition of fruits and vegetables and milk products.[29] In both production and marketing the greatest stability of wheat was assured by a system of established rotation—corn and livestock, for example.

In all modern small-grain production, mechanization has exercised a

---

[28] An informing but highly colored account of wheat improvement is given in Paul de Kruif, *Hunger Fighters,* Book I. New York: Harcourt, Brace and Company, 1928. A scholarly exposition is given in U. S. Dept. of Agriculture, *Yearbook, 1936,* pp. 207-302.

[29] The most scientific findings on this subject are in the publications of the Food Institute of Stanford University.

The ironically fallacious prophecy of Sir William Crookes in 1898 that by 1931 the western world would be confronted by a serious deficit in the wheat supply failed to take account of the changed nature of demand resulting from modern working and living conditions as well as of increased efficiency in production. See J. S. Davis, "The Specter of the Dearth of Food: History's Answer to Sir William Crookes" in *Facts and Factors in Economic History,* pp. 733-754. Cambridge, Mass.: Harvard University Press, 1932. For the changes in crop adjustment in California, C. B. Hutchinson, ed., *California Agriculture.* Berkeley, Cal.: University of California Press, 1946.

determining influence. The chief addition to the basic harvester principle was the perfected self-binder. After unsatisfactory trials of wire binders, the twine binder was invented by John F. Appleby in the late seventies. The next step in mechanization integrated the processes of harvesting and threshing by means of the time- and labor-saving combine, which was adjustable to different crops and scales of production.

Power was the unique mechanical contribution of this period. The practicability and availability of the gasoline tractor in all stages of cereal production was demonstrated both in the medium-scale enterprise of the humid areas and the vast undertakings of the Plains. Large-scale, mechanized agriculture reached its height in the 50,000-acre wheat farms of Montana, exceeding even the old bonanza ventures that had been dependent upon horse power.

The extension of wheat production into the Northwestern Plains area was directly related to the localization of the milling industry. The invention of the roller process to grind the hard durum varieties was a vital development for the producer of the grain as well as for the manufacturer of the flour.

Grazing Belt—The Range and the Ranch [30]

Large-scale wheat growing, as a more or less speculative enterprise, was extended into the semiarid region beyond the 98th meridian, in normal or dry-farming cultivation. Unfortunately, the planless and carelessly administered public-land system encouraged the extension of general family-unit farming into the danger zone with resulting periodic crop failures, varying mainly in the degree of disaster. But the general region came into line as a vast grazing belt—a cattle and sheep country.

Following the open range stage for a couple of decades after the Civil War, the ranch became the typical form of enterprise. The ranching region furnished stock for the central markets and supplied feeders for the Corn Belt. Systematization of the modern meat-packing industry in Chicago, St. Louis, Kansas City, and Omaha in the seventies and eighties opened regular livestock markets.

The effective utilization of the Plains, as well as of the open Prairies, for individual farming or stock raising was made possible by the introduction of barbed wire fencing. The invention of J. F. Glidden at De Kalb, Illinois, in 1874 provided a satisfactory product, and, after a long struggle over patent rights, the price was put within the reach of the average farmer. Meantime, breeds of beef and sheep were systematically improved. State and Federal control of animal diseases, the regulation of shipping rates, and the formation of marketing associations gave a

[30] For fuller discussion of both the cultivation and ranging of the region, see Chapter 21.

measure of stability to an industry that had been entered upon with little plan or system and had been marked by extensive fluctuations.

The Corn Belt

Indian corn, or maize, because of its wide cultivation and basic position in crop systems and stock raising, remained the unchallenged monarch of American cereals. It was grown in all cultivable belts: in those of cotton, winter wheat, and dairying it had an essential place both as a feed and as a variant in crop rotation. Like wheat, corn moved westward, but, unlike the other cereal, its cultivation became localized in the strategically situated Prairie Plains. The crop's prevalance and dominance throughout the region was recognized in the designation of the belt. The Corn Belt, of somewhat variable bounds, in general coincided with the prairies. It stretched from western Ohio to southeastern South Dakota and southward along the Missouri River where it overlapped the belt of winter wheat. The region thus included most of Indiana, Illinois, and Iowa, southern Minnesota, eastern Kansas and Nebraska, and northern Missouri.[31]

Its use as feed, rather than the cash sale of the bulk of the great crop, exercised an unusual stabilizing and conserving influence on the economy. In this garden spot of the nation hogs and cattle were fattened for the home and foreign trade. When grown in combinations with oats, clovers, and winter wheat, and when cultivated with reasonable care and by the best established methods, corn gave the fullest assurance of a dependable return.

With corn and hogs the main products of cultivation and husbandry, and with the current relations between the two the key to the financial return of a given season, special consideration was given to the nature and nurture of both. From the nineties selection and improvement of corn received increasing attention. For a long time the standard of the form of the ear—uniformity and symmetry—falsely guided the efforts of breeders and determined the ratings in corn shows and demonstrations. Perry G. Holden of the Iowa State College extension service became famous as a champion of these standards in his corn-demonstration trains, in regional short courses, and in farmers' mass meetings. These prelim-

[31] Two survey essays provide an excellent introduction to the study of this region: E. E. Edwards, "Middle Western Agricultural History as a Field of Research," *Mississippi Valley Historical Review,* Vol. XXIV (1937), pp. 315-328; L. B. Schmidt, "The Agricultural Revolution in the Prairies and the Great Plains of the United States," *Agricultural History,* Vol. VIII (1934), pp. 169-195. State histories of agriculture are beginning to appear: Joseph Schafer, *A History of Agriculture in Wisconsin,* Madison, Wis.: State Historical Society of Wisconsin, 1922; Staff members of Iowa State College, *A Century of Farming in Iowa.* Ames, Iowa: Iowa State College Press, 1946. A more general history of Iowa agriculture by the present writer is shortly to be issued by the State Historical Society of Iowa.

inary efforts at selection, along with increased attention to seed germination, helped to create an interest among farmers and prepare the way for the application of scientific corn breeding.[32]

Dr. William J. Beal of the Michigan Agricultural College conducted sound but premature research in corn breeding as early as the seventies, but the effective basis of the modern hybrid strains, with their resistant and high yielding qualities, was laid in the first decade of the new century by George H. Shull at the Cold Springs Harbor Laboratory, by Edward M. East at the Connecticut experiment station, and by R. A. Emerson at the University of Nebraska and at Cornell. Henry A. Wallace of Iowa played a prominent role in the practical utilization of these findings. These scientific findings were not applied in commercial production until the 1930's. In addition to breeding, corn diseases and pests were among the leading concerns of the experiment stations in the Corn Belt.

No less care was bestowed on the lineage and development to marketable maturity of the hogs for which most of the corn was grown. From crosses of native and imported stock of the leading breeds, the most desirable combinations of qualities were secured. The change from the old heavy, lard type of hogs to the lighter, bacon animals in response to consumer desire marked a turning point in the industry. Whatever the breed or type, the traditional lowly hog had become an animal of increasing value, and consequently the epidemics of virulent diseases that attended the concentration of the industry were major calamities to the entire Corn-Hog Belt.

Hog cholera especially presented a mortal threat to the whole Corn Belt economy with a yearly loss reaching 144 per thousand in 1897. After long and patient experiment in a laboratory at Ames, Iowa, Dr. Marion Dorset, biochemist for the Federal Department of Agriculture, with the assistance of veterinary colleagues, developed a preventive serum that was given practical application in 1913. By the time the nation entered the First World War, the losses of the pork supply had been cut by more than half.[33]

In general, progressive methods, early, varied, and wide adoption of machinery, prevalence of occupational organizations, and relatively high living standards were characteristic of the region in its maturity. Continuing fertility, in spite of serious erosion spots, the rising price level from the late nineties, and the limited extent of the true Prairies, along with speculative estimates of future trends, steadily raised the value of land. By the first decade of the new century, the high price of farm land

---

[32] Paul de Kruif, *Hunger Fighters,* Book III; U. S. Department of Agriculture, *Yearbook, 1936,* pp. 455-522.

[33] de Kruif, *Hunger Fighters,* Book II, has a readable story, but the fullest and most authoritative account of the long and patient struggle to combat animal diseases is in the U. S. Department of Agriculture, *Yearbook,* 1942.

was causing large numbers of prospective young farmers to migrate from the region to the American or Canadian Northwest or to the South.

A direct accompaniment of and, in considerable part, a result of the appreciated land values was a marked increase in tenancy. In the three leading Prairie states, the percentage of tenant holders increased from 26.3 in 1880 to 36.4 in 1910. Tenancy in the Corn Belt offered a marked contrast to that in the Cotton Belt. The high and mounting value of land made it increasingly difficult for a young farmer without adequate capital to buy and equip a farmstead. On the other hand, the success of an undertaking made possible relatively high cash rentals and enabled older farmers to rent their holdings, frequently to relatives, and to retire to an adjoining town or to the mild climate of southern California. There was in this generally favorable situation the obvious menace of an inflationary land boom, and a pressing credit need that limited and hampered the development and best utilization of the rising investment in a corn farm.

With all the risks and uncertainties inseparable from a highly capitalized and increasingly commercialized enterprise, the relative longtime advantages of this peculiarly favored environment were evident. Its dominant position in the nation's bulk food production seemed permanently established. In national leadership the primacy of the region was recognized in the influence of its representatives in agricultural organizations and in the continuous selection of the head and key administrators of the Department of Agriculture from these states. In Congress the equality, at least, of Corn Belt with Cotton Belt was steadily maintained.

Thus, in its localizing as well as in its other tendencies the agricultural industry was attaining a coordinate position with other industries. Consequently, farming for the first time was confronted, within the natural limitations of this branch of the economy, with the opportunities as well as the liabilities of modern business. Certainly as compared with earlier tentative and more or less subsistence ventures, the "new agriculture" was relatively permanent and systematized. The period from about 1898 to the World War I era has generally been regarded as one of exceptional stability and relative well being for the American farmer. Scientific findings and verified practices had removed or reduced many of the uncertainties and devastating losses in production. The growth of population and the expansion of industry were creating strong and steadily growing demand. Marketing agencies and systems were becoming more efficient and economical. In the more prosperous and progressive areas rural standards of living were rising markedly. Farm and home mechanization and modernization were removing or alleviating primitive drudgery and discomfort. Rural delivery of mail, local telephones, daily newspapers, improved roads, and consolidated schools and "functionalized" community churches were breaking up the isolated situation and bringing the countryside into the full current of modern industrial society.

Unhappily, there was a darker side to rural America as it appeared in the first decade of the new century. For the agricultural as for all other modern businesses, specialized and intensified output along with its possibilities of increasing gains brought corresponding hazards and maladjustments. Credit necessities not adequately met by the initial state and Federal land banks; speculative land values; the mounting burden of the general property tax; changing consumer demands at home and the decline of the market for most agricultural commodities in the always precarious export trade; the menace of the depletion of soil resources by cropping and erosion; the ever-present diseases and pests of plants and animals, intensified by the high degree of cultivation and breeding; the economical and social limitations of a steadily mounting tenancy and the physical and human wastes of the croppers and other underprivileged inhabitants of the nation's "rural slums"; all these were emergent and immediately pressing problems in the adjustment of the basic occupation to an industrialized business, and the answers to most of them seemed not forthcoming.

Consequently, the assumption that the relative stability and parity position would have persisted but for the catastrophe of world war is wholly contrary to the long time trend and the immediate condition of the economy. When the international storm broke on the fateful July day in 1914 the pendulum of the business cycle was definitely moving toward a depression in which agriculture as always must have met disorganization and retardation.

Agricultural Participation in the First World War

The period of relatively well-adjusted and balanced conditions in American agriculture from the recovery of the late nineties was brusquely interrupted by the outbreak of war in Europe.[34] So far as agricultural production and marketing are concerned, the war period extended from the fall of 1914 to the spring of 1921; and comparisons may most helpfully be made with the preceding five-year average. During the first two years, neutral trade did not stimulate agricultural production to any marked degree. In fact, with the cessation of regular European trade certain commodities, notably cotton, were depressed. But with the large loans to Great Britain and France, followed by the entry of this nation into the conflict as the provisioner of the Allies, basic agricultural commodities were given unprecedented public stimulation. In the spirit of the popular slogan, "Food will win the war," the main effort of the Department of

[34] B. H. Hibbard, *Effects of the Great War Upon Agriculture in the United States and Great Britain.* New York: Oxford University Press, 1919; U. S. Dept. of Agriculture, *Yearbook, 1940,* pp. 277-296.

Agriculture was directed to increasing the production of cereals and meat.

The program was put into action largely through a new extension service created by the Smith-Lever Act of 1914 and implemented by the county-agent system with a co-operating farmers' organization, most frequently the Farm Bureau. Owing to the suddenness and the unprecedented magnitude of the demand along with the unusual need for certain products the undertaking "was inevitably an uneven, faulty expansion which threw out of gear no little of the favorable adjustment that had been achieved before the war." [35]

With the emergency food requirements of the Allied armies and populations, and with the cutting off or sharp curtailment of ordinary sources of supply in Russia and South America, wheat came to be the cultivated product most urgently in demand. The production program thus centered on this enterprise, and the price was pegged at what seemed, in comparison with past levels, a most attractive return. As a result the wheat acreage was increased over 50 per cent and wheat production 38 per cent. The bulk of this increase was in winter wheat, and the added acreage was provided at the expense of other small grains, corn, and grasslands. Over one-quarter of the new wheat lands was located in the Corn Belt and most of the remainder in the pasturage and forest areas of the Great Plains. In livestock industries the demand for fats gave the greatest boom to hog production. In comparison with the pre-war 5-year average of 450,000,000 pounds in exports of pork and lard, over 1,000,000,000 pounds were shipped abroad in 1918.

The remarkable increase in the export of concentrated milks, together with the larger domestic consumption of milk and its products resulting from the increased purchasing power of workers, added more than 1,500,000 head to the country's dairy cows and led to a general expansion of the dairying enterprise. Even on the basis of war demand such expansion was often unsound; for in general dairy prices were unfavorable in comparison with the cost of feed. Much the same condition prevailed in the poultry business where increased war demand was met at an unfavorable ratio of costs of production.

Following an overextension and overproduction of the cotton crop in 1914, exports were reduced during the war period by about one-fourth. In spite of this reduction, general business stimulation, increased industrial demand, and inflation brought a record crop in 1919 valued at $2,000,000,000. Tobacco acreage expanded gradually and the price rose threefold, mainly by reason of the increased demand of soldiers and civilians for cigarettes; the period marked the beginning of the present-day spectacular consumption of this product.

The conclusion reached by the most reliable statistical studies is that

[35] U. S. Dept. of Agriculture, *Yearbook, 1940*, p. 292.

the farmers' return in the war years was by no means excessive. The three years, 1917–1919, were the only ones of the period that could be characterized as relatively good, and returns varied greatly for different enterprises. Thus, while prices of wheat, tobacco, and hogs were relatively high, those of horses, cattle, butter, and eggs ranged relatively low. Inflated values were largely responsible for the general high level of prices and this influence increased markedly, and at times disproportionately, the farmers' production and living costs. A special element in mounting costs for the new or extending proprietor was that of land values, which for the country as a whole went up as much as 70 per cent from 1913 to 1920. This rise was most spectacular in the Corn Belt. Meantime, intensified and extended mechanization added to capital charges.

For agriculture two of the most positive results of the war were thus the greatly multiplied rent, interest, and tax charges, and the expansion and in certain cases the derangement of production belts, as illustrated most strikingly by the extension of wheat growing in the Corn Belt and the Great Plains. Both of these developments endangered regional balance and security.

These danger signs were little heeded amid the seeming, if wholly spurious, evidences of indefinitely continuing post-war prosperity. The postponment of a general market break due to the temporary stimulation of extended European credit, an accumulated backlog of purchasing power, and a liberal discount rate all helped to create the delusion that a continued high output from the farm would find profitable outlet. In spite of disturbing trends in the market early in 1920, at late as the season of fairs in the fall the outlook appeared promising and predictions were generally optimistic. Hence, the drop in wheat prices in December that started a general break caught individual farmers, marketing organizations, and governmental agencies quite unprepared. It was all too evident that the "new agriculture," with all of its efficiency in production, was hopelessly ineffective in providing security for its markets.

Selected References

Barger, Harold and H. H. Landsberg, *American Agriculture, 1899-1939*. New York: National Bureau of Economic Research, 1942.

Buck, S. J., *The Granger Movement*. Cambridge, Mass.: Harvard University Press, 1913.

Eliot, Clara, *The Farmer's Campaign for Credit*. New York: D. Appleton, 1927.

Hibbard, B. H., *Marketing Agricultural Products*. New York: D. Appleton, 1921.

Hicks, J. D., *The Populist Revolt*. Minneapolis: University of Minnesota Press, 1931.

Nourse, E. G., *American Agriculture and the European Market*. New York: McGraw-Hill Book Company, 1929.

Rogin, Leo, *The Introduction of Farm Machinery In its Relation to the Productivity of Labor in the Agriculture of the United States During the Nineteenth Century*. Berkeley, California: University of California Press, 1931.

Ross, E. D., *Democracy's College: the Land-Grant Movement in the Formative Stage*. Ames, Iowa: Iowa State College Press, 1942.

Shannon, F. A., *The Farmer's Last Frontier*. New York: Farrar and Rinehart, 1945.

United States Department of Agriculture, *Reports of the Commissioner, 1862-1888*. Washington: Government Printing Office.

———, *Reports of the Secretary, 1889-1920*. Washington: Government Printing Office.

———, *Yearbook of Agriculture, 1894-1920*. Washington: Government Printing Office.

21 · THE PASTORAL ECONOMY OF THE WEST

CATTLE AND SHEEP RAISING comprised the first major economic enterprise of our western pioneers, although fur traders and Santa Fe traffickers had preceded them by several decades. When Juan de Oñate moved with his colonists up the Rio Grande Valley to plant Spain's northernmost outpost at San Juan, New Mexico, he drove before him cattle and sheep, as did Spanish settlers entering southern California a little more than a century and a half later. Indeed, a pastoral economy was well advanced in Spain's northern borderlands by the time the Anglo-Americans arrived there during the early nineteenth century.

The Great Plains was the first geographic province of the Far West occupied by the westward advancing Anglo-Americans. Here were vast prairies imperceptibly rising from 1,000 feet along their eastern border to 6,000 feet at the base of the Rocky Mountains. They comprised about two-thirds of the Louisiana Territory acquired from France by the United States in 1803 and were unlike any other geographic province heretofore settled.[1]

In 1804 Meriwether Lewis and William Clark began their crossing of the northern plains while enroute to the Oregon coast, and in 1806–1807 Z. M. Pike transversed the Kansas and Texas parts of the southern plains. Thirteen years later, Major Stephen H. Long visited the same general area, journeying from the Missouri River to the Rocky Mountains via the South Platte, thence southward to New Mexico, and then descending the Canadian River to Fort Smith, Arkansas. Pike thought that the Great Plains was a desert, too arid for the white man's settlement, and Long concurred in this opinion. He wrote "Great American Desert" across the Great Plains part of a map in his report to the Department of War. And for many years geographers accepted this designation.

Cattlemen were among the first Great Plains visitors to believe that this area was not a desert. To them, the region was a rancher's paradise—

[1] The most authoritative book on The Great Plains is W. P. Webb, *The Great Plains.* Boston: Ginn and Company, 1931. See also Willard D. Johnson, "The High Plains and Their Utilization," in twenty-first and twenty-second annual reports of the United States Geologic Survey, Part IV of both volumes. Washington, D. C.: 1901-1902.

a vast sea of mesquite, blue-stem and grama grasses, enough perennial streams of good water, and free government land upon which to graze their cattle. Saddle horses and equipment, a dugout or sodhouse for a home, and sod or pole corrals, sheds, and a barn completed a rancher's simple needs. Vast herds of fat antelope (pronghorns), bison, deer, and elk grazing the prairies were proof enough that the ranges would also support cattle.

But the bison, or "wild cattle," as the *conquistadores* called them, must first be destroyed before the cattlemen could move in. Formerly, these great shaggy animals had been the red man's commissary. Now they were to afford the white pioneer a temporary but ready means of employment.

Destruction of the American Bison [2]

During the period 1820–1880, both red and white hunters reduced the ranks of Great Plains bison, for both hides and meat were media of exchange. Buffalo robes were in demand along the frontier, and large quantities of meat were also needed by Federal troops stationed at Great Plains posts.

There is little doubt that millions of bison were killed by hunters from 1820 to 1870, yet millions of them remained, even though emigrants passing over the Mormon, Oregon, and other trails increased the rate of destruction. In 1849 Captain Howard Stansbury commented on the trail hunters' deadly work, stating that to find bison his own hunters had to travel great distances on either side of the Mormon Trail. Three years later Colonel Alexander Doniphan encountered the southern herd in southwestern Kansas. His chief hunter, Thomas Forsythe, computed the herd at 300,000 bison and other hunters with him estimated it at from 200,000 to 800,000. But they could not see the herd's outer edge in any direction.

Four years earlier Colonel John C. Fremont wrote of American Fur Company figures showing that for over a decade the Upper Missouri Indians had annually sold to white traders 90,000 robes. Since buffalo were killed for this purpose only four months in the year, he believed that the Indians' yearly slaughter of bison approximated 120,000; but another contemporary authority placed it at 400,000 annually or about 5,000,000 within the period 1835–1845. During the next twenty-five years the slaughter was intensified, but it was only an earnest of what was to follow.

American and English tanning tests during the early 1870's proved that buffalo hides could be used in shoe and harness manufacture; so within the next few years hundreds of hunters, in parties large and small, moved into the buffalo country to supply this new market. Buffalo hunting was

---

[2] Douglas Branch, *The Hunting of the Buffalo*. New York: D. Appleton-Century Company, 1929. John R. Cook, *The Border and the Buffalo*. Topeka: Crane and Company, 1907.

now quite profitable, since hides sold at $1 to $3 each and a party of six hunters could kill and skin upward of 100 bison a day.

Within three years, 1872–1874, western dealers shipped 1,374,359 hides, 6,751,200 pounds of meat, and 32,380,850 pounds of bones to eastern markets over the Santa Fe, the Union Pacific, and the Kansas Pacific railroads. Large caravans moved additional thousands of buffalo hides, meat, and bones to nearer markets. With their Springfield rifles ("Big Fifties") the hunters followed the herds from watering place to grazing ground, slaying hundreds of thousands. On one occasion, Colonel Dodge rode for more than 100 miles along the South Platte without being free of the stench of dead buffaloes.

The great slaughter reached its peak in 1877. On an early January day the F. E. Conrad general merchandise store at Fort Griffin, Texas, sold goods worth more than $4,000, of which $2,500 represented buffalo guns and ammunition. In this same year Reynolds City, seventy-five miles farther west, boasted a $1,000,000 hide trade, and other neighboring hide-buying stations were almost as successful.

General Nelson A. Miles, who saw much of the "Great Kill," [3] stated later that 4,373,730 bison were slain during the early 1870's, while another observer placed the number at a million more. At best, however, available data are incomplete. Conservative figures indicate that during the 13-year period, 1870–1883, hunters killed a grand total of 10,000,000 bison, the approximate value of whose hides was about $25,000,000.

Texas legislators talked of hunting restrictions during the early years of the "Great Kill," but Lieutenant General P. H. Sheridan dissuaded them, warning that only by killing the bison could the Indians be tamed and the Great Plains opened for "speckled cattle." So the enactment was not passed and the slaughter went on. By 1880 the last of the southern herd was gone, and by 1883 Sitting Bull and his Sioux warriors had killed those remaining in the northern herd. Then, with their "wild commissary" destroyed, the nomadic Indians accepted the reservation way of life offered them by the Federal Government, and ranchers moved their cattle onto the grassy High Plains.

The Range Cattle Industry [4]

"Speckled cattle," of which Sheridan had spoken, had grazed the Texas timbered and brush-covered ranges long before the bison were destroyed.

---

[3] M. S. Garretson, *The American Bison, the Story of Its Extermination as a Wild Species and Its Restoration Under Federal Protection*. New York: New York Zoological Society, 1938. See also Carl Coke Rister, "The Significance of the Destruction of the Buffalo," *Southwestern Historical Quarterly*, Vol. XXXIII (July, 1929).

[4] For dependable, early-day accounts of western ranching, see Joseph G. McCoy, *Historic Sketches of the Cattle Trade of the West and Southwest*. Kansas City: J. T. Reton and Company, 1874 (reprinted, Washington: 1932); Joseph Nimmo, "Range and Ranch Cattle Traffic," in *House Executive Documents*, No. 267, 48th Cong. 2nd session.

As in New Mexico and California, Spanish settlers had driven cattle and sheep to pasturelands in southern Texas throughout the first half of the eighteenth century, and after the independence of Mexico was established in 1821 these pastoral pursuits were encouraged. For example, in 1825 the new Mexican State of Coahuila-Texas promulgated a land law offering each prospective settler one *labor* (177 acres) of land for farming and one *sitio* (4,428 acres) for ranching. Such encouragement by 1836 brought cattle grazing to about four-fifths of the settled but unplowed parts of this State. Yet many years were to elapse before the Texas range cattle industry gained great importance.

Anglo-American pioneers had started the cattle industry in other western areas. In Oregon, Dr. John McLaughlin had imported bulls and milch cows by the 1820's and had permitted settlers near Fort Vancouver to use his cows with the understanding that he was to retain their permanent ownership, as well as the annual calf crop. But finally the settlers broke up this monopoly when they drove their own cattle from California. When the Mormons arrived in Utah in 1847 they bought Miles Goodyear's Great Basin ranch with its 75 cattle, 75 goats, 12 sheep and 6 horses; these they added to herds they had driven over the Mormon Trail, and grazed them on their pasturelands. But in neither area did ranching gain the major importance that it did on the Great Plains.

It was not until after the Civil War that the western range cattle industry became nationally significant. Hundreds of thousands of "mavericks," [5] or unbranded wild cattle, then grazed Texas grasslands and offered employment to many ex-soldiers. In Kansas, a fat two-year-old steer was worth $40; on the Texas range, only $6 or $7. Here was an opportunity hardly equalled during pre-war days. If an adventurous cowman could round up 1,500 of the longhorn steers ranging along the border and drive them through the lawless Indian country to market in Missouri or Kansas, he could sell them for $60,000. Of course, he would have to pay the expenses of the "Long Drive"—a small sum for flour, soda, bacon and beans; the monthly wages ($25 to $40) of his cowboys and $125 for a trail boss; and additional expenditures for other minor needs. But even when these costs were subtracted the cowman still had left a handsome profit.

The first "Long Drive" was made during the late summer of 1865, when a Texan sold his steers at Sedalia, Missouri, for $35 each. When he brought home the electrifying news of his accomplishment, many excited, penniless neighbors sought to duplicate his success; and they succeeded.

Westward building railroads supplied markets at their termini—at Sedalia, Missouri, and at Abilene, Ellsworth, Newton, and Dodge City, Kansas, towns that also became the rendezvous of gamblers, gunmen, and

[5] During the pre-Civil War period unbranded cattle on Samuel A. Maverick's Conquista farm were marked and claimed by enterprising neighbors, thus starting the use of the term "Maverick."

prostitutes. These railroads furnished new shipping points farther west as farmers moved out to claim free government land along the border, thus making necessary new cattle trails. At first the East and West Shawnee trails, running from Texas through eastern Indian Territory to Sedalia and Kansas City, were used by Texas drovers. But Missouri and Kansas farmers forced them to seek routes farther west when it was found that Texas trail herds left along the way a mysterious fever that infected their own cattle, although Texas cattle were immune to it. This was "tick fever" but Missourians and Kansans did not know its cause. Later, the true cause of the fever was known and state laws providing for cattle "dipping" were enacted.

In 1867 Joseph G. McCoy, an Illinois cattle dealer, opened another major trail across Indian Territory by building stock-pens at Abilene, Kansas, at the terminus of the Kansas Pacific Railroad in north central Kansas, and by sending riders southward to invite drovers to trail their herds to this new shipping point. Texas cattle soon crowded Abilene's stock-pens and celebrating cowboys gave local merchants and citizens many uneasy moments by shooting up the town by day and by thronging the "cesspools of iniquity" (saloons, bawdy houses, and gambling dens) at night. Only mining towns rivaled the Kansas cattle-shipping towns in lawlessness.

Cattle driven to Kansas markets numbered 75,000 in 1868; 350,000 in 1869; and more than 600,000 in 1871. The Chisholm Trail, over which cattle were driven to Abilene, lost its importance when home seekers took up and fenced their claims astride it. Then the Western Trail, crossing the Red River at Doan's Store and extending to Dodge City via Camp Supply, was still another major route used. Joseph Nimmo reported that over a period of nineteen years, beginning in 1866, more than 5,200,000 cattle were driven from the Texas ranges to Kansas, Missouri, and Nebraska markets over these northern trails. At an average price of $20 per steer, the sale of these cattle would have netted their owners almost $100,000,000.

But all the cattle driven northward were not sold at the cowtowns; thousands were fattened on corn in Kansas and Nebraska or used to stock northern ranges. Many thousand steers were also driven over the Goodnight-Loving Trail, from Fort Concho, Texas, to Horsehead Crossing of the Pecos, and then up this river to new ranch country in New Mexico, or farther north to other states and territories. Of more than 100,000 cattle passing over this trail in 1870, 20,000 animals were driven to Montana, 8,000 to Wyoming, 11,000 to Idaho, 7,000 to Nevada, 8,000 to Utah, and 10,000 to California. The remaining 36,000 or more cattle were driven to the Pecos and Rio Grande ranges of New Mexico.

From Texas, by the 1870's, bonanza ranching had fanned out to the Laramie Valley of Wyoming, to the Beaverhead of Montana, and to the

Dakotas, Idaho, New Mexico, Colorado, and Arizona. Within these areas cattle ranching prospered in spite of drought and blizzard, and at the same time the Texas frontier was checkerboarded with ranches for a depth of 100 miles. So pressing were the cattlemen's common problems that by 1877 the Northwestern Texas Cattle Raisers' Association was organized to oversee roundups upon these generally unfenced properties, to guard against cattle "rustling," and to provide other necessary safeguards. And as the industry spread northward and westward other similar organizations appeared: the Cherokee Strip Livestock Association, the Colorado Cattle Raisers' Association, and the Wyoming Stock Raisers' Association, for example.

Not uncommonly, the early-day rancher was a tenant-at-will squatting on the public domain or leasing his land at a nominal rental. In either case his expenditures were small. He built his own sodhouse or dugout and appurtenant corrals and sheds; he hired his cowboys at modest monthly wages, and his expenditures for supplies each year were also small. At the end of the year he could ordinarily sell enough cattle to meet these expenditures and still have enough of his original herd and his calf crop left to give him more cattle than he had the preceding year. By thrifty management he could normally expect to gain financial independence within a few years.

News of such successes quickly spread to every part of the nation, and even to Europe, and hundreds of would-be cowmen came to the West to make investments. They, too, squatted on the public domain and bought cattle for their ranges. As a consequence, the market felt this enlarged demand for range stock. Cattle that had sold in Texas at from $10 to $20, now brought from $40 to $60 on the northern ranges. Presently every likely grass range was crowded to the point of overstocking and seasoned ranchers could plainly see the handwriting on the wall, for the spiraling market and over-grazed ranges must surely bring disaster.

Great Plains promoters advertised far and wide the fabulous returns to be made in ranching. By 1880 the development of western ranching was such that range-fed beef even threatened the English market, and Parliament sent a committee to America to find the reasons why this was so. The committee brought back a report showing that the maintenance cost of Great Plains ranching was negligible and that profits of 30 per cent or more were not uncommon. This report caused a wave of speculation in England and Scotland. Edinburgh, Scotland, became an investment center and both English and Scotch corporations were formed to exploit what were thought to be New World opportunities in cattle ranching. In 1882 the Wyoming Stock Raisers' Association estimated that foreign investments, largely in Texas and Wyoming, amounted to $30,000,000; and two years later, Representative N. W. Nutting of New York reported to Congress that foreign interests controlled 20,000,000 acres of Great Plains ranch lands and threatened to absorb the entire western ranching industry.

Titled Europeans sought to create baronial estates in the American West. The Marquis de Mores, a Frenchman, built the town of Medora on the Union Pacific Railroad in western Dakota and bought up a nearby acreage. Farther south, in Colorado, Baron von Richthofen, a German, acquired a large property, with the Earl of Dunraven, an Englishman, as his Estes Park neighbor. John George Adair, an Irishman who owned a large estate at Rathdairs, Ireland, bought part interest in Charles Goodnight's Palo Duro Canyon Ranch, near present-day Amarillo, Texas.

The Scottish American Mortgage Company controlled three large properties: the Arkansas Ranch, extending from the Arkansas River in Colorado on the north to the Colorado-New Mexico line on the south, comprising 2,240,000 acres; the Cimarron Ranch, in northeastern New Mexico, extending 24 miles from the Colorado line to the south line of Mora County, an area of 2,580,000 acres; and the Canadian Ranch, in Potter and Oldham counties of Texas, of 256,000 acres. More than 140,000 cattle grazed these three properties. Other English and Scottish investments were in the Espuela (Spur) Land and Cattle Company of western Texas, the Wyoming Ranches Limited, and the Western Land and Cattle Company with interests in California, Montana, and Wyoming, and the Swan Land and Cattle Company of Wyoming.

In contrast, most of the earlier American ranches were individual enterprises. For example, in 1870 the John King Ranch on the Santa Gertrudes River in southern Texas was an important property of 84,032 acres and supported 65,000 cattle and thousands of horses, sheep, and goats. Mifflin Kennedy's Robideaux Ranch, on a peninsula of the Gulf of Mexico, embraced 142,840 acres and grazed 30,000 cattle. Yet there were a few corporate American ranches. In the 1880's a Chicago syndicate agreed to build the Texas capitol at Austin in exchange for 3,050,000 acres of land in nine Texas Panhandle counties. This huge property, known as the XIT Ranch, required a three-strand wire fence of 781¼ miles to inclose it; it ranged more than 150,000 cattle.

The 1880's saw notable changes. The cattle trails to Kansas markets were abandoned. Recently invented barbed wire was used widely in the prairie country. Farmers claiming free government land strung wire athwart the cattle trails, and the westward-building railroads made possible new cattle-shipping towns well within the cow country.

The range cattle industry, too, presently came on evil days. Overstocking the range and the annual marketing of far more cattle than the normal rate of consumption required depressed prices. While the Kansas, New Mexico, and Texas ranges were already overstocked, the Department of the Interior made matters worse by forcing cattlemen ranging their herds in Indian Territory to drive them out. More than 200,000 cattle were driven onto contiguous ranges, where, half-starved, they were caught by the fierce blizzards of 1886-1887, many thousands dying along a drift fence built across the Texas Panhandle. By the following spring bondholders took over many hard-hit ranches. Some cattlemen escaped disaster by breaking up their properties into 160-acre tracts and selling them to farmers; others turned to sheep ranching.

These years of depression marked the beginning of a new era in cattle raising and the end of the distinctly pastoral era. The first period was characterized by the longhorns, grazing the public domain, the long drives, and cattle trails. The new era was marked by improved cattle (Herefords, Shorthorns, and Polled Angus), fencing of properties, corporation-owned ranches, and by railroads furnishing cattle-shipping points well within the ranching country. The average ranch of this period was smaller than that of the free range era, but it was better equipped and organized and to some degree it was mechanized. Quantity in cattle raising gave place to quality.

The Sheep Industry [6]

Many of those cowmen who turned to sheep raising during the hard years of 1885–1887 met with surprising success. In some respects the sheep industry was as well suited to the semi-arid mountain and plateau regions of the West as the cattle industry was to the Great Plains grasslands. In the plateau and mountain country were water holes and swift streams, along which was fine pasturage. Shepherds knew the location of every green oasis, vega, grassy hillslope, mountainside, and valley and led their sheep from one to the other so that they could have adequate pasturage.

Although sheep raising differed in many respects from cattle raising, there were a few similarities. Like the cattleman, the sheep rancher started with poor-quality animals—the *chaurros.* And in some instances he also had princely properties, drove his sheep in flocks of several thousand to market over well-traveled trails, and encountered many of the problems of the cattlemen. In other respects sheep ranching was quite unlike cattle ranching, and life was different from that on a cattle ranch. Spanish tradition and practice strongly influenced the sheepman. Indeed, a large per cent of the sheepmen of New Mexico, Texas, Arizona and California were Spanish-Americans.

Oñate, previously mentioned, brought sheep to New Mexico at the close of the sixteenth century, and *conquistadores* and *padres* had driven numerous other flocks into Texas, Arizona, and California. Later, the

---

6 The most complete study on the sheep industry is Edward Norris Wentworth, *America's Sheep Trails.* Ames, Iowa: Iowa State College Press, 1948. See also Winifred Kupper, *The Golden Hoof.* New York: Alfred A. Knopf, 1945.

Anglo-American fell heir to the Spanish *chaurros,* lean, gaunt sheep of coarse wool and tough, strongly flavored flesh, and by cross-breeding he soon improved the flocks on the former Spanish-American ranges. In addition, he imported other breeds—Cotswolds, Lincolns, Merinos, Shropshires, and Southdowns.

Occasionally western sheep ranches were more highly organized than cattle ranches. An example was the Callahan ranch of southern Texas which employed four grades of workmen. The *pastor* (shepherd) was the lowest in rank. He was directly in charge of a flock of 1,000 or more sheep over which he kept watch, assisted only by his dog. A *vaquero* (a rider), next in rank, supervised the work of two or three *pastores,* selected each day's grazing range and attended to other minor duties. A *caporal* (range boss) had charge over about the same number of *vaqueros* and was directly responsible to the *majordomo* (superintendent). The far-spreading acreages of New Mexico *ricos* (wealthy landowners) lent themselves to large-scale sheep raising and to patronistic control.

Within the chaparral-mesquite-pricklypear country of Texas, Anglo-American settlers early found sheep ranching profitable, but it was not until after the Civil War that it was developed on a large scale. For many years the border was unsettled and Mexican and Apache outlawry constituted a serious handicap. Military commanders of the Department of Texas often reported sheep rancher losses, both in property and lives. But the death of Victorio, the Apache renegade leader of Rio Grande raiders, finally brought comparative security to this distracted region. After these troublous years southern Texas sheep ranching prospered. From 1880 to 1884 Texas sheep increased from 5,940,700 to 8,035,700, or an increase of about 33 1/3 per cent.

In southern and western Texas the Merino was favored. It was a better herd sheep and its mutton and wool were superior to those of the *chaurros.* Ranchers paid their Mexican herders as low as $12 per month, with an additional $6 for food. Thus, with a few herders at low pay handling large flocks of Merinos, the rancher could expect more than average profits. From 1,000 ewes he could count on more than 800 lambs annually and an average of 5,000 pounds of wool which sold at thirty cents a pound, or more.

But New Mexico was best suited to sheep raising. This territory had been the incubator of the southwestern sheep industry as Texas had been of the range cattle industry. Annually, from 1821 to 1846, New Mexicans drove to Mexico, via the Rio Grande Valley, not less than 200,000 sheep. About four-fifths of these sheep came from the ranches of the *ricos,* of whom Colonel Chaves was a leader. In 1839 he drove 75,000 sheep to Mexico. Later, he estimated that the general New Mexican annual drive southward reached about 1,000,000 sheep, although other available sources indicate that his estimate was too liberal.

By 1865, thousands of long-legged, short-wool New Mexican sheep grazed the green meadows, mountainsides, and valleys of Las Animas, Huerfano, and Conejos counties in southern Colorado. Then this penetration was deepened and widened; Colorado's eastern plains region, from Las Animas to Weld county, was dotted with the flocks of the New Mexican *pastores*. In 1876, the year in which it achieved statehood, one authority believed that Colorado gave pasturage to 2,500,000 sheep, sold 7,000,000 pounds of wool, and had a crop of 1,000,000 lambs annually.

Anglo-American settlers gave impetus to New Mexico's sheep industry by improving the herds and by finding new markets. They drove tens of thousands of Merinos to neighboring states and territories—as far west as California and as far north as Montana. The federal census of 1880 listed 2,990,700 sheep in New Mexico, not as large as a normal increase would have made possible. However, surplus flocks had been driven to distant ranges.

A static sheep industry in California, inherited from the Spanish settlers, finally came to life during the hectic days of the gold rush. Tens of thousands of eager argonauts poured into California's gold regions, congesting towns and communities and consuming food surpluses. A consequent demand for all kinds of meat created a healthy market for mutton, and presently New Mexicans appeared with their flocks. But it was not until 1853 that the price of wool became an added market stimulus. In this year W. W. Hollister devoted his attention to woolgrowing in southern California. His success encouraged other ranchers to turn to sheep raising, for chances for profit in both mutton and wool were excellent. By the end of this decade the many ships putting in at Pacific ports had landed thousands of Cotswolds, Lincolns, and Shropshires to stock California ranches.

There were also other reasons for California's excellent start in sheep ranching. Its climate was salubrious, its rainfall adequate, its soil fertile, and its green fields could supply the ranches with fodder to supplement range grasses. In summer the shepherds drove their flocks to the hills, where pasturage was sufficient; when the autumn rains began they returned to the foothills and plains, now covered with green grass. There was little danger of depressing the market, because every ship putting in at Los Angeles, Monterey, or San Francisco brought many other immigrants, and this caused food prices to remain high.

By 1875, Fresno, Los Angeles, Mendocino, San Joaquin, Colusa, Merced, and Sonoma counties each grazed from 100,000 to 300,000 sheep. Five years later Californians drove 40,000 Merinos to New Mexico (and many other thousands to other western states and territories), thus returning the favor that the New Mexicans had done them during gold rush days. Other neighboring territories also profited from these drives. The Governor of Utah, however, complained that Californians had driven "immense herds . . . of fifteen, twenty, and thirty thousand sheep" onto his already overstocked ranges and that they would "poison and kill" the buffalo grass and leave the range bare.

In this territory sheep ranching was already a major industry. The Mormons imported improved breeds of sheep, although the Merino predominated. Up to 1870 New Mexicans had driven their flocks from the south into Utah, and others from Kansas, Nebraska, and Missouri were brought over the Mormon Trail. The Utah legislature encouraged this movement by exempting sheep from taxation for the first few years. This state's yearly increase of population was an added stimulus; immigrants not only brought flocks of sheep but, in order to be independent of Gentile industry, they also brought spinning wheels, looms and cards. Woolen mills, too, presently appeared. By 1882 Utah possessed 10 woolen mills, one of which was equipped with 3,000 spindles. Others were cooperative enterprises; the Provo Manufacturing Company, for instance, reputed to be the largest woolen mill west of the Missouri River. But the Mormons found that their mills could process only one-fourth of their annual wool crop; the remaining three-fourths was sent east, to be returned as clothing and blankets.

Not uncommonly, Mormon sheepmen owned large ranches, as in Millard, San Pete, and Emery counties in central Utah, and in Jaub, Utah, and Wasatch counties farther north. Others ranged their flocks along the Colorado and Green River basins. In this manner, Arizona and Nevada profited from Utah's overflow, although the industry in these two areas was never large. From 1875 to 1880 Utah's wool clip averaged 1,500,000 pounds annually, the fleece running about four pounds for ewes and six for wethers.

Farther north, in Montana, Idaho, Dakota, Washington, and Oregon, ranchers had to guard their flocks against prolonged and severe winters by providing warm shelter and adequate fodder. Such close supervision and requirements militated against large ranches, although there were many prosperous small ones.

In 1876, while Montana was still Sioux country, a Mr. Burgess drove a mixed Cotswold-Merino flock of 1,400 sheep from California to this territory, having consumed two seasons on the trail. He located on the Tongue River, not far from Miles City. In the following fall he sold his sheep to George M. Miles, who moved them to a point about 14 miles above the mouth of the Tongue. The new owner could not entirely guard his flock against predatory animals and cold weather; consequently he had little increase. He profited by experience, however, and in 1879 he was able to ship to Philadelphia 3,000 pounds of wool for which he received 32 cents per pound, or $960. This success caused Miles' neighbors to engage in sheep ranching and, presently, many thousand sheep to stock the ranches were driven to Montana from California, Oregon, and Washington. Yet sheep ranching in Montana had its limitations, the most formidable of which was that cowmen had largely preempted the best ranges.

Elsewhere in the West the meeting of the frontiers of these two industries engendered rivalry and strife. The cowman bitterly resented the sheepman's encroachment upon his range. He complained that the sheep's cutting hoofs destroyed the grassy turf and that cattle would not drink at watering places where sheep had been. Nor were shepherd traditions to his liking. Many shepherds were Spanish-Americans, and their way of life differed from that of the Anglo-American cowman. Along the cowman-sheepman range border, from Mexico to Canada, frequent clashes occurred.

Violence was common. For example, New Mexicans drove their flocks onto the Goodnight Ranch, and aggressive cowboys promptly drowned 400 sheep in the Canadian River. A serious clash was averted when Goodnight and the *pastores* agreed on a division of the range. But elsewhere settlements were not made so peacefully. In Arizona, Colorado, Nevada, Idaho, Wyoming, and Montana, there were struggles for range ownership. During the eighties and nineties sheepmen controlled the Arizona range from Ash Fork to Seligman and seriously encroached on the properties of cowmen. A bitter range war, known as the Graham-Tewksbury feud, followed and twenty-six cowboys and six sheepmen lost their lives before the range problem was solved. In Wyoming, cowmen drove encroaching shepherds from their ranges and stampeded more than 10,000 sheep, forcing them into the mountains to be eaten by wolves; near North Rock Springs, 12,000 sheep were plunged to their death over a cliff.

But sheepmen had certain advantages in these border rivalries. The maintenance costs of their sheep ranches were less than those of cattle ranches. Prices of wool and mutton were more stable than those of beef, and the fact that the sheepmen derived yearly returns from mutton, wool, and lamb crops gave them a triple advantage over the cowman, who sold only beef. By the mid-1880's, therefore, many a cattleman turned his range to sheep grazing. Generally, sheep ranching did not suffer the depression that came to cattle ranching during the last half of the 1880's. In 1903 the western mountain and plateau country ranged more than 30,000,000 of the nation's 63,964,876 sheep.

By 1900 the pastoral West gave place to a more complex era. The farmer with his gang-plow, reaper, dry-farming, and irrigation techniques helped to bring a transition from the old era to the new. Millions of ranch acres became prosperous farms. But the springing up of towns and cities, the increasing use of automobiles by 1910, and the consequent good roads movement; the construction of a network of railroads, telephone, and telegraph lines—all were equally significant. Mechanization ushered in a new period. By reading their livestock journals and by attending county and state fairs and livestock expositions, the ranchers, former leaders of the pastoral West, could now learn the ways of the new period.

Selected References

GENERAL WORKS

Billington, Ray Allen, *Westward Expansion,* Chap. XXXIII. New York: The Macmillan Company, 1949.

Bowles, Samuel, *Our New West,* p. 49. New York: Hartford Publishing Company, 1869.

Hafen, LeRoy R., and Carl Coke Rister, *Western America.* New York: Prentice-Hall, Inc., 1941.

Henry, Stuart, *Conquering Our Great American Plains; a Historical Development.* New York: E. P. Dutton and Company, 1930.

Humphrey, Seth, *Following the Prairie Frontier.* Minneapolis: University of Minnesota Press, 1931.

Paxson, Frederic L., *History of the American Frontier,* Chap. LVI. Boston: Houghton Mifflin Company, 1924.

Richardson, Albert D., *Beyond the Mississippi.* Hartford: National Publishing Company, 1867.

Webb, W. P., *The Great Plains.* Boston: Ginn and Company, 1931.

SPECIAL TOPICS

Adams, Andy, *The Log of a Cowboy.* Boston and New York: Houghton Mifflin Company, 1903.

Allen, J. A., "History of the American Bison," *Ninth Annual Report of the United States Geological and Geographical Survey.* Washington: U.S. Government Printing Office, 1875.

Branch, Douglas, *The Hunting of the Buffalo.* New York: D. Appleton-Century Company, 1929.

Brockett, L. P., *Our Western Empire: or the West Beyond the Mississippi.* San Francisco: William Garretson and Company, 1881.

Bureau of the Census, "Statistics on Agriculture," in *Tenth Census of the United States,* pp. 965-1102. Washington: U.S. Government Printing Office, 1880.

Burton, Harley True, *History of the JA Ranch.* Austin, Texas: Press of Von Boeckmann-Jones Company, 1928.

Chittenden, Hiram, *The American Fur Trade in the Far West* (2 vols.). New York: Press of the Pioneers, 1935.

Cook, John R., *The Border and the Buffalo.* Topeka, Kan.: Crane and Company, 1907.

Craig, John A., *Sheep Farming in North America.* New York: The Macmillan Company, 1920.

Dale, E. E., *The Range Cattle Industry.* Norman, Okla.: The University of Oklahoma Press, 1930.

———, *Cow Country.* Norman, Okla.: The University of Oklahoma Press, 1942.

Dobie, J. Frank, *A Vaquero of the Brush Country.* Dallas: The Southwest Press, 1929.

Dodge, Richard Irving, *Hunting Grounds of the Great West.* New York: G. P. Putnam's Sons, 1877.

Garretson, M. S., *The American Bison, the Story of Its Extermination as a Wild Species and Its Restoration Under Federal Protection.* New York: New York Zoological Society, 1938.

Grinnell, G. B., "Sheep on the Prairies," in *Report of the United States Commissioner of Agriculture.* Washington: U.S. Government Printing Office, 1862.

Haley, J. Evetts, *The XIT Ranch.* Chicago: The Lakeside Press, 1929.

———, *Charles Goodnight.* Boston and New York: Houghton Mifflin Company, 1936.

Hamner, Laura V., *Short Grass and Longhorns.* Norman, Okla.: The University of Oklahoma Press, 1943.

Johnson, Willard D., "The High Plains and Their Utilization," in annual report of the United States Geologic Survey, Vols. XXI, XXII. Washington: U.S. Government Printing Office, 1901-1902.

Kupper, Winifred, *The Golden Hoof.* New York: Alfred A. Knopf, 1945.

McCoy, Joseph G., *Historic Sketches of the Cattle Trade of the West and Southwest.* Kansas City: J. T. Reton and Company, 1874.

Osgood, E. S., *The Day of the Cattleman.* Minneapolis: The University of Minnesota Press, 1929.

Peake, Ora Brooks, *The Colorado Range Cattle Industry.* Glendale, California: Arthur H. Clark Company, 1937.

Pelzer, Louis, *The Cattleman's Frontier.* Glendale, California: Arthur H. Clark Company, 1936.

Randall, Henry S., *Sheep Husbandry.* New York: Orange Judd and Company, 1860.

Richthofen, Walter Baron von, *Cattle Raising on the Plains of North America.* New York: D. Appleton Company, 1885.

Thayer, William M., *Marvels of the New West,* pp. 535-626. Norwich, Conn.: The Henry Bill Publishing Company, 1888.

Wentworth, Edward Norris, *America's Sheep Trails.* Ames, Iowa.: Iowa State College Press, 1948.

Wheeler, Colonel Homer Webster, *Buffalo Days.* Indianapolis: The Bobbs-Merrill Company, 1925.

Wilcox, E. V., "Sheep Ranching in the Western States," in *Nineteenth Annual Report, Bureau of Animal Industry.* Washington: U.S. Department of Agriculture, 1902.

22 · PROCESSING OF AGRICULTURAL PRODUCTS AFTER 1860

AFTER 1860 the agricultural processing industries pretty generally passed into the factory stage. At the same time, they expanded in number and importance, in variety of products, and in volume of output. Industries unknown before 1860, such as candy manufacture, the bottling of carbonated beverages, and the production of vegetable oils, appeared on the scene. Other industries that had started before 1860, such as factory production of dairy products and commercial baking, now grew to major importance. Still others, well established before the Civil War, experienced radical changes in techniques of production and in business organization and management. In all these industries, large-scale production, increasing mechanization, a tendency to concentrate in certain cities or areas, and some elements of monopoly appear after 1860.

Meat Packing

Rise of the Chicago Meat Industry

Up to 1850, Chicago was not an important center of the meat packing industry. The territory north and west of the city was as yet but sparsely settled. There were no railroads into that area and only the lake steamers to give access to Eastern markets. In 1848 there were only six packing houses in Chicago, and their combined output was less than one-tenth that of the Cincinnati packers.[1]

In 1848 the Illinois and Michigan Canal was completed, and in the same year the Chicago and Galena Railroad was opened to service. Together they brought prosperity to Chicago. Hog-raisers who formerly had driven their animals to local markets in central and northern Illinois now shipped them to the new center. The immediate financial success of the Chicago and Galena line inspired the building of other railroads to the Eastern markets and westward into new territory being opened up beyond the Mississippi. Improved transportation not only drew

[1] See H. C. Hill, "The Development of Chicago as a Center of the Meat Packing Industry," *Mississippi Valley Historical Review*, Vol. X (1923-4), pp. 253-273, for a detailed study of this topic.

larger supplies of cattle and hogs to the Chicago market, but it stimulated shipments of meat to distant Eastern markets. Between 1852 and 1860 the number of cattle packed in Chicago doubled and the number of hogs slaughtered tripled. By 1864 Chicago had become the leading packing center of the country.

Of course, this growth was not due solely to the influence of transportation. In the decade after the Civil War many of the farmers in the Chicago territory changed from wheat raising to corn growing. The change-over was accelerated by the chinch-bug, by wheat-rust, and perhaps by "wheat-sick" land. Many farmers in the western part of the new Corn Belt found it profitable to buy range cattle and fatten them for the market. Pigs are a good side line for the cattle raisers: they can be combined with cattle because they eat what cattle waste and they can be pastured with the cattle. Consequently, the popularity of corn growing caused a phenomenal growth in the number of hogs raised in the Corn Belt states, especially after 1860.

By that date the railroads had opened up large areas west of the Mississippi for cattle raising. Cattle ranching has always been associated with frontier life. Great herds raised in Texas moved over the cattle trail to the northern ranges and then were shipped to Chicago for sale to the packers.

A minor but not unimportant cause of the growth of packing in Chicago was the development of the Union Stock Yards. The slaughter-houses at first provided their own storage facilities: pens for the hogs, and pastures at the outskirts of the town for the cattle. Then the railroads established stockyards in various sections of the city, each railroad for a time having its own yard. In 1865 nine railroads combined to establish the Union Stock Yards. Covering 300 acres and containing facilities for unloading 500 cars at a time, they were the largest stockyards in the world. Both as a market for buying and selling livestock and as a system of physical distribution, they became a model for other yards that were established later in the newer centers.

In Chicago, as in Cincinnati, the packing industry was at first almost exclusively interested in hogs. Before the development of refrigeration, fresh beef could not be shipped any considerable distance except during the winter months. The demand for packed beef seldom exceeded 10 per cent of the beef supply. But anywhere from one-half to two-thirds of the hogs could be packed. Thus there was a larger steadier market for pork, and this was the more attractive branch of the industry, until refrigeration changed the picture.

New Leaders in the Packing Industry

New developments in packing are associated with the rise of the captains of industry in this field. Some of them were immigrants who had acquired experience in packing in Ireland, Germany, and other countries. Some were men who had started as cattle traders or packers in Eastern cities and then migrated to the West. Still others got their start in the Middle West. Perhaps the ablest of them all was Gustavus F. Swift, who had started as a New England cattle dealer and butcher. Located originally in Boston, he moved west as a cattle buyer first to Albany, then to Buffalo, and finally to Chicago. He started cattle buying in Chicago in 1875 and in 1877 established a packing plant.[2]

Philip Armour started a produce and commission business in Milwaukee in 1859. Some three years later, with his brothers as partners, he started a grain business in Chicago, and at the same time became a partner of John Plankinton in a packing plant in Milwaukee. During the Civil War, Armour progressed rapidly, partly from the profits of a rising pork market and partly through speculative dealings in grain. In 1867 the firm of Armour & Company started packing hogs in Chicago. The partnership with Plankinton continued for a number of years longer, and then the firm was consolidated with Armour & Company.[3]

A third notable packer was Nelson Morris, who came to Chicago in 1859. When the Chicago stockyards were established, he became an important cattle dealer. In the 1870's he made large shipments of live cattle to the European market and presently established a packing house.[4] His was one of the first packing houses to be built near the Union Stock Yards. Gradually almost all the plants were moved into that neighborhood.

Whereas Armour and Morris were primarily interested in pork-packing, Swift concerned himself with the marketing of beef in the Eastern consuming centers. Boston, New York, and Philadelphia had local firms engaged in slaughtering and distributing fresh beef. These naturally tried to get shipments of live cattle from the West, but transportation was slow and facilities for handling livestock bad. A large proportion of the animals died on the way, and the shrinkage in the rest caused serious loss. Nor did the Eastern slaughterers operate on a scale sufficiently large to enable full utilization of by-products. Only about half of the animal could be used for meat; the rest (except the hide) was wasted. Swift saw that the remedy for these conditions was to be found in doing the slaughtering at Western centers and shipping fresh beef to the Eastern markets. For a time he confined his efforts to shipments during the winter

---

[2] A. Van Vlissingen and L. F. Swift, *The Yankee of the Yards* (Chicago: A. W. Shaw Company, 1927), is an interesting and valuable account of Gustavus Swift.

[3] H. Leech and J. C. Carroll, *Armour and His Times* (New York: D. Appleton-Century Company, 1938), gives a detailed account of Philip Armour's life with many quotations from his letters.

[4] He first secured employment in the stockyards, "then began buying smothered hogs for rendering purposes, and finally engaged in the slaughtering of cattle." Hill, "The Development of Chicago as a Center of the Meat Packing Industry," p. 268.

months. It was the development of refrigeration that brought a revolution in the industry.

Refrigeration Revolutionizes the Industry

Refrigeration began in the slaughterhouses. Up to about 1860 even the slaughtering of hogs was confined to the winter months. Then the packers found it possible to slaughter successfully in warm weather by placing crates of ice and salt about the slaughterhouses. Wherever ice was cheap, it was possible to build large refrigerator chambers, so by 1870 all the larger plants had cooling rooms chilled with natural ice. Thus slaughtering could be carried on continuously through the year.

By that time Swift and other packers were experimenting with shipments in freight cars iced in various ways. Repeated failures did not daunt the persistent "Yankee of the Yards." Finally one of Swift's engineers discovered the principle of air circulation, as applied to refrigeration, and designed a practical refrigerator car.[5] As soon as Swift had demonstrated its practicability, the other Chicago packers adopted it. By 1880 this type of car was being regularly used for shipments from the West. As a result, sales of fresh beef to Eastern markets rose with great rapidity. In 1875 Chicago packers had slaughtered 250,000 cattle. The number was doubled in 1880 and doubled again by 1890.

The packers had need to be persistent, for the new development met with a great deal of opposition. The Trunkline railroads refused to build refrigerator cars. They did not want to take the risk and undergo the expense while the cars were still an experiment. If the experiment proved successful, they would lose a large volume of traffic in cattle cars and in stockyards in Eastern markets. So Swift found it necessary to build his own refrigerator cars, and for some years he ran them to the Atlantic Seaboard over the Grand Trunk Railway of Canada, which was not a member of the Trunkline Association. Opposition came also from the local butchers. Many of them refused to handle Chicago beef. They tried to convince their customers that the refrigerated beef was inferior in quality if not altogether unfit for consumption. In some states the legislatures were induced to pass hostile legislation. Virginia, for example, required that all fresh meat offered for sale in that state must be slaughtered within one hundred miles of the place of consumption.

Shrewd management was able to overcome this opposition. Swift met the antagonism of the local butchers by setting up distributing firms in Eastern centers, in which he took local men into partnership. Armour and Morris set up branch houses from which to distribute their products.

---

5 The principle of car refrigeration is to keep a current of fresh chilled air in constant circulation about the meat, which is hung in the car in such fashion that the air currents can reach every part. Hill, "Development of Chicago as a Center of the Meat Packing Industry," *op. cit.*, p. 273.

"The Swift partnerships were the best for immediate results but the branch house proved superior in the long run so that eventually Swift also adopted that method."[6] Careful and persistent advertising slowly overcame the prejudice against Western beef, although for years it had to be sold in Eastern markets at lower prices than native beef. The opposition of the railroads was overcome by the payment of proportionately higher freight rates on beef than on live cattle and by the willingness of the packers to assume the burden of providing and servicing the refrigerator cars.

The introduction of the refrigerator car accelerated the revolution in the packing industry. The packers could now set up an all-year industry and sell to a national market. To meet the demands of that market, they had to develop slaughtering and packing capacity to meet sudden or unusual demands. This meant large cold-storage facilities in which supplies could be accumulated for peak periods or withheld from the market when demand unexpectedly fell off. All these things involved heavy outlays, large capital, and an increase in the size of the business unit. Armour & Company, for example, showed a net worth of $200,000 in 1870. By 1880 this had risen to $2,500,000, and by 1890 the figure was $10,500,000. Large-scale production, in turn, created serious marketing problems for the packers. The refrigerator car put them into the transportation business. In order to avoid the waste of hauling empty cars back to their plants and in order to provide a full load for outbound shipments, it was necessary for the packers to engage in the buying and selling of various other products. Fruit, butter, eggs, cheese, and many sorts of vegetables were brought from every part of the country in the returning refrigerator cars. A marketing and storing organization had to be built up to handle these products, and thus the packers became produce merchants on a very large scale. Meantime the system of branch houses had been expanded, so that Armour, for example, had 40 such branches by 1890. To reach retailers distant from their branches, "peddler cars" were put in service and later automobile trucks were used.

The introduction of refrigeration also meant an expansion in the utilization of by-products. The local butcher threw away almost half of the animal because he had no plants to utilize such waste products. His scale of production was too small to justify an effort to use them. But the large-scale packer saw an opportunity in this waste. Even before 1875 there were plants in Chicago processing lard, lard oil, tallow, soap, glue, and fertilizer. These were allied industries rather than an integral part of the packing industry. After 1875 the packers took the manufacture of by-products into their own hands. Armour took over an established glue factory in 1884; somewhat later he began to make soap. A new invention made it possible to use fats, hitherto useless, for the making

[6] Malcolm Keir, *Manufacturing*, p. 270. New York: Ronald Press, 1928.

of oleomargarine. This became a thriving part of the industry by 1880. Then the packers set up research laboratories to study the problems of waste utilization. As a result one line of research has developed some 50 pharmaceutical and medical preparations. To find a market for some by-products, it was necessary to combine them with products of other industries, a development that led to further expansion. For example, to utilize the large quantities of glue they were producing, the packers engaged in the manufacture of sandpaper. In utilizing wastes, other wastes were created which, in turn, became raw materials for other by-products. Including merchandised as well as processed products, a modern packing house may sell nearly 700 different items.[7]

New Centers of Production after 1890

Once the shipment of fresh meat had become the main business of the packers, it became economical for them to establish their plants as close to the sources of supply of livestock as possible. After about 1890 new centers of packing developed rapidly on the western edge of the Corn Belt. In the Southwest the practice of fattening cattle on cottonseed meal, a by-product of the cottonseed oil industry, helped the new centers. The use of mechanical refrigeration also made it easier to carry on packing in the Deep South. In 1890 the centers of packing, ranked by value of product, were Chicago, Kansas City, New York, Indianapolis, and St. Louis, all but Kansas City east of the Mississippi River. By 1914 three out of the five states leading in packing were west of the Mississippi River: Kansas, Nebraska, and Missouri. Omaha after 1885, St. Joseph after 1897, and Fort Worth, Dallas, and South St. Paul after 1900 had become important centers.

Flour Milling

Growth of the Minneapolis Mills (to 1890)

There were no important technical changes in flour milling in the decade of the Civil War. In the East, Baltimore, Richmond, and Rochester were the principal centers of production. In the West, St. Louis outshone all the rest, although Chicago and Milwaukee were important. New York, Pennsylvania, and Illinois ranked first, second, and third among the states in the value of flour produced in 1870. The mills were generally small and widely scattered. Soft red winter wheat was the chief variety grown in those states and was considered to make the best bread flour.[8]

In 1870 Minneapolis flour mills were beginning to attract national attention. The first mills at the Falls of St. Anthony ground wheat for

---

[7] See R. A. Clemen, *By-Products in the Packing Industry* (Chicago: University of Chicago Press, 1927), for a detailed discussion.

[8] The soft red winter wheat area extends from Pennsylvania westward to the Mississippi River.

the logging crews and sawmill workers of Minnesota's pioneer days. At first grain was brought up the Mississippi by boat from older settlements. When wheat growing became well established in Minnesota, the farmers grew spring wheat, for the more popular winter wheat was not able to stand the rigors of the Minnesota winter.[9] Spring wheat presented new problems for the millers. While richer in gluten and making a "stronger" flour, its hardiness made it less easy to grind. The millstones had to be run at higher speed with greater pressure. The heat thus generated discolored the flour, and the husk of the wheat kernel broke into fine powder that was difficult to sift out. The germ of the wheat berry ground into the flour injured the flour's keeping qualities. Thus, up to 1870, winter wheat flour was whiter, kept better, and was generally preferred in the Eastern markets. Yet by 1870 there were 13 flour mills in Minneapolis producing some 250,000 barrels of flour a year. There were also important mills in some of the river towns of Minnesota south and east of Minneapolis. The leading millers of the state were all experimenting with improved methods of milling designed to overcome these objections to spring-wheat flour.

Out of their experiments developed "New Process" milling. Essentially it involved multiple grinding with slower speed and reduced pressure on the millstones to prevent discoloration of the flour. The process increased the production of "middlings," which when purified and reground produced the best flour. The problem of purifying the middlings stumped the experts for a time, until in 1871 a miller named La Croix built a machine (apparently based on a French design) that performed the operation successfully.[10] The middlings purifier made the New Process a commercial success, and this fact in turn gave spring-wheat flour a dominant position in consumer markets. For a time the Minneapolis mills could hardly turn out flour fast enough to satisfy their customers. The Washburn "A" Mill in that city is said to have been built out of two or three years' profits of the "B" Mill.

Their experience with the middlings purifier induced the leading Western millers to turn to Europe for further ideas. They studied French and German milling practices, in particular, Hungarian milling, because their mills were dealing with similar problems. The Hungarian wheat was also hard with a brittle husk. Their millstones wore out rapidly and the quality of their flour was injured by the fine grit from the stones. The Hungarian millers were the first to experiment with roller grinding machines as a substitute for millstones.

---

[9] In recent years new hardy varieties of winter wheat have been introduced and grown successfully.

[10] See C. B. Kuhlmann, *Development of the Flour Milling Industry in the United States* (Boston: Houghton Mifflin Company, 1929), pp. 115-120, for a description of the La Croix invention.

The first roller grinders were introduced in Minneapolis in 1873. Used originally to regrind the purified middlings, their use was soon extended to all grinding operations. The first complete roller mill in America was set up in Minneapois by Governor Washburn in 1878. The superiority of the rollers was quickly recognized, and their use spread rapidly along with the multiple grinding process. The roller grinders took up less space, used less power, and required less oversight. Millstones had to be "dressed" every three or four days, while the rollers could run for months without change. The flour yield from a given amount of wheat was somewhat larger and, owing to the absence of millstone grit, it was of better quality.

The Minneapolis millers took the lead in introducing these improvements and reaped the greatest benefits. By 1882 the 13 mills of 1870 had doubled in number and were turning out over 3,000,000 barrels of flour a year. Not only did these mills dominate the domestic market but they were making rapid progress in conquering the markets of northern and eastern Europe: "As early as 1878 a solid train of cars carrying 2,500 barrels of flour reached New York after an unbroken trip fom Minneapolis, to make connection with a steamer which would deliver the consignment in London sixteen days from the time it left the Falls of St. Anthony." [11]

By 1885 the Minneapolis mills were producing over 5,000,000 barrels of flour annually; by 1890, over 7,000,000. They had outdistanced all their rivals. Certain causes of their extraordinary success may be pointed out. One was the growth of large-scale production. In 1876 the average capacity of the Minneapolis mills was 242 barrels a day; by 1890 it was 1,837 barrels. In the 1880's the trade papers were pointing out the superior advantages of the larger mills: advantages in buying and selling, in better superintendence, in ease of securing capital, and in filling the large orders customary in foreign trade. Except perhaps in Richmond, this enlargement of the scale of production was most prominent in Minneapolis. There was also a concentration of ownership, so that by 1890, seven-eighths of the milling capacity of the city was combined in four large corporations.

These mills required large wheat supplies: much larger than could be obtained from local territory. The Minneapolis millers, therefore, found it necessary to push the westward expansion of the railroads into the wheat-producing area. How far the millers were responsible for the development of the Twin Cities as a transportation center is debatable; but unquestionably they benefited from the fact. To free themselves from any domination by the railroads centering in Chicago, millers promoted the building of the Minneapolis, St. Paul, and Sault Sainte Marie (the "Soo line") eastward across Wisconsin and the upper peninsula of

[11] V. S. Clark, *History of Manufactures in the United States,* Vol. II, p. 504. New York: McGraw-Hill Book Company, 1929.

Michigan to a connection with the Canadian Pacific Railway in 1888. Rival centers subsequently claimed that the Minneapolis millers used their strong position to secure discriminating freight rates for themselves.

When the production of wheat spread from Minnesota into the Dakotas, the marketing of wheat also had to be organized. Subsidiary companies organized by the millers built up lines of elevators along the railroads throughout the wheat area. An effort, as early as 1869, to prevent competition in wheat buying by forming a single buying agency to purchase for all the mills (the "Millers Association") was successful for a time but created a good deal of enmity against the millers among the farmers. The milling interests took the lead in developing the Minneapolis Chamber of Commerce, organized in 1881. Through its efforts Minneapolis became the marketing center for wheat of the Northwest.

The mills required large amounts of capital, much of which came in the early days from the lumber industry of Minnesota. By the 1870's the millers were securing funds from Eastern financial institutions. Then the building of a group of strong local banks, in which the flour manufacturers played a leading part, made them secure in their capital needs. It was stated in 1889: "Nearly all the money paid for grain in the interior is sent from the city by elevator companies and millers, to their agents in the country. Thus Minneapolis is not only the market to which the grain is shipped and where it is sold, but the financial center from which the money is sent out to purchase and move the grain crops of the Northwest." [12]

Rise of Milling in the Hard Red Winter Wheat Area

After 1890, Minneapolis mills were faced with competition from new milling centers. The settlement of the territory west of, and tributary to, Kansas City was roughly contemporaneous with that of the Minneapolis area. Mennonite settlers from Russia are said to have brought the Turkey Red wheat into Kansas as early as 1872. This hard red winter wheat was improved as other varieties of the same general type were introduced or developed by experiment. Because these wheats gave a heavy yield and produced a good bread flour, they spread rapidly. As a result, Kansas by 1892 led all the states in wheat production. Kansas City, important as a wheat market by 1880, began to grow as a milling center after 1890 as the excellent qualities of Turkey Red wheat were generally recognized. By 1901 the city was producing over a million barrels of flour annually. Millers from St. Louis, Philadelphia, and New York erected large new plants there, the development culminating in 1922 when Washburn-Crosby of Minneapolis acquired a Kansas City mill.

Meantime the new hard red winter wheats were spreading beyond Kansas into Oklahoma, Texas, Colorado, and other states. In 1923 the

[12] Minneapolis Chamber of Commerce, *Annual Report,* 1883, p. 120.

total production was 241,000,000 bushels: almost double the Northwest's hard red spring wheat crop of 126,000,000. Many new mills of large size were built to process this grain, notably in Wichita, Salina, Hutchinson, and Topeka in Kansas; in Dallas, Fort Worth, and San Antonio in Texas; and in Oklahoma City, Oklahoma. In marketing their rapidly expanding output, these producers came into competition, not only with Kansas City mills, but also with those of the older centers in Minnesota and the East. For a long time the Kansas millers had to accept lower prices on their flour than was paid for the Northwestern flours. Even now spring-wheat flours, grade for grade, are slightly higher in price. As against this, Kansas millers are able to buy wheat at somewhat more advantageous prices and their costs of operation are somewhat lower. Because of a rapidly expanding demand, they were for years able to get better prices for mill-feeds. As a result, millers operating simultaneously in the Minnesota, Kansas, and Buffalo districts have testified before the Interstate Commerce Commission that Kansas flour is laid down in New York at the lowest cost, Buffalo at the next lowest, and Minnesota at the highest.

Buffalo as a Milling Center

Buffalo had a flour mill as early as 1832, and a number of other mills were put into operation before the Civil War. By 1885, Buffalo had 10 mills producing annually about 750,000 barrels. In the following decades milling languished, and Buffalo seemed destined to be a distributing point for lake shipments from the Minneapolis mills because of the practice by which the railroads granted the Western millers free storage for their flour at Buffalo. Appeals were made to the Interstate Commerce Commission against this practice, and it may be that the decision of the railroads in 1901 to withdraw the privilege was the turning point in the struggle. At any rate, Buffalo flour production increased rapidly after that date, not because of the expansion of old, established companies, but because Minneapolis millers moved to Buffalo. First of these was the Washburn-Crosby Company, which built a large mill in Buffalo in 1903, later enlarged to 22,000 barrels' capacity—the largest mill in the world. Ultimately all the larger Minneapolis companies acquired mills in Buffalo. With the withdrawal of the free-storage privilege, and since the lake rates were relatively lower on wheat than on flour, the Minneapolis mills were at a disadvantage. Buffalo is favorably situated for distribution to Eastern markets. Not only can Buffalo mills get Northwestern wheat by lake steamer at low rates, but low-cost Canadian wheat as well. Canadian wheat can be milled in bond and the flour exported. This privilege has caused Minneapolis millers to transfer virtually all their export orders to their Buffalo mills. Lastly, cheaper power is available in Buffalo. As these advantages became generally recognized, new mills were built and

Buffalo production increased steadily. Minneapolis production, on the contrary, decreased rather rapidly after about 1922. In 1930 Buffalo passed Minneapolis in output, and it is now the nation's largest milling center.

Decline of Minneapolis as a Milling Center

The decline of milling in Minneapolis merits, perhaps, some further comment.[13] Some of the causes for this decline have been noted above. To these might be added the fact that after the First World War freight rates rose generally throughout the country, tending to decentralize the industry. Minneapolis millers moved not only to Buffalo and to Kansas City; they also acquired mills in the soft wheat area, the Pacific Coast area, and the Inter-mountain territory. The growth of the chain stores, which promoted their own private brands, was unfavorable to the heavily advertised brands of the big Minneapolis mills. The shift from home baking to the buying of bakery products and the rise of large-scale baking had a similar effect. These bakeries in their flour purchases were likely to consider price rather than quality. They could not afford to pay higher prices for widely advertised manufacturers' brands.

The main cause of the decline of Northwestern milling, however, is to be found in the decrease of Northwestern wheat both in quality and in quantity. In part this decrease is due to the use of inferior varieties of wheat, which have been adopted because they were supposedly more rust-resistant. In part it is the effect of the replacement of bread wheat by "durum" wheat, which is used not for bread but for macaroni and similar products. Northwestern farmers have been unable to rotate their crops as successfully as the farmers of the Southwest, and consequently weeds keep down the yield. To the extent that the farmer has practiced diversification, it has cut down the acreage devoted to wheat. In Minnesota especially, the wheat raiser has given way to the dairy farmer over a large area.

Diversification of Products and Advertising

The breakfast-cereal industry, which arose shortly before 1900, was at first a separate enterprise from flour milling. The early millers were disposed to dispute the exaggerated claims for the new breakfast foods. It was not until these controversies were forgotten and breakfast food firmly established in the American diet that the large milling companies invaded the field. Washburn-Crosby, for example, built a cereal mill in Chicago in 1923, and since that time all the leading mills have been active in that field. At the same time, they have diversified the products of their flour mills, making corn meal, rye flour, and other products.

[13] See V. G. Pickett and R. S. Vaile, *The Decline of Northwestern Flour Milling.* Minneapolis: University of Minnesota Press, 1933.

In similar fashion, the millers strongly opposed the introduction of durum wheat which the Department of Agriculture brought over from Russia about 1900 and induced the Dakota farmers to grow. It was drought and rust-resistant and a good yielder, but was not a good bread wheat. The areas devoted to durum cut down by so much the production of the hard red spring wheat on which the Northwestern millers had made their reputation. But when the farmers persisted in growing durum the millers were forced to use it and found a market in the increased popularity of macaroni products. So the semolina ground from durum wheat became an important product of the mills of the Northwest.

Once the revolution in milling methods was accomplished, the millers turned their attention more and more to promoting consumption. As a result there were some important marketing changes between 1870 and 1920, notably (1) the growth of advertising, and (2) the growth of selling direct to retailers and bakers. Selling direct involved the use of a great deal of capital—much more than the small mill could afford—in setting up branch houses, carrying warehouse stocks and sending out traveling salesmen. Since, in general, selling direct meant a larger volume of business for the large mills, it was one factor in the growth of the large companies and the decline of the small.

Advertising of sorts was used by millers even in colonial times. But large scale advertising in the modern manner dates back only to about 1885. At that time the Minneapolis millers began to advertise in the trade journals and the local newspapers and gradually extended the field of advertising to take in billboards, the national magazines, and just about every other medium open to them. Up to about 1900 they had the field pretty much to themselves. Leadership again brought larger volume and larger profits.

The Baking Industry

Many of the Colonial flour mills also operated bakeries, a considerable part of their exports being bread, probably mainly a "hardtack" that would not deteriorate on long sea voyages. In the following period, the baking industry was split into two divisions—one producing biscuits and crackers, the other bread and pastry. The former was first to develop into the factory stage and large-scale production, since its goods were less perishable and could, therefore, be distributed over a larger area. By the 1890's the factories turning out biscuits and crackers were combining into corporations of considerable size. In 1898 the National Biscuit Company was formed by the merger of four large companies. The new company, it was claimed, would control the cracker and biscuit trade from the Atlantic to the Rockies, operating 139 plants and about 90 per cent of the total capacity of the industry. By putting its products into attractive, sanitary packages and by extensive advertising, it was able to expand its markets greatly, so that in 1900 the company was using over 2,000,000 barrels of flour annually and was preparing to mill its own flour. The National Biscuit Company disclaimed any intention to exercise monopoly control, and, in fact, did not achieve a monopoly position, for, although today it has about half of the total business in its hands, there are several large competing companies and many smaller firms with more restricted markets.

The other branch of the baking industry produces more perishable products: bread, cake, pies, and pastry. In value of output it is much more important than the older division. Since most people insist on delivery of their bread on the same day it is baked, bread baking is a local industry. "The geographical distribution of bakeries is practically identical with the distribution of urban population." [14] Commercial bread bakeries existed in Colonial times and all through our history. Until the First World War, however, the greater part of the population ate bread baked in the home. Conditions during the First World War turned many people from home baking. The improvement of commercial bakery products, resulting from increased mechanization and scientific processes, doubtless helped to promote their popularity. Except in the South, where there is still a pronounced demand for hot breads baked in the home, the swing was decidedly toward bakery products after 1914.

The Canning Industry

It has been pointed out [15] that the period of the Civil War brought prosperity to the canners. Gail Borden's first factory for manufacturing condensed milk was opened in Wassaic, New York, in 1861, and almost immediately its whole output was taken over by the National Government for army use. Soldiers acquired a taste for the product that gave it a popularity that otherwise might have taken many years to develop. Army demands also stimulated the canning of fruits and vegetables. The discovery that higher temperatures could be attained by the use of calcium chloride extended the range of fruits and vegetables that could be packed successfully and increased the dependability of the product. The growth of the industry led to the establishment of various subsidiary industries.

Machine-made cans were introduced about 1885, and thereafter the manufacture of cans became a separate industry. Machines for filling and sealing cans were invented. A machine for removing corn from the cob, developed about 1880, gave impetus to corn canning. Viners for picking pods from vines and shelling peas were introduced about 1893; and the "iron chink," which revolutionized the process of salmon canning, was brought in about 1903. The first developments in canning

---

[14] E. B. Alderfer and H. E. Michl, *Economics of American Industry*, p. 437. New York: McGraw-Hill Book Company, 1942.

[15] See above, Chapter 9.

had been made in Europe, but now America took the lead in making it a machine industry.

Some progress was also made in chemical and bacteriological control in the decade of the nineties. As a result, the canneries were enabled to extend further the range of their products, because they could now can almost all food products with safety. During this period canneries were built in almost all parts of the country. Maryland was still the leading state, but California had taken second rank.

After 1900 canning grew more rapidly than any of the other food industries. Improved processes, resulting in higher-quality products and breaking down the prejudices that had deterred many from purchasing, were at the same time bringing lower costs and hence lower selling prices. The canners supervised the production of crops and furnished pure seed so as to insure a high-grade product. Scientifically determined standards of temperatures, pressure, and processing time now assure uniformity of quality for each type of food. New labor-saving machinery reduced the costs of production of raw materials.

The growing urbanization of American population also stimulated the industry. City people cannot store food and therefore cannot purchase it in large quantities. This has been the fundamental cause of the decline of home baking, canning, and preserving. Another cause of growth was the increasing number and variety of products processed. This led to a concentration on certain products in each region or state: sweet corn had made Maine important in canning; Wisconsin led in canning peas; peaches were put up largely in Maryland and California, pineapple in Hawaii, salmon in Alaska. Each has tended to be localized where soil and climatic conditions provide best and cheapest materials.

Save for a few notable exceptions, such as Campbells, Heinz, and Libby, McNeill and Libby, the perishability of the raw materials has also tended to limit the size of the canneries. Doubtless the seasonal nature of the process also operates to the same effect because of the number of laborers available in any given locality.

Nevertheless, canning has always been a highly competitive industry. Its chief problems arise from the fact that its supplies of raw materials may fluctuate greatly in quantity, quality, and price from year to year, so that control of production is almost impossible. Although the industry has grown faster than any other food industry, it is improbable that that rate of increase will continue. As standards of living continue to rise, it is possible that increased consumption of fresh or frozen vegetables and fruits will at least slow down the rate of increase of canning production.

The Soft-Drink Industry

Until the beginning of the present century, the manufacture of soft drinks, mainly carbonated beverages, was a small-scale local industry operated by hand labor. Thereafter automatic machinery was introduced. Conveyors carried the bottles from one machine to another. New machines to wash and sterilize the bottles, to fill, cap, and label them, all operating at higher speeds than older equipment, revolutionized the industry. Mechanical refrigeration, new methods for pasteurizing the fruit juices, which allowed producers to store raw materials, and motor transportation enabled them to operate on a much larger scale and reach a much larger territory. The prohibition era aided the larger producers by expanding per capita consumption of their products. There was a great growth in the sales of root beer, ginger ales, and other products of that type.

Most of the producers are small companies serving a limited local territory. They may have a franchise from some large company, such as Coca-Cola, from which they buy their syrups, and use the company's name for the product they sell. A small local manufacturer who has no franchise from a big national company buys his ingredients from independent manufacturers and puts his own name on the bottle. In that case, he does not have the national company's advertising and good will to help him sell his output.

With this development may be associated the increasing popularity of fruit and vegetable juices, although these are products of the canning industry. The only fruit juice commercially important before 1925 was grape juice. In 1926 canned grapefruit juice was first produced on a commercial scale. Tomato juice was introduced on a large scale in 1928. Recently "nectars" prepared from apricots, peaches, and pears have become important. Changing food habits have popularized other vegetable juices as well. They link the soft-drink industry with the canning industry and create an increasing competition for the manufacturers of alcoholic liquors.

Dairy Products

The increase in the number of dairy cows provides a simple measure of the growth of the dairy industry. In 1860 there were some 8,000,000, by 1920 there were over 19,000,000, and by 1939 over 25,000,000 dairy cows in the United States. Up to 1860 dairying had made but little progress in getting away from century-old methods. After that date change began. Cheese factories began to multiply; creameries and condensed-milk plants got under way. The development of the refrigerator car by the meat packers aided dairying also by providing efficient transportation of butter and cheese to distant markets. State associations were established by the dairymen for the improvement of the industry, first in Vermont (1869) and then in the seventies in New York, Illinois, Wisconsin, and Minnesota. In 1870 *Hoard's Dairyman* was established in Wisconsin.

From the first it exerted a powerful influence for the progress of the industry.

The westward expansion of dairying brought it into territory that had carried on staple wheat growing until soil exhaustion, insect pests, and the competition of newer lands farther west made wheat growing a losing venture. The shift to dairying was often difficult, since it required considerable capital and great agricultural skill. But by 1920 that change-over had been completed in Wisconsin.[16] Whereas in 1860 New York led all the states in the number of cows, by 1920 Wisconsin was first.

Since 1890 milk production has been aided by a number of important developments: the cream separator, invented in Sweden in 1877 and brought to America soon after; the introduction of the silo, also from Sweden (1882); the invention of the milking machine; and the development of pasteurization. The separator and the milking machine are labor-saving devices. Mechanized milking also prevents contamination and deterioration of the product, as also does pasteurization. The milk test enables the farmer to discover the profitable and unprofitable members of his herd and thus to eliminate the latter. By 1931, there were only 15 per cent more cows in the United States than there were in 1914, but the increase in milk production was over 50 per cent.

The dairy industry has two main branches (or three, if the raising of animals for breeding purposes is included): the production of milk for direct consumption (fluid milk), which absorbs nearly half of the total output; and the milk that is to be processed before being sold to the consumer. Butter making takes about 36 per cent of the total milk output, and cheese, ice cream, condensed milk, and other products take 3 or 4 per cent, leaving 6 or 7 per cent to be used on the farm.[17]

Milk for direct consumption is usually sold to city distributors, by whom it is pasteurized, bottled, and delivered to domestic and other users. Because the distributors are small in number and strong financially, and since mechanization and large-scale operations require large capital, the milk producers have been forced in many instances to organize themselves co-operatively in order to bargain successfully.

Whereas production of fluid milk is necessarily concentrated near the great consuming markets, the manufacture of butter and cheese is much more decentralized. Butter and cheese can be stored for considerable periods and shipped long distances to market. Their manufacture, therefore, can be carried on in regions where conditions are most favorable. Wisconsin and Minnesota seem at present to be the most favorable re-

---

[16] For the beginnings of dairying in Wisconsin see F. Merk, *Economic History of Wisconsin During the Civil War Decade,* pp. 22-30. Madison: The State Historical Society of Wisconsin, 1916.

[17] The estimates are for 1926. See *Biennial Census of Manufactures,* 1927.

gions. In those states butter and cheese are manufactured in thousands of local creameries scattered over the countryside so that the skimmed milk, buttermilk, and whey may be returned to the farmers to feed their calves and pigs.

It has been pointed out [18] that the first cheese factories were started in Oneida County, New York, in 1850. Ten years later the first creamery was started in the same state. From New York the idea spread into other dairy states. Descendants of English dairymen moved from New York to Wisconsin and there introduced the art of making Cheddar cheese. Swiss immigrants popularized the making of Swiss cheese. In another 10 years Wisconsin cheese was winning prizes in competition with that of older states. In Minnesota creameries developed more rapidly than cheese factories. Many of these were of the co-operative type. Historically, it was the dairy farmers who were the first to set up cooperative associations in the United States. By 1934-1935, 35 per cent of the butter produced in this country and 21 per cent of the cheese was marketed by co-operative associations. Up to 1919 these cooperatives were scattered, disunited, small-scale, local organizations. Marketing difficulties plus uneconomical management caused a high mortality rate. After 1919 these difficulties were remedied by the establishment of a number of regional federations, such as the Land O'Lakes Creameries, Inc., formed in 1924.

Naturally, not all the creameries and cheese factories are co-operatives. The Chicago meat packers own chains of them, and there are a number of other chains operated by stock companies. But the co-operative is the dominant form of organization in this branch of dairy production. In contrast, the production of condensed, evaporated, and powdered milk is a field in which the co-operatives have had little success as yet, except where large co-operative milk-producers associations have entered the field to find an outlet for their surplus fluid milk. In the production of canned milk, as well as in ice cream manufacture, increased mechanization, the need for large capital, and the advantages of quantity production have permitted private proprietorship corporations to take the lead.

It would seem that, for the future, co-operative associations should make a greater effort to increase American consumption of dairy products. The United States now ranks only sixth in per capita consumption of milk, although consumption is increasing markedly. We rank no better than ninth in the consumption of cheese. Butter is relatively more popular than cheese in America; but when the price of butter rises, the substitution of oleomargarine increases. Our dairy industry may lead the world in efficiency, as it is claimed; but when the per capita milk consumption is only half the minimum considered necessary by experts to maintain the highest level of public health, it would seem that the biggest job left for the co-operative associations in dairying is to promote by every pos-

[18] See above, p. 169.

sible means the expansion of the market. This, rather than restriction of output, should be the long-term goal.

Tobacco Manufacture

The Civil War encouraged Northern tobacco manufacture, especially in New York, but Richmond recovered the place of leadership as soon as the war was over. Perhaps the most important development in that decade was the introduction of the cigarette. Cigar making remained a small-scale, hand-labor, widely dispersed industry until after 1900. The first cigarettes were also handmade, but soon after 1880 machines were developed and the processes of cigarette making became mechanized and standardized. This development resulted in the familiar round of large-scale production, cutthroat competition, and combination. In 1890 the five principal producers of cigarettes united to form the American Tobacco Company. Within a few years of hard fighting it managed to achieve a monopoly control of cigarette manufacture. At the same time it extended its activities into the plug and smoking tobacco fields. The manufacture of snuff and cigars was subjected to at least partial control, and the company even entered the retail field by means of the chain of United Cigar Stores, which it controlled.

Meantime there came an increasing mechanization of the smoking and plug tobacco field that accelerated large-scale production. The Trust was able to close out smaller plants, erect larger and more efficient ones, and thus adopt modern manufacturing economies. The American Tobacco Company also attempted to extend its control over foreign fields as well, building or acquiring cigarette factories in Canada, Australia, Japan, Mexico, and Germany. Havana cigar factories were taken over and Great Britain was invaded, "where a long struggle ended in a compromise with the British producers and the creation of what was virtually an international tobacco trust." [19]

By 1907 the American Tobacco Company controlled 75 per cent of the American trade in cigarettes, chewing and smoking tobacco, and snuff, and about 25 per cent of the cigar industry. That control had been built up "with brutal energy upon ruthless competition and unfair practices," [20] but it is also true that no other industry had developed an organization so complete and so efficient.

During this time important changes in the geographical distribution of the industry had taken place. In 1890 Richmond was still an important manufacturing center. St. Louis, Louisville, and Cincinnati had become important in the manufacture of plug tobacco. New York City was the first important cigarette-manufacturing city, but after 1890 Dur-

---

[19] J. W. Jenkins, *James B. Duke, Master Builder* (New York: Geo. H. Doran Company, 1927), describes this interestingly.

[20] V. S. Clark, *History of Manufactures in the United States,* Vol. III, p. 280.

ham and Winston, North Carolina, together with Richmond, became the chief centers for that branch of the industry.

The consumption of tobacco increased gradually after the Civil War. Whereas in 1863 only 1.6 pounds per capita was consumed, by 1935 we were using over 6 pounds per person, a consumption higher than that of any other country. Much of this increase was due to the remarkable popularity of the cigarette, beginning with the introduction of the blended cigarette just before the First World War and its popularization by the Tobacco Trust and its successor companies.

The American Tobacco Company had been brought into court in 1911 and the Supreme Court had ordered its dissolution. Some 14 separate companies were formed, with an arrangement that provided for at least two companies in each of the branches of tobacco manufacture. In the cigarette field it was these new companies that brought out the new type of cigarette, on which they concentrated their promotional efforts. Large-scale production in highly mechanized plants, the exercise in the tobacco markets of their superior buying strength, which allowed them to purchase raw materials at low prices, and, above all, a tremendous campaign of advertising to increase the consumption of the cigarettes, particularly among women—those were the causes of the rapid expansion of cigarette production.

Cigars, as has been said, were made by hand until about 1919 when the American Tobacco Company (one of the concerns arising out of the dissolution of the Trust) began to produce machine-made cigars. The demand for the more expensive brands fell off: only the five-cent cigar could compete against the increasingly popular cigarette.

Some Effects and Tendencies

The products of the industries discussed are among the most important American manufactures. Not only are the food industries large, but they are growing, owing to a wide variety of factors. Population growth has enlarged markets for all. The shift of population to the large cities has also moved some of these industries from the home to the factory: baking, canning, and dairy products, for example. The increasing employment of women in industry has operated toward the same effect. A higher standard of living for the masses has enabled them to add variety to their diet. Changes in living conditions, such as less strenuous manual labor, better-heated houses, closed automobiles, and so forth, have enabled us to cut down our consumption of certain foods. The flour mill and the bakery have suffered from a decrease in per capita consumption of their products, and so has the packing house; but the consumption of milk and milk products has increased. The demand for a greater variety in diet has benefited the canning industry to no small extent.

While the industries discussed all show a tendency toward increased mechanization and large-scale production, most of them are carried on in both large-scale and small-scale establishments. Especially is this true for canning, in which the perishability of the raw materials is a dominant factor. It is not so true in packing, where large capital is needed to carry large inventories, to process by-products, and to provide complicated and expensive machinery.

There has been a notable tendency toward consolidation and concentration of control in these industries. The savings in cost of distribution resulting from consolidation, the savings in overhead expense when allied lines are entered, and the ability to develop new processes and new products have all promoted this development. The growth of large-scale retailing has had a similar effect on those manufacturers producing consumer goods. Technological change has been an important factor in the development of most of these industries, notably in four: milling, meat packing, dairy products, and tobacco. Even more important has been the shift in the geography of raw materials.

Since the raw materials of these industries all spring from agriculture, there are necessarily wide fluctuations in supply and price. This variable factor creates a degree of instability. In most cases, the consumer demand for their products is elastic, and the retailers cannot readily adjust their prices to the changes in the prices of the raw material. In flour milling, the producers can protect themselves from these fluctuations by the process of hedging, but for the others this method is not available. On the other hand, in most of these industries, the demand is much more stable than the supply, a fact that favors stability in earnings.

Selected References

GENERAL WORKS

Alderfer, E. B., and H. E. Michl, *Economics of American Industry*. New York: McGraw-Hill Book Company, 1942.

Bogart, E. I., and C. E. Landon, *Modern Industry*. New York: Longmans, Green and Company, 1927.

Clark, V. S., *History of Manufactures in the United States,* Vol. II (1860-1893), Vol. III (1893-1928). New York: McGraw-Hill Book Company, 1929.

Glover, John G., and William B. Cornell, *The Development of American Industries,* rev. ed. New York: Prentice-Hall, Inc., 1941.

Keir, Malcolm, *Manufacturing* (*Industries of America Series*). New York: Ronald Press, 1928.

Malott, D. W., and B. F. Martin, *The Agricultural Industries*. New York: McGraw-Hill Book Company, 1939.

Pound, Arthur, *Industrial America. Its Way of Life and Work*. Boston: Little, Brown & Company, 1936.

Warshow, H. T., ed., *Representative Industries in the United States*. New York: Henry Holt & Company, 1928.

SPECIAL TOPICS

Baking industry:

Alsberg, Carl, *Combinations in the American Bread Baking Industry.* Food Research Institute: Stanford University Press, 1926.

Federal Trade Commission, *Report on Competition and Profits in Bread and Flour.* Washington, D. C.: U.S. Government Printing Office, 1928.

Kyrk, Hazel, *The American Baking Industry, 1849-1923.* Stanford University: Stanford University Press, 1925.

Encyclopedia of the Social Sciences, "Baking Industry—U. S." New York: The Macmillan Company, 1930-1935.

Beverage industries:

George S. May Business Foundation, *Analysis of the Brewing Industry,* Report 103. New York: 1940.

Persons, W. M., *Beer and Brewing in America.* New York: United Brewers Industrial Foundation, 1940.

Temporary National Economic Committee, *Hearings: The Liquor Industry.* Washington, D.C.: U.S. Government Printing Office, 1939.

Encyclopedia of the Social Sciences, "The Beverage Industry." New York: The Macmillan Company, 1930-1935.

Canning industry:

Carothers, Neil, *Some Phases of the Canning Industry.* Washington: National Canners Association, 1942.

Collins, J. H., *The Story of Canned Foods.* New York: E. P. Dutton & Company, 1924.

Lyon, L. S., *Some Trends in the Marketing of Canned Foods.* Washington: Brookings Institution, 1929.

May, E. C., *The Canning Clan.* New York: The Macmillan Company, 1937.

Dairy industries:

Bakken, H. H., and M. A. Schaars, *The Economics of Cooperative Marketing.* New York: McGraw-Hill Book Company, 1937.

Gras, N. S. B., *A History of Agriculture.* New York: F. S. Crofts & Company, 1925.

Schmidt, L. B., and E. D. Ross, *Readings in the Economic History of American Agriculture.* New York: The Macmillan Company, 1925.

U. S. Department of Agriculture, "The Dairy Industry," *Yearbook, 1922.* Washington: 1923.

Encyclopedia of the Social Sciences, "Dairy Industry." New York: The Macmillan Company, 1930-1935.

Flour milling:

Edgar, W. C., *The Medal of Gold.* Minneapolis: The Bellman Company, 1925.

Federal Trade Commission, *Report on the Wheat Flour Milling Industry.* Washington, D.C.: U.S. Government Printing Office, 1924.

Kuhlmann, C. B., *The Development of the Flour Milling Industry in the United States.* Boston: Houghton Mifflin Company, 1929.

Pickett, V. G., and R. S. Vaile, *The Decline of Northwestern Flour Milling.* Minneapolis: University of Minnesota Press, 1933.

Meat packing:

Clemen, R. A., *By-Products in the Packing Industry.* Chicago: University of Chicago Press, 1927.

———, *The American Livestock and Meat Industry.* New York: Ronald Press, 1923.

Federal Trade Commission Report on the Meat Packing Industry. Washington, D.C.: U.S. Government Printing Office, 1918-1920, Parts 1-3.

Leech, H., and J. C. Carroll, *Armour and His Times.* New York: D. Appleton-Century Company, 1938.

Van Vlissingen, A., and L. F. Swift, *The Yankee of the Yards.* Chicago: A. W. Shaw Company, 1927.

Encyclopedia of the Social Sciences, "Meat Packing and Slaughtering." New York: The Macmillan Company, 1930-1935.

Tobacco manufacture:

Commissioner of Corporations, *Report on the Tobacco Industry.* Washington, D.C.: U.S. Government Printing Office, 1909-1911, Parts 1-2.

Cox, Reavis, *Competition in the American Tobacco Industry, 1911-1932.* New York: Columbia University Press, 1933.

Federal Trade Commission, *Report on the Tobacco Industry (1920).* Washington, D.C.: U.S. Government Printing Office, 1922.

Gottsegen, J. J., *Tobacco: A Study of the Consumption in the United States.* New York: Pitman Publishing Company, 1940.

Jenkins, J. W., *James B. Duke, Master Builder.* New York: Geo. H. Doran Company, 1927.

23 · PRODUCTS OF THE EARTH 1866-1918

NO ASPECT OF the growth of the American economy in the half century that followed the Civil War is more striking than its rapidly increasing dependence on the mineral industries. Never impressive either for value of output or for numbers employed, the mining industries nonetheless became and have remained in a very literal sense the foundations on which the entire economy has increasingly rested. The substantial beginnings of industrialism, as already noted, date from the second quarter of the century. By 1850, much progress had been made in the mechanization of manufacturing processes, in the replacement of muscular by mechanical power, and in the organization of production on a large scale and with an extensive subdivision of labor. At the middle of the century, however, the raw materials for American industries were still drawn for the most part from field and forest rather than from mine, quarry, and well.

On the eve of the Civil War, wood was still, in a quantitative sense, the most important raw material of manufacturing industry. Its cheapness and wide distribution, the ease with which it could be shaped and fastened, the wide variety of kinds and qualities available, its adequacy under most conditions in articles and equipment of common use about the home, farm, and small workshop, enabled it to resist the advances of the metals. Wood was, in 1850, still the principal fuel in use, both for domestic and industrial purposes. It was more used than coal in the smelting, refining and forging of metals; it was the principal source of steam power, whether applied to driving the machinery of factories or the wheels of locomotives and steamboats.

Next to the forest, the farm was the most important source of the raw materials of industry. From field, pasture, and range came fibres for textiles, hides for tanneries, and grain and livestock for the food-processing industries. Even the lubricants that greased the rapidly multiplying wheels of industry and commerce had their source on the farm when they did not come from the sea *via* the whaling industry. Sperm oil, lard oil, and tallow were the principal reliance of mechanic, millwright, and engine-driver.

The New Role of Minerals in the Economy

During the generation following the Civil War the raw material base of the American economy underwent significant changes. Heretofore, in the exploitation of our material resources, we had, in an almost literal sense, hardly more than scratched the surface of the earth. Compared with the decades ahead, most mining before this time consisted of little more than surface diggings. Many of the largest mines in the older states were simply open excavations. In the new mineral age, industry went underground in its search for a steadily widening range of materials, and the mine took its place beside the steam engine and the factory as a symbol of industrialism.

Between 1870 and 1920, the value of all mineral products in the United States rose from less than a quarter billion dollars annually to nearly seven billion dollars, a twenty-one fold increase (allowing for changes in the value of money) compared with an eleven fold increase in the value of all manufactured products and an increase in population of less than three times. During this same period lumber production, in board feet, increased less than three times, and wood as an industrial and domestic fuel ceased to be important. On the other hand, a number of new minerals acquired economic significance after 1850. Gold mining assumed importance first with the discoveries in California in 1848 and 1849, and thereafter it spread from one mining district to another in the Far West. Silver mining as an independent rather than a by-product industry dates from the discovery of the Comstock Lode in Nevada in 1859. The commercial development of petroleum begins with the drilling operations in western Pennsylvania shortly before the Civil War. Copper production rose so rapidly between 1865 and 1914 as to reduce the earlier activities in copper mining to minor proportions. The other non-ferrous metals underwent a less spectacular but yet important expansion. The alloy metals, such as vanadium, chrome, and manganese, played but a slight role prior to 1900, and as late as 1890 aluminum and magnesium had advanced very little beyond laboratory curiosities. Of the nonmetallic minerals, phosphate rock production dates from shortly after the Civil War; sand, gravel and the raw materials of cement did not enter the significant period of their growth until about 1870. Salt had been in production, principally for nonindustrial purposes, from an early date, but the spectacular rise of sulphur did not get under way until after 1900.

The causes of this tremendous growth of mineral output are to be found chiefly in the circumstances that ushered in the age of machines and mechanical power. Only the metals with their durability, tensile strength, and capacity for taking the most complex forms and shapes could meet the requirements of rapidly moving machinery driven by powerful prime movers. Metals could be shaped with greater precision than wood; they were less subject to distortion by weather, less affected by fire; they could be joined in firmer bonds by means of casting, riveting, and welding; they permitted higher speeds and greater strains; they were more compact in relation to their weight. In various combinations, the metals, basic and alloy, could be given wide variations in characteristics to adapt them to a wide variety of requirements. To mine, smelt, forge and transport metals and to drive the equipment and machinery into which they were fabricated required proportionately greater quantities of fuel—especially fuel to supply the power mechanisms of steam engine, electric generators, and internal combustion engines. The other nonmetallic minerals rose sharply in importance, in part in response to the general expansion of industry and in part to such direct influence as the rapid growth of the chemical and construction industries and the developing needs of agriculture for fertilizer. Although the actual number of persons engaged in the various mining industries has never been large, and in recent years has amounted to only two per cent of the total working population, in many of the western states, as well as in substantial districts in many other states, mining has been from the beginning the principal, sometimes almost the only, important industry.

Scientific and Technological Advances

The expansion of mineral production in this period became peculiarly dependent upon advances in the science and technology of mining. The prospector with his rule of thumb knowledge and pick and shovel methods continued to play an important pioneering role so long as outcroppings and other surface indications of the more obvious kind served as the chief guide to the presence of minerals. The location of mineral bodies at depths of hundreds and thousands of feet and the estimation of their probable extent required vastly greater resources in knowledge and equipment.

The foundations of a systematic knowledge of geological structures and minerals distribution had been laid by 1850 for most of the states east of the Mississippi by the state geological surveys, staffed chiefly by college and university professors. In the states and territories of the Far West, responsibility for the systematic exploration and mapping of the mineral areas was assumed by the Federal Government. Beginning in the late sixties, a series of geological surveys were carried out, and these were followed by the establishment in 1879 of the United States Geological Survey, which became the leading organization of its kind in the world. The resulting intensive studies of the genesis of ore deposits, ore structure and occurrence, and the general character of underground geology, combined with the preparation of detailed topographic-geologic maps of the mining districts, provided an indispensable basis for the effective development of the mineral industries of the West. By the end of the First World War, many of the larger mining companies carried on their own geological work, and in later years the scientific exploration for and mapping of new mineral bodies became fundamental features of all large scale commercial mining operations.

In the nature of things, the most accessible and the richest of the known mineral bodies were exploited first. As these became exhausted and as market conditions warranted, lower grade bodies were brought under development, mining operations were carried to greater and greater depths, and the problems of utilizing ores of lower metallic content received more and more attention. This gave rise to new and difficult problems of mining—of sinking shafts and excavating and securing underground passages, of drainage and ventilation, of detaching, removing and hoisting the minerals, and of dressing operations to separate the ore proper from associated refuse materials as a preliminary to smelting or other refining operations. There were variations upon and exceptions to this general development in mining. The extraction of minerals in liquid or gaseous form, of which petroleum, natural gas, salt, and sulphur were the chief examples, presented its own peculiar problems, and these were met by the progressive development of drilling and related techniques. In the case of the two most basic minerals, bituminous coal and iron ore, the fortunate discovery of vast deposits at or near the surface, aided by the development of highly efficient earth-moving equipment, made possible in some districts a reversal of the general trend in mining. By means of giant power shovels, drag lines, bulldozers and similar equipment, the overburden of earthy materials is removed in stripping operations, making possible the removal of the mineral by open pit methods which have the advantages of greater mechanization and lower costs. Stripping methods have been introduced in the case of other minerals to some extent, particularly in the case of low grade copper ores. A specialized form of stripping using powerful streams of water, known as hydraulicking, was early introduced in the gold regions of the West and for some twenty-five years played an important role.

Progress in underground mining operations was marked by the fairly steady advance of mechanization. At the close of the Civil War, hoisting, pumping, and ventilating were the only operations performed mechanically; steam power was employed in nearly all instances. All other underground operations—shaft-sinking, tunneling, ore digging and loading, and, where the use of animals was not feasible, even hauling—were carried on by hand with hand tools, aided only in the initial separation of mineral from the earth by blasting. The problem of mechanization was a two-fold one of devising machines to perform mining operations—especially drilling, cutting, and carrying—under the limitations imposed by the restricted space of mines, and of obtaining power in a form that could be used underground and in the constantly changing locations required by advances within the mine. The story is one of improvements in power drills and blasting explosives, in mechanical cutting, loading and hauling, in the machinery for pumping, hoisting, and ventilating, and in methods of power transmission.

Progress was long limited by the circumstance that steam boiler units could not be placed underground because of combustion fumes and gases. The transmission of steam over the necessary distances through pipes was usually attended by prohibitive heat losses. The piping of compressed air from surface compressors into the mines, however, proved feasible, and its use in power drills was the first important advance, being inaugurated in the 1870's and undergoing steady improvement. The general employment of machines in underground operations had to await the coming of electric power and its application to mining machines. Underground lighting, surprising as it may seem, was supplied principally by candles down to the nineties; candles gave way gradually to kerosene lamps, which in turn were replaced by carbide lamps, and these in their turn by electric cap lights and underground wired lighting systems.

These improvements in mining equipment and machinery were accompanied by the development of underground mining systems of excavation and removal. The purpose here was to devise methods by which to obtain maximum extraction of minerals, to minimize handling, and to facilitate removal with the least expense for tunneling, timbering, and other preliminary work, subject always to the requirements of safety of operations which in recent decades have received increasing emphasis. Much practical ingenuity and engineering skill went into this phase of mining operations, although the results have been less spectacular since the methods are less readily understood than those in the field of mechanization.

Development of Iron Ore Fields

Iron ore was much the most important, quantitatively, of the ores produced throughout this period. National output increased from an annual average of more than ten million tons, 1881–1890, to nearly 70,000,000 tons, 1916–1920, a figure thereafter exceeded in only one year prior to 1940. The outstanding development of the years following the Civil War was the great expansion of production in the Lake Superior ore fields, marked especially by the rise to prominence of the rich Mesabi ranges and the thoroughgoing mechanization of the handling of ore from mine to furnace-mouth.[1] The Michigan and Wisconsin ores, which comprised

[1] The best account of the Superior ore fields on the historical as well as the organizational side is H. R. Mussey, *Combination in the Mining Industry: A Study of Concentration in Lake Superior Iron Ore Production* (New York: Columbia University Press, 1905). For the Mesabi field, see F. P. Wirth, *The Discovery and Exploitation of the Minnesota Iron Lands* (Cedar Rapids, Iowa: Torch Press, 1937).

practically all the Superior ores in use prior to 1890, were hard and rock-like in character and had to be mined by drilling and blasting. After the first few years operations were almost entirely underground. The Mesabi ores of Minnesota, on the other hand, were soft and crumbly and lent themselves admirably to the stripping and steam-shovel techniques of mining. Tracks were laid in the open pits and railroad cars loaded at the excavation. These advantages more than offset the greater distance from the Mesabi field to the major lake ports of delivery. Once the technical difficulties of handling this dustlike ore had been overcome, its use increased rapidly, and by 1913 70 per cent of the 50,000,000 tons of ore mined in the Lake Superior district (out of a total of some 62,000,000 tons for the entire country) came from the Mesabi field. Improvements in ore-handling facilities made it possible to unload 10,000 tons from specially designed ore freighters in less than two hours and loading from gravity docks was effected with equal rapidity. The freight charges on Lake Superior ores to Cleveland and Buffalo were reduced even before the First World War to one dollar and less a ton.

A new and important source of ores in the last quarter of the century was the Alabama-Tennessee district centering in Birmingham. Despite their unsuitability for Bessemer purposes, the proximity of these ores to cheap coal and their usefulness for foundry iron encouraged their active development. By 1892 they constituted nearly one-fourth of all the ore raised in the country. Eastern ores still played an important, if minor, part in the industry and ores in steadily increasing quantities were imported from Spain, Cuba, and elsewhere abroad for use in the furnaces of the interior as well as along the Seaboard.

Opening of the Western Copper Fields

Here, as in the case of iron ore, the principal developments of the post-Civil War decades are associated with the rise of new ore districts in the West. Down to 1880 the bulk of the copper produced in this country came from the Michigan district where during the seventies some 85 per cent of the national product was mined. Michigan's dominance was challenged and within a few years overthrown when discoveries in the seventies and eighties brought into production the rich copper districts of Montana and Arizona. By 1885 Montana's ore output nearly equaled and five years later had passed that of Michigan. By 1910 Montana and Arizona ores together accounted for 54 per cent of the national output as compared with Michigan's 20 per cent. The Butte district of Montana was the first of the new copper fields to come into production.[2] Butte

[2] The more spectacular features of the development of the Butte district are treated in C. B. Glasscock, *The War of the Copper Kings: Builders of Butte and Wolves of Wall Street* (New York: Grosset and Dunlap, 1939). For a fuller and more thorough discussion consult Robert G. Raymer, *A History of Copper Mining in Montana* (Chicago: Lewis Publishing Company, 1930).

began as a gold- and silver-mining camp but disappointments in these metals turned attention to the exploration of copper lodes. With the striking of rich copper ore in the Anaconda mine and the completion of a railroad connection to the East, production in this area shot upward.

By 1887 the Anaconda was the chief producing mine in the United States and a competitive struggle between it and Calumet and Hecla, leading Michigan producer, cut copper prices in half. Arizona followed more slowly, beginning with the development of the Globe and Copper Queen districts in the seventies and eighties. In 1890 this state was producing but one-eighth of the national product, but by 1925 it had moved into the leading position among the copper-producing states, accounting for 43 per cent of the country's total as compared with 30 per cent for Montana and Utah combined and 8 per cent for Michigan.

Development of Low-Grade Ores

While many of the Western ores first exploited showed as high a copper content as those of the Michigan field, native copper excepted, and were concentrated without difficulty by the customary methods of stamping and washing, the general yield steadily declined in quality as the higher-grade ores were exhausted. Within a few years producers were faced with the problem of reducing bodies of ore assaying but four to six per cent copper. Even with improvements in the older methods of concentration, four-per-cent ore ordinarily proved profitable only because of the gold and silver associated with it. A revolution in mining and concentration methods was necessary before the enormous and long unknown porphyry deposits of the West, assaying for the most part between 0.75 and 2.5 per cent, could be successfully exploited.[3] Their recovery was a technological and engineering feat of the first order. It was effected in part by the adaptation of the stripping and open-cut methods of the Mesabi iron ranges but in greater part through the development of the oil flotation method of concentration. In this ingenious process the heavier minerals are made to rise to the top of a mass of water by mixing them, after a preliminary fine grinding, with oil and driving air through the mixture. The metal-bearing froth that forms is readily skimmed off and the oil then separated from the ore concentrate by the application of heat. This flotation method made possible a high recovery of metal from very low-grade ores. In some instances ores containing as little as 11 pounds of copper to the ton were exploited successfully. Production in the porphyry mines got under way about 1905 and 10 years later 6 of them accounted for nearly 30 per cent of the total copper product of the United

[3] On the technical problems involved in the handling of the porphyry ores and details of their solution, see A. B. Parsons, *The Prophyry Coppers* (New York: American Institute of Mining and Metallurgical Engineers, 1933).

States. By 1923 the average recoverable content of copper ore mined in the United States was estimated at but 1.58 per cent.

Mining of Other Non-Ferrous Metals

Gold and silver mining, following the initial upsurge of operations in the fifties and sixties, held the lead in the non-ferrous field down to the end of the century; their products exceeded the aggregate value of copper, lead, and zinc mining combined until about 1900. A few years after the early discoveries in California, gold mining left behind hand methods of placer mining with pan or rocker in the sands and gravels of stream beds. As the richer surface deposits accessible by manual operations were exhausted, gold mining took two directions, both involving heavy capital expenditures for development: hydraulic and quartz mining. Hydraulic mining was developed to make possible the large scale exploitation of low-grade alluvial deposits. It was simply the mechanization of placer mining and required heavy expenditures, running into hundreds of thousands of dollars, to bring water to the deposits by means of elaborate systems of "ditches" (canals) and flumes. As early as 1860 these "ditch" systems totaled thousands of miles in length in California alone. Hydraulic mining passed its peak within a few years, digging its own grave by the success of its operations. The washing away literally of whole hills led to the silting up of rivers below, causing much damage and culminating in legal restrictions that placed strict limits on hydraulic operations.

Quartz mining had its beginning in the search for the rock formations in which the alluvial deposits of gold had their origin. The surface outcroppings of quartz veins were quickly exhausted and underground operations presented problems of shaft sinking, tunneling, and extraction that required the greatest skill of the mining and mechanical engineer and heavy investment of capital. The great physical bulk of the ores made preliminary processing in the mining region necessary, despite the scarcity and high cost of fuel. Stamp mills and smelters were erected to concentrate and reduce the ores, and the production of precious metals and the baser ones associated with them assumed a leading place in the economies of the mountain states of the Far West. In the mining of gold, California, Colorado, and South Dakota early became and remained the leading states; in the mining of silver, Montana, Utah and Idaho.

The great expansion of lead production in this period is associated with development of the silver-bearing ores of the Rocky Mountain region and the large deposits of low-grade disseminated ore of southeastern Missouri. Exploitation of the Rocky Mountain area dates from the discoveries of lead ores in Nevada and Utah in 1869–1870 and was made possible on a significant scale by the completion in 1871 of railroad connections that enabled the ore to reach a market. The eighties were marked by the development of the Leadville, Colo., district, which for a few years supplied one-third of the total United States product. In the next decade the Coeur d'Alene district of Idaho entered upon the development that was to make it one of the principal lead areas of the United States.

Of even greater importance were operations in southeastern Missouri and adjacent Oklahoma and Kansas, the "tri-state" district, where rich, near-surface ores had long been exploited. The really big development of the district dates from 1869 when a lead company began prospecting for deep deposits with a diamond drill, and uncovered extensive areas, hundreds of feet thick, of a low-grade ore with a metallic content of between four and six per cent, the practical extraction of which called for large-scale operations and a heavy investment of capital. This district became the largest producing area in the United States, contributing in 1921 about one-third to the national output. It also became the principal center of zinc production in this country; the two metals were to an important extent taken from the same mines.

Coal

The coal industry that in the preceding period established so firm a position for itself both in the domestic and in the industrial economy of the nation strengthened that position step by step with the advance of industrialization.[4] The power and heat supplied to industry by coal increased rapidly in the second half of the nineteenth century. By 1870 steam coal passed water power in importance as a source of industrial energy and by this time, too, coal had become the most important metallurgical fuel. For a generation the position of coal in our economy was unchallenged and even with the rise of competing sources of energy coal continued to supply the greater part of the nation's requirements. Anthracite, steadily displaced by bituminous coal for most industrial purposes, was confined increasingly to domestic use. Its production leveled off about 1913 and began to decline about 1920. Bituminous coal reached its peak during the First World War and thereafter declined, subject to marked fluctuations in annual output.

Changes in the use and consumption of coal were not many in this period but they were important. Although the use of charcoal for metallurgical purposes continued to increase, in an absolute sense, down to the last quarter of the nineteenth century, coal rapidly reduced it to a position of negligible importance in this field. Coal in general supplanted

[4] There is a great need for a history of the coal-mining industry in this country, especially for the bituminous fields, that has been met only in part by the recent work of H. N. Eavenson, *The First Century and a Quarter of American Coal Industry* (Pittsburgh: Privately printed, 1942). Within its scope, Eliot Jones, *The Anthracite Coal Combination in the United States* (Cambridge, Mass.: Harvard University Press, 1914), is excellent.

wood as fuel and was used in increasing amounts to manufacture gas for domestic uses of a population in rapid process of urbanization. Undoubtedly the most important of the new demands for coal were made by the railroad locomotives that had so long been stoked with wood. Railroads reached a peak consumption of 28 per cent of the total output of bituminous coal in the first decade of the twentieth century. Although this percentage fell off to about 20 per cent in the thirties, the railroad was long the greatest single consumer of coal. Only in recent years have coke ovens, the next most important outlet for bituminous coal, approached and at last equaled locomotives.

The most significant developments in the technology of coal mining can be summed up in the word mechanization. Progress was slow until the close of the century, principally because of the difficulty of applying steam power to underground operations. Electricity and compressed air altered the situation and after 1900 the introduction of mechanical devices for cutting and undercutting as well as hauling proceeded rapidly. Mechanical loading devices did not attain importance until the 1930's.

The Geography of Production

No radical changes in the geographical distribution of the coal-mining industry took place in this period. Anthracite production, except for negligible amounts, continued to be confined to northeastern Pennsylvania and gave way to bituminous coal as the major industrial fuel. In the bituminous industry the center of production moved slowly westward, owing to the rising importance of the Middle Western fields. In the trans-Mississippi region the most notable development occurred in Colorado, but Kansas, Iowa, Wyoming, and several other Western states eventually added some millions of tons each to the national coal output. More important was the rise in the South of the Birmingham district, where the demands of the iron and steel industry made Alabama one of the leading coal states in the country. Despite developments elsewhere Pennsylvania continued to lead the field in bituminous production until West Virginia forged ahead after 1930. In recent years Pennsylvania, West Virginia, and Illinois have together accounted for more than three-fifths of the national output.

Depression in Coal

The most interesting developments in the coal industry during this period are found not in the field of technology or in regional-production trends but rather in the organization and general economic condition of the industry. The production of coal, basic as it has been in America's industrial structure, attained the unenviable distinction of becoming America's first depressed industry, suffering from chronic overproduction and disorder during the past half century. The causes of the industry's troubles have been above all the enormous extent of coal lands suitable to commercial development, the decline in the use and demand for coal, and the system of private ownership that permits owners of this basic resource to develop or withhold it at will and to extract it in the manner most advantageous to private profit. These factors have resulted in the development of mining capacity far in excess of demand, a high degree of plant and labor idleness, excessive competition aggravated by high fixed charges, much labor-management trouble, and very wasteful methods of extraction. There have been at all times favored districts and mines that have enjoyed a good measure of prosperity and some stability. In the slump that set in after the First World War, the bituminous industry was more seriously affected than the anthracite.

The Anthracite Combination

With respect to many features of its organization and development the anthracite industry belongs in a class by itself.[5] The disorder and instability characteristic of the bituminous industry have largely been lacking. The localization of industry within a small and compact territory and the early concentration of ownership in the hands of a few large companies made possible and encouraged an orderly development. The railroads, which in the years following the Civil War came to own the great bulk of the anthracite fields and to engage directly or indirectly in the mining of coal, were faced for a time with the problem of active and uncontrolled competition, both among themselves and with independent operators. Prices, profits, and wages were beaten down with resulting disorder at times approaching chaos. Relief from this situation was secured by the adoption and extension of pooling agreements that fixed the total quantity of coal shipped from the region, allotted percentage quotas to members, established penalties for noncompliance, and in many instances fixed prices.

Eventually, the anthracite combination was able to perfect its arrangements with such skill that disorder and instability were a thing of the past. Each railroad was made responsible for seeing that the coal carried by it, including that mined by independents, did not exceed its quota. The larger independent companies were tied up with contracts for their entire output at a definite and attractive percentage of the selling price, thus eliminating one source of competition and barring traffic from rival railroads. By combined action the pool succeeded in blocking the construction of new railroads that would provide independent access to

[5] In addition to the Jones study cited above, see the accounts of the findings of the United States Coal Commission in E. C. Hunt and others, eds., *What the Coal Commission Found* (Baltimore: Williams & Wilkins, 1925) and E. T. Devine, *Coal* (Bloomington, Ill.: American Review Service, 1925).

markets. Annual production was stabilized at the amount that the market would profitably absorb. In these ways the development of the anthracite region was carefully regulated and the extremes of competition and over-development that plagued the bituminous industry were thereafter unknown to it. If such measures did nothing to prevent and possibly aided the eventual decline in production, there was some compensation—at least, for the producing interests—in the steady upward trend in prices.

Competition Is the Death of Trade

Quite different conditions emerged in the bituminous industry. The area of bituminous production spread steadily until some 30 states were engaged regularly in the commercial mining of coal and others were ready to join in when market conditions were favorable. There was no typical operator, as in the anthracite field. At one end of the scale were the great corporations, including the "captive mines," owned and operated by steel companies, railroads, and other enterprises to supply their own needs, and producing by 1920 one-fourth of the national output. At the other end were the "wagon mines" and "country banks" that often turned out less than 1,000 tons annually. In addition to the mines that within the limits of normal demand operated more or less regularly throughout the year there were hundreds of "snow-birds," the little mines with high costs of production that began working at the height of the season's demand each winter to take advantage of a favorable market and high prices. In marked contrast with the 174 producers operating in the anthracite fields in 1920 there were 12,212 bituminous producers operating 14,766 mines of which 5,845 were wagon mines and country banks operating on a small scale.

The Age of Oil

The rise of the petroleum industry is one of the outstanding industrial developments of the generation following the Civil War. The successful drilling of Drake's well on Oil Creek in western Pennsylvania in 1859 is a useful peg on which to hang the beginnings of the growth of this industry. Petroleum had often been encountered in drilling for salt brine in earlier decades. While generally regarded as a nuisance, both "burning fluid" and lubricants had been manufactured from it through distillation before 1859. Natural gas, too, had been used for years in the manufacturing of salt in the Kanawha salt region of western Virginia. The significance of Drake's well was that it was drilled purposefully to obtain petroleum. Within twelve years, petroleum production for the country had reached 15,000 barrels daily and the foundations of the new industry were solidly laid.

The causes of this extraordinary growth are found in the growing pressure of the demand for better and cheaper illuminants and lubricants. A rising standard of living, the spread of public education and literacy, and the popularization of newspapers, periodicals and books, together with the rapid increase of population and its concentration in urban communities, underlay the need for more and better illuminants. The situation with respect to lubricants was, in some respects, even more pressing. By the 1850's, the advance of mechanization had reached the point where lubricants had become one of the critical raw materials of industry. The rapid multiplication of machines in the extractive industries, in manufacturing, and in transportation, the increase in the speed of their operation and in the ruggedness and weight of their construction, and the inadequacy of existing oils necessitated the obtaining of better and cheaper lubricants. The most satisfactory of the animal fats and oils heretofore relied upon—the oil derived from the sperm whale—could not meet the rapidly increasing demands of industry, and its high cost encouraged the search for cheaper substitutes.[6] The 1850's were a period of experimentation, and a variety of illuminants and lubricants were placed on the market, of which the most important were those obtained from the distillation of bituminous coal. This thriving new industry had its spectacular growth brought quickly to an end by the mushrooming of the petroleum industry, which provided better products at lower cost.

The Westward March of Oil

The oil boom in western Pennsylvania in the sixties was soon followed by a continuous series of discoveries and developments as the search for petroleum was extended to other states, especially in New York, West Virginia, northwest Ohio and the adjoining region in Indiana, and even in far off California. The wide distribution of petroleum, the ready clues of surface seepage as a guide to discovery, and the relatively low cost of reaching the shallower reserves through simple drilling methods, resulted in rapid increases in output. Pennsylvania's production reached 26 million barrels in 1881 and an all-time high of over 31 million barrels in 1891. Ohio forged ahead of Pennsylvania, becoming the nation's leading producer in 1895 and holding this position until displaced by California in 1903. Texas, Oklahoma, Louisiana, and Illinois in turn followed with spectacular developments. California's production rose from less than five million barrels in 1900 to 73 million in 1910. By this last date the total United States production had reached the 200 million barrel mark, and by the end of World War I this figure was nearly doubled.

---

[6] A typical comment of the period may be cited: "The whale oils which have hitherto been much relied on in this country to furnish light, are yearly becoming more scarce, and may in time almost entirely fail, while the rapid increase of machinery demands a large portion of the purest of these oils for lubricating." *Scientific American,* Vol. XII, p. 329 (June 27, 1857).

New Methods of Extraction, Refining, and Use

This development was aided by advances in the techniques of extraction and refining. The simple method of drilling by means of tools attached to the end of cables was satisfactory for the shallow wells of the early decades. The introduction of the rotary system (first developed in water well drilling) in oil drilling in the nineties and the invention of the rock bit in 1908 made possible the drilling of wells to depths and under conditions that were impracticable with the older system. The important role of gas pressure in the expulsion of petroleum was slow to be recognized, with the result that there were tremendous losses from the free escape of natural gas and the output and production life of wells were reduced. By 1918 the Federal Bureau of Mines was giving much attention to sources of waste in the petroleum industry and its studies provided the basis for conservation measures in the years ahead.

The development of refining techniques was influenced especially by the changing emphasis in the demand for petroleum products. At the end of the first two decades of the industry, kerosene still comprised three-fourths of the products of refining, with gasoline and lubricants accounting for two-fifths and three-fifths, respectively, of the remainder. By 1900 the kerosene yield had fallen to one-half, while gasoline yield was virtually unchanged. The fuel oil yield increased rapidly after the turn of the century and by 1918 reached a peak of 55 per cent of the total products of refining. The use of fuel oil first became important in California, presumably because of the expense of bringing in coal from a distance, and by the nineties was in extensive use by locomotives. Its use spread to industrial fields, for the heating of buildings, and for marine and naval purposes. By 1912 the railroads alone were consuming over 33 million barrels of fuel oil and the total national consumption amounted to one-third of all petroleum products.

The important rise of gasoline as a petroleum product did not begin until about 1910, an outgrowth of the rapidly mounting use of the internal combustion engine, particularly in automobiles. Not until after World War I did gasoline become the major product of the refining industry, and its rise in importance was accompanied by a sharp upward turn in the overall production of petroleum. Up to 1918, refining was accomplished by the physical separation of the components of the crude oil through simple distillation, and stills of very small capacity were operated at atmospheric pressure on a batch (noncontinuous) method. Following separation, the products were treated with sulphuric acid and alkalies to improve color and reduce odors. Although the industry made little use of science and engineering prior to the First World War, improvements were made in both distillation and treatment. It was not until the demand for gasoline assumed primary importance that the newer process of thermal conversion (called "cracking"), followed in the late thirties by catalytic conversion, was developed.

Salt and Sulphur

The well-drilling technique of extraction, on which the petroleum industry was based, was also employed, with some variations, in the case of two other materials that rose to a position of industrial prominence in the period between the two wars. These were salt and sulphur. Salt is one of the oldest products of industry in this country, but prior to the Civil War its uses were principally confined to the preservation of meat and to its use as a condiment for both human and livestock food. Although found in many districts, the principal sources before 1865 were the Syracuse-Salina district in New York and the Kanawha-Pomeroy district of the upper Ohio Valley. The drilling method of reaching the salt brines, supplemented by pumping to bring the brine to the surface, was employed virtually from the beginning in these districts. Evaporation by solar or artificial heat was then employed to obtain the different commercial grades of the finished article. Beds of rock salt were discovered and brought into production after the Civil War in New York, Michigan, Louisiana and other states, but in most instances, because of the high solubility of salt, drilling and pumping continued to be the simplest and cheapest means of extracting. When the salt beds were reached by drilling, water would be forced down and circulated and then pumped out as brine.

The most important factor in the expansion of salt production, however, was the growth in new industrial uses of salt resulting from the rise in the importance of the chemical industries in the last quarter of the 19th century. The sodium and chlorine of which crude salt is principally composed were basic constituents in a number of materials used in steadily mounting quantities by industry, especially soda ash, caustic soda, bicarbonate of soda, and chlorine, and chemicals made from or with these products. Between 1890 and 1920 the per capita consumption of salt, in all its uses, increased three times.

Sulphur occupied a different position from salt in that our needs had to be met almost entirely by imports prior to 1900, chiefly in the form of pyrites from Spain, with some native sulphur brought from Sicily, the principal source of the world's supply of native sulphur before 1900. After 1860, sulphur acquired numerous and important industrial uses, chiefly in the form of sulphuric acid. This acid was used primarily as a reagent in the manufacture of fertilizer and petroleum products and in a variety of other manufacturing processes. Large quantities were used in many branches of the chemicals industry, especially in the manufacture of other acids. Its production increased fiftyfold in the United States between the Civil War and 1900. Native sulphur came into extensive use in the manufacture of paper, rubber, insecticides and many other products.

The sulphur industry was revolutionized in the United States by two developments: the discovery of immense beds of native sulphur overlying the salt domes in Louisiana and Texas and the invention of the Frasch process of sulphur mining. In this method, large quantities of superheated water were forced down into the sulphur bearing formations. Here it reduced the sulphur to a liquid form that was pumped to the surface. Even after the technical difficulties of this process were solved, it did not become a commercial success until the discovery and opening up of rich petroleum fields in adjacent areas provided the huge quantities of cheap fuel required for its use. Production shot up from less than 8,000 tons in 1903 to 220,000 tons only two years later and to more than a million tons in 1917. The United States shifted overnight from a sulphur-importing to a sulphur-exporting nation. The First World War with its heavy demands for sulphur, resulting chiefly from the tremendous expansion of explosives production, completed the change in the conduct of the sulphur industry by reducing greatly the importation of pyrites from Spain, thereby stimulating the shift in the acid industry from pyrites to sulphur as a raw material. The native pyrite industry, despite the spectacular rise of sulphur, had its beginnings in the years 1875–1900 and continued to expand till a peak of nearly a half million tons was reached in 1917.

Energy Resources and Their Application

The relationship between the mining industries and the development of our energy resources in this period (1866–1918) was one of close interdependence. The extraction of minerals and the preliminary processing of ores at or near the minehead employed increasing quantities of power. More important was the steady shift to mineral products as the major sources of power in the new industrial age. The coal mine and the oil well overtook and then left far behind forest and falling water as sources of the mechanical energy necessary to meet the rapidly expanding demands of industry for power. The replacement of hand tools and processes by machine, the increase in the size and speed of machines, the centralization of manufacturing in large urban centers, and the concentration of manufacturing operations in plants of increasing size were among the more important factors responsible for the change. Finally, problems in the transmission and application of power, especially the need for a compact and mobile motor with a high ratio of power to weight, were solved by the introduction of the electric generator and motor and the internal combustion engine.

So long as industry was decentralized and the typical industrial plant was small, the falling water available in innumerable streams provided a source of mechanical power that in most respects was quite adequate to the needs of the earlier age. There were tens of thousands of stream sites, widely distributed over the country, at which power sufficient for the needs of the typical industrial establishment of the pre-Civil War decades could be obtained. The typical water power installation required but modest expenditures for mill dam, race, water wheel and other appurtenances, and relatively simple skills and equipment for construction, repair, and maintenance.

With the growth in the scale of industrial operations and in the size of plants, the number of stream sites that could meet the enlarged power requirements became progressively limited. Moreover, such sites were often unfavorably located with reference to markets, sources of raw materials, and transportation facilities, situated as they too frequently were in districts whose remoteness and rugged terrain hampered both settlement and the growth of industry. Even in the districts most favored with water power, there were few developments that could support industrial communities of more than 25,000 population. From the nature of things, the growth of manufacturing industries at commercial centers on the larger navigable rivers, on the seaboard and the Great Lakes, and at most inland points was dependent almost wholly, prior to the coming of electric power, upon the use of steam power. The expansion of industry at such important water power sites as Lowell, Holyoke, and Paterson before long reached the point where it could proceed only through the introduction of steam engines. Seasonal irregularities and unseasonal interruptions in the supply of water were other factors that tended increasingly to discourage reliance on water power, even where available. The introduction and improvement of the hydraulic turbine, with its superior efficiency, was insufficient to check the trend toward steam power.

A major influence favoring the shift to steam power was the increased availability of fuel, resulting from the development of old and the opening of new coal fields. Prior to 1850, total annual United States coal production did not exceed eight million tons and an output of twenty million tons was not reached until 1860. Three-fourths of the total at both dates was produced in a single state, Pennsylvania, and one-half of the national output and over two-thirds of that of Pennsylvania came from the anthracite district within this state. Coal production doubled between 1860 and 1870 and again in the following decade, reaching an estimated national total in 1885 of 110 million tons. Of this amount, only one-third was anthracite and less than three-fifths came from Pennsylvania. Even before the Civil War, Ohio, Illinois, and Maryland had become important coal producing states, and after 1865 they were joined by West Virginia, Kentucky, Indiana, and Missouri, with Alabama, Colorado, and even Kansas attaining positions of some importance after 1880. Before 1860 the coal trade had been confined chiefly to water routes—canals and coastal waterways in the East and the rivers in the West—but, with the improvement and cheapening of rail service in the post-war decades, the spreading railroad network made possible a much wider distribution and use of coal as an industrial fuel.

While the expansion of fuel production was under way, improvements in steam power plants provided the technical basis for the shift from water to steam power which advanced so rapidly after 1860. The small, crude and inefficient plants of the early industrial period gave way to boilers and engines that not only were larger and more efficient, but were designed to meet the specialized requirements of the variety of purposes to which they were put. This development proceeded along several lines. The increasing importance of fuel economy where large quantities of power were required led to experimentation and advances in the design of furnaces and boilers and their equipment. Simple cylindrical boilers, often without internal flues, gave way eventually to a variety of forms of the water tube boiler, which combined high efficiency with rapidity of steam generation and was far safer than the older types. These large and complicated vessels, with their banks of tubing and their elaborate arrangements of headers, drums, and combustion chambers, supplemented frequently by superheaters, mechanical stokers, and forced draft, were made possible only by improved qualities of iron and steel and by advances in metal working techniques and in the methods of forming and fitting boiler shells and tubes.

Parallel developments in steam engine design were equally important. Engines increased in size and power, in speed, in economy of steam, and in smoothness of operation. Progress in the larger types of engines was related especially to the development of new types of valves and valve gears, of governors to regulate speed by changing the admission or expansion of steam in response to variations in load, and of additional cylinders in which steam of initially high pressure underwent successive expansion. Special types of engines were designed to meet the specialized requirements of such varied works as textile mills, blast furnaces, water works, and mine hoists. For the smaller manufactory, simple and rugged engines were developed that combined the advantages of low initial cost and attendance expense with simplicity of operation and fair economy of fuel. At the other extreme were the huge power plants of many hundreds of horsepower supplying power at a cost that bore favorable comparison with the best water power installations.

The only major innovation in the application of steam power was the introduction of the steam turbine, first brought to this country from Europe about 1890. Because of its extraordinarily high speed of operation, the steam turbine was unsuited to most industrial uses and found its principal application in driving dynamos for the generation of electric power. The other important power developments in the closing decades of the century were the introduction of electric power and the internal combustion engine. The first internal combustion engines were introduced in the late sixties but it was not until the coming of the Otto silent gas engine, first produced in 1876, that this type of engine became a practical success. Prior to 1900 this engine, of small horsepower and using gas as fuel, was confined to a limited number of industrial uses. The tremendous expansion in the number and the horsepower of internal combustion engines is associated with the extraordinary rise of the automobile after 1900 and with the use of gasoline and other petroleum products as fuels.

Although one of the earliest applications of the electric motor was to traction in urban transit systems, its revolutionary effects were felt principally in the field of manufacturing industry. Introduced first about 1880, electric power made its way slowly for the next twenty years; thereafter it increased rapidly. In combination with the electric generating station, in which steam engines, steam turbines, or hydraulic turbines were the prime movers, the electric motor provided a compact, noiseless and mobile source of power, free from the annoyances and inconveniences attending the provision and operation of furnaces and boilers in the plant. Motors could be placed directly where needed, reducing and eventu ally eliminating the elaborate, noisy, wasteful, and space-consuming systems of overhead shafting and belting. Moreover, the motor permitted the introduction of new and more efficient arrangements of machines and processes not feasible under the old system. By World War I, the trend from direct steam to electric power in industry was well advanced.

The full extent of the power revolution is revealed by a comparison of the relative importance of prime movers in all fields. Total horsepower capacity increased twenty times between 1869 and 1919. Excluding pleasure automobiles, steam engines and turbines accounted for two-thirds of the 1919 total, internal combustion engines for one-sixth, work animals for one-seventh, and, bringing up the rear, water wheels, which accounted for only one twenty-fifth. Nearly two-thirds of the electrical energy was generated at steam plants and most of the remainder at hydro-electric plants. If energy in all its forms and not simply that coming from prime movers is considered, the dependence upon mineral sources of energy is even more striking. As late as the First World War, four-fifths of our energy was derived from coal and four-fifths of the remainder from oil and natural gas.

Selected References

GENERAL WORKS

Barger, Harold, and Sam H. Schurr, *The Mining Industries, 1899-1939. A Study of Output, Employment and Productivity.* New York: National Bureau of Economic Research, Inc., 1944.

Cressy, Edward, *Hundred Years of Mechanical Engineering.* New York: The Macmillan Company, 1937.

Eavenson, H. N., *The First Century and a Quarter of American Coal Industry.* Pittsburgh: Privately printed, 1942.

Jones, Eliot, *The Anthracite Coal Combination in the United States.* Cambridge, Mass.: Harvard University Press, 1914.

Parsons, A. B., ed., *Seventy-Five Years of Progress in the Mineral Industry, 1871-1946.* New York: The American Institute of Mining and Metallurgical Engineers, 1947.

SPECIAL TOPICS

Cushman, Robert E., *The Independent Regulatory Commissions.* New York: Oxford University Press, 1941.

Daugherty, C. H.; A. H. Horton; and R. W. Davenport, *Power Capacity and Power Production in the United States,* U. S. Geological Survey, Water-supply Paper 579. Washington, D. C.: Government Printing Office, 1928.

Hunt, E. E., *et al., What the Coal Commission Found.* Baltimore: Williams and Wilkins, 1925.

Ingalls, W. R., *Lead and Zinc in the United States.* New York: Hill Publishing Company, 1908.

Parsons, A. B., *The Porphyry Coppers.* New York: American Institute of Mining and Metallurgical Engineers, 1933.

Raymer, Robert G., *A History of Copper Mining In Montana.* Chicago: Lewis Publishing Company, 1930.

Wirth, F. P., *The Discovery and Exploitation of the Minnesota Iron Lands.* Cedar Rapids, Iowa: Torch Press, 1937.

24 · THE HEAVY INDUSTRIES

INDUSTRIALISM CAME OF AGE in the post-war decades, and the heavy industries laid the foundations for the new economic structure.[1] Peripheral in their position and importance in the agricultural economy of the earlier years the heavy industries occupied a position of central importance in an economy resting solidly on iron and coal. The capital equipment of our industry assumed a scale, complexity, and cost in comparison with which that of the period before 1850 has the appearance of small-scale working models. In the new industrial technology man was changed from a direct manipulator of materials and tools to a pusher of buttons, reader of dials, and puller of levers controlling giant mechanisms, a metamorphosis that proceeded fastest and furthest in those branches of manufacture concerned with the production of metals and heavy equipment.[2] This is the period when blast furnaces were raised 100 feet in the air, making pygmies of the men who served them; of trains of rolls extending hundreds of yards and capable of reducing in a single operation an eight-ton ingot to a ribbon of sheet steel several feet wide and many hundreds long; of cranes powerful enough to carry the heaviest locomotives; of ore-handling equipment that emptied freight cars by turning them upside down.

In organization as in equipment the heavy industries did much to introduce the age of giantism. If the trust was conceived in oil, it came of age in U. S. Steel and Anaconda Copper; although bituminous coal resisted the consolidation in wide sectors, in the anthracite field there early developed one of the most compact and powerful monopolies the country has known. Concentration of ownership and control, far from universal, was peculiarly characteristic of this field of enterprise. The heavy indus-

1 For the period covered by this chapter there is a dearth of specialized literature dealing with the history of particular industries. The standard general work on manufacturing for this as for the earlier period is V. S. Clark, *History of Manufactures in the United States,* 1929 ed., Vol. 2 (1860-1893) and Vol. 3 (1893-1928). Washington, D. C.: Carnegie Institution, 1929.

2 For a stimulating discussion of the implications of electricity for the industrial age ahead, see Walter N. Polakov, *The Power Age: Its Quest and Challenge.* New York: Covici, Friede, Inc., 1933.

tries, dispelling the haze of anonymity that clouded industrial growth of the earlier years, contributed their full share of colorful personalities to the new age of big business: Carnegie and Schwab in steel; Daly, Heinze, and Guggenheim in copper; Frick in coal and coke; Merritt and Oliver in iron ore.

Led by men of bold imagination, organizing genius, and, very often, buccaneering morals, equipped and directed by engineers and technicians who achieved remarkable results in mass manipulation and processing of materials, favored by natural resources of extraordinary extent and richness, sustained by an ever-replenished supply of cheap immigrant labor and by tariffs protecting the weakest and least efficient companies from foreign competition and enabling the sounder and better-managed to reap profits that at times were literally fabulous, the heavy industries in the generation following the Civil War laid solidly the foundations for the development that by the turn of the century had made the United States in many respects the leading industrial nation of the world.

The Age of Steel

The new industrial age was, above all, an age of iron and steel. The main emphasis in this, as in the earlier period, necessarily falls on the keystone of the whole structure of industry, for although the gap between the ferrous and other heavy industries narrowed appreciably as nonferrous enterprises spurted forward under the stimulus of new and extraordinary demands, iron and steel continued to dominate the scene. The major demand for iron continued for some years to come from the railroads, but important new commodities were pushing to the fore, especially structural iron for the new age of skyscrapers, pipes and tubes to serve as the arteries of industry, armor plate for an expanding navy, and, later, vast quantities of sheet metal to supply the mushroom growth of the automobile industry. Merchant bar, once the chief product of the rolling mills, was reduced to a position of minor importance.

Technical advances in this period were many and varied, but without question those of most far-reaching significance were those associated with the Bessemer and open-hearth processes of making steel.[3] Despite certain misleading connotations of the phrase, the "age of iron" truly became the "age of steel," and the whole economy felt the impact of the change. It is important at the outset to avoid the misconception that this new kind of mass-produced steel resembled at all closely the kind of steel used traditionally in cutlery and edge tools and heretofore manufactured with much difficulty and at high cost. Bessemer and open-hearth steel fell

[3] Fuller accounts of the technical aspects of the making of iron and steel may be consulted in Waldemar Kaempffert, *A Popular History of American Invention* (New York: Charles Scribner's Sons, 1924) and H. M. Howe, *The Metallurgy of Steel* (New York: The Engineering and Mining Journal, 1904).

midway in chemical composition and qualities between wrought iron and tool steel, lacking the softness and weldability of the one and the hardness and brittle quality of the other. The new steel was a low-carbon steel, soft as steels go but having a much greater tensile strength and hardness than the wrought iron that had been the staple product of the puddling furnaces and rolling mills. Admirably suited to a country-blacksmith, horse-and-wagon age, wrought iron for all its toughness was lacking in the qualities demanded to withstand the high speeds, heavy strains, and punishing treatment of the age ahead. Moreover, with the new methods steel could be produced on a large scale quickly and at low cost, not only far more cheaply than edge and tool steel but before very long more cheaply than the wrought iron that it was so largely to supplant.

The Bessemer Process

The Bessemer and open-hearth processes were methods of refining the product of the blast furnace, using molten pig iron in the early years and later the hot metal taken directly or by way of a mixer from the blast furnace. The refined product in each case was given the character of steel by the addition of carefully measured amounts of carbon in some form; it was then cast into ingots preliminary to reduction in the rolling mill to the proper size and shape. The Bessemer or pneumatic process was the more radical and spectacular of the two processes, and the first of them to be introduced in this country. The charge of metal, weighing from 3 to 20 tons, was poured into the familiar eggshaped converter and a blast of air was blown through it from the bottom. In the resulting combustion not only were the carbon, silicon, and other elements associated with the metal removed, but their oxidation supplied the heat necessary for the refining process.

Sir Henry Bessemer was not only responsible for the central idea of the process but he designed elaborate equipment and hydraulic machinery that contributed much to the practical success of the new method. The introduction of the process in this country was delayed for a time by a controversy growing out of conflicting patents of Bessemer and William Kelly, an American who had devised and patented without developing to the point of practical success a pneumatic method of refining iron.[4]

The Open-Hearth Process

A major limitation of the Bessemer process was its failure to remove two elements having a deleterious effect upon the refined product: sul-

[4] The fact that Kelly was an American is evidently the principal reason why certain writers have made much of an invention that, had not Bessemer developed his process, would never have attracted notice. Kelly's patent proved very useful to industrial interests in this country as a bargaining weapon in negotiations with the Bessemer group for the exchange of patent rights.

phur, and, especially, phosphorus. The process was consequently limited to refining pig metal made from the so-called Bessemer, that is, free of phosphorus, ores that comprised but a part of the ore reserves of this country. The problem of refining non-Bessemer pig iron cheaply was solved by the introduction of the open-hearth process, which, like that of Bessemer, was developed first abroad. In this process, scrap iron and steel were charged with pig metal into a reverberatory furnace of a type not unlike the old puddling furnace. The metal was reduced to a molten state and kept so without physical manipulation until the impurities had been removed through various chemical reactions. The lining of the furnace was composed of a chemically basic material that combined with the phosphorus, removing it and other impurities with the slag.

Although the open-hearth process was slower than the Bessemer process—and for many years more expensive—that slowness permitted testing the metal at various stages, thereby making possible much closer control over the final product. Another advantage of great importance for the future was the possibility of using scrap metal as part of the charge, thus providing an important outlet for materials otherwise difficult to utilize. Moreover, while the open-hearth process could be carried on with much smaller units and less equipment than the Bessemer process, furnace capacity was steadily increased until the handling of 250 tons per heat was possible.

Although made experimentally in this country as early as 1864, Bessemer steel was not produced commercially until several years later when several plants were established in the East and Middle West. The principal use to which Bessemer steel was put in the early years was in rails, where its superior wearing power was soon demonstrated. Despite their much greater cost Bessemer rails were adopted rapidly, particularly for main-line use where traffic was heavy. Of nearly 900,000 tons of Bessemer steel made in 1880, 741,475 tons were rails. Five years later, iron rails accounted for only 15,000 tons of a total of something over 1,000,000 tons.

As steel proved itself in use and as methods of manufacture and control of quality and characteristics improved, the factor of cost turned in its favor. Wrought iron was confined to a narrowing range of uses, although for some purposes it continued to be superior.[5] Efforts made to reduce the cost and enlarge the scale of wrought iron production by mechanizing the puddling process were not particularly successful and the methods devised for this purpose were not widely introduced. Open-hearth steel gained steadily in favor, attaining preference first in the manufacture of sheet and plate steel and steel castings and eventually entering the rail field. By 1908 its production topped that of Bessemer steel and thereafter ad-

5 The greater resistance of wrought iron to corrosion, for example, makes it preferable for products such as pipe when used under given conditions or for certain purposes.

vanced with such rapidity that by 1930 the ratio of open-hearth steel to Bessemer was seven to one.

Bigger and Better Blast Furnaces

In the blast-furnace department changes of equal magnitude were taking place. The old square masonry structure, which in ruin took on so picturesque a character, built against a hillside to facilitate hand charging by wheelbarrow at the furnace top (tunnel head), began to be replaced in the sixties by cylindrical boiler-plate shells lined on the inside with refractory brick and elevated on supporting pillars for convenience of access. Within a few years automatic skip hoists carried charges to the top and emptied them, completing the mechanization of operations. Hot-blast stoves were removed from the tunnel head and placed in a row upon the ground near by. Using gases piped from the tunnel head, these immense stoves, approximating in size the blast furnace itself, under the improved regenerative technique made possible air-blast temperatures of twice the 600° (F.) reached by the older method.

Higher temperatures and increased pressure supplied by powerful blowing engines greatly accelerated the smelting process and, combined with the use of larger furnaces, raised production to phenomenal figures. The lead was taken by the Pittsburgh district and by the Carnegie works where rivalry fostered by Carnegie brought extraordinary results. Whereas before the Civil War few furnaces reached an output of 300 tons a week and 50 to 100 tons were good average yields, and whereas in the seventies 600 tons was the maximum, by 1880 there were furnaces at Pittsburgh turning out 1,200 tons a week. Ten years later this figure was doubled and in 1905 a prewar record of 918 tons a day was set by a furnace at the Edgar Thomson works. Average furnace output increased sixfold between 1874 and 1892. British ironmasters were amazed at these achievements.

Rolling Mill Practice

Developments in the rolling mill were no less extraordinary. The typical practice in the merchant-bar and early rail mills was to pass the slabs and bars through the rolls by hand and then carry them back to repeat the process from the same side as many times as might be necessary. Such methods were hardly practical for handling the rails of increasingly heavy section and the structural shapes that were demanded by new industrial requirements. The three-high mill, introduced in the late fifties and permitting the bar to be passed back and forth through the rolls without waste motion or handling, was the first of an important series of innovations that eventually eliminated, save for the hand at the controls, human muscle. Mechanical devices pushed the ingot from the furnace or raised it from the soaking pit on to the roll tables, passed it back and forth through the rolls, turned it over when necessary and carried it to the shears or trimming saw at the conpletion of the process.

Of the newer products of the rolling mill, none was more exacting in its requirements than the structural shapes that were acquiring such importance. Prior to the decade ending 1860, most of the iron made for structural purposes took the form of cast-iron girders and pillars. The earliest demand for structural iron and steel came from the railroad bridges needed to sustain the loads of increasingly heavy locomotives and rolling stock. When in the last decade of the century mounting land values and the concentration of business in the larger metropolitan centers brought in the age of the skyscraper, structural steel received a new impetus that was greatly to expand this branch of production and to take up some of the relative slack resulting from the completion of our railway network and the stabilization of rail demand.

The total output of rolled products, which by 1860 had just passed 500,000 tons, reached an annual average of more than 5,000,000 tons in the late eighties, rose to 16,000,000 in the years 1900-1910, 32,000,000 by 1920, and a peak figure of 41,000,000 tons in the boom year of 1929.[6] Indicative of the developing requirements of the new industrial age was the course of production figures for the major products of the rolling mill. Rails reached a peak annual average of 3,250,000 tons from 1906 to 1910 and thereafter leveled off at about 2,750,000. Structural shapes, which in the early nineties averaged less than 500,000 tons, overtook and passed rails in the period from 1911 to 1915 and advanced to a peak of nearly 5,000,000 tons in 1929. Plates and sheets, starting from an average annual figure of less than 700,000 tons in the late eighties, mounted steadily to more than 8,000,000 tons between 1916 and 1920, slumped for a few years, and rose to 12,500,000 tons in 1929. While the growth of the automobile industry was the most important single factor in the development of this class of rolled products, the extraordinary expansion of production indicated by these figures reflected the replacement of wood by sheet steel not only for innumerable industrial uses but also in a wide variety of consumers' goods ranging from filing cases and refrigerators to children's toys.

The Geography of Iron and Steel

The geographical distribution of the industry, in the meantime, underwent important changes. Although the erection of new and enlarged plants along the Seaboard more than counterbalanced the decline of the old charcoal industry of the East, and although Pennsylvania continued to lead all other states by a wide margin with the Pittsburgh district maintaining its position, there was a westward trend among new estab-

[6] The annual *Statistical Abstract of the United States,* compiled under the direction of the Bureau of the Census, contains a wealth of statistical data on our industrial growth, frequently going back as far as 1850.

lishments of larger scale. A preference was shown for shore sites on the Great Lakes with convenient access to ore supplies. This trend was demonstrated by the transfer of the 60-year-old Lackawanna works from Scranton to a site near Buffalo where a $40,000,000 plant was erected at the turn of the century, and by the United States Steel Corporation's establishment of a $50,000,000 plant on Lake Michigan in Gary, Ind.

The Chicago district showed the most substantial growth in the period between 1865 and 1914. Some of the first Bessemer steel in the country was made and rolled there and a thriving blast-furnace industry based on Superior ores and Connellsville and Illinois coal developed in the seventies and eighties. A single company owning works in both Chicago and Milwaukee increased its production from 60,000 tons in 1875 to more than 1,000,000 tons in 1888, and formed the nucleus of an organization that 10 years later was to rival the largest steel enterprise of the Pittsburgh district. The early hopes of St. Louis for prominence in this industry faded with the failure of the Missouri mines to yield the anticipated amount of ores and the only important development west of the Mississippi centered in Colorado, where the dominant organization had an output in 1900 of 150,000 tons.

Pig Iron and Birmingham

What was in some respects the most astonishing development of the industry in the post-Civil War decades took place in the hitherto industrially retarded South with the Birmingham district of northern Alabama and adjacent Tennessee as the center of greatest growth. The rise of Birmingham began with a speculative townsite boom in the seventies when the iron industry was in that castles-in-the-air stage in which limitless possibilities are envisaged.[7] Vast resources of coal and iron ore, in notable instances mined from the same hill, held out the promise of unusually low production costs and prompted the undertaking of scores of projects to realize this potential wealth. Wide publicity was given to the prediction of Sir Lowthian Bell, the British iron expert, that the low cost of assembling raw materials was destined to make the district one of the cheapest iron centers of the world. Substantial development got under way in the eighties when the Alabama blast-furnace industry outgrew that of every state except Pennsylvania. By 1894 Alabama and Tennessee together produced over 800,000 tons of pig iron, more than one-third of the metal produced in the nation, exclusive of that used for making steel. Large quantities were sent to Northern markets and there were considerable exports as well. After this promising beginning, the growth of the Southern iron industry slowed down to a pedestrian

[7] Ethel Armes, *The Story of Coal and Iron in Alabama* (Birmingham: Published under the auspices of the Chamber of Commerce, Birmingham, Ala., 1910) gives a colorful picture of this phase of Birmingham's development.

pace that in the years between the panic of 1893 and the First World War failed to keep up with even the rate of growth for the country at large. The South's production of pig iron in the years 1893-1903 virtually stood still and its share in the total pig iron product of the country declined by 50 per cent. The distance to Northern markets that provided the chief outlets for its products, the cost of reaching these markets, and the unsuitability of most Southern pig iron for Bessemer use both limited Northern demand and held back the manufacture of steel in the vicinity. Even though the bright promise of the early years was realized only in part, an iron and steel center of major importance had been added to the industrial resources of the country.

The Rise of Big Steel

It goes without saying that the extraordinary technical achievement and enormous expansion of production described above could hardly have occurred within the framework of the industry as organized in the years preceding the Civil War, when the typical industrial establishment was a small firm, organized as a partnership and operated with the caution and conservatism characteristic of the small-scale enterprise of that day. Pittsburgh's rolling mills, much above the average in size and investment, had an average capitalization of but $156,000 in 1857 and the Cambria Iron Works, probably the largest in the country at that time, had an authorized capital of only $1,000,000. Sums such as these were but petty cash in the finances of the giant corporations that within a few years came to dominate the scene. The vast plants required for efficient operation under the new techniques, combined with the advantages of owning ore and coal lands and transportation facilities, called for an outlay of tens of millions of dollars before a ton of metal could be turned out. Not least among the techniques indispensable to the functioning of the new iron and steel industry was that of managing bigness. Andrew Carnegie led the way and marked the path for others in this talent.

Carnegie

From bobbin boy to messenger to assistant railroad superintendent and spare-time venturer in profitable speculative schemes, Carnegie's rise to industrial leadership was an epic of the new industrial America.[8] His connection with the iron industry began during the years of civil war with an investment in a Pittsburgh mill, and was enlarged shortly after by an interest in a new blast-furnace plant. When, in 1874, Carnegie

[8] There is no adequate biography of Carnegie. B. J. Hendrick's *Life of Andrew Carnegie* (New York: Doubleday, Doran & Company, 1932) is good so far as Carnegie's social and cultural activities are concerned. For a useful antidote to this semiofficial life, see J. H. Bridge, *The Inside History of the Carnegie Steel Company* (New York: The Aldine Book Company, 1903).

became the leading partner in the firm that erected the first Bessemer plant in the Pittsburgh district, the Edgar Thomson Steel Works, he was fully launched on the career that made his company within a few years the greatest steel producer of the country. Acquisition of the Edgar Thomson plant was followed by the purchase of Homestead, and later of Duquesne—all three major steel works occupying virtually adjacent sites on the banks of the Monongahela a few miles above Pittsburgh.

The Carnegie enterprises presently included iron works, blast-furnace properties, and a bridge company as well. Alliances, which were equivalent to absorption, with the Oliver Mining Company on the one hand and with the Frick Coke Company on the other brought within the Carnegie orbit extensive ore properties in the Superior fields and the largest and richest coke properties in the country.[9] Finally, in absorbing the Lake Superior Iron Company the Carnegie organization became an important shipowner and the largest shipper of ore on the Great Lakes. These facilities, together with a controlling interest in the Pittsburgh, Bessemer, and Lake Erie Railroad, made the company independent in the matter of ore transportation. The capital of the parent organization in the meantime mounted from $5,000,000 in 1879 to $25,000,000 some 12 years later, and when the company was at last incorporated in 1900 it had a capital stock of $160,000,000, of which Carnegie controlled over $86,000,000.

Carnegie's contributions to this development were of central importance. As an ironmaster he contrasted sharply with the typical Pittsburgh millowners of the previous generation. He knew little of iron and steel and spent little time in plant or mill. He did not get down to the works before his men in the morning nor did he pride himself on hard labor and long hours. His summers were usually spent vacationing abroad; and in the social life of New York and Pittsburgh he was an active participant, combining thoroughgoing pleasure with not a little business profit. Carnegie was a supersalesman and customer's man who cultivated with great success the friendship of men of financial and industrial prominence; a skillful judge and manager of people, with the ability to select highly competent plant superintendents whom he bound to him with fractional interests in the company and spurred on by a system combining rivalry with detailed, personal reports forwarded to him wherever he might be; and a leader who, without technical knowledge, had the imagination and foresight to exploit to the utmost the newer technological developments of proved worth.

---

[9] Henry Clay Frick was the stormy petrel of the Carnegie organization. For an account of his relations with Carnegie and his role in the industry, see the authorized biography by George Harvey, *Henry Clay Frick, the Man*. New York: Charles Scribner's Sons, 1928.

Unhampered by the craftsman's respect for his tools and the petty capitalist's reluctance to abandon a machine so long as it served well, Carnegie was one of the first industrialists to discover the profits of a policy of hard driving and early scrapping of equipment. So skillfully were the Carnegie properties managed under his direction, so efficiently were blast furnaces, rolling mills, and converters operated, that production costs were driven far below those of most other companies, and in a bitterly competitive field great fortunes were piled up for Carnegie and his associates. In prosperous years profits amounted to $20,000,000 and more.

Consolidation Is the Life of Trade

Carnegie was but the leader in a trend that was general throughout the industry in these years, although there were few indeed who found or made the sailing so smooth as he. For most men, indeed, the long and bitter competitive struggle, intensified by high fixed charges and by the marked fluctuations in business conditions felt with particular severity in the iron and steel industry, ended more often in disaster and defeat than in success. The years between 1865 and 1900 were filled with many and varied attempts to restrain and relieve competition. Pools that divided the market, allotted production quotas, fixed prices, or served as marketing agencies were common, but in most instances did no more than blunt the edge of competition, serving chiefly to hasten the trend toward large-scale, integrated operations through consolidation, either along the line followed by the Carnegie company or by combinations of plants of the same kind.

No major iron and steel district escaped the influence of this powerful trend. Bethlehem Steel and Pennsylvania Steel on the Seaboard, Tennessee Coal, Iron and Railroad in the South, Colorado Fuel and Iron in the Far West, and Illinois Steel, later absorbed by Federal Steel, in the Chicago district—all these were giant organizations, integrating in varying degrees the manufacture of iron and steel products from raw material to finished commodity. Organization of a great number of combinations or trusts of the horizontal kind brought together companies engaged in the production of similar goods—iron, ore, forgings, tin plates, steel hoops, barbed wire, steel pipes and tubes, cast-iron pipes, and the like.

There was room too for outstanding independent companies such as Jones & Laughlin, Cambria Steel, and Lackawanna Steel. At least as large as and even more diversified in its activities than Carnegie Steel was the Federal Steel Company with properties and major operations centering in Chicago. In 1899 this giant company with its 21,000 employees produced nearly 3,000,000 tons of ore and 1,500,000 tons each of pig iron and Bessemer ingots. Extensive ore and coke lands, railroads, steamships, and docking facilities, as well as the usual blast-furnace, Bessemer, and rolling-mill plants, were among its properties.

The Billion-Dollar Business

All these earlier combinations were dwarfed in 1901 by the organization of the United States Steel Corporation, a combination of combinations that brought together 12 of the largest companies in the United States, including the Carnegie properties and the Federal Steel Company.[10] Only this union of interests forestalled the impending renewal of the battle of the giants on a vaster scale than hitherto. Carnegie, who had achieved glory and profit enough and was ready to retire to the more leisurely pursuits of social intercourse and philanthropy, had no taste for the struggle. Elbert H. Gary, moving spirit in Federal Steel and later chairman of the board of the Corporation, had earlier proposed a combination of this kind. Charles M. Schwab, chief lieutenant of Carnegie and soon to become the dominant spirit of Bethlehem Steel, succeeded in prodding J. P. Morgan to assume the role of an architect of a colossus that would impart to steel the order, stability, and profit that made up the trinity of the great financier.[11]

The blast furnaces of the new $1,400,000,000 corporation produced one-half of the pig iron output of the country and its rail mills over one-half of the steel rails. It controlled some 60 per cent of the national output of structural steel and of wire and wirerods, virtually all the barbed wire and woven fence wire, wire nails, tin plate and steel tubes, and large proportions of other major steel products. It built some nine-tenths of all the bridges in the country. It dominated the Superior ore fields and ore traffic on the Lakes and produced more than half the coke made in the United States.

The policy of absorption and expansion did not stop with the organization of the Corporation; within a few years the largest iron and steel firm in the South, the Tennessee Coal, Iron & Railroad Company, was taken over in a transaction that threatened to become a national scandal, and on the swampy shores of Lake Michigan not far from Chicago a $50,000,000 steel works and industrial town was erected bearing the name of Chairman Gary. Despite these and other expansions of plant, the Corporation's hold on the market gradually fell off in the decade following its organization but without fundamentally altering its influence as a stabilizing force, exercised through the power of example and sugges-

---

[10] For interesting accounts of the circumstances leading to the formation of U. S. Steel, see H. R. Seager and C. A. Gulick, Jr., *Trust and Corporation Problems* (New York: Harper & Brothers, 1929), Chapters 13 and 14; and Lewis Corey, *The House of Morgan* (New York: G. Howard Watt, 1930), Chapter 23.

[11] Corey's *House of Morgan* is a stimulating interpretation of a dominant business firm and should be read by all interested in understanding the course of industrial development in the late nineteenth century.

tion and facilitated by the growing feeling of community of interest that marked the maturity of this fundamental heavy industry.[12]

One final merger of major importance rounded out this phase of the steel industry's development. This was the absorption by the Bethlehem Steel Company during the First World War and post-war years of a number of other large independent companies in the East, notably the Cambria, Pennsylvania, Lackawanna, and Midvale steel companies. The result was to make Bethlehem Steel the dominant organization in the East and the largest independent company in the country. In 1930 six great steel combinations controlled 75 per cent of the national output.

Ordnance and Armor Plate

In the field of heavy machinery the chief developments in the latter part of the nineteenth century centered in railroad equipment, stationary and marine power plants, and naval ordnance and armor. Foundry and forging techniques advanced to new levels in the effort to cope with the problems of shaping iron and steel in large masses.

The Civil War brought not only demands for heavy ordnance but called on industry to supply iron plates of unprecedented thickness for the monitor fleet and for armored gunboats. At the opening of the war one and one-half inch plates were the largest that could be rolled in any existing mill, but before its end plates up to five inches thick had been made by both rolling and forging. Nothing permanent came out of this activity, for in the retreat from steam and armor that marked the post-war navy there was no business for heavy industry. In the 1880's a program of naval expansion called for large armored battleships and laid the foundations for a naval-construction industry on a permanent and expanding basis, favored by legislation requiring the use of American materials. By 1909 naval appropriations reached the unprecedented peace-time figure of $140,000,000 and the bulk of this went into the enlargement of our rapidly growing battleship fleet.[13]

The specialized nature of the demand and the heavy investment for the necessary equipment, much of which had to be imported in the early years, confined the production of armor plate and ordnance to a handful of firms. The two major steel companies to engage in the manufacture of armor plate were Carnegie and Bethlehem, each of which in 1886 began the erection of armor-plate plants. Bethlehem got its first order in 1887

---

[12] By 1929 the percentage of the national output of crude steel produced by the Corporation had declined from a onetime figure of 65 per cent to 40 per cent. The effort of the Federal Government to dissolve the Corporation as a combination in restraint of trade came to an unsuccessful end in 1920 with a Supreme Court decision favorable to the Corporation.

[13] For the political and international background of this significant development the reader should consult the illuminating study of Harold and Margaret Sprout, *The Rise of American Naval Power, 1776-1918*. Princeton: Princeton University Press, 1939.

and by 1891 the Carnegie works were able to roll nickel-steel ingots weighing 50 tons. These developments quickly freed the United States from dependence on foreign makers of armor plate. The most important technical improvement in this field came with the substitution of powerful hydraulic forging presses for rolls in the production of the heavier plates.

The heavy ordnance of the period of the Civil War, including cannon up to 20 inches in bore and throwing shot weighing as much as 1,000 pounds, was made by casting. The Fort Pitt Foundry in Pittsburgh, long a leading producer of ordnance, delivered more than 2,000 heavy pieces to the Government during the war. The lathe required for finishing the larger pieces weighed more than 100 tons. The trend of the post-war years was away from cast ordnance to breech-loading guns forged from wrought iron and steel. Owing to the limitations of American forging equipment the Government arsenals were for many years dependent on foreign makers for heavy gun forgings, but by importing ordnance machinery from abroad our own manufacturers were able by 1893 to produce the largest guns required by our expanding navy. The use of the hydraulic forging press in place of the heavy steam hammer was of great importance, turning out a better product at lower maintenance cost and handling material with greater facility.

Heavy Machinery

In the field of heavy industrial equipment the most significant developments of this period lay not so much in the expansion of existing lines as in the great increase in the variety of equipment and in the rise of specialized branches of industry to produce it. In the early stages of our industrial growth, specialized equipment required by a new branch of industry usually had to be designed and built by the using company or by general foundry and machine shops that made equipment to order. Some of the largest and best known of the early builders of industrial machinery originated as machine shop departments of the great cotton textile companies founded in New England in the second quarter of the 19th century.

When the demand became sufficiently great, companies were organized to produce exclusively a given class of equipment. The building of steam engines—stationary, steamboat, and marine—and locomotives provides outstanding examples of this trend in the period before 1865. The growth of specialization continued in the postwar years. The manufacture of textile machinery is an interesting case in point. On the one hand, the complete separation of this industry from the large-scale production of textiles was achieved; on the other hand, the leading members of the industry confined their attention increasingly to textile machinery, abandoning the production of other types of machinery in which some had long participated.

In the postwar decades many new branches of the machinery industry arose to supply the equipment demanded by the extension of industrialization to new areas, especially for handling and processing materials efficiently in large volume.[14] Included among these products were heavy-duty cranes of many kinds; dredging and excavating equipment; conveying and elevating machinery; mining, oil-well, and refining equipment; and many others. To steam engines of the older reciprocating type were added steam turbines. With the coming of electric power a whole new class of generating and motor equipment was introduced and the production of electrical machinery became a major industry. In 1929 manufacture of locomotives was exceeded in value by both dredging and excavating equipment and by oil-well machinery, and was nearly equaled by electric motors and dynamos. The value of mining machinery and of conveying and elevating machinery produced in this year was greater by at least one-fourth than that of steam engines and turbines, and the value of steam turbines to that of reciprocating engines was in the ratio of five to one.

Locomotives and Rolling Stock

Although railroads ceased to dominate the heavy industries, their equipment requirements nonetheless continued to make them one of the major outlets. Only in comparatively recent years has the demand for locomotives and rolling stock tended to level off. Increase in size as well as numbers has been characteristic of both branches of equipment. A 30-ton locomotive at the close of the Civil War was regarded as exceptional, but by 1900 a 70-ton engine was quite common and the largest built up to this date weighed 133 tons. Production of locomotives followed the trend of other commodities toward concentration in fewer hands. The Baldwin Company, long the largest in the country, continued to dominate the field, increasing its output from 500 locomotives in 1873 to more than 2,600 in 1907. The early years of the new century, which witnessed the formation of so many giant consolidations, brought all the locomotive manufacturers of the country, save only Baldwin, together in a $50,000,000 corporation, the American Locomotive Company, whose nine works, located chiefly along the Atlantic Seaboard, produced a slightly larger number of locomotives in the aggregate than Baldwin.

In rolling stock the small wooden cars of the fifties and sixties eventually were replaced by steel cars of many times their capacity. During the Civil War, the normal capacity of railroad cars was 7 to 8 tons; by 1885 the figure had risen to 30 tons, and at the turn of the century cars of 40 to 50 tons were in common use and larger ones were still to come. The increasing adoption of the steel car was a major development of the period. In 1880 a steel car cost several times as much as the usual

[14] Material on this subject is buried for the most part in census reports and trade journals.

wooden one, but by 1900 the cost was reported to be the same for cars of equal capacity. By 1906 45 per cent of the cars in the country were either made entirely of steel or steel was used for all parts except the body. Mergers brought this branch of industry into the hands of a few large companies of which the Pressed Steel Car Company of Pittsburgh was the most important. Using 1,600 tons of steel daily this company was said in 1900 to be the largest single consumer of steel in the world. In 1906 the Pennsylvania Railroad placed the first regular order for all-steel passenger coaches, beginning a trend that was to relegate the old-fashioned wooden coaches to minor branch lines and local service. By the end of the century the production of sleeping cars had been concentrated in the hands of the Pullman Company.

Shipbuilding in the Age of Iron and Steel

While the railroad continued to provide a major source of demand for heavy goods and equipment, developments in the field of ocean transportation gave rise in the closing years of the nineteenth century to what in all logic should be classed with heavy industry, the building of iron and steel ships.

The building of wooden ships, which had long brought much profit and no little fame to this country, could hardly be so described, despite the ponderous character of the materials used—single spars and masts often weighed many tons—and the large dimensions of the product. Down to 1860 shipbuilding had advanced little beyond the handicraft-small-shop stage of organization. Although there were some large concerns, employing 100 men or more, the typical *ante bellum* shipyard represented but a small investment of capital and possessed little in the way of plant and equipment, employing relatively few men and turning out only a few ships of modest tonnage each year. With ships small in size and abundant timber available along a large part of the Eastern Seaboard, shipyards were set up easily and operated to advantage on many a small inlet and tidal stream. Decentralization was a characteristic feature of an industry dominated by the individual proprietorship and the partnership, with the master carpenter typically serving as the directing head. The corporation was almost unknown and consolidation a thing of the future.[15]

Already at mid-century the days of the wooden sailing ship were numbered as ships built of iron and driven by steam demonstrated their effectiveness. The trend from sail and wood to steam and steel resulted in radical changes in the organization and conduct of the shipbuilding

---

[15] Much the best treatment of the history of shipbuilding in the United States is the careful and comprehensive study of John G. B. Hutchins, *The American Maritime Industries and Public Policy, 1789-1914: An Economic History*. Cambridge, Mass.: Harvard University Press, 1941.

industry. Where 40 years earlier 500-ton vessels were few in number, in the sixties ships of 2,000 tons became common and capital investment mounted from $20,000 to $140,000. The construction of iron and, later, steel ships presented problems and demanded organization, techniques, and equipment differing markedly from those characteristic of wooden shipbuilding. Elaborate and costly equipment, a heavy capital investment, and large-scale operations were the distinctive features of shipyards building steel steamships of large tonnage. Moreover, the new industry required at its base a supporting structure of heavy metal and engineering industries to supply the essential raw materials, fabricated parts, and machinery that went into the modern ship.

The building of the new class of ships developed slowly in the United States. This was due in part to the decline of the American merchant marine and to the greater attractions in other fields of capital investment. But it was also due to the earlier start obtained by the industry in Great Britain and to the advanced state of the metal and engineering industries in that country. The advantages possessed by the United States in its rich timber resources and its craftsmen skilled in the technology of wood could not readily be transferred to the new industry. The shift of major centers of iron and steel production inland in this period, together with steel pricing policies, introduced freight charges with which British shipyards did not have to reckon; labor rates were high; and the protecting umbrella of the tariff added further to construction costs. Engineering industries capable of supplying machinery and equipment for steamships of rapidly mounting tonnage were in a stage of crude beginnings.

Under these conditions the tonnage of iron ships built in the country prior to 1860 was negligible. In the post-war decades production mounted slowly as experience was gained in the new methods, but activity was confined to a few shipyards and to steamships of modest tonnage, chiefly for use in the protected coastal trades. In the eighties came the stimulus of naval construction, leading to the establishment of a few large yards, elaborately equipped with special machinery for handling and fabricating materials and with a capacity for ships of large tonnage. The capital investment of iron shipbuilding yards mounted from an estimated $50,000 in 1886 to $1,000,000 in 1900. A companion industry arose on the Great Lakes in the eighties and nineties where, at various points from Buffalo to Chicago, yards were established to build vessels for the rapidly expanding grain and ore trade. Sixty per cent of the steam tonnage built in the United States in the decade, 1891-1900, was turned out from these yards.

A protected market and marked progress in the organization and techniques of production were insufficient to overcome the handicaps of high costs, due particularly to the monopolistic situation in the steel industry, and the low wage rates enjoyed by foreign shipbuilders. Total output in the nineties was little more than one-tenth that of British shipyards. Output mounted from an annual average tonnage of about 100,000 in the years 1891-1900 to 250,000 tons in the period 1910-1914 and then shot up abruptly under the pressure of war demands.

The Rise of Copper

In the nonferrous-metal industry, the most notable development in this period took place in the copper industry. Annual output rose from some 8,000 tons just prior to the Civil War to more than 900,000 tons during World War I, a rate of increase several times that of iron and steel. In contrast with the earlier period, when it found its principal outlet in sheathing and fastenings for ships and in the manufacture of brass, copper now became a vital industrial metal with a wide range of conversions into capital and consumer goods alike. The most important of these new uses, accounting for from one-third to nearly one-half of the total copper product in the twenties, were those associated with the coming of the age of electricity. Electrical equipment and machinery of all kinds, transmission lines, and wire rapidly claimed the lion's shares of copper. Other important industrial uses were found in the numerous brass and bronze products, and in bearing metal and automobiles. The increase in copper production was relatively slow up to 1880 with an annual average for the period 1876-1880 of just under 25,000 tons. By 1890 output was up to 130,000 tons and the period of greatest growth lay just ahead. By 1895 the United States had deprived Great Britain of the position she long held as the world's leading producer of copper and after 1910 this country usually produced one-half or more of the world output.

New Refining Methods

The important developments of the late nineteenth century were associated with the discovery and exploitation of new ore districts, invention of new techniques of reduction and refining, and concentration of ownership and control in the several branches of the industry.[16]

In the smelting process the trend was from the shaft type to the reverberatory type of furnace. The reasons for this change lay chiefly in the difficulty of handling in the shaft furnace the finely divided ores required by the flotation process. Eventually the great bulk of copper ores in the country was reduced in great reverberatory furnaces with a capacity of 100,000 tons and more per year. In the later stages of refining, two innovations were of chief importance: the adoption of the Bessemer process for reducing to crude or blister copper the matte produced in the smelting operation and containing 40 to 50 per cent copper, and the use

---

[16] The best study of the copper industry in this period is F. E. Richter, "The Copper Mining Industry of the United States, 1845-1925," *Quarterly Journal of Economics,* Vol. XLI, pp. 236 ff., 684 ff.

of electrolysis in the final stage. The first technique resulted in a great saving of time, labor, and fuel and has been described as doing almost as much for copper as it had for steel. Electrolysis, applied in vats of great size, not only gave a purer copper than obtainable heretofore, but resulted in a virtually complete recovery of the copper contained in the crude metal. This method, introduced in the eighties, spread until in recent years more than 80 per cent of the copper in this country has been refined by it.

Big Business in Copper

The organization of the copper industry in this period was marked by a continuation of trends already evident in the Michigan field before 1850. The cost of deep-mining operations and the advantages of large-scale operations called for a heavy capital investment that the smaller companies were unable to obtain. Again and again the smaller producers in a district were squeezed out or absorbed by larger companies, not so much by such practices as price cutting and local underselling, so effectively used in other industries, as by their sheer inability to approach the production costs of the big companies. Technological improvements calling for progressively larger operations and more costly equipment to handle ores of lower grade added to the already heavy capital requirements of the industry and promoted concentration of ownership.

The wide range between costs and selling price that was customary with the larger companies prior to the First World War meant high and often extraordinary profits. The Calumet and Hecla Mining Company, for example, paid total dividends of nearly $28,000,000 in the years 1871-1886, or an annual average of 144.5 per cent. While production costs of Calumet and Hecla in this period ranged between 5 and 10 cents a pound, copper brought 20 cents most of the time in New York City. The wide margin between cost and selling price not only served as a cushion in the occasional competitive wars between the larger companies but, prior to 1900, provided the basis for expansion of production largely without resort to the public security markets and tended to keep control within the industry.

A trend toward consolidation of properties and interests appeared early in the copper industry, and in few other branches of manufacturing has this development been carried further. The four companies with the largest holdings of ore in 1925 controlled 45 per cent and the 16 leading companies over 83 per cent of the estimated ore reserves of the country. In each of the major copper districts the tendency was to concentrate production in the hands of one or two large companies whose interests in most instances did not extend to other districts. The big four in the mining of ore—Anaconda, Kennecott, Phelps Dodge, and Calumet and Arizona—produced 51 per cent of the national output in

1929. Of this amount Anaconda alone accounted for more than half, or 27 per cent. In the smelting of copper the big four in this year were American Smelting and Refining, Phelps Dodge, United Verde, and Anaconda. In contrast with the earlier period nearly all the larger companies not only mined ore but concentrated and smelted it in the immediate vicinity. Beyond this point integration was not often carried.

In general, fabrication was separated from the production of raw metal, and similarly the greater part of copper was refined not by the companies producing it but by refining companies operating on a toll or contract basis. The outstanding exception was the Anaconda Copper Mining Company, which not only operated great refining plants in Montana and New Jersey but in its subsidiary, the American Brass Company, controlled the greatest consumer and fabricator of copper in the world. With total assets in 1929 of more than $750,000,000 Anaconda owned, besides ore reserves, mines, and smelting and refining plants, collieries, timber reserves, and sulphuric-acid, zinc, lead, and oil works, as well as a railroad and numerous foreign mining properties. The dominant organization in the refining of copper has long been the American Smelting and Refining Company, organized in 1899 and soon brought under the control of the Guggenheim group.[17] Primarily a horizontal combination, American Smelting and Refining soon established itself as the foremost refiner of copper in the world and was for years its greatest seller. With Anaconda it stood out as one of the two largest nonferrous organizations in the world. Between them they disposed of from two-thirds to three-fourths of all the copper refined in the United States and Latin America.

The Production of Lead

As with copper the large-scale development of the lead industry, as well as the closely associated manufacture of zinc, has taken place chiefly since the Civil War and the pattern of organization and technology in the two industries has been much the same.[18] After leveling off during the fifties and sixties, production mounted rapidly after 1870 until in the years 1920-1929 the annual output of the United States averaged close to 600,000 tons, about two-fifths of the world product. The principal new uses to which lead was put with the advance of industrialization were, as in the case of copper, those arising from the electrical age. Storage batteries and cable sheathing in recent years have accounted for nearly half the total supply of lead. Of the older uses, white lead for paint continued

[17] The story of the role of this family in copper has been told in popular biographical style by Harvey O'Connor in *The Guggenheims: the Making of an American Dynasty.* New York: Covici, Friede, Inc., 1937.

[18] Although old, W. R. Ingalls' *Lead and Zinc in the United States* (New York: Hill Publishing Company, 1908), is still the only work that gives much attention to the historical side of the industry's development.

in top place, Zinc also increased substantially in output; its principal uses were in galvanizing and in the manufacture of brass and of paint.

With respect both to technical aspects of concentration, reduction, and refinement, and to the organization of the industry, lead and zinc present substantial similarities to copper. Varying amounts of silver, gold, and other metals in association with many of the ores affect appreciably and often markedly the cost of production. Smelting and refining operations were carried on in the larger industrial centers of the Middle West and the Atlantic Seaboard with San Francisco occupying a leading position on the Pacific Coast. Active and at times bitter competition among smelters and refiners led here, as in other areas, to agreements and associations and eventually in 1899 to the formation of what was once known as the lead trust, the American Smelting and Refining Company, which acquired a dominant position in the lead as well as in the copper industry. The bulk of mining and reduction of lead ores came to be concentrated in the hands of a small number of large-scale organizations.

Selected References

GENERAL WORKS

Barger, Harold, and Sam H. Schurr, *The Mining Industries, 1899-1939, A Study of Output, Employment and Productivity*. New York: National Bureau of Economic Research, Inc., 1944.

Bureau of the Census, United States Department of Commerce, *Historical Statistics of the United States, 1789-1945*. Washington, D. C.: U.S. Government Printing Office, 1949.

Clark, V. S., *The History of Manufactures in the United States,* 1929 ed., Vols. II and III. Washington, D. C.: Carnegie Institution of Washington, 1929.

Eavenson, H. N., *The First Century and a Quarter of American Coal Industry*. Pittsburgh: Privately printed, 1942.

Hendrick, B. J., *Life of Andrew Carnegie*. New York: Doubleday, Doran & Company, 1932.

Jones, Eliot, *The Anthracite Coal Combination in the United States*. Cambridge, Mass.: Harvard University Press, 1914.

Kaempffert, Waldemar, *A Popular History of American Invention*. New York: Charles Scribner's Sons, 1924.

Richter, F. E., "The Copper Mining Industry of the United States, 1845-1925," *Quarterly Journal of Economics,* Vol. XLI, pp. 236 ff., 684 ff.

SPECIAL TOPICS

Armes, Ethel, *The Story of Coal and Iron in Alabama*. Birmingham: Published under the auspices of the Chamber of Commerce, Birmingham, Ala., 1910.

Bridge, J. H., *The Inside History of the Carnegie Steel Company*. New York: The Aldine Book Company, 1903.

Corey, Lewis, *The House of Morgan*. New York: G. Howard Watt, 1930.

Cushman, Robert E., *The Independent Regulatory Commissions*. New York: Oxford University Press, 1941.

Gibb, George Sweet, *The Saco-Lowell Shops: Textile Machinery Building in New England, 1813-1949*. Cambridge. Mass.: Harvard University Press, 1950.

Glasscock, C. B., *The War of the Copper Kings: Builders of Butte and Wolves of Wall Street.* New York: Grosset and Dunlap, 1939.

Harvey, George B. M., *Henry Clay Frick, the Man.* New York: Charles Scribner's Sons, 1928.

Howe, H. M., *The Metallurgy of Steel.* New York: The Engineering and Mining Journal, 1904.

Hunt, E. E., *et al., What the Coal Commissions Found.* Baltimore: Williams and Wilkins, 1925.

Hutchins, John G. B., *The American Maritime Industries and Public Policy, 1789-1914, An Economic History.* Cambridge, Mass.: Harvard University Press, 1941.

Ingalls, W. R., *Lead and Zinc in the United States.* New York: Hill Publishing Company, 1908.

Mussey, H. R., *Combination in the Mining Industry: A Study of Concentration in Lake Superior Ore Production.* New York: Columbia University Press, 1905.

O'Connor, Harvey, *The Guggenheims: The Making of an American Dynasty.* New York: Covici, Friede, Inc., 1937.

Parsons, A. B., *The Porphyry Coppers.* New York: American Institute of Mining and Metallurgical Engineers, 1933.

Raymer, Robert G., *A History of Copper Mining in Montana.* Chicago: Lewis Publishing Company, 1930.

Wirth, F. P., *The Discovery and Exploitation of the Minnesota Iron Lands.* Cedar Rapids, Iowa: Torch Press, 1937.

25 · LIGHT MANUFACTURES

The Scope of Light Manufactures

The definition and classification of light manufactures, as distinguished from heavy industry, must of necessity be made on an empirical basis; and their treatment, for practical limitations of space, can scarcely be exhaustive. While light manufactures may be defined by various criteria, the chief relevant factor is that they embody consumers' goods of different degrees of durability. They entail, moreover, the conversion of materials in raw or partly manufactured form into finished products by the addition of a considerable amount of labor and through a complex series of mechanized processes, for which the substantial value added by manufacturing provides a general measure. But none of these production characteristics is an absolute, applying exclusively or completely to all examples of what may be described as light manufactures.

This category embraces, furthermore, the staple essentials of consumption as well as the expanding variety of specialty goods that are an index both of a rising standard of living and of the inventive ingenuity and enterprise of modern industry in applying machine methods of manufacture to the familiar products of old skills or to the creation of new products and utilities. Briefly, light manufactures, as they have developed particularly since 1860, supply the wants of the whole man: his food, his clothing, and his shelter. They include also to an increasing degree the goods serving his recreational and leisure-time consumption needs. In all of these, but especially in the last, lie some of the most distinctive contributions of American industrial and social evolution since 1860. The principal classes or types of light manufacture include such broadening complexes of industrial production as textiles and clothing, leather and rubber goods, furniture and furnishings, and metal wares ranging from watches and jewelry to household appliances. Food and tobacco products by definition belong to, and constitute indeed a basic part of, the total consumption pattern, but their peculiarly close relation to agricultural production warrants their separate treatment elsewhere. Toward these so-called light manufactures is ultimately directed a large part of heavy industry proper, whose vast output of materials, machinery, and power has become increasingly fundamental to the production of consumption goods and services, both for domestic use and foreign export.

The Textile Industries

The establishment of cotton and woolen manufactures on a factory and machine basis had been a major manifestation of early industrialization in the United States, and by 1860 New England had won a substantial leadership in both branches of the textile industry. The products of the cotton and woolen factory had virtually displaced household manufactures; and, even with the modest degree of protection available during the 1850's, they were sufficient to supply the major share of domestic needs, particularly in the more common varieties of fabrics then in general use. By 1860, some eleven hundred cotton mills, operating more than 5 million spindles, consumed approximately 800,000 bales of cotton, and produced goods valued at one hundred and fifteen million dollars. Imports, at this time, accounted for approximately 25 per cent of total domestic consumption. The value of domestic woolen manufactures in 1859 was some sixty-five million dollars, the product of 1,476 establishments, and imports worth thirty-three million dollars added approximately a third to domestic consumption.

The Civil War years had a mixed effect upon the textile industry, both temporary and permanent. The interruption of cotton supply contributed to a crisis and curtailment of cotton manufacture, while the woolen industry received a special impetus arising out of wartime demand for uniform cloth and blankets to supply the armies, coupled with the inflation of prices and profits. By 1869, there were nearly 3,000 woolen factories, and the industry employed twice as many persons as it had a decade earlier. More significantly, wartime tariff acts brought high protective rates on both cottons and woolens, and in the half-century following the Civil War these averaged over 40 per cent in value and virtually gave the textile industry a monopoly of the home market. Except for a few specialties, exports of cotton fabrics exceeded imports; and in the case of woolen goods, imports fell steadily from one-third of domestic consumption in 1859 to approximately six per cent by 1914, and to under two per cent in 1919.[1]

Within the framework of an expanding domestic market, the generation following the Civil War witnessed a number of significant trends in the evolution of the textile industry in its several branches. In the first place, the changing nature of demand, marked by rising consump-

---

[1] A. H. Cole, *The American Woolen Manufacture,* Vol. II, pp. 39 ff. Cambridge: Harvard University Press, 1926; M. T. Copeland, *The Cotton Manufacturing Industry of the United States,* pp. 17 ff. Cambridge: Harvard University Press, 1923; V. S. Clark, *The History of Manufactures in the United States,* Vol. III, p. 190. Washington, D. C.: The Carnegie Institution of Washington, 1929.

tion standards and the development of new types of quality fabrics, affected the rates of growth in different parts of the complex textile industry and produced shifting relationships among its principal components. In the woolen industry, for example, the phenomenal rise and growth of worsted manufacture after 1870 overshadowed that of the older types of woolen fabrics. While the value of woolen goods reached a peak in 1869, and thereafter declined to scarcely three-fourths that value in 1909, worsted products increased fourteenfold in the same period. In volume of raw material consumed, worsted production multiplied nine times, while woolens in general accounted for somewhat less than in 1869.

As between the woolen and the cotton branches of the industry, a significant shift of position in favor of the latter also revealed the effect of unequal rates of growth. As late as 1889, the value of domestic cotton manufactures was just under that of wool products, reported at two hundred and seventy million dollars. By 1914, cotton goods were valued at seven hundred and one million dollars as against four hundred and sixty-four million dollars for all woolen manufactures, and in 1919 the value of cotton fabrics was almost double that of woolens. Moreover, after 1900 both cotton and woolen production was expanding at a slower rate than the relatively new branches of knit goods and silk manufactures. While the volume of both cottons and woolens about kept pace with population growth and rose by 63 and 45 per cent, respectively, between 1899 and 1919, silk and knit goods grew more than three times as fast, increasing by 168 and 169 per cent, respectively. The pattern of textile manufacture was thus assuming its modern complex character and displaying internal changes and competitive pressures that combined with other factors to contribute to the instability and retardation particularly of the older branches and areas of the textile industry. Nevertheless, the entire group of textile manufactures occupied third rank in value of production, after foods and iron and steel products, and held first place in number of persons employed in 1919 among major industrial groups.

Apart from the factor of sheer growth, with its complicated variations, the several branches of the textile industry were subject after 1860 to the common and fundamental impact of mechanization, which brought them to industrial maturity, and this in turn had an important effect upon the structure and equipment of the industry, as well as upon the size and scale of operation of the individual establishment. Added to this were significant trends in the geographical distribution and localization of the industry, affecting each of its many parts differently, according to their respective conditions and needs.

Cotton and Woolen Manufactures

In the older and well established cotton and woolen manufactures, the basic machinery and methods employed in all the different processes, from carding to finishing, continued to be the object of progressive and cumulative improvement in the half-century following the Civil War, thereby enhancing their productivity gradually rather than by any sudden, revolutionary transformation of technology. Chief among the mechanical advances in the textile industry was the shift from the mule to the lighter ring-frame for spinning. Capable of continuous spinning at speeds up to 10,000 revolutions per minute by the close of the century, ring spinning employed less skilled operatives, in large proportion women, and increased the output of yarn per worker by one-third. In weaving, the major innovation was the Northrop automatic loom, developed during the 1890's, and its adoption tripled the number of looms attended by a single weaver, from 8 to 24 within a decade. A third basic advance occurred in the field of power equipment. The increased use of steam power after 1860 freed the textile industry from the limitations of size and location imposed by the earlier dependence upon water-power. It favored the expansion of the industry and particularly the development of its younger branches in new areas: in the middle and western parts of the country, for instance, which had an advantageous access to coal, as well as to new sources of labor supply and growing markets. Even in New England, steam power and access to coal brought by sea reinforced the considerable post-Civil War shift of cotton manufacture to Southern Massachusetts, as exemplified by the rise of New Bedford and Fall River to the front rank between 1870 and 1890, particularly in the expanding production of print fabrics and finer yarns. Toward the close of the nineteenth century, the introduction of electric power, first in some of the early southern ventures in cotton manufacturing, brought further technical advantages, and hydro-electric power became a major factor in accelerating the growth of the industry in the Southern Piedmont after 1900. In general, the rate of technical progress was greater in the newer branches and areas of the industry.

The cumulative effect of mechanization was revealed, between 1870 and 1890 alone, in the actual reduction of the number of cotton factories from 956 to 905, which, however, had twice as many spindles and looms. With an increase of 64 per cent in persons employed, cotton manufactures had tripled their consumption of raw cotton, although the value of production increased only by 51 per cent in the same period, in part as a result of declining prices coupled with monetary deflation.

The most significant transformation the cotton industry underwent after 1890 was a geographical one quite as much as a technological one. As late as 1890, New England was still the predominant center of production, with 76 per cent of the nearly 15 million spindles then in operation, and only one per cent less than in 1870. Outside of New England, Cohoes, in upper New York State, was an important center of cotton spinning, and it boasted the largest single establishment in the country, the Harmony Mills with 275,000 spindles, supplying yarn for the knitting industry of the Mohawk Valley. Cotton manufacture was also well established in the other Middle Atlantic States, particularly in Pennsylvania, and the Philadelphia area was a major consumer of yarns in its expanding hosiery and other knitting industries.

The principal redistribution of cotton manufacture, however, affected the post-Civil War South, where a great awakening had begun by 1880, and the foundations of a new cotton industry were laid in the form of numerous small establishments scattered through the Southern Piedmont. Exploiting its many advantages of access to raw material, power, and especially labor, as well as the market for coarser fabrics and yarns, the southern branch of the industry expanded rapidly, repeating in many respects the experience of New England in the earlier development of the industry. Between 1880 and 1900 it multiplied the number of spindles in operation eightfold, to more than four million, or a fourth of the entire industry, while New England's share increased by scarcely 50 per cent. By 1912, with eleven and a half million spindles out of a total of some thirty and a half million, the southern cotton industry was using more than half the raw cotton, or nearly two and three-quarters of a million bales. Already in 1889 there had occurred the first migration and removal of an entire plant from New England to Spartanburg, South Carolina, and this was the ominous token of a future interregional competition, the source of great economic displacement and discomfort to New England, particularly after the first World War. In the beginning, however, and for a long time, the basis of the competition was a regional division of labor between the finer and coarser branches of cotton manufacture, with the latter located in the Southern states.[2]

In the woolen branch of the textile industry, the principal change after 1860, as already indicated, was the introduction and rapid expansion of worsted manufactures, which had technical as well as economic and social significance. Technologically, it entailed the importation and widespread adoption of both the French and the English types of combing machinery and methods of preparation of long-fibred wool for spinning and weaving. Economically and socially, it signified a drastic shift in consumption to the lighter worsted fabrics, and in turn this was accompanied by the development of a virtually new group of industrial plants, operating on a much larger scale than the existing woolen mills and requiring an increased importation of the finer, long-fibred wool for worsted manufacture. The expanding ready-made clothing industry, moreover, introduced a factor of relatively large and constant demand for the new types of cloth, which tended to favor the more fully standardized production

[2] P. H. Buck, *The Road to Reunion,* p. 103. Boston: Little Brown & Co. 1937. Clark, *History of Manufactures,* Vol. II, pp. 393 ff.; Vol. III, p. 172. Copeland, *The Cotton Manufacturing Industry,* pp. 27 ff.

of staple fabrics, as compared with the smaller volume and more diversified character of woolens.

This contrast was reflected in the fact that both the average number of persons employed in the worsted mill and the value of output were consistently greater than in the woolen mill. Already in 1869, the workers in the few worsted plants averaged 127 per establishment, as against 28 for the average woolen mill. By 1919, both types had increased in size, but employment in the average worsted factory numbered 355, as compared with 112 for the woolen mill. In value of product both worsted and woolen factories had grown at nearly the same rates between 1869 and 1919, eleven and twelvefold, respectively, but in 1919 the output per worsted mill was nearly four times as great ($2,400,000 as compared with $650,000) as that of woolen mills.

Geographically, the two divisions of the woolen industry displayed a high degree of concentration in New England and the Middle Atlantic States between 1869 and 1919, as contrasted with the drastic redistribution of the cotton industry. In number of woolen establishments, New England increased its proportion of a dwindling number from 21 to 51 per cent, the Middle Atlantic States remained constant with one-fourth, while the large number of small mills scattered throughout the rest of the country, more than half the total in 1869, shrank to approximately one-fourth by 1919. In number of spindles, as a measure of size and capacity, the proportion of New England and the Middle Atlantic States was even greater and stood at nearly 85 per cent by 1919. Six eastern states then accounted for approximately three-fourths of the spindles employed in the manufacture of woolens, while an even higher degree of concentration was indicated by the fact that 93.7 per cent of the worsted spindles were located in six states—three-fourths of them in the three leading states of Massachusetts, Rhode Island, and Pennsylvania.[3]

As one of the major industries, but to a lesser degree than most, textiles felt the broad influence of integration in the latter part of the nineteenth century. There was, in the first place, technological integration, affecting the size and internal structure of the individual establishment and involving the combination and closer coordination of the various production processes from raw material to finished commodity, although even in this respect there continued to be a certain traditional separation as regards the production of yarn and the finishing and printing of cotton cloth. The great variety of textile products, subject to seasonal and secular changes of fashion and demand, coupled with the complex character of competition in the industry, tended to impose, however, limitations upon the degree and kind of integration possible among plants. The principal interest common to the industry as a whole was largely political, and the efforts of manufacturers' associations in the different

[3] Cole, *The American Wool Manufacture,* Vol. II. pp. 183 ff., 209.

fields of textile production were largely directed toward the maintenance of tariff protection.

Financial integration, in the sense of corporate ownership or control of multiple plants, had a relatively modest place, falling short of the monopolistic tendencies so notorious an object of public concern and criticism in other industries by the end of the nineteenth century. Large and interlocking absentee ownership interests had figured prominently in the early development of the cotton industry, particularly in the Boston area, and continued to play a part in the later growth of the industry. In the 1890's for example, B. B. and R. Knight of Providence, owned and controlled the considerable aggregation of 14 mills, with 420,000 spindles, reported to be the largest in the field. Of the modern type of combination, however, the American Thread Company, organized in 1898, was a major, if special, illustration, and this was, moreover, closely linked financially with a similar British combination. In the woolen industry, the most significant consolidation, reflecting the contemporary trend of business organization, was the American Woolen Company, founded in 1899, which merged 26 mills with some 300,000 spindles, representing approximately ten per cent of the total number. Expanded from 26 to 59 mills by 1919, this combination, under the leadership of William M. Wood, its founder, attempted, not entirely successfully, to stabilize, if not to dominate, the market for staple woolen fabrics by the familiar methods of internal reorganization and external control of selling policies. In the textile industry as a whole, in 1919, not quite 10 per cent of the total number of establishments, 2,832 in all, were linked with 923 central-office, multiple-plant concerns, all but 17 of which controlled ten or fewer plants, and only two of which operated 26 or more establishments.[4]

The Carpet Industry

Although part of the general development of the textile industry, the growth of carpet manufacture after 1860 presented somewhat different and special features. In this instance, the principal impetus came mainly from the mechanization of the key process of weaving in the period between 1845 and 1875. The initial step was the invention and improvement of a power loom for weaving ingrain carpet by Erastus B. Bigelow of Lowell, Massachusetts, during the 1840's. This he adapted a decade later to the manufacture of the Brussels and Wilton types of carpet. By the 1870's, power weaving was applied also to the manufacture of Axminster and Moquette types of carpet through the inventive efforts and enterprise of Alexander Smith and Halcyon Skinner of Yonkers, New York. The establishments growing out of these ventures early became among the largest in their respective fields and reflected the early trend of

[4] W. L. Thorp, *The Integration of Industrial Operation*, p. 107. Washington: Government Printing Office, 1924. Cole, *American Wool Manufacture*, Vol. II, pp. 231 ff.

the industry toward large-scale production, particularly in the New England and New York areas, although Philadelphia long continued to be a major center, its relatively numerous plants operating on a smaller scale and more dependent upon outside sources of yarn supply.

Between 1869 and 1919, the number of plants manufacturing the various grades and types of carpets fell from a high of 215 to 75. These employed nearly 23,000 wage-earners, almost double the number in 1869, and the volume of output had grown from some 20 million to nearly 52 million square yards, disregarding, however, significant increases in the value and quality of the different kinds of carpets that had occurred during the period in response to changing demand and standards of consumption. The substantial relative decline in the per capita use of wool carpeting since 1900 was in itself evidence of changing fashion, and indicated in part the rising importance of new types of floor covering, such as linoleum, and a developing indirect competition with many other new goods for the attention of the American consumer. The carpet industry reached maturity rapidly, and after 1900 tended to display a retardation of growth, as measured by the fact that the index of production rose from 100 to 1899 to a high of 131 in 1909, and declined to 119 in 1914, and to 102 in 1919.[5]

The Apparel Industries

A fundamental part of the evolution of so-called light manufactures after 1860, and indeed one of the most significant phenomena in this age of industrialization, was the development of a composite and considerable group of industries engaged in the conversion of textile materials into ready-made clothing on a machine and factory basis. The individual products of traditional household, custom, and craft methods of manufacture were thereby transformed into standardized wear supplied to an expanding national market and "fit for a free, democratic people." Literally the whole man, woman and child as well, came to be thus clothed in the ready-made products of the apparel industries, including underwear and hosiery, machine-made hats, shirts, collars, and other furnishings, as well as factory-made outer clothing, to which may be added boots, shoes, gloves and other products of the leather and rubber industries. The apparel industries developed into a major segment of the American industrial structure, combining in a special way the elusive element of changing style with the more standard requirements of quantity production. Sometimes by the accident of an early start, but more often under the influence of special factors of labor supply, capital needs, and access to market and materials, these industries acquired a distinctive pattern of

5 A. H. Cole and H. F. Williamson, *The American Carpet Manufacture*, pp. 53 ff., 94 ff., 144 ff. Cambridge: Harvard University Press, 1941. E. W. Martin, *The Standard of Living in 1860*, p. 100. Chicago: University of Chicago Press, 1942.

geographical distribution. Their growth, moreover, contributed greatly to the total volume and scope of national business, not only in relation to production, but particularly in respect to merchandising, advertising, and other aspects of distribution. In a peculiarly sensitive way, the apparel industries became an index of the general trend of national standards, habits, and fashions of living, whose influence was in turn reflected in the changing fortunes of the underlying textile industries and their respective products.

Ready-Made Clothing

Men's clothing began to undergo the process of standardization and production for a general market in the generation preceding the Civil War. It came about first and most readily in the special field of cheap working garments, the so-called "slops," which presented no problem of quality or style and which supplied the simple wants of such groups as sailors, slave field hands in the South, and miners in the West. The business was largely developed through merchants in eastern seaboard cities, such as New Bedford, Boston, and New York, who combined manufacturing, generally on a domestic basis, with merchandising. An early example of this type of firm was that founded by John H. Browning, originally a dry goods jobber in New York City, and his son, William C. Browning, which supplied the southern market. During the Civil War it manufactured uniforms for the government, and it turned to civilian clothing for returning soldiers after the war. By the 1890's, this old concern, under the name of Browning, King and Company, still retained some of its earlier characteristics; it embraced a factory in New York City, a wholesale branch in Chicago, and retail stores in fifteen cities.

The manufacture of men's ready-made clothing expanded after the Civil War by capturing the market for higher grades and better quality; by the close of the century "store clothes" supplied perhaps nine-tenths of the demand, and more than three-fourths of the woolens produced in the country, including particularly the newly developed worsteds, went into their manufacture. By 1890, the value of men's clothing had reached a quarter of a billion dollars, and it doubled by 1909. Paralleling this development was that of the manufacture of shirts, collars, and other furnishings, which reached a value of more than one hundred million dollars by 1909. The manufacture of women's wear gathered momentum more slowly, its products having a value of approximately sixty-eight million dollars in 1889. It grew more rapidly thereafter, approaching four hundred million dollars by 1909. A decade later, in 1919, men's and women's clothing each had a value in excess of a billion dollars, of which nearly one-half represented value added by manufacturing. Both branches of the industry were among the principal employers of labor, with approximately 200,000 persons in each.

A number of factors combined to accelerate the development of the ready-made clothing industries. The technological factor was, of course, of primary importance, as in industry generally. It was represented, first and foremost, by the introduction of the sewing machine, in foot-operated form, in the 1850's. Subsequently it became power-driven and, moreover, was adapted to numerous special operations, such as button-hole making and button-sewing. Cloth-cutting and steam-pressing machinery gave added impetus to the mechanization of processes and to the trend toward concentration of production in the factory, which tended, however, to remain relatively small in size and scale of operation. Peculiarly important, however, in the case of the clothing industry was the stimulus of a new labor supply, made available particularly after 1880 by the new immigration from eastern and southern Europe, chiefly of Jews and Italians. While many of these were tailors, the greater number, both men and women, were unskilled, and these were incorporated into the growing clothing industry, with its newly developed sub-divided and mechanized operations. The somewhat peculiar structure and organization of the industry were shaped by the common resort of jobbers and manufacturers to the contract system of production, under which numerous small establishments operating in tenement or other inadequate facilities and a considerable amount of homework long continued to be characteristic features of production. Capital investment was relatively small, and the work had a highly seasonal character. As late as the 1930's the ratio of fixed assets to total net worth in selected clothing factories was estimated at ten per cent or less, as compared with fifty per cent or more for the paper and chemical industries.

Coupled with the technical and labor elements, the sensitive style factor and the concentration of distribution and materials supply agencies contributed to the localization of the needle trades in the larger eastern cities. New York in particular became the predominant center of the women's wear branch of the industry, while men's clothing was manufactured more widely in such cities as Boston, Baltimore, Philadelphia, Rochester, and Chicago. Significantly, one of the most distinctively American industrial developments, the manufacture of ready-made clothing, was closely linked with the enterprise, skill, and labor of special immigrant groups, and was, moreover, accompanied by peculiarly unhappy and unhealthy conditions of labor exploitation and tension, especially in the formative period between 1880 and 1910.[6] But the needle trades also became, after 1910, with equal significance, the scene of noteworthy experi-

[6] J. E. Pope, *The Clothing Industry in New York,* pp. 45 ff. Columbia, Mo.: University of Missouri, 1905; C. M. Depew, ed., *One Hundred Years of American Commerce,* Vol. II, pp. 561 ff. New York: D. O. Haynes & Co., 1895; *The Men's Factory-Made Clothing Industry,* pp. 9 ff. Washington: Government Printing Office, 1916.

ments in labor organization and contract negotiation, aimed at the improvement and stabilization of working conditions.

Boots and Shoes

Even more than in the case of clothing, the manufacture of common varieties of footwear for distant markets in the South, on the frontier, and on the West Coast had become an established enterprise of substantial scope and size in the half-century preceding the Civil War. It had, moreover, acquired a high degree of concentration in the area of which Boston was the hub, favored by the fact that the importation of hides from South America and the shipment of the finished commodity were an important part of the trade of that port. The development of tanning in the area supplied the leather, and the near-by towns and countryside furnished the labor. While methods were still fundamentally manual and production was organized on the domestic system, there had already evolved a considerable division of labor, particularly in Lynn, to the north of Boston, and operations were divided between the central shops cutting and supplying the materials and the so-called ten-footers, or domestic shops, in which small gangs of workers assembled the shoes. The census of 1860 reported some 12,487 shoe-working establishments, employing 123,000 persons, with an output valued at ninety-two million dollars.

The transformation of shoe manufacturing into a factory and machine industry occurred primarily in the period following 1855; by the close of the century it had achieved its modern form. The chief impetus came from the introduction of machinery to perform the numerous operations into which shoe-making was sub-divided. Already in the 1850's a pegging machine became available for attaching soles, and many other machines for other processes followed, such as leather-rolling, lasting, and finishing. The key development was, however, the adaptation of the sewing machine to shoe manufacture after 1860. The machine was used for sewing uppers, and there was a sole-stitching machine, improved and promoted by Gordon McKay, that could sew at the rate of 500-600 pairs daily. During the 1870's the Goodyear welt-sewing machine was introduced and was especially suitable for the manufacture of better quality shoes. Power application began in the 1860's, and by the 1870's shoe-making was completely a factory process, divided into some 100 separate operations, fifty of which were performed by machinery. It was estimated that by 1895 the labor cost of a pair of shoes had been reduced to one-ninth of what it had been in 1865.

A special feature of the shoe industry almost from the start of its mechanization was the lease and royalty system for the new machinery developed and employed by the enterprise of McKay and Goodyear. This had two quite different effects upon the evolution of the industry. On the one hand, it tended to foster the growth and continuance of many relatively small establishments, which were particularly suitable to the more highly specialized branches of manufacture in which style and quality were important, since little original capital investment was required. The centralization of machine ownership, on the other hand, favored further consolidation, which was accomplished on a virtually monopolistic basis by the formation of the United Shoe Machinery Company in 1899.

The scale of shoe manufacturing thus ranged from quite small to very large. The total number of establishments in the industry, however, declined from 1,959 to 1,449 between 1879 and 1919, while the number of workers doubled in the same period, amounting to approximately 211,000 persons in 1919, and the output grew from 125 million in 1879 to 331 million pairs in 1919. The shoe industry, moreover, underwent a significant geographical redistribution especially after 1900. The long-established predominance of Massachusetts was weakened, and its share of national output declined from one-half to one-third between 1890 and 1914. New centers of large-scale production were developed at St. Louis, Milwaukee, Chicago, and other western cities, where access to domestic materials and markets overweighed the long-established factors of tradition and skill.

Boston also became an early center in the production of rubber footwear. Already before the Civil War the Boston Rubber Shoe Company was developing the so-called "Boston" goods, and the war added further demand for rubber products. The value of rubber production rose from three to one hundred million dollars between the Civil War and 1900, principally in rubber wear. Only the pneumatic rubber bicycle tire and the emergence of Akron, Ohio, as a producing center by 1900 gave prophetic indication of the phenomenal expansion of the industry after that year as an adjunct of the automobile industry. But already in 1892, the formation of the United States Rubber Company represented a merger of 18 factories, which had a daily capacity of 150,000 pairs of rubber footwear, supplying about 70 per cent of the market,[7] and thus inaugurated the process of consolidation in the industry.

Diversification and Multiplication of Light Manufactures

The pervasive influence of business and mechanical enterprise in the generation after the Civil War, combined with the opportunities presented by an expansion in market, material, and labor supply, made itself

---

[7] Clark, *History of Manufactures,* Vol. III, p. 235; H. T. Warshow, *Representative Industries of the United States,* pp. 577 ff. New York: Henry Holt and Co., 1928; J. L. Bishop, *A History of American Manufactures,* Vol. III, p. 307. Philadelphia: E. Young & Co., 1868.

felt in many other fields and transformed the production of diverse consumers' goods into industries of considerable size and scope by the turn of the century. The chance of a headstart achieved through an early venture or technical innovation promoted the trend toward localization but did not altogether prevent the diffusion or redistribution of particular industries under the impact of changing conditions. Limitations of space permit only the mention of such developments as the high degree of concentration of the manufacture of collars and cuffs at Troy, estimated at 80 per cent of total output in 1909, of knit goods in the Mohawk Valley, and of gloves at Gloversville, all in New York State. Already in the 1860's, Danbury, Connecticut, was the center of an expanding hat manufacture, although new machine methods for the quantity production of hat forms had been developed in the New York City area. Connecticut, in particular, was already then noted for "the manufacture of the lighter articles in metal," which "for cheapness and ingenious workmanship are the Wonder of the World." Among these were the clocks of Bristol, the brass manufactures and buttons of Waterbury and Ansonia, the guns of Hartford, the hardware of New Britain and Meriden, and the sewing machines of Bridgeport.[8]

New Jersey and Pennsylvania also were the seats of a diversified list of light manufactures, especially of the expanding woolen, silk, and knit goods industries; carpets, silk fabrics, and machine-made hosiery figured prominently among them. The "silk stocking age" was ushered in with an increase in production of that item from 12,572 to 2,354,648 dozen pairs between 1899 and 1914, and to nearly twice the latter figure by 1923. The introduction of synthetic fibres and the rapid expansion of rayon output from 300,000 to 15 million pounds between 1911 and 1921 announced the beginning of a new revolution in the textile industry, altering consumption and production ratios among its principal components.

Two new items of machine and factory production, developed before 1900, bore witness to the inventive ingenuity of American industrial enterprise and its impact upon standards of consumption. One of these was the machine-made jewelled watch, introduced in the decade of the 1850's through the efforts of A. L. Dennison and Edward Howard, founders of the Boston Watch Company, first at Roxbury and subsequently at Waltham, both near Boston. Based on the standardization of parts and the application of precision tools and machine methods to their manufacture, these early ventures long experienced technical and economic difficulties and began to prosper only during the Civil War; thereafter the industry expanded with the migration of mechanics westward and the establishment of new factories in Illinois and Ohio. In 1882, two pro-

[8] Bishop, *A History of American Manufactures,* Vol. III, pp. 448, 496 ff.; D. R. Fox, *Ideas in Motion,* p. 11. New York: Appleton-Century Co., 1935.

ducers, the Waltham and Elgin companies, reported the employment of 2,000 and 1,600 persons respectively, and accounted for two-thirds of domestic output. The Waltham plant exported one-third of its production. By the close of the century the American Watch Company at Waltham had a daily capacity of 2,500 watches, and was described as an outstanding example of the American System of Interchangeable Manufacture.[9]

The second example of a new item of machine production was the achievement largely of George Eastman at Rochester, New York, and is an early illustration of a combination of industrial research and business enterprise resulting in the creation of a major industry. Beginning in the 1870's as a kind of amateur investigator and producer of photographic materials, Eastman had developed a "stripping film" and machine-coated photographic paper by 1885; in 1888 the Kodak made its appearance as the people's camera and as a voracious consumer of photographic film. George Eastman, moreover, was one of the first manufacturers in the United States to "formulate and to put into practice the modern policy of large-scale production at low costs for a world market, backed by scientific research and extensive advertising." [10]

Significantly, the single year 1895 witnessed three separate events that were prophetic of three vast new fields of industrial production catering to the recreational and consumption needs of people on a mass scale. One of these events was the display of moving pictures on a screen at the Cotton States Exposition at Altanta, Georgia. The second event was the first motor vehicle race in the United States, held at Chicago on Thanksgiving Day, 1895. The third event was the more remote demonstration in Italy of the miracle of wireless communication, out of which was ultimately to emerge the radio industry.[11]

In the 1890's the creation of the General Electric Company by merger, the establishment of its principal rival, the Westinghouse Company, and the completion of the first large-scale hydro-electric installation at Niagara Falls announced the birth of a new industry. This was followed by the introduction and mass production of a versatile list of appliances that literally electrified the household by the 1920's. This substantial new group of light manufactures helped to swell the physical volume of production after 1899 at a rate "considerably in excess of the growth of population." Comprising electric lamps and household appliances, these manufactures grew in value from less than two million dollars to over 84 million dol-

---

[9] Clark, *History of Manufactures,* Vol. II, pp. 364 ff.; Bishop, *A History of American Manufactures,* Vol. III, pp. 292 ff.; *Engineering Magazine,* Jan. 1900, pp. 530 ff.

[10] C. W. Ackerman, *George Eastman,* pp. XIV, 33 ff. Boston: Houghton, Mifflin Co., 1930.

[11] F. R. Dulles, *America Learns to Play,* p. 287. New York: Appleton-Century Co., 1940; W. R. Maclaurin, *Invention and Innovation in the Radio Industry,* pp. 31 ff. New York: Macmillan Co., 1949.

lars between 1899 and 1919, and this was merely a start.[12] Thus, the years 1860-1919 constituted a truly middle period in American industrial evolution, middle in the sense that during it manufactures already in existence reached their maturity, and middle also in the sense that it witnessed the birth and continuous development of new products and manufactures that were to reach their full fruition in the period following the First World War.

Selected References

GENERAL WORKS

Clark, V. S., *History of Manufactures in the United States* (3 vols.). New York: McGraw-Hill Book Co., 1929.

Committee on Recent Economic Changes, Herbert Hoover, Chairman, *Recent Economic Changes in the United States* (2 vols.). New York: McGraw-Hill Book Co., 1929.

Day, E. E., and Woodlief Thomas, *The Growth of Manufactures, 1899 to 1923*, Census Monograph VIII. Washington: Government Printing Office, 1928.

Depew, C. M., ed., *One Hundred Years of American Commerce* (2 vols.). New York: D. O. Haynes & Co., 1895.

Glover, J. G., and W. B. Cornell, eds., *The Development of American Industries*. New York: Prentice-Hall, Inc., 1941.

Keir, Malcolm, *Manufacturing*. New York: Ronald Press Co., 1928.

Martin, E. W., *The Standard of Living in 1860*. Chicago: University of Chicago Press, 1942.

National Industrial Conference Board, *A Graphic Analysis of the Census of Manufactures, 1849-1949*. New York, 1923.

Shaw, W. H., *Value of Commodity Output Since 1869*. New York: National Bureau of Economic Research, 1947.

Warshow, H. T., ed., *Representative Industries in the United States*. New York: Henry Holt Co., 1928.

SPECIAL TOPICS

Allen, F. S., *The Shoe Industry*. New York: Henry Holt Co., 1922.

Burgy, J. H., *The New England Cotton Textile Industry*. Baltimore: Waverly Press, 1932.

Cole, A. H., *The American Wool Manufacture* (2 vols.). Cambridge: Harvard University Press, 1926.

Cole, A. H., and H. F. Williamson, *The American Carpet Manufacture*. Cambridge: Harvard University Press, 1941.

Copeland, M. T., *The Cotton Manufacturing Industry of the United States*. Cambridge: Harvard University Press, 1923.

Hazard, B. E., *The Organization of the Boot and Shoe Industry in Massachusetts Before 1875*. Cambridge: Harvard University Press, 1921.

Mitchell, Broadus, *The Rise of Cotton Mills in the South*. Baltimore: Johns Hopkins Press, 1921.

---

[12] W. H. Shaw, *Value of Commodity Output Since 1869*, p. 42. New York: *National Bureau of Economic Research*, 1947; E. E. Day and W. Thomas, *The Growth of Manufactures, 1899-1923*, p. 12 ff. Washington: Government Printing Office, 1928; D. L. Cohn, *The Good Old Days*, pp. 401 ff. New York: Simon and Shuster, 1940.

Pope, Jesse, *The Clothing Industry in New York*. Columbia, Mo.: University of Missouri, 1905.

Selekman, B. M., and others, *The Clothing and Textile Industries in New York*. New York: Committee on Regional Plan of New York, 1925.

Thorpe, W. L., *The Integration of Industrial Operation,* Census Monograph III. Washington: Government Printing Office, 1924.

U. S. Bureau of Foreign and Domestic Commerce, *The Men's Factory-Made Clothing Industry, The Shirt and Collar Industries.* Washington: Government Printing Office, 1916.

26 · DOMESTIC TRADE AND MARKETING

Marketing and Trade Before 1865

INTER-REGIONAL COMMODITY movement during the early nineteenth century was channelled through communities on natural waterways, particularly seaboard cities on navigable rivers. Merchants in such seaboard cities had a dominating influence over the commerce of interior communities, purchasing or accepting on consignment the produce that had been assembled and forwarded by retail storekeepers up the river and furnishing such retailers with imports or domestic manufactures.

Wholesale organization at the seaboard centers was adapted to serve both the country merchants, who came semi-annually to make purchases, and the local shopkeepers. Imports were received by shipping merchants or importers with shipments at one time arriving from the East Indies, and at other times from China, England, France, or Germany. The retailer wished an assortment of such goods and required long term credits. It was in serving the retailers that the jobbers found a function, an 1829 description indicating they "are an intermediate grade of merchants, between the wholesale and importing merchants and the retail shopkeepers." [1]

These jobbers found, in time, other suppliers in addition to the merchant shippers. There were specialized importers and commission merchants receiving foreign goods on consignment and there were auctions at which foreign wares were sold. In purchasing domestic manufactures, the jobbers generally dealt with commission merchants, or agents, that represented American manufacturers in the seaboard markets. In some instances merchant shipping houses or prosperous importers solicited com-

[1] *New York House Journal,* 1829, p. 393; quoted by Arthur H. Cole, *The American Wool Manufacture* (2 vols.), Vol. I, p. 214. Cambridge: Harvard University Press, 1926.

The several categories of intermediaries or middlemen were from time to time designated in different ways. In the early nineteenth century the term jobber was used to distinguish a merchant who bought smaller lots from large importers, and in the fruit and vegetable produce line the term was subsequently retained for this designation of a man intermediate between the large dealer and store proprietor. To the extent distinction between jobber and wholesaler is made, the practice in this chapter will follow the early usage.

mission business and utilized available capital in financing expansion of manufacturing activity.

Some of the country merchants who made semi-annual trips East came to Philadelphia or New York from near-by communities. They usually operated purely retail general stores in villages in which their establishments were without local competition, except such as was offered by itinerant peddlers. Merchants from rising interior cities such as Pittsburgh, Cincinnati, or Louisville were not in so fortunate a monopoly position. Such firms often had an advantage of another sort, however, in that they specialized in some such general line as dry goods, hardware, or groceries and purchased in adequate quantity to obtain jobber prices, reselling part of their stock to general stores in neighboring small communities and disposing of the balance at retail prices.

The general stores provided the chief retail outlet, particularly in rural areas, during most of the nineteenth century. In the first half of the century, these establishments and the merchants managing them often provided the chief commercial tie between the rural community and the metropolis. It was at the local store that all purchases were made, whether of provisions, metal manufactures, or dry goods.

A large portion of sales were charged on open book account, with a closing of the books taking place only once a year. Such infrequent settlement was suited to the shortage of cash and the confused currency conditions prior to 1865, already described in Chapter 10. But the extension of credit to purchasers added to retailing costs and it increased the local merchant's dependence upon credit from jobbers. The merchant also accepted produce, particularly butter, cheese, and eggs, for which there was a local market, and credited the customer with the price of these goods. In many areas the storekeepers also served as concentrators of farm products for shipment to the metropolitan markets.

In the older communities of the East that boasted manufacturing industries, the general stores were frequently operated in conjunction with a local factory, and this facilitated payment of wages in truck. A manufacturer might, in fact, barter some of his product for a wide variety of consumer items that could be disposed of at the store. The same procedure was followed by lumber mill proprietors, or mine operators, in other parts of the country.

The local storekeeper served much more in the capacity of a trader than does a retailer today. Goods were not sold by brand and it was, therefore, the storekeeper's standing that was damaged if he procured a barrel of inferior flour or a hogshead of defective molasses. The one-price system had not been established, and on many items the sales usually involved considerable haggling over price.

Agricultural produce used for local consumption in towns and cities in the early nineteenth century did not necessarily pass through any of the wholesale or retail trade channels. This was often sold directly by the farmer to consumers, either at private sale or in municipally controlled open markets. Sometimes sale was through middlemen who rented stalls at public markets and operated with relatively small capital. The role of public markets differed very much from one community to another, but a diminishing proportion of farm produce and foodstuffs was retailed through such markets by the 1860's. Specialized retailers and hucksters carried produce to the consumer's neighborhood or doorstep and offered it for sale at a convenient place and at a reasonable time of day. Thereafter it was only the most thrifty housewife who set forth at dawn to "go to market."

Wholesale Marketing After 1865

The Movement of Goods in Commerce

The predominant direction of inter-regional movement of domestic and imported manufactured articles in 1860 was westward and southward, mostly from New England and the Middle Atlantic states but with some goods moving downstream from such rising centers as Pittsburgh or Cincinnati. During this same period the major commodity movements eastward, or down the Mississippi, consisted of agricultural products or other raw materials for use at downstream points or for export. Changes that occurred in this movement by the time of World War I reflected both the growth of manufacturing output sold in national markets and changes in location of manufacturing activity. The westward and southward movement of goods from the industrial Northeast continued. In dollar or tonnage terms it showed a marked increase and it was matched by a return flow of farm products and raw materials. Manufacturing industry also developed, however, in the Central states, and in the South and West, and produced goods for national as well as local markets. The greater part of such manufacturing output consisted of processed foods and fibres, such as flour, meats, or cotton, and steel and mineral products. The location of manufacturing in these areas shortened the haul from developing raw material sources to processors or industrial users. The manufacturing growth in the newer areas, particularly the Central States, was at a much more rapid rate than that in the East. Already by 1910 the railroad tonnage of manufactures originating in the West and South together was more than half the magnitude of such tonnage originating in the East.[2]

Wholesaling Farm Produce vs. Wholesaling Manufactures

A contrast may be drawn between the task of marketing manufactures and that of marketing farm products. The problem of assembly was

[2] Emory R. Johnson, *et al., History of Domestic and Foreign Commerce of the United States* (2 vols.), Vol. I, p. 200. Washington, D. C.: Carnegie Institution of Washington, 1915.

generally greater in the case of the latter. In grain and livestock marketing, for example, this task was generally performed at interior subordinate points of commerce, by local merchants or buyers from the central markets, before shipments moved to such metropolitan centers as Chicago of St. Louis or, later, to Minneapolis-St. Paul and Kansas City. Local merchants might assume the middleman function in this assembly, and rail lines and extensions made new areas accessible. One measure of successful progress in the conduct of produce assembly is a narrowing of the spread between prices at local and central markets. Analysis of wheat prices at a number of local markets during post-Civil War years indicated a definite narrowing of this margin.[3]

In the marketing of cereal crops, and of a number of other staples such as cotton, development of formal exchanges provided open competitive pricing for standardized grades, thus conforming to the economist's dream of perfect competition, and corners on such markets were generally short-lived. Formalization of futures trading in the exchanges facilitated shifting of risk. The operation of warehouses in metropolitan centers, open trading on the exchanges, formalized grading, and futures transactions were all in due course subjected to rules imposed by the exchanges or dealers' associations and by government regulatory bodies.

In the handling of fresh fruits and vegetables the problem of assembly was of major importance, as in the case of the staples. Formal trading did not develop in the same manner, and numerous overlapping types of intermediaries found a function in expediting the movement of perishable goods that were often offered for sale in a wide variety of qualities not subject to standard classification. As a consequence there was not, in this field, a narrowing of marketing costs. In fact, in 1918 it was observed: "The fruit and vegetable trade used to be handled on a five per cent basis. Then seven per cent became the normal rate, and it is now becoming established at the ten per cent level—though commissions of fifteen per cent are not unknown." [4]

Wholesale Channels in the Distribution of Manufactures

By the time of the Civil War a major part of our manufactures were sold beyond local markets and moved through the wholesale trade channels of the larger cities. The dominating role of wholesalers and jobbers

[3] A general statement concerning this trend was made in the introduction to Vol. VI of the *Report of the Industrial Commission* (Washington: U.S. Government Printing Office, 1901), p. 6: "The facts examined," it was stated, "show that in the course of the past 25 years there has been a constant tendency toward a reduction in the difference between what the producer receives and what the consumer pays." Specific data are presented by Henrietta M. Larson in, "The Wheat Market and the Farmer in Minnesota, 1858-1900," Columbia University *Studies in History, Economics and Public Law,* Vol. CXXII, No. 2 (1926), pp. 53, 94. New York: Longmans Green & Company.

[4] Edwin G. Nourse, *The Chicago Produce Market,* p. 116, Boston: Houghton Mifflin Company, 1918.

in the distribution of manufactured products continued for some years after the Civil War. "Nine-tenths of all American commerce is in the hands of various commission men and brokers," wrote a foreign business man who had come to this country and operated a furniture factory and general store in North Carolina during the 1880's. His account continues, perhaps, with more vividness than accuracy: [5]

> It is almost impossible to buy anything directly from the producer; every factory sells off its entire production to some sort of broker, who then resells it to retail merchants throughout the entire Union. Furthermore, as soon as the broker has some degree of monopoly over a given branch of production, he designates local wholesalers for a given territory—sometimes a state, sometimes several counties, sometimes one large city. It is then completely useless to try to deal directly with the producer. The purchaser must buy third-hand and pay two commissions. Among the goods thus distributed are Minneapolis flour, California canned fruits, the better kinds of soap, the best candies, agricultural and other machinery, glass, pianos, and organs, cheeses, good boots and galoshes, and the best hats. On all these one is forced to pay excess charges, sometimes twice the original value, for the maintenance of the middlemen. The commission men even control the commerce in such merchandise as cotton and woolen fabrics, although these are made in factories dispersed throughout the country.

Within the wholesale market there was, during the latter half of the century, a further shift away from general commission merchants either to wholesalers proper, to sales through brokers or manufacturers' agents, or through branches or sales departments of the manufacturers.[6] The shift to wholesaling may have been furthered by the establishment of quality standards that made it possible to order goods with some assurance they would measure up to samples.[7] In some lines there was an asso-

---

[5] P. A. Demens (Pseud. Tverskoy) as quoted in Oscar Handlin, *This Was America,* pp. 350-351. Cambridge: Harvard University Press, 1949.

In commenting on the series of middleman intermediaries the Commissioner of Internal Revenue observed, in the 1860's, that the marketing of manufactures was less direct than that of agricultural produce. The extreme case was that of textile fabrics which were "sold five, six or seven times before being consumed." He concluded: "It has been assumed by competent calculators, that, on a general average, productions of the country are sold four times." U. S. Treasury Department, *Report of the Secretary of the Treasury on the State of the Finances for the Year 1864,* p. 60. Washington: Government Printing Office, 1864.

[6] Throughout the half century after the Civil War, some transactions continued to pass through merchants operating on a commission basis, though perhaps not actually to the extent thus described, in the same manner as prior to the War. In some lines, *e.g.* in the growing Western flour industry, commission merchants served a function comparable to that which such merchants had earlier served in Eastern textile marketing.

[7] The change was well under way already before the Civil War. A rough date for the transition from predominance of commission agency to predominance of the wholesaler proper has been suggested by Professor N. S. B. Gras to be around 1840. See his *Business and Capitalism,* pp. 195-207. New York: F. S. Crofts, 1939. The new form is illustrated in the textile field by such a firm as H. B. Claflin and Company, which grew from a partnership started in 1843, and in the hardware line by such a firm as Simmons Hardware, founded in 1864.

ciated reduction in the number of times a product was resold before reaching the final consumer. With the development of greater specialization in wholesaling the commission merchant's services in extending credit to manufacturers provided the basis for the business of factors who advanced funds to manufacturers on the basis of accounts receivable, which were collected by the factor.

Toward the latter half of the nineteenth century there was also a more rapid growth of general service wholesalers and of jobbers in the interior cities, especially those of moderate size, than occurred in large seaboard centers as New York or Philadelphia. In the larger centers the wholesaling function was assumed in part by the buying departments of chains or department stores, special line wholesalers, or cooperative buying agencies created by independent retailers.

The wholesalers and jobbers of the 1860's carried general lines of groceries, dry goods, hardware, drugs, etcetera. Some special line jobbers of a later period carried a narrower line; for example, foreign food specialties for a particular racial group or, in textiles, ready-to-wear lines or knit underwear.

Wholesale Enterprises

With some exceptions, most of the wholesale establishments were first started as retail institutions and grew through plowing back of profits. The mortality of business ventures engaged in the general wholesale trade was probably lower, and longevity greater, than that of the brokers. In all establishments in the wholesale trade category, mortality was possibly lower and longevity greater than in either manufacturing or retailing. Yet the wholesale field retained a competitive character after trusts and combinations had provided restraints on price competition among manufacturers.

The capital requirements for the several classes of wholesaling activities ranged from a negligible figure for the broker to a very much larger sum for either the commission merchant who financed his suppliers or the old style general line wholesaler proper. Most of the established wholesale houses in the 1860's or 1870's did an annual business and had capital requirements that were small by today's standards. In the New York grocery line James E. Nichols observed that in the 1870's "an annual trade of $1,500,000 was rare, and large houses were looked upon as having a comfortable sales account when it ran above $750,000 per annum." [8] By 1895, he reported, there were by contrast six large grocery wholesalers in the Chambers Street vicinity, and two who did about $25,000,000 annually.

---

[8] Chauncey M. Depew, ed., *One Hundred Years of American Commerce* (2 vols.), Vol. II, pp. 598-9. New York: D. O. Haynes & Co., 1895.

Manufacturer Initiative in Merchandising

Shifts That By-Passed Wholesalers

In many lines of manufactures wholesaling, during the period between the Civil War and World War I, there was a shift in initiative and control from the wholesalers to the manufacturers. "The old-line wholesaler," observes Professor Copeland, "typically was a trader. He performed a valuable service in seeking out sources of supply of dependable goods at reasonable prices." Subsequently, however, "as more and more manufacturers have trade-marked their goods and advertised them to consumers, the services called for from the wholesaler have become less of a trading character and more of a distributing nature." [9] This was reflected, in part, in increased direct selling by manufacturers or their representatives to industrial or institutional consumers and to large scale retailers, including chains and department stores. The initiative in thus by-passing wholesalers was generally taken by a firm of large size that advertised directly to consumers. Associated with this shift in marketing channels and arising in part from the same causes, there was a change in the role and a weakening in the bargaining position of the wholesaler.

Furthermore, the wholesalers and jobbers of the latter nineteenth century shared in the risks of distribution by placing advance orders and by stocking goods in anticipation of orders, while those in the early twentieth century, who rely more and more upon the manufacturers' ability to supply goods promptly on short notice, avoid these risks. By that fact, however, they render themselves more easily dispensable.

Manufacturer Merchandising, Brand Advertising, and Packaging

In the latter nineteenth century a number of manufacturers undertook to service retailers directly, and some concerns undertook retailing operations. This entry of manufacturers into merchandising was associated in some cases with a greatly increased amount of manufacturer advertising directed to both retailers and final consumers of brand-name packaged products, employment of traveling salesmen and missionary salesmen, and the opening of sales depots or branch offices to by-pass middlemen.

The packaging of articles under a nationally advertised brand name had its earliest general vogue in the sale of patent medicines that were widely sold prior to the Civil War. In the sale of groceries trade names were of some importance by the 1860's, but in that period it was the retailers who valued the trade names and to whom any advertising of trade names was directed. In the year 1860, for example, a grocer in

[9] Melvin T. Copeland, "The Present Status of Wholesale Trade," *Harvard Business Review,* Vol. VI, No. 3 (April, 1928), pp. 257-263, see p. 262.

Leominster, Massachusetts, returned coffee to his Boston wholesaler with the complaint, ". . . this box of Coffee has not the Stickney and Poor Mark upon it." [10] In the same year a California grocer also wrote this Boston wholesaler that he wished to be certain that his sugar was from the East Boston Sugar Refinery. Advertising in the subsequent period was more and more directed toward consumers as well as dealers.

An advertiser who showed initiative in reaching ultimate consumers in the 1870's and early 1880's was Vogeles, owner of St. Jacobs Oil, an ointment. He began advertising in 1876, and by 1881 his appropriation had grown to $600,000. "There was hardly a township in the United States in which the words 'St. Jacobs Oil for Rheumatism' or just 'St. Jacobs Oil' were not carried on barns, fences, trees, or anywhere they could be placed, and hardly a newspaper that did not have the small but ever-present advertisement." [11] Castoria was another such item publicized in the 1870's, 1880's, and 1890's through magazine and outdoor advertising that impressed mothers with the catch phrase "children cry for it." This product was sold without salesmen, all sales effort taking the form of such advertising. In the 1880's and 1890's advertising was also undertaken on a larger scale by manufacturers of soaps, foods, and novelties in addition to patent medicines.

The function of advertising as an instrument in facilitating innovation is suggested by the variety of new products advertised by manufacturers or producers of moderate scale. Professor Hower in his history of N. W. Ayer & Son, an advertising agency, refers to the advertisement of products that represented "new developments in agriculture, education, and general living conditions." He adds: "Seeds and nursery stocks, for example, were widely advertised by Ayer along with agricultural implements and machinery—hay forks and knives, self-acting cow-milkers, chilled-steel plows, horsepower threshers and separators, grist mills, and tools of all kinds." [12]

The consolidation and combination that took place toward the end of the century brought enough production under the control of one management to warrant large scale expenditures on advertising. In the consumer goods lines there was concentration of control in the output of foodstuffs—flour milling, meat packing, sugar refining, salt production, and biscuit baking—in the output of hardware and enamel ware, and in the manufacture of cigarettes. This concentration was a necessary condition to large scale advertising; but it is also true that the increase in advertising and the adaptation of the distributive organization to the

---

[10] Jonas Colburn to Stearns & Co., December 3, 1860. (Baker Library.)

[11] Frank S. Presbrey, *The History and Development of Advertising,* pp. 389-90. New York: Doubleday, Doran & Company, 1929.

[12] Ralph M. Hower, *The History of An Advertising Agency,* rev. ed., p. 47. Cambridge: Harvard University Press, 1949.

handling of advertised products placed an even greater premium on large scale organization.

Whatever the nature, or the immediate message, of advertisements they grew to be an accepted instrument in merchandising. Manufacturers who did not advertise could process or manufacture components or finished goods for others that owned an established trade name. Small firms in this category, or large firms selling their own branded products but with surplus capacity, might contract to prepare goods sold by chains, department stores, or wholesalers under private brand names.[13]

The chief media for brand advertising in the 1860's were the religious papers or journals, local newspapers, and outdoor advertising. When such periodicals as *Harpers Weekly* and the *Saturday Evening Post* were started they were at once used in the program. Advertising directed to the trade was placed in such trade journals as *American Grocer* and *Hardware Age*. Advertisements in newspapers and periodicals in the 1860's conformed to the regular newspaper print and style, were one column in width, and generally only several lines in length. By the end of the century most publications offered quarter and half pages for advertisements that broke column rules, illustrations were frequently used, and some periodicals carried multi-colored lithograph advertisements on their back covers.

Outdoor advertising, including posters, provided an alternative or supplement to newspaper or magazine advertising, and St. Jacobs Oil was at one time even advertising by lettering in huge size on a rock at Niagara. Stunt advertising, which had been given an impetus by Barnum, still had wide appeal. Other media were the county fairs and such expositions as the Columbian. Business cards, which had served as an advertising medium for many years, were made more ornate and bore rhymes or appealing illustrations.

The packaging of food under brand labels became more common with the development of brand-name advertising. Packaging as such for the sake of sales appeal had always been an important aid in merchandising. American manufacturers who sold in competition with imported items took pains, for example, to wrap and package their goods in conformity with established custom.

Several changes in the distribution of manufactures after 1860 were made by manufacturers for the express purpose of providing for more aggressive merchandising of their products. A growing number of manufacturers sent their own salesmen or missionaries direct to the retailers

[13] There is a presumption that profits were greater in marketing a branded product under one's own label and that sales were more stable. The business opportunity that was thereby opened was aptly expressed by a motto that hung in the office of the H. J. Heinz Company: "Any common thing well done and properly advertised will bring success."

over the protests of established jobbers. There were also, prior to the Civil War, a considerable number of manufacturers' sales depots in the principal markets, such as New York. Some even created a marketing organization prepared to service the numerous retail stores. This was reported to be the case with the Loose-Wiles Biscuit Company. A manufacturing concern that undertook retail distribution on a national scale at an early date was the W. L. Douglas Company, manufacturer of shoes, which opened a chain of retail outlets as early as 1876. The manufacturer policy of by-passing intermediaries had particular appeal in the sale of fashion goods, and it was followed by millinery and other clothing firms. The establishment of manufacturer-controlled retail outlets, even if on an agency basis, was of importance also in the marketing of products that required subsequent servicing, such as typewriters.

An alternative to such direct retailing was afforded in the practice of sending out missionaries to publicize and win favor for the product without making sales, which were to pass through the regular channels. This practice was followed by a number of the firearms manufacturers by the turn of the century, if not earlier.[14] Possibly the Standard Oil policy was comparable. In areas of sharp competition, company representatives might clean lamps and trim wicks for the customer.[15]

A manufacturer that advertised widely often included the price in the message to the public, as was the case in advertising of the Ingersoll watches. Even where price was not explicitly included in advertising statements there developed on many branded articles a conventional price that the consumers considered normal, and a charge in excess of this would have been regarded by the consumer as an indication that the retailer's prices were exorbitant in general. By the same token, it was on branded articles that price cutting was most telling in its effect. As a consequence of these several forces, the margin on branded articles was progressively narrowed and led to some dealer opposition to advertising in general.[16] A counter-move by manufacturers was taken in setting up procedures for maintaining resale prices. Contracts with dealers might re-

---

[14] Harold F. Williamson, *The Story of Winchester. A History of the Winchester Repeating Arms Company, passim.*, Unpublished manuscript. Winchester supplied expert marksmen with ammunition and paid them retainers provided they would publicize the fact that they used Winchester rifles and ammunition.

[15] Ida M. Tarbell, *The History of the Standard Oil Company* (2 vols.), Vol. II, pp. 33 and 51. New York: McClure, Phillips & Company, 1904.

[16] A tally of dealers made in the years prior to World War I by the Curtis Publishing Company was reported to show that of the dealers opposed to manufacturer advertising 45 per cent of the wholesalers and 54 per cent of the retailers were opposed because the mark-up on advertised goods was so much less than on unbranded articles. It is pertinent to add, however, that those opposed to such advertising were a minority of those in trade. Source: Mac Martin, *Planning An Advertising Campaign For A Manufacturer* (3 parts, General Series No. 10). Part 1, p. 50, Part 3, pp. 81-2. Minneapolis: University of Minnesota, February, 1914.

quire forfeiture of a fixed sum as liquidated damages in the event goods were sold below the price fixed by the manufacturer, or a rebate might be allowed at the year's end to dealers who had maintained prices at prescribed levels. Some publicity was attached to court decisions in which these procedures were held a violation of the Sherman Anti-Trust Act. A more significant observation is that such contracts prevailed generally.

Marketing and Manufacturer Competition

The prevalence of ever fewer sellers, the practice of selling under advertised brand names and often through controlled retail outlets, and the number of missionary salesmen of one form or another all contributed to conditions in which price competition was in some measure replaced by service or other forms of competition. The formation of dominant monopolies was often attended by predatory tactics. International Harvester tied up all local firms that might have marketed farm equipment of its competitors. National Cash Register bribed agents or dealers to damage their competitor's product.

Manufacturer cooperation as an alternative to predatory competition took the form of price agrements or of agreements assigning quotas. The agreement among producers of cast iron pipe condemned in the Addyston Pipe Case is an example. Occasionally cooperation took the form of cooperative selling, such as that used by the Michigan salt industry after 1876 or by the oil industry under Standard Oil Company domination about the same time. In the wall paper line, the Continental Wall Paper Company formed in 1898 controlled marketing of 98 per cent of the wall paper manufactured in the United States.

Once monopoly or leadership was established, however, many of the large concerns recognized the importance of good public relations and generally refrained from the more overtly destructive policies on the one hand or extreme predatory tactics on the other hand.

Retail Trade After 1865

Retailing and Commodity Movement

Tryon has characterized the period 1830 to 1860 as that of industrial revolution, because factory output replaced home industry. While for some lines the major transition occurred somewhat later, the process of change conformed to what Tryon, speaking of the earlier period, characterized as "the transfer from family- to factory-made goods." He added that "the end of the period found family-made goods the exception rather than the general rule as formerly." [17]

Associated with this change was an increase in retail sales. A contrast

---

[17] Rolla M. Tyron, *Household Manufactures in the United States 1640-1860,* p. 303. Chicago: University of Chicago Press, 1917.

can be drawn between the relation of retail trade to realized national income in the years just after the War of 1812 and in the 1920's. Sales by retail trade establishments in 1816 were probably less than one-tenth of realized private production income. In 1929 the magnitude of such sales was more than 80 per cent of realized private production income.[18]

The extension of markets for manufactures and farm products after 1865 was reflected in a corresponding extension of the area serving as the ultimate source of goods consumed in each locality. By the time of the First World War there was a truly national market for such varied items as fresh fruit or hardware. The consumer could find at the retailer's products from every part of the country. Hundreds of thousands of food retailers carried citrus fruits from Florida and California. Some of these establishments carried perishable fruits from different regions as the season progressed, strawberries from Florida or Louisiana in March and from Delaware or Maryland in May and June. The tens of thousands of retailers who stocked hardware offered locks and brass goods from Connecticut and nails and iron and steel products from Pennsylvania.

Retail Establishments as Business Enterprises

In the retailing field the form of ownership continued to be largely that of proprietorship or partnership, and incorporation was rare for the individual-unit, old-style retail establishment. Capital requirements for most such retail establishments were small, ranging from a minimum of a few hundred dollars for smaller confectionaries or grocery stores to somewhat more for a butcher shop, dry goods store, or hardware store. The average investment in retail units was probably several thousand dollars; this may have risen during the period, partly due to increases in the variety of goods handled. Due to the ease of entry into business on a small scale and the readiness with which entrepreneurs of mediocre capacity turned to this field, the bulk of the stores did only a very small annual business, although exact data on the distribution or change in the distribution are not available. It was suggested by contemporaries that business mortality of retail enterprises was high.[19] The great number of

[18] For the year 1816 available data on retail sales comes from an estimate made by the Collector of Revenue which is cited in Fred M. Jones, "Middlemen in the Domestic Trade of the United States, 1800-1860," *Illinois Studies in the Social Sciences,* Vol. XXI, No. 3 (May 25, 1937), pp. 55-56. Urbana, Ill.: University of Illinois. Jones cites from *American State Papers,* Finance III, pp. 182-183. Realized private production income for 1819 was estimated by Martin for the National Industrial Conference Board and is published in *Historical Statistics of the United States, 1789-1945,* Series A-154, p. 14. Washington: Government Printing Office, 1949. For 1929 the retail sales are from *Statistical Abstract of the United States, 1948,* Table 1050, p. 964. Washington: Government Printing Office, 1948. Realized private production income for that year is from *Historical Statistics* as cited above.

[19] A report presented at the meetings of the American Economic Association that was tallied from inquiries sent to retailers chiefly in Kansas, Iowa and Minnesota indicated high turnover, as follows: "That in localities reporting, during five years fifteen per

new starts that must have occurred each year can only be accounted for in terms of some attraction this field must have had. Perhaps it was due to the narrowing of opportunities for profitable self-employment in manufacturing industry.

The changes in retailing that occurred during the period provide an example of gradual replacement of old forms and establishments by more efficient organizational forms conducting business on a large scale. The individual unit retailers sought protection, however, through legislation. They provided the major political support for so-called fair-trade, resale-price maintenance laws.

Data covering the retailer's mark-up are rather sketchy, and any general statements must fail to indicate the wide variation in retail mark-up. Comments in trade journals and scholarly periodicals suggest that the retailer received half, or more, of the spread between producer and consumer; and that this gross spread was well above forty per cent of retail price. Perhaps, therefore, as a crude figure it may be suggested that the retailers' share of the consumer's dollar amounted to between twenty to thirty cents. One study of shoe retailers indicated that expenses, and the corresponding mark-up necessary in order to earn a profit, comprised a larger share of retail price in 1913 than it had in the 1880's. At the later date the retailers' costs were generally between fifteen and twenty per cent, whereas in the 1880's it was claimed that many retailers' costs were less than ten per cent. In this line the rise in cost was partly due to the greater variety of stock it was necessary to carry after 1908 when new styles were introduced to aid in making sales.

There was, of course, no consistent procedure for determining retail price or the retailers' mark-up. In the grocery trade sugar was sold at little or no profit, and one grocer observed that to make ends meet "we practically rob customers on teas and coffees to make up the balance." [20] In the hardware line nails sold at an inadequate margin, as was true for the sugar sold by grocers. The hardware dealers were also reported to make little or nothing on barn door hinges but to recoup their loss by a high mark-up on fancy butts. Generally, it was on trade marked items that the margin was narrowed. Pear's soap, for example, was reported in 1901 to be retailing at ten cents rather than at the former price of fifteen cents even though the dealer was obliged to pay $1.20 to $1.25 per dozen.[21]

---

cent of the retailers have failed, about seventeen per cent have changed localities by removal and twelve per cent have withdrawn from business, leaving but about fifty-six per cent that can be called stable." Report of Committee on Trade, *Publications of American Economic Association,* Vol. III, No. 3 (July, 1888), pp. 202-4; see p. 203.

Data are not readily available for comparison of turnover in retailing with turnover in other fields, nor for changes in the turnover in this field during the period to 1917.

[20] *Grocers' Review* (July, 1910), p. 246 as quoted in E. M. Patterson, "The Cost of Distributing Groceries," *Annals,* Volume L (November, 1913) p. 75.

[21] Emily Fogg-Meade, "The Place of Advertising in Modern Business," *Journal of Political Economy,* Vol. IX (March, 1901), p. 242.

General Stores and Specialization in Retailing

The general store continued to serve as an important retail outlet in rural regions throughout this period. In the South the breakdown of the plantation economy created enlarged opportunities in retailing and in the concentration of the cotton crop. Lien laws passed after the Civil War formalized the storekeepers' claim on crops as security for store credit, and thus led to a system that held many store customers in perpetual debt. The southern general store thus served as a focus of economic life. "Perhaps, no other southern institution more nearly embodied so much of the intimate story of the New South." [22] In mining or factory towns the employers often continued to operate stores at which they expected their employees to spend their wages. In western communities storekeepers occasionally accepted local produce, such as wheat or corn, offering "store pay" or marketing the products on a commission basis.

Changes in the goods carried by general stores reflected somewhat tardily the new factory output of finished consumer goods. Canned soups and vegetables slowly found a place alongside mason jars used for home canning. Ready-to-wear dresses, shirts, and suits were stocked in addition to bolts of cotton and woolens. Factory made saddles and harness, and horse drawn plows, cultivators, and tedders assumed new importance as these replaced equipment and implements made by local artisans.

Retail grocery stores often evolved from general stores, and in many rural regions differentiation did not take place until after the First World War. In seaboard cities the grocery trade found a market in provisioning ships; or, on occasion, grocers started as dealers in tea and other imported products. In 1895 a member of the trade contrasted the typical retail grocery stores of that year and of 1870.[23]

> The retail store was still distinguished by many of the characteristics familiar to the early traders. . . . Staples in bulk, doled out in brown-paper parcels to customers, were still the rule; the "shelf goods" of to-day were almost unknown. Fruits in barrels and casks, sugar in boxes, and molasses in hogsheads still stood in unsightly cumbersomeness in the middle of the floor. The sun-cured fruits of California were unknown, the vast resources of that State in this direction being still undeveloped. Evaporated stock, too, was still of the future. The stores were small dingy places compared with the great establishments of to-day; the old sugar-mill, the back-breaking "fall," and stuffy little offices, in place of light and airy counting rooms, were prominent features. Despite all this the spirit of progress had entered, and innovation in one form or another was an almost daily event.

In the twenty-five year interval covered by this contrast, and in the years following, grocers marketed an ever larger part of their staple stock

---

[22] Thomas D. Clark, *Pills, Petticoats and Plows*, p. 22. Indianapolis: Bobbs-Merrill Book Company, 1944.

[23] Depew, *op. cit.*, Vol. II, p. 598.

in packaged form under manufacturers' brand labels—Pillsbury's Best flour, Kellogg's corn flakes, and Franco-American canned soup. On the other hand there was some tendency to include perishable fruits and vegetables formerly peddled by hucksters, and except for citrus fruits these were not subject to standardization and labelling. The tendency of the grocery store to become more inclusive in its stock, illustrated by the handling of produce, was the predominant one and overbalanced the counter-trend toward specialization seen in the growth of special line delicatessens or dairy product stores. Indeed the line often included wooden ware, household utensils, washboards, and step ladders.

The number of stores carrying groceries in Chicago and in Philadelphia was tallied shortly before World War I. In Chicago it was estimated that in 1914 there were 8,929 retail stores carrying groceries as a general practice, or one store for every 268 persons.[24] In Philadelphia, in 1911, there were 5,723 retail stores carrying groceries as a general practice, which amounted to approximately one for every 270 people.[25]

The large number of stores and the ease of entry may have narrowed trading margins. As of 1913 Professor Patterson commented on the problems of grocery retailers as follows: [26]

> . . . . it is estimated that the grocer must make from 15 per cent to 20 per cent gross profit in handling his goods and that "any one whose expenses do not run over 17½ per cent has cause to congratulate himself." But this margin of gross profit is hard to secure.
>
> Butter and eggs together are said to represent about 36 per cent of the grocer's total sales and yield about 10 per cent profit. Sugar represents 7 per cent and always sells on a very narrow margin. Flour yields 16 per cent profit, but ham, bacon and lard less than 5 per cent. Eggs, butter, sugar, smoked meats, lard, bread, flour and potatoes represent about 60 per cent of the total sales and show the retailer an average gross profit of only about 9 per cent. Evidently a large profit must be derived from other lines of goods if the grocer is to survive.

Patterson did not mention perishable produce, which comprised only a small part of the grocer's sales at that time. The retail mark-up on perishables was large and it may have been this fact that led grocers to carry more and more perishables in spite of spoilage losses. Nourse indicated, for years prior to World War I, that the retailers mark-up on oranges was 33.3 per cent and on strawberries from 10 to 30 per cent.[27]

The differentiation of retail establishments during the years prior to the Civil War had provided most cities and towns with apothecaries, hardware stores, queen's-ware, and housefurnishings stores, and in the dry goods line with general dry goods stores and a variety of specialty shops.

---

24 *Preliminary Report to the Mayor and Aldermen of the City of Chicago* by the Municipal Markets Commission (Chicago, April 27, 1914), p. 23.

25 Patterson, *loc. cit.*, p. 76.

26 *Ibid.*, pp. 75-76.

27 Nourse, *op. cit.*, p. 122.

In the larger cities there were specialty shops in the hardware or clothing lines, shops handling "Yankee Notions," or even bargain shops. During the period ending with the First World War the differentiation and specialization was carried further only in a few specialty lines. The main drift was toward constant adaptation of each type of store to include new lines that afforded a wide profit margin or that drew customers into the store. The introduction of the soda fountain in the apothecary's shop was designated by one writer as a "rather notable economic revolution." [28]

At the middle of the nineteenth century there were dry goods retailers that handled largely bulk cloth from the bolts. With the development of the ready-to-wear clothing industry the retail sale of cloth did not grow as rapidly as other lines, and dry goods firms "intermixed dry-goods proper with many other lines of merchandise." [29] Some of the general dry goods stores in the seaboard cities expanded business both in terms of the quantity and variety of dry goods they stocked and by stocking additional types of merchandise, such as novelties and notions, jewelry, or even trunks or valises. Such firms as Lord and Taylor or Arnold Constable and Company carried wide assortments of dry goods, both imported and of domestic manufacture. Buyers from such firms generally visited Paris, London, and other world markets. Business could be done on a large scale by these concerns in the first place because the goods handled were items for which the customer shops, for which he is willing to travel some distance, and in the second place because the growth of cities brought vast numbers of prosperous customers within shopping distance of the stores. It was from such ventures that department stores grew.

New Forms In Retail Organization

The striking and constructive innovations in marketing during the period between the Civil War and World War I were generally made by entrepreneurs who found a means of administration by which they could extend the scope of operations under their supervision and subject to their policy decisions. It might be said that separation of policy determination and top level management from clerking involved an "administrative revolution" in retailing. This feature was common to all three of the new forms that were initiated during the period by enterprising merchants, the department stores, the chains, and the mail order houses. Another common feature, but necessarily a development subsequent to a moderately large scale operation, was the assumption of the jobber function by the retail management, or by an affiliate, which purchased in quantity from wholesalers, wholesale brokers, or producers, and either undertook or arranged for storage, transportation, grading, re-packaging in smaller

[28] A. W. Douglas, *Traveling Salesmanship*, p. 108. New York: Macmillan Company, 1919.

[29] Depew, *op. cit.*, Vol. II, p. 558.

lots, and other functions previously considered in the province of the jobber.

These new forms in large-scale retailing afforded the enterprising merchant avenues for promotion and expansion within the field of retail trade. As such men found adequate challenge and scope for their talents they brought to retailing constructive innovations, many of which were adopted by small establishments. The size and scale of business conducted under the new forms led eventually to the first wide use of the corporate form of organization in retailing.

There were some changes in practice that were already under way by 1865 but were effected more quickly as a consequence of the new large scale retailing ventures. The one-price policy, for example, became a necessity where large numbers of clerks made the actual sales. R. H. Macy had followed this policy in his dry goods store at Haverhill in 1854, emphasizing in his advertising that his first price was the lowest, and he continued the policy when he started a dry goods specialty store in New York in 1858. This policy, already practiced by a number of New York merchants in the 1840's, appears to have gained general favor by the late 1860's, although rural general stores still followed a multiple price or haggling system at that time and for some years subsequently.

Large scale business in retailing also made possible more extensive advertising and hence there came now a further transfer of strategic power and initiative in marketing. Whereas the wholesaler had dominated in our distributive organization prior to the Civil War, and the manufacturer of branded, advertised products assumed a major role by the turn of the century, the retail organizations that advertised to consumers were just on the threshold of assuming strategic importance in mass marketing by the time of the First World War. The growth of large scale business in retailing eventually posed some of the same problems of monopoly and competition that had been faced by industry; for example, to what extent could the consumer have the benefits of large scale organization without being denied the advantages of vigorous competition among the sellers?

Department stores had their most phenomenal growth early in the twentieth century. The principle of arranging store plan and store accounting by department permitted specialization of buyers and of sales clerks in one line of merchandise, while each line of goods could be marketed with the advantage of specialists' services in such activities as advertising or display. The policy followed by the larger department stores was to offer a wide variety of goods in one establishment, to emphasize such services as delivery and credit, and such conveniences as attractive lunch rooms. These stores might operate with a part of the business conducted by leased departments. At Macy's, in the 1870's and 1880's, for example, leased departments included the restaurant, women's shoes, silver, china, and glassware, and it was as a lessee that Straus, subsequently its president, first became connected with the Macy store. Characteristically, the stores of this type developed in large urban centers, but departmentizing was also profitable in moderately large stores in the smaller cities.

While a large part of the department store supplies came through regular wholesale channels, the larger stores were in a position to make purchases in such quantities that manufacturers or selling agents were induced to sell directly rather than through established jobbers. Often this innovation was made in depression times, as during the middle seventies. Related to this direct purchase was the deliberate effort to increase the rate of stock turnover and the seeking out of novel items that would sell quickly. A contrast may be drawn between department store buyers who made monthly purchasing trips directly to the manufacturers and the rural individual retailers in the South who made yearly trips to intermediary jobbers at Louisville or Cincinnati. The new form provided more direct communication. "In short, the integrated firm was in a better position than the specialized wholesaler to coordinate the manufacturer's production with actual consumption." [30]

Success in the separation of managerial and clerking functions while maintaining accountability on the clerking level is, perhaps, best illustrated in the retail chain form of organization as it had developed by 1900. General policies with respect to opening or closing of separate units, with respect to merchandising or advertising procedures, and with respect to procurement were centralized. Each separate retail establishment was, however, a distinct unit for accounting purposes. The development of this form gave adequate scope to the ambitions of such men as George F. Gilman, George Hartford, B. H. Kroger, or F. W. Woolworth, and they focussed their attention upon developing improvements in retail merchandising or procurement. It is not an exaggeration that, "with the advent of the grocery chain store, the retail distribution of staple groceries received for the first time the sustained attention and direction of administrators of a high order of business ability." The success of chains was, therefore, "that of efficient business organizations in a trade notoriously inefficient." [31] A number of procedures in retailing gained wide acceptance after their introduction in the chain systems. These included the packaging of tea blends for retail sale under trade-marked labels, the use of premiums or trading stamps as inducement to purchasers, and the later scrapping of such inducements and all other frills or services in the effort to pare costs when this offered greater appeal to buyers. In the

---

[30] Ralph M. Hower, *History of Macy's of New York, 1858-1919,* p. 154. Cambridge: Harvard University Press, 1943.

[31] Bullock, *op. cit.*, pp. 83-4. The greater part of the material on food chains is from Professor Bullock's unpublished manuscript. This material was summarized in two articles in the *Harvard Business Review* which are shown in the Bibliography.

years just before and during World War I the "economy stores" of the Atlantic & Pacific system may have cut retailing costs by a third, and their service to the consumer was attested to when an official Markets Commission of Chicago, studying high living costs, reported favorably on the lower costs of distribution through chain stores.

The expansion of retail units under such chain operation in food and later in variety store and drug lines was more rapid than the increase in independently operated units, and in some cases the gross sales of the larger systems showed an even sharper rise than the number of chain-operated units. "Growth was slow until after 1900;" Copeland has suggested, adding, "in fact 1910 is probably a better date for marking the acceleration in chain-store expansion in this country." [32] The emergence of this new form brought to public attention problems in retailing that had earlier been recognized in manufacturing; for example, absentee ownership, so-called "unfair" local price cutting, and business concentration that threatened to reduce competition.

The inception of chain stores was attended by a great outcry against them. The early tea companies were condemned in the first issue of the *American Grocer* that appeared in 1870, the charge in that and subsequent issues being that the tea sold by such companies was of inferior quality and included some tea already used. These charges were reprinted in some of the local newspapers. The connotation "price cutter" was frequently given to chain stores in general conversation, and the charge of discriminatory price cutting aimed at restraining or monopolizing trade provided grounds for legal action by independents and the government under the anti-trust laws. Furthermore the retail price of many advertised items was fixed by manufacturers in the late nineteenth century and, while such resale price clauses were held unenforceable under Federal law, the first of the state fair trade laws was passed by New Jersey in 1911. The reaction to the price reductions offered by the Atlantic & Pacific "economy stores" in the years prior to World War I is significant for what it reveals of the degree to which price cutting violated prevailing practice.[33]

The mail order house provided a third form of retail organization that developed in this period and that afforded opportunity for separation of clerking from policy formulation. The firms of Montgomery Ward and Sears, Roebuck both were started in the last quarter of the nineteenth

[32] Melvin T. Copeland, "The Managerial Factor in Marketing," *Facts and Factors in Economic History*, p. 615. Cambridge: Harvard University Press, 1932.

[33] Suit was brought by the Cream of Wheat Company over a drop in price from fourteen cents to twelve cents. Great Atlantic & Pacific Tea Company *vs.* Cream of Wheat (CCA, 224 Fed. 566; affirmed 227 Fed. 46) . Bon Ami objected to a price reduction on its product. The independent merchants complained concerning price reductions on Campbell's soups although the manufacturer apparently took no action. Bullock, *op. cit.*, p. 93. Some so-called fixed prices cut by these stores or by chain or department stores were evidently fixed merely by custom in the trade rather than by contract with the manufacturer.

century, at a time when department stores were also soliciting orders that were filled by mail. This type of business grew rapidly in furnishing goods to rural customers and the mail order houses provided, by 1917, a channel for the mass marketing that was to grow phenomenally in the post-war period.

Conclusion

Description of the diverse functions of middlemen and retailers has indicated the complexity of distributive functions in an economy of specialization. The increase in scope and extent of the marketing task during the period after the Civil War was probably associated with a widening distributive mark-up. Probably, also, for the entire period 1869-1919 this margin, rising slowly, was less than in recent times.[34] A contrast between marketing and such activities as manufacturing and transportation points up the absence of significant "economies of scale" in the "trade" segment of our economy.

One measure of the burden of marketing upon the entire economy is provided by data on the portion of our labor force engaged in marketing and on the related portion of national income derived from marketing. Between 1870 and 1920 the percentage of the total labor force 10 years of age and over engaged in trade rose from 6.1 per cent to 9.8 per cent.[35] In corresponding measure, the middleman function absorbed a significant and increasing portion of national income. The percentage of realized private production income that was tallied as earned in trade rose from 5.24 per cent in 1799 to 12.05 per cent in 1859. It rose further to 16.52 per cent in 1869 and continued at approximately this percentage of the total during the ensuing fifty years being, for example, 16.47 per cent in the year 1920.[36]

The role of middlemen and the power of middlemen in the bargaining process was significantly altered during the latter nineteenth century as a part of the changes associated with development of factory production and the sale of factory produced goods under advertised brand names and frequently at prices that were advertised. While the wholesaler in the early nineteenth century was often a key figure with power to initiate manufacturing ventures, by the twentieth century strategic bargaining power in the market generally was held by the enterprises controlling

[34] In a director's comment to Simon Kuznets, *National Product Since 1869* (New York: National Bureau of Economic Research, 1946), Oswald Knauth, who was for many years an active executive in retailing, observes: "The assumption is made that the distributive mark-on was the same in the decades 1869 to 1919 as in the period 1919-35 on which considerable data are obtainable. My observations would lead to a guess that distributive mark-on increased in the later decades as compared to the earlier."

[35] National Bureau of Economic Research, *Studies in Income and Wealth,* Vol. XI, p. 47. New York: 1949.

[36] This is based on National Industrial Conference Board data. *Historical Statistics, op. cit.,* Series A-161, p. 14.

popular brand names. These were generally manufacturers and, in a few cases, the new types of retail units, such as department stores, chains, or mail order houses.

In the bargaining process consumers were at a disadvantage in terms of their information about products and marketing conditions. Consumer cooperation, however, never gained popularity in this country except among closely-knit homogeneous groups or among a few farm groups where it was incidental to cooperative marketing. Consumers did receive legislative protection against fraud and adulteration in the early nineteenth century legislation concerning the U. S. Pharmacopoeia and in the pure food and drug legislation of the twentieth century.

Perhaps a final measure of the increased services performed by those engaged in trade is provided by the increase in per capita real product, described in Chapter XXXIV, an ever increasing portion of which passed through trade channels. The rising real income received by consumers was accompanied by changes in its composition. During the period after the Civil War there was a marked increase in per capita consumption of sugar, but decreases in per capita consumption of meat and flour. Also, the form in which these commodities were purchased was changed. The sugar consumed, for example, came to the consumer increasingly as an ingredient in confectionaries, preserved foods, and beverages. The increase in range of finished goods retailed was thus but a counterpart of the larger shift in our economy that involved a transfer of economic functions out of the home and into manufacturing and commercial establishments. By the time of World War I the trade organization for distributing such goods as sugar, meat, flour, confectionaries, preserved foods, and beverages was adapted to serve customers of widely differing tastes and incomes. Most significant, perhaps, both trade and customers in 1917 were more responsive to change and innovations than in 1865. This responsiveness, achieved at the cost of added expense devoted to communication and seller advertising, provided the basis for the new developments in styles and in marketing procedures that took place after World War I.

Selected References

GENERAL WORKS

Cochran, Thomas C., *et. al.*, "Historical Aspects of Imperfect Competition," *Journal of Economic History*, Vol. III (December 1943), Supplement pp. 27-50.

Depew, Chauncey M., ed., *One Hundred Years of American Commerce* (2 vols.). New York: D. O. Haynes & Company, 1895.

Hotchkiss, George B., *Milestones of Marketing*. New York: The Macmillan Company, 1938.

Johnson, Emory R., *et. al., History of Domestic and Foreign Commerce of the United States* (2 vols.). Washington: Carnegie Institution of Washington, 1915.

SPECIAL TOPICS

Annals of the Academy of Political and Social Sciences, Vol. XXXVIII (September, 1911), "American Produce Exchange Markets."

———, Vol. L (November, 1913), "Reducing The Cost of Food Distribution."

Atherton, Lewis E., "The Pioneer Merchant in Mid-America," *The University of Missouri Studies,* Vol. XIV, No. 2 (April 1, 1939).

———, *The Southern Country Store, 1800-1860.* Baton Rouge, La.: Louisiana State University Press, 1949.

Beckman, Theodore N., and Nathanael H. Engle, *Wholesaling,* rev. ed. New York: Ronald Press Company, 1949.

Bullock, Roy J., "The Early History of the Great Atlantic & Pacific Tea Company," *Harvard Business Review,* Vol. XI, No. 3 (April, 1933), Part I, pp. 289-98.

———, "A History of the Great Atlantic & Pacific Tea Company," *Harvard Business Review,* Vol. XII, No. 1 (October, 1933), pp. 59-69.

Clark, Thomas D., *Pills, Petticoats and Plows.* Indianapolis: Bobbs-Merrill Company, 1944.

Cole, Arthur H., *The American Wool Manufacture* (2 vols.). Cambridge: Harvard University Press, 1926.

———, and Harold F. Williamson, *The American Carpet Manufacture.* Cambridge: Harvard University Press, 1941.

Federal Trade Commission, *Report on the Wholesale Marketing of Food.* Washington: Government Printing Office, 1920.

———, *Chain Stores: Growth and Development of Chain Stores,* Senate Document #100, 72d Congress, 1st Session. Washington: Government Printing Office, 1932.

Gibb, George S., *The Whitesmiths of Taunton.* Cambridge: Harvard University Press, 1943.

Hartsough, Mildred L., "The Twin Cities As A Metropolitan Market," *Studies in the Social Sciences,* Research Publication No. 18, University of Minnesota, December 1925.

Hower, Ralph M., *History of Macy's of New York, 1858-1919.* Cambridge: Harvard University Press, 1943.

———, *The History of an Advertising Agency,* rev. ed. Cambridge: Harvard University Press, 1949.

Industrial Commission, *Report on Capital and Labor in Manufactures and General Business,* Vol. VII. Washington: Government Printing Office, 1901.

———, *Final Report,* Vol. XIX. Washington: Government Printing Office, 1902.

Jones, Fred M., "Middlemen in the Domestic Trade of the United States, 1800-1860," *Illinois Studies in the Social Sciences,* Vol. XXI, No. 3 (May 25, 1937).

Kuhlmann, Charles B., *The Development of the Flour-Milling Industry in the United States.* Boston: Houghton Mifflin Company, 1929.

Marburg, Theodore F., "Commission Agents in the Button and Brass Trade a Century Ago," *Bulletin of the Business Historical Society,* Vol. XVI, No. 1 (February, 1942), pp. 8-18.

———, "Manufacturer's Drummer, 1832" and "Manufacturer's Drummer, 1852," *Bulletin of the Business Historical Society,* Vol. XXII, Nos. 2 and 3 (April and June, 1948), pp. 40-56 and 106-14.

Martin, Edgar W., *The Standard of Living In 1860.* Chicago: University of Chicago Press, 1942.

Martin, Margaret E., "Merchants and Trade of the Connecticut River Valley, 1750-1820," *Smith College Studies in History,* Vol. XXIV, Nos. 1-4 (October, 1938—July, 1939).

Nourse, Edwin G., *The Chicago Produce Market.* Boston: Houghton Mifflin Company, 1918.

Nystrom, Paul H., *Economics of Retailing* (2 vols.), Vol. I, *Retail Institutions and Trends.* New York: Ronald Press Company, 1930.

Porter, Kenneth W., *The Jacksons and The Lees* (2 vols.). Cambridge: Harvard University Press, 1937.

Presbrey, Frank S., *The History and Development of Advertising.* New York: Doubleday, Doran & Company, 1929.

Williamson, Harold F., *The Story of Winchester. A History of the Winchester Repeating Arms Company.* Unpublished manuscript.

27 · FOREIGN TRADE AND COMMERCIAL POLICY

Institutional Changes in the Organization of Foreign Trade

BUSINESS ORGANIZATION for the conduct of American foreign trade continued, after 1850, to show gradual modification along lines already indicated in the preceding period of our development. The role of the old-fashioned overseas merchant as an independent middleman buying and selling goods at his own risk continued to shrink; he was superseded by trading houses that conducted business on a narrower and surer margin of profit by taking commissions for executing orders of either foreign or domestic buyers and sellers. In theory it is possible to distinguish between foreign trade houses that (1) acted on a commission basis in filling foreign orders, (2) acted as sellers of manufactured goods on the basis of specific arrangements with manufacturers, and (3) acted on their own account like the old-style merchant house. In practice, however, all these functions were frequently performed by the same organization, with the emphasis shifting to the first two types of activity. In addition, the foreign trade house would frequently use its facilities to aid foreign business interests in disposing of their goods in the American market.

Alongside the commission houses and the agents, brokers, and banks operating in the highly organized markets for international staples, new institutional arrangements came into play with the growing export opportunities for American manufacture. This has been called the development of direct foreign trade, to distinguish it from the indirect methods of trading through the use of a variety of independent intermediaries. The reasons for this structural change are not far to seek. As long as the export trade of American industry was casual, intermittent, and geographically widely dispersed, it was best served by utilizing established export firms with their specialized knowledge and equipment. These firms would arrange the details of engaging shipping space and marine insurance, delivering the goods to the customer, negotiating credit terms, and securing conformity with the many Government regulations at home and abroad. But in many cases such a purely passive policy did not appeal to manufacturing concerns, accustomed in the domestic market to aggressive policies of demand creation for their specialties. The export firms were frequently unsuited, if not hostile, to special sales efforts on behalf of branded products and trade names. Hence, when the volume of sales in particular foreign markets showed prospects of great increase, industrial corporations proceeded to set up their own marketing organization abroad, complete from facilities for the physical storage and handling of the product to the building up of "good will." The advantages of such a course were substantial, particularly in the case of products requiring service after sales.

Sewing machines, petroleum products, cash registers, steel products, agricultural and other specialized machinery, shoes, soap, and the products of the meat-packing industry were prominent early examples of American goods that were sold in foreign markets in this way.[1] In order to facilitate more systematic control over foreign market possibilities, Congress passed the Webb-Pomerene Export Trade Act in April, 1918. This act permitted producers to combine their resources and activities in the quest for foreign markets, though similar combinations in the domestic market remained subject to the restraints of anti-trust legislation. At one time or another in the entire period from 1918 to 1939, 120 associations, with a total membership of 2,074 companies, were formed to operate under the terms of this act. The total exports of these associations rose to a peak in 1929, when they accounted for a total export of $724,000,000.

The Triumph of Protectionism

The pattern of United States commercial policy in the latter part of the nineteenth century was fixed in substantial measure during the Civil War years and the period that followed. The war marked a decisive turn in the history of tariff policy. During the 30 years preceding the outbreak of the war, there had been a partial reversal of the protectionist trend that had been evident in the period from 1816 to 1832. On the eve of the conflict the Morrill Act set the stage for the rapid rise in rates that was to follow. The need for revenue became more urgent as the war progressed, and Congress responded to this need by setting up an elaborate system of excise taxes and greatly increasing tariffs on imports. In part, the higher tariff rates were meant as an offset to the new internal excise taxes; but as the war progressed, protectionist aspirations and private cupidity played their part in raising duties indiscriminately. The most extensive revision of the tariff occurred in 1864, when, after scanty discussion and under the stress of war, Congress passed a bill raising the average rate on dutiable commodities to 47 per cent, as compared with about 20 per cent in 1860.

[1] In 1929 it was estimated that a total of 938 American branch houses were operating abroad in foreign selling, with an aggregate investment of $362,000,000. These figures exclude the large investment of the petroleum industry in foreign distribution estimated at $500,000,000.

For a period of nearly 20 years, this war tariff remained the basic public regulator of our foreign trade. The act was frequently amended and the protectionist features of the legislation became more prominent as the war excise taxes were dropped, while tariff rates remained what they were. On several items, such as wool, steel rails, copper, nickel, and marble, the duties were raised. In 1872, a flat 10 per cent reduction in all protective duties was agreed to by the protectionist elements in Washington to head off the more drastic revision then impending; but this proved to be a purely temporary reduction, because the earlier rates were restored in 1875. Ultimately the public ceased talking about the "war tariff" and adjusted itself by and large to the fact that the wartime expedient of extremely high import rates had became a permanent institution. As the foremost student of the American tariff reminds us, this new system fostered its own peculiar theory and dogma to justify its existence, and ideas that had been held to be the exploded errors of a small school of economists became the foundation of the policy of a great people.[2]

Throughout these years and subsequently, there were frequent occasions for renewing public debate over the tariff. Until the First World War, the tariff duties were the backbone of our Federal revenue system, and the varying fortunes of the public treasury offered many opportunities for suggesting changes in the tariff structure. Moreover, the remarkable growth of business combinations and the evidence of monopolistic practices greatly agitated the public mind, and these phenomena were frequently linked with the protective tariff. But on the whole, the protective system stood off these assaults, as in the general tariff revision of 1883 and toward the close of the first administration of President Cleveland, and even succeeded in moving to higher ground, as in the McKinley Act of 1890 and the Dingley Act of 1897.

In 1892 the election of Grover Cleveland for the second time seemed to give him a clear mandate for seeking the enactment of a lower tariff, but his intentions were frustrated in the Wilson-Gorman Act of 1894. Although this act temporarily checked the advance of protection and brought some reductions, it was such a severe disappointment to the President and his followers that he allowed the bill to become law without his signature. The history of the entire episode of Cleveland's frontal attacks on protectionism has lingered on as a reminder of the great difficulties of securing congressional assent to a downward revision of the tariff.

The only serious interruption in the forward movement of the protective system was the passage of the Underwood bill of 1913. This act was a consequence of the unusual combination of circumstances that lifted Woodrow Wilson to the presidency of the United States, and fol-

[2] See F. W. Taussig, *The Tariff History of the United States,* pp. 174-175. New York: G. P. Putnam's Sons, 1931.

lowed four years after the inconclusive Payne-Aldrich Act of 1909. The outbreak of the First World War in 1914, however, produced such abnormal trading conditions that the act never received an adequate trial. The aftermath of the war brought the disintegration of Wilson's national liberalism and a resumption of "normalcy" in tariff policy.[3]

In reviewing the history of tariff policy during this period, little credence should be given to the exaggerated and sweeping language frequently used in discussing this subject. The purely historical record of the economic effects of the tariff yields only limited and tentative results, and makes necessary inferences based on generally accepted economic principles. Most students of the problem would agree that the policy of high protection accelerated the process of industrialization and, in particular cases, aided the establishment of branches of manufactures that subsequently were able to stand on their own feet.[4] It would be wrong to conclude from such cases, however, that the policy of protection was a necessary prerequisite to the development of manufactures in the United States, or that a net increase in real national wealth and income was the result.

Another aspect of the question concerns the extent to which commercial policy harmonizes with the requirements of the international monetary system and the fulfillment of freely contracted international obligations. From this point of view, it might be argued that the protective tariff policy was not inconsistent with our status as a mature debtor nation in the period between 1873 and 1914. At any rate, the international financial position of the American economy required an export balance of trade in goods and services, and the protective tariff might have facilitated this by restricting imports. It cannot be proved, however, that the protective tariff was necessary for attaining this result, nor, indeed, that the tariff was responsible for it. The coincidence of our restrictive tariff policy and the requirements of our international financial position was probably more adventitious than planned. In the post-war period, however, the disparity between our growing creditor status and the intensification of our high protective policy threatened the breakdown of the network of international financial and monetary relationships whenever the process of American capital export was interrupted. This lesson had to be learned by bitter experience.

The Quest for a "Scientific" Tariff

In practice, modern protection has been in some ways precisely the opposite of what its theoretical exponents pretended it to be. Their arguments have run in terms of the general national interest, as distinct from

---

[3] See Chapter 41.

[4] See F. W. Taussig, *Some Aspects of the Tariff Question,* 3rd enlarged ed. Cambridge, Mass.: Harvard University Press, 1931.

private interest; but in reality the practice of protection had the effect of placing the sovereign taxing power at the disposal of organized special interests to help themselves at the expense of other elements in the national community. Down to the Civil War, except for the Act of 1842, tariff acts were statutes running to less than ten pages. Under such circumstances Congress could reasonably be expected to master the substantive content of the legislation and to devote its intelligence to a discussion of the general principles underlying it. After the Civil War, a seemingly irresistible tendency to expand the detailed rate structure set in; the Smoot-Hawley Act ran to nearly 200 pages of print. What this really meant was that an expanding array of producer interests had attained well-nigh undisputed initiative in suggesting rates and writing the paragraphs of the act that concerned them most, while the role of Congressmen was confined to preserving the ceremonies of the democratic legislative process, working out compromises between competing pressure groups, and seeing to it that the sectional interests they represented were appropriately recognized. Respectable elements in both political parties increasingly looked upon the prospects of new tariff legislation with feelings of dread and embarrassment.

Such uneasy feelings ultimately crystallized in a set of affirmations that "the tariff should be taken out of politics," that the tariff should be made "scientific," and that a tariff commission should be set up to aid Congress in realizing these objectives. From as early as 1865, individuals and boards had occasionally been appointed to give temporary and limited assistance to Congress in its tariff-making duties. In 1909 a Tariff Board was created, but it went out of existence in 1912, when Congress refused to vote its appropriation. In 1916 a bill setting up a United States Tariff Commission was passed; it provided for a bipartisan, fact-finding body of six members, who were charged with duties of investigation regarding the operation of the tariff. It was not, at that time, granted any powers over actual rates.

Meanwhile the so-called "scientific" principle of tariff making had been in its period of gestation. For many years party platforms had contained clauses declaring that a proper tariff rate was a rate equalizing differences in wages or in cost of production at home and abroad. Frequent repetition appears to have attached the odor of sanctity to this formula, and in due course of time it came to be known as the "scientific" principle of tariff making. In the Fordney-McCumber Act of 1922 Congress granted the President power to change individual tariff rates on recommendation of the Tariff Commission, provided the Commission found that the prevailing rate was in excess of, or below, the ascertained difference between foreign and domestic costs of production. This so-called "flexible provision" of the act limited administrative changes in the rates to 50 per cent of the congressional rates.

The operation of the Commission under its new powers proved a bitter disappointment to those who construed the flexible provision as an important step in the right direction. Far from taking "the tariff out of politics," it put the Tariff Commission squarely in politics and made it the center of unsavory political intrigue. Outstanding tariff lobbyists were appointed to membership on the Commission and severe pressure was brought to bear upon the Commission to prevent it from recommending a reduction in the existing duty on Cuban sugar. The futility of the new procedure was painfully illustrated when President Coolidge finally refused to take any action upon the recommendation of the Commission that the duty be reduced from 1.76 cents to 1.23 cents per pound. As a fitting climax, Congress finally raised the duty to 2 cents per pound in the Act of 1930. All told, the Commission's recommendations in the period 1922-1929 led to 37 changes in individual rates, of which five were downward and the remainder upward. Such a trifling and unsatisfactory record justified the conclusion that the incorporation of the flexible provision in the acts of 1922 and 1930 was used by the high protectionist group as a device to deflect possible popular resentment over congressional logrolling tactics, and to gratify the aspirations for formal decorum in the rate-setting process. As long as the Commission was hamstrung in the exercise of its power over rates by the cost-equalization formula, the dominant protectionist group had its opponents blocked.

Commercial Treaty Policy

In order to understand the full implications of the shift in commercial policy that was in the making in the years following 1930, it is necessary to consider the role of commercial treaties in the shaping of commercial policy. From the beginning of our Federal history, the United States had pursued a tariff policy that left no discretion with the executive branch of the Government and that imposed uniform rates on particular imports, regardless of the country of origin. Such a policy is referred to as an *autonomous* tariff policy, as distinct from the policy of *conventional* tariffs (tariffs determined in the process of negotiating trade conventions). We stood aloof from the movement that swept Europe following the Anglo-French commercial treaty of 1860; this movement made bilateral negotiation of commercial treaties the vehicle for securing an all-around reduction of tariff barriers and joined this to an acceptance of the principle of equal treatment for all foreign goods. When the tide turned toward renewed protectionism in the last quarter of the nineteenth century, the sectional pressures for high protection, as registered in European parliaments, were checked somewhat by a continuation of this active commercial treaty policy, which left with the executive authority considerable discretion to modify rates in the course of negotiating trade treaties with other nations. There was also a disposition, notably in

France after 1892, to become less open-handed in pledging equal treatment in respect to all foreign imports and to pursue instead a more mixed policy, in which the same goods from different countries might be taxed at different rates. This was known as the "conditional most-favored-nation" or "preferential" policy, as distinct from the "unconditional most-favored-nation" or "equal-treatment" policy. Theoretically, the United States had adhered to the conditional most-favored-nation principle since 1778; but this had been of little practical significance, because we granted the same tariff to all comers as a matter of course and, on the other hand, encountered for most of the nineteenth century little disposition to withhold from our export goods unconditional most-favored-nation treatment. The predominance of crude materials in our export trade and the high repute of the equal-treatment principle in Europe were two factors contributing to this absence of discrimination. By the same token, however, the increasing importance of manufactures in our export trade, and a new disposition to withhold the equal-treatment pledge from nations who came to the conference table empty-handed, raised in the United States a demand for a more active commercial treaty policy. The United States had made special reciprocity treaties with Canada (1854-1866) and Hawaii (1875-1900), but these were isolated episodes in our commercial history with other nations and tinged with political implications. Apart from these reciprocity treaties, the issue was brought to the fore in this country during the last decade of the nineteenth century.

In the tariff acts of 1890 and 1897, the President was given power to place penalty duties on a small list of products on the free list, mostly South American products like coffee, to give him leverage to obtain special trade concessions for American goods. In 1897, the President was also empowered to reduce congressional rates on a small list of products, known as the "argol" list, and to offer tariff concessions on these products in exchange for special concessions or a promise of minimum tariffs abroad. Though a number of agreements were signed as a result of these provisions, the first policy is remembered primarily for the irritation it produced in Latin America. The bargaining power given to the President was too small to leave any perceptible imprint on trade. Of potentially greater significance was the delegation to the President of power to reduce any dutiable items in the Dingley Act by 20 per cent in the course of negotiating trade treaties with other powers. On paper this constituted a greater departure from our traditional procedure, but its practical significance was nil, because the so-called "Kasson treaties" negotiated under this provision of the Act of 1897 required Senate ratification by a two-thirds majority, and none had a chance of approval. The fate of these treaties in the Senate was remembered many years later, when the so-called Hull Trade Agreements Program of 1934 was under consideration.

After these few half-hearted and futile gestures, there was no further disposition on the part of Congress to delegate to the President any power to reduce the congressional rates in the course of trade negotiations until 1934, although the aftermath of the Spanish-American War did lead to special preferential tariff arrangements between the United States and Cuba and the Philippine Islands, respectively. The attempt to conclude a much publicized reciprocity treaty with Canada during the Taft administration failed, owing to Canadian opposition.

TABLE 1

UNITED STATES BALANCE OF INTERNATIONAL PAYMENTS, BY PERIODS

(in billions of dollars)

Period	Goods and Services Net	Income on Investment Net	Capital Transactions Net	Unilateral Transfers	Gold	Errors and Omissions
1850-1873 (24 yrs.)	— 1.9	— 0.9	1.0	0.3	1.1	0.4
1874-1895 (22 yrs.)	1.2	— 1.9	1.0	— 0.3	0.1	— 0.1
1896-1914 (19 yrs.)	4.8	— 3.0	1.0	— 2.6	— 0.2	—
1914-1919 (6 yrs.)	14.7	1.0	— 14.1	— 1.5	— 0.8	0.7

(Based on *Historical Statistics of the United States, 1789-1945*, a supplement to the *Statistical Abstract of the United States*. Washington: 1949, page 242-243. The subdivision "unilateral transfers" includes personal and institutional remittances, and relief shipments.)

The Balance of Payments

The balance of international payments of the United States measures, in terms of dollars, the total inpayments and outpayments across the frontiers of the American customs area over a stated period of time. By grouping the various items of the balance of payments under relatively few headings, it is possible to secure some insight into the interrelations existing between our trade in commodities and services, our international capital accounts, and the flow of monetary metals. A knowledge of the changes occurring in the main subdivisions of the balance of payments is an indispensable basis for the appraisal of the logic and the timeliness of the international commercial, financial, and monetary policies of the government. In the table given above, the essential relationships in the United States balance of payments over four successive periods from 1850 to 1919 are summarized.[5]

The Period 1850-1914

Down to the outbreak of the First World War, the United States was a capital-importing nation; by 1914 the total foreign stake in the United

[5] See Chapter 41 for a continuation of this table through 1945.

States had risen to $7,200,000,000. The process of building up this foreign investment had a rather uneven character for most of the second half of the nineteenth century, in which periods of active investment alternated with years of partial liquidation of the newly acquired securities. This was particularly true in the first two periods covered by the table. In the third period, 1896-1914, the flow of new capital to the United States had a more even and sustained character, but in these years the great inflow of foreign capital was offset in part by the acquisition of foreign properties by American enterprise. It is estimated that the total American investments abroad had reached the $3,500,000,000 mark by 1914.

As long as the net interest and dividend payments arising out of the accumulated foreign investment were less than the net inflow of new capital, the simple arithmetic of the balance of payments left the door open for an import balance in the trade of goods, services, and precious metals. This was actually the case in the first of the four periods shown in the table above. In the second and third periods, however, the net annual outflow of interest and dividend payments normally overbalanced the net inflow of new foreign capital; such a transition is sometimes referred to as the change from the status of immature debtor nation to that of mature debtor nation. A mature debtor nation must find the necessary foreign exchange with which to meet its annual interest obligations, either by exporting precious metals or by developing an export balance in its trade of goods and services. This is precisely what happened to the United States. Beginning with the fiscal year 1874, an export balance in merchandise became a characteristic of our foreign trade, and prevailed thereafter, with the exception of small import balances in the fiscal years 1875, 1888, 1889 and 1893. The export balance in goods was sufficient, together with small gold exports, to offset the balance of payment deficits arising out of shipping, tourism, and immigrant remittances and still leave enough to meet our international financial obligations. The unprecedented expansion of agricultural exports to Europe was a great factor in shaping the size of this export balance in the last quarter of the nineteenth century, and subsequently the export balance of trade was further enhanced by the rapid growth of our exports of manufactures.

The Period 1914-1919

The period of the First World War brought a drastic overturn of the existing international financial relations of the United States. In the decades preceding the conflict, there had been occasional predictions that the United States would ultimately become a creditor nation, but these prophecies could hardly have been expected to foretell the rapidity and extent of the transition that took place. The character of the balance of payments during these years was determined by the needs of the Allied Powers for goods. Over the entire period from July, 1914, to December,

1919, the active balance on goods and services came to $14,700,000,000. To this credit balance, another billion dollars had to be added for net interest payments to the American economy. Against this huge active balance stood a net gold inflow of $800,000,000, and the remainder had to be financed by the liquidation of foreign-held securities, by the acquisition of new foreign investments by Americans, and by United States Government loans or unilateral transfers to its Allies. The public loans amounted to $9,600,000,000, and changes in the private capital account and unilateral transfers took care of the remainder. Estimates of America's international financial position in 1914 and 1919, respectively, sometimes show an even greater change than the foregoing figures would indicate, because the book values of the assets acquired on private account were frequently in excess of their actual cost. A study of recent data by the Brookings Institution gives the following estimate of American private investments abroad and foreign investments in the United States.

	1914	1919
Private American assets abroad	$3,514,000,000	$6,956,000,000
Foreign assets in the United States ...	$7,200,000,000	$3,985,000,000

Trends in Our Merchandise Trade [6]

The general trend of our foreign trade from 1850 to 1946 may be studied in the accompanying (semilogarithmic) chart. The export and import curves of this chart measure the rate of change of export and import values over successive averaged five-year periods. A comparison between these curves and the line measuring the rate of American population growth shows that the per capita value of exports and imports has grown fairly steadily, at least until the decade following 1929. Generally speaking, the fluctuating appearance of the export and import curves since 1914 stands in rather striking contrast to the more even rate of growth in the preceding period of time. It must be remembered, however, that these relate to the value rather than the volume of trade, and that fluctuations in prices may cause the dollar value figures of trade to oscillate more sharply than the volume. It has been estimated, for instance, that in the years 1911-1914 and 1919, respectively, the quantity of our exports increased by 40 per cent, while the dollar value figures more than tripled. The index of United States wholesale prices offers a crude device for correcting possible misunderstanding concerning the quantity significance of changes in the dollar values of foreign trade. A line representing the rate of change in the wholesale price index has therefore been included in the chart, and it suggests that the increase in the volume of trade from

[6] The material in the following three sections of this chapter include data for 1919-1946 in order to present the major trends more clearly.

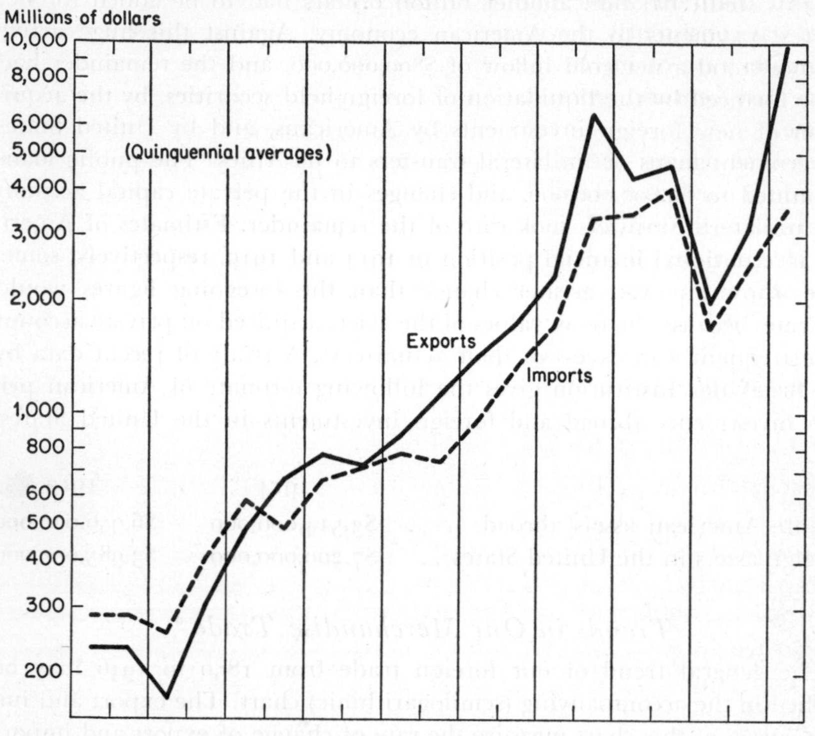
Millions of dollars
10,000
8,000
6,000
5,000
4,000
3,000
2,000
1,000
800
600
500
400
300
200
(Quinquennial averages)
Exports
Imports

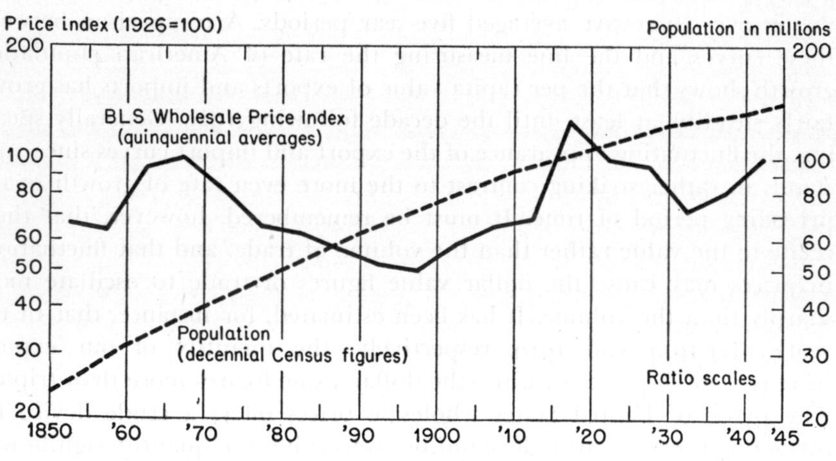
Price index (1926=100)
Population in millions
200
100
80
60
50
40
30
20
BLS Wholesale Price Index
(quinquennial averages)
Population
(decennial Census figures)
Ratio scales
1850
'60
'70
'80
'90
1900
'10
'20
'30
'40
'45

FIGURE 1.

the Civil War until the end of the nineteenth century was more pronounced than the value figures would indicate, because the trend of prices was consistently downward after 1865. On the other hand, part of the greater rate of increase in the value of trade since the closing years of the last century represented higher prices rather than increase in volume.[7]

Measured against the growth of the American economy, foreign trade showed no particular trend, but maintained a more or less constant ratio. At any rate, the official figures measuring the ratio of export values to the value of total output of movable goods produced in the United States show only minor fluctuations around the average ratio of 10 per cent. The most marked departures from this ratio occurred in 1919 when it rose to 16 per cent, and in the depression year of 1933 when the ratio dropped slightly below 7 per cent.

The Commodity Composition of Foreign Trade

The pattern of products entering into our export and import trade during this period changed in a steady and persistent fashion. Tables 2 and 3 show these changes in the composition of our export and import trade, respectively, by averaged five-year periods. Three striking characteristics stand out in the export table. First, the relative decline in the importance of raw material exports. At the beginning of the period, these constituted three-fifths of total exports, largely by virtue of large exports of raw cotton. This proportion declined until crude materials accounted for less than one-fifth of our total exports. Second, as crude materials lost ground, finished manufactures began their great and sustained rise to pre-eminence among our exports. From a modest 12 per cent of total exports in the decade preceding the Civil War, they forged ahead until more than one-half of our total exports are accounted for in this category alone. This development becomes even more impressive when viewed in conjunction with the parallel rise in the exports of our semi-manufactures. Third, the history of foodstuffs in the export trade of this period appears to run in a broad cycle. The significance of crude and manufactured foodstuffs built up to a crest in the final quarter of the nineteenth century, and then gradually diminished in relative significance. The period of the First World War was marked by a temporary reversal of this downward trend, but it again became very marked in the final decade from 1931 to 1940. During the Second World War and its

[7] The United States Department of Commerce publishes trade statistics in which the trade values are corrected for price changes in the articles exported and imported respectively. Thus it obtains a table of index numbers measuring the trend of the quantity of exports and imports. The principal result of this procedure is to demonstrate that the volume of exports and imports is relatively more stable than the value figures might lead one to suppose.

TABLE 2

PERCENTAGE DISTRIBUTION OF UNITED STATES EXPORTS BY ECONOMIC CLASSES, 1851-1946

Yearly Average	*Crude Materials*	*Crude Foodstuffs*	*Manufactured Foodstuffs*	*Semi-Manufactures*	*Finished Manufactures*
1851-60	61.7	6.6	15.4	4.0	12.3
1861-65	20.0	22.1	34.4	5.7	17.8
1866-70	57.6	9.0	13.8	4.7	14.9
1871-75	44.9	15.5	19.6	4.7	15.3
1876-80	32.2	23.9	24.4	4.6	14.9
1881-85	33.8	21.0	25.5	4.8	14.9
1886-90	38.1	15.0	25.0	5.5	16.4
1891-95	33.7	17.2	27.2	6.3	15.6
1896-1900	26.1	18.9	24.0	9.6	21.4
1901-05	30.3	12.2	22.1	11.3	24.1
1906-10	31.7	8.9	18.1	14.2	27.1
1911-15	30.8	8.8	14.3	15.4	30.7
1915-20	18.2	9.2	17.7	15.4	39.5
1921-25	27.6	9.7	13.9	12.5	36.3
1926-30	24.4	6.4	9.7	14.1	45.4
1931-35	30.2	3.9	8.8	14.5	42.6
1936-40	19.0	3.8	5.5	19.3	52.4
1941-45	5.9	1.6	11.6	9.4	71.5
1946	14.9	6.9	16.0	9.4	52.8

(*Statistical Abstract of the United States, 1941,* page 533; *Historical Statistics of the United States, 1789-1945,* page 246.)

aftermath, food exports once more assumed—temporarily at least—a more important place in our export trade.

As to imports, the statistical trends of crude materials and finished manufactures were the reverse of those described above for the export trade. Finished manufactures declined from one-half to one-fifth of total import trade, and industrial raw materials rose from 10 per cent to from 35 to 40 per cent of total imports. Years of business depression in the United States were likely to bring a temporary reversal of this trend and might yield a relative as well as an absolute decline in the figures for raw materials imports, just as years of intensive industrial activity, as in the First and Second World Wars, accentuated the raw material character of our import trade. In years of normal business activity, the total value of imported crude materials exceeds the value of exported crude materials by a good margin. Among the raw materials imported, either in the raw state or partly processed, the most important are rubber, wood pulp, hides and skins, furs, wool, silk, copper, tin, jute, petroleum, nickel, vegetable oils, and a variety of steel alloys, the latter of great strategic importance in industrial processes, though the quantities and values used are of relatively minor significance. The columns on imported crude and manufactured foodstuffs show a downward trend since the decade 1871-

TABLE 3

PERCENTAGE DISTRIBUTION OF UNITED STATES IMPORTS BY ECONOMIC CLASSES, 1851-1946

Yearly Average	*Crude Materials*	*Crude Foodstuffs*	*Manufactured Foodstuffs*	*Semi-Manufactures*	*Finished Manufactures*
1851-60	9.6	11.7	15.4	12.5	50.8
1861-65	14.1	14.3	17.5	13.6	40.5
1866-70	11.7	13.2	19.9	13.9	41.3
1871-75	16.1	14.1	20.1	13.6	36.1
1876-80	18.6	18.2	21.5	12.4	29.3
1881-85	20.0	14.9	19.1	13.7	32.3
1886-90	22.6	15.8	16.5	15.8	29.3
1891-95	23.6	18.7	17.9	14.4	25.4
1896-1900	29.5	15.1	15.9	13.3	26.2
1901-05	33.4	12.9	12.4	16.6	24.7
1906-10	34.6	11.0	11.8	17.8	24.8
1911-15	34.9	12.8	12.5	17.4	22.4
1915-20	40.1	12.2	16.2	17.1	14.4
1921-25	37.4	11.1	13.0	17.6	20.9
1926-30	36.8	12.5	9.9	18.9	21.9
1931-35	28.9	15.6	13.8	18.7	23.0
1936-40	33.1	13.1	14.2	20.9	18.7
1941-45	32.9	16.4	11.5	21.2	18.0
1946	35.5	17.0	10.5	19.4	17.6

(*Statistical Abstract of the United States, 1941,* page 533; *Historical Statistics of the United States, 1789-1945,* page 246.)

1880, which, in the case of manufactured foodstuffs, was reversed in the last decade. Imported foodstuffs include, in substantial measure, products that cannot be grown in the United States except at prohibitive cost, such as coffee, tea, cocoa, tropical fruits, and nuts, as well as cane sugar, edible vegetable oils, and alcoholic beverages. In addition, sizable importation of various grains occasionally took place when crop failures in the United States, as in 1936 and 1937, made it profitable to import wheat and corn into the United States over the tariff wall.

The Geographic Distribution of Foreign Trade

The expansion of foreign trade and the changes in the composition of the exports and imports brought with them great changes in the geographic dispersion of our international economic contacts. Tables 4 and 5 bring out the extent to which the commercial relationships with different continents have changed with the passage of time. At the outset United States foreign trade was primarily trade with Europe. Three-fourths of our exports found their market on that continent, and the rapid development of food exports in the last quarter of the century raised this percentage even higher. But the European market did not maintain this position with the continued expansion of our exports, and a steady relative decline set in that had not yet run its full course in the decade 1931-1940. Even in this last decade, however, the European market accounted for over 40 per cent of our total export trade, far ahead of any other continent in its ability to absorb American products. On the import side, European trade likewise suffered relative diminution. This decline was not pronounced in character until the period of World War I, when Europe's share fell from 50 per cent to 30 per cent and less. This sudden drop is partly explained by the influence of the war in causing the United States to establish direct trade relations with the Asiatic sources of supply in place of using European countries as intermediaries.

TABLE 4

PERCENTAGE DISTRIBUTION OF UNITED STATES EXPORTS BY CONTINENTS, 1860-1940

Yearly Average	*Northern North America*	*Southern North America*	*South America*	*Europe*	*Asia*	*Oceania*	*Africa*
1860	6.9	8.8	4.7	74.8	2.4	1.5	1.0
1871-75	6.4	7.2	4.0	80.2	1.0	0.8	0.4
1876-80	5.0	5.4	3.3	83.1	1.7	1.1	0.6
1881-85	5.4	5.7	3.6	81.1	2.2	1.6	0.5
1886-90	5.2	5.8	4.3	79.3	2.8	2.0	0.5
1891-95	5.5	6.8	3.7	79.5	2.3	1.6	0.6
1896-1900	6.9	5.6	3.1	76.7	3.9	2.3	1.5
1901-05	8.6	6.7	3.2	72.3	5.3	2.0	1.9
1906-10	10.2	8.7	4.6	68.2	5.5	1.8	1.0
1911-15	14.2	7.7	5.2	64.0	5.6	2.2	1.1
1915-20	12.0	7.7	5.5	63.2	8.6	1.7	1.3
1921-25	14.3	10.1	6.8	52.7	11.3	3.2	1.6
1926-30	17.4	8.4	9.4	46.8	12.0	3.7	2.3
1931-35	14.8	8.0	7.0	47.4	17.3	2.4	3.1
1936-40	16.2	9.0	9.8	41.4	16.6	2.8	4.1
1941-45	13.1	5.6	4.9	56.9	7.9	3.5	8.3
1946	15.1	11.0	11.8	42.1	13.8	1.3	5.0

(*Statistical Abstract of the United States, 1941,* page 542.)

As American trade gradually swung free from its European orbit, the trade with other continents necessarily gained in relative importance. The Asiatic continent, with its important island fringe in Japan, the Philippines, and Indonesia, began to equal and even surpass Europe as a supplier of products for the American market and grew more rapidly than any other area in its ability to absorb American exports, at least until the outbreak of World War II. Next to Asia, our commercial relations with Canada showed the greatest vitality. Here we are dealing with a vast area of rich resources, geographically contiguous and inhabited by people similar to our own in standard of living and consumption habits. In the decades between World Wars the Canadian market had grown to the point where its annual share of American exports was almost equal to the amounts annually taken by all of Latin America, with a population roughly ten times as large as Canada. The South American areas, however, likewise accounted for growing percentages of our export trade, and they maintained their relative position in the growing import trade of the United States. Considered separately, the Caribbean area appears to have lost some ground, relatively speaking, as a source of supply and South America, below Panama, to have held its own with the passing years. During World War II the Latin American countries assumed a new and special importance as areas of supply for American needs. Finally, our trade with Africa and Oceania appears to be growing somewhat more rapidly than total trade, but the amounts involved are still very small.

TABLE 5

PERCENTAGE DISTRIBUTION OF UNITED STATES IMPORTS BY CONTINENTS, 1860-1940

Yearly Average	*Northern North America*	*Southern North America*	*South America*	*Europe*	*Asia*	*Oceania*	*Africa*
1860	6.7	12.5	9.9	61.3	8.3	0.3	1.0
1871-75	5.9	16.6	11.0	55.6	9.7	0.7	0.6
1876-80	5.6	17.6	13.8	50.3	11.3	0.9	0.5
1881-85	6.3	14.4	11.4	55.1	10.5	1.7	0.6
1886-90	5.6	13.8	11.5	56.0	10.4	2.3	0.5
1891-95	4.6	16.3	14.9	50.6	10.8	2.1	0.6
1896-1900	5.0	10.3	13.2	52.6	14.6	3.1	1.3
1901-05	5.4	13.3	12.5	51.3	15.4	0.9	1.1
1906-10	5.9	13.4	11.7	51.3	15.2	1.2	1.2
1911-15	7.7	14.5	12.8	46.6	15.8	1.1	1.4
1915-20	12.7	17.5	17.6	20.3	27.1	2.1	2.7
1921-25	11.5	14.9	12.2	30.4	27.3	1.6	2.1
1926-30	11.9	11.4	13.5	29.9	29.7	1.3	2.3
1931-35	13.8	10.3	14.3	30.1	28.7	0.9	1.9
1936-40	14.9	10.0	13.6	25.3	31.6	1.4	3.2
1941-45	27.4	16.8	22.8	8.1	13.7	5.3	6.2
1946	18.7	14.9	22.3	16.2	18.0	3.7	6.2

(*Statistical Abstract of the United States, 1941,* page 542.)

Summary and Conclusions

The foregoing analysis of our foreign trade in its overall statistical aspects has emphasized certain basic changes in the character of our economic relationships with the rest of the world. In Chapter 41 the implications of these fundamental trends will be more fully discussed, particularly with respect to the issues of United States foreign policy. Down to the outbreak of World War I our participation in international economic life may be said to have been important, but its significance for the functioning of the world economy was, nevertheless, still comparatively modest. For the most part our role in world affairs was a passive one, though the decades before 1914 did see the development of a more active foreign policy in the Caribbean and the Pacific. This new interest in foreign policy is seen most clearly in the sharp challenge of President Cleveland to Great Britain in the British Guiana-Venezuelan boundary dispute of 1895, the Spanish-American War, the building of the Panama Canal, the assumption of colonial responsibilities, and the first stirrings of a greater interest in a bargaining commercial policy. It could not yet be said, however, that our foreign policies and international economic behavior were a decisive factor in determining the course of world events and the performance of the world economy. The upheaval of World War I produced sharp changes in the distribution of military and economic power between nations and brought the United States to the center of world affairs. This carried with it new responsibilities and thrust upon the United States the necessity of making grave decisions. The way in which we discharged these new responsibilities will be discussed in Chapter 41.

Selected References

GENERAL WORKS

Culbertson, W. S., *International Economic Policies.* New York: D. Appleton-Century Company, 1925.

Johnson, E. R., and others, *History of Domestic and Foreign Commerce of the United States* (2 vols.). Washington, D. C.: Carnegie Institution, 1915.

Taussig, F. W., *Some Aspects of the Tariff Question.* Cambridge, Mass.: Harvard University Press, 1931.

Williams, B. H., *Economic Foreign Policy of the United States.* New York: McGraw-Hill Book Company, 1929.

SPECIAL TOPICS

Bidwell, P. W., *The Invisible Tariff.* New York: Council on Foreign Relations, 1939.

Gordon, M. S., *Barriers to World Trade.* New York: The Macmillan Company, 1941.

Huebner, G. G., and R. L. Kramer, *Foreign Trade: Principles and Practices.* New York: D. Appleton-Century Company, 1942.

Hutchins, J. G. B., *The American Maritime Industries and Public Policy.* Cambridge, Mass.: Harvard University Press, 1941.

Lewis, C., *America's Stake in International Investments.* Washington, D. C.: Brookings Institution, 1938.

Taussig, F. W., *The Tariff History of the United States.* New York: G. P. Putnam's Sons, 1931.

28 · MONEY AND BANKING 1865-1919

The Monetary Standard and the Money Supply

THE RAPID INDUSTRIALIZATION during the decades following the return of peace in 1865 required a sound banking system and a money supply responsive to seasonal, cyclical, and secular changes in the volume of transactions. To this end a dependable monetary standard was needed to provide the basis for a healthy domestic and international trade and to facilitate the borrowing from abroad that would promote expansion. If the banking system was to make its maximum contribution to economic progress the banks must be soundly and honestly managed, with the individual units large enough to command competent personnel and to effect a reasonable diversification of investment. Moreover a bank note must be established that would be universally acceptable without discount.

On a number of grounds the nation required a continuous growth in the money supply. The growing population (greatly augmented during the last half of the century by immigration), the increasing complexity of business and commercial relationships, the growth of financial institutions like the stock market, and steadily rising industrial and agricultural output, all implied a rapid and prolonged increase in the number of transactions for money. Not only this, but the gradual rise in per capita real income resulting from the constant stream of inventions and innovations increased the ability and the desire of the public to hold assets in the form of money, and therefore required a still further increase in the quantity of money to counteract the fall in velocity.[1]

The Need for a Flexible Money Supply

But seasonal and cyclical changes in the demand for money also had to be met. If pressure on lending and the interest rate was to be avoided, the increased demand to hold cash at certain seasons of the year must be satisfied through the creation of additional bank notes. Furthermore, the variations in seasonal monetary requirements in different types of industry and agriculture in the several parts of the country necessitated a free movement of reserves from region to region, and particularly between

[1] Alvin Hansen, *Monetary Theory and Fiscal Policy*, Chapter 1. New York: McGraw-Hill Book Co., 1949.

New York and the interior. Cyclically, rises and falls in business activity and prices would require an appropriate response on the part of the monetary system. The greater danger was the possibility of a failure of the monetary system to supply additional cash in the event of sudden demand by the public. The problem was to avoid the panics and crises arising out of an internal cash drain. Much of the danger of panic cash withdrawals from the banking system could be obviated if the public were to be satisfied with the soundness and liquidity of the banking system. But the latter could not always be liquid if individual banks lent too freely during the optimism of a business upswing. After a certain lag the higher incomes and prices would tend to lead to both a drain of gold abroad and an internal drain of cash into circulation. Thus the true solution to the problem of achieving both soundness and liquidity would have been a central bank, with effective supervisory powers over the commercial banks, capable of mobilizing the country's cash reserves, and endowed with the power to put a timely brake on excessive credit expansion. One further power would confer the final required degree of elasticity on the money supply: the central bank should be constantly in a position to create new reserves for the commercial banks in any amount necessary to meet a cash drain. In other words, while centralization of the reserves of the banking system would provide part of the answer to banking liquidity, there would be circumstances in which additional reserves might have to be created.

Inelasticity of the Money Supply under the National Banking System

The creation of the National Banking System accomplished a part, but by no means all, of this objective. The achievement of a uniform currency was an encouraging step. The state bank notes were secured by obligations of the states. Since these obligations fluctuated widely in value, the state bank notes circulated at varying discounts. National bank notes, backed by Federal obligations, were, on the contrary, generally acceptable. National banks were subject to supervision by the Federal Government, and minimum reserve requirements were established in order to afford protection to depositors. But, as will be seen, the National Banking System did not provide the country with an elastic currency; furthermore, it assured neither adequate centralization of reserves nor the type of central control required for either a completely sound or liquid banking system. Indeed, the method employed resulted in the pyramiding of reserves in New York, which magnified the disturbances that a banking system ought to minimize. Despite the 10 per cent tax on note issues of state banks, moreover, the desired conversion of state to national banks was not long sustained (owing to the growth of deposit banking and the resulting decrease in the importance to a bank of the note issue privilege), and central control over bank practices therefore continued inadequate. The money supply was affected, during this period, not only by the banking operations of the national and state banks, but also by the action of Congress with respect to the standard. Therefore, before evaluating the operations of the National Banking System it is necessary to discuss the effect on the money supply of this factor.

The Greenbacks

At the close of the Civil War the country found itself suffering from the effects of a highly inflationary method of war finance. Greenbacks had been issued to the extent of over $400 million, and in addition a part of the war had been financed through sales of government securities to the national banks. It was at first quite generally agreed that the greenbacks ought to be retired quickly in order to permit a return to price and income levels appropriate to a return to the pre-war gold standard. In 1866 Congress authorized the Secretary of the Treasury to retire $10 million of the greenbacks within six months, and an amount not to exceed $4 million per month thereafter. But this proved to be the beginning of a long struggle between those who wished to lower the price level and those who would benefit from rising prices. A falling price level would not only affect the debtor class adversely, but a constant discouragement would be exerted on output, since producers would be continually incurring costs at a higher price level than that at which they would have to sell their products. Prices began to fall after the war (as has always been the case) and less than $50 million of the greenbacks had been recalled when Congress had to yield to anti-deflation sentiment. The panic of 1873 caused the usual currency drain, which was alleviated by the reissue of $26,000,000 of greenbacks to make up for the decline in revenue.[2] This tendency on the part of the government to issue greenbacks in time of emergency stiffened opposition to allowing them to remain a part of the money supply, but they were retained in circulation because of the highly deflationary policy pursued in connection with the resumption of the gold standard, and this gave the Greenback Party significant strength in the elections of 1872.

Inflation vs. Deflation

It was the return to a metallic standard that brought to a head the conflict between the inflationists and the deflationists. During the war, the large issue of paper currency had driven gold and silver from circulation. Wholesale prices had more than doubled, and a return to gold or silver at the old ratio would have meant the immediate loss abroad of our monetary metal supply. A sufficient devaluation of the currency in terms

[2] For a discussion of this episode, see W. C. Mitchell, *A History of the Greenbacks*. Chicago: University of Chicago Press, 1903.

of gold and silver would have made our exchange cheaper in relation to foreign currencies, thus offsetting the effect of our higher price level on imports and exports. A combination of devaluation and reduced prices might have been tried. But it was decided to return to the pre-war dollar gold content. Since we would not cheapen our currency in terms of foreign currencies, there was no practical alternative to pushing down the price level by the extremely painful method of diminishing the money supply.[3] The process was made the more difficult by the fact that prices were also falling abroad. Nevertheless, success was finally achieved in the act of January 14, 1875. Resumption of specie payment was scheduled for January 1, 1879 at the prewar gold content of the dollar.[4] But the cost of this success in terms of output, employment, structural maladjustments and political disquiet was very great. The encouragement given by this policy to the Greenback Party has already been mentioned, and the presence in Congress of members sympathetic to an expansion of the currency forced a halt in the reduction of the greenbacks at $347 million (Act of May 31, 1878). No further change has been made to the present time.

The Struggle to Monetize Silver

In the 90's the Populists, who made the most determined efforts to inflate the currency, took up the greenback issue again, but despite the depressed state of agriculture during the early part of the decade their efforts failed.[5] Of more permanent importance to our monetary and fiscal systems was the alliance of the silver interests with the inflationists. Because of undervaluation of silver at the mint, silver coins had not circulated since 1837. Little notice was taken when the silver dollar was dropped from the coinage in 1873, but almost immediately thereafter the market value of silver began to decline. This decline was caused by the release of silver by the newly organized German states when the German Empire adopted the gold standard, new discoveries in America, and the suspension in 1873 of unlimited coinage of silver by the Latin Monetary Union, which had been the major champion of bimetallism. As a result, the market ratio of gold to silver declined from about 1 to 16 in 1873 to

---

[3] The extraordinary difficulties facing British attempts, after World War II, to stimulate exports by cutting costs through increasing efficiency may be cited in this connection.

[4] The Act also provided that United States notes were to be retired up to 80 per cent of new national bank notes, provided the volume of the former did not go below $300 million.

[5] It should be pointed out that the elections did not turn on a single issue. The Populists also opposed the existing distribution of wealth and income. The hot debate over a progressive income tax, which was taken by many of its opponents as the first step toward a complete leveling of income, solidified opposition to the entire program of the inflationists. To the extent that an inadequate money supply was responsible for depression, the inflation parties had a strong case, though they have always received a bad press from the economists.

1 to 17.8 in 1876, and ultimately to 1 to 33. Consequently the silver interests became retroactively alive to the "Crime of 73," which had removed the standard silver dollar from the coinage. Unlimited coinage of silver would amount to a pegged demand for their produce at a time when its market value was rapidly falling.

The attempts of the silver interests to monetize silver occupied much of the monetary history of the last twenty-five years of the century. The fall in the market price of silver depreciated the heavier "trade dollars" (coined for use in foreign trade) to such an extent that they began to appear in circulation. This was the reverse of the process that obtained during the Civil War, when large issues of paper had driven silver and gold out of circulation. The inflationists joined the silver interests in calling for bimetallism at a ratio of 16 to 1. With a lower market ratio for silver, this metal would have flowed to the mint, and, in accordance with Gresham's law, it would have paid to sell gold in the market. But with unlimited coinage of silver, the money supply would have increased. The free coinage issue became so acute as to be a factor in the election of 1876, and in 1878 the Bland-Allison Act was passed, which compromised by requiring the Secretary of the Treasury to buy and coin into dollars silver in the amount of not less than $2 million or more than $4 million a month. Like most compromises this one angered both sides. The Secretary of the Treasury bought as little silver as the law allowed, but, even so, nearly $400 million of new silver certificates were added to the money supply. In the following year the country returned to the gold standard, a feat made more difficult by the inflation of the currency through silver purchase. The unpopularity of metallic silver standard coins caused the public constantly to return them to the mint. Since under a gold standard other forms of currency must be kept at a parity with gold, this resulted in a gold drain that threatened the standard.

The Outcome of the Struggle for Bimetallism

The movement for bimetallism encountered growing opposition during the 1880's. The adoption of gold by important countries during the previous decade made it seem unlikely that the United States almost alone would be able to maintain bimetallism. The "compensatory action" of bimetallism, by means of which, it is argued, market and mint ratios can be kept reasonably close together, requires international monetary cooperation, and this was not forthcoming so long as independent American silver purchases were supporting the market.[6] Despite the growing feeling that bimetallism was becoming impractical, the continued decline in prices and the clamor of the silver interests for a government subsidy worked on Congress until, in 1890, the Sherman Silver Purchase Act was

[6] W. J. Shultz and M. R. Caine, *Financial Development of the United States,* p. 380. New York: Prentice-Hall, Inc., 1937.

passed. This Act directed the Secretary of the Treasury to buy as much of 4.5 million ounces of silver each month as might be offered, to be paid for in legal tender Treasury notes redeemable in either gold or silver. The result was the addition of $156 million of these Treasury Notes of 1890 to the money supply, leading to an export of gold that threatened the maintenance of the gold standard. To these effects was added the combination of an unfavorable trade balance, a decline in Federal revenues as a result of the passage of a tariff act that reduced imports and customs revenues, and a downturn in business. It became increasingly difficult to pay out gold for other forms of currency. Congress repealed the Silver Purchase Act on November 1, 1893. The Treasury had to sell bonds to obtain gold, but the reserve continued to fall and the process had to be repeated, finally with the aid of the investment bankers. An upturn in business confidence ultimately put an end ot the gold drain, but the difficulties experienced during this episode lent weight to the view that the maintenance of convertibility would require more careful control over the currency than hitherto. A sound money sentiment developed in time to be pitted against the final onslaught of the free silverites and the Populists in the campaign of 1896. With the victory of the former, the gold standard act was passed in 1900.

The effects on business of a mismanaged money were particularly apparent in the crisis and depression of 1893. It was an opinion commonly held that the increase in the money supply in the form of the Treasury notes had caused the panic and depression of 1893. (The President was said to hold this view.) The slump in business had been produced by a complex of forces. But one of its effects was to put a strain on a precarious gold standard, and this in turn increased pessimism and retarded recovery. Thus, sentiment in favor of passage of a gold standard act grew as much out of impatience with continually recurring crises of confidence, panics, and depression, as out of fear of the inflationists. With the growth in the relative importance of demand deposits in our money supply, the time was passing, however, when tinkering with the standard or the currency could continue to have the important effects that it exerted during the last quarter of the nineteenth century.

Free coinage of silver would have increased the volume of money; and, in so far as the trend of falling prices was due to the inadequate money supply, relief would have been felt, provided sufficient silver was brought to the mint. This would have been facilitated by the overvaluation of silver at the mint (which was the objective of Bryan's 16 to 1 ratio). No one now doubts that a reversal of the downward trend in prices was desirable, and, indeed, many Republicans saw the merit in attempting to obtain a world agreement in favor of bimetallism. Nothing came of the idea; but happily, in view of the adoption of the gold standard, world output of gold began to rise rapidly, owing to a number of gold discoveries and to the development of more efficient processes for extracting gold.

The National Banking System, 1865-1919

Inelasticity of the National Bank Note

The National Banking System gave the country a sound currency but not one that was elastic. In view of the magnitude of the government debt at the end of the Civil War, it seemed obvious that adequate bond-backing existed for whatever volume of currency might be needed. The volume of currency, however, depended not on the magnitude of the government debt, but on the amount of eligible government securities held by the banks. Unfortunately, these holdings bore no positive relationship to the demand for money. The circulation of national bank notes was at first limited to $300 million, but this provision was removed by the resumption act in 1875.[7] The removal of the ceiling did not alter the profitableness to the banks of issuing bond-backed currency. A bank was permitted under the law to issue notes up to 90 per cent of par or market value, whichever was lower, of its holdings of eligible government securities. There was no reason to suppose that the total of the notes thus issued would coincide with the needs of the country. During prosperous periods, when Federal tax revenues were high, repurchase of bonds drove up their price, making it unprofitable for the banks to increase the currency supply in accordance with the increased volume of transactions. This was because of the provision that notes could be issued only up to 90 per cent of par, which in these circumstances was lower than market value. During the prosperous eighties, when the currency supply should have expanded, the volume of national bank notes declined substantially.[8] The retention of a bond-backed bank note was also contingent upon the existence of a large national debt. Thus a consequence of debt repayment, which was made possible by the recurrent surpluses of the eighties, would be either to reduce the securities available for backing or to drive the bonds to a premium, thus making it unprofitable for the banks to hold them for purposes of note backing.

Not only were the national bank notes unresponsive to cyclical and long term changes in the needs for currency, but they were very unresponsive to changes in seasonal requirements. Additional notes were needed by the public during the Christmas season, and during crop movements. But there was nothing in these changing currency needs of the public that would affect the bond holdings of the banks or of the

---

[7] D. R. Dewey, *Financial History of the United States,* p. 387. New York: Longmans-Green, 1934.

[8] From $359 million in 1882 to $168 million in 1891. Dewey, *op. cit.,* p. 412.

currency issued by them. Even more serious was the fact that there was no mechanism whereby a bond-backed currency would respond to an increase in the demand for hand-to-hand currency during a panic.

The Need for a Central Bank

The note-issue deficiencies of the National Banking System remained serious throughout the entire period, but the growth of deposit banking partly alleviated what would otherwise have been an unendurable deflationary force. The gradual increase in the importance of check currency caused more and more attention to be focused on the significance of the reserve requirements under the National Banking System. These requirements had been set at a high level, because under the National Bank Act little was done to bring about the centralization of reserves that would have permitted low reserve requirements. Banks in central reserve cities were required to maintain reserves of 25 per cent against deposits, and other banks, 15 per cent. But since only 40 per cent of the latter had to be in cash (the remainder, if desired, in the form of deposits with reserve or central reserve city banks), the result was double counting of a part of the reserve of the latter banks. The city banks were profit-making institutions, and were thus impelled to lend out the reserves deposited with them by the country banks. The banking system lacked a non-profit-making "lender of last resort," which would always allow enough of its assets to remain in the form of cash reserves so that it could come to the rescue of the commercial banks when either panics, or simply too high a rate of lending, threatened to drain reserves down to the legal minimum.

The New York banks not only were unable to provide needed reserves to the country banks during times of stress, but they contributed to the instability of the system by themselves lending these reserves to the stock market. Reserves held by the country banks with the New York banks were in the form of demand deposits. A seasonal need for cash in the interior of the country, or a sudden wave of cash hoarding, resulted in sudden calls upon the stock market for repayment. During times of panic (there were four serious panics between 1870 and 1910) the pressure on the stock market was so great as to precipitate a catastrophic fall in stock prices. Sharply falling stock prices have usually ushered in a period of liquidation and a decline in business activity. Because of purely institutional defects, remediable by an overhauling of the reserve system of the country, the economic system had to suffer periodic deflations. Consequently, sentiment grew for an entirely new type of banking system, which would eliminate these defects.[9]

[9] The possibility of amending the National Bank Act was debated as early as 1880. Cf. L. W. Mints, *A History of Banking Theory,* Chapter 11. Chicago: University of Chicago Press, 1945. Once the silver question had been removed from the center of

Other Defects of the National Bank Act

In the absence of a central banking institution, no adequate provision existed for the collection of checks. The rapid growth in the use of demand deposits called attention to this lack, and one of the most important conveniences to be contributed by the Federal Reserve Act in 1913 was an efficient system of check collection. Again, under the National Banking Act no provision was made for the establishment of branches by national banks. As a result of this extreme decentralization there were far more banks than there were competent men to manage them.[10] Restrictions on the activities of the national banks diminished their usefulness and their popularity: an example was the prohibition on loans on real estate (which was later relaxed). Another was the bar to the setting up of savings and trust departments. In an effort to popularize the Federal Reserve System these restrictions were relaxed under the Federal Reserve Act. But as will be seen below, even this Act did not succeed in eliminating the advantage of remaining outside of a centralized banking system.[11]

Treasury Influence on the Money Supply

Under the National Banking System the Federal Government had no fiscal agent. Thus, a great convenience for effecting the day-to-day business of the Treasury was sacrificed. During the entire period 1865-1913 the Federal Government made use of the Independent Treasury as its main depository. The National Bank Act permitted the Treasury to deposit with the national banks, and transfers of deposits to and from these banks gave the Treasury influence over their reserves. The lack of a fiscal agent, coupled with the absence of central bank control over credit policy, led the Treasury to exercise consciously a portion of the control that would otherwise have been left to the banking authorities.[12] The consequence was that the financial activities of the Treasury often ran counter

---

the stage after 1896 the tempo of the debate accelerated. But as Mints points out, not until around 1910 was it understood that the major problem was not the note issue, but the establishment of a central bank, with full recognition of the major importance of the treatment of reserves, their concentration, and the availability of a central bank constantly ready to aid the commercial banks while at the same time regulating their lending policies and capacities.

[10] In 1913 there were 25,993 independent unit banks which, so far as matters of soundness and liquidity are concerned, were operating independently. Ray Westerfield, *Money, Credit and Banking*, p. 929. New York: Ronald Press, 1938.

[11] Minimum capital requirements tended to be higher for the national banks, and state laws were more lenient with respect to reserve requirements. Not until the passage of the Federal Reserve Act was the difficult position of the national banks recognized, with the setting of lower reserve requirements for time than for demand deposits, already a characteristic of state banking laws.

[12] Esther Taus, *Central Banking Functions of the United States Treasury, 1789-1914*. New York: Columbia University Press, 1943.

to the monetary interests of the country. On the other hand, frequent Treasury attempts to fill the role of a central bank raised doubts as to the proper function of the Treasury in the monetary system. Thus, in 1871 and 1872 the Treasury responded to a demand for currency with $6,000,000 of paper currency, a step that excited criticism on the ground that control over the money supply was vested in Congress and not in a single official.[13] Again, different Secretaries had different opinions on the propriety of depositing Treasury funds with the national banks. Treasury control was at its maximum under the Secretaryship of Leslie M. Shaw (1902-1907).[14] By this time the instruments of control at the disposal of the Treasury included: the deposit and withdrawal of funds in the national banks, transfer of cash from and to the Independent Treasury, prepayment of interest and principal of bonds (Secretary Windom tried to ease the effects of gold outflow in 1890 by buying bonds and prepaying quarterly interest dues), open-market bond dealings, currency issue, gold and silver purchase, and changing collateral and reserve requirements behind government deposits.[15] It was logical that doubts would arise concerning the appropriateness of the assumption of central banking techniques and policies by the Treasury and that these doubts, coupled with dissatisfaction with the National Banking System and the example of successful central bank control in England, would cause a rise in sentiment for the establishment of a central bank in the United States. It was not a long step from the informal exercise of many central banking functions by the Treasury to the establishment of the Federal Reserve System in 1913.

The Federal Reserve System

The failure of the banking system to provide an adequate money supply, particularly in the panics of 1884, 1890, and 1893, set in motion the political forces that culminated in the passage of the Federal Reserve Act. The spark that set off the train of events leading to the establishment of a central banking system was the panic of 1907. The Aldrich-Vreeland Act of May 30, 1908, provided for an investigation of the monetary system by a National Monetary Commission, and Senator Aldrich introduced a bill embodying its suggestions.[16] But the Republicans lost control of

---

[13] Dewey, *op. cit.*, pp. 360-1; Taus, *op. cit.*, p. 67.

[14] Taus, *op. cit.*, p. 82. Taus argues that the Independent Treasury operated as a real central bank from 1890 to 1912. Quoting from the *Commercial and Financial Chronicle* she states (p. 88) that since the Treasury was, by the nineties, counted upon as a lender of last resort, the banks ceased building up reserves for the annual fall cash drain.

[15] Taus, *op. cit.*, p. 131.

[16] The Commission published a series of studies, including several which have become classics. Among others may be mentioned Sprague's *History of Crises Under the National Banking System,* and Kinley's *The Independent Treasury.*

Congress, Aldrich's bill was shelved, and a Democratic version was passed as the Federal Reserve Act on December 2, 1913.

In place of the single central bank recommended by the Commission, and invariably adopted by other countries, the Act made its peace with sectionalism and the fear of the money power of New York by providing for the establishment of not less than eight nor more than twelve regional banks. They were to be owned by the private banks in each district, but policies were to be coordinated by the Federal Reserve Board. National banks were required to become members of the system, but state-chartered banks were, of course, outside the jurisdiction of Congress. Thus a dichotomy that had weakened the banking system since 1863 was perpetuated, and to the present time the Board of Governors of the Federal Reserve System is plagued with the problem of attracting state banks to become and remain members of the System. Each of the twelve Federal Reserve banks was to have nine directors, equally divided among Class A (selected from the stockholding banks), Class B (selected from commerce and industry), and Class C (appointed by the Federal Reserve Board). The Federal Reserve Board was empowered to designate one of the Class C Directors as Chairman of the Board of Directors and Federal Reserve Agent. A Federal Advisory Council was also established to maintain contact between member and Federal Reserve banks in each district with the Board in Washington. After the System was established, the Board empowered the boards of directors of the Federal Reserve banks to elect a chief executive officer to be called Governor, whose responsibility was to assist in formulating policy.

Although the National Monetary Commission had concluded that the Treasury possessed too much power over the monetary system, the Federal Reserve Act did not go as far as it might have done in reducing Treasury influence. The Federal Reserve Board was to consist of seven members, of which five were to be appointed by the President from different Federal Reserve districts and two, the Secretary of the Treasury and the Comptroller of the Currency, were to hold office *ex officio*. The latter provision, coupled with the stipulation that the Board's offices be located in the Treasury building, started the Board off under the domination of the Treasury. The necessity of integrating monetary policy with fiscal and other policies of the Federal Government during World War I, moreover, established a tradition of Treasury dominance at the outset. Again, the fact that Board members were to be appointed by the President made them sensitive to political influence, which on a number of occasions has been reflected in policy. Possibly the criticism directed at the Board on the latter ground should have recognized that monetary policy must be based on political reality. The question was, rather, whether the Board should make the political decisions or leave them to a higher authority.

The Federal Reserve Banks as Lenders of Last Resort

The Federal Reserve Act provided the banking system with a lender of last resort. A true central bank must be spared the incentive to make profits. It was largely the circumstance that the New York banks were under a profit incentive to lend the reserves entrusted to them in the call market that had made the National Banking System an inadequate solution. To make certain that the reserves of the system would be available when needed, the Federal Reserve banks were required (after certain payments to surplus, and the payment of a 6 per cent dividend to their stockholders, namely the member banks in their district) to turn over the excess to the government as a franchise tax. Provided the Reserve banks remained in possession of sufficient earning assets to cover expenses and these limited dividends, they would not be averse to holding excess reserves, and consequently, by rediscounting their eligible paper, could assure the banks of relief in time of need.[17] The Federal Reserve banks were required to carry reserves of 35 per cent against deposits, and 40 per cent against the new Federal Reserve notes.[18] The significance of the reserve requirements of the Federal Reserve banks has been the limitation on the volume of money rather than the safety to noteholders or depositors. The latter is adequately safeguarded by making the Federal Reserve note an obligation of the government, and by the centralization of reserves in the system. A Reserve bank whose reserves have fallen to the minimum can rediscount with other Federal Reserve banks, so that from the point of view of centralization of reserves a true central bank had been established.

The Federal Reserve System also performs efficiently the various administrative functions of the typical modern central bank. The concentration of reserves in the Federal Reserve banks has facilitated the collection of checks, although the failure to attract all state banks into the System has made it impossible to enforce universal par collection. The Federal Reserve Board acts as a clearing house for the Federal Reserve banks, and the latter perform the same function for the member banks. Nonmember banks also benefit from the Federal Reserve check clearing system but the Board has forbidden the Reserve banks to accept any check that is drawn on a nonpar bank. Again, the possession of reserves by an essentially nonprofit-making bank has provided the assured market for

---

17 During the early years of the Federal Reserve System there were occasions when insufficiency of earning assets prompted the System to acquire Government securities, thereby increasing member bank reserves independently of credit policy. This defect has not continued to be important despite the preference of the banks to remain free of indebtedness to the Reserve banks.

18 It was vainly hoped that these would drive the national bank note out of circulation.

government securities vainly hoped for under the National Banking System. Not only have the Federal Reserve banks acted as fiscal agent of the government by assisting in the distribution of government securities, but they have also carried large amounts in their own portfolios. The Federal Reserve Act perpetuated the practice of allowing the Treasury to deposit its cash outside the banking system by permitting it to deposit directly with the Federal Reserve banks. Thus the power remained with the Secretary to affect the money suppiy either incidentally, as part of tax-expenditure operations, or directly, through conscious usurpation of part of the powers properly belonging to the central bank. The close integration of Treasury and Federal Reserve policy has prevented their working at cross-purposes, but the former has retained effective control over monetary policy during the crises of war and depression.

Member Bank Reserves and the Currency under the Federal Reserve System

The Federal Reserve Act recognized that under a more centralized banking system the commercial banks would not require reserves as high as the requirements in effect under the National Banking System. Therefore lower rates were set, though the same distinction was made as before between central reserve city, reserve city, and country banks. The rates were originally placed at 18, 15, and 12 per cent respectively, and 5 per cent (after three years) against time deposits. But from June 21, 1917, to August 15, 1936, the rates stood at 13, 10, and 7 per cent against demand deposits, and 3 per cent against time deposits.[19] Although at first the member banks were to carry one-third of their required reserves in their own vaults, they were later permitted, and then required, to deposit them with the Federal Reserve bank.

One of the primary objectives of the Federal Reserve Act was to free the monetary system from the rigidities of a bond-backed currency. The substitution of commercial paper for government bonds as backing for the currency was intended to provide a currency that would respond to the needs of trade. The rise in the volume of commercial paper during periods of prosperity would provide the basis for increased issues of Federal Reserve notes. But the wartime necessity for Federal Reserve rediscounting of large amounts of notes backed by government obligations eliminated the intended close tie between self-liquidating commercial and agricultural loans and the volume of Federal Reserve notes.

[19] Since the latter date, changes in required reserves of member banks have been frequent. This policy has not been without effect on the willingness of state banks to become and remain members of the System, since an increase in required reserves for a state member bank would place it at a disadvantage with a non-member state bank in the same city.

The commercial loan was likewise originally assigned a strategic role in the granting of credit to the member banks by the Reserve banks, and thus in the creation of deposit currency. Bank lending and the creation of deposits were to increase only in response to the needs of trade, and repayment would be made automatically as the goods produced on the basis of the loan were sold.[20] This provision proved too restrictive, however, and the Amendment of September 7, 1916, permitted advances by the Reserve banks against government securities. Despite the preference originally given to notes, drafts, and bills of exchange based on trade, the promissory note has become much the more important basis for Federal Reserve credit in recent years.[21] Thus the attempt by the framers of the original Act to reduce the popularity of the collateral loan has not met with success.

The power to engage in certain types of open market operations, which included dealings in Federal Government securities (also the short term securities of states and localities issued in anticipation of taxes) and foreign exchange and domestic bills of exchange, was at first regarded as useful largely in providing the Reserve banks with earning assets during periods when the member banks were making little use of rediscounts. The privilege of dealing in the open market was also a means whereby the Reserve banks could make their rediscount rates effective beyond their own immediate customers, the member banks. Sales of securities would involve the drawing of a check in favor of the Reserve bank, and the consequent reduction of the reserves of a member bank. If the banks were loaned up, under a fractional reserve system this would involve a multiple contraction of loans and deposits. To the extent that the member banks were thus forced to rediscount with the Federal Reserve banks, the rate published by the latter would affect the rate charged the customers of the banks. Conversely, purchases of securities on the open market by the Reserve banks would increase the reserves of the member banks, thus encouraging lending at cheaper rates. The development of the technique of open market operations took place gradually over a number of years.

---

[20] W. R. Burgess, *The Reserve Banks and the Money Market,* p. 46. New York: Harper and Brothers, 1946. The fallacies of the commercial loan theory were the following: It was an error to suppose that the banks could safely grant credit only in an amount determined by the volume of commercial paper. Furthermore, in an emergency, when the banks must be provided reserves by the Reserve banks, commercial loans are no more liquid than any other form of loan.

[21] Banks holding large amounts of government paper naturally use it as collateral, whereas country banks have made greater use of eligible paper, owing to their relatively small holdings of government securities. Cf. R. G. Thomas, *Our Modern Banking and Monetary System.* New York: Prentice-Hall, Inc., 1950. The Act specifically prohibited the rediscount of loans secured by stocks and bonds. The spirit and provisions of the original Act are discussed by O. M. W. Sprague, "The Federal Reserve Act of 1913," *Quarterly Journal of Economics,* February, 1914.

The Monetary Standard, 1900-1919

The Gold Standard Act of March 14, 1900 made the gold dollar the standard unit of currency. The Act established a Treasury gold reserve of $150 million, which was to provide assurance that all United States money would be maintained at par with gold. The practice indulged in earlier (1893), when the gold reserve had been used for government expenses, was proscribed; in the event that redemptions of Treasury notes brought the reserve below the $150 million minimum, the notes were to be kept out of circulation. If paid out again, as formerly, they could again be presented for further gold withdrawals.[22] The background of economic and financial circumstances, both at home and in the world at large, proved particularly favorable to the adoption of gold. The years 1900 to 1914 saw the closest approach at any time to the relatively automatic operation of the automatic gold standard. In general the world accepted the leadership of the pound sterling in international financial dealings, and capital movements largely reflected the normal flows of trade. Moreover, new gold discoveries and more efficient processes for extracting gold removed fears that there might be a world gold shortage. The gold standard operated relatively uneventfully, therefore, until 1914.

World War I and the Gold Standard

The declaration of war in Europe in the summer of 1914 was the signal for a general *de facto* abandonment of the gold standard abroad. But despite the strong pressure on the standard at home, the United States did not embargo the export of gold until our entry into the war in 1917. On that occasion we experienced the same sharp rise in imports from neutrals that had occurred in 1914 with respect to the original belligerents, and large gold losses resulted. Under a proclamation issued on September 7, 1914, gold exports were permitted only for imports directly or indirectly contributing to the war effort. The immediate reason for the abandonment of gold, in the United States as abroad, was the loss of gold and the possibility of adverse psychological effects on public confidence. If reserve ratios were maintained, it was thought, the fact that we were actually off the gold standard might seem relatively unimportant. But for the task of financing the war the gold standard had to be abandoned (or greatly modified) in order to allow the expansion of the money supply necessary for financing the tremendous increase in production. The restriction of the money supply that has been regarded as a desirable attribute of the gold standard during normal times becomes a clog on the transition to a war economy. It is not feasible to finance the entire cost of a war by taxation or borrowing from savers only. Therefore either paper currency must be issued, or, as under modern conditions, the

22 Shultz and Caine, *op. cit.*, p. 444.

Treasury must sell securities to the commercial banks for new money. The resulting rise in the income stream, and the attendant rise in imports and decrease in exports, require the effective embargo of gold exports.

The prohibition on the export of gold was maintained until the summer of 1919. A large part of the inflationary effects of war finance was experienced after the war came to an end. But the transition back to a full gold standard was facilitated by the relatively extensive inflations in other belligerent countries and by the strong position of the dollar at the end of the war, owing to our favorable economic situation and the urgent demand for dollars to finance the import of goods to the slowly reviving European countries.

The widespread economic and financial upheavals that attended the First World War were such as to make extremely difficult a worldwide return to the gold standard after 1919. The breakdown in orderly international economic relations prevented the assertion of currency leadership by any single country, and the mutually cooperative trade and financial practices prerequisite to successful operation of the standard were lacking. Furthermore, after four years of independent management of their monetary systems, many countries showed a desire to make use of recently learned techniques of monetary management, as well as to go their own ways with respect to domestic economic programs. Despite attempts to bring about a workable degree of monetary cooperation through international conferences, and despite sincere attempts on the part of many countries to return to gold in the decade following the war, success was very limited because of the almost hopeless economic chaos produced by the war and the nationalistic programs adopted to restore economic health in the various nations.

The Monetary and Banking System in World War I

The years 1914 to 1919 were crucial for the development of a centralized banking system in the United States. During this period a number of changes were made in the Federal Reserve Act, and, on the basis of experience with the extraordinary conditions of war finance, important practices were inaugurated early in the life of the Federal Reserve System. The fact that the Federal Reserve banks were already in existence when war broke out in Europe provided the banking system with the elasticity, soundness, and centralized control that was to prove indispensable in a modern war. In turn, the experience gained during the war accelerated the development of a central banking philosophy and central banking techniques.

The Federal Reserve Note

One of the first tests that the Federal Reserve Act had to meet was the question whether it could provide the nation with a truly adequate and elastic note issue. The founders of the System had assumed that if the Federal Reserve note were backed 100 per cent by rediscounted paper (in addition to the 40 per cent gold backing), the amount in circulation would vary automatically with the rate of commercial bank borrowing from the Reserve banks. But a combination of events restricted the volume of rediscounting of open market paper by the commercial banks.[23] The result was an inadequacy of commercial paper available for Federal Reserve note backing. The Federal Reserve banks responded by replacing the maturing collateral behind Federal Reserve notes with gold from their excess reserves. So much gold flowed into the country before we entered the war (over $1 billion in 1915 and 1916) that by 1916 the circulation of notes was nearly triple the volume of discounted paper held by the Reserve banks.[24] In the Act of June 21, 1917, the Federal Reserve banks were given the specific power to issue Federal Reserve notes on the basis of gold as well as of discounted paper.[25] The effect of this change in the backing of the Federal Reserve note was to insure its adequacy to meet the needs of the public for hand-to-hand currency, and to surrender the unnecessary tie to the commercial loan.[26]

The Reserve Banks and the Credit Supply in World War I

The Federal Reserve banks were assigned an essentially passive role by the Act of 1913. They were expected to respond with credit facilities to the member banks when this was called for by the needs of trade. Before this policy criterion could be put to a test the European war interfered, and the operations of the Reserve banks were subjected to forces other than the needs of trade alone. The gold inflow commencing in 1915 made it unnecessary for the banks to forward paper for rediscount, thus reducing the earnings of the Reserve banks and forcing them to buy securities in order to increase their earning assets. The profit motive thus con-

---

[23] Shultz and Caine, *op. cit.*, pp. 488 ff. The Act lowered the required reserves of the national banks, thus releasing reserves and obviating discounting. Banks in some agricultural areas, moreover, possessed insufficient eligible paper for rediscounting.

[24] Alexander Noyes, *The War Period of American Finance, 1908-1925*, p. 133. New York: G. P. Putnam's Sons, 1926.

[25] This amendment was intended to facilitate the centralization of gold reserves in the Reserve banks. Cf. Frederick Bradford, *Money and Banking*, p. 209. New York: Longmans, Green, 1949.

[26] In 1931-32 the backing of the Federal Reserve note again proved inadequate, and owing to an outflow of gold the method used in World War I to support the issue was unavailable. The Glass-Steagall Amendment permitted the deficiency to be made up with government securities, thus reintroducing the principle that had been rejected in the Act of 1913. The Amendment of June 2, 1945, made this provision permanent. Since the notes are obligations of both the issuing Reserve bank and the United States Government, and since present collateral provisions rightly make no attempt either to limit their issue or to make their issue depend on any automatic device such as the commercial loan, it is apparent that the collateral requirements have no significance.

flicted with credit policy, since purchases of securities put more reserves into the member banks, and, by exerting a downward pressure on the interest rate, added fuel to the inflation that was already beginning to make itself felt.

The needs of the Treasury after the country entered the war forced the Reserve banks to abandon all thoughts of playing a passive role in the credit system. It was desired to negotiate war borrowing at low rates of interest, and to make certain of an adequate market for the securities issued under the successive Liberty loans. Federal Reserve purchases of securities consequently had the combined effect of facilitating the marketing of government obligations, pushing down the interest rate, and providing the commercial banks with reserves out of which they could directly purchase government securities or lend to those who were encouraged to do so in the Liberty Bond campaigns. After 1916, the expansion of business activity began to put pressure on the reserves of the member banks, and the volume of rediscounting at the Federal Reserve banks increased. This released the gold that had been substituted for eligible paper behind the Federal Reserve notes, a circumstance which, coupled with the continued inflow of gold from abroad, formed the basis for a tremendous expansion of bank loans. Rediscount rates were held down so that loans at low rates of interest might be made to those who had been urged to borrow from the banks in order to purchase government securities. Since the member banks could thus borrow reserves cheaply on the basis of their customers' notes backed by government bonds, the low rate could be passed on to the market.

The contribution necessarily exacted by the Treasury from the Federal Reserve banks in expediting the financing of the war proved to have particularly inflationary effects. This was because the mechanism adopted for marketing government securities paid insufficient attention to the need for effecting a corresponding reduction in individual purchasing power. It was in this respect that the financing of World War I was carried out in an even more inflationary fashion than that of World War II. Although in both wars a large part of government expenditures was financed through direct or indirect sales of securities to the banks ("monetizing the debt"), the fact that in the earlier war the public was urged to "borrow and buy" de-emphasized the importance of reducing consumption. It was discovered that many of those who borrowed from the commercial banks on the security of government obligations failed to extinguish their debt before the next Liberty loan drive was initiated. But this weakness in the financing of the First World War should not obscure the indispensable contribution made by the Federal Reserve system. The attitude of the Treasury toward the System during its early years was that its functions could be pretty well handled by the Treasury. This view was changed when the great task had to be undertaken of paying for over half the cost of the war through government borrowing.

In order to assist the Federal Reserve banks in their function of providing the reserves needed for the forthcoming expansion of loans and deposits, Congress undertook to effect a greater concentration of the monetary gold stock than had been provided for under the original Act. Although over a billion dollars worth of gold had entered the country up to the time we entered the war, the Reserve banks possessed a gold reserve of little more than half a billion dollars.[27] Two amendments were made to the Act. The first (June 22, 1917) required that the entire amount of member bank's legally required reserves be kept at the Federal Reserve banks, and thus added a quarter of a billion of new reserves to the latter's vaults. The second, passed the same day, was designed to release the excess gold tied up against Federal Reserve notes. This it accomplished by allowing a Federal Reserve bank to count as part of its own lawful reserves the gold that it was holding as collateral in place of commercial paper. The combined effect of these two amendments was to raise at a single stroke the active gold reserve of the Reserve banks from approximately $600 million to nearly $1,300 million. This raised the actual reserve ratio of the system from 40 to 75 per cent, and provided the basis for a considerable expansion of member bank reserves. The exigencies of the war thus hastened the centralization of reserves contemplated in the original act.[28]

Conclusion

At the end of the First World War the United States had achieved a predominant position among the world leaders in political and economic affairs. Henceforth, its economic and monetary policies would exert significant, and, at times, even definitive effects on the world economy. Thus monetary and banking institutions were needed that could assist the nation in withstanding external shocks, such as sudden withdrawals of capital, panics, and sharp declines in the level of international trade. But more than this, our monetary system would have to make a maximum contribution to stability of prices, employment, and income at home, in order that the United States might play its part in preserving world-wide economic stability. The events of the inter-war period made it clear that the great strides in banking and monetary control from 1865 to 1919 were not sufficient to bring about this desirable objective. Even within the limits of what is possible through monetary policy alone, and thus excluding the instruments of fiscal policy and direct controls, a further period of experiment was necessary with respect to both credit control and

[27] Noyes, *op. cit.*, pp. 206 ff.
[28] *Ibid.*, p. 210.

the monetary standard. This experience was to be gained in all its facets during the prosperous twenties, the depression thirties, and the war and post-war years of the forties.

Selected References

Dewey, Davis R., *Financial History of the United States*. New York: Longmans, Green, 1934.

Hepburn, A. B., *History of Coinage and Currency in the United States*. New York: The Macmillan Company, 1903.

Kinley, D., *The Independent Treasury of the United States*. Washington, D. C.: National Monetary Commission, 1910.

Laughlin, J. L., *The History of Bimetallism in the United States*. New York: D. Appleton and Co., 1896.

Noyes, A. D., *Forty Years of American Finance, 1865-1907*. New York: G. P. Putnam's Sons, 1909.

Shultz, W. J., and M. R. Caine, *Financial Development of the United States*. New York: Prentice-Hall, Inc., 1937.

Sprague, O. M. W., *History of Crises under the National Banking System*. Washington, D. C.: National Monetary Commission, 1910.

Taus, E. R., *Central Banking Functions of the United States Treasury*. New York: Columbia University Press, 1943.

Westerfield, R. B., *Money, Credit and Banking*. New York: The Ronald Press, 1938.

Willis, H. P., *The Federal Reserve System*. New York: The Ronald Press, 1923.

29 · THE INVESTMENT MARKET AFTER THE CIVIL WAR

THE MARKET FOR long-term or capital funds had developed very slowly during the first half of the nineteenth century, and had reached only a low degree of specialization when the Civil War broke out. The war gave an impetus to this process, greatly accelerating the rate of development, first by reason of the need of the Government for funds with which to carry on the war, and second by reason of the expansion of industry that accompanied and followed the war. Usually, in the case of individuals, and occasionally in the case of corporations, the process of transferring funds from the saver to the borrower requires the services of an intermediary. This intermediary, in a highly industrialized society like the United States, is the investment market, with its array of specialized investment banks for underwriting new issues and brokerage houses for distributing them. Like most other financial institutions, this market developed slowly by a process of gradual specialization of function, and in its early stages can hardly be distinguished from other forms of financial operations. By the time of the Civil War, a number of merchant bankers had given up mercantile activity and concentrated upon finance, and a number of new firms had been organized specifically for that purpose. The large-scale financial operations necessitated by the war merely accelerated a process of evolution that had been going on in previous years at a more moderate rate.

The sources from which funds were provided for the long-term needs of business enterprise and governments in the period after the Civil War were various and widely scattered. The small individual enterprise or partnership continued to be the form under which production and trade were most often carried on, and they secured their capital funds from their own savings or those of friends and neighbors, without any financial intermediary. This was true even for many small corporations that operated within a limited area and had little need for, or access to, the organized security markets of the great financial centers. The large corporations that were growing in size and importance throughout this period formed the demand side of the capital market. Railroad builders and factory owners took the place of the canal and road builders of the earlier period. Even these large corporations, however, frequently resorted to the investment market for only part of their capital funds, and added to their equipment out of their own profits.

It is difficult to estimate the total amount of all these forms of capital investment; even the volume of new securities issued by the larger corporations was not adequately reported in the earlier years. Such indirect evidence as is available indicates that the wealth of the country was increasing steadily and that the national product, whether considered as goods and services or as money income, was also increasing.[1] Only large amounts of new borrowing and a steady flow of new capital into production could account for such a rapid increase in national income.

An important addition to the supply of working funds for business enterprise of whatever size was the open account or open-book credit that permitted delays in payment for merchandise, raw materials, and the like sometimes running into months. This type of open-book credit seems to have superseded the commercial credit based upon the trade acceptance or the promissory note that had been the customary forms of commercial credit before the Civil War.[2] The length of such credits varied with business conditions. Many firms offered a discount for bills paid within a minimum time, usually thirty days. The type of commercial credit, offered to all business firms wherever located, offset to a certain extent the higher cost of bank loans that prevailed in the southern and western states as compared with the northeastern.

Another form of credit that developed in the period after the Civil War was the so-called one-name promissory note, which enabled the larger and better known firms to borrow at very favorable rates. These notes, drawn in round sums, were signed and endorsed by the borrowing firm, then sold to the commercial paper brokers who in turn sold them to banks and other institutional investors. Both the open-book account and the single-name note were American innovations that had no counterpart in European money markets, where the trade acceptance was the preferred form of commercial credit instrument.

These various forms of short term commercial credit helped to keep business enterprise provided with funds during a period when the demand for long term capital funds seemed always to be pushing ahead of the supply. The United States was still a relatively new country with great natural resources awaiting development, and the native population, in spite of its high per capita savings, was not able to supply all the capital that could be used productively. Individual investors gradually became accustomed to investing directly in stocks and bonds rather than

---

[1] For a summary of early estimates of national wealth and income see *Historical Statistics of the United States, 1789-1945*. Washington: United States Bureau of the Census, 1949.

[2] See Chapter 14.

in real estate mortgages. Besides the individual investors whose savings were placed in securities, there were many institutional investors—banks, savings banks, life insurance companies, and others—whose function it was to gather together the funds of many small savers and invest them. All of these together were able in the first decades after the Civil War to meet only a part of the demand for long-term funds.

In the years before 1900, foreign investors provided a large part of such funds, although the proportion was declining steadily throughout the period. Before the Civil War, canals and railroads had often been built with foreign capital, and by 1860 the Secretary of the Treasury estimated that $400,000,000 worth of American securities was held abroad. The outbreak of the war was a rude shock to these investors. Many of them sold their American securities, and nearly all of them refused to buy more. It was for this reason that the financing of the war became a domestic problem that gave Jay Cooke his unique opportunity.

As soon as it became apparent from the course of the war that the Northern Government would be the victor, however, European investors recovered their confidence and began to buy Federal and other issues in large amounts. By 1869 a Congressional committee estimated that Europeans were holding $1,000,000,000 in United States Government bonds, $243,000,000 in railroad stocks and bonds, and $223,000,000 in municipal, mining, canal, and other securities, making a total of $1,466,000,000. Some of the Government bonds had been bought from American investors who had taken them during the war, and this purchase freed American funds for investment in railroad and industrial issues. But many railroad stocks and bonds were also bought directly by foreigners, some of the bonds being issued in denominations of the English pound rather than the dollar and made payable in London, in order to facilitate English investment. Several of the roads built at this time were practically owned in England, and others were controlled by foreign stockholders who owned a majority of the stock. It was not until the period of railroad mergers around 1900 that railroad securities were bought back by American investors in large amounts.[3]

Industrial securities were never as popular with European investors as the rails and the governments. One reason for this was that a large proportion of industrial issues was in the form of common stock of uncertain earning power, rather than in bonds with a fixed rate of interest. This fact made industrials seem rather speculative to far-off investors whose chief concern was the income to be derived from placements. Moreover, the bankers refused to accept industrial securities on the same terms as rails, as security for loans. Federal issues were the safest of all and were preferred by conservative investors.

---

[3] Margaret G. Myers, "Origins and Development to 1913," *The New York Money Market*. New York: Columbia University Press, 1931.

The total volume of foreign holdings of United States issues continued to increase until the outbreak of the First World War in 1914, but at a decreasing rate. The total was estimated at $3,000,000,000 in 1890, had risen to only $3,300,000,000 by 1899, and by 1914 stood at $4,500,000,000. These figures must be judged in the light of the rapidly expanding population of these years and the rapidly expanding industry. The United States was becoming self-sufficient with respect to its own capital needs, and indeed was soon to reach the point of providing capital funds for other nations.

The Post-War Boom, 1865-1873

The technique that had been so successful in selling Government bonds during the Civil War [4] was applied in the following period to corporate securities, especially to railroad issues. Up to this time the number of industrial issues available for investors had been extremely limited. But when the business enterprise became so large that no single person or group of partners could provide enough capital to set it in operation, it became necessary to sell stocks and bonds to a wide public, which often lacked any direct contact with or knowledge of the enterprise. The new type of investment banker filled this gap.

The years between 1865 and 1873 were boom years in the victorious states of the North. Moreover, the West was growing rapidly in population and in wealth. The great need of the times was better transportation facilities, and 30,000 miles of new track were laid in those years. The funds with which these lines were built were raised largely by such houses as Jay Cooke and Company, using the methods developed during the war bond campaigns to persuade investors to take the bonds issued by the Northern Pacific, the Chesapeake & Ohio, the New York, Ontario & Western, and other roads. In some cases the clients were even urged to sell their Government bonds and invest in railroad bonds, which offered a higher return.

Many of these railroad issues were bought not by investors, but by speculators who had little interest in the good management of the railroad and were concerned only with immediate profits to be made out of Stock Exchange trading. As a result the Exchange became the arena for historic conflicts between the "bulls," who tried to make profits by forcing stock prices up, and the "bears," who made profits by selling short what they did not yet own, forcing prices down, and then buying at the lower price what they had already sold at the higher. The New York Stock Exchange in this period had little control over the trading carried on under its roof. It was organized as a partnership and was conducted almost like a private club, with each new member buying a "seat," which represented his right to carry on trading in the Exchange.

[4] See Chapter 14, above.

The roll of listed securities was read out at stated times each day and prices noted, but most of the trading was actually carried on between roll calls. Corporations made no regular reports to stockholders or the Exchange. There were not even listing requirements until a series of scandals in connection with Erie Railroad issues finally gave the Exchange the courage to rule that after January 30, 1869, no company might have the privilege of listing unless it kept a registry of all its outstanding issues with an approved agency, bank, or trust company.

In the absence of any effective regulation, and in the existing state of business morals, traders in securities were able to manipulate prices through corners, pools, and other devices now illegal. The most prominent individuals in this group of speculators were Daniel Drew, Jim Fisk, and Jay Gould. Daniel Drew[5] entered the New York scene by bringing droves of cattle into the city from upstate, feeding them salt on the way, and not allowing them to quench their thirst until just before this "watered stock" was weighed for purchase by the city butcher. This sort of unscrupulous ingenuity soon enabled him to gain a fortune and become a stock trader. He sometimes worked with, and sometimes against, Gould and Fisk, was prominent in the Erie scandals, founded a theological seminary, and in his old age complained that even his own grandchildren would not trust him to invest their money for them. Jim Fisk was involved, not only in the manipulations of Erie stock, but also in the attempted gold corner of "Black Friday" in 1869, which involved Government officials as well as stock market operators.

Jay Gould was the only one of this group who evidenced any constructive ability as a businessman. He too came from a small town in upper New York State; but he spent his spare time in studying accounting and surveying, and got his start in the railroad business by reorganizing a small railroad, making it pay, and then selling it at a profit. Unlike his associates, he understood the operation of railroads as well as the manipulation of their securities. In 1859 he set up as a stockbroker in New York City, and with Drew and Fisk soon gained control of Erie. He then proceeded to make himself wealthy at the expense of the railroad and of his associates. When the outraged stockholders finally forced him out of the Erie management, he turned his attention to the new railroads of the West. By depressing stock prices and then buying, he had gained control of 10,000 miles of road at the peak of his power. His methods remained unchanged in this new field, and the new series of scandals associated with his roads led eventually to Government investigation and reform legislation.

One other figure of this period who figured prominently in the speculative markets was Cornelius Vanderbilt, but he differed from the others

[5] An interesting account of his life is given in Bouck White, *The Book of Daniel Drew.* New York: George H. Doran Company, 1910.

in being an entrepreneur as well as a speculator. His early life was spent in sailing, first a ferryboat between Staten Island and New York, then a coastwise trader. He was one of the first to recognize the possibilities of the steamboat, and after serving a long apprenticeship under another owner, finally launched out for himself. In the face of violent opposition he established a line of Hudson River steamboats that won him the title of Commodore; then he went upward in the nautical scale and operated boats to Panama during the California gold rush and eventually ocean liners to Europe. It was not until 1857 that he turned his attention to railroads. As director and then president of the New York & Harlem road, he came into conflict with Drew and was obliged to engage in stock market activities in order to prevent Drew from buying up all the stock in the market and wresting control from Vanderbilt. By 1873 he had gained control of the Hudson River line, the New York Central, and the Lake Shore & Michigan, and welded them into the new and integrated New York Central, which was one of the first of the big railroad systems. In this later period Vanderbilt was as arrogant and unscrupulous as his opponents, resorting even to bribery of judges when it served his purpose.

Much of this unprincipled manipulation of stock prices would have been impossible if the issue of new securities, the refunding operations, and the conversion of bonds into stock had been subject to legal regulation or had been disapproved by the public opinion of the time. But the mores of the period set the making of money above all other considerations, and the successful man was judged to be the man who made a fortune. The investment bankers themselves rather encouraged than discouraged such manipulation, and even a highly respected house like that of Jay Cooke was not above speculating on its own account.

The orgy of speculation came to an end with the panic of 1873 and the collapse of Jay Cooke's banking house and the Northern Pacific bonds which he had sponsored. Several other banking houses which had grown up since the Civil War also collapsed in this panic. Financiers interested in railroads after this period were obliged to pay somewhat more attention to the development and operation of the lines, since the disillusioned public was less ready to accept securities without regard to the underlying values. Some of the roads never recovered from the financial mismanagement of that early period, which loaded them with debt. Erie paid no dividends on its common stock until three-quarters of a century later, in 1942.

An important factor in the type of stock market speculation described above was the existence in New York City of large amounts of funds available for short term loans to brokers. They consisted for the most part of balances of interior banks placed on deposit with banks in New York City during periods of the year when they were not needed at home.

Such deposits had long served as a kind of unofficial reserve fund for the interior bankers, and were even recognized as such by the National Banking Act. Such deposits were by their very nature of temporary duration and fluctuated widely in amount during the year, tending to be drawn down especially during the autumn when farmers needed currency with which to pay off their hired hands and merchants needed funds with which to buy stocks of goods for the winter season.

The New York City banks quite rightly refrained from placing such short term deposits in long term loans. The alternative that they adopted however was the call loan on security collateral. Since the demand for such loans came almost entirely from stock brokers, the result was that at certain seasons of the year large amounts were available for speculation in securities, and at other seasons the funds would be quickly withdrawn. Some interior banks made such loans directly in the call market, sacrificing the interest that would have been paid on their deposits but gaining the interest on the call loans, which was generally higher than the rates they could get from the New York banks.

The amount of such loans increased most rapidly in the period from 1879 to 1904, accounting in some periods for half of all the loans reported by New York national banks. Six of the largest banks in New York were the most active in the call loan market, competing most actively for the bankers' deposits, and placing about two-thirds of all the loans. Other less important lenders were the life and fire insurance companies, the trust companies, and even the savings banks of New York until they were forbidden by the legislation of 1875 to invest their funds in this way. Large corporations also sometimes used call loans as a way of investing their surplus funds, either directly or through the agency of a New York City bank. These loans made by others than banks greatly increased the instability of the call loan market, since they were withdrawn at the first hint of tightness or danger, leaving the New York banks to carry the full responsibility for meeting the needs of brokers and preventing a collapse of security prices. During these years there was no central bank to which the banks could turn, and their own resources were often inadequate to support the burden thus thrust upon them. The Secretary of the Treasury, in spite of hindering legislation, frequently came to the aid of the market, either by selling gold as in the famous "Black Friday" episode of 1869, or by making deposit of public funds in national banks, or by other measures devised for the occasion.[6] In nearly every autumn there was a minor crisis in the money market, and in some years, notably in 1873, 1884, 1890, and 1907, this crisis developed into a "panic" with serious repercussions in the security markets. At such times the rates charged for call loans rose

[6] Further details of Treasury intervention in the money market may be found in Margaret G. Myers, "Origins and Development to 1913," *The New York Money Market,* Chap. XVII.

to extremely high levels. In 1884, for example, the call loan rate was no longer publicly quoted after it passed three per cent per *day*.

The close connection that existed between the commercial banks and the security markets as the result of the call loan market gave a color to the investment institutions of the United States that distinguished them from those of other countries. Daily settlements that are used on the New York Stock Exchange could hardly have been possible without the call loan, and they are seldom used in other large security markets of the world, where monthly or fortnightly settlements are the rule. It is difficult to decide whether or not the reputation of the American securities market as a center for speculative activity of a peculiarly unbridled sort must be ascribed to the call loan. Certainly the call loan did not contribute to stability in the market.

The Beginning of Large-Scale Industries

The period after 1873 was marked by a great increase in the number of corporations among industrial enterprises. With the widening of the market due to the increasing population of the country and the improved transportation facilities, and with the steady progress of invention stimulated by the possibility of large-scale production, big business became possible and profitable. The selling of corporate securities for industry was taken over by investment bankers, who had already become accustomed to handling Government and railroad issues. It is true that some small enterprises were still able to raise funds locally, but the larger units were obliged to turn to the great financial centers for aid.

The effect of this development may be seen in the listings on the New York Stock Exchange. Before the Civil War, the list had consisted largely of Government issues and the securities of banks, insurance companies, canals, and a few railroads. By 1867 there were 15 industrial stocks and 63 rails; in 1913 the industrials had risen to 191, while the rails had risen only to 147—a thirteenfold increase for industrials as compared with little more than doubling for rails. Other stock exchanges throughout the country showed the same trend.

Although the industrial issues gained a place beside the rails in the listings of the Exchanges, they were at first viewed with considerable suspicion by bankers and investors. The bankers refused to allow industrial securities to be used as collateral for loans on the same terms as rails until well into the twentieth century, while conservative investors continued to prefer rail issues, leaving the industrials to the speculators. Toward the end of the century mining shares began to be bought and sold on the market, but they also were viewed with suspicion, much of it justified. Some of these issues were refused listing by the New York Stock Exchange, either because they were too speculative, or because they were not widely enough distributed to provide a broad market; consequently, these shares were often traded on the "Curb" market, which was held in the street outside the Exchange until it acquired a roof over its head in 1921.

Types of Securities in the Investment Market

Although stocks are far more important than bonds in trading on the exchanges, where old issues are bought and sold, the reverse is true in the investment market, where new issues are distributed. Stock is normally issued only once and usually remains outstanding during the life of the corporation. Bonds, on the other hand, are a form of debt that must be periodically repaid or refunded, and each renewal or increase of the debt means a new issue in the market. In addition to this reason for the preponderance of bonds, there has been a preference for bonds among certain groups of investors. Many banks and insurance companies are not permitted by law to buy common stocks, but are able to purchase bonds of good quality, so that bonds often find a market that would be closed to the stocks of the same corporation. Corporations themselves, when faced with a choice between increasing their capital stock or borrowing, often choose the latter course, either because the majority stockholders do not wish to share control with outsiders, or because they do not wish to share the expected high earnings. The tax laws of the United States and many states have furthered this tendency by permitting corporations to count interest on bonds as an expense to be deducted from net income in computing taxes, while dividends on stock are regarded as corporation income and therefore subject to taxation.

Types of Investment Banks

The investment banking houses that functioned in the period after 1873 may be considered in two groups. In the first place, there was a rather small number of strictly domestic firms, located not only in New York City but also in such rising centers of the West as Chicago and St. Louis. N. W. Harris & Company of Chicago, for example, the forerunner of Harris, Forbes & Company, handled municipal securities and mortgages as well as the usual rails and industrials. Other companies in this domestic group issued their own debentures secured by mortgages. There had not previously been a systematic market for mortgages in the United States, and the public response to this type of security was at first favorable. A considerable volume of such securities was placed in the market, chiefly in the West, during the 1880's. Some of the companies took out licenses for selling in New York as well, but this attempt to invade the strongholds of Wall Street was not very successful. In the panic of 1893 some of the mortgage companies failed, and the volume of trading in such securities declined, never to revive in that form. The companies that carried on more varied activities were more successful in weathering the panic.

A second group of houses that came into prominence after 1873 had important international connections. The American security market had always been dependent upon Europe for help in floating large issues; in the period before the Civil War, Baring of London, Hottinguer of Paris, and Hope of Amsterdam had been in close touch with the bankers of the United States, and many American bonds had been sold through their offices. In these early years the relation had often taken the form of a representative of the foreign house stationed in New York City. After 1873, however, the Americans began to establish branches in foreign cities, thus shifting the center of gravity and preparing for the day when the United States would cease to borrow abroad and begin to be a lending nation.

Outstanding among American investment bankers was the house of Morgan. The family had been engaged in the brokerage business in New York City since 1853, when Junius Spencer Morgan became a partner of Peabody & Company, but it was not until 1871 that an association with the Drexels gave the firm important foreign connections in London and Paris in addition to those in New York and Philadelphia. With this added strength, the firm was able to force the Rothschilds and Jay Cooke to share with them the $300,000,000 Government loan of 1873; and when Cooke & Company failed, later in that year, the Morgan firm was left in undisputed leadership of the investment field.

By this time young Pierpont Morgan was active in the firm. He had been educated abroad, specializing in mathematics in Germany. His particular talent for finance first became apparent when William Vanderbilt, the son of the Commodore, found himself unable to keep control of the railroad empire built up by his father and appealed to Morgan for aid. Morgan was able to make a sale of 250,000 shares of New York Central in England without breaking the market, and so saved Vanderbilt; but in return Morgan received $3,000,000 and the right to put his nominee on the Board of Directors of the railroad. He then proceeded to build up the system by buying up the West Shore Railroad, which operated on the other side of the Hudson, thus giving the New York Central a virtual monopoly of rail traffic along the river.

This device of insisting upon a share in managerial control before granting credit was used many times by investment bankers. Another financial device by which bankers were able to gain control of industries for which they had floated security issues was the voting trust, by which a special corporation was set up for the purpose of holding the securities of a number of related companies and securing unified management and policy. The reorganization of the Richmond & West Point Terminal Railway & Warehouse Company was accomplished by this measure in 1894. The frequent railroad bankruptcies of the 1890's provided a strong firm like Morgan's with many opportunities for lucrative reorganization, by means of voting trusts, interlocking directorates, and the like.

The technique that had been worked out for railroads was later applied to industrial companies and resulted in the formation of a number of important mergers. The most important of the operations carried out by the aid of the Morgan firm was the formation of the United States Steel Corporation out of a group of smaller enterprises. The tangible assets of the combined companies were valued at $682,000,000, but the new merger was capitalized at $1,400,000,000. The Morgan firm received not only the fee of $12,500,000 for underwriting the issue, but also a share of $50,000,000 in the profits of the syndicate that supported the issue when it was first put on the market. Other combinations sponsored by Morgan were the General Electric Company, which gradually extended its operations into many foreign countries as well as throughout the United States, the International Harvester Company, which controlled many types of farm machinery, and the International Mercantile Marine Company, which was a conspicuous failure in its effort to dominate the transatlantic shipping business.

Morgan's was not the only investment banking house that was active in the combination movement. Many other bankers co-operated with Morgan or took the lead on their own account in floating securities of this sort, and in the peak years, 1899-1901 inclusive, 200 industrial combinations were formed, with a total capitalization of $10,000,000,000. This activity in the flotation of new issues was inevitably accompanied by an increase in trading on the New York Stock Exchange, which rose from a total of 57,000,000 shares in 1896 to 266,000,000 in 1901, while bond dealings in the same period rose from a total of $394,000,000 par value to $999,000,000 par value.

During the combination era there developed that close integration of the whole financial system that on the one hand led to many abuses and complaints of banking monopoly and on the other hand greatly facilitated the formation of large-scale enterprises. Investment bankers extended their interests into the fields of commercial banking, insurance, and industry itself. Partners in the investment banks became directors of industrial corporations that floated their new issues through the banks; others became vice-presidents of commercial banks and trust companies that bought new issues from the investment banks; others became officers of insurance companies that were heavy buyers of securities. These interlocking directorates, reinforced by such devices as holding companies and bank trustees for corporate issues, created what was popularly known as the "Money Trust." [7]

[7] Many examples of these are given in Louis D. Brandeis, *Other People's Money and How the Bankers Use It*. New York: Frederick A. Stokes Company, 1914.

Criticism of this financial hierarchy became more severe after the panic of 1907 and brought about an investigation in 1908 by a committee appointed by Governor Hughes of New York State. The report of this committee did little but point out the difficulty of effective regulation. Several years later the subject was taken up by a committee of the United States House of Representatives under the chairmanship of Mr. Pujo, who carried on a much more searching inquiry in response to the order to lay before the public "full and complete information on the banking and currency conditions of the United States for the purpose of determining what regulation is needed." The report of this committee was published in 1912 and gave impetus to the public demand for drastic regulation of banking. The election of Wilson to the presidency and the ensuing passage of the Federal Reserve Act were the results of this agitation, although in fact the situation with respect to investment banking was little changed by the new legislation. The Federal Reserve System was designed to control expansion in the commercial banking field and almost ignored the close connection between commercial and investment banking. The failure to establish some sort of control over the capital market at this time left the way open for the difficulties of the 1920's, which followed the financing of the First World War.

The Financing of the First World War

The outbreak of the First World War in 1914 marked the beginning of another period of rapid change in the investment market of the United States. The country was shifted violently and with inadequate preparation from a borrowing to a lending position among nations, and became in the course of a very few years the world's greatest creditor nation. The war was hardly under way before the Allied nations began to borrow and spend in the United States. By the end of 1916 the total of loans to the Allied governments amounted to nearly $2,000,000,000, and the resources of private credit were about exhausted. If no further credit had been extended to them, their purchases in the United States would have been greatly reduced and a serious depression would have resulted; how much this had to do with the entry of the United States into the war on the side of the Allies in 1917 is still a hotly debated question. At most, however, it was only one of a number of factors that affected the decision.

The declaration of war by the United States put at the disposal of the Allied governments the public credit of the country as well as the private credit of a host of banks and investors. The loans that were floated by the Treasury in the next 30 months carried the American public debt from $1,300,000,000 in April, 1917, to a peak of nearly $27,000,000,000 in August, 1919—in per capita figures, from about $13 to about $250. About one-third of this total arose from loans by the United States Government to the Allied governments.

In order to clear the way for the war issues by reducing to a minimum the issue of industrial securities, the War Finance Corporation Act provided for a Capital Issues Committee to be appointed by the President. This committee had no punitive powers under the Act, but depended upon the co-operation of the financial community for its effectiveness. It disapproved about one-fourth of the issues presented for its scrutiny. Perhaps the most important aspect of the committee's work was that it set a precedent for Federal regulation of security issues.

The task of distributing such an unprecedented volume of securities among the investors of the United States taxed to the utmost the facilities of the investment market and led to a revival of the methods used by Jay Cooke in the Civil War. Newspaper and billboard campaigns, rallies on street corners, and public meetings were used to supplement the usual procedures for selling bonds to the public. Banks not only bought bonds and short-term Treasury notes and certificates of indebtedness for their own portfolios, but they also loaned on easy terms to individuals who wished to buy. Nearly 12,000,000 persons subscribed to the Victory Loan of 1918. Many who bought these bonds had never before been owners of securities, and the habit of direct investing rather than of making deposits in a savings bank undoubtedly facilitated the wide public participation in the boom of the late 1920's.

Conclusion

In the years from the Civil War to the conclusion of World War I, the increasing wealth of the United States made possible a shift in its position from that of an international borrower to an international lender. This was accompanied by an increasing specialization of function among financial institutions, among which the investment banker played an important and at times a dominant role. It must not be forgotten however that all of these institutions—commercial banks, Stock Exchange, investment banker, and the rest—developed within the existing legal framework and in answer to the changes in the economic situation; they were the result, not the cause, of the growth of large corporations, the increased industrialization of production, the large-scale market, and the increasing wealth.

Selected References

GENERAL WORKS

Adams, Charles F., Jr., and Henry Adams, *Chapters of Erie, and Other Essays.* Boston: J. R. Osgood and Company, 1871.

Brandeis, Louis D., *Other People's Money and How the Bankers Use It.* New York: Frederick A. Stokes Company, 1914.

Meeker, J. Edward, *The Work of the Stock Exchange,* rev. ed. New York: Ronald Press, 1930.

Myers, Margaret G., "Origins and Development to 1913," *The New York Money Market*, Vol. I. New York: Columbia University Press, 1931.

Ripley, William Z., *Main Street and Wall Street*. Boston: Little, Brown and Company, 1927.

SPECIAL TOPICS

Corey, Lewis, *The House of Morgan*. New York: G. H. Watt, 1930.

Larson, Henrietta, *Jay Cooke, Private Banker*. Cambridge, Mass.: Harvard University Press, 1936.

White, Bouck, *The Book of Daniel Drew*. New York: George H. Doran Company, 1910.

30 · THE CHANGING STATUS OF LABOR

The Nature of Unionism

UNIONISM MAY BE VIEWED as a formalized social-group response to certain conditions faced in common by workers below the rank of supervisor. These conditions were the changes in the status of low-income persons brought about by the "revolutions" of the seventeenth and eighteenth centuries. The commercial and ideological revolutions changed the organization of society from one in which the main emphasis was on collective security of status under a relatively simple technology to one that gave free reign to intellectual, religious, and economic adventure. Rich new resources were discovered and technological inventions multiplied enormously. But the material benefits of the expanding private-enterprise system were very unevenly distributed. Workers came to believe that they would have to fight for larger, more equitable shares. And they found themselves, as individuals, in very poor bargaining positions. Most of them had lost control of the tools of production. They had got out of touch with the people who bought the products they helped to make. The relationships with their employers had become more and more impersonal. They had little or no control over where and when they worked. They found, in short, that under the new system they had given up security for a freedom that meant very little in terms of benefit.

Workers as individuals wish to have a number of things: (1) They wish to obtain increasing amounts of the good things they know their society is equipped to produce. (2) They wish to have leisure in which to enjoy the goods. (3) They wish to be able to obtain jobs and job income when they look for them. That is, they wish their rising incomes to be secure and certain as long as they live. (4) They wish not to work under unpleasant and unsafe conditions. (5) They desire secure tenure in particular jobs. They wish not to be subject to arbitrary discharge or other discipline by their supervisors. (6) In terms of the jobs they have and the way they live, they wish to have an accepted, respected social status.

These are normal human urges. And if the environment is such that little outlet is provided for them through individual effort, the normal reaction frequently is combination to improve the outlets, that is, to get the things the workers want. Organization is regarded as the only effective means.

Unions are "formal" associations of workingmen. Whether confined to particular crafts, as in the building trades, or covering all occupations, as in most of the manufacturing industries, they have constitutions and by-laws, elected executives and judges, and prescribed legislative procedures. It would be a mistake to believe, however, that in shops or offices where there are no formal unions there is no worker organization. Numerous studies have demonstrated that there are very few unorganized workers. Somehow common problems evoke common responses. Non-union workers are found to have informal leaders and spokesmen, standards of output and behavior, and means of enforcing the standards. But the informal sort of organization has been found to be much less effective than the formal. Its discipline and control is much weaker.

It is not to be expected that workers' efforts to establish formal unions would be regarded with favor by the "bosses"—those who owned the tools of production or those who represented the owners. There was, in fact, considerable resistance and opposition from the owners and managers of industry, who, wishing to be free of all restrictions in their efforts to produce and sell their products at a profit, considered the labor movement to be a challenge to their prerogatives and their position in society. Employers used a variety of measures, some peaceable and some not so peaceable, to fend off unionization. In so doing they frequently had as willing allies many members of the executive and judicial branches of government at various levels.

This opposition, together with the absence of respected social status, was a main reason why the drive for organization became known as a *movement*. Most movements—the abolitionist movement, the women's suffrage movement, and the prohibition movement, for example—are in behalf of "causes," usually (at least at first) unpopular, underdog causes. The objectives are "noble" ones and often "inspire" their followers with "religious" fervor. The movements have their martyrs, saints, scriptures, and hymns. One has only to read early union documents or listen to recordings of old union songs to understand how and why unionism was a movement.

A union is also, internally, a *political* organization. This is another thing for the reader to hold in mind as he undertakes the study of this book's chapters on labor. Many union attitudes and tactics, perhaps irrational from the economic standpoint, make sense when unionism's political nature is understood. Union leaders are always in some degree responsible to the rank-and-file members. There are often rival cliques maneuvering for the seats of power. In dealing with "outsiders," such as employers, union officials must almost always consider the effects of their actions, speeches, and bargains on their positions vis-a-vis the members or rival factions.

Thus, a union is usually considerably more than an economic unit, more than a mere cooperative-marketing association interested only in selling its members' labor energies and skills at the highest possible price in the labor markets. It is a way of life, a way of thinking and behaving and living together, a possible way of practicing the principles of democracy day by day.

From all the above it is evident that unionism's first task was to win acceptance or recognition from employers and from society in general. Its efforts in this direction constituted the social-group response mentioned at the beginning of this section. In a sense this response was a passive one of adaptation to a hostile environment for the purpose of survival. But once this adaptation was made, unionism could become a more active agent: It could do more than adapt itself to an environment that had been a given datum; it could try to mold and control the environment to its own uses. This stage has been reached in recent years with the advent of "big unionism" in America. It has led many people to ask, "What does organized labor want? Where is it headed? What are its ultimate political and economic goals?"

To these questions two kinds of answers are possible: (1) A labor movement may wish ultimately to change the organization of society; it may wish to have the government own and control all productive activity, and it may wish to *be* the government. (2) Organized labor may accept the existing private-enterprise system and try, within this social framework, to improve its economic and social status. Thus far, the American labor movement has chosen the second way.

Earlier in this section were listed a number of things desired by workers as individuals. Union leaders, to keep themselves in power, have to work to satisfy these desires of the membership. Much can be done by dealing with employers directly. Sometimes the problems seem so big that the unions choose to work through government.

In dealing with employers, unions have two main economic objectives: (1) A solid, united front must be presented to employers. Employers must not be able to get workers to compete among themselves. There must be standard rates of pay, lengths of work periods, physical working conditions, and rules of employee-employer conduct and relations. Unions try to hold members in line with union policies by means of various welfare measures, such as medical benefits, recreation, workers' education, housing, and the like. These devices, along with the economic benefits such as wage increases, help unions control the supply of labor to employers. Restrictions on work periods, membership (where possible), and output (including the so-called featherbedding measures) have the same effect. (2) Employers must, so far as possible, be deprived of access to alternative productive agents, such as non-union workers and labor-displacing machines. Herein lies the economic rationale of the closed shop and the union shop.

If a problem—the mass unemployment that comes with serious business depressions, for example—seems so huge that individual employers or associations of employers, no matter how friendly to organized labor, are powerless to cope with it, unions may decide that the government must act through, for instance, its budget control over total spending in the economy. In this case the labor movement must first decide whether to form a political party of its own and try itself to become the government or to work through existing political parties by nominating and electing friendly legislators and administrators and by lobbying to influence the decisions of these officials.

These, then, are among the important matters to be held in mind as our story of American unionism unfolds below. In relating this story (in the present chapter and in Chapter 44) three main periods will be considered: (1) The early formative period (roughly from 1800 to 1890), (2) the predominance of the American Federation of Labor (1890 to 1935), and (3) the rise of the Congress of Industrial Organizations (1935 to date). The general outline of discussion to be used for each period will be: (1) A sketch of the economic, technological, and political conditions existing during the period, and (2) the efforts, in terms of organizational activities and policies and tactics, of unions to adapt themselves to or to control the environmental conditions that were mentioned above.

The Early Formative Period

The technological revolution got under way somewhat later in America than in England. In the earliest days of the republic, goods were produced, mainly by simple techniques in small establishments, and product and labor markets were mainly local in scope. For example, products made in Boston usually did not compete in a common market with similar items made in, say, Philadelphia. Nor was the skilled labor of those days sufficiently mobile to make Philadelphia shoemakers worry about the conditions under which the shoemakers of Boston worked. Consequently, the first labor organizations were independent, unconnected local unions of skilled workingmen such as shoemakers, printers, tailors, and carpenters.

In the local markets, however, competition among firms was sharp enough for the workmen to believe that they were bearing the brunt in the form of wage reductions and lengthened work periods. This was a main reason for the formation of the local craft unions.

When these unions attempted to obtain recognition from their employers in order to get them to hire only union members and in order to bargain over demands for higher wage rates and shorter work periods, they ran afoul of a very important employers' ally of those days—the courts of government. The American common or court law was based almost entirely on that of England. And this meant that the legal obstacle to organization and to strikes (workers' refusals to work) and boycotts (refusals to buy employers' products)—economic weapons used by the unions to enforce their demands—was the doctrine of criminal and civil conspiracy.

This doctrine in practical application to particular cases is a rather complicated thing, but in essence it amounts to this: In a criminal action brought by a governmental unit or in a civil action or suit for damages brought by an aggrieved private party (such as an employer), a conspiracy is said to be a combination of two or more persons who set out to achieve an unlawful objective by any means (lawful or unlawful) or who seek a lawful objective by unlawful means. In the earliest days the mere combination of workers stamped them as conspirators. But this rule was soon discarded by the courts, and consequently, under the doctrine stated above, it was necessary that the judge determine the objectives of a strike or boycott and the means used to make it effective. In general, it was held that (1) if the main purpose of the union was to benefit itself, with only incidental injury to (interference with the rights of) other parties (such as the employer and non-union workers), the objective was lawful, and (2) measures involving violence or fraud certainly (and measures involving more subtle devices of coercion and intimidation possibly or probably) constituted unlawful means.

These principles for interpreting the conspiracy doctrine were found to be so general that in actual cases the biases and prejudices of particular judges about unionism had great latitude. In Massachusetts and New Jersey, for example, the unions had to be very careful lest they be judicially condemned as conspirators, while in New York the courts were much more lenient.

In spite of employers' and judges' disfavor, unionism made headway on a small scale. By 1830 the economic scene had begun to shift. With technological improvements and under government encouragement (such as tariff protection) manufacturing developed. Transportation media (not yet including railroads) were improved, and there was some widening of markets. About this time also, there was a monetary inflation in the banking system. All these things, plus other conditions (such as the lack of universal suffrage and the lack of equal opportunity to settle new land) led to efforts by local unions to combine. These combinations took one or both of two forms: (1) Local federations of local unions in various trades, such as the New England Association of Mechanics; and (2) regional associations of local unions in the same trade or craft, such as those among the shoemakers, printers, and weavers. In short, the abovementioned conditions presented problems common to all unionists, and combination was a natural structural response. Functionally, the response was to add political activity to the economic measures focused on employers; a number of Workingmen's Labor Parties were organized to exert political pressure at various levels of government.

The panic of 1837 saw the temporary eclipse of unionism. Almost none of the unions managed to survive the rigors of depleted treasuries and memberships brought on by the prolonged depression. Thereupon the country began to be caught up by the backwash of the revolutionary movements that had begun to surge in Europe. The forties were the decade of the American humanitarian movements. Thoughts about day-to-day, bread-and-butter unionism yielded to political allegiance to bizarre reforms and utopias offered by so-called intellectuals and do-gooders who had never been a part of the labor movement. Cooperative societies were formed in the fields of production and consumption; working-class congresses were organized for political action; and a few collectivist (truly communist) communities were formed (as at New Harmony, Indiana, and Brook Farm, Massachusetts).

Almost all these efforts fell short of their objectives, and the cycle of utopianism ended in the failure and dissolution of the organizations. A number of events conspired to swing most American workmen back to the more practical and conservative kind of unionism during the fifties. The discovery and use of California's gold helped to establish an industrial revival. With further improvement in transportation, including the railroads, the commodity and labor markets widened considerably. Technological developments in manufacturing began to displace labor and change the skills and abilities needed by workmen in particular occupations. And the first of the great waves of immigration began to beat upon the nation's shores.

During this decade (1850) the first national craft union of permanence was formed. It was created by the printers—the union long known as the I.T.U., the International Typographical Union of North America. By 1857 five others—the Stonecutters, Hat Finishers, Molders, Machinists, and Blacksmiths—had organized nationally. Each of these craft unions tried not only to control its members as they moved from market to market but also to achieve the general union objective of uniform conditions of employment in all labor markets, that is, to take wage rates out of employers' competition in the various product markets.

There was another depression beginning in 1857. Only the I.T.U. and the Molders survived it. But recovery from the depression came as the country was plunged into civil conflict. And, as in all wars, labor became scarce in relation to the greatly increased demand for it. Men were needed for the armies. Some workers took advantage of the Homestead Act of 1862 and moved west. Once more, unions were formed, and some twenty were national in scope. Of these, the Cigar Makers, the Bricklayers, the

Plasterers, the Locomotive Engineers, and the Railway Conductors survive to this day.

During the war and postwar periods these national unions for the most part adopted narrowly selfish "business" or conservative policies and tactics. The further development of transportation and broadening of markets saw to that. But there were common problems for these unions, for the large group of workers still in local unions, and for the mass of the unorganized. These problems included a severe inflation of the price level before 1873, competition from immigrants who had been brought over during the war, and a serious depression beginning in 1873. Consequently we still find in this period—in the land of hope and free ideas and freedom to keep hope alive by trying out the ideas—flirtation with "panaceas" and with broad organizational forms. Small business, farmers, and other nonunion workers were usually invited to join. Three of the objectives were: (1) legislative enactments providing universally for a reduction in daily hours from ten or eleven to eight (this was the pet hobby of Ira Steward, a famous member of the Machinists), and (2) a cheap money policy (easily obtainable loans at low interest rates) by the Federal Government so that workers could freely establish producer and consumer cooperatives or could set up in business for themselves. It is noteworthy that for the most part, these aims, while visionary from the standpoint of workability, were not radical in the sense that they betokened a desire to do away with the private-enterprise system. Rather were they an expression of the desire to give reality to the American dream of an equal chance for all common men to acquire economic independence and security. (Cooperatives also had an especially practical appeal to local union members who had lost strikes and had later been unable to obtain work because of employers' blacklists against them).

The objectives met no permanent acceptance or realization. A few states passed eight-hour laws, but they lacked enforcement teeth and were not effective. The Federal Congress stopped issuing "greenback" money; there was to be no cheap currency of this sort. And the cooperative movement exhibited no signs of durable virility.

Three organizations of this period (the post-Civil War years up to about 1880) may be singled out for brief mention: (1) The National Labor Union was a conglomerate national association that convened for the first time in Baltimore in 1866 and met annually thereafter until 1872. The delegates at these conventions represented a variety of constituent organizations—city assemblies (loose local federations of local craft unions), national craft unions, farmers' organizations, women's rights groups, and various other "reform" associations. Peak membership amounted to about half a million. (2) The Knights of St. Crispin was a national craft union of shoemakers that began in 1867 as a response to the threat of labor-saving machinery and the competition of "green hands." The word

"Knights" is suggestive of the idealism of the times. The union experienced a phenomenal growth, claiming the allegiance of some 50,000 by 1870. Miscalculations in political maneuvering and untrustworthy leadership led to just as rapid a decline, and the organization went under in the 1873 depression. (3) Just before the depression began and soon after the decline of the National Labor Union, the national craft unions, which numbered about thirty by this time and which had never been much of a factor in the N.L.U., organized a loose federation called the Industrial Brotherhood. As might be expected, the more skilled workmen of these unions took a more hard-headed view of attainable objectives. They decided to abandon political activity and to confine themselves to the more immediate issues, such as exclusion of immigrants and regulation of apprenticeships.

This organization and all but eight of its constituent national craft unions collapsed during the long, severe depression beginning in 1873. Once more a serious business recession took a heavy toll in the labor movement. During the five years of low-level employment, financial resources of unions were sapped, and the membership of the organizations that managed to survive dwindled greatly. There were successive rounds of wage-rate reductions against which workers protested with numerous bitter strikes. Most of these conflicts were lost, employers (sometimes with the aid of government, as when Federal troops were used to break the violent railroad strike of 1877) having consistently the greater staying power. And when the unions lost their strikes, they usually lost "recognition" from the employers. Blacklisting of active unionists was common.

The Predominance of the Knights of Labor

Under these conditions—plus other important circumstances, which included further invasion of skills by technological progress in manufacturing and further widening of markets through technological advancement in transportation and through settlement of lands to the west—American workmen doubtless felt the need for strong unionism as never before. But it was not until the end of the depression in 1879 that most of them were able to find fulfillment of the need. When the demand for labor had picked up sufficiently, they found an organization ready and anxious to receive them—a curious association unique in American labor annals that, begun in 1869 by a Philadelphia garment cutter named Uriah Stevens, had managed, by dint of great secrecy (including the use of ritual, signs, passwords, "grips," etcetera), to survive on a small scale the rigors of the depression. This was the Noble Order of the Knights of Labor.

Before reviewing the organizational make-up and the aims and tactics of the Knights, let us pause to consider the beliefs of American workmen at the end of the eighth decade of the century. The country was still young; there were still frontiers to be settled, rich new resources to be exploited, new claims to be staked. Workmen were far from being unanimous in feeling that they were rooted in the worker class with no chance of escape. All that many asked was a fair chance to become self-employed, to go into business for themselves. Those who entertained little hope of rising out of the wage-earning class were not of one mind about how to improve their positions. And the workers in the East might well have views different from those held by workers who lived farther west.

There were, in fact, at this time, as there had been in previous decades, a number of alternative, competing notions about how labor organizations should be organized and about what they should do. Most of the skilled craftsmen believed that they were in sufficiently strategic market positions to be able to help themselves, provided that the courts and other government agencies did not raise serious obstacles to organization and provided that the government would pass laws restricting the competition of hard-to-organize workers, such as immigrants, women, and children. These skilled craftsmen for the most part wished to be organized in national craft unions and wished these unions to be bound together in a federation for the purpose of influencing government on the abovementioned common problems. A second group of workers—the less skilled and the less strategically situated of the skilled group—were susceptible to the broad, sometimes visionary measures advocated by various non-labor, middle-class reform groups—measures that, as we have seen, included monetary and banking legislation, anti-trust proposals (the combination or trust movement had begun among firms), producers' cooperatives, and free-land laws. These workers believed mainly in an all-inclusive form of organization. A third group, relatively small and composed mainly of recent immigrants in the East, had socialistic aims (labor government ownership of basic productive facilities) and leaned also to the broadly inclusive organizational type. In addition to the above, there was a small number of anarchists, who believed in no government at all, complete freedom of worker enterprise, and in violent dispossession of employers; and there was to develop a little later an organization favoring syndicalism (operation of industries by workers' corporations, with government nonexistent or negligible).

During the remainder of the nineteenth century the first two of these groups were by far the largest and most important. But the other three made up somewhat for their lack of numerical, economic, and political weight by a disproportionate amount of noise, agitation, and, sometimes, violence. It should also be noted that, as we have already had cause to see, many of the groups' members were not irrevocably committed to their structural and functional ideals for the labor movement. That is, they changed their minds and passed from group to group (at least from group one to group two and back again) fairly frequently. Such shifts often depended on which phase of the business cycle the workers were living in; we have seen that the broader reform goals frequently became more popular during periods of severe business deflation (or inflation), whereas high-level, stable economic activity often evoked the conservative, business type of unionism. Nevertheless, during the formative periods under consideration here, with social and economic conditions still very much in flux, there was by no means a precise and exclusive coordination between business-cycle phases and the structural and functional manifestations of the American labor movement. This last statement is borne out by the period when the Knights of Labor was the country's outstanding labor organization. Most of the years of its ascendancy (1879-1890) were prosperous ones. Yet, as we shall see, this union was far from typifying the strictly "business" sort of function.

The Knights began to move after 1881, when, under a new leader ("grand master workman" T. V. Powderly), they abandoned their rituals and other elements of secrecy. The year of peak membership was 1886, when they numbered about 700,000. By 1890, the organization had dwindled to about 100,000. Its popularity in 1886 may be ascribed mainly to two circumstances: (1) The public got a highly exaggerated idea of the Knights' strength from the press, especially after their success during 1885 in conducting strikes against the railroads controlled by Jay Gould, one of the most powerful business moguls of the period, who was temporarily in a weak financial and competitive position. (2) The rapidly growing and spreading sentiment among workers for a universal eight-hour day reached a climax in 1886. Although the Knights' leadership had given no official support to this drive and was in fact, because of the union's financial flabbiness and organizational looseness, cool to it, the mass of workers rallied to the Knights' local units as the only groups that could lead them to victory. In May of that year more than 300,000 workers were out on strike for the eight-hour day. Most of these conflicts were lost. And when the official attitude became known, many workers angrily withdrew their membership and support. (But, as will be shown, there were more basic reasons for the subsequent demise of the union.)

The Knights were in part blamed by the general public for another happening of early May, 1886—the Haymarket affair. This was a violent two-day outbreak, involving severe rioting, bombing, and gunfire between mobs and the police, centering in Haymarket square of Chicago. More than two hundred on both sides were killed or wounded.

The organizational make-up of the Knights was, as already indicated, loose and conglomerate. As a whole, they were "one big union," including almost any person who wished to join, regardless of craft, degree of skill, creed, sex, or color. Even "fair" employers were allowed to join; one of the Knights' cardinal principles was the brotherhood of man, and they did not hold that being an employer automatically put a person beyond the pale of polite labor society. Many people in the professions were also admitted. In fact the only exclusions were stockbrokers, bankers, lawyers, gamblers, and those producing or selling intoxicants. The local units of the national organization were called *local assemblies*. These were of two kinds—*mixed* and *trade*. The former was heterogeneous in membership, admitting anyone except those in the excluded groups. The trade assemblies were composed of members from only a single craft. (Occasionally even a national craft union was constituted as a local assembly.) Five or more locals made up a *district assembly*. The latter were then united in the General Assembly, the supreme law-making body of the Knights' organization. This Assembly and its officers exercised, at least in theory, a complete and centralized control over the district and local assemblies. It had final jurisdiction on the granting and revocation of charters, calling and terminating strikes, and other matters.

The general objective of the Knights was not to replace the private-enterprise system with socialism. Rather did they aim to replace the wage and banking systems with a society of cooperatives. Their methods for the most part involved political action and education instead of collective bargaining and strike action against employers.

After the great upheaval of 1886 the popularity of the Knights began to decline swiftly. In 1886 many of the skilled craft unions of the country, dissatisfied with the broad reform goals, the ineffective tactics, and the confused structure of the Knights, banded together in a new association, the American Federation of Labor, which was committed to the observance of craft-union autonomy and exclusive jurisdiction and to the immediate objective of improving workers' conditions of employment through the tactics of business unionism. After a bitter struggle with the Knights over membership, centering mainly in the New York cigar-making industry, the Knights were thoroughly beaten and proceeded to disintegrate. By 1900, to all intents and purposes they were no more.

The reasons for the demise of this unique organization are of large importance to the student of the development of the American labor movement. First, its membership was too polyglot and its organizational structure too mixed. It was impossible to weld a cohesive, smooth-functioning machine out of these elements. The Knights' leaders wrongly believed that the interests of all classes and groups of workmen were harmonious under the American conditions of those years. Second, the local and district assemblies and the member craft unions became rebellious because they were not given enough freedom of action; there was too great a concentration of authority in the General Assembly and its officers, at a time when a good deal of autonomy was needed. Third, the aims and methods of the Knights were ill suited to the day-to-day needs of the membership. The reform goals were too broad and idealistic. The program of political action was ill-conceived and ill-executed. The cooperative ventures were mismanaged and they failed.

The Predominance of the American Federation of Labor

The A. F. of L. was to demonstrate that its organizational structure and its tactics (briefly mentioned above and explained at greater length below) had much greater survival value, that is, they were a much better adaptation to environment than those of the Knights. Before considering the manner of its survival and reviewing its rise to predominance, we must look at the environment itself.

By the middle eighties the pace of the technological revolution had been stepped up. Most workers became acutely aware of the machine's threat to their particular jobs and to their physical welfare. New materials and products were being developed, the former blurring the lines of demarcation among particular crafts (the use of steel instead of wood in building, for example) and the latter causing shifts in employment from declining to expanding industries. The country had been spanned east-west and north-south with a network of railway lines. The markets of many products for a rapidly expanding population (this expansion coming partly from an accelerated immigration) had now become truly national. Large, powerful, integrated corporations and combinations of corporations (trusts) were being formed—in petroleum, steel, and railroading (for example—whose monopolistic and discriminatory practices were to lead Congress to pass the Sherman (Anti-Trust) Act of 1890. Employers in some localities and industries were beginning to organize associations for the purpose of presenting a united front in dealing with organized labor or of preventing the unionization of their employees.

All these problems were common to almost all wage-earners. This was one reason for the temporary success of the Knights. But they affected the various industries and crafts in different degree and in different ways. And the effects on the skilled workmen were different from those on the unskilled.

In the decades after the Civil War an increasing number of national craft unions were formed in response to the above-mentioned conditions. Railway train operation was becoming highly organized. So were the building trades and the printing industry. In the metal industries the Blacksmiths, the Boilermakers, and the Iron, Steel, and Tin Workers were added to the Molders. There was substantial organization also in glass, pottery, and miscellaneous manufactures.

Now, as already suggested, these craft unionists, almost without exception, had never been more than lukewarm about the Knights of Labor. The Knights' leaders issued charters to assemblies rather indiscriminately, and the jurisdictions or coverages in the charters were seldom clearly defined; there was much overlapping. This was exceedingly irksome to skilled workmen who had invested considerable time, energy, and money in learning their trades. Many of the craftsmen thought of themselves in a sense as small businessmen. They had not a little of contempt for the masses of unskilled laborers so eagerly sheltering under the wings of the parent body. And, as small businessmen, the craftsmen wished to deal in a business way with the employer-buyers of their labor, rather than go off on wild-goose chases after utopian reforms. True, many of the skilled workmen—like Gompers and Strasser of the Cigar Makers, who were to become leaders in founding and promoting the growth of the A. F. of L. —inherited from European backgrounds a belief in socialism. But they were not believers in revolutionary violence; they wished to work with the private-enterprise system while it existed (and in time they worked themselves out of their original beliefs). Furthermore, each national craft union wished to run its own internal affairs and to develop its own tactics for dealing with employers, free of interference or dictation from a central union authority. It wished, in other words, to enjoy what is known as autonomy, and it desired to federate with other, similar unions only on common problems (such as legal restrictions on union activities) that were broader than those involved in bargaining with employers or employers' associations.

An abortive attempt to organize a federation composed of national and local craft unionists holding the views outlined above was made in 1881 by the Federation of Organized Trades and Labor Unions. For various reasons that need not concern us here, this move failed. But five years later Samuel Gompers and Adolph Strasser launched a successful revolt against the Knights and took the lead in establishing the American Federation of Labor. Gompers was elected first president by his fellow craft unionists and, until his death in 1924, he held this office every year except during 1894-1895.

The path of the new federation was thorny at first. Not all the leaders of member unions wanted war with the Knights; some wanted unity. Gompers' view prevailed, however. Then came the fight; and for a while it was bitter. But the A. F. of L. emerged victorious. There was another split on policy within the Federation; the socialists were strong at first and demanded a political program that included government ownership and operation of the means of production. In 1896 many of the A. F. of L.'s members were attracted by the Bryan free-silver-coinage campaign and wished to hitch the organization to the Democratic bandwagon. It was not until after 1896 that the business, non-political unionists prevailed. The organization of the two great political parties (Republican and Democratic) had crystallized two decades earlier, and Gompers recognized that it would be most unwise to attach labor to either party or to form its own party. Rather, he believed, labor should try to elect friendly legislators and executives from each party. Still another obstacle was the severe depression in business activity that began in 1893. But more than ever before, the trade union movement gave evidence of its staying power; it successfully weathered the economic storm. The opposition of powerful corporations such as the Carnegie Steel Company and the Pullman Company also confronted some of the constituent unions. Carnegie beat the Iron, Steel, and Tin Workers badly in 1892, and the strike of 1894 against the Pullman Company was also lost.

The latter defeat is especially noteworthy because it involved a new form of assistance to employers by government—the court-in-equity injunction restraining unions from exerting economic pressure through strikes or through boycotts. The injunctive weapon came to be utilized with increasing frequency and effectiveness by employers in later decades. Its effectiveness lay in the ease and promptness with which it could be obtained from friendly judges and in the severe penalties attached to disobedience of the court orders. Failure to obey an injunction meant "contempt of court"; that is, union violaters (such as Eugene Debs, a leader in the strike of 1894) could be sentenced to fine and/or imprisonment by the judge who issued the injunction, thus depriving the union of its leadership and breaking up the collective action. It is clear that the injunction, although based on an application of essentially the same common law principles (the conspiracy doctrine) as those governing ordinary criminal and civil suits, was calculated to give much swifter and fuller relief to anti-union employers than would criminal and civil suits.

Not all the events of the Federation's first fifteen years were unfavorable. By 1900 an increasing number of employers and employers' groups had begun to deal and sign collective-bargaining agreements with the constituent unions. The first agreement of real substance was concluded in 1891 between the Molders and the firms in the stove foundry industry. This was truly a business deal of far-reaching significance. During the period of the agreement, whether during prosperous or depressed years, it gave unprecedented security to the union in respect to all the conditions of employment covered by the agreement. Here, then, were tangible benefits that solidified the resolve of craft unionists to avoid chasing the rainbows of broad, vague reform. They could now concentrate on tactics for improving the conditions of employment (wage rates, hours, and so forth) for organizing the non-union plants in their crafts and industries, and for making uniform among all plants (in order to minimize inter-worker competition) these terms of employment. These immediate business things became the chief goals of the A. F. of L. unions.

Up until about 1904 the Federation's success was, on the whole, notable. By that year the membership of its constituent unions totaled about 1.6 millions, whereas 15 years earlier it had numbered less than a quarter of a million. But it was not until 1915 that the 2.0 million point was attained. In other words, the rate of growth after 1904 dropped off sharply. This retardation was in part due to the business recession of 1907. But mostly the cause lay in other conditions. The member unions seem pretty much to have reached the end of the list of employers willing to deal with them. The violent, prolonged strike of 1902 by the Mine Workers in the anthracite coal mines, which required the intervention of President Roosevelt and his "big stick," served to alienate unionism from the esteem of a large portion of the middle-class public. Many employers became fearful of the strength of the labor movement. Besides, they wished to be free of union restrictions in order to play freely with the newly discovered technological toy known as scientific management, which promised large reductions in production costs and much higher profits. So a variety of union-resisting measures, such as vigilante groups, citizens' committees, and strike-breaking organizations, were used with considerable success. And, as was usual in those days, most Federal and state courts interpreted the common and statutory law to the disadvantage of the unions. Great was the alarm of the A. F. of L. when, in 1908, the United States Supreme Court, in the Danbury Hatters case (*Loewe* v. *Lawlor*), judged the Hatters' union to be liable under the provisions of the Sherman Act to triple damages of almost $300,000 for conducting an effective secondary boycott in some 20 states against the hats produced by the Loewe company. Consternation mounted when in 1911 the Court approved an injunction against the A. F. of L. for helping the Molders to prosecute an effective secondary boycott against the Buck Stove and Range Company of St. Louis. Samuel Gompers was sentenced to jail for contempt of court when he disregarded the injunction.

The A. F. of L. decided to marshal its non-partisan political program against such court actions. By 1914 it thought it had achieved success when the Congress included, in the Clayton Act amendments to the Sherman Act, provisions legalizing peaceably conducted strikes and secondary boycotts. Gompers hailed the Clayton Act as organized labor's Magna Charta. But, as we shall see in a later chapter, the courts interpreted these provisions in such a way that labor was no better off than before.

In 1914 World War I began in the midst of a business slump in America. But, as various commodities became scarce under war conditions, business revived. When the United States entered the conflict in 1917 business boomed. The labor market became "tight." This circumstance is always favorable to union organizing activity, and the A. F. of L. unions rose to the opportunity. By the end of the war and the subsequent inflation they were above the four million mark.

We may summarize this period of union history as follows: (1) In spite of growing opposition by employers and courts, the strength and influence of the American labor movement, as typified by the A. F. of L., rose considerably during the period from 1886 to 1918. The A. F. of L.'s structural and functional features for that period appear to have represented the most appropriate response thus far discovered to the changing American environment. (2) Structurally, the Federation was composed mainly of national craft unions, organized on the principles of exclusive jurisdiction and union autonomy. In addition to the national unions (mainly craft) there were other structural units: (a) the *federal local,* that is, a local union, usually recently organized, for which there was as yet no national union to join; (b) the *city central body,* a local federation of all local units of national unions, plus federal locals, existing in a given community; (c) the *state federation* of all the local units in a given state; (d) the *local department council,* a federation of local units of national craft unions in a particular industry (the local printing trades and building trades councils, for example); and (e) the *national department,* a federation at the national level, within the A. F. of L. itself, of all the national unions organized in a given industry or having a common national interest (there are now four of these—the building trades, metal trades, railway, and union label departments). The A. F. of L. was (and is) governed legislatively by an annual convention and administratively and judicially by an Executive Council. The big craft unions were (and are) the predominant influence within the Federation. (3) Functionally, during this period the A. F. of L. developed its program of opportunistic business unionism, (a) concentrating on the control of job opportunities and uniform terms of employment through trade agreements and economic pressures; (b) avoiding reliance on government except for (i) removal of court restrictions and (ii) removal of competition from groups hard to organize, such as women, children, and immigrants; and (c) avoiding alliance with any political party as such.

Our story of unionism during this period would not approach completeness without mention of certain non-A. F. of L. groups. An average of about 25 per cent of the total union numerical strength was in non-affiliated national and local unions (mainly national) from 1886 to 1918. These were chiefly in railroad train operation—the "big four" Brotherhoods—and in government service. One union—a "labor" or all-inclusive union called the Industrial Workers of the World (the I.W.W. or "Wobblies")—was of unique interest in the history of American labor. Formed in 1905 from such various dissident, left-wing elements as the Western Federation of Miners, the Socialist Trade and Labor Alliance, and other "splinters" dissatisfied with A. F. of L. craft exclusiveness and conservatism and sharing a hatred of the private-enterprise system, this loose organization was the cause of much turmoil in the mining communities of the West and the textile centers of the East with its program of sabotage and general or sympathetic strikes. It persisted through World War I but finally yielded to the "anti-red" campaigns of 1918-20.

Selected References

Adamic, Louis, *Dynamite* (rev. ed.). New York: Viking Press, 1934.

Bakke, E. W., and Clark Kerr, *Unions, Management, and the Public*. New York: Harcourt, Brace and Co., 1948.

Beard, Mary R., *A Short History of the American Labor Movement*. New York: G. H. Doran Co., 1924.

Brooks, R. R. R., *When Labor Organizes*. New Haven, Conn.: Yale University Press, 1937.

Commons, J. R., *et al., History of Labor in the United States* (4 vols.). New York: Macmillan Co., 1918-1935.

Dankert, C. E., *Contemporary Unionism in the U. S.* New York: Prentice-Hall, Inc., 1948.

Doody, F. S., ed., *Readings in Labor Economics*. Cambridge, Mass.: Addison-Wesley Press, Inc., 1950.

Gregory, C. O., *Labor and the Law*. New York: W. W. Norton & Co., 1949.

Hunter, Robert, *Violence and the Labor Movement*. New York: Macmillan Co., 1919.

Lester, R. A., and Shister, Joseph, eds., *Insights into Labor Issues*. New York: Macmillan Co., 1948.

Miller, G. W., *American Labor and the Government*. New York: Prentice-Hall, Inc., 1948.

Perlman, Selig, *A History of Trade Unionism in the United States*. New York: Macmillan Co., 1922.

———, *A Theory of the Labor Movement*. New York: Macmillan Co., 1926.

Seidman, Harold, *Labor Czars*. New York: Liveright Publishing Co., 1938.

Seidman, J. I., *Union Rights and Union Duties*. New York: Harcourt, Brace and Co., 1943.

Slichter, S. H., *Union Policies and Industrial Management*. Washington, D. C.: Brookings Institution, 1941.

———, *The Challenge of Industrial Relations*. Ithaca, N. Y.: Cornell University Press, 1947.

Taylor, G. W., *Government Regulation of Labor Relations*. New York: Prentice-Hall, 1948.

Twentieth Century Fund, *Collective Bargaining*. New York: 1941.

———, *Trends in Collective Bargaining*. New York: 1946.

31 · BUSINESS ORGANIZATION AND MANAGEMENT

BUSINESS MANAGEMENT may be defined as the deciding upon and carrying out within a unit of business organization of policies designed to result in a maximum profit to the owners of the enterprise.[1] This objective is achieved by utilizing the so-called factors of production: land, labor, and capital. The business may take the form of a corporation, partnership, or individual proprietorship, depending upon various factors such as taxes, publicity, the need for capital, or the desire for limited liability.

From a survey of the changing scene of American economic development from the Civil War to 1919, two conclusions can be drawn. First is the fact that throughout these years there have been alternate periods of "buyers' markets" and "sellers' markets." In some years the products of American business were easy to sell because of general prosperity and rising demand, while conversely there were times when goods were difficult to get rid of at profitable prices. Naturally, these situations were reflected in the varying policies of business management. The second conclusion is that, despite these alternating trends, fundamental changes occurred in the economic, social, and political background of the American scene. German writers call these "structural changes" or "Strukturwandlungen," and they have important repercussions upon the decisions of business management. One of the most important of the recent changes, for example, has been the steady trend since the 1860's toward greater and greater Government intervention in the affairs of business. Another is the decline in the rate of growth of the population in the United States. Reference will be made to these two types of changes as the discussion progresses.

Business Management and the Civil War

Many of the most important trends in the post-Civil War period had their beginnings during previous decades.[2] Yet the quickening effect of

[1] There may, of course, be other goals in business besides maximum profits, such as prestige for owners or management, enlarged size, maximum employment, reputation of product, and so forth, but in most cases profits are certainly the main consideration.

[2] See Chapter 15.

the war years should not be minimized. Some important changes took place that were destined to make their influence felt in the post-war years. From the point of view of the businessman, the most important contribution of the war was its spurring of a tremendous increase in demand. It created a "sellers' market" in which selling problems gave way to the problem of producing enough to satisfy the great needs of private consumers plus the Government. Fortunately for business (and perhaps unfortunately for the interests of the nation as a whole) few if any attempts were made by the state to limit prices and profits or to restrict the demand of the general public. Inflation was left to run its course. The important immediate cause of the increased demand was, of course, the need of the Federal (and, in the South, of the Confederate) Government for war supplies. The manufacturers and distributors of woolen textiles, shoes, and iron and steel products apparently benefited the most.[3] Another factor was the protective tariff and the extensive internal revenue duties that added to the price and profit rise. Furthermore, in the North the settlement of the West continued at a rapid pace and served to support business activity. Finally, the issuance of greenbacks added fuel to the already high flames of inflation. The net result of all these conditions was to assure a market to almost any business that could obtain capital, labor, and raw materials. The war with its demand for large quantities of standardized goods for the use of the armed forces also helped to hasten the trend toward large-scale machine industry. More and more businessmen became acquainted with the problems and potentialities of mass production.[4]

A further result of the war that was to make its influence more strongly felt in the last quarter of the century was the rise of the magazine and especially the newspaper to satisfy the demand for war news. Their increased popularity was aided by the decline in publication expenses due to the invention of the curved stereotype plate and the use of the cheaper wood pulp paper.[5] People had become "news conscious." All that remained was for business to become aware of the possibilities of large-scale advertising.

[3] E. D. Fite, *Social and Industrial Conditions in the North During the Civil War*. New York: Macmillan Co., 1910.

[4] On the other hand, a few industries found themselves handicapped by the war conditions because of a lack of materials or of labor absorbed by the war effort or because of high taxes or a decline in demand for their products. Thus railroad and building construction were almost halted during the war, and the production of cotton goods suffered from a lack of raw material and sales of beer declined apparently because of the inability of working class consumers to pay the high war-time price. See Copeland, M. T., *The Cotton Manufacturing Industry in the United States*. Cambridge, Mass.: Harvard University Press, 1912; and Cochran, T. C., *The Pabst Brewing Company; The History of an American Business*. New York: New York University Press, 1948.

[5] F. Presbrey, *The History and Development of Advertising*. New York: Doubleday, Doran & Co., 1929.

Before 1860 there existed an increasing tendency to divide up the functions of business management among various specialists in transportation, wholesaling, retailing, insurance, banking, and so forth. In earlier times the average manufacturer very often undertook to perform these functions himself as a part of his job.[6] The war undoubtedly accelerated this trend toward specialization through its emphasis upon production problems, through its contribution to the rapid growth in the geographic size of markets, the great expansion in demand itself, and the increased size of the typical business firm. All these factors encouraged greater concentration of the manager upon manufacturing or production problems and dependence upon the outsider to take care of marketing and financial problems. The day of the "merchant prince" and the "captain of industry" was declining.

Finally, an important and lasting effect of the war years was the establishment of close relations between business and Government. As always in wartime, the desire to procure lucrative Government contracts brought many businessmen to Washington. Closer contacts were also induced by the lobbying necessary to push through the protective tariffs of 1862 and 1864. The Government land grants and loans that were deemed so important for the construction of the transcontinental railroads exercised a beckoning influence. Last but not least, relations between the two groups were solidified by the rise to power of the businessman's political organization: the Republican Party.

The Impact of Depression upon Business Management

The 35 years between the end of the war in 1864 and the opening of the present century were vital years in the development of American business. In the first place, price trends until 1896 were distinctly downward, making profitable operations extremely difficult during many of these years. The problem was complicated by the greatly increasing production of manufactured goods during this period. In the second place, the long years of severe depression that punctuated the period added to the difficulties of a falling price trend and rising production. Two of the worst depressions in American history were ushered in with the panics of 1873 and 1893. In the third place, there arose out of the unstable economic situation an uncertain political condition. These were the years of the "revolt against big business" by farmers and laboring classes. Weighty financial questions were argued, including the matters of whether or not to pay war bond issues in gold, whether to resume specie payments or resort to bimetallism, whether to regulate railroads

---

[6] See Chapter 15 and N. S. B. Gras and H. Larson, *Casebook in American Business History*, pp. 3-15.

and break down monopolies or remain faithful to the principles of *laissez faire*. Such uncertainties probably had some effect upon the formulation of business policies.

Closer study of the situation reveals that the effects of the depression years were particularly severe upon business because of the nature of American enterprise at this time. Markets in general were expanding their demands except during the years of most severe depression. Population was increasing at the rate of about 25 per cent a decade until 1890, and somewhat less thereafter. The costs of transportation were falling as the railroad network stretched across the country, and improved its service.[7] Cutthroat competition among the various over-built lines brought down rates and developed markets still further. Meanwhile, the ocean steamship helped to cut the costs of exports. Yet business management, strangely enough, met these changes with divided feelings. The combination of declining prices and widening markets coupled with long periods of severe depression subjected individual firms to what appeared to be a ruinous type of competition. Competition was becoming nationwide, even worldwide, and no longer merely local in scope.

But it was especially the state of affairs within the structure of costs of production that served to make such competition ruinous. The war-speeded tendency toward mechanization and large-scale business placed greater importance on fixed expenses in the costs of operating a business. These fixed costs included depreciation on the important fixed assets of the factories, interest on the larger quantity of capital now needed, rent on the expanded plants, and salaries of a larger administrative staff of experts in production, record-keeping, and selling. When sales declined, as they frequently did because of depression or the influx of competing firms, these costs grew larger and larger when figured on a unit of output basis. At the same time, toward the end of the period the growing strength of labor unions made it more difficult than usual to cut expenses by reducing wages, at least in time to keep up with the decline of sales and income. The result was a race to secure by price-cutting as much of the declining market as possible. When indulged in by all, the effect was indeed ruinous and only made a bad matter worse. Such a situation had become common among the railroads with their fixed-costs structure even before 1860, but now as a result of the rise of mass production it had become all too common among industries in general. The question naturally arose: what could be done to restore profits?

It should be added that this period was by no means a period of continual depression, although two of America's worst sieges of bad business fell before 1900. In fact, there was considerable prosperity in

[7] Between 1880 and 1890 some 70,000 miles of railways were constructed, a record never again reached in the United States.

the years 1869, 1871-73, 1879-82, 1887, 1889-90, and 1892.[8] But the combination of a downward price trend and alternating periods of good and bad business certainly affected most business firms in the manner described above.

Attempts to Restore Profits in Depression

The first thought of business enterprise naturally was to place the price structure upon a profitable level again. Such efforts took two forms: the simple, time-tested remedy of control of supply (monopoly or duopoly) and the more complicated remedy of differentiation of product (monopolistic competition).[9] Monopoly was attempted in those industries burdened with an especially high level of fixed costs such as the railroads, iron and steel mills, and mining companies. The relatively small number of competitors also aided such attempts in these and other industries such as petroleum and tobacco products. The result, which is well known to all followers of the trust problem, was a series of gentlemen's agreements, pools, trusts and outright mergers. In many other industries either bankruptcy overtook the weaker firms or the second method, product differentiation, was resorted to. The subject of monopolistic competition has drawn considerable attention from economic theorists in recent years and only a brief explanation is necessary.[10] Among other things, it involves the use of brand names, trade marks, advertising, or special services in an effort to persuade the customer of the superiority of the products of the differentiating firm over those of its competitors. If successful, sales are bolstered or expanded at the expense of the firm employing less effective methods of differentiation or even none at all.

It has been shown above how events during the war years had served to encourage the use of the cheap daily or weekly periodical. The medium was there; now businessmen were beginning to appreciate its value for their advertising in these years of expanding markets or of depression. The public actually seemed to like this new method of cut-throat competition, although it rather unlogically condemned the more naïve method of monopolistic cartels and trusts!

One other method of dealing with embarrassing competition was adopted: diversified production. Businessmen discovered that, particularly during times of depression when demand fell off, concentration upon the production or sale of only one item or a few related items could become very risky. They attempted to take their eggs out of the one basket

---

[8] See W. L. Thorpe, *Business Annals*, pp. 77-80. New York: National Bureau of Economic Research, 1926.

[9] See Chapter 32.

[10] For a concise, elementary discussion of the problem see A. L. Meyers, *Elements of Modern Economics*. New York: Prentice-Hall, Inc., 1941.

and distribute them among many baskets by developing new products and sidelines.

The Bankers, the Corporation, and Business Management

Behind the rise and fall of business conditions changes were taking place that were destined to put a new face upon the American economic situation. One of these was the continued rise of the investment banker. Even before the war the average business enterprise had begun to turn to outside sources for its capital but the movement became more pronounced as big business rose to a more dominating position in American economic life. This was quite in conformance with the tendency described above of specialization in production, selling, transportation, and financial problems but the result was far-reaching, for in these years was laid the foundation for the much-condemned, much-discussed "banker control" of business. In other words, the investment banker was to become not a mere specializing servant of business enterprise, but sometimes a ruler of it.

A good case could have been made for intervention of the banker in the problems of management. Presumably he possessed a broader knowledge and viewpoint gained through his contacts with many firms and entire industries in similar circumstances, in contrast to the narrow point of view of the management of a particular firm. Furthermore, a firm embarrassed by a temporary lack of cash could seek aid from its favorite banker without publicity or an examination of its financial affairs by numerous outside banking interests. The favorite banker could also gain great familiarity with the condition of his clients by means of exclusive access to records, and contacts with managing officers. From the point of view of the investor the rise of the investment banker assured a thorough examination of the securities before their sale, a tacit guarantee of their quality after sale, and a continued conservative influence by the banker upon the actions of management.

But to many observers the control exercised by the banker did not appear to be an unmixed blessing. There was too great a possibility of conflict among the interests of management, banker, security-holder, and the general public. It was possible for banker, management, and investor to profit from the monopolies so commonly created in the nineties by pools, trusts, and mergers, but they were hardly beneficial to the public interest. Desire for the profits and commissions of security sales often led bankers to advise the sale of unnecessary issues of stocks and bonds, leaving corporations overburdened with watered stock and excessive fixed charges from interest on bond issues. In this case, both the corporation and the security purchaser were harmed. Despite these disadvantages, criticism of the situation was slow to develop and the voices of famous critics such as Louis D. Brandeis and William Z. Ripley were to be heard only later as bankers' control became more widespread and conspicuous.[11] The earliest examples of the misuse of big business powers appeared in the actions of men of the Wall Street speculator type, such as Jay Gould and Jim Fisk, rather than the banker specialist.[12] Some of these men were railroad operators or entrepreneurs, some bankers, and others unscrupulous speculators. Fortunately they were a rare breed appearing largely as a result of the low level of business ethics in the years immediately following the Civil War, and their places were eventually taken by more subtle if not less unscrupulous persons.

The rise of the investment banker to a key position in the business world tended to shift the emphasis on personalities from the businessman who spent most of his time working on the management problems of his own firm to the banker who had a controlling hand in the affairs of many companies. Without a doubt, the leader of this new race of business moguls was the much-maligned, much-praised John Pierpont Morgan. The story of his accomplishments is told elsewhere, but it should be stressed here that he received his early training in an environment of banking in a time when foreign exchange was one of the chief interests of bankers. Like that of other bankers his interest in foreign exchange expanded into U. S. and foreign government financing and finally into private industry, beginning with the railroads, the chief consumers of the nation's savings in those years. In order to be sure that his "suggestions" were adopted Morgan was forced to take over the control of reorganized railroads by means of the voting trust. By the close of the century the capital needs of the manufacturing industries began to press for attention, and this situation, together with the dangers of cutthroat competition, drew the attention of Morgan to this field, so that manufacturing firms controlled by Morgan soon began to make their appearance.[13] His example of banking service coupled with control was soon followed by other bankers, and a new era had begun in the field of business management.

The appearance of the investment banker was closely accompanied by the growing popularity of the corporation as a form of business organization. There is considerable evidence that the corporation was being used

[11] The earlier critics tended to condemn the capitalistic sytsem in general, rather than the actions of the bankers alone. See, for example, E. Bellamy, *Looking Backward, 2000-1887* (Boston: Houghton, 1888); and H. D. Lloyd, *Wealth Against Commonwealth* (New York: Harper, 1894).

[12] See F. C. Hicks, ed., *High Finance in the Sixties*. New Haven, Conn.: Yale University Press, 1929.

[13] For a careful appraisal of Morgan's work in the railroad field see: E. G. Campbell, *The Reorganization of the American Railroad System, 1893-1900*. New York: Columbia University Press, 1938. General biographies of Morgan are less satisfactory although interesting: J. Winkler, *Morgan, the Magnificent* (New York: Garden City Press, 1930); and L. Corey, *The House of Morgan* (New York: G. H. Watt, 1930).

more and more, especially in the 1850's by business enterprise outside of the field of public service industries (railroads, turnpikes, bridges, and so forth) and of banking and finance. After the war, however, there developed not only an increased demand on the part of business enterprise for such an institution but also a greater tendency on the part of Government to grant its use. New circumstances increased the need for the corporation. Business firms were becoming larger in volume of output, number of workers employed, and, most significant, capital needs. In such industries as iron and steel, textiles, mining, chemicals, liquor, and nonferrous metals, the proprietorship and the partnership proved inadequate means of obtaining the large amount of capital needed by these gigantic mechanized firms. Other and less important attractions offered by the corporation probably included its permanence as a legal entity separate from the stockholder-owners; the limited liability of the owners, which facilitated the widespread sale of stock; the ease of administration arising out of the separation of investment from management, so that persons with managerial ability and no capital could join forces with persons with capital and little managerial ability. Large firms were also able to decentralize administration by setting up subsidiary companies with separate managing staffs and even stockholders, over which the parent companies could retain control by reserving substantial blocks of stock. This arrangement also permitted combinations aimed at reducing costs or building up monopolistic control. All of the advantages bestowed by the corporation were especially appealing during a period when capital needs were expanding and competition becoming keener.

But the needs of business would have had an indecisive effect had they not been strengthened by a public opinion favorably disposed toward the corporation. Here again, even before 1860, the old hostility toward the corporation as monopolistic and special privileged showed signs of weakening. More and more special acts of incorporation were passed for a growing variety of purposes, and some states even resorted to general incorporation laws in order to relieve the burden of their legislatures and "equalize" opportunities of firms to incorporate. But it was during and after the Civil War that corporations really began to appear in large numbers.[14] Furthermore, the movement toward incorporation by general act became more widespread and, once the ball started rolling, other states were forced to fall in line or run the danger of losing revenue derived from the granting of charters and watch the migration of capital to states less strict.

The softening attitude toward the corporation thus took two lines of development: The first was a continuing expansion of incorporation

[14] The experience of Vermont may have been typical: the largest number of firms incorporated by special act in any single year before the war was 42 in the boom year of 1836. In 1865, 58 corporations were created and in 1870, 66, and so on.

by general act instead of by special legislation for each charter. The new system was considered more democratic because it opened up incorporation to all on equal terms. A hardly less important feature of general incorporation law was the relief from congestion [15] and attempted corruption that it afforded a hard-pressed legislature. The second concession to business was a general lowering of the standards of corporation law. These standards seem to have remained fairly high until about the last decade of the century, when the combined needs of business for the corporation and of the state for revenue after long years of depression soon produced a sweeping change in the hitherto rigorous attitude of the state governments. As is well known, the first state to weaken was New Jersey. This state had introduced a limited form of general incorporation as early as 1849, but incorporation by special act continued until prohibited by a constitutional amendment in 1875.[16] In 1888 a radical departure allowed New Jersey corporations to hold stock in other corporations, a privilege that until then had been permitted by any state only under special circumstances. This move made New Jersey a popular state with companies participating in the trust movement, but apparently it was not yet enough, for in 1896 New Jersey companies were expressly granted the right to do business anywhere, incorporation taxes were greatly reduced, and amendments to articles of association by majority vote were made easier. After about 1890 the movement toward easing corporation laws spread to other states, partly as a measure of self-defense, partly as a means of increasing revenue.

The "Corporation Problem" Appears

The basic problem of the corporation in modern economic life has been succinctly defined by Professor Wright as follows:

> The corporation problem may be said to consist in the need for devising a form of business organization suited to meet the wants of modern large-scale enterprise with the specialization of functions that this requires, which will at the same time provide adequate safeguards to protect all the different groups of interests concerned. At present the chief evils have arisen from the failure to provide such safeguards.[17]

Such safeguards had probably been lacking to some degree before the last quarter of the twentieth century, but at no previous time had the demand for incorporation been so insistent and widespread and the state so anxious to satisfy it. Incorporation had ceased to be looked upon by

---

[15] For example: Maine in one year (1836) issued 150 separate charters in contrast to an annual average of 16 in the period 1820-1860.

[16] H. W. Stoke, "Economic Influences upon the Corporation Laws of New Jersey," *Journal of Political Economy,* Vol. XXXVIII, No. 5 (October, 1930), pp. 551-579.

[17] Chester W. Wright, *Economic History of the United States,* p. 673. New York: McGraw-Hill Book Co., 1941.

grantor and grantee as a special privilege and had come to be regarded almost as a right. Not only did this change in view weaken the protection set up for investor, worker, and general public: the corporation became a vehicle for monopoly and unfair competition. But at the same time it was making possible mechanization and mass production that, with the natural wealth of the country, became the basis of the famous American standard of living.

Meantime a definite break occurred in the relations between business management and the public. The combination of two serious depressions, a falling price level (especially for agricultural products), and the abuse of powers of monopoly by railroads and manufacturing interests raised a public uproar. The situation was not at all improved by the tactics used by business leaders to break strikes, nor by the growing influence of business in Washington and the various state capitals, nor by the general indifference of some businessmen toward public relations as expressed by William H. Vanderbilt's famous "The public be damned." The public reaction was to reach its climax later in the anti-trust drives of Presidents Roosevelt, Taft, and Wilson. Perhaps only the price rise and the improvement in economic conditions after 1896 "saved" American business from a New Deal then and deferred its appearance until another time of somewhat similar conditions.

The Period of Steady, Slow Growth: 1900–1913

The years from the opening of the century to 1913 were a period of quiet growth unmarked by serious and complicated problems in manufacturing and marketing. In fact, some observers are prone to call this a period of that elusive "normalcy" so often described and so seldom realized. Prices rose steadily, markets and sales (both domestic and foreign) expanded, and only one serious depression, in 1907-1908, marred the scene but only for a relatively short time. From the point of view of business management the only serious problems were the growing power of organized labor, the "trust-busting" activities of the Federal Government, and a growing intensity of non-price competition.

But many leaders began to realize that in addition to these problems large-scale business brought with it the disadvantage of absence of personal contacts and incentives that were present in the days of smaller business units. A problem of immediate importance in those years was how to manage big business with the greatest amount of efficiency and the least amount of red tape. A vital part of this problem was management's relations with labor. Rising wages and a greater use of expensive capital equipment per worker made labor a key figure in manufacturing industry. The result was the scientific-management movement fathered by F. W. Taylor and limited at first to the technical problems of production but expanded later to form the basis of better business management as a whole. Scientific management originally undertook studies designed to test the operations used by workers and devised new ones to take their places if the old ones proved inefficient. Out of this process grew personnel administration intended to improve relations between management and labor by trying to restore something of the personal element that had formerly existed, by seeing to it that the worker was given the job best suited to his abilities, and by improving working conditions in general. On the whole, however, only the foundations of the personnel-administration movement were laid during these years and it gathered greater momentum during the World War years and after than at this time.

In the sphere of office management, scientific management was aided by the development of better accounting methods, greater accuracy in keeping of records by means of the card index, and a tendency toward organization of business more and more on a departmentalized or staff basis whereby specialists in various fields were set up in their own departments with their own staffs to aid the enterprise as a whole. Many firms soon had entire departments with managers devoted to accounting and auditing, buying and selling, warehousing, advertising, or handling personnel problems. Specialists outside the firm set themselves up in business to act in consulting capacity. Mechanized methods also invaded business administration, led, of course, in these early years by the typewriter. It became recognized, furthermore, that business management might benefit from rationalized study in higher education just like any other subject, and university schools of business presently began to make their appearance, offering a variety of courses ranging from statistics and accounting to business economics and problems of top management control.

Another problem faced by business management was the growing power of organized labor noted in the preceding chapter. As a result, business management began to organize itself into powerful bodies designed to present a united front to labor, the most important being the National Metal Trades Association formed in 1899, and the National Association of Manufacturers founded in 1895. Both were increasingly active up to 1913.

As a matter of fact, the activities of trade associations were not confined to labor relations nor even to trust-building or monopolistic matters. Beginning in the eighties of the past century and especially after 1900, American businessmen showed a greater and greater desire to co-operate with each other in affairs of mutual interest. Perhaps the main reason for this trend was that business problems were fast getting beyond the ability of the average firm to solve; besides, the tactics of such organizations in restricting prices and production before the more rigid enforcement of the antitrust laws probably pointed the way to the advantages of such co-operation in more legal and innocuous fields. Such co-operative undertakings included joint research and advertising, patent pools, joint insurance, and similar programs.[18]

A final problem was that of marketing the product of business enterprise. Under the stress of depression conditions and increasing competition more and more business firms in the last quarter of the nineteenth century found themselves forced either to resort to some form of monopoly or to concentrate upon other aspects of the product they were selling besides price. Consequently, since outright monopoly was frowned upon by public opinion this period witnessed a great expansion in advertising. In contrast to previous years, the methods became more refined and subtle. Photographs and colored pictures were used in the increasing number of magazines available.[19] Whether this type of competition was of benefit to the consumer or not is, of course, a moot question. It could be said that it resulted merely in a shifting of demand from one advertiser to another. On the other hand, it could be regarded as being highly informative to the consumer and as stimulating the seller to keep up with his competitors.[20] Whatever the influence of advertising was during these years, it is certainly true that the rise of the practice coincided with a rapid growth of production goods and services in the United States and a consequent rise in the standard of living.

The First World War

In wartime the first effects of conflict usually are not clear and they vary from industry to industry. As a war continues confusion gives way to unfavorable trends that apply with equal intensity to all business. As far as the American effort was concerned, the First World War was too short for this second stage to develop to an appreciable degree. The chief effects upon the decisions of business management seem to have been in the field of labor relations and in the costs structure.

Employers were almost immediately faced with a rise in labor costs together with a rise in the costs of raw materials. The change in raw material costs, however, was of significance chiefly to those firms that were tied down by custom, consumer resistance, or Governmental regulation to more or less rigid prices for their products. Railroads, public utilities, and to a less extent manufacturers of consumers' goods, were the chief sufferers in this respect. Firms that were combined vertically (from raw material to finished product) probably were able to avoid buying in the higher-priced, open market so that the war tended to encourage such combinations, But there remained the problem of the unions and the

---

18 See *Trade Associations, Their Economic Significance and Legal Status.* New York: National Industrial Conference Board, 1925.

19 See Presbrey, *The History and Development of Advertising.*

20 For a detailed study of the subject see N. H. Borden, *The Economic Effects of Advertising.* Chicago: Irwin, 1942.

progress they were making in organizing workers and extending the closed shop, as well as securing a shorter basic working day. Membership in labor unions began to rise at a rapid rate in 1915 until a record high was reached in the early post-war years (1920: 5,047,000).[21] For a time rising costs were absorbed by many industries through the high prices of wartime inflation [22] and a real encounter with the unions was postponed until after the war.

Certainly business benefited greatly from the flood of Government orders arising out of the war and from the fact that price regulation was so long postponed and so ineffective.[23] Furthermore, the war, as always, performed the function of a protective tariff which barred competitive products from the belligerents of both sides: the unfriendly powers for obvious reasons and the friendly because of their preoccupation with the war. New markets that had been the preserves of the warring nations were found, especially in Latin America. Finally, owing to the non-enforcement of the antitrust laws and because of advantages to business and Government alike, combinations, both horizontal and vertical, were greatly encouraged. Membership in the looser trade associations expanded with the need for co-operation among business firms in obtaining Government contracts and fulfilling Governmental regulations.[24]

Selected References

GENERAL WORKS

Beard, Miriam, *A History of the Business Man*. New York: The Macmillan Co., 1940.

Berle, Adolph A., Jr., and Gardiner C. Means, *The Modern Corporation and Private Property*. New York: The Macmillan Co., 1934.

Clark, Victor S., *History of Manufactures in the United States*, Vols. II and III. Washington, D. C.: Carnegie Institution of Washington, 1929.

Cochran, Thomas C., and William Miller, *The Age of Enterprise*. New York: The Macmillan Company, 1942.

Edwards, G. W., *The Evolution of Finance Capitalism*. New York: Longmans, Green & Co., 1938.

Gras, N. S. B., *Business and Capitalism*. New York: F. S. Crofts & Co., 1939.

———, and Henrietta M. Larson, *Casebook in American Business History*. New York: F. S. Crofts and Co., 1939.

Wright, Chester W., *Economic History of the United States*. New York: McGraw-Hill Book Co., 1941.

[21] L. Wolman, *Ebb and Flow in Trade Unions*, p. 16. New York: National Bureau of Economic Research, 1936.

[22] Wholesale prices rose from 98 in 1914 to 214 in 1918 and a peak of 231 in 1920. (1910-1914 = 100).

[23] The Governmental price-control program did not take form until the summer of 1917. See C. O. Hardy, *Wartime Control of Prices*, p. 121. Washington: The Brookings Institution, 1940.

[24] See H. R. Seager and C. A. Gulick, *Trust and Corporation Problems*, p. 306. New York: Harper & Bros., 1929.

SPECIAL TOPICS

Dimock, M. E., and H. K. Hyde, "Bureaucracy and Trusteeship in Large Corporations," *Temporary National Economic Committee Monograph No. 11.* Washington, D. C.: 1940.

Handlin, Oscar, "Laissez Faire Thought in Massachusetts, 1790-1880," *The Journal of Economic History,* Supplement (December, 1943), pp. 55-65.

Knight, Frank H., *Risk, Uncertainty and Profit.* London: London School of Economics, 1937.

Sombart, Werner, "Capitalism," *Encyclopedia of the Social Sciences,* Vol. III.

———, *The Quintessence of Capitalism: A Study of the History and Psychology of the Modern Business Man.* New York: E. P. Dutton, 1915.

32 · INDUSTRIAL CONCENTRATION AND ANTI-TRUST POLICY

IN THE UNITED STATES AFTER THE CIVIL WAR, the rapid expansion of population and of industrial activity was accompanied by an increasing concentration of the control of business operations in the hands of a limited number of relatively large individual firms. Such concentration was first met in the railroad field, previously discussed in Chapter 19, but after 1870 it also developed rapidly in the areas of mining, processing, and manufacturing. In a great many industries individual firms expanded so as to control significant fractions of their markets, and, in addition, groups of firms within industries combined or merged into one or a few business units that were frequently of such a size as to dominate their respective industries.[1]

This movement progressed so rapidly in its early stages that as early as 1905 the control of a large proportion of the major industrial markets was concentrated in the hands of a relatively few large firms.[2] The movement of course did not terminate in 1905; it was continuing, although at a reduced and declining pace, as late as the middle 1930's. Between 1890 and 1905, and again at a lesser rate during the 1920's, however, the process of industrial concentration via consolidations moved so rapidly that it has often been referred to as a *merger movement.* This merger movement, and more broadly the progressive movement toward concentration through individual firm expansion, acquisitions, and mergers, are primary aspects of the recent development of the American economy. Accordingly, some attention must be devoted to its principal origins, to the details of its development, to its effects on the structure of the modern economy, and to the problems it has raised for public policy toward industry.

---

[1] Instances of such developments in processing and manufacturing industries are discussed in Chapters 22, 23, and 24, above.

[2] Thus, by 1904, there were at least 318 large industrial combinations in the United States, which had accumulated no less than 5200 original plants. Collectively they are estimated to have controlled over two-fifths of the manufacturing capital in the country, and a great many controlled over half the output of their respective industries. (See John Moody, *The Truth About the Trusts,* pp. 485-487. New York: Moody Publishing Company, 1904).

The analysis of the concentration movement herein and in Chapter 46 will be principally concerned with the phenomenon in mining and manufacture, since it is there that it has been most important. Agriculture, which has not been significantly affected, is not discussed, and the regulated public utilities fields are also neglected. The distributive trades have been less affected by a concentration or merger movement than many fields of manufacture, and then largely following 1920, but the rise of chain-store and other mass distribution since 1920 may be viewed as another phase of the broad concentration movement herein discussed. The discussion will therefore deal generally with the concentration movement in the American economy, excepting the areas of agriculture, rails, and public utilities.

The Rise of Large-Scale Industrial Firms

The development of industrial concentration, or in a narrower sense the rise of "monopolies" or "trusts," does not appear as an independent or abnormal phenomenon in economic evolution; it is readily explicable in terms of technological and other forces shaping the path of economic development in all of its phases. In some considerable part, at least, it appears as one of the several phases of the adaptation of economic life to the primary stimuli of technological innovation that had influenced the industrial development of the preceding century. Improvements in methods of textile making, a revolution in the technique of iron and steel manufacture, the development of steam power, and the building of railroad systems had provided the technological basis for the shift of production to factories, for the movement of population to the cities, and for the organization of the production of more and more goods under the direction of business enterprise. As this reorganization of the economy was proceeding, a further implication of these and of a growing mass of smaller technical innovations became evident, namely, that industrial firms would very frequently find it both more economical and more profitable to expand, to integrate, and to combine.

The growth in the scale of individual plants was rapid in the years immediately following the Civil War. In the 1870's, while the number of manufacturing establishments was virtually constant, capital investment in manufacturing rose 65 per cent; and the value of industrial output, 58 per cent. The strong firms in many industries, moreover, grew much more rapidly than the average, driving out of business or reducing to relative unimportance their weaker competitors. In the 1880's the principal establishments in many industries had attained, as judged by current standards, moderately large-scale production.

This growth of large-scale plants was in part attributable to the superior efficiency or enterprise of certain manufacturers. In large part, however, it was the result of the fact that, with the developing techniques of manufacture, large-scale, mass-production plants in many industries became more efficient than small ones. Producers expanded their plants in order to lower their costs and enhance their profits. The rise of machine techniques of production and the development of factory routines involving extensive specialization of both labor and machines were the basis of the increasing economies of large-scale plants. Labor tasks could often be specialized and simplified, and strategic machinery effectively employed only in quite large-scale plants. The pursuit of the economies of machine production and of labor and machine specialization was a principal factor in the rise of mass-production plants and large firms.

The vertical integration of plants performing successive steps in an industrial process was another phase of industrial concentration, and it was in part motivated by the technical economies that such integration offered. Successive manufacturing processes could often be carried on more effectively in a single plant than in a succession of independent plants. In steel making, for example, integration of blast furnace, steel converter, steel furnace, and rolling operations into a single plant made possible the avoidance of the loss of heat entailed when the pig iron or steel ingots were cooled for shipment between separate plants and led to considerable savings in fuel cost. Furthermore, placing several successive operations under a single control made possible the co-ordination of interdependent production schedules, and also eliminated marketing costs. Technological development was thus the basis both of integration and of growth of industrial plants.

The Merger Movement

The rise of large-scale plants and firms was accompanied in the seventies and eighties by the emergence of particularly severe competition. In part this was evidence of the fact that firms with new, large-scale plants were driving smaller and less efficient rivals from business. In many industries, moreover, general expansion of facilities led to a temporary surplus of capacity, and therefore to competitive price cutting among large rival firms. Competition was intensified by the continuing growth of the railroad systems, which tended to bring all of the principal firms together in direct competition for a single national market. Many industries in the economy were passing from a situation where a fairly large number of small manufacturers sold their products, each in a limited local market somewhat protected by high costs of transportation, to a situation where a few large firms vied among themselves for sales in a single market. In the new environment, price competition was potentially ruinous to all.

As this tendency developed, the competing firms in many industries sought to avoid the ravages of unrestricted price rivalry by forming combinations or mergers. Slowly between 1879 and 1896, much more rapidly from 1897 to 1904, and again more slowly thereafter, there developed a merger movement of major proportions. The usual merger combined several firms in an industry into a single corporation or holding company, after which it closed down inefficient plants, expanded others, and sometimes effected various types of vertical integration. In a few industries a single firm gained a virtual monopoly of its field, but in most cases the result of combinations was to place a fairly high proportion of the capacity of an industry under the control of a single firm and to concentrate much of the remainder in the hands of a few large rivals.[3]

The scope of the merger movement was so great that by 1904 it had basically altered the structure of American industry. By the beginning of that year there were over three hundred large industrial combinations, with a combined capitalization in excess of $7,000,000,000. They controlled more than two-fifths of the manufacturing capital of the country and had affected about four-fifths of important American industries. Since 1904, mergers have occurred less frequently, perhaps because the outstanding opportunities for mergers had already been rather fully exploited, and, although concentration has on the average increased somewhat since 1904, the increase has been much more selective, gradual and at an apparently declining average rate. The major exception to this tapering off process is that there was during the 1920's a considerable wave of mergers affecting new industries like the automobile, radio, and moving picture industries, and some others like food processing, metals, and petroleum. The combination movement, particularly that part of it occurring up to 1904, was the climactic phase in the development of concentration in American markets. Once it was accomplished, the previous pattern of competition gave way to the complicated rivalry of gigantic industrial estates.

The Rationale of Industrial Combination

The motivating forces in the combination movement were in part technological. Many mergers enabled the combining firms to achieve further economies of large-scale production and of vertical integration. But the rise of highly concentrated industry must be explained also in other terms. The most evident of these further motives for combination was the desire to eliminate or control competition. The rivalry of a relatively small num-

---

[3] The largest combine in point of capitalization was the United States Steel Corporation, capitalized for $1,370,000,000, which merged most of the important iron mines and iron and steel manufacturing facilities in the country. Other prominent combinations were the Standard Oil Company, American Sugar Refining Company, Consolidated Tobacco Company, American Smelting and Refining Company, and the United Shoe Machinery Company. Of the 92 largest combinations in 1904 (of the 318 then listed), 78 controlled 50 per cent or more of their industries, 57 controlled 60 per cent or more, and 26 controlled 80 per cent or more. (Moody, *The Truth About The Trusts,* pp. 485-487.) For a general discussion of the combination movement, see Seager and Gulick, *Trust and Corporation Problems,* pp. 49-71. New York: Harper & Brothers, 1929.

ber of large firms in a national market was seen in the latter part of the nineteenth century to be potentially of such a character as to destroy profits for all. The combination of a firm with the stronger of its potential competitors was an obvious means of protecting profits. Although the stage for combination was thus set by the technologically induced rise of large-scale plants and firms, combination itself had a more complex rationale.

As indicated in the previous chapter, a strategic concomitant of industrial mergers was the rise of the large corporation and of the holding company. The formation of the ten-, fifty-, or hundred-million-dollar enterprises that resulted from many combinations required the amassing of large amounts of funds, and the right of incorporation made this necessary financing relatively easy. The legalization in several states of holding companies (corporations formed to acquire the stock of several other corporations) likewise greatly facilitated the combination of existing firms. The new large firms and mergers typically took the form of corporations and holding companies. With the rise of incorporated industry, moreover, a financial community including the New York stock market, stockbrokers, and investment bankers acting as middlemen in selling corporate securities assumed a position of dominant importance in the American economy. Not only were the services of this financial community required in most combinations, but bankers or financiers often took the lead in the promotion of mergers. Since the commissions received by investment bankers and other financiers for the flotation of combinations were often very large, it seems probable that their pursuit of financial profit was at least a contributing cause of the formation of many mergers.

Certain aspects of the American legal system are also significant in the explanation of the merger movement. The Federal patent law, as judicially construed, grants to inventors the exclusive right for 17 years to make, sell, lease, license, or confine to absolute disuse any useful, original invention, and these rights are acquired in full by a business firm purchasing a patent. In certain industries, the acquisition by one or a few firms of a group of patent rights covering strategic industrial processes enabled them to exclude competitors for a considerable period and to establish firmly a monopolistic or highly concentrated control of their industries.[4] Protective tariff laws also provided a favorable climate for combination. Finally the Federal antitrust law, as embodied principally in the Sherman Act, contributed somewhat paradoxically to the formation of mergers. The act, passed in 1890, specifically forbade loose agreements, cartels, or pools among independent firms but, as construed during the periods of most intense merger activity, did not seem to outlaw the

[4] See Walton Hamilton, *Patents and Free Enterprise,* Temporary National Economic Committee, Monograph No. 31. Washington, D. C.: 1941.

actual merger or combination of firms. This construction of the Sherman Act seems definitely to have encouraged firms to *combine* with their competitors rather than to agree with them to limit competition. In countries where no such law was in force, cartels were more frequent and outright combinations less common.

The fact that strategic resources furnishing their raw materials were located in limited areas within the national boundaries was a contributing factor to integration and combination in certain industries. In some of these instances one or a few firms gained control of virtually all desirable resources and, as a result, were able to build upon them integrated and combined firms dominating their fields. A final factor conditioning the development of integration and large size in American industry was the tremendous extent of the American market, protected always by distance from foreign sources of supply and often by tariffs. Effective exploitation of such a market implied the development of firms selling on a national scale and in many cases also the acquisition by manufacturers of integrated facilities for distribution. Distributive integration and combination for effective marketing, probably oriented more toward the protection of profit than to the pursuit of low costs, were thus final phases of the movement to concentration.

The American combination movement, although it was indeed an orderly phase in the evolution of industrialism, was thus considerably more than an adaptation of market structure to technological change in pursuit of the greatest economies of production. Combinations were formed by private enterprises in order to increase or protect their profits. They accomplished this in a degree by reducing their costs, but also by maintaining or raising their prices, controlling competition, excluding potential competitors from access to resources or to industrial techniques, and availing themselves of the possibilities of nationwide sales promotion. Their ability to do so depended not only on the potential economies of combination, but also on the availability of the corporate form of organization, the existing framework of law, and the geography of markets and resources. Distinctions between "good" and "bad" combinations that turn upon the question of whether they were intended to economize or monopolize are idle. Mergers in general had a multiple motivation and were productive of a multiplicity of results. Whatever the subjective intent of the promoters may have been in individual cases, the general effect was to create highly concentrated markets in the heart of American industry.

Evolution of Industrial Price and Market Behavior

As a large proportion of markets came to be dominated by a few very large corporate firms, certain significant developments appeared in the competitive behavior of the economy. The initial developments were transitional in character. In the formative years of many mergers, ruthless tactics were employed to drive remaining competitors out of business or to harass them so as to induce them to sell out to the combinations. The rise of the old Standard Oil Company, for example, to a position where it controlled about 85 per cent of the American petroleum industry was greatly facilitated by secret agreements with railroads whereby the Company received substantial rebates, not only on its own shipments of oil but also on those of its competitors, and by local price cutting designed to drive small competitors out of business.[5] The Consolidated Tobacco Company, a combine that controlled 90 per cent of the American tobacco industry, was alleged to have resorted to predatory price cutting, to the imitation of competitors' brands, and to inducing boycotts by jobbers and dealers of its competitors' products, all as a means of forcing competitors to sell out to the combination. Mergers that gained virtual control of their industries in some cases raised their prices and proceeded to reap unusually large profits at the expense of buyers.

This phase had largely passed by 1920. In interpreting the Sherman Act, the courts had frowned on predatory market tactics and on obviously exploitative pricing policies, but had shown tolerance of better behaved combinations. At any rate, the jungle warfare stage of combination had passed and predatory competition was no longer in order.

The competitive pattern that emerged as concentrated market structures became firmly established was one in which open rivalry in pricing was restricted or absent, and where the emphasis was rather on competition through product differentiation and development, advertising, and other types of sales promotion. Large firms in concentrated industries were not at the mercy of a market price, and were able to quote their prices and to establish long-term pricing policies. They found it futile to engage in open and active price rivalry with equally strong competitors, and avoided it as a means of securing custom. Avoidance of price competition was implemented in a number of ways. The firms of some industries tacitly recognized the strongest member firm as a "price leader" and changed quoted prices only in unison and in accordance with the price changes of the leader. Many industries formed trade associations through which trade information was exchanged, selling policies were standardized, and prices were filed for the inspection of all members. Secret or semi-secret agreements concerning price, output, and market territories were not infrequently made. Some of these techniques for the limitation of price competition were found illegal under the Sherman Act, but the desire to avoid unrestricted price rivalry was so deeply seated that the basic behavior was not much altered by sporadic antitrust prosecutions. Competition in terms of price by no means vanished, but free-

---

[5] See Ida M. Tarbell, *History of the Standard Oil Company* (2 vols.). New York: The Macmillan Company, 1925.

moving and uncontrolled market prices became rare.[6] Price rivalry became deliberate rather than automatic, and thus more sparingly used; it tended to take the form of secret and limited concessions rather than of open price cutting; it tended to be sporadic rather than persistent. Under such a system, prices evidently tended to lie or to move somewhat unpredictably between the levels associated respectively with monopoly and atomistic competition.

The restriction of price competition was compensated for by a growing emphasis on non-price competition. Product improvement, mere product variation, extensive advertising, and direct selling became, by the 1920's, the accepted modes of soliciting custom in many industries. Concerns tended to establish a conventional price, and then to vie for the market by competitive expenditures on sales promotion. This was still competition but a distinctly different sort of competition. The shift in competitive behavior was accompanied by the rise of new business ethics that justified it. "Live and let live" was the keynote of the emergent philosophy regarding competition, and it was accompanied by censure for the cut-price producer and praise for the "fair" competitor. Whether or not all this represented a decline in competition is not a very meaningful question. Competition was unquestionably less vigorous than during the period of market warfare preceding and accompanying the main merger movement. If we look before that time, however, we find an economy much less industrialized, and with smaller local or regional markets instead of large national ones as the arena for potential competition, and direct comparisons are indeed difficult.

The Sherman Act and the Enforcement of Competition

Prior to the merger movement, the basic policy of the Federal Government toward industry was one of laissez faire. The right of private individuals to own and control personal goods, productive facilities, and resources was an integral part of the basic American law, and it was accepted as a matter of course that economic activity would be conducted by profit-seeking private enterprises. A minimum of governmental restrictions was imposed upon the activities of private enterprise. Acceptance of this policy of "hands-off" by the Government rested not only on the philosophy of individual liberty, but also on the generally accepted belief that competition among private enterprises would provide an adequate sort of automatic regulation that would ordinarily redound to the benefit of all.

This belief and the policy based upon it survived the merger movement and, indeed, survive today. Specific regulations limiting particular aspects

[6] See Gardiner Means, *Industrial Prices and Their Relative Inflexibility* (Senate Document 13, 74th Congress, First Session), for an early discussion of the changes in the character of competition.

of private business activity, like labor policies of employers and credit policies of banks, have become increasingly numerous. Except as an emergency expedient, however, no general alternative to the automatic regulation provided by competition has been tried in the United States. Laissez faire is still the basic principle, albeit a principle to which more and more exceptions are made.

This basic reliance on competition is reflected in the fact that the chief general type of regulation of industry has consisted of the attempt to maintain or enforce competition among business enterprises. The attempt is represented principally in the so-called anti-trust legislation of the Federal Government—in the Sherman Act, and less importantly in the Clayton Act and the Federal Trade Commission Act. The enforcement of these laws has constituted the main line of industrial regulation in America for the past sixty years. They were originated in the early phases of the merger movement and reflected the misgivings of certain groups concerning the effects on competition of the rapid rise of industrial combinations. As enforced, they have brought before the Federal courts instances of the evolving pattern of modern competition and have given the courts the opportunity to decide whether this new variety of competition has satisfactorily fulfilled its social function. Because competition has been a flexible and changing concept, however, no fixed standard of adequately competitive behavior has been developed. Because the legal conception of competition is narrower than the economic, enforcement of anti-trust legislation has frequently turned more on the observance of the form of the law than on the socio-economic consequences of market behavior. And because of lax enforcement at strategic times, the anti-trust policy has probably failed to attain its full potentialities. The history of anti-trust policy that follows is accordingly an account of administrative and judicial attempts to maintain "competition" and forbid "monopoly" in an evolving free-enterprise economy where each of these conceptions was susceptible to a multitude of interpretations.

Political Origins of the Sherman Act

The broad implications of the concentration movement for the structure and behavior of the American economy were not often foreseen or appreciated by its early contemporaries. Nor does the general public in the seventies, eighties, and nineties seem to have been violently concerned with the general problem of trusts and monopolies. The early phases of the concentration movement, however, involving predatory competitive tactics of growing firms and the experimental formation of competition-limiting agreements and pools in industries in the process of concentration, did draw the censure of at least two groups—small businessmen, who were injured by predatory tactics, and farmers. The concern of the former over the growth of great combinations was a matter of direct self-interest, whereas, for the agrarian group, opposition to combinations was a facet of a political program featuring opposition to high railroad rates, opposition to the protective tariff on industrial goods, and the advocation of inflationary monetary reforms. Industry and agriculture were clearly divided on these principal issues; the farm group's opposition to "monopolistic" big business was only one aspect of its political enmity for the industrial group.

Nevertheless, the agitation of these directly interested groups was sufficient to induce 21 states, mostly in the South and Middle West, to pass statutory or constitutional prohibitions of "monopoly" and of agreements "in restraint of trade" by 1890. In practice these laws did little more than to reaffirm prevailing common-law doctrines against monopolization and restraint, since the laws of a single state could seldom impede the activity of a combination operating on a national scale but incorporated in some state with more lenient laws.

The passage by Congress of the Sherman Act as a Federal anti-trust statute in 1890 was apparently a minor measure of appeasement to the farm group. The presidential campaign of 1888 had been fought on the tariff issue, and it was a Congress primarily preoccupied with protective tariff legislation (opposed by farmers) that passed the Sherman Act almost unanimously and with little debate. It was not passed in response to a noticeable clamor by any considerable group in Congress for action with respect to combinations, and for the time being served principally to put Congress on record as opposed to monopoly as it probably was also to sin and the common cold. Yet it was this Act with its very inauspicious beginnings that served for the ensuing sixty years as the principal basis for Federal regulation of monopoly, combination, and the restriction of competition.

Early Enforcement and Interpretation: 1890–1905

The substantive provisions of the Sherman Act are simple and general, declaring illegal "every contract, combination in the form of trust or otherwise, or conspiracy, in restraint of trade or commerce among the several States," and declaring guilty of a misdemeanor "every person who shall monopolize, or attempt to monopolize, or combine or conspire . . . to monopolize any part of the trade or commerce among the several States." The Act provided fines and imprisonments for violations of its provisions, allowed private damages to injured parties, and invested the Attorney General with the duty of enforcement by bringing either criminal or civil proceedings in the courts. The Federal courts were given jurisdiction over enforcement procedures. Because of its very general phrasing, leaving the way open for multiple interpretations of the ideas of "restraint" and "monopolization," and because enforcement was to be through case-by-case litigation in the courts, the Act was in many senses a blank check written jointly to the Attorney General and to the courts. Each Attorney General could bring such actions as he saw fit, and the courts in each action, drawing upon but not unequivocally guided or strictly bound by such definitions of monopolization and restraint as had been developed in the common law, could define these crucial concepts as they were relevant to the cases that arose. In a broad sense, the Act was perhaps a congressional affirmation of the desirability of preserving a competitive economy, but in a more specific sense it was a prohibition of certain actions the legal definition of which was to be discovered by the courts when and as litigations were brought before them.

In view both of the character of the Act and of the lack of widespread interest in its enforcement, it is not astonishing that in the first 15 years of its history it was almost unused. From 1891 through 1905 only 22 cases were brought under it, of which only 18 concerned industrial combinations. Partly as a consequence, it was nine years before the general scope of the Act as applied to restraining agreements was made reasonably clear, and fourteen years before its applicability to monopolization by merger was even tentatively established.

This delay in establishing the scope of the Act resulted in substantial part, however, from the first important case to come before the Supreme Court, *U. S. vs. E. C. Knight Co.*, in 1895. Here the Court declined to apply the Act to a monopolistic combination under one ownership of nearly all the sugar refineries in the country, primarily on the narrow ground that the monopolization of *manufacture* was not the monopolization of interstate *commerce,* the effect on commerce being only indirect and incidental, and that the prohibitions of the Act thus did not apply. In addition, the Court remarked that Congress had not attempted to limit the right of corporations in the acquisition, control, or disposition of property, a statement that was widely held to mean that the Act could have no force as applied to monopolization or restraint by consolidations or mergers, which necessarily involved property transfers. The possibility of blanket exemption to all sorts of restraint was effectively removed in subsequent cases affecting loose-knit agreements, strategically in the *Addyston Pipe and Steel Co.* case, where an agreement restraining competition among iron pipe manufacturers was found illegal in 1899. (Fairly broad prohibition of such agreements among independent firms was thereafter rather consistently sustained.) But it was not until 1904, in the *Northern Securities Co.*[7] case, involving a railroad merger, that it was decided that the Act would definitely apply to restraints promulgated by

[7] The Northern Securities Company, a holding company, had acquired control of the stocks of the Great Northern and Northern Pacific railroads, competing lines. The court found that there was an illegal combination in restraint of interstate commerce and that holding companies formed under state corporation laws were in no wise thereby exempt from the prohibitions of the Sherman Act.

merger or other property transfer, and it was several more years before it was clinched that monopolization of manufacture by such a device could be in violation of the law.

"Trust-busting" Under the Sherman Act—1906–1920

The Roosevelt administration that took office in 1905 had made a campaign issue of "trust-busting"—dissolution of monopolistic mergers—and was the first administration committed to a vigorous prosecution of the then 15-year-old Sherman Act. Public interest in its enforcement was rallied in the election campaign. Moderately active enforcement of the Act was accordingly begun in 1906 and was carried on in the succeeding Taft and Wilson administrations. Thirty-seven cases were brought under the Roosevelt regime, 43 under Taft, and 53 in the first Wilson administration. Although many of these were minor cases involving restraining agreements, a number of the major cases of the era from 1905 to the close of World War I were concerned with the attempt to dissolve existing mergers that seemed to monopolize their respective industries.

The total effects of these prosecutions on the structure of American industry and on the character of competition was not very great. A few prominent mergers were indeed found in violation of the Sherman Act and were dissolved—notably the original Standard Oil Company, which had practically monopolized the refining of petroleum, and the Consolidated Tobacco Company, which occupied a similar position in tobacco manufacture. In a succession of cases decided at the conclusion of World War I, however, it became clear that the Court would dissolve established mergers only in exceptional circumstances. In the critical cases of *U. S. vs. United Shoe Machinery Co.* (1918) and *U. S. vs. United States Steel Corporation* (1920) the courts found that a merger controlling all or a substantial proportion of an industry was not in violation of the Sherman Act, provided that it was not currently either harassing or agreeing with its remaining rivals nor excluding others from the market. Size alone was no offense, and past sins were forgiven if current market behavior seemed orderly and there remained at least a hypothetical freedom to compete.

The judicial interpretation of the Act that underlay these decisions was, in effect, that its prohibition of monopolization was not directed at the phenomenon of industrial concentration or market control or at its implicit effect on competition, but rather at specific actions designed to exclude competitors or to restrain their ability to compete. The adverse decisions in the Oil and Tobacco cases turned strongly on the evidence of oppression of competitors, predatory pricing tactics, and "intent" to monopolize by the combinations in question. In the later cases where the Court found no violation, the combinations in question had long since abandoned predatory tactics and were following a "live and let live" policy with remaining competitors. The court declared that these combinations were neither monopolizing nor restraining trade; the modified sort of competition characteristic of highly concentrated industries constituted in the eyes of the Court no violation of the Sherman Act. The legal conception of monopoly, in short, drawn as it was from the common law, referred to specific overt actions of large firms and took little cognizance of the alteration of the character and effectiveness of market rivalry that accompanied the concentration of industrial markets.

The courts showed no disposition, therefore, to apply the penalties of the Sherman Act to the already typical American case of a highly concentrated industry, the ruthless tactics of whose member firms were in the past, their purpose having been accomplished, and the market behavior of whose members evidenced some limited degree of rivalry. Concentration was accepted as a *fait accompli*; further concentration was not discouraged, but large firms were perhaps admonished to avoid predatory tactics and to stop short of complete single-firm monopoly. For nearly two decades after 1920, therefore, few cases were brought to dissolve mergers. The Sherman Act had lain idle when it might have been employed to prevent concentration; it now appeared that it could not be used to dissolve most well-established combinations. As a result of their interpretation of the Act, it may be noted, the courts have largely spared themselves, and also the Attorney General, the task of solving the perplexing economic question of how far, in the interests of more vigorous competition, dissolutions of large firms could be carried without serious loss of the efficiencies of large-scale organization.

Although the meager results of anti-merger enforcement of the Sherman Act were attributable principally to the judicial construction of the law, and perhaps ultimately to the common-law definition of monopolization upon which the courts draw, there were other factors contributing to its inefficacy. By the time merger cases were brought to trial in any number, most combinations had been established for 20 or 30 years; their stock issues represented widely held investment values, and dissolution would have been quite disruptive of economic activity. In a number of industries, combination furthermore rested on patent control and licensing, and many of these combinations, because of the inclusiveness of the patent right, appeared to be immune to prohibitions of the Sherman Act. In cases like *U. S. vs. Standard Oil,* where relief was granted by the courts, the remedies granted by the courts altered only the surface appearance of the industry and took few of the steps essential to the real revival of competition. When the Standard Oil Company was ordered dissolved by the court, for example, it was directed that the shares of each of the 33 constituent corporations whose stock had been held by this holding company be distributed pro-rata to each of the stockholders of the holding company. As a result, the group of men who had held a controlling majority of stock in Standard Oil retained individual control of each of its member firms, and the "co-operation" of these members was not immediately impaired. Finally, the original phrasing of the Act was obviously such that it was not ideally adapted to the real regulation of market structure and competition. This, together with the timing of its enforcement, its narrow interpretation by the courts, and the espousal of an economic philosophy that found little amiss in the competitive behavior of concentrated markets, contributed to the manner in which mergers fared under the Sherman Act.[8]

Conclusion

At the close of the First World War, American industrial markets had assumed the typically concentrated form with which we are familiar today. The great wave of the merger movement was fifteen years past, and new patterns of competitive behavior appropriate to the revised industrial market structures were taking definite form. Avoidance of price competition, emphasis on non-price competition, and the development of intra-industry cooperation through trade associations were common trends, and a philosophy of market-sharing and live-and-let-live among rival firms tended to replace that of predatory market warfare. To this latter tendency the interpretation of the Sherman Act in merger cases probably contributed, since the courts had singled out overt acts of suppression and coercion of competitors as prime evidences of monopolization. The major movement toward monopoly or oligopoly in the economic sense—that is, toward domination of a market by one or few large firms—had not been arrested by the application of the anti-trust law, however. With the *Steel* and related decisions it appeared that established paterns of concentrated market control would not be disturbed, although there were some evident deterrents to the establishment by merger of complete or substantial single-firm monopoly in any industry. As the economy entered the post-war-period, therefore, a principal economic issue concerned the character and economic effects of the price and output policies that would be followed in the major industrial markets. A principal regulatory issue concerned the manner in which the anti-trust law might be used thereafter, either to influence behavior within concentrated markets or to influence the further development of their structures. We will turn to the development of that period in Chapter 46.

Government anti-trust policy in this postwar period had at its disposal two additional pieces of legislation passed in 1914—the Clayton Act and the Federal Trade Commission Act. Since the principal applications of these laws developed after World War I, we will postpone discussion of them also until Chapter 46.

---

[8] See Seager and Gulick, *Trust and Corporation Problems,* for a discussion of the leading merger cases under the Sherman Act.

Selected References

GENERAL WORKS

Berle, A. A., Jr., and G. C. Means, *The Modern Corporation and Private Property*. New York: Commerce Clearing House, Inc., 1932.

Burns, A. R., *The Decline of Competition*. New York: McGraw-Hill Book Company, Inc., 1936.

Fainsod, M. and L. Gordon, *Government and The American Economy*. New York: W. W. Norton & Company, Inc., 1941.

Hoover, E. M., and J. Dean, eds., *Readings in the Social Control of Industry*. Philadelphia: The Blakiston Company, 1942.

Laidler, H. W., *Concentration of Control in American Industry*. New York: The Thomas Y. Crowell Company, 1931.

Purdy, Harry L.; Martin L. Lindahl; and William A. Carter, *Corporate Concentration and Public Policy*. New York: Prentice-Hall, Inc., 1942.

Ripley, W. Z., *Main Street and Wall Street*. Boston: Little, Brown and Company, 1927.

Seager, H. R., and C. A. Gulick, *Trust and Corporation Problems*. New York: Harper and Brothers, 1929.

Watkins, M. W., *Industrial Combinations and Public Policy*. New York: Houghton Mifflin Company, 1927.

SPECIAL TOPICS

Hamilton, W., *Patents and Free Enterprise* (Temporary National Economic Committee, Monograph No. 31), 1941.

Handler, M., *Construction and Enforcement of the Federal Anti-Trust Laws* (Temporary National Economic Committee, Monograph No. 38), 1941.

Lyon, L. S.; M. W. Watkins; and V. Abramson, *Government and Economic Life*, Vol. I, Chapter 10. Washington, D. C.: Brookings Institution, 1939.

Moody, John, *The Truth About the Trusts*. New York: Moody Publishing Company, 1904.

33 · PUBLIC FINANCE AND FISCAL POLICY, 1866-1918

THE FURLING OF THE CONFEDERATE COLORS at Appomattox marked the beginning of a new era in all parts of the economy, both North and South. Manufacturing had undergone a great expansion under the stimulus of war and increased tariff protection. Agriculture was entering a new stage of development with the freeing of the slaves in the South and the impetus given the westward movement of population by free homesteading. The building of the railroads, greatly accelerated after the Civil War, was soon to alter the face of the country and to play an essential part in its development.

Federal Finances

For the Federal Government the return of peace meant reabsorbing into the Union the Southern states that had seceded. The Confederate debt ceased to exist as an economic factor at the end of the war, and the Union debt of $2,300,000,000 became the responsibility of North and South alike. Expenditures dropped sharply with the end of hostilities, but never approximated their pre-war level. Larger outlays for pensions and interest and a greatly inflated price level that affected all governmental costs were the war's legacy. When it became apparent that the Federal Government would need less revenue, Congress appointed a commission to study the revision of the tax system. The Special Revenue Commission objected particularly to the diffuseness of existing taxes and their duplication and recommended that taxes be concentrated on a few commodities, that all taxes on manufactures except those on liquor and tobacco products be abolished, but that excises on luxuries be retained. A surplus of $133,000,000 in 1867, equal to more than one-third of Federal expenditures in that year, emphasized the need for lower taxes. Although various excises were removed in 1867 and 1868, surpluses continued and that of 1870 was again over $100,000,000. Excises were further reduced in 1870, the inheritance tax was abolished, and the income tax was limited to two more years, although the Revenue Commission had regarded the latter as a tax on "realized wealth" and had favored its retention as a permanent feature of the tax system. The debates and the Congressional vote on continuing the income tax reflected both the sectional interests that resulted from the concentration of wealth in the Northeast—as indicated by the payment of 60 per cent of the tax of 1864 by the three states of New York, Pennsylvania, and Massachusetts—and the fact that this tax, paid by only somewhat more than 1 per cent of the population at its peak in 1866, had always been limited to a small group.

Efforts to reduce customs duties, which approximated 50 per cent of Federal revenue by the end of the decade, encountered more resistance as protectionist sentiment remained very strong. With southern representation absent from Congress during the war, northern industrialists succeeded in raising tariff duties to a new high level. But opposition to the tariff was growing among westerners and among consumers in general, and the uninterrupted succession of annual surpluses made existing tariff rates increasingly indefensible. A few rather unimportant reductions were made in 1870, and two years later, as part of their election propaganda the Republicans came out for lower tariffs. Various duties that gave no protection, such as those on tea and coffee, were abolished and protective duties were reduced 10 per cent, but no serious alterations were made in the protective system. When customs receipts dropped significantly during the depression that followed the crisis of 1873, protectionists seized the opportunity to restore the 10 per cent cut in duties in 1875. Revenue declined somewhat more than expenditures after the crisis of 1873, and smaller surpluses during the rest of the decade were absorbed by the need for redeeming fractional currency in silver and building up a gold reserve for the redemption of greenbacks.

The Problem of Surpluses

But surpluses became a problem again in the 1880's, averaging more than $100,000,000 annually. While there was some growth in civil expenditures and a great increase in pensions, interest payments declined as the debt was paid and there was little change in total expenditures, which fluctuated around $265,000,000. With a view to decreasing revenue, miscellaneous excises and taxes other than those on national banks were abolished in 1883, and the tobacco tax was cut in half. Revenue did not decline as much as anticipated, however, because the lower rates on liquor and tobacco gave less stimulus to evasion. In view of large surpluses it was difficult to deny the need for some sort of tariff reform, and Congress, therefore, appointed a special Tariff Commission in 1882, made up of representatives from agriculture, manufacturing, and commerce, to study revision of the existing system. The Commission recommended a 20 to 25 per cent reduction of duties on raw materials and articles of general consumption, but the act of 1883 showed little, if any, effect of the Commission's studies and, while it followed no consistent principle, made the system as a whole slightly more protective.

Since the laissez-faire conception of government still dominated the scene, there had been little growth in expenditures. Although President Arthur endorsed the building of a new steel navy as advisable from the standpoint of both protection and promotion of commerce and industry, he vetoed a bill for river and harbor improvements on the grounds that the amount called for was excessive and because he did not believe that the expenditure was for either the common defense or the general welfare. His successor, Cleveland, vetoed a bill repaying to the states the direct tax collected during the Civil War, since he did not believe such windfalls would be put to proper use. Cleveland also vetoed a bill granting more liberal pensions to disabled veterans and to veterans' dependents, and, although he signed more private pension bills than he vetoed and more than any of his predecessors had signed, his vetoes were so numerous as to discourage this continuous and indiscriminate drain on the Treasury. Furthermore, his veto of bills giving free seeds to farmers in distress was in line with his belief that "Though the people support the government, the government should not support the people."

On the other hand, taxes could not be collected and entirely withheld from the income stream without causing a tightening of the money markets. Depositing revenue from customs duties in national banks was felt to be questionable, inasmuch as such revenue was legally required to be set aside for paying the interest and principal of government bonds. Nevertheless, the policy of depositing government funds in national banks, secured by deposits of United States bonds with the Treasury, was followed to an increasing extent during Cleveland's term to ease the currency situation. This in spite of the fact that the practice had such serious disadvantages as opportunities for favoritism, the injustice of letting the banks have the free use of government funds and at the same time paying them interest on the bonds they had pledged as security, and the disturbing effect on credit and business in general of any withdrawal of government funds. The government also resorted to prepaying the interest on its bonds and to buying them in the open market, in order to keep down its surplus and to put its collections back into circulation again during the seasons when the credit and monetary stringency was most serious. The use of surplus funds to repay the debt, however, not only raised problems of governmental economy and of equity between taxpayers and bondholders, but also had a very direct effect on the currency. Reduction of the debt could not be viewed with complete equanimity insofar as bank notes were issued on the basis of government bonds and a reduction of the latter forced a contraction in the volume of circulating currency. Furthermore, bonds had been at a premium since shortly after the refunding of the Civil War debt had been completed in 1879. The 4 per cent thirty year bonds had gone to a premium of 25 per cent as early as 1883, and before they were due the government could borrow at 2½ per cent.

By 1888 the debt stood at $940,000,000 and all the bonds that were callable had been paid. In using the surplus to buy its own bonds the Treasury paid premiums as high as 30 per cent, and this procedure of using taxpayers' funds to pay a profit to bondholders naturally evoked violent protest.

The surplus was thus not only an economic, but a political issue as well. The Democrats did not take advantage of the opportunity to reduce duties after the election of 1884, in spite of the fact that the Treasury was experiencing an unprecedented succession of large surpluses. Cleveland became seriously concerned about the situation near the end of his first term, however, and devoted his entire message to Congress in 1887 to the problem of surplus revenue and to the necessity of reducing the tariff. The campaign of 1888, therefore, centered around the issue of the tariff, with the Democrats promising to reduce revenue by lowering and abolishing duties, and the Republicans promising to accomplish the same objective by revising the tariff to make it more protective. Harrison was elected and the Republicans, preferring to ignore the fact that 100,000 fewer popular votes had been cast for their candidate than for Cleveland and the lower tariff platform, raised duties still further in the McKinley Tariff of 1890, with a view both to greater protection and to the reduction of revenue. This act also introduced the principle of commercial reciprocity to be exercised by the President in bargaining with other countries, a principle that was to receive more emphasis in the twentieth century. The reduction in customs revenue was prompt and much greater than anticipated because of a slump in world trade. Internal revenue increased, in spite of a 25 per cent reduction of the tax on tobacco and the repeal of license taxes on the sale of tobacco in 1890, but not in sufficient amount to compensate for the decrease in customs receipts. Mindful of its campaign promise of greater expenditures, the Republican administration provided for repayment to the Northern states of the direct tax collected during the Civil War, a sum amounting to $15,000,000. While the decline in interest payments continued, outlays for rivers and harbors increased and expenditures for the navy mounted as the number of steel ships increased from three in 1889 to twenty-two in 1893. Pensions increased rapidly after the more liberal law of 1890 was passed, and by 1893 more than twice as many Northern veterans were receiving pensions as in 1889. When Cleveland was re-elected for a second term in 1892, the Democrats had an opportunity once again to lower tariff rates. But after arguing that the prevailing high level of prices and the growth of trusts stemmed from the protective tariff, they passed the Wilson-Gorman Act providing for rather mild reductions. Cleveland felt that the bill was much too protective and allowed it to become law without his signature.

The crisis of 1893 and the severe depression that followed during which more than four million were unemployed, put a damper on trade and decreased revenue sharply with the result that in 1894 the Treasury showed the first deficit since the Civil War. The Federal debt had been reduced to less than $600,000,000, but the simultaneous occurrence of a deficit and serious monetary difficulties, which were being reflected in a drain on the government's gold reserve, made it necessary for the Treasury to borrow for other than refunding purposes for the first time since the Civil War.

The Income Tax

Agitation for an income tax had been almost continuous after the expiration of the Civil War tax in 1872. The depression in industry and commerce following the crisis of 1873 was especially favorable to the development of this movement, and beginning with 1874 one or more bills were introduced at almost every session of Congress, with most of the support coming from southern and western Congressmen. The Democrats and other proponents of an income tax had long objected to the high tariff on both social and economic grounds and saw the income tax as at least a partial substitution for it. Since frequent changes in tariff rates were held to be disturbing to trade, they proposed levying more constant duties on imports and varying income tax rates according to the need of the government for revenue. An income tax was also more equitable, some maintained, because it would require contributions from individuals according to the protection and benefits they received from the government. Others argued that an income tax would be more equitable because it would impose a levy on individuals in proportion to their ability to pay, and would tax them on their surplus only, unlike tariff duties which impinged on necessities. Furthermore, the adoption of an income tax was favored because the effect of the tariff in fostering the growth of trusts and monopolies was held to be increasingly apparent. The Republicans and those opposed to an income tax, on the other hand, claimed that it would injure business by discouraging savings, that it would be harmful to capital values such as real estate and stocks, and that it would be practically unenforceable in peacetime because of lack of cooperation from the taxpayers. Far from promoting democracy they argued that it would have the opposite result, since, by exempting taxpayers with incomes under $4,000, it became class legislation and weakened the feeling of responsibility for government among the lower income groups. The reduction in revenue that would have ocurred under the original version of the Wilson-Gorman Act provided the opportunity for attaching a rider calling for a tax of two per cent on incomes over $4,000. Although the income tax was not needed to compensate for any reduction in customs receipts under the tariff bill as finally passed, agitation for it was so great that it was retained, with support coming again primarily from the South and the West. The question of constitutionality, which had been hotly argued by both sides, was soon brought before the Supreme Court where it was settled in the negative. In spite of the fact that the Supreme Court had declared the Civil War income tax to be an excise, it construed that of 1894 as a direct tax, and since the latter was not apportioned among the states according to population as direct taxes were required to be by the Constitution, the law was declared unconstitutional.

The war with Spain that broke out in 1898 created no serious financial problems for the government. Expenditures somewhat less than doubled as compared with a twenty-fold increase during the Civil War. Tariff rates had been raised shortly before the war by the Dingley Tariff Act of 1897, which the Republicans had passed at a special session of Congress called to consider the need for further revenue, the Democrats having been defeated in accordance with what has been the usual pattern of a change of administration following a depression. As soon as war was declared Congress authorized the Treasury to borrow and at the same time levied heavier internal revenue duties. The 3 per cent loan of $200,000,000 brought forth a subscription of $1,400,000,000, indicating both popular endorsement of the war and the need of the national banks for more government bonds as a basis for note issue. Tax rates on fermented liquors and tobacco were doubled, and many new excises were levied on commodities, businesses, occupations, commercial transactions, and financial instruments. For the third time during an emergency a tax was levied on the transfer of property at death, with the Supreme Court ruling that the rate was to be determined by the size of the beneficiaries' shares rather than by the size of the entire estate as Congress had intended. Both customs duties and internal revenue taxes were so productive that the deficit of $127,000,000 for the two war years was more than covered by the bond issue of $200,000,000. The various war excises were repealed with the decline of expenditures after the war and the reappearance of Treasury surpluses.

Increasing Public Expenditures and Revenues

Expansion of Federal activities became more marked after the opening of the twentieth century. Federal expenditures, which had fluctuated around $350,000,000 during the 1890's, never reached $500,000,000 before 1900 except in wartime. After 1900 Federal expenditures were less than $500,000,000 in only one year, and before the middle of the second decade of the century they were exceeding $700,000,000. Military expenditures became larger as the country added to its colonial possessions and the international situation made better defense seem imperative. Pensions expanded as veterans of the Spanish-American War were added to the rolls. Salaries were raised generally to meet the increased cost of living. The Panama Canal became an actuality and many new public buildings were erected. Civil expenditures increased as the government broadened its scope of activities with the creation of new agencies and departments and the expansion of old ones. The operations of the Post Office Department were greatly enlarged with the establishment of parcel post and postal savings systems and the extension of rural free delivery. More attention was given to assisting and encouraging agriculture, conserving natural resources, enforcing pure food laws, collecting better statistics, regulating railroads, and promoting measures designed to benefit commerce and labor.

Revenue likewise increased, since customs duties and excises on tobacco and liquor were very productive until World War I, but the recurrence of annual surpluses was interrupted by the crises of 1903 and 1907. The suffering of both individuals and businesses in the crisis of 1907 and the depression that followed evoked renewed outcries against the tariff. In their campaign platform in 1908 the Republicans promised a tariff that would equalize differences between the cost of production at home and abroad, although their candidate, Taft, made it clear that he favored a lower tariff. Having won the election, the Republicans passed the Payne-Aldrich Act of 1909 which made extensive changes in tariff rates, but on the whole made the system slightly more protective than before. Under this Act the principle of reciprocity—which according to the Dingley Tariff Act was to be exercised by the Senate rather than by the President, but which the Senate refused to exercise—was abandoned in favor of the so-called maximum and minimum principle. Minimum rates were to be those set forth in the Act and maximum rates 25 per cent higher were to be imposed at the discretion of the President on goods coming from countries that discriminated against the United States. Since Taft was anxious for lower duties, he used his influence to have the minimum duties put into effect immediately. The Payne-Aldrich Act also provided for the re-establishment of a Tariff Board to facilitate the administration of the maximum and minimum clause by the collection of data on costs of production at home and abroad.

The demand for more emphasis on direct taxes and less on indirect taxes had continued after the adverse decision of the Supreme Court on the income tax of 1894, but proposals for new taxes met with little success in view of Treasury surpluses. The slump in revenue after the crisis of 1907, however, and the obvious need for some sort of new revenue bill gave fresh impetus to the movement. Theodore Roosevelt had recommended both an income and an inheritance tax in his message to Congress in 1908, and in the presidential campaign later that year Taft spoke with favor of the income tax. The fact that in his message to Congress after the election Taft recommended the adoption of a graduated inheritance tax as a means of eliminating the deficit and did not mention an income tax can be accounted for at least partially by the loss of prestige he feared the Supreme Court would suffer if a new income tax law should be declared constitutional before the adoption of a constitutional amendment. While a graduated inheritance tax was attached to the Payne-Aldrich Tariff Act as passed by the House, in accordance with Taft's recommendation, the Senate rejected it and substituted a personal income tax. When it became clear that the continued opposition on the part of the administration to a personal income tax would result in a split in the Republican party, Taft sent a message to Congress recommending a tax on corporate income and an amendment to the Constitution that would permit the taxation of personal incomes without apportionment among the states. Congress agreed to this proposal, and levied a tax of 1 per cent on corporate incomes over $5,000, designating it an excise on the privilege of doing business in order to ensure its constitutionality. This tax on corporations was to be very productive of revenue in later years, but its other merits were to become the subject of prolonged debate in view of its uncertain incidence and economic effects. At the same time a coalition of Democrats and progressive Republicans succeeded in putting a resolution for an income tax through Congress in July 1909. Conservatives helped to pass the amendment in the belief that ratification by the states would not be forthcoming, but by February 1913 the amendment had been ratified by the necessary thirty-six states. Thus at last Congress was authorized to redistribute the costs of government by means of an income tax unhampered by court decisions.

Democratic Reforms

When the Democrats won the election of 1912 after four terms of Republican administration, both an income tax and tariff reform seemed within grasp. Inasmuch as it had long been argued that the income tax would make possible both a more equitable distribution of the costs of government and a reform of the protective tariff system, it was perhaps not illogical that Congress sought to accomplish both objectives in the Underwood-Simmons Tariff Act of 1913. The enactment of the personal income tax, a milestone in the development of Federal taxation, not only provided a more equitable basis for distributing the costs of government, but also brought into use a source that was to become the mainstay of Federal revenue. The tariff reform of the Underwood-Simmons Act had also been a long time in the making. Although the Act did not do away with protection, the free list was extended and rates were reduced somewhat more than 25 per cent on the average, or more than at any time since the Civil War. The maximum and minimum clause of the previous bill was dropped, and, since the Democrats had objected to the cost of production theory both in principle and in practice, they substituted the competitive tariff theory, according to which rates were to be set at a level such as to encourage foreign competition. The existing Tariff Board was thought to be superfluous and was abolished, but upon reconsideration another Tariff Commission was established in 1916 to undertake a continuing study of the fiscal, administrative, and economic aspects of the tariff.

Financial Aspects of World War I

Although the United States did not enter World War I until 1917, it was constantly under its shadow from the beginning. Even before our active participation in 1917, expenditures had started to increase rapidly as better military defense seemed imperative, and once hostilities were declared men and armaments were mobilized as quickly as possible. Expenditures totalled $1,978,000,000 in 1917 compared with $734,000,000 the year before, and by 1919 they were more than $18,500,000,000, a figure not to be equalled again until World War II.

Taxes

The disruption to trade after the outbreak of war in 1914 and the drop in customs receipts led to adoption of an emergency revenue measure in that year which levied new taxes and increased the rates of old ones. Excises were imposed on toilet articles, chewing gum, telephone and telegraph messages, and freight and express charges. Although taxes on liquor were increased, the adoption of the eighteenth amendment in 1916 resulted in a great loss of liquor excises. License taxes were imposed upon certain occupations, and stamp taxes were levied on various commercial transactions. Once the country was seriously engaged in active combat it was obvious that more drastic revenue measures would be necessary. For the fourth time during an emergency transfers of property at death were taxed, this time with rates determined according to the size of the entire estate. A capital stock tax was added and both corporate and personal income rates were increased.[1] Taxes on profits, an innovation of the war years, reflected the feeling of the time against the growth of a class of war millionaires. The profits of munitions manufacturers were made subject to tax in 1916 with the thought that it was only proper that the government should share in gains that resulted directly from the war. It was apparent very soon, however, that munition manufacturers were not alone in benefitting from the war, and since it seemed appropriate that all profits in a wartime economy should be shared generally, an excess profits tax was imposed in 1917. The base for the tax was a combination of normal earnings and invested capital, emphasis being given to the lat-

[1] The normal rate of the personal income tax was increased from a flat one per cent in 1913 to six per cent on the first $4,000 and 12 per cent on income over $4,000 in 1918. Surtax rates which had ranged from one per cent on income over $20,000 to six per cent on income over $500,000 in 1913, extended from one per cent on income over $5,000 to 65 per cent on income over $1,000,000 in 1918. The corporate income tax was increased from one per cent in 1913 to 12 per cent in 1918.

ter with the thought that if the tax was successful it could be retained permanently.

Borrowing

But it was not to be expected, of course, that taxation could furnish all the necesary funds or that it could provide them quickly enough, and consequently borrowing was inevitable. The Federal debt increased from somewhat more than $1,000,000,000 in 1916 to $25,000,000,000 in 1919, and the per capita debt, which had fallen from $75 during the Civil War to less than $12 in 1915, stood at $242 in 1919. While nearly three-quarters of the Federal debt bore 2 per cent interest in 1916, under war conditions the Treasury found it necessary to pay 3½ to 4¾ per cent on the four Liberty Loans and the Victory Loan that were floated, the variations in interest being due in part to differing tax exemption privileges. Without the Federal Reserve system, established in 1913, the successful prosecution of the war would have been much more difficult. Bonds were sold mainly through the Federal Reserve banks, which distributed them to their member banks, and the latter sold them to the public. An attempt was made to tap the savings of the lower income groups by the issue of war savings certificates that had a maturity value of $5 and bore interest at 4½ per cent and war savings stamps that had a value of 25 cents and bore no interest, but could be exchanged in sufficient volume for certificates.

World War I is estimated to have cost the United States about $35,000,000,000, including loans of $9,000,000,000 to the Allies. Although the Treasury had hoped in the beginning that half of the cost could be met by taxation, about one-third of the direct outlay of $26,000,000,000 was actually met by taxes and the remainder by loans. The financing of this war, however, was definitely superior to that of the Civil War, because the government relied to a greater extent upon taxes and thus lessened both the amount of inflation and its inevitable inequities and other consequences and the postwar problem of transferring funds from taxpayers to bondholders. Furthermore, the revenue measures adopted were more progressive. Almost one-third of Federal revenue was derived from income and profit taxes in 1917, and under the heavier rates levied in 1918 and 1919, these taxes contributed about three-fifths of all Federal revenue.

State and Local Finances

State and local expenditures were of much greater magnitude after the Civil War, reflecting the higher price level, heavier interest charges on expanded debts, the wider scope of governmental functions, and the prevalence of graft throughout the country, but especially in the South. Rabble from the North known as "carpetbaggers" and Southern "scalawags" obtained control of government in the South and inaugurated a period of great extravagance and corruption. Although they left some roads and bridges to their credit and advanced the cause of common education, on the whole there were few benefits to show for the large debts incurred, many of which were later repudiated. With the decline in revenue after the crisis of 1873, many local governments in both the North and the South repudiated their debts. But once prosperity returned, state and local obligations were gradually reduced until the turn of the century, when states began to borrow considerable sums for the construction of highways. State and local expenditures doubled in the last decade of the nineteenth century and continued to increase rapidly in the twentieth century, stimulated by the growth of population, the expansion of governmental functions, and the more intensive development of old functions, until by 1915 they constituted 75 per cent of all governmental expenditures. The steady progress of industrialization led to greater concentration of population and increased urbanization, which were reflected in higher governmental costs for police and fire protection, sanitation, roads, and streets. The movement of population away from rural areas to cities and towns was given increased impetus by floods of immigrants who settled in urban areas, and made the costs of various municipal services greater than they would have been for a homogeneous population. In the ten years preceding World War I, more than 10,000,000 immigrants came into the country, or almost one-third of the total number admitted in the previous century. Greater industrialization also made old standards of service outmoded and necessitated larger expenditures to achieve satisfactory results. Education, the largest item of expenditure, was much more firmly established at the end of the Civil War in the North and West, where elementary schooling was practically universal, than in the South. Reconstruction governments set up the first public school systems in several southern states and made provision in the constitutions of a number of them for common schools and their support. Gradually longer attendance came to be required and the curriculum was broadened as the movement for high schools spread throughout the country by the end of the nineteenth century.

Sources of Revenue

In the years between the Civil War and World War I, the major source of state revenue and practically the only source of local revenue was the general property tax. State boards of equalization were established in an effort to improve and supervise the administration of the tax, to equalize assessments, and to provide for state assessment of railroads. Boards of equalization were finally replaced by state tax commissions, which were entrusted with all the functions of the old boards and were also given supervision over the new taxes on business. Assessment and evasion became increasingly difficult problems as intangible property such as mortgages, stocks, and bonds multiplied. By 1913, twelve states had adopted classified property taxes with law rates on intangibles, which were more equitable and gave less stimulus to evasion.

As for other sources of revenue, taxes on state banks became less important after the establishment of the national banking system. Various kinds of special taxes were imposed on business after the Civil War—such as taxes on the so-called corporate excess and on capital stock—as well as on railroads. New impetus was given to the adoption of state inheritance taxes by the New York law of 1885 that taxed collateral heirs. Seven years later New York levied a tax on direct heirs, which is often regarded as the first modern direct inheritance tax, since the North Carolina tax of 1855 was abolished in 1874. Progressive rates were generally adopted, and only three states had not levied inheritance taxes by 1913. The most important innovation of the period, however, was the adoption of an income tax by Wisconsin in 1911, that, contrary to popular opinion as to the feasibility of a state income tax, proved very successful. When revenue from liquor excises was lost after the ratification of the eighteenth amendment, several more states turned to using an income tax.

Aid from one level of government to another also began to be significant in these years, as states began granting increasing amounts to their subdivisions for education. When the country caught its breath after the Civil War and abundant surpluses began appearing annually during the 1880's, the general lack of educational facilities in the South led to pressure for Federal aid for education to be distributed to the states on the basis of illiteracy. The Freedmen's Bureau, a branch of the Army, sometimes called the Federal government's first big venture in relief, had established special courts and relief centers and had opened special schools for the Negroes immediately after the war. There was considerable feeling that, even aside from the economic incapacity of the South, the education of the Negro was the responsibility of the entire country and that such education might very largely solve many aspects of the problem of the Negro in contemporary society. Sectional feeling over the proposal for Federal aid was somewhat assuaged by the fact that the North had long been receiving pensions paid in part by southern taxes. But the measure was out of tune with the political philosophy of the times. Its opponents argued that it would result in less local initiative and effort, might make future demands on the Federal Treasury more difficult to resist, and would probably be declared unconstitutional. In the end the bill did not even have the support of the southern senators. The Federal Government had actually begun extending some aid to the states for education during the Civil War under the Morrill Act of 1862, which donated lands to the states for the endowment of colleges of agriculture and mechanical arts. The Second Morrill Act of 1890 granted annual funds for the same purpose, and the Hatch Act of 1887 granted annual funds for agricultural experiment stations. The whole question of Federal aid for education, however, was to receive much more attention during the middle of the twentieth century. Grants to the states from the Federal Government were of little significance before World War I, constituting only 1 per cent of all state revenue in 1915. But the rapid growth of motor transportation was already foreshadowing the importance that intergovernmental aid for highways was to have in the future for all levels of government.

Conclusion

During the latter half of the nineteenth century the principal financial problem of the Federal Government continued to be that of surpluses. Revenue exceeded expenditures for a quarter of a century after the Civil War. The Federal Government weathered the severe crisis of 1873 and the subsequent depression without a deficit, and in the following decade surpluses assumed larger proportions, amounting in one year to more than 50 per cent of expenditures. During the next twenty years, which encompassed the crisis of 1893, the Spanish-American War, and the crises of 1903 and 1907, surpluses became intermittent and of smaller magnitude, approximating 10 to 15 per cent of expenditures or less. As in the first half of the nineteenth century, Treasury surpluses might have had a more restricting effect in these years if practically all segments of the economy had not been undergoing a very rapid expansion.

It was not until the last decade of the century that changes in both political philosophy and economic conditions began to be reflected in a more favorable attitude towards governmental activity, which led in turn to more generous expenditures. Historically, laissez-faire had developed as a reaction against the mercantilist system under which the mass of the people had little control over governmental operations, which were seldom undertaken in their behalf. As democratic control over government gradually became better established with the extension of the vote, the direct primary, the popular election of senators, the use of the Australian ballot, woman suffrage, and the use of the initiative and the referendum, wider government activity met with greater approval. It was no mere coincidence, furthermore, that the scope of governmental functions expanded simultaneously with the disappearance of the geographical frontier. Nearly all of the good land was privately owned by 1900, and a subsistence was no longer available to anyone who might stake out his claim, as had been true earlier when almost all land west of the Alleghenies had been publicly owned. Nor is it surprising that in an economy that was largely agrarian, one of the first indications of the changing attitude towards governmental activity was the establishment of a department of agriculture in 1862, which was given cabinet rank in 1889. Indicative of the growing feeling that the government should take an interest in wage earners as a group was the creation of a Bureau of Labor in the Department of Interior in 1884 and the establishment of a separate department without a cabinet seat in 1888. The development of a new type of governmental activity was presaged about the same time by the establishment of the Interstate Commerce Commission in 1888 and the passing of the Sherman Anti-Trust Act in 1890. Although the railroads had received liberal public assistance in the form of loans and grants of land, their operation became so discriminatory as to make regulation by the government seem necessary. Similarly, the growth of trusts and monopolies, fostered in part by the high tariff, brought forth such violent criticism that Congress was impelled to provide for government investigation and prosecution. On the other hand, the concern of the Government for the welfare of business and industry in general was recognized by the establishment of a Department of Commerce and Labor in 1903 with full cabinet rank, and its division ten years later into two separate departments. Gradually the interests of the various segments of the economy came to be represented in the government, and the doctrine of laissez-faire and non-interference began to be modified more and more in favor of a broadening of governmental activity.

Budgetary considerations were not decisive in the determination of Federal revenue policy during most of the period. Excises on liquor and tobacco were retained after the Civil War and—together with customs duties, previously the mainstay of the Treasury—accounted for practically all Federal revenue until World War I. No great protest arose against excises, perhaps because they did not result in profit to any special group, they were looked upon as being shared fairly evenly, and they were considered to be sumptuary in nature. But the tariff had long been the cause of great dissension; it impinged heavily on various necessities, it was much more burdensome to some groups than others, and it granted special privileges that resulted in large profits to certain industries. Protectionist forces were so strong, nevertheless, that they succeeded in maintaining high tariff rates in spite of ample surpluses. With the ratification of the Sixteenth Amendment and the enactment of an income tax, the long struggle for Federal tax reform was won. But, inasmuch as the structure of the tariff during most of the nineteenth century, had not been determined primarily by the need for revenue, it was hardly to be expected that the protective system would be swept away with the introduction of the income tax. Although tariff rates were reduced in 1913 to a lower level than at any time since the Civil War, certain industries continued to enjoy the privileges of protective rates. The income tax law of 1913 culminated the growing feeling that Federal taxation should be based more largely upon ability to pay. In the past various indirect means had been used to increase the income of particular groups, such as agriculture, labor, industry, and commerce. Regulatory measures had been adopted, on the other hand, to prevent large accumulations of wealth, by railroads, trusts, and monopolies, that were considered socially unjustifiable. But henceforth, Congress could directly affect the distribution of income by levying a tax on personal income to finance the activities of the Federal Government.

Selected References

Beard, C. A., and M. R., *A Basic History of the United States.* New York: Doubleday and Co., Inc., 1949.

———, *The Rise of American Civilization.* New York: The Macmillan Co., 1947.

Buck, P. H., *The Road to Reunion, 1865-1900.* Boston: Little, Brown and Co., 1947.

Dewey, D. R., *Financial History of the United States,* 11th ed. New York: Longmans, Green and Co., 1931.

Leland, S. E., *The Classified Property Tax in the United States.* Boston: Houghton Mifflin Co., 1928.

Lutz, H. L., *The State Tax Commission.* Cambridge, Mass.: Harvard University Press, 1918.

Noyes, A. D., *Forty Years of American Finance, 1865-1907.* New York: G. P. Putnam's Sons, 1909.

Ogg, F. A., *National Progress, 1907-1917.* New York: Harper and Brothers, 1918.

Ratchford, B. U., *American State Debts.* Durham, N. C.: Duke University Press, 1941.

Ratner, Sidney, *American Taxation.* New York: W. W. Norton and Co., Inc., 1942.

Shultz, W. J., and M. R. Caine, *Financial Development of the United States.* New York: Prentice-Hall, Inc., 1937.

Shultz, W. J., *The Taxation of Inheritance.* Boston: Houghton Mifflin Co., 1926.

Annual Report, Secretary of the Treasury.

Financial Statistics of States, Bureau of the Census, U. S. Department of Commerce.

Financial Statistics of Cities, Bureau of the Census, U. S. Department of Commerce.

34 · THE PERFORMANCE OF THE AMERICAN ECONOMY 1866-1918

IN THE PERIOD that elapsed between the end of the Civil War and the end of World War I, the structure of the American economy underwent a profound change, although the change was a gradual one and was not crucially influenced by the Civil War itself. Not until some time later, in fact, did it become evident that American economic development had entered a new era in which manufacturing was beginning to make a greater contribution to national income than agriculture.[1] But the war probably hastened the movement by reducing the influence of the agricultural, low-tariff South. This internal change meant that a predominantly open, world-dependent, and relatively undeveloped economy had become a predominantly closed, self-sufficient, and intensively organized economy. The trend of the country's economic growth was fundamentally altered thereby and so was its performance in war and peace.

[1] The change in the relative importance of agriculture and manufacturing may be observed in Figure 1, which traces the percentage shares of these two industries in realized private production income. From 30.8 per cent for agriculture and 12.1 per cent for manufacturing in 1859, the proportions change to 12.3 per cent for agriculture and 30.3 per cent for manufacturing in 1937. (Robert F. Martin, *National Income in the United States, 1799-1938*, pp. 60-61. New York: National Industrial Conference Board, 1939.)

The declining relative importance of agriculture may be traced to the passing of the frontier—that is, the extensive frontier in terms of free land in the West. With the elimination of free land, the rate of growth of agriculture became stabilized and the drainage of labor and capital from the potential manufacturing areas of the East was reduced. This does not mean that agricultural development had reached a stationary condition. Intensive development took place, of course, and has continued to this day.

The changes in the field of manufacturing may be traced largely to the influence of the Industrial Revolution on the United States. The growth of population through immigration and natural increase created an enlarged market and increased the labor supply. Improvements in transportation, mainly in the building of transcontinental lines, increased the accessibility of the market and made the various sections of the economy more interdependent. These developments, together with improved financial and distribution facilities, made possible the extensive introduction of machine technology and mass production in manufacturing. Manufacturing contributed an increasing share of the national income, and it surpassed agriculture in income production even before the end of the nineteenth century. The number of persons employed in manufacturing exceeded that in agriculture somewhat later because of the high labor productivity in mechanized factory production. These developments automatically meant a more self-sufficient economy.

Peacetime Crises and Cycles

In those parts of the period following the Civil War in which this country was at peace, the economy showed evidence that it was maturing out of one cause of instability and into another. In the period before the war, economic crises had resulted mainly from a combination of frontier land speculation and an inadequate and unreliable currency supply. These were a function of the rapid growth of the economy and

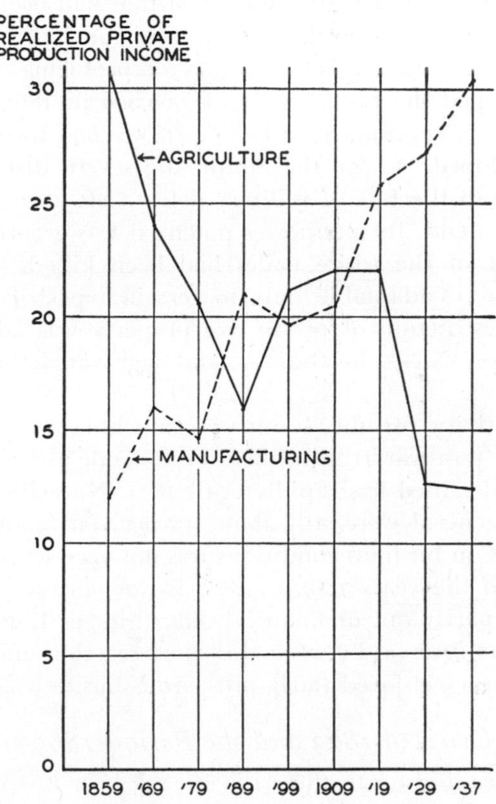

FIG. 1. *Percentage Shares of Agriculture and Manufacturing in Realized Private Production Income, 1859-1937.* (Source of basic data: National Industrial Conference Board.)

found their origin largely in outside factors, such as agricultural conditions and wars. Now the speculation that took place was based on investment in plant and equipment, such as is involved in railroad building and the opening up of factories; the expansion was geared to the supply of deposit money rather than to that of currency. The country also now became more sensitive to internal, regional fluctuations as a national, interdependent economy grew up. Any change in one part of the country was felt in other parts sooner and more seriously than a decade before. The gradual passing of the extensive or geographical frontier thus changed the type of problem but did not produce less serious problems.

Post-War Reconstruction

The end of the Civil War necessitated a sharp readjustment in the North. War demands had overexpanded both manufacturing and agriculture. A much lower level of activity was adequate for peacetime purposes. On the financial side, the great public debt that had been incurred necessitated a heavy transfer burder of taxation, and the depreciated fiat money, still in circulation, left a legacy of problems. Government expenditures dropped sharply from $1,300,000,000 in 1865 to $536,000,000 in 1866, while tax revenues rose from $348,000,000 to $572,000,000 and a surplus developed. As for the South, the severe disruptive effects of the war, added to the fact of military defeat, left a very different economy at the war's end. Its manpower potential was greatly reduced, since a large number of the white males had been killed. The slave labor was, unfortunately, adaptable only to certain types of production. Actual physical destruction of productive property was added to the economic dislocation caused by the war, and aggravated the post-war problems of the South.

Economic activity for the country as a whole was not too greatly affected by the post-war readjustment. Wholesale prices fell sharply in 1865 and then declined less rapidly until 1871. Nevertheless, at the later date prices in general were still about 35 per cent above their pre-war level. The effect on business conditions was not very severe. Such reaction as took place in the years 1865 to 1867 is not entirely traceable to the war, but arose partly out of financial difficulties in England during the year 1866. In the interval between this short reaction and the end of the decade, the country enjoyed fairly prosperous business conditions.

The Crisis of 1873 and the Period 1869–1879 [2]

The factors leading up to the crisis of 1873 bear a strong resemblance to those surrounding the several crises of the pre-war period: financial disturbances precipitated the decline, and overinvestment (in railroads, now, instead of land) was the major weakness in the underlying situation. The crisis is frequently regarded as part of a postponed readjustment arising out of the Civil War and its attendant inflationary disturbances.[3] It is difficult, however, to discover disruptive forces that were

[2] See Willard L. Thorp, *Business Annals,* pp. 130-133 (New York: National Bureau of Economic Research, 1926); and O. M. W. Sprague, *History of Crises under the National Banking System,* pp. 1-107 (Washington: National Monetary Commission, Sen. Doc. No. 538, 1910).

[3] See, for instance, *First Annual Report of the Commissioner of Labor, 1886: Industrial Depressions,* p. 60. Washington: Government Printing Office, 1886. The reader

created by the war and then lay dormant for nearly a decade before coming to the fore. Rather, the war interrupted the gathering railroad boom and thereby postponed the sharp reaction to be expected from the hectic financing and the overbuilding that had taken place. The behavior of prices and business activity during this period is portrayed in Figure 2.

The decade of favorable business conditions following the war was geared mainly to investment activity in the railroad industry, the financing of which was facilitated to some extent by considerable inflows of foreign capital. A general boom developed, but it carried with it the seeds of its own destruction. At that time the economy displayed two characteristics that have since lost their relative importance. First of all, the "marginal propensity to import" was high: an increase in national income resulted in greatly increased imports, since many desirable products, particularly luxuries, were of foreign manufacture. Second, the stability of the country's financial structure, both monetary and banking, was dependent on the supply of specie. The increased national income resulting from the railroad boom brought about an increase in imports and led to a capital outflow, in the form of gold. This loss contributed to a financial crisis, which broke in September, 1873. Although in looking back it is apparent that the breaking point was near, the panic when it actually occurred took the economy unawares.[4]

The financial crisis, from rather small beginnings, soon spread throughout the economy. When the important Jay Cooke and Company failed as a result of its attempts to finance the Northern Pacific,[5] bankers and brokers in general felt the pinch, and many went bankrupt. The New York Stock Exchange had to close its doors, and bank suspensions were widespread.[6] Again the country's delicate financial structure had been set off-balance, with disruptive effects on the whole economy.

In the depression that followed the financial crisis, the only favorable developments lay in the financial sphere and in international trade. The financial situation soon improved, largely because of expansive Treasury measures. The developments in international trade consisted of the

---

may also find interest in the section on "Causes of Depression as Elicited by Committees of Congress," pp. 61-63.

[4] The signs of trouble were there nevertheless. "The crisis of 1873 did not come without loud warnings. In the two preceding years, at the autumn season, money was scarce and rates of interest were high. On the 2nd of October, 1871, bank reserves in New York city exceeded requirements by only $3,666,943. On the 3rd of October, 1872, there was a deficiency in reserves of $1,131,436. On the 28th of February, 1873, a deficiency appeared again, and although there was an increase of reserves in June, rates of interest were high and displayed abnormal fluctuations." (Theodore E. Burton, *Financial Crises,* p. 288. New York and London: D. Appleton-Century Company, 1931.)

[5] For a vivid description of the events surrounding this failure, see Charles A. Collman, *Our Mysterious Panics: 1830-1930,* pp. 98 ff. New York: William Morrow & Company, 1931. See also, "Panic in Wall Street," *Harper's Magazine,* Vol. XLVIII, p. 128. New York: Harper and Brothers, 1874.

[6] Collman, *Our Mysterious Panics,* pp. 103-107.

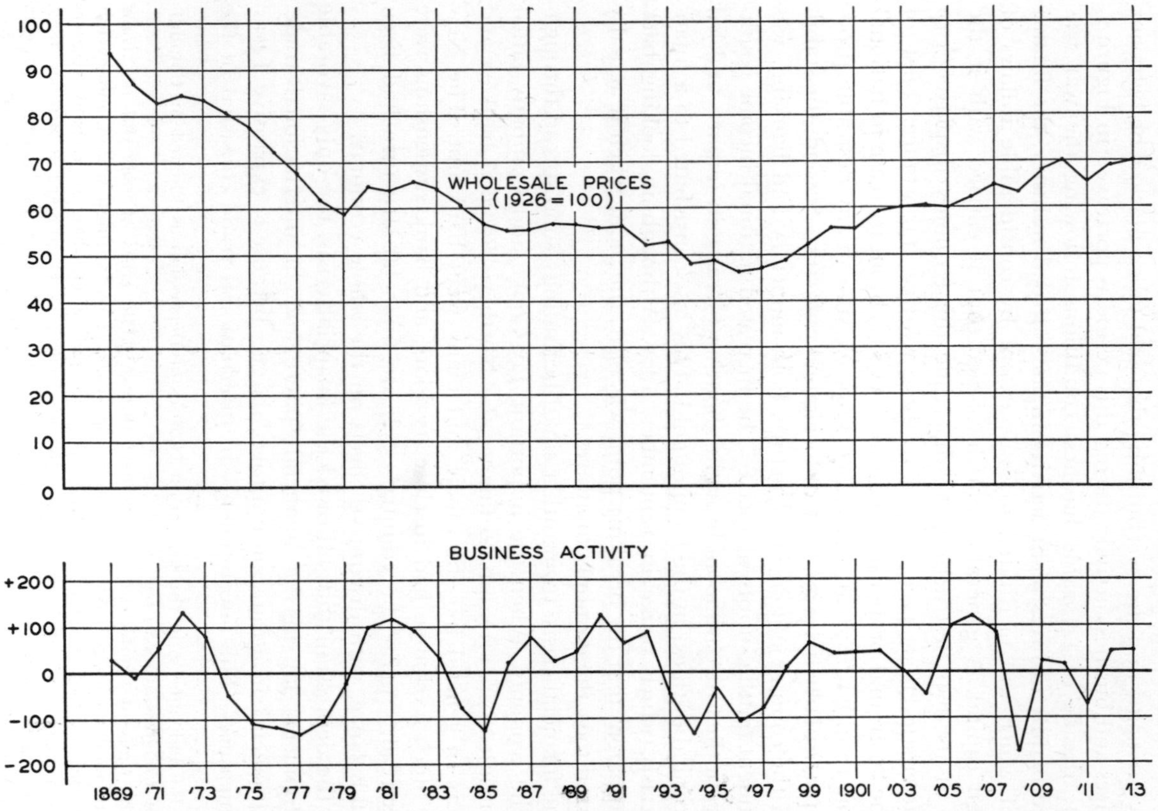

FIG. 2. *Wholesale Prices and Business Activity, 1869-1913.* (Sources of basic data: "Wholesale Prices," United States Bureau of Labor Statistics; "Business Activity," Cleveland Trust Company.)

establishment of a "favorable" balance of commodity trade, which removed one cause of the gold outflow. This "favorable" balance was partly achieved, however, by a reduction of imports, and so cannot be regarded with unmixed approval. The decline in imports was a reflection of a downward revision of both domestic prices and national income, the elasticity of the demand with respect to price and income for imported goods having been very high. Hence, the decline in domestic prices relative to world prices, and the decline in national income accompanying the depressed state of business activity, reduced the demand for imported goods. At the same time, the relative price adjustments improved the position of the export industries and led to an increase in exports. The country as a whole was, however, in the depths of a business depression that lasted four years. It has been customary to consider this depression as comparable to that of the 1930's but a recent study suggests that the relative degree of unemployment in the earlier period was much less than in the more recent period.[7]

The recovery became noticeable toward the end of 1878, and the level of business improved during that year and the one following. The recovery may be traced largely to an exogenous factor—the coincidence of record wheat and corn crops here with European crop failures in 1879 and 1880. Agriculture prospered and expanded, and the increased exports led to gold imports, which facilitated the resumption of specie payments. Railroad building and general manufacturing were stimulated. The country entered upon a period of exhilarating prosperity.

The Crisis of 1884 and the Period 1879–1889 [8]

The crisis of 1884 was an almost purely financial reaction with only minor repercussions on the economy as a whole. Again the hectic financing of the railroads was at the root of the difficulties. This, added to a series of business failures and a state of general uncertainty over the country's ability to remain on the gold standard, tightened up the money and capital markets. The main feature of the brief depression period was the scarcity of funds on the money market,[9] but it took only a few weeks for the financial crisis to pass, and the subsequent depression in general business activity lasted barely more than a year.

The recovery in business activity took place in the second half of 1885, and by 1887 the country was once again enjoying prosperity. Railroad building was resumed and led to a renewal of speculation in Western

---

7 Rendigs Fels, "The Long-Wave Depression, 1873-97," *Review of Economics and Statistics*, February 1949, pp. 69-73.

8 See Thorp, *Business Annals*, pp. 133-135; and Sprague, *History of Crises under the National Banking System*, pp. 108-123.

9 For a description of the fall of many prominent men and firms in the crisis of 1884, see Collman, *Our Mysterious Panics*, pp. 132-150.

land, a buying movement that was accentuated by the increasing scarcity of undeveloped areas. The heavy industries that were geared to railroad expansion, particularly iron and steel, also boomed, and manufacturing and agriculture were favorably affected.

The Crisis of 1893 and the Period 1889–1899[10]

Once more, in the crisis of 1893, monetary factors played a major role in creating panic and depression. In the period surrounding the crisis, the major point of financial uncertainty was the status of the gold standard.[11] This uncertainty resulted in an outflow of capital through the sale of American investments by foreigners. The loss of capital, together with the bankruptcy of several railroads, placed an unbearable strain on the banks, and they finally had to suspend. The volume of bank loans contracted, currency rose to a premium, and substitutes for it were used.[12]

The crisis passed rather soon but an unfortunate combination of monetary and fiscal factors kept the country in an unstable financial condition. The growing movement favoring free silver renewed the uncertainty regarding the maintenance of the gold standard.[13] At the same time, the Government found it increasingly difficult to stay on the gold standard. Because of a great amount of imports and a reduction of investments by foreigners in this country, there was an outflow of gold from the country. In addition to this outflow, a considerable amount of gold was being hoarded within the country because of the uncertain monetary situation.

The financial stringency of 1893 prefaced three and a half years of business depression similar to that which followed the crises of 1837 and 1873. By the end of the crisis year itself, a large number of business and banking failures had taken place. The whole state of depressed business activity was beclouded by continued uncertainty regarding the maintenance of the gold standard and the results of the presidential election.

The turning point came in the latter part of 1896, when a number of favorable events improved the financial situation and paved the way for a business recovery. The uncertainty arising out of the presidential election was removed with the defeat of the Free-Silver party. A favorable movement in exchange rates reversed the outflow of gold, and an

---

[10] See Thorp, *Business Annals,* pp. 135-138; and Sprague, *History of Crises under the National Banking System,* pp. 124-215.

[11] See Frank Weberg, *The Background of the Panic of 1893,* pp. 59-60. Washington, D. C.: The Catholic University of America, 1929.

[12] See Collman, *Our Mysterious Panics,* pp. 168-174.

[13] Weberg gives the silver-purchase policy a more direct place and claims "that the inflation of currency through silver legislation with no assurance that it could be controlled, and with no method of contraction provided for, was an important cause of the panic of 1893 and of the years of depression that followed." Weberg, *The Background of the Panic of 1893,* p. 58.

improvement in the Government's fiscal position permitted the Treasury to put an end to the loss of gold. Both agriculture and industry improved.

The Crises of 1903 and 1907 and the Period 1899–1913[14]

The crises of 1903 and 1907 were financial in their origin and had only brief repercussions on the economy as a whole. In this they resembled strongly the reactions that had occurred in 1857 and 1884. The financial difficulties of 1903 were largely a result of speculation in securities that had begun with a rise in stock values in 1897. During the period 1898 to 1902, a great trust movement was under way, and the country swarmed with promoters who were able to foist watered stock on an unsuspecting public. The reaction came in 1903, when some of the trusts failed. Apart from the steel industry, which suffered greatly, prices remained steady and business activity was affected only to a slight extent. The whole business recession had run its course by the end of 1904. As indicated in Figure 2, a favorable level of business activity was maintained in the years 1899 to 1902, and then a decline occurred in 1903 and 1904. The level of realized national income did not drop, although the rate of increase declined. There was an increase of $1,200,000,000 from 1902 to 1903 and of only $500,000,000 from 1903 to 1904.[15] A brisk recovery then took place.

The overexpansion of the trust companies lay at the bottom of the difficulties in 1907 just as it had in 1903. The panic broke when the Knickerbocker Trust closed in October.[16] A tight money market ensued, and all the characteristics of a banking crisis appeared. Call money advanced to 70 per cent.[17] An indirect and favorable result of the unfavorable monetary developments was an increase in gold imports resulting from the premium on specie. The most noteworthy characteristic of the depression was its brief duration. As revealed by Figure 2, however, the decline in business activity was quite severe. Industry and trade were stagnant, business failures took place, and there was widespread unemployment. Numerous railroads went into receivership, and foreign trade declined. Realized national income fell nearly a billion dollars from 1907 to 1908.[18] Commodity prices fell from their high level of 1907 to a low in the summer of 1908.

The crisis itself was relieved in part by a number of Federal activities. The Government established a fund for extending credit and also au-

---

14 See Thorp, *Business Annals,* pp. 138-141; and Sprague, *History of Crises under the National Banking System,* pp. 216-320.

15 See Robert F. Martin, *National Income in the United States, 1799-1938,* p. 6. New York: National Industrial Conference Board, 1939.

16 Collman, *Our Mysterious Panics,* pp. 235-243.

17 See *Annals of the American Academy of Political and Social Science,* Vol. 31, 1908, p. 309.

18 Martin, *National Income in the United States,* p. 6.

thorized the issuance of clearinghouse loan certificates. The financial stringency passed by the end of the year, and in 1909 business revived and the country enjoyed mild prosperity. Then followed a recession in 1910, a mild recession in 1911, followed by revival and prosperity for the next two years. Prices also recovered in 1909 and rose to a peak in the spring of 1910. Then prices declined to a low level in May, 1911. Thereafter prices rose to the end of the period, and in 1913 the general level of wholesale prices was 34 per cent above 1899.

Economic Changes During the First World War: 1914–1918 [19]

During World War I the American economy was severed from one part of the world economy and was allied with the other part in destroying the common enemy. The war years, 1914-1918, had a very uneven effect on the country as a whole. A panic and depression at the outbreak of war were turned into a period of prosperity when the temporary maladjustments were corrected and when it became evident that the war would last for some time. Then the United States' entry into the war propelled the economy into wartime boom and inflation. During this war period the country exhibited great sensitiveness to influences exogenous to the private domestic economy, both from foreign countries and from the Government.

The general state of indecision that prevailed because of uncertainty regarding the length of the war hampered business during the major part of the first two years of war. This unsettled condition may be seen in the low level of the index of business activity in 1914 and, to a lesser extent, in 1915,[20] as shown in Figure 3. Then, in the summer of 1915, when it became evident that at least another year of war was to be expected, business activity improved on the basis of war orders. The actual entry of the United States into the war brought with it new financial as well as military responsibilities. It was necessary to furnish funds to support the war effort of this country and of the Allies. Here again, as in preceding wars, the Government resorted to inflationary finance. The great release of purchasing power through expenditures was only in small degree offset by the taxation and borrowing program, which impinged very slightly on consumer purchases. The taxes in force [21] had

[19] See Thorp, *Business Annals,* pp. 142-143; E. L. Bogart, *Direct and Indirect Cost of the Great World War* (Carnegie Endowment for International Peace, *Preliminary Economic Studies of the War,* ed. by David Kinley, No. 24, New York: Oxford University Press, 1919); J. M. Clark, *The Costs of the World War to the American People* (New Haven: Yale University Press, 1931); and B. M. Anderson, Jr., *Effects of the War on Money, Credit and Banking in France and the United States* (Carnegie Endowment for International Peace, in the series cited above, No. 15).

[20] See Clark, *The Costs of the World War to the American People,* p. 22.

[21] See Bogart, *Direct and Indirect Cost of the Great World War,* p. 170.

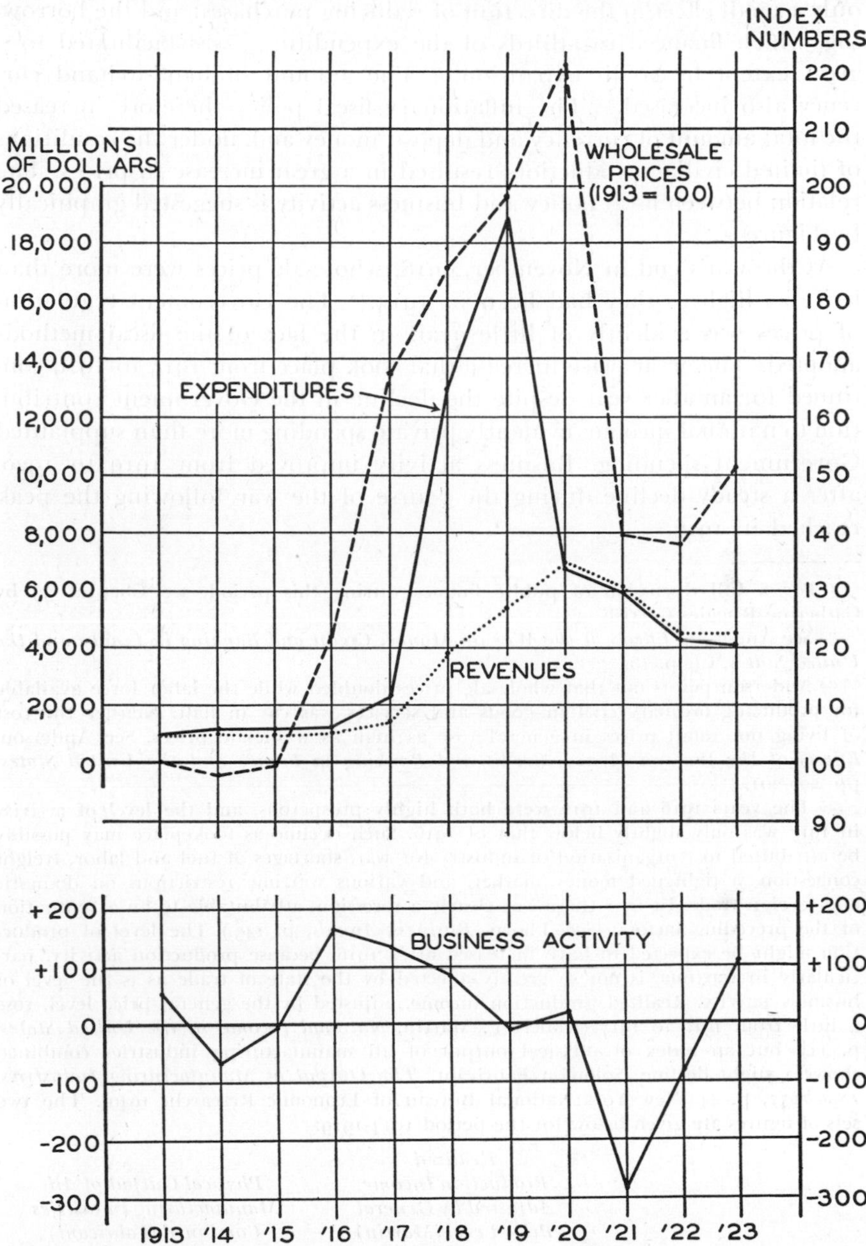

FIG. 3. *Fiscal Policy and Business Activity, 1913-1923.* Expenditures and revenues in fiscal years; wholesale prices and business activity in calendar years. (Sources of basic data: "Expenditures" and "Revenues," United States Treasury Department; "Wholesale Prices," United States Bureau of Labor Statistics; "Business Activity," Cleveland Trust Company.)

only a small effect in the direction of reducing purchases; and the borrowing, which financed two-thirds of the expenditures, was facilitated to a great extent by credit expansion.[22] The amount of hand-to-hand currency also increased.[23] The inflationary fiscal policy therefore increased the total amount of currency and deposit money and, under the conditions of limited civilian production, resulted in a great increase in prices. The relation between fiscal policy and business activity is suggested graphically by Figure 3.

At the war's end in November, 1918, wholesale prices were more than twice as high as they had been in 1913.[24] The Government regulation of prices was evidently of little avail in the face of the fiscal methods adopted. The great price increase that took place from 1915 to 1919 continued for another year despite the decline in the Government contribution to national income: evidently private spending more than supplanted Government spending. Business activity improved from 1919 to 1920, after a steady decline during the course of the war following the peak reached in 1916.[25]

---

[22] For a full discussion of public finance during this period, see Chapter 33 by Catherine Ruggles Gerrish.

[23] See Anderson, *Effects of the War on Money, Credit and Banking in France and the United States,* Chap. 16.

[24] Anderson points out that wholesale prices doubled while the labor force available for producing ordinary civilian goods and services was cut in half. Neither the cost of living nor retail prices in general rose as high as wholesale prices. See Anderson, *Effects of the War on Money, Credit and Banking in France and the United States,* pp. 200-201.

[25] The years 1916 and 1917 were both highly prosperous, and the level of activity in 1917 was only slightly below that of 1916. Such decline as took place may possibly be attributed to reorganization of industry for war, shortages of fuel and labor, freight congestion, a tightened money market, and various wartime restrictions on domestic and foreign trade. In 1918 there was clearly a recession, attributable to an accentuation of the preceding factors. (See Thorp, *Business Annals,* p. 143.) The level of production might be expected to have increased after 1916, because production activity, particularly in wartime, is not so greatly affected by the state of trade as is the level of business activity. Realized production income, adjusted by the general price level, rose a little from 1916 to 1917 (Robert F. Martin, *National Income in the United States,* p. 11), but an index of physical output of all manufacturing industries combined shows a slight decline (Solomon Fabricant, *The Output of Manufacturing Industries, 1899-1937,* p. 44. New York: National Bureau of Economic Research, 1940). The two sets of figures are given below for the period 1914-1919:

	Realized Production Income Adjusted by General Price Level (Martin) (In billions of 1926 dollars)	*Physical Output of All Manufacturing Industries Combined (Fabricant)* (1899 = 100)
1914	50.8	186
1915	51.4	218
1916	54.1	259
1917	54.8	257
1918	59.8	254
1919	59.9	222

Economic Trends

An examination of the trends in the economy's performance during the period since the Civil War centers around the study of various measures of economic activity and economic well-being. The most valuable and at the same time the most difficult of such measures is the "standard of living." An enumeration of the material goods and services enjoyed by a representative American family in 1866 and a comparison with the condition of a corresponding representative family of 1918 (or thereabouts) is only the first step in making generalizations about the trend in the standard of living. Even if a "representative" family could be defined and discovered, the difficulty immediately arises that the standard of living is somehow related to the satisfactions derived from the enumerated goods and services. Is it possible to compare the satisfactions derived from two different sets of goods and services consumed at two widely separated dates? Such inter-temporal comparisons of utility are extremely difficult for a single individual even when the length of time involved is short and the items considered remain the same. The difficulties are multiplied many times when instead of the single individual there is a changing group of many individuals, when the time lapse is of considerable length, and when the commodities and services consumed are radically different. The subject is too indefinite to lend itself readily to economic analysis.[26]

This section must confine itself to a less ambitious project than that of determining the change in the standard of living. The analysis is confined to objective indicators of the trends in the performance of the American economy. Two main groups of such indicators are considered: (1) national income per capita and the composition of the national income; (2) length of the working day and length of life. The first gives us some indication of the quantity and composition of goods and services available to the members of the community. The second suggests the length of time that people have in which to enjoy these goods and services.

---

26 For a highly courageous and successful attempt to obtain concrete results in this field, the reader is referred to Chester W. Wright, *Economic History of the United States,* Chapter 45. New York: McGraw-Hill Book Company, 1941.

"If we are to approach economic history by way of the standard of living, how are we to measure economic progress? Can we reduce the standard of living . . . at any one time to an index number and focus our attention on the trend of these index numbers? Our desire to be 'scientific,' to avoid vagueness and abstraction, makes this tempting. Such index numbers, however, become meaningless if comparisons are to be made between levels of living widely separated in time or space: qualitative differences are as significant as quantitative differences. What sort of index number could we use to compare the level of living in 1860 with that of 1940? In 1860 there were no telephones, radios, electrical refrigerators, washing machines, vacuum cleaners, or electric lights, no automobiles and no hard-surfaced roads. The list of consumers' goods which are in common use now but were not available to anyone in 1860 is a long one, and expenditures on these goods now make up a large part of consumers' expenditures." (Edgar W. Martin, *The Standard of Living in 1860,* pp. 2 and 3.)

National Income and its Composition

A good objective measure of the performance of the American economy is the real income per capita, that is, the average amount of goods and services available. However dangerous averages may be, they nevertheless aid in obtaining an indication of changes in the item that they represent. Figure 4 shows the fluctuations in realized national income per capita in constant (1926) dollars.[27] Real income per capita evidently has risen greatly in the era since the Civil War.

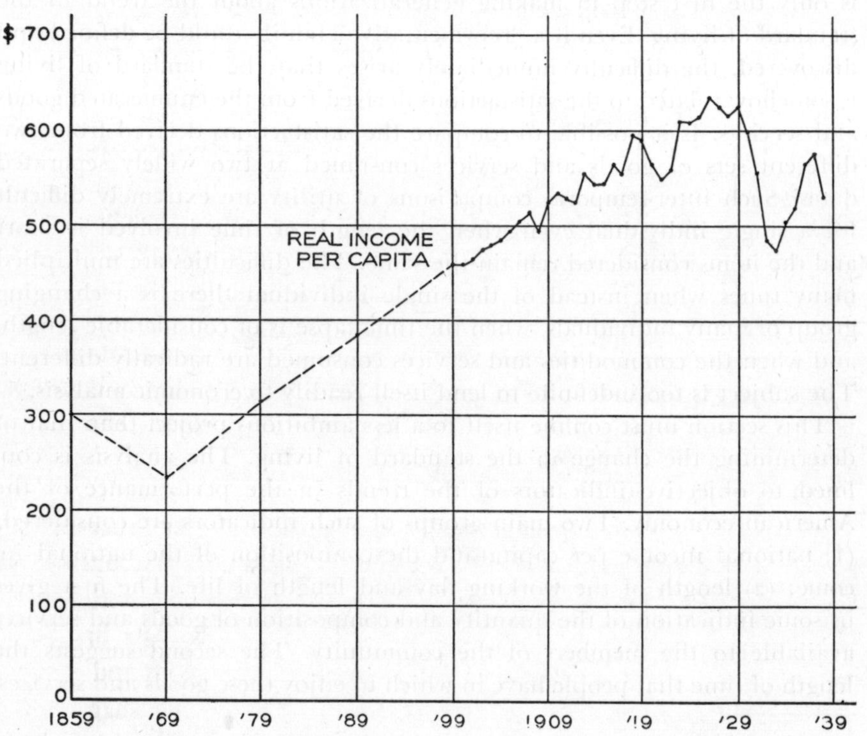

FIG. 4. *Real Income Per Capita.* (Source: Robert F. Martin, *National Income in the United States, 1799-1938,* pp. 6-7. New York: National Industrial Conference Board, 1939. Cf. Simon Kuznets, *National Product Since 1869,* Part II; and *National Income: A Summary of Findings,* Part II. New York: National Bureau of Economic Research, 1946.)

According to one (necessarily rough) estimate that has been made, the real income per capita in 1859 was $300, while in 1918 it was $599. Although these two years are not strictly comparable in terms of cycle phase, the figures are nevertheless suggestive of the rise that has taken place.

[27] The data are taken from Robert F. Martin, *National Income in the United States,* pp. 6-7. Income figures are deflated by an index of the general price level. Realized national income is not quite the same as the total of goods and services available, but is a sufficiently close approximation for the purposes of this analysis.

This great rise did not take place without rather violent fluctuations. There was a substantial drop in real income per capita from 1859 to 1869, the figure for the later year being $233. There was then a steady growth in terms of decades to the end of the century, and then, after minor fluctuations, a prewar peak of $557 was reached in 1913. Then there was a slight decline in 1914 and 1915, a slight upturn in 1916, another dip in 1917 and then a peak in 1918. The rise in real income per capita over the period as a whole was therefore by no means continuous.

Since one test of the performance of an economy is its ability to recover from serious internal and external shocks, it is important to consider more fully the behavior of real income per capita before and after serious wartime or peacetime disturbances.[28] It was noted above that the decade of the Civil War left the economy worse off than before in terms of real income per capita, a decline having taken place from $300 in 1859 to $233 in 1869. In the following decade, however, the economy improved greatly despite the crisis of 1873 and the prolonged depression that followed it. Real income per capita in 1879 stood at $315. The crises of 1884 and 1893 likewise failed to impair the growth of the economy, the figure for 1889 being $385 and for 1899, $456. Similarly, the decade that saw the crises of 1903 and 1907 ended with a real income per capita of $530 in 1909. And the decade that suffered through World War I ended with a real income per capita of $592 in 1919.

Length of Working Day and Length of Life

One of the most reliable and persistent trends in factors affecting the standard of living since the Civil War is that which has taken place in the length of the working day.[29] About 1860 some of the stronger crafts had secured a 10-hour day, but most city workers had longer hours; the same was true of those in factories.[30] Seventy hours a week was probably fairly typical. By 1870 the 10-hour day was the rule in crafts, but employees in bakeries, transportation, cotton mills, and others worked 11 to 14 hours. Two decades later, the carpenters won an 8-hour day in 137 cities and a 9-hour day in most other places.

In 1909, 76 per cent of the workers in manufacturing industry worked from 54 to 60 hours a week, and nine per cent worked over 60 hours. During World War I, labor organizations grew in strength, and the War Labor Boards favored shorter hours.[31]

---

[28] Owing to the nature of the data, it is not possible here to insure a comparison between corresponding cycle phases.

[29] See L. T. Beman, *Five Day Week* (New York: H. W. Wilson Company, 1928); and *The Five-Day Week in Manufacturing Industries* (New York: National Industrial Conference Board, 1929).

[30] Dr. Martin points out that the average working day in 1860 was around 11 hours. (Edgar Martin, *The Standard of Living in 1860*, p. 343.)

[31] See the table given in Beman, *Five Day Week*, p. 44.

An increase in the number of legal holidays also took place, and vacations became much more common among the great mass of the population. Compulsory education meant that the average child did not begin full-time work until he reached the age of 16 or 18 years. Social security legislation increased the number of people financially able to retire before death. Finally, the expectation of life at birth has increased greatly. Figures based on Massachusetts experience show an increase from 38.7 years in 1855 to 54.1 years in 1919-20 and to 58.1 years in 1929 for males, and from 40.9 years in 1855 to 56.6 years in 1919-20 and to 61.4 years in 1929 for females.[32] Virtually all of the increase in the expectation of life at birth is attributable, however, to a reduction in infant mortality rather than to an actual increase in the length of life for adults.[33]

The general conclusion to be derived from these figures is that the increase in real income per capita was coupled with a reduction in the hours of work and a lengthening of life. Leisure time increased, and there was a greater amount of goods and services available for enjoyment during the leisure time. More output per capita was produced with a smaller number of hours of effort per worker. Although temporary setbacks were suffered in time of war or serious peacetime disturbance, the improvement in the material basis for a higher standard of living continued.

Basic Conditions of Future Growth

The instability of the American economy in this period again left its valuable contribution to posterity. Although the national banking system had improved the situation greatly over the preceding era, it nevertheless tended to aggravate financial difficulties once they arose. And it was irritatingly inflexible when called upon to render assistance in time of crisis. The result was the establishment of the Federal Reserve System, which has since been an important aid to progress and stability in both war and peace. The railroads, conceived though they were under conditions that nurtured panic, gave an important stimulus to economic activity[34] and provided the basis for economic unity to parallel the political unity that had been established by the Civil War. The domestic market was thereby enlarged and the division of labor was encouraged precisely as Adam Smith might have forecast. The result was the mass production of goods, which raised the standard of living in peace or maximized the

---

[32] Warren S. Thompson and P. K. Whelpton, *Population Trends in the United States,* p. 240. New York: McGraw-Hill Book Company, 1933. See also Louis I. Dublin and Alfred J. Lotka, *Length of Life.* New York: The Ronald Press Company, 1936.

[33] Edgar Martin, *The Standard of Living in 1860,* p. 220. Dr. Martin also points out that in 1879 the expectation of life at 60 was 14.80 years for males and 16.10 years for females, while in 1929 it was only 14.01 years for males and 15.35 years for females.

[34] See Leland H. Jenks, "Railroads as an Economic Force in American Development," *Journal of Economic History,* May 1944, pp. 1-20.

economic potential in war. Both the free and trustified enterprise of this period left a sizeable legacy which the subsequent period invested in sound industrial ventures that ultimately yielded a return in the form of world-wide economic pre-eminence.

Conclusions

The peacetime crises of 1873, 1884, 1893, 1903 and 1907 indicated that the American economy was far from attaining stability. Its performance was still defective. During these crises and attendant periods of depression the economy lost much of what it had gained under prosperous conditions. Although there was a net gain during the period it was far less than might have been. But the magnitude of real investment, especially in railroads, was such that some disturbances were inevitable. Perhaps the financial methods that were used to build the railroads and the frequent crises that resulted were indispensable to progress. However, the financial weakness and immaturity of the Federal Government—as evidenced by the gold crisis of the nineties—can claim no offsetting merit. The country just had to learn "high finance," which it finally did. By the time of World War I it had learned a little. Nevertheless it employed inflationary methods of war finance that had repercussions in the subsequent period. The performance of the economy was noteworthy in the ability to recover in spite of policies and basic institutional conditions that impaired the rate of progress.

Selected References

GENERAL WORKS

Burton, Theodore E., *Financial Crises.* New York and London: D. Appleton-Century Company, 1931.

Collman, Charles A., *Our Mysterious Panics, 1830-1930.* New York: William Morrow & Company, 1931.

Eckler, A. R., "A Measure of the Severity of Depressions, 1873-1932," *Review of Economic Statistics,* May, 1933.

Martin, Robert F., *National Income in the United States, 1799-1938.* New York: National Industrial Conference Board, 1939.

Mitchell, Wesley C., *Business Cycles, The Problem and Its Setting.* New York: National Bureau of Economic Research, 1928.

Schumpeter, Joseph A., *Business Cycles: A Theoretical, Historical, and Statistical Analysis of the Capitalist Process.* New York: McGraw-Hill Book Company, 1939.

Sprague, O. M. W., *History of Crises under the National Banking System.* Washington: National Monetary Commission, Senate Document No. 538, 1910.

Thorp, Willard L., *Business Annals.* New York: National Bureau of Economic Research, 1926.

Wright, Chester W., *Economic History of the United States.* New York and London: McGraw-Hill Book Company, 1941.

SPECIAL TOPICS

Anderson, B. M., Jr., *Effects of the War on Money, Credit and Banking in France and the United States*. New York: Oxford University Press, 1919.

Bogart, Ernest L., *Direct and Indirect Costs of the Great World War*. New York: Oxford University Press, Preliminary Economic Studies of the War, No. 24, 1919.

Burns, Arthur F., and Wesley C. Mitchell, *Measuring Business Cycles*. New York: National Bureau of Economic Research, 1946.

Clark, John M., *The Costs of the World War to the American People*. New Haven, Conn.: Yale University Press, 1931.

Fabricant, Solomon, *The Output of Manufacturing Industries, 1899-1937*. New York: National Bureau of Economic Research, 1940.

Fels, Rendigs, "The Long-Wave Depression, 1873-97," *Review of Economics and Statistics*, February, 1949.

Frickey, Edwin, *Economic Fluctuations in the United States*. Cambridge, Mass.: Harvard University Press, 1942.

Kuznets, Simon, *National Income: A Summary of Findings*. New York: National Bureau of Economic Research, 1946.

———, *National Product Since 1869*. New York: National Bureau of Economic Research, 1946.

Weberg, Frank, *The Background of the Panic of 1893*. Washington, D. C.: The Catholic University of America, 1929.

PART 5

1919-1950

PROSPERITY, *depression, recovery, World War II, and postwar boom; these were the chief episodes of American economic history between 1918 and 1950. The country took its part in World War I more or less in stride. The problems of postwar adjustment, aside from the sharp price deflation of 1920-21, were comparatively simple. Then followed the prosperous 20's, which ended abruptly with the onset of the depression in late 1929. For a decade the primary concern was to get the economy functioning on a reasonably efficient basis again; a decade that was marked by an acrimonious debate over the merits of the New Deal in this direction. This argument had scarcely been resolved when World War II started in 1939. There was a noticeable acceleration in economic activity as the United States began to supply an increasing amount of aid to the allies; active participation after December 1941 resulted in the feverish activity of a war economy that, contrary to many expectations, was little diminished between 1946 and 1950. All these events left their mark on the various segments of the economy. They also affected the general structure, although in many respects the changes that came after 1918 were but a continuation of trends established earlier.*

Population grew during the decade of the 1920's at the decennial rate (around 15 per cent) that had characterized the previous ten years. This rate of growth was cut approximately in half during the1930's, only to be restored by a war-time lowering of the marriage age in the 1940's, much to the astonishment of many prognosticators who had visualized the early approach of a stationary population. The net result was a population of around 150 million in 1950, nearly half again as large as the figure thirty years earlier.

There was a noticeable shift in age distribution of the population after 1920. A continuing decline in the death rate and the fall in the birth rate during the 1930's combined to increase the percentage in the upper age brackets. In 1920, persons 45 years and older made up about 21 per cent of the total; in 1945 they constituted over 27 per cent. These changes had significant economic as well as social implications that were just beginning to be recognized by the late 1940's.

The population was also becoming more and more native born. Following World War I the United States practically closed its doors to foreigners seeking residence in this country and the flood of immigrants was reduced to a trickle.

There was, however, no cessation of the movement of population within the country. With the automobile and highways, in addition to the railway network, internal mobility was even further increased. To be sure, the frontier, with its free or cheap land, had largely disappeared and no longer caused the distinctive westward trend in the population movement that had marked our earlier history. Urban centers, however, continued to attract a larger portion of the population, and by 1947 there were three residents in places with 2500 or more inhabitants for every two who lived in rural areas.

Data on the percentage distribution of the labor force indicate that the patterns of economic opportunity had changed somewhat between 1920 and 1940. During these years the total number of gainfully employed rose from some 41.6 million to 53.3 million. (Population in 1940 was around 131.6 million compared with 105.7 million in 1920.) Of this number, the employment in Agriculture had shown the largest percentage decline, from 25 per cent in 1920 to 17 per cent in 1940. Manufacturing and Construction dropped from 32.3 per cent to 27.1 per cent during the same period, and Transportation and Public Utilities from 10 per cent to 8.5 per cent. Increases were registered in Trade, Finance, and Real Estate, from 12 per cent to 16.5 per cent; in Educational and Other Professional Services, from 5.4 per cent to 7.5 per cent; Personal Services from 4 per cent to 5.8 per cent; and Government from 2.4 per cent to 3 per cent.

The data implicitly show the increased capacity of our economic organization to produce goods and services, a capacity that was dramatically revealed by output during World War I and in the years immediately following. Most striking was the reduction in the amount of human resources devoted to agriculture without any diminution in the flow of agricultural products; indeed the use of production quotas and price supports in this field suggests that even fewer farmers could have adequately supplied our needs. The reduction in the percentage employed in manufacturing and construction and transportation and public utilities are a further indication of greater efficiency in these fields without, however, the acute threat of occupational overproduction that affected agriculture. The reduction in the percentage needs for labor in the more basic parts of the economy freed others for occupations, mostly in the service type, which showed expanding percentages.

These categories on the shifts in employment are too broad and incomplete to serve any more than a rough skeleton of American economic development during this period. Moreover, such an examination fails to give an adequate impression of the dynamic character of American development. The chapters that follow put substance on the bare bones and breathe life into the body of our history. Essentially they follow the same arrangement that was used in the preceding sections by considering transportation, agriculture, industry and commercial policies, money and capital, labor, business organization, management, trust policy, and public finance. The section, like the preceding ones, ends with an appraisal of the performance of the economy.

35 · TRANSPORTATION SINCE WORLD WAR I

IN 1920, JUST AFTER WORLD WAR I, the national transportation system comprised four types of carriers: steam railroads, electric railways, steamship lines, and pipe lines. The highways were essentially local in character and in that year aviation could claim only a first experiment in regular transportation.

The railway network included some 253,000 miles of line of which a seventh was two or more tracks. There were 35,000 railroad owned passenger cars, less than half all steel, and over 2,800,000 freight cars, of which almost one tenth were owned by other than railroads. The investment in road and equipment had reached a book value of twenty billion dollars. There were a little over two million railroad employees, an inflated number growing out of the vicissitudes of the war and government wartime control. In 1920, passenger service amounted to forty-seven billion passenger miles, half again as much as pre-war years, and freight service to four hundred and fourteen billion ton-miles. Only the speed of the passenger service can be presented in quantitative terms. The fastest trains between New York and Chicago were scheduled for 20 hours and between Chicago and San Francisco for 67½ hours.

The electric railways of the country had become the important interurban carriers and the value of their total capital equipment for some 43,000 miles of line totalled approximately five billion dollars. About one-half of the mileage belonged to companies engaged to some extent in interstate commerce. It was possible though not expeditious to go from Boston to New York or from New York to Chicago by electric railway alone.

No complete statistics are available concerning the water carriers at this time. Scheduled coastwise vessel movements were numerous up and down the Atlantic and Pacific coasts and between the Gulf and the largest Atlantic coast ports. The Great Lakes were traversed by many well established lines. Bulk carriers of coal, iron ore, grain, and petroleum operated both in coastal and lake waters. Many passengers, along with very substantial volumes of freight, moved over these routes in preference to the railroads.

The pipe-line network of the country had become substantial by 1920, with some 25,000 miles of trunk and a somewhat greater mileage of gathering lines. The investment was nearly half a billion dollars, although employment was small and traffic was confined to crude oil.

As was suggested, the rural highway network carried only local traffic. Total mileage was over 3,000,000, but only a fraction more than 1 per cent was high type, hard surface concrete or bituminous compound, and 10 per cent was low type surface of oil or waterbound macadam. The 8,000,000 passenger cars and 1,000,000 trucks were limited to short hauls. Pneumatic tire and engine failures were frequent, trucks were equipped with hard rubber tires, and maximum speeds for cars over rural highways rarely exceeded 45 miles per hour.

While the highways, electric lines, and pipe lines were of considerable importance in the national transportation system, the period immediately following World War I was dominated by steam propulsion. Between them the railroads and the steamships carried the vast bulk of freight and the greatest number of passengers. Few contemporary observers could imagine any basic changes occurring in the structure of the transport organization.

Technology

By 1920, however, the United States transportation system was already entering an unprecedented phase of technological change that even by 1950, thirty years later, had yet to complete its course. The basic factor bringing about the change was the development of the internal combustion engine, which had been invented several decades before the turn of the century and which had been initially applied to highway vehicles just before and during the 1890's and to the airplane in the subsequent decade. Up to World War I, neither of these types of equipment had achieved the reliability or serviceability that would warrant making it a basic part of the general transportation system. But a few years thereafter the highway motor vehicle was improved to a point where engines could be run thousands of miles by anyone without trouble, tires were no longer a source of frequent delay and repair work, and the complementary development of year-round smooth surface highways of concrete or bituminous compounds enabled vehicles to operate at the speeds of which they were capable. Not many years later, the airplane also arrived at the stage where operability and reliability of commercial planes were sufficient to make it a full-fledged member of the nation's transportation network.

The period of gestation of any radically new technology for transportation has always been long. During this interval it is never apparent just how well the new methods will satisfy existing demands or to what degree they will create new demands for transport service. The process of adaptation is essentially one of trial and error. This was true of the introduction of the internal combustion engine. It largely accounts for the failure of the operators of the older systems of transportation to realize the full significance of the new innovation. Yet, as will be brought out more fully below, the new types of transportation were to create forces that far overshadowed the labor, financial, and regulatory problems facing the old.

This emphasis on the emergence of new means of transportation after World War I, critical as it was, should not obscure the further refinements in the older types. The railroads continued to increase rail weights, car capacities, and locomotive sizes, with consequent improvement primarily of freight hauling efficiency. They experimented with the principle of internal combustion in the form of gasoline engine rail cars, but without much success, and it was not until the diesel engine was applied that any revolutionary refinement was forthcoming. Pipe lines were expanded and their efficiency improved, while a further adaptation of diesel engines led to increased possibilities of inland waterway transportation utilizing self-propelled barges.

Capital Growth

To be utilized, technical achievements must be followed by the actual production of the new transportation facilities, which requires plant and equipment to manufacture them and means of financing their purchase. In the United States, private firms have produced most of the capital equipment needed for all types of transportation. Prior to the coming of highway motor vehicles, this meant primarily supplying other companies that operated railroads, street railways, vessels, and pipe lines. The subsequent rise of two other groups of purchasers, however, introduced as radical a change in the economic structure of transportation as occurred in its physical aspects.

The biggest new category included private individuals and non-transportation firms who purchased automobiles and trucks to provide their own transportation. Annual expenditures for this new equipment exceeded gross capital expenditures for the railroads after World War I, and in some years have amounted to three times as much. The other category comprised the government, which since the early canal days had done little more than maintain the status quo of the road system. The motor vehicle demanded something much more, and in essence forced the government to become an active participant in the transportation field as the only feasible provider of a network of roads adequate for the potentialities of that vehicle. Less important in total, though just as revolutionary in its effects on the economic structure of transportation, has been the similar demand from aviation, with government agencies again supplying the ground facilities by way of airports and basic ground communication equipment. In this case there was the additional interest of the government in the subsidy of mail and providing for military needs.

The new types of purchasers of transportation facilities were also responsible for new arrangements for financing. The private vehicle owners used substantial funds directly saved from their incomes acquired from non-transportation activity. They also relied on short term installment credit, especially after World War I. While installment credit used to purchase motor vehicles has sometimes reached a level of several billion dollars, it has, nevertheless, always remained low relative to the total investment in vehicles. In the eleven years from the end of World War I to 1929, these types of financing were used to add 20,000,000 motor vehicles to the country's stock, representing a net depreciated additional investment in transportation facilities of more than ten billion dollars. In terms of an economy's ability to provide its participants with new capital goods, this was an almost unprecedented achievement. In the ten non-war years between 1936 and the end of 1950, some 20,000,000 motor vehicles had been added to the previous total.

Exclusive of city streets, it proved more difficult to channel funds for building a network of modern roads. Initially the general funds of governmental units were used, but special taxes upon vehicles, accessories and gasoline soon became the accepted means of raising money for the operation and for a large share of the construction of roads. On occasion, large bond issues supplied funds for the improvement of the road systems of individual states, and between 1920 and 1950 some three to four billion dollars of debt were issued for this purpose. In the main, however, it was a matter of "pay as you go." The special taxes produced some hundred million dollars in 1920, over eight hundred million a year by 1929, and more than two billion in 1949. Because of the diversion of funds for other purposes, capital expenditures for highways did not rise commensurately. The early 1920's saw around six hundred million of gross capital outlay, exclusive of city expenditures, with an increase to a peak of a billion in 1930. During the depression years the level receded to around six hundred million annually, and in 1941 only eight hundred million was being spent. During World War II, as part of providing war resources, the amount was reduced to a three hundred million dollar level. By 1949, a new high of a billion and a half was being spent, but because of higher costs this produced no more physical plant than the 1930 level of expenditures.

In the meantime, traditional financing of the private operating company type in the railroad field had been applied to gross capital expenditures of around eight hundred million dollars a year in the 1920's. Roughly, half of this amount came from reservations of operating profit and half from sale of securities. In the subsequent depression this class of expenditure dropped to some 75 per cent and had risen to only five hundred million by 1940 and 1941. Meanwhile, the volume of both passenger and freight traffic handled by the railroads had dropped considerably from the levels reached during the 1920's. During World War II the railroads maintained their gross capital expenditures at an increased average annual rate of just below six hundred million. By the late 1940's the rate was increased to over a billion dollars, although in terms of physical units this did not equal that of the 1920's.

Just before and following World War II there was an unprecedented volume of capital expenditures financed through private operating companies for oil, gasoline, and gas pipe lines. During the war major oil pipe lines from the Southwest to the Atlantic were financed by the government. In the fifteen years from 1935 to 1950, on the order of three billion dollars were invested in this new type of transportation facility. Air carriers too developed their investment through private financing, though the magnitudes were not comparable with other types of transportation. In the postwar period they were able to get sufficient capital to change over their major route equipment to new standards of speed and capacity.

The Problem of Leadership

Because of the importance of entrepreneurship and management in the performance of economic organizations, economic history should include some characterization of this area even though it must be of an exploratory nature because of the difficulty of obtaining complete data. For this purpose the field of transportation offers an interesting example. At the beginning of the period under consideration the railroads represented by all odds the biggest share of transportation service performed by economic organizations whose primary purpose was to offer that service. By that time, however, the pioneering and empire building days of the railroads were largely over. No more dynamic geniuses rose to the fore at an early age, such as Hill who built the Great Northern or Harriman who welded the Southern and Union Pacific together into the biggest of all railroad networks. The key individual companies had become very big, the bureaucratic aspects of their organizations had been established, and the higher officers were primarily men who had gradually worked up through the hierarchy of those bureaucracies. The size and complexities of the individual companies were often such that the top executive was quite removed from actual operating, sales, and the market conditions in which service was offered. The stock ownership of companies was generally so widespread that few individuals owned large enough proportions to be able to exert a really dynamic influence from outside, even if they were able to push through the bureaucracy. The public utility aspects of the railroad industry had come to a peak with an emphasis upon the obligation of government regulatory bodies to lend a hand both toward making ends meet and providing a return on capital. Technology seemed to be stabilized, with gradual improvement of existing facilities the likely trend. It appeared unlikely that anything could challenge the supremacy of the railroads in the field. The chief executives of the railroads were essentially conservative, and unwilling to break with tradition.

During the 1920's and 30's the whole restrictive environment in which the leaders lived seems to have been little changed. The inertia of their own organizations, the limitation, supposed as well as real, of regulation, the trade association influence toward uniformity and stability, the demands upon management's time in dealing with unions, and the lack of any inter-industry competition were all against the rise of dynamic leadership. So were the general procedures in promotion, with insistence on long training in the lower ranks with its tendency to wear down potential initiative and to favor those who patiently accepted tradition and were not unduly critical. Bringing in of personnel from outside seldom occurred in the larger, dominant railroad systems, in any case not from sources other than the railroad industry.

There is some indication that with the advent of the newer forms of competition certain of these factors began to have less influence in the railroads, although bureaucratic inertia and involvement with unions continued to weigh heavily. The leadership rose to the occasion of World War II and produced a splendid performance when the job to be done was along traditional lines. But afterwards that leadership found itself faced with a most vigorous motor truck carrier industry to which it seemed not fully prepared to adjust. Many railroad innovations that came after the mid-thirties and again after the war appeared to be forced on top management by outside competitive pressures. By 1950 a number of major rate readjustments, particularly that for steel, indicated a belated willingness to break with tradition. The general adoption of the diesel locomotive was an example of a willingness to accept a major change in physical plant. But the railroad managements had yet to demonstrate an aggressive spirit and willingness to undertake further radical changes.

Meanwhile the coming of motor and air carriers brought quite a different group of leaders into the transportation field. Firms were small to start with, top officers were intimately familiar with current details of operation, of selling, and of shippers' needs. Many of the officers were the owners of the companies and they had the independent attitude of the man who has built up his own business. Making changes was the order of the day and the organizations were small enough to facilitate such changes. Unsuccessful firms were liquidated or new leadership was relatively quickly brought in to improve matters. Initially there was freedom from undue trade association and regulatory pressure for keeping in line. The size of most organizations remained relatively small and the tradition of change was carried on so that the tendency has been for the continuance of a more dynamic type of leadership in the new fields. At the same time a number of outside restrictive factors had begun to show their influence by the 1940's. The gradual pulling away of the men who built up the firms took some toll of dynamic qualities. Increased restriction by way of added government regulation, decreasing possibilities of radical technical improvement, and declining opportunities for expansion tended to deflate the aggressive attitudes of management. Yet, so long as the individually operated passenger car and privately operated truck continued to operate, the managements of the motor carrier companies could not escape the influence of strong competitive forces pushing for active leadership qualities.

Trade Associations

By 1920 the railroad industry had behind it a quarter of a decade of legally approved trade-association participation in rate making. Substantial proportions of rates were published jointly for various companies by regional freight and passenger associations or bureaus, as they were called, and competitive rate changes were presented to them for hearings and vote. These organizations had their origins in the great trust building days of the 1880's and 90's. The courts ruled under the subsequent antitrust legislation that such associations were not illegally monopolistic if they eliminated pooling of traffic and allowed individual companies the option of publishing rates independent of association action.

After 1920 the new types of carriers universally adopted the association pattern of industry organization. Numerous regional associations were established in the bus and truck field, drawing for their initial personnel on individuals who were familiar with the old railroad procedure. It is not astonishing, therefore, that many of the detailed aspects of the railroad rate pattern were introduced into the rate structure developed by the highway associations for rationalizing the chaos of their original rates. Nor were the regulatory agencies of government adverse to the growth of such association, since it simplified the seemingly impossible job of supervising the rate making of tens of thousands of firms engaged in motor transport. Regional associations in close contact with their member firms could be counted on to discipline members more readily than could, for instance, the limited staff of the Interstate Commerce Commission from Washington. The air carriers, too, developed an association on a national basis, as was consistent with the scope of their company objectives. Due to the differences between ordinary common carriers, contract carriers, and other forms, the new types of transportation were also forced to devise various classes of the associations to handle divergent problems. Not only were the standard common carrier organized, but the contract truckers had their groupings—even dump truck operators were organized—and in the aviation field non-scheduled air lines had a separate association from the scheduled lines.

There was one particular aspect of the association pattern that came out of the transportation revolution of this period. The formalized railroad association processes of administrative handling, hearings, and committee action on rate changes were valuable in bringing conflicting interests into agreement without government regulatory participation. But the rigidity and time-consuming aspect of this whole administrative process seems to have delayed the adaptation of railroad rate-making to the new competition. It was too easy for one railroad company successfully to oppose a change suggested by another railroad in the course of the procedure. Peace in the family of the association members seemed more attractive than fighting over new experiments. At a time when innovations were especially needed, association practices limited the introduction of changes and discouraged any individual initiative in experiments that might disturb existing member-relationships.

Government Regulation

In addition to self-imposed regulation, the transport industry was also subject to increasing governmental control after 1920. Before World War I the major share of active government regulation of transportation had been confined to the railroads. The general philosophy behind this regulation was negative in character, being aimed at undoing what the railroads had practiced by way of discriminatory charges and service over the preceding half century. Railroad managements had strongly resented this interference and vigorously opposed it at every step, but by 1920 the paramount power of the Federal Government over interstate commerce had been confirmed by the Supreme Court and the basis for wide regulatory powers to be exercised by the Interstate Commerce Commission was established. Following the war there was a complete reversal of the old philosophy on the part of those active in the railroad industry. When it came to the writing of the Transportation Act of 1920 they gave general support to the legislative grant to the Interstate Commerce Commission of general overall control, including limitation of the construction of new lines and the abandonment of old ones, supervision of financing, fostering and control of consolidation and pooling, together with affirmative and broad rate and service regulation.[1] Apparently both financial and managerial leaders thought they had much to gain by such a policy. Competition from new lines would be limited and the reduction in the number of independent firms by consolidation would make for a more stable type of competition between existing lines. There was an obvious

[1] It must be emphasized, however, that even the added power over rates still left the great bulk of rate adjustments to be made by the railroads with no need for Commission action unless someone complained.

appeal in the assumption that the Commission had a major responsibility for the financial success of the railroads through the requirements in the law that its general control over rates include an attempt to achieve a fair return on capital. The complementary supervision of labor disputes by another government agency—the Railroad Labor Board—provided for in the new legislation, seemed to offer help against the more militant phases of union activity. It was in these terms that the comprehensive Transportation Act of 1920 came into existence.

The following ten years gradually undermined most of the hopes placed in the new era of regulation. The Act's Railroad Labor Board had failed by 1925, the expected general consolidations were not forthcoming, and the fair return seemed impossible to achieve. Some of the other phases of regulation, which had to be accepted in order for the legislation to be politically acceptable, proved onerous. The more profitable roads were burdened with the purchase of marginal lines when the former integrated their systems. The potential recapture of excess earnings took away some of the stimulus to keep costs down. Control over abandonment, which was the counterpart of limitation on construction, made it difficult to get rid of unprofitable branches.

These disappointments, however, did not bring about a reversion to the earlier philosophy of opposing regulation. On the contrary, with the growth of highway competition during the late 1920's and the 1930's, the railroads advocated a further entry of government in the regulatory field with the expectation that regulations would prove helpful in tempering the new competition. First at the state level and then at the federal, railroad management, with the active assistance of railroad labor, insisted that regulation of the growing truck and bus carriers be as strict as that of railroads. In 1935 the final objective of having the Interstate Commerce Commission take on the job was achieved.[2]

While the legislative pattern of the new phase of regulation generally reflected the provisions applying to the railroads, in important respects the truck carrier regulation proved more complicated. The fact that, unlike the railroads, not all highway carriers were simply general common carriers prepared to haul whatever and wherever the shipper asked led to a more detailed control of the entry into business of the individual firm. This, in turn, put far greater power over economic success or failure in the hands of the Commission. Active restrictions imposed by the Commission on the exact commodities that might be carried, and sometimes on the direction of allowed haul, illustrate both the detail and the importance to the firms of such regulation. The problem was further complicated by the emergence of contract carriers who confined their operations

[2] It is only fair to point out that the railroads were not alone in the advocacy of all this; the established motor carriers were as interested in the possibility of restricting new entry and independent rate cutting in their field as the railroads were in theirs.

to a limited number of customers and who, though also under regulation, were controlled to a lesser degree than the common carriers.

By 1940 a similar combination of interests brought coastal water carriers under the same regulatory tent. The railroads were equally anxious to have the same patterns established for the air carriers, but the youngest member of the transportation family was firmly opposed because of a fear of restriction upon their growth and of a less favorable attitude toward government aid and subsidy. Actually the new and independent regulatory agency, the Civil Aeronautics Board, born in 1940, established a degree of control over the regular air carriers that dealt with the minutiae of economic operation to an extent never dreamed of by the older agency, including detailed specification of what cities on a route may be stopped at, which may be passed over, and even limits on the number of flights.

It was by these processes that public transportation came under comprehensive governmental regulation between 1920 and 1950. This regulation was tempered, however, by a vast amount of unregulated transportation by private vehicles on the highway that competed with the regulated portion. In the last analysis, if a shipper thought rates were too high he could buy a truck and transport his goods himself, or if an individual did not like the fares and service of public passenger transport he could drive his own automobile. This was an important aspect of the motor vehicle revolution that was bound to circumscribe some of the possibilities of regulation.

The persistence of an unregulated portion of the industry was a major factor behind the question, growing in the minds of railroad managements, of whether there should not be a reversal of the trend and a relaxation of regulation. Furthermore, what had the appearance of protection when the railroads asked for extension of rate and other regulations to highway and water carriers proved to have reverse possibilities. The newer carriers became equals before the Interstate Commerce Commission in their demand for protection. Their protests brought regulatory limits on railroad strategy in the general struggle for traffic. Further, the slowness of the Commission in matching rates to rapidly rising costs during and after World War II also raised doubts as to effectiveness of the control. The failure of the 1920 provisions for setting rates at levels that would permit a fair return (which had been repealed in 1933) may have had a part in convincing the railroads that there should be some freedom from rate regulation. With as many alternate ways of transporting things, with the possibilities of decentralization simply cutting out transportation, and with rapid changes in price level, it was hard for the regulatory agencies to keep up with necessary general adjustments in rates. There was a real question whether even the general adjustments of rate levels should not be left largely to managerial direction.

Labor

A summary of the history of labor in the transportation industry following World War I must begin with railroad labor, because labor unions had one of their earliest origins in the train and engine services and had already become an accepted institution. During the war there had been great strides in union organization of the rest of the railroad employees, but during the early 1920's much of this ground was lost. In the 30's the trend was again reversed and, with the aid of new legislation, railroad labor became completely unionized along craft lines. It is noteworthy that the railroad unions did not initially demand a formal closed shop; only at the end of the 1940's did they come to ask for such enabling legislation, including provision for the checkoff of dues.

The period under consideration was characterized by relatively peaceful relations between railroad management and labor. Throughout there were federal agencies active in dealing with disputes. From the end of the Railroad Labor Board in 1925 until the late 1940's, the Federal machinery had achieved results that were pretty generally credited by both sides as being illustrative of exemplary relationships between management and labor. After World War II the results obtained under the complicated provisions for dealing with minor disputes established in 1935 and by the Presidential Emergency Boards for resolving the later stages of major disputes began to raise doubts. The vast number of minor issues carried to the federally created machinery for adjustment became so great as to delay decisions beyond limits tolerable to either side in the cases. From management's point of view, the "impartial" representatives called in to break stalemates seemed too generally to side with labor to be considered fair. In connection with the major cases, there have been several instances where labor has refused the decisions of the Emergency Boards and gone on strike. After a long previous history of acceptance by both sides of such decisions, these actions lessened confidence in the effectiveness of the bargaining machinery and suggested the need for drastic changes.

One of the unique aspects of transportation labor has been the pattern of pay and working conditions for vehicle operating employees. Roughly, a quarter of the railroad's payroll has gone to the train and engine employees. It is within this group that a system of pay, starting in the 1880's, became entrenched. In essence, this system set a certain number of hours—for example, in freight service originally 10 and subsequently 8—or 100 miles as the basis for a day's pay. If a crew exceeded the limits in either category, it was paid proportionately more, even though in the other category it fell short of reaching the day's limits. For instance, a freight crew going 200 miles in 5 hours would get two basic days' pay for the five hours' work. In other words, standards of speed and mileage established during the 1880's were still being followed some 70 years later. Although vast increases in overall speed had been achieved, there had been no adjustments in the standards to bring them up to date. It has even been demanded that the 150-mile standard day for passenger train crews be set back to 100 miles in spite of recognized increases in speeds of passenger service. In addition, there has been an expansion in the number of rules that make for increases in number of men to perform service or for higher earnings for those who continue doing certain tasks as before if the added men were not hired. For instance, with the introduction of diesel locomotives, whose increased capacity has led to longer trains, have come demands for a second fireman and even a second engineman in addition to the usual complement of the steam locomotive. In train service new rules have been obtained that require an extra day's pay if over three sets of hoses between cars have to be coupled by a trainman, even though previously that task had always been accepted as part of the regular duties of the job. This type of wage structure with its never-ending accretions of a unit-cost-increasing character has seriously handicapped the railroads in competition with newcomers in the transportation field. Together with the rapidly increasing rates of pay in the other categories of employees, they have made it impossible to pass on to users as substantial a share of the savings from technological advance as might be expected.

As the other fields of transportation have developed, the railroad pattern of separate craft unions has been generally followed. The vehicle-operating employees have tended to form separate unions from the maintenance, clerical, and station employees. Some effort was made by railroad unions to obtain control over competitive fields, but only with inter-city bus operators was any headway achieved. Even so, there has been a tendency with other than railroad carriers to follow the railroad union pattern of establishing working condition rules that would either increase employment or add to earnings by other than straightforward increases in hourly or piecework rates of pay. The truck unions have required extra men in the driver's cab within some of the larger cities and limits have been put on city delivery work by inter-city drivers, all in much the same fashion as the railroad unions have tried to get extra firemen for diesel locomotives and have limited switching work by road crews. For air carriers the railroad pattern of giving a choice between an hourly or mileage calculation of pay was amplified by basing first-pilot pay on hourly, mileage, and basic monthly rates.

As for the general character of the new transportation union organizations, some have been small and powerful, such as the Air Lines Pilots Association. In contrast, the million-member Teamsters Union, covering truck drivers, became almost as large as all the railroad unions put together. The pattern of bargaining in the highway field has been regional, with subdistricts for large cities, reflecting both the nature of the transportation service and the geographical coverage of the firms. For the airlines, bargaining has been on a national basis in line with the extended operation of the major firms.

All in all, the transportation industry has become solidly unionized, with its character developing along the general lines of unionization in railroads. Over and above regular increases in pay there have been throughout the period under consideration continued accretions to the bases for pay, chiefly by way of more restrictive working-condition rules. These have further prevented passing on to the customer a substantial share of the benefits of the parallel improvements in technology.

Price and Service

Any summary of the performance of a sector of the economy should attempt to portray the sequence of price changes, even though such price data must be interpreted with caution. In a service-producing sector like transportation, where there is no physical product of a relatively constant standard, this is especially true because prices alone can be quite misleading. A ton-mile of service rendered in carrying freight can vary as to speed of transport, convenience of loading and ease of packing, and amount of ancillary expenses. The price attached to a ton-mile, then, does not remain the price of a uniform unit. This variation applies particularly to the years of rapid technological change after World War I when, for example, the advent of the motor truck provided door-to-door delivery of shipments and at the same time reduced packing requirements and provided more flexible and sometimes faster service.

Even with these limitations the changes in rates during the period are worth noting. World War I had seen a rate increase under government control of about 25 per cent, which was followed in the postwar inflation in 1920 by further increases of 25 per cent to 40 per cent, depending upon the regions covered. In the short deflation of 1921 general reductions were in order, which left the rates anywhere from 12½ per cent to 26 per cent higher than at the end of the War. Subsequently during the 1920's and early 30's there were numerous modifications of rates, but at the same time the character of traffic changed. The latter factor invalidates possible comparisons of average revenue per ton-mile as an index of price levels. During the latter 1920's there were no over-all country-wide rates changes as there had been earlier. The rates that were generally available for the less heavy or regular flow of goods, called class rates, were generally increased during this period. The so-called commodity rates, those established separately for a class of goods in terms of its particular commercial and locational factors, remained fairly constant. In the depression of the 1930's there were small over-all increases which were followed by a series of larger increases during the latter 40's, averaging over 50 per cent. At the same time there were many cuts in those commodity rates that were subject to motor-truck and, in special cases, water competition. The complexity of these conflicting trends of increase and decrease defies effective statistical summarization.

In general, after regulation was established for motor-truck common carriers there was a tendency for their rates to stay close to the level of the railroads. It was in respect to standards of service that the principal change was to be found. For one, overnight delivery was furnished by trucks where it had not before been offered by the railroads, from Buffalo to New York, for instance. In turn the railroads established new freight train schedules during the 30's in an attempt to meet this competition. The railroad offering was limited to service between their freight stations or central yards in the large cities and was not extended to private sidings of shippers located in other parts of the cities. The trucks, as far as truck-loads were concerned, could provide the scheduled service to any part of the city. As trucking developed further with better highways and vehicles, trucks pushed into longer-haul traffic; from Florida to New York and Chicago to New York, for example. For this latter distance the railroads had long scheduled third-morning delivery, but the trucks were often able to achieve second-morning deliveries. In 1950 the first move on the part of the railroads to meet this latest competition came in the form of a second-morning schedule for less-than-carload shipments.

The new competition also spurred advances in loading and in the protection of shipments against damage in the course of transportation. Improvements were made in springing of freight cars, devices were incorporated in car design for easier stowing of articles, and special cars for easier loading and unloading were also developed. In response to the trucks' widespread door-to-door delivery service, the railroads, for less-than-carload traffic, initiated truck service from their freight stations, or, in the case of rural areas with small towns, substituted trucks instead of way-freight trains for this type of shipment. For a considerable time this store-door pick-up-and-delivery service was provided without increase in rates, but increasing costs forced the railroads to impose added charges. All in all, the improvements in service characteristics for many types of freight have been as important as rate changes in the past decade and a half.

The history of passenger fare and service changes between 1920 and 1950 can be divided into two periods. During the first ten years railroad service was little changed and basic fares remained at their peak of 3.6 cents per mile for coach and Pullman, with a surcharge for the railroad added to Pullman fares. During this decade came the growth of bus carriers, whose rates were generally below rail rates. The vast network of bus lines actually came to provide more widespread service than the railroad and, on branch lines and across main-route lines, faster and more frequent schedules. At the same time the increased use of private automobiles for longer journeys brought new possibilities for travel to the public. As a result of these factors the coach traffic of the railroads dropped 40 per cent between 1923 and 1929, even though economic activity was comparatively constant. Pullman traffic remained practically unchanged.

The depression of the 1930's, along with the increased highway competition, brought a radical change in railroad fares. By 1932 and 1933, rail travel had decreased roughly to a half of what it had been in 1929. In response, fares were reduced drastically, the southern and western carriers being the first to inaugurate changes and the ones to cut the most. In the South the basic coach fare was cut in 1933 to 1½ cents and Pullman to 3 cents. In the West the new fares were 2 cents and 3 cents. The East followed the Western levels. With the boom of 1936 and 1937 the fares were increased some, typical being the level of 2 cents for coach travel in the South and the level of 2½ cents in the East. In 1939, with a reversal in trends, fares were reduced again, and then came the gradual rise during and after World War II to a final level of nearly 3 cents for coaches and roughly four cents for Pullman, to both of which had to be added a 20 per cent Federal tax.

Meanwhile, there had been vast changes in passenger service inaugurated during the depression. For one thing, the railroads were not unwilling to let the buses take over in the case of lightly travelled or abandoned passenger train operation. By the end of 1949, out of the country's 225,000 miles of railroad only 155,000 were operated in passenger service. On the positive side, the railroads adopted air-conditioning on a large scale and trains running between major cities were speeded up. A full day and night was taken off Chicago-Pacific Coast train schedules, overnight service was extended to distances as great as from Chicago to Denver, and trains that had taken all day were speeded up to allow a round trip in a day. Finally, by 1950 new, streamlined, modern equipment was provided for nearly all regular main-line trains. Bus carriers concurrently improved their service with air-conditioning and better riding equipment.

The airplane, too, came into its own, primarily as a passenger and mail carrier. In the course of the 20-year life span of the principal scheduled air carriers in operation in 1950, there had been almost constant and marked improvement in comfort and speed and a gradual decrease in fares. It took 31 hours for the flight from New York to San Francisco in 1931, 12 in 1950. The fare in 1931 was $200; twenty years later it was $158 for first class and $110 for coach, with a reduction for round trip and for family groups. After World War II the newly formed non-scheduled airlines were active advocates of low fares, and the establishment of a coach service by the older lines to meet such competition brought the airlines as a whole to a price level and structure, for a service far more valuable in terms of speed, that was quite comparable to the railroad charges. By 1949 the scheduled air lines had reached a passenger mileage equal to a fifth of that of the railroads, excluding commuters.

Wartime Transportation

No history of transportation of the period subsequent to World War I would be complete without a review of the wartime performance of the transportation system from 1941 to 1945. The demands on transportation in the Second World War were of an altogether different order than they had been during World War I. From 1916 to 1918 railroad freight tons originated increased only four per cent, freight ton-miles 11 per cent, and passenger miles but 21 per cent. From 1940, which was not unlike 1937, to the peak year of World War II, 1944, tons originated increased 49 per cent, ton-miles 100 per cent, and passenger miles 300 per cent. In the World War I years railroad service, together with the physical and financial condition of the railroads, deteriorated rapidly, and government administration inaugurated in December 1917 only helped to relieve the freight congestion. In World War II, under private administration and with added governmental regulation, negligible congestion appeared, finances improved, and physical condition was maintained astonishingly well in the face of war demands for military use of labor and materials.

The basic reason for this achievement lay in the ability to increase the utilization of facilities. Traffic demands were not only such as to allow better use of equipment, but certain government controls were established to insure improvement in use immediately. More specifically, the haul of war production and military materials tended to be longer than in peacetime and commodities could be loaded more heavily. The westward flow for operations in the Pacific utilized cars that would have gone empty under ordinary conditions. The heavy movements of petroleum by rail in lieu of coastwise movements could be handled in full trainload lots. Freight loading and unloading was expedited by around-the-clock and seven-day-week operation of the industry. The wartime regulatory agency, the Office of Defense Transportation, insisted on increasing the tonnage of less-than-carload shipments placed in a car. Other shipments were ordered to be loaded to full car capacity. Short haul movements were diverted to trucks. Export shipments were not allowed to be loaded unless vessels were planned to be available.

From 1940 to 1944 average loads in freight cars increased 18 per cent, average haul for a load was 35 per cent longer, and the proportion of empty car mileage dropped from 38 per cent to 34 per cent. There was an increase in tons of freight per train of 37 per cent, and in daily mileage run by freight cars of 42 per cent.

The improved performance with passenger service was even more spectacular. The change in character of demand, with an increase of 100 per cent in the average length of a journey and a patriotic tolerance of crowding and standing, accounted largely for the ability to expand traffic. The average passenger load of a car increased 140 per cent and of a train by 230 per cent. Daily passenger-car mileage increased 165 per cent. In all, the doubled freight and tripled passenger traffic was handled by only 38 per cent more employees and with only two-thirds more fuel.

In contrast, highway transportation was rigorously curtailed by government rationing of vehicles and gasoline. From 1941 to 1944 passenger automobile mileage dropped some 40 per cent, truck mileage dropped 25 per cent, and gasoline consumption by almost a third. Intercoastal and coastwise water traffic was reduced to practically nothing by enemy action and by commandeering of vessels. To make up for the loss of petroleum transportation by water to the east coast, substantial additions to the pipline system were made during the war. Commercial air traffic increased over threefold largely because, as with railroad passenger service, the air lines were able to utilize equipment more fully.

The experience of World War II was a demonstration of the effectiveness of the decentralized operation of numerous private firms in an industry when overall protection and guidance with respect to the abnormalities of war demands is provided by government. At the same time, the controlling importance of the improvement in the character traffic demands in wartime relative to utilization of capacity stands out. As has already been indicated, it was doubtful whether the railroad managements, especially, would be able to achieve anything approaching the same efficiency during peacetime operation.

Transportation in Relation to Other Economic Activity

Transportation after 1920 could scarcely escape some effects of the important changes in the structure and location of economic activity as well as in the changed demands of consumers. Rearrangements and rationalizing of distribution and marketing practices, such as direct delivery without warehousing or direct selling by manufacturer to retailer or to a manufacturer-operated store, led to changed demands for transportation service. Substitution of different raw materials in manufacture of many articles or the shifts in the type of energy sources used made for different origins of traffic. Changing origins of raw material, though not a new factor, brought significant shifts in use of particular transportation routes. The vast increase in proportion of coal produced in the West Virginia region as compared to Pennsylvania and Ohio had important effects on the finances and growth of particular railroads. So did the shift in wheat from the north central to the southwestern states. In later years the generally increasing economic activity and income level of the southern and southwestern states had a major impact on the fortunes of the carriers of those regions. The accelerated tendency for industry to decentralize its operations, either by establishing branch plants or separate firms in each region, played a part in reducing transportation of numerous raw or semi-finished products. The radical changes in consumer demand, for instance the decreasing use of flour in the average diet and the increase of fruits, made important differences to transportation companies in particular regions. The movement of population to suburbs and of industry away from urban centers were additional factors of importance.

Many of these changes have favored one type of transportation over another. The substitution of gas and petroleum for coal in heating and power production transferred traffic to the pipeline and coastwise water carrier. Suburban and rural locations have favored trucking against railroads. So have some of the direct shipment of products from factory to retailer, because the smaller, more frequent lots for each consignee lend themselves to effective handling by the truck, which can stop with little delay for partial unloading. Where most effective distribution can be obtained by quick changes of destination of relatively short-haul commodities, the flexibility of truck movement also proved superior. Transportation by no means played a passive part in the changes that affected the structure of the economy. The advent of motorized highway transportation was the major factor in suburban development, for all except the largest cities, and in the rural movement of industry. As will be brought out in more detail in Chapter 39, below, it brought a vast increase in the mobility of people in relation to job opportunities and enjoyment of the resources of the country.

The total influence of the interplay of these various changes may be summarized by a comparison of tons of different classes of freight originating in various parts of the country in 1920 and in 1949. The statistics are available for comparison between the East (defined as the territory north of the Ohio and Potomac Rivers, and east of a line connecting St. Louis and Chicago and the west side of Lake Michigan), the South (defined as the territory east of the Mississippi and south of the above area) and the West (defined as the rest of the United States).

Of the tonnage of all the railroad-carload freight originated in 1920, 43 per cent came from the East and 33 per cent from the West. By 1949 the East accounted for but 37 per cent, the West rose to 37 per cent, and the South came up from 23 to 26 per cent. The total for the country dropped 8 per cent. Comparing ton-miles of railroad service for the same period, the West, with 44 per cent by 1949, exactly took over the position held earlier by the East, while the South remained practically constant at just over 22 per cent. The total ton-miles hauled was some 19 per cent larger in 1949 than in 1920, reflecting the increasing length of rail haul.

For particular classes of commodities there were important variations from the over-all pattern of tonnage originated. The East's proportion of forest products was halved in the 29 years, the West's stayed roughly the same, and the South's increased by a quarter. Total shipments of these products for the country as a whole decreased 34 per cent. For products of mines, the East dropped a sixth and the South gained a seventh in their shares, with the country's total declining 13 per cent.

The tonnage of shipments of agricultural products for the United States rose 26 per cent in the period from 1920 to 1949, with no great change in regional shares. Manufactured and miscellaneous products increased 13 per cent in total tonnage originated, but the East's share declined from almost two-thirds to one-half. The South increased its share by 36 per cent, and the West by 23 per cent. The volume of railroad less-than-carload traffic, particularly susceptible to truck competition, dropped by 72 per cent.

The Product of 30 Years of Progress

Taking into account the newly offered forms of transportation along with the old, the span of time between World War I and 1950 witnessed an unparalleled improvement in price (adjusted for changes in standards of service and general price levels), speed, coverage of the country, and comfort. Man's mobility increased immeasurably in this period, due largely to the application of the internal combustion engine to the highway and air and to economic institutions and a philosophy that, despite the efforts of the older types, allowed the new means of transportation to develop and exert a competitive impact on the previously established transportation agencies.

There had been significant changes in the relative importance of the various transport services. The steam railway mileage had dropped to 225,000, and passenger service was offered on only two-thirds of that. There were 20,000 railroad-owned passenger cars, almost all steel, and about two million freight cars, of which a sixth were not owned by railroads. The investment in road and equipment was up to twenty-five billion dollars in book value. The employees numbered around 1,400,000, a little less than three-quarters of 1920. The passenger-miles were thirty-five billion, only three-fourths of 1920's, but the ton-miles were 526 billion, a quarter again as much. Passenger service had been speeded up so that between New York and Chicago the best time was 14 hours, and between Chicago and San Francisco, a little over 39 hours.

The electric railways had practically disappeared, except in the largest cities. The remaining total of 10,000 miles of line represented a decline of almost 80 per cent in thirty years. The bus had taken over with a much greater coverage, with inter-city bus companies operating some 30,000 buses over 400,000 miles of highway.

The position of scheduled coastwise and lake water carriers for transportation of passengers and general merchandise had constantly receded, the final blow coming during World War II. Unscheduled bulk water carriers originally confined to hauling oil, grain, ore, and coal did expand their operations to rivers and canals, spreading as well into handling of other commodities such as sulphur, molasses, and phosphate rock.

The expansion of pipe lines was one of the spectacular developments of the period, though the lines, being buried under the ground, were little noticed by the public. Gasoline and natural gas were added to crude oil as the items carried. The gas pipe-line network alone reached a mileage in excess of that of the railroads and petroleum lines increased two fold. The increased size of pipe resulted in an even greater growth of tonnage handled.

Obviously the great change was in highway transportation. Near the end of 1949 the country had 36,000,000 passenger cars and 8,000,000 buses and trucks registered, 44,000,000 all told. Of around 3,600,000 miles of rural roads, some 10 per cent were paved with a high type concrete or bituminous surface, something over 10 per cent more with low type bituminous, and a third with stone or gravel surface. It is estimated that in 1949 almost 400 billion passenger miles were travelled in passenger cars in inter-city travel, nearly eight times the mileage reported by the railroads for the peak year of 1920. Ton-miles of freight trucks in inter-city traffic reached 88 billion, or one-sixth of that handled by the railroads in the same year.

Air traffic, non-existent in 1920, had reached six and a half billion passenger miles in 1949. This was equal to a fifth of the non-commuter passenger business of the railroads in that year. Mail and express by air had reached substantial volumes, but was not comparable in ton-miles to the corresponding land transportation.

In total, as far as inter-city movement of people was concerned in 1949, the highway vehicles accounted for over 90 per cent, the railroads for 8 per cent, and air carriers for 1½ per cent of the movement. For inland transportation of goods, the railroads still accounted for the bulk of the traffic, 61 per cent; trucks provided 11 per cent; water carriers 15 per cent; pipe lines (excluding gas) 12 per cent; and air carriers 0.03 per cent. In 1920, a guess would be that railways had handled 95 per cent of passenger travel and 75 per cent of commodity movements. The per capita travel of people increased fourfold in 30 years, and the volume and movement of commodities increased about twofold.

As already noted, these changes in the structure and the performance of the transportation system not only reflected the dynamic character of the economy during the period, but were in themselves an important element in affecting the operation of the entire economic system. It is no overstatement to say that in the 30 years following World War I the motor vehicle was a major force in the economic and social changes in the United States. Few of the wealth-getting and wealth-using activities of the country were unaffected. Together with the improvements in pipe lines and steam propulsion, the internal combustion engine gave a further stimulus to territorial division of labor and to the mobility of the population, basic factors in the material growth of the American economy.

Selected Readings

Bureau of Public Roads, United States Department of Commerce, *Highway Statistics* (1945-48). Washington: United States Government Printing Office.

Fair, M. L., and E. W. Williams, Jr., *Economics of Transportation*. New York: Harper & Brothers, 1950.

Healy, K. T., *Economics of Transportation in America*. New York: Ronald Press, 1940.

Interstate Commerce Commission, *Statistics of Railways in the United States* (1920-1949). Washington: United States Government Printing Office. (Includes selected data for electric railways, water carriers, oil pipe lines and motor carriers.)

Wilson, G. L., and L. A. Bryan, *Air Transportation*. New York: Prentice-Hall, Inc., 1949.

36 · AGRICULTURE IN AN INDUSTRIAL ECONOMY

Post-War Deflation and Depression

THE PRICE DECLINE THAT SET OFF the primary depression in 1920 came first and fell farthest in agricultural products. When credits were withdrawn the foreign markets collapsed, while the production equipment to supply it retained its high costs of maintenance. Added acreage, mechanization, and improved methods created a surplus for which there was no outlet at a remunerative price. With his large proportion of fixed costs, the farmer sought to better his position by increased production for a low price rather than to raise the price by curtailment of his output.

The recovery of business in the middle twenties and the resulting industrial and financial boom brought to agriculture an improvement that was limited and spotty.[1] At the peak of the boom in 1929 the index of agricultural prices was only 91 per cent of the pre-war level. With the Great Depression the ratio fell to 50 by February, 1933. Gross farm income, which had risen from $7,000,000,000 in 1914 to $17,000,000,000 in 1919, fell to the low of slightly over $5,000,000,000 in 1932.

Regional Responses to Distress

The distress came at different periods and with varying degrees of intensity in the different regions. From 1920 to 1922 hard times and their resulting protest centered in the spring wheat region. By 1923 the slump of the hog market brought widespread bank failures and farm foreclosures in the Corn Belt; hence this region was accorded first place in relief proposals. Southern interests that had sought relief for specific commodities individually in the early years of the depression were ready for a more general program by 1926. By 1932-1933 all regions and all farm commodities were directly involved in the general and complete collapse.

Relief Efforts, 1921–1933

Owing to the traditional and still prevalent attitude toward the relation of government to economic problems, the early efforts at relief were made by commodity co-operatives aimed at restoring a profitable return

[1] George Soule, *Prosperity Decade*. New York: Rinehart and Company, 1947.

by controlling output. Successive administrations from 1921 to 1933 placed main reliance upon co-operative action, with governmental policy strictly incidental or supplementary. The main relief act—the establishment of the Farm Board in 1929—was drawn up chiefly to support and promote co-operative marketing associations. The limitations and inadequacies of these highly desirable agencies were soon manifested. Group consciousness and loyalty were not strong enough to insure united action; general problems vital to the entire agricultural occupation necessitated public provision and direction. Recognizing the urgent needs and, more or less adequately, the opportunities of the situation, the leading general agricultural organizations, the Grange, the Farmers' Union, and the American Farm Bureau Federation (formed in 1920) initiated programs of national relief.

In 1921 the Farm Bureau backed an "Agricultural Bloc" of Western and Southern Senators and Representatives in sponsoring and propagating emergency and long-time measures of relief and stabilization. The central objectives of such legislation were the disposal of farm surpluses and provision for credit.

With the renewal and elevation of protective tariff rates for industry, in spite of the change of the nation from a debtor to creditor status, there was a persistent agitation to utilize this venerable protective and promotive device to establish and maintain a cost-of-production price for the leading farm products in the home market. The most publicized of such proposals was the McNary-Haugen plan to dispose of the surplus (above domestic demands) abroad, the costs to be borne by an equalization fee assessed on the producers. This particular application of the "domestic allotment" principle was favored by the Farm Bureau, while the Grange was partial to a protective tariff in the export debenture scheme, and the Union advocated a guarantee of cost of production. All of the proposals were too great departures for the administration. Twice passed by both houses of Congress, the bill embodying the Bureau plan of financing the exportation of surpluses by an equalization fee assessed on producers, was in each case vetoed by President Coolidge.

Credit needs were recognized in this period by the provision in 1923 of intermediate credit banks to make short-term loans on livestock and farm commodities. Next to the Farm Board Act, this was perhaps the most important agricultural measure of the decade. The dozen years of continuous agitation for farm relief before 1933 focused attention on the problem as a major national issue, stimulated the search for remedies, and put into operation preliminary tests of policies; in this way the period before 1933 helped to prepare the way for the more complete and elaborate program that followed.[2]

[2] Broadus Mitchell, *Depression Decade.* New York: Rinehart and Company, 1947; U. S. Dept. of Agriculture, *Yearbook, 1940,* pp. 298-314.

Agriculture in the New Deal

To appraise fairly and realistically the agricultural as well as the other branches of the recovery program,[3] it is necessary to take account of the wholly unprecedented degree and extent of the collapse and the consequent emergency that confronted the new administration. For the farmer, the primary and secondary depressions converged and the resulting shock was devastating beyond all precedent. With vastly increased investments and obligations, the prices of agricultural staples fell even below the previous all-time low of the ill-famed nineties. Many who retained possession of their lands slipped back generations to a primitive subsistence. Large numbers of substantial proprietors fell to the status of tenants or even to farm laborers. Still others joined the city unemployed. At the same time there was a steady return from the city to once-despised old farm homes. Both movements obviously complicated recovery efforts. Like other parts of the program, the agricultural measures involved the three stages of emergency relief, reform of abuses and discriminations, and long-time planning. Naturally the main controversy centered about the last objective.

Unfortunately for a rounded out program, all of these objectives had to be given a certain attention at once. In large part the weaknesses that developed in the original adjustment act were due to the fact that it was being frantically worked out by all available advisers at a time when a desperate constituency was demanding in forceful manner immediate measures of relief and security. The seemingly erratic and inconsistent policies of these hectic days are explained in part at least by the pressure for immediate concrete action.

To offset the emergency of price collapse in 1933, extreme measures were included in the first Agricultural Adjustment Act to reduce production drastically and to provide for compensation payments secured by a tax upon processors and by a devaluation of the currency. State and Federal moratoriums upon foreclosures and cotton and corn loans helped further to tide over the immediate crisis. These measures of relief were hastened by the violent demonstrations of the farm holiday movement. The immediate desperation measures for removing obstructing surpluses of key commodities led to the slaughter of sows and little pigs and the plowing under of cotton plants. These practices, emphasized in public discussion out of all proportion to their importance, had a discrediting effect on the whole program of emphasizing restricted production rather than balanced output and fuller utilization. After a year of trial the re-

3 The most impartial study of the agricultural recovery program is E. G. Nourse, J. S. Davis, and J. D. Black, *Three Years of the Agricultural Adjustment Plan*. Washington, D. C.: The Brookings Institution, 1937. Most other writings to date are strongly pro or con.

duction program was upset by a series of droughts culminating in 1935-1936 in the dust storms of the Southern Plains. The problem of surplus was changed to one of shortage. At this point, in 1936, the Supreme Court held the A.A.A. to be unconstitutional as an unwarranted invasion of state jurisdiction and an improper use of the taxing power.

The policy now shifted to an emphasis upon bettered production and the provision for an "ever-normal granary." The new Agricultural Adjustment Act of 1938 was a synthesis and a cumulation of proposals dealing with the basic problems of the producers of the main agricultural commodities; it comprised legislative machinery for soil conservation and balanced output, loans, marketing quotas, parity payments, marketing aid and promotion, and crop insurance for the precarious wheat-growing enterprise. Special acts dealt with the problems of tenancy, credit, and rural social security.

Regional differences presented the most difficult and complex problems of adjustment and security. Wheat, corn and hogs, cotton, and other leading enterprises had their special needs and interests. Whatever its limitations and questionable features, the program as completed by 1939 marked, in its inclusiveness of policy and elaborateness of organization, a real farmers' charter.

But before the full program could have adequate trial, agriculture, like the other branches of national economy, was involved fully in a war that was global in extent and magnitude. Production demands, under pressure of military requirements and the lend-lease program, again were to be extended and speeded to potential capacity.

Global War Tests Agricultural Resources and Systems

World War II made demands upon the productive and distributive capacity of the American economy such as no nation hitherto had been called upon to fulfill.[4] For agriculture it was the acid test of resources and of organization and techniques of cultivation, husbandry and management. In place of redundant surpluses, the disposal of which taxed commercial and governmental ingenuity, there were requirements for staples and specialties that dwarfed those of the former conflict. Instead of counsels of restricted and carefully balanced production, the farmer heard the call to produce to the full capacity of his land and capital. Furthermore this unexampled task was entered upon under the handicaps of an all-time shortage of farm labor and of competition with the defense agen-

[4] The most informing studies of American agriculture in the 1940's are W. W. Wilcox, *The Farmer in the Second World War*. Ames, Iowa: Iowa State College Press, 1947; Bela Gold, *Wartime Economic Planning in Agriculture: A Study in the Allocation of Resources*. New York: Columbia University Press, 1949; S. E. Johnson, *Changes in Farming in War and Peace*. Washington, D. C.: U. S. Dept. of Agriculture, 1946. A realistic report of typical areas of the farming front is given in John Dos Passos, *State of the Nation*, pp. 254-282. Boston: Houghton Mifflin Company, 1943.

cies and industries for priorities of essential equipment and distributive services.

Contrasting Conditions of Agriculture in 1917 and 1941

In many respects the social and technical advances between the wars were commensurate with the increased size of the latter involvement. In public attitude, in country as in town, there existed from the start an awareness of issues and obligations and a consequent unity of purpose. The emotional crusading zeal of past struggles that alternated from unwarranted confidence to hysterical depression was little in evidence.

In mobilization of resources and allocation of services the experiences of the former war and of the recovery program could be drawn upon. Organizations and directing agencies that had to be improvised suddenly and inadequately in 1917 were now ready at hand for the expanded functions. The specialized talents and equipment of the land-grant colleges and the research facilities of the Department of Agriculture and the experiment stations were all focused on the war effort. The now inclusive and elaborate extension service brought the redirected program directly to the farm through the participating Farm Bureau or other dominant organization membership. Leaders of the Grange and of the Farmers Union gave their counsel and kept their constituencies in line. The stronger commodity cooperatives gave system and stability to the distribution end. The Federal Triple A and the loan and marketing agencies reaching from Washington to the local representatives were directly available. The average farmer was becoming accustomed to group activity and governmental aid and direction. Ordinarily he might resent a seeming tendency toward "regimentation," but in a crisis he was prepared to "stand in his place" and take orders. There could be no question of the existence of a crisis, and in order to concentrate authority most fully a special War Food Administration to have control of both production and distribution was created early in 1943.

Technological changes were no less strategic and timely. Mechanization, which had been so determining in the Civil War and in World War I, was still more significant in helping to offset the depletion of "hands" by the demand of the services and the attraction of war industries. In fact, the inter-war years marked some most basic attainments in the extension and adaptation of farm machinery.[5] The all-purpose tractor on rubber tires proved the best solution to the general power needs of the average farm. Airplanes were already being utilized for spraying and doing emergency errands. Midget combines; practicable corn pickers, and field hay choppers, bailers, and ensilage cutters brought key labor saving devices to the medium sized undertaking. Large-scale enterprises,

[5] Interbureau Committee, U. S. Department of Agriculture, *Technology on the Farm*. Washington, D. C.: U. S. Government Printing Office, 1940.

like their counterparts in manufacturing, rested to a high degree upon mechanical processes. Even the cotton plantation, the last great survival of the hand labor system, was invaded by a fairly practicable mechanical cotton picker which magnified many fold the exploitive possibilities inaugurated by Whitney's initial invention. The supplying of the equipment needs was one of the major problems of the allocation of materials, but, while the need was never fully met, these essential "machine tools" were kept high on priority lists.

Agronomists and animal husbandrymen in their varied lines kept step with the engineers and technologists.[6] The hybridization principle, applied most fully and effectively to maize until the entire commercial acreage of the Corn Belt and four-fifths of the nation's total was so planted, was being extended increasingly in both plant and animal breeding. Soybeans, utilized as a source of oil, became a major addition to corn belt rotation. "Magic" plants such as Kudsu and lespedeza brought renewed productivity to areas wasted by erosion, while contour plowing and terracing cultivation preserved vast areas from draining or blowing into waste lands. Commercial fertilizer, given high priority, was used more fully and understandingly.

Progeny testing was proving a surer basis of animal breeding than the herd book entry or the judging ring, and artificial insemination was multiplying the progeny of proved sires. Experiments in cross breeding had gone far enough to create superior strains. These appliances and techniques were utilized in the war economy, and in not a few cases they were hastened and further improved by such applications. The concern of these years, however, was not in long-time possibilities but in immediate results. The test of the whole program of "technology on the farm" was in supplying the demands of the war for food at home and abroad.

Productive Achievement

The effectiveness of the changes in scientific method and management was demonstrated conclusively by the record of production throughout the war years. In the spring of 1945 the food administrator reported that, with 10 per cent fewer farm laborers, 50 per cent more had been produced than in the previous war. The increase in total production from 1939 to 1944 was twice as large as it had been during the entire preceding twenty years. Twice as much was sent to the forces overseas, and at the same time there was a 10 per cent increase in civilian consumption of food.

Actually, the war years set a new standard for nutritional improvement in the general population—"a fact," as Professor Wilcox observes, "without precedent for a large nation at war." The Department of Agriculture,

[6] *Ibid.;* U. S. Department of Agriculture, *Yearbook,* 1943-1947, 1948.

under the lingering New Deal emphasis on improved living for the masses, took advantage of the war prosperity to push this dietary reform. Significantly, the Department's Bureau of Home Economics was reorganized in 1943 as the Bureau of Human Nutrition and Home Economics. The extensive use of lockers and home freezers contributed to the economical preservation of food and to the added enrichment of the diet. This greatly increased output was effected without a marked addition of acreage in the staple crops; cotton acreage actually declined. The main extensions and shifts were in the areas of oil bearing crops and of vegetables for processing. Due largely to the abundant supply of wheat at the beginning of the war, but also to better planning and foresight, there was less disruption of rotation systems than in the previous war.

The Return to the Farmer

In general and for most commodities, the return to the farmer was unusually favorable. With a combination of record high production and relatively high prices, the net income for farm producers jumped from $5.3 billion in 1939 to $13.6 billion in 1944. This, with the moderate increase of marketing costs, probably gave the farmer a larger proportion of the consumer's dollar than he had ever received. The aid rendered by the Farm Security and Credit Administrations, along with high prices, enabled such a large number of tenants to rise to the status of ownership during the war that the percentage of tenancy fell to the lowest point in a generation.

General Effects on the Economy

These great achievements with relatively liberal returns to the producers were made at tremendous immediate cost, the creation of long-time obligations, and the emergence of doubtful precedents. The greatest of wars made larger drains upon extractive and agricultural resources than had ever been experienced. The over-extension of tillage with the curtailment of soil building and protective crops intensified the liabilities of erosion. The marked increase in intertilled crops made large areas of the prairies and high plains especially liable to the losses of washings and blowings.

Control and subsidy policies, always difficult to adjust in practice, led to a considerable unbalancing of production. Livestock production was undoubtedly overstimulated, and consequently too large a proportion of cereal crops went into feeds for live stock rather than into food for starvation areas abroad. Dairy products as compared with meat were given inadequate support. The precedents of price support as war measures, like similar gains of industry and labor, were certain to be occasions of conflict both inside and outside the occupation in the postwar years.

Problems of Postwar Adjustment

In the midst of the stimulated prosperity of the 1940's, the average farmer was haunted by the all too vivid memories of the market collapse of the 1920's. Such memories led to a certain prudential restraint in extending operations and in contracting indebtedness. Land values, while increasing materially, did not reach the fantastic heights or involve the speculative tendencies of the previous boom. The increasing control of governmental agencies upon credit tended further to stabilize investments.

The most pronounced reaction to the feeling of insecurity, however, was the insistent demand of farm organizations for a permanent policy of price support. The main concession during the war was in the guarantee of supports up to 90 per cent of parity for two years following the war. As it proved in the case of most commodities, the support was not needed in the early years of peace. Continued high industrial employment, an assured large export under the Marshall Plan, and benefit payments along with inflated values after the removal of controls brought in 1947 the highest farm income on record, with prices at 120 per cent of parity. Relative returns were later reduced by concessions to labor and the consequent rise in costs of equipment and in the charges of utilities. Near the end of the decade the index remained well above the old parity level, but the future was most uncertain and the proposal for a system of permanent guarantees became a major national issue. All parties and responsible leaders favored the general objective, but the method and extent of the support were matters of sharp disagreement.

The chief differences were between those who advocated high parity supports, either by price increase or by subsidy payments, in the supposed interest of the consumer, and those who favored a flexible adjustment in accord with the supply of the commodity involved. As a practical financial consideration, supports without an effective reduction and readjustment of production would involve a cumulating burden. Parties divided on the issue along regional and commodity interest lines and, as usual on important policies, the three main national farm organizations were in disagreement. While each of them sponsored, directly or through subsidiaries, extensive cooperative enterprises, their main efforts were directed to the determination of governmental policies. In general emphasis the modern Grange has represented the most conservative position, opposing extensions of Federal control and departures from traditional foreign relations.[7] The Union has been at the other extreme in advocating a

---

[7] The official history of the Order is by the high priest emeritus, C. M. Gardner, *The Grange—Friend of the Farmer . . . , 1867-1947*. Washington, D. C.: National Grange, 1949. Much source material is contained in the writings of a former national lecturer, T. C. Atkeson, *Semi-Centennial History of the Patrons of Husbandry*. New York: Orange Judd, 1916; and *Pioneering in Agriculture*. New York: Orange Judd, 1937.

large measure of Federal relief and protection and public enterprises. especially in the interest of the underprivileged elements in the farming population.[8] The Farm Bureau has occupied somewhat a midway position between the other groups, but has generally appealed to the well established proprietary interest.[9] The semi-official relationship which the local bureaus in certain states occupy to the extension service and the influence that this has given the organization in the administration of the various programs has been subjected to increasing criticism and demands that the service be freed from its dependence on this particular interest group. Since the 1930's the national Farm Bureau has come increasingly into conflict and rivalry with the Department of Agriculture.

The general recognition of the security of the farming enterprise as of vital concern to the whole national economy and the struggle of powerfully organized groups within it to advance their special interests give further and conclusive evidence of its full establishment as a coordinate industrialized business. As such it was shortsighted and futile to emphasize the traditional conflicts with the other branches of the economy. Whatever the measures employed to provide a "parity" of opportunity, the ultimate influence in its stability and progress would depend upon the soundness of the economy as a whole and most especially upon a high level of employment. [10] The view of the "embattled farmers" aligned against the other interests has thus become wholly unrealistic. In many ways the basis of conflict is within the occupation itself rather than with outside interests.

Whatever its relative rating, the agricultural enterprise, in its various specialties, has been a distinct and coordinate phase of "modern industrialism." The tendency to treat the farm and its problems as something apart and essentially different from the characteristic phenomena of business enterprise runs counter to the basic facts and conditions of modern rural economy. A typical farm undertaking, in its essential area of the national economy, is as fully and characteristically a participant in modern technology and enterprise as is an integrated manufacturing combination, a key utility, an imperial banking house, or a chain distributor or servicer. It has the same central problem as the others of adjusting expanding production to a fluctuating demand at home and abroad. The farm and the farm home, when meeting recognized standards, have become fully mechanized in every operation and service; the expression, "the farm, a factory," is neither fanciful nor wishful, but a reality. The three fairly distinct stages in the Industrial Revolution, distinguished by meticulous students, have

---

[8] C. B. Fisher, *The Farmers Union*. Lexington, Ky.: University of Kentucky, 1920.

[9] O. M. Kile, *The Farm Bureau Movement*. New York: Macmillan Company, 1921 (Origins and foundation); and *Farm Bureau through Three Decades*. Baltimore: Waverly Press, 1948 (development to recent times). More critical views of the organization are given in H. R. Tolley, *The Farmer Citizen at War*. New York: The Macmillan Company, 1943; and A. L. Moore, *The Farmer and the Rest of Us*. Boston: Little, Brown, 1945.

[10] For a clear and thoughtful elaboration of this point, see T. W. Schultz, *Agriculture in an Unstable Economy*. New York: McGraw-Hill, 1945.

had corresponding and equivalent attainment in the transformation of agricultural technique. As a matter of fully verified record, technology, that all-embracing term for the impact of science upon the world's work and play, has taken over the progressing farm at every point, as it has all other typical forms of satisfying economic wants, and with the same general sets of problems: specialization, standardization, labor displacement, capital apportionment, credit provision, and market adjustments. As with all other modern businesses, managerial and entrepreneurial functions have of necessity been increasingly emphasized. Thus, like other enterprises, the farmer has passed from the securities of a simple primitive economy, such as they were, to the risks and hazards of a matured, complex, and geographically and functionally interrelated world order.

In an age of combination and consolidation, agriculture, as a whole and by commodity groups, was forced to provide its own equivalent in organized effort. As in the experience of the other leading interests, early crude and faltering trial-and-error in types and methods of collective action was to be replaced by increasing effectiveness in associated controls and in the determination of governmental policies. An evidence of the extent of the influence of farmers' organizations has been in the opprobrium that at times they have shared with other "big business" interests. Hence today there is a peculiar irony in the dictum of elemental economics of a generation ago that the combination movement had and would extend to all lines of business except two—retail merchandising and farming.

Organized efforts, general and special, regional and national, reflected and in turn accentuated the tendency, inevitable under capitalistic enterprise, toward class divisions within the occupation. As in other undertakings, such divisions have been accelerated and intensified by the readjustments from war and depression. Rural economy and society, no less than urban, has its problems of small business and big operators. The countryside has its underprivileged, indigenous or migratory, its fringe of unemployed, and its slum dwellers.[11]

Concentration Tendencies in Agriculture

Concentration of capital and consequent control over output has been a tendency in agriculture as in other businesses. Mechanization and scientific methods have enabled an ever decreasing number of the gainfully employed to produce the nation's food supply. The number of producing units has decreased accordingly, and the average size of units has shown a marked increase. If subsistence and marginal holdings that contribute an insignificant proportion of the total are eliminated from the calculation, the degree of concentration becomes decidedly pronounced. The later statistics show a much larger rate of increase for large-sized than for medium-sized farms. Aside from large-scale speculation in farm lands, there have been capitalistic investments in enterprises, both large and medium, that involve tenancy or chain supervision. With narrowing outlets for investment, such investments may very likely increase.[12] With all

[11] E. D. Ross, "Agriculture in Our Economic History," *Agricultural History,* Vol. XXII (1948), p. 67.

[12] Descriptions of outstanding exhibits are Walter Goldschmidt, *As You Sow.* New York: Harcourt, Brace, 1947 (large-scale enterprises in southern California); J. K. Howard, "Tom Campbell: Farmer of Two Continents," *Harper's Magazine,* Vol. CXCII (Mar. 1949), pp. 55-63 (mechanized wheat cultivation in Montana and New Mexico).

of these evidences, the tendency toward large-scale, mass production, and "corporate farming" may be easily exaggerated. The frontier bonanza farms did not persist, and the most spectacular cases of modern giant enterprises have been in regions best adapted to the production of a certain crop on a scale that reduces the unit cost. Obviously the size of the area and the amount of the capital investment limit the number of such enterprises.

The Outlook for the Family-Sized Farm

The confident prediction of superficial observers that the family-sized farm is "doomed" by technology is not verified by the actualities of the rural scene. The great proportion of commercially producing units are still of medium size and the great bulk of the leading staples are produced by them. Mechanical appliances and long-time systems of cultivation have been more and more adapted to this type. For the most profitable utilization of modern equipment the size of the unit has increased moderately, but not to the point requiring appreciable additions of labor. No less scientific adaptations are bringing essential conveniences, comforts, and informational and recreational agencies into rural homes. Farm organizations and redirected schools and churches are providing economic and social stability to community life.

Social institutions and standards of the countryside have been transformed through the years by the same general technological and intellectual influences that were making over the cities, physically and psychologically. With waning of home processing and the extension of utilities and other services, the farm is decreasingly a peculiar unit of living. The family-sized farm is being steadily adjusted by modern technology to the desires and standards of the farm-size family.

With all the emphasis of rural social leaders through the years upon a distinct open-country culture, the prevailing town ways and standards, perhaps one might better say the common national ways and standards, prevail. Well may the national advertisers ask, "Which is the country girl"? The crossroads settlement is bypassed and its function superseded or subordinated by the trunk and market highways, and city and country are increasingly merged in activities and interests. The old general store becomes a filling station and possibly a curio shop; chautauqua and camp-meeting grounds, tourist camps; the village tavern, a roadhouse; and many a big meadow of ancestral pride, an airport, golf course, ball ground, or amusement park. David Grayson, in wanderings in "modernized" rural areas, would seek in vain for freedom from either physical or social turbulence. The traditional "rural versus urban" basis of conflict—never as clear-cut as represented—thus becomes a factor of decreasing influence, with the more realistic interests and motives, economic, social, and political—that cut across any such an alignment.[13]

The decentralizing tendency that manufacturing industries have been undergoing for some time past may well operate in farming to counteract

[13] Ross, "Agriculture in Our Economic History," pp. 67-69.

the unit concentration. "Subsistence farming" offers little for agriculture as such, whatever it may do to promote the comfort and security of the industrial worker. But by reason of its economic and social adaptability the technologically-adjusted family-sized enterprise may well be perpetuated as the optimum unit in general farming, and all reasonable public policies to attain that end would seem to be justified.

In 1882, General Francis A. Walker in an analysis of current census statistics of agriculture observed that, in contrast to the backward peasantry of Europe, "The actual cultivators of the soil here have been the same kind of men precisely as those who filled the professions or were engaged in commercial and mechanical pursuits." As a result of this superior skill and initiative, he was convinced that there was "no other considerable country in the world where the same mental activity and alertness have been applied to the cultivation of the soil as to trade and so-called industry." [14] Whether or not fully consonant with realities, then or later, Walker expressed the great objective for agriculture as a coordinate branch of a progressing American economy.

Selected References

Committee on Recent Economic Changes, *Recent Economic Changes in the United States.* New York: McGraw-Hill Book Co., 1929.

Committee on Social Trends, *Recent Social Trends in the United States.* New York: McGraw-Hill Book Co., 1933.

Kile, O. M., *The Farm Bureau Through Three Decades.* Baltimore: Waverly Press: 1948.

Lord, Russell, *The Wallaces in Iowa.* Boston: Houghton Mifflin Company, 1947.

Mitchell, Broadus, *Depression Decade.* New York: Rinehart and Company, 1947.

Moore, A. L., *The Farmer and the Rest of Us.* Boston: Little, Brown, 1945.

Nourse, E. G., *Government in Relation to Agriculture.* Washington, D. C.: Brookings Institution, 1940.

Nourse, E. G.; J. S. Davis; and J. D. Black, *Three Years of the Agricultural Adjustment Plan.* Washington, D. C.: Brookings Institution, 1937.

Norton, L. J., *Financing Agriculture.* Danville, Illinois: The Interstate, 1948.

Soule, George, *Prosperity Decade.* New York: Rinehart and Company, 1947.

United States Department of Agriculture, *Technology On The Farm.* Washington, D. C.: Government Printing Office, 1940.

United States Department of Agriculture, *Yearbook of Agriculture,* 1921-1948. Washington, D. C.: Government Printing Office.

---

[14] "General Characteristics of American Agriculture," reprinted from the Tenth Census in C. J. Bullock, *Selected Readings in Economics,* p. 81. Boston: Ginn and Company, 1907.

37 · INDUSTRY IN THE TWENTIETH CENTURY

THE YEARS SINCE 1919 HAVE witnessed important developments in industry no less than in other sectors of American economic life. Post-World War I adjustment was followed by boom, boom in turn by depression of unprecedented severity and extent, depression by an equally unprecedented and altogether astonishing wartime expansion, and this expansion in turn by readjustment of employment and production at a level far above the expectations of the most sanguine observers. Each of these phases was reflected in and influenced by industrial developments. Running like a bright band through the kaleidoscopic pattern of economic change was a closely woven series of innovations in technology, resulting in the creation of new industries and in raising old industries to new levels of productive achievement.

The major production trends in manufacturing industries during the three decades following World War I are indicated in the accompanying table. Starting with 1923, the first year of postwar "normalcy," industrial production rose steadily to the climax of 1929, reached the depth of depression in 1932 and then underwent slow recovery, barely reaching in the last pre-war years the level attained ten years earlier. The contrasting behavior of the durable and nondurable goods industries, revealed in these figures, is particularly noteworthy, production of the former declining much more sharply and recovering more slowly than that in the non-durable goods field. Then came World War II. Under the driving stimulus first of defense needs and Lend-Lease and then of our own colossal war requirements, industrial production soared high above all previous levels as the United States became, in the slogan of the period, the "arsenal of democracy." During the war years American industry displayed a vigor and flexibility and achieved goals that surprised even the most ardent supporters of the "free enterprise" system.

The rate of growth was unevenly distributed (see table). In several of the basic industries, especially coal, cotton, and lumber, the expansion characteristic of the nineteenth century gave way to recession, due primarily to competition from substitute products; petroleum, natural gas, and hydroelectric energy in the case of coal, synthetic fibres in the case of

MANUFACTURING: PRODUCTION INDEX
1923-1945

COMMODITY	1923	1929	1932	1939	1943	1947
TOTAL, *Manufactures*	*100*	*128*	*66*	*127*	*300*	*226*
TOTAL, *Durable goods*	*100*	*128*	*40*	*106*	*350*	*214*
Lumber and products	100	102	36	74	90	100
Iron and steel	100	121	29	105	190	179
Stone, clay, and glass products	100	126	59	131	199	237
Non-ferrous metal and products	100	151	56	126	297	208
Machinery	100	151	50	121	515	322
Transportation equipment	100	122	35	94	668	209
TOTAL, *Non-durable goods*	*100*	*129*	*97*	*151*	*244*	*239*
Cotton spindles	100	90	75	65	65	—
Coal	100	93	55	68	104 †	92 ‡
Leather and products	100	96	77	106	124 **	117
Printing and publishing	100	141	100	143	172 **	195
Textiles and products	100	113	86	135	189 *	196
Manufactured food products	100	123	96	132	185 †	191
Paper and products	100	147	76	197	259 **	272
Petroleum and coal products	100	171	123	196	441 †	345
Chemical products	100	156	119	196	674	440
Rubber products	100	159	102	180	371 †	359

† 1944 ‡ 1946 * 1942 ** 1941

cotton textiles, and the metals, plastics, and concrete in the case of lumber. In still other industries, especially if the war years are excluded, the evidence suggested a levelling off of growth, as for example in the case of iron and steel, the older non-ferrous metals, and leather. On the other hand, there were industries, some with roots in the nineteenth century and still others of more recent origin, which during and after World War I underwent extraordinary expansion. Of these the automobile industry provides the most familiar and in many respects the most striking example, not only because of its own rapid growth, but because of its influence on its supplier industries, especially petroleum, rubber, steel, and glass. Developments in the field of industrial chemistry gave rise to a remarkable complex of related industries, both transforming such established industries as petroleum refining, rubber, and paper, and giving rise to new ones engaged in the production of such articles as synthetic fibres, plastics, and light metals.

The electric power industry and the new communications industries, such as radio and the elaborate cluster of electrical equipment and machinery industries to which they gave rise, entered the period of their greatest expansion following World War I. The internal combustion engine in its various forms—gasoline, gas, and diesel—found increasing applications in industry, in land transportation, and in civil and military aviation. Taken in the aggregate, the extension of the new forms and applications of power, together with the penetration of industry by chemical methods and processes and by electrical and electronic techniques of measurement and control, caused a revolution in production and in ways of living fully as significant (and far more directly felt by most people) as the changes associated with the introduction of the steam engine and the new techniques of metal and textile fabrication a hundred and fifty years earlier. Especially noteworthy as an index of industrial change during the past generation has been the rapid expansion of the machinery industries. This exceeded that of every other branch of industry in the durable goods field.

Iron and Steel

Between the wars steel continued to maintain its preeminence as an industrial material and its place as the most important of the basic industries. In spite of the many remarkable qualities of such new materials as the light metals and plastics, their output could not be compared with the tremendous tonnages turned out by blast furnace, rolling mill, and foundry. The steel industry, too, developed its own new materials in the important ferro-alloys, of which stainless steel is the best known, having special qualities adapted to special uses. New product qualities derived from alloying metals, physical manipulation, and heat treatment, together with new and improved techniques of fabrication, strengthened and extended the use of steel for many purposes.

In raw materials, the most important developments after World War I were related to the problems of ore supply resulting from the approaching depletion of the high grade ores hitherto chiefly used. Ores continued to be drawn principally from the Lake Superior region. Of some 71 million tons of iron ore produced in 1946, 59 million tons or 83 per cent came from the Lake Superior fields, with the Mesabi range alone supplying 46 million tons. More than one-half of the remaining production came from the Birmingham district, while the Adirondack ores ranked third in importance.

The extraordinary requirements of World War II resulted in the accelerated depletion of the easily mined open pit ores of the Mesabi range and focused attention upon the problems of utilizing ores of lower grade. At the end of the war it became clear that, in the case of the high grade Superior ores, another ten or twelve years would see the approaching exhaustion of reserves. During the 1940's the larger steel companies, with some government assistance, gave much attention to the development of commercially practicable beneficiation processes for raising the quality of low grade ores. The vast deposits of taconite in the Mesabi range present the greatest development opportunity. To raise the metallic content of this ore—25 to 30 per cent iron compared with 50 per cent in the Superior ores now mined—and to make it suitable for furnace use present many difficulties. In recent years approximately one-fifth of United States production has consisted of beneficiated ores, based on ores of intermediate grade. Another evidence of the changing ore position of this country has been the growing interest in and acquisition of foreign ore properties by the larger steel companies, in places as far separated as Canada, Labrador, Africa, and South America.

World War II underscored the threat to national security of our dependence upon foreign sources for other raw materials essential in steel production. In quantity, the most important of these materials is manganese, of which the United States normally has obtained 90 per cent of its supplies from abroad, from places as widely scattered as South America, India, Chile, and the U.S.S.R. Equally vital to the manufacture of the varied kinds of steel required by industry, in peace as in war, are the alloy metals, of which chromium, molybdenum, nickel, titanium, tungsten, and vanadium are the most important. Despite extended efforts to discover and develop domestic supplies of these metals, our requirements are, in most instances, supplied principally from other countries.

Another important raw material development of the past generation has been the increasing proportion of scrap metal used in the manufacture of steel, chiefly in the open hearth and electric furnace processes and in foundries. As late as 1900 the amount of scrap metal used in the industry was only two million tons. By 1929 the consumption of scrap had risen to twenty-five million tons and in the next twenty years the amount nearly doubled. In recent years the amount of scrap used as raw material for making steel and castings has frequently been greater than the pig iron and hot metal products of the blast furnace. This development discouraged scrap metal losses that might otherwise have become a major source of national waste and has prevented the depletion of ore reserves from assuming more serious proportions.

In smelting and refining processes there were no spectacular developments during this period. Some interest was shown in the direct reduction of the ore by the sponge iron process, but primary reduction of the ore has continued to be carried on almost entirely in the blast furnace. During the twenty-five years prior to 1950, blast furnace capacity doubled. In an effort to meet the extraordinary steel requirements of World War II, increased attention was given to obtaining further increases in output from blast furnaces by raising the top pressure within the stack and by the use of oxygen for combustion. Experiments with the use of oxygen in open hearth furnaces for the purpose of increasing output and reducing fuel costs met with some success. The shift from the Bessemer to the open hearth process, which began actively about 1890, continued between the two World Wars. The unsuitability of iron made from our more important ores for refinement by the Bessemer process, together with the better control of product qualities and the ability to use large amounts of scrap in the open hearth furnace, were the factors chiefly responsible for the shift. Open hearth steel increased its share of total steel output from nearly 75 per cent in 1915 to 93 per cent in 1940.

Paralleling the decline of Bessemer steel was the gradual replacement of crucible steel by that made in the electric furnace. Down to the First World War tool and other cutting steels were produced chiefly by the old crucible process, operated on a small and inefficient batch basis by predominantly hand methods. First introduced in this country in 1908, electric furnace production increased rapidly during World War I to meet military requirements for the special alloy steels demanded by many types of military equipment. Continued improvement in electric furnace production resulted in the steady displacement of crucible steel, whose output declined from 114,000 tons in 1915 to some 2,200 tons in 1930. In recent years, electric furnace steel has nearly equaled the output of the Bessemer process, the two methods together accounting for about nine per cent of total steel production.

The development of special alloy steels, made possible principally by advances in the metallurgy and chemistry of steel, aided by the introduction of the electric furnace, has been the most important innovation in steel products during the past generation. Between World Wars I and II, alloy steel tonnage rose from two to eleven millions, or from four to twenty per cent of the total output of steel. The development of these special steels was an outgrowth of the increasing need for steels having qualities of hardness, resistance to corrosion and high temperatures, high tensile strength, and other qualities possessed neither by the ordinary carbon steels nor by the high-cost crucible steel. Familiarity with the production and use of the alloy steels increased through their military applications in the First World War. In the postwar years these finer steels found increasing use in automobiles, machinery, and other industrial equipment. The demands of turbines using steam of mounting pressures and temperatures, of aircraft engines with their high ratios of power to weight, and of gas turbines, culminating in the jet propulsion power plants of the nineteen forties, were met only through the continued development of the alloy steels.

Steel plates and sheets continued to rise in importance, owing especially to their increasing use in a widening range of consumer durable goods, such as automobiles and household equipment. Between the First World War and 1940, the production of steel rails declined about 40 per cent in amount and structural steel rose 50 per cent. Production of steel plates and sheets, on the other hand, increased from five to nearly fifteen million tons during the same period. The outstanding technical development in the fabrication of sheet steel was the introduction in 1927 of the continuous strip mill for rolling ingots into long strips of sheet steel in a single and continuous operation, a remarkable advance over the older method of sheet rolling.

The geographical and organizational pattern of the industry underwent relatively little change during this period. With the growth of steel production centers on the Great Lakes, the Pittsburgh district lost something of its onetime preeminence. There were no major shifts in location, chiefly because there were no important changes in sources of raw materials or in markets and because heavy plant investments discouraged such shifts. Access to cheap fuel of the proper grade probably remained the principal factor in determining location, not only because of the tremendous amounts used in the reduction and refining processes, but also because of the heavy power requirements of steel plants. Yet the locational influence of fuel declined somewhat, owing to a steady reduction in the amount required per ton of pig iron produced and to the rising importance of steel scrap as a raw material, extensive supplies of which added weight to the growing desire of market areas for their own steel plants. Construction by the Federal government during World War II of the large Geneva and Fontana steel works in Utah and California to meet the needs of West Coast war industries—chiefly shipbuilding—has not materially altered the national picture, although these plants are of great importance to western industry.

Steel production declined from a peak of over 56 million tons in 1929 to a low of less than 14 million tons in 1932, rose again to 52 million tons in 1939 and then soared to a wartime peak of 90 million tons in 1944. During 1940 and 1941 the industry was reluctant to expand capacity to supply defense and war needs and only did so after much prodding from the defense agencies and with the aid of government financing. The unexpectedly high level of industrial production maintained in the reconversion period following the defeat of Germany and Japan brought a revival of the controversy over steel capacity, centering this time on the ability of the industry to supply the steel essential for the continuance of employment and national income on a high level.

The Chemical Industries

The seventy-five years ending in 1950 witnessed the rapid rise in the importance of chemicals and chemistry in industry and, through industry, in everyday life. Before 1860 the chemist and the chemical laboratory were virtually unknown in industry, the chemical industries were of minor importance, and the industrial uses of chemicals were relatively few. The marked development of the role of chemistry and chemical processes in industry got under way about 1880; the First World War gave it a decided stimulus, with many of the most spectacular developments coming during the succeeding thirty years. The index of physical output for chemical products (1929: 100), which stood at only 19 in 1899 and 42 in 1914, rose to 133 in 1939, thereafter more than doubling under the impact of war demands. In scores of industries chemical processes came to occupy a central role and in a far greater number chemicals constitute an important class of raw materials.

The chemical revolution as it affected industry has been marked by three major developments: (1) the rapid increase in the use of chemicals in industry, accompanied by a corresponding expansion of industries engaged in the manufacture of these chemicals, (2) a steady penetration of most branches of industry by chemical techniques and processes, and (3) the introduction of methods and processes by which such familiar materials as fertilizers and rubber are produced artificially and entirely new materials, such as coal-tar dyes, plastics, fibres, and explosives, are created synthetically. The spectacular developments in synthetic creation have been much in the public eye, owing to the popularity of rayon and nylon fabrics, to the wartime expansion of synthetic rubber production, and to the innumerable applications of the plastic resins in household gadgets and a wide variety of consumers' goods. Less apparent but not less substantial have been the contributions of chemistry to everyday living through such media as the soap, paper, and fertilizer industries.

Among the early industrial users of chemicals the textile industries were outstanding, consuming large quantities of bleaching agents, detergents, and dyes. As the production of other basic commodities passed from the handicraft stage and small-factory fabrication to production on a large scale, chemicals found new and enlarged applications. Sulphuric acid offers an interesting example of this development. Only 60,000 tons were produced in this country as late as 1867 when it was beginning to be used in the manufacture of fertilizer and steel and in the refining of petroleum. Production increased to 380,000 tons in 1878, rose another million tons by 1900, and by 1925 passed the six million ton mark.

Another of the heavy chemicals to attain industrial significance was soda ash (sodium carbonate), manufactured chiefly from common salt. This chemical was itself used in industry and was also the source of such other soda products as caustic soda, sodium bicarbonate, and washing soda. Soda ash is important in the manufacture of glass, soap, pulp and paper, nonferrous metals, textiles, water softeners, and other chemicals. Before 1880 there was virtually no soda industry in the United States. By 1914 self-sufficiency had been attained, and production increased until by 1940 the three million ton mark had been passed. Among other heavy chemical industries to attain importance were the mineral acids—hydrochloric, nitric, and phosphoric—and the artificial fertilizers—phosphates, nitrates, ammonium sulphates, and potash.

Prior to World War I, despite the rapid growth of the chemical industries since 1880, there was little general awareness of the key role of chemicals in industry and in agriculture. Few understood that vast quantities of acids, alkalies, chlorine, nitrates, and other chemicals were required in the conduct of modern war. For the production of such powerful explosives as cordite, lyddite, and TNT, which had replaced black powder, the manufacturers required unprecedented quantities of the major acids, caustic soda, toluol, phenol, cellulose, and ethyl alcohol. Prices for nitrates soared; imports from Chile, the principal source heretofore, more than doubled in three years, and an elaborate program for the fixation of atmospheric nitrogen was launched, costing the government over one billion dollars and producing no nitrates before the end of the war and chiefly political controversy thereafter.

By-product coke making was another industry that felt the heavy impact of war demands. The abundance and cheapness of coal and natural gas had retarded the replacement of the wasteful beehive oven process by by-product coking, and even in existing by-product plants the recovery of chemical by-products had been neglected owing to the limited demand for them. The skyrocketing of explosives requirements during the war resulted in the building of thousands of new by-product ovens to supply these chemicals. When at the end of the war the demand for explosives collapsed, the resulting surplus of coal tar crudes provided the raw material basis for a new synthetic chemicals industry, especially the new plastics.

Another serious wartime shortage was in potash, heretofore obtained almost entirely from Germany. The cutting off of supplies was followed by a tenfold rise in prices, creating a shortage that was particularly serious in agriculture since there were no substitutes for potash as a fertilizer. There followed a feverish search for native sources of potash. Brine wells and lakes, wood ashes, kelp, distillery waste, and cement dust were the principal sources exploited, but the total production in 1918 came to but one-fourth of our pre-war consumption. Most of the war-born potash plants failed to survive the peace and the renewal of imports from Europe, but a small remnant of the industry continued and during the next two decades grew to substantial proportions. Dyes were another class of chemical products obtained chiefly in Germany before the war. Fantastic price increases, aided by a protective tariff and the confiscation of German patents, produced a mushroom growth in the dye industry. Output of dyes in 1917 was in excess of 140,000 tons, and the new industry had obtained a permanent footing.

World War I experience not only resulted in a marked expansion of the chemicals industry, but it awakened the American people both to the potentialities of chemistry in industry and to our dependence upon foreign sources for many essential raw materials. The period between the two World Wars was marked by the rapid expansion of the chemicals industry, the penetration of industry in general by chemical techniques, and by outstanding developments in creative chemistry.

After 1919 there was a steady expansion of the production of such war-born industries as potash and nitrates. Potash output, reduced to less than 5,000 tons in 1921, increased steadily until, by 1939, production was approximately 400,000 tons and was much in excess of our imports. Nitrogen production rose unevenly from some 100,000 tons in the early twenties to a half million tons in 1940, by which date net imports amounted to but one-fourth of the domestic production.

The rise of synthetic fibers and plastics was the most spectacular development of the between-war years. Those products are peculiarly the product of the chemist and the chemical engineer. Sometimes described as artificial silk, the synthetic fibers are more commonly grouped under the generic term "rayon," which was given to filaments made by any one of several processes from solutions of modified cellulose. The basic raw materials are wood pulp and cotton linters, and in their processing the rayon industry consumes large quantities of sulphuric acid, caustic soda, carbon bisulphide, and other chemicals.

The growth of the plastics industry paralleled that of synthetic fibers in many respects, but the wide variety of the applications of plastics gives them a much greater industrial significance. Plastics are materials of a non-crystalline character which when heated become soft and pliable and can be given any desired shape when molded under pressure. Their lightness, toughness, colorability, resistance to corrosion, and ease of fabrication into either simple or intricate forms are the qualities that have led to their use for innumerable purposes in the general industrial and durable goods fields. Prior to World War I, the principal synthetic plastics materials used were celluloid (trade name for cellulose nitrate), originating in 1869, and Bakelite, first of the synthetic resins, discovered in 1909. The uses of the early plastics were rather limited, but the search for new kinds of plastics and the development of desired qualities and characteristics continued. The result was a steady increase in the types of plastics and a multiplication of their practical applications. Manufactured from such common materials as coal, petroleum, gas, salt, and wood, the extension of plastics use depended chiefly on the ingenuity of chemists and the reduction of prices.

The rise of plastics to industrial prominence did not come until the decade before World War II. As late as 1935 total output in this country did not exceed 50,000 tons, but by 1939 this figure had increased to 170,000 tons. During World War II the numerous applications of plastics in military equipment and the extreme scarcity of metals resulted in a rapid expansion in plastics production, with the total output in 1945 nearly five times that produced in 1939 and equal to nearly one-half the tonnage of aluminum produced in 1945.

The Rise of Rubber

While the manufacture of rubber products in the United States goes back to the middle of the nineteenth century, the attainment of major industry status awaited the coming of the automobile age. The soaring output of motor vehicles—25,000 in 1905, 970,930 in 1915, and 2,227,349 in 1920—had far-reaching consequences for the rubber industry. The value of rubber products increased from $100,000,000 in 1899 to $700,000,000 in 1921, with tires accounting for nearly three-fourths of the latter figure; an extensive industry arose in Malaya to fill the mounting requirements for crude rubber; and the rubber manufacturing industry in this country was transformed from one composed of numerous small companies to one dominated by a handful of great corporations.

Long the world's principal consumer of crude rubber, the American industry down to World War II was much affected by the repeated efforts of the producing countries to restrict the amount and raise the price of crude rubber. This situation led to some international ill feeling and prompted the larger rubber companies to invest in plantation properties for their own protection, but without altering the supply picture materially thereby.

The outstanding development of the decade ending in 1950 was the creation of a huge synthetic rubber industry. Our gradual involvement in the war during 1940 and 1941 and the extension of Japanese control over the principal rubber producing areas of Malaya compelled the government to embark on a synthetic program capable of supplying military and essential civilian requirements. The execution of this program, financed by the government but with private operation of the new plants, was one of the outstanding industrial achievements of the war years. Synthetic production, which in 1939 had been less than 2,000 tons, mostly special purpose rubber, rose from 10,000 tons in 1941 to 260,000 tons in 1943 and 930,000 tons in 1945. The natural rubber required for mixing with the synthetic product for many purposes came from stockpiles accumulated at the beginning of the emergency and supplemented by small supplies obtained during the war, chiefly from Latin America. By the end of the war 85 per cent of United States rubber requirements were met by the various general and special purpose synthetic rubbers, as compared with but 1 per cent in 1941. While the use of natural rubber increased markedly after 1946, it was clear that synthetic rubber had made a permanent place for itself in the market.

Light Metals

The most spectacular metallurgical development since the First World War has been the rise of light metals to a position of industrial prominence. Although the commercial production of aluminum in Europe dates from the 1850's, the difficulties and high costs of production long narrowly limited its use and kept output low. The improvement of the electrolytic method of refining, together with the availability of cheap hydroelectric power, led to a rapid expansion of aluminum production after 1900. Yet, on the eve of World War I, production in the United States was only 29,000 tons. Wartime needs greatly increased the demand for the new light metal, both for miltary and civilian uses, and production reached 69,000 tons in 1920, thereafter increasing at a much slower rate and reaching a total of 163,000 tons in 1939.

The qualities of aluminum that favored its growing use were not simply its light weight—only one-third that of steel—but also its resistance to corrosion, high conductivity of heat and electricity, high tensile strength when alloyed with other metals, and ease of shaping and fabrication by a variety of methods, such as casting, forging, rolling, machining, extrusion, spinning, and stamping. Its usefulness in cooking utensils was early demonstrated, with the result that aluminum rapidly replaced copper utensils. After 1920 it largely displaced tin in the production of foil and came into increasing use in electrical equipment, in automobiles, and in a wide variety of industrial apparatus, transportation equipment, and other durable goods. It became the material par excellence for the production of aircraft and played an important role in the expansion of commercial and military aviation in the nineteen twenties and thirties.

The most striking development of aluminum, and of its sister metal magnesium, came during World War II when the enormous requirements of military aircraft led to a sixfold increase in primary aluminum production within a period of four years. As a result of this extraordinary growth, aluminum took its place as the third of the nonferrous metals in tonnage, passing lead and closely approaching zinc in production. If volume rather than weight is considered, aluminum actually headed the list of the nonferrous metals, exceeding even copper in quantity.

Until the Second World War aluminum production in this country was entirely under the control of the Aluminum Company of America (Alcoa). An anti-trust action, begun in 1937, culminated in 1945 with a verdict declaring Alcoa in certain respects to be a monopoly, but it remained for the war itself to loosen Alcoa's complete control of the industry. As in the case of steel, there was some reluctance during the defense and early war years to expand aluminum capacity to the extent made necessary by military requirements. Congressional prodding plus a gradual awakening to the tremendous demands of our war machine eventuated in a vast program of plant expansion. Although most of the new capacity, built with government funds but operated under private contract, was managed by Alcoa, several independent companies entered the field, beginning with the erection in 1940 of a primary aluminum plant by the Reynolds Metals Company.

By 1944 total plant capacity had been increased to well over a million tons, of which more than half was owned by the government, much of it located in the Pacific Northwest to take advantage of the abundant hydroelectric power available in that region. At the end of the war the two independents that continued in operation accounted together for less than ten per cent of primary aluminum production. This situation was changed at the end of 1946 by a partial disposal of government-owned reduction facilities which brought about a marked shift in the pattern of control. Alcoa now controlled but 51 per cent of primary capacity, the Reynolds Company 29 per cent, and the Kaiser-controlled Permanente Metals Corporation the remaining 20 per cent.

The development of the magnesium industry followed a course similar in many respects to that of aluminum except that its growth was much slower, not exceeding an output of 2,500 tons until 1939. Control here, too, came to center in the hands of a single producer, the Dow Chemical Company, after its principal competitor, an Alcoa subsidiary, withdrew from magnesium production by agreement between Dow and Alcoa in 1927. From this date to 1942 Dow produced all the primary magnesium in this country. Under the pressure of war needs, plant capacity was expanded at a cost of more than a third of a billion dollars to the government. Plants operating by different processes were built in various parts of the country. The peak of wartime production was reached in 1943 with a total output of 170,000 tons; by the end of 1944 magnesium capacity had been increased to 240,000 tons.

In the case of both of the light metals, production at the end of the war fell off sharply from the wartime peak and some of the new plants remained idle in the hands of the government. Yet output was maintained at levels far higher than the greatest prewar production. Wartime needs had stimulated technical advances, resulting in new and improved light metal alloys, in improved production and application techniques, and in many new uses. When price ceilings were removed in the winter of 1946, the price of aluminum for the first time in history fell below that of copper. The prospect for the continued expansion of the light metals in competition with the older nonferrous metals appeared to be good.

The Fuel Industries

In the field of industrial fuels, the major developments following World War I were the decline in the relative importance of coal and the sharp rise of petroleum and natural gas as sources of energy.[1] Within the coal industry three developments are outstanding during this period: technological advances in mining operations, the rise in importance of organized labor, and attempts to stabilize production. Technological advance took the form principally of mechanization of mining operations.

[1] See below, p. 736.

The proportion of coal mined by machine rose from 60 per cent in 1920 to 76 per cent in 1944; output per man-hour between 1929 and 1939 increased almost a third in bituminous and nearly four-fifths in anthracite mining. Mechanical loading of coal, introduced commercially at the end of World War I, in 1944 accounted for approximately half of bituminous and one-third of anthracite production. Mining of coal by stripping off the surface cover of earthy materials expanded steadily during these decades, due especially to improvements in the size and efficiency of excavating machinery. It became feasible to remove from seven to fifteen feet of barren material for every foot of coal thickness recovered. By 1945 approximately one-fifth of the total anthracite and bituminous product was obtained by stripping operations, with sorry results for the appearance and usefulness of the land surface.

The First World War had brought prosperity for a time to the coal industry, but the postwar years found the industry burdened with excess capacity and falling prices, accompanied by a depressed rate of return on investment. Between 1920 and 1929, the average price of coal declined more than 50 per cent. Thousands of mines closed and employment and wages fell. Labor troubles, the growth of competing sources of energy, and mechanization which increased effective capacity added to the difficulties of coal operators. Distribution of bituminous production among a very large number of mines effectually discouraged the resort to the methods of restraining competition so popular in other fields of industrial enterprise. Recurring stoppages in production from strikes and transportation difficulties had led to numerous government investigations of the industry and to proposals for government supervision of coal production.[2]

No effective action was taken to relieve the situation until the National Industrial Recovery Act of 1933 made available to the bituminous industry some relief from the extremes of competition. When the NIRA was declared unconstitutional, special relief for the coal industry was provided by the Guffey-Snyder and Guffey-Vinson acts. The latter, the Bituminous Coal Conservation Act of 1937, set up the machinery by which it was hoped that, through the enforcement of minimum prices and fair trade practices, a measure of stability could be established in the industry. The difficulties and complexities of the task delayed the establishment of minimum prices, and when the amended act of 1937 expired in 1943 only limited progress toward stabilizing the industry had been made.

The petroleum industry continued its rapid growth in the years following World War I. National output rose from some 400 million barrels in 1919 to over a billion barrels in 1929. As discovery of one flush field followed another, especially in Texas, Oklahoma, and California, the

---

2 See below, p. 847.

industry was faced with an embarrassment of riches. In oil as in coal, chronic overproduction was the bane of the industry during the twenties. This condition arose from the peculiarities of oil production and ownership. Ownership of an oil property does not carry with it title to a fixed amount of oil proportionate to the extent of the land, but only the right to draw upon the fluid and highly fugitive oil in the extensive underlying reservoir that constitutes the oil field. Under these conditions a premium was placed on maximum exploitation, since each producer in the field sought to take out as much oil as possible from the common pool before depletion set in. As each new field came into production an upsurge of output flooded the market and prices fell. The onset of the depression after 1929 accentuated the difficulties of the industry and hastened the search for adequate methods of relief.

Excessive production in relation to demand had plagued the crude petroleum industry from the beginning. Although a number of states early took steps to discourage the more flagrant forms of waste associated with excessive production, it was not until after 1920 that government intervened to regulate production as such in the oil fields. An increasing number of states, at first independently and then in varying degrees of cooperation with the Federal government and each other, undertook to check the unrestrained output that had such a depressing effect upon the market. The public interest centered primarily in the conservation of a valuable natural source by preventing wasteful methods of extraction. Oil producers understandably were more concerned with the effect that government intervention might have in stabilizing the market and in supporting prices. The result was the establishment through Federal and state legislation of an intricate system of regulatory controls, described as *prorationing,* by which production in most of the leading oil producing states was restricted.

In general, state prorationing laws sought to limit the production of each well to a fraction of its potential output by means of quotas based on monthly estimates of market demand. The Federal government not only cooperated actively in the administration of prorationing, but under the Connally Act of 1935 forbade the shipment in interstate commerce of oil produced in violation of state conservation laws. While the value of prorationing as a method of conserving oil resources is debatable, the system has had considerable success as a method of restricting output and stabilizing the market.

With the rapid increase in automobiles, it became important to obtain from petroleum a higher proportion of gasoline than was obtainable through simple distillation. To meet this need the process of thermal conversion, or "cracking," was developed by means of which the heavier components of the crude oil were broken down chemically into the lighter gasoline components. This new process, operating under pressure and soon placed on a continuous flow basis, was introduced commercially during World War I and was improved and extended steadily in the succeeding years. A further important advance was made with the introduction in the mid-thirties of catalytic cracking, which gave much greater control over the kind and quality of the products of refining. It enabled the industry not only to increase further the yield of gasoline but also to vary the proportions of the several products of refining and to produce from crude petroleum a variety of chemical products for other industrial uses, as for example the butadiene essential for the production of synthetic rubber.

World War II and Aftermath

American industry entered the period of World War II with much idle plant capacity, despite some recovery from the recession of 1937. Many months before Pearl Harbor, most of the industrial slack had been taken up as a result of defense armament and foreign aid (Lend-Lease) programs. Industry was faced with the dual task of greatly expanding capacity to meet the nation's requirements for civilian and military goods and of converting plants, equipment, and labor force from producing the familiar goods of peacetime to producing the unfamiliar, often complex, and always exacting materiel of modern war. Prior to Pearl Harbor there was considerable unwillingness in industry to carry out the essential conversion and expansion of industrial capacity. Industries enjoying rapidly growing demands for their peacetime products showed little enthusiasm for making the difficult changeover to war production. Other industries, plagued with substantial excess capacity in peacetime, were unwilling to add materially to that capacity in order to meet the requirements of what appeared to many as a temporary emergency. Such attitudes did not long survive Pearl Harbor and the measures adopted thereafter by the government to speed war production.

The resulting upsurge in production exceeded all expectations of the capabilities of industry. Munitions production showed the greatest expansion of any class of products, rising from a monthly rate of less than a quarter billion dollars in value early in 1940 to a wartime peak of more than five billions at the close of 1943, after which there was a slow tapering off until VE Day, followed by a precipitous descent. The most spectacular increases were in airplanes and in merchant ships, where output multiplied fifty- and seventyfold, respectively, and in the light metals and synthetic rubber, with results referred to elsewhere. In the tonnage metals the most impressive increases were in iron ore, whose output doubled, and in pig iron and steel ingots, each of which increased by four-fifths. Machinery production multiplied six times and the number of locomotives more than eightfold. Even in the non-durable goods fields, least affected by military demands, there were substantial rises in production.

Such increases in industrial production were a tribute to the resourcefulness, the ingenuity, and the adaptability of American industry—management, engineers, and labor alike. With consumers' purchasing power rising sharply, civilian goods production likewise rose to new heights despite wartime restrictions on the production of less essential goods. These unprecedented results were possible only through the overall direction and coordination of the national economy by the Federal Government. The expansion and conversion of industrial facilities was to a large extent financed by Federal funds, mounting in the aggregate to 18 billions of dollars. The distribution of scarce materials, equipment, and manpower among essential industries and services in the amount and in the order necessary to insure maximum and balanced production was accomplished only through the elaborate priority systems administered by the war agencies. Finally, it was through Federal price and production controls that the powerful inflationary pressures resulting from the unbridgable gap between supply and demand were kept under control and the balance and stability essential to maximum production maintained.

One of the most important consequences of the war was a substantial addition to industrial capacity. Of some 32 billions of dollars expended in enlarging productive capacity, approximately half went into new plants for the production of such direct war materiel as ships, aircraft, tanks, guns and ammunition, synthetic rubber, aviation gas, and chemicals. The other half was distributed among a dozen civilian-type industries, especially the metals, machinery and automotive vehicles, food, lumber and textiles, and mining. An additional 9 billions were applied to the expansion of transportation, communications, power, and commercial facilities. Much of this new plant capacity, as in the case of explosives and ammunition loading plants, had slight if any use in peacetime. In the case of shipyards and airplane factories, more than 90 per cent of the wartime capacity was in excess of peacetime needs and, except where set aside for standby emergency use, could in most instances be adapted to other uses only at considerable expense. There remained, however, a net addition of new and highly efficient plant capacity estimated as equal to one-sixth the value of our prewar manufacturing plant and equipment.

The war left behind also a legacy of important technological advances. A great stimulus had been given to the production and use of light metals, plastics, synthetic fibres, and synthetic rubber. Important advances were made in aircraft and communications equipment and in electronic devices as applied to industrial processes. Wartime production needs led to the extension and perfecting of many industrial techniques and processes and to the introduction of others. The harnessing and application of atomic energy opened a new frontier of industrial potentialities.

Against these gains, which were unevenly distributed through industry, must be balanced substantial losses, especially in respect to the national resource base. The extension of industrialization since the turn of the century resulted in a rapid acceleration of the demands made upon our mineral resources. The tremendous raw material requirements of a war economy further accentuated these demands, resulting in some instances in a serious depletion of the highest grade deposits. While the over-all position of the United States with respect to mineral resources continued to be enviable, with respect to certain categories of raw materials this country has either joined the have-not nations or is faced with the imminent prospect of doing so. Although reserves of iron ore are still immense, the metallic content of the ores used has been slowly declining for years and war demands greatly accelerated the depletion of the high grade open-pit ores. Within the near future it will be necessary to rely increasingly upon foreign sources for high grade ores. Coal reserves likewise are immense, yet the heavy inroads made in recent decades, especially during World War II, upon reserves of high grade coking coal have created a serious problem of depletion. Industry is faced with the problem of developing techniques for the utilization of the poorer coking coals.

In petroleum, too, the future is not bright. The war increased the already rapid drain on our oil reserves, and in the postwar years our consumption has been at a rate equal to the entire world output in 1938 and has exceeded production. In lumber, the principal forest product, the United States has been on a net importing basis since 1941. In the major item of pulpwood we have for some years imported from one-third to one-half of our requirements. The overall forest situation has long been a subject of criticism because of the wasteful methods of "cut-out-and-get-out" exploitation. While some progress has been made in operating forests on a sustained-yield basis, the forests in many parts of the country are badly run down and for the nation as a whole saw timber drain has been 50 per cent greater than growth.

The situation in respect to nonferrous metals is even less satisfactory. For many years we have been dependent in part upon imports for our copper, and in the past decade net imports have at times equalled domestic production. In both lead and zinc, too, domestic sources have been increasingly inadequate to supply domestic requirements in recent years. The aluminum industry has been mainly dependent on foreign ore (bauxite) and, while domestic supplies of low grade aluminum ores are abundant, the problems of their commercial utilization have not yet been solved. A similar situation prevails with respect to the ores of manganese and vanadium. In other essential metals, such as tungsten, antimony, and mercury, domestic reserves are quite inadequate for either present or future needs. The recent war dispelled the widely held view that our mineral resources were virtually inexhaustible. Many minerals that have become essential to American industry must be obtained largely or entirely from foreign sources, with implications for national security as well as production costs.

In only a few instances are resources abundant in relation to probable future needs, and even in these instances industry faces the prospect of steadily rising costs as the richer and more accessible mineral bodies are depleted. Increasing attention is given to problems of resource conservation, although little has been accomplished in this direction, and to the development of methods by which low grade deposits can be made commercially available. Many are confident of the ability of scientists and technologists to overcome mounting resource deficiencies, drawing support from the man-made miracle of harnessing atomic energy. How far such confidence is justified only the future will reveal. One thing at least seems clear, American industry in the years ahead will not continue to enjoy the competitive advantage so long derived from its superior resource base.

Selected References

GENERAL WORKS

Barger, Harold, and Sam H. Schurr, *The Mining Industries, 1899-1939. A Study of Output, Employment and Productivity.* New York: National Bureau of Economic Research, Inc., 1944.

Dewhurst, J. Frederic, and others, *America's Needs and Resources.* New York: Twentieth Century Fund, 1947.

Haynes, William, *The American Chemical Industry. World War I Period: 1912-1922* (2 vols.). New York: Van Nostrand, 1945.

Jerome, Harry, *Mechanization in Industry.* New York: National Bureau of Economic Research, Inc., 1934.

Muller, Charlotte, *Light Metals Monopoly.* New York: Columbia University Press, 1946.

National Resources Committee, *Technological Trends and National Policy.* Washington, D. C.: U. S. Government Printing Office, 1937.

Rostow, Eugene V., *A National Policy for the Oil Industry.* New Haven, Conn.: Yale University Press, 1948.

United States Bureau of the Budget, *The United States at War. The Development and Administration of the War Program by the Federal Government.* Washington, D. C.: U. S. Government Printing Office, 1947.

SPECIAL TOPICS

Daugherty, Carroll R.; Melvin D. De Chazeau; and Samuel S. Stratton, *The Economics of the Iron and Steel Industry.* New York: McGraw-Hill Book Co., 1937.

Krug, Julius A., *Wartime Production Achievements and the Reconversion Outlook. Report of the Chairman of the War Production Board.* Washington, D. C.: 1945.

Nelson, Donald M., *Arsenal of Democracy. The Story of American War Production.* New York: Harcourt, Brace and Co., 1946.

United States Bureau of the Census, *Historical Statistics of the United States, 1789-1945. A Supplement to the Statistical Abstract of the United States.* Washington, D. C.: U. S. Government Printing Office, 1949.

United States Civilian Production Administration, *Industrial Mobilization for War. The History of the War Production Board and Predecessor Agencies.* Washington, D. C.: U. S. Government Printing Office, 1947.

38 · MASS PRODUCTION AND THE USE OF ENERGY

What is Mass Production?

"Mass production" has become a kind of catch-all conveying diverse connotations. In its widely publicized popular sense, the term has acquired a social import far transcending its more precise technical meaning. It has come to be regarded as a distinctively and almost exclusively American phenomenon, embodying the essence of all past industrial achievement and containing the promise of all future industrial progress. It appears to supply the secret to the winning of modern wars and to the attainment of the great goals of economic prosperity and social well-being in peacetime. Indeed, it seems to have become a major weapon in the contemporary ideological competition between rival economic and social systems, serving both as an instrument and symbol in the struggle toward ultimate victory. It epitomizes the whole complex set of forces that form the material basis of the "American way of life."

Apart from this broad popular connotation, however, the concept of mass production is undoubtedly a convenient one, since by means of it one may attempt to integrate and to coordinate the many complex processes that comprise the technological and industrial development of the United States since the Civil War, and particularly since 1900. It provides a framework within which he who is rash may undertake to compress the principal trends of modern industrial history. But what are the essential ingredients of this concept that may best serve this purpose? It is noteworthy that the very name, as well as the initial attempt at a definition of mass production, appeared first in an article credited to Henry Ford, who was himself the presiding genius over one of its most spectacular early achievements, that in the automobile industry. The chief constituent of mass production, according to Ford, is method rather than magnitude of output: "Mass production is not merely quantity production . . ., nor is it merely machine production. . . . Mass production is the focusing upon a manufacturing project of the principles of power, accuracy, economy, system, continuity, and speed. . . . And the normal result is a productive organization that delivers in quantities a useful commodity of standard materials, workmanship, and design at minimum cost." [1]

Significantly, this authoritative definition of mass production also sharpened the distinction between the technical and financial aspects of modern industrial development, presenting them almost in opposition to each other. Mass production Ford held to be a triumph of engineering and management: "Beginning with management, . . . there is a noticeable increase of industrial control, as distinguished from financial control. The engineer's point of view has gained the ascendancy, and this trend will continue until finance becomes the handmaid instead of the mistress of productive industry." The ultimate economic and social possibilities of the new methods were, moreover, linked with the "capacity, latent or developed, of mass consumption, the ability to absorb large production. The two go together." Other factors, outside the scope of mass production technology proper, have, of course, combined to complicate and to obscure the actual trends of costs, prices, and total output. Among them certain restrictive tendencies in business organization and policy, as well as fluctuations of political and economic conditions, have hampered or retarded the realization of the advantages inherent in mass production, and may have, indeed, intensified many modern social problems, chief among them being continuous employment and the maintenance of full production through mass consumption.

Basic Conditions of Mass Production

Such formal definition as Henry Ford gives of a process in an advanced stage of development tends to abstract it from reality and to simplify unduly its actual evolution. Three principal questions, all of them interrelated, are involved in the history of mass production: namely, what made it possible, how it was achieved, and what have been its effects, insofar as they can be measured. It should be noted that, although the principle, and some of its constituent elements, germinated early, their full and effective combination came slowly and ripened late. This was because, in the actual historical process, the conditions that made mass production possible did not appear together and all at once; their impact was gradual and cumulative rather than immediate. The progress of mass production, in fact, generated its own favorable conditions as well as new problems and continuing difficulties.

---

[1] Quoted from an article by Henry Ford on "Mass Production," first published in the Thirteenth Edition of the *Encyclopaedia Britannica* (1926), Vol. II, p. 821. Mass production was also the subject of two monographs prepared by William Butterworth and Pierre Gounod respectively, dealing with its American and European aspects. Written under the auspices of the Europe-United States Committee of the International Chamber of Commerce, these studies provided background material for an Industrial Congress held in Washington in 1931, and were published in the third volume of *Europe-United States of America*. Paris: International Chamber of Commerce, 1931.

Three sets of conditions have contributed to the rise and growth of mass production. There was first, of course, the progress of technology and invention, determining the rate at which the machinery, the methods, and the very materials essential to mass production became available. Secondly, the secular trends of the national economy and business also exercised an important influence, since these affected the rate at which the requisite capital funds, the forms of business organization, and the skills of management were able to support and promote the expanding structure of mass production technology.

A third set of factors fostering the development of mass production had its source in the character of American society proper, and the latter was in turn shaped and conditioned by industrial progress, both psychologically and practically. American society proved to be peculiarly congenial to the requirements and the results of mass production. There was, in the first place, the factor of a population that grew from 31,000,000 to 76,000,000 between 1860 and 1900 and nearly doubled between 1900 and 1950, rising to a total of more than 150,000,000. Quantitatively, this provided both a labor and a consumption market for an expanding volume and variety of capital and consumers' goods. The vast home market was, moreover, being created during this period by the happy combination of improved means of communication and an elaborate machinery of distribution functioning within a national system of internal free trade.

Mass consumption was the main support as it was the prerequisite of mass production, and it was the principal index and evidence of the rising standard of living that became the distinctive mark of American society and the object of universal admiration and envy. The purchasing power of the American people, on an average per capita basis, increased nearly threefold between 1869 and 1929; to this material measure should be added the increase of leisure resulting from a shortened working day, which provided further incentive and opportunity for a broadened pattern of consumption, apart from and in spite of recurring periods of depression and contraction. In 1928 the total national income of the American people was estimated as being one-third greater than the combined incomes of the twenty-odd states of Europe with three times the population. It is noteworthy, in this connection, that the philosophical and practical relation between mass production and mass purchasing power was perceived early by Henry Ford. By 1929, it had become a commonly held business opinion that "Wage earners . . . are the spenders of the nation, and upon their ability to spend freely the general business of our country depends." [2] The experience of the ensuing depression dur-

[2] D. D. Lescohier, and E. Brandeis, *History of Labor in the United States, 1896-1932*, p. 89. New York: The Macmillan Company, 1935; Henry Ford, *My Life and Work*, pp. 116 ff. New York: Doubleday, Page & Co., 1923. The growth of purchasing power is summarized in R. F. Martin, *National Income in the United States, 1799-1938*, p. 6. New York: National Industrial Conference Board, 1939.

ing the 1930's reinforced this conviction and served to convert it into a major national policy of relief and recovery.

The American home market, in the words of Andrew Carnegie, was, "a vast homogeneous market"; and this factor, too, was a major influence affecting the evolution of mass production. Across the horizontal plane of its great geographical extent, as well as up and down the vertical social scale, the American market underwent a standardization of taste and consumption that bore profound psychological and economic significance. In part, the demand for great quantities of identical or similar commodities was built up by the subtle suggestions of salesmanship and advertising that were a parallel and logical accompaniment of mass production itself. In part also, such ready standardization of consumption was due to the scarcity of craft skills in a new country. The products of such skills had always figured prominently among American imports, and these fell an easy victim to the process of mechanization and mass production, which added, moreover, many new commodities to an expanding catalogue of consumers' goods.

This basic compatibility between mass production and standardized mass consumption was, furthermore, a practical manifestation of that democratic equalitarianism that was distinctively American. Certainly it was a useful and powerful instrument of Americanization, and by means of it men of widely different racial and cultural origins took on at least the superficial similarity of common tastes, satisfied by the common goods of mass production, and were reinforced in their common conceptions of equality and opportunity. Whether and to what extent mass consumption and mass production also contributed to the supposed stereotyping of the American way of life and to the growth of big business is, of course, a broad philosophical and cultural question more easily raised than answered. Equally broad and controversial are the issues of speed-up, monotony, fatigue, and other labor problems that have been associated with mass production. Added to this is the over-all question of the degree of rigidity inherent in the technological and economic structure of mass-production industry, and the relative facility with which it may be adapted to changing needs. The experience of two world wars since 1914 has demonstrated its capacity for conversion and reconversion within a remarkably short time to the purposes of war and peace. There remains, however, the long-run factor of changing demand and the spectre of a saturated or contracting market in relation to the expanding potential of mass production; this appeared to loom up as early as the 1870's.[3]

[3] D. A. Wells, "How Shall the Nation Regain Prosperity?" *North American Review*, July, 1877, p. 126; also by the same author, *Recent Economic Changes*, p. 63. New York: D. Appleton and Company, 1890. The same pessimistic note was echoed by Carroll D. Wright in his first report as United States Commissioner of Labor: *Industrial Depressions*, p. 257. Washington, D. C.: 1886. Compare, however, the prediction of an economy of abundance in Edward Atkinson, *The Industrial Progress of the Nation:*

Essential Elements of Mass Production

If the conditions and characteristics of the American market provided both incentive and opportunity for the development of mass production, the process itself evolved gradually and haltingly from faint beginnings. It was compounded of a number of separate elements arising in the nineteenth century but for the most part attaining their effective and conscious integration into a unified coherent pattern after 1900. Mechanization was, of course, the central core of the pattern as it was also the outstanding phenomenon of the Industrial Revolution generally; the problem is, indeed, one of differentiating mass production from the progress of modern industrialism as a whole. Chief among the other elements in the pattern of mass production is the principle of standardization. Stemming from the rudimentary division of labor, standardization involved the continuous pursuit and progressive realization of uniformity of the materials, operations, and products of industry, which made possible the further subdivision and mechanization of labor.

The culminating achievement of mass production technology after 1900 was the combination of the system of interchangeable parts and the principle of mechanized transport into a unified or progressive system of production, popularly known as the assembly line. This development was the conscious outgrowth of industrial organization and management and thus constituted another integrating element in the pattern of mass production. Industrial management aimed at the most efficient utilization of both machinery and labor in an over-all program of planning, maintaining, and coordinating the smooth flow of production. It was an essential condition of mass production, precisely as the parallel art of business management became a necessary adjunct of the large-scale corporate organization of business.

Industries on the Interchangeable System Before 1900

Most directly in the genealogical line of evolution of mass production technology was a group of metal-fabricating industries developed in the United States during the nineteenth century. First and chief among these was the manufacture of firearms, both guns and pistols. In the generation following the Civil War a number of other new products based upon the machine tool technology of interchangeable parts won considerable prominence and discovered large potential markets both at home and abroad. Among them were agricultural machinery, the sewing machine, the typewriter, and the bicycle. Like the rifle and the pistol, these were relatively

---

Consumption Limited, Production Unlimited. New York: G. P. Putnam's Sons, 1890. For a modern version of these questions, see H. G. Moulton, *Capital Expansion, Employment and Economic Stability,* pp. 162 ff. Washington, D. C.: Brookings Institution, 1940.

complex metal mechanisms that could best be assembled from uniform parts, which were manufactured with the same machine tools and in some cases even in the same machine shops. In the case of agricultural machinery, as in that of the sewing machine, quantity production was being achieved in the Civil War decade, following a preliminary period of pioneer invention and industrial experimentation and development.

The major triumph of mass production technology prior to 1900 was the bicycle, which reached the height of its popular vogue and its peak of production at about 1900, just as the automobile was emerging from the experimental into the industrial stage. Introduced from England, the industry by the close of the century was one of the largest in the country, employing 70,000 workers and having an annual output of more than a million bicycles; bicycle factories had become a special object of interest both for their machinery and for their high degree of standardization of methods and product. Like the automobile at a later date, the bicycle commanded a large and devoted public, estimated at 4,000,000 persons in 1900; it had become the nucleus of a broad cultural complex that reached out to a good-roads movement and to new habits of life and fashions in dress. The American Bicycle Company of 1899, merging 56 plants into one of the principal industrial combinations of the period, was only some 20 years removed from the first factory established by Col. Albert Pope at Hartford, which had sold 92 bicycles in 1878.[4]

The Machine-Tool Industry

At the turn of the present century two distinct lines of industrial evolution had sprung from the original general machine and metal product shops located principally in New England. One of these was the machine-tool industry proper, in which a high degree of specialization became characteristic both of particular plants and localities. It provided machinery for the expanding technology of mass production, and, indeed, the "master tools" of all industry. The second trend comprised the various industries fabricating interchangeable parts and assembling them on a quantity basis into finished products. The automobile industry was to be, after 1900, a major example of the second trend, starting with the prevailing methods of fabrication and assembly but contributing significantly and spectacularly to the further evolution of mass production.

[4] *Scientific American,* July 25, 1896; November 6, 1897. On the evolution of the interchangeable system before 1900 and of the industries dependent upon it, consult C. H. Fitch's "Report on the Manufacture of Interchangeable Mechanism," in the second volume of the tenth census (Washington, D. C.: 1883); the second volume of V. S. Clark's *History of Manufactures;* also C. H. Cochrane, *Wonders of Modern Mechanism* (Philadelphia: J. P. Lippincott Company, 1895) ; C. M. Depew, ed., *One Hundred Years of American Commerce* (New York: D. O. Haynes & Co., 1895); E. W. Byrn, *The Progress of Invention in the Nineteenth Century* (New York: Munn & Co., 1900); and F. W. Wile, ed., *A Century of Industrial Progress* (New York: Doubleday, Doran & Co., 1928).

Accompanying and affecting these trends was, of course, the phenomenal development of the metal industries, especially those producing iron and steel, that supplied the essential materials for the manufacture of metal products in expanding volume and with increasingly reliable uniformity of quality. It was reinforced by an increasing awareness of the role of scientific research; the research and testing laboratory tended to become an integral part of industry after the turn of the century, particularly in the expanding metallurgical, chemical, and electrical fields.

The principal achievement of the American machine-tool builders of the nineteenth century was in meeting the varied requirements of "the modern system of manufacturing." The basic machine tools, such as the lathe, the planer, the drill, and the borer were given a multiplicity of form and adapted to a variety of special purposes in shaping metal into uniform parts. By 1900 the turret lathe had been made fully automatic, thereby enabling one man to tend a number of lathes. The multiple tool principle, combined with automatic action, was applied also to the drill and gear-cutter, accelerating repetitive operations and constituting "the commonplaces of American shops."

With repetitive automatic action of the machine tools went increased accuracy and precision of workmanship, as the holding parts and measuring devices underwent continuous improvement; these included jigs, limit gauges, rules and particularly the micrometer caliper developed by Browne & Sharpe in 1867. By means of these the mechanic was enabled to achieve "accuracy to a thousandth of an inch" at the close of the century, and an even higher degree of precision, to one ten-thousandth of an inch, in the more delicate machine-tool operations of the watch industry. The speed and accuracy of machine-tool operation were advanced still further by the improvement of the tool metal used for cutting. An early venture in modern industrial research, originally sponsored by William Sellers and engaging the services of Frederick W. Taylor, Maunsell White, and Henry L. Gantt, had resulted in the development of a new high-speed carbon steel that more than doubled the cutting rate. As part of their experimentation, these men also undertook the first systematic investigation of the metal-cutting process, and their findings were published in a significant paper on the "Art of Cutting Metal." Simultaneously they were also laying the foundations of what became highly publicized as "scientific management."

The evolution of machine tools was accelerated after 1900 in a number of directions. Their durability, speed, and cutting power were increased by the use of new metals, including molybdenum, tantalum, and tungsten-steel, and particularly by the introduction of carbide alloys after 1928. It was estimated that the cutting tools of 1940, made from the new nonferrous materials, had a productivity nine to fourteen times that of the machines of 1900. Moreover, finer finish and precision of work were achieved with the development of new tools for honing, broaching, and lapping processes. The increased importance of the frequent inspections made necessary by the employment of less skilled labor stimulated the further improvement of gauges and other measuring instruments; the Johannson blocks, introduced from Sweden by Henry Ford during the 1920's, brought the precision standards of the laboratory into the factory. Statistical theory and methods were evolved for quality control, and automatic self-recording instruments, employing air pressure or electronic devices, permitted multiple inspection as an integral part of the production process. As an example, one such machine was capable of measuring the bores of an eight-cylinder automobile engine at thirty-two points simultaneously.[5]

The introduction of the electric motor imparted greater flexibility to machine tool operations; power units of appropriate size were incorporated into the individual machine, offering the advantages of closer control and synchronization of automatic actions. One of the most significant applications of electrical power was to portable hand tools, which added greatly to the convenience and speed of assembly. Where the large-scale repetitive production of uniform parts made them economically feasible, special purpose tools of considerable complexity were employed, culminating in the multiple-station type of machine that was really several units linked into a series, which performed successive processes automatically and operated simultaneously on a number of parts. One multiple-spindle drill, for example, was able to make 98 holes at one time in a single tractor crankcase assembly, while another machine, equipped with 152 tools, executed 31 separate operations on parts conveyed through 24 successive stations.[6]

A development of particular importance in the automobile and similar mass-production industries was the increased use of methods of fabrication other than metal cutting, such as pressing, stamping, and punching, as well as the increased use of welding of sheet metal. Such processes were performed by machines that could be made fully automatic and continuous in operation and with less skilled labor as well. Especially significant was the extensive application of electrical welding, invented before 1900 by Elihu Thomson, one of the founders of the American electrical industry. Spot and seam welding, in one instance at the rate of 100 welds per minute, displaced many operations that had formerly required riveting and bolting by hand. These processes, moreover, played a large part in

---

[5] *Business Week,* May 1, 1948, p. 42; *Machine Tool Industry* (New York: George S. Armstrong and Co., 1941), p. 11; Temporary National Economic Committee, *Technology in Our Economy* (Washington, D. C.: U. S. Government Printing Office, 1941), p. 114; *Wartime Technological Developments* (Washington, D. C.: U. S. Government Printing Office, 1945), pp. 17 ff.

[6] *International Industry Yearbook,* p. 257. New York: Kristen-Browne Publishing Co., 1948.

the extension of mass production technology to such complex products as aircraft and shipping during the 1940's.[7]

Since it supplied the required mechanical equipment in increasing volume and ingenious variety, the machine-making industry, deriving from the machine shops of the nineteenth century, was basic to the progress of mass production. Already in 1899, it employed more than 400,000 persons, nearly nine per cent of all industrial workers. By 1929, it employed more than one million workers, or about one-eighth of all wage earners in industry. The machine-tool branch of the industry, in particular, while comparatively small, employing less than 50,000 in 1929, had become one of the most sensitive indices of the progress of mass production and of the state of business generally. Its expansion was a prerequisite to conversion and preparation for war.

The Automobile Industry and Progressive Line Production

The very progress of machine tools and other mechanical equipment facilitating and accelerating the repetitive manufacture of uniform parts accentuated other aspects of production. The assembly of parts into the finished product was a particularly critical problem; it entailed much manual labor in the handling and transporting of materials and parts, as well as relatively large inventories of stock in process of manufacture. There was, furthermore, a distinct limit on the degree of division of labor possible, even with the system of fixed stations by which such products as carriages and railroad cars were assembled at the turn of the present century. The full realization of mass production, therefore, hinged upon the acceleration of the assembly process. This, however, demanded more than technical or mechanical improvements; it was essentially a problem in organization and control of production, belonging to the non-mechanical or management aspect of mass production.

In supplying a solution, the automobile industry became peculiarly important, both as a promoter and as a model of mass production; its history, in fact, epitomizes the triumph of mass production in the United States, in the strictly technical as well as in the broader economic and social aspects of the concept. Like the earlier bicycle, the automobile was European in origin and initial experimentation, and it entered the stage of practical industrial development in the United States during the 1890's, first achieving recognition in the Census of 1900, in which year its output of some 4,000 cars was valued at just under $5,000,000. In this first stage of the industry, manufacturing ventures were numerous, small, and hazardous, often scarcely more than assemblers of parts supplied by machine shops and other fabricators. By 1910 the new industry had won position

[7] C. R. Walker, "American Productivity in World War II," *Fortune,* Vol. XXXIII (Jan., 1946), pp. 150 ff.; also *Monthly Labor Review,* Vol. LIV (Jan., 1946), pp. 34 ff.; *International Industry Yearbook,* pp. 260 ff.

as a major industry, with an output of 187,000 cars valued at more than $200,000,000.

In the next decade, 1910-1920, the industry completed the transition to mass production, the full fruits of which were to become manifest during the prosperous 1920's, serving indeed as a major symbol and evidence of that prosperity. The process of integration and consolidation into a few major producers had made great headway, and the industry had become, on the eve of the depressed 1930's, the largest single one in the country in the value of its product, as well as the central core of a large complex of related industries, all subject to the same pressure for large-scale output by mass production methods.

In the automobile industry, mass production was linked with mass distribution and consumption through new intensive methods of advertising and salesmanship, as well as through steadily declining prices made possible by the economies of production that were estimated to have reduced the labor cost of the average car to one-sixth between 1900 and 1929. During the 1920's, the automobile even showed that it could defy a basic condition of mass production; it witnessed a trend in design and fashion that raised the automobile to standards of comfort and aesthetic appeal far beyond the essentials of a mass-consumption utility. The industry now also undertook to surmount the critical problem of market saturation that tends ultimately to confront mass production, especially in the durable-goods field, quite apart from such sharp contractions of demand as that which accompanied depression in the 1930's. According to one commentator, "Wear alone made replacement too slow for the needs of American industry. And so . . . business elected a new god to take its place along with . . . other household gods. Obsolescence was made supreme. It could be created almost as fast as the turn of the calendar." [8]

Many factors combined to make possible this phenomenal development within scarcely more than a quarter of a century, and the principal achievement of the automobile industry was their integration into a single, unified production system. Among them was the long established method of manufacture of interchangeable parts, and underlying it was the increasingly conscious philosophy and policy of standardization and simplification peculiarly suitable to a new industry that drew many of its parts from independent and specialized fabricators for assembly.

The initial step in the mass production of automobiles was taken in 1908, and was essentially an entrepreneurial policy adopted by the Ford Motor Company as part of its decision to manufacture thereafter only a single standard type of car. This celebrated Model T was continued in production without significant modifications up to 1927, or until new conditions of market demand compelled a shift to an entirely new model.

[8] P. M. Mazur, *American Prosperity*, p. 92. New York: The Viking Press, 1928.

More than 15,000,000 Model T cars had been manufactured in less than 20 years, during which time the base price had been reduced from $950 to a low point of $290 in 1924. The expanding production of a single standardized commodity such as the Model T car offered, of course, enormous possibilities for the design and use of specialized machinery and for the subdivision of labor to a high degree. Here was, indeed, a kind of industrial laboratory in which were developed a business policy and an art of industrial management peculiarly suited to mass production, as well as a whole school of industrial managers and "masters of mass production." This school included such noteworthy figures as Carl Emde, William Knudsen, and Charles Sorensen, through whom the principles and skills of mass production were diffused through the industry generally, culminating in its mass mobilization for war purposes during the 1940's.[9]

The most significant advance under the Ford auspices was made between 1913 and 1914 when the assembly process was reorganized on novel and revolutionary principles. Down to this time assembly was of a stationary type; at the Ford plant there were 100 stations, at each of which a team of five assemblers literally constructed the car out of component parts manufactured and assembled in other departments. During 1913, experiments were begun with some of the minor assemblies by the introduction of the sliding line, subsequently mechanized into a power-driven conveyor system carrying the work at the right level and speed past workers performing single specialized tasks. In 1914 these methods were extended to the assembly of the motor, chassis, and body as well, with amazing economies of time and labor. The labor required for the chassis assembly, for example, was reduced from 14 to under 2 man-hours. The rudimentary idea of the mechanized conveyor was not new; it stemmed from Oliver Evans's flour-milling machinery, which dated as far back as 1790, and it had received many industrial applications during the nineteenth century. The Ford experiments, however, incorporated the principle of power-driven conveyors as an integral and vital part of a new type of "continuous-flow production" in which the progressive assembly line was only the spectacular end-result.

This innovation, moreover, had an impact upon the entire manufacturing process, involving a more elaborate division of labor and drastic changes in the plant layout. With emphasis on the orderly and planned flow of work, this new philosophy of industrial management analyzed all phases of production and arranged the necessary machinery and processes in proper functional order, rather than in conventional separate de-

[9] Christy Borth, *Masters of Mass Production* (Indianapolis: Bobbs-Merrill Co., 1945), especially chapters 2, 3, 10; R. C. Epstein, *The Automobile Industry* (Chicago: A. W. Shaw Co., 1928), pp. 30 ff.; Keith Sward, *The Legend of Henry Ford* (New York: Rinehart & Co., 1948), pp. 32 ff.

partments. Thereby was effected a great saving of labor previously consumed in the criss-cross transportation of materials and parts as well as in the storage and handling of surplus inventory. As early as 1914, this principle of "progressive production" was hailed as an "ultimate achievement," but it received an even more impressive demonstration during the 1920's in the Ford River Rouge plant, which literally converted coal, iron ore, and other materials into a finished automobile by a consecutive and continuous series of operations centered at a single site. The Ford methods were, moreover, given early emphasis and publicity by the adoption in 1914 of an equally spectacular labor policy, in the form of a five-dollar minimum daily wage for certain categories of workers and the reduction of the working day from 9 to 8 hours. Aside from its practical purpose of winning labor support for the speed-up of the new methods, it also had broader social significance in dramatizing the new accomplishment and in linking this model example of mass production with a philosophy of high wages.[10]

Diffusion of Mass Production

The period after 1900 was a fertile one, both in the expansion of the concept and methods of mass production and in their extension to the broadening pattern of American industry. Mass-production methods were of an infinite variety adapted to particular purposes, and their effect was cumulative. But essentially they were of two principal kinds. There were, in the first place, the technical methods, entailing the increased use of machinery and power wherever products and processes were sufficiently standardized for quantity production. Of equal importance were the non-mechanical or organizational elements that effected a better control and more efficient utilization of the materials, machinery, and manpower engaged in production. The ultimate objective of mass production was, in Henry Ford's words, "the planned orderly progression of the commodity through the shop."

On the whole, these trends were most prominent in industries characterized by a large and relatively constant and uniform market demand. From the technical standpoint, too, the methods of mass production were best adapted to two classes of industry. One of these classes embraced the heavy industries in which large masses of materials could be handled

---

[10] In 1914, the Ford plant served as the theme of a series of articles in the *Engineering Magazine*, by H. L. Arnold and F. L. Faurote, also published in separate form as *Ford Methods and Ford Shops* (New York: Engineering Magazine Co., 1915). In 1936, the still greater River Rouge plant was the subject of a similar series of articles in *Mill and Factory*, also published separately as *Ford Production Methods*. (New York: Harper and Brothers, 1936.) Aside from a certain quality of overeloquent zeal, both of these volumes give perhaps the best available specific portrayal of mass-production technology in the early and advanced stages, as developed in its modern form. For a more critical review of Ford policies, see K. Sward, *Legend of Henry Ford*, Chapter 4.

in a continuous and almost automatic sequence of processes, as exemplified by iron and steel, paper, cement, petroleum, and a growing number of chemical products. The second class included those industries that produced finished commodities in quantity by means of a consecutive series of mechanized operations under the straight-line system of production. Aside from the automobile, the latter category embraced the equally new electrical industry, with its expanding list of industrial and household appliances, such as the motor, the electric iron, the washing machine, the mechanical refrigerator, and the radio, which assumed large-scale importance in the decades following World War I. Food processing proved equally adaptable to mass-production technology, under the impact of automatic machinery developed for the manufacture and packaging of food and tobacco products. Originating before 1900, the machine-made and packaged commodity supplied the link between large-scale mass production and mass consumption in convenient, small-scale, and individually differentiated form, which, however, provoked a stream of criticism during the 1920's as an undue exaltation of "the magnificent technique of selling the package rather than what the package contains." [11]

The First World War imparted an immediate practical stimulus, as well as a broader political and social significance, to the already prominent trends toward mass production, accentuating in particular the movements for standardization, industrial research, and scientific management. Systematic industrial research facilitated, in the words of C. E. Kettering, himself a pioneer figure in this field in the automobile industry, "the transition . . . from the individual as an inventor to the group as an inventor." [12] Nor were the trends inaugurated during World War I allowed to lapse thereafter. Under the official sponsorship of Herbert Hoover, an engineer by training and Secretary of Commerce during the 1920's, standardization and simplification of industrial products became a national policy; in 1922 a Division of Simplified Practice was established in his Department as a branch of the Bureau of Standards, in existence since 1901, and a program of conferences was launched for voluntary collaboration with industry and trade associations in the direction of continued standardization of products and practices.

---

[11] Stuart Chase and F. S. Schlink, *Your Money's Worth* (New York: Macmillan Co., 1927), p. 17. On the development of packaged products and canned foods, see above, Chapter 20; Clark, *History of Manufactures,* Vol. III, pp. 278 ff.; R. O. Cummings, *The American and His Food* (Chicago: University of Chicago Press, 1941), p. 68; *International Industry Yearbook,* Chapter 10.

[12] *Technology in Our Economy,* p. 211; R. H. Lansburgh, ed., *Standards in Industry* (Philadelphia: American Academy of Political and Social Science, 1928), pp. 3 ff.; Committee on Recent Economic Changes, *Recent Economic Changes,* Vol. I, pp. 89 ff.; Maurice Holland, *Industrial Explorers* (New York: Harper and Brothers, 1928).

Measures of Mass Production

Mass production, in its germinal form and in some of its basic methods, had made its appearance in American industry by 1900. Thereafter the diffusion of mass production was more general and its evolution more dramatic, particularly in the newer industries, under the favorable influences of expanding markets, progressive technology, the stimulus of war needs, and more advanced forms of business organization and management.

From a statistical standpoint, certain aspects of the growth of American industry illustrate and reflect the broad trend toward mass production. The total volume of industrial output and, in particular, the productivity of labor increased considerably faster than did the population, the number of industrial workers, and the number of industrial establishments. Thus, between 1899 and 1939, the growth of population was approximately 75 per cent; the physical volume of production, however, increased by 273 per cent. While the number of wage earners in industry nearly doubled in the same period, industrial output rose almost fourfold. If allowance is, furthermore, made for the shortened working week, the productivity of labor, on a comparable man-hour basis, more than doubled during this period. As compared with an estimated increase of 30 per cent in productivity in the years 1899-1914, the middle period, 1914-1929, witnessed a rise of nearly fifty per cent, and even the depressed 1930's brought an increase of about 20 per cent in labor productivity.

During the same period the number of industrial establishments showed decline, indicating a trend toward greater size and scale of plant. In 1899, the Census reported 207,514 plants with an annual output of $500 or more; in 1919, there were 290,105 such plants, of which 214,188 had a production of $5000 or more. By 1937 only 166,794 establishments were reported with a production of $5000 or more. Even among these plants, the larger ones, those with an annual output of $1,000,000 or more, while representing only 4 per cent of the total number, accounted for 70 per cent of the gross value of industrial production.[13]

Such measures of the number and size of industrial plants, to be sure, support only a general presumption as to the predominant influence of

[13] Statistical data measuring major industrial trends are given abundantly in the *Statistical Abstract of the United States, Historical Statistics of the United States, 1789-1945* (Washington, D. C.: Bureau of the Census, 1949); and in Solomon Fabricant, *The Output of Manufacturing Industries, 1899-1937* (New York: National Bureau of Economic Research, 1940); F. C. Mills, *Economic Tendencies in the United States* (New York: National Bureau of Economic Research, 1932); *Machinery, Employment, and Purchasing Power* (New York: National Industrial Conference Board, Inc., 1936); and especially in the monograph, *Technology in Our Economy,* No. 22 in the series prepared in connection with the investigation of concentration of economic power by the Temporary National Economic Committee (Washington, D. C.: 1941.)

mass production among other factors. A similar presumption may be offered with respect to the connection between mass production and the process of industrial consolidation and integration that was another significant trend of this period. The motives, the methods, and the controversial issues concerning the merits of the combination movement fall outside the scope of mass production in its strictly technical sense; it has even been argued that mass production is primarily a "matter of internal arrangements and economies within a single plant. It is technical, . . . not financial or commercial." [14]

World War II and Mass Production

The climactic measure and test of mass production capacity was provided by the demands of defense and war after 1940. World War I had accelerated the evolution of mass production, then in its formative stage; during World War II the fully developed managerial, technical, and manpower resources of the nation were mobilized and converted to war with remarkable speed and amazing results in terms of new capital plant, new methods, large output, and even in the increased productivity of labor, particularly in the defense industries. Primarily this was accomplished by the existing system of industrial technology and business organization, influenced by the fact that emergency needs transcended all normal considerations of cost and ultimate utilization. With an increase of 50 per cent in factory employment, the physical volume of production was doubled between 1939 and 1945.

The chief opportunities for expanding both production and productivity were, of course, present in the war industries, while the peacetime industries lagged behind because of low priorities and the employment of marginal labor. To the war industries went new plant and equipment, the new machine tools and materials, and an intensive application of the methods of standardization and continuous production characteristic of mass production. In two of these industries, the manufacturing of Liberty ships and of airplanes, the resulting gains in output were phenomenal. In the peak year of 1943, 1200 Liberty ships were produced by assembly-line techniques, and man-hour expenditure per ship was cut in half as compared with 1941. The manufacture of airplane frames witnessed a rise in productivity of nearly 250 per cent between 1941 and 1945. The production of the airplane industry, with a total capacity of scarcely 10,000 planes in 1940, and hampered, moreover, by a great variety of types that changed rapidly in design, was multiplied more than tenfold by the end of the war. This was accomplished by an enormous expansion and conversion of plant and equipment and, even more important, by a revo-

[14] Quoted in *The Relative Efficiency of Large, Medium-Sized, and Small Business*, Monograph No. 13 of the T.N.E.C. Series on Concentration of Economic Power, p. 95, Washington, D. C.: 1941.

lutionary application of mass production principles and methods, supported by the accumulated skills and facilities of the automotive and other machine industries. This was illustrated dramatically in the case of the Willow Run plant, near Detroit, built and operated under the auspices of the Ford Motor Company for the mass production of the Liberator bomber, which attained a scheduled output of a plane per hour by 1944. As a classic example of wartime mass production in its rigidity as well as in its potentiality, it presented, moreover, the characteristic problem of reconversion and use in peace.[15]

There was also the further development of conveyor equipment for materials and products, affecting as it did the key problem of handling and transport, which was estimated to constitute 70 per cent of the average production cycle and to account for one-fifth of the industrial payroll. Especially significant was the research and application made in the relatively new field of electronics. Among its contributions were new types of inspection and control instruments that promised to advance the technology of mass production by facilitating automatic and continuous production, particularly in the chemical industries. Among the latter, the attainment of an annual capacity of 900,000 tons by the synthetic rubber industry was a major wartime achievement.

War needs mobilized, furthermore, the scientific resources of the nation. Research, expanding steadily after the impetus it received during World War I, enlarged and confirmed its role in the growth of industry. The production of the atom bomb was merely the most spectacular wartime accomplishment of scientific research combined with engineering and industrial technology; but atomic energy research, continued under the Atomic Energy Commission, promised to become a major factor in correlating scientific with future technological and industrial progress. Aside from this and other public research agencies, the National Research Council reported 2450 laboratories in existence by 1947; these employed nearly 133,000 scientific and other personnel. This was nearly double the number so engaged in 1940 and represented an enormous increase over the 9,300 persons employed in some 300 industrial laboratories at the close of World War I. The expenditure by industry alone for research was estimated at half a billion dollars in 1947. Scientific research had become an integral part of the newly developed concept of the systematic pursuit and promotion of new products and processes; it paralleled the pursuit and promotion of standardization, mechanization, and continuous production, which were the essentials of mass production.[16]

[15] C. Borth, *Masters of Mass Production,* Chapters 9 and 10; C. R. Walker, "American Productivity in World War II," *Fortune* (Jan., 1946) pp. 150 ff.; *The Aviation Industry* (New York: George S. Armstrong & Co., 1940).

[16] *International Industry Yearbook,* pp. 71 ff., 207 ff.; *Wartime Technological Developments,* pp. 28 ff., 153 ff.; *Industrial Research and Changing Technology,* pp. 5 ff.; "Revolution in Mass Production," *Fortune,* Vol. XXVII (Feb., 1943), pp. 131 ff.

The Energy Pattern in Mass Production Economy

The pivotal place of power in the development of modern industry generally and of mass production in particular is a commonplace that scarcely needs to be labored or elaborated. The abundant availability and the lavish utilization of energy in many forms have become, indeed, the fundamental feature and indispensable condition of American economy, supporting the requirements of mass production technology and powering its chief products, whether the automobile or the many appliances and services of the household and community. It is estimated that between 1870 and 1950 the total power consumption of the United States multiplied more than twentyfold, and per capita consumption increased seven times. It is further noteworthy that the largest proportion of the principal energy resources in the United States has been produced since 1900—80 per cent of all the coal and more than 94 per cent of all the oil, as well as 99 per cent of the electricity generated.

Two types of trends have combined to give direction to the development of the power pattern of industry and of the American economy generally since the turn of the present century, and their cumulative effects became manifest particularly during the period between the two World Wars. One of these trends is quantitative and is revealed in expanding power capacity and in the increased production of the principal energy resources supplying that capacity. The second is qualitative and embraces the changing ratios and relationships of the principal components of the power pattern. These stem from significant technological advances in power generation and constitute indeed a broad power revolution, accompanied by problems and adjustments of an economic, social, and political nature. In a quantitative sense, the power equipment of American industry trebled between 1899 and 1919, from 10 million to nearly 30 million horsepower, and increased still further to a total of more than 51 million horsepower by 1939. Industrial power capacity rose from 2.24 horsepower per wage earner in 1899 to 3.5 horsepower in 1919, and to 6.5 horsepower per wage earner by 1939. The immediate needs of the war years brought a further addition and, even more important, an intensive and continuous utilization of existing power equipment.

The principal changes, however, occurred in the forms of power equipment comprising this pattern and in the methods of power generation. In 1899 industrial steam and water-power equipment still accounted for more than 95 per cent of the total; by 1919 this was down to 64 per cent, and to 38 per cent by 1939. Purchased power, on the other hand, grew from approximately 3 per cent in 1899 to 32 per cent in 1919, and to 59 per cent of the total power consumed in industry by 1939. This expanding factor of purchased energy in manufacturing establishments was a partial measure of the power revolution by which electricity, generated in steam and water turbines, came increasingly to supply the multiple needs, in the form of light, heat, and power, not only of industry but also of the household and the community. Electric power generation on a mass production basis became the specialized function and business of an expanding public utility industry characterized by the familiar trends toward large-scale operation and integration of central plants.

In quantitative terms, electric power production had reached a total of 40 billion kilowatt hours in 1919 and rose to 97 billion by 1929; in 1939 production was 161 billion kilowatt-hours, and it attained a wartime peak of 280 billion in 1944. It grew to more than 300 billion kilowatt-hours in 1947. Electrification reinforced the trend toward mass production technology by bringing to it the advantages of flexible and individual power-driven mechanisms and automatic precision instruments for the control and inspection of operations; from the outset it provided cheap and abundant power to large energy-using industries, such as those manufacturing non-ferrous metals, like aluminum and magnesium, steel, paper, and a host of chemical products.

In the energy pattern that resulted from this and other phases of the power revolution, coal continued to occupy the central and dominant position it had won during the nineteenth century; but it came, nevertheless, under the increasing pressure of competition from other energy resources, particularly after World War I. Production of coal, both anthracite and bituminous, experienced its greatest rates of growth prior to 1910 and reached a wartime peak of 678 million tons in 1918. Thereafter, it sagged to an average level of less than 600 million tons even during the prosperous decade of the 1920's, and annual output sank to a low point of under 400 million tons during the depressed 1930's. Recovery and unusual wartime demand raised production to a new high of nearly 683 million tons by 1944. Moreover, the ratio of coal to total energy consumption tended to decline steadily, from nearly 90 per cent in 1900 to 84 per cent in 1913, to 60 per cent in 1929, and to approximately 50 per cent by 1947. The principal uses of bituminous coal were displaying an inelastic or declining tendency during this period. By the 1940's approximately one-fifth of the coal was absorbed by the railroads, one-fifth went into metallurgical and chemical channels, one-sixth into electrical power, and the rest into domestic and other industrial uses.

The major factors that combined to account for the instability of the coal industry have been noted in the preceding chapter. Special attention should be given, however, to the increased efficiency and economy in coal utilization. This was particularly pronounced in electric power generation, in which coal continued to account for more than half of the total output. The trend toward large central steam plants employing higher steam pressures and temperatures effected a reduction of average coal consumption per kilowatt-hour from 7 pounds in 1899, to 3 pounds in 1929, and to 1.3 pounds by 1945. Economies in coal consumption were also achieved in the by-product processing of coke, in the manufacture of iron and steel, and in railroad operation. Another significant factor derived from the relatively large expansion of water-power as a component of the power pattern after 1900. Although rapidly eclipsed by the steam engine in the latter part of the nineteenth century, water-power in the new form of hydro-electric generation experienced a revival, beginning with the spectacular Niagara Falls project of the 1890's. By 1921 hydro-electric development had attained a capacity of 8 million horsepower. This figure was more than doubled by 1938, reaching a total of more than 17 million horsepower, and a decade later it had reached 22 million horsepower. Water-power early achieved and maintained a ratio of about one-third in a steadily growing output of electrical energy, although its contribution to total energy consumption of the nation remained relatively low and constant, at under 4 per cent.

The fluctuations and pressures of the coal industry were related most dramatically to the revolutionary expansion of petroleum and natural gas as constituents of the power pattern, particularly since the First World War. As was noted in the preceding chapter, the domestic output of crude oil rose rapidly after 1900, reaching a total of over 2 billion barrels by 1948. At the same time technical innovations were increasing the amount and proportion of usable refined products; especially in the form of gasoline and other fuels. The portion of the total energy consumption that was supplied by oil rose from 14 to 32 per cent between 1918 and 1947, while natural gas contributed another 13 per cent at the later date. Of the major products of the oil industry, fuel oil, amounting to approximately 40 per cent of its total output, became directly competitive with coal in such varied fields as shipping, railroad transportation, domestic heating, and to a lesser degree in the generation of electrical power. The expanding production of gasoline, however, representing another 40 per cent of the industry's output by 1929 and thereafter, bore testimony to a major feature of the power revolution since 1900—the introduction of the internal combustion engine and its triumphant capture of large new fields of transportation on the road and in the air. It was a parallel accompaniment of the new automobile and airplane industries, the first of which figured so prominently in the evolution of modern mass production. Together with these and other related industries, the oil industry constituted a major factor, not only in the new power pattern, but also in the newly developed and enlarged segment of the American industrial complex to which the principles and methods of mass production were peculiarly adaptable and in which they flourished extensively. These industries not only contributed to its actual evolution, but also gave to mass production a broader meaning as the embodiment of past American industrial achievement and future promise, both in war and peace.

Despite the present strategic importance of oil in our energy supply, rapid depletion and uncertainty regarding the long run supply of petroleum, at home and abroad, may cause an eventual return to coal on an expanded scale. Methods are known and available for the conversion of coal into oil and its products. A possible advance in more effective utilization of coal is also indicated in the development of gassification by combustion in the mine and in other forms of economic power generation at the mine. Atomic energy is still too new and undeveloped to offer more than distant prospects for a limited and specialized role in the broad and evolving power pattern with which the progress of industry, mass production, and the national economy as a whole is intimately associated. Indeed, as Gilbert and Pogue, pioneer students of America's energy resources, put it: "The progress of democracy is measurable in terms of the advancing use of mechanical work in place of human labor." [17]

Selected References

GENERAL WORKS

Alderfer, E. B., and Michl, H. E., *Economics of American Industry*. New York: McGraw-Hill Book Co., 1942, 2nd ed., 1950.

Borth, Christy, *Masters of Mass Production*. Indianapolis: Bobbs-Merrill and Co., 1945.

Brown, P. S., ed., *The Second Industrial Revolution and Its Significance*. Philadelphia: Annals of the American Academy of Political and Social Sciences, Vol. CXLIX, 1930.

Burlingame, Roger, *Engines of Democracy*. New York: Charles Scribner's Sons, 1940.

———, *Backgrounds of Power*. New York: Charles Scribner's Sons, 1949.

Burns, A. F., *Production Trends in the United States Since 1870*. New York: National Bureau of Economic Research, 1934.

Chase, Stuart, *Men and Machines*. New York: The Macmillan Co., 1929.

Clark, Victor S., *History of Manufactures in the United States* (3 vols.). New York: McGraw-Hill Book Co., 1929.

Fabricant, Solomon, *The Output of Manufacturing Industries, 1899-1937*. New York: National Bureau of Economic Research, 1940.

Gideion, S., *Mechanization Takes Command*. New York: Oxford University Press, 1948.

Glover, J. G., and Cornell, W. B., *The Development of American Industries*, rev. ed. New York: Prentice-Hall, Inc., 1941.

Mumford, Lewis, *Technics and Civilization*. New York: Harcourt, Brace & Co., 1934.

[17] C. G. Gilbert and J. E. Pogue, *America's Power Resources* (New York: Century Co., 1921), pp. 10, 87 ff.; John Ise, *The United States Oil Policy* (New Haven: Yale University Press, 1926), pp. 489 ff.; *Transactions of the Third World Power Conference* (Washington, D. C.: Government Printing Office, 1938), Vol. II, pp. 672 ff.; Vol. IV, p. 471; Vol. VI, p. 675; *Energy Resources and National Policy* (Washington, D. C.: National Resources Committee, 1939), pp. 9 ff.; 148, 376; *Scientific American*, Vol. CLXXVI (May, 1946), p. 220.

Recent Economic Changes in the United States (2 vols.). New York: McGraw-Hill Book Co., 1929.

SPECIAL TOPICS

Technology and specific industries:

Arnold, H. L., and Faurote, F. L., *Ford Methods and Ford Shops*. New York: Engineering Magazine Co., 1915.

Barclay, H. W., *Ford Production Methods*. New York: Harper and Brothers, 1936.

Epstein, R. C., *The Automobile Industry*. Chicago: A. W. Shaw Co., 1928.

Jerome, Harry, *Mechanization in Industry*. New York: National Bureau of Economic Research, 1934.

Roe, J. W., *English and American Tool Builders*. New Haven, Conn.: Yale University Press, 1926.

Sward, Keith, *Legend of Henry Ford*. New York: Rinehart & Co., 1948.

Temporary National Economic Committee, Investigation of Concentration of Economic Power, especially Monograph No. 22: *Technology in Our Economy*, and Monograph No. 27: *The Structure of Industry*. Washington, D. C.: 1941.

Standardization, research, and scientific management:

Alford, L. P., *Principles of Industrial Management for Engineers*. New York: Ronald Press, 1940.

Drury, H. B., *Scientific Management*. New York: Columbia University Press, 1915.

Holland, Maurice, *Industrial Explorers*. New York: Harper and Brothers, 1928.

Lansburgh, R. H., ed., *Standards in Industry*. Philadelphia: American Academy of Political and Social Sciences, Vol. CXXXVII, 1928.

Person, H. S., ed., *Scientific Management in American Industry*. New York: The Taylor Society, 1929.

Taylor, F. W., *Principles of Scientific Management*. New York: Harper and Brothers, 1911.

Works Progress Administration, National Research Project monographs, Philadelphia, 1939-1940. Especially: *Industrial Research and Changing Technology; Industrial Instruments and Changing Technology; Effects of Technological Development upon Capital Formation.*

Power and energy resources:

Energy Resources Committee, *Energy Resources and National Policy*. Washington, D. C.: United States Government Printing Office, 1939.

Gilbert, C. G., and Pogue, J. E., *America's Power Resources*. New York: Century Co., 1921.

Parsons, A. B., ed., *Seventy-Five Years of Progress in the Mineral Industry*. New York: American Institute of Mining and Metallurgical Engineers, 1947.

Polakov, W. N., *The Power Age*. New York: Covici-Friede, 1933.

39 · INTERNAL MOBILITY AND THE LOCATION OF INDUSTRY*

THE COMPLEX GEOGRAPHIC PATTERN of our economy was not planned, but has evolved almost entirely as the result of countless decisions by individuals in what they have believed to be their own interest. These decisions are, of course, rarely made in the light of complete information and wisdom. Moreover, even if a businessman miraculously knew all about the profit prospects of all possible locations, he would give some weight also to personal and family considerations such as preference for living in a particular community.

The existence of competition, however, means that those who either ignorantly or deliberately select high-cost locations are less likely to succeed and expand. Thus, an analysis of the economic advantages of a given kind of location for any line of business indicates the kind of location toward which that line of business gravitates through more or less rational personal decisions and the impersonal forces of competition.

General Principles of Location [1]

For any productive activity—whether it be smelting iron ore, selling hardware, mining coal, raising hogs, or assembling aircraft—the relative desirability of possible locations hinges on two considerations: (1) the cost or difficulty of carrying on the process itself at any given location, and (2) the cost or difficulty of bridging the distances that separate the given location from its markets and sources of materials. For convenience these may be called simply "processing cost" and "transfer cost" respectively. The choice of a desirable location for any type of business takes account of the relative advantages of possible locations in terms of differences in processing costs, plus differences in the transfer costs involved in collecting the necessary materials and in marketing the product.

1 A somewhat more detailed presentation of locational theory will be found in E. M. Hoover, *The Location of Economic Activity* (New York: McGraw-Hill Book Company, 1948). The most complete and systematic treatment is in August Lösch, *Die räumliche Ordnung der Wirtschaft* (Jena: Gustav Fischer Verlag, 1940; second edition, 1944; Ann Arbor, Mich., University Microfilms, Inc., 1942). An English translation, to be published by the Yale University Press, is in preparation.

* The author of this chapter wishes to acknowledge the valuable assistance of Miss Marion Hayes in making revisions for the present edition.

For some types of activity, the pattern of locations that has evolved shows mainly the influence of processing costs, with transfer costs playing a minor role. Thus mines are found where the cost of extraction of the ore is lowest. In some lines of manufacturing, too, the economies in processing cost at certain locations are so large in comparison with any possible differences in transfer cost that they determine the location almost wholly. This is true, for instance, when a process requires some particular quality in such local natural resources as climate or water. In such a case, the manufacturing operation shows a certain kinship to the extractive type of industry (mining, farming, forestry, or fishing) in that it exploits physical features of the site other than position; consequently the choice of a site is made with such features in mind. In still other industries, labor costs or tax rates have been significant factors in determining the choice of location. Finally, in locating a given activity within an urban area the cost of land is often the dominant factor.

In some other types of economic activity, location patterns have evolved primarily on the basis of easy access to markets or sources of materials. The accessibility of different sources or markets depends not only on distance, but also on the kind of transport service available. A route that permits cheaper service, such as a navigable waterway, may be said to bring the points it serves "economically closer." From Lake Superior ports iron ore is shipped a thousand miles by water for less than it would cost to ship it a fraction of that distance by land.

When materials are bulky, fragile, perishable, or dangerous to ship, it is usually cheaper to process them near their source. This factor explains the characteristic location patterns of such establishments as canneries, sawmills, ore concentrators, cotton gins, cheese factories, beet sugar refineries, glass factories, wineries, and cement plants.

The same qualities in the product of a process make it advantageous to locate the process near the market. Ice cream, for instance, is distributed only short distances from any one plant. Daily newspapers are printed within the city they primarily serve, since speedy delivery and speedy collection of local news are essential for this highly perishable product. In order to maintain the close commercial contacts required, manufacturers of fashion garments find it important to be located close to established market centers where buyers congregate. The same holds true, often in still greater degree, with businesses that retail personal services, such as barber and shoe-repairing shops and movie houses. Customers will come to them to receive the service, but not very far. Fifty yards may spell the difference between success and failure in the location of an establishment selling a "convenience" type of product or service that is bought on the run.

At any given location, the processing costs of any kind of business as well as its transfer costs depend partly on the scale of operations. Economic forces can thus favor concentration of an industry in a few large establishments or at a few places. Even if resources and markets were initially distributed over the globe with perfect uniformity, economic forces would lead to varying degrees of clustering of production in specific industries and for economic activity as a whole.

Several factors favor concentration of production in large plants. Units of highly specialized equipment or personnel performing small parts of a production process operate more effectively when the overall scale of output is large enough to employ each unit fully. A large plant is also likely to be able to get along on a closer margin of reserve stocks, supplies, and spare capacity. Finally, the large establishment can receive, handle, and market commodities in larger lots, and thus generally at lower cost. It may, for instance, get cheaper and quicker service by receiving and shipping by the carload, trainload, or shipload.[2]

Analogous factors favor concentration of production in as few areas as possible. Thus the close geographical concentration of the fashion garment industry—despite the fact that small plants are involved—makes possible and in turn rests upon an elaborate system of parceling-out of the processes of manufacture and distribution to minutely specialized manufacturers, factors, contractors, and subcontractors. In a smaller producing center, such elaborate specialization could not be practiced because some of the subsidiary functions would be on too small a scale to keep a minimum-sized unit (say even one man, or one machine) fully employed. Skills developed in a specialized industrial center are another cumulative advantage offered by concentration.

A large city can often provide more economical service functions than can smaller places. Capital is usually more readily and cheaply available. The ready and flexible labor supply in a large, diversified employment center constitutes a powerful attraction, especially for irregular and seasonal businesses. Finally, transport service is often cheaper and better in a large industrial center than in a small one. This advantage reflects the fact that transportation itself enjoys the benefits of large-scale operation, so that routes of heaviest traffic are generally cheapest. The consequent tendency to canalize traffic on as few routes as possible puts a special premium on locations at the junctions of heavy-traffic routes where low-cost and prompt service in many directions is available.

In addition, a special incentive to concentration applies to industries

---

[2] For more detailed discussion, see National Resources Planning Board, *Industrial Location and National Resources* (Washington, 1942); P. Sargant Florence and W. Baldamus, *Investment, Location, and Size of Plant* (Cambridge, England: University Press, 1948); and Joseph Steindl, *Small and Big Business*, Oxford Institute of Statistics, Monograph No. 1 (New York: Oxford University Press, 1945).

selling shopping goods: those in which the buyers like to compare various offerings before choosing. In this case, buyers will prefer to shop in centers offering the largest possible variety of goods. Consequently, the best location for any seller to display his wares is next door to his competitors, in as large a center as possible. A large market becomes a Mecca for buyers and sellers alike, and so grows cumulatively larger. For some types of fashion goods, the bulk of the trade funnels through one district in New York City.

All these powerful cumulative forces have played a part in the trend toward greater urbanization of the American economy. It is obvious, however, that there must also be forces operating in the other direction, tending to keep production dispersed in smaller units and more scattered locations. Otherwise we should all be New Yorkers by now.

The primary influence in favor of scatter is the familiar principle of diminishing returns in land use. Even in manufacturing and commerce, where land represents merely space or "standing room," there is a limit to the degree of intensity of land use that is worthwhile. In general the cost of land is a measure of the intensity of competition among different users for a particular site; a highly desired site commanding a high rent or price will evoke a skyscraper superposing dozens of layers of use on the same ground area. Among individual users, the high rent serves as a sieve, keeping out all except those who can profit sufficiently from such a location to afford the rent.

Since markets and sources of material are necessarily scattered to some extent, a geographically concentrated industry may have long hauls on its materials or products, or both. Despite the economies of large-scale transportation, this distance factor sets another limitation on the concentration of economic activity. Breweries are scattered, because the possible economies of production realizable from greater concentration would be more than offset by the inordinate added costs of delivery of the product. Newspaper production is likewise scattered, in close conformity with the distribution of readers. Cheese factories and cotton gins are scattered because the mass production economies of further concentration would not balance the extra costs of bringing the materials long distances.

The significance of all the factors of location discussed above has varied considerably at different stages of our economic history. Better transport and communication have reduced the handicaps of distance, bringing to light the economies involved in servicing the unrivalled American mass market. In the past generation, electricity, automobile transport, and new production techniques have opened up wider areas of locational choice and have made for still more efficient and flexible mutual adjustment of people and productive activities.

The location of population is dependent on the location of economic opportunities, to the extent that people actually migrate in the direction of more and better jobs.[3] But geographic mobility is quite imperfect, and at any given time the consumer market and the labor supply—both important locating factors—are where the population happens to be, not where it might like to be. Areas where employment opportunities fail to keep up with increase of population offer a supply of low-wage labor that attracts some types of industry in which labor costs are important and skill requirements low. This condition has prevailed rather generally in rural areas of this country, particularly in the Southeast.

Within the range of income levels found in the United States, lower incomes are generally associated with more rapid rates of natural increase of population. To overcome this differential and to provide any net shift of population to areas of expanding opportunity, continuous heavy migration from poorer regions (including most rural areas) is required.

In general the movement of population within the United States has been from lower income areas to higher income areas, and the regional and rural-urban differences in income have diminished. Ignorance and inability to move on the part of many (especially during depressions) have prevented a rational geographic distribution of our population at any particular time, but these limitations should not obscure a tendency in this direction. Indeed this tendency, however imperfectly realized, offers the key to an understanding of the actual changes that have taken place. The dynamic character of our economy has constantly changed the character and location of economic opportunities, which largely explains the extensive mobility that has characterized the American population.

Even though migration may be said generally to go in the right direction, it cannot be relied on as a cure-all for regional economic ills. One important complication is that uncontrolled migration is *selective*. Mobility is greater among the more productive age groups and income groups in the labor force. As a result, a region with heavy emigration may lose just the people who might contribute most to raising its level of output.

Overall Characteristics and Basis of the 1919 Locational Pattern

The distribution of population and economic activity at the end of World War I illustrate the general principles just set forth. Especially noteworthy was the uneven distribution of population. Half the people lived in 14 states and the District of Columbia, which had in all only an eighth of the area of the country. Manufacturing industry was more concentrated still, with half its workers in the five states of New York, Pennsylvania, Massachusetts, Illinois, and Ohio.

Within regions, the concentration of population and economic activity

[3] For the best discussion of this tendency, and of some related problems of public policy, see Carter Goodrich and others, *Migration and Economic Opportunity*. Philadelphia: University of Pennsylvania Press, 1936.

took the form of urbanization. Only 30 per cent of the population lived on farms in 1920. Over half lived in cities and towns of 2,500 or more, and over a quarter in cities of over 100,000; a third of the population was in the 33 chief "industrial areas" which employed 58 per cent of the manufacturing workers but occupied only 1.7 per cent of the area of the United States.

Associated with the great variety in occupational patterns in different parts of the country were great differences in the economic well-being of the population. The most conspicuous features were the lower levels of per capita wealth and income in the Southeast as compared with other regions and in rural as compared with urban territory within any given region.

In the development of these regional and local concentrations of population and economic activity, cheap rail and water transportation had played a major part for several generations. These means of carriage had made it possible to concentrate industries at particularly advantageous points where processing costs or transfer costs were low, and to supply large areas more cheaply than local enterprises could.

Thus, the iron industry, originally scattered through forest areas in small units and serving scattered markets, had come to be concentrated in a relatively small number of establishments strategically located as to major deposits of coal and ore and major markets. Toward the end of the nineteenth century, a large proportion of the Nation's furniture was being made in Grand Rapids; giant plants in a handful of midwestern rail centers commanded the meat-packing industry; and Brockton shoes and Danbury hats were worn in all parts of the world.[4]

New means of freight transportation, however, were not solely responsible for the concentration of industries. Cheaper transportation merely permitted extension of the market areas of individual producing centers. Wider markets provided an incentive for the adoption of revolutionary new large-scale methods of manufacture, illustrated by Pittsburgh's rise to pre-eminence in iron making and Chicago's growth as a meat-packing center. Ingenious machines were indispensable also in the development of the specialized textile and shoemaking industries in New England that served nationwide markets.

Somewhat analogous advantages led to the concentration of many similar plants in one community or area as soon as cheap transportation made it feasible. Several factors tended for a time to make concentration cumulative, so that a community acquiring a certain reputation for production

[4] The industrial specialization of particular areas, and the localization of particular industries, had become so marked as to attract general attention by the end of the nineteenth century. The Census of 1900 included a long special monograph on the subject, pointing out the chief instances of extreme local concentration of industries and of specialized "one-industry towns." See 12th Census, 1900, *Manufactures,* Part I, "The Localization of Industries."

in a particular line often became more and more specialized and finally dominated the industry, as the industry conversely dominated the community.

One such factor was labor supply. Acquired skills handed down from one generation to the next and attracting immigrant groups with similar skills played a strong part in building up the shoe industry in New England and a few midwestern cities, the clothing industry in New York City, the knitting industry in the Mohawk Valley and in southeastern Pennsylvania, instrument-making in Rochester, the hardware and machinery industries in southern New England and later in Cincinnati and other midwestern cities, and the jewelry industry around Providence.

Another basis of cumulative specialization in certain lines was the development of highly specialized and centralized auxiliary and marketing services in larger centers. Thus, New York City became the fashion clothing market and Boston the leading shoe market for the country as a whole, while other cities performed a similar function for more limited areas. Once these cities had been recognized as market outlets where wholesale buyers congregated to compare the wares of rival sellers, they logically became still more desirable as locations for the sellers themselves and thus the foci of considerable clusters of the industry.

The high degree of concentration of population, of industry, and of specific industries observable in 1919 does not mean that the trend was necessarily running in the direction of still further concentration. For several decades at least prior to 1919, it seems clear that the trend had run toward more equal regional distribution of both population and industry and a more nearly equal degree of industrialization of different regions.[5] With respect to local concentration in and around cities, population had grown steadily more urban but manufacturing had not. The share of total manufacturing employment accounted for by the 33 chief industrial areas had remained remarkably stable at around 55 per cent ever since 1869, the date of the earliest available figures.[6] Within metropolitan areas, there was already a tendency by 1919 toward industrial "suburbanization." For reasons to be discussed later, industry, and particularly heavy industry, tended to shift to the edges of the built-up area while the urban core came to be more specialized in trade, service, financial, and other non-manufacturing activities.

---

[5] For further details, see Table I below; Edgar M. Hoover, "Interstate Redistribution of Population, 1850-1940," *Journal of Economic History,* Vol. I, No. 2 (November, 1941), pp. 199-205; and George C. Smith, Jr., "Lorenz Curve Analysis of Industrial Decentralization," *Journal of the American Statistical Association,* Vol. XLII, No. 240 (December, 1947), pp. 591-596.

[6] See Glenn E. McLaughlin, *Growth of American Manufacturing Areas,* Table 22, p. 100 (Pittsburgh: University of Pittsburgh, Bureau of Business Research, 1938). See also Bureau of the Census and Bureau of Agricultural Economics, *Changes in the Distribution of Manufacturing Wage Earners, 1899-1939,* Table 10, p. 36 (Washington, D. C.: 1942).

Factors in Locational Change Since 1919

In the analysis of changes in the locational patterns of population and economic activity during the 30 years ending in 1950, particular significance attaches to certain developments in transportation, industrial technology (especially in the conversion and utilization of energy), natural resources, and population growth and mobility. These factors will be examined separately.

Transportation

In the three decades following 1919 the two changes in transportation most important from the standpoint of location were the Panama Canal and the automobile. Both were actually in use some years earlier, but neither began to exert its real effect on locational patterns in the United States until the 1920's. On the other hand, air transport, which developed phenomenally, had scarcely begun to change the location pattern.

Even before the Panama Canal was built, the competition of trans-Isthmian routes had brought rail rates from the east coast to Pacific ports below some intermediate rates. Completion of the canal in 1914 further lowered the cost and improved the quality of intercoastal transport. In 1914, for example, the cost of shipping farm implements from New York to the Pacific Coast was 12 per cent less than the rate from Chicago to the same destinations; in 1926, the rate from New York was 43 per cent below the rate from Chicago. The rate from Chicago to the Pacific Coast rose 37 per cent during this interval, while the rate from New York fell 12 per cent.

Beginning in the 1920's, the relation of transcontinental to intermediate rail rates was greatly altered in response to Canal competition, though the railroads were not permitted to go as far as they wished in this adjustment. The principal locational effects, as might be expected, were the following: [7]

1. In the case of manufactured goods shipped from other sections of the country to the Pacific Coast, the East benefited at the expense of the Midwest. Cheap water rates from the East also probably retarded the development of some of these manufacturing industries on the Pacific Coast.
2. In the case of products shipped from the Pacific Coast—particularly the bulky and non-perishable ones such as lumber—low rates to East Coast and European markets aided Pacific Coast industry at the expense of competing areas elsewhere in the United States.
3. Pacific ports lost some of the import and export trade between the

[7] See Calvin Crumbaker, "The Panama Canal and the West," *Journal of Business,* Vol. II, No. 2 (April, 1929), pp. 151-176.

Far East and the eastern part of the United States, which now took the canal route and used Atlantic ports.

4. Pacific Coast wholesalers were given an increased competitive advantage over intermountain wholesalers in distributing eastern products. This fact doubtless has much to do with the striking relative underdevelopment of wholesaling in the intermountain area.[8]

As was pointed out in Chapter 35, the outstanding transport development following World War I was the automobile (including the bus and truck).

It is significant that the automobile is particularly adapted to the short and medium haul, in which the railroad had made the least advance over still earlier means of transport. Automotive transport, moreover, calls for a relatively small fixed investment in fixed ways and structures. That investment happens to be of a type long accepted in this country as being in the legitimate sphere of public works, and has, therefore, enjoyed a larger and cheaper supply of capital. Highways are so much cheaper than canals or railroads that they can be built in far greater mileage and reach every community of economic significance. Although it is probably true that the unit costs of automotive transport are lower on highly developed routes of heavy traffic than on other routes, this is a less significant factor than in the case of railroads, particularly since the costs of highway transport have not been in general assessed on a toll basis. The automobile, therefore, has not exerted the strong canalizing and concentrating influence on locations that was previously noted in the case of railroads. Big junction points have less advantage in costs or quality of service from the standpoint of automotive transport than from that of rail or water shipment.

Another feature of automotive transport is that the economies of large shipments have been less significant than is the case with water or rail carriers.[9] One of the former advantages of concentrating production in large plants and around large terminals consequently disappears when truck transport is substituted for rail. Finally, along any one highway route the stops can be much more frequent than along a railroad route, so that the number of possible plant locations becomes practically limitless from the standpoint of availability of transport service.

The motor truck, then, by increasing the number of locations to which satisfactory transport service can be rendered and by reducing the differential advantage of large plants and of location near major terminals, has

[8] Census figures available for the period since 1929 show that the Mountain region has a far lower ratio of wholesale sales to retail sales than any of the other regions of the United States.

[9] For further details see Board of Investigation and Research, *Comparisons of Rail, Motor, and Water Carrier Costs,* 79th Congress, 1st Session, Senate Document No. 84. Washington, D. C.: 1945.

permitted a much looser scattering of productive establishments. The location of industrial plants in and around cities is an indication of this factor at work. Locations away from congested freight-yard districts have become feasible, as have also the extensive specialization of parts manufacturers and specialty subcontracting. The Detroit area is an example. Trucks of many specialized types are used almost exclusively in shuttling back and forth across this huge industrial district carrying parts and subassemblies from one plant to another.

The locational effects of the automobile as a passenger carrier are twofold, since it can carry either the producer or the consumer according to circumstances. Seasonal mobility of transient labor has been of greater importance since the advent of the automobile, and the migration of labor in search of jobs has also increased. Differentials in economic opportunity between regions and between country and city have persisted, but have tended to be reduced by virtue of this increased mobility of population.

Most important of all, however, has been the effect of the passenger automobile on the structure of cities and metropolitan areas. When travel between home and work was on foot or by trolley car or suburban train, factories, large stores, and other establishments had to be located in the immediate vicinity of their labor supply or clientele, or in a district easily accessible by public transit. Long tentacles of built-up territory extended from the centers of large cities along the lines of public transit that furnished the only practicable means of going any great distance. The economic structure of cities was highly concentrated at the central nucleus where the various transit routes came together and where the chief shopping and office buildings were located. Compact means of transportation developed a highly intensified use of building space at the heart of the city, and the advantage of transacting various businesses in close proximity fostered concentration.

While our cities have continued to follow the main lines of this pattern, they also began to develop a quite different pattern on the basis of the widespread use of automobiles. With the automobile came a vast increase in the mobility of labor, particularly in daily commutation. It became possible to locate a plant not merely with respect to the immediately surrounding labor supply or that available by public carrier commutation, but also with respect to that within a radius of 20 to 30 miles around the plant. In any territory with reasonably high density of population, these possibilities created a potential labor supply for very large plants in a suburban or even rural environment.

The fact that the automobile can be used to transport the buyer as well as the producer is reshaping the geography of retail trade and service industries, as is manifest in the development during the last decade of supermarkets and large department store branches along suburban commuters' routes. These new departures in location, as already noted, depend on the ability of customers to come by the thousands in their own cars, for which special parking facilities are provided.

Near the center of the city, conversely, the major effect of the automobile was one of blight. With all its merits, the automobile is a great waster of space. Not only does it take up far more street space than public transit does in getting the traveler to his destination, but also (being a private vehicle) it has to be parked somewhere to await the owner's return. A vehicle so space-consuming is ill suited to serving the central areas of cities where space is at a premium. These central areas, built for an age in which street space requirements per person were much smaller than now, make poor locations for catering to customers who want to come by automobile.

Retail trade and specialty service establishments, and even some office buildings, have naturally tended to move out from the congested central districts of large cities. Together with the loosening of the ties of manufacturing and storage establishments through the use of trucks instead of direct rail connections, this transition goes far to explain the vexing problem of urban blight. Property owners, municipalities, and utilities are left with enormous investments in downtown facilities that, under automobile-age conditions, can perhaps never be utilized in such a way as to make a fair return on the investment.

Major Developments in Energy Utilization

In addition to the improvements of transportation described above, the same period witnessed important changes in the ways in which energy was obtained, transmitted, and put to use. These changes were reflected in correspondingly important locational trends.

The most obvious change was the shift from major dependence of the non-energy-producing sectors of the economy upon coal to an increased degree of dependence on oil, natural gas, and electricity, as noted in the preceding chapter. The shift from coal to oil was particularly evident in transportation, being reflected not only in the rapid growth of highway and air transport as compared to rail and water, but also in the shift to diesel motive power on the railroads. In space heating too, oil and gas made inroads on the market formerly served almost entirely by coal. Finally, many industrial processes, especially in the metallurgical and chemical fields, substituted electricity, oil, or gas for coal.

One definite locational effect was a stimulus to industrial development in the oil and gas surplus regions, particularly in the Gulf Southwest. Cheap mineral fuels helped to put that region in a leading position in postwar industrial expansion in the chemical and other industries, despite the fact that both oil and natural gas were being transmitted to other parts of the country on a rapidly increasing scale.

Recent developments in energy use seem on the whole to have lessened geographical differences in the cost and availability of energy. In part, this has been due to the replacement of the rail transport of coal by the transmission of electricity over cables (for relatively short distances) and the transportation of oil or gas by pipeline (over both long and short distances). The resulting patterns of energy cost have shown reduced geographic differentials. Within the distribution area of a power system, for example, rates are generally uniform, giving the user no special incentive to locate near the generating station. Important further economies in the transmission of electricity are promised by recent technological developments. More efficient use of fuels and energy, described in Chapter 38, has also lessened the locational pull of fuel resources.

There are of course some specific industries, of great and growing importance, that have continued to be located primarily with reference to cheap energy supply. The industries most responsive to the lure of low-cost energy are those using great heat or electrochemical reactions (metallurgy, heat-treating, artificial abrasives, caustic soda and chlorine, and ferro-alloys). When using electricity, these processes have generally been concentrated at the best hydroelectric power sources; but it is noteworthy that at least one postwar aluminum plant has been designed to use electricity generated with locally-produced natural gas.

It has sometimes been argued that the availability of electricity in small or large quantities anywhere on a distribution network at uniform cost would produce a general scattering of industry to small rural plants or even back into workers' homes. No such shift has occurred, and none seems in prospect. Energy rates are considerably lower for large users, reinforcing the other economies of concentrated production previously described.

The layout and local choice of sites of individual industrial plants, however, have been modified by electrification. Electric power can be bought so conveniently that small factories are at less of a disadvantage than they would be if forced to set up a steam or water power unit. Within the plant, energy flows through wires rather than along shafting and belts, so one reason for the old compact, quasi-cubical factory structure is eliminated. The modern electric-driven plant is more likely to be a spreading structure of one or two stories. Such a layout obviously calls for a more suburban location, which is now feasible for other reasons already mentioned.

Natural Resources and Locational Change

In addition to improvements in the techniques of transport and use of energy, changes in the availability and use of natural resources had also produced significant shifts in economic activity and population by 1950.

Areas dependent on mining are notorious for their mushroom growth and sudden decay. This period provided many instances of both. The spectacular economic advance of the southwestern oil and gas region has already been noted. On the reverse side of the picture were the unfortunate cases of declining economic opportunity in the copper mining district of Michigan, in the Tri-State lead-zinc area (where Missouri, Kansas, and Oklahoma meet), and in some older coal regions of the Appalachians. In the Montana copper workings and in the main iron ore producing district in northern Minnesota, high-grade deposits were approaching exhaustion. Preparations were made for utilizing lower-grade ores in the same localities, which could help to maintain output and employment. But it appeared likely that foreign sources would be called on to supply a larger share of our iron and copper ore needs in the future. The partial shift to new sources of iron ore supply would probably encourage the development of steel making at coastal points.

Most of the lumber industry was already in the Pacific Northwest and the Southeast by 1919 as a result of previous shifts from the depleted forest areas of the Northeastern and Lake states. The three decades after 1919 brought some further shift to the Northwest and an apparent stabilization of northeastern production at reduced levels. Wood-processing industries moved toward the southern and western sources of their material. The expansion of furniture, paper, and rayon production in the Southeast was noteworthy, and the use of fast-growing tree species of that region provided a basis for further industrial expansion.

By 1950, water supply had already become a factor limiting economic growth in many industrial areas, being a major regional problem in the Far West. California, which added seven million to its population between 1920 and 1950, was in no position to provide for further large population increases or industrial growth without heroic steps to provide more water.

Climate is probably an increasingly effective determinant of migration, in view of the increased mobility and leisure of the population. A substantial part of the consistently heavy migration to the Pacific Coast and Florida in recent decades [10] reflects simply the desire to live in a more agreeable climate.

Agricultural land use displayed some significant trends during the period after 1919, partly based on natural resources factors and partly in response to technological developments. A rapid extension of cultivation into the western Great Plains was followed in the 1930's by disastrous droughts, with permanent soil depletion through wind erosion and a sharp curtailment in the ability of the area to support a farm population. Overgrazing led to somewhat similar consequences in other western areas. In the Southeast there appeared a promising tendency toward agricultural diversification as livestock raising increased in importance in a region intensely specialized in cotton. The production of cotton in turn spread

[10] See Fig. 1 below.

farther west, making California by 1949 one of the leading cotton states. This shift was due in large part to the development of more mechanized techniques of cultivation and harvesting, which could more easily be applied in the Southwest than in the old southeastern Cotton Belt. The effect in the Southeast was to increase the surplus farm population and to give further impetus to past trends of migration from farm to city and from the Southeast to the North and West.

Public Policies and Promotional Efforts

Although the United States has had no integrated national policy regarding location of economic activities or people, every major public activity has affected the relative economic advantages of different areas. Farm price support programs, for example, have helped to maintain the incomes and economic activity of the less industrialized states. Public and private policies regarding wage determination and collective bargaining affected the relative labor costs of different regions and communities. Public placement agencies helped to increase labor mobility and population adjustment. The allocation of supply contracts and construction of new facilities in wartime has played a part in advancing the spread of industry into hitherto non-industrial areas in the South and West.

At state and local levels, there has appeared a locational policy, which in its crudest manifestations has been simply an effort by public and private interests to attract more industry into their area without regard to broader considerations. Local industrial promotion during the past few decades has become more active, better organized, and more soundly conceived.[11] Under favorable auspices, this activity can perform a useful service for the national economy in at least three ways, though its effect is confined to a rather narrow range of industries. It can provide the informational basis for more informed choices of location, hence more efficient production. It can promote an improved balance of activities to stabilize the economy of an area. And finally, it can help new enterprises to overcome financial and other handicaps in getting established.

Concentration and Redistribution of Population and Industry

The long-established trends toward more equal interstate distributions of population and manufacturing continued after 1919, but so slowly following 1930 that they should be regarded with considerable reservations as indicators of the future. Table 1 sets forth some overall measurements of concentration and redistribution, using states as the unit. It shows that the steadily diminishing degree of concentration of population relative

[11] See Richardson Wood, "The Community Goes Into Business," *Harvard Business Review,* Vol. XXXVI, No. 2 (March, 1948), pp. 144-155.

TABLE 1

COEFFICIENTS OF CONCENTRATION AND REDISTRIBUTION OF POPULATION AND MANUFACTURING, BASED ON STATE DATA, 1900-1950

(All Coefficients are Expressed in Percentages)

	1900	1910	1920	1930	1940	1947	1950
COEFFICIENTS OF CONCENTRATION							
Population relative to area	48.0	44.8	43.8	42.7	42.1	42.4	42.2
Manufacturing [1] relative to area	63	62	61	59	60	58	N.A.
Manufacturing [1] relative to population	27	25	25	22	22	21	N.A.
	1900-10	1910-20	1920-30	1930-40	1940-47	1940-50	
COEFFICIENTS OF REDISTRIBUTION DURING INTERCENSAL INTERVAL							
Population	4.1	2.4	3.6	2.0	3.4 [2]	3.8	
Manufacturing [1]	3.8	6.2	6.0	4.4	4.4 [3]	N.A.	

[1] The manufacturing data used for the various years were those of the nearest Census of Manufactures, which was one year earlier than the date shown in the table in all cases except 1947.

[2] Interval of only 7 years.

[3] Interval of only 8 years.

NOTE: The coefficient measuring concentration of population relative to area is computed as follows. For each state, the difference between its percentage share of the total U. S. population and its percentage share of the total U. S. area is calculated. The coefficient of concentration is the sum of all the positive differences in percentages (which is also equal to the sum of all the negative differences). Coefficients of concentration of manufacturing relative to area, and manufacturing relative to population are calculated similarly from the appropriate data. Coefficients of redistribution are derived in the same way by comparison of percentage distributions at two different dates.

All these coefficients may range from zero (indicating identical geographic distributions of the two series compared) to maximum values approaching 100 percent. Other applications of such coefficients, and further discussion, may be found in National Resources Planning Board, *Industrial Location and National Resources*, Chapter 5 (Washington, D.C.: U. S. Government Printing Office, 1943); E. M. Hoover, *The Location of Economic Activity*, pp. 155-161 (New York: McGraw-Hill Book Co., 1948); and P. S. Florence and W. Baldamus, *Investment, Location, and Size of Plant*, Chapter IV (Cambridge, England: Cambridge University Press, 1948).

to area reached a low point at the 1940 Census and appears to have turned up a little by 1947.[12]

The concentration of manufacturing relative to area, by states, reached a new low at the 1947 Census, indicating a resumption of the slow trend toward equalization or "interregional decentralization".[13] The concentration of manufacturing relative to population (i.e., the "inequality of industrialization" of the various states) has also continued to decline since 1919, but very slowly since 1930.

Rates of shift in the geographical distribution of both population and industry since 1919 are measured by the "coefficients of redistribution"

TABLE 2

PERCENTAGE OF UNITED STATES POPULATION IN URBAN PLACES, BY SIZE, AND IN RURAL NONFARM AND FARM TERRITORY, 1920-1949

Area	1920	1930	1940	1944 [1]	1946 [1]	1949 [1]
Total United States	100.0	100.0	100.0	100.0	100.0	100.0
Urban places, total	51.2	56.2	56.5	59.6	60.0	58.7
By size classes:						
500,000 and over	15.5	17.0	17.0	31.0	N.A.	N.A.
100,000-500,000	10.5	12.6	11.8			
25,000-100,000	9.8	10.5	11.2	28.6	N.A.	N.A.
2,500-25,000	15.5	16.0	16.5			
Rural territory, total	48.8	43.8	43.5	40.4	40.0	41.3
Nonfarm	18.8	19.3	20.5	20.0	19.9	22.3
Farm	30.0	24.6	22.9	20.4	20.1	19.0

1 Percentages for 1944, 1946, and 1949 are estimates (based on samples for the civilian population only).

NOTE: The 1940 Census definitions of "urban," "rural nonfarm," and "rural farm" territory have been applied for 1920 and 1930 as well. Consequently the percentages here shown for those earlier years may differ from the ones originally published for them.

Percentages shown for 1944, 1946, and 1949 are based on a classification of places according to their urban, rural nonfarm, or farm status and their populations in 1940. In areas that would have been classified in 1944, 1946, and 1949 as urban and in the larger classes of cities the percentages of civilian population would presumably be larger than the figures shown.

SOURCE: United States decennial Census figures through 1940. Census Bureau estimates for later years, from published releases.

---

12 This upturn reflects in part the interesting fact that California, which has led all other states in its population increases, has since 1940 attained a density of population per square mile greater than that of the United States as a whole. Further shifts of population to California since 1940, therefore, tend to increase the overall index of concentration of population, rather than to reduce it as earlier California increases did.

13 The concentration indicated in 1947 might have been even a little less than is shown in Table 1 had the 1947 Census not excluded certain industries, such as logging camps, retail bakeries, and repair shops, which were covered in previous Censuses and are presumably less concentrated in the leading industrial states than is manufacturing as a whole.

in Table 1. Locational change is slower in depression periods. Allowing for this factor in the 1930's and for the shorter time intervals involved after 1940, the rates of shift since 1940 seem roughly in line with earlier historical experience. This table does not support the assertion that either population or industry is shifting with unprecedented rapidity. On the other hand, the patterns show no signs of becoming frozen.

Urbanization

The steady trend toward urbanization of the population continued, apparently, through World War II. According to the rather fragmentary recent data set forth in Table 2, however, this trend was checked during the postwar reconversion and boom, and the percentage of population living in urban places may have shown an actual decline.[14] The striking upturn in rural nonfarm population after 1946 reflects renewed activity in

TABLE 3

MANUFACTURING IN STANDARD METROPOLITAN AREAS AND MAJOR CITIES, 1939-1947

Area	Number of Production and Related Workers (Thousands)		Percentage Increase	Percentage of U. S. Total Workers	
	1939	1947	1939-47	1939	1947
United States, total	7,863 [1]	11,918	51.7	100.0	100.0
48 Standard Metropolitan Areas (each including at least one city over 100,000 population in 1940)	4,347	6,679	53.8	55.2	56.0
Cities of over 100,000 (in 1940) included in the 48 Standard Metropolitan Areas	2,951	4,492	52.3	37.5	37.6
Remainder of Standard Metropolitan Areas	1,396	2,187	56.6	17.8	18.3
United States outside 48 Standard Metropolitan Areas.	3,516	5,239	49.0	44.7	44.0

1 Originally-reported Census total adjusted to exclude employees of logging camps and logging contractors (not operating sawmills). Such establishments were not covered in the 1947 Census, and presumably were not found in Standard Metropolitan Areas to any significant extent in 1939. A few other types of establishment covered in 1939 were omitted in 1947 (*e.g.* retail bakeries) but no adjustment has been made in the 1939 figures here shown. As a result, the 1939 and 1947 figures are not perfectly comparable, but the discrepancy involved is believed to be too small to affect significantly the indications of this table.

SOURCE: Bureau of the Census, preliminary releases of 1947 Census of Manufactures.

14 Final judgment on the extent and significance of this apparent reversal in the urbanization trend must await analysis of the results of the Census of 1950. See note under Table 2.

suburban development as automobiles and housing again became available.

The major metropolitan industrial areas continued to account for about the same proportion of total manufacturing employment as they had for many decades, though as Table 3 indicates they slightly increased their share between 1939 and 1947. Within metropolitan areas, as the same table also shows, growth of manufacturing was particularly rapid in the territory outside the boundaries of large cities. This statistical fact in itself is not conclusive evidence of any real suburban "decentralization." As any cluster of industry grows, it naturally expands in area and the percentage rate of growth is fastest in the outer parts. None the less, there appears to have been a real outward shift of manufacturing in metropolitan areas, with non-manufacturing activities assuming a larger relative share in the inner urban zones. The chief factors responsible for this suburbanization have been discussed.

Migration and Income Levels

A major factor in the continuing redistribution of population is internal migration.[15] The spread of automobile ownership since 1919 has resulted in a high degree of mobility. Table 4 indicates the impressive volume of migration since 1935, which is as far back as reasonably comparable estimates extend. Over the five-year period 1935-1940, nearly 16 million people, or more than an eighth of the population, moved to a different county.[16]

After 1940 the rate of migration was even greater. In both the wartime and the immediate postwar migration, a much higher proportion of the moves covered longer distances. Of the 1935-40 migrants, only 41 per cent were interstate and 59 per cent moved within states; in the migration of 1940-46, these proportions were reversed. After the initial postwar shakedown in 1945 and 1946, however, postwar migration seems to have returned to a slight predominance of intrastate over interstate moves. The rate of migration continued high during the postwar boom, evidencing in part the apparent trend toward greater mobility and in part the effects of general business prosperity, which has regularly tended in the past to stimulate migration.

Migration has followed a reasonably consistent pattern of flows, as the three maps in Figure 1 show. Seven northeastern industrial states (Connecti-

---

[15] The two other factors are geographic differences in rates of natural increase and net foreign migration. Both are now of much less importance than they were as recently as the 1920's, and seem likely to become still less important.

[16] The total is really an understatement, since it does not include the people who were born during the period and then moved, nor those who died during the decade, nor those who moved more than once but ended up in the same county where they began the period. Moreover, other multiple migrants are counted only once regardless of the number of moves.

TABLE 4

MIGRATION IN THE UNITED STATES, 1935-1949

Period	Population [1] Covered in Survey (Born Before Beginning of Period and in U. S. at End of Period) (Millions)	Migrants (in Millions)				Migrants as Per Cent of Population Covered			
		Between Counties			Within a County [2]	Between Counties			Within a County [2]
		Total	Between States	Within a State		Total	Between States	Within a State	
April 1935-April 1940	120.0	15.7	6.5	9.2	N.A.	13.1	5.4	7.7	N.A.
April 1940-Feb. 1946	118.8	19.5	11.4	8.1	N.A.	16.4	9.6	6.8	N.A.
April 1940-Feb. 1947	122.6	25.5	12.4	13.1	44.4	20.8	10.1	10.7	36.2
Dec. 1941-Mar. 1945	116.9	15.3	7.8	7.5	N.A.	13.1	6.7	6.5	N.A.
April 1947-April 1948	141.7	9.0	4.4	4.6	19.2	6.4	3.1	3.3	13.6
April 1948-April 1949	144.1	8.3	4.3	4.0	18.8	5.8	3.0	2.8	13.0

1 The migration estimates for 1935-1940 are based on returns of the 1940 Census of Population, covering the entire population. Those for later periods are based on sample surveys and covered only the civilian non-institutional population.

2 Persons not living in the same house at the end of the period that they occupied at the beginning, but living in the same county. The Census does not count such persons as migrants.

SOURCE: Bureau of the Census, Current Population Reports, Series P-S, Nos. 5, 11, and 24; Series P-20, Nos. 22 and 28.

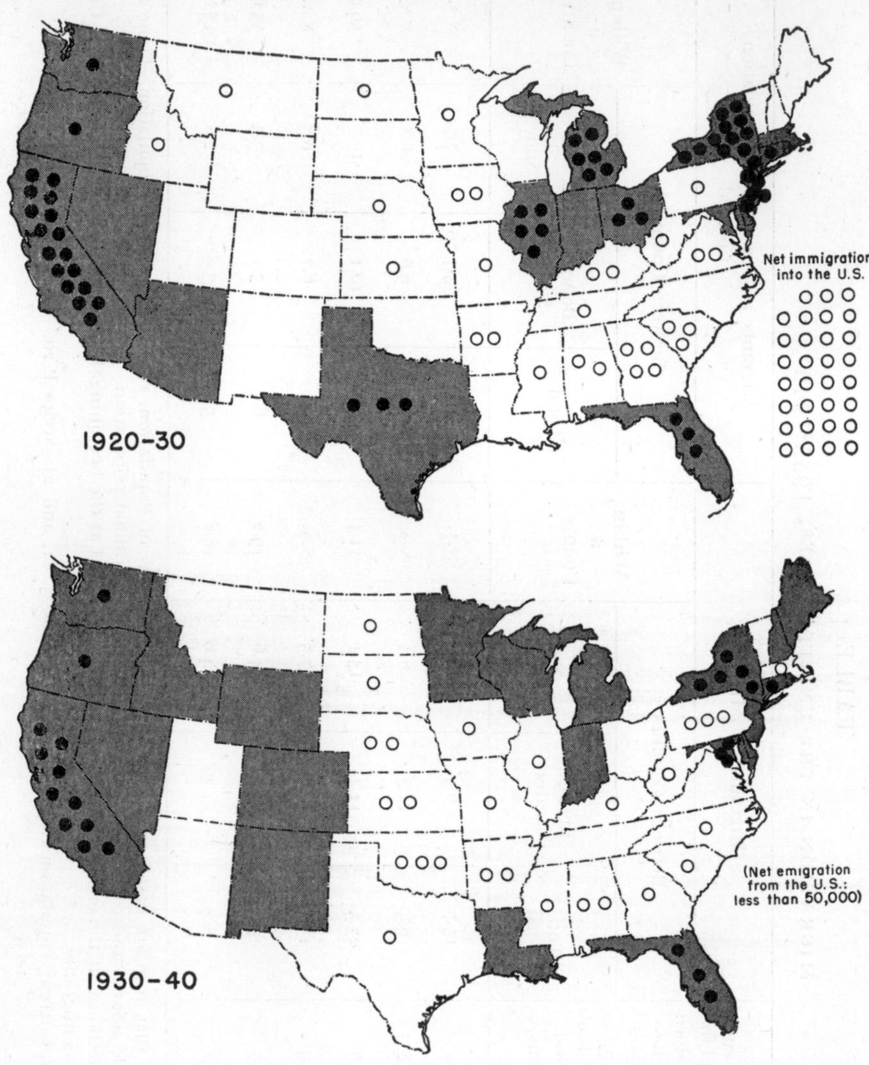

cut, New York, New Jersey, Delaware, Maryland, Michigan, and Indiana) made a net gain by migration in each of the three periods 1920-30, 1930-40, and 1940-47. The same is true of Florida and of the three Pacific Coast states and adjacent Nevada. On the other hand, in each of the three periods there was net emigration from a broad swath of states including the whole Southeast (except Florida) and extending northwestward through Montana. The remaining states experienced periods of both net emigration and net immigration between 1920 and 1947. To a considerable extent, reversals in the migration currents represent the movement out of certain heavily industrialized states (such as Ohio, Pennsylvania, Massachusetts, and Illinois) during the depressed 1930's. Nearby, less industrial states

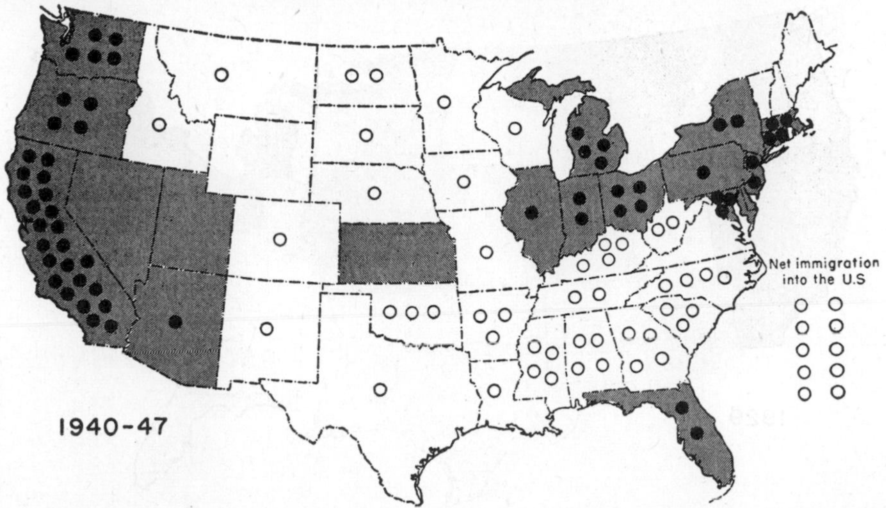

FIG. 1. *Net Migration by States, 1920-47.* States with net inward migration are shaded and states with net outward migration unshaded. Amounts of net migration are shown by circles, in units of 100,000 or major fractions thereof; states without circles had net migration of less than 50,000 during the period in question. Total net migration into or out of the United States is shown by the circles at the right; the migration indicated for individual states includes both domestic and international. (Source: 1920-30, C. Warren Thornthwaite, *Internal Migration in the United States,* Plate VII-D, p. 22 (Philadelphia: University of Pennsylvania Press, 1934); 1930-40 and 1940-47, U. S. Bureau of the Census.)

such as Maine, Vermont, Wisconsin, and Minnesota gained temporarily by migration during the 1930's, though losing in both other periods. A surge of migration out of "Dust Bowl" areas of the Great Plains after the droughts of the 1930's also helped to put some other states, such as Idaho, New Mexico, and Colorado, temporarily in the net-immigration category in that decade.

In reasonably prosperous times, people move predominantly to areas of higher income levels. This is true of both interregional and farm-to-city migration. In depressed periods, on the other hand, migration dwindles and is attracted more by security or cheapness of subsistence than by the average income levels of the employed. It is striking to observe that the period 1930-47, despite the fact that it included several depression years, showed a pattern of migration consistently away from low-income states toward high-income states.[17]

Migration during at least the latest decade appears to have played some part in relieving the disparity of income in various parts of the country.

[17] If we take the 19 states in which the ratio of net emigration to population was highest in 1930-47 (in each case, more than 5 percent), we find that all these states had had average per capita incomes at least 9 per cent below the United States average in 1929. Conversely, the states with lowest income levels in 1929 showed high rates of

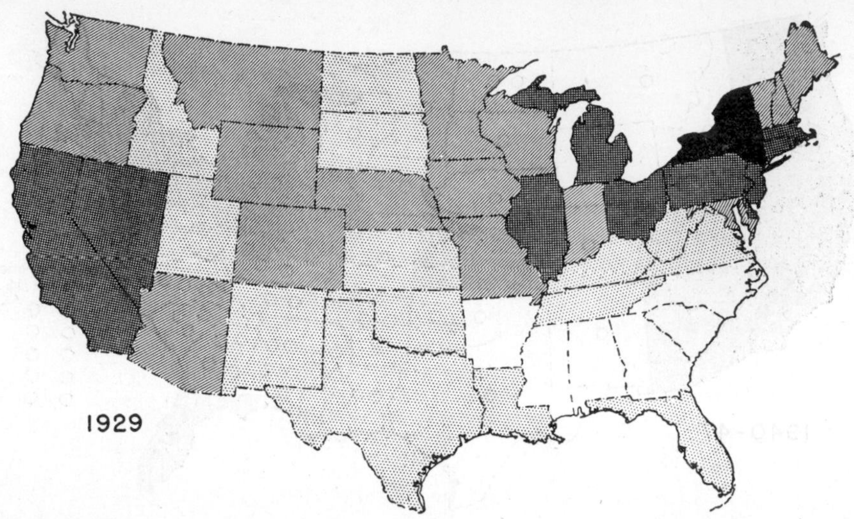

come in various parts of the country. Between 1929 and 1947 there was a notable tendency toward equalization. All states gained substantially in per capita income, but the gains were greater in the poorer states.[18]

FIG. 2. *Per Capita Income by States, as Ratio to United States Per Capita Income, 1929, 1940, and 1947.* (Source: Charles F. Schwartz, "Regional Trends in Income Payments," *Survey of Current Business,* September, 1948, Vol. 28, No. 9, Table 4, p. 17.)

A part of this remarkable shift in the direction of equalization of income levels undoubtedly reflects the rise in farm prices and the consequent rapid income gains of agricultural states, which had generally ranked low in per capita income. Farm income was 9.3 per cent of total national income in 1947 as against 8.9 per cent in 1929, and, moreover, was divided among considerably fewer farmers.[19]

---

emigration from 1930 to 1947. Nine out of the 10 lowest-income states had net emigration of 15 per cent or more of their respective 1930 populations. The remaining one, Tennessee, with only 8 per cent net emigration, is an interesting exception for which the activities of TVA may doubtless claim some credit.

[18] For example, in 1929 there were 20 states with per capita incomes less than 80 per cent of the national average (shown in white and the lightest shading on the top map of Fig. 2). Every one of these increased its per capita income faster than the country as a whole between 1929 and 1947—in other words, they all made headway toward overtaking the standards of living of the rest of the country. Conversely, the states best off in 1929 showed a smaller increase than the national average between 1929 and 1947. The 13 states, including the District of Columbia, with per capita incomes 10 per cent or more in excess of the national average in 1929 (shown in black and the darkest shading on the top map in Fig. 2) all showed a smaller-than-average increase from 1929 to 1947, with the sole exception of Nevada.

[19] Edward F. Denison, "Industrial Composition of National Income," *Survey of Current Business,* Vol. 28, No. 12 (December, 1948), Table 1, p. 12.

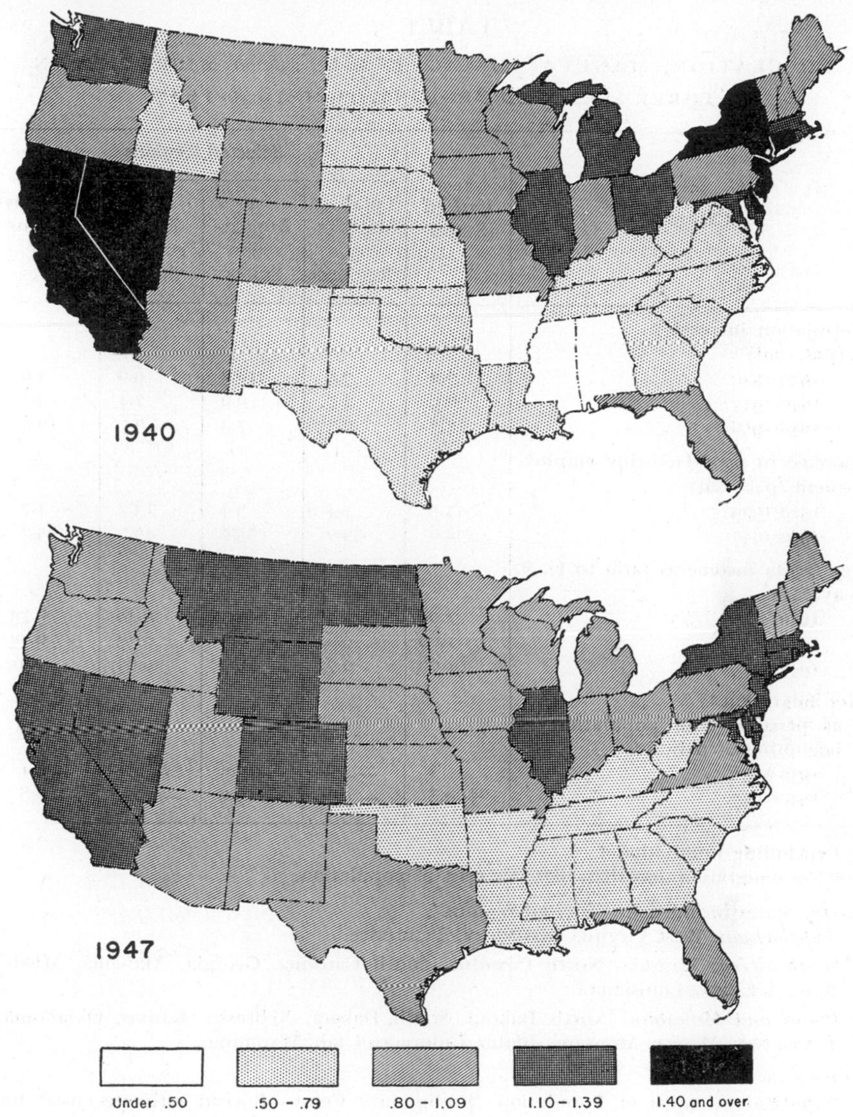

Some further detail on the experience of specific areas after 1929 is shown in Table 5. Three groups of states characterized by low income and chronic emigration have been compared with the country as a whole.[20]

[20] The "regions" assembled for comparison in Table 5 are of course only crude approximations to "problem areas"—partly because they are marked out along state lines, and partly because they are not internally homogeneous. A few of the 23 states included in them showed small net inward migration in one of the two periods covered (1930-40 and 1940-47), and a few of the "Plains and Mountain" group had per capita incomes above the national average in 1947.

TABLE 5

POPULATION, MANUFACTURING, INCOME, AND MIGRATION IN THREE SELECTED REGIONS, 1929-1940-1947

Category	United States	Selected Regions			
		Total, 23 States in 3 Regions	3 Appalachian States	8 Southeastern States	12 Plains & Mountain States
Population increase (per cent)					
1930-1940	7.2	7.5	10.2	9.6	3.9
1940-1947	8.9	2.7	0.9	2.4	3.8
1940-1950	14.3	9.7	7.2	9.7	10.9
Increase in manufacturing employment (per cent)					
1929-1939	— 5.5	7.4	3.4	13.2	— 4.7
1939-1947	52.6	53.0	53.8	43.7	85.2
Per capita income as ratio to U. S. average					
1929	1.00	0.59	0.57	0.48	0.73
1940	1.00	0.62	0.58	0.53	0.73
1947	1.00	0.75	0.70	0.64	0.91
Net migration [1] as percentage of population at beginning of period					
1930-1940	[2]	— 4.8	— 3.5	— 4.3	— 6.1
1940-1947	+ 0.8	— 9.3	— 10.2	— 10.1	— 6.8

[1] Including international.

[2] Net emigration, less than 0.05 per cent of population.

NOTE: States included in "selected regions":

Appalachian: West Virginia, Kentucky, Tennessee.

Southeastern: Virginia, North Carolina, South Carolina, Georgia, Alabama, Mississippi, Arkansas, Louisiana.

Plains and Mountain: North Dakota, South Dakota, Nebraska, Kansas, Oklahoma, Texas, New Mexico, Montana, Idaho, Colorado, Utah, Wyoming.

SOURCE OF FIGURES:

Population: Census of Population (preliminary Census Bureau estimates used for 1947 and 1950).

Manufacturing employment: Census of Manufactures. The 1929-39 percentage changes are on the basis of "wage earners" and the 1939-47 percentage changes are on the basis of "production and related workers." The industries covered differ slightly between the two intervals but it is unlikely that this significantly affects the figures here shown.

Income: Charles F. Schwartz and Robert E. Graham, Jr., "State Income Payments in 1947," *Survey of Current Business,* August, 1948, pp. 10-21; Charles F. Schwartz, "Regional Trends in Income Payments," *ibid.,* September, 1948, pp. 10-21.

Migration: Bureau of the Census. The 1930-1947 estimates are preliminary.

All three groups raised their per capita income levels considerably toward the national average after 1940. The "Appalachian" and "Plains and Mountain" regions acquired an increasing share of the national total of manufacturing, but the Southeast lagged in this respect after 1940. One factor explaining this lag is the extent to which manufacturing in the Southeast is still largely confined to certain lines, such as textiles and tobacco products, for which demand in the war and postwar period expanded less than was the case in, say, the metal and metal products fields.

Table 5 and the bottom map in Fig. 2 show that despite the considerable equalization that occurred up to 1947, there still existed wide interregional disparities in living standards at that time. Per capita money income, though admittedly a very crude measure of economic well-being, was 2.7 times as high in New York State as in Mississippi. The poorer states can hardly expect to hold their relative gains without both continued farm prosperity and increased development of their potentials for industrialization.[21]

Conclusion

Many of America's most serious economic and social problems have been and are associated with the changes outlined above. The modern metropolis with its difficulties of traffic congestion, zoning, and provision for public services represents a stage of evolution in response to new means of transport, production, and marketing. Poverty descends on whole regions as a result of depletion of resources or migration of industry. The economic and social structures of some communities may become vulnerable through intense specialization in a single industry, and diversification is urged as a remedy. Regions and communities bid against one another for new industries, and in such matters as freight rates, public power development, and wage regulation the heat of controversy rages fiercest. Finally, a special series of locational problems is posed by the vulnerability of present industrial concentrations to military attack.

Only the future can reveal the impact of such new factors as mass transport by air, utilization of atomic energy, conversion of coal at the mines into liquid and gaseous fuels, and multifarious new industrial techniques. The one thing certain is that such developments, and others not yet even envisaged, will call for continued shifts and adjustments in the location of people and their economic activities.

---

[21] It is appropriate to direct attention here to the penetrating and constructive analysis of Southern economic development pursued in recent years by the National Planning Association's Committee for the South. Two recent studies of the Committee are *Why Industry Moves South*, by Glenn E. McLaughlin and Stefan Robock (Washington, D. C.: National Planning Association, 1949), and *The Impact of Federal Policies on the Economy of the South* (issued as a report of the Congressional Joint Committee on the Economic Report, 81st Congress, 1st Session. Washington, D. C.: 1949).

Selected References

GENERAL WORKS

Florence, P. S., and Baldamus, W., *Investment, Location, and Size of Plant.* Cambridge, England: Cambridge University Press, 1948.

Goodrich, Carter, and others, *Migration and Economic Opportunity,* Report of the Study of Population Redistribution. Philadelphia: University of Pennsylvania Press, 1936.

Hoover, E. M., *The Location of Economic Activity.* New York: McGraw-Hill Book Company, Inc., 1948.

Hawley, A. H., *Human Ecology.* New York: The Ronald Press Company, 1950.

McLaughlin, Glenn E., *Growth of American Manufacturing Areas.* Pittsburgh: University of Pittsburgh, 1938.

Paullin, C. O., *Atlas of American Historical Geography.* Washington: Carnegie Institution and American Geographical Society, 1932.

Semple, E. C., *American History and its Geographic Conditions.* Boston: Houghton Mifflin Company, 1903.

U. S. National Resources Committee, *Our Cities: Their Role in the National Economy.* Washington, D. C.: 1937.

———, *The Structure of American Economy,* Part I. Washington, D. C.: 1939.

U. S. National Resources Planning Board, *Industrial Location and National Resources.* Washington, D. C.: 1942.

Whittlesey, Derwent, *The Earth and the State.* New York: Henry Holt and Company, 1939.

SPECIAL TOPICS

Bogue, D. J., *The Structure of the Metropolitan Community.* Ann Arbor: University of Michigan, 1949.

Canoyer, H. G., *Selecting a Store Location.* U. S. Bureau of Foreign and Domestic Commerce, Economic Series No. 56. Washington, D. C.: 1945.

Hoover, E. M., *Location Theory and the Shoe and Leather Industries.* Cambridge, Mass.: Harvard University Press, 1937.

Isard, Walter, "Some Economic Implications of Atomic Energy," *Quarterly Journal of Economics,* Vol. LXII, No. 2 (February, 1948), pp. 202-228.

———, "Some Locational Factors in the Iron and Steel Industry Since the Early Nineteenth Century," *Journal of Political Economy,* Vol. LVI, No. 3 (June, 1948), pp. 203-217.

———, "Transportation Development and Building Cycles," *Quarterly Journal of Economics,* Vol. LVII, No. 1 (November, 1942), pp. 90-112.

———, and William Capron, "The Future Locational Pattern of Iron and Steel Production in the United States," *Journal of Political Economy,* Vol. LVII, No. 2 (April, 1949), pp. 118-133.

———, and Caroline Isard, "Economic Implications of Aircraft," *Quarterly Journal of Economics,* Vol. LIX, No. 2 (February, 1945), pp. 145-169.

Lösch, August, *Die räumliche Ordnung der Wirtschaft.* Jena: Gustav Fischer Verlag, 1944. An English translation is in preparation, to be published by the Yale University Press.

McLaughlin, G. E., and Stefan Robock, *Why Industry Moves South.* National Planning Association, Committee for the South, Report No. 3. Washington, D. C.: National Planning Association, 1949.

Magee, Mabel, *Trends in the Location of the Women's Clothing Industry.* Chicago: University of Chicago Press, 1930.

Ogburn, W. F., *The Social Effects of Aviation.* Boston: Houghton Mifflin Company, 1945.

U. S. Bureau of the Census and Bureau of Agricultural Economics, *Changes in Distribution of Manufacturing Wage Earners, 1899-1939.* Washington, D. C.: 1942.

40 · MASS MARKETING OF CONSUMERS' GOODS

IN THE PERIOD FOLLOWING World War I, changes in marketing took place so rapidly that some have referred to the period as the post-war marketing revolution. Actually, most of the changes that occurred were merely continuations of those that were taking place before the war, the essential difference between the two periods being the rate of change. It was the rapid acceleration of developments in the post-war period that made them conspicuous.

As already indicated in Chapter 26, wholesalers and manufacturers, in that order, had occupied the dominant role in guiding the production and marketing of consumer goods in the American economy prior to 1919. Until early in the twentieth century the retailer was, therefore, at a disadvantage in dealing with the wholesaler or manufacturer. The importance of the retailer in guiding production and marketing increased significantly, however, after World War I. Large-scale retail organizations and groups increased in number and size, until at the close of the period they accounted for a substantial share of retail sales. In addition to greater bargaining power, large-scale retailers gained influence by introducing merchandise bearing their own brands, which tended to transfer consumer loyalty from the manufacturer to the retailer. To some degree the wholesaler also established private brands, but generally the wholesaler, being less aggressive than either the retailer or the manufacturer of consumers' goods, declined in importance in promotional work although he continued to remain important in the physical distribution of consumers' goods.

Manufacturers attempted in several ways to meet the new marketing conditions brought about by the growth of large-scale retailers and the generally more severe competition of the period, and they were able to retain an important place in the market during the period under consideration, even though large-scale retailers gained considerable ground.

The marketing changes that occurred after World War I were brought about, in large measure, by a great increase in the intensity of competition, a more rapid rate of technological development, and greater freedom of choice, the latter the result of the changing pattern of income and the higher scale of living brought about by an increased level of general education and a world made small by new avenues of intercourse. In general, there was a continuation of the shift from a seller's to a buyer's market, already marked prior to 1914.

The Retailer Assumes New Importance

The transition away from small-scale shop-keeping toward large-scale retailing enterprises commenced before 1900, but it was after that date, particularly after World War I, that the most important developments occurred.[1]

The growth of large-scale retailing brought new importance to the retailer. Bargaining between retailers and manufacturers became less one-sided as a result of the amazing growth of corporate chains, the rapid expansion of chain systems by mail-order houses, and the attainment of real stature by cooperative groups of independent retailers. The manufacturer was no longer able to dominate the retailer; in fact the large-scale retailer was frequently able to dictate to the manufacturer.[2]

It has been estimated that in 1947 about 50 per cent of the dollar volume of over-the-counter retail sales of merchandise was accounted for by approximately 400 retail companies and groups.[3] Included among these organizations were some of the larger voluntary chains, which represent buying and promotional rather than ownership arrangements. Thus, on the basis of ownership, the 400 largest retail organizations would probably account for a smaller proportion of all retail sales. There is little doubt, however, that there was an increase in the volume of retailing concentrated in the hands of an infinitesimally small proportion of the over 1,500,000 retail enterprises that operated some 1,700,000 stores at the close of the period.

Conspicuous Types of Large-Scale Retailing Organizations

The Chain Store

The first decade of this century saw the department stores make their greatest development; the second, mail order houses; the third, chain stores; and the fourth and fifth, supermarkets. The development of the

1 "The economic historian of the future is likely to put his finger on the first three or four decades of the 20th century as the time when the marketing of commodities to consumers definitely developed away from the small-scale shop-keeping basis, parallel to the home industry or handicraft phase of manufacturing, toward a large-scale, fully capitalistic basis." M. P. McNair, "Trends in Large-Scale Retailing," *Harvard Business Review*, Vol. X, No. 1 (October 1931), p. 30.

2 See D. R. Craig and W. K. Gabler, "The Competitive Struggle for Market Control," *Annals* of the American Academy of Political and Social Sciences, Vol. 209 (May 1940), pp. 84-107.

3 E. B. Weiss, "400 Retailers Make Half of All Over-the-Counter Sales," *Printers' Ink*, Vol. 222, No. 8 (February 26, 1948), p. 34.

chain store was one of the outstanding institutional changes in modern marketing, particularly after 1920. So rapid was the development of this type that the decade of the twenties has been referred to as the "chain-store era." The dollar volume of chain store sales in relation to total retail sales rose from about 4 per cent in 1919 to 22 per cent in 1929 and remained somewhere near that figure in subsequent years.

A few chains had become quite large by 1918, notably the A. & P., with 3,799 stores and annual sales totalling $152,000,000, and Woolworth, with 1,037 stores and annual sales of $107,000,000. In 1929 the A. & P. had 15,418 stores and sales of $1,053,693,000. Several others counted their stores in the thousands and their sales in the hundreds of millions. In 1918, there were some 29,200 chain-store units in twenty-six fields. In 1929, chain-store units in all fields numbered 159,638. Many of these chains grew from single-store operations and expanded by using profits for further expansion.

Beginning in 1929 conditions changed. The total number of store units declined; many of the poorer stores were eliminated and emphasis was put on fewer stores with greater volume. In the period 1929-1939, chain-store units to total retail stores declined from 10 per cent to 8 per cent. There was a definite tendency for chains to be concentrated in fewer hands and national and sectional organizations gained at the expense of local enterprises. Chains became more important in some kinds of business and less important in others in the thirty years preceding 1950. They gained slightly between 1929 and 1948 in food, apparel, and hardware stores, moderately in variety stores, and substantially in drug stores.[4] Census data for 1929 and 1939 indicate that between those dates the most striking gains made by chains were in department stores, women's ready-to-wear, shoes, radios, and jewelry. The most striking losses were in family clothing stores. The sharp rise in chain store operations of department stores reflected primarily the opening of a large number of department stores by Sears, Roebuck & Company and Montgomery Ward and Company.

The Supermarket

The supermarket was the most conspicuous development in the 1930's. It commenced as a depression period type of retailing, but remained to occupy an increasingly important role in retailing. In 1940 there were 6,175 food supermarkets with sales of 2 billion dollars; by 1948 the number had grown to 11,885 and sales volume to 8.4 billion dollars. The expansion of the supermarket type of store, in the late 1930's and subsequently, was closely tied to chain store operations. Recognizing the soundness of supermarket methods, chain store organizations adopted many of

[4] N. H. Engle, "Chain Store Distribution Vs. Independent Wholesaling," *Journal of Marketing*, Vol. XIV, No. 3, p. 242.

them. This was in line with the policy of emphasizing large units, which had grown out of the various anti-chain store laws and the search for greater efficiency. Moreover many of the supermarket operations developed from a single store into a local or regional chain. Thus, by 1939, 80 per cent or more of the total supermarket business in the country was accounted for by chains of four or more stores.

Supermarkets added further confusion to the already confused channels of distribution by their addition of non-related merchandise. Thirty-five per cent of the food supermarkets included in a study in 1948 had a drug department, 31 per cent carried cosmetics, 22 per cent wine and liquor, 21 per cent stationery, and 20 per cent magazines. Other departments included housewares, small appliances, hardware, and variety goods.[5] The tendency for retail types to make an entrance based upon price appeal and then gradually adopt more elaborate operations and quarters, which of course increases the operating cost ratio, is well illustrated by the development of the supermarket.[6] The inconveniently located barnlike warehouses and industrial buildings in which supermarkets first saw light were cleaned up and redecorated or forsaken for better locations and buildings, in some cases especially constructed for the purpose. The initial low ratio of operating costs to sales increased following these improvements, but it was still low enough to continue to appeal in part on a price basis.[7]

The Department Store

This type of retail store was first to rise to prominence among the large-scale retailers, but it was also first to complete its major growth. The position of the department store in the retailing structure showed little change in the twenties and thirties. During World War II substantial gains in sales were made, and in 1947 about 10 per cent of all retail sales were accounted for by department stores, in contrast to about 8 per cent in both 1929 and 1939.

Originally the department store was an independent store. This type dominated the field up to about the middle of the 1920's. Following this, Sears, Roebuck and Montgomery Ward opened a number of large retail stores, many of which were department stores. These stores and others of

---

5 "Supermarkets Expanding in Numbers, Volume and also in Non-Food Products Carried," *Printers' Ink,* Vol. 226, No. 1 (January 7, 1949), p. 72.

6 The tendency of new types to enter the field on the basis of price, as did department stores, chain stores, mail order houses and supermarkets, has been called the retail "cost cycle." For discussion of this point see M. P. McNair, C. I. Gragg, and S. F. Teele, *Problems in Retailing,* pp. 17-22. New York: McGraw-Hill Book Company, 1937. Also see McNair, *op. cit.,* p. 39.

7 Much of the appeal of the supermarket, however, proved to be the desire to shop in one place, the attractive displays, and, in some cases, the wide variety of perishable goods. Self service, originally thought to be undesirable from a consumer point-of-view, proved otherwise, and in the late forties was extended to meats.

similar type made an impressive number of chain department stores. The depression of the early thirties favored low-price department store chains and in part accounted for an increase in their share of the dollar volume department store sales from 19 per cent in 1939 to slightly over 30 per cent in 1943.

In the forties, chains such as W. T. Grant commenced to diversify their merchandise lines and included a greater number of high-price items. While this and similar organizations could not be classified as department stores, they certainly moved in that direction. Likewise, many of the limited-price variety store chains took on higher-priced merchandise and increased the size of individual stores.

Developments in the period between the two World Wars tended to handicap rather than benefit the non-chain department store. Among the more important of these were: (1) the greatly increased traffic congestion in central city areas, (2) the tendency for suburban areas to grow more rapidly than the cities proper and the consequent growth of suburban shopping centers, (3) the rise of limited-line specialty stores in style-goods lines, and (4) the growth of chain stores in the apparel, dry goods, and the department store field.

The limitations of central city, non-chain department stores were recognized by the executives of such stores. In an effort to improve their competitive position, branch stores were opened, ownership groups formed, buying of some lines was done cooperatively, certain lines of merchandise were expanded and new lines added, telephone and mail-orders were encouraged, and even house-to-house selling was employed.

By 1949 only a few of the large non-chain department stores in the country remained unaffiliated with one of the buying organizations in New York City. Cooperative buying assumed importance in the twenties, and, while advantageous, it did not help the independent department store to overcome completely the advantages of better buying and better management enjoyed by the chains in some instances. Such buying led to such further cooperation among stores as the establishment of private brands, which were sold by member stores,[8] and the exchange of operating information.

The desire to gain even greater advantages than those found in cooperative buying and selling, coupled with the desire for promoters' profits, led to the creation of ownership groups. These organizations brought under common ownership several well established stores, which usually retained their individual names and were operated with far less central control than characterized chain store organizations. The economies visualized in the formation of ownership groups were not realized to any

---

[8] For example, the Associated Merchandising Corporation established private brands for staple and fashion goods as well as household appliances. The promotion of these private brands by a large number of stores gave them some of the advantages of a nationally advertised brand.

great extent during the 1930's. They accounted for some 28 per cent of the dollar volume of sales of all department stores in 1929, but only 23 per cent in 1939. During and immediately following World War II, however, ownership groups showed better promise and began to acquire more stores. During the close of the period several networks of department stores in smaller cities were being developed.

Toward the close of World War II, and immediately following, there was a great increase in the number of branch stores in suburban shopping centers, for by that time it was apparent that department stores could no longer maintain their position solely through their central city stores. There is little doubt that the proportion of all non-chain department store sales occurring outside the central shopping districts increased greatly following World War II although it is clear that the downtown area was still the principal shopping center.

The Mail-Order House

Mail-order retailing, as such, accounted for roughly one per cent of retail sales in each year during the period between the two world wars. As communication and transportation facilities improved and shopping centers developed in the smaller cities, rural areas became less dependent upon mail-order buying. Consequently, some of the mail-order houses established retail stores. In 1928 and the following years, Sears, Roebuck & Company established almost 300 retail stores, and Montgomery Ward about 530. Other mail-order houses also acquired retail stores in the years that followed. World War II caused Sears to embark on a great expansion program that proved eminently successful. Montgomery Ward also engaged in some expansion, but on a smaller scale and only after it was clear that no recession would accompany the postwar adjustment.

In the early 1930's, the retail store volume of sales of mail-order houses exceeded the volume of mail-order sales. In the late 1940's, mail-order sales probably amounted to about one-third of the total sales of such firms. This type of business was still eagerly sought and several means were used to encourage mail-order sales. Catalog stores were located at places convenient to customers, telephone orders were solicited, and credit extended. Moreover, orders were sent from catalog stores to warehouses by means of teletype, and the merchandise was then delivered by truck. Such activities helped mail-order retailing to retain a share of retail sales. The persistence of this type of retailing in the face of the great changes that have occurred in retailing indicates that it is still a useful method of retailing. Nevertheless, it is probably true, as one authority points out, that mail-order need no longer be considered as a separate type of large-scale retailing.[9]

[9] M. P. McNair, "Trends in Large-Scale Retailing," *Harvard Business Review*, Vol. X, No. 1 (October, 1931), p. 31.

Large-Scale Cooperative Action by Small Independent Stores

Despite the many developments in retailing over the years, the small independently owned store continued in 1949 to be the most important type on the basis of number of stores. It was also the most important type on the basis of dollar volume of sales.

The operator of the small independently owned store became less independent following World War I. Of necessity he entered into cooperative arrangements with other independent retailers, with wholesalers, and even with corporate chains through agency agreements. The rapid progress made by chains in many lines made it imperative that he find means of competing with them. At first cooperation took the form of buying; later joint promotion proved successful.

Retailer-owned wholesale establishments and wholesaler-sponsored voluntary chain organizations, through their members, accounted for an insignificant share of the total market in 1918. During the middle 1920's they commenced to develop at a rapid rate. In 1939 there were 638 voluntary chains and 136 retailer cooperative chains in the grocery field, with sales of $658,000,000 and $155,000,000, respectively. It has been estimated that retailers affiliated with voluntary chains or retailer cooperatives accounted for 50 per cent of the food sales of independent stores in the closing years of the 1940's.

The largest voluntary group, the Red and White group, in 1948 accounted for over one billion dollars in sales through its 8,500 members in the food trade, which compared favorably with that of the largest corporate chains, other than the A. & P. Group activities among retailers had grown important in other fields by 1949, and in the hardware, drug, and dry goods fields real progress was made.

In still another way independent stores became less independent. They became agencies for corporate chains, such as the Walgreen Company and the Western Auto Supply Company. Rexall also had a number of agency stores operated by independents, many of which were in the smaller towns and cities.

It is clear that by 1950 the small-scale independent in general had lost ground to the chain store. This development, and especially the tremendous growth of chains during the 1920's, led to predictions that independents will disappear from the scene within the next few decades. This prediction is of doubtful validity. It is clear that in some fields they can more than hold their own. In others they can hold their own if they operate efficiently and are served by efficient wholesalers. One effect of the chain store has been to raise the level of efficiency throughout marketing. Even in the fields handling staple goods, independents have found that they can achieve many of the chain stores' advantages while retaining their own. It is probable that the independent merchant, through group activity and cooperation, will continue for a long time, and possibly permanently, to play a large part in marketing in the American economy.

Reasons for the Recent Rapid Growth of Large-Scale Retailing

The rapid growth of large-scale retailing during and since the second decade of the twentieth century can be explained as the result of the adjustment of retailing institutions to fundamental changes in the size and distribution of the population; the buying habits and motives of consumers; and the availability of goods in greater volume and variety.

Population Changes

In the thirty years following 1920 the population increased by some 44,000,000 people, a gain of over 41 per cent. Moreover, the trend away from home production and toward the purchase of finished goods continued. These two factors contributed toward the purchase of a much larger volume of goods from retail institutions. The major shift in population from rural to urban areas, which had been nearly completed by 1920, laid the foundation for large-scale retailing by bringing more and larger concentrations of population. As metropolitan areas grew in population, and the shift from city to suburban living became important, the need for community shopping centers increased. Moreover, automobile traffic became badly congested in the downtown districts of large cities. These factors led to the establishment of secondary shopping districts. From the early twenties these suburban shopping centers increased in size and number at an accelerated rate. Department stores commenced to establish suburban branches in the late 1920's. Chain stores handling shopping goods, also, located units in these centers as well as in the central city districts. By 1928 Sears, Roebuck had established a chain of 37 department stores in the outskirts of large cities. While some non-chain department stores were quick to sense the importance of the developing suburban shopping centers, there were many more who did not believe that the development was of great significance.

The trend toward community shopping centers presented a problem for independent department stores with central city locations but, in general, favored large-scale retailing, particularly chain operations. Greater urbanization of population made possible a more effective use of advertising and displays and permitted less costly transportation and physical handling. An indirect factor favoring large-scale retailing was the less personal service of independent stores in population centers.

Buying Habits

World War I and the short boom following its completion caused consumers to break away from many of their old buying patterns. They were more than usually receptive to new products and improved types of old ones. Moreover, as a result of the increased income created by the war and the boom that followed, consumers had more money to spend. Prices after 1920 declined at a more rapid rate than wages. Many new products gained acceptance and several old ones experienced rapid increases in the rates at which they were purchased. The materialistic spirit prevailing in the 1920's brought about a fertile market for those who had something new to offer. Novelty items had great appeal. Fads were commonplace. Country clubs and other forms of amusement grew at tremendous rates. All of these developments were evidence of very fluid consumer demand.

Underlying these factors were more basic ones—improved transportation, new types of merchandise, wider selections of old types, the greater importance of style, the increased tendency to buy finished products in the food, apparel and other lines, and smaller families and more crowded living quarters, which brought new patterns of buying habits. These factors composed the ground swells upon which the whitecaps caused by World War I appeared.

The automobile, together with hard surfaced roads, was perhaps the most important single factor accounting for the development of urban trading centers to a degree of importance far greater than that indicated by population alone. The average trading area for consumers outside urban districts was increased from 5 or 6 miles to 30 to 150 miles and even farther.

These geographical shifts in trade were of major economic significance. To some extent these changes had begun prior to World War I, but their progress was markedly accelerated by World War I and continued so until 1929.[10] The volume of trade occurring in villages and small towns greatly diminished.

By 1940, according to census reports, 38 per cent of the population lived in cities of over 30,000, and these accounted for 57 per cent of total retail sales. About 17 per cent of the population dwelt in places of 2,500 to 30,000, yet such places accounted for nearly 26 per cent of the sales. The small town and rural areas of the country contained some 44 per cent of the population, but less than 20 per cent of total retail sales.

Retailers, wholesalers, and manufacturers all felt the impact of this shift in trade. The concentration of sales in fewer trading centers afforded chain stores an opportunity to increase their sales volume. Previously it had not been economical for them to establish stores outside of trading centers, but now they were able to obtain even grocery business from those who came to such a center. The increase in importance of trading areas worked against the mail-order business of mail-order houses, which until 1926 had no retail stores. There is reason to believe that the sub-

[10] See Melvin T. Copeland's discussion of this subject in *Recent Economic Changes in the United States,* Vol. I, pp. 331-342. New York: McGraw-Hill Book Company, 1929.

sequent opening of retail stores by the mail-order houses, at least in some instances, accelerated the shift toward trading centers.

Self-service also represents a basic change in buying habits during the past thirty years. Limited price variety stores quite early adopted semi-self-service through the open display of merchandise. A more thorough type of self-service developed during and following World War I, when the number of sales clerks was greatly reduced by many of the food chain stores. The advent of the supermarket in the early thirties, however, greatly increased the speed with which self-service was adopted. From that point on it made rapid headway. By 1949 almost all chains, supermarkets, and independent food stores, except the very small ones, were operated at least partially in this manner. Packaging and package display became more important from the manufacturer's point of view. Following World War II developments in prepackaging and refrigeration made possible extension of self-service to perishable items, including meat. In fact, the extremely rapid growth of self-service meat departments in supermarkets was little short of amazing, although in some areas, particularly Chicago, labor unions delayed this development. Drug stores tended more toward open displays in the sale of non-drug items. Even department stores adopted open displays and self-service to some extent. Sale through vending machines also became important.

Originally, self-service was introduced in an effort to reduce operating cost; but as consumers became accustomed to serving themselves, they soon found certain advantages in this system. It permitted them to handle merchandise, read labels, and make their comparisons without pressure from a waiting salesman. One of the great surprises of self-service came in connection with meats, for many women shoppers found they could obtain greater satisfaction by a careful inspection of the various cuts, with the price plainly marked on each, than was possible when pressed by the presence of a butcher and waiting customers.

The lower operating costs of self-service stores is sometimes pointed out as an evidence of improved efficiency in retailing. Such evidence is far from conclusive because, among other considerations, the transference of some of the work to the consumer must be considered.[11]

Buying Motives

Style became increasingly important in the purchase of many consumers' goods during this period. Before about 1920, styles changed quite slowly and their influence was largely confined to limited groups of people and limited kinds of merchandise; styles moved slowly from style centers to the outlying areas. In the middle 1800's apparel styles remained in vogue for several years. During the 1920's and following, this period was

[11] See D. F. Blankertz, "Consumer Actions and Consumer Nonprofit Co-operation," *Theory in Marketing*, p. 163. Chicago: Richard D. Irwin, 1950.

greatly reduced. Fall and spring styles became distinct and somewhat independent. Styles became more uniform over the entire country and the progression of style from group to group speeded up tremendously. This was true of not only apparel, but a wide range of other goods.

In 1914 only about 20 per cent of cotton goods were affected by changes in style. These changes came about slowly enough to require no violent readjustments. By 1932 "practically all fabrics from flour bags to sheets and automobile upholstery were subject to changes in style." [12] Style gradually assumed importance in the sale of such products as electrical appliances, home furnishings, automobiles, foods and beverages, and even cosmetics. Few manufacturers and middlemen could escape the style consciousness of consumers as time and space barriers became less important and style consciousness seemed to increase.

It is clear that the changes in demand were closely related to changes in trading areas. Consumers who went to trading centers to shop came in contact with the latest styles through displays of merchandise and in their social intercourse. They became increasingly interested in obtaining a wide selection of those goods in which style was an important element, particularly women's apparel and home furnishings. This resulted in a cumulative increase in the demand for style goods and worked toward a shortening of the time lag in the spread of new styles. Purchases of jewelry, toilet goods, dry goods, men's clothing and shoes tended to shift toward trading centers. Essentially, trade centers became concentrations of shopping goods, highly specialized goods and services, as well as amusements.

Price consciousness on the part of the consumer worked to the advantage of large-scale retail organizations and groups during and after World War I because they were able to lower the cost of goods to the consumer in a number of ways.

The high cost of living, during and following World War I and following World War II and the depression periods that succeeded the 1920 and 1929 crises and the slump of 1938, caused people to give considerable weight to price in buying goods. This was true particularly throughout most of the thirties. Even during the so-called "golden twenties" courses in consumer economics and provocative literature such as *Your Money's Worth* by Chase and Schlink attracted attention.

The increased importance of consumer durable goods in the American economy as well as the availability of increasingly great varieties of goods and services also increased the price consciousness of the consumer. While consumer credit helped to spread the burden of buying consumer durables, such purchases nevertheless reduced the proportion of current in-

---

[12] C. T. Murchison, "Stabilization in the Cotton Textile Industry." *Proceedings,* Forty-fifth Annual Meeting of the American Economic Association, 1932, p. 75. Cited by A. R. Burns, *The Decline of Competition,* p. 408. New York: McGraw-Hill Book Co., 1936.

come available for food, clothing, and the other basic requirements of the consumer. This favored large-scale retailers.

Mass Production Calls for Mass Retailing

Trade publication articles appearing in the twenties frequently dealt with the need for new marketing methods and institutions that could take the huge outputs of mass-production industries and market them on a large-scale basis. Manufacturers of consumer goods saw in large-scale buyers, such as chain stores and mail-order houses and, later, super markets, an opportunity to sell huge volumes of goods, to reduce their distribution costs, and to take up slack capacity. Department stores of the regular independent type represented less attractive opportunities since, while their total purchases were impressive, the amounts of individual items were not large. So anxious were some manufacturers to get this type of business and be relieved of the usual marketing costs that they were often willing to sell unbranded or retailer branded merchandise at less than full cost. This practice gave large-scale retailers a real price advantage. It should be recognized that not all of such savings were retained; goods bearing the retailer's brand or no brand at all required extra sales effort on the part of the retailer. Also, the retailer often assumed some of the physical handling and warehousing duties that in recent years have been performed quite efficiently by most of the retailing giants.

Improvements in Retail Enterprise Management

Developments in management have been of extremely great importance in making possible the growth of large-scale marketing organizations.[13] One of the chief disadvantages of large-scale organizations is the personnel problem. Selection, training, compensation, and supervision pose heavy problems. The standardized methods that make possible the effective use of specialized management result in a degree of inflexibility that makes it difficult to adapt to local conditions. It should also be recognized that costs relative to sales do not necessarily diminish as the volume of sales increases.

Only by improvements in management have large-scale retail organizations and groups been able to take advantage of the opportunities presented by the changes in the size and location of the population, the changes in buying habits of consumers, and the changes in the volume and varieties of merchandise that occurred during and following World War I.

---

[13] An excellent discussion of this point is found in M. T. Copeland, "The Managerial Factor in Marketing," *Facts and Factors in Economic History*, pp. 596-619. Cambridge, Mass.: Harvard University Press, 1932. See also H. S. Dennison, "Management," *Recent Economic Changes*, Vol. II, pp. 531-544. New York: McGraw-Hill Book Company, 1929; and S. F. Teele, "Logics and Emotions," *Business and Modern Society*, pp. 295-312. Cambridge, Mass.: Harvard University Press, 1938.

During the period under consideration great strides were made toward large-scale retailing. Mass buying, mass display and mass advertising helped to bring this about. But, in spite of these developments, the actual sale of merchandise remained small-scale. The individual consumer continued to buy in lots that were infinitesimally small when compared with the retailers' purchases.

Changes in the Wholesaling of Consumers' Goods

After World War I the rise of large-scale buying by retailers made it easier and more satisfactory for manufacturers to deal directly with such buyers. In time the smaller manufacturing organizations found themselves at a disadvantage in dealing with large-scale buyers, and many resorted to combination. On the other hand, many manufacturing organizations were developing into giants simply by sales expansion. Direct sales became more prevalent as a result of both of these developments.

Decline of the Orthodox Wholesaler in the Jobbing Trades

World War I brought technological advances and increased productive capacity. The intensity of competition increased. Manufacturers needed increased promotional effort. Full-line, full service wholesalers were unable or unwilling to promote specific products to the extent manufacturers thought they should. The thousands of items carried by wholesalers and retailers made it difficult for them to know the benefit-giving characteristics of each product handled. Moreover, wholesalers were willing to give a manufacturer's line only the amount of selling effort warranted by profit possibilities. The great increase in the volume of consumer and trade advertising following World War I was in part the result of the efforts of the manufacturer to present his product in a much more dramatic, forceful, and complete manner than he had previously. Nevertheless, it was still necessary to use wholesalers to handle the physical distribution of a wide variety of convenience goods.

Another reason why wholesalers were circumvented by manufacturers was the latters' insistence on hand-to-mouth buying, especially after they took substantial inventory losses in connection with the drastic decline in wholesale prices in 1920. For a period of about thirty years prior to 1920, wholesale prices had gradually risen, thus affording small inventory profits. Under these circumstances wholesalers were agreeable to carrying large stocks of goods. Buying was done in quantity some time in advance, and wholesalers had adequate stocks to meet the demands of their customers. Hand-to-mouth buying on the other hand resulted in small frequent purchases by wholesalers, which increased marketing and in some instances production costs. Moreover, the maintenance of small inventories increased the chances of being unable to meet unusual demands. The establishment of branch offices and better transportation facilities enabled the manufacturer to control the availability of physical product as well as sales promotion efforts.

It can be seen that, as manufacturers and retailers became larger in size and better able to obtain market information, the advisory and financial services of the wholesaler became less important. Further, in many instances, his promotional value was not great. Frequently, then, the independent service wholesaler was to the manufacturer essentially a warehouseman. But, to many small independent retailers, independent service wholesalers constituted a source of supply for all or a part of their requirements.

The struggle of the full-line service wholesaler during the transition period is a dramatic one. Upon finding their competitive position threatened, full-line service wholesalers in the jobbing lines at first tried to resist the underlying changes that were occurring. Manufacturers who sold direct were boycotted. Attempts were made to coerce retailers who bought direct from manufacturers. But the futility of such resistance soon became apparent and means were sought whereby full-line service wholesalers of consumer goods could adjust to the changes being encountered. Various plans were tried. Lines of merchandise were narrowed, services were curtailed, private brands were promoted, and horizontal and vertical integrations were effected. There was no uniformity of attempts or results. Some firms were quite successful, while others using the same plan failed.

The Increase of Specialty Wholesalers in the Jobbing Trades

Accompanying the decline of the full or general line service wholesalers in the consumer goods field, there was a rise in the importance of the limited-line service wholesaler or specialty house. While specialization among wholesalers came into being much earlier, the increased intensity of competition in wholesaling following World War I caused a considerable shift from general line to specialty lines among service wholesalers. By 1939 the share of total business of service wholesalers accounted for by limited-line houses was 70 per cent for dry goods, 54 per cent for groceries, 31 per cent for drugs, and 9 per cent for hardware. In the same year, of the total of specialty and full-line service wholesaler establishments, 93 per cent in dry goods, 83 per cent in drugs, 79 per cent in groceries, and 42 per cent in hardware were specialty houses.[14] Specialization also took place in the wholesaling of tobacco, jewelry, household appliances, and automobile supplies and accessories.

Specialty wholesalers grew because they were able to (1) acquire expert knowledge of the products they sold, (2) handle a wide assortment of merchandise within the special lines they stocked, and (3) supply fresher

[14] T. N. Beckman and N. H. Engle, *Wholesaling*, p. 203. New York: The Ronald Press Co., 1949.

stock because of their high turnover rates. It must be recognized, however, that, along with these advantages, specialty wholesalers brought with them higher operating expenses than were customary among general-line wholesalers.

For many years the idea that the wholesaler is disappearing from our marketing system has been prevalent. While it is true that in recent years wholesalers have become less important in the marketing of consumers' goods, there is certainly no indication that they will pass from the scene. They will continue to exist so long as they perform worthwhile services. In 1950 there were a large number of independent retailers obtaining the bulk of their needs and a large number of buying groups and retailer-owned wholesale organizations buying "fill-in" items from service wholesalers. In some areas, particularly sparsely populated areas, the service wholesaler played a major role.[15]

Manufacturers' Marketing Activities

The growth of large-scale retailers and the increased intensity of competition among sellers made it necessary for manufacturers to give more attention to their marketing activities. Production was no longer the dominant problem. In recognition of this fact, marketing executives assumed more important duties in the management of manufacturing organizations. It became much less common to find the marketing function handled by the president, the production manager, or the treasurer. This was due in part to the fact that some firms had grown in size, but to a large measure it resulted from the closer attention that competition in the market place required. Moreover, the severity of competition led, in some cases, to integration. Product planning, and advertising were given much greater attention. Channels of distribution became less clear-cut and selling direct to the retailer gained new importance. Formal marketing research became more important as a tool of management.

Integration

Certain marketing advantages were expected to result from the mergers, which occurred in great numbers in the 1920's.[16] In the food and other fields the small manufacturer found that he could combine with three or four other manufacturers and thereby obtain a growth overnight that would otherwise have taken years to achieve. It is said that one of the objectives of the General Foods Corporation merger was to gain a more effective size for dealing with the chains. The same objective was involved

---

[15] H. A. Mitchell, *Wholesale Buying Centers for Retailers in the Deep Central South.* New Orleans: Tulane University Press, 1949.

[16] See J. A. Murphy, *Merchandising Through Mergers.* New York: Harper and Brothers, 1930.

in the consolidating activities of the Kraft Cheese Company and of the Quaker Oats-Aunt Jemima-Muffets combination.

Where competing lines were combined, duplicate selling effort was eliminated and a greater degree of specialization by product and customer type resulted. But where geographical expansion occurred or a number of different lines of products, each requiring a separate sales force, were combined, smaller savings, if any, resulted from marketing activities. Where combinations resulted in a national market, firms were fortified against local variations that might have proved disastrous to a firm whose market was confined to a single locality or to a limited number of purchasers. Many companies sought to develop more complete lines and to diversify the range of goods they offered, feeling that these measures would help to reduce marketing costs. By consolidating two or more firms, a full line could be acquired quickly without the hazards of developing and introducing new products. The increasing importance of fashion appears to have been influential in causing firms to widen their lines. On the other hand, some mergers were made with but little consideration of the marketing implications.

Product Planning

Product planning, with the consumers' needs and wants prominently in mind, was greatly emphasized in the period immediately following World War I. This was brought about by the increasing instability of the manufacturers' competitive position, on the one hand, and the increasing instability of consumer preferences and purchasing power on the other. The increase in production capacity and the technological advances engendered by the war strengthened the long-run trend toward more intense competition and gave industry the impetus to develop new and improve old products in an aggressive manner. Also bringing about the need for greater attention to product planning was the unusually fluid condition of consumer demand.

Manufacturers found it difficult to meet this new condition. They were not prepared for the rapid changes in demand that were experienced. Aggressive large-scale retailers, on the other hand, were quick to sense such changes. This permitted them to stock the goods people wanted. In addition, their large individual orders permitted them to sell at low prices. Thus, consumers looked to large-scale retailers for satisfaction of their needs at low prices. This new loyalty to large-scale retailers made the manufacturer less important in the eyes of the consumers in the purchase of many types of merchandise.

Advertising

The volume of advertising had been growing steadily prior to World War I, but it remained for the tremendous activity during and immediately following the war to bring great increases in the amount of advertising. The volume of business of one of the leading advertising agencies of the time leaped from $6,528,000 in 1918 to $13,734,000 in 1919, fell to $10,882,000 in 1922, but rose to over $38,000,000 in 1930.[17] After 1933, advertising expenditures increased gradually each year through 1948, except for the years 1938 and 1942.[18]

The immediate causes of the great increase in the volume of advertising expenditures following World War I were: (1) the obvious success of advertising in the promotion of the war effort, (2) the resumption of peace-time trade,[19] (3) the desire of some manufacturers to increase advertising appropriations rather than pay large federal excess profits taxes, and (4) perhaps the most important, the increasing intensity of competition that marked the postwar period.

During the 1920's several industries awakened to the value of branding and advertising. The Wamsutta Mills cut out all private brands and through advertising increased sales and built a stable year-round demand for their percale. The Cannon Mills scored a real success for their towels. The name Jantzen became closely associated in the minds of consumers with bathing suits. The zipper, in existence before 1900, was not demanded by the public until it was aggressively advertised beginning in 1926. Kraft commenced to advertise processed cheese. Public utilities and insurance companies jumped on the advertising bandwagon, and, in 1927, the Model A Ford was introduced with what was then the greatest advertising effort ever exerted over a corresponding period of time. Previously Ford had abandoned advertising as an "economic waste."

The development of large-scale retailing brought about a tremendous volume of advertising, particularly in newspapers. Where small independents were previously unable to consider metropolitan dailies, chain stores, supermarkets, and cooperative groups of independents commenced to take pages. Department stores had already been doing this.

Marketing Research

Before 1920, marketing efforts were carried on with little actual information and a great deal of guesswork. It became necessary to improve the marketing operation. To accomplish this it was necessary to obtain more factual information upon which to base decisions. It was necessary

---

17 R. M. Hower, *The History of An Advertising Agency*, p. 536. Cambridge: Harvard University Press, 1949. While not strictly representative of the rate of change in advertising volume generally, these figures tell a dramatic story.

18 Hans Zeisel, "The Printers' Ink Advertising Index Expands," *Printers' Ink*, Vol. 226, No. 11 (March 18, 1949), p. 64.

19 It should be recognized that many companies at that time figured their advertising appropriations on the basis of a percentage of sales and consequently the boom immediately following the war led to larger advertising expenditures.

also to improve marketing methods, particularly selling and distribution, and to develop techniques for measuring the effectiveness of these efforts.[20]

There were several reasons why the application of scientific method to marketing occurred later than its application to production. The number of variable elements was considerably greater. Selling did not lend itself to standardization. People could not be dealt with as machines. Marketing activities were more intangible and dispersed. In contrast to the limited area involved in the operation of a factory, wide geographical areas had to be considered. The main reason for the late attention to marketing was, of course, the comparative ease with which goods had been sold prior to the early twenties.

As the need for information increased, specialized personnel and departments took over this work, previously done on a hit-or-miss basis by salesmen or others untrained in research work. This new acceptance of research was far from universal, but it represented an important forward step. Statistics of production and consumption were studied as a means of determining potential sales volumes. Markets for new products and new uses for old ones were analyzed more systematically than before. Also subject to analysis were problems involving the sales force. The selection, training, compensation, and control of salesmen were greatly improved as a result of research effort. While some of the activities that passed as research were crude, there was certainly an awareness of the potential value of research. Some attention was given to advertising appeal, copy, and media selection in the 1920's, but the major advances in this field did not come until the thirties.

Advertising agencies and media did much to foster marketing research, particularly with respect to locating the market and promoting the sale of the product. The Curtis Publishing Company pioneered in marketing research by establishing a department for that purpose in 1911. Although other such departments came into being prior to World War I, the ground swell did not appear until the twenties. During and following the depression of the 1930's, research was given even more attention and departments and specialized professional organizations devoted to this function greatly increased in number and importance. By 1938 over $2,000,000 annually was being spent by manufacturers for marketing research, and by 1948 this sum had increased to $30,000,000. This amount, however, was extremely small in relation to that spent for manufacturing and technical product research.

[20] Teele indicates "the five most important paths along which management has sought to go in the application of logics to marketing: (1) specialization of the individual by function; (2) specialization of institutions themselves; (3) transfer and recombination of functions among institutions; (4) transfer of commodities among institutions; and (5) application of statistical and psychological methods." S. F. Teele, "Logics and Emotions in Marketing," *Business and Modern Society*, p. 305. Cambridge: Harvard University Press, 1938.

Conclusion

Large-scale retailing made tremendous strides following World War I and in 1950 its growth had not come to a halt. Corporate chains, voluntary chains, supermarkets, and to a more limited extent department store groups all shared in this development toward mass marketing. The mail-order type of business dropped out of the ranks of large-scale retailers. Manufacturers found it necessary to adopt mass marketing methods to avoid domination by large-scale retailers. Wholesalers and independent retailers became less important, but showed no signs of being eliminated despite such predictions. Independent retailers became much less independent in action, though they remained independent in ownership. The struggle for control of the market and the transition to mass marketing affected the consumer as did the advent of mass production. While the consumer continued to buy in very small quantities (the mass aspects of marketing occurring within the channels of trade), he was offered a wider selection of merchandise and lower prices than would probably have prevailed had small-scale marketing continued.

Selected References

Cassady, R., Jr., and W. L. Jones, *The Changing Competitive Structure in the Wholesale Grocery Trade*. Berkeley: University of California Press, 1949.

Copeland, M. T., "Marketing," *Recent Economic Changes in the United States,* Vol. I, pp. 321-424. New York: McGraw-Hill Book Company, 1929.

Copeland, M. T., "The Managerial Factor in Marketing," in *Facts and Factors in Economic History,* pp. 596-619. Cambridge: Harvard University Press, 1932.

Emmet, B., and J. E. Jeuck, *Catalogs and Counters*. Chicago: University of Chicago Press, 1950.

Engle, N. H., "Chain Store Distribution vs. Independent Wholesaling," *Journal of Marketing,* Vol. XIV, No. 3, pp. 241-252.

Federal Trade Commission, *Chain Store Inquiry*. Washington, D. C.: U. S. Government Printing Office, 1932-35.

Hotchkiss, G. B., *Milestones of Marketing*. New York: The Macmillan Co., 1938.

Hower, R. M., *The History of an Advertising Agency,* rev. ed. Cambridge: The Harvard University Press, 1949.

McNair, M. P., "Trends in Large-Scale Retailing," *Harvard Business Review,* Vol. X, No. 1 (October, 1931).

Weiss, E. B., *Selling to and Through the New Department Store*. New York: Printers' Ink Publishing Corp., 1948.

"Fifty Years, 1888-1938," *Printers' Ink,* Vol. 184, No. 4, Section 2 (July 28, 1938).

41 · FOREIGN TRADE, INVESTMENTS, AND COMMERCIAL POLICY

WORLD WAR I marked an important turning point in the development of the United States as a world power. It terminated the debtor status that had characterized our international economic relations since independence and made us a creditor nation on international account. In a still broader sense, World War I could be said to have ended the period of British leadership and predominance in the world economy and to have opened the way for the assumption of leadership by the United States. We had emerged from the war unmatched in productive power, capacity for economic expansion, and ability to accumulate surpluses for investment at home and abroad. We had a skilled and adaptable industrial population, dynamic leadership in business and industrial technology, and an immense variety of natural resources.

The Expansion of American Industry Abroad

The vitality and expansibility of American business is illustrated in Table 1, which shows the growth of direct foreign investments by American corporations.

This table emphasizes the extent to which American industrial corporations had already become prominent in international business by 1919 and their further expansion after that date. They have reached out and secured for themselves control over essential raw materials, such as petroleum, copper, aluminum, lead, nickel, zinc, iron ore, manganese, vanadium, molybdenum, tungsten, tin, nitrate, cane sugar, rubber, wood pulp, and a variety of agricultural products. In part, these raw-material resources supplemented deficiencies in our domestic resources, in part they were shipped to the United States for refining and subsequent re-export, and in part they never reached American shores at all, but entered foreign markets directly. But whatever the objectives in view, corporate management straddled national frontiers and began to exercise control over production and the channels of distribution on both sides of such frontiers.

Apart from the truly cosmopolitan reach of American industrial corporations in the field of raw-material production, the establishment of

American-controlled manufacturing enterprises abroad calls for special consideration. This development was very rapid in the three decades preceding 1929 and was basically inspired by the desire to find the most profitable adjustment to the political and economic conditions of the world market. These enterprises fell into two broad categories—those producing primarily for the American market, and those producing for foreign consumption. As far as the first group is concerned (illustrated by American units in the Canadian pulp industry and marine foods industry, by cork factories in Spain and Portugal, and by jute factories in British India), their location abroad was dictated for the most part by the location of the foreign materials processed; judged by their contribution to the American economy, American investments in such manufacturing enterprises have been quite similar to the investment in foreign mines and plantations whose output supplemented a deficient domestic supply.

TABLE 1

UNITED STATES DIRECT FOREIGN INVESTMENTS, 1897-1935 [1]
(In Millions of Dollars)

Investor	1897	1914	1919	1929	1935
Sales Organizations	56.5	169.5	243.0	362.0	325.0
Purchasing Organizations	5.0	9.0	11.5	16.1	20.0
Banking	10.0	30.0	125.0	125.0	125.0
Oil Distributors	75.0	200.0	275.0	487.0	509.0
Oil Production	10.5	143.0	328.5	854.0	872.5
Mining:					
Precious Metals	88.0	232.7	219.0	262.3	259.3
Industrial Minerals	46.0	487.0	657.3	964.5	958.8
Agricultural Enterprise	76.5	355.8	587.0	985.8	586.6
Manufacturing	93.5	478.0	795.0	1,821.0	1,870.0
Railways	143.4	255.1	297.3	308.7	260.5
Public Utilities	22.1	133.2	137.9	1,025.2	1,088.0
Miscellaneous	8.0	159.0	203.0	341.7	344.5
Total Direct Investment	634.5	2,652.3	3,879.5	7,553.3	7,219.2

[1] Based on C. Lewis, *America's Stake in International Investment,* p. 605. Washington, D. C.: Brookings Institution, 1938.

The situation with respect to the second group was quite different. Here was a group of expanding American industries whose ability to supply the domestic market was unquestioned, and whose competitive power in world markets was increasingly respected. Their decision to establish assembly plants and manufacturing subsidiaries abroad was motivated usually by a combination of factors, such as (1) cost factors, (2) tariff policies and other forms of restriction, (3) the national peculiarities and prejudices of ultimate consumers in foreign markets, and (4) patent exploitation and market control. In setting up assembly or finishing plants abroad, for example, the savings in transportation costs were frequently an important consideration. Occasionally, the availability of cheap labor was a factor, though popular discussion greatly exaggerated its significance. Foreign tariffs constituted a special kind of cost factor confronting the American manufacturer and were of growing importance in prompting the decision to produce abroad within the protected markets. By producing inside the Canadian frontiers, for instance, better access could be gained to the greater part of the British Empire than by marketing directly from the United States.

In addition to the pervasive influence of trade barriers, American industry sometimes had to contend with other difficulties that could be overcome successfully only by producing on the spot. Consumer tastes and requirements in the foreign markets were not always identical with those of the American market. The list of American products—such as automobiles, agricultural machinery, cash registers, and heating and plumbing supplies—that required some modification to fit the demand of the foreign market, was large.[2] Moreover, the American concern might have to contend with popular suspicion of, or hostility to, foreign products, sometimes played upon by organized propaganda to "buy British" or "buy German." Under such circumstances, its choice might lie between giving up the prospect of foreign sales altogether, or of adjusting itself to these conditions by production inside the foreign market.

The patent laws of certain countries have exerted some influence on the establishment of American subsidiaries abroad. For instance, the Canadian patent regulations of 1903, subsequently modified, declared a patent null and void after two years, unless the patentee produced the patented product in Canada and made it available at a reasonable price. Apart from the quasi-compulsion of foreign patent legislation, there is evidence to suggest that American companies proceeded of their own choice to enter into patent agreements with their foreign competitors with a view to exerting some form of world market control over the sale of their products and obtaining a voice in the system of international cartels and combines of Europe. The acquisition of minority interests in existing foreign companies has at times been the device used to cement such understandings. The evidence on this point is usually rather difficult to appraise, but, to say the least, it suggests that the expansion of American industry abroad has lent added strength to the growth of corporate instruments of control over world production and world marketing.

Brief mention should also be made of the development of international cartels and combines, which appear to have become an important element in the control of international trade in the last quarter of the nineteenth century, at which time the rapid industrial growth of Germany raised

[2] For a detailed discussion of this point, consult F. A. Southard, *American Industry in Europe*. New York: Houghton Mifflin Company, 1931.

new problems of international competition. At the outbreak of World War I, 114 international combines and industrial agreements were known to be in existence, and the aftermath of the war saw a rapid resumption and extension of this trend.[3]

Though many of these cartels and combines were still of a restricted character, and frequently suffered from internal stresses arising out of the divergent interests of its members, it is likewise true that the trend to such integration and coordination of effort in respect to national and world markets was a process that had by no means run its full course at the outbreak of World War II. On the contrary, the attitude underlying private industrial agreements has repeatedly received the tacit or open approval of the public authorities, particularly in the field of internationally marked raw materials. Rubber, coffee, tea, sugar, cotton, wheat, tin, nitrates, and potash may be cited as outstanding examples of commodities made subject to control schemes with active governmental support in recent decades. National tariff policies and other governmental forms of import control have played an important part in buttressing private international industrial agreements. Relevant also in this connection is the Webb-Pomerene Export Trade Act of 1918, under the terms of which the United States Government permitted the organization of export cartels by American producers, thereby facilitating, as in the notorious case of Copper Exporters, Inc., the formation of an international sales cartel.

In general, it may be said that American business and the American Government alike have become frequent participants, if not leaders, in the efforts to establish instruments of control over world production and world consumption. What still remains in doubt, however, is the compatibility of such a mixed and uneven system of producer combines with the potentialities of world-wide expansion of production resulting from technical progress.

The Balance of Payments

Before turning to the international economic policies pursued by the United States Government in the years following World War I, it is desirable to draw attention to the essential statistical magnitudes of the United States balance of international payments for the periods 1920-1933, 1934-1940, and 1941-1945. These are given in Table 2.

The dividing line beween the first and second period has been chosen because the net creditor status of the United States on private account appears to have been at its highest point in the early 1930's and a remark-

[3] For a good general survey of international business combinations, see A. Plummer, *International Combines in Modern Industry*. London: Isaac Pitman and Sons, 1938. Also, G. W. Stocking and M. W. Watkins, *Cartels in Action*. New York: Twentieth Century Fund, 1946.

able change in the capital account occurred thereafter. In the period 1920-1933, the total active balance on goods and services amounted to 7.8 billion dollars. Net income on investments abroad, including war debt payments to the United States, was 8.5 billion dollars, and this raised the total credit balance of 16.3 billion dollars. Offsetting this were unilateral transfers of 5.1 billion dollars, a net gold inflow of 1.4 billion dollars, and a net increase in the international investment of the United States of 7 billion dollars. The actual investment in foreign securities and properties in the years 1920-1930 was greatly in excess of the foregoing amount, but the resumption of foreign investment in the United States partly cancelled out this larger total investment. After the collapse of 1929, a process of liquidation brought the total stake of foreigners in the United States and of Americans abroad to lower figures. Our total foreign investments in 1930 have been estimated at 17.2 billion dollars, exclusive of the so-called war debts, and foreign investments in the United States at 8.4 billion dollars; in 1931, the figures are 15.9 billion dollars and 3.8 billion dollars, respectively. The bulk of the 2.8 billion dollars in the item "Errors and Omissions" is usually assumed to be the result of omissions and errors in calculating the capital movements.

TABLE 2

UNITED STATES BALANCE OF INTERNATIONAL PAYMENTS, BY PERIODS

(In Billions of Dollars)

Period	Goods and Services Net	Income on Investment Net	Capital Transactions Net	Unilateral Transfers	Gold	Errors and Omissions
1920-1933 (14 yrs.)	+ 7.8	+ 8.5	— 7.0	— 5.1	— 1.4	— 2.8
1934-1940 (7 yrs.)	+ 2.8	+ 2.3	+ 7.4	— 1.3	— 14.9	+ 3.7
1941-1945 (5 yrs.)	+ 36.7	+ 1.8	+ 0.8	— 41.6	+ 1.9	+ 0.4

Based on *Historical Statistics of the United States, 1789-1945,* A Supplement to the *Statistical Abstract of the United States,* pp. 242-243. Washingon, D. C.: 1949. The subdivision "unilateral transfers" includes personal and institutional remittances, lend lease, UNRRA, and other relief shipments.

The period 1934-1940 shows highly abnormal characteristics. The active balance on Goods and Services stood at 2.8 billion dollars for the seven-year period. Personal and institutional remittances at 1.3 billion dollars still left a credit balance of 1.5 billion dollars. To this credit balance another 2.3 billion dollars must be added for net interest and dividend payments. Under more normal circumstances than actually prevailed, the offset to these credit balances might have been found in a resumption of foreign investment by American interests or in a liquidation of foreign holdings in the United States. But instead, the uncertainties of the world political situation and the demoralization of the world economy brought a major flow of capital funds to the United States. The net change in the capital account aggregated, according to the official figures, over 7 billion dollars, and the large item of 3.7 billion dollars for errors and omissions meant that the net inflow of funds was in all probability several billions above this amount. Thus, from a balance of payments point of view, the offset to the large credits on current and capital account was found in an unprecedented inflow of gold and silver, jointly recorded as in excess of 15 billion dollars. This colossal inflow of precious metals was a symptom and a symbol of the interrelated political chaos and economic frustration of the entire world.

The final period 1941-1945 covers the years of our participation in World War II. The international economic transactions of the United States during these years were dominated by our Lend-Lease policy of March, 1941, under which the United States made itself into the "arsenal of democracy" and supplied huge quantities of goods to its allies without charge. The active balance on goods and services during these years was 36.7 billion dollars, net gold flows were outward, foreign dollar balances increased, and the offset to these credit items in the United States balance was found in the 41.6 billion dollars of unilateral transfers abroad by the United States.

Isolation at High Tide

The history of American policy following World War I revealed that the American people were largely unprepared to assume the burdens and opportunities of world leadership that events had thrust upon them. From the enactment of the emergency tariff act of 1921 to the dollar devaluation program of late 1933, American leadership in world affairs lacked even the rudiments of effectiveness, and was, for the most part, a depressing mixture of incompetence, irresponsibility, and inertia. As a consequence, the world economy—already severely strained by the war itself—was to be exposed to destructive forces that in the end undermined even the very idea of world community.

The Republican party was returned to power after the election of 1920, at a time when the American economy was in the midst of the short, but drastic postwar slump of 1920-1921. Promptly on assuming power, the new Congress voted the Emergency Tariff Act of 1921 in the hope of remedying the collapse of agricultural prices. In 1922 there followed the Fordney-McCumber Act. In these two bills the United States Congress came out flatfootedly for a return to high protection. The legislation emphasized agricultural protection, lifted the rates on many manufactured products, and added a number of so-called "war babies" to the lists of protected industries. Among the war babies, coal tar products and dyestuffs were the most important, but the list also included such items as toys, imitation jewelry, buckles, buttons, vanity cases, cotton gloves, lace window curtains, chinaware, penknives, pocketknives, and so forth. In many instances the protection on these items was inordinately high, varying from 60 per cent to well over 100 per cent ad valorem. In general, the Fordney-McCumber Act was a reaffirmation of the old and somewhat naive faith that a policy of paying off all articulate economic minorities at home would somehow miraculously add up as the true national interest.

The Inter-Allied War Debts

In the same year Congress set up the World War Foreign Debt Commission to negotiate settlements of the war debts with our former allies. Congress ruled that no part of the indebtedness could be cancelled except through payment, and further stipulated that repayments should be completed within 25 years and that the rate of interest on outstanding indebtedness was not to be less than 4½ per cent. These congressional standards proved highly impractical, and the Commission was forced to modify them even in the case of the most solvent debtor. The total amount advanced to its allies by the United States Government between April, 1917 and November, 1920 was approximately 10 billion dollars at five per cent interest. Under the several debt-finding agreements negotiated between 1922 and 1926, the United States modified its insistence on the precise letter of the bond and employed in varying degree a yardstick of "capacity to pay" in working out particular agreements. Thus, for instance, it is estimated that, on a basis of 4½ per cent interest, the agreements with the United Kingdom involved cancellation of about 20 per cent of the debt. In the French and Italian agreements, the amount of "forgiveness" is similarly calculated at 53 per cent and 75 per cent respectively.[4] Debt payments were stretched out over a period of some 60 years, to be concluded in the 1980's. Over this period of time the United States was to receive a grand total of 22 billion dollars in return for the original advances made.

Under these agreements the United States received amounts normally in excess of 200 million dollars a year until July, 1931, when the collapsing world economy forced a suspension of German reparations and interally debt payments. After the expiration of the so-called Hoover moratorium, most debtor governments paid one further semi-annual installment in December, 1932, but thereafter receipts dwindled into insignificance. As a final gesture of futility, Congress passed the so-called Johnson Act, sponsored by Senator Hiram Johnson, under which United States citizens and corporations were forbidden to lend to, or buy the

[4] Hal. B. Lary and associates. *The United States in the World Economy,* p. 84. Washington, D. C.: 1943.

securities of governments in default to the United States government. This legislation was still on the statute books, when Congress—in a very different mood—enacted the Lend-Lease policy into law in March, 1941.

In the years of prosperity following the postwar slump of 1920-1921, the critics of American economic foreign policy had difficulty in making themselves understood by the American people. These critics emphasized the wide discrepancy between our power and our performance in contributing to the reconstruction of a viable and cooperative world community, especially our failure even to join the League of Nations, the International Labor Organization, and the World Court. They deplored the relapse of our national import policy to a policy of private and sectional privilege, when the interests of the American people as a whole seemed to require the stimulation of imports. They spoke of the inconsistencies of preaching to the world the virtues of the international gold standard, while pursuing national policies which, on balance, set up strong suctions on the world's monetary gold.

The Policies of Herbert Hoover

Against these criticisms of our international economic policies, the successful Republican candidate for President in 1928, Herbert Hoover, spoke in confident tones. American policies, he said, should be judged on the basis of their practical effects, and by that test they were a remarkable success. The tariff had not ruined import trade; on the contrary, United States imports had risen faster than world imports, faster than our exports, and both exports and imports faster than at any other peacetime period in our history. Import tariffs had not restrained indirectly the rise of our export trade. Foreign trade was of growing importance to the United States, a fact that the government had recognized by its encouragement of the work of the Department of Commerce under his own direction as Secretary of Commerce.

According to Hoover, these satisfactory results did not just happen; they were the result of deliberate government policies in guiding trade with full regard to the necessity of protecting the American standard of life from the destructive competition of cheap labor and floods of cheap agricultural imports. Protecting the American standard of life meant maintaining the purchasing power of the community, which, in turn, meant prosperity and high levels of United States imports. Thus, in the final analysis, the rest of the world also benefitted from American protection. Immigration restriction, enacted in 1924, was endorsed on similar economic grounds as rounding out the American protective system. As long as we exported more than we imported, it was sterile theorizing, in Hoover's view, to complain that foreigners could not discharge their debt obligations to the United States. The facts were, he contended, that the American economy was making available—apart from payments on our large imports of merchandise—some two billion dollars annually in the so-called "invisible services" of the balance of payments.

If there was a skeleton in the closet of United States economic foreign policy, there was no hint of it in the solid satisfaction with which the President-elect surveyed the immediate past and confronted the future. We would continue to push exports, we would bar all imports that were "competitive" and threatened to undermine the American standard of life. We would subsidize the American merchant marine and we would get full payment on every dollar of the debt settlements. Future adjustments would be relatively painless, because of the flexibility and expansibility of the "invisible services." [5] Hoover did not greatly expatiate upon the fact that perhaps one half of the "invisible services" were new private loans to the rest of the world, which, year by year, were rapidly increasing the total accumulated financial obligation of the world to the United States economy. Also, it was perhaps just as well for the new President's peace of mind in 1928 that he did not know that at the time of his speeches these new dollar loans had about come to an end.

The upshot of the matter seemed to be that as long as (1) the American economy was willing to absorb large new foreign bond issues and American corporations were willing to continue programs of direct investment abroad, and (2) industrial production with its attendant demand for imports continued at high levels, the flow of dollars into the world market was adequate to sustain the level of American exports, permit the servicing of foreign debts to the United States, and keep the international exchanges reasonably level. But if either or both of these conditions should fail, the pressure upon the exchanges would become intense and international monetary stability and the entire framework of international commercial relations might be destroyed.

In the year following Hoover's election, as Congress opened the door wide to another general upward revision of the tariff, these two conditions were beginning to fail. It was the culminating year of the New York stock market boom, and foreign and domestic funds were being drawn to the New York market while interest in new foreign investments lagged. In 1928 the United States economy had made available 1.2 billion dollars net in international capital transactions; in 1929 this balance of payments item shrank to less than 300 million dollars. The spectacular crash of the bull market in the autumn of 1929, was the signal for the beginning of a chaotic process of economic recession and disintegration that did not reach its lowest point until 1932. In between these two dates the world economy suffered a series of blows from which it has, in many ways, never fully recovered.

The outflow of private United States funds for purposes of long-term

[5] See *The New Day—Campaign Speeches of Herbert Hoover.* Stanford University Press, 1928.

foreign investment was reversed in 1931, and it was superseded thereafter by a process of partial liquidation of acquired holdings. Defaults on outstanding dollar bonds—floated only a few years previously in the United States capital market—ran to nearly 40 per cent of the total amount outstanding in private American hands. The system of German reparations payments, revised only in 1930, was swept away in 1931 along with the payments on inter-ally war debts. Industrial depression in the United States brought with it a decline of imports from 4.4 billion dollars in 1929 to 1.3 billion dollars in 1932. Gold flows became chaotic as international confidence in the financial stability of nations disappeared and defaults multiplied. The international gold standard began to crumble in 1930 as certain raw materials exporting nations were forced to suspend under the pressures of falling prices, shrinking demand and the drying up of the flow of dollar credits. In 1931 the United Kingdom abandoned the gold standard. Foreign exchange control and quota and license systems of import control reappeared and spread rapidly as debtor nations strove hard to regain a measure of control over the values flowing in and out of their economies. Bilateral and discriminatory payments agreements in lieu of the hitherto prevailing system of multilateral payments, mushroomed rapidly.

In all this headlong retreat from the insecurities of the world economy, the lack of world-wide leadership to counteract the rapidly growing forces of economic restriction was conspicuous. The best that the United Kingdom could do, following its departure from the gold standard, was to extend its tariff system and to stage the widely advertised Ottawa Conference of 1932, at which the constituent elements of the British Commonwealth entered into special and discriminatory trading arrangements with one another. Though hailed by British statesmen as a great step to world recovery, it obviously was merely another effort to benefit the contracting nations at the expense of the outsiders.

As far as the United States was concerned, there was not even the pretense of world leadership. In March, 1930, the Smoot-Hawley Tariff Act became law. It raised the average rates of all the fifteen schedules of the Act and made substantial changes in several of them. The average rate on agricultural products, for instance, was raised from 19.8 per cent in 1922 to 33.6 per cent in 1930; the average rate on spirits, wines and other beverages went up from 36.4 per cent in 1922 to 47.4 per cent in 1930. On wool and woolen manufactures the increase in average rate was from 49.5 per cent in 1922 to 59.8 per cent in 1930; on earthenware and glassware the average rate rose from 45.6 per cent to 53.6 per cent. Senator Smoot, widely hailed for his wisdom and experience in tariff matters, predicted that the new law would restore prosperity to the United States in a few months. Thereafter, the government's international economic policy appeared to be based on a conviction that there was hardly anything that could usefully be done, either by ourselves or in collaboration, to overcome the strong tide running to disaster.

The New Deal

This barren record of negation and inaction was not much improved in the first year of the Roosevelt "New Deal." Franklin Roosevelt had made political capital out of attacking "Smoot-Hawleyism" in the presidential campaign of 1932, and his selection of Cordell Hull as secretary of state gave promise of greater world-mindedness in the economic policy of the United States government. This expectation was not borne out by events. President Roosevelt's first New Deal took an unexpected and sharp turn towards economic nationalism. The United States delegation to the World Economic Conference in the summer of 1933 arrived in London without a program. It had no authority to make agreements on tariffs and other trade barriers and it would not discuss the question of war debts. After much backing and filling, the United States delegation would not even agree to a temporary stabilization of exchange rates. Though Roosevelt had endorsed the gold standard in the campaign of 1932, he cabled the World Economic Conference that exchange rate stabilization was merely one of the "old fetishes of so-called international bankers." The President's message was a unique and mystifying document. It stressed the importance of national self-help and of a commodity dollar with stable purchasing power. It also lectured the Conference on the necessity of reducing the cost of government, the virtues of a balanced budget and the ability to service government debts, and the sin of dissipating gold reserves. To the conference this message could only signify that the President of the United States was still in the process of clarifying his own thoughts on basic issues, and, pending the outcome of this process, there was little to be done. The Conference was a grandiose failure.

Roosevelt continued to show his contempt for the methods of international bankers in the autumn of 1933, when he launched the United States upon a drastic devaluation of the dollar. On assuming office in the Spring of 1933 the government had been forced to suspend gold convertibility, and Congress had conferred sweeping powers on the President to deal with the emergency. In the course of 1933 the President became convinced that the quickest and most promising road out of economic depression was to raise the dollar price of gold. It would, he had been led to believe, raise prices, especially agricultural prices, and would stimulate exports. The dollar was, therefore devalued to something less than three-fifths of its former gold equivalent. This policy proved highly disappointing to the President, because it neither raised prices nor stimulated exports. Its effects on the world economy were adverse, except for the boon conferred on gold-producing areas by the rise in the price of gold. It also served notice on the rest of the world that the United

States was determined to use strong and aggressive measures of economic nationalism to help itself, even at the expense of other nations. In 1934 the emergence of George Peak, farm leader and former Undersecretary of Agriculture, as the President's "Foreign Trade Adviser" likewise indicated that the President was still weighing in his own mind the possible benefits of a hard-hitting and aggressive policy of bilateral bargaining, using the world market as a convenient dumping ground for embarrassing domestic farm surpluses, without worrying overly much—in the manner of Cordell Hull—about the stability and orderly processes of the world economy as such.

The Reciprocal Trade Agreements

Not until after the hectic first year of the Roosevelt administration had run its course did the tariff policy of the New Deal finally take shape. The risks of attempting a general Congressional tariff revision were held to be too great, especially in the light of historical experience with such general tariff revision. Instead Congress delegated to the President limited powers to alter the Smoot-Hawley tariff structure. He was authorized to enter into trade agreements with other governments for a period of three years and to reduce individual tariff rates by as much as 50 per cent in the course of such negotiations. These trade agreements did not require Congressional ratification and were to be based on the unconditional most-favored-nation principle.[6] In making tariff reductions, the President did not need to consider himself bound by the cost-equalization principle of the Acts of 1922 and 1930. From 1934 through 1949, Congress did not fail to renew this delegation of power to the President.

The inauguration of this policy may be said to mark a turning point in the method of handling of our international economic policy, but it did not mean the abandonment of the policy of protection. On that score the professed fears of the protectionist groups in Congress were wholly unfounded. In the first place, Congress had set definite limits to administrative power; furthermore, the State Department and other agencies concerned with the program showed considerable caution in granting concessions in the twenty-one agreements signed prior to the outbreak of World War II. This cautious policy is illustrated, for instance, by the occasional use made of so-called tariff quotas to guard against a sudden,

[6] In 1922 Congress had clarified one aspect of our international commercial policy when it came out with a straightforward declaration in favor of the principle of equal treatment. In conformity with this objective the United States gave up the minor special favors it had for many years extracted from Brazil under the threat of a penalty duty on coffee and emerged alongside the United Kingdom as the champion of the unconditional most-favored-nation clause. Although world public opinion welcomed this American sponsorship of equal commercial treatment, there was general agreement that it was devoid of economic significance as long as the principle was not implemented by a policy of trading concessions.

or sharp, increase of imports following a particular tariff reduction and by the employment of narrowed tariff classifications in granting some reductions. It became apparent that the administration was counting on the cumulative effects of a steady succession of carefully circumscribed tariff concessions over a period of years, rather than on a spectacular and drastic exercise of its power. Nevertheless, an appreciable modification of the American tariff level resulted. By January, 1939, 1,077 out of the estimated 3,200 rates in the American tariff schedule had been reduced, and nearly one-half of these reductions had amounted to from 40 to 50 per cent of the congressional rates. But many of these reductions were more impressive on paper than in their immediate economic consequences in stimulating imports. At any rate, the program appears to have been more successful in stimulating exports than imports, judging from the trade returns of the few years preceding 1939.[7] With the outbreak of war in that year, our foreign trade and commercial policy were subordinated once more to the military and political exigencies of world conflict.

As a counteroffensive against the world-wide forces of economic restriction and government-dominated international trade, the trade agreements program was definitely "too little and too late." Its principles were impeccable and its methods a great improvement over the hitherto customary methods of tariff-making in the United States. Moreover, the experience with the program in the half dozen years before the outbreak of the Second World War could be said to have laid the basis for a more broad-gauged and comprehensive international economic program in the postwar years. But beyond that, its substantive effects on the course of international economic relations were largely cancelled out by a lack of confidence in the future of the world economy and by the expectation of war. To be sure, world trade revived, but this fact was overshadowed by the massive preparations for war and the unprecedented flight of capital to the United States. Nothing testified so eloquently to the disordered state of the world as the 15 billion dollars worth of gold and silver that flowed into the United States in the years 1934-1940.

Neutrality

When World War II began in the late summer of 1939, the relations of the United States with the belligerents were subject to the neutrality legislation of the mid-thirties. This legislation was a product of the confused thinking of the American people on the subject of war and peace

---

7 For detailed analysis and interpretation of the trade agreements policy, the reader is referred to. G. Beckett, *The Reciprocal Trade Agreements Program* (New York: Columbia University Press, 1941); F. B. Sayres, *The Way Forward* (New York: The Macmillan Company, 1939); W. Diebold, *New Directions in Our Trade Policy* (New York: Council on Foreign Relations, 1941).

in general, and of our participation in the First World War in particular. Senator Nye's munitions inquiry of 1934 had popularized the view that we had been drawn into the conflict as a result of the greed and profit-seeking manipulations of international bankers and munitions makers. This was a crude and superficial version of the theories about war and imperialism propagated by Hobson and Lenin and their respective fol-followers. Traditional isolationist sentiment and the spirits of disillusionment bred by the depression combined to make this view plausible and acceptable. In order to make sure that the United States would be kept out of another world war, the neutrality legislation of 1935, 1936, and 1937 imposed prohibitions on foreign loans and security sales, forbade the export of munitions, and stipulated the so-called cash-and-carry principle in supplying other goods to the belligerent nations. This policy was supported by overwhelming majorities in Congress and acclaimed by a substantial majority of the American people. It was looked upon as a panacea to end all danger of war for this country.

Even after the war had begun this flimsy make-believe of economic insulation from war was reaffirmed in the legislation of November 4, 1939, except for one important change, namely the repeal of the embargo on the export of munitions. Under this revision of the neutrality laws it was possible for the Allies to place large war orders in the United States as far as their mobilized dollar resources permitted. Following the collapse of France in the spring of 1940, the United Kingdom took over French procurement contracts, but not the French dollar assets with which to pay for them. As the year drew to a close, it became apparent that a fateful decision would have to be made by the United States, because British dollar resources were limited and shrinking while British requirements for continuing its struggle were vast and virtually limitless.

Lend-Lease

Finally, in the conviction that the survival of the British Commonwealth and its allies was a primary security objective of the United States, the Roosevelt administration introduced legislation that would enable the British and its Allies to draw deeply upon American resources and industrial power without regard to their ability to pay for such aid. The adoption of this so-called Lend-Lease policy in the spring of 1941 must be rated as one of the most far-reaching decisions of modern times in its boldness, imagination and determination to avoid new disasters of "too little, too late." It proposed to make the United States the "arsenal of democracy." It smashed the incubus of neutrality towards the world conflict. It offered us additional time to prepare our own war economy, while supplying large scale material aid to the Allies. It was unrealistic only to the extent that the policy was adopted, in part, in the conviction or hope that the United States would not be drawn into actual military participation in the conflict.

Under the Lend-Lease policy down till the end of 1945, the United States government transferred 39.5 billion dollars of goods and 8.5 billion dollars of services to its Allies. In reverse lend-lease the United States received 4.2 billion dollars in merchandise and nearly 3 billion dollars of services. In round figures, therefore, some 40 billion dollars net of goods and services were supplied free to our allies over and beyond what was actually paid for by them. Such transfers accounted at their peak in 1944 for over 80 per cent of all merchandise and over 60 per cent of all services furnished to foreign countries. In 1943 and 1944 lend-lease goods poured across the waters in such a mighty flow that the United States incurred a passive balance on merchandise account of 1.3 billion in the first of the two years and 0.7 billion dollars in the second, after deducting lend-lease transactions from total exports and imports.

Apart from the direct contribution of Lend-Lease to the winning of the war, another result was to enable the rest of the world to increase its dollar balances and its gold holdings. There was indeed a wide difference in the experience of individual nations, but several of the Latin-American countries, Canada, certain European neutrals, and others improved their gold and dollar exchange position substantially. It is estimated that the short-term dollar assets of foreigners increased from 3.3 billion to 7.8 billion dollars over the years from 1939 to 1945. This gain provided a valuable cushion of dollar purchasing power once the war had ended and countries could once again freely purchase American goods for peacetime purposes.

Long before the war had risen to its military climax the United States and its partners indicated the kind of world economic order that they would seek to establish after the conclusion of hostilities. In Article VII of the Lend-Lease Master Agreement it was laid down that in the final settlement of Lend-Lease claims, "the terms and conditions thereof shall be such as not to burden commerce between the two countries, but to promote mutually advantageous economic relations between them and the betterment of world-wide economic relations. To that end, they shall include provision for agreed action between the United States and the United Kingdom (or other contracting party), open to the participation by all other countries of like mind, directed to the expansion by appropriate international and domestic measures, of production, employment, and the exchange and consumption of goods, which are the material foundation of the liberty and welfare of all people; to the elimination of all forms of discriminatory treatment in international commerce and to the reduction of tariffs and other trade barriers. . . ."

The basic ideas of this paragraph—(1) the necessity for renewed world economic expansion, (2) the dependence of political freedom and material welfare alike upon such expansion, and (3) the insistence upon the methods of economic liberalism—can be said to be the characteristically American contribution to the discussion of what the postwar world ought to be. Throughout the remaining years of the war and thereafter, American policy strove hard to bring them nearer to realization, in spite of many obstacles and discouraging circumstances.

One formidable difficulty was the extent of social upheaval, economic dislocation, and material damage caused by the war itself. Another was the great stimulus given to socialist and nationalist programs of economic organization by wartime economics. Still another was the alleged disparity between the international competitive ability of the United States and the rest of the world, which was presumed to have outmoded the simple methods of economic liberalism as a means of achieving world economic balance.

International Cooperation

As the war drew to a close it became apparent that the American program for international economic cooperation called for an imposing array of international organizations. A conference of the United Nations at Hot Springs in 1943 had laid the groundwork for the Food and Agricultural Organization (FAO), devoted to world problems of agriculture, nutrition, and conservation. In 1944, at Philadelphia, the International Labor Organization (I.L.O.), a holdover from the interwar period, prepared to carry on its activities in the field of social legislation and labor problems and for a while seemed intent on assuming a position of leadership in handling future problems of world employment and world economic stability. The United Nations Relief and Rehabilitation Administration (UNRRA) was set up to cope with the postwar relief problem, the cost to be financed by contributions of 1 per cent of the national income of such countries as had not suffered directly from the ravages of war. This organization functioned until 1947 and distributed supplies valued at nearly four billion dollars, of which the American share was approximately 70 per cent. These and other so-called "specialized agencies" were to be brought into coordination with one another under the supervision of the Economic and Social Council of the United Nations.

Of special importance among the specialized agencies promoted by the United States in these years were the International Monetary Fund, the International Bank for Reconstruction and Delevopment, and the projected International Trade Organization (I.T.O.). They were the means by which, it was hoped, a new order of international cooperation might be established and maintained in the field of monetary policy, international investment, and international trade, respectively.

In July, 1944, representatives of forty-four countries signed two agreements at Bretton Woods, New Hampshire. The first agreement laid down the principles of postwar monetary cooperation and set up a joint agency to promote their observance; the second established the International Bank to promote constructive international investment. Both institutions began their operations in 1946.

The monetary agreement provided for free convertibility of all member currencies after a transition period of not more than five years, subject to two important exceptions. The first exception allows member governments to exercise permanent control over their international capital flows; the second permits members to exercise exchange control over currencies that the Monetary Fund has formally declared to be a "scarce currency." This exception was generally held to be aimed at the prospect of a "shortage" of United States dollars in the postwar world.

The agreement made stability of exchange rates an important objective of international monetary policy, but nevertheless provided for flexibility of exchange rates to meet changing conditions in the international economy. In this respect the Fund agreement could be said to be a reasonable compromise between the two schools of thought that had struggled with one another over the international gold standard and its alleged propensity to sacrifice domestic stability to stability of the exchange rates. Like the gold standard, the Fund agreement makes an ideal of exchange rate stability; at the same time, however, it recognizes that variations in exchange rates might be highly desirable under certain conditions of economic disequilibrium, especially if such changes were internationally agreed upon rather than unilaterally carried through.

The contracting governments agreed to subscribe sizeable quotas to the Monetary Fund, aggregating over 8 billion dollars, and this pool of foreign exchange was to be administered as a revolving stabilization fund to enable members to meet temporary balance of payments deficits without serious strain on the exchange rates. The United States quota in the Fund was set at 2¾ billion dollars, and its voting power was roughly proportional to the size of its quota.

The establishment of the Bank for Reconstruction and Development was regarded as an important step in restoring the confidence of investors in foreign investment and in promoting a higher rate of international lending. The authorized capital of the Bank was 10 billion dollars, not all subscribed at the outset, and the total loans and guarantee of other loans could not exceed that amount. Its purpose was not to supplant private lending, but rather to supplement or bolster private lending activities. It was expected that the bulk of its operations would consist of the guarantee of loans that met stipulated conditions. The Bank would stand in the same general relation to private foreign lenders that the FHA occupies in relation to lending institutions in the domestic housing field. It was expected to establish reasonable interest rates and other loan conditions, to develop the multilateral character of international investment, and to eliminate the imperialistic overtones that from time to time have accompanied international investment in the past. At the same time it would create an international stake in the regular servicing of loans and counteract modern tendencies for the international debtor to exploit the creditor.

Among the many plans for permanent international organization none was more important to the ultimate destinies of United States international economic policies than the projected International Trade Organization. The plans for the I.T.O. had been in process of gestation since 1943. First developed with the United States State Department, then discussed with the representatives of the United Kingdom and Canada, and finally published to the world at the time of the negotiation of the United States-United Kingdom loan agreement in the autumn of 1945, it was pushed through many revisions at successive international conferences. Finally a draft charter was signed at Havana in March, 1948. Two years later, however, the Havana charter still awaited ratification by the United States Congress and there was considerable doubt whether such action would ever be taken.

Initially, the I.T.O. was the brain child of those who sought to make the United States trade agreements program a more effective medium for the reduction of world trade barriers. As matters stand the charter provides a framework for economic cooperation within which the import policies of governments can be harmonized and common policies developed to deal with international cartels, intergovernmental commodity arrangements, and world employment. In the course of its evolution it had lost much of its original simplicity; amendments, qualifications, and exceptions to general principles multiplied and gave rise to the suspicion that the charter might actually bolster rather than weaken the restrictive policies of economic nationalism. At any rate, the I.T.O. charter threatened to become sharply controversial at home and abroad. To many socialists and national economic planners it was suspect because its basic principles reflected an allegedly outmoded economic liberalism. To the more uncompromising adherents of free trade and private enterprise the completed charter was offensive, because it conceded too much to government planning and supervision. In between was a school of "realists" who defended the charter as the most practicable means of securing cooperation between nations whose economic systems embodied varying mixtures of private enterprise and government control.

While the ratification of the Havana charter lagged and became the object of ideological crossfires at home and abroad, the United States Government was forced to declare itself on world problems of the most urgent character. It had enlarged the lending capacity of the Export-Import Bank in order to accommodate the world's needs for additional dollars for reconstruction purposes. It had negotiated a financial settlement with the United Kingdom in the fall of 1945, ratified in the summer of 1946, whereby the United States closed out the Lend-Lease account with England and extended a loan of 3.75 billion dollars on moderate and flexible terms as an aid in the solution of Britain's difficult balance-of-payments problem.

It was hoped in many quarters that these measures, together with our contributions to the Bretton Woods agencies, to UNRRA, and other forms of relief, would suffice to enable the war-torn world to turn the corner towards a balanced and expanding world economy. But the actual course of events was disappointing. It became apparent that the U.S.S.R. was not interested in the development of a healthy world economy, either in Europe, Asia, or elsewhere. The Soviet looked upon the active interest of the United States in promoting world economic recovery and developing the specialized agencies of economic and social cooperation with suspicion and interpreted this interest as evidence of the imperialistic designs of American "monopoly capitalism." From the non-Russian point of view, Russian diplomatic tactics made sense only on the theory that the Soviet wanted to perpetuate and extend world chaos and disorder. Military tension and military expenditures began to increase, and strikes and domestic unrest paralyzed economic recovery in several European areas. The revolutionary conditions in Asia and the continuation of Germany as a kind of economic vacuum in Central Europe weakened the Western European struggle for recovery. The severe winter of 1946-1947 and the partial crop failure in Europe brought a new crisis in Europe's international economic relations. The problem of restoring Europe to a condition of economic order and balance in its relations to the rest of the world was proving more difficult than anticipated.

The Marshall Plan

Under these circumstances the United States launched a vast new program known as the Marshall Plan, or European Recovery Program (E.R.P.). It came into operation in April, 1948, and was expected to run for four years until 1952. Under this policy Congress made available 6 billion dollars in foreign aid, of which 5.3 billion was earmarked for the sixteen participating countries and Western Germany. In the following year, Congress appropriated another six billion dollars in total foreign assistance, including military aid. At the end of 1949 total United States government postwar aid in outright grants, loans, and investments was in excess of 30 billion dollars and was still rising. Though the United States had terminated Lend-Lease rather abruptly after V-J day, it seemed to some observers as if the United States were settling down to a kind of peacetime Lend-Lease under a different name. In the language of the politician, the justification for the continuation of large scale aid was largely in terms of the "cold war" we were waging with the U.S.S.R. for the heart and the mind of the peoples of the world lying between Moscow and Washington. In the language of the economist, the vast discrepancy between the values exported and imported by the United States since 1945 created a dollar shortage, which was remediable only by large scale loans or gifts (see accompanying table).

Year	*Exports* (in millions of dollars)	*Imports* (in millions of dollars)
1936-38	2.925	2.461
1939-41	4.026	2.680
1942-44	11.669	3.346
1945	9.586	4.075
1946	9.503	4.792
1947	15.162	5.643
1948	12.494	7.038
1949	12.004	6.623

To some observers the discrepancy between exports and imports in recent years was but a new chapter of the old story of economic imbalance in United States international economic relations since 1914. To others it meant that there could be no further delay in the drastic downward revision of the barriers to United States imports. Whether or not such a drastic downward revision would suffice to bring import values into a more balanced relationship to export values, was a moot question. The trade figures for the first five months of 1950 showed a narrowing of the gap between exports and imports. According to the preliminary figures for these months, exports were running at an annual rate of 9.7 billion dollars, while imports were running at an annual rate of 7.5 billion dollars. If continued, this trend would result in reducing the balance between exports and imports to the smallest figure since Pearl Harbor.

The American Merchant Marine

Another segment of the problem of "dollar shortage" in the years following 1945 was the remarkable shift in the dollar balances arising from our international transactions in shipping. One of the noteworthy events associated with World War I was the revival of the American merchant marine. Following the Civil War there had been a decline in the number of ships flying the American flag. In 1860, American ships still carried about two-thirds of our total ocean-borne foreign trade, but this figure declined to 10 per cent in 1914. A basic factor in this decline was the American policy of limiting the registration of the national merchant marine to American-built ships. This policy, laid down in the law of 1789, began to handicap the American shipping business even before the Civil War, the initial advantages of low-cost materials in American shipbuilding having disappeared at that time. In the period following the war, this disadvantage became more pronounced with the displacement of wooden sailing vessels by metal sailing vessels and then by steamships. The unfavorable cost differentials arising out of construction were further enhanced by the comparative operating costs of labor, subsistence, and repairs. Under such conditions American capital showed a tendency either to withdraw into the protected coastwise shipping lanes or to be invested in foreign ships.

The outbreak of World War I opened a new phase in American shipping. The period was dominated by the huge shipbuilding program launched by the Government under the Shipping Act of 1916. Total American tonnage in foreign trade rose from about 1,000,000 tons in 1914 to 11,000,000 tons in 1921, of which the greater part was in Government hands. In the Act of 1920, the Government sought to lay down a long-range policy, the essential aspects of which were: (1) the sale to private enterprise of the Government's accumulated tonnage on extremely favorable terms, and (2) the establishment of Government-owned services on selected foreign trade routes, to be operated by private charterers. Under these conditions, the percentage of our foreign trade carried in American ships was maintained at considerably higher levels than before the war, varying between 30 per cent and 40 per cent. The policy failed to provide, however, for replacements of our merchant fleet, and with every passing year the total tonnage engaged in sea-borne trade continued to shrink. The White-Jones Act of 1928 was passed to remedy this situation; it provided mail subsidies for ship operators on a more generous scale than had ever been the case before in our history and offered cheap loans for new ship construction. The act failed to stimulate any considerable amount of new construction, however, and the operation of the mail subsidy system, under which $176,000,000 had been paid out by 1937, became the source of a public scandal.

A new start was made by the Merchant Marine Act of 1936. This legislation provided for comprehensive subsidies in shipbuilding and ship operation. The government undertook to provide shipping companies with new ships at a cost not in excess of the cost of construction abroad. These ships were to be built in the United States, and the differential in cost of construction was to be absorbed by the government up to one-third, and possibly one-half, of the American cost. Moreover, ship operators were allowed easy terms in paying for the ships. The ship-operating subsidies were to offset all differential cost advantages enjoyed by foreign shippers, including also subsidies paid to foreign competitors by their governments. The United States Maritime Commission was set up to administer the act. If, in the judgment of the Commission, the interest of the United States required government ownership and operation, it was authorized to proceed with such a program.

In 1938 the Commission began a long-range program for the replacement of over-age cargo and passenger-cargo vessels with new ships at the rate of 50 ships a year for a ten-year period. After the outbreak of war in 1939, this program was greatly expanded, until, towards the close of 1946, the United States government owned an ocean-going merchant fleet of approximately 60 million dead weight tons, including some 5,000 vessels of 2,000 tons or over. This represented an investment of over 16 billion dollars, and was over 60 per cent of the world's total tonnage of merchant ships. In 1939, the United States merchant marine was less than 12 million dead weight tons or 15 per cent of the world's total.

In spite of this enormous and lopsided growth of American shipping, there was little reason to suppose that there had been any fundamental improvement in the economic capacity of the American merchant marine to compete in world trade on an unsubsidized private enterprise basis. National defense considerations and the private interests of shipbuilders, ship operators, and organized labor mingled to perpetuate a government policy of subsidy and protection. At first, American policy was to sell off government-owned ships to domestic and foreign buyers alike, but in 1948 Congress, in response to objections by domestic shipping interests, refused to extend the Commission's authority to sell to foreign buyers. At the end of 1948 domestic buyers had purchased some 700 vessels and foreign buyers had obtained 1,100 ships.

In May, 1949, 1881 vessels of nearly 19 million deadweight tons were laid up in the reserve, and 1,566 vessels of about 18 million tons were in the active American fleet. According to a recent Brookings study, "ocean trade was becoming more and more the concern of governments and was threatening to become entangled again in the restrictions from which it had been freed a century ago." The United States was in a delicate position in its endeavors to check this tendency, since it was itself using government-owned ships in private operation, operating government-owned ships as government projects, subsidizing both the construction and operation of privately owned ships, and controlling the allocation of cargoes.[8] Meanwhile, from a balance of payments point of view, transportation has become a sizeable credit item in the United States balance of payments, as contrasted with the debit balances prevailing in former years.

The General Agreement on Tariffs and Trade

In order to facilitate imports into the United States, the Government was accelerating its trade agreements program. In 1945 the administration had secured renewal of the President's power to cut tariffs by 50 per cent, with the added proviso that the President could exercise this power over

---

[8] *Major Problems of United States Foreign Policy, 1949-1950,* pp. 235 ff. Washington, D. C.: The Brookings Institution, 1949.

tariffs as they stood on January 1, 1945, not merely as they were fixed in the Smoot-Hawley Act of 1930. In 1948, Congressional forces opposing the lower tariff program theatened for a while to upset it, but this effort failed, except for some minor limitations placed upon the President's powers. In 1949 the program was once again restored to its full vigor.

Meanwhile the State Department had developed a new technique for promoting international agreement on the lowering of trade barriers. In 1947 there assembled at Geneva a conference of twenty-three governments, and after seven months of negotiations this conference concluded the General Agreement on Tariffs and Trade (G.A.T.T.). This agreement established rules for the conduct of trade between the contracting parties and fixed the tariff treatment, item by item, for products that aggregated about one-half of the world's international trade. The consolidated tariff schedule of the participants in this low tariff club included the results of over one hundred separate negotiations among them. These negotiations ran parallel to the negotiations over the terms of the I.T.O. charter, and the agreement among the signatories of the G.A.T.T. was sometimes referred to as "the little I.T.O." In 1949 at Annecy, France, similar negotiations took place with ten additional countries and in September, 1950, it was expected that a still larger list of countries would join the G.A.T.T.

No one can foretell with assurance what the future might hold in store as a consequence of the tremendous efforts of the United States to restore conditions for peaceful expansion of the world economy and to promote a better economic balance between itself and the rest of the world. The forces unleashed by two global wars in one generation are so vast and unpredictable in their scope and intensity that facile optimism seems out of place. The basic political conflict for world order or world dominion is unresolved. Yet, whatever the outcome of this political struggle, and whatever the fate of particular programs of action sketched in the above pages, it may fairly be said that the policies of the United States following World War II testified to a high, and newly won, sense of responsibility for the functioning of world society, and to the remarkable vitality of American initiative and leadership.

Selected References

GENERAL WORKS

Buchanan, N. S., and F. A. Lutz, *Rebuilding the World Economy*. New York: The Twentieth Century Fund, 1947.

Gordon, M. S., *Barriers to World Trade*. New York: The Macmillan Co., 1941.

Lary, H. B., *The United States in the World Economy*. Washington, D. C.: Government Printing Office, 1943.

Williams, B. H., *Economic Foreign Policy of the United States*. New York: McGraw-Hill Book Company, 1929.

SPECIAL TOPICS

Harris, S., *The European Recovery Program.* Cambridge: Harvard University Press, 1948.

———, *Foreign Economic Policy for the United States.* Cambridge: Harvard University Press, 1948.

Lasswell, H. D., *World Politics Faces Economics.* New York: McGraw-Hill Book Company, 1945.

Lewis, C., *The United States and Foreign Investment Problems.* Washington, D. C.: The Brookings Institution, 1948.

Schattschneider, E. E., *Politics, Pressures and the Tariff.* New York: Prentice-Hall, Inc., 1935.

Southard, F. A., *American Industry in Europe.* Boston: Houghton Mifflin Co., 1931.

Wilcox, C., *A Charter for World Trade.* New York: The Macmillan Co., 1949.

42 · MONEY AND BANKING, 1919-1950

The Federal Reserve System at the End of World War I

DURING THE WAR THE Federal Reserve System had amply proved its ability to offer monetary support to the transition from peace to full war-time output. More than this, through its assistance in mobilizing the reserves of the banking system and in stimulating the creation of new deposits, it had given indispensable aid in forcing the pace of conversion from peace to war. But this had not been done without economic and social cost. The price rise initiated before the entry of the United States into the war continued into 1919, and, though the Federal Reserve System's reserves were still above requirements, the reserve ratio had declined by nearly half. Some of the Reserve banks had lost a relatively great proportion of their excess reserves, and at the initiative of the Board the reserves of the system were equalized.

The Banking System and "Back to Normalcy"

The Armistice made little difference in the underlying economic situation: the tempo of output and the level of incomes and prices continued to rise. Another big tax bill and another flotation of government bonds, the Victory loan, had to be engineered before the fiscal and monetary transition to peace could be made. Thus, the Federal Reserve banks were forced to continue the support of the government bond market—that is, continue the policy of easy money rates—until the success of the new issue was assured. Since it was only a matter of time before a cutback to a peacetime rate of output would be inevitable, the Federal Reserve banks were eager to restrict the credit supply. Until late 1919, however, the Federal Reserve System was effectively out of touch with the money market, just as it would be again after World War II, and for the same reason. The banks and the public were loaded up with government bonds, the price of which had to be maintained.[1] But the maintenance of their

[1] Institutions and individuals who have invested their savings in government securities need to be protected against fluctuations in their prices, which may involve the investor in loss if he finds it necessary to dispose of them before maturity. Since the interest rate varies inversely with the market price of the security, a fall in the market price of the security implies a rise in the interest rate. This affects adversely the market

price required the Reserve System to lend its support to the demand for the government securities. Furthermore, for fiscal reasons the System was constrained to continue for many months the preferential buying rates on short term government paper.

When the System at the end of the year and during 1920 abolished preferential rates and attempted to put a brake on member bank borrowing, the boom was hardly in control. On both economic and monetary grounds the Board was eager to reverse the trend. During the war, gold production had declined because of the manpower scarcity and because the general rise in prices, coupled with the fixity of the dollar price of gold under a gold standard, had made the production of gold unprofitable. The war itself had caused a maldistribution of gold, and the scramble of nations for the available supplies to support their standards had given rise to a search for means whereby gold output could be increased. In this country the rise in incomes and prices, which by 1919 was reaching boom proportions, threatened an external drain of gold. Therefore, as soon as possible, the Federal Reserve banks attempted to put an end to the boom.[2]

Federal Reserve Attempts to Restrain the Boom

A general tightening of Federal Reserve discount and lending rates in late 1919 and 1920 was unsuccessful in stemming the tide of member bank borrowing. The great increase in bank loans had naturally resulted in a loss of bank reserves, and bank borrowing at the Reserve banks increased. The Victory loan (1919) tied the hands of the Federal Reserve banks, since their support of this loan at the same time put reserves at the disposal of the commercial banks and reduced the reserves of the Federal Reserve banks. The drain on their reserves was intensified by the increased member bank borrowing. The latter continued a trend that was initiated during the war, largely in connection with the methods used in marketing government securities. During the two years before our entry into the war the member banks had possessed ample reserves and

---

for future government issues, and to the extent that it spreads to the general market for capital funds, increases the cost of private borrowing and discourages investment. On both these counts the Federal Reserve System is under pressure to assure a market for government securities. The problem is made more acute by the natural tendency of the commercial banks to dispose of government securities after a war as they turn to the more profitable market for private loans and discounts.

[2] It will be observed that the warring nations looked forward to a return to the gold standard after World War I. During the interval between the wars, however, many countries had come to the conclusion that internal price and output stability was preferable to stability of exchange rates and adherence to the gold standard. It required much argument by the United States, as well as the promise of dollar aid to support weak currencies, to convince some nations of the desirability of a return to stable exchange rates and even a qualified gold standard in 1945.

had not, therefore, done much rediscounting with the Federal Reserve banks.[3] Reserve requirements were reduced in 1917, which still further delayed the need for member bank borrowing. But loans and discounts were increased by half between the date of our entry into the war and the end of the boom in mid-1920. The centralization of reserves under the Act of June 21, 1917 provided the Federal Reserve System with the elasticity needed to play its part in war finance, but it also encouraged the commercial banks to fill their portfolios with government bonds on the basis of borrowed reserves, without sufficient curtailment of private lending.[4] The addition of government spending to a large volume of private spending, which was not adequately curtailed through taxation or by government borrowing, set in motion an upward price spiral that encouraged business to superimpose its bank borrowing upon that of the government. The result was a rising inflationary pressure. In some respects the boom and inflation that followed upon the end of World War I were similar to those experienced in the years 1945-1947. But the difficulties of reconverting to peace time production after World War II at least put a brake on the extent of industry's recourse to commercial bank loans, and although inflationary pressure was exerted through the lack of goods available for sale on the market, the creation of deposits characteristic of 1919 and 1920 was obviated. Furthermore, the years after the end of the second war were marked by a rather extraordinary disposition on the part of the public to retain command over the very large volume of their liquid assets.

Treasury Influence over the Federal Reserve System

The inadequate financial methods of the First World War led to a boom and collapse for which the Federal Reserve System was held to blame. But Federal Reserve policies during and after the war were dictated largely by the Treasury, in line with decisions already made with respect to the ratio of taxation to borrowing. Federal Reserve support of the government security market immediately after the war, which unduly eased interest rates and encouraged expansion of commercial bank loans, could only be withdrawn with the concurrence of the Treasury. In November 1919 the Treasury saw the necessity of curbing the boom despite the advantage of low interest rates in servicing the debt, and a rediscount rate as high as 7 per cent was set by the Board in June 1920.[5] By this time, however, the inventory boom that had developed as a result of the diffi-

[3] W. J. Shultz and M. R. Caine, *Financial Development of the United States*, p. 553. New York: Prentice-Hall, Inc., 1937.

[4] By 1919 three-fifths of the bank's investment portfolios were in the form of government securities. Shultz and Caine, *loc. cit.*

[5] Ray B. Westerfield, *Money, Credit, and Banking*, p. 731. New York: The Ronald Press, 1938.

culty of obtaining goods was suddenly reversed, and the Board was subjected to the accusation of having precipitated the crisis.[6]

The Federal Reserve Contributes to Early Recovery in 1921

The rapid recovery made from the sharp but brief depression of 1921 has special interest from the points of view of (1) the soundness of the banking system, (2) the role of the Federal Reserve System in alleviating a downswing, and (3) business cycle theory. With respect to the first of these, the financial panics associated with earlier depressions were absent. The reserves of the Federal Reserve banks were placed at the disposal of the commercial banks, and through the latter to firms whose liquidity had been destroyed by the fall in values. It was demonstrated that the Federal Reserve System was able to avoid a panic that under the National Banking System would probably have been inevitable.[7] Because the banks were protected from collapse, and because unnecessary business failures were minimized, the basis was quickly laid for a recovery. Time was provided for making the necessary readjustments in a manner that avoided accentuating the downswing. Finally, this experience demonstrated that a sharp decline in inventories and consumption is possible without setting in motion such a pronounced reduction in investment and production that a deflationary spiral becomes inevitable. It provides one instance, at least, in support of the view that the proper remedy for depression may in some circumstances be the readjustment of costs and prices rather than immediate recourse to expanded public works and government deficits.

Federal Reserve Policy, the Gold Standard, and the Money Supply

The war had brought to an end an era in which the international gold standard had operated fairly smoothly, an efficiency which was due to the

---

[6] This political attack on the Board was extremely serious from the point of view of independence of action. It is pointed out by W. Randolph Burgess, (*The Reserve Banks and the Money Market,* p. 271. New York: Harper and Brothers, 1946) that Governor Harding was not reappointed at the end of his term, an example which could not be without effect in subsequent cases in which strong Board action was required.

[7] This did not mean that under any and all circumstances the Federal Reserve banks could prevent the banks from closing their doors. In the crisis of 1933 the public was in such a state of panic that a widespread *de facto* closing of the banks was ultimately sanctioned by Presidential proclamation of a four day bank holiday. The authorities did not feel in a position to meet the demand of the public for hoarding by providing an unlimited supply of new currency, and the potentialities of the Federal Reserve bank were not exploited. Furthermore, it was the RFC rather than the Federal Reserve System that restored liquidity to the banks after the bank holiday. But it remains true that in the Federal Reserve System the country possesses an instrument capable of meeting any monetary crisis, provided only that a sufficiently bold policy is politically feasible.

relatively high degree of international monetary cooperation under the leadership of the British pound. Among the factors making for smooth operation were the extensive use of British bills of exchange for financing foreign trade, the fact that British loans dominated the international lending scene and were adapted to the natural flows of trade, the dominance of the Bank of England among central banks, the relative lack of trade barriers, and the movement of international short-term funds primarily in response to interest rate differentials rather than to seek safety. With the postwar emergence of the United States as an international lender, the new Federal Reserve System was required almost over night to function as one of the world's two leading central banks. The great domestic success of the System in facilitating the financing of the war followed logically from the experience gained in internal central banking problems under the Independent Treasury and the National Banking System. But little or no experience had been gained in the problems of international finance and the management of the gold standard. It was here that trouble threatened. Not only did the Reserve authorities inherit little practical experience in these external problems, but during the interwar period the United States did not possess the undisputed central financial position enjoyed by Britain before 1914. The situation was further complicated by the fact that American private and public loan policy was uncoordinated during the twenties. Foreign loans were not primarily Treasury loans (as has been the case after World War II) but were made ostensibly on the basis of business considerations. But the world interest rate structure had been completely upset by the cataclysm of war, and loans made in response to high interest rates received no assurance that export of capital goods would follow the loan. Moreover investment houses placed too much stress on high foreign interest rates and not enough on the productivity of the proposed investment. Conversely, with an uncoordinated lending policy, areas needing equipment and materials for construction and development could not be assured of a continuation of needed loans. The upshot of all this was that American monetary policy could hardly be consistent after World War I. Banking policy had not had time to solidify, experience was lacking, and a conflict was evidently inevitable between criteria of domestic stability and those of international stability.

Certain steps were consciously taken in the early years of the Federal Reserve System to prepare for its international role. The Reserve banks were given the power to support the acceptance market, in order to establish such a market in the United States. The Federal Reserve Act had empowered the national banks to set up foreign branches and to create foreign trade bankers' acceptances. On the other hand, the System refrained from directly financing foreign trade, limiting itself to financing dollar acceptances. The relative unimportance of international trade in so large and self-contained an economy as that of the United States obviated the international banking outlook that had made Britain such a logical supporter of the trade and financial mechanisms required for managing an international gold standard. With the cooperation of the Federal Reserve System an attempt was indeed made by New York to replace London as the international financial center. But Britain played the role of middleman in international finance, and, despite the rapid increase in the number of foreign branches by American banks, trade was again to become largely financed in sterling. Retention of this role, however, did not leave Britain in the undisputed central position occupied by her before the war. The war aftermath of upset currencies and distorted trade flows brought about an inflow of gold into the United States. Although Federal Reserve policies could not bring order into international currency relationships, they were to exercise independent influences that prevented integrated international monetary cooperation, and the disturbing effects of our own independence of action were added to those of the nationalistic policies of other nations. In the latter part of the twenties unilateral currency devaluations and independent domestic economic policies led to the complete breakdown of the gold standard.

The Gold Inflow and Federal Reserve Policy

During the years 1921 to 1924 there was an enormous inflow of gold into this country. The magnitude of this gold inflow made impractical the adoption of the passive policy called for under the automatic gold standard and actually adhered to during the first years of the Federal Reserve System. The country had just passed through a boom and price inflation, and the sharp price fall in 1921 did not remove fears of another inflation. Furthermore, the example of the German hyper-inflation of 1923 was heeded. Consequently, Federal Reserve policy was directed toward moderating the effects of the gold inflow. This was to be accomplished by paying into circulation gold certificates instead of Federal Reserve notes, thus artificially inducing an internal cash drain. Since the inflow of gold had raised actual reserves of the Federal Reserve banks well above required reserves, no restriction of credit was in fact brought about. But the steps taken to prevent a rise in actual reserve ratios were evidence of a determination of the Board to prevent a price rise.[8] In any event it would not have been feasible to try to halt the gold inflow by allowing it to have its full effects on prices and incomes. Excess reserves at the Federal Reserve banks and the commercial banks are a necessary, but not a sufficient, condition to increasing business activity. To the extent that the Federal Reserve banks purchased government securities, the

[8] R. G. Thomas, *Our Modern Banking and Monetary System.* New York: Prentice-Hall, Inc., 1950.

member banks were enabled to pay off their indebtedness, with little net effect on the money supply and incomes. The Reserve banks undertook these purchases, be it noted, in order to increase their earnings, which is an example of a partial failure of the System as a central bank. For, as has already been noted, central bank earnings should be subsidiary to credit policy.[9] But the fright that the Board and the Federal Reserve banks had received when accused of having caused the 1921 recession militated against the immediate adoption of more constructive policies.

Declaration of a New Federal Reserve Policy in 1923

Federal Reserve policy during the remainder of the decade became, however, much more positive. The Federal Advisory Council had censured the Reserve banks for gearing open market policy to their own profits. In 1923 a permanent open market committee was set up to coordinate the purchases and sales of all twelve reserve banks. The new objectives of credit policy were set forth in the Annual Report of the Federal Reserve Board for 1923. Clearly, in view of the unmanageable influx of gold, watching reserve ratios had failed as a basis for credit policy. Criticism of the type to which the System was subjected in 1921 and 1922 was forestalled by explicit rejection of the view that the Federal Reserve Board could affect the price level through credit policy, or should regulate credit with reference to prices. The original intent of the Federal Reserve Act was reaffirmed by asserting that Federal Reserve credit should be used only for accommodating the needs of trade. The System was to avoid making its reserves available in support of speculative activity. Admitting that frequently the System must find itself out of touch with the market and that the magnitude of its operations would be inadequate to enforce control over the entire market, the Board satisfied itself with a rediscount and open market policy aimed at stimulation of credit during depression and restriction during boom periods. In consequence, Federal Reserve policy was passive during much of the next two years, until in 1927 changed circumstances caused a new criterion of policy to be temporarily adopted.

Partly to encourage business recovery but partly also to assist Britain to go back on the gold standard, the Board decided in 1927 to favor an easier money policy. An immediate effect of a fall in the interest rate would be the encouragement of a gold flow to Britain and other countries desiring to stabilize their exchanges in preparation for a return to the gold standard. More remotely, lower interest rates might raise incomes

[9] In the particular case, the loss of incomes from rediscounts offset the gain in incomes from government securities, with little net effect on either earnings or the volume of demand deposits. Westerfield, *Op. cit.* p. 734.

and prices in the United States, thus encouraging an increased demand for foreign exchange and an outflow of gold.[10]

The Federal Reserve System and the Stock Market Crash

The role of the banking system in the circumstances that led to the stock market boom and collapse and the beginning of depression, in 1929 is difficult to evaluate. Moreover, differences of opinion exist concerning the influence of corporate profits, the level of personal incomes, and the rate of consumer spending on the demand for consumers' goods, and therefore on the maintenance of a high level of derived demand for investment goods. The mid-twenties was a period of rapid growth in instalment credit and finance companies, and therefore in consumer spending. Corporations were building up surpluses and thus required less recourse to the banks. The rapid growth in business profits tended to inhibit the growth in consumer incomes. Loans for account of others increased in importance, and diminished somewhat Federal Reserve control over the credit supply. Though commodity prices were relatively stable through to 1929, stock prices rose rapidly, and a boom psychology developed. In these circumstances the Board became increasingly concerned lest its resources be used to support stock speculation at the expense of production and trade. It was thought in some quarters, however, that bank credit to business, which had not substantially increased, was inadequate to the maintenance of prosperity. On this subject a cleavage of opinion developed between some of the Reserve banks (notably New York) and the Board. The former favored rising rediscount rates, while the latter wished to continue granting credit to productive industry while attempting to bar it from speculation. Owing to the integration of the market for loans, selective credit policies, operating through pressure on the banks to reduce brokers' loans in favor of loans to business, proved unsuccessful. Moreover the stock boom had developed so far by 1929 that higher Reserve bank discount rates were without effect. Critics of Federal Reserve policies maintained that the rises in the rediscount rate during 1928 were always too slow to be effective. In any event, a really restrictive discount policy was obviated by the fear of attracting gold from abroad so soon after a number of countries had returned to gold, and by the belief that credit to the stock market could be segregated from that to business and agriculture. Also, in view of the fact that there appeared to be no production boom,

---

[10] In view of the doubtful connection between the rise in business activity in 1924 and the open market purchases and lowered rediscount rates in that year, most of the effect would probably have had to come through the impact of the short-term interest rate on gold flows. Also, the Board was influenced by the prevalent view that nothing must be done to threaten our export surplus, which for the last fifty years has been perennial.

the System feared that a substantial rise in interest rates might precipitate depression. The 1921 experience was much in the minds of the Board and the Reserve banks. When crisis and depression did strike in the fall of 1929, the Reserve System naturally reversed its policy, purchasing government securities and lowering discount rates in an attempt to encourage business borrowing and rising income and employment. The experience of the next few years was to demonstrate to the satisfaction of all that low interest rates and conditions favorable to the creation of demand deposits are inadequate to stimulate recovery when the inducement to invest is lacking. On the other hand, during a depression the task of the banking system and the control authorities is simple: merely provide the necessary bank loans on easy terms when business shows a disposition to borrow.

Banking and Monetary Policy during Depression and Recovery: 1930–1940

The importance of Federal Reserve policy during the twenties, evidenced by the prominent headlines devoted to its decisions throughout the decade, and particularly in the years 1927 and 1929, was not sustained after the beginning of the depression. An era had commenced in which it began to be recognized that the powers of the monetary authorities over income, employment, and prices are severely limited. More direct measures, while based on appropriate monetary policy, supplanted the latter in importance. These measures took the form of a multitude of separate, often unrelated, and sometimes inconsistent, acts of the Federal Government, partly aimed at stimulating recovery and partly at effecting the adoption of the concepts of social welfare of the New Deal. In a world of constantly increasing centralization of power, the Federal Reserve System could not escape Treasury dictation. But this was not a new phenomenon. During World War I the Secretary of the Treasury had dealt directly with the individual Federal Reserve banks. Though the Secretary of the Treasury did not long remain chairman of the Board, and though the Secretary and the Comptroller of the Currency were dropped from the Board in the Banking Act of 1935, Treasury influence has necessarily dominated during both time of war and depression. Legislation aimed in this direction has been enacted in both periods. The Overman Act in 1917 gave the President the power to reorganize government agencies in the interest of the war effort. The Thomas amendment in 1933 conferred much discretion with respect to the money supply on the Secretary of the Treasury,[11] and in the recent war greater powers than ever were exercised by the Treasury.

The vast increase in the portfolio holdings of government securities by

---

[11] Westerfield, *op. cit.,* 722.

both the Federal Reserve and the commercial banks during the recovery program and, to a much greater extent, during war, meant that the fiscal policy of the government determined the rate of interest and the money supply. This development was inevitable as banks increased their holdings of government securities. But it was also consistent with the fact that in the last analysis control of the money supply is a political matter, and must be vested in an essentially political authority. An example of the power of politics was the criticism of the Board by agricultural groups in 1921-2, which brought about an amendment to the Federal Reserve Act requiring the specific representation of agriculture in monetary decisions, and thus focused attention on the axiom that the control of the money supply must remain with a central agency responsible to the electorate. More normally the power is exercised through congressional decisions concerning the level of expenditures and taxes.

Loss of Control of the Money Market by the Federal Reserve System

After 1933 the Federal Reserve System remained more or less out of touch with the money market. Only if the banks must borrow from the Reserve banks at rediscount rates that can be raised to penalty levels can a real brake be put upon the creation of deposits by the banking system. Early in the 1930's the banks began to amass excess reserves. Despite the obvious advantage of lending these out, even at a low rate of interest, inflowing gold from abroad, coupled with a low level of business activity at home, gave rise to a steady increase in reserves, which finally reached a maximum of $7 billion in 1940. The excess would have been still greater had the Board not taken advantage of a provision in the Banking Act of 1935 authorizing it to raise reserve requirements up to double those of the Act. The rise in commercial bank holdings of government securities to $91 billion by December 1945 greatly reduced reserves. But the Federal Reserve System still remained out of touch with the money market because of the bond support program, which required the Reserve banks to establish fixed buying rates on short term government securities, thus opening up unlimited member bank access to the System's reserves.

With the eclipse of the influence of Federal Reserve credit policy on the money supply after 1933, the history of monetary policy was written largely in terms of New Deal economic measures. One of the first tasks was to restore confidence in the banking system, which had proved itself unable to survive the rapid deflation from a period of excessive lending and stock market speculation. Although the banks cannot be accused of sole, or even major responsibility in the circumstances leading to the collapse of values that began in 1929, certain unhealthy characteristics had gradually become apparent in the twenties. For example, the decline in the importance of the commercial loan encouraged the banks to expand investments in less liquid assets. The failure rate of the banks under the Federal Reserve System had proved disappointingly high.[12]

Increasing dependence by corporations on their own liquid reserves for financing expanion limited outlets for investments by commercial banks and other institutions; growth in "loans for account of others" (lending of these reserves for the corporations by the banks as agent only) not only reduced Federal Reserve control over the money supply but also injected elements of unsoundness into lending practices. Opposition in the United States to branch banking unnecessarily weakened the banking system through its limitation on the scope for diversification of bank business and recruitment of able personnel. Although relaxation of restrictions in recent years has permitted branch banking on a state-wide scale by national banks as well as state banks, not much scope exists under present legislation for an integration of banking by this device. An elaborate system of bank examination by the Federal Reserve banks, the Comptroller of the Currency, and the state banking authorities cannot correct an unhealthy underlying economic situation or remedy the effects of an excessively decentralized banking system.[13]

The Collapse of the Banking System

The gathering forces of deflation finally so weakened the banking system that at the very bottom of the depression, when nourishment to the return of business confidence was indispensable, the whole banking structure collapsed. A substantial part of the responsibility for the accelerating run on deposits throughout the country that led to the banking moratorium has been laid at the door of the political situation. The election of 1932 was carried out in an atmosphere of gloom, and the delay (at that time) in inaugurating a newly elected President left the country without a helmsman at a most critical time. Rumors that President-elect Roosevelt might abandon the gold standard accelerated the internal cash drain. Bank closings spread from state to state, culminating in a general

[12] O. W. Wright, *Economic History of the United States,* p. 845. New York: McGraw-Hill, 1949. Wright points out that there were 4300 failures from 1923-1929, of which 550 were national banks and therefore members of the Federal Reserve System. With respect to the national banks, this rate of failure was greater than during the whole period of the National Banking System. Wright ascribes this in part to the loss of population from the towns due to the rise of the automobile, and to the agricultural depression in the early twenties. The consequence was a substantial decline in the number of banks during the decade (though part of this was owing to consolidations).

[13] As part of the remedial legislation of the thirties, the Federal Deposit Insurance Corporation was established in 1933. It examines all insured non-member banks. (Federal Reserve Board, *Banking Studies,* 1941, p. 195.) The Reconstruction Finance Corporation has certain supervisory powers over banks in which it has made an investment. The Trust Indenture Act of 1939 gave the Securities and Exchange Commission the power to examine certain trust activities. Though the standards and coverage of bank examination have thus vastly improved, it is obvious that the activities of the various supervising agencies should be coordinated.

moratorium on March 4, 1933. Reserves of the Federal Reserve banks, which had stood at well over $1 billion in February, had been quickly drawn down as member banks borrowed to replenish the drained cash. A rise in the rediscount rate of the New York Federal Reserve bank failed to diminish the pressure, relief finally being accorded by the banking moratorium. The uselessness of required reserves for a central bank was amply displayed by this episode. They should be regarded as a device for sounding a warning at the proper time and to assure careful scrutiny of proposed changes in reserve requirements by Congress or those to whom Congress may delegate the power.

Much legislation was required to clear up the debris of the banking system and to pave the way for the establishment of a sound financial basis for business recovery. As always, the first step was the dissipation of unreasoning fear. This was aided greatly by the calmness and self-assurance of the new administration. The gradual back-flow of cash to the banks enabled them to repay their borrowing at the Reserve banks, and by the end of the year the member banks had excess reserves of nearly $1 billion.[14]

Remedial Banking Legislation

Unfortunately the accumulated defects of the banking system required a remedy more thorough-going than a mere willingness on the part of the public to redeposit its cash in the banks. The strain on the banking system had become pronounced in 1930 and matters substantially worsened in 1931. In an effort to restore liquidity to borrowers and the banks, the Reconstruction Finance Corporation had been established by the Act of January 22, 1932; but this agency could not stem the tide of security sales as banks strove to meet withdrawals by depositors. After the banking holiday the administration immediately sought Congressional aid in establishing a legislative basis for banking reform. The Emergency Banking Act of March 9, 1933 gave the President power to prohibit the export and hoarding of gold, authorized the Treasury to call in gold coin, bullion, and certificates, provided for the appointment of a conservator for closed national banks, enacted a number of provisions for liquefying the banks' assets, authorized the issue of emergency currency,[15] and allowed

[14] It must be clearly borne in mind that excess reserves months after the crisis are of no use. An unreasoning bank run requires unlimited willingness on the part of a central bank to create reserves for the banking system so long as the public demands greater than normal supplies of cash.

[15] This emergency currency took the form of Federal Reserve bank notes. In order to provide all banks, non-member as well as member, with the currency needed to satisfy any conceivable cash drain that might arise during the period when the banking system was being set in order, banks were allowed to borrow, on the basis of adequate security, Federal Reserve bank notes backed by United States bonds, notes, drafts or bills of exchange. The breadth of these alternatives assured that the Reserve banks would have adequate collateral in either depression or prosperity.

banks to borrow temporarily on non-eligible paper. The R.F.C. played an important part in furnishing the reserves necessary to reopen the closed banks. Though two-thirds of the country's 18,000 banks were quickly reopened, progress thereafter was gradual. To facilitate restoration of more nearly normal conditions, this institution advanced funds to the closed banks and invested in their preferred stock and debentures. Total loans and investments by the R.F.C. to the banks had reached nearly $3 billion by the end of 1935, over half of which had been repaid by that time.[16]

New Deal Legislation and the Money Supply

Once the banking system had been set on the road to recovery, the financial problem facing the administration was how best to adapt the money supply to the complex program for recovery and social reform adopted by the New Deal. A veritable spate of monetary legislation during the early thirties gave the administration all the tools that could be conceivably required. From that time the major problem was that of proper criteria for monetary policy. The administration did not make use of all the enabling legislation designed to increase the money supply. The power to devalue the dollar was exercised later under the Gold Standard Act of 1934, but no effort was made to expand the currency supply on the basis of the released gold.

The monetary inflation policy of the New Deal helped provide the basis for the gradual rise in incomes and prices from 1934 to 1937, but was not the main factor in that rise. Some use was made of the inflationary powers granted by Congress. In addition, part of the Federal deficit incurred in connection with the decline in revenues and the cost of the various public works programs from 1933 to 1937 was financed through sales of securities to the commercial banks, in other words, with the aid of new money. Moreover, the abortive gold buying policy accepted by the President in the latter part of 1933 on the advice of Professor Warren was intended to raise prices directly.[17] It is not possible to say how far infla-

---

Consequently this device assured complete elasticity of the currency. Since the period of hoarding had already passed, these notes were not much used at the time. They were used during World War I in order to save the cost of printing the new currency required in connection with the expansion of the money supply at high level employment.

16 Shultz and Caine, *Op. cit.*, 673.

17 Apparently Warren thought that if the price of gold was raised in terms of dollars the prices of all other goods would likewise be raised. This view overlooks the several points at which the chain can be broken between changes in the dollar price of gold and changes in the dollar price of goods. If the gold profit from devaluation is utilized as bank reserves, if these reserves are lent to business, and if there is full employment so that increased spending takes the form of a rise in prices instead of increased output, the nexus would be approximately established. None of these provisos operated in 1933. The purpose of trying to raise prices instead of operating directly on investment and employment was partly to restore the price cost relationship that had obtained in earlier prosperous years, partly to relieve the position of debtors, and

tionary monetary policies were responsible for the upturn that commenced as early as 1933. Total industrial production, which had declined to a low of 58 (1935-39=100) in 1932, rose steadily from 69 in 1933 to 113 in 1937, whereupon it declined sharply to 89 in the depression year 1938. Wholesale prices were likewise lowest in 1932. The index of the Department of Labor (1926=100) had declined to 64.8 by that year, but rose slightly to 65.9 in 1933, and sharply to 74.9 in 1934. After reaching a peak (86.3) in 1937 it, too, declined (to 78.6) in 1938. Employment followed the same trend as output and prices. After reaching a low of 66.3 in 1932, the Department of Labor index (1923-25 = 100) rose to 73.4 in 1933 and 85.7 in 1934, reaching a maximum of 105.8 in 1937. Factors other than monetary policy in effecting this partial recovery were the annual deficits, which averaged about $3 billion a year, the complex structure of remedial legislation, prior recovery abroad, and the recovery of free private enterprise that has always followed depression. Finally it is noteworthy that measurable recovery was made in 1933 before most of the New Deal measures had had much time to take effect.

Conflict between National and International Objectives of United States Monetary Policy

United States monetary policy during the thirties was very largely insular, which seems strange in view of the recent fervor with which international economic and financial cooperation has been advocated in this country. A determination to pursue an independent policy was asserted at the outset of the new administration. The London Economic Conference in July, 1933, was intended to provide the basis for stabilization of currencies. Unfortunately, as has been noted in the preceding chapter, Roosevelt was in the midst of his price-raising program. Any plan for stabilizing international currency ratios would be difficult to inaugurate while one of the major sponsoring nations was making every effort to depreciate the internal value of its currency. Thus the United States announced its embarkation upon a unilateral currency program, which, though probably unavoidable in the upset conditions then obtaining in economic relations, is of interest in view of the subsequent American sponsorship of international monetary cooperation.

The sabotaging of the London Monetary Conference was followed in January, 1934, by the Gold Reserve Act, which vested title to all gold bullion in the Treasury, forbade the circulation of gold coins and certificates, permitted devaluation of the dollar to between 50 and 60 per cent of its then weight, and set up a stabilization fund of $2 billion out of the profit from devaluation. The effect of the devaluation, while not at all

partly because the public and the administration apparently believed that a restoration of the price *level* of 1926 would bring with it the prosperity of 1926. This experiment was relatively brief, and efforts were soon directed correctly at raising income and employment rather than prices.

justifying Professor Warren's hopes that general prices would rise by as much as devaluation raised the gold price of the dollar, was to place an export premium on American goods. Consequently gold flowed into the country in response to increased exports, an increase that was not abated by the gradual rise in prices. Rather, the flow was accentuated by the upset conditions in Europe, together with the fact that a stable United States dollar might now be anticipated. Operations of the stabilization fund were carried out in secrecy, but weakness first in the pound sterling and, in 1936, in the French franc led ultimately to the announcement of a Tripartite Monetary Agreement, among Britain, France, and the United States, asserting the desirability of stability of exchange rates. Belgium, Switzerland, and the Netherlands later announced their adherence, and the basis was established for a permanent form of monetary cooperation. The International Monetary Conference at Bretton Woods paved the way for postwar international monetary cooperation on the basis of limitations on the freedom of individual countries to alter their exchange rates and a large rotating fund of international currencies to stabilize exchange rates.

Money and Banking from 1941 to 1950

Monetary policies of the Federal Reserve system, subordinated to the exigencies of depression finance during the greater part of the period 1933 to 1941, continued to play a passive role during the period of Treasury dominance of the money market during and after the war. The reserve position of both the Federal Reserve banks and the commercial banks was peculiarly strong in 1941. A steady inflow of gold since early 1934 (due to the combination of export surpluses and flight of capital from war-threatened areas) had increased the monetary gold stock from 4 billion to 22 billion dollars by the end of 1940, and, despite occasional countering measures by the Treasury and the Federal Reserve Board, member bank excess reserves had reached seven billion dollars by the year 1940. Thus, the banking system was in a position to manage the money supply freely in response to the policies adopted for financing the war. The decision to finance a large proportion of war expenditures by sales of government securities to the commercial banks ensured a large rise in the money supply. Their holdings of United States government obligations rose from 22 billion dollars at the end of December, 1941, to a high of over 90 billion dollars at the end of December, 1945. During the same period loans increased only from 22 billion to 26 billion dollars which reflects the fact that the great bulk of the expansion of output during the war was financed by direct lending to the government. "Total deposits adjusted and currency outside banks" rose from 78 billion in 1941 to 175 billion dollars in 1945. Of this increase, 26 billion dollars was in demand deposits adjusted and 17 billion dollars in currency outside banks. Time deposits increased by 21 billion dollars. Yet the wholesale price index of the Department of Labor rose only from 87.3 to 105.8. The much greater rise in the money supply than in prices is accounted for by (1) the vast increase in transactions, which absorbed much of the increase in the volume of money, (2) the decline in velocity of money owing to the willingness of the public to hold money idle in circumstances of an increasing scarcity of goods, and (3) O.P.A. price controls, which could be reasonably well maintained so long as the public was willing to build up liquid balances. But this "hidden inflation" was quickly converted into outright price inflation on the lifting of price controls and the increased rate of spending of liquid assets by the public when goods again commenced to appear in volume on the market. The wholesale price index had risen from 105.8 in 1945 to 166.6 by the second half of 1948.

Steering a Course between Inflation and Deflation after World War II

Until well into 1948 it appeared that the major economic problem faced by the United States was price inflation, and this inflation was largely ascribable to the use that the Treasury made of the banking system both during and after the war. Plans were proposed on all sides for absorbing excess liquidity and correcting the course of inflation. In the second half of 1948 and the first half of 1949, however, the situation was reversed. The proportion of personal incomes spent on consumption declined, inventories were shortened, and unemployment rose. The Reserve Board, therefore, reversed its earlier policy of limited credit restriction. Member bank reserve requirements were twice lowered in the summer of 1949, with the intention of releasing about 2.5 billion dollars of reserves, and restrictions on installment credit were removed. The events of the recession of 1948-1949 bore out earlier experience that the banking system is substantially limited to assuring the economy of an adequate money supply. In the absence of an outright collapse, the signs of an approaching depression are not sufficiently uniform to justify the adoption of a bold monetary policy aimed at preventing depression.

By financing a large proportion of government war costs through borrowing, Congress virtually committed the Treasury and the Federal Reserve System to a policy of supporting government securities and low interest rates. In order to lessen the burden of interest transfer payments it was in the interest of the budget to achieve low interest rates, and hence, the depressive effect of taxation on consumer spending and business incentive after the war. Thus, the rate on long term, partially tax exempt government bonds, which had already declined from 3.60 in 1929 to 2.41 in 1939, fell to 1.98 in 1943 and 1.66 in 1945.[18] In order to stabilize the market by conferring complete liquidity upon commercial bank holdings

[18] *Economic Report of the President,* January, 1949, Table C-27.

of government securities, the Federal Reserve system in 1942 inaugurated a policy of fixed buying rates on Treasury bills (3/8 of one per cent, certificates of indebtedness (7/8 of one per cent), and bonds (to yield different amounts up to a maximum of 2 1/2 per cent, the 2.9 per cent yield on Series E bonds involving a subsidy to the small saver. The purpose of these fixed buying rates was to guarantee the banks against market fluctuations in their prices. The effect was to simplify greatly the problems of Treasury finance and to assure the willingness of the banks to purchase whatever volume of government securities might be offered to them by the Treasury. But this convenience was purchased at the cost of a loss of control by the Federal Reserve System over the credit policies of the banks. For by guaranteeing to buy government securities at any time at fixed buying rates, the Reserve banks lost the initiative to the member banks. That is, the latter were placed in a position in which they could exercise control over their own reserves.

The Federal Reserve System during and after World War II

The role and objectives of the Federal Reserve System in the financing of the war can perhaps be best stated in the words of the *Annual Report* of the Board of Governors for 1943 (p. 12). The Federal Reserve System:

> Cooperated with the Treasury in the two major war loan drives....
>
> Took measures to assure sufficient reserves to the banking system to enable banks to purchase such Government securities as had to be issued *in excess of those taken by other investors.* [Italics are the author's.]
>
> Maintained stable conditions in the United States Government security market and kept prices and yields within a pattern agreed upon with the Treasury. This policy facilitated the sale of securities by removing all incentive for delaying investment and by encouraging purchasers to hold the securities they had acquired.
>
> The Board recommended to Congress that United States Government deposits with banks arising out of war loans be exempted from reserve requirements. Congress adopted this recommendation.

The loss of initiative by the Reserve System during the war was a necessary corollary of a financial policy designed to stimulate the rapid increase in output required to fight a major war. Thus "Federal Reserve operations in the open market were directed toward the objectives of supplying banks with reserves sufficient to purchase such Government securities as were not bought and held by other investors, and of maintaining stable prices and yields on marketable Government securities." [19]

[19] (*Annual Report,* 1944, p. 3.) By 1945 the Reserve authorities were concerned with the effects of this process on the money supply, the interest rate, and the price level. Owing to the greater demand for the higher-yield long term securities, the Reserve banks found themselves purchasing Treasury bills and certificates and selling long term bonds. The commercial banks were purchasing new long term government bonds with reserves placed at their disposal through sales at fixed rates of short term securities to the Federal Reserve banks. This process, known as "monetizing the debt," laid the basis for multiple credit expansion.

The maintenance of a fixed pattern of rates on government securities naturally encouraged the purchase by the banks of long term rather than lower-yielding short term securities and thus, by monetizing the long term debt, stimulated an increase in the money supply at a time when the major credit policy objective of the Reserve System was inflation control.

Reserve Board Attempts To Strengthen Instruments of Monetary Control

From the point of view of control over the money supply by the Federal Reserve System, the legacy of the methods employed in World War II was the sacrifice of the major function of central banking to the narrower Treasury problem of debt management. This was argued by the Board in its *Annual Report* for 1946 (p. 4):

> Under existing powers of the Federal Reserve System and with the necessity for maintaining stability in the market for the vast and widely distributed public debt, it is not possible for the Reserve System to maintain the same degree of control over the supply of bank reserves, and hence over potential credit expansion, that it formerly had.

The Board suggested that by giving up the Federal Reserve policy of purchasing short term government securities at low rates the incentive to monetization of the debt could be reduced. A much more vigorous step had been advocated in the annual report for 1945, and was repeated in subsequent reports. This was the requirement that member banks either be required to hold additional legal reserves, or that, in connection with a rise in reserve requirements, they be allowed to hold certain assets not previously eligible, for example, Treasury bills and certificates and short term notes. The latter alternative would have avoided the necessity for the banks' disposing of short term government securities, thereby depressing their prices; but it would have prevented their monetization. In effect this policy would have partly insulated the market for government securities from the market for private loans, inhibiting inflation by forcing up rates of the latter without at the same time driving down the price of government securities.

The recession of 1949 temporarily eliminated fears that the redundant money supply, coupled with the huge volume of liquid assets, would encourage inflation. Indeed, it was regarded as a favorable element for the maintenance of a high level of income and employment that the banks were in a position to expand loans to business without difficulty. But the inconsistency between a Federal Reserve policy aimed at guaranteeing the market for government securities and maintaining a fixed pattern of interest rates, on the one hand, and control over the ability of the banks to lend, on the other, remains to plague the economy whenever the problem again becomes one of inflation control.

The significance of the limitation on the independence of Federal Reserve credit policy that was exerted by the greater importance assigned to debt management was illustrated during 1948 when a large Treasury surplus (8 billion dollars) might have been used to reduce bank reserves. The Federal Reserve System was, indeed, enabled to sell securities back to the Treasury, but this drain on bank reserves was more than offset by the System's purchases of securities in accordance with the market support policy. In order to minimize the growth in deposits and therefore inflationary pressure, a number of deflationary steps were taken by the System. These included the acceptance of cash for maturing securities, a rise in the rediscount rate and in the interest rates on short term government securities (thus shifting some of the latter from the Federal Reserve banks to the commercial banks), increased reserve requirements for member banks in order to absorb reserves created by the gold inflow and by Reserve purchases of government securities in support of that market, reimposition of controls over consumer instalment credit, and retention of high margin requirements despite the inactivity of the stock market. The recession of 1948, however, brought about a reversal of Federal Reserve policy. Consumer credit regulations were terminated in June, and reserve requirements were lowered on three separate occasions.

The Report of the Board for 1948

The Federal Reserve continued to advocate legislative changes that would tend to increase central bank control over the reserves and lending policies of the banks. In its report for 1948 the Board requested the power to increase reserve requirements, not for member banks alone, but for all commercial banks. The temporary authority granted earlier expired at the end of June, 1949, and was not renewed. The Board subscribes to the formation of a National Monetary Commission for the study of all problems relating to the roles of banking and the government in the financial system. Increased powers are requested with respect to the System's open market operations in their relation to the public debt and the use of selective credit controls over security loans and consumer instalment credit. In order to simplify and make more effective the supervision of the banks, it is requested that a review be made of the distribution of bank regulatory and supervisory powers among the competent government agencies. The Board is also interested in improving the degree of coordination of domestic financial policy in somewhat the same manner as that in which the National Advisory Council operates on the international side. Among the most urgent reforms, finally, is the rationalization of bank reserve requirements. The Board advocates a change from basing reserve requirements on the size of the city in which a member bank happens to find itself. This holdover from the National Banking System has little meaning today. Differences in reserve requirements ought to be based "more largely" on the nature and activity of deposits. Furthermore, over-all monetary control requires that not merely member banks, but all insured commercial banks, should be subject to any requirement that banks hold additional reserves. Member banks number somewhat less than half of all commercial banks, and account for about 85 per cent of all deposits. Nonmember banks have advantages with respect to their reserves that work against a growth in the coverage of the Federal Reserve System. The member banks carry higher reserves, since they may not count vault cash or balances with city correspondents as part of their legally required reserves. Nonmember banks, moreover, obtain indirectly most of the advantages of the Federal Reserve System, but are not subject to controls introduced in the national interest.

Conclusion

In conclusion, it may be stated that after nearly forty years of operation the Federal Reserve System still lacked a number of powers ordinarily associated with a modern central bank. Much of the difficulty derives from the failure to subject all commercial banks to centralized control. More of it, perhaps, stems from the excessive use made of the System for the essentially narrow function of debt management and undue influence of the Treasury over the policies of the Board. Granted that complete understanding between the two authorities is necessary, and that in essential matters the Treasury's views must prevail, yet it is nevertheless true that the Treasury should assure the System the freedom it requires to perform adequately its function of providing the economy with an amount of purchasing power appropriate to stable and high level income, output, and employment.

Selected References

Annual Reports of the Board of Governors of the Federal Reserve System.

Board of Governors of the Federal Reserve System, *Banking Studies*. Washington, D. C.: 1941.

Burgess, W. R., *The Reserve Banks and the Money Market*. New York: Harper and Brothers, 1946.

Currie, L., *The Supply and Control of Money in the United States*. Cambridge: Harvard University Press, 1934.

Hardy, C. O., *Credit Policies of the Federal Reserve System*. Washington, D. C.: Brookings Institution, 1932.

Harris Institute Lectures, *Gold and Monetary Stabilization*. Chicago: University of Chicago Press, 1932.

Paris, J. D., *Monetary Policies of the United States, 1932-34*. New York: Columbia University Press, 1938.

Shultz, W. J., and M. R. Caine, *Financial Development of the United States*. New York: Prentice-Hall, Inc., 1937.

Westerfield, R. B., *Our Silver Debacle*. New York: The Ronald Press Co., 1936.

Willis, J. B., *The Functions of the Commercial Banking System*. New York: King's Crown Press, 1943.

Youngman, A., *The Federal Reserve System in Wartime*. National Bureau of Economic Research, 1945.

43 · THE INVESTMENT MARKET AFTER 1919

THE END OF WORLD WAR I found the organization of the investment market strengthened as a result of floating large amounts of government bonds. Moreover, the widespread holding of these bonds had accustomed many small investors to purchasing and holding securities instead of making deposits in savings banks, and the methods used by the Treasury in selling the bonds ("Borrow and Buy") had accustomed individuals of relatively low income to purchasing securities on credit.

The strong organization of the investment market was enhanced by the relatively strong position of the economy as a whole. The war period and the immediate postwar period were marked by a great expansion of industry and agriculture as the United States was called upon to feed and equip her allies during the war, and her former enemies as well as allies after the war. National income had increased with rising employment. Prices had risen during the war and continued to rise at a still more rapid rate after the war until May of 1920. Farm lands increased in value as the price of raw materials and foodstuffs rose. Business firms were expanding and were anxious to obtain the funds that they had been unable to raise while the war was in progress. The stage was therefore set for an expansion of activity in the investment market.

The expected boom did not at once get under way, however, because of a decline in prices, production, and employment that occurred in the early part of 1920 and was accompanied by a sharp decrease in the volume of new securities put on the market. It was not until 1922 that the volume of new corporate issues began to rise, and every year thereafter there was an increase until 1929. The total of all new issues, which had stood at 4.4 billion dollars in 1919, had passed that figure by 1922, after the short depression of 1920-21, and reached a high point of 11.5 billions in 1929. Nearly two-thirds of all the issues were offered by corporate borrowers, including investment trust offerings and refunding issues. The Federal Government was practically out of the market throughout this period, and state and municipal borrowings accounted for only one-sixth.[1]

1 Board of Governors of the Federal Reserve System, *Banking and Monetary Statistics*, p. 487. Washington, D. C.: 1943.

The remaining sixth of the issues during these eleven years emanated from foreign sources, and consisted of borrowing that in large part paid for the purchases of American goods by customers abroad. The war-developed mechanism for bond distribution in the United States was put to active use. Bond house representatives from this country toured the continents of Europe, Asia, also of South America, offering the opportunity, and sometimes giving inducements, to public officials to borrow on easy terms in the American market. The public at home, excited by the rise in stock prices, did not trouble to examine closely the offerings from abroad. In addition to the bonds actually floated in the United States, American investors purchased many securities originally offered abroad, and by 1929 were holding an amount of foreign securities estimated at 15 billion dollars.

Sales of foreign securities were only one phase of the boom of the 1920's. There was a boom in Florida real estate that attracted erstwhile stock market speculators as well as many inexperienced investors. This boom collapsed in 1926, pulling down with it a number of Florida banks. The speculators who retrieved their funds in time turned to the New York Stock Exchange where the increase in stock prices was already attracting attention. The average of 402 stock prices as computed by Standard and Poor (on a base of 1935-39 = 100) had stood at about 80 during 1919 and had fallen with commodity prices during 1920 and 1921. By the latter part of 1921 the average again turned upward and, except for a brief period in 1923, continued steadily and at times steeply towards a high point of 237 in September 1929, when the break in prices began. The turnover of securities was very rapid during the latter part of the boom, taxing the facilities of the Stock Exchange to the utmost, as buyers ignored the basic earning power of the stocks and considered only the possibility of buying one day and selling the next day at a higher price.

Some of the responsibility for the unhealthy development of this boom must be placed upon the great increase in call loans on security collateral by which brokers financed the transactions of their customers. Such loans had long been made by New York banks for their out-of-town correspondents,[2] and during this period they were made also for the account of corporations. This added further instability to an already top-heavy financial structure, since on the first hint of a decline in stock prices the lending corporations withdrew their funds from the market without warning, leaving the banks with the full burden of carrying their broker customers as best they could. The decline in prices, once started, was therefore more precipitous than it would otherwise have been. The Securities Exchange Act of 1934 forbade brokers to borrow on call from any but member banks, and thus took corporate funds out of the call loan market.

---

2 See Chapter 29.

There was another link between the investment market and the commercial banks in this period that was no more fortunate in its effects than the call loan. This was the security affiliate, or investment banking corporation, which was usually owned by the shareholders of the commercial bank, but which could nevertheless engage in underwriting and distribution of new issues without any of the restrictions to which the commercial bank was subject. The origin of such affiliates seems to have been the First Security Company, organized by the First National Bank of New York in 1908, with all of its capital stock owned by the shareholders of the mother bank. Other large banks followed this example, until by 1927 there were so many security affiliates that they were handling one-eighth of all originations of security issues, and by 1930, one-half.

The break in stock prices reduced the value of the securities owned outright by the affiliates, and also reduced their earning power by making new issues difficult to float. A commercial bank that found its affiliate in a difficult position was under heavy temptation to make loans to the affiliate on "frozen" stocks, and to help it out by purchasing such issues for the accounts in its trust department. The collapse of the United States Bank in New York City in 1930 and several other large failures in other cities, brought the matter of affiliates sharply to the attention of the banking authorities. As a result, the Banking Act of 1933 contained as one of its chief provisions a clause requiring all member banks to dispose of their affiliates within a year's time, and forbidding all investment banks to receive deposits. This dictum amounted to the complete separation of commercial and investment banking. Some of the older houses chose to retain the deposit side of their business. J. P. Morgan for example became a commercial bank and turned its investment business over to a firm consisting of former Morgan partners, Morgan, Stanley and Company. On the other hand Kuhn, Loeb and Company retained the investment business in which it had been engaged for three-quarters of a century and divested itself of its demand deposits.

It must not be thought that the United States was the only country which suffered an unhealthy postwar boom and slump. The great money markets of the world are closely linked, as may be seen in the career of the Swedish "Match King," Ivar Krueger. He had started life as a builder, but went into the match business in 1913. Under his management, the Swedish Match Company, owned by Kreuger and Toll, obtained a monopoly of match manufacture in 15 European countries, and *de facto* monopoly or market dominance in 24 others. His enormous wealth and financial power was extended into banking, real estate, telephones, iron and gold mining, and newspapers. He loaned 400 million dollars to 15 countries between 1926 and 1930, and on his favor virtually depended the life of governments. A total of 250 millions of Kreuger securities was floated in the United States, and his principal agents, the respected firm of Lee, Higginson in Boston, held eight millions. The debacle began when it was discovered in 1931 that nine million pounds of Italian bonds, which he had offered as security for a loan, were forgeries. When auditors began to go over the books of his companies with the care which should have been exercised earlier, it was found that his accounts had been juggled as early as 1923, that securities had been issued for non-existent companies, and that the whole great financial structure was built upon the myth of his probity. Kreuger committed suicide in Paris in 1932, but his death was of no avail to the companies that he dragged down with him.[3]

The Securities and Exchange Commission

In addition to the divorce of commercial and investment banking under the banking legislation of 1933-35, there were other clauses that directly affected the investment market. These gave power over margins for security trading to the Board of Governors of the Federal Reserve System, and permitted the Reserve Banks to limit the rediscounting of a member bank if it was too heavily involved in security loans. There still remained however a number of problems that did not fall within the province of the central banking authorities and were too urgent to be left to the voluntary action of the stock exchanges. A new device for direct control was therefore established by the Securities Act of 1933, the Securities Exchange Act of 1934, and the Public Utility Holding Company Act of 1935. Such direct control had some precedent in the "blue sky" laws of a number of states, beginning with that of Kansas in 1911. The Federal legislation did not follow the model of any state laws, but turned rather to the English Companies Act, in operation since 1900, which was based on the principle that adequate publicity for all pertinent facts is the best protection for the investor. The Securities Act of 1933 put into effect somewhat more drastic penalties on a somewhat wider group of responsible individuals than did the English law, and entrusted the administration of the Act to the Federal Trade Commission. After a great deal of discussion and criticism, the Act was amended in the Securities Exchange Act of 1934. The penalties were made less drastic and less widely applicable, and a special Securities and Exchange Commission was created to administer the law.

The larger security exchanges were required to register with this Commission and furnish information regarding their members, their rules, and their operations. By 1947 there were nineteen such exchanges, and there were in addition five exchanges exempt from registration because of their limited operations. New public offerings of securities had also to be registered with the Commission, except for Federal and state obligations, and those of railroads, which were under the control of the Inter-

[3] *Fortune* for May and June 1933 contains a detailed account of his widespread activities.

state Commerce Commission, and banks, which were under the control of Federal or state banking officers. Any small issue (at first defined as less than $100,000, later as less than $300,000) was also exempt from registration. After filing the registration statement, the investment banking house or consortium must wait for a maximum of twenty days while the Commission investigates the offering and makes any revisions in the statement. Then it may be offered to the public in an approved prospectus. Individual brokers are also subject to regulation by the Commission with the general object of maintaining a genuine market for securities without manipulation, wash sales, matched trading, or rigging of the market for the benefit of insiders. In 1939 the National Association of Security Dealers was established under the supervision of the Commission to give dealers a large measure of responsibility for self-regulation and to raise the level of competition within the market.

One of the important activities of the Securities and Exchange Commission was the carrying out of the provisions of the Public Utility Holding Company Act of 1935 requiring geographical integration and corporate simplification of public utility companies—the so-called "death sentence." The Act was passed in order to eliminate the obvious evils of such organizations as the "Insull Empire" which had reached their climax in the boom period. Samuel Insull Sr., after several years with the Edison Company of Chicago, organized the Middle West Utilities Company in 1912. He bought up a number of operating companies, combined them, organized holding companies for them, and regrouped them. Some of the operating companies were also holding companies of other holding and operating companies. The financial relationships became so confusingly crisscrossed that it was almost impossible to evaluate the real position of a company. The Insull organization finally included the brother and son of Samuel Insull Sr. and extended over a wide geographical and industrial area. It seemed to be enormously successful until the decline in security prices involved one of the constituent companies after another. Many of the transactions by which the Insull organization had been built up were not illegal under the legislation existing at the time, but the frantic efforts to save his wealth as his empire tottered led Insull to take steps that were viewed askance by the authorities. In order to avoid prosecution he fled the country in 1934 and died in Greece, a broken man.

Although the Act of 1935 had specified that all reorganizations were to be completed within two years, it was soon evident that a much longer period would be necessary to unscramble the complicated legal relations of the interlocked companies. The Associated Gas and Electric Company, for example, had twenty different classes of securities outstanding when the Act was passed. It was not until the late 1940's that the work was substantially completed. By that time it was generally admitted that the results had been beneficial, both to the corporations which had undergone a streamlining of their financial structure and to the investors whose holdings were greatly improved in quality. The consumer also benefitted by elimination of excessive service charges and high costs arising from uneconomic capital structures. Holding companies had sometimes been of service in the early days of the utility industry by providing small operating companies with expert guidance, but the large operating companies of modern times are not in need of outside financial or technical aid. The Act of 1935 does not affect the use of holding companies by industrial concerns.

Among the most controversial rulings of the Securities and Exchange Commission was that which required competitive bidding rather than direct negotiation with underwriters in connection with the issue of public utility securities. This device has been required in Massachusetts since 1919 for offerings of gas and electric company bonds, and since 1926 it has been required by the Interstate Commerce Commission for railroad equipment trust certificates, and since 1944 for railroad securities. It was therefore not an untried experiment when the Commission in June 1941 ruled that thereafter public utility issues should be offered under competitive bidding. Experience with this method has not yet yielded conclusive results as to its effect on monopoly control of investment banking and cost of securing new funds.[4]

Although at first there was suspicion on both sides and little disposition to cooperate, the financial community and the Commission soon realized that it was to their mutual interest to cooperate. The Commission's emphasis on sound capital structure and an amount of equity capital in proportion to indebtedness is in the long run beneficial to everyone. Problems connected with war financing, accounting practices, uniform reporting by corporations, and the like have been studied by joint committees of businessmen and Commission experts, to the advantage of both.

The Issuing of New Securities

The technique for placing new issues of securities in the hands of investors has continued to develop in response to changes in market conditions and in legislation. The main outlines of the method are fairly standardized, although the details vary. The investment market may be thought of as divided into underwriters, wholesale dealers, and retail dealers, although many firms act in more than one of these capacities. Very few issues are underwritten by one house acting alone. Usually a syndicate or group is formed, not only for the sake of reducing the liability of each house but also for the sake of ensuring a wider basis for

[4] A summary of the problems involved in competitive bidding may be found in an article, "Competitive Bidding in Sale of Securities," by Sidney M. Robbins in the *Harvard Business Review* for September, 1949.

distribution. The house that takes the initiative in the organization of the group receives the fee for management, about one-fourth of a point, whether the issue is a success or not. The underwriters obtain their return on the transaction from a "spread" of two to four points which covers all costs of investigation and distribution as well as the risk of not being able to pass the issue on to the wholesale dealers promptly and at the desired price. Occasionally the issue is handled on a commission basis.

The underwriting houses must file a registration statement with the Securities and Exchange Commission, and await its approval before going on to the next step in the distribution, which is the organization of the selling group. The members of this wholesaling group are carefully chosen on the basis of their working capital, their standing in the market, and their past performance. In many cases an invitation to join the group is in the nature of a royal command, since refusal to participate in the less attractive offerings may mean exclusion from the next, possibly more lucrative, issue. Before 1933 the dealers in the selling group had a firm commitment to take a definite amount of the issue; since that date, under the new legislation, these dealers sell on commission, getting a lower return for their services but subjecting themselves to a smaller risk.

The third level in the distribution of the issue is reached when the bond houses of the selling group make their offer to dealers in their district, often by telegraph on the issue date. Under the new legislation, copies of the prospectus must accompany the offer to the dealers and must be made available to all prospective investors. The retail dealers, who may number several thousand for any one issue, then make the sales to the individuals, banks, trust companies, and other investors. The members of the original underwriting group frequently support the market for a limited time by buying if the price starts to fall.

Concentration of Investment Banking[5]

The business of investment banking is inevitably concentrated in the larger cities of the country, especially in New York City. Many investment firms with a head office in New York have branches in Chicago, Boston, Philadelphia, San Francisco, and other places, while many firms with head offices in these cities have also a branch office in New York City, which has been the undisputed leader in the financial field for more than a century.

There is concentration of underwriting not only in New York, as compared with other cities, but also in a few firms in New York City. Of the $9,200,000,000 of securities issued for cash which were registered with the Securities and Exchange Commission between January 1934 and July

[5] The recent activities of the investment banking houses are described in detail in Parts 23 and 24 of the *Hearings before the Temporary National Economic Committee* of the Seventy-sixth Congress, Third Session, 1939-1941.

1939, 57 per cent were handled by 6 firms in New York City, and another 21 per cent by 14 other firms, making a total of 78 per cent, or more than three-quarters, handled in New York. Of the remaining 22 per cent, 12 per cent was accounted for by the 18 largest firms outside of New York, and the final 10 per cent was shared by all the other firms in the country. Morgan Stanley and Company was the largest single participant in the market during these years, accounting for nearly one-fourth of all the registered issues. In general, the higher the quality of the security issued, the larger the proportion handled by New York firms. The large and strong firms have the pick of the market, and the smaller firms outside New York take the local offerings. This situation prevails also with regard to the management of the issues; Morgan Stanley acted as manager for the issuing group of houses in four-fifths of the bond flotations of the 38 leading borrowers of that period, and no issue of these leading borrowers was managed by an underwriting firm outside of New York.

This concentration in the investment banking business continued to characterize the market in the decade that followed. Of the 254 well-recognized investment banking houses in the United States, 17 had handled two-thirds of all the business between 1936 and 1945, leaving only one-third to be shared by the remaining 237 houses. Thus was raised again the question of what constitutes monopoly and how it can be most effectively dealt with.[6]

The problem in banking, as in industry, is largely one of optimum size of firm. The large investment banking houses that can handle the larger issues have an important advantage over smaller firms, since the cost of flotation of new issues varies inversely with the size of the issue. A study made by the Securities and Exchange Commission of 715 new issues marketed in 1945 through 1947 indicates that, for issues of less than half a million dollars, the total cost of flotation reached the high figure of 24 per cent of the proceeds, of which 20 per cent was commission and discount. As the size of the issue increased the proportionate cost decreased, falling to 4.64 per cent of the proceeds for issues between five and ten millions in amount and to 1.23 per cent for issues of more than fifty millions. The average cost of flotation for all securities in the group was 2.83 per cent; 2.18 per cent of this cost represented commission and discount, .01 per cent represented expenses attributable to registration of the issue with the Securities and Exchange Commission, and the remaining .64 per cent represented miscellaneous expenses. The cost of flotation varied also with the type of security being offered, from 1.33 per cent of the gross proceeds for bond issues, to 4.16 per cent for preferred stock and 10.03 per cent for common stock. Although the cost of flotation still seems high, especially for smaller issues, it had declined by more than 50 per

[6] See Chapter 46 for discussion of this problem in connection with corporations.

cent for bond and preferred stock issues between 1939 and 1947, and by 45 per cent for common stock offerings.

Capital Funds for Small Business

The new issues that are underwritten by investment bankers, although comprising the most conspicuous part of the market, are not by any means the whole market and are outnumbered, although not outvalued, by the small issues that never appear in the central money markets at all. Small corporations would find it far too expensive to raise their capital funds through the specialized investment banking houses, and the bankers themselves would find it not worth their while to handle such small issues.

Moreover, although the corporate form of organization is used by nearly all large and many small business enterprises, the partnership and individual enterprise forms are still used by an enormous number of small concerns, especially in the retail and service lines. They need relatively small amounts of capital funds but the obtaining of even those small amounts is often a serious matter. Since the great financial markets cannot help him, the small businessman is thrown back upon local resources and finds only too often that the locality in which there is the greatest opportunity for small industry is the very one in which local savings are inadequate to finance him.

Banks have been sometimes criticized for their unwillingness to aid in providing capital funds for small local borrowers. In general, the history of bank failures would seem to indicate that commercial banks have rather erred on the side of too great leniency in making long-term loans for capital purposes. It is no solution of the problem to foist it upon institutions unfitted by their very nature to handle it. Commercial banks, which have primarily demand obligations to meet, must maintain their assets in short form if they are to avoid failure. The volume of term loans made by commercial banks has increased in recent years and thus provided capital funds for business. Such loans, however, are usually made to large corporations. The loans of mutual savings banks are restricted by law in most states to the more conservative forms of highly rated bonds and mortgages, but some small businessmen are able to give mortgage security, which makes it possible for them to borrow. The banking legislation of 1933-35 integrated the savings banks into the banking system of the country by granting them the privilege of membership in the Federal Reserve System and the Federal Deposit Insurance Corporation. Building and loan associations and other similar institutions function in much the same way as the savings banks, accepting small sums from many individual savers and making them available to borrowers. These associations were organized to meet the need for loans on mortgages to homeowners, but they serve also the small business that can borrow in that form. Their usefulness has fluctuated widely from one period to another; they were very active during the real estate booms of the 1890's, the early 1900's, and the 1920's, but less important in the intervening years.

The available facilities are still inadequate to meet the genuine need of small business for capital funds. Because of the failure of private enterprise to solve the problem, the Federal Government has made several attempts to fill the gap, either by the creation of special institutions or by widening the scope of institutions created originally for another purpose. In the first category are the various agricultural credit banks and mortgage credit institutions that have been of great service to farmers and small homeowners but to few businessmen. In the second category falls such legislation as the permission granted to Federal Reserve Banks after 1932 to lend directly to businessmen if the latter could give evidence of sound credit but inability to borrow elsewhere. Many applications were made to the Reserve Banks under this legislation but few loans were made, and it became evident that the inability of most applicants to borrow elsewhere had been due to poor credit standing rather than to the lack of lending institutions.

The Reconstruction Finance Corporation was created in 1932 with its capital stock of half a billion dollars subscribed entirely by the United States Treasury. It was designed to fight the depression by making direct loans to, or by purchasing the obligations of, any business enterprise that could not obtain long or short term funds from private sources. In its early years it functioned chiefly as a lender to large banks, insurance companies, and railroads. During the war its powers and activities were enormously extended, largely by means of a host of subsidiary corporations organized for specific war purposes, such as the Rubber Reserve Corporation. Although the greater amount of the funds loaned by the R.F.C. went to large enterprises, the number of loans made to small firms was very large. Nearly half of all the loans made up to 1945 were for $10,000 or less, while 90 per cent of all loans were for less than $100,000. The total of such loans authorized was nearly $400,000. In 1945 a new device was put into operation, the Blanket Participation Agreement, under which the R.F.C. guaranteed 75 per cent of the amount of the loan made by a commercial bank to a small business. Nearly one-half billion dollars was loaned to small business under this arrangement before it was abolished in January, 1947, although many of these loans were for short periods and did not meet the need for capital.

During the war a special agency, the Smaller War Plants Corporation, was set up by the government to provide funds needed by small businesses with war contracts. In the fiscal year 1944 a total of $135,000,000 was loaned, about three-fourths for working capital, and one-fourth for long term purposes. The functions of the Corporation were taken over by the R.F.C. in 1945. None of these efforts, in spite of their value, has solved the vital problem of aiding the small business to get equity capital without sacrificing control to those who supply the capital funds.

The Investment Market and the Second World War

As in every war in which the United States has engaged, the financing of the needs of the Treasury became a major preoccupation of the investment market, and the exigencies of the war left their mark upon the organization of the market. The war brought the national debt to a new high point of 278 billion dollars, and at the same time the offering of corporate securities was reduced to a negligible figure.

To offset the impossibility of raising new capital funds in the securities market, businessmen were enabled to finance a large part of the war production by direct loans from the government or its agencies, on short or long term, or by loans guaranteed by a government agency. For such loans it was unnecessary for the borrower to pass through the screening process ordinarily required by commercial and investment banks. Since the economic function of the bankers was thus reduced to a minimum, they were able to concentrate their energies on placing Treasury issues in the hands of private and institutional investors.

Institutional investors, especially the life insurance companies and the savings banks, which had always played an important role as suppliers of funds in the money market, continued this role in relation to the government debt. By 1948 the life insurance companies were holding more than one-third of the long term bonds, worth more than 15 billion dollars. Savings banks at that time held about 6 billions of the long term Treasury issues.

With Treasury issues playing so large a part in so many security portfolios, it was inevitable that the method of managing the debt in the years that followed the war should be watched with care and even with anxiety by the investment market. In order to keep the demand for capital funds by business enterprises from pushing up interest rates, a development which would have tended to depress the price of the government bonds since they bore a fixed return, the government agreed to buy all government bonds that were offered to the Reserve banks. This resulted at times in large holdings of long-term governments by the Reserve banks. As more remunerative issues came into the market, many institutional and private investors sold their government obligations in order to make a shift, and this increased the downward pressure on the bonds.

Since the debt was so large, the policy of the Treasury with regard to refunding and repayment was also of vital concern to the investment market. In the first three years after the war, partly because of large balances still held by the Treasury on current account and partly because of budgetary surpluses, it was possible to reduce the total of the outstanding debt by about ten per cent. The petering-out of the inflationary boom during 1949 turned the budget surplus into a deficit and made it clear that continued debt reduction would be difficult.

Sources and Uses of Capital Funds

Individual investors continue to furnish a large part of the funds needed by business enterprise to maintain and expand the industrial plant, the basis for the stream of goods and services that comprises our national income. The sale of government securities during World War II, as in World War I and the Civil War, gave an impetus to individual ownership of government bonds that carried over after the war into a stimulus to own other bonds and stocks. Few small investors hold real estate mortgages, although these were formerly considered the typical and appropriate medium for them. Some corporations and particularly the public utilities, which are desirous of cultivating good public relations, make a special point of encouraging small investors and rewarding their attendance at stockholders meetings by special attention and recognition. The American Telephone and Telegraph Company boasts of the fact that there are 765,800 owners of its stock, and the Du Pont Company made a public ceremony of the purchase of its shares by the millionth shareholder.

An interesting new feature in the investment activity of the small investor was the rise of the investment trust. This type of corporation had developed in England during the last third of the nineteenth century, but did not become popular in the United States until after World War I. The management trust, the preferred form in this country, issues its own stock and places the proceeds in all kinds of securities at the discretion of the trust managers; in this way the owner of a share of investment trust stock spreads his risk by owning a cross section of many different kinds of issues. Unfortunately, some of the investment trusts became involved in the hysteria of the 1920 boom period and did not survive the crash, but the more conservatively managed were able to keep going during the depression years and become a permanent addition to investment facilities. Under the Investment Company Act of 1940 they are required to register with the S.E.C.

Many individuals still prefer to make their savings in the form of deposits in savings banks or of life insurance policies. These savings banks and life insurance companies, along with charitable and religious foundations, are thus enabled to channel large amounts of funds into business uses by their purchase of securities. Their importance in the government bond market has already been indicated. Total assets of the legal reserve life insurance companies in the United States in 1948 amounted to $56 billions, of which more than one-third was invested in securities of business and industry. The state laws under which insurance companies operate regulate their investments very strictly, giving preference to bonds rather than to stocks because the latter do not have a guaranteed rate of return. Laws regulating investments of savings banks have the same effect. One result of the increase in assets of these institutions has been, therefore, to discriminate against equity issues (common and preferred stock) in favor of bonds that represent corporate debt.

The great amount of funds at their disposal—one large company sometimes has a million dollars of new funds to be invested each day—gives them an enormous amount of influence in the investment market. It was formerly the custom for insurance companies like other investors to make their purchases of securities through the regular channels, but in recent years it has become common for insurance companies to buy up whole new issues of securities directly from the borrowing corporation, even bidding against the investment bankers in some cases. In October, 1941, the American Telephone and Telegraph Company asked for competitive bids on its $90 million offering of debenture bonds. Two groups of investment bankers entered bids but saw the whole issue taken by a group of insurance companies that had been able to outbid them. In other cases the insurance companies lend directly to industrial concerns with investment bankers playing the part of intermediary, as in the $20 million loan made to the Continental Can Company in 1949 by insurance companies through Goldman, Sachs and Company. In some recent years the total of this type of private financing has amounted to more than one-third of all corporate financing.

In addition to the funds provided by investors, individual and institutional, business enterprises use very large amounts of capital funds provided out of their own earnings. The large automobile manufacturers have increased their capital stock very largely by plowing back their own earnings into the business. By means of stock dividends the original investors have found their holdings greatly increased, although they have done no conscious saving or investing. This tendency to reinvest corporate earnings rather than to pay them out to stockholders in cash dividends seems to be increasing, perhaps because of the Federal tax laws that set high surtax rates on personal income and lower rates on long-term capital gains, perhaps also because reinvestment is easier and less costly than flotation of new stock issues in the open market. In 1929 two-thirds of the earnings of non-financial corporations were paid out as dividends, in 1939 almost three-fourths, in 1946 slightly more than half, and in 1947 less than forty per cent.

As a result of this conservative dividend policy, the corporations have a better ratio of equity to debt than they had just before the war, in spite of an increase in the dollar total of their debt. The volume of new securities issued in the postwar years increased rapidly, even though it did not reach the peaks of the 1927-29 boom.

Another source of relatively long-term funds for business is the so-called "term loan" made by commercial banks for periods of three to ten years.

These loans are usually made to large borrowers with first-class credit standing, and in such large amounts that a group of banks will often be involved, or a group of banks with one or more insurance companies.

Conclusion

It is clear that a considerable portion of the capital funds needed by the business community is now provided in ways that by-pass the investment banker. The earlier tendency to blame this situation on the Securities and Exchange Commission has largely given way to a realization that the whole economic situation has changed and that the good old days of the investment market are probably gone forever. The ability of many large corporations to finance themselves out of their own profits, or by private placements with insurance companies, or through long term loans from commercial banks has eliminated a large part of the demand for the services of the investment banker. The real need for such service arises among the smaller business enterprises, which have always had difficulty in providing themselves with capital. The role of the investment banker in the industrialization of the American economy was an important one, but changing conditions require a new type of service if the savings of the future are to be put at the disposal of the industries that promise most for the production of socially useful commodities.

Selected References

GENERAL WORKS

Berle, A. A., and Gardiner C. Means, *The Modern Corporation and Private Property*. New York: Commerce Clearing House, Inc., 1932.

Bonbright, James C., and Gardiner C. Means, *The Holding Company*. New York: McGraw-Hill Book Company, Inc., 1932.

Ripley, William Z., *Main Street and Wall Street*. Boston: Little, Brown and Company, 1927.

Fundamentals of Investment Banking. Sponsored by the Investment Bankers Association of America. New York: Prentice-Hall Inc., 1949.

SPECIAL TOPICS

Annual Reports of the Securities and Exchange Commission, starting with 1934.

Hearings before the Temporary National Economic Committee of the 76th Congress, 3rd Session. Part 10, "Life Insurance." Parts 23, 24, "Investment Banking."

Allen, Frederick Lewis, *The Lords of Creation*. New York: Harper and Brothers, 1935.

44 · LABOR

The Pre-New Deal Period

As shown in Chapter 30, organized labor fared well in the "artificial" environment of World War I when the demand for labor rose much faster than the supply (immigration having ceased and many able-bodied workmen having entered the armed forces). Unions expanded rapidly in membership and power, a fair percentage of the gain coming among the hitherto untouched (some critics were unkind enough to say "untouchable") unskilled class. In large part, employers abandoned their anti-union tactics during this period, and union leaders were members of the councils that advised government officials about prosecution of the war on the home front.

After the armistice there were almost two years of severe price inflation. Unions held and increased their wartime gains and total membership rose to above 5 millions in 1920. But in that period of labor unrest caused by the rapidly rising cost of living, there were ominous forebodings of what was to happen to the labor movement in the "natural" environment of the next decade or so. First, there were two great labor conflicts in 1919 —the steel strike and the coal strike. The basic steel industry had long been regarded (since the Homestead strike) as a citadel in the defense of the country's big manufacturing industries against unionization and against collective bargaining between unions and employers. The steel companies were foremost among the proponents of the so-called "open shop" (a term that, although ostensibly used to designate a condition under which union members and non-unionists worked harmoniously and democratically together for a benevolent employer, actually cloaked a situation in which an anti-union employer was free to weed unionists out of his plant and operate without collective bargaining). Some fifteen unions of the A.F. of L. banded together to unionize the racially conglomerate work force of the steel industry, concentrating mainly on the United States Steel Corporation. Apart from vigorous efforts of the steel companies and local government agencies to break the strike and apart from the problem of communicating with and uniting these immigrant groups of varying languages and backgrounds, the conditions were propitious. The demand for steel labor was high and there were significant issues for arousing the workers, such as the exhausting twelve-hour day and the poor working and living conditions. But the A.F. of L. unions were not up to the task. In the face of the above-mentioned unfavorable conditions the drive fell apart from lack of unity among the participating unions, lack of financial resources, and lack of imagination and energy.

In the same year the coal strike, conducted by durable, experienced, united leaders and members of the United Mine Workers, was also lost. This time the cause was the government. Under the still-existing war powers, Federal Judge Anderson issued a memorable injunction forbidding most of the activities (even to the payment of strike dues) that are necessary to success in striking.

These two big labor upheavals raised public apprehension over the matter of unionism. The public had recently also been disturbed by the strikes and unrest caused by the I.W.W. during the war. Added to these causes of anxiety was the post-war spread of "radicalism" in Europe, centering mainly, of course, in the new Bolshevik state, the Soviet Union. A "red scare" developed in the United States, with witch-hunting on a considerable scale led by Attorney General Palmer.

This scare, together with the steel and coal victories, fortified most of the employers in manufacturing and metal-mining in their resolve to resist unionism. There was further fortification from government. Kansas passed a compulsory arbitration law for public-interest industries in 1920. In 1917 the United States Supreme Court, in a case arising long before the war in the nonunion West Virginia coal fields, had declared it unlawful for union organizers to try to get nonunion workers to break their so-called "yellow-dog" contracts with employers. (These contracts required that, as a condition of obtaining and retaining employment, a worker signed an agreement not to join or help organize a union.) This decision strengthened one of the principal anti-union weapons. Then, in the midst of the 1921 depression, came two other Supreme Court decisions that left unionists in no doubt as to whose ally this branch of government was. So far as organized labor was concerned, Congress' friendliness in passing Sections 6 and 20 of the Clayton Act (which, it will be remembered, presumably legalized peaceably conducted strikes and secondary boycotts in labor disputes broadly defined) was wholly nullified in the *Duplex* case (where a boycott of printing presses had been made effective in New York City by a machinists' union that had struck the manufacturer in Michigan) and in the *American Steel Foundries* case (where mass picketing in furtherance of a strike had occurred).

Perhaps nowhere was the adamant anti-union attitude of most employers more pointedly revealed than at the national labor-management conferences called by President Wilson in 1919 and 1920 for the purpose of developing constructive principles and procedures of sound, harmonious labor relations for the postwar years. The employer and union delegates to these conferences split wide apart over the issue of union recognition and collective bargaining versus the open shop.

Of all the early postwar events unfavorable to unionism, the rather severe (if relatively brief) depression of 1921 possibly did the movement the most immediate injury. In this period of unemployment and reduced worker incomes, union membership fell off sharply, perhaps mainly among the recently organized unskilled laborers. Many additional employers declared for the open shop. Thus was the usual story of unions during depressions retold.

Ordinarily, in previous decades, business recovery had brought union recovery. It was not so this time. When economic activity became high-level again in 1923, total union membership was about 3.6 millions. By 1929, after seven fat business years, the total was about 0.2 millions less. Existing union strength was concentrated in certain industries—such as railroad train operation, water transportation, street railways, construction, coal mining, and, within the manufacturing group, clothing and printing. But most of metal mining and almost the entire field of large-scale mass-production manufacturing—steel, automobiles, rubber, petroleum refining, chemicals, metal fabricating, lumber, and textiles, for example—were nonunion.

The main reason for this "stagnation" of the labor movement has already been suggested—employer opposition, with considerable assistance to employers from government. This continued throughout the decade. Employers' positions were strengthened by a greatly accelerated rate of invention and technological change; improvements in production methods further diluted or altered skills, making it easier for employers to dismiss union members and hire nonunionists. Part of the technological development came in the field of human relations. The techniques of so-called "personnel management" and industrial psychology, which had received much stimulus in the selection and training of soldiers during the war, came to have important peacetime uses. The smarter firms adapted them to industrial uses for the purpose of making more careful selection of employees and for maintaining them in contentment on their jobs. These techniques could be used effectively and subtly against unionism in two ways: (1) to keep unionists out as employees, and (2) through various "welfare" measures (such as employee representation plans or "company unions," bowling leagues, soft-ball teams, pensions, group insurance, and housing), to make existing employees so well satisfied that they would not care to join unions. (Wage-rate increases were also sometimes part of the drive to take workers' minds off unionism.)

As already suggested, the structural and functional responses of unionism to this environment were inadequate for progress and barely enough for survival or maintenance of the status quo in the industries where craftsmen were still in a strategic position. There were a few unions, such as those in men's and women's clothing, that developed new policies and techniques for winning and holding new members and for gaining and retaining recognition from employers. These unions duplicated and even improved on employers' "welfare" programs; that is, by means of such measures as workers' education, housing, banks, recreation centers, medical and dental service, and summer camps these unions tied their members loyally to them by filling almost every corner of their lives and providing outlets for almost all the basic human drives. As the Amalgamated Clothing Workers demonstrated in their unionization of the nonunion Philadelphia market, these unions had learned smart new tactics for limiting employers' alternatives, while broadening their own alternatives and developing a favorable attitude on the part of the public. But such things were exceptional. That the organizational and functional devices of craft unionism were obsolescent in respect to the task of organizing the big manufacturing and metal-mining industries cannot be doubted. Moreover, the attitude of the public as a whole remained in general hostile to unionism, being fed from material supplied by both pro- and anti-labor critics of the union movement. It was a rare month when some story of labor extortion or racketeering, lack of democracy within unions, or jurisdictional bickering and strikes between craft unions was not told to the public. Much too often these stories appear to have been true.

One matter that received favorable publicity and attention was union-management cooperation. This term referred to joint programs worked out by local unions and their employers for the purpose of improving production methods and efficiency, thereby lowering costs, improving the employers' competitive positions in the product markets, and increasing the employment opportunities and security of the union members. This was undoubtedly a constructive, socially beneficial development—a far cry from other unions' policies of output-restriction and of opposition to technological advancement. Unfortunately, it was practiced by only a very small minority of local units of national unions. There were some notable examples, as in the shops of the Baltimore and Ohio Railroad and in a number of textile and hosiery mills, but by and large the actual application of union-management-cooperation principles was extremely limited, being confined almost entirely to partially unionized, rather competitive industries in which the job security of union members depended importantly on the ability of union-recognizing employers to develop some offset to the competitive advantage enjoyed by nonunion employers because of the latters' much greater freedom to reduce wage rates.

Another noteworthy, constructive functional feature of unionism in the twenties was the A.F. of L.'s enunciation of a "social wage policy." This policy emphasized labor's wish to raise the incomes of union-members in proportion to the increases in the national income occasioned by productivity-raising technological improvements. The A.F. of L. did not care who was responsible for the technological and output gains; it wanted the members of its constituent unions to share in them. But no noteworthy practical techniques were developed for measuring and sharing these gains.

The political program of organized labor remained, in general, as it was in recent decades. True, just after the war, when the government had virtually taken over the railroads, the Railway Brotherhoods came out for permanent government ownership and operation of the lines. The Mine Workers similarly wanted nationalization of the mines, and the A.F. of L. in general talked about nationalizing all public utilities. But these proposals met with only hostility from the rest of the nation and came in time to be dropped by labor itself. With respect to political parties, the A.F. of L. maintained its traditional policy of not tying itself to any one group, choosing, rather, to elect friends and purge enemies from all parties. With respect to the legislation to be sought from friendly legislators, the program was also, with one exception, the traditional one—pass laws to curb the courts and pass laws to curb the wage competition of the hard-to-organize. In short, give us no help except that which we need in order to be able to help ourselves. The exception was in the field of old-age security; by 1927 the A.F. of L. was forced to admit that the old-age benefits systems of its unions were entirely inadequate to cope with the income problems of superannuated union members and that a government system would have to be developed.

It was during this decade that international communism made its appearance in the American labor movement. This is the form and direction of labor radicalism that by 1949 (and actually much earlier) had come for the most part to supplant all other kinds of revolutionary unionism in America. During most of the twenties the official "line" was to bore from within the existing conservative unions in an effort to elect communist party members or sympathizers to important policy positions within these unions, to make the unions adopt more progressive and militant policies, and to instil class-consciousness among the rank and file. There were fair-sized communist minorities in some of the unions—in clothing, textiles, and lumber, for example—and these were given organizational direction through the Trade Union Educational League. These minorities became sufficiently vocal and annoying to lead the conservative majorities to conduct purges in 1926 and 1927. As a result of the expulsions, the communist leaders were compelled in 1928 to form a separate, rival federation of labor. But, in this form, "commy" unionism turned out to be almost wholly ineffective.

To sum up the position of organized labor in the twenties, it may be said that, while the country as a whole was completing its transition from the horse-and-buggy era to the automobile age, the labor movement as a whole—though undeniably handicapped by employer opposition and government unfriendliness, with some notable exceptions—remained in the horse-and-buggy stage.

Then came the great depression. The events of this period of economic cataclysm may well have done more than the happenings of any other time to change the face of American unionism and to make it what it is today—a big, powerful economic-political force. One of the most important things that happened by the end of 1932, when unemployment had reached the staggering total of 15 millions or about 30 per cent of the national labor force, was a de-deification of the American big business man, a questioning of the rightness of his attitudes and decisions on many matters, including those on labor unions. All groups, including most of the business community itself and most of the members of the political party in power, participated in this questioning. There is some indication also that important parts of the organized labor movement were questioning the wisdom of their own previous policies. Moreover, many workers were questioning why they should not be free to organize unions.

Perhaps the chief piece of evidence on the changing attitude of the public toward unionism during these last months of the pre-New Deal period was the enactment in 1932 of the Norris-La Guardia Act by the Republican-controlled Congress. There had been a forerunner to this event in 1926 and 1930. In 1926 the Congress passed the Watson-Parker Act, dealing with labor relations on interstate railroads, where unionization had been almost complete in train operation but very spotty in maintenance and repair. One significant provision was aimed at banning the employers' anti-union activities, such as the previously legalized and protected yellow-dog contract. Railroad companies were forbidden to discriminate, in hiring or firing, against employees who joined or organized unions for the purpose of collective bargaining. There had been a similar provision in the Erdman Act of 1898 for railroads. The Supreme Court had invalidated it, however, in the case of *Adair* vs. *U.S.* But in 1930 the court reversed itself; in the *Texas and New Orleans Railroad* case it upheld the protective clauses of the Watson-Parker Act.

This decision was encouraging to those favoring the enactment of the Norris-La Guardia Act. It showed that even that ultimate legislator, the United States Supreme Court, was being affected by the change in men's thinking. The Act stated it to be public policy that workers should be free to unionize. It forbade Federal courts to issue injunctions protecting employers' use of yellow-dog contracts and, by various substantive and procedural provisions, it sought (1) to undo most of the previous nullification by courts of the labor provisions of the Clayton Act, which had legalized peaceably conducted strikes and boycotts in labor disputes broadly defined, and (2) to remedy a number of other abuses into which the use of the labor injunction had fallen, such as "blanket" provisions, acceptance of *ex parte* evidence, and too easy issuance.

This Act was not enough to assuage the distaste of the voters for the political party under which economic catastrophe had befallen the country. In November, 1932, the Republicans were voted out of office. The New Deal was about to take over.

The New Deal Period

The trend that had begun in the last days of the Republicans was greatly accelerated under the Democrats. The first half of the thirties clearly marks a momentous shift in the attitude of government toward unionism. A century and a half before, government's attitude had been one of suppression. During the previous century the attitude may be said to have been one of toleration. But now it was to be one of encouragement. Whereas previously government officials' hearts in the main had bled for employers, now for many years they were for the most part to bleed for labor. All branches of government exhibited this new point of view, but the change seems to have been most marked in the administrative branch.

In the early days of the New Deal there was no noteworthy alteration in employers' attitudes toward unionism. Here and there came a defection from the ranks of the anti-union group, but it took about five years for most of them to be convinced that the tide had turned for an indefinite period and that consequently they had better learn to live with their labor partners.

Early in 1933 the National Industrial Recovery Act was passed to help bring the country back from the state of economic-financial collapse into which it had fallen at the time President Roosevelt was inaugurated. One of its sections (*7a*) was a forerunner of what was to come. Section *7a* repeated in essence the policy previously enunciated for railway workers in the Watson-Parker Act of 1926 and in the public-policy statement of the Norris-La Guardia Act of 1932. Under its stimulus a number of unions launched vigorous and successful organizing movements. Conspicuous among these was the drive of John L. Lewis, president of the United Mine Workers, whose membership—as a result of the competitive pressure of non-union operators during the twenties, the competition of other sources of energy, and the later depression conditions—had fallen to an unprecedented low of less than 100,000. By 1934 virtually all the mines had been rewon to unionism and the membership was close to 500,000.

Many other unions, however, did not do so well, partly because of their own ineptitude or lack of interest, partly because of continued employer opposition, and partly because the N.I.R.A. provided no adequate means for enforcing the policies stated in Section *7a*. In 1935 two new events of great moment for organized labor took place. In that year, after the Supreme Court junked the N.I.R.A. (for reasons not directly connected with labor matters), the Congress passed the National Labor Relations Act, and, when it became clear that the Executive Council of the A.F. of L. did not intend to try seriously to unionize the big nonunion manufacturing and metal-mining industries, John L. Lewis of the Miners and seven other union presidents formed within the A.F. of L. a Committee for Industrial Organization to undertake the task.

The National Labor Relations Act of 1935, as it was conceived by its sponsors and as it was administered by labor's friends on the National Labor Relations Board, was one statute that truly deserved to be called the Magna Charta of organized labor. It contained two main sets of provisions. (1) Upon complaint by unions and after hearings by the Board, the Board was authorized to issue cease-and-desist orders to employers found guilty of the unfair labor practices of interfering with the freedom of workers to form unions, discriminating in hiring, firing, or tenure, against union members, fostering or dominating labor organizations (this was the anti-company union clause), or refusing to bargain collectively with a bona fide, duly certified labor organization. In cases of noncompliance with its orders the N.L.R.B. was empowered to obtain enforcement from an appropriate federal Circuit Court of Appeals (here were "teeth" at last). (2) On its own motion or upon request by a union, the N.L.R.B. was authorized to hold a secret, free election among an employer's workers to determine or "certify" which union, if any, was the proper representative of the workers for collective dealing with the employer.

The C.I.O. was formed because the A.F. of L. majority (composed of craft unionists) refused to take advantage of the organizing opportunities afforded by the successive favorable statutes culminating in the N.L.R.A. The craft unionists refused to surrender their jurisdictional rights in the highly mechanized mass-production industries, while the progressives headed by Lewis argued that the inclusive *industrial* form of union organization was much more appropriate than a conglomeration of loosely federated crafts. Calling upon the combined financial and human resources of the eight member unions, the C.I.O. set up a number of organizing committees for these industries, concentrating first on basic steel. New organizing methods were employed with marked success. In 1936 the A.F. of L. suspended most of the C.I.O. unions, the suspension taking effect at the local and state levels as well as at the national. But the C.I.O. members were undeterred from their task.

The year 1937, the least unfavorable in a decade of economic depression and stagnation, was another notable one in American labor history. There were at least four major events. First, the National Labor Relations Act was declared constitutional by the Supreme Court in the *Jones &*

Laughlin case. Many anti-union employers, on advice of counsel, had been disregarding the Act's provisions in the belief that it would be held invalid. Now the supreme authority on such matters had spoken. Second, a month earlier the United States Steel Corporation, the very core of the country's previous anti-unionism, agreed, without one shot being fired, to bargain collectively with the steel union. The psychological impact of this about-face was shattering. The same year witnessed the capitulation of another major industry, automobiles. Third, there were many union-employer contests in which shots *were* fired. The steelworkers' union fought a very difficult and unsuccessful battle with the big "independent" steel companies during a series of bitter strikes in the summer. This also was the year in which the new techniques of slow-downs and sit-down strikes were most widely practiced. In the end, in spite of court disapproval of the sit-downs and in spite of other temporary reversals, the unions were victorious. Fourth, peace negotiations between the A.F. of L. and the suspended C.I.O. unions to work out arrangements whereby the labor movement might be united on mutually accepted principles of structure and function broke down. This had three main results. (1) In self-defense the A.F. of L. was compelled to try to organize the mass-production industries itself. Willy-nilly it usually had to accept the industrial form of unionism. (2) The Committee for Industrial Organization was forced to organize its members into a rival federation of labor, known now as the Congress of Industrial Organizations. (3) The National Labor Relations Board, employers, and the general public got caught between the rival claims and drives of the two federations. The provisions of the N.L.R.A. came to be used as much for settling disputes between the A.F. of L. and the C.I.O. as for handling issues between organized labor in general and employers.

The Congress of Industrial Organizations developed internal organizational and governmental forms not very different from those of the A.F. of L. The C.I.O. is a federation mainly of industrial unions. Legislative work is accomplished at the annual convention. Administrative and judicial functions are performed by an executive board. There are state and local councils that deal at these levels with the problems common to the C.I.O. local units in the respective areas.

It is in its functional aspects (objectives and tactics) that the C.I.O. came to differ most markedly from the A.F. of L. Like the latter federation, it accepted the private enterprise system and tried to practice the precepts of business unionism within it. But in general it appeared somewhat more militant, had a much larger communist-led element, and depended much more on government. With its main strength in the mass-production industries, where the unskilled and semi-skilled workers outnumbered the more strategically placed skilled craftsmen, it was unable or unwilling to utilize the restrictive (and occasionally racketeering) practices that characterized some of the A.F. of L. organizations. During its first five years most of the C.I.O.'s energies were devoted to organization drives, in which it not only showed uncommon imagination and vigor but also an unusual ability to use effectively for its purposes the administration of such statutes as the N.L.R.A., the Fair Labor Standards (Wage and Hour) Act, and the Walsh-Healey (government contracts) Act. The C.I.O. followed the A.F. of L. in its relation to political parties; that is, it too adopted the non-partisan principle and tried to elect labor's friends and defeat its enemies. But it spent much more effort on building effective organizations (political action committees) to get out and influence the vote than did the A.F. of L. at this time. And in general it was much more of an ally of the Democratic Party than was the rival federation.

By 1940 there were about nine million members in the ranks of American unions. Almost half of these were in A.F. of L. affiliates, about 40 per cent in C.I.O. unions, and a little more than 10 per cent in non-affiliated organizations. Thus, under the encouraging conditions of the New Deal, union membership almost trebled from 1932 to 1940, and most of the manual workers in the country's major industries were becoming organized.

The War Period and Its Aftermath

Great as were the numerical gains of organized labor by the end of the thirties and much as it grew in economic and political strength, there was one environmental condition lacking in those days, a condition that prevented even more sweeping conquests. This was a "tight" labor market, a condition of full employment. In 1940 there were still about 8 million unemployed—almost 15 per cent of the total labor force. In earlier years, except during the 1936-37 upswing, the percentage of unemployed had been even higher.

It is a commonplace that workers are more likely to organize when labor is relatively scarce, and this was the kind of labor market that existed throughout almost all of the forties. First came the defense program, with government beginning to supplement total private spending with large expenditures for war materials. By 1941, unemployment came to only about 5.5 million. Then came the war, with government spending on a staggering, unprecedentedly large scale. By 1944, with the greatly increased demand for goods and with about 12 million men withdrawn from the labor supply for service in the armed forces (and with these men not wholly replaced by the entrance of women into the labor market or by increases in labor productivity), unemployment had fallen to less than a million.

This sort of labor market continued during most of the months after the war through 1950. There was a short period of temporary increase in unemployment in the early part of 1946, when many firms paused in their operations to convert from war to peacetime productive equipment and products. There was also a temporary business recession during the first half of 1949, with a rise in unemployment. But in general the postwar years were high-employment ones; for the most part the total demand for products kept pace with the "natural" increase in the country's labor force.

Under these circumstances—and with no significant diminution in government encouragement of unionism—the A.F. of L., C.I.O., and unaffiliated unions prospered. By 1950 total union membership was about 15 millions, with roughly 50 per cent in the A.F. of L.'s affiliates, 30 per cent in the C.I.O. unions, and 20 per cent in the unaffiliated organizations.

The economic and political potency of organized labor rose with the increase in numerical strength. The ordinary middle-class citizen seemed to become aware for the first time of the existence and potency of big unionism and of the problems raised by its growth. Each of the ten largest unions had more than 300,000 members. Three had about a million or more. Their treasuries bulged with dollars counted in the millions. Seventy per cent and more of the employees in mining, manufacturing, construction, and transportation (plus public utilities) were working under collective-bargaining agreements. (As usual, the percentage of unionization in agriculture and in the white-collar fields of trade, finance, and public and private service were low—20 per cent or less.) Labor leaders were making, with appropriate publicity, pronouncements on various economic and political issues in the domestic and international areas. Nonpartisan political action was undertaken on an unprecedented scale, particularly by the C.I.O. and usually in behalf of Democratic candidates and proposals.

But the thing that seemed most to draw the attention of the man in the street to the new position of unionism was the ability of the big unions to shut down all or major portions of the country's basic industries. This economic power was first manifested in 1946, when there were more strikes, more strikers, and more man-days lost from strikes than in any other year of our history (including 1919, also a postwar year, which had previously led in these respects). The later years (1947-49) were also ones of uncommon labor conflict. The indirect effects, on employment and business, of stoppages in industries like coal and steel were also evident, if hard to measure. As a result, there was much questioning about how to make collective bargaining work in a manner that would eliminate such stoppages, and how to direct the power of unionism into channels that would be constructive in terms of the common welfare.

Broadly conceived, the problem of obtaining successful collective bargaining is the problem of developing successful, harmonious human relations between managerial personnel, who wish to be secure and free to organize the nonhuman and human factors of production, and union officials (from the shop representatives or stewards or business agents up to the top leadership) who wish to advance the economic interests of the membership, to keep themselves in power, and to obtain respected social status. These respective interests, sometimes identical and often conflicting, must be composed without substantial impairment of communication between management and the rank and file of employees and between union leaders and the rank and file of union members. Thus conceived, the problem of socially desirable collective bargaining involves much more than the successful negotiation, every year or two, of new labor contracts; it involves also living harmoniously together during the life of the contract.

The general problem can be better understood if two environmental conditions—one during the war and the other during the first few postwar years—are considered. Both had considerable influence on the course of collective bargaining during the forties.

Unionism had just come to many of the big, basic industries before the defense effort started. There had been very little time here to develop procedures, techniques, and attitudes for successful and harmonious living-together. Such things take time, and just at the time when such things might have gotten underway the war began. The country, desiring speedy total victory, could not afford to risk strikes in basic industries; the home front had to be stable, all out for continuous high production to support and supply the armed forces. Therefore, the government, recognizing the inevitability of inflationary pressures and knowing that price inflation brings labor unrest and low, interrupted production, resulting from high labor turnover (as workers shop around for higher-paying jobs) and from strikes (as workers quit collectively to enforce demands for higher pay), instituted price control through the Office of Price Administration and wage-rate control through the National War Labor Board. Recognizing also that price-wage rate stabilization would not itself be a complete guarantee against work stoppages, the President got management and unions voluntarily to agree to give up the strike and lock-out and other major forms of economic coercion in return for representation on the War Labor Board which, if government mediation failed, was in effect to act as an agency of compulsory arbitration for unsettled labor disputes.

Now this no-strike, no-lockout agreement and the creation of the N.W.L.B. meant in essence that, in the national interest, much of the collective bargaining that normally would have been successfully conducted day by day between the parties themselves would be carried on in Washington or in regional offices by the tripartite Board or its subsidiary regional counterparts. There would be some bargaining at the "bench level" of course, and there would be bargaining in Board offices by management and labor representatives on the Board, with the public members casting the deciding votes when necessary. But by and large there would not be the free, peacetime sort of relationship. In short, during the war many disputes came to the Board that ordinarily would have been settled at "home," peacefully or by economic force, and many times one side or the other came to the Board, believing that it could get a better break there than at home. Such practices meant the atrophying of the practices of two-party bargaining. In the newly organized industries, real collective bargaining had very little chance to develop normally.

Then came the second—the postwar—circumstance referred to above. There was a severe price inflation, and all the labor unrest and strife that had been controlled during the war broke out in the wave of strikes described above. After V-J day, in the fall of 1945, the War Labor Board—with the agreement, even urging, of most of its members—was abolished. In effect the wage-rate controls were largely removed (in spite of their nominal continuance under a Wage Stabilization Board), and the collective-bargaining game was given "back to the boys" in the hope that they would restore their collective-bargaining muscles and develop harmonious relations. But, with the removal of the product-price controls a year later and the resulting rises in living costs, there was much less restoration and development than had been anticipated.

There were other postwar obstacles to the growth of stable, equable labor relations. Most of these remained after the price inflation ended (at least temporarily) in 1949. And most of them were evident at the National Labor-Management Conference called by the President in November, 1945. The employer representatives at this Conference showed an attitude toward unions that was in marked contrast to the attitude of employer representatives at the Wilson conferences of 1919 and 1920. They indicated an acceptance of unionism and collective bargaining that was almost wholly absent 25 years before. But they did have some grievances against unions, and they wanted the union representatives to agree to redress the grievances, voluntarily or through legislation amending the National Labor Relations Act. The employers wished labor to agree to remedy abuses—such as strikes against the results of elections conducted by the National Labor Relations Board to determine the proper collective bargaining agency—which arose out of the A.F. of L.-C.I.O. conflict or out of jurisdictional disputes among A.F. of L. unions. Employers were tired of being innocently caught in the middle of rival union disputes. They also wished labor to limit its demands to items that would not further "infringe on the prerogatives of management," and they asked in general that unions be reasonable in the nature and number of their demands. Third, employers wished labor to cease its drive for industry-wide or multiple-employer bargaining; the employers wanted the bargaining area no broader than the individual company. Fourth, employers asked unions to agree to curb certain "unfair practices," such as the coercion of nonunionists into membership, the use of secondary boycotts, and bad-faith bargaining. Fifth, there was the question of what the proper role of government should be in respect to the handling of unsettled labor disputes in basic industries. Some employers wanted the government to have the power to settle such disputes.

The union representatives refused to give ground on these matters. Like the conferences of 1919 and 1920, the conclave of 1945 broke up without agreement on major issues. It will be seen, however, that, whereas 25 years earlier the basic employer-union issue was the desirability of unionism and collective bargaining, the fundamental cleavage of 1945 came on the nature and permissible scope of collective bargaining and union activities. There had been a notable change in the attitude of employers since 1919. Unionism had won an unprecedented degree of acceptance. But the possibility remained that failure to reassure and give security to employers on the matters troubling them might in the end lead them to revert to some form of anti-unionism.

Upon the break-up of the conference, each side had the alternatives of (1) trying to develop the kind of relations it desired through peaceful collective bargaining, or (2) trying to get what it wanted through economic and political pressure. As is usual in American democracy, each side tried some of each. The employers drew first blood in the political field. In the 1946 elections the Republicans wrested control of the Congress from the Democrats, and by 1947 there was on the statute books a National Labor Relations Act that had been significantly amended by the so-called Labor-Management Relations (Taft-Hartley) Act.

Organized labor (A.F. of L., C.I.O., and unaffiliated unions) were and continued to be united in bitter opposition to the amendments, which, employers claimed, would merely restore a measure of balance between management and organized labor. Employers argued that under government encouragement the pendulum had swung too far in favor of unions; the employers were now the underdog. Government must be neutral and evenhanded in union-employer relations. The power of each side must be kept in balance. This, they said, would truly be in the public interest.

The original Act of 1935, it will be remembered, had three main sets of provisions: (1) those empowering the N.L.R.B. to proscribe unfair labor practices of employers, (2) those empowering the Board to hold elections and certify the collective-bargaining agency in a bargaining unit or area determined by the Board, and (3) those enabling the Board to obtain enforcement of its orders and decisions in the Federal Circuit Courts of Appeals. The Act of 1947 substantially retained these provisions. The amendments of 1947 that are important here may be grouped under five heads: (1) limitations on what unions can do to exert pressure on employers, (2) limitations on what unions and employers can agree on, (3) limitations on unions' relations with individual workers, that is, with non-unionists and union members, (4) limitations on unions' exercise of political pressure, that is, on unions' influence on government, and (5) procedures for bringing the power of the Federal Government to bear on unsettled labor disputes affecting national safety and welfare.

Upon hearing after complaint by an aggrieved party, the N.L.R.B. was authorized to order unions (1) not to strike against an employer to obtain recognition if the union has not been chosen by a majority of voting employees themselves, (2) to stop refusing to bargain in good faith with employers, (3) to cease striking in behalf of a jurisdictional claim if the work has properly been assigned to another union, (4) to cease conducting secondary boycotts against employers' products, and (5) to cease exacting money from an employer for work not performed (featherbedding). In cases where termination or modification of an existing agreement were desired by unions, they were also required to give 60 days notice to employers and, if agreement on a new contract was not reached in 30 days, to notify Federal and state mediation agencies to that effect. Foremen and plant guards were also removed from the purview of the Act.

Unions and employers were forbidden to agree on a closed shop (under which only union members can be hired). Union shops (see below) were permitted only under certain conditions. Certain restrictions on welfare plans put still another limitation on what unions and employers might bargain about.

Non-unionists were protected by a statement establishing their freedom not to join unions. As just stated, the closed shop was banned, and the union shop (whereunder workers need not belong to unions to obtain jobs but must join the union after some such period as 30 days) was made allowable only if a majority of eligible voting employees chose such a shop in an election supervised by the N.L.R.B. The Act forbade unions to strike or otherwise coerce employers into discharging or refusing employment to nonunionists unless the latter had been expelled from the union for nonpayment of initiation fees or dues.

Union members were protected (1) directly by the Act's provision that dues or fees need not be paid in excess of amounts found reasonable by the N.L.R.B., and (2) indirectly by the above-mentioned provision that, if expelled for any reason other than nonpayment of dues, they need not lose their jobs.

The Act's limitation on union use of political pressure came in the section forbidding labor organizations (and business corporations) to make certain kinds of contributions and expenditures in Federal elections.

These, then, were the chief amendments aimed at redressing the balance of labor-relations power. That in the remaining years of the forties organized labor suffered a loss of strength because of these changes would be difficult to discover or prove. But labor did not cease to work for their elimination. By the end of 1950, however, the Congress had not altered the Act.

The N.L.R.A. attempted to handle unsettled "national-emergency" labor disputes by resort to delay or "cooling off," temporary Federal injunctions against work stoppages, and compulsory investigation of the dispute by *ad hoc* fact-finding boards, which were to have no power to make recommendations in respect to settlement. This measure was invoked by the President a number of times from 1947 to 1950, with fair success.

With or without the amended N.L.R.A., no one could say by 1950 that labor relations had reached a stage of reasonable stability and maturity. The issues that split the President's Conference of 1945 remained unresolved in the minds of management and unions. Unions were still afraid that employers had not been converted to the gospel of the labor movement. Unionism had come a very long way, indeed, from its humble beginnings. But there was still the feeling of insecurity, the lack of full social acceptance, the fear that employers (during the next depression or Republican administration) would backslide into union-smashing. On their side, employers also felt insecure. Unions were beginning to ask for things far beyond their demands during the horse-and-buggy days. Guaranteed annual wages, pensions, medical benefits, and a host of restrictions on freedom to manage—plus the C.I.O.'s outspoken desire to guide government policies on such matters as income taxation, control of the business cycle, and corporation price policies—were among the things that made management wary and fearful.

In short, by the end of the forties the development of harmonious relations and mutual good faith and confidence between employers and unions remained one of the major domestic problems of the country.

Selected References

Adamic, Louis, *Dynamite,* rev. ed. New York: Viking Press, 1934.

Bakke, E. W., and Clark Kerr, *Unions, Management, and the Public*. New York: Harcourt, Brace and Co., 1948.

Beard, Mary R., *A Short History of the American Labor Movement*. New York: G. H. Doran Co., 1924.

Brooks, R. R. R., *When Labor Organizes*. New Haven: Yale University Press, 1937.

Commons, J. R., *et al., History of Labor in the United States* (4 vols.), New York: The Macmillan Company, 1918-1935.

Dankert, C. E., *Contemporary Unionism in the United States*. New York: Prentice-Hall, Inc., 1948.

Gregory, C. O., *Labor and the Law,* revised and enlarged edition. New York: W. W. Norton & Co., 1949.

Hunter, Robert, *Violence and the Labor Movement*. New York: The Macmillan Company, 1919.

Lester, R. A., and Joseph Shister, eds., *Insights into Labor Issues*. New York: The Macmillan Company, 1948.

Miller, G. W., *American Labor and the Government*. New York: Prentice-Hall, Inc., 1948.

Perlman, Selig, *A History of Trade Unionism in the United States*. New York: The Macmillan Company, 1922.

———, *A Theory of the Labor Movement*. New York: The Macmillan Company, 1926.

Seidman, Harold, *Labor Czars*. New York: Liveright Publishing Co., 1938.

Seidman, J. I., *Union Rights and Union Duties*. New York: Harcourt, Brace and Co., 1943.

Slichter, S. H., *Union Policies and Industrial Management*. Washington, D. C.: The Brookings Institution, 1941.

———, *The Challenge of Industrial Relations*. Ithaca, N. Y.: Cornell University Press, 1947.

Taylor, G. W., *Government Regulation of Labor Relations*. New York: Prentice-Hall, Inc., 1948.

Twentieth Century Fund, *Collective Bargaining*. New York: 1941.

———, *Trends in Collective Bargaining*. New York: 1946.

45 · BUSINESS ORGANIZATION

IN TRADE, SERVICE AND, SOME BRANCHES of manufacturing the small business unit persisted, and the total number of such enterprises remained fairly constant from 1920 to 1950. But the progress of technology tended toward ever larger plants and companies. By 1930 the two hundred largest corporations in manufacturing and transportation came to produce more than half of these types of goods and services.

The owners of these big companies, the common stockholders, made up a large part of the top fifth of income receivers who were, in turn, the nation's chief consumers of manufactured goods. Such an army of stockholders, often equally interested in competing firms, could exercise none of the directing functions of the classic "risk-taking" entrepreneur. These functions were largely surrendered to professional management, and the "owners" became merely "consumers" of dividends, whose interests management had to balance against those of "consumers" of wages and consumers of the company's products. Managing such companies required a new "political science" of internal administration, and a new psychology of external or public relations.

These changes made the business community increasingly complex. The very little businessman still remained in the corner store, repair shop, gas station, or lunch counter; the medium sized businessman also remained in department stores, wholesale houses or factories, but the only rapidly growing group were the new professional managers controlling large complex corporate structures. As a result, business organizations had to assume new relations with government, labor, stockholders, and consumers, and few of the parties involved had similar conceptions of the ideal character of the new relations. Since history is concerned particularly with the process of change, the following discussion will focus attention on the evolution of big business forms and practices as the emergent force, and in doing so, it will neglect some of the minor alterations that have appeared only in the conduct of small and medium sized concerns.

Technology and Big Business

Technology, which contributed to the size of producing units, also increased bigness by facilitating the management of large concerns. Communication, the nervous system of business, was improved in the twenties and thirties by the teletype, telephoto, microfilm, automobile, and airplane. All types of office equipment from electric typewriters to punch-card machines made it easy to keep, and to multiply records. These various devices allowed management to maintain a central office in New York or Chicago, close to their chief markets and financial connections, and from there effectively to control plants located in lower cost areas, or closer to raw materials.

While in some industries technology led to larger plants, it also facilitated the decentralization of operations. The shift from coal as source of power to oil and electricity and the perfection of the concrete highway and the motor truck often made several strategically located medium sized plants preferable to one gigantic one. Meanwhile, more exact scientific controls over materials and processes lessened the risk from variable quality in multi-plant operations. It became possible to manufacture exactly the same product, even one as delicate as beer, in plants three thousand miles apart. Big companies, such as Container Company of America, for example, might have over thirty plants located throughout the country. As a result, corporations and their managements grew ever larger while operations were conducted by medium sized units.

The Market and Big Business

But technological advance was only one of the factors leading to bigger business organizations. In the period after 1920 better adjustment to the market was often regarded as more important.[1] The bigger a company became the more influence it could exercise over the total sales of its types of products, and in conjunction with a few other big companies it might largely eliminate price competition. In addition, unit costs for advertising and other marketing expenses generally fell as volume increased. Large volume also reduced the unit cost of research, public relations, and other long-run activities needed for maintaining a market position.

Just as in the case of the technological pressure toward bigness, the market trend also showed some notable exceptions. In the city slums where price competition and the pressure on costs were intense, small family-run shops continued to operate in competition with big chain stores. In trades such as garment making, moderate sized factories successfully marketed through small independent outlets. Many large companies bought from medium-sized suppliers and sold through small distributors rather than risk managerial difficulties, ill will, or anti-trust prosecution by absorbing these independent units. In short, if one looked at the American economic scene, even in 1950, on the basis of variety of activi-

[1] U. S. Temporary National Economic Committee, *Monograph No. 13*. Washington, D. C.: Government Printing Office, 1941.

ties rather than volume of products, only a minority of the activities were controlled by giant corporations. While less than 600 big organizations, each with assets over $50,000,000, might do a majority of all business reckoned in dollar volume, 3,800,000 independent enterprises still shared the remainder. Furthermore, surveys based on data of the 1920's indicated that, except for some types of retail selling, the small business that was able to keep going at all was likely to earn a higher return on invested capital than the large corporation.

Controlling Price Competition

The cost of building up special brands through advertising and direct selling interested big and small business entrepreneurs alike in stable prices. In Europe this goal had been largely achieved by contracts and cartels, but in America the Sherman Anti-Trust Law of 1890 condemned such formal agreements among competitors. In spite of the law, however, the increasing need of highly capitalized concerns for price stability and the growing interest of professional management in long-run security produced support for the medieval or mercantilist concept of a "just" price. The allied ideas of fair and uniform standards spread to all types of trade practices. As A. J. Eddy wrote in 1912, in a book called *The New Competition:*[2]

> The basis of the old competition is secrecy, the strength of the new is knowledge; the essence of the old is deceit, the spirit of the new is truth. Concealment characterizes all the dealings of the old; frankness is vital to the new.
>
> The old looks with suspicious eye on all associations and combinations; without cooperation the new is impossible.

In industries dominated by a few large companies, informal understandings usually led to cooperation. Cross-licensing of patents between companies offered another means of controlling prices and trade practices. But in the large group of industries in which competition was vigorous, uniformity required some type of formal action. The trade association was the obvious agency for cooperation in pricing and for exchanging other information that might lead to "fair" competition. There were already both regional and national trade associations for most industries, but some of them were not very active. In World War I the government's use of the associations as agencies to estimate and apportion production put life into the existing groups and aided the formation of new ones. By 1918 there were perhaps one thousand trade associations with pretensions, at least, to national influence, and ten or fifteen per cent of these were experimenting with open price policy. Under this system each member firm posted its prices with the association, and the latter

[2] Arthur Jerome Eddy, *The New Competition,* p. 100. New York: D. Appleton and Company, 1912.

circulated them, along with other pertinent information, in letters or periodicals.

This advance toward a theory and practice of non-price competition was retarded by a series of Supreme Court decisions that first appeared to rule against all open price policy,[3] and then held that it was not illegal, in itself, if not used as a means of controlling prices.[4] But, in any case, the relatively prosperous years of the twenties removed severe competitive pressure from prices and lessened the desire of many firms for trade association supervision.

The depression from 1930 on, however, produced the greatest attack on price competition in American history. Both businessmen and politicians thought that the economy should not be allowed to go through a spiral of deflation with price cuts that would eliminate all but the strongest firms. The idea of maintaining a just price was incorporated in the National Industrial Recovery Act of 1933 and its resulting codes. These codes, largely drawn up by trade associations, went several steps beyond anything that they had previously attempted. Not only were prices set, but wages and hours as well. And while, within two years, vital parts of the NRA were declared unconstitutional, the close cooperation of businessmen in trade associations had a lasting effect.

Another approach to the idea of a just price, during the depressed thirties, was by "fair trade" laws in the states. Starting with the California Act of 1931, forty-four states passed laws permitting contracts between producers and distributors to regulate the prices of sale and resale of branded commodities. In 1937 a federal statute, the Miller-Tydings Act, amended the Sherman Anti-Trust Law to the extent of permitting such contracts in interstate commerce where they were legal in the state in which the commodity was to be sold. In addition, the Robinson-Patman Act of 1936 prohibited a seller from discriminating as to price among his various customers who bought for resale. These state and federal laws were more important in illustrating trends in business thought than in their effect on business organization. They were applied only to certain lines of branded commodities, not over fifteen per cent of total retail trade, and probably had only a slight effect upon general prices.[5]

As a result of these various factors tending toward price stability, the major incidence of the business cycle—of changes from sellers' to buyers' markets—was shifted between 1921 and 1941 from prices to volume of production. In the downswing of depression from 1930 to 1933 many industrial producers were able to avoid deep price cuts. While this provided

---

[3] *U. S.* vs. *Linseed Crushers' Council.* 1923.

[4] *Maple Flooring Manufacturers' Association* vs. *U. S.* 1925.

[5] In the inflation after World War II, when price maintenance of branded commodities became embarrassing to both producers and sellers, several state courts held such contracts to be illegal.

greater stability for invested capital, it reenforced relatively firm wages as an element of rigidity in the economic system. And as business lost elasticity, depressions appeared to be losing their tendency toward self-correction.

The gradual change in many industries from competitive to administered price altered the pressures on management. Survival in price warfare had depended on efficiency and economy in production. Frugality and careful figuring were the watchwords. But success under relatively high, uniform prices, depended on gaining more of the market through ingenious advertising and selling. Frugality and an eye for detail were less vital than a flare for choosing the right product and understanding the market.

Increasing Rigidities

Price stability was only one of a number of increasing rigidities in the business structure. The very basis of mass production was a large commitment to a particular way of doing a job. This applied not only to machines and buildings, but to the office work as well. A filing system might become obsolete, but to refile fifteen or twenty million letters, in, say, an insurance office, was as staggering a task as to completely retool an assembly line. Even communication suffered from rigidity. The smooth functioning of a vast organization required established channels of information and control. But such elements introduced a time lag and a chance that an idea for improvement might get lost on the way. The expression "so and so is too large a company to move rapidly" became commonplace.

The old ideal of the "innovating" entrepreneur who gained an advantage over his competitors by secretly developing new ways of doing things became largely meaningless in the big company. There could be few "trade secrets" where hundreds of men had to be informed and where new methods could only be introduced after long testing and preparation. Not that one company might not be more progressive than another, but it was rare that their new ideas were unknown to their competitors.

Most of all, entrepreneurs deplored a sharply increasing rigidity in wage rates. Up to 1933 managers in most of the mass production industries had set wages according to their own judgment. Strikes in these companies had been infrequent and generally unsuccessful. The rise of industrial unionism backed by federal legislation (noted in the preceding chapter) put an end to this situation. Management now had to fix wages in conference with the executives of the national unions. The result, greatly magnified by wartime shortages of labor, was the beginning of a higher wage economy than the world had ever seen.

The increasing bureaucratization of business arrangements was paralleled in other parts of society. Supported prices for farm products, high military, pension, and debt-servicing budgets, and consequently high tax rates, all produced a society that could not stand violent economic ups and downs. The "unfit" could no longer be eliminated by drastic pressure on prices, and the "fit" would think twice before committing themselves to new ventures.

Business Forms

No basically new development in the legal characteristics of firms took place between 1918 and 1950. Proprietorships, partnerships, simple corporations, and holding companies continued to be the legal units for the nation's business activities. But in the holding company an elaboration occurred that for a few years promised to be of great significance. The early holding companies, created following the New Jersey general act of 1888, were generally of the single stage variety. That is, the parent company owned stock in a number of operating subsidiaries. The addition to this simple form, appearing rapidly in the twenties, was the multi-stage or pyramided holding company.

The pyramid was generally designed for the purpose of controlling more real assets with the same amount of venture capital or, its corollary, to attract more capital from the general public without endangering the control of the managing group of entrepreneurs. The mechanics of the structure were built around the fact that a bare majority, or even less, of the voting stock of a corporation carried control of all of its operations and assets. It was possible that one dollar invested in the stock of the topmost company of a six- or eight-stage pyramid might control one thousand dollars in the assets of an operating company at the base. This so-called "leverage" depended, of course, on the fact that the public was willing to buy the non-controlling blocs of securities in all the intermediate, non-operating companies. During the 1920's investors were not only willing but eager to "get in" on what were judged to be business empires of great potential profitability.

In practice most of these structures soon ceased to be orderly pyramids proceeding from many operating companies at the base through intermediate holding companies to one parent corporation at the top. The intermediate companies borrowed from each other, bought each other's securities and those of outside corporations, issued bonds, and often produced such a tangle of intercompany connections that no officer could keep them all in mind.

The depression of the thirties checked the use of the pyramided holding company as a general business form. The overcapitalized multi-stage companies revealed so much financial mismanagement when falling revenues forced reorganizations that they became anathema to many investors, while the Federal Government in the Public Utility Holding

Act of 1935 placed so many restrictions on such companies that most of them were forced to liquidate, and new ones appeared uneconomic. Partly as a result of the spectacular collapse of the Van Sweringen pyramid of trunk-line railroads, the I.C.C. also came to frown on control acquired through complex financial structures.

Such multi-stage holding companies are to be distinguished from occasional double layers of subsidiaries created for productive purposes. Almost all large companies owned the stock of operating subsidiaries, as A.T.&.T., for example, held that of the various state telephone companies. These subsidiary companies, in turn, might own the stock of other units set up for special functions. But here the stages were merely incidental to the effective control of operations, not a financial device for increasing the leverage of an inside entrepreneurial group.

The flexibility of the holding company type of structure has led in practice to several clearly distinguishable types of big company organization: simple monolithic types like the Ford Motor Company where subsidiaries, aside from those in foreign countries, are for specific functions; closely federated types like General Motors where there is considerable autonomy allowed to the presidents of the producing units, but where major policies are closely coordinated; and loosely federated types like Weyerhaeuser Timber Company where the top unit represents ownership, but takes little direct part in the management of the subsidiaries.

The Entrepreneur in Big Business

In corporations of even moderate size, those with assets of five to twenty-five million dollars, the twenties was a period of rapidly increasing divorce of ownership from control. This occurred as more and more of these companies decided to sell stock to the public. The motives behind such sales were to expand working capital without borrowing from the banks, to permit the old owners to diversify their holdings, or, as will be discussed below, to increase public interest in the welfare of the company. By 1930 the management group had come to be much less associated with ownership than in the previous generation. The great majority of stockholders had ceased to view their companies as property they could administer, or their votes as instruments of power.

Where, then, was the ultimate power in the widely owned corporation? Who performed the entrepreneurial function? Was there any longer a man or a group who directed the enterprise and took calculated risks in order to maximize profits? Since the equity owners, the stockholders, no longer constituted such a group, the next place to look for ultimate leadership would be to their elected representatives, the board of directors. In the early twentieth century, investment and commercial bankers had exercised so much authority on the boards of the largest companies that the title "finance capitalism" was applied to the situation. In railroads, public utilities, and other enterprises with large indebtedness or continual need for refinancing, this financial influence continued. Possibly it represented the ultimate power if such a force existed at all, but it should be noted that these directors representing banks, trustees, and insurance companies were themselves "managers" of institutionalized money rather than old-fashioned owner-entrepreneurs.

In manufacturing and trade, financial power, which had never been so great as in the railroads and public utilities, probably declined during the twenties and thirties. The easy money market from 1923 to 1929 made the bankers more eager for securities to market than the more successful companies were to issue them, and with high profits in many industries the relatively mild rate of expansion that prevailed could be financed from earnings. In the depression, the government's Reconstruction Finance Corporation took over the responsibilities for aiding big companies that had previously rested upon the shoulders of the investment bankers. In 1933 the Federal Banking Act struck a still heavier blow at the strength of investment houses by forcing them to cease commercial banking activities. Furthermore the Federal Government never withdrew from the business of financing and money lending. Certainly in 1950 the ability of financial managers to wield the ultimate power in big business was distinctly less than it had been thirty years earlier.

Additional examination of large company boards indicated that, in general, only a few members kept well enough informed regarding company affairs to take a hand in guiding the organization, and that these members were usually salaried officers of the company. Along with this decline in supervision by the board there arose the theory that the director's function was merely advisory, that he should not try to form or veto policy or to interfere in the operation of the concern. This de-emphasis of the board as the direct representatives of the owners of the property, the supreme council for which management worked as hired hands, reached its ultimate extreme in boards like those of the American Tobacco Company or Standard Oil Company of New Jersey, composed entirely of salaried officers. But on all large company boards officers had long since come to play a leading role.

This shift in practical power from independent stockholder-directors to manager-directors had been taking place gradually from the end of the nineteenth century. In 1941 philosopher James Burnham applied the name "managerial revolution" to the change, and argued that henceforth the administrators would wield economic and political power. The shift may also be seen, however, as a diffusion of ultimate power or sovereignty in the corporation. In some matters, particularly those connected with financial policy, important board members may have overruled management. And, in addition, representatives of "outside" financial interests were often placed in key executive positions. But on routine matters board members necessarily trusted the managerial decisions. Whether important stockholders, institutional financial interests, or company executives would triumph in any absolute disagreement depended on the particular firm, and such irreconcilable quarrels were so rare and so carefully concealed in this period that it is hard to generalize.

The highest entrepreneurial functions in a company, therefore, were generally shared by several of the directors and managers, and had to some degree lost their connection with either ownership or profits. Both the professional manager, the man who, without investing any capital, had made his way up through the organization to the top level, and the representatives of institutional money who favored secure investments were presumably more interested in a strong, progressive, going concern than in paying unusually large dividends to stockholders. The president of the company, in theory its most important entrepreneur, was apt to be primarily interested in keeping a satisfactory balance among the various claimants to the company income. Labor, management, customers, cash reserves, the physical plant, and the stockholders represented essentially contending interests in that if one got more in any given division the others received less. It was not astonishing that the modern professional entrepreneur tended, perhaps unconsciously, to favor the financial claims of those closer to him than those of the mass of stockholders.

Even where entrepreneurs had a large investment in their own company, federal tax policies furthered the preference for harmony and security rather than added profit. Not only would corporation taxes take a large part of any gains resulting from unusual risks, but personal income taxes would operate against the part distributed to themselves as stockholders. To put it another way, since ultimate net gain to individuals could not be more than about one-third of the original profit, the risks involved in any new venture had to be assessed on this basis. An even chance was no longer a good gamble.

The Science of Business Administration

The new conditions of entrepreneurship, the growing size of companies, and the complexity of organizational forms created new managerial situations. As some companies grew to have administrative groups running into the thousands, it became clear that they were encountering the same types of problems that had existed for centuries in public administration. As one well qualified critic saw it, business growth had "resulted in concentrating in relatively few hands a degree and scope of economic power which transcend the limits of effective administration." [6] Obviously, business needed its own political science.

As noted earlier, there were several types of response in the early twentieth century to the need for more efficient business administration. Frederick W. Taylor and other writers on scientific management had tried to rationalize the lowest levels of administration through dividing the supervision of workers along functional lines. On an intermediate administrative level, cost-accounting techniques were elaborated in an effort to detect inefficiency. After World War I, management made greater use of industrial engineers, theoretical economists, lawyers, and business consultants who might provide new knowledge or perspective on business problems. Increasingly complex relations with government necessitated more legal experts to analyze proposed legislation, more trained lobbyists or public relations men to forestall harmful acts, and more reliable analysts to learn or forecast government policy. In order to guard against or prepare for disruptive changes in technology, big companies established research laboratories employing scores of scientists.

But at the very top level, that of chairmen, presidents, and major vice-presidents, the problems seemed most difficult of all. The inefficiencies of single departments or weak administrators might be detected and eliminated by the devices just discussed, but how were men to be trained, selected, and inspired to undertake the task of coordinating and directing the enterprise as a whole? How were men to translate power into effective administration?

The rise of the university business school was one effort to provide the proper training. A few such schools antedated World War I, but their great spread came in the twenties. By the end of the decade most large universities were offering undergraduate or graduate courses in both the essential techniques of business and in academic subjects that might contribute to sounder and broader viewpoints.

Methods of selecting executives, however, remained hit or miss, and, as organizations grew bigger, success for the man without influential connections depended on having his abilities brought to the attention of someone in top management, usually by a fortunate conjunction of circumstances. The individual competitive struggle for success in such companies, therefore, was couched in terms of how one distinguished oneself as a desirable leader rather than in the quest for wealth or market advantages. There was nothing new in the basic situation. Men in the bureaucracies of Egypt, Greece, and Rome had competed under these conditions, but the return toward a bureaucratic career for the country's most able citizens was a notable departure from historic American conditions and conflicted with a good deal of the nation's cultural heritage.

---

6 Myron W. Watkins in T.N.E.C. *Monograph No. 13*, p. 99.

While the top executives of the large companies continued to talk the language of profits for the stockholders and to have their superficial behavior profit-oriented, most of them had relatively little personal stake in the size of the dividends paid by their companies. Maximization of profits was still a slogan, but one without much emotional force. In many companies, therefore, substitute incentives seemed desirable. This led to bonus plans and management funds. Again, as in the case of the other palliatives for bigness, the earliest of these antedate World War I, but they were particularly characteristic of the prosperous twenties and forties. Part of the year's earnings would be divided among management either on a fixed percentage, or by vote of the board of directors or the chief officers. In good years, like 1928 and 1929, these payments might considerably exceed the regular salary of the executive, and a few companies paid bonuses even in 1932. Efforts to encourage management buying of stock were probably a less successful stimulant for managerial incentive, as the desire for a wise diversification of personal investment in order to achieve added individual security was likely to impel officers to hold only a reasonable amount of stock in the companies for which they worked.

The very unevenness of the use of bonus and stock plans indicated that they were imperfect solutions to the problem of stimulating energy and devotion to the company. Even in the early twenties it was becoming clear that the problems were not exclusively monetary, but involved prestige, security, and general morale. Seen in this way, the problems could be met partly by introducing the incentives of competition for prestige within the big company and using refined techniques of cost accounting to test efficiency. Alfred P. Sloan, Jr., of General Motors was one of the leading exponents of these new theories of management. Not only were the individual car producing subsidiaries put in competition with each other through broad price overlaps and considerable managerial autonomy, but, to the extent that figures were available, the companies were also rated in relation to the efficiency of their outside competitors. Thus, a company like Cadillac in the 1930's might be a small money maker, but its officers gained prestige as successful entrepreneurs both from a cost accounting standpoint and from a comparison of the profits of Cadillac with those of other companies making expensive cars. General Motors could, therefore, in theory, preserve the advantages and incentives of competition, even in a semi-monopolistic situation. In order to counteract the centrifugal forces of such internecine warfare, Sloan developed a system of coordination through committees made up of board members and officers of the various constituent companies.[7]

[7] See Peter F. Drucker, *Concept of the Corporation*. New York: John Day, 1946. General Motors and A.T.&T. have been taken as examples because they have been more carefully studied than other large corporations.

A.T.&.T. under the leadership of Walter S. Gifford pursued somewhat similar policies. Other big companies with multi-plant systems have in varying degrees introduced such techniques for artificial or "book" competition.

For successful administrators personal recognition could come through higher titles. In this way the need for labelling officials in a large formal organization could also be used to improve morale. The functional vice-president had arisen in the railroad field in the mid-nineteenth century, but in the first half of the twentieth century the increasing size of businesses led to more minute division of functions at the top level and to the creation of many officerships in subsidiaries. The typical big organization came by 1930 to have from ten to fifty vice-presidents of the parent organization and an equally large number of assistant vice-presidents as well as assistant secretaries and assistant treasurers. There might also be assistants to the chairman of the board, the president and the vice-presidents. Usually these assistants were staff officers, specialists, or intermediaries for better communication. The subsidiaries would have their presidents, vice-presidents and other officers. Often the chief officers of the parent company divided among them the topmost posts in the subsidiaries, but the lesser positions were filled by additional officer personnel. Under the officers in rank, but not always in salary, were managers, assistant managers, department heads, agents, supervisors, and their various assistants. While no exact research has been done on the question, it seems probable that the increase in administrators kept up with the growing quantity of business, or, in other words, that there was not much saving in unit cost of administrative salaries and expense accounts as volume increased.

Officers' clubs aided the *esprit de corps* of executives in large companies. The club was generally built around a comfortable restaurant where they could assemble for lunch. In many companies officers also spent much of their social life entertaining each other. By such means the company might become an engrossing interest in both work and recreation. So far did this go in some companies that an opposite danger began to develop, that of losing independence of judgment and viewing problems only in terms of group clichés. The dilemma is inherent in group activity. The self-centered individualist with deviant ideas tends to cooperate poorly and to disrupt the smooth functioning of the organization, while the out-going type, hungry for the friendship and support of his fellows, may cooperate excellently but lack the ability to originate ideas. Many critics inside the ranks of business thought that the normal mechanics of company promotion advanced too many men of this latter type.

The problems of prestige, security, and morale ran from top to bottom of the large company. Sample surveys indicated that workers as well as executives were generally more interested in security and personal recognition than in additional money.

Increased security could be achieved by pension and insurance plans to which the company made the whole or a partial contribution. Such plans spread slowly in the twenties, but more rapidly after the depression of the thirties, illustrating that the instability of personal savings and higher taxes and lower interest rates made it difficult for either workers or executives to save enough to provide an adequate income for old age. While some firms, such as A.T.&.T., where pension money was supplied entirely by the company, had extended the plan to ordinary workers, in most companies the system applied at first only to the administrative staff. In the forties, under pressure from labor unions, more companies set up pension plans for workers.

Personal recognition could be provided in several ways. For the workers and lesser administrative employees the company magazine and company club were means to both individual distinction and closer group cooperation. Company periodicals devoted to internal news began as early as 1870, but there were only about thirty-five in 1916. Between that date and 1921 the number increased tenfold, and grew steadily thereafter. By 1925 it is safe to assume that practically all of the three or four hundred biggest corporations had some type of house organ.[8] Company clubs achieved somewhat the same purpose on a more general level. The employee was given a chance to build friendships and become a recognized personality within the company atmosphere. He graduated from being number 7,046 in the finishing plant, to being the best first baseman or a good bowler. Many executives hoped that magazines, clubs, and other welfare devices, such as cafeterias, swimming pools, athletic equipment, and employee representation plans for dealing with management, would reduce labor turnover and lessen the appeal of outside trade unions. To a degree such welfare devices probably achieved both of these aims, but in most cases the workers proved ready to join national labor organizations when given the opportunity.

The failure of the welfare and morale programs to check the rise of A.F. of L. or C.I.O. unionism in the middle thirties illustrates, paradoxically, the general soundness of the approach. A large part of the appeal and strength of national unionism is psychological and social. The union is built up as the workers' own organization, while the company is seen as the organ of the bosses; the union, it is claimed, truly seeks the welfare of the worker, the company only pretends to in order

[8] The magazines reported promotions, social events, athletic contests, marriages, and other family news, and published fiction and poetry by company employees. Editorially they served as media for indoctrination in company policy and ideals. The fact that there was a company reading public or community also gave a feeling of added importance and responsibility to the chief executive officers. National Industrial Conference Board, *Employee Magazines in the United States*. New York: The Board, 1925.

to make higher profits. This psychological conflict, first brought home forcibly to the managers of American big business in the period of the New Deal, introduced a subtle and frequently misunderstood element into collective bargaining. The management group at the bargaining table spoke in terms of economic considerations, the labor group had to consider as well the social and psychological factors that held their organization together and gave it strength.[9] Management learned these things, and reluctantly recognized that entrepreneurial decisions would have to be modified to take such considerations into account.

External Relations of the Large Company

Meanwhile, external forces were making the problems of entrepreneurship more complex than ever before. From 1910 on there was a multiplication of state regulatory laws affecting labor and factory conditions in various industries and controlling rates for public utilities. For many industries, World War I produced complex relations with the Federal Government. And events in Europe indicated unmistakably that government regulation of and participation in business were in a rising trend.

But knowledge of how to meet these threats to business autonomy had also grown. Ivy Lee's successful public defense of the Rockefeller family after the Colorado Fuel and Iron Company strike in 1913-14, George Creel's handling of World War I propaganda, and new psychological theories of the subconscious all combined to create the modern public relations counselor. The larger advertising agencies also set up public relations services. The basic aim of these services was to create a public opinion favorable to business in general and to the client's business in particular. The chief techniques were distribution to editors of news items that displayed business or industry in a favorable light, the preparation of magazine articles, to be signed by prominent citizens, recounting the achievements of business, and paid advertising designed to create good will rather than to sell a particular product. Moving pictures, lectures, and popular books were additional means for emphasizing the contributions of business to the public welfare. All these devices became particularly important during labor disputes or attacks by government.

During the prosperity of the twenties such information was readily absorbed by the public and was no doubt responsible to some degree for a slowing down of the trend toward government regulation. But in the depression of the thirties, public relations men found that glorification did not work when the standard of living was sinking and millions were unemployed. From the soul-searching of these years there emerged new concepts. The public relations expert learned that he must convince his

[9] E. Wight Bakke, *Mutual Survival The Goal of Unions and Management,* p. 3. New Haven: Yale University Labor and Management Center, 1946.

client that business had public responsibilities and that businessmen should act in the public interest. The counselor had to operate on a "two-way street," explaining business attitudes to the public and public responses to the businessmen.

The Securities Exchange Act (1934) regulating the raising of capital, the Wagner Act controlling labor relations, and the continued activity of the Works Progress Administration and various government lending agencies all forced businessmen, slowly and reluctantly, to face the fact that their continued freedom of economic action depended on educating public and political opinion. The National Association of Manufacturers and some of the Chambers of Commerce pursued such education in the conventional way of harping on the virtues of the free enterprise system. But, judged by election results, these campaigns were not very effective.

No one seemed able to discover the correct approach. It appeared that the change from the happy, traditional situation of the twenties, when even big business seemed popular, to the desperate straits of the thirties was too fast for businessmen or their professional advisors to follow. Business philosophies were in a state of confusion. Some favored government regulation to check price competition—certain intercoastal shipping lines, for example, carried on a successful campaign to get themselves regulated by the I.C.C.; others were prepared to see what could be gained by accepting government favors and promoting a closer union of business and government; a few even accepted the Keynesian ideas that more or less continuous government spending might be necessary to insure a stable economy; but the great majority appeared to be beaten and confused by the sudden turn of American politics and opinion and uncertain as to what to think. The war boom and postwar inflation temporarily relieved the situation by substituting old fashioned military activity for newfangled relief and public work projects, and gave businessmen a decade in which to readjust their thinking.

From the twenties on a few companies were experimenting with more indirect and basic forms of public relations. An early effort of this kind —an attempt under utility company sponsorship to get the writers of school textbooks to condemn government ownership—aroused so much public criticism when discovered that it was dropped. By the thirties, some leaders realized that the scandals of the depression and the anti-business literary trends, present from the nineties on, had produced a bizarre and distorted picture of the history and practices of business. This picture built by textbooks, teachers, and general reading could not be destroyed by propaganda. It would have to be altered by reeducating the teachers and authors. In other words, business leaders with the greatest insight realized that they were faced with the problems of modifying a cultural tradition with deep roots in the agrarian past. History seemed an obvious tool with which to alter traditions, and gradually a handful of business companies opened their records to scholars commissioned by universities to write objective accounts. Of a similar nature were studies by academic scholars of the nature of entrepreneurship and of different business processes. The needs of these studies, as well as the demands of government relations, put a new emphasis on the preservation of business records and led a few companies to place their older records in libraries open to the public. Ultimately the effect of these movements might be profound, but it would necessarily be slow and indirect, and by 1950 they were still in their infancy.

A more direct and tangible type of public relations could be carried on with stockholders. Nearly a century of corporate history had demonstrated that widely held stock offered no menace to the control of company elections by the principal entrepreneurs and that stockholders were loyal supporters against government encroachments. As a result, a number of large companies, particularly the public utilities, carried on active campaigns for new stockholders. Cities Service Company, for example, increased its stockholders from 100,000 in 1928 to over 500,000 by 1932, and A.T.&.T. increased the number of stockholders owning five shares or less from some 50,000 in 1920 to 210,000 in 1930.

Part of the problem was to attract the small stockholder, another part was to keep him. Public relations experts, therefore, turned their attention to stockholder relations. Presidents were persuaded to sign form letters welcoming new members to the stockholder family and, from time to time, other notes conveying special news; annual reports were made attractive and more informative; pamphlets and periodicals describing company activities were distributed to the stockholders. It is doubtful whether all of this literature added much to the stockholder's precise knowledge of the state of his investment, but it did give him a feeling of belonging to an organization and that his importance as a property owner was recognized.

Conclusion

In the thirty years from 1929 to 1950 a number of economic tendencies, noticeable in earlier periods, became dominant realities. The result was rather rapid changes in American attitudes and ideas. The potential effect of the corporation on property relations had been foreseen by thinkers like Daniel Raymond and Nathan Appleton as early as the eighteen-thirties, but the reduction of ownership of the means of production to a functional claim against income, somewhat inferior to those of labor and management, was not the general rule until about 1920. This constituted the basic "revolution" inherent in corporate industrialism. The increasing size and cost of machinery required ownership by large groups, and this form seemed inevitably to make owners into passive *rentiers*. The practical control of economic activity meanwhile passed into the hands of the professional entrepreneur. These elements of size and professional administration underlie the business changes of the period between the two World Wars.

As technology solved production problems with increasing ease, it added to the human problems involved in distribution. Equating supply and demand in such a way as to provide full employment seemed the chief problem of the society, and this was a problem in business entrepreneurship. Perhaps because of premature government action, or perhaps because of a new stage of the economy, processes that hitherto had been regarded as governed by natural economic laws became the subject of planning and control. In consequence, entrepreneurs had to develop a new consciousness of their places and roles in a subtly interconnected social democracy.

All these factors—bigness, problems of distribution, and administrative responsibility—led to new study of the political science of large business organizations, and of the relations of such organizations with the public. Deeply stirred by the economic debacle of 1932 and the new attitudes of government, entrepreneurs and their advisors increased their interest in these studies. They evolved new organizational forms calculated to stimulate incentive and improve morale. They cultivated better relations with stockholders and consumers. But they discovered and accepted few new major principles applicable to business as a whole. The situation in 1950 was still essentially confused. Businessmen had, as always, solved new production problems with creditable speed, but their relations with society, which were now of vital importance, were still uncertain. The Henry W. Taylor or Charles F. Kettering who could find a reconciliation between the entrepreneurial ideal of the autonomous economy and the twentieth century trend toward government sponsored order and security had not yet appeared.

Selected References

GENERAL WORKS

Berle, A. A. Jr., and G. C. Means, *The Modern Corporation and Private Property*. New York: The Macmillan Company, 1932.

Burns, Arthur R., *The Decline of Competition*. New York: McGraw-Hill Book Company, 1936.

Copeland, M. T., and A. R. Towl, *The Board of Directors and Business Management*. Boston: Harvard Graduate School of Business Administration, 1947.

Danielian, N. R., *A. T. & T.* New York: Vanguard Press, 1939.

Drucker, P. F., *Concept of the Corporation*. New York: John Day, 1946.

Gordon, R. A., *Business Leadership in the Large Corporation*. Washington, D. C.: The Brookings Institution, 1945.

Knauth, Oswald, *Managerial Enterprise*. New York: W. W. Norton and Company, 1948.

Nourse, E. G., *Price Making in a Democracy*. Washington, D. C.: The Brookings Institution, 1944.

Watkins, M. W., *Public Regulation of Competitive Practices in Business*. New York: National Industrial Conference Board, 1940.

SPECIAL TOPICS

Baker, J. C., *Executive Salaries and Bonus Plans*. New York: McGraw-Hill Book Company, 1938.

Bakke, E. W., and K. Clark, *Unions, Management and the Public*. New York: Harcourt, Brace and Company, 1948.

Barnard, Chester I., *The Functions of the Executive*. Cambridge, Mass.: Harvard University Press, 1938.

Bernays, Edward, *Propaganda*. New York: Horace Liveright, Inc., 1928.

Cochran, T. C., *The Pabst Brewing Company*. New York: New York University Press, 1948.

James, Marquis, *Metropolitan Life*. New York: The Viking Press, 1947.

Larson, H. M., *Guide to Business History*. Cambridge, Mass.: Harvard University Press, 1948.

Sloan, A. P. Jr., *The Adventures of a White Collar Man*. New York: Doubleday, Doran & Company, Inc., 1940.

Temporary National Economic Committee, *Final Report and Monographs* (44 vols.). Washington, D. C.: Government Printing Office, 1941.

46 · INDUSTRIAL CONCENTRATION AND ANTI-TRUST POLICY

IN CHAPTER 32 ABOVE, the rise of industrial concentration prior to World War I was described, as were the evident consequences of this for competitive behavior and pricing within industrial markets. A large proportion of industrial markets came to be dominated by a few large firms; at the same time, price competition was restricted and non-price competition emphasized. The manner in which the functioning of the economy was affected by these developments in competitive behavior cannot be precisely ascertained in all respects. Certain distinct tendencies, however, are evident. Industrial prices after the merger movement were relatively inflexible in many cases; they were changed infrequently and fluctuated much less over the course of business cycles than did agricultural prices. Since these prices were controlled by the policies of large firms, they may have become less persistent regulators of the rates of economic activity. The amount of expenditure on and the proportion of resources invested in product development, advertising, and sales promotion was substantial. To the extent that greater productive efficiency did not result from advertising and sales promotion, non-price competition led to higher costs and possibly higher prices. Prices were established far enough above costs in many industries to yield relatively high profits in the 1920's, and again in the comparatively prosperous years of the later 1930's. With the concentration of industrial control, freedom of enterprise for the small investor was reduced. Small capital could purchase corporate securities but found difficulty in establishing independent firms in most industries.

The most evident changes were that the control of much of the nation's industries had become centered in the hands of a few large firms—200 of them controlled 57 per cent of corporate wealth outside of the financial field in 1933—and that their competitive behavior was of a different sort than that observed in the later nineteenth century.[1] Whether the economy functioned less efficiently than it might have because of this concentration, whether consumers paid too much for their goods, and whether

[1] National Resources Committee, *Structure of the American Economy,* Part 1, Ch. 7. Washington, D. C.: 1939.

labor received enough were controverted issues not susceptible of easy resolution. The economy had become much more productive while it was becoming concentrated. In what degree this increase in productivity was due to concentration and in what degree in spite of it, was an unsettled question.

Some writers refer to the development from 1887 to the present as a "decline" of competition.[2] There is no question that the whole structure of the economy, and the associated pattern of competitive behavior, underwent a basic change during this period. The term "decline," however, is perhaps unfortunate. There is still much rivalry for custom apparent in most American industrial markets. It is frequently of a character that does not emphasize price rivalry, and it may be productive of unique market results, but it *is* competition. Comparison with the behavior typical of the period from 1870 to 1890 is perhaps misleading. Although price competition—even price wars—typified the earlier interval, this was certainly a transitional period in the evolution of concentrated markets. Competition did not simply decline; it developed and changed. Except in periods of rapid transition, private enterprise has shown a tendency to limit, to regulate, or to eliminate price competition, and to confine rivalry to its milder forms. This is implicit in the pursuit of profits. The history of the merger movement and its results in modern market structure and behavior are primary evidence of this tendency.

The courts, in cases decided at the end of World War I, interpreted the Sherman Act in such a way that concentration of control of an industry in the hands of one or a few firms, in and of itself, seemed immune from legal attack; dissolution of quasi-monopolistic firms apparently could not be secured in the usual case so long as rivals were not overtly excluded or oppressed and an ostensible freedom to compete remained. (Even here, the remedy might be elimination of oppressive tactics rather than dissolution.) It is thus not surprising that most actions brought under the Sherman Act after 1920 were directed not against mergers but against restraints of trade arising out of agreements among independent competitors designed to limit competition. The courts from the outset had not hesitated to declare such agreements unlawful, regardless of the reasonableness of their results, and had found violations of the Sherman Act in the leading cases of *Addyston Pipe and Steel Co.* vs. *U.S.* (1899), *Swift & Co.* vs. *U.S.* (1905), and others. Prosecution under the Act of collusion in restraint of competition was potentially fruitful even if mergers were relatively immune, since the limitation of competition in concentrated industries was commonly implemented by explicit or implied argreements concerning output or price, by exchange

---

2 See A. R. Burns, *The Decline of Competition* (New York: McGraw-Hill Book Company, 1936) for the development of this point of view.

of information through trade associations, and by tacit acceptance of price leadership.

In the three Republican administrations from 1921 through 1932 (after which the Sherman Act was temporarily suspended) an average of 14 cases per year were brought under the anti-trust laws. The decisions of the courts in the leading cases of this period substantiated their previous stand against agreements restraining competition. In *American Column & Lumber Co.* vs. *U.S.* (1921), *U.S.* vs. *American Linseed Oil Co.* (1923), *Maple Floor Manufacturers Association* vs. *U.S.* (1925), *U.S.* vs. *Trenton Potteries* (1927), and other cases the courts maintained the attitude that any collusive agreements or activities either fixing price or having the substantial effect of fixing price were illegal, regardless of the intent of the agreeing parties and regardless of the reasonableness of the prices fixed. The same prohibition apparently applied to agreements to limit output or to share the market. Mere failure to compete actively, exchange of information, and price leadership, however, if unsupported by evidence of consensual action, were in general found not to constitute violations.[3]

The courts thus adhered to the practice of finding violation of the Act in overt actions of competitors rather than in the character of price and competitive behavior. Their definition of violations was nevertheless sufficiently broad and unequivocal to give considerable scope to the application of the law in the form of policing the competitive practices of concentrated industry. In spite of this, enforcement of the Sherman Act in general did not secure either the complete elimination of collusive activity or the institution of vigorous and unrestricted competition in the period from 1921 through 1932.

The limited effectiveness of the Act during this period was, perhaps, in part attributable to a lack of vigorous enforcement. It has been suggested that the administrations of the 1920's were, in general, sympathetic with the aims and policies of big business, and the attorneys general were consequently indisposed toward widespread anti-trust litigations. Consistently prosperous business conditions seemed to imply that interference with an efficient system was unnecessary. In any event, the number of cases brought was so small in relation to the probable number of violations that, at the most, the enforcement agency could make a few "examples" and hope that the rest of the violators would take the hint. Violators faced the possibility but not the probability of prosecution. The penalties for being found in violation of the Act, moreover, were not severe. The permissible fines were not important to large enterprise, so that the principal penalty to be faced was the entering of a decree enjoining the violator from continuance of the activities that were

[3] See Milton Handler, *Construction and Enforcement of the Federal Anti-Trust Laws*, Washington, D. C.: Temporary National Economic Committee, Monograph No. 38, 1941.

found illegal. Finally, the remedies secured frequently had the tendency to eliminate technical violation of the Act rather than to effect any substantial revision in market price and competition.

Although the temper and scope of enforcement in the 1920's hampered the development of whatever potentialities the Sherman Act may have had, it was by no means certain that even a more vigorous enforcement would have had a much greater effect on the character of competition. The extent to which the pattern of restrained competition depended on the employment of collusive agreements is not known, nor is it known whether the natural tendency to collusive action could have been checked by any enforcement of the Sherman Act.

The Revival of Sherman Act Enforcement: 1937

From 1933 to 1935 the operation of the Sherman Act was largely suspended by the National Industry Recovery Act. Under the N.R.A., industries were requested to form so-called codes of fair competition, to be approved and enforced by the Government. Many of these codes were essentially cartels or agreements in restraint of trade designed, indirectly or directly, to limit output, raise price, or otherwise restrict competition. Adoption of the N.R.A. plan reflected not only the latent desire of concentrated business to limit competition further, but also a growing general belief arising out of the depression prolonged from 1929 to 1933 that competition was unworkable and should be replaced by centralized planning either by private business or by government. There was at least temporarily an abandonment of that basic faith in competition as a regulator of the economy, of which the Sherman Act was the principal representative. Economic opinion in the post-N.R.A. period continued to regard enforcement of the Sherman Act as of questionable value, while business interests desired its repeal or modification in order to allow closer co-operation and greater restriction of competition.

In this light, the revival of the Sherman Act in 1937 with a program of vigorous enforcement was astonishing. Its renascence seems attributable at least in part to the personality of a newcomer to the administration, Thurman W. Arnold, who took charge of the anti-trust division of the Justice Department in the second Roosevelt administration. With a background in the legal profession, with his roots in the liberal and agricultural West, but with a highly sophisticated appreciation of the intricate working of markets dominated by large-scale corporate enterprise, Arnold undertook anti-trust enforcement with an attitude that was unique in the history of the Sherman Act.

The aim of the Arnold program was to increase substantially the degree of competition and, correspondingly, to reduce prices through elimination of "private seizure" of the control of markets or private control of competition. Enforcement was to be in the public interest and was to emphasize greater over-all production of the necessities of life rather than mere technical compliance with the provisions of the Act. The basic tenet of the program was that restraints of trade tended to emerge naturally in most industries and therefore required continual policing. The Sherman Act was like a traffic speed law—nearly everyone tended to violate it and widespread and continued enforcement was necessary to insure compliance. Compliance, it was felt, would increase price competition and this, in turn, would lead to greater employment and production. The program itself was accordingly one of very numerous litigations under the Act, directed against strategic industries (and simultaneously against various parts of the same industry) and oriented primarily to the revision of price and other market behavior regarded as socially undesirable. Prosecutions were primarily against collusive agreements, and no general attempt to disintegrate established combinations was proposed. This program was accompanied by the recommendation of revision in patent and fair trade laws, which sponsored collusive agreements legally exempt from the provisions of the Sherman Act. These changes in the traditional policy of Sherman Act enforcement, it was argued, would greatly enhance its effectiveness.[4]

Thus, beginning in 1937, the Sherman Act was applied to the task of enforcing competition with greater vigor and perhaps more realistically than at any time in its history. In 1940, for example, the first year of the expanded program, 85 cases were instituted under the anti-trust law; from 1940 through 1948, more cases were instituted than in the previous 50-year history of the act. Cases were brought against industries producing goods important in the cost of living, and were oriented toward substantially revising competitive behavior. The potentialities of the Arnold program, in part because of the special circumstances of the war and postwar years, are as yet not entirely clear. The high proportion of convictions obtained in the many cases brought before the courts substantiate the claim that restraints of trade are very numerous and can be reached only through an expanded enforcement program. It is not clear from available evidence, however, whether restraints can be really eliminated by such enforcement, or whether, if they are eliminated, competitive behavior will be much revised.

In the current postwar period, after the resignation of Arnold from the anti-trust post, the philosophy and policy that he initiated seems to guide the activity of his successors. In addition to numerous cases against collusive agreements, several significant cases have been brought to decision affecting concentrated or monopolistic control of industries.

[4] The philosophy of the Arnold enforcement policy, as well as his critique of past anti-trust enforcement, is developed in Arnold's *Bottlenecks of Business*. New York: Reynal and Hitchcock, Inc., 1940.

The significance of these cases, which include those against Aluminum Company of America and American Tobacco Company and several involving motion picture producers and exhibitors, is that the courts appear at last to be revising their interpretation of the Sherman Act to find illegal monopolization not only in predatory action toward competitors, but also in the simple attainment and persistent maintenance by normal business means of a dominant control of an industry either by a single firm or by several firms acting in concert. The finding of such violation of the law largely in possession and exercise of monopoly power rather than simply in oppressive tactics, and further that monopoly power may be exercised by several firms as well as by one, suggests that the government may be able to attain revisions of market structure through enforced dissolutions of dominant firms in concentrated industries, even if overt acts of oppression and exclusion are not apparent. Some of the recent decisions in motion picture cases, in fact, sustain this thesis. If this line of interpretation is sustained and extended, the Sherman Act may finally give the government powers of control over concentration in industry that it so significantly lacked between 1890 and 1950. The precise character of the revisions in established market structures that could and should be secured, however, and their effects on competitive behavior, are quite uncertain. As of the present writing, it appears that a vigorous pursuit of anti-trust action against both collusive restraint of trade and unduly concentrated market control offers no certain guarantee of securing the socially most desirable degree of competition; on the other hand, it should be beneficial to some as yet unascertained extent, and it does offer the principal alternative to some scheme of centralized direct regulation.

The Federal Trade Commission and the Clayton Act

Since 1890 the Sherman Act has been the cornerstone of the government policy of anti-trust regulation and enforcement of competition. The policy was elaborated and implemented in a degree in 1914 with the establishment of the Federal Trade Commission and with the passage of the Clayton Anti-Trust Act. The Commission was established as an administrative body to investigate the competitive practices of business and to proceed, through hearings and the issuance of orders subject to review and enforcement by the courts, to enjoin firms from pursuing unfair methods of competition. The Clayton Act was intended to supplement the Sherman Act by outlawing certain specific practices restraining trade or conducive to monopoly. Because of the narrow scope, weak original construction, and subsequent judicial interpretation of the Clayton Act, and because the powers of the Federal Trade Commission to deal with restraint of trade have not extended much beyond those already bestowed by the Sherman Act, these supplements to the basic anti-trust law have made relatively limited additions to the power of the government to regulate or enforce competition.

The substantive provisions of the Clayton Act made illegal certain specific business practices that had been employed in eliminating competitors, limiting competition, and forming combinations, but which were not forbidden under the prevailing interpretation of the Sherman Act. Price discrimination among buyers was subjected to certain restrictions if it would tend substantially to lessen competition or create monopoly; tying and exclusive-dealing contracts as a condition of the sale or lease of goods were outlawed where they would have a similar effect. Acquisition by one firm of the stock of a competitor was forbidden, and certain limitations were placed upon interlocking directorates among competing firms. The newly established Federal Trade Commission was charged with the enforcement of the act through the issuance of cease and desist orders, backed by reference to the circuit courts. Litigation under the act could also be brought into the district courts by the Attorney General.

The Federal Trade Commission Act established a commission of five appointive members. In cooperation with the President, Congress, and the Attorney General, it was empowered to make investigations of firms and industries and to make recommendations based thereon. Its only regulative powers were to enforce the substantive provisions of the Clayton Act and to prevent "unfair methods of competition." This it could accomplish only by the issuance of cease and desist orders, which could be appealed to the circuit courts either by the Commission or by those affected by the orders.

The Clayton Act never became a very important weapon in the anti-trust arsenal. Dealing only with a few specific practices among the many available to business, poorly drafted, and handicapped by the flexible proviso that some of these were illegal only where they substantially lessened competition or fostered monopoly, it was largely emasculated through strict judicial interpretation. The courts nullified the section of the act dealing with intercompany stock acquisitions, by holding that intercompany acquisition of assets was a legal alternative to stock acquisition, and that mergers which had acquired the assets of the combining firms at the time proceedings were instituted were not in violation of the act even if stock acquisition had been undertaken as an initial step. The provision forbidding price discrimination contained so many loopholes and frequently was so narrowly construed as to have little regulatory scope. The provision prohibiting tying contracts was restricted largely to cases involving dominant firms without strong competitors, but has served a useful regulatory function within this limited sphere.

The more significant activities of the Federal Trade Commission, therefore, came to center largely around its remaining powers—making investigations and preventing unfair methods of competition through the use of a cease-and-desist procedure. Its investigations were often well conducted and its recommendations to Congress in some instances influenced the drafting of legislation applying to specific industries. Positive action under the power to prevent unfair methods of competition, as time passed, resolved itself principally into action to maintain an ethical "plane of competition" by proceeding against misbranding and misrepresentation, and so forth. In this field its powers were considerably enhanced by the passage in 1938 of the Wheeler-Lea Act, which extended the Commission's authority to attack unethical competitive practices simply on the basis of injury to consumers. Numerous actions of this character designed to maintain the morals of businessmen for the protection of both their competitors and consumers have been undertaken to some public advantage. The emphasis, however, was neither on the enforcement of competition nor on its restriction, but rather on the establishment of the ethical level on which business rivalry might take place. As such, it was not the most vital part of the public policy toward monopoly and competition. Certain actions have also been taken by the Commission against collusive agreements and various practices restraining trade, over which it shares jurisdiction with the Sherman Act as enforced by the Department of Justice, and a few of these have resulted in important additions to our anti-trust law.

Legislation Conflicting with the Policy of Enforcing Competition

Although the maintenance of competition and the prevention of monopoly within the field of business enterprise has been and is the avowed and active policy of our government, there are increasing areas of exception to this policy, and some of these stand in more or less direct conflict with the philosophy of maintaining competition wherever possible. In certain industries, competition has been traditionally found to be unworkable and a direct governmental regulation of prices and outputs, subject to certain constitutional limitations, has been imposed. The railroad and the electric, gas, urban transport, and other public service industries have thus long been declared to be natural monopolies; firms have been granted monopoly franchises and their rates and service subjected to regulation by federal or state authorities. The "natural monopoly" sphere, discussed in other chapters, has thus come to stand as a recognized exception to the rule of competition.

Two other areas of major exception are those of labor and agriculture. The tendency of our modern law, discussed in Chapters 29 and 43, has been to guarantee to labor the right of collective bargaining, subject to numerous additional protections, and thus to assist laborers through unions to escape the processes of unrestricted competition and to establish such monopoly bargaining power as they may be able to in particular instances. This departure from universal dependence on competition has been justified on the ground that labor is less able to withstand the pressures of competition than enterprise—personal incomes being directly involved—and that at any rate it should be enabled to offset the buyers' monopoly power of strong employers. It is not necessarily inconsistent in logic or unworkable in practice to foster concentrated economic power in labor and to combat it in business, but certain conflicts may tend to arise if the the two policies are not carefully controlled and coordinated. In the field of agriculture, excessive competition, together with exposure to the superior bargaining power of industrial buyers, has again been adduced as reason in part for systematic interference with competition. Beginning with the early 1930's, our policy toward agriculture, discussed in Chapters 20 and 36, has become increasingly one of minimum price fixing, crop control, and elimination of competition in marketing. So far as this has extended to the direct governmental fixing of the prices of processors and marketers—as in the case of many state milk control schemes—competition within nonagricultural areas of business enterprise has been suppressed in rather clear inconsistency with our basic policy of maintaining competition in the economy.

Aside from the bituminous coal industry, which was for a time subjected to minimum price regulation by the Guffey-Vinson Act of 1937, again because of the plea of excessive competition, the principal remaining area where restriction of competition has been legally supported is that of the distributive trades. The primary stimulus to control of competition in the distributive fields was the rise of chain stores and other mass-distribution firms, which after World War I brought relatively big business, with superior efficiency and aggressive competitive tactics, into the traditionally small-business fields of local wholesaling and retailing of groceries, drugs, drygoods, hardware, and so forth. Although in such fields the position of a few dominant chains ordinarily did not rise above control of a substantial minority of the trade, their aggressive competition and low-price policies reduced the earnings of small competitors; further they tended to displace the independent wholesaler firms whose functions they subsumed. A primary reaction of small retailers and wholesalers to this threat to their welfare was to organize for political action to reduce the competitive advantages of mass-distributors. The most direct attack was carried forward through punitive taxation of chain stores, passed in a number of states. But in addition to these, and more generally adopted, were several items of legislation aimed at the competitive advantages of chain stores or simply at reducing price competition in the distributive trades. On the federal level, the principal legislation was the Robinson-Patman Act (1936), which amended the Clayton Act, principally to prohibit price discriminations in favor of large buyers (chain stores buying from manufacturers, for example) except where such concessions were based on demonstrable cost savings.

On the state level, in all but two states, the principal legislation secured by organized independent distributors since 1930 is found in the fair-trade or resale price maintenance laws. These generally permit a distributor and a manufacturer to enter into a contract fixing the minimum resale price of any branded item, and thereupon to make this price binding upon any competitor of the distributor, whether or not the competitor has signed such a contract. When applied to each item of a full line of merchandise, such contracts permit, in theory at least, overall private price fixing, without public supervision or representation, of the retail prices of goods—in effect, some approximation to publicly sponsored private collusion. Major limitations on the full effectiveness of such control are the competition of brands not under resale price maintenance contracts and the difficulty of enforcement, but these laws have had an apparently substantial effect in some lines in raising or maintaining price and suppressing distributive price competition.

Representing a clear departure from our traditional policy of fostering competition within the field of enterprise, the enactment of these laws has created a paradox—to counteract the alleged threat of monopolistic chain store distribution we suppress competition in the threatened area. Some commentators would hold that the preservation of small business and small business earnings is the paramount aim and justifies the measure; others would hold the cure to be worse than the disease and the dangers of the disease to be badly overrated. In any event, it would appear that public sponsorship of unsupervised private price fixing is a doubtful measure even should some public interference be advisable.

Viewing our policy toward competition in retrospect, it appears that the policy of fostering competition has become increasingly a qualified one. The result of conflicting political pressures is that we seem to seek competition but not too much of it. In the major industrial fields, where concentration is common, we attempt, though not too successfully, to increase or maintain competition. In labor, agriculture, the distributive trades—and potentially in any small business field—a plea of subnormal earnings or excessive competition is likely to be considered as serious ground for restriction of competition. It is quite possible that the restrictions of competition already have reached or will reach so far as to render the maintenance of competition in remaining spheres infeasible, meaningless, or ineffective. Meaningful pursuit of the basic anti-trust policy requires a careful scrutiny of every plea for exception and a careful application of adequate safeguards and standards wherever exception to the rule is granted.

Conclusion

The anti-trust policy since its inception in 1890 may be viewed as an adjunct to the basic policy of laissez faire; its ostensible aim has been to preserve the conditions under which competition will serve as an adequate regulator of economic activity. In the accomplishment of this aim it has had to rely on the legal prohibition of what the courts and the attorneys general chose to regard as monopolization and restraint of trade. On the whole its influence on competitive behavior is thought by many not to have been significant. Concentrated market structures favorable to the limitation of competition have developed in spite of it, and it has certainly been less than completely effective in elimination of industrial cooperation or collusion through attacks on restraint of trade. Critics emphasize that its alleged weakness is attributable mainly to the absence of any generally accepted standard of a desirable form of competition or market structure, and to the existence of a legal standard that emphasizes the maintenance of a freedom to compete rather than the observance of some particular degree or form of competition. Others charge laxity of enforcement, but also conclude that the anti-trust laws have been relatively ineffective.

On the other hand, it is argued that if they have not provided a panacea in economic policy, the anti-trust laws have accomplished much more than meets the eye—that under their pressure we have neither private cartels in the European style nor mergers to the extent of full monopoly, and that competition is in general more effective and active than if they had not been passed or had not been even lightly enforced. To this line of argument it was added by Arnold that, with more vigorous and better directed enforcement (together with repeal of conflicting legislation), the anti-trust laws could be much more effective than in the past and could preserve competition as a fairly adequate automatic regulator of the economy. Certain changes in the judicial interpretation of the anti-trust laws, which now seem incipient, together with some statutory revisions, might appreciably contribute to this end. The relative merits of these and related positions must be weighed in the development of future economic policy in this country.

Selected References

GENERAL WORKS

Arnold, T., *The Bottlenecks of Business*. New York: Reynal and Hitchcock, Inc., 1940.

Fainsod, M., and L. Gordon, *Government and the American Economy*. New York: W. W. Norton & Company, Inc., 1941.

Lyon, L. S.; M. W. Watkins; and V. Abramson, *Government and Economic Life,* Vol. I, Chapter 11. Washington, D. C.: Brookings Institution, 1939.

Purdy, Harry L.; Martin L. Lindahl; and William A. Carter, *Corporate Concentration and Public Policy.* New York: Prentice-Hall, Inc., 1942.

SPECIAL TOPICS

Adams, W., ed., *The Structure of American Industry.* New York: The Macmillan Company, 1950.

Edwards, C. D., *Maintaining Competition.* New York: McGraw-Hill Book Company, Inc., 1949.

Federal Trade Commission, *Report on Resale Price Maintenance,* 1945.

Mason, E. S., "The Current Status of the Monopoly Problem in the United States," *Harvard Law Review,* Vol. 62, No. 8 (June, 1949), pp. 1265-1285.

National Resources Committee, *The Structure of the American Economy,* Part I, 1939.

Nourse, E. G., and H. B. Drury, *Industrial Price Policies and Economic Progress.* Washington, D. C.: The Brookings Institution, 1939.

47 · PUBLIC FINANCE AND FISCAL POLICY, 1919-1950

THE COURSE TAKEN BY FEDERAL FINANCE during the decade of the twenties can best be understood in the light of the forces that produced the tax system of World War I. Much of the debate over fiscal policies during the succeeding decade turned on the question whether the trend toward progressivity established with the passage of the first permanent income tax in 1913 should be continued or reversed. Tax developments during the war had continued and had strengthened the trend toward greater progression, first embodied in legislation in the so-called corporation excise tax of 1909. This effort to stimulate the introduction of the income tax principle was part of a running battle between those who resented the increasing concentration of wealth and monopoly in the latter half of the nineteenth century and those who regarded graduation of tax rates as a breach of democratic equality of treatment.

The Fiscal System at the End of World War I

The passage of the 16th Amendment to the Constitution and the income tax act of 1913 were regarded by their proponents as indispensable steps in a national program to halt the growth of socialist sentiment that had been nourished by an ever-clearer separation of the public into class groups. It should be borne in mind that the intent of the advocates of progressive taxation was not to redistribute income in the downward direction, but to call a halt to an increasing inequality of income. On the other hand, it is true that once the principle of progressive taxation of incomes and inheritances comes to be accepted as a permanent feature of a tax system, a trend to an ever larger degree of progression may be established. The vast revenue needs of World War I brought this possibility quickly into the foreground and set in motion the still unresolved struggle over how much redistribution of income should be accomplished through the tax instrument. Indeed, it will be a continuing struggle so long as private enterprise economy is retained.

The Controversy over the Degree of Progression of the Income Tax

Since the income tax had hardly been introduced before Europe was at war, President Wilson was doubtful of the advisability of increasing rates despite the sharp fall in Federal revenues caused by the dislocation of trade. Not until 1916 was the question of what proportion of the war cost should be paid by the various income groups really faced. The Republicans wanted to revert to the higher tariffs prevailing before the Democratic administration had succeeded in shifting the emphasis from customs to the income tax in 1913. On the other hand, the administration offered a program under which over half of the new revenue was to come from the income tax. The significance of this struggle must be inferred from the fiscal background of the time. In 1915 only 80 million of total internal revenues of about 700 million dollars was accounted for by the income tax. Much of the rest came from customs, excises, and miscellaneous taxes, the incidence of which was almost entirely on the consumer. Since the vast bulk of total consumption is accounted for by those in the lower income groups, this tax system was still highly regressive despite the passage of the income tax of 1913. The need for revenue brought about a revolution in Federal taxation, however, and ultimately the bulk of the taxes levied for war purposes was provided by the income tax and the taxes on profits. The income tax itself, and of course the new estate tax which was developed during the war, impinged for the most part on the middle and upper income groups rather than the lower.

Taxes vs. Borrowing To Pay for the War

Another aspect of war finance that exerted an important influence on fiscal policy for a dozen years after the Armistice was the proportion of the cost of the war paid out of taxation. Economists had written extensively on the economic evils that ensued from the financial mistakes of the Civil War. A highly vocal group argued in favor of financing the whole (or a very large part) of the war out of taxes. This was, of course, politically and economically impossible. Tax bills take months to pass, and spending must commence immediately upon adoption of an armament program. Rates of tax become unbearably high if much over 50 per cent of a major war is to be financed out of taxation, exercising a discouraging effect on willingness to invest and to work. The Secretary of the Treasury, McAdoo, originally wished to see one-half of the cost of the war paid for through taxation, but later revised his estimate downward to one-sixth.[1] Ultimately 32 per cent of the total expenditures of the Federal government between April 6, 1917 and October 31, 1919 was paid for out of tax revenues.[2]

---

[1] W. J. Shultz and M. R. Caine, *Financial Development of the United States,* p. 526. New York: Prentice-Hall, Inc., 1937.

[2] D. R. Dewey, *Financial History of the United States,* p. 511. New York and London: Longmans, Green and Co., 1934. Total expenditures during this period amounted to $35,413,000,000.

Economic Effects of War Borrowing and Taxing

The effects on the postwar fiscal system of the war financial system were the following: *First,* the higher the proportion borrowed, the lower the tax revenue needs. Thus if a relatively heavy proportion of the costs of the war were borrowed, the issue of progression to that extent could be deferred. This may account for the view of some wealthy men that only a relatively small part of the war costs should be met out of taxation. In order to cover a third of the expenses of the war out of taxes, Congress was forced to enact a sharply progressive income tax. The top surtax rate under the Revenue Act of 1918 was 65 per cent on that portion of income over $1,000,000. *Second,* the greater the proportion of war costs raised by taxation, the less is the inflationary pressure. A greater amount of private spending would thereby be eliminated as government spending increased. Since inflation hits the small income receiver hardest (wages lag behind prices), a sound financial policy would minimize the diversion of purchasing power from them to profits. Moreover, the greater the inflation the more difficult the postwar readjustment. *Third,* a high rate of borrowing intensifies the problem of debt repayment after the war. A high rate of debt repayment affects the level and nature of taxes and thus raises the issue of which income groups should bear the main brunt of taxation during the postwar period. Even if no serious effort is made to repay debt, the burden of the interest payments is felt in terms of increased tax levies. Since the debt has been held by savers, that is, primarily the higher income groups, the issue inevitably arises whether the annual interest payments (which average a billion dollars a year from 1920 to 1924) ought not to be recaptured from these groups by means of income and inheritance taxes.

The Difficulty of Reducing Federal Expenditures After the War

The ending of hostilities in 1918 by no means permitted a return to the low level of government expenditures of the prewar days. The attitude of the public toward the role of the Federal government in the economic system, which had increasingly favored various forms of intervention since 1850, took further strides in this direction after the war despite President Harding's advocacy of a policy of "back to normalcy." For several reasons expenditures were to remain permanently higher. (1) The price level had more than doubled. (2) Population had increased. (3) A large transfer expenditure in the form of interest payments would continue until the increase in the debt had been eliminated. (4) The United States had to play its part in the reconstruction of Europe. (5) Payments to veterans would be large, and would increase as the veterans' lobby began to make itself felt. (6) The great decline in farm income focussed attention on the need for farm subsidies. (7) The twenties were a period of great multiplication of government agencies. (8) The growing complexity of economic life promised to require a great increase in the role of government. As late as the nineties Cleveland could say that it is not the role of the Federal Government to relieve the distress of its citizens. But both political parties rejected this view after World War I. Thus there was a steady increase in Federal Government expenditures, and therefore in taxes.

Fiscal Policies in the Decade After World War I

The fiscal policies of the Federal Government during the twenties were determined by a few simple considerations. *First,* as has been noted, it was not possible to bring the cost of government down to prewar levels. The cost of the war did not end with the armistice; the country was left with a legacy of veterans' payments and government bureaus. *Second,* though the level of expenditures remained relatively high, it was possible to minimize them to a degree not attainable after World War II. The watchword of the administration under President Coolidge was economy, and the establishment of the Budget Bureau in 1921 had eliminated some of the possibilities of waste. In contrast with our experience after World War II, the government rapidly curtailed loans to European countries in response to the public desire for a return to isolation. The prospect of another war did not seem sufficiently imminent, moreover, to require the enormous expenditures for national defense necessitated by the division of the world into two antagonistic parts after World War II.

Third, the debates over the distribution of the tax burden among income groups, and over the appropriateness of placing a significant portion of the burden on business, raged almost continually for two decades. Business in general was eager to see the elimination of the excess profits tax and the high income surtax. Coolidge and his Secretary of the Treasury, Andrew Mellon, supported the contention of the wealthy in favor of a low level of public spending and correspondingly low income tax rates. But the ranks of business were split over the advocacy by a group of rich men of a general sales tax. The merchant class naturally opposed this disability on sales of consumer goods. Although Mellon and his supporter, Senator Smoot, argued that a high surtax discourages business enterprise, there was little economic argument brought forward on either side of the debate during the twenties. Those who admired the productivity of a general Federal sales tax had no conception of its possible discouraging effects on consumption, and indirectly on the very investment that they supposed to be discouraged by a high surtax.[3] The

[3] The twenties constituted a period of high profits, and an increasing tendency of corporations to free themselves from dependence on the banks by ploughing back profits into the business. The result was, on the one hand, a rapid increase in investment and the capacity to produce consumers' goods, and, on the other, a diversion of part of the

liberal groups, which had succeeded in forcing Congress to make substantial use of the income and excess profits taxes to finance the war, could not prevent repeal of the Excess Profits Tax (1921). They did manage, however, to limit the reduction of the maximum rate of surtax in the Revenue Act of 1924 to 10 percentage points. But the Revenue Act of 1926 effected a further reduction in surtax rates. Increasing prosperity and national income provided annual surpluses (which were applied to the national debt) despite these decreases and the elimination of the excess profits tax.

Fourth, the struggle over business taxation emphasized the differences in point of view between those who either wished for greater redistribution of income and reduction in monopoly power or thought of the excess profits and corporate profits taxes as a means of stemming the socialistic tide, and those who regarded these taxes as the first step in an inevitable trend toward a socialist economy.

Fifth, in line with the Republican philosophy of relatively low expenditures went a policy of debt repayment. But this officially adopted policy was in practice carried out rather mildly. An important part of the reason for the surpluses was the persistent tendency of the Treasury during those years to underestimate revenues, but the main cause was the high level of income throughout the decade.

Sixth, agriculture had joined with liberal and labor opinion in opposing the repeal of the excess profits tax and reduction in surtax rates, although it had allied itself with industry on the tariff question. Since the problem of the farmers was to export surpluses, and since they bought the manufactured goods subject to high tariffs, their interest in protection was mistaken. Their action contributed to the maintenance of a Federal tax system that was much more favorable to the higher income groups than they intended.

The Federal fiscal developments in the decade after the war may be summarized by saying that generally prosperous conditions so eased the revenue problem that a reversal was brought about in the trend toward greater progressivity in income and business taxation. It is true that Mellon and the conservative wing of the Republican party strove in vain for the repeal of the Federal estate tax (they nearly succeeded in 1926), and that the gift tax, necessary for making the estate tax effective, was actually eliminated. Income tax rates, though made less burdensome for all groups in the Revenue Act of 1926, were adjusted to favor the wealthy. Given prosperity and a philosophy of low government expenditures and limited debt repayment, a reduction in taxes was inevitable.

---

stream of purchasing power into deposits with a relatively low velocity. Thus many economists have argued that part of the cause of the depression of the thirties was the failure of the economy to provide the consumer with adequate purchasing power. A sales tax would have strengthened this tendency.

The party in power was psychologically oriented to the wealthier classes and regarded the maintenance of prosperity as essentially a matter of avoiding discouragement to the formation of capital. Consequently, the reduction in taxes offered greater concessions to the higher income groups than to the lower. But the general prosperity of all classes gave the public a much greater feeling of solidarity than had been felt at any time (except during war) in the previous fifty years. A manifestation of this was the decline in the strength of the Progressive movement in the latter part of the decade.

State and Local Financial Problems, 1919–1950

During the interwar period, state finance continued the growth in relative importance that had already become marked in the nineties. States accounted for 10 per cent of total government expenditures in 1890 and the percentage had doubled by 1939. This growth in state expenditures was part of the trend toward centralization that was also noticeable in the growing contribution of the Federal government to the national income. Both were at the expense of the rural and smaller localities. The rapidly growing expenditures and tax receipts of the states reflected in part the extension of the state road network as the public became increasingly impatient with the inefficiency of local road building. Moreover, a rising consciousness of the value to the community of the benefits of a high standard of education, welfare services, adequate relief programs, centralized police force, and the like, dictated a much greater role for the states in regional government.

The financing of these multiplied services required the states to make every effort in their search for suitable revenues. During World War I the states had attempted to find means of making the traditional property tax more productive, but the situation was somewhat relieved by the relative reduction in state and local expenditures as many normal projects were suspended. During the twenties, however, came the great development of the automobile, and with it the general adoption of gasoline and motor vehicle taxes. The productivity of these taxes in an expanding era prompted their use for the general tax fund, despite vigorous attempts by the motor interests to restrict the use of the proceeds to highways. The adoption of a permanent Federal income tax encouraged the states to follow suit. Nearly a third had income taxes by the end of the twenties. State sales taxes had as yet hardly put in an appearance.

Local Financial Problems in the Twenties

Although local government expenditures have decreased in relative importance, in absolute terms they have quadrupled. The flow of population to the cities has greatly increased the expense of police and fire protection, and standards of education, social services, and physical equipment have risen. During the twenties local expenditures (of cities rather than rural localities and small towns) actually increased more than did state expenditures (while Federal expenditures decreased between 1924 and 1929). Thus the problem of financing became acute, and the use of the property tax was expanded to the utmost. Assessments and tax rates rose along with the rise in property values. As the states turned to other taxes they tended to leave the property tax more and more to the localities. By the end of the decade, in view of the unhealthiness of the underlying economic situation, too great a burden had been put on property, and the property tax collapsed in the general economic debacle of 1929.

The Continued Growth in State Functions

Following 1930, despite temporary fluctuations due to war and depression, the states continued their trend toward increased spending. This tendency reflected their growing importance as units of regional government. The depression forced the states to take over much of the responsibility for relief expenditures from the localities, and the passage of the Social Security Act (1935) coerced all the states to establish their own unemployment insurance legislation. Other forms of state relief have been old age assistance, child welfare aid, and relief to the blind. State expenditures on roads remained high until the mid-thirties, and, although the completion of projects might have brought about an eventual decline in state capital expenditures on roads and state institutions, the virtual cessation of these expenditures during and for some time after the war ensured the importance of this item in state budgets for a long time to come. Another factor that promised to sustain the rate of state spending was the growing interest, accelerated by the war, of the Federal government in coordinating the welfare activities of the states.[4] Corresponding to the foregoing changes in the magnitude and relative importance of state expenditures were the changes in those of the cities and towns. During the thirties relief expenditures rose and capital expenditures declined. The effect of World War II was to reduce local expenditures substantially, but this temporary advantage was more than offset after the war when worn-out roads and equipment had to be replaced at a much higher price level.

By 1950, per capita total state revenue had increased nearly tenfold since 1915, the rise being virtually continuous despite alternations of

---

[4] Federal grants-in-aid to states have risen from about $100 million a year in the twenties to over $1.7 billion in 1948. Formerly the chief purpose of Federal aid was to stimulate or control state activities, but more recently increasing account has been taken of the differences in the wealth and needs of the various states. *Cf.* Shultz and Caine. *Op. cit.*, pp. 746-8.

periods of rising and falling prices. The most striking change was the rise in "Aid received from other governments" (mostly Federal) from 5 million dollars in 1915 to 1,154 million dollars in 1947.[5] Over 350 million dollars of the increase occurred between 1946 and 1947. The bulk of Federal aid to the states during the 1930's was for highways, but after 1937 grants for this purpose declined continuously, their place being taken by grants for education and public welfare. State tax collections likewise increased rapidly and steadily, and substantial changes occurred in the relative importance of state tax revenues. The property tax declined greatly in relative importance after 1919. In 1930 the first important use was made of the state sales taxes, and they rose steadily in importance. The tax on motor vehicle fuels likewise became one of the most important state taxes. The income tax (corporate and personal) is now a major revenue yielder for the states, and taxes for unemployment compensation have gained increasing importance.[6] Death and gift taxes were never a very important source of state revenues.

Recent Trends in Local Finance

Local tax collections, after quadrupling from 1913 to 1927 (a substantial part of the increase due, of course, to higher prices), remained surprisingly stable until 1944, except for a 15 per cent drop during the depression. After 1946, however, the rise in local collections of property taxes was extremely rapid, and assessments were substantially increased. Despite rising postwar expenditures by the localities, the property tax remained their major source of revenue, though many cities introduced (among other tax sources) the sales tax. A few resorted to a crude form of income tax.

State and Local Borrowing

During the twenties both states and cities borrowed for road construction, the cities on a large scale. Again, the depression necessitated increased borrowing by both states and localities, this time for relief. Had it not been for the rapid decline in interest rates during the depression (owing to a low demand for investable funds and to a low interest rate policy by both the Federal Reserve System and the Treasury), difficulties would have been even more acute than was actually the case. By forcing a reduction in expenditures, the war provided the opportunity for a reduction in debt, but the trend was again reversed as expenditures increased after 1945. For example, many states have financed their veterans' bonuses by borrowing.

---

[5] The Tax Foundation, *Facts and Figures on Government Finance, 1948-1949,* p. 69. Based on data of the Department of Commerce.

[6] The Tax Foundation, *Op. cit.,* p. 73.

Federal Finance and the Depression

Federal financial policies relate to any depression both as cause and effect. Secretary Mellon in part attributed the prosperity of the twenties to the encouragement to investment provided by tax policies favorable to business and to the upper income groups. Yet this tax incentive to a high rate of saving, coupled with the high tariff, contributed to a relative decline in spending and therefore to depression. Debt repayment, made possible by low Federal expenditures and high revenues, exercised a deflationary effect, which some observers find evidenced in stability of prices during a period in other important respects thought to be a boom.[7] During this period, moreover, foreign loans had supported the export surplus demanded by American business. Growing difficulties on the Continent finally frightened the American investor, and the absence of compensating foreign loans by the United States Government, coupled with the discouraging effect on imports of our high tariff, forced France, England and Germany to default on their loans.

It would, of course, be erroneous to ascribe the crisis and depression solely to American financial policies. All that can fairly be said is that more enlightened Federal fiscal policies might have served to delay the crisis. There was, for example, no positive assurance that the more far-sighted policies of the post-World War II years could forestall a similar collapse, or, if a collapse were avoided, that these policies would be responsible.

Conflicting Views on Fiscal Policy Early in the Depression

Whatever weight is to be attached to fiscal policy in the multitude of forces that finally resulted in the collapse of the prosperity of the twenties, the effect of that collapse on fiscal policy and fiscal theory ultimately proved to be revolutionary. The Hoover administration became hopelessly involved in inconsistent "recovery" policies. As incomes and employment fell off, tax revenues automatically declined, which, combined with the necessity for growing relief payments, converted the surplus into a deficit. To reduce the deficit the administration recommended to Congress a rise in tax rates. It was thought that discouragement to business would be avoided if the burden was placed on the lower income groups through a sales tax. Actually of course, this would have magnified any tendency to underconsumption to which the regressive trend of the tax

[7] The Federal government paid off $9.3 billion of debt between the high point in 1919 ($25.5 billion) and the low point in 1930 ($16.2 billion). To the extent that debt repayment was effected by taxes on those who would have spent, the money had a lower velocity in the hands of the interest receivers, who were savers. But it must be remembered that between 1922 and 1932 local debt increased from $7.75 billion to $15.2 billion. This virtually offset the effect of Federal debt repayment on the purchasing power stream. Cf. *Statistical Abstract of the United States*, 1939, Tables 206 and 229.

system of the twenties might have contributed. Thus, the battle between the liberal and conservative elements with respect to what income groups should bear the brunt of the tax burden was taken up again after a temporary victory, during a disarming period of prosperity, for those who favored the higher income groups. But the sales tax failed, and in 1932 estate tax rates were raised and a gift tax was enacted.

On the international side, Congress had increased tariff rates still further in the Hawley-Smoot tariff of 1930. With depression becoming world wide, however, it was obvious that employment at home could not be maintained by insisting on a favorable balance of trade. Retaliatory measures abroad were at once forthcoming, and the net effect was to slow down the rate of economic activity in all countries.

In view of the obviously discouraging effect on the rate of economic activity of all attempts to increase tax rates, the attempt to balance the budget now seems foolish. But it must be borne in mind that a long tradition of governmental noninterference in economic life could hardly be reversed over night, and in the light of events and the development of economic theory in the decades before 1929 it is quite clear that no administration could have advocated deficit spending. Indeed, one of the planks in the Democratic program in 1932 was to balance the budget, which itself forced Hoover's hand in his search for satisfactory recovery measures.

Fiscal Policies of the Roosevelt Administration

Despite some initial groping by the Roosevelt administration, it soon became apparent that an entirely new philosophy would supplant the Hoover program of consolatory advice to business, conservative public finance, and the leaving of relief and public works primarily to the states and localities. The financial program of the New Deal can be understood only in the framework of its entire economic legislation. In so broad a program inconsistencies were inevitable. Thus, the National Industrial Recovery Act (1933) took the initiative in encouraging business to prevent downward spiraling of prices, and indeed to reverse the trend. Yet one of the fundamental tenets of New Deal economics was the support of consumer purchasing power as a prerequisite to recovery. Again, the Agricultural Adjustment Act of the same year sought to support farm purchasing power through subsidies financed by taxes, the incidence of which was largely on the industrial consumer. Both of these measures were means of augmenting the purchasing power of certain sections of the community at the expense of others. To the extent that strategic importance could be assigned to stopping downward price spirals in certain industries and in farm purchasing power as compared with the purchasing power of other sectors of the economy, the net effect on the income stream would be favorable. There was in fact, some substance in this argument, although the shortcomings of a program devoted to supporting weak spots in the economy by subsidies and government-encouraged monopoly are apparent. Constitutionally, the levying of taxes for the special benefit of a particular group was inadmissible, as evidenced by the decision of the Supreme Court against the processing tax on certain agricultural commodities, the proceeds to be used for the support of their prices. Economically, short of virtual certainty as to the location of the weak spots, a more effective means of stimulating employment and income would appear to be to force an increase in the income stream. The latter is most effectively performed through a combination of a monetary policy aimed at increasing the supply of money, and a fiscal policy devoted to getting the new money into the hands of those who will either spend it on consumers' goods or invest it in plant, equipment, and inventories.

The Economic Effects of Depression Deficits

During the early months of the Roosevelt administration, fiscal policy was aimed at economy rather than at increased employment. But it proved impossible to balance the budget. A deficit, however, means that the government is injecting purchasing power into the income stream by borrowing and spending either new or idle money. There arose, therefore, the possibility of conscious Federal deficits aimed at increasing the income stream and, as a result, restoring the economy. This was the thesis advanced by J. M. Keynes in his *Means to Prosperity,* published in 1933, which was accepted by a large number of American economists. The gist of the program was the encouragement of private investment through public spending. It was argued that if the government would spend enough, the net increase in the flow of income would put industry in a profit position, which would induce a further rise in incomes as private investment responded.

The severe doubts attending the success of a fiscal program aimed at encouraging business to undertake investment during a period of retrenchment prevented outright acceptance of the Keynesian thesis by the administration. First, no one could say how much purchasing power the government would have to inject in order to convert losses into profits. It was clear, however, that the figure would have to be very large.[8] Second, even if sufficiently large deficits were created, investment (beyond inventories) would hardly be expanded without assurance that the spending would be continued. Third, during the 1930's businessmen were quite as

---

[8] The administration announced as its policy the financing of ordinary expenditures out of tax revenues, and public works and relief expenditures out of borrowing. The aggregate deficit from fiscal 1932 through fiscal 1939, was $25.5 billion, an average of $3.2 billion a year. *Statistical Abstract of the United States,* 1939, p. 167. These deficits, while large enough to focus attention on our inability to balance the budget, are generally agreed to have been very inadequate to convert business losses into profits throughout the economy.

likely to be discouraged as encouraged by an announced policy of pump-priming. The rising strength of socialism from the 1890's onward had not been forgotten, and a government that succeeded in restoring the economy to full employment through fiscal policy might well use fiscal policy as an entering wedge to a socialized economy. Fourth, the problem of government finance itself was sufficiently difficult to impel the administration to return to a balanced budget as soon as possible, and thus there was lacking the outright acceptance of pump-priming required for an adequate test.

Pump-Priming vs. New Deal Social Philosophy

The social philosophy of the New Deal conflicted with attempts at pump-priming, which favors the businessman and higher income receiver. The Revenue Act of 1934 was an indication that Roosevelt had not accepted pump-priming as an instrument of recovery, for this Act placed a greater portion of the tax burden on the higher income groups. Regardless of the justice of this move, its effect must have been to nullify in some degree the beneficial effects on profits and investment exerted by deficit spending. Increases were made in the steepness of the progression of the income, estate, and gift taxes, and steps were taken to reduce tax avoidance. These changes did not satisfy the depression-born share-the-wealth people (Long, Coughlin, Townsend), and in 1935 the President was forced to go much farther in his attempt to reduce the concentration of wealth. The Revenue Act of 1935 increased surtax rates. Though many businessmen maintained that the higher rates discouraged investment as well as the savings out of which investment was made, there was no way of testing the contention.

Probably the tax regarded by businessmen themselves as most discouraging to investment was the undistributed profits tax, the major change effected by the Revenue Act of June 27, 1936. A graduated tax was imposed on undistributed profits of corporations, with the object of forcing them to distribute dividends. Advocates of this tax desired to increase the importance of the stockholder and to reduce corporate savings and stimulate consumption. Businessmen argued that the tax penalized the accumulation of surplus and discouraged investment. The quarrel over this tax emphasized the collision between the views of those who saw high level income and employment achieved through greater distribution of income and consumer spending, and those who believed recovery possible only if care was taken to encourage investment.

The Federal Fiscal System on the Eve of World War II

New Deal fiscal policies were finally dissolved in a mixture of preparation for war and a reaction against several years of what many regarded as wasteful public spending. In his budget message in April, 1937, the

President continued his fight against tax evasion through such instruments as the personal holding company, multiple trusts, and so forth. Congress went part of the way, but the Revenue Act of 1937 did not eliminate the tax avoidance made possible by tax exempt securities, failure to distribute profits, and the treatment of capital gains. On the other hand, in the face of violent attacks by business, Congress in effect repudiated the principle of undistributed profits taxation. Furthermore, the capital gains tax provisions were liberalized, so that taxes were levied on only 50 per cent of gains made on capital assets held for over 24 months. The disposition seemed to exist on the part of both business and government to exaggerate the role of the tax system, as then constituted, in affecting the level of economic activity. This may explain in part the high rate of activity in the realm of Federal taxation in the late thirties.

Fiscal policy in the months before the outbreak of war in Europe became extremely complex. The President had apparently accepted the stagnation philosophy set forth by J. M. Keynes in his "General Theory of Employment, Interest, and Money" (1936). That is, pump priming could not work out; the government must actually replace private investment with public investment when, as in 1937, income and employment fell off. The President, in the spring of 1939, requested Congress to vote recovery and relief expenditures of 9 billion dollars. Though Congress rejected the spending philosophy, it actually authorized 2 billion more in expenditures (including relief and defense expenditure) than for 1938. Congress repealed the undistributed profits tax in 1939, a carryover of five years was enacted for long term capital losses, and a conciliatory attitude toward business was implied by the announcement in February, 1939, by Secretary Morgenthau that no new taxes were contemplated.[9] In view of the proximity of war, and the certainty of almost unlimited demand for the products of industry, it may seem strange that so many fiscal concessions were made to business. Part of the explanation appears to be the pendulum swing away from the earlier New Deal policies, which manifested itself in a growing Congressional conservatism. The momentum was carried into the period immediately preceding the war, when the rate of economic activity was already beginning to be stimulated by increased exports to Europe. The approach of war naturally diminished the importance of the class struggle, and the depression economics and the attacks on the "economic royalists" of the thirties gave place to the very different fiscal problems of total war.

Federal Fiscal Policies During the War

The primary objective of tax policy during the war was, of course, the provision of adequate revenues. Like Secretary McAdoo, his predecessor

---

[9] Sidney Ratner, *American Taxation*, p. 485. New York: Norton, 1942.

of World War I, Morgenthau hoped that the war might be financed to the extent of two-thirds by taxation. Ultimately the proportion was nearer one-third. The bond financing was carried out with care, and in such a way that as little as possible was left to the whims of the market—issues were tailored to the needs of different types of savers and payroll deductions for bond purchases were widely instituted in government agencies, the armed forces and private businesses. A large proportion of bonds was sold to the Federal Reserve and the commercial banks, however, and thus formed the basis for deposit expansion. Although a rise in the supply of money was needed to support the enormous increase in transactions associated with wartime production, at least a part of the inflationary pressure could have been relieved by even higher increases in taxes on spending and through a more thoroughgoing program of forced savings than could be provided by semi-voluntary payroll deductions for bonds and social security taxes.

Fiscal Policy and Inflation Control

The controversy continued as before between those who wished to put most of the burden of the war on business and the higher income groups and those who wished to see most of it put on consumption and the lower income groups. But in World War II there was a greater understanding of the role of fiscal policy in the control of inflation, and political decisions could be made on the basis of a reasonably accurate knowledge of their economic effects. Thus, the necessity of restraining consumption was clearly appreciated, as it had not been in World War I. This was accomplished by lowering exemptions under the income tax to the point where 50 million people were brought under the tax [10] and by the enactment of heavy excises on commodities the consumption of which affected the war effort.[11]

The Treasury also proposed a graduated tax on spending in 1942, but it was rejected by Congress, partly because of its unfamiliarity and partly because of a reluctance to introduce further complications into the tax system. Yet a graduated tax on spending would have had one great advantage over excises and lowered income tax exemptions. Granted reason-

10 The Revenue Act of 1942 accomplished this through reduced personal exemptions, higher rates, and a 5 per cent Victory Tax with the low exemption of $624. The combined taxes brought the top surtax above 90 per cent, and the Act provided that this figure be taken as a limit. R. E. Paul, *Taxation for Prosperity,* p. 106-7. New York: Bobbs-Merrill, 1947. From the point of view of inflation control, the introduction of current tax payment in 1943 represented a step forward. Top rates were reached in 1944, but were reduced slightly after the end of the war, and substantially in the Revenue Act of 1948, with effective bracket rates running from 16.6 to 82.1 per cent. The Korean war sharply reversed this downward trend.

11 Federal excise tax collections rose from $1.7 billion in 1939 to $7.4 billion in 1948. Despite much pressure Congress did not reduce the high war excises in the revenue revision of 1948.

able exemptions, the tax could be avoided by reducing consumption. Thus, goods and factors of production would be released to the war effort and the lower income groups would have been left in possession of their purchasing power. This would have provided a cushion of demand in the postwar period when output and employment might be falling rapidly.

The spendings tax would also have been superior to a general sales tax, since the low income groups could not avoid a tax which would apply to virtually everything they bought except, perhaps, some exempted foods. Excises during wartime, on transportation and long distance telephone calls, for example, served the purpose of reducing the demand for services needed in the war effort, and to that extent the consumer was left in possession of his money. Their retention after the war was far less logical. They reduced inflationary pressure, but at the expense of a limited number of commodities and by permitting an unnecessary degree of regression in the Federal Tax system.

One way to reduce consumption during the war, while avoiding a permanent transfer of income away from the lower income groups, would have been a system of compulsory loans. This could have taken the form of an increase in social security or other payroll taxes, as advocated by the President and rejected by Congress. Compulsion is not agreeable to a democracy, however, and it was preferred to rely on incentives to save. In addition, the reaction of labor to payroll deductions has been to regard them as a permanent reduction of income; effective pay is regarded as "take-home" pay only. Compulsory saving might, therefore, have proved inflationary, since pressure would have been set up for wage rises to compensate for the payroll deductions.

Sentiment was naturally strong during the war for sharply increased taxes on business in order to compensate for the regressivity of the consumption taxation required on revenue and anti-inflationary grounds. Consequently, an excess profits tax was levied (in 1940) and increases were enacted in the corporate profits tax. The latter yielded 1.1 billion dollars in 1939 and 5 billion dollars in 1945. The excess profits tax yielded 11.1 billion dollars in the latter year. Although the excess profits tax was abolished after the war, corporate profits continued to increase during the postwar inflation; the yield of the corporate profits tax reached nearly 10 billion dollars in 1948, which compares with a combined yield from the excess profits and corporate income taxes in the peak year (1943) of about 14 billion dollars, when the price level was lower.

Main Features of World War II Finance

The salient features of Federal finance in World War II may be summarized as follows. The Federal government devoted close to 300 billion dollars to war expenditures between the years 1940 and 1945, which was over 86 per cent of total Federal expenditures.[12] The national debt rose from 36 billion dollars at the end of 1940 to 270 billion dollars at the end of the fiscal year 1946. Congressional opinion lagged behind that of the Treasury, and evidently of the country at large, with respect to the proportion of war expenditures that might be paid out of taxes. In World War I much impetus had been given to price inflation through the practice of encouraging the purchase of Liberty bonds by the public out of the proceeds of loans from commercial banks, with the bonds used as security. This was patently inflationary, since, simultaneously, the newly established Federal Reserve System provided the commercial banks with additional reserves. Although this crudity was avoided in World War II, not only was a large proportion of the war issue sold directly to the commercial banks, which increased the money supply, but the circumstances of issue facilitated bank borrowing by individuals in order to purchase securities. As of December, 1945, the commercial banks held 279 billion dollars in bonds. In addition, purchases of Federal securities by the Federal Reserve banks amounted to 22 billion dollars since the end of 1941 (a ten-fold increase) provided the commercial banks with adequate reserves for their own purchases as well as their loans to individual purchasers. The consequence was an increase in the money supply (total deposits adjusted and currency outside banks) from 78 billion dollars in 1941 to 175 billion in 1945. This more than doubling of the money supply considerably exceeded the rise in the price level, but the removal of price controls after the war allowed the impact to be felt in the form of a marked rise in prices. By constantly standing ready to purchase government securities from commercial bank portfolios at fixed buying rates, the Federal Reserve banks placed effective control of the money supply in the hands of the private banking system. In other words, a sufficient proportion of the increased government debt was monetized so that interest rates were kept low (thus reducing the interest burden to the Treasury), but at the cost of a considerable amount of monetary inflation and decreased Federal Reserve control over the banking system.

The Postwar Period

Federal fiscal problems after the end of World War II were intensified by the failure of the world to achieve a stable peace. During the last year of the war economists and businessmen alike underestimated the size of the postwar budget. Most expenditure estimates were around 20 billion dollars, whereas, after falling to 36 billion dollars in the fiscal year 1948, expenditures again rose, chiefly in connection with European aid. At the same time a movement developed in favor of tax reduction. As victory became certain in 1943-44, several postwar tax plans were evolved which

[12] See *Annual Report of the Secretary of the Treasury*, especially 1946.

stressed the necessity of lightening the burden of taxation on business after the war. Corporate income taxes and the excess profits tax were to be reduced or eliminated entirely. Thus, the same conflict developed as after World War I between those who emphasized the need for profits to stimulate production and employment and those who stressed the role of consumer purchasing power. A new complication was added, however, by the great growth in the strength of the trade unions, which took the form of an uncompromising opposition to allowing corporations to retain their large postwar profits. The corporations thus had to face both high corporate income taxes and higher wage rates. Several rounds of wage increases removed some of the pressure for a return to the high business taxes that obtained before the excess profits tax was repealed in 1945.[13] Although the threat of depression in the spring of 1949, accompanied by a sharp decline in corporate profits, temporarily silenced the advocates for higher corporate taxes and further general wage increases, labor nevertheless resumed its agitation for the latter in the summer of 1949. But it should be borne in mind that the ultimate cause of these inflationary moves was the great rise in purchasing power brought about by the methods used in financing World War II.

The major problems facing the Federal fiscal system after the war may be briefly summarized. The President was sharply opposed to tax reduction in 1948, on the ground that the best time to repay debt is at full employment and a high price level, when the burden of repayment is relatively small. Furthermore, he recommended the reenactment of the excess profits tax because of the profit showing of corporations since the war. The recession that started early in 1949 had developed by July to such an extent as to lead the President to restrict his tax recommendations to increases in the Federal estate and gift taxes and to the elimination of the transportation tax. He also evidenced his concern over business incentive by advocating liberalization of loss carry-over provisions under the corporate income tax. In January, 1949, his interest had been centered on inflation control and social insurance programs; in recommending additional taxes aggregating 4 billion dollars, the President recommended to Congress that it increase the levies on corporate profits and on estates and gifts (receipts had been reduced by one-third by the action of Congress in 1948 allowing estates to be divided between husband and wife). He also recommended the study of increased income tax rates on the middle and upper income brackets. Particularly anti-inflationary aspects of his recommendations would have been the enactment of the requested

---

13 Contrast the views of Sumner Slichter and Seymour Harris as expressed in the Hearings before the Joint Committee on the Economic Report, 80th Congress, 2nd Session, December 6-21, 1948.

increases in excises (except for that on oleomargarine, which he recommended to be reduced), increased social security contributions, and extension of social insurance programs.

Current Opinion on the Role of Fiscal Policy in the Stabilization of Employment

The administration has continued the practice established by Roosevelt of acknowledging the role of the government in filling any gap in private expenditures that might lead to unemployment. The Employment Act of 1946 expressed the interest of the Federal government in the maintenance of high levels of income and employment.[14] It established the Council of Economic Advisers, whose function is to continually assess the economic situation, on the basis of which the President makes a report to Congress twice a year. In his report for January 7, 1949, the President stated that "we must now look to an improved combination of basic private action and supplementary government action to develop still better remedies and safeguards" against unemployment and inflation.[15] It will be noted that the government contribution is regarded as supplementary. It is hoped that the major role will be assumed by the private sector. But if not, then compensatory government spending must be relied upon. This point of view derives directly from the Keynesian revolution in economics, which has focused attention on the need for a level of national income adequate to maintain full employment. Budgets are to be drawn up, no longer primarily with respect to the objectives of matching revenues with expenditures, but rather to the achievement of the net contribution by the Federal government to national income necessary to accomplish full employment and to avoid inflation.

One would naturally suppose it difficult, even if the executive branch had become convinced of the desirability of a national budget for full employment rather than a budget primarily designed to govern the size and direction of revenues and expenditures, to convince a body of complex opinion like the Congress of the validity of this aim. And so it has proved. Despite threats of inflation, Congress has been interested in reducing taxes. Conversely, public opinion accepts with reservations the view that substantial unemployment should be met with purposely created Federal deficits. Federal spending and taxing policies are likely to remain, despite recent developments in theories concerning the role of government in stabilizing the national income, in large measure opportunistic, adapted to changing conditions as they arise.

---

14 The Murray Full Employment Bill had stated it to be the much stronger objective to maintain *full* employment. See the *Introduction* to the *Economic Report of the President to Congress,* January 7, 1949, pp. VII ff.

15 *Report,* January 7, 1949, p. xvi.

Selected References

Annual Reports of the Secretary of the Treasury.

Beveridge, W. H., *Full Employment in a Free Society*. New York: W. W. Norton and Company, 1945.

Dillard, D., *The Economics of John Maynard Keynes*. New York: Prentice-Hall, Inc., 1948.

Groves, H. M., *Viewpoints on Public Finance*. New York: Henry Holt and Company, Inc., 1947.

Hansen, A. H., *Fiscal Policy and Business Cycles*. New York: W. W. Norton and Company, 1941.

Mellon, A. W., *Taxation, the People's Business*. New York: The Macmillan Company, 1924.

Noyes, A. D., *The War Period of American Finance, 1908-1925*. New York: G. P. Putnam's Sons, 1926.

Paul, R. E., *Taxation for Prosperity*. New York: The Bobbs-Merrill Company, 1947.

Ratner, Sidney, *American Taxation*. New York: W. W. Norton and Company, 1942.

Twentieth Century Fund, *Financing American Prosperity*. New York: 1945.

48 · THE PERFORMANCE OF THE AMERICAN ECONOMY SINCE 1919

THIS PERIOD OF OUR ECONOMIC HISTORY (1919-1950) included the prosperous twenties, the depressed thirties and the mobilized forties; it saw the introduction of the atomic age with its fears and uncertainties. It was a period of extremes—each phase of economic life appearing in larger measure than it ever did before. The prosperity was greater, the depression more severe, the mobilization more extensive, and the uncertainty more pervasive than ever before.

Readjustments After World War I

The return to peacetime conditions after World War I was expected to bring the usual depression and price deflation.[1] These expectations were confirmed for a short time in the early part of 1919, when general business uncertainty prevailed and a fall in prices of some goods took place. This was a false alarm, however, because a short but intense boom developed.[2] The cessation of the demand for war materials was offset by civilian demand for both consumption and investment purposes. The high-cost industries encouraged by the war were thus able to survive in large part.[3] This fact is indicated by the continued rise in income. National income in current prices rose from $64,200,000,000 in 1919 to $74,200,000,000 in 1920.[4] The sale of consumption goods was stimulated by the European need for foodstuffs and by postponed domestic demand for both durable and nondurable goods. Investment was facilitated by low interest rates, which formed part of the Treasury's policy of maintaining "easy money" conditions to keep down the cost of Treasury borrowing. Private borrowing from the banks increased, and in the period

1 See Willard L. Thorp, *Business Annals* (New York: National Bureau of Economic Research, 1926), pp. 143-144, and J. M. Clark, *The Costs of the World War to the American People* (New Haven: Yale University Press, 1931), pp. 52-68.

2 See Charles O. Hardy, "Adjustments and Maladjustments in the United States after the First World War," *American Economic Review,* Supplement, March, 1942, pp. 24-30.

3 See Curtis P. Nettels, "Economic Consequences of War: Costs of Production," *Journal of Economic History,* Supplement, December, 1943, pp. 1-8.

4 Simon Kuznets, *National Income and Its Composition: 1919-1938,* Vol. I, p. 137. New York: National Bureau of Economic Research, 1941.

from the last quarter of 1919 to the middle of 1920 loans and discounts of all banks showed an increase of nearly $6,000,000,000, or nearly 25 per cent.

So active was this post-war boom that a severe inflation developed. Government regulation of prices was abandoned at a time when underlying inflationary pressure persisted. As a result, the price level reached a peak that even exceeded that attained during the war. Not even in the Civil War had such a sharp price increase taken place; it is necessary to go back to the War of 1812 for a comparable situation.

The boom did not last long, however, and several signs of trouble soon appeared. The great and rapid price increase led to what has been called a "buyers' strike"—consumers held off until prices should reach a more reasonable level. This condition led to excessive business inventories and price cutting. As reconstruction measures rehabilitated European countries, or as these countries ran out of borrowed funds, exports also dropped and the whole economy suffered. On top of all this, the credit situation grew threatening. Banks were reaching their reserve limits despite the Federal Reserve System's easy money policy and the large gold inflow. When the major part of the Treasury financing was over, by November, 1919, the Federal Reserve System took steps to tighten credit and raise interest rates. The rediscount rate was raised, at first slightly and then rapidly in January and May, 1920. The combination of all these circumstances ended the boom early in the summer of 1920.[5]

With the boom at an end, the wholesale price level fell sharply. The inflationary bubble had been pricked. There took place the sharpest drop in our history, with the possible exception of prices in terms of Continental currency after the Revolutionary War.[6] Farm prices were hardest hit of all. The ensuing business depression was severe, although the banking situation generally was good. National income fell from $74,200,000,000 in 1920 to $59,400,000,000 in 1921, and commercial failures reached a new peak. The postponed reaction to wartime conditions had set in.

Prosperity and Depression, 1922–1933[7]

The period between the postwar depression ending in 1921 and the introduction of new fiscal policies in 1933 includes the greatest peacetime boom and the deepest depression in this country's history. The "Golden Twenties" from 1922 to 1929 raised the economy to unheard-of heights

[5] See E. A. Goldenweiser, *Monetary Management,* pp. 46-49. New York: McGraw-Hill Book Company, Inc., 1949.

[6] The extensive decline in prices after the War of 1812 took place, it will be recalled, over a period of about five years.

[7] For the early part of this period, see Thorp, *Business Annals,* pp. 144-145; and for statistical data covering the entire period see Kuznets, *National Income and Its Composition, 1919-1938.*

of business activity, only to be followed by a sharp drop to the depths of business inactivity and stagnation from 1929 to 1933.

The economy recovered quickly from the depression of 1920-1921 and experienced a cumulative improvement in business conditions up to 1929. A major basis of the improvement lay in the amazing expansion of the modern motor-car industry, which gave impetus to the iron and steel trade. A business boom with subsidiary land booms and building booms resulted. National income rose from $59,400,000,000 in 1921 to $87,200,000,000 in 1929. Capital formation rose from $3,300,000,000 in 1921 to $10,000,000,000 in 1929. Wholesale prices reached their postwar peak in 1925 and declined thereafter, except for a slight rally in 1928, as shown in Figure 1. Marked differences existed in the contributions made by various industries to the national income in this period of expansion.[8] Manufacturing enjoyed fair prosperity and profits rose, at a moderate rate but with considerable acceleration from 1928 to 1929. The improvement in manufacturing is reflected in the trend of factory payrolls and employment shown in Figure 2. The most important distinguishing feature of the developments in the field of agriculture during this period was the failure to achieve a recovery in any way comparable to the high level reached during the war. The main difficulty lay in the altered world-market situation.[9]

The spectacular stock market crash [10] of 1929 was followed by a rapid deterioration of virtually every branch of economic activity. The immediate causes were the speculative boom of 1927-29, the weakness of the banking system, and the heavy burden of mortgage debt.[11] The underlying economic conditions were conducive to a downswing in business activity. The dislocations created by World War I still remained in large part, and the world economy was likely to react unfavorably to shocks that might otherwise have had little effect.[12] Other underlying factors weakening the economy's ability to withstand shocks may have been the rapid pace of technological change and the growing rigidities in some segments of the price structure. Another factor, seriously suggested by some students of the period, is that at this time the short-, intermediate-, and long-term business cycles were due for a downswing.[13]

---

[8] See Kuznets, *National Income and Its Composition, 1919-1938,* p. 163, for the behavior of construction, trade, and other industries.

[9] See Vladimir P. Timoshenko, *World Agriculture and the Depression,* Michigan Business Studies, No. 5, p. 69. Ann Arbor: 1933.

[10] See National Industrial Conference Board, *Major Forces in World Business Depression* (New York: 1931), p. 40; and Irving Fisher, *The Stock Market Crash—And After* (New York: The Macmillan Company, 1930).

[11] Joseph A. Schumpeter, "The Decade of the Twenties," *American Economic Review,* May 1946, pp. 9-10.

[12] See discussion by Garfield V. Cox, *Ibid.,* pp. 28-32.

[13] See Joseph A. Schumpeter, *Business Cycles,* Vol. I, pp. 161-174. New York: McGraw-Hill Book Company, 1939.

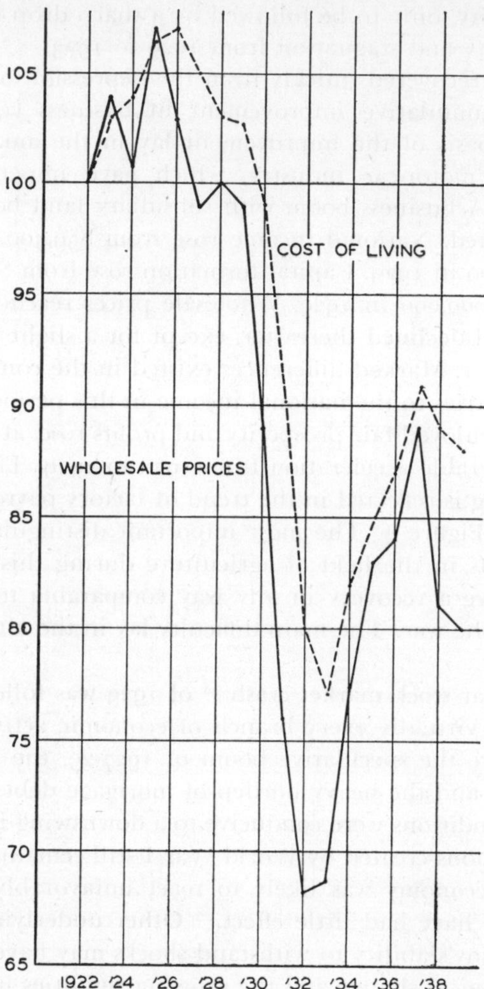

FIG. 1. *Price Changes, 1922-1939* (converted to 1922 base). Sources of basic data: "Cost of Living," National Industrial Conference Board; "Wholesale Prices," United States Bureau of Labor Statistics.

The decline in business activity was associated with a general economic collapse.[14] National income dropped to \$42,900,000,000 in 1932 and to \$42,200,000,000 in 1933. Net capital formation dropped to –\$4,200,000,000 in 1932 but turned up slightly to –\$3,600,000,000 in 1933, thus anticipat-

[14] See Kuznets, *National Income and Its Composition, 1919-1938*; and D. Yoder and G. R. Davies, *Depression and Recovery* (New York and London: McGraw-Hill Book Company, 1934).

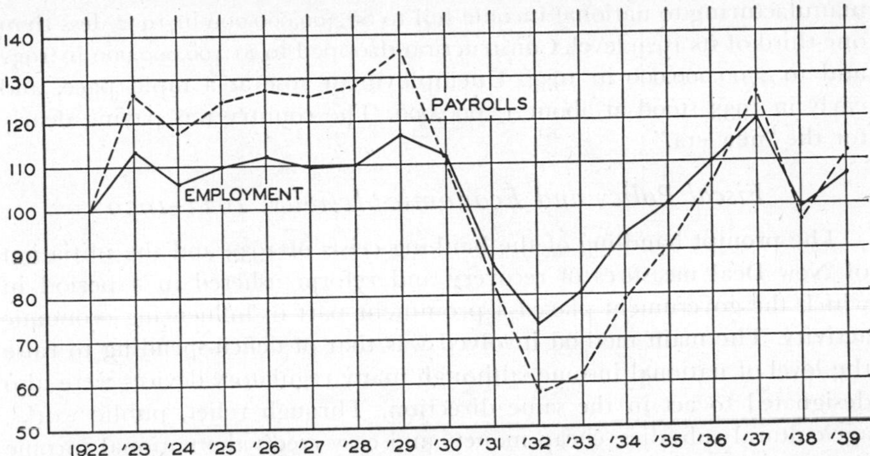

FIG. 2. *Employment and Payrolls in Manufacturing Industries, 1922-1939* (converted to 1922 base). Source of basic data: United States Bureau of Labor Statistics.

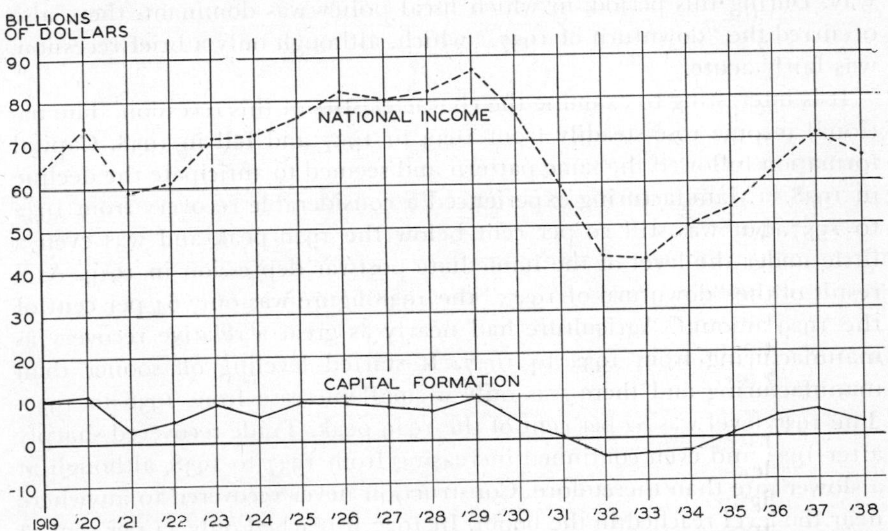

FIG. 3. *National Income and Capital Formation, 1919-1938.* Source of basic data: National Bureau of Economic Research (Kuznets).

ing the subsequent rise in national income.[15] These data are depicted in Figure 3. Agriculture's contribution to national income dropped from its none-too-high level to $2,800,000,000 in 1932, and agricultural exports also declined sharply in both value and volume.[16] The contribution of

[15] Timing relations of this sort have been made the basis for designating capital formation as a primary causal factor in explaining income fluctuations. See A. H. Hansen, *Fiscal Policy and Business Cycles* (New York: W. W. Norton & Company, 1941), Chapter 2. See, however, William J. Fellner, *Monetary Policies and Full Employment* (Berkeley: University of California Press, 1946), pp. 32-42.

[16] See V. P. Timoshenko, *World Agriculture and the Depression*, p. 69.

manufacturing to national income fell to $6,300,000,000 in 1932, less than one-third of its 1929 level. Construction dropped to $1,100,000,000 in 1932 and to $700,000,000 in 1933. Unemployment rose at a rapid pace, and early in 1933 stood at about 15,000,000. The country was paying dearly for the "new era."

Fiscal Policy and Economic Activity, 1933–1939

The prompt handling of the banking crisis of 1933 and the initiation of New Deal measures of recovery and reform ushered in a period in which the government played a prominent part in influencing economic activity. The main method involved was that of deficit-spending to raise the level of national income, although many regulatory devices were also designated to act in the same direction. Through relief, public works, agricultural subsidies, cheap money, and easy credit the national income was forced up from its low level of 1932 and 1933.[17] Between the beginning of 1935 and the middle of 1937, an unmistakable recovery was under way. During this period, in which fiscal policy was dominant, there also occurred the "downturn of 1937," which, although only a brief recession, was fairly acute.

It is interesting to examine the characteristics of this recession. The national income rose steadily from 1933 to 1937 and fell in 1938. Capital formation followed the same pattern and seemed to anticipate the decline in 1938.[18] Manufacturing experienced a considerable recovery from 1932 to 1937, but was still 20 per cent below the 1929 peak and was even a little under the level of the immediate postwar depression in 1919. As a result of the "downturn of 1937," the 1938 figure was only 64 per cent of the 1929 amount. Agriculture had nearly as great a relative recovery as manufacturing from 1932 to 1937. It started leveling off sooner than manufacturing and there was only a small increase from 1936 to 1937. The 1937 level was 82 per cent of the 1929 peak. Trade recovered sharply after 1933 and even continued increasing from 1937 to 1938, although at a slower rate than theretofore. Construction never recovered to anywhere near the level reached in the boom. In 1937 it reached only 44 per cent of its 1929 figure.

The improved level of business activity greatly reduced the rate of commercial failures between 1933 and 1937. There was some increase of failures in 1938, but after that the situation improved a little. Foreign trade recovered somewhat in the upswing, although it did not nearly approach the 1929 level. In the subsequent downturn, imports dropped sharply while exports fell only slightly. This fact demonstrates the mainly domes-

---

[17] See Arthur Smithies, "The American Economy in the Thirties," *American Economic Review,* May, 1946, pp. 11-27, and Gardiner C. Means' dissenting comments, pp. 32-35.

[18] This is consistent with the analysis, previously noted, that gives a prominent causal place to fluctuations in capital formation.

tic nature of the downturn. Imports dropped in sympathy with the decline in national income, while exports, dependent in the first instance on foreign economic conditions, did not suffer so much. With the rise in domestic economic activity in 1939, imports also jumped. Exports, however, rose only slightly. Again the largely domestic nature of the recession and subsequent recovery is demonstrated.

There are some significant impressions to be gained from the national-income figures of the period. Agriculture and manufacturing responded to the increase in government contribution from 1932 to 1933, but the other industries continued their decline. Then all private industrial groups continued their increase from 1934 to 1935 virtually unabated, despite the decline in government contribution. This fact is consistent with the pump-priming theory, since economic activity in the private sphere continued its improvement after the stimulating effect of government had been removed to a large extent. On the other hand, no such influence persisted from 1937 to 1938. Here almost all parts of the private sector of the economy suffered a decline while the government contribution did not fall, although, to be sure, its rate of increase slowed down almost to a standstill. The great decline in the rate of the increase of the government contribution might conceivably provide an adequate explanation of the absolute decline in private activity through the "acceleration principle," broadly interpreted.

The relation between fiscal policy and economic activity during this period is shown more explicitly in Figure 4. Fiscal policy is represented by the series known as "Total Net Income-Increasing Expenditures of All Governments," [19] and economic activity is represented by a series based on the entire national income minus the share contributed by the government.[20] Here can be seen particularly the sustained rate of increase in economic activity from 1933 to 1937, despite the fall in net government income-increasing expenditures in 1935 and again in 1937. This evidence again tends to substantiate the impression that the government contribution actually "took," that is, that private business was able to carry on under its own power for some time. The private sector was able to withstand completely the relatively small decline in the government impact in 1935, but the drastic fall in 1937 showed its effects in due course.

The downturn of 1937 should not, however, be interpreted solely in terms of the decline in deficit-spending. The other major factors that have been suggested as contributing to the recession are [21] the development of

---

[19] H. H. Villard, *Deficit Spending and the National Income,* p. 323. New York: Farrar & Rinehart, Inc., 1941.

[20] Kuznets, *National Income and Its Composition, 1919-1938,* p. 163.

[21] See J. W. Angell, *Investment and Business Cycles,* Chapter 12 (New York: McGraw-Hill Book Company, 1941); A. H. Hansen, *Full Recovery or Stagnation?,* Part IV (New York: W. W. Norton & Company, 1938), and *Fiscal Policy and Business Cycles,* Chapter

a number of bottlenecks and price increases, which resulted in some curtailment of economic activity, and an increase in reserve requirements leading to a reduction in member bank investments. As an underlying influence, there was also the fact that the recovery had been mainly one of consumption—both durable and nondurable—and the continuance of government "investment" (since private investment was inadequate) may have been necessary to maintain the recovery. Nevertheless, the existence

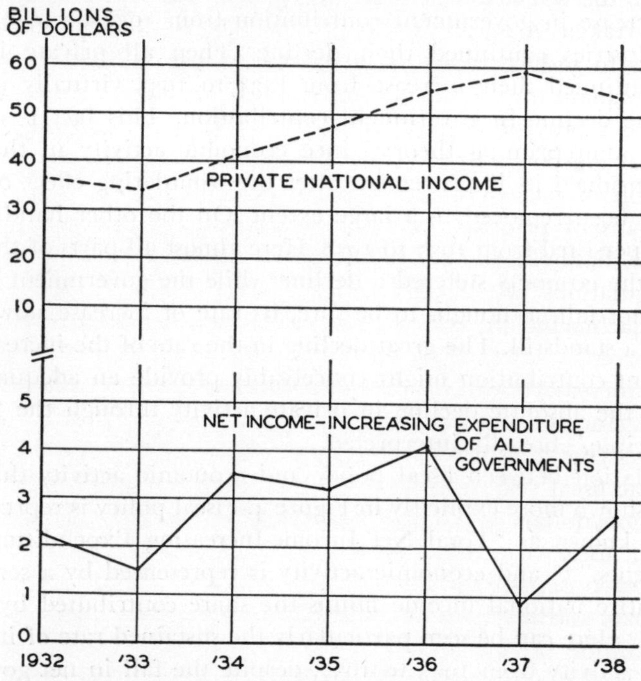

FIG. 4. *Government Expenditures and Private National Income, 1932-1938.* (Source of basic data: "Net Income-Increasing Expenditures of All Governments," H. H. Villard, *Deficit Spending and the National Income;* "Private National Income (total minus government)," Simon Kuznets, *National Income and Its Composition, 1919-1938.*)

of a considerable lag between the drop in Federal deficit-spending and the drop in income has been taken as a reason for relegating the fiscal policy element to a secondary position. This view holds that the recession might have been avoided by fiscal methods, but that the causes are probably the other two specified above. The recovery after the 1937-1938 recession is associated with an increase in deficit-spending (although the initiating factor is not clear), and, later, with the outbreak of the war.

---

4 (New York: W. W. Norton & Company, 1941); and H. H. Villard, *Deficit Spending and the National Income,* Chapter 25.

Economic Changes During World War II: 1939–1945

The United States felt the economic impact of World War II, which began in Europe in September 1939, through English and French purchases of war materials. In the middle of 1940, this country launched a defense program of its own. This brought immediate effects in increasing government expenditures, national income, and prices.[22] With America's entry into the war at the end of 1941, a full-scale economic mobilization was undertaken. A major problem immediately confronting the government was to induce industry to convert its peacetime facilities and to expand its plant for wartime production. Among the inducements offered finally was a provision for the five-year amortization of emergency facilities for tax purposes. Blanket orders, such as the one which stopped the production of passenger cars, were required in some cases. Thoroughgoing plans of priorities and allocations were required to ensure the adequate channeling of materials and manpower to war use. Stringent draft regulations, with exemption for persons in war employment, also aided in achieving the transfer of personnel into war production or the armed forces.

Sharp increases took place in Federal expenditures, revenues, and the deficit during the war years.[23] As may be seen in Figure 5, Federal expenditures rose to unprecedented heights. From a level of 9.2 billion dollars in the fiscal year 1940 (ending June 30) they reached a peak of over 98.7 billion dollars in 1945. Revenues fell far behind. From 5.3 billion dollars in fiscal 1940 they rose to only 44.8 billion dollars in 1945. The largest deficit occurred in fiscal 1943 when, with expenditures of 79.6 billion dollars and revenues of only 22.2 billion dollars, there was a deficit of 57.4 billion dollars. The Federal debt rose from 43.0 billion dollars at the end of fiscal 1940 to 258.7 billion dollars at the end of fiscal 1945 and 269.4 billion dollars at the end of the following fiscal year. The peak in the debt was reached in February 1946 when a level of 279.8 billion dollars was attained.[24]

The national income rose from 72.5 billion dollars in 1939 to a high level of 183.8 billion dollars in 1944 and 182.7 billion dollars in 1945.[25] The index of industrial production rose from 89 in 1938 (1935-39 = 100)[26] to 109 in 1939 and to a high level of 239 in 1943. It dropped to 235 in 1944 and 203 in 1945. The total number of employees (full and

---

22 See Meyer Jacobstein and Harold G. Moulton, *Effects of the Defense Program on Prices, Wages and Profits*. Washington: Brookings Institution, 1941.

23 *Treasury Bulletin*, August 1949, p. 1.

24 *Treasury Bulletin*, August 1949, p. 15.

25 Department of Commerce, *Survey of Current Business*, July 1947, Supplement, p. 19, and July 1949, p. 10.

26 Board of Governors of the Federal Reserve System, *Federal Reserve Bulletin*, August 1949, p. 975.

part-time, wage and salary earners) in all industries rose from an average of 39.1 million for the year 1939 to a high level of 57.0 million in 1944 and 55.3 million in 1945. The military forces rose from 342 thousand in 1939 to 11.4 million in 1944 and 11.3 million in 1945.[27]

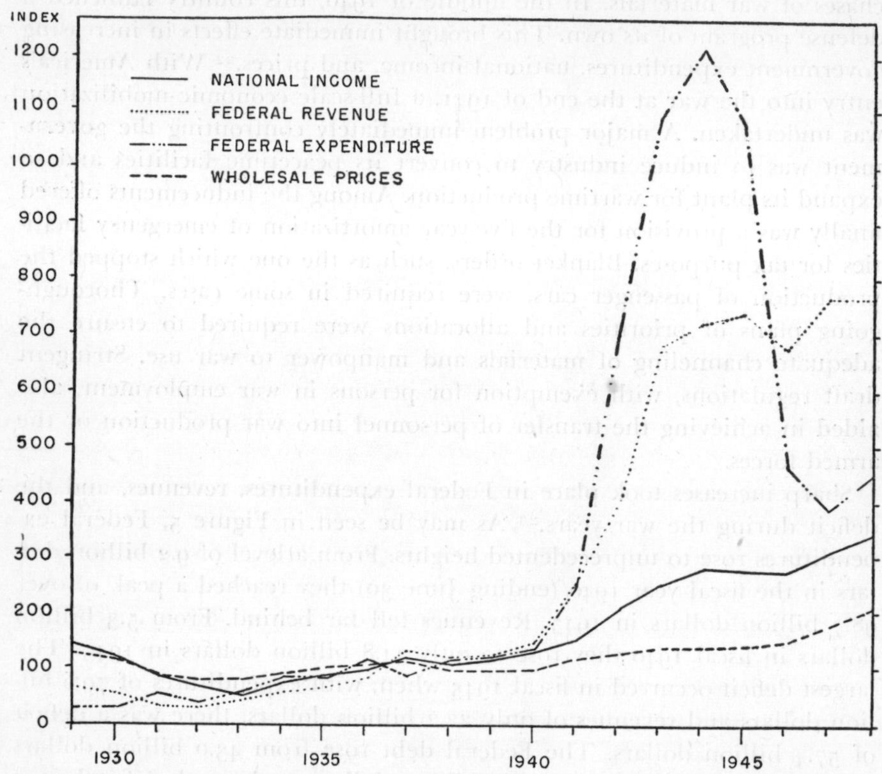

FIG. 5. *National Income, Federal Revenue, Federal Expenditure, and Wholesale Prices, 1929-1948.* (Source of basic data: "National Income," Department of Commerce; "Federal Revenue" and "Expenditure," Treasury Department; "Wholesale Prices," Bureau of Labor Statistics. All data converted to index numbers with 1935-1939 base.)

The perennial problem of war—an inflationary increase in prices—presented itself. The average of wholesale prices of all commodities rose from 77.1 in 1939 (1926 = 100) [28] to 105.8 in 1945. The cost of living was at 99.4 in 1939 (1935-39 = 100) [29] and 100.2 in 1940. It rose to 128.4 in 1945. The price increases that took place during this period were dispersed widely. An analysis of 367 commodities that appeared in the United States Bureau of Labor Statistics wholesale price index in both

[27] *Survey of Current Business,* July 1947, Supplement, p. 37.

[28] Bureau of Labor Statistics, *Federal Reserve Bulletin,* August 1949, p. 975.

[29] Consumers' Price Index for Moderate Income Families in Large Cities, Bureau of Labor Statistics, *Federal Reserve Bulletin,* August 1949, p. 975.

1939 and 1946 has been made.[30] A comparison of the monthly average for 1939 and the figures for August, 1946 (the first full month following the general removal of government price controls) shows that the percentage changes ranged from a decline of 9.7 per cent in the price of calcium carbide to an increase of 442.6 per cent in the price of shellac. About one-sixth of the total number of prices rose more than 100 per cent, and an approximately equal number rose less than 10 per cent. The (unweighted) average increase in these items was 53.4 per cent.

From a basic economic, as opposed to a purely financial, point of view, a large part of the war was "free" for the United States in that an overall curtailment in the pre-war level of consumption was not required. The major portion of war output, in the aggregate, was produced through: (1) the utilization of manpower and equipment that was unemployed before the war began; (2) the employment of persons who were previously not part of the working force (whether employed or unemployed), such as housewives and persons who might otherwise have been considered too old or too young to work; (3) the using up of capital through inadequate maintenance and replacement. Consumption, in fact, was at a higher level than before the war. Individual commodities that were needed for war purposes, or which used materials or man power diverted to war production, did become scarce, of course. The pressure of high wartime national income on the available consumption goods gave the impression of relative scarcity, hence there was a tendency for prices to rise. Rationing and price control were instituted in order to reduce the inequalities that occur when prices of commodities, including necessities, are permitted to rise sharply while many individual incomes are fixed or rise slowly. War bond campaigns, designed to siphon off spendable funds to the Treasury, also were undertaken in order to achieve the same counter-inflationary effect.

Readjustments Since the War

The end of hostilities in 1945 came while the American war machine was in full swing. One of the crucial issues that then arose was concerned with the rate at which demobilization should take place. The payment of unemployment benefits to workers and of readjustment allowances to veterans modified considerably any unfavorable impact of a rapid demobilization. A sharp drop-off in retail trade was prevented by the maintenance of purchasing power. Speedy settlement of war contracts and loans to finance reconversion acted similarly. The rapid upsurge of private business to take the place of declining government expenditures cushioned the impact of demobilization of service personnel, the cancellation of war contracts, and the sale of war assets. Freed ultimately from wartime con-

30 Ralph C. Epstein, "Price Dispersion and Aggregative Analysis," *American Economic Review*, June 1947, pp. 402-407.

trols on wages and prices, encouraged by the sustained high level of business, provoked by the rising cost of living, and attracted by large profits, organized labor sought and achieved three rounds of wage increases by 1948. A fourth round with primary emphasis on pensions and health benefits was negotiated in some of the major industries in the latter part of 1949.

The postwar years were characterized by a volume of Federal expenditures and revenues far above the prewar level.[31] Expenditures dropped from 98.7 billion dollars in fiscal 1945 to 60.7 billion dollars in 1946 and 39.3 billion dollars in 1947. Revenues, fed by a high national income, fell very little. From 44.8 billion dollars in fiscal 1945 they slipped to 40.0 billion dollars in 1946 and 1947. In the latter year a major fiscal event took place—a surplus was recorded for the first time since 1930.

There was no great change during the next few years. A surplus of 5.4 billion dollars occurred in 1948, but by 1950 a deficit again appeared in the budget estimates. The debt was reduced to 252.8 billion dollars at the end of the fiscal year 1949.

The national income fell slightly from its high level of 182.7 billion dollars in 1945 to 179.6 billion dollars in 1946. It then rose to 201.7 billion dollars in 1947 and 226.2 billion dollars in 1948.[32] It was running at the annual rate (seasonally adjusted) of 225.3 billion dollars in the first quarter of 1949. The index of industrial production fell from 203 in 1945 (1935-39 = 100) [33] to 170 in 1946, and then rose to 187 in 1947 and 192 in 1948. From a high level of 199 (seasonally unadjusted) in October 1948 it fell to 170 in June 1949.

The total number of employees (full and part-time, wage and salary earners) in all industries fell from an average of 55.3 million in 1945 to 49.2 million in 1946. It then rose to 49.4 million in 1947 and 50.5 million in 1948. The military forces fell from 11.3 million in 1945 to 3.4 million in 1946, 1.6 million in 1947, and 1.4 million in 1948.[34]

The average of wholesale prices of all commodities rose sharply from 105.8 in 1945 (1926 = 100) [35] to 121.1 in 1946, 152.1 in 1947, and 165.1 in 1948. For the month of August 1948, the index stood at 169.8 (seasonally unadjusted). It then declined, with only slight interruption, to 154.4 in June 1949. The cost of living index rose from 128.4 in 1945 (1935-39 = 100) [36] to 139.3 in 1946, 159.2 in 1947, and 171.2 in 1948. From its level

---

[31] *Treasury Bulletin,* August 1949, p. 1.

[32] Department of Commerce, *Survey of Current Business,* July 1949, p. 10.

[33] Board of Governors of the Federal Reserve System, *Federal Reserve Bulletin,* August 1949, p. 975.

[34] *Survey of Current Business,* July 1949, p. 20.

[35] Bureau of Labor Statistics, *Federal Reserve Bulletin,* August 1949, p. 975.

[36] Consumers' Price Index for Moderate Income Families in Large Cities, Bureau of Labor Statistics, *Federal Reserve Bulletin,* August 1949, p. 975.

of 174.5 (seasonally unadjusted) in August and September 1948, it fell to 169.0 in February 1949, and, after slight fluctuations, stood at 169.6 in June 1949.

A striking aspect of the postwar economy was the failure of predictions of postwar depression made by most economists.[37] In general, the effect of deferred demand, financed by accumulated liquid holdings, was underestimated. The postwar boom lasted until the latter part of 1948 when it was replaced by a mild recession.[38]

At the international level, several steps were taken to restore world trade and rehabilitate war-devastated economies. These included the renewal of the Trade Agreements Act, permitting tariff reductions by executive action, the establishment of the International Monetary Fund, designed to stabilize exchange rates, the International Bank for Reconstruction and Development, to make productive loans, the chartering of the International Trade Organization, to stimulate international trade, and the establishment of the Marshall plan, to ensure political stability by raising the level of economic well-being. As a result of these measures, trade between the United States and the rest of the world rose to a high level. For instance, in 1945 purchases from United States business firms were 4,944 million dollars and sales to United States business firms were 4,413 million dollars. In 1948 the figures were 12,280 million and 8,464 million dollars, respectively.[39] There were indications that balances in international transactions of the United States with Europe and the rest of the world in 1948 changed in the direction of their prewar pattern.[40]

At the end of the war, rapid demobilization had been demanded and effected. But this policy was reversed when the international good will of 1945 turned into the fear and recrimination of 1946. Since then, efforts have been made to maintain a strong national military establishment.[41] A military budget of about 15 billion dollars, the stockpiling of critical and strategic materials, and the maintenance of service personnel at a high level through use of the draft and voluntary enlistments are indications of this policy. Even the campaign to sell United States Savings Bonds, which was pressed in 1949 when the immediate economic consequences were probably undesirable, is evidence of an attempt to maintain a state of readiness on all fronts.

---

37 See Michael Sapir, "Review of Economic Forecasts for the Transition Period," *Studies in Income and Wealth,* Vol. XI. New York: National Bureau of Economic Research, 1949, pp. 275-329.

38 See "The Inflationary Process" (papers by Abba P. Lerner and Seymour E. Harris; comments by Fritz Machlup, Harold M. Somers and Henry H. Villard), *Review of Economics and Statistics,* August 1949, pp. 193-216.

39 *Survey of Current Business,* July 1949, p. 13.

40 *Survey of Current Business,* June 1949, pp. 4-7.

41 See *Economic Mobilization* (mimeo.), p. 2. Washington: The Industrial College of the Armed Forces, June 1948.

Basic Characteristics of America's Economic Growth

It is difficult to single out those forces that have been responsible for the peculiar nature of America's economic growth. The major factors were probably ample natural resources, an enterprising population, and an economic system that resulted from and, in turn, facilitated the fuller utilization of both. There are several basic characteristics of this growth that help us understand more fully the nature of the underlying forces. These are the rising standard of living, the broadening scope of governmental activity, the growing and changing population, the country's increasing predominance in the world economy, and the economy's instability coupled with resilience in the face of disturbing forces.

The Rising Standard of Living

The problems involved in drawing inferences concerning changes in the standard of living have been indicated in earlier chapters.[42] Changing customs and habits, changing populations and differences in tastes make any intertemporal-interpersonal comparisons of the standard of living highly tenuous. Considering, however, the very large increase that has taken place in real income per capita it is hard to resist the temptation to assert that in some, perhaps undefinable but nevertheless significant, way there has been a large rise in the standard of living. The shortening of the working day and the increasing length of life are indirect indications of the improvement that has taken place. The main measure, however, is the rise in real income per capita. It will be recalled that real income per capita was estimated (with a necessarily wide margin of error) to be $211 in the year 1799, using dollars of 1926 purchasing power.[43] By 1929 it had reached $625.

Can this increase in real income per capita be expected to continue? The decade of the great depression altered the continued progress that had taken place. In no year during that decade did real income per capita reach $600.[44] Can this mean that the American economy has marred its record of performance—its continuous progress in real income per capita, decade by decade?[45] This is, perhaps, the most important problem in the consideration of the performance of the American economy. Productivity has continued to rise. This is demonstrated by the following indexes of output, employment, and output per worker covering six major industrial segments, which employed two-thirds of the country's labor force in

---

[42] See Chapter 17, p. 328, and Chapter 34, p. 657.

[43] Robert F. Martin, *National Income in the United States, 1799-1938*, pp. 6 ff.

[44] The figure for 1939 is not available, but other physical indexes suggest that it at least did not exceed the 1929 figure.

[45] The decade of the Civil War constitutes an exception to the record of continuous progress. Several exceptions also exist in the era before that war.

1899 and slightly less than one-half in 1939.[46] For the period since 1919, both man-hour output and average hourly earnings (in manufacturing) have approximately doubled.[47] With a growing population and labor force, the national income has, of course, increased as well. It is necessary, however, to examine the composition of the national income and seek some clue to the alteration of trend in real income per capita.

	1899	*1909*	*1919*	*1929*	*1939*
Output	100	146	195	283	289
Employment	100	129	153	150	130
Output per worker	100	113	127	189	222

The most significant development in the composition of the national income lies in the changing relative importance of consumers' outlay and capital formation. There is no consistent trend for the whole period, but rather a sharp alteration of trend in the latter part of the period. In view of the crucial importance of capital formation in the maintenance of a high level of income and employment, any such change in trend deserves the most careful attention.

It can be seen from Figure 6 that gross national product increased by increasing amounts every decade with the exception of the most recent one. The villain of the piece appears to be gross capital formation, which rose every decade from 1879 to 1928 but actually declined in the decade 1929-1938. The consistent upward trend to 1928 is clearly broken in the 1929-1938 decade. Consumption rose throughout the period, although the rate of increase slowed down in the last decade. Since a decline in the rate of increase of consumption is here associated with an actual decline in capital formation, there is some possibility that the acceleration principle was in operation and that the change in behavior of national income may actually be traced to the behavior of consumption.

The change in trend is even more evident when percentage figures are used. In the five decades from 1879 to 1928, the share of gross capital formation in the national product did not fall below 20 per cent. In the decade 1929-1938, however, the figure fell to 15 per cent. Thus, in the decade 1929-1938 the economy was much more a "consumption" economy than it had been before. In the past, a larger part of the real income per capita consisted of goods to be used for the production of other goods and not to be used for immediate consumption. Thus, the leveling off in real income per capita does not necessarily represent an immediate decline in rate of increase of consumption per capita; but it might presage a decline in rate of increase in income-producing wealth, and thus in the output of consumers' goods at some future date. The decade of the 1940's,

---

[46] George J. Stigler, *Trends in Output and Employment.* New York: National Bureau of Economic Research, 1947, p. 3.

[47] See Clark Kerr, "The Short-run Behavior of Physical Productivity and Average Hourly Earnings," *Review of Economics and Statistics,* November 1949, pp. 301-2.

which was characterized by an "extraordinary" state of economic mobilization, does not provide evidence that can be used for any long-run evaluation.

A natural question that arises at this point is whether the development of atomic energy will materially alter the prospects for continuous improvement in the standard of living. A first impression might be that the harnessing of atomic energy for industrial and domestic use might bring

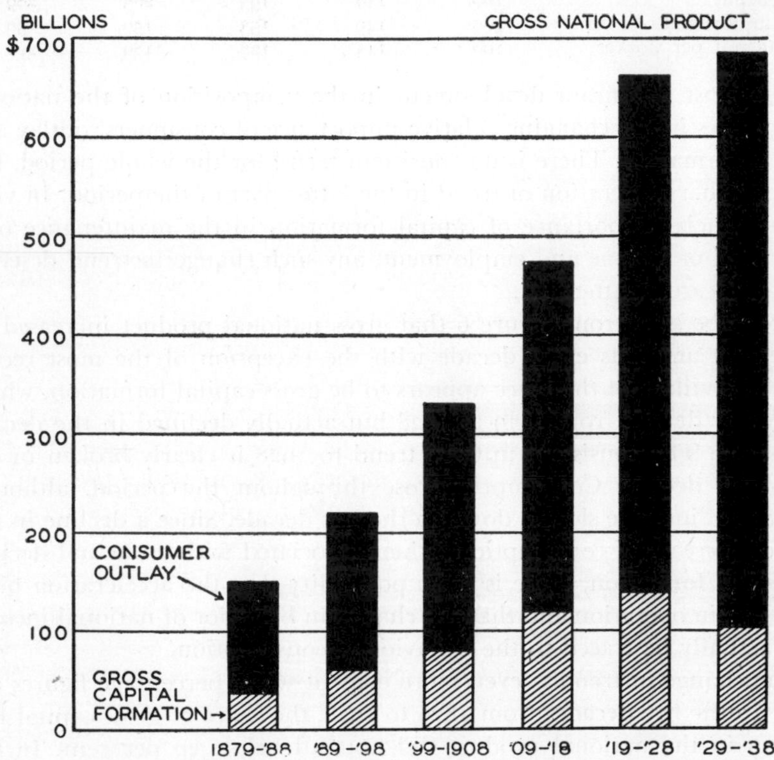

FIG. 6. *Gross National Product and Its Components, by Decades, 1879-1938* (Values in 1929-1938 prices). Source of basic data: Simon Kuznets, "Capital Formation, 1879-1938" (mimeo.).

about a large increase in the real income per capita or, at least, make possible a great reduction in hours of work. Economic analyses of the potentialities of this source of power have indicated, however, that a conservative outcome is likely. The currently large size of the atomic pile requires central power generating stations. The power must then be distributed in the usual way, in the form of electric energy, for example. Since the cost of transmission is a major element in the final cost of power to the user and is unaffected by a cheapening of the cost of the primary power (that is, in the cost of coal, water-power, or atomic energy), the prospect is against any radical change in cost of power or in the location of industry.[48]

The Broadening Scope of Governmental Activity

The growing role played by governmental activity in America's development is one of the most striking aspects of her history. From the provision of a few minimum essential services, governmental functions have grown to the point where they touch virtually every phase of an individual's life.[49] Government expenditures include[50] protective activities (war and defense, veterans' administration, police, militia, fire, corrective institutions, health); cultural activities (education, libraries, parks, and museums); welfare activities (relief and general welfare, hospitals and other institutions, social security); public works (highways, sanitation, and other works); miscellaneous activities (such as conservation of natural resources); and interest on the public debt.

One indicator of the expansion of government is given by the number of public employees. In 1900 governmental units in the United States employed more than a million persons; in 1949 there were more than six million.[51] In 1900 one out of twenty-four workers was a government employee; in 1949 the ratio was one out of eight or nine.[52]

Another way of indicating the position of government is to compare governmental expenditures with gross national expenditure. In 1948, governmental expenditures were 51.8 billion dollars while the gross national expenditure was 262.4 billion dollars.[53] Comparable figures for the earlier period are not available, but one estimate places realized income from government at 1 per cent of total realized income in 1799. The same source places the percentage at 16.7 per cent in 1937.[54] The percentage relation between governmental expenditures and the gross national expenditure in 1948 was 19.7 per cent. This may be taken as a rough index of the "mixed economy," that is, a measure of the extent of the government's participation in economic activity. It understates the case, however, for included in governmental functions are many regulatory and supervisory activities whose effects on the citizenry are more

---

[48] See A. J. Brown, *Applied Economics* (New York and Toronto: Rinehart and Company, Inc., 1948), pp. 227-243; Walter Isard and John B. Lansing, "Comparisons of Power Cost for Atomic and Conventional Steam Stations," *Review of Economics and Statistics,* August 1949, pp. 217-226; and Sam H. Schurr, "Atomic Power in Selected Industries," *Harvard Business Review,* July 1949, pp. 459-479.

[49] See Harold M. Somers, *Public Finance and National Income,* Ch. 3. Philadelphia: Blakiston Company, 1949.

[50] Classification derived from *Tax Policy,* published by the Tax Institute.

[51] Solomon Fabricant, "The Rising Trend of Government Employment," p. 3. New York: National Bureau of Economic Research, 1949. Occasional Paper 29.

[52] *Ibid.,* p. 5.

[53] *Survey of Current Business,* July 1949, pp. 10, 13.

[54] Robert F. Martin, *National Income in the United States: 1799-1938,* p. 87. New York: National Industrial Conference Board, 1939.

extensive than the dollar amounts of expenditures indicate. A few examples of these are licensing of certain trades, supervision of security issues, prosecution of monopolies, control of foods and drugs, enforcement of fair trade prices, supervision of industrial relations, support of agricultural prices, and tariff barriers. These activities, together with outright expenditures on goods and services on a large scale, suggest that the influence of government in the modern American economy is an all-pervasive one.

The Growing and Changing Population

The growth of population to a prevailing level of about 150 million has left its mark on the structure of the American economy and will have an important influence on its future development. Key factors are the rate of growth of population, the number of the aged, and the size of the labor force.

One set of estimates [55] puts population at 162.3 million in 1975. This represents an annual increase of 498,000 over the 1970 estimate, compared with an increase of 876,000 forecast for the 1950-55 period.

Associated with this increase in population is the problem of caring for the growing number of the aged.[56] The percentage of persons over 65 has risen from 2.6 per cent in 1850 to 7.7 per cent (estimated) in 1950. The number of persons 65 years and over in 1975 is estimated to be 17.6 million, or more than 10 per cent of the total. Since social thinking seems more and more inclined to make adequate provision for the aged, a large consuming and nonproducing group must play a significant part in the economic policy of the future.

The growth of the labor force represents another major challenge to the private economy and a test of its ability to maintain a high level of employment without compensatory spending. In the middle of 1949, the labor force stood at over 65 million.[57] This was broken down approximately as follows: armed forces, 1.5 million; government, 6.0 million; agriculture, 8.5 million; other workers, 45.5 million; unemployed, 3.7 million. Prior to World War II, the labor force had increased at the rate of about 600,000 a year. The rate of increase since the war has been much greater. By January 1949, the labor force had increased by one million over the previous year. By the middle of 1949, the labor force had in-

---

[55] "Forecasts of the Population of the United States: 1945-1975," U. S. Department of Commerce, Bureau of the Census, 1947, pp. 41, 49. (Assumptions: medium fertility, medium mortality, no immigration). Another estimate (made by the Bureau of Agricultural Economics) places the figure for 1975 at 188,500,000. (*New York Times,* November 27, 1949, p. 44.)

[56] See Seymour E. Harris, "What To Do With 18 Million Aged?" *New York Times,* Magazine Section, July 10, 1949.

[57] *Survey of Current Business,* August 1949, p. S-10; *New York Times,* September 11, 1949, p. E-7.

creased several million more. The belated entry of many veterans into the labor market was an important factor in this development. Employment and unemployment were increasing at the same time, with the former outstripping the latter.

This points up sharply the problem that faces the economy. Can industry's capacity to provide jobs grow quickly enough to absorb the increasing labor force? The rate of growth in capacity may be limited by a physical inability to provide resources and skilled labor to expand productive facilities at a sufficient pace.[58] This is a problem of supply. Or it may be limited by a demand for goods and services that will be inadequate to warrant the needed growth in productive facilities.[59] This is a problem of demand. Both types of problems can exist side by side and may face the American economy in future years.

To summarize, the population picture, which holds a key position in the outlook for the economy, is as follows: an increase in population but at a declining rate, an increase in the labor force, an increase in the number and proportion of the aged. This combination of developments may solve its own problems; the aged may form the basis for a high-consumption economy that will absorb the growing working force which might otherwise encounter employment difficulties owing to the declining rate of population growth.

America's Dominant Role in the World Economy

America's contemporary role as the dominant economic and political power of the Western world has given her new responsibilities in maintaining peace and stability. This was pointed up almost painfully in connection with Great Britain's postwar financial difficulties, which came to a head in 1949. As a result of a shortage of dollars (that is, an insufficiency of exports in terms of dollars compared with imports that had to be paid for in dollars), Britain was dependent on American generosity to prevent economic collapse, not only of herself but also of a large part of the sterling area. That the United States had it within its power to alleviate Britain's financial situation may be taken as an indicator of the new state of affairs.

How did the United States achieve such a dominant world position? The fact that the United States escaped war damage in the sense of devastation of property is a major factor in its postwar economic strength. It even built up capital for peacetime production. An example of this is the Willow Run plant near Detroit, which is being used for the produc-

---

[58] See Evsey D. Domar, "Expansion and Employment," *American Economic Review,* March 1947, pp. 34-55; "Capital Accumulation and the End of Prosperity," abstracted in *Econometrica,* January 1948, pp. 98-101.

[59] See Alvin H. Hansen, *Fiscal Policy and Business Cycles.* New York: W. W. Norton and Company, 1941.

tion of automobiles. Also, by giving employment and income to many who would otherwise have been either unemployed or outside the working force, there was probably on balance a favorable effect on the physical condition of the population. Offsetting this there is the loss of life and health of the members of the armed services. America's resulting postwar economic strength compared with that of other belligerents helps place it in a dominant position in world affairs.

From a broader point of view, America's international strength has been a result of its high productivity, which has created an investible surplus. This has made possible a greater and greater international role in both peace and war. It does not follow from this that large net exports must continue in order to maintain a high level of domestic activity—there may be many potential outlets for investment at home. Nevertheless, net exports represent a convenient way for the nation to invest part of its current output. Thus, a program for the development of backward areas (known as the "Point Four" program) fits readily into a policy of maintaining a high level of production and income at home. The inevitable result is an even more dominant place in the world economy and an increased interdependence of the United States and the rest of the world.

Instability and Resilience of the Economy

The outstanding conclusion to be drawn from the analysis of wartime and peacetime fluctuations and long-time trends is that the American economy has demonstrated an abounding resilience. The wars seem to have had no enduring effects of a retarding nature.[60] There is an almost continuous record of growth in spite of serious internal and external shocks. This is true to a large extent even of the decade of the thirties, around which some of the most heated controversy rages. The conditions surrounding the progress that has taken place have changed radically, however, and our real lessons can be learned from an examination of these conditions rather than merely from their results.

The main cause of concern regarding the interwar period lies in the severity of the depression of the thirties and the possibility that bigger and better depressions are in the offing. No such pessimistic conclusions seem warranted on the basis of the cyclical history of the American economy.[61] The main characteristic of this history is the prominent part played by monetary and banking instability. The progressive improve-

---

60 See Chester W. Wright, "The More Enduring Economic Consequences of America's Wars," *Journal of Economic History,* Supplement, December 1943, pp. 9-26, esp. p. 25.

61 See W. C. Mitchell, *Business Cycles, The Problem and Its Setting* (New York: National Bureau of Economic Research, 1927), pp. 343-349; A. R. Eckler, "A Measure of the Severity of Depressions, 1873-1932," *Review of Economic Statistics,* May 1933; and Arthur F. Burns and Wesley C. Mitchell, *Measuring Business Cycles* (New York: National Bureau of Economic Research, 1946).

ment in the monetary and banking structure of the economy augurs well in this respect. Another observation derived from cycle history is that the government invariably played some part in relieving depressed conditions or in promoting recovery after a major reaction. And in every case the economy ultimately glided into a private-enterprise prosperity apparently with very little difficulty. Even the three major wars that occurred since 1860 confirm this general impression. All three strained the economy to the utmost, although only the most recent was favored with the epithet "total war." In every case the required transition was drastic and a large part of the national income had to be devoted to the prosecution of the war. In all cases the country ultimately returned to a high level of peacetime employment.

The depression following 1929 presents a special case, but the significant fact is that by 1937 the economy had, in a real and important sense, recovered from the deep depression that it had experienced. It had once more demonstrated its resilience. The recovery was, however, associated with large-scale deficit-spending by the government. This mars the achievement if something vital has been given up in the process—for instance, if the heavy government debt incurred during this period comes to plague us at some later date, or if the private-investment economy has permanently lost its ability to produce and distribute effectively a large volume of goods and services under its own power. Neither of these questions can be settled conclusively for some time, if ever. Owing to the war, it is particularly difficult to say whether the economy could have glided into a prosperity sustained by private industry alone.

It is true, nevertheless, that the crash of 1929 pulled down with it some of the generalizations based on the preceding era. The long-time trend of progress was altered in rate and in composition. The consistent growth of manufacturing compared with agriculture remained, but national income barely held its own and capital formation actually lost out. Fiscal policy played a greater and greater part in influencing economic activity. Here, more than ever, it is difficult to disentangle effect from cause. Some observers claim that the private sector of the economy must be given the lion's share of blame for the crash and that the government sector must be given at least some share of credit for the recovery. The main question, however, is whether the recovery would have been quicker or "healthier," or both, if the government had not intervened so fully. Basically, the question is whether the economy has undergone a profound change—whether it has reached a state of maturity and perhaps stagnation. Those favoring a continuation of fiscal and other intervention by the government say that past progress has been geared to a rapid population growth and the development of heavy industries—such as railroads and automobiles—and that neither of these conditions will persist in the future; those who favor a reversion to the predepression state of affairs can point to the fact that, one way or another, the economy has recovered and progressed in the past. The record of the New Deal period is used by one side to indicate the necessity of continued government intervention and by the other to demonstrate the dire consequences of interfering with the natural behavior—the ups and downs—of free enterprise.

More important, however, than distributing praise or blame for past events is to insure a favorable state of business activity in the future. Whether the steps taken by the government have been for good or ill, one thing is certain—those steps can never be fully retraced. The economically and, in some cases, politically strong groups that exist today cannot suddenly be removed. That being the case, fiscal and other government intervention cannot suddenly be eliminated without calamitous consequences. In such circumstances it seems unavoidable (regardless of whether it is desirable) that the government should stand ready to counteract any serious dip in employment in the event that business enterprise is unable to maintain a high level of employment. In view of the virtually unalterable rigidities that have been set up, even those economists who are generally in favor of severe business reactions in order to readjust the price structure and lay the basis for healthy recovery must yield. A high level of national income and employment must be maintained.

Conclusion

Both internal and external factors point emphatically to the crucial importance of maintaining economic stability within the United States if she is to fulfill her new obligations as leader of the Western world.[62] Internally, the many rigidities that exist, although they tend to "cushion" a slight decline, would tend to aggravate the difficulty of any automatic readjustment should a substantial decline in employment and prices take place. For instance, the maintenance of wage rates in the face of a substantial decline in prices and employment may tend to accentuate the decline in employment. The maintenance of farm prices in the face of a substantial decline in income may tend to accentuate declines in retail food sales. The maintenance of industrial prices in the face of a general decline of purchasing power may accentuate the reduction in output and employment. Since such rigidities, by and large, are here to stay, it is folly to permit any substantial decline in income and employment in the hope that market forces will automatically bring about a readjustment. Competition cannot be relied on to achieve generally accepted social objectives.[63] The government must accept responsibility for preventing

[62] See Alvin H. Hansen, *America's Role in the World Economy* (New York: W. W. Norton and Company, 1945), and Sumner H. Slichter, *The American Economy: Its Problems and Prospects*, esp. pp. 157-158 (New York: Alfred A. Knopf, 1948).

[63] See J. M. Clark, *Alternative to Serfdom* (New York: Alfred A. Knopf, 1948) and *Guideposts in Time of Change* (New York: Harper and Brothers, 1949).

sharp declines in national income if the American enterprise system as we know it, with its mixture of flexibility and rigidity, is to be preserved.

At the international level, the issue is even more clear-cut. With Britain and a large part of the rest of the world dependent on the American market for goods and services to obtain the dollars with which to buy the American goods and services they need, the most drastic political consequences may be occasioned by an economic collapse in the United States. Even what may be called the "prosperous recession" of 1948-49, with its change from a seller's to a buyer's market, caused considerable embarrassment abroad. Goods and services could not be sold to Americans as easily as before; dollars became scarcer than ever; a serious threat to the standard of living of Britain and other countries arose. It is not difficult to visualize what would have been the political consequences of a depression on the order of the 1932 holocaust.

The essence of this discussion is that a "mixed economy" is here to stay; it cannot be wished away. A reasonable and necessary amount of government expenditures is not any more likely to lead to totalitarianism than is completely unfettered competition. Dangers exist in both directions, but there is no reason to believe that a "mixed economy" is necessarily unstable and must inevitably lead to a growing role of government; the opposite tendency is also likely. For instance, a withdrawal of veterans' services and benefits, the removal of all aid to Western Europe, the curtailment of various monopoly controls, the collapse of orderly processes of collective bargaining—to mention only a few aspects of our economy—might have the most devastating repercussions in a totalitarian direction. The mixed economy, provided that the mixture is carefully concocted, safeguards freedom of enterprise in a world of powerful domestic and international forces eager to destroy it.[64] The future growth of the American economy will depend on the realistic appraisal of this fundamental fact.

Selected References

GENERAL WORKS

Burns, Arthur F., and Wesley C. Mitchell, *Measuring Business Cycles*. New York: National Bureau of Economic Research, 1947.

Dewhurst, J. Frederic, and Associates, *America's Needs and Resources*. New York: Twentieth Century Fund, 1947.

Moulton, Harold G., *Controlling Factors in Economic Development*. Washington: The Brookings Institution, 1949.

Slichter, Sumner H., *The American Economy: Its Problems and Prospects*. New York: Alfred A. Knopf, 1948.

Snyder, Carl, *Capitalism the Creator*. New York: The Macmillan Company, 1940.

---

[64] See O. H. Taylor, "Free Enterprise and Democracy," Chapter 28 in *Saving American Capitalism*. (S. E. Harris, ed.) (New York: Alfred A. Knopf, Inc., 1948); and David McCord Wright, *Democracy and Progress* (New York: The Macmillan Company, 1948).

Somers, Harold M., *Public Finance and National Income.* Philadelphia and Toronto: The Blakiston Company, 1949.

Stigler, George J., *Trends in Output and Employment.* New York: National Bureau of Economic Research, 1947.

Thorp, Willard L., *Business Annals.* New York: National Bureau of Economic Research, 1926.

Wilson, Thomas, *Fluctuations in Income and Employment,* 3rd ed. New York and London: Pitman Publishing Corporation, 1948.

Wright, Chester W., *Economic History of the United States.* New York and London: McGraw-Hill Book Company, 1941.

Wright, David McCord, *Democracy and Progress.* New York: The Macmillan Company, 1948.

SPECIAL TOPICS

Angell, James W., *Investment and Business Cycles.* New York: McGraw-Hill Book Company, 1941.

Bogart, Ernest L., *Direct and Indirect Costs of the Great World War.* New York: Oxford University Press, Preliminary Economic Studies of the War, No. 24, 1919.

Brown, A. J., *Applied Economics.* New York and Toronto: Rinehart and Company, 1948.

Clark, John M., *The Costs of the World War to the American People.* New Haven: Yale University Press, 1931.

———, *Guideposts in Time of Change.* New York: Harper and Brothers, 1949.

Fabricant, Solomon, *The Output of Manufacturing Industries, 1899-1937.* New York: National Bureau of Economic Research, 1940.

———, *The Rising Trend of Government Employment* (Occasional Paper 29). New York: National Bureau of Economic Research, June, 1949.

Fisher, Irving, *The Stock Market Crash—and After.* New York: The Macmillan Company, 1930.

Hansen, Alvin H., *Fiscal Policy and Business Cycles.* New York: W. W. Norton and Company, 1941.

Kuznets, Simon, *National Income and Its Composition, 1919-1938,* Vol. I and II. New York: National Bureau of Economic Research, 1941.

———, *National Product Since 1869.* New York: National Bureau of Economic Research, 1946.

Lange, Oscar, "Is the American Economy Contracting?" *American Economic Review,* September, 1939.

Timoshenko, Vladimir P., *World Agriculture and the Depression,* Michigan Business Studies, No. 5. Ann Arbor: University of Michigan, 1933.

Tinbergen, J., *Business Cycles in the United States of America, 1919-1932,* Vol. II. Geneva: League of Nations, 1939.

United States, *Midyear Economic Report of the President* (Message of the President) and *Economic Situation at Midyear 1949* (Report of the Council of Economic Advisers). Washington: Government Printing Office, 1949.

United States Department of Commerce, "National Income," *Survey of Current Business,* Supplement, July, 1947; "National Income and Product Statistics of the United States, 1942-48," *Survey of Current Business,* July, 1949.

Yoder, Dale and George R. Davies, *Depression and Recovery.* New York and London: McGraw-Hill Book Company, 1934.

INDEX

A

G

H

I